Complete Guide to
HUNTING
ACROSS
NORTH
AMERICA

An Outdoor Life Book

Complete Guide to

HUNTING
ACROSS
NORTH
AMERICA

Byron Dalrymple

Maps by Delos D. Rowe Associates
Basic maps courtesy of Rand McNally & Company

OUTDOOR LIFE • HARPER & ROW
NEW YORK • LONDON

To MY WIFE, ELLEN, who put in as many months of work on this project as I did, often when it seemed the mass of information could never be dominated. And, to those thousands of hunters whose outdoor world has seen swift encroachment by the growth of our population—in the hope that they may discover here new kinds and sources of enjoyment and healthful recreation.

CONTENTS

ACKNOWLEDGMENTS

My sincere thanks and appreciation to the following persons for their help in gathering information about their states, provinces or particular localities: Thomas H. Bell, Dept. of Conservation, Montgomery, Alabama; Amos Burg, Dept. of Fish & Game, Alaska; Bill Sizer, Arizona Game & Fish Dept., Phoenix; George M. Purvis, Arkansas Game & Fish Comm., Little Rock; George D. Seymour, Dept. of Fish & Game, Sacramento, Cal.; Peter Hansson, Dept. of Game, Fish & Parks, Denver, Colo.; Elizabeth T. Caulk, I. & E. Chief for the Board of Game & Fish Commissioners, Dover, Delaware; James T. Floyd, Game & Fresh Water Fish Comm., Tallahassee, Fla.; Jim Morrison, I. & E. Coordinator, and Hubert Handy, Game Management Chief, State Game & Fish Comm., Atlanta, Ga.

E. Kliess Brown, Idaho Fish & Game Dept., Boise; Jim Lockart, Dept. of Conservation, Springfield, Ill.; Herbert R. Hill, Dept. of Natural Resources, Indianapolis, Ind.; A. Claude Ferguson, Supervisor, Hoosier National Forest, Bedford, Ind.; Julius Satre, State Conservation Comm., Des Moines, Iowa; Thayne Smith, Forestry, Fish & Game Comm., Pratt, Kansas; Robert F. Collins, Supervisor, Daniel Boone National Forest, Winchester, Ky.; Harry Towles, Dept. of Fish & Wildlife Resources, Frankfort, Ky.; Steve Harmon, Louisiana Wild Life and Fisheries Comm., New Orleans; Wm. C. Mincher, Dept. of Inland Fisheries & Game, Augusta, Maine; Malcolm E. King, Dept. of Game & Inland Fish, Annapolis, Maryland; Bryant R. Chaplin, Div. of Fisheries & Game, Westboro, Mass.

John Gray, Dept. of Natural Resources, Lansing, Michigan; Charles Shick, game biologist, DNR, Lansing, Mich.; David J. Langowski, Section of Game, Dept. of Conservation, St. Paul, Minn.; Lewis W. Bays and other biologists and Medora Hall Sharp, Game & Fish Comm., Jackson, Miss.; James F. Keefe, Missouri Dept. of Conservation, Jefferson City; Richard J. Munro, State of Montana Dept. of Fish & Game, Helena; E. K. Hornbeck, Nebraska Game, Forestation & Parks Comm., Lincoln; Gene McDowell, Nevada Game & Fish Comm., Reno; Richard G. Seamans, Jr., and Denton H. Hartley, Fish & Game Dept., Concord, N.H.; Robert McDowell, Dept. of Conservation & Economic Development, Trenton, N.J.

Wm. S. Huey, E. M. Lang, Levon Lee and others of the New Mexico Dept. of Game & Fish, Santa Fe; of the New York State Conservation Dept., all of the Regional game managers, who were exceedingly helpful, and in addition A. W. Bromley, Conservation Education, and Ralph B. Colson, Bureau of Game, both at the Dept. in Albany; Rod Amundson, North Carolina

Wildlife Resources Comm., Raleigh; Joel Arrington, North Carolina Dept. of Conservation & Development, Raleigh; Pershing Carlson, North Dakota Game & Fish Dept., Bismarck; Dan C. Armbruster, Dept. of Natural Resources, Columbus, Ohio; W. H. Oldfield, *Ohio* magazine, Columbus; Dean G. Graham, Dept. of Wildlife Conservation, Oklahoma City, Okla.

R. C. Holloway, Oregon State Game Comm., Portland, and Milt Guymon, press relations officer for the Oregon Game Comm.; Roy W. Trexler, Pennsylvania Game Comm., Harrisburg; Ronald Anderson, Dept. of Natural Resources, Providence, R.I.; Eddie Finlay, South Carolina Wildlife Resources Comm., Columbia; Robert P. Morris, Dept. of Game, Fish & Parks, Pierre, South Dakota; S. Hillard Brown, Jr., Anson Galyon, and all of the Regional game managers, who were extremely helpful, Tennessee Game & Fish Comm., Nashville; Paul D. Hope, news editor for the Texas Parks & Wildlife Dept.; Larry Eyre, Division of Fish & Game, Salt Lake City, Utah.

W. Robert Candy, Vermont Fish & Game Dept., Montpelier; James F. McInteer, Jr., Comm. of Game & Inland Fisheries, Richmond, Virginia; Frank Hill, Jan Riffe, Richard L. Hall, all of the Dept. of Natural Resources, Charleston, W. Virginia; Clar Pratt, Dept. of Game, Olympia, Washington; A. W. Jorgensen, Dept. of Natural Resources, Madison, Wis.; George A. Kaminski, Game & Fish Comm., Cheyenne, Wyo.

W. G. Smith and I. D. Smith, Fish & Wildlife Branch, Victoria, B.C., Canada; S. B. Smith, Fish & Wildlife Div., Edmonton, Alberta; K. H. Doan, Wildlife Branch, Winnipeg, Manitoba; W. A. Klassen, Wildlife Branch, Regina, Sask.; Gordon R. Kerr, biologist, Dept. of Lands & Forests, Edmonton, Alberta; H. Etienne Corbeil, Wildlife Service, Quebec City, Quebec; Merrill Prime, Dept. of Lands & Forests, Nova Scotia; Stanley Vass, Div. of Fish & Wildlife, Prince Edward Island; C. H. D. Clarke, Dept. of Lands & Forests, Ontario; John Power, Ontario Dept. of Tourism and Information, Toronto; D. G. Pike, Director of Wildlife, Newfoundland and Labrador; P. A. Kwaterowsky, Superintendent of Game, Government of the Northwest Territories; John C. Baird, Fish & Wildlife Branch, New Brunswick; J. B. Fitzgerald, Director of Game, Yukon Territorial Government.

There were many others from both the U.S. and Canada, some of whom compiled requested information but failed to send covering letters with names signed. Surprisingly, many readers of magazine contributions of mine, learning I was involved with this large project, proffered local information. To all, again, my thanks.

Byron Dalrymple

Complete Guide to
HUNTING
ACROSS
NORTH
AMERICA

INTRODUCTION

PLANNING A SUCCESSFUL HUNTING TRIP

This book is designed chiefly to tell readers what game is available in each state, and where. It also tries to show hunters, in as fine focus as possible, where their best chances will be over broad areas of the range of any game species. However, there are many facets of a successful hunting trip. Just heading off to a strange state, or a distant area of your own state, looking for the place where the deer or pheasants are most abundant may not always be the most successful trip approach for you as an individual. Thus, you must know how best to utilize the information placed here to assist you.

What hunters yearn most for are two things: a reasonable *abundance of game* and *room to hunt*. The space is often more important than the level of abundance, for hunters, unlike fishermen, cannot swarm into small areas and operate either pleasantly or safely. In addition, while the angler finds his quarry tied to a specific habitat—a stream course or lake it cannot leave— the hunter, possibly excepting some waterfowl hunters, must often roam rather widely in order to locate his targets.

As you read the material on each state, you will discover that in each case the *size* in square miles of that state is given in the text. That can be important to you, especially when posed against the *population* of the same state. Population figures quite obviously are rising. Those given are in round numbers. They will allow you to make a choice in some cases between crowded and less crowded regions. A state covering 50,000 square miles, with a population of 7,000,000, quite plainly doesn't have as much room for game or hunters, given proper terrain for a certain species, as a state with similar good habitat that covers 80,000 square miles and has a population of only 500,000. Much depends, too, on *where* in each state the most people reside. Conceivably, plush accommodations might be easier to find in the more heavily populated, smaller state, or in one portion or section of the less populous one. And there certainly might be very good hunting. But if you wanted the most wide-open spaces, and small towns with sparse accommodations, or you wished to camp out, the thinly populated state or section might be best for you.

You will discover, too, that in the material about each state the average number of hunting licenses annually sold is also given. These also steadily grow, but with no drastic upswing. In some instances, where figures were available, and important, resident and nonresident license sales are given separately. And in some others, big-game hunters are noted by gross numbers. A state that shows a sale of 900,000 hunting licenses is, regardless of size, fairly well saturated with hunters. If it is also a populous state, it is easy to visualize this great number of hunters crowded into only a nominal amount of territory. If 500,000 of that 900,000 hold deer licenses as well as small-game licenses, it is obvious that deer hunting will be crowded and competitive.

Some states draw a tremendous number of nonresident hunters for deer. This is usually because the deer hunting has proven very good there. Sometimes it is abetted by heavy advertising by the states. Such places may be precisely where you will want to go. Or they may not. Much will depend on a look at some of the other material, to see how much public hunting land is available to the great number of hunters. Several million acres of National Forest, for example, can soak up a lot of hunters—*if* it is accessible. If it is only easily accessible around the fringes, then you might deduce that the hunting would be crowded, unless you were able to get into the interior via horseback or 4-wheel-drive.

There is another figure that is important, and you will find a good many references to it in the material on each state. This is the average percentage of success in activities like deer hunting. Percentages, to be sure, fluctuate year to year somewhat, dependent upon the game crop that year. But they remain reasonably similar on a broad average. Percentages are often important because of easy, or difficult, hunting conditions. Some states may have ample room, and really a good deer herd, but they may also show a low kill percentage compared to the number of hunters. By plotting the places against percentages, often you can win. As an example, one of the northern plains states is large, lightly populated, sells comparatively few deer licenses, does a meager amount of advertising, is hardly ever visited by nonresident deer hunters, and is seldom mentioned as a "good deer state." Yet its hunter success annually runs around 80 percent, while many a famed deer state highly touted and advertised runs 25 to 35 percent.

One should of course check figures on what sex the deer are. That is, a certain state may show a kill of 100,000, and a high success ratio for hunters. But a closer check of the kill will determine that of that 100,000 deer, 65,000 were antlerless animals. An any-deer hunter would be in clover here. But a buck hunter would perhaps be better off going elsewhere.

This gets us to trophies. Some big-game hunters look specifically for trophy animals. This is an intriguing business, and while there may be a trophy buck almost anywhere, there are areas that year after year produce trophy bucks, and it is wise to try to locate such a place—if you are a trophy hunter. You might well avoid an area where the kill is high. It is a good bet the old bucks are skimmed off fast here, or never get a chance to grow old. A careful check of the Boone & Crockett Club and the Pope & Young Club records is a good way to find where the big-antlered deer have come from.

Paradoxically, you will often discover that some of the largest deer, both in antler and body, are taken in places that do not have a very high deer kill and even in places that have a low percentage of success. In some of the farm country in deer range, for example, where there are few deer and few hunters, some tremendous old bucks hang on. Some very large bucks come every year from several of the states that are not renowned as deer hot spots. Some of this is because certain of the farm states and the populous mid-continent states have growing deer herds that have learned to get along with civilization. Seasons are brief, and in some cases there have been no seasons for some years. When a season is opened, some tremendous bucks are available.

There are numerous items that bird hunters, too, should take into consideration. Right within your own state there may be bonanzas of bird hunting that you do not know about. Or, you may not realize that, though you have found a good area, some other may be far better. Many states claim, with complete truth, that a certain game bird ranges "throughout the state." Many years ago game biologists had already found out that the *soil types* hold the fundamental key to production of all living things, plants and animals alike. For example, studies done years ago on the vanishing prairie chicken in Illinois showed that on the black prairie soils the most birds had existed. On the gray prairie soils there was a good population, but not the abundance found where the black soils were. The fewest birds were found on the sandy prairie soils.

Thus, if you were looking for a new spot to hunt pheasants, you might well discover by carefully evaluating the material in a certain chapter that the northwest corner of a certain pheasant state has the best habitat and consistently the most birds. The remaining three-fourths of the same state, let's say, does have pheasants in varying abundance, but always that northwest corner—and specifically within that good area a certain county or half of a county—has the heaviest concentration. Obviously such pinpoint information is valuable to the planner of any hunting trip. Really it's a matter of shopping around and comparing values and possibilities.

This gets us to the importance of a phrase used a moment ago about the place that "consistently has the most birds"—or any other kind of game. No matter how carefully a book like this is put together, unfortunately no one can predict nature's influences from year to year upon game, especially on the smaller game that has drastic ups and downs in population. Many hunters are still not fully aware of how fragile are populations of game birds and small animals. These creatures are prolific. They are also prone to crushing debacles because of nature's complex influences.

Ruffed grouse may be phenomenally abundant in a state or certain portion of a state for several years, then suddenly all but disappear. Snowshoe hares appear in overwhelming numbers, and two seasons later are hardly in evidence at all. The populations of most game birds and small game are cyclic. They build slowly, given good nesting and breeding and rearing seasons, and then often suddenly explode into fantastic numbers in certain ranges. This occurs because all breeding, nesting, and rearing conditions happened that year to fall into almost perfect place. It can almost invariably be predicted that when this occurs a low cycle is also certain to be on the way. Crowded populations skim the food down fast. Disease and parasites spread swiftly. Or, a smashing blow by weather may be dealt by nature. As this is written, the once numerous pheasant population of the Dakotas has been in serious trouble for several years, due chiefly, it is thought, to several bad winters that killed off millions of birds. In the Edwards Plateau area of Texas, one of the finest of wild turkey ranges, two severely dry springs in a row have resulted in an almost complete lack of nesting success. Only old birds, growing older each season, are left.

However, game men nowadays do not become unduly disturbed about these natural cycles and difficulties. With whatever assistance is possible, and a switch in the weather, the game populations will come back. A normal breeding season plus a good acorn crop may suddenly bring squirrels into super abundance in some chain of hills. A normal nesting spring may skyrocket the quail. But now go back to that phrase again and the word "consistently." The places that had the greatest abundance in the first place will undoubtedly be the hot spots again, unless in the brief interim something drastic has occurred to change the quality of the habitat. In other words, these areas of great game populations will *consistently* have the highest numbers, even during the lows and the build-back period.

Thus, *abundance* is a relative matter. The wise hunter will check with the game department people at the last possible moment, when he is planning his trip. This book may state, correctly, that some specific area of a certain state offers some of the best quail hunting in that state. Yet a die-off in process as you read this might mean you should not go there expecting—this year— a high concentration of birds. The hunting might still be the best available in the area, but on a relative basis. A check with the game people could save you a poor hunt for that year, or just as possibly gain you a better one by your discovery that a fabulous high cycle was in progress or was about to bloom.

Big game is not subject to quite such swift and drastic ups and downs. However, a severe blizzard can at times literally decimate an antelope herd, or a hard winter cause in a particular area a deer die-off that all but sweeps that region clean. No one can predict these disasters. But you can avoid getting caught in the middle of one by checking the information in this book, at the latest possible moment before your trip, with game department people.

Most of the time the game people know fairly well ahead what can be expected so far as a *crop* is concerned. They can tell if the nesting season for quail, for example, seemed good. By midsummer they can judge quite well if the young birds seem to be doing all right. They will know if the deer or elk wintered well, and if the fawn drop appeared average. Yet there is one more hurdle that the trip-planning hunter must still manage to surmount, and how successfully he does it depends upon how well he uses his sources of knowledge. This last hurdle is again based on *weather*.

For example, an early ruffed grouse season in the Great Lakes country or New England, or a later season but with an unusually mild fall, may mean that the leaves are so thick that regardless of grouse population density you would come back empty in the game pockets. It would be wise, in such an event, to wait until the end of the season to make your trip, when the leaves are down. If you were planning an elk hunt in the west, and the summer and fall in your selected area had been extremely dry, even the best elk areas where animals usually concentrate would probably have the herds scattered hither and yon over the hills. They would not be seeking water only, but ample food. By a careful check you might be able to switch your plan to another area or state. Conversely, it occurs occasionally that some of the best big-game ranges—again we might use elk as an example—will get several weeks of rain before the season opens. There may be scores of big bulls waiting—but the area is primitive and, alas, hunters cannot get in.

Such hazards, of course, cannot always be overcome even by the most careful planning. The point to be made here, however, is that a thorough study of your sources beforehand, plus use of sound judgment, can often make a hunt far more enjoyable and successful than just running pell-mell to some spot that is highly publicized.

Today, you see, game management is a very precise art. Much is still to be learned. But a great deal already is known—and works. It is now well known that game population patterns are changing on this continent. Land use, rising population, and game management all combine to change these patterns. Some states hardly ever heard of a few years ago as mecca for hunters of one sort or another are today among the top areas. This is especially true for such game as quail and deer. Wild turkeys, because of expert management, exist today in huntable populations in more places than before the white man came to this country. By wisely using the material gathered for you here, you may have a *more* successful hunt for your favorite game in another state, instead of returning to the region where the same game has been standard fare for centuries.

HOW TO USE THE MAPS

The maps of the forty-eight contiguous states were prepared especially for this book to enable the reader to locate the hunting areas referred to in the text. Numbers in the text correspond to numbers on the maps, pinpointing the locations of Management Areas, State Forests, State Parks, and other public hunting grounds. National Forests are numbered, and are also labeled on the maps. Counties are shown on all maps and are repeatedly referred to in the text as the basic units for evaluating hunting prospects. Adjacent to each map is a list of all the public hunting areas, with their numbers, to aid the reader in locating the areas. With a few exceptions, this is the system that has been followed throughout. The exceptions are those states that don't lend themselves to this treatment because of the way their hunting areas are managed. Maine, for example, has few Management Areas of Hunting Units as such, but offers hunting on lumber company lands and in its wilderness areas. Thus there are no numbers on the map of Maine; best hunting areas have been located by counties. A reading of the text will quickly reveal to the reader how a state is managed for hunting, and how to use the map.

SHOOTING PRESERVES

Today it is well known that the shooting preserve, or as some sportsmen have called it, "artificial hunting," is a very popular form of gunning recreation throughout most of the United States. On some of these preserves, where for example pheasants and chukars or quail are shot, the hunting is indeed a very close approximation of hunting birds raised in the wild. On some others, birds are released for the gun under conditions that are too easy for the sportsman. Yet, some like it this way, and go home happy.

In this book shooting preserves are not dealt with in the chapters because we are concerned here chiefly with the available public lands and those private lands on which wild game is hunted by permission of the landowner, but a list of the preserves is included at the back of the book. There will be a few exceptions. These will concern the existence of fee hunting in several states, a practice that is growing extensively. Also, there are today some possibilities, especially in Texas, for hunting for a fee numerous exotic big-game animals, many of them existing on large tracts of land in a completely wild condition.

However, the shooting preserve as such on a grand scale is not properly a part of this volume's domain. To be sure, the preserves do fill a much needed place in U.S. gunning. Most of them are located within easy reach of the large metropolitan areas. Here sportsmen with only brief hours to spend can go afield for a quick hunt and for a set fee bag a few birds, or in some instances a feral boar or goat, or perhaps even a whitetail deer. The bird hunting preserves are the most numerous. These, along with offering recreation and surefire bags to busy city-dwelling gunners, also take some pressure off the public lands, to which those thousands who can ill afford preserve shooting must go.

Thus, we do not take a stand against shooting preserves. On the contrary, we are all for them. They are distinctly a part of today's shooting scene, and are here to stay. There are as this is written at least forty states and two Canadian provinces in which such preserves are located. There are several hundred of them, all told, the majority of course in the areas of heaviest population.

All hunters should know that certain states require a special license to allow hunting only on regulated shooting preserves. This is not common, but one should be aware of the existence of such laws in certain states. In at least one eastern state this applies only to nonresidents. Check the regulations.

MAINE

The state of Maine forms the extreme northeastern corner of the United States. It touches only one other state, New Hampshire, and shares over two-thirds of its border with the Canadian provinces of Quebec and New Brunswick. Maine is envisioned by most sportsmen as one vast northern forest. This is not far from literally true. This largest of the half-dozen New England states, with slightly more than 33,000 square miles, has almost 90 percent of its area forested.

The coastal area of Maine is well developed, and so are portions of the interior. However, much of northern Maine is still authentic wilderness, unspoiled and with some portions extremely remote and meagerly accessible. Several thousand miles of streams course down across the state, reaching toward the Atlantic. Lakes are everywhere. The coast runs a straight-line distance of roughly 250 miles but is rough, rocky, indented continuously so that the total coastline is over 2300 miles. From the coast the terrain rises inland and becomes rolling and hilly. In the west and parts of the north there are mountains with steep slopes, and with a number of peaks reaching to 4000 feet and at least one to over 5000.

Maine is famous for its lobsters, fisheries, blueberries, its potatoes and granite. But basically it is a lumbering state furnishing vast amounts of wood products from pulp for paper to lumber for the building trades. Upon the vast forest is based much of the excellent hunting for which Maine has long been famous.

Roads in the coastal sector, in the southwest and in the lower central region are good, and abundant. But a tremendous expanse of the north is all but roadless, so far as fast highways are concerned. The eastern border, with New Brunswick, has U.S. 1 running north through Caribou and on to Van Buren and to Edmunston, New Brunswick. There is also Route 11 angling up across the northeast and north-central region to the Canadian border. However, a large part of the north and interior northern half of the state is reached only by secondaries, and in the more remote parts by lumber roads and trails.

Air transport to all the larger cities is adequate, and there are numerous hunting lodges and camps where fly-in trips are available, with airstrips or lake landings for small planes on or near their premises. Although hunting in the accessible portions of the state can be reached easily by passenger car, a pickup or 4WD transport is best, and in some instance mandatory, for much of the north. For late seasons, during snow time, the snowmobile is now offering a popular and useful method of off-trail access.

Much of Maine is sparsely populated. Population totals less than one million, the great share of it along the coast and in the south-central and southwest regions. Hunting is exceedingly popular, indeed traditional among a large percentage of Maine residents. Some 200,000 persons hunt here annually. Among adults, at least 25 percent are hunters. Maine is also popular with nonresidents, most of whom enter the state for deer hunting. On the average between 30,000 and 35,000 nonresidents annually purchase licenses.

Hunting is excellent. Chief targets are whitetail deer, black bear, ruffed grouse (popularly called "partridge" in Maine), black ducks, snowshoe hares, woodcock. There are also some pheasants, cottontails, gray squirrels, other varieties of waterfowl besides the popular black duck, fair goose hunting, a scattering of snipe, plus predators such as foxes and bobcats.

Oddly, with its excellent hunting and its over seventeen million acres of forests, Maine has very little public land. About 98 percent, 16,953,000 acres, of the Maine forests are in private ownership. Most of this is in commercial forests. However, over many years Maine hunters have had access to the great share of these lands almost as freely as if they were in public ownership. Therefore, finding a place to hunt in Maine is not at all difficult.

There are approximately 77,000 acres of the White Mountain National Forest within the western boundary of the state. This Forest is chiefly in New Hampshire. There is good hunting for deer, bear, and small game within the Maine section of this Forest. The Forest headquarters is at Laconia, New Hampshire, where requests may be directed to the Forest Supervisor for maps and details.

There are also a number of state-owned Game Management Areas, some eighteen at a recent count, plus upwards of thirty presently under lease agreement with the landowners and under game management control of the state. Most of these are not large, the largest approximately 5000 acres, and many are set up as refuges or are not open, or at least not open every season, to public hunting. Thus, on a statewide scale these GMAs, which will be touched to some extent under the various species headings, are not as important or urgently needed for hunting here as similar lands are in other more heavily populated states.

Hunters should have a basic understanding of how the paper companies and commercial forest owners operate regarding public use of their lands. A good example is the policy of Great Northern Paper Company, which owns over two and a quarter million acres of Maine forests. Roughly 85 percent of these lands is open for public recreational use, and much of this area is accessible over some 800 miles of company roads. Hunters may be excluded at any time during fire hazard periods, or from specific locations during logging operations. About half the roads are open to use without charge. Remaining roads may be used by payment of a use fee, and a camping fee if one intends to camp for a period of time. These fees are set by the company and are listed in a folder available from it. The land use fees are set by week, month, and season.

This same firm also leases out some hundreds of camp lots, most of them accessible via company road, the remainder via water. There are also numerous campsites on company lands maintained by the Maine Forest Service. A "Sportsman's Map of Northwestern Maine," and the use-fee folder, are available from the Woodlands Department, Great Northern Paper Company, 6 State Street, Bangor, Maine 04401. The same map can be had from the Maine Department of Inland Fisheries and Game, address at chapter end.

Great Northern is of course only one of numerous firms owning forests in Maine that are open for recreational use. American Forest Products Industries is a good source of material about commercial forests and may be contacted at 1835 K Street, NW, Washington, D.C. 20006. Some firms with acreage in Maine and offering printed information about their recreational facilities are as follows: Dead River Co., 55 Broadway, Bangor, Maine 04401;

Georgia Pacific Corp., St. Croix Woodlands Div., Woodland, Maine (Washington Co.) 04694; International Paper Co. (over a million acres), Public Relations Dept., 220 E. 42nd St., New York, N.Y. 10017; St. Regis Paper Co., 150 E. 42nd St., New York, N.Y. 10017.

Game Department surveys in Maine show that the majority of Maine resident hunters hunt locally, within their own county and in fact chiefly within an area of moderate size around their homes. Nonresident hunters, and those residents wishing to go into other parts of their state not well known to them, will be far better off to book a guided hunt or stay at one of the many lodges and hunting camps for which Maine is famous, and hunt with a guide. The Game Department has available a list of Maine guides. A listing does not mean recommendation, since obviously the state cannot recommend individuals. Where-to-go ads in outdoor magazines have numerous hunting camps in the state listing what they offer, and their fees. The Department of Economic Development, State House, Augusta 04330, offers a folder, "Maine Hunting," free upon request. Queries to Chambers of Commerce in any of the sizable towns of the state can gain hunters invaluable local information, too.

Hunters wishing to camp find few problems in this state. As already mentioned there are a number of campsites on the commercial forest lands. A booklet, "Forest Campsites," can be obtained from the Maine Forest Service, Forest Recreation Development, Augusta. Another, "State Parks and Historic Sites" can be had from the Department of Economic Development, address above. There are also campsites in the Maine portion of the White Mountain National Forest. Other accommodations, in motels and hotels, are numerous in the more heavily settled areas along all main highways. But in the "north woods" in general hunters will either camp out, or stay at one of the numerous lodges and hunting camps.

Hunters should go prepared for cold weather. Most seasons do not open until early or mid-October. Weather at that time can be exhilarating, with frosty nights and sunny, invigorating days. But Maine weather is whimsical, and October can also be very cold. November is virtually certain to see snow on the ground, sometimes a lot of it. Coastal waterfowl hunters will want warm clothing and rain gear at any time of season. Check recent laws in some sections of Maine regarding necessity of wearing blaze orange.

Nothing special in arms and ammunition are needed. The bird hunter will deal mostly with grouse and woodcock, with shot size No. 7½ a good compromise for both. Duck hunters will step down to highbase sixes or No. 4. Some snowshoe hare enthusiasts like No. 4s, too, but ordinarily No. 6 is used. A .22 rifle is a good arm for hares, too, and for squirrels. Deer and bear hunters use traditional calibers, such as the .30/06, .30/30, .270, and others comparable. Most deer and bear hunting, it should be remembered, will be done in dense cover, with few long shots available.

RUFFED GROUSE

Without question the ruffed grouse, or as Down Easters call it, "partridge," is the king of the game birds in Maine. By numbers bagged each season it is topped only by the snowshoe hare among all the state's game species, and then only by a rather small margin. Probably at least a fourth of the state's hunters hunt ruffed grouse annually. This bird is notoriously cyclic in its radical ups and downs of population. However, over a recent ten-year survey period the kill never ran below 134,000, had a general level of around 180,000 and in one peak year was 232,000.

Ruffed grouse range throughout Maine in all suitable covers. The climate is precisely suitable to this bird, and lumbering practices, which with their cuttings have created much ideal habitat, have helped keep grouse in abundance. In addition, abandonment of farms, and the occurrence of burns that have opened dense timber stands and left brushy "edges," have both contributed to forming in Maine one of the highest ruffed grouse densities of any place in the range of the species across the continent.

It is not possible to give locations of the best grouse hunting in Maine. As always with this bird, it may be excellent in one region and spotty in another during the same season. Or the cycle may be at peak, with birds in abundance everywhere, or at its low with them scarce, or only moderately abundant over most of the state. However, in any good season ruffed grouse hunting is of top quality over almost the entire state and it matters little which area one selects.

Along any stream course, around the woodlot edges of abandoned farms, where there is some brush and second growth and a mixture of deciduous and evergreen forest, grouse will be found. In the easily accessible settled portions of the state, dogs are popularly used for grouse hunting. However, a majority of native hunters "walk up" their birds. A favorite method is walking the lumber roads and trails. Particularly in the north this is a successful practice, for in the heavier forests the openings of the trails and roads are favorite places for grouse.

Over 50 percent of the total kill of grouse comes from western and southwestern Maine. Another 20 percent, approximately, are bagged in the eastern strip of Aroostook County, in the northeast, through which run U.S. 1 and 2 and State 11. These high percentage portions of the state remain so simply because of hunter density in the southwest and accessibility in the northeast. The southeast, and the central coast sectors furnish the smaller portion of the bag. The highest success percentage per hunter is had in the northwest, in the western half of huge Aroostook Co. This is the more remote country, gets few hunters, but a high kill per hunter. The northeast is almost as high. Central and west-central Maine come third. Hunters should bear in mind that some of the higher success percentage in the north is due to the fact that ruffed grouse, when under little hunting pressure, are far less wild than in settled regions where they are hunted hard.

PHEASANT

Pheasants were first released in southern Maine at the end of the last century. A few may have crossed into southwestern Maine even earlier, from releases in Massachusetts and New Hampshire. By the early 1900s pheasants were established in modest numbers near Portland, and they spread to the Auburn and Lewiston area later. By 1931 all of Maine's coastal counties had been stocked.

However, Maine cannot be considered a good pheasant state. There is enough farm cover to furnish nesting and food during summer, but winter food is scarce and winters are severe. Thus the winter carry-over of birds is low. Almost all of the hunting is furnished by birds annually stocked. The carry-over during winter is placed at less than 4 percent of the number of birds released. Birds wild-bred therefore are a minor percentage of the annual bag.

Ordinarily about 20,000 birds are raised and released by the state, and another 10,000 are farmed out for rearing and release by sportsmen and clubs. The annual total release averages about 30,000. During one recent season

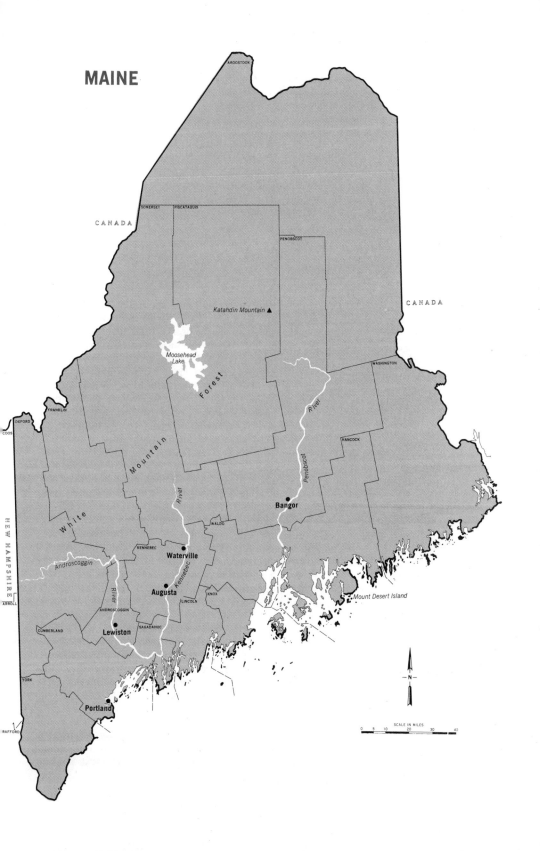

MAINE

CANADA

AROOSTOOK

SOMERSET PISCATAQUIS

PENOBSCOT

CANADA

Katahdin Mountain ▲

Moosehead
Lake

Forest

WASHINGTON

FRANKLIN

OXFORD

COOS

Mountain

HANCOCK

River

Penobscot

Bangor

White

River

WALDO

NEW HAMPSHIRE

Androscoggin

KENNEBEC

Waterville

River

Kennebec

Augusta

KNOX

Mount Desert Island

CARROLL

ANDROSCOGGIN

LINCOLN

SAGADAHOC

Lewiston

CUMBERLAND

YORK

N

Portland

RAFFORD

SCALE IN MILES
0   5   10   20   30   40

29,300 birds were taken by hunters. Over a period of years the average kill has run between 25,000 and 30,000. The release program attempts to place birds where hunters have shown most interest in them, and to place them in huntable and suitable cover.

The southwestern fourth of the state gets the preponderance of the birds, and accounts for from 80 to 90 percent of the kill. The southwestern coastal counties of York, Cumberland, Androscoggin, Kennebec, Lincoln, Knox, Waldo, plus portions of the tier above these, running from the New Hampshire border east across from about the city of Rumford to Bangor takes in the best of the pheasant region. The majority of the birds are found on privately owned farmlands. Permission to hunt is usually not especially difficult to obtain.

WOODCOCK

Maine is an excellent state for woodcock hunting. There is a large nesting population, offering shooting on birds raised in the state. And there is a heavy migration of flight birds raised in Canada. As a rule the season is six or seven weeks. This gives hunters an opportunity to shoot local birds early in the season. As hard frosts occur farther north, flight birds pour in. If weather in southern Maine stays moderate, occasionally both local and flight birds will be in coverts at the same time. Then shooting is exceptional. Ordinarily, however, the migrating woodcock from Canada arrive as local birds are departing, thus giving Maine hunters the equivalent of two seasons.

Many woodcock are shot as incidentals by grouse hunters. Most Maine woodcock enthusiasts use dogs, hunting the stream courses where alders give cover and soft earth allows the birds to probe for earthworms with their long bills. Edge cover on abandoned farms is also excellent. A number of nonresidents bring their dogs to Maine purposely for the combined woodcock and grouse shooting. Depending on the season, Maine woodcock hunters harvest from 20,000 to 45,000 birds. The tally for one recent season was 46,700. This shows an abundance of birds when compared to number of woodcock hunters, which is less than 10,000. And, of those, many are one-time-per-season hunters.

Better than 90 percent of the woodcock are bagged in the southern half of the state. This is not necessarily an indication of poor hunting in the north, but rather a matter of accessibility. The southwestern counties—York, Cumberland, Androscoggin, Kennebec—account for the largest percentage of the kill, but coastal counties to the east offer a higher success ratio. For example, southeastern Maine—the southern halves of Hancock and Washington Cos.—gets about half as many woodcock hunters but has chances of good shooting twice as high.

The region immediately to the north, east of the Penobscot River and between it and the St. Croix forming the border between Maine and New Brunswick, also can be rated as excellent. In the central and central-west sector, the southern half of large Piscataquis Co., the central portion of Somerset Co., the northern portions of Franklin and Oxford Cos. in the west are on a par with the region east of the Penobscot.

SNIPE, RAILS, WATERFOWL

Maine hunters could have quite good snipe hunting by seeking the proper expanses of marshlands. But there is little interest shown in this bird. Fair flight populations are found in the duck marshes and bogs. Harvest studies indicate that very few hunters pursue this small game bird diligently and that the kill probably is no more than 2000 annually.

Although rails are on the game bird list each season, very few are shot, and rail hunting as a sport in its own right is all but unknown.

For a modest number of duck hunters, shooting in Maine is excellent. For many years such places as Merrymeeting Bay have been famous for duck hunting. In fact, in studies the state has been divided into Inland, where the duck kill is low, Coastal, and Merrymeeting Bay. Duck hunters throughout the state probably number around 12,000. While there is a fair amount of shooting available on the lakes and along the streams of the interior, the Maine coast gets the major share of the flight.

The black duck is the number one target. About half the ducks killed in Maine are black ducks. The annual duck kill ranges from 50,000 to around 70,000. Green-winged teal and wood ducks make up possibly 25 percent. Sea ducks such as the scoters and eiders are also important, probably about 10 percent of the annual bag.

One of Maine's most vital waterfowl problems is the loss of coastal wetlands. The coast has been so continuously developed that wetlands are swiftly gobbled up. Recently an inventory of coastal wetlands was completed and throughout the immense length of coastline authorities were astonished to find there were only about 16,000 acres of tidal marshes in blocks over ten acres in size.

Nonetheless, there is still ample opportunity for the duck hunter, even though the amount of habitat for ducks is swiftly dwindling. Over half of Maine's duck hunters concentrate in the southwestern coastal region. Here success is highest, too. The mid-coast and the southeast coast get about 25 percent of the hunters, with success also excellent. Up in the strip of Aroostook Co. along the New Brunswick border duck hunters are few, but success is invariably high. A strip of the state from Rumford to Bangor in the southwest-central region stacks up about equal.

Along the coast there is not much problem finding a place to hunt, for most of the hunting is done from boats on the bays. Here both the black duck, and off rocky points and peninsulas the various sea ducks, mostly scoters, offer good shooting. The average hunter will be well served to hunt with a guide who knows the territory.

There are a number of GMAs dedicated to waterfowl management. Some are open to shooting under specified regulations, and some are utilized as refuges. All are likely to have concentrations of ducks in their vicinities. Because these are not necessarily open to hunting, they are only named here and their general locations given. Check with the Department as to hunting possibilities.

In the southwest section are: Scarboro; Brownfield; Chesterville; Swan Island (refuge). South-central: Fahi Pond near Emden; Ruffingham Meadow near North Searsmont; St. Albans; Madawska Marsh near Palmyra; Sandy Point. In the east central: Manuel near Hodgdon. In the southeast Old Pond Farm near Howland; Pokey near Crawford; Pennamaquan near Pembroke; Great Works near Edmunds. There is also the Weskeag area on the south-central coast near Thomaston, managed for both waterfowl and upland game.

While Maine cannot be considered a top goose hunting state, at times the kill is fair. And, local breeding flocks of Canada geese are now becoming established. Maine has in recent years concerned itself in a determined manner with goose management. At the Moosehorn National Wildlife Refuge near

Calais in the southeast, a resident flock is launched. Geese have been brought in from New York and New Jersey and liberated at Brownfield, Swan Lake, and Ruffingham Meadow GMAs, to attempt to establish breeding flocks at those locations. Up in the northeast, below Edmunston, New Brunswick, in northern Aroostook Co., one of the best of the Maine goose management areas for migrating birds has been established. In parts of this county potatoes are a prime crop, but the land use is rotated, with hay and grains crops. It is ideal for geese. They even feed during migration on small potatoes left in the fields after harvest. In fact, goose hunting in the Aroostook potato fields is some of the best to be had in the state.

Other locations are along the coast, and especially in the Merrymeeting Bay region. Coastal geese feed on eel grass to some extent, and in Merrymeeting Bay on wild rice, bull rushes, and other aquatic plants. Maine geese are hunted over decoys in grain or potato fields and in the shallow rice-filled bay waters. The annual bag is certainly not large at present. A few fortunate hunters take from 500 to 1000 birds in a season. The highest kill in recent years was 1700. However, the future of goose hunting in Maine, if management practices are as successful as they appear to be at present, should be much better.

For specialists with proper equipment, or hunters using guides, there is good brant hunting along the Maine coast.

DEER

Maine has long been famed for its whitetail deer hunting, and for the large size of some of the deer taken each season. As many as a dozen deer each year have estimated live weight of well over 300 pounds, and dressed weight from 200 to 270. Deer hunting is exceedingly popular. In fact, practically all license buyers hunt deer. Over two recent seasons figures showed nearly 150,000 adult resident deer-license buyers, 17,000 junior residents, and approximately 33,000 nonresidents. Annual total kill runs from 30,000 to 35,000 but occasionally passes 40,000. Success figures on the average run around 20 percent, but it is known that some licensed hunters do not hunt. Thus the success figure is probably close to 25 percent of hunters who actually participate. This is thought to be the highest deer-hunt success anywhere in the eastern U.S., and compares well to whitetail success almost anywhere in the U.S.

The state is divided into two zones, north and south. The season is earlier in the north. The line divides the state about evenly, beginning in the west at about where the border with Quebec begins, and running with some deviation across to the east. The south zone kill is much the largest. Generally it reaches about 26,000 while the north zone averages somewhere over 6,000. Much of the north zone hunting is wilderness hunting, and while hunter pressure is far less, numerous areas of the dense forest do not have as large a deer population as the mixed forest and farmlands of the south zone. However, the main reason for the heavy southern kill is that the human population, and hunter numbers, are much greater here. There are plenty of deer, and the majority of hunters hunt near home.

Hunting is excellent almost everywhere, and as has been noted, places to hunt are not at all difficult to find. Kill per square mile is a good indication, when it occurs fairly consistently, of good deer herds, regardless of pressure. It is interesting that the counties rating highest in this respect are generally in the southwest—York, Waldo, Lincoln, Oxford, Androscoggin. However, these and most of the southwest get a lot of hunters and success percentage is not as high as in some other parts of the state.

A survey averaged over several years shows that success up in the wilderness northwest is very high, from 34 to 46 percent. The southeast has shown up to 35 percent for nonresident hunters, the central coastal region 37 percent. However, throughout the state both residents and nonresidents have for many years found quality hunting and there is no great choice. Visitors could be wise to shy from the southwest, however, where numerous residents hunt and have only a modest success percentage.

Some of the state's best deer range has been in the south-central coastal region, but recent years have seen land use changes that have dampened the quality. The north-central part of the state and west to the border has long been popular with nonresidents as well as many residents. Success is usually good. However, the northwest, covering northern Somerset and Piscataquis Cos. and western Aroostook Co. offers some of the best chances for bagging deer and at the same time seeing few other hunters. Much of the northeast—which actually is eastern Aroostook Co.—is in farmlands and has good deer hunting, about statewide average so far as success is concerned.

Some of the high-kill counties, but also in the southwest high-pressure counties, are generally as follows: 3500 to 4000 or more deer, Oxford, Aroostook, Somerset, Penobscot; over 2000, Franklin, Hancock, Piscataquis, Waldo, Washington, York.

BEAR

Black bears are plentiful in Maine. Prior to 1957 in fact they were considered nuisance animals and were bountied. Over recent years, however, more and more interest has been shown in bear hunting for sport by both residents and nonresidents. Many hunting camps and lodges now offer bear hunting, and the animal has become a much sought trophy. The annual kill averages around 1850. Interesting is the fact that prior to removal of the bounty only about 1700 bears a year were brought in. Thus the state saves nowadays some thousands of dollars in bounty payments, and lodges and guides take in thousands more in service to hunters.

The season is long, running as a rule from about June 1 through until the end of the year. Thus spring hunting over bait, and fall hunting with dogs or by still-hunting are all available. The Game Department publishes a folder, "Bear Hunting in Maine," which is invaluable to prospective bear hunters. It lists by counties various camps offering bear hunts, gives addresses, accommodations, and services furnished to hunters. These are not recommended by the Department, but simply listed as a service to hunters. This folder may be had free by request. See Department address at chapter end. Prospective bear hunters are well advised to book with a camp that has guide service. Many such operations have reputations for very nearly 100 percent kills for customers.

Total number of bear hunters averages around 7000 to 8000. Thus by average annual kill approximately 40 percent chance of success is normal. Following are some of the recommended general locations for bear hunting. Aroostook Co.: best hunting along the western edge of the farming lands. Franklin Co.: best on abandoned farmlands of the southern part. Hancock Co.: inland portions of this coastal county provide good hunting. Oxford Co.:

the edge of the wilderness in the northern portion. Penobscot Co.: northern parts. Piscataquis Co.: central and southern parts. Somerset Co.: central part. Washington Co.: wilderness portions inland from the coast.

RABBITS

Cottontails are not abundant in Maine. They are found locally in the southern and coastal portions, but limit of cottontail range is about in northern Waldo Co. The species cannot be considered common and in fact is not much hunted. Natives seldom use the word "cottontail" but instead call this rabbit the "cooney."

It is the snowshoe rabbit, more properly snowshoe hare, that is the prime small-game animal in Maine. These big hares of the evergreen and alder swamps and of the forest are brown in summer, white in winter, do not hole up when chased by hounds, as cottontails do, and weigh as much as four pounds or more. They are exciting game animals, can be hunted either with hounds or by stalking, and are excellent eating.

The rabbit kill, which means almost entirely snowshoes, runs from 150,000 to 300,000. All rabbits and hares show definite cycles, lows periodically followed by seasonal peak populations. While the major share of the kill occurs in the south, this is simply because hunters are concentrated there. Snowshoe hare hunting is excellent over most of Maine and there is no problem finding places to hunt, and good rabbit populations.

SQUIRREL

The gray squirrel, predominantly a species of the forest and its edges, is the squirrel hunted in Maine. But it is about at the fringe of its range here, not especially abundant nor of great interest to Maine hunters. It occurs chiefly in the southern half of the state. In some places squirrels are fairly abundant around villages and towns, and are seldom bothered by hunters. In southwestern Maine gray squirrels reach peaks of abundance in hardwood forests and receive a fair amount of hunting pressure. The average annual kill stays fairly consistent, averaging from 25,000 to 30,000. Any area with mature food-bearing trees such as beech, in a forest situation, will offer fair to good squirrel hunting. But Maine cannot be considered an important location for the species.

OTHER ANIMALS

Maine has a fair number of red foxes and bobcats. There is at this writing no closed season except nights and Sundays. There are a few lynx, which definitely should be protected as an endangered animal, and may be as this is read. Foxes and bobcats are popular as hound-chase game, and are becoming ever more so. Animal calling has made no great strides here to date, but could. Bobcats and red foxes come readily to a call. An indication of bobcat population can be gained from bounty payments over a period of years. It has averaged about 600 per year. Fox kills probably average somewhat less than 10,000. There are some raccoons, but this is not an important game animal, although it is protected by a dog-hunt and trapping seasons. Porcupines, which are certainly not game animals but are considered pests because of destruction to coniferous plantings, have been bountied in Maine for some years and may still be as this is read. The annual pest kill exceeds 30,000. Woodchucks in the farm country are fairly plentiful, with a kill of over 40,000 on the average.

MOOSE AND CARIBOU

Neither of these species is on the hunting list as this is written. Caribou almost certainly will not be for many years if at all. The woodland caribou, once native to Maine, was re-introduced to the Mt. Katahdin area in 1963. These animals—twenty-three in all—were thought to have disappeared, but have over recent seasons been seen in small numbers. No prediction can be made at this time as to the possible success of this experiment, but several animals have been observed and it is remotely possible that a herd may become established. At this time it is exceedingly important that hunters use caution in identification of big-game targets in the area.

Moose are native to Maine but have not been on the open-season list for many years. Careful, and continuing, surveys seem to indicate that the present population may be over 6000 animals. About two-thirds are in the northern deer zone. The Game Department feels that a limited, controlled season, probably with a few permits issued by drawing, is feasible. At each session of the legislature bills urging such a season are in evidence. To the date of this writing, none has been passed. It may reasonably be predicted that within the next few years a very carefully controlled moose season may be set, with an extremely limited, and experimental, number of permits available.

REGULATIONS

Game laws pertaining to seasons, bag and possession limits, areas to be hunted, special hunts, license fees all may have numerous changes from year to year. For current regulations, and for other specific queries, write to: Department of Inland Fisheries and Game, Augusta, Maine 04330.

NEW HAMPSHIRE

Although New Hampshire is a small state, with the modest total of 9304 square miles, it is one of the most scenic, with stunning mountains, swift and beautiful rivers, lakes large and small scattered everywhere, and with five-sixths of its area forested. It borders Maine in the east, with the exception of an eighteen-mile frontage in the southeast on the Atlantic. Massachusetts is to the south, placing New Hampshire near the densely populated Boston region, and not far from New York City. The western border, with Vermont, is formed within U.S. borders by the Connecticut River. But the far northern, and narrow, tip of New Hampshire pushes back the Quebec border in an uneven triangle.

The northern half of the state is ruggedly mountainous, with numerous peaks above 4000 feet, several over 5000 and at least one, Mount Washington, above 6000. Most of this portion of the state is over 2000 feet. Southward, in the broader half below large Lake Winnipesaukee, the terrain is less rugged, but with hills, and a few mountains. A preponderance of the population is here.

At present New Hampshire has upwards of 700,000 residents. The far north is sparsely settled. Because New Hampshire is blessed with tremendous sources of water power, its economy has for many years been based chiefly on manufacturing. From a hunter's viewpoint, this is in one respect fortunate: the climate, and the soil, are not conducive to concentrated agricultural use. Following manufacturing, recreational tourism is the next largest industry.

The highway system is excellent. Interstates course north clear to the Canadian border. Over all of the southern half of the state there is a heavy network of good roads. In the northern half the system diminishes. A large expanse in the center of New Hampshire is in National Forest, and here there is much wilderness. Above the Forest the several main highways continue but throughout the interior of the Forest and the far north secondaries and side trails are the hunter's access. Almost anywhere else a passenger car easily takes one to the good hunting, and in fact it will in the north, if the hunter elects to stay near easy access. But for back-country northern New Hampshire a 4WD or pickup truck is essential.

Air travel to the southern cities is adequate. In the north regular flights are few, but there are some fly-in hunting camps with charter or private planes. Air transport here is not too important anyway. The state at its widest in the south is less than 100 miles. From the southern border to Quebec is roughly 200.

Considering the amount of forest opportunities for hunting, hunter numbers are modest. A recent season showed a total of slightly more than 85,000. Of these, only 63,000 were residents, and visiting nonresidents made up a whopping 21,000-plus, or almost 25 percent of the total. Hunting is chiefly for the forest-based species, deer, black bear, ruffed grouse, woodcock.

There is also some pheasant hunting, good duck hunting, some shooting for geese. There are cottontail rabbits, snowshoe hares, gray squirrels, raccoons, woodchucks, foxes, and in one area a very few wild boars.

Although specific locations are at times overcrowded with hunters, finding a place to hunt is not difficult. Slightly more than 12 percent of the land area of New Hampshire is in public ownership. This is mostly in the White Mountain National Forest. This Forest overlaps in the east into Maine. The acreage within New Hampshire is about 600,000. The Forest runs from the eastern border almost across to the western border, and lies just north of the center of the state. Several main highways cross it: Interstate 93 (U.S. 3), State 16, U.S. 302.

This Forest is basically in two blocks, the largest one crossed by the highways mentioned. Separated to the north by U.S. 2 is another block. State 110 runs along its northern border. Key towns to the northern block are Berlin in the east, Groveton on the northwest. For the other block, Conway is near on the southeast corner, Gorham in the northeast, Plymouth to the south, Littletown and Whitefield nearby in the northwest. The headquarters of the Forest Supervisor is at Laconia. Queries requesting maps and hunting details should be directed there.

More than four million acres of New Hampshire forests of over ten square miles in size are in private ownership. Most of the vast acreage is in commercial forests, and a large percentage of these forests are open to hunting under regulations specified by the firms owning them. The bulk of this land is in the north. Some firms have printed material available about their recreational facilities. The New England Power Service Co., Public Information Director, 441 Stuart Street, Boston, Massachusetts 20016, and the St. Regis Paper Co., 150 E. 42nd Street, New York, New York 10017, are two of these. Contacts regarding commercial forests can also be made through American Forest Products Industries, 1835 K Street, NW, Washington, D.C. 20006.

There are numerous small State Forests and a number of State Parks, some of good size. Some public hunting is allowed on these lands, but not on all. It is therefore advisable for interested hunters to check directly with the Fish and Game Department, address at chapter end, regarding these lands. The total acreage, compared to other public-access lands already mentioned, is minor.

The state also has a number of Waterfowl Management Areas, many of them small, a few of good size, and on most of these hunting is allowed. They will be mentioned later under "Waterfowl." However, it is best for waterfowlers to make a last-minute check with the Department regarding these, to ascertain what regulations are currently in effect. In southern New Hampshire, where population density is highest, and where visiting hunters are likely to concentrate, there are some minor problems with posting of land. However, in most instances permission to hunt is granted to those who are courteous in their requests.

Accommodations for hunters in New Hampshire are no problem. There are numerous camps and lodges in the north, some in the south. In addition, there are plentiful motels and hotels along the highways. Camping hunters will find sites in the State Parks, State Forests, and the National Forest. Booklets titled "Family Camping in New Hampshire" and "New Hampshire State Parks" may be obtained from the Department of Economic Development, Concord 03301.

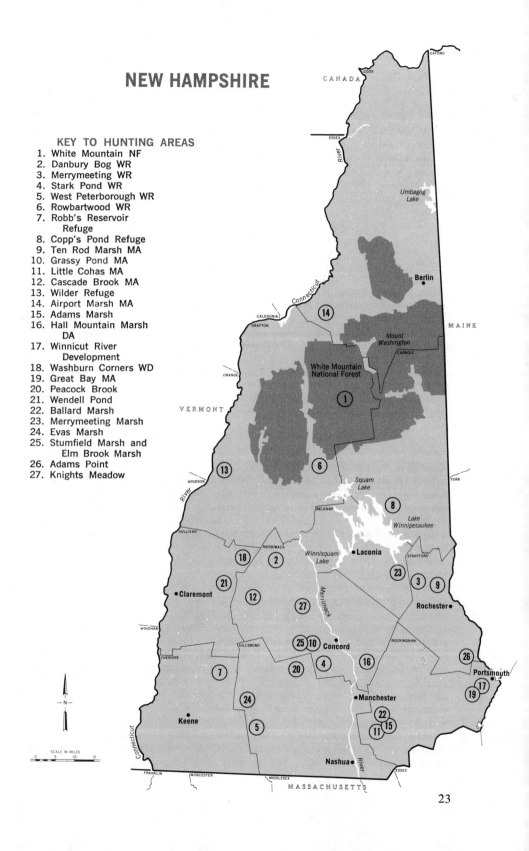

NEW HAMPSHIRE

KEY TO HUNTING AREAS

1. White Mountain NF
2. Danbury Bog WR
3. Merrymeeting WR
4. Stark Pond WR
5. West Peterborough WR
6. Rowbartwood WR
7. Robb's Reservoir Refuge
8. Copp's Pond Refuge
9. Ten Rod Marsh MA
10. Grassy Pond MA
11. Little Cohas MA
12. Cascade Brook MA
13. Wilder Refuge
14. Airport Marsh MA
15. Adams Marsh
16. Hall Mountain Marsh DA
17. Winnicut River Development
18. Washburn Corners WD
19. Great Bay MA
20. Peacock Brook
21. Wendell Pond
22. Ballard Marsh
23. Merrymeeting Marsh
24. Evas Marsh
25. Stumfield Marsh and Elm Brook Marsh
26. Adams Point
27. Knights Meadow

23

New Hampshire weather is crisp and invigorating in early fall, but as the season progresses there is snow in the mountains and it may be particularly heavy in the north. Hunters should go prepared with clothing for both mild and rather severe weather.

Arms for New Hampshire hunters should be any of the rifles of standard caliber for deer and black bear. For the very occasional wild boar, a heavy caliber is needed. These animals can be dangerous. There are special seasons for muzzle-loader hunting for deer. A .22 is a good weapon for squirrels. However, hunters should carefully check the laws. In some towns (townships) rifles may not be used. Shotgun ammunition in sizes No. 7½ and No. 6 will do for all shotgun game except ducks, sea ducks, and geese, for which No. 4s at least should be used.

RUFFED GROUSE

The ruffed grouse is the most important game bird in New Hampshire. The game department does not collect kill figures on small game, and so no indication of average seasonal bag can be given. Also, hunters must bear in mind that ruffed grouse are extremely susceptible to high and low population cycles. A poor nesting season, or a poor year for grouse food, drastically cuts the grouse population and usually it requires several seasons to build back up again. Thus, before planning a ruffed grouse hunt here it is important that a hunter check the prospects with the Game Department. Summer surveys generally give game men a good idea of what may be expected in any given season.

There is another most important consideration related to ruffed grouse. Since these are birds of the forest and forest edges, when foliage is heavy shooting is poor. It makes little difference whether the cycle is high or low. There may be many birds present, but if one can get little chance at them there may as well be few. A good example occurred during a recent New Hampshire season. Reports coming in during the week of October 15 showed foliage creating tough shooting conditions even in the far northern part of the state. The week of October 22 showed foliage conditions not a major hindrance in the northern and central portions of the state but still a hurdle toward success in the south. The following week, of October 29, indicated foliage nearly gone in the north, mostly so in the central area, but still heavy in the south. This happened to be during a season of low grouse population. However, by November 5 hunters were doing quite well in the north because of fallen leaves, even though birds were not really plentiful.

This same picture may not be presented each season. Hard early frosts can change conditions. But because New Hampshire covers several degrees of latitude north to south but is narrow east-west, foliage in any given part of the state is an important consideration. This, and the condition of the grouse cycle, can make or break a hunt.

The ruffed grouse is so well distributed over the state that it is not possible to note specific areas where the best hunting is located. During high population cycles, ruffed grouse may be found in good numbers literally anywhere one elects to hunt. So little land is posted that no problems are involved in locating a place to hunt. The White Mountain National Forest (1) and the commercial forest lands offer excellent opportunities particularly in areas where cutting has been done and mixed cover is available.

The entire state has a covering of forest, with openings and abandoned farms interspersed. Without any question the stream courses where alders and various grouse foods grow, the beech, oak, and maple woodlands which also furnish food, plus the birch and poplar forest intermingled with conifers and often with patches of wild clover, are ideal. Abandoned farms surrounded by such cover are among the best grouse habitats of all. As a general rule it is a good idea to select a hunting area away from the more heavily populated sectors. Nonetheless, southern New Hampshire has some very good grouse hunting, when the cycle is up, although it is likely to be more crowded than farther north. By and large, the northern half of the state is the best choice. Also, during the lower cycles or cycles building from low to high the north generally has the most birds. Coos County, which encompasses the upper portion of the White Mountain NF and all of the remainder of northern New Hampshire, is one of the best ruffed grouse counties, and offers season to season the least foliage trouble. For visitors who do not have contacts with local hunters, this is a good place to plan a hunt.

PHEASANT

Pheasants were introduced to southern New Hampshire in the early 1900s. There is actually little good pheasant habitat in the state and the birds are not and never have been truly successful. Nevertheless, demand by sportsmen keeps some pheasant hunting, almost entirely of released birds, available. Annual release totals from a high of around 15,000 to an average of around 10,000 birds. The major share are birds raised by the state. However, some birds are released by individuals and various groups. During a recent release state birds totaled 5100 cocks, 3600 hens. An additional 400 roosters were privately released.

At one time either sex might be shot. Presently only cocks are legal. New strains, of wilder birds, have been introduced and the present regulations are in the hope that carry-over pheasant populations of importance may occur and pockets of the birds become better established in suitable cover. What results may be in future years is questionable. At this writing the carry-over is very small and wild pheasant populations are sparse indeed.

The Merrimack River Valley gets the preponderance of the birds released. As one moves up the valley from the Massachusetts line, stocking becomes lighter. The better habitat is in the lower section. Best counties can be considered as Rockingham, Hillsboro, Merrimack. Some choice spots, however, are found farther north and west, in Sullivan and Grafton Cos., and in the central region. The southwestern county, Cheshire, also gets some birds.

QUAIL

The New Hampshire game laws as this is written continue year after year to list the bobwhite quail as a game species, with a two-month season, and a 5-a-day bag limit. Hunters should not be misled. New Hampshire has no quail hunting. Some years ago quail were tried. They were not successful. The project was abandoned. The continued listing of the species, apparently, is to inform hunters that if they happen to find remnant flocks still hanging on it is legal to hunt them, but with restrictions as noted in the law.

SPRUCE GROUSE

This bird is mentioned here only as a caution to readers that they do exist, but are not legal game at this time. The spruce grouse, a dark-meated grouse of relatively the same size as the ruffed grouse, is fairly common in northern New Hampshire. It is invariably found in association with the tree for which it is named, and in dense and often boggy stands. Presently there is no open season and none at this time is planned. The overall appearance of the male bird is darker than the average ruffed grouse. The female is lighter.

WILD TURKEYS

Early settlers found plentiful wild turkeys in what is now New Hampshire. But by the late 1800s the birds had been exterminated. Agriculture as well as hunting had played an important part. Early settlement and continuing settlement destroyed all but about 15 percent of the primeval forest. But in this century, with changing land uses and a streamlined agriculture, New Hampshire could not compete and so today the state is back to approximately 85 percent forest, or right where it was when the wild turkey was abundant.

Sentiment has been strong to reestablish the wild turkey. Conditions seem most favorable. Several years ago New Hampshire conceived the idea of trading some of its species that are rare elsewhere for wild turkeys. Eventually a deal was made with West Virginia. The trade was to be for fishers from New Hampshire, where they are still fairly common in the northern area, so that they might be tried in the mountains of West Virginia. The first of the wild turkeys arrived in New Hampshire in late February of 1969. More have been brought in since. While no predictions can as yet be made, and no hunting is even remotely in sight, there is a very good possibility that within the coming decade the wild turkey may get a solid foothold and once more appear on the hunting list.

WOODCOCK

The woodcock is avidly hunted in New Hampshire, and is second in importance only to the ruffed grouse among game birds. There are a substantial number of resident nesting birds, and the state is on the migration route for birds moving south from Canada and some southwest from Maine. As with other game birds, and small game, the state has no kill figures available.

Woodcock are very common throughout all of New Hampshire, especially along the stream courses and in moist places around abandoned farms that have good overhead cover and open ground cover. Incidentally, hunters should beware of the foliage problem (see "Ruffed Grouse"). Also, hunting after the leaves fall is usually better anyway because frosts drive the flight birds down and this is the time when the top shooting is available literally statewide.

By and large there are two portions of New Hampshire best for a planned woodcock hunt. These are the seacoast area and the northern counties, particularly Coos. The leaves fall earlier in the north, and generally about when the big flights pour in. Thus, a plan to hit the northern sector during the migration is the very best that can be made. The Game Department's local Conservation Officers are the most important contacts for setting up such a hunt. They know almost exactly when flight birds will appear and precisely where the most will be found. A list of these officers can be obtained from the Department, address at end of chapter. The best of the woodcock hunting is without question dependent upon being there at the right time. This is not predictable, season to season, but as a rule will fall sometime between mid-October and November 1.

SNIPE AND RAILS

Jacksnipe are available in most of the waterfowling marshes and along creeks and around beaver ponds. There is very little hunting interest. See "Waterfowl" for possible locations.

Some rail hunting is occasionally available. This is an unimportant variety of hunting for two reasons: New Hampshire has a short coastline and thus rail hunting in marine marshes is extremely restricted; there is not always a rail season. At this writing a fall has just passed with no rail hunting offered by federal regulations. It is doubtful even during open seasons if more than a scattering of birds are killed as incidentals by hunters after other game.

WATERFOWL

Waterfowl hunting can be quite good in New Hampshire, particularly for the experienced native who knows the waterways well. However, this cannot be considered as a great waterfowl state. The black duck and the wood duck are the two most important species. There are also goldeneyes. These three species nest in the state. More of the same, and other species such as mallards, migrate through.

New Hampshire has a tremendous amount of water in lakes and streams, and on the smaller streams especially there are, scattered everywhere over the state, hundreds of beaver ponds. These and the streams furnish some of the most important waterfowling. Jump-shooting on the streams, for blacks and wood ducks, is a prime sport. Making a "sneak" from beaver pond to beaver pond is also a common method, and effective, but requires a very intimate knowledge of the hunting area.

The New Hampshire coastline is brief. But fortunately Great Bay, Little Bay, and the estuarine region there near Portsmouth form a perfect resting and feeding place for waterfowl. This is one of the state's best locations for black duck hunting, and there is some goose shooting here, too. A good many geese stop in the bays, but they are extremely wary here, and goose hunting is not easy, nor is the kill high. Some cornfield shooting and blind shooting for miles on up the tributary rivers is available. Again, this requires a good local knowledge of conditions, or else a guide.

Sea duck shooting, for scoters, eiders, etc., often called "coot" in New England, is good during the migration at several places along the short New Hampshire coastline. The Hampton Beach area is one of the best. This is down almost to the Massachusetts line. There is also more of the same in Great Bay. Brant are also found along the coast and in the Bay region. During proper flights there is good brant shooting in the same places as for sea ducks.

Quickly reviewing duck shooting from north to south, in the north, which means Coos Co., best is to be had along the beaver flowages which can be sought out along any of the streams, and as a rule on and around Umbagog Lake. This lake is on the border with, and partially in, Maine. State 16 and 26 take one close to it. In the central region, good duck shooting can be found along the Connecticut River, which is the border with Vermont, and also in numerous of the interior lakes. The entire area in which lie huge Lake Winnipesaukee, Squam Lake, and Winnisquam Lake is one of the best spots. There have been, lately, special restrictions on Winnisquam. Hunters should check before shooting. In the south the small lakes and the beaver ponds offer shooting, and in the southeast the estuarine and marine possibilities have already been noted.

The hundreds of beaver ponds are among the most important waterfowl resting and breeding—and hunting—locations in the state. To help keep them so, the state has fashioned structures that assure keeping the ponds in proper condition to serve as waterfowl habitat. During past years well over a hundred such projects have been completed. Local conservation officers can direct hunters unfamiliar with the area to any of these.

In addition there are at least twenty-seven Waterfowl Management Areas built and operated by the state. Some of these are refuges. Most are small. The smallest has only one and a half acres flooded. The largest has slightly under a square mile flooded. However, most, but not all, have a surrounding land area. It is best to check the list with the Department to make certain hunting is allowed, and precisely where. Also, other varieties of hunting may be available on surrounding lands. A list of these Management Areas is given below with their map key numbers. The portion of the state and the nearby village is listed for each.

WATERFOWL MANAGEMENT AREA	AREA	NEAREST TOWN
2. Danbury Bog Waterfowl Refuge	West-central	Danbury
3. Merrymeeting Waterfowl Refuge	East-central	New Durham
4. Stark Pond Waterfowl Refuge	South-central	Dunbarton
5. West Peterborough Refuge	Southwest	Peterborough
6. Rowbartwood Waterfowl Refuge	West-central	Campton
7. Robb's Reservoir Refuge	Southwest	Stoddard
8. Copp's Pond Refuge	Central	Melvin Village
9. Ten Rod Marsh Management Area	Southeast	Farmington
10. Grassy Pond Management Area	South-central	Hopkinton
11. Little Cohas Management Area	Extreme south-central	Londonderry
12. Cascade Brook Management Area	Southwest	Sutton
13. Wilder Refuge	West-central	Lyme
14. Airport Marsh Management Area	Upper west-central	Whitefield
15. Adams Marsh	Southeast	Derry
16. Hall Mt. Marsh Dev. Area	Southwest	Allenstown
17. Winnicut River Dev.	Southeast, near coast	Greenland
18. Washburn Corners Waterfowl Dev.	Upper southwest	Springfield
19. Great Bay Waterfowl Management	Southeast, near coast	Greenland
20. Peacock Brook	Southwest	Weare
21. Wendell Pond	Upper southwest	Sunapee
22. Ballard Marsh	Southeast	Derry
23. Merrymeeting Marsh	East-central	Alton Dam (Alton)
24. Evas Marsh	Southwest	Hancock
25. Stumpfield Marsh and Elm Brook Marsh	South-central	Hopkinton
26. Adams Point	Southeast	Durham
27. Knights Meadow	Upper southwest	Webster

Hunters should also check Corps of Engineers public lands, for ducks and also for grouse, woodcock, pheasants, in the Blackwater Dam region near Concord, south-central, and the Surry Mountain Dam area near Keene, southwest.

DEER

Whitetail deer are plentiful in New Hampshire and avidly hunted with good success. The kill averages from about 10,000 to 14,000 annually. There is hunting (check regulations) for either sex. Bucks make up over half the kill, usually running about 100 more than does. However, in some seasons the figures are almost even. The season is statewide. Prior to the general season there is a brief muzzle-loader season. Earlier there is a special archery season. All kills in any season must be checked in at the nearest registration station. There are other special pertinent regulations. Drives are limited to no more than six persons, deer may not be killed on islands except as specified, and in certain towns (townships) no rifles may be used. Uniquely, there is a special season on Long Island, Lake Winnipesaukee, for paraplegics.

Deer hunting is good over the entire state. Average kill per square mile throughout the state is from 1 to 1.50 or better. For some seasons Grafton Co., which encompasses the western central part of the state, has had the highest kill. It runs from over 2000 to as high as 3215 in one recent season. The three northern counties—Grafton, Carroll to the east of it, and Coos taking in all of the far north—consistently furnish well over half the kill for the entire state. There are ten counties in the state. Note that all of the White Mountain NF is within these three counties. Thus, finding a place to hunt, in the Forest or on commercial forest lands of the north, presents no difficulties.

In order to spot deer concentrations within counties, it is important to check the towns (townships) with highest kill per square mile. While these do not remain the same season to season, several are fairly consistent. Almost without fail the highest are located within the three northern counties. In Coos Co., Dummer township is usually one of the top locations. The kill per square mile in one recent season was 4.81, a total of 232 deer! Also in Coos Co., the following towns have recently furnished exceptionally high kills, from 3.00 to almost 4.00 per square mile: Green's Grant, Jefferson, Lancaster, Whitefield. During the same season, in Grafton Co., those towns with 3.00 or over were as follows: Bath, Canaan, Haverhill, Monroe (usually very high season after season and during this illustrative one 4.98), Orford (another consistently exceptional township). In Carroll Co.: Madison, Moultonboro, Ossipee, Tuftonboro were the high ones. Ossipee is one of the consistently high concentration points here.

BEAR

Black bear are fairly common in the northern part of the state. Almost the entire kill comes from Coos, Grafton, and Carroll counties. Kills in other counties are negligible, from 1 to 5 per county on the average. Of the three counties, generally Grafton and Coos are somewhat higher than Carroll, and over four recent consecutive seasons, Grafton was highest in three seasons, with kills of 54, 80, 123, and 82 during the four hunts. Coos Co. ran: 31, 64, 90, 91. Carroll was: 23, 55, 65, 56. These figures give a rather good picture of bear hunting in New Hampshire.

Hunting with a guide and dogs is probably the most consistently successful method, although more bear are killed as incidentals during deer season. The Game Department can assist hunters in locating guides with dog packs. Studies show that the highest kills come during November. This is without question because so many deer hunters are then in the woods, due to a November deer opening. Over two seasons just prior to this writing, 179 out of 199 kills and 90 out of 106 kills were by deer hunters during November.

Kills by towns do not remain very consistent within these high-kill counties. Best bet is to check prior to planning with local Conservation officers within one of the three counties. As a rule they will know where concentrations may be. In addition, some interesting and important food studies have been done in New Hampshire. For some years now a pattern of heavy utilization of beechnuts during even-numbered years and apples during odd-numbered years has occurred. This is probably because of weather patterns which produced the good crops. Apples in one season made up 46 percent of the food. Apples, beechnuts, and acorns are primary food sources for bear here. The animals, fattening in fall before winter hibernation, are certain to be found in proximity to whichever food source is most abundant. In poor food years, bear depredations are more severe and many are found hanging around forest-farm boundaries where livestock may be raided.

WILD BOAR

Some years ago some wild boars escaped from a New Hampshire private preserve in Sullivan Co. They are legal game, with no closed season or bag limit, although a hunting license is required. These animals are exceedingly scarce. Very occasionally, one is taken with dogs. However, chances of success on a hunt are slim indeed and it is difficult to find a bear guide with dogs who is willing to chance a boar killing or maiming his dogs.

MOOSE AND ELK

There is a small and steadily growing moose population in northern New Hampshire. It is estimated that there may be as many as 300 animals. There is no open season. To date there is no official sentiment for trying a controlled token hunt, and no hunt is likely to materialize in the foreseeable future.

Elk are mentioned in the law digest with the notation "no open season." There are apparently no elk roaming free in New Hampshire, but there are some on a private preserve.

SMALL GAME

The most important small-game animal is the snowshoe hare, which wears a white coat in winter. It is abundant throughout the northern part of the state, particularly in areas where coniferous swamps offer dense winter cover. There is no difficulty in finding a place to hunt in the National Forest or the commercial forests. Coos Co. probably offers the highest hare populations.

Cottontails are plentiful throughout the southern part of the state. There is no great hunter interest. Most hunters prefer the much larger snowshoe, chiefly because it does not hole up when chased as does the cottontail.

In suitable forest areas of the south there are fair gray squirrel populations. However, squirrels are by no means abundant and New Hampshire hunters are not much interested in squirrel hunting. Coos and Carroll counties allow no open season.

OTHER ANIMALS

Foxes are fairly plentiful throughout the state. A few gray foxes are taken in the south. Red foxes are the dominant species. Some fox hunting is done with dogs. Fox calling is not so far practiced widely, but could be most effective.

Bobcats are quite common, particularly in wilderness pockets and dense evergreen swamps in the snowshoe hare range. They are most often hunted with hounds, and there is presently a bounty on them. Very occasionally a lynx is taken with hounds in the northern mountains.

There may be a few wolves left in the extreme north, but they are exceedingly scarce, if any exist at all. They are not protected. Some years ago it is believed that coyotes pushed their way far enough east to get a foothold in New Hampshire and some, according to common belief in New Hampshire, have crossed with dogs and are called "coy-dogs." Some biologists have even identified the animals as three-way crosses, of wolf, coyote, and dog. A few have been killed when caught marauding livestock.

Woodchucks are fairly plentiful and there is a fair interest in hunting them. There is no closed season. The Connecticut River Valley is considered perhaps the best area of the state for this endeavor.

There are also abundant raccoons. In fact, they have reached pest proportions in some parts of the state, even though there is a long hunting season (with dogs) and a trapping season. Some farmers have urged that raccoons be bountied. Game personnel are extremely cool to the suggestion, for bounties have never proven worthwhile.

REGULATIONS

Game laws pertaining to seasons, bag and possession limits, areas to be hunted, special hunts, license fees all may have numerous changes from year to year. For current regulations, and for other specific queries, write to: Fish and Game Department, 34 Bridge Street, Concord, New Hampshire 03301.

VERMONT

Vermont is a small state, but it makes up in handsome mountain scenery what it may lack in size. The state is long and narrow, almost like a wedge thrust down from the north between New York State and New Hampshire and blunted against Massachusetts in the south. The northern border is with Quebec. The top of the wedge is roughly 130 miles wide, the bottom little more than 50. But from north to south the straight-line distance is about 230 miles.

The striking topographic feature of Vermont is its backbone, the Green Mountains, running north-south from border to border, with a number of peaks over 4000 feet. From the top of the rugged and forested backbone the land slopes steeply down on the east to the Connecticut River, which forms all of the eastern boundary. The west slope drops to become at last a kind of plain along the shores of large, long Lake Champlain, which forms about two-thirds of the western border.

Of Vermont's 9609 square miles, roughly 60 percent is forested. In fact, forest industries, including the renowned maple syrup, plus the quarrying of its famed granite and marble, are economically among the most important activities in the state. Mountain-based recreation, especially skiing, has also brought fame and fortune to Vermont.

Small villages are scattered everywhere across the southern half of the state, and though the northern half is well settled the preponderance of population is in the south. Considering its nearness to the high-density population centers of the east, however, Vermont is still uncrowded and rural, and this is readily reflected in the quality of hunting available. Total population is slightly below half a million. There is still plenty of room, and there is an astonishing amount of back-country wilderness.

Roads are excellent throughout the state, with several U.S. and Interstate highways supplying fast travel all the way to the northern border. Air transport to the larger cities is adequate, but few hunters will need it in a state of this modest size. Although most of the best hunting of all kinds can be reached by passenger car, for those who wish to explore the rugged mountains and get away from the crowd a short-coupled 4WD vehicle is prime equipment.

Hunting is extremely popular. Roughly 25 percent of the entire population —over 100,000 residents—buy hunting licenses each fall. This indicates that the adult hunter percentage is still higher. Interest by nonresidents reflects quality of the hunting, too. An additional 35,000 visit Vermont each season, most of them for the top-notch deer hunting. There is also good hunting for black bear, for ruffed grouse, woodcock, snowshoe hares, and cottontails. There are gray squirrels, ducks, geese, pheasants. Raccoons and foxes are plentiful, and there are bobcats scattered through the forests. Deer, grouse, hares are the primary targets, with the black bear in a trophy class of its own.

Finding a place to hunt is not difficult. The largest expanse of public land

33

is in the handsome Green Mountain National Forest (1). There are almost 235,000 acres here, lying across the backbone in southern and central Vermont. The Forest is not in a solid block. It begins well above central Vermont and reaches southward to a short distance above Rutland. It begins again some miles south of Rutland and reaches in scattered tracts south to the border. Nearby towns, reading from north to south are: Waterbury, Middlebury, Rochester, Brandon, Rutland, Manchester. The Forest headquarters is at Rutland, and maps and details are obtainable there from the Forest Supervisor.

Commercial forests cover nearly 3.5 million acres in Vermont. Ownership is in small part in public lands, somewhat larger among forest industry. Farmer ownership, though sizable, is steadily dropping. The remainder is in various private ownership. Large lumber and paper firms own about half a million acres. Numerous small firms own anywhere up to 10,000 acres individually. Most of this land is open to hunting, but many small firms, while not discouraging such use, do not publicly encourage it. Printed material dealing with some of these lands is available from: St. Regis Paper Co., West Stewardstown, N.Y.; International Paper Co., Glen Falls, N.Y.; Brown Paper Co., Berlin, N.H.; New England Electric, Concord, N.H. Some other firms that may be able to answer queries: Glastonbury Timber Lands, Bennington, Vt.; Atlas Plywood, Morris-

KEY TO HUNTING AREAS

1. Green Mountain NF
2. Missisquoi NWR
3. L. R. Jones SF
4. Camels Hump SF
5. Putnam SF
6. Mount Mansfield SF
7. Groton SF
8. Roxbury SF
9. Lyndon SF
10. Mathewsen SF
11. Maidstone SF
12. Jay SF
13. Willoughby SF;
    Willoughby WMA
14. Washington SF
15. Thetford Hill SF
16. Charles Downer SF
17. Proctor Piper SF
18. Coolidge SF
19. Williams River SF
20. Okemo SF
21. Hapgood SF
22. Arlington SF
23. Emerald Lake SF
24. Rupert SF
25. Townshend SF
26. Grafton SF; William C.
    Putnam SF;
    J. J. Durand SF
27. Aitken SF
28. West Rutland SF
29. Mount Carmel SF
30. Darling SP
31. Hagens Notch SP
32. Elmore SP
33. Monroe SP
34. Brighton SP
35. Grand Isle SP
36. Lake Carmi SP
37. North Hero SP
38. Ainsworth SP
39. Granville Gulf SP
40. Allis SP
41. Button Bay SP
42. Mount Philco SP
43. Gifford Woods SP
44. Wilgus SP;
    Ascutney SP
45. Molly Stark SP
46. Emerald Lake SP
47. Bomoseen SP
48. Fort Dummer SP
49. Woodford SP
50. Howe Pond SP
51. Mud Creek WMA
52. Little Otter WMA
53. South Bay WMA
54. Fairfield Swamp WMA
55. Sand Bar WMA
56. Dead Creek WMA
57. Cornwall Swamp WMA
58. Pond Woods WMA
59. Whipple Hollow WMA
60. Otter Creek WMA
61. Rock Landing WMA
62. DAR SP
63. Burton Island SP
64. Maquam Bay WMA
65. East Creek WMA
66. Richville WMA
67. South Stream WMA
68. Fred Johnson WMA;
    Lewis Creek WMA
69. Snake Mountain WMA
70. Stamford Meadow
    WMA
71. Bald Hill WMA
72. Calendar Brook WMA
73. Roy Mountain WMA
74. Levi Pond WMA
75. Robbins Mountain
    WMA
76. Huntington Gap WMA
77. Hurricane WMA
78. Elm Brook WMA
79. Gilson Mountain WMA
80. Averys Gore WMA
81. East Hill WMA;
    East Hill PHA
82. Wild Branch WMA
83. Washington WMA
84. Malmquist WMA;
    Clover Hill WMA
85. Howe PHA
86. West Fairlee WMA
87. Willoughby Falls WMA
88. Pittsford PHA
89. Brandon Swamp WMA
90. Vernon WMA;
    Vernon PHA
91. Atherton Meadow
    WMA
92. Les Newell WMA;
    Les Newell PHA
93. Reading-Plymouth
    WMA
94. Hawk Mountain WMA
95. Ottauquechee WMA
96. White River WMA
97. Skitchewaug WMA
98. Rochester WMA
99. Little Ascutney WMA;
    Little Ascutney
    PHA; Weathersfield
    WMA

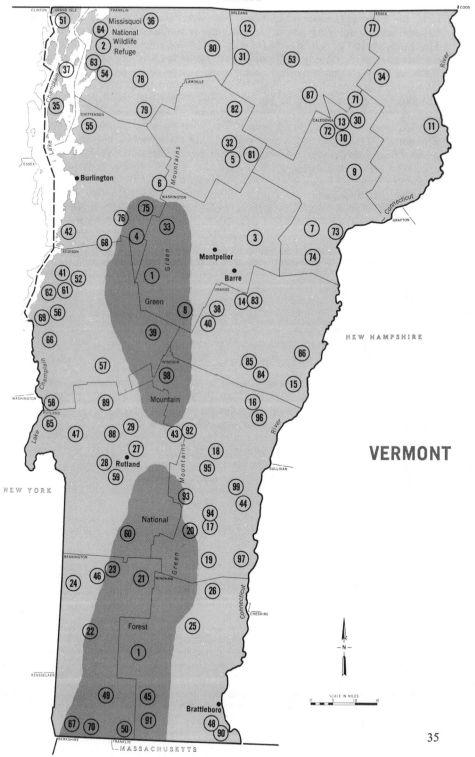

CANADA

CLINTON GRAND ISLE FRANKLIN ORLEANS ESSEX COOS

⑤① ③⑥

⑥④ Missisquoi ①② ⑦⑦
② National
Wildlife ⑧⓪ ③① ⑤③
⑥③ Refuge
③⑦ ⑤④ ③④
⑦⑧ LAMOILLE ⑧⑦ ⑦①
③⑤ ⑦⑨ CALEDONIA ①③ ③⓪
CHITTENDEN ⑧② ⑦② ①①
⑤⑤ ①⓪
③② ⑨
⑤ ⑧①
● Burlington ⑥
WASHINGTON
⑦⑤ Connecticut
⑦⑥ ③③ GRAFTON
④② ④ ⑦ ⑦③
⑥⑧ ③
ADDISON ● Montpelier ⑦④
① ● Barre
④① ⑤② Green ORANGE ①④ ⑧③
⑥② ⑥① ⑧ ③⑧
⑥⑨ ⑤⑥ ③⑨ ④⓪ NEW HAMPSHIRE
⑥⑥ ⑧⑥
⑤⑦ WINDSOR ⑧⑤
⑨⑧ ⑧④
WASHINGTON Mountain ①⑤
⑤⑧ ⑧⑨ ①⑥
RUTLAND ⑨⑥
⑥⑤ ④⑦ ②⑨ ④③ ⑨②
⑧⑧ ①⑧
②⑦ ⑨⑤
②⑧ Rutland
⑤⑨ ⑨⑨
NEW YORK ⑨③ ④④
National ⑨④
⑥⓪ ①⑦
②⓪
BENNINGTON ①⑨ ⑨⑦
②④ ④⑥ ②③ ②① WINDHAM
②⑥
②② Forest ②⑤ CHESHIRE

VERMONT

① Connecticut

②④ ④⑥ ②③ ②①

④⑨ ④⑤
⑥⑦ ⑦⓪ ⑤⓪ ⑨① ● Brattleboro
BERKSHIRE FRANKLIN ④⑧
—M A S S A C H U S E T T S ⑨⓪

— N —

SCALE IN MILES
0 5 10 15

35

ville, Vt.; Ward Lumber Co., Waterbury, Vt.; Bardill Land and Lumber, Wolcott, Vt.; A. Johnson Co., Bristol, Vt.; Groveton Paper Co., Groveton, N.H.; Franconia Paper Co., Lincoln, N.H.

There are several types of state-owned public lands. Fully controlled by the Fish and Game Department are some forty-eight Wildlife Management Areas with a total of almost 60,000 acres. Other lands with leased rights or other state management are called Public Hunting Areas. There are about 6000 acres in these. Lands under control of the Department of Forests and Parks are State Forests, open to hunting, and portions of State Parks also open to hunting. These total about 120,000 acres. Some WMAs are within the above lands, managed on a cooperative basis between the two departments. As this is written, a detailed brochure showing all state lands open to hunting is soon to appear, obtainable from the Fish and Game Department.

There is also some hunting for the public at the 4226-acre Missisquoi National Wildlife Refuge (2) in the extreme northwest, on the shore of Lake Champlain, Franklin Co. Waterfowl, upland game, and deer are hunted, but the open portions vary from season to season so anyone planning a trip there should contact the Refuge Headquarters, Swanton, ahead of time. Especially in the less populous north, obtaining permission to hunt on privately owned farm and other lands is not difficult, if one makes the request politely and minds his shooting manners. Also, the large expanse of Lake Champlain and portions of its shoreline offer hunter access.

Camp-out hunters will find ample opportunity in the State Parks, in the National Forest, and in the State Forests. There are also numerous private campgrounds. Other accommodations are abundant. Vermont is well oriented toward tourism. In addition, there are a good many lodges and camps that cater especially to hunters. It is not amiss, however, to make reservations ahead for the opening of deer season, which brings many hunters into the state at one time.

Hunting-season weather in Vermont is delightful during late September and as a rule up to mid-October. It is light-wool-shirt or light-hunting-jacket weather. There will be nightly frosts, and bright, crisp days. But there can also be early storms and one is well advised to go prepared. Later in October and on through the seasons snow may be expected, and much colder weather.

Guns and ammunition requirements are quite standard. For deer and bear a rifle such as the favorite .30/30 or the .30/06 or popular calibers in that category are most common. Bird hunters, who will be after grouse and woodcock for the most part, will require No. 7½ shot or an approximation. This, or No. 6, will do for rabbits. For ducks heavier shot should be used. Hunters should check the regulations carefully as to where rifles may or may not be used.

In Vermont, townships are called "towns." In all following material please note that this local terminology will be used.

RUFFED GROUSE

The ruffed grouse is Vermont's most important game bird. It is usually called "partridge" here. Grouse are distributed throughout the state in all suitable habitats. While the Department has no harvest figures and the total average bag is thus unknown, it is considered to be high. Almost all Vermont hunters do at least some ruffed grouse hunting.

The Green Mountain National Forest is a prime range offering public access over a vast acreage. There is also some grouse hunting on the Missisquoi Refuge. Both these are described above, in chapter opening.

The State Forests all offer grouse hunting, and they are numerous. Dividing the state by north, central, and south, the State Forests are located below by county and town.

In the north are the following: Washington Co.—L. R. Jones SF (2), 642 acres, town of Plainfield; Camels Hump SF (4), .11,244 acres, in towns of Duxbury, Fayston, and Waitsfield of Washington Co., but also in towns of Bolton and Buells Gore of Chittenden Co. and Starksboro of Addison Co.; Putnam SF (5), 4239 acres, Worcester and Middlesex, and town of Elmore in Lamoille Co.; Mount Mansfield SF (6), 22,956 acres, Waterbury, but also in town of Bolton and Underhill, Chittenden Co. and towns of Stowe, Morristown, Johnson in Lamoille Co.; Groton SF (7), 20,026 acres, Marshfield, and also in towns of Peacham and Groton in Caledonia Co.; Roxbury SF (8), 4197 acres, Roxbury.

Caledonia Co.—Lyndon SF (9), 80 acres, Lyndon; Mathewsen SF (10), 589 acres, Sutton and Wheelock. Essex Co.—Maidstone SF (11), 469 acres, Maidstone. Orleans Co.—Jay SF (12), 1110 acres, Jay and Westfield; Willoughby SF and WMA (13), 5360 acres, Sutton, Westmore.

Located in the central part of the state are the following: Orange Co.— Washington SF (14), 392 acres, Washington; Thetford Hill SF (15), 262 acres, Thetford.

In the southern counties there are these State Forests: Windsor Co.— Charles Downer SF (16), 705 acres, Sharon; Proctor Piper SF (17), 1557 acres, Cavendish; Coolidge SF (18), 11,667 acres in towns of Bridgewater, Reading, Plymouth, Woodstock of Windsor Co., but also in towns of Shrewsbury and Sherburne in Rutland Co.; Williams River SF (19), 108 acres, Chester; Okemo SF (20), 4513 acres, Ludlow, but also in town of Mount Holly of Rutland Co.

Bennington Co.—Hapgood SF (21), 118 acres, Peru; Arlington SF (22), 225 acres, Arlington; Emerald Lake SF (23), 510 acres, Dorset; Rupert SF (24), 336 acres, Rupert. Windham Co.—Townshend SF (25), 856 acres, Townshend; Grafton SF, 203 acres, Grafton; Wm. C. Putnam SF, 148 acres, Grafton; J. J. Durand SF, 560 acres, Grafton and Rockingham (26). Rutland Co.—Aitken SF (27), 918 acres, Mendon; West Rutland SF (28), 344 acres, West Rutland; Mount Carmel SF (29), 263 acres, town of Chittenden.

As noted in the first portion of the chapter, a number of State Parks allow hunting. There are restrictions around the developed portions, but the other parts open to hunting are plainly marked. Grouse are found in all.

In the north are the following: Darling SP (30), 1076 acres, towns of Kirby and Burke, Caledonia Co.; Hagens Notch SP (31), 197 acres, town of Westfield, Orleans Co.; Elmore SP (32), 545 acres, town of Elmore, Lamoille Co.; Monroe SP (33), 228 acres, town of Duxbury, Washington Co.; Brighton SP (34), 152 acres, town of Brighton, Essex Co.; Grand Isle SP (35), 226 acres, town and county of Grand Isle; Lake Carmi SP (36), 445 acres, town and county of Franklin; North Hero SP (37), 399 acres, town of North Hero, Grand Isle Co.

The central counties have the following State Parks: Ainsworth SP (38), 884 acres, towns of Williamstown and Brookfield, Orange Co.; Granville Gulf SP (39), 1171 acres, town of Granville, Addison Co.; Allis SP (40), 487 acres, town of Brookfield, Orange Co.; Button Bay SP (41), 236 acres, town of Ferrisburg, Addison Co.

In the south, the State Parks with grouse hunting are: Mount Philco SP (42), 163 acres, town of Charlotte, Chittenden Co.; Gifford Woods SP (43), 112 acres, town of Sherburne, Rutland Co.; Wilgus SP, 121 acres, town of Weathersfield, Windsor Co. and Ascutney SP (44), 1779 acres, towns of Windsor and Weathersfield, Windsor Co.; Molly Stark SP (45), 158 acres, town of Wilmington, Windham Co.; Emerald Lake SP (46), not to be confused with State Forest of like name, 462 acres, town of Dorset, Bennington Co.; Bomoseen SP (47), 1190 acres, towns of Castleton and Hubbardton, Rutland Co.; Fort Dummer SP (48), 207 acres, towns of Vernon and Guilford, Windham Co.; Woodford SP (49), 400 acres, town of Woodford, Bennington Co.; Howe Pond SP (50), 266 acres, Readsboro town, Bennington Co.

As stated earlier, the WMAs are numerous, and there are a few PHAs (see opening for designation). All but a few of these are managed primarily for deer, with resultant good grouse habitat as a bonus. Thus, all of these public tracts described under "Deer" (which see) offer grouse hunting also. Three not notable for deer are mentioned below.

The Mud Creek WMA (51), of 1050 acres, is primarily for waterfowl but has a scattering of grouse. It is in the town of Alburg, Grand Isle Co., in the extreme northwest. The Little Otter WMA (52), 1150 acres, has good grouse hunting, is in the town of Ferrisburg, in Addison Co., west-central part of state. South Bay WMA (53), of 650 acres, is primarily for waterfowl, has some grouse. It is in the town of Coventry, Orleans Co., in the north.

PHEASANT

Vermont has no wild, self-sustaining pheasant population. There is some shooting for a modest number of birds game-farm reared and released, most of them on some of the Management Areas. This is strictly "put-and-take" hunting, with virtually no carryover. The kill is estimated to average about 2500 birds each season. Most of the hunting is in the Champlain Valley region. Although in the past it was hoped pheasants might establish themselves, there appears little hope that they ever will.

Pheasants are occasional on the following public lands covered under "Grouse": West Rutland SF (south); Bomoseen SP (south); Button Bay SP (central); Grand Isle SP and North Hero SP (north); Little Otter WMA, Addison Co., west central.

Although none of the WMAs or PHAs are primarily pheasant hunting grounds, some of them offer fair shooting each fall. Fairfield Swamp WMA (54), 1200 acres, is one, located in the towns of St. Albans, Swanton, Fairfield, in Franklin Co. in the northwest. Sand Bar WMA (55), with 300 acres open to hunting and a waterfowl refuge of 1300 closed, is in the town of Milton, Chittenden Co., in the southwest. Dead Creek WMA (56), chiefly for waterfowl and with a closed refuge portion, has approximately 2500 acres open to hunting, with pheasants stocked. It is in the towns of Addison, Panton, Bridport, in Addison Co., west-central. The Cornwall Swamp WMA (57), 1350 acres, towns of Salisbury and Cornwall, is also in Addison Co. Pond Woods WMA (58) has 2000 acres in the towns of Benson and Orwell, on the border between Addison and Rutland Cos. Whipple Hollow WMA (59), 500 acres, is in Rutland Co., towns of Pittsford and West Rutland. Otter Creek WMA (60) has slightly over 1000 acres in Mount Tabor and Danby towns, Rutland Co. Rock Landing WMA (61) is small, 135 acres, town of Ferrisburg, Addison Co.

Hunters interested in pheasants should check each season with the Department to ascertain where releases are to be made.

QUAIL AND CHUKAR

At this writing the Vermont game regulations still list quail, with a season, bag, and possession limit. There are no quail in Vermont. This fact is noted here to avoid confusion for hunters.

HUNGARIAN PARTRIDGE

Some Huns have apparently drifted into Grand Isle County in the north-west, and perhaps into other Vermont locations, from New York State and Canada. There is at this time no open season on these birds. The small population appears to be expanding, and the Department is currently interested in monitoring growth of the nucleus and in possibly launching a program to assist it. Forecast at this time is that a season is not to be expected in the near future.

WILD TURKEYS

The wild turkey situation in Vermont might well confuse hunters reading regulations that may not be completely up to date. At least until very recently the wild turkey was listed with an open season and bag limit. Presumably this was because certain clubs and individuals had attempted to stock wild turkeys, and those birds—if any—found on public lands came under state regulation. Vermont is probably marginal turkey habitat at best, and the private stockings have produced no results. Officially the Department claimed there were no wild turkeys in Vermont until the winter of 1968–69, when seventeen wild-trapped birds were brought in. The plan at that time was to keep a closed season at least until about 1974.

SNIPE AND RAILS

Good concentrations of snipe, and in places of rails, occur in lowlands of the Champlain Valley in fall. The upland edges of waterways in Franklin, Grand Isle, and Addison Cos. offer good shooting, but there is almost no interest among local or visiting hunters in either species. A handful of specialists pursue these sports. More might.

WOODCOCK

Vermont has an excellent local woodcock population, and a good fall flight from the north in addition. Though no harvest figures are available, the woodcock is exceedingly popular and the annual bag substantial. Birds are well distributed over the state during the season, although the northern counties may have an edge when the heavy fall migration begins from Canada.

In all suitable places in the Green Mountain NF, such as around ponds, along streams and timber edges and openings, woodcock hunting is good. The Missisquoi Refuge also furnishes some woodcock shooting on its open upland acreage. With very few exceptions all of the State Forests and State Parks located under "Grouse" offer woodcock hunting. So do Little Otter and South Bay WMAs under "Grouse." As most shooters know well, woodcock and grouse are very commonly found in similar coverts. Under "Pheasant," Fairfield Swamp, Cornwall Swamp, Pond Woods, Whipple Hollow, Otter Creek, Rock Landing WMAs all have most seasons better woodcock than pheasant shooting.

Practically all of the WMAs and PHAs where deer are the primary game offer, as mentioned under "Grouse," fine small-game hunting. This is particularly true of grouse and woodcock. Since all of these tracts will be covered under that heading, see "Deer" for numerous additional good woodcocking grounds.

WATERFOWL

Compared to kills in numerous other states, the harvest of ducks and geese in Vermont is not high. The duck bag averages around 20,000, geese 500. There is a small flock of captive geese at Dead Creek Waterfowl Area and WMA in

Addison Co., and their returning progeny are slowly building up a flock. There is a fair to good goose flight early in fall along Lake Champlain, with flocks stopping on farms to feed and resting in marshes.

In the Lake Champlain region duck hunting is on the average better than elsewhere in the state. Access to these waters is open to hunters. There is also good jump-shooting along the streams and around the many beaver ponds. The Lake Memphremagog region along the northern central border, with several large rivers emptying into this lake shared with Canada, is one of the better duck hunting locations. Much good hunting is also to be found along the Connecticut River, which forms the eastern boundary.

The small (85-acre) DAR State Park (62), Addison Co., town of Addison, furnishes some waterfowling. So does Lake Carmi SP ("Grouse"). Burton Island (63), a 253-acre State Park in the north, town of St. Albans, Franklin Co. is primarily a waterfowl spot. Under "Pheasant" several WMAs primarily for waterfowl or with at least some waterfowling were noted: Fairfield Swamp; Sand Bar; Dead Creek, Cornwall Swamp; Rock Landing. Mud Creek WMA, Little Otter WMA, South Bay WMA under "Grouse" also are waterfowl areas.

Four WMAs not so far covered are set up as waterfowl management tracts. Maquam Bay WMA (64) contains 368 acres, town of Swanton, Franklin Co. The 830-acre East Creek WMA (65) is in Orwell and Benson towns on the border between Rutland and Addison Cos. Richville WMA (66) has 200 acres in Shoreham and Bridport towns, Addison Co. And South Stream WMA (67) is a 130-acre shooting site, town of Pownal, Bennington Co. in the southwest. The Vermont Department of Water Resources has at least two flood-control dams forming pools that furnish some duck hunting. These are Wrightsville, and Waterbury.

CARIBOU, ELK, MOOSE

These animals are usually mentioned in the game laws as having closed seasons. To avoid confusion hunters should know that Vermont has no elk, and just possibly never did have. Woodland caribou were recorded as visitors to the north over a century ago. No plans are in progress for programs with either species. There are a very few moose. The present estimate is twenty-five. It is doubtful that there will ever be a moose season.

DEER

Vermont is an excellent deer hunting state. In fact, it has deer problems, with too many deer. In 1966 first attempts were made toward control, with a season of antlerless deer. It was estimated that year that Vermont had 25 deer per square mile of land area, and a state herd, in this small state, of at least 250,000. The buck kill that season was almost 18,000, and more than 2500 additional deer were harvested during the antlerless season. The following year adult buck kill was 16,425 and antlerless season accounted for about 5000 more. Each year also Vermont has a deer kill by resident owners of farmland, under statutory rights, of 500 to 700 animals. The 1968 season was about like the foregoing. Thus, Vermont is harvesting between 20,000 and 22,000 deer on the average each season.

By density of kill, which shows where the most deer are, Orange Co. in the central part of the east and Windsor Co. directly south of it, have for some years roughly tied for first and second place. Kills have run as high as 3.5 animals per square mile! Down the central and south center of the state, about fitting the position of the National Forest, Rutland, Washington, and Windham

Cos. have for some time run almost even and next in order. While these counties are outstanding in deer density to date, this does not mean that the others are lacking in good hunting. In general the counties with lowest density of kills have been Franklin, Grand Isle, Orleans, Essex. Deer hunting is exceedingly popular, and by license sales overall success percentage has averaged about 12 percent for a number of years.

There is no problem whatever in finding a place to hunt. The Green Mountain NF has been covered early in the chapter. So have paper company lands. These are all excellent. The many State Forests and State Parks located under "Grouse" offer deer hunting and on most the primary species is deer. There is some deer hunting on the Missisquoi National Wildlife Refuge, also mentioned early in the chapter. The WMAs noted under "Pheasant" and "Grouse" also almost without exception furnish at least some deer hunting. All of these lands in total would be ample. But added to them are a large number of WMAs and PHAs where deer are plentiful. They are listed below alphabetically by county, with all those in the same county placed together and further located by towns in which they occur.

In Addison Co., west-central part of state, the 1076-acre Fred Johnson WMA, Starksboro town, and across the border in the town of Hinesburg, Chittenden Co.; Lewis Creek WMA (68), 1720 acres, town of Starksboro; Snake Mountain WMA (69), 966 acres, towns of Addison and Weybridge.

In Bennington Co., southwest, the 4756-acre Stamford Meadow WMA (70), towns of Stamford and Pownal.

In Caledonia Co., northeast, the 1150-acre Bald Hill WMA (71), in the town of Newark, and partly across the Orleans Co. border in Westmore town; the 320-acre Calendar Brook WMA (72), town of Sutton; Roy Mountain WMA (73), 927 acres in towns of Barnet and Ryegate; the 200-acre Levi Pond WMA (74), town of Groton.

In Chittenden Co., in the lower northwest, the Robbins Mountain WMA (75) of 818 acres, towns of Richmond and Bolton; the 1248-acre Huntington Gap WMA (76), in the towns of Hntington and Buells Gore and the town of Fayston in neighboring (to the southeast) Wash. Co.

In Essex Co., northeast, a large one of 9275 acres, Hurricane WMA (77), in the towns of Warrens Gore, Warners Grant, Norton, and across the county border in the town of Holland, Orleans Co.

In Franklin Co., the 210-acre Elm Brook WMA (78), town of Fairfield; 380-acre Gilson Mountain PHA (79), town of Fletcher; Averys Gore WMA (80), 300 acres in Montgomery town.

In Lamoille Co., East Hill WMA with 230 acres, town of Wolcott, and East Hill PHA (81) with 705 acres; Wild Branch WMA (82), 410 acres, town of Eden.

In Orange Co., 260-acre Washington WMA (83), Washington town; Malmquist WMA, 924 acres, and Clover Hill WMA (84), 506 acres, both in town of Strafford, and Howe PHA (85), 882 acres in Strafford and Turnbridge; West Fairlee WMA (86), 100 acres, town of same name.

In Orleans Co., 130-acre Willoughby Falls WMA (87), town of Barton. In Rutland Co., the Pittsford PHA (88), 687 acres, in like-named town, and the Brandon Swamp WMA (89), in Brandon.

In Windham Co., 900-acre Vernon WMA and 400-acre Vernon PHA (90), both in towns of Vernon and Guilford; two tracts of Atherton Meadow WMA (91), one of 925 acres, one of 242 acres, both in town of Whitingham.

In Windsor Co., the 6409-acre Les Newell WMA (92), in Stockbridge,

Barnard, and Bridgewater towns and across the Rutland Co. border in town of Sherburne, that county; the Les Newell PHA (92), Barnard and Stockbridge towns, 1777 acres; Reading-Plymouth WMA (93), towns of similar names, 7844 acres; Hawk Mountain WMA (94), 2183 acres, Cavendish and Baltimore; the 256-acre Ottauquechee WMA (95), town of Bridgewater; White River WMA (96), 325 acres, Sharon; Skitchewaug WMA (97), 287 acres, Springfield; Rochester WMA (98), same town, 251 acres; Little Ascutney WMA (99) of 412 acres and matching PHA of 709 acres, both town of Weathersfield; and the Weathersfield WMA (99), same town, of 85 acres.

BEAR

Black bears are reasonably plentiful in most of Vermont's forests. In 1955 mandatory reporting of bear kills was begun. Over the years since, the average annual kill has been 317. Highest kill to date: 449. County averages over a period of the past seven years place the counties by highest kill in the following order: 1. Essex; 2. Rutland; 3. Addison; 4. Bennington and Windsor tied; 5. Lamoille and Orleans tied; 6. Washington; 7. Caledonia, Franklin, Windham all about equal; 8. Chittenden. The Orange Co. kill is consistently lower than the others, although from five to fourteen bears have been bagged annually there.

The National Forest, the State Forests and many of the State Parks covered under "Grouse," and all but a few of the smaller WMAs and PHAs covered under "Deer" offer bear hunting. The larger tracts, in the counties consistently furnishing the higher kills, will in general be the best hunting grounds.

SQUIRRELS

The gray squirrel ranges over much of the Vermont forest country, but is not generally plentiful throughout the northern half of the state. In the south, where oaks furnish better food supplies, there are more squirrels. No figures are available on the squirrel kill. It is believed to be moderate. Only a scattering of hunters are avidly interested.

Public lands for squirrel hunting are numerous. Among the State Forests and State Parks with fair to good squirrel hunting are the following: Charles Downer SF; West Rutland SF; Mount Philo SP; Thetford Hill SF; Williams River SF; Wilgus SP; Ascutney SP; Emerald Lake SP; Emerald Lake SF; Grand Isle SP; Button Bay SP; Bomoseen SP; Rupert SF; Fort Dummer SP. All these are noted under "Grouse." Some others have low squirrel populations. The National Forest also is a good location for squirrels, especially in its southern portion.

Some of the better WMAs and PHAs for squirrel hunting: Fred Johnson WMA; Lewis Creek WMA; Snake Mountain WMA; Pond Woods WMA; Malmquist WMA; Clover Hill WMA; Whipple Hollow WMA; Otter Creek WMA; Hawk Mountain WMA; White River WMA; Pittsford PHA; Brandon Swamp WMA; West Fairlee WMA. See "Deer" for locations of all of these.

RABBITS

Both cottontails and snowshoe hares are found in Vermont. In the Lake Champlain region, including the islands, cottontails are plentiful. In the northeast cottontails are found in the Connecticut River Valley beginning at about Wells River and growing in abundance southward. Throughout southern Vermont cottontails are fairly abundant in most lower elevations with non-forest cover. Snowshoe hares are abundant in the higher northern elevations. Essex

Co. and the eastern half of Orleans Co. are good locations. These hares are in good supply throughout most of the mountain country running down through the center of the state and clear to the border.

Most of the State Forests, State Parks, WMAs, and PHAs offer hunting for snowshoe hares, as does the National Forest. See chapter opening, also "Grouse" and "Deer." Cottontails are not as abundant on the public lands, because most such lands are managed primarily for the forest species. The best cottontail hunting is on private lands in farming sections.

OTHER ANIMALS

Raccoons and foxes are found in varying abundance over much of the state. They are in general more plentiful in the south, are hunted to some extent with dogs and by varmint hunters but there is no high popular interest. Some woodchuck hunting is available, by permission, in the farming sections. A few bobcats are scattered through the forest regions.

REGULATIONS

Game laws pertaining to seasons, bag and possession limits, areas to be hunted, special hunts, license fees all may have numerous changes from year to year. For current regulations, and for other specific queries, write to: Vermont Fish and Game Department, Montpelier, Vermont 05602.

MASSACHUSETTS

Massachusetts is a kind of enigma. Scene of some of the oldest settlements in the United States, and today one of the most heavily populated states, it still has over 65 percent of its land area forested. It is a leader in the manufacture of electrical equipment, in shoes and in textiles. But it also is the largest U.S. producer of cranberries, and is well known for its maple syrup. With teeming cities, and a welter of colleges and universities, it was still necessary recently for the Massachusetts Game Department to tranquilize and move to a remote State Forest a bull moose that was pestering a farmer's cattle.

Sandwiched in among New York State on the west, Vermont and New Hampshire on the north, Connecticut and Rhode Island on the south, Massachusetts bursts out upon the Atlantic with an irregular shoreline that stretches all told some 1800 miles. Here portions of the state are the islands of Nantucket and Martha's Vineyard. Above these is the long sweeping hook of Cape Cod. From the marshes and coastal lowlands of the east, where waterfowl flights ply the bays offshore and others settle in marshy ponds, the land rises quickly to glacial hills, valleys, and some marshlands. Then to the west it rises more and becomes an area of modest-sized mountains, the Berkshires, with a high point atop Mount Greylock of nearly 3500 feet.

These western highlands are heavily forested with conifers, birch, maple, and beech. Eastward the woodlands and forests become less grand, but still often dense, made up of hardwoods, and with scrub oak, bull briars, and pine in the southeast and on the Cape, tough hunting cover unique in such a populous region. Notwithstanding the mass of population, there are, especially in the west, areas of forest that are surprisingly reminiscent of true wilderness.

Good roads of course crisscross the state, for traffic is heavy. With coastal Boston as the focal point, Interstates and other roads fan out in every direction. Hunters can get by car to any point in the state swiftly, by utilizing the arteries and then the secondary roads. Air transport, though hardly needed by resident sportsmen because of the state's small size, swiftly links all of the larger cities.

It is little short of amazing that good hunting can still exist in Massachusetts. Nonresidents, and even many residents, are unaware of the quality and variety that has been zealously guarded. This is especially surprising considering that Massachusetts covers only 8257 square miles. From Boston west to the New York line is roughly a hundred miles, and most of the west is a mere fifty or sixty miles north-south, although on the east there is a large expansion to the south especially and also north, along the coast and out upon Cape Cod where, incidentally, excellent roads take one to all points, and ferries offer transport to the islands.

Into this small state are packed at this time approximately 5.5 million people. By far the majority are in the east-central area surrounding Boston. Other large centers are to the west, in the Worcester and Springfield complexes.

Some of the far southeast is not deluged with people, and the Berkshire region of the west, though of course with its share of settlement, is comparatively rural and, in the hills, quite removed from the bustle of the east.

Partly because of the urban quality of life in much of Massachusetts for so many decades, there is no vast interest in hunting among the majority of the people. This is fortunate for the avid hunter. An average of little more than 130,000 hunting licenses are sold annually, and of this number no more than a couple of thousand are from out of state.

Game attractions are varied. There are ruffed grouse, pheasants, bobwhite quail, woodcock, waterfowl. Gray squirrels, cottontails, and snowshoe or varying hares are found in many parts of the state. Though Massachusetts is not a top deer state, it has surprisingly good hunting and for its size a fair annual harvest. There are raccoons, foxes, woodchucks.

Quite obviously, with a high percentage of the land privately owned, most of the hunting must be done on these lands. Realizing this, the Game Department has worked out cooperative arrangements with many landowners whereby the Department furnishes "Safety Zone" signs and other warning signs to be posted properly, and the landowner in turn allows hunting as long as the hunters stick to the rules involved.

But in addition to private lands, the Division of Fisheries and Game and the Department of Natural Resources have in ownership and under management numerous lands for public hunting. The Game Department owns or leases at this writing approximately 35,000 acres in Wildlife Management Areas. There are over twenty of these, well scattered across the state. Hunters should note well that a determined land acquisition program is in progress. Wildlife Management Areas that will be described and located later in this chapter may, as this is read, have had additions. There is an excellent booklet available from the Department (address at chapter end) titled "Guide to Wildlife Management Areas." As new ones are added, this booklet will be brought up to date. It is an excellent source of information for hunters.

Added to the WMAs are 160,000 acres of State Forests. The State Forests are utilized in differing ways. Some are developed for varied kinds of recreation from skiing to horseback riding. Many have large campgrounds. But some are undeveloped, and of course these are among the better hunting lands. On some, also, the Game Department does some stocking and management work, particularly in the several instances where a WMA is situated within a State Forest. Another booklet, "State Forests and Parks of Massachusetts," can be obtained from the Department of Natural Resources, 100 Cambridge St., Boston, Mass. 02202. From either the Game Department or the Department of Natural Resources, or from the Department of Commerce and Development, Division of Tourism, 150 Causeway St., Boston 02114, one may also obtain an excellent publication, "Massachusetts Outdoor Vacation Guide." This gives a vast amount of information on hunting, as well as serving as a guide to state-operated campgrounds.

There is in fact no lack of camping places for hunters who elect to use them. The state has an excellent State Park system, and as noted many of the State Forests and other public areas also offer camping. There are several Corps of Engineers campgrounds, and there are numerous private ones. Other accommodations for food and lodging are legion, in or near any sizable city or town. Hunters might bear in mind that the only really crowded times on the public hunting lands are on opening days, holidays, and Saturdays. Weekdays often find almost no hunters afield, and it is thus wise when possible to plan hunts then.

During the upland bird and small-game seasons in October and November, Massachusetts weather is usually lovely. It is crisp, New England fall weather, with the forests ablaze with color. Light wool shirts, and a hunting jacket for early and late in the day, are all that one needs. Late in November and on through the winter, however, weather can become severely cold at any time, and one should plan accordingly. Coastal waterfowl seasons usually call for very warm clothing, for the coast can be damp and raw, with bitter breezes.

There is very little rifle shooting in Massachusetts. Only shotguns and bow and arrow are legal for deer hunting, and no rifles of any kind may be used on the WMAs during upland bird seasons. Check the laws carefully pertaining even to use of a .22, and for use of rifles for such off-trail hunting as for woodchucks. Indeed, the Massachusetts hunter is primarily a shotgun man. Loads for the uplands are standard at anywhere from No. 8 or No. 7½ for quail and grouse to No. 6 for pheasants. For ducks, heavier loads are of course mandatory, and for heavy sea ducks and any goose shooting No. 4, No. 4 short magnums, or No. 2 are a good choice.

RUFFED GROUSE

Some years ago it was believed that the ruffed grouse, a bird of the forest and its edges, could not survive the push of civilization. It has turned out to be the only game bird in its range that *can* cope with civilization, as long as it has some natural habitat left, and maintain fair abundance without more than rudimentary assistance from game managers. In fact, in experiments to determine what effect long seasons may have on a ruffed grouse population, biologists have found that it is virtually impossible to remove all grouse by hunting, even with the assistance of hired professional hunters.

Thus it is that Massachusetts, with a dense human population but still with a good amount of forest, has some excellent ruffed grouse shooting. Some annual estimates have put the number killed as high as 80,000. While this may be a somewhat optimistic figure, it is probable that at least half that many or more are annually taken in Massachusetts, and this, for the size of the state, is a remarkable kill indeed.

The great share of grouse hunting here is in the high woodlands. This takes in a greater part of the state than is at first obvious. Perhaps Berkshire County, which is farthest west and reaches from north-south clear across the state, may be considered the prime grouse county. East of it, Franklin and Hampshire Cos. share the honors. Worcester in central Massachusetts is also good range, and so is the northern part of Middlesex, the county where Boston is located. A glance at the map shows that these counties take in the west and much of the north. Southern Massachusetts is not as good for grouse. But in the far southeast, Barnstable Co., which includes Cape Cod, is the surprise. There is rather good grouse hunting here. It is interesting to note, too, that ruffed grouse have been transferred in some numbers recently from the mainland to Martha's Vineyard.

So many public lands offer grouse hunting that they will be covered as concisely as possible here. Williamstown WMA (1) contains 2000 acres of abandoned farms, woodlands, moors in the northwest corner of Berkshire Co., near Williamstown at the junction of U.S. 7 and State 2. Peru WMA (2) is in east-central Berkshire Co., contains 2360 acres of mixed conifers and hard-

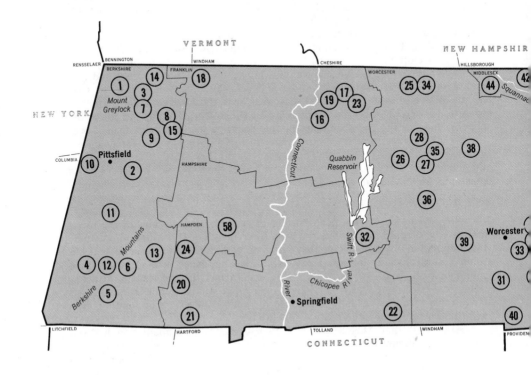

KEY TO HUNTING AREAS

1. Williamstown WMA
2. Peru WMA
3. Clarksburg SF
4. East Mountain SF
5. Cookson SF
6. Otis SF
7. Savoy Mountain SF
8. Mohawk Trail SF
9. Windsor SF
10. Pittsfield SF
11. October Mountain SF
12. Beartown SF
13. Chester WMA
14. Monroe SF
15. Hawley SF
16. Wendell SF
17. Warwick SF
18. Colrain SF
19. Erving SF
20. Tolland SF
21. Granville SF
22. Brimfield SF
23. Mount Grace SF

24. Chester-Blandford SF
25. Birch Hill WMA
26. Phillipston WMA
27. Barre Falls WMA
28. Hubbardston WMA
29. Fort Devens WMA
30. Quaboag WMA
31. Hodges Village WMA
32. Swift River WMA
33. West Hill WMA
34. Ashburnham SF
35. Hubbardston SF
36. Oakham SF
37. Upton SF
38. Leominster SF
39. Spencer SF
40. Douglas SF
41. Pantry Brook WMA
42. Townsend SF
43. Wrenham SF
44. Willard Brook SF
45. Harold Parker WMA
46. Harold Parker SF

47. Crane Pond WMA
48. Northeast (Downfall) WMA
49. Georgetown-Rowley SF
50. Willowdale SF
51. West Meadows WMA
52. Myles Standish WMA
53. Myles Standish SF
54. Fall River WMA
55. Freetown-Fall River SF
56. Otis Air Force Base WMA
57. Martha's Vineyard SF
58. Knightville WMA
59. Westborough Field Trial Area
60. Squannacook WMA
61. Crane WMA
62. Parker River (Plum Island) National Wildlife Refuge
63. Mill Creek WMA

48

MASSACHUSETTS

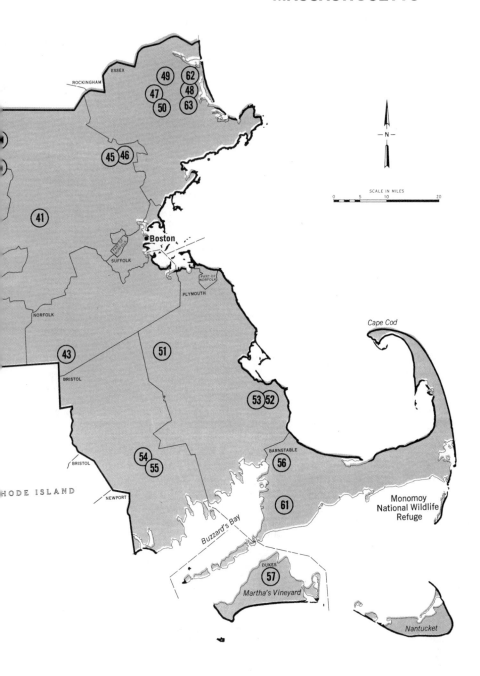

woods, perfect grouse habitat, near the town of Peru, east of the city of Pittsfield, on State 143.

Several undeveloped State Forest tracts in this county also offer grouse
shooting. Clarksburg SF (3) has almost 3000 acres in the northwest corner of the
county near North Adams. East Mountain SF (4) near Great Barrington in the
southwest of the county has 1387 acres near the junction of U.S. 7 and State 23.
Cookson SF (5) is 2387 acres of near wilderness southeast of the above, near
New Marlboro and Sandisfield, both of which are on State 57. Otis SF (6) has
3468 acres to the north of Cookson SF, near Otis, which is at the junction of
State 23 and 8.

There are also several large State Forests with various developments in the
Berkshires that hunters should check. Ordinarily they are open to hunting. All
are well detailed in the booklets of State Forests and Parks and the Vacation
Guide mentioned earlier in this chapter. These are: Savoy Mountain SF (7)
near North Adams and Savoy with over 11,000 acres; Mohawk Trail SF (8),
6542 acres near Charlemont; Windsor SF (9), 1558 acres near Windsor and
Savoy; 7914-acre Pittsfield SF (10) between Pittsfield and Hancock; October
Mountain SF (11) with over 14,000 acres near Lee and Becket. All of these
are in northwestern Berkshire Co. There is also Beartown SF (12), 8207 acres
near Great Barrington and Monterey in the southwest.

Moving east a bit in the Berkshire Hills, there is Chester WMA (13),
which contains over 1000 acres of mixed timber, with access via State 112 out
of Worthington and Chester. There are also several good State Forest locations.
Monroe SF (14) has 4000-plus acres near Monroe, reached out of Florida on
Route 2. Hawley SF (15) has 7497 acres accessible via Route 116 and 8A
from the towns of Hawley and Plainfield. Wendell SF (16) covers better than
7000 acres located near town of like name with access via Routes 2 and 2A.
Warwick SF (17) is wild country without development, with 6520 acres in same
general region with access from 2A and 78. Colrain SF (18) is to the north, out
of Colrain, access from State 112, with over 1500 acres.

As in Berkshire Co., in this section of Massachusetts there are also some
developed State Forests with campsites and various recreational uses, but
usually open to hunting. These can be located easily in the Guides noted. Their
names: Erving SF (19) near Erving, with better than 5000 acres; Tolland SF
(20) near Otis and Tolland with almost 3000; Granville SF (21), near Granville, 2247; Brimfield SF (22), near Brimfield, 3129; Mt. Grace SF (23) near
Warwick, 1390; Chester-Blandford SF (24), same towns, 2537. It should be
remembered that the WMAs are especially managed for game, while most of
the State Forests are simply in their wild, unmanaged states.

As was mentioned in the opening material about ruffed grouse, Worcester
Co., with its high hills, is one of the better grouse areas. There are a number
of public lands here, both WMAs and State Forests. Birch Hill WMA (25) has
over 4000 acres, in the north out of the town of Winchendon at the junction of
U.S. 202 and State 12. This WMA is under lease by the state from the Corps
of Engineers. Some distance south, out of Barre and Petersham on State 122
is a 1146-acre tract of mixed conifers and hardwoods, Phillipston WMA (26).
East of Barre, in the vicinity of Rutland and Hubbardston, State 56 and 68, is
1000-acre Barre Falls WMA (27), with some open fields and marshes as well as
woodland. Also near Hubbardston is Hubbardston WMA (28) with 2200 acres
of comparable terrain and cover.

Farther east, partly across the line in Middlesex Co., is Fort Devens WMA
(29) with 2000 acres of woodlot and abandoned farm habitat, and some marsh,

accessible from Shirley via Route 2 and out of North Lancaster on 117. To the south, and west of the city of Worcester, is Quaboag WMA (30), somewhat smaller, with 730 acres of marsh and woods, in the vicinity of Brookfield on Route 9. Almost straight south of Worcester on State 12 is the town of Oxford, with access to Hodges Village WMA (31), 785 acres. West of Worcester along Route 9 past the Quaboag WMA is another, 800-acre Swift River WMA (32), in the vicinity of Ware and Belchertown, both on State 9, the latter at the intersect with U.S. 202. This is south of Massachusetts' largest inland body of water, Quabbin Reservoir on the Swift River. West Hill WMA (33), the last of the Worcester Co. WMAs, contains 475 acres of forested uplands accessible from Whittinsville via Route 122. This is a few miles southeast of Worcester.

State Forests of note for grouse here, each named for the town which is near it, are: Ashburnham SF (34), 1574 acres; Hubbardston SF (35), 1397 acres; Oakham SF (36), 1000 acres; Upton SF (37), 2639 acres. There are also several other State Forests under the day-use category, which means with varied recreational developments but not for overnight camping. These are: Leominster SF (38), near town of like name, with almost 4000 acres, reached via Route 31; Spencer SF (39), near same town, with 1088 acres also accessible from Route 31, and 3232-acre Douglas SF (40), near Douglas, via Route 16 to the west of the town.

All of the lands so far covered of course have numerous other species, and this will be noted under those species. Also, there are some WMAs and Forests that offer fair grouse hunting but on which grouse are not considered primary. One such is Pantry Brook WMA (41), a smaller tract, of 377 acres in Middlesex Co. Primarily a waterfowl area, it does offer a bit of grouse hunting. It is in the Sudbury and Concord area northwest of Boston, off Route 117. Two State Forests named for the towns near them are also at times productive. These are 2916-acre Townsend SF (42), off Route 119 and 1101-acre Wrentham SF (43), southwest of Boston, the village at the intersect of State 11 and 140. Another State Forest, with high development for varied recreation is 2247-acre Willard Brook SF (44), in the Townsend-Ashby area, reached via Route 119.

Although Essex, the northeasternmost county of the state, is not in general as good for grouse as some of the area already covered, it does have several spots with fair to excellent shooting. One of the best is the Harold Parker WMA (45), a 2906-acre tract within the Harold Parker State Forest (46). It is forest with openings and some low, marshy portions, east of the city of Lawrence, near North Andover. Crane Pond WMA (47) also has good grouse hunting on its 1569 acres. This Area is a bit northeast of the one just mentioned, in the vicinity of Groveland, West Newbury, and Georgetown. I 95 runs north-south (old U.S. 1 also) east of the Area, and State 113 out of Groveland reaches it. Also in the vicinity is the Northeast WMA (48) (known as the Downfall Area also) located near Newbury, with 1317 acres of brushy fields and woodlots. This lies on the east side of I 95. Georgetown-Rowley SF (49), near those towns, with over 1000 acres, and Willowdale State Forest (50) of twice that acreage near Ipswich, should not be overlooked.

As was stated early in this section, surprisingly good grouse hunting is found in portions of the southeast. Plymouth, Bristol, and Barnstable Cos. have a fair amount, and a substantial acreage of public lands. A small (218 acres) WMA primarily for waterfowl, West Meadows WMA (51) has a few grouse also. It is near the intersect of Routes 28 and 106 near West Bridgewater. This is in Plymouth County. In the same county is Myles Standish WMA (52), a 2000-acre tract within the Myles Standish State Forest (53). This is a woodland of pine and oak, with some openings, ponds, marshes. It is near the coast, south of the city of Plymouth, about halfway down toward Wareham and Buzzard's Bay, and east of Route 58. The Forest itself contains almost 12,000 acres.

To the east, in Bristol Co., northeast of the city of Fall River, is the Fall River WMA (54). There are 2000 acres here with some grouse hunting, with the terrain wooded swamp and upland woods. This is in the Freetown-Fall River State Forest (55). Route 24 lies to the northwest, running roughly north-south. The WMA is actively managed. The surrounding Forest totals 5441 acres, with access from Route 24.

Barnstable Co., the Cape Cod county, has one excellent bet for grouse, in a large tract. This is the 3000-acre Otis Air Force Base WMA (56), a stretch of woodland with numerous scattered openings and edges perfect for grouse. U.S. 6, the big highway that runs out the Cape, locally called the Mid-Cape Highway, gives access. Cities in the vicinity are Bourne and Sandwich.

While ruffed grouse have only recently been introduced to Martha's Vineyard, the island south of the Cape, there is Martha's Vineyard State Forest (57), with over 4000 acres. Hunters may wish to keep track of grouse progress here, or to hunt the Forest, which is open for other game.

PHEASANT

The pheasant kill in Massachusetts is estimated at from 100,000 to 150,000 annually, cocks only. This makes the pheasant all told the most popular game bird in the state. It is not, however, by any means a self-sustaining species. Each year three game farms raise and release 55,000 or more. Some are adult releases in spring and summer, others are young birds. Without these releases it is well known that the pheasant, in its present strain, would undoubtedly disappear, or at best become only remnant.

Although pheasants are distributed across the state, areas where there are any agricultural lands are best. The Connecticut River Valley is one good example. The river runs down across Franklin, Hampshire, and Hampden Cos. in the west. However, Worcester, Middlesex, Essex, Plymouth, Bristol, and Barnstable Cos. also offer good shooting. Many of the WMAs are well stocked.

Presently the state is trying to "fashion" a pheasant suitable to its habitat. The only places where self-sustaining pheasant populations hang on—and they've been stocked ever since the early part of the century—are in the agricultural areas. Most of Massachusetts' habitat is woodland. A forest-type pheasant that would perhaps utilize tree buds for part of its diet much as ruffed grouse do, and one that might even roost in trees, would be desirable. There is hope that by crossing numerous strains over a period of some years such a bird can be bred and established. Experiments of this nature are under way.

In the far west, in Berkshire Co., the Williamstown WMA is stocked ("Ruffed Grouse"). Another western WMA not so far mentioned is 500-acre Knightville WMA (58). This is near the Knightville Reservoir, which lies on the east side of State 112 just north of its junction with Route 66. Pheasants are stocked here by the Game Department. In the central part of the state, the following WMAs, all located under "Grouse," are stocked with pheasants: Birch Hill; Barre Falls; Hubbardston; Fort Devens; Quaboag; Hodges Village; West Hill. There is also in the central region the small (175 acres) Westborough Field Trial Area (59) that has limited stocking of pheasants, although it is not primarily a hunting area. It is near Westborough, with access from Routes 135 and 9.

Farther east, in Middlesex Co., Pantry Brook WMA, chiefly for water-fowl, and not stocked, has some pheasants (see "Grouse"). There is a new WMA in northwestern Middlesex Co. reached off Route 119 between the villages of Groton and Townsend. The Squannacook River is here and the area is named for it, Squannacook WMA (60). As this is written it contains 300 acres but attempts to add more land were in progress. A limited amount of pheasant stocking is done here.

In Essex Co., in the northeast, Harold Parker, Crane Pond, and North-east WMAs (see "Grouse") are stocked. To the south, in Plymouth Co., pheasants are stocked also on West Meadows and Myles Standish WMAs, and in Bristol Co. on Fall River WMA (see "Grouse"). There is one other, Crane WMA (61)—not to be confused with Crane Pond WMA in the northeast—in Barnstable Co. on the Cape, where pheasant stocking is done. This is an Area of 1562 acres located near Falmouth, with open fields and with some scrub oak and pine. It can be reached either from Route 151 or Route 28.

Some pheasants may be found in edge cover and open abandoned farm-lands of the State Forests, but the stocked WMAs are best. Aside from these, the remainder of the pheasant hunting is by permission on private lands. Hunters should check the farms with Safety Zone signs (see opening portion of chapter) for possible locations.

QUAIL

Quail shooting is surprisingly good, but it is confined to the southeast. As this is written, the counties of Plymouth and Bristol on the mainland are open, plus Barnstable (Cape Cod), plus Dukes Co. (Martha's Vineyard) and Nantucket (Nantucket Island). The quail hunting on the Cape is often as good as any in the Deep South. But it is also exceedingly difficult hunting. The cover is oak scrub and pine, plus dense briars. Pressure is seldom heavy and hardy hunters can have good shooting here wherever permission can be arranged.

In Plymouth Co., the Myles Standish WMA has been developed for quail hunting and the department stocks quail there. In Barnstable Co., the Otis A.F.B. WMA has quail without stocking necessary. Both these Areas are noted under "Ruffed Grouse." The Crane WMA in Barnstable Co. also has quail shooting, with birds stocked (see "Pheasant").

WATERFOWL, SNIPE, RAILS

Although snipe and rails are legal in Massachusetts, there is virtually no hunting for either, except very occasionally as incidentals by waterfowlers.

There is good shooting for ducks, some for geese, and much for sea ducks (scoters, eiders, etc.), but it must be understood that in a state so densely populated by far the major share of available sites are in private hands. Inland there are numerous opportunities for jump-shooting along rivers and ponds and small marshes, and there is also shooting over decoys on some of the impoundments and other lakes. Much of both of these can be arranged by the public, if a careful search of possibilities is made. Such inland shooting is best early in the season, and the prize species here is the renowned black duck, although wood ducks and others are also available.

The coast offers the greatest number of opportunities. Hunters who will acquire U.S.G.S. topographic maps can locate numerous marshes and bay contours that will offer shooting from a boat. The Parker River National Wildlife Refuge (62), also known as Plum Island NWR because headquarters are located there, has some public hunting, too. This is under the Bureau of Sport Fisheries and Wildlife. The Refuge is located near Newburyport, in the extreme northeast, contains 4650 acres, attracts many black ducks, broadbills (greater scaup) and Canada geese, as well as shorebirds, including snipe.

Waters along and near Cape Cod offer excellent opportunities. The Barnstable Marshes, Plymouth Bay and harbor, and Pleasant Bay, which is out at the crook of the Cape, south from Orleans and north of Chatham, are all prime waterfowl areas. There is a 2700-acre Refuge, Monomoy, in the Chatham region. It is not open to hunting, but is a haven for many black ducks and sea ducks.

Sea duck hunting (with some brant also) is one sport that anyone with boat and decoys can participate in here. And the various sea ducks are among the most abundant of waterfowl. A recent winter survey showed them most numerous of all, with over 100,000 counted in January. Sea ducks are not as a rule very wary. Decoys can be set out around a boat within shooting range and often the flights will come right in, even returning after some of their number have been shot. Any of the waters offshore from Cape Cod are likely to furnish good sea duck shooting. So do coastal locations such as waters off Duxbury on the north shore of Plymouth Bay, the outer harbor at Boston, and in the north off Plum Island. There is also good shooting in numerous coves and bays off Martha's Vineyard and Nantucket.

The WMAs also offer some waterfowling. Hubbardston, Fort Devens, West Hill are among those with fair opportunities. West Meadows has a good number of wood ducks and black ducks. Pantry Brook also has good shooting for teal, black ducks, wood ducks, and is primarily managed as a waterfowl area. All these WMAs are located under "Ruffed Grouse." One other, Mill Creek WMA (63) in Essex Co., also is a waterfowl ground. This is south of Newburyport, east of I 95 and north of State 133, with key nearby towns Newbury and Rowley. There are 529 acres.

WOODCOCK

A fair number of woodcock are raised in Massachusetts each nesting season. The state is also on a major flyway and gets good flights in fall. Alder runs and all damp or moist woodlands with thin ground cover and scattered or dappled overhead shade hold groups of birds.

This bird, like the ruffed grouse, is found in such a large number of places across the west, central, north, and northeast that any hunter who wishes may partake of good shooting on public lands. Virtually all of the WMAs and State Forests in Berkshire, Franklin, Hampshire, Worcester, Middlesex, and Essex Cos. offer either native birds or flight birds. For information about all of these, see "Ruffed Grouse" and "Pheasant." Although there are scattered woodcock in the south and the Cape region, the best shooting will be as listed.

OTHER BIRDS

The wild turkey is not at this writing on the game list, but plants have been made and the Department hopes to establish it in suitable areas across the state. It appears at this time that turkeys are firmly established in the Quabbin Reservoir area, and transplants have been made to the Barre area and several others. Some transplants have slightly increased, others appear static.

Many years ago the heath hen, relative of and similar to the prairie chicken, was abundant in parts of the state. It has been extinct for many years. In an effort to establish a similar bird in possibly suitable habitat, Massachusetts imported sharptail grouse from South Dakota, and during a recent season ninety-one birds were released on Nantucket Island. It is far too early at this time to guess what the outcome may be.

DEER

Massachusetts has long had a deer season, until recently for any deer as a rule, the hunting with shotguns and bow and arrow. In the early fifties the season kill ran about 3500 animals. It climbed to a peak in the late fifties of around 5000. Since that time there has been a steady decline in deer kills, and a noticeable decrease in the herd. Estimates place the entire deer population of the state at 8000 to 10,000 animals. During a recent season 3404 deer were harvested.

There are probably about 50,000 deer hunters. The sport is avidly followed. Recently during an antlered deer season but with a limited number of permits available for antlerless deer (2000), there were 27,800 applications for these. Success estimates on deer of any sex range from 1 in 15 to 1 in 20. The Game Department hopes to be able to regulate and manage deer hunting and herd so that a stable annual kill of from 4000 to 5000 is possible. It is doubtful that it can ever be higher than that and still keep the herd in balance with its food supply and range. Best of the deer range is in the Berkshires, Franklin Co., northern Worcester Co., and on Cape Cod. During one recent season the three top counties, in order, were Franklin, Berkshire, and Worcester.

There are ample opportunities for deer hunting on public lands. Of the WMAs, reading from the west, the following, noted under "Ruffed Grouse," all furnish deer hunting: Williamstown; Peru; Chester; Birch Hill; Phillipston; Barre Falls; Hubbardston; Fort Devens; Northeast. Note that these start in Berkshire Co. in the far west and sweep across the central and northern parts of the state into the northeast. Then there are in the south: West Meadows and Myles Standish in Plymouth Co.; Fall River in Bristol Co.; Otis A.F.B. in Barnstable Co. Crane WMA ("Pheasant") in Barnstable Co. also has deer.

In addition to the WMAs, all of the sizable State Forests open to hunting are among the best bets for the deer hunter. These also have been listed and described under "Grouse."

On the island of Martha's Vineyard there is a small herd of fallow deer. During 1968 five more were released there, a cooperative action with the Game Department, a sportsman's club, and a private individual involved. Currently fallow deer are not hunted. Whether a herd of huntable surplus will evolve is questionable.

SQUIRRELS

The gray squirrel is the species found throughout almost all of the state. Oddly, though rather abundant it is lightly hunted. The gray squirrel is basically a forest species. All of the State Forests offer fair to excellent hunting. These can be checked under "Ruffed Grouse." WMAs with some of the best gray squirrel hunting are as follows: Peru; Birch Hill; Phillipston; Barre Falls; Hubbardston; Fort Devens; Hodges Village; West Hill; Harold Parker; Crane Pond; Northeast; West Meadows; Fall River—all under "Ruffed Grouse"— and Knightville WMA under "Pheasant."

RABBITS

Cottontails are abundant and range throughout the state. They, like squirrels, receive very light pressure and are even considered nuisances in some areas. However, an interest in beagling over recent seasons is making rabbit hunting more popular. Virtually all of the WMAs offer cottontail hunting. Many of the forests where edge cover, fields, brush, and abandoned farmland are available also have abundant cottontails.

Another extremely popular game species is the varying hare, snowshoe rabbit, or as it is colloquially known in Massachusetts, "white hare." The state even stocks a good many white hares annually on some of the WMAs. Among those where stocking is done, or where this species is self-sustaining, are the following WMAs: Peru; Chester; Birch Hill; Phillipston; Barre Falls; Hubbardston; Hodges Village; Harold Parker; Northeast; Myles Standish, all listed under "Ruffed Grouse." Because of stocking, most of these places will ordinarily furnish the best hunting. The State Forests also may be fair in up-cycle seasons.

OTHER ANIMALS

The black bear is on the game list but there is very little hunting for it. There are a few in some of the larger, undeveloped forest tracts.

Raccoons are plentiful, considered a game species with a season, hunted to some extent by hound enthusiasts. Most of the Forests and the WMAs have raccoon populations from fair to good. Among the WMAs where the raccoon is listed as a common species: Peru; Birch Hill; Phillipston; Barre Falls; Hubbardston; Fort Devens; Harold Parker; Crane Pond; Northeast; Myles Standish. All these are covered under "Ruffed Grouse."

Foxes are not protected except for trapping regulations. There are also woodchucks on forest edges, abandoned farms, and agricultural lands. There is a modest amount of hunting for them. Woodchuck hunters should carefully check rules regarding use of rifles.

REGULATIONS

Game laws pertaining to seasons, bag and possession limits, areas to be hunted, special hunts, license fees all may have numerous changes from year to year. For current regulations, and for other specific queries, write to: Massachusetts Division of Fisheries and Game, Information and Education Section, Westboro, Massachusetts 01581

RHODE ISLAND

Nestled in between Massachusetts and Connecticut along the coastal northeast of the U.S. is one of our most unusual states, Rhode Island. It is at once the smallest and most densely populated of all the states. But oddly, even with its small size, it has a saltwater coast that with all its bays and meanderings covers enough miles to belong to a state of much greater size. Actually Rhode Island is not as a state an island at all, but among the islands of Narragansett Bay is one, the largest, which is named "Rhode Island."

Because of its coastal position and large areas of marine bays, plus the rivers that empty into them, this is a lowland state. The highest point is a hill in Providence that is a bit over 800 feet in altitude. Because of the dense population—over 800 average per square mile—there is little true "countryside" as it is known in less populous areas. This is a kind of urban state, heavily industrialized, and hemmed in by other states also with concentrations of industry and populations. Thus there is certainly no wilderness, but a number of inland areas have been stubbornly saved nonetheless for the hunter.

There is little hunting on private lands so far as the general public or a visitor is concerned. However, the Management Areas and State Forests do offer a substantial amount of shooting, and the saltwater coasts offer some.

Good roads are everywhere, many of them large, fast highways. Air transport to Providence and other cities is excellent, but distances are so short within the state that it is faster to drive from point to point than to attempt to fly. Over the main portion of the state the east-west dimension is seldom over twenty-five miles, and north to south roughly not quite three times as far. The land area is only 1214 square miles. But uniquely, if all the shorelines of the saltwater bays are added they total some 400 miles.

Population is over 900,000. But not many of this number are hunters, possibly because of crowded conditions. During a recent season 10,578 hunting licenses were issued. Of those, only 304 were to nonresidents. There is shooting for ruffed grouse, and some for pheasants and quail. Rhode Island is also one of the northernmost of the northeastern states to have dove hunting, which is fair. There is a reasonable amount of hunting for small-game animals such as rabbits and squirrels, and a modest amount of deer hunting.

The migratory birds, waterfowl, woodcock, a few rails and snipe also offer opportunities, because so much protected bay water and river-mouth water, plus some tidal marshes, are available for wintering and migrating habitat for these birds. As more and more land is urbanized, the Rhode Island authorities feel that it is possible the best hope for the future of hunting here may be dependent upon good waterfowl management.

Inland there are, however, a scattering of public lands open to hunting. These are areas of modest size, chiefly in the northwest and the southwest. They come under three headings: Wildlife Reservations; State Forests; State Management Areas. A Recreation Map of Rhode Island available from the

Department of Natural Resources shows all of these areas.

Accommodations for hunters are no problem here. There are numerous motels and hotels along all the highways. Camping is limited. One state park—Burlingame—in the south has numerous sites. There is also a growing number of private campgrounds. There are numerous public beaches on salt water, and of great importance to the waterfowler, a number of public boat-launching sites. Some of these are on fresh waters and some on salt. A list of them is offered on the Recreation Map previously mentioned.

September and October weather for upland hunting is mild. Because of the coastal emphasis, and waterfowl seasons during November and December, it is best to go prepared for nasty weather—chilly, rainy, foggy—the kind so often perfect for the best of waterfowling. Also, much of the best of this is offshore or in exposed positions along shore. Thus rain gear, woolen clothing, and rubber boots or waders are important.

There is virtually no rifle hunting in Rhode Island, none during the game seasons with anything larger than a .22 long rifle. Thus one should take only a shotgun, even for deer. Loads for the smaller birds can be in the class of No. 7½. Waterfowling loads, especially for coastal shooting where pass shooting and long-range shots may be the rule, should be heavy. Also, brant and sea ducks are heavy, strong birds and require loads to match. No. 4 short-magnum should in general be the minimum.

GROUSE

One of the surprises in this state is that ruffed-grouse hunting is still available in such a densely populated region. Because everything here is in miniature, the kill does not appear large. An average good season supplies 2500 ruffed grouse to hunters' bags. However, that is substantial, compared to the small number of hunters. There is virtually no grouse hunting for the public on private property. But amazingly, of the thirteen public hunting sites in Rhode Island, eleven of them offer ruffed grouse. And, of these, the hunting on seven can be considered good, with the other four at least fair.

Providence County is the northernmost, and largest, of Rhode Island's five counties. In the far northwestern corner of Providence Co., bordering Massachusetts on the north and Connecticut on the west, is Buck Hill State Management Area (1). It is open to hunting, and is one of the good ruffed grouse areas. State Route 100 runs northwest from Pascoag and through Bridgeton toward the Area. The road forks four miles from the Connecticut border, with Route 100 turning north and Buck Hill Road skirting the southern end of the SMA. This Area covers 1290 acres. Most of it is woodland. There is a small marsh of perhaps thirty acres and roughly twice that much in openings. The Area is thus large enough to accommodate a number of hunters, and grouse shooting is quite good. There is also a public rifle range here.

East of this hunting ground, and near the Massachusetts line, is Black Hut State Management Area (2). It is easily reached out of Harrisville via

KEY TO HUNTING AREAS

1. Buck Hill SMA	7. Carolina SF	12. Woody Hill SF
2. Black Hut SMA	8. Great Swamp Wildlife	13. Seapowet Marsh
3. George Washington	Reservation	Wildlife Preserve
SMA	9. Indian Cedar Swamp	14. Point Judith
4. Durfee Hill SMA	SMA	15. Conanicut Island
5. Wickaboxet SF	10. Burlingame SF	16. Sakonnet Point
6. Arcadia SF	11. Burlingame SP	17. Newtown Swamp

RHODE ISLAND

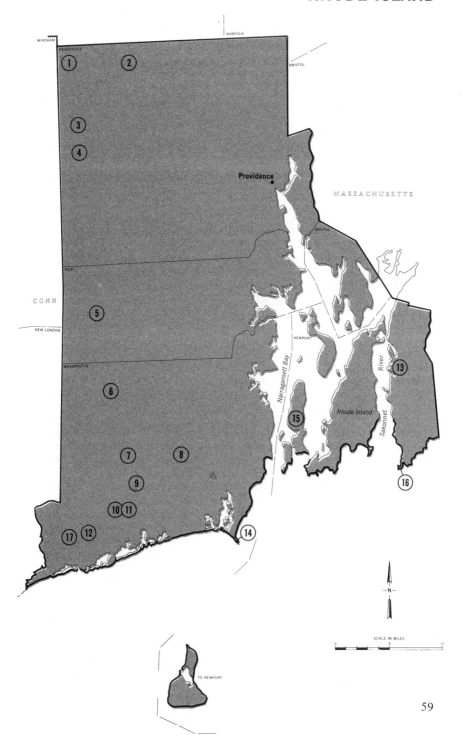

Providence

MASSACHUSETTS

CONN

Narragansett Bay

Rhode Island

Sakonnet River

TO NEWPORT

SCALE IN MILES

State 107, or Glendale via 102. A secondary named Lake Road cuts across the Area, and numerous other small roads reach it from every side. Black Hut SMA has 1208 acres, chiefly woods, with a small amount of marsh and field terrain. It is considered one of the better ruffed grouse Areas.

Directly south of the first named—Buck Hill SMA—lies the George Washington SMA (3). This is another excellent ruffed grouse possibility, and somewhat larger than the ones to the north. It is 3341 acres, almost entirely woodland, with a small marsh and openings comprising approximately fifty acres all told. Secondary roads cross it in several places. It can be reached via U.S. 44 from Chepachet and a turnoff to the north on a secondary, or via State 100 from or near Bridgeton with a turn south on a secondary. A portion of this Area borders in the west on Connecticut.

Directly below this Area, on the south side of east-west running U.S. 44, is the Durfee Hill SMA (4). It is in two sections. The eastern one can be reached directly from U.S. 44. The one to the west, on the Connecticut border, is reached by a turn south from U.S. 44 on Reynolds Road, or from the south by Sheldon Road out of the village of North Foster on State 101. Ruffed grouse hunting here is labeled "good." The SMA covers 740 acres, with most of it woods and with approximately 150 acres in fields and marsh.

The next county to the south is Kent. It is the center county of the main or "inland" portion of Rhode Island. In the western part of Kent Co., about midway down across it from the north, is Wickaboxet State Forest (5). Grouse hunting here is good. This is a smaller area, of 425 acres, all woodland. A secondary road runs through it. Access is from the nearby village of West Greenwich Center, or from State 102 a short distance to the east.

Two or three miles south is Rhode Island's largest public hunting area, Arcadia State Forest (6). Portions of it are open to hunting, and the ruffed grouse is the top game. The southern Kent Co. line (with Washington Co.) bisects it east-west. The area is 7500 acres, almost all woodland, with a bit over 300 acres in fields and marsh. It is accessible from any direction. State 165 runs east-west across it, 102 runs to the east, and there are numerous secondaries. Coming down from the north, Plain Road, out of West Greenwich Center reaches it. The village of Hope Valley is a short distance south of the Forest.

Approximately two miles south of Hope Valley, with the Hope Valley Road skirting its western border, is Carolina State Forest (7). It is wholly in Washington Co. This is the southernmost of the three "mainland" counties. Carolina SF has 1460 acres, about 1000 in woods, the remainder in fields and marsh. It is excellent grouse habitat. It can be reached along the same road from Wood River Junction to the south, or from State 112 which runs east of it.

The tracts so far mentioned are the best of the ruffed grouse habitat. The following areas may be considered fair. Much of course depends on seasonal cycles. Largest of the "fair" locations is Great Swamp Wildlife Reservation (8). It covers 2775 acres. Of this, about 900 acres are woods. There are at least 1400 acres of wooded swamp, the rest in fields and marshy openings. Great Swamp is directly east of Carolina SF. State 2 runs along its western edge and State 110 between Tuckertown and W. Kingston is on the east side. On the southern border of Great Swamp is Worden Pond.

In southwestern Washington Co. are three other fair areas. South a couple of miles from Carolina SF is Indian Cedar Swamp SMA (9). Wood River Junction just north of it is a good access point. Or one may come up from the south via Kings Factory Road, which branches off U.S. 1 along the coast to the south. This is a 900-acre tract chiefly in maple and cedar woods.

Burlingame State Forest (10) all but borders Indian Cedar Swamp, on the south. There is a fairly large area here that contains Burlingame State Park (11) as well as the Forest. Thus hunting boundaries must be observed. The hunting ground can be reached from U.S. 1 to the south, or from State 91 on the west, or out of Wood River Jct. to the north. It covers 800 acres, mostly woods.

Southwest of Burlingame SF, and directly south of the village of Bradford, from which a secondary reaches it off State 216, is Woody Hill SF (12). This is in almost the southwestern corner of Washington Co. It has 725 wooded acres, with a few openings of small size.

PHEASANT

There is a small self-sustaining pheasant population in Rhode Island, but the greater share of the pheasant hunting over most of the state is put and take, using stocked birds. Much pheasant hunting, because of the farmland habitat required by the species, is on private lands. There is a modest amount of pheasant shooting, however, on the public sites. The total annual kill averages around 3000 birds for the entire state.

Pheasant hunting may be termed "fair" on a number of the public lands covered under "Grouse." These are: Buck Hill SMA; Black Hut SMA; Durfee Hill SMA; Arcadia State Forest; Carolina SF; Great Swamp Wildlife Reservation; Indian Cedar Swamp SMA.

Best of the pheasant hunting in Rhode Island is on a public area not so far mentioned. This is Seapowet Marsh Wildlife Preserve (13). It is in the southeast, across Narragansett Bay and the Island of Rhode Island and on the east side of the Sakonnet River which branches north as a bay off Rhode Island Sound. This places it on the small, narrow southeastern corner portion of Rhode Island that borders Massachusetts. This is a part of Newport Co., in the town (township) of Tiverton. Seapowet MWP borders the Sakonnet River on the west, lies just north of the village of Tiverton Four Corners on State 77. West Road out of Tiverton Four Corners circles it on the west. The area is small, 156 acres of fields and marsh.

QUAIL

Quail are considered, in light of modern use, fairly plentiful on private lands. This is not to say they are abundant. There is not a great deal of room for agriculture in Rhode Island today. Nonetheless, there is fair though spotty quail shooting and a bit of it on public as well as private property. The kill by standards in larger and less populous states is of course small. Probably around 700 birds are taken in good seasons.

A few quail coveys are found on some of the public tracts noted under "Grouse," with the hunting graded as fair. These are: Durfee Hill SMA; Arcadia SF; Carolina SF; Great Swamp WR; Indian Cedar Swamp SMA; Woody Hill SF. There is also a bit of quail shooting on the Seapowet Marsh Wildlife Preserve noted under "Pheasant."

SNIPE, WOODCOCK, RAILS

There is very little shooting of either snipe or rails. The harvest of these birds is almost nil. The small Seapowet Marsh WP ("Pheasants") offers a small amount of shooting for each.

Woodcock shooting is better. There is a fairly good woodcock migration down across the state, and some fairly good hunting may be had. Some of this is in the north, but the best concentrations are usually in the south and west. The annual kill averages around 1000 birds.

Grouse and woodcock are quite often found, in numerous states, in similar coverts. Here, the "Grouse" areas already mentioned where fair woodcock shooting may be had are as follows: Buck Hill SMA; Black Hut SMA; Geo. Washington SMA; Durfee Hill SMA; Carolina SF; Great Swamp; Indian Cedar Swamp SMA; Burlingame SF; Woody Hill SF.

Best of the woodcock shooting is furnished by the 7500-acre Arcadia State Forest in the southwest. This was also noted as an excellent area for grouse.

MOURNING DOVES

Rhode Island offers rather good dove shooting. During the split season the early segment is likely to be best, for the birds may begin to migrate south. In a mild winter, the late season may hold birds and turn up the best concentrations. Annual dove kill is estimated at about 47,000. Because of the feeding needs of doves, almost all of the better shooting is on private property. There is a substantial amount of potato raising in Washington (the southernmost) Co. The major share of the good shooting is in these potato fields.

Several of the public areas offer surprisingly good dove shooting. The best is found on the following: Black Hut SMA; Carolina SF; Great Swamp. Fair dove hunting can be found on: Durfee Hill SMA; Arcadia SF. All of these are located under "Grouse." There is also some dove hunting on Seapowet Marsh Wildlife Preserve ("Pheasant").

WATERFOWL

Many years ago Rhode Island was a prime waterfowling ground, with geese, puddle and diving ducks, sea ducks, brant, as well as numerous shore birds, in almost limitless abundance. The years have of course brought changes because of civilization's pressures. Diminishing marshlands and pollution have been serious menaces. Notwithstanding all the difficulties, there is still some good waterfowling here for those who avidly seek it and are willing to work for it.

The days of offshore pass shooting from open boats and of elaborate off-shore blinds with scores of decoys are almost entirely gone. Some hunters pass shoot the diving ducks along the coast from breakwaters or points of land, or along Narragansett Bay they hide among rocks with a few decoys set out. There is some early-season jump-shooting inland. The offshore blind is still undoubtedly the most successful method for those willing to do all the hard work of setting it up. Access to open waters is easy and there are numerous launching sites. The map referred to early in this chapter gives locations. The saltwater hunting offers the widest choice of opportunity for waterfowlers.

Brant hunting is exceedingly spotty, but hunting for the sea ducks (scoters, eiders) is fair. Estimates place the kill of sea ducks at around 750 birds annually. This interesting—and to inland waterfowlers who may visit here, unusual— sport is best from some of the points of land jutting into or overlooking open salt water. To the south, offshore, in Block Island Sound and Rhode Island Sound are the main hangouts of the sea ducks. The best shooting is either directly from points here, or else by boat offshore from them.

Point Judith (14) is a good spot. This is the southeasternmost tip of Washington Co. State 108 and Scenic 1A run to it, at the village of Point Judith. Northeast from here, long, narrow Conanicut Island partially blocks the southern end of Narragansett Bay. The southern tip of the Island is called

Beavertail. Access from Washington Co. is via the Jamestown Bridge halfway up the island. The turnoff to the bridge is from Routes 138 and Scenic 1A. From the east, via the island of Rhode Island, access is by the Newport-Jamestown ferry.

Still farther east, on the southern tip of that portion of Rhode Island bordering Massachusetts, there is Sakonnet Point (16). State 77 runs from the north down to the village of Sakonnet just above the Point. This is an excellent bet for sea ducks.

There is some fair duck shooting primarily for the puddle ducks on the public units previously mentioned. Durfee Hill SMA has some. So does Arcadia SF. Carolina SF is also fair. Great Swamp Wildlife Reservation has shooting for both ducks and geese. So does Seapowet Marsh Wildlife Preserve, with ducks rated good and geese fair. These areas have been previously located under "Grouse" and "Pheasant."

A small but good waterfowling spot not mentioned so far is in the southwestern corner of the state. Both ducks and geese are here. This is Newtown Swamp (17). It is directly west of and close to Woody Hill SF ("Grouse"). State 91 crosses it, giving access either from Bradford to the northeast or from Westerly to the west. The public acreage is slightly under seventy-five acres.

An average duck kill in Rhode Island totals around 3500 birds, and usually approximately 200 geese are taken.

RABBITS AND HARES

By numbers killed—some 15,000 annually—cottontails are the most popular of Rhode Island's game species. The major share of the kill is from private lands, but the public lands offer satisfactory hunting. All of the tracts mentioned throughout the chapter, with the exception of Newtown Swamp immediately above under "Waterfowl," have cottontail hunting from fair to good.

Rhode Island also has a scattering of snowshoe hares. While the kill is not large, these big hares that turn white in winter wherever snow is on the ground are avidly sought by sportsmen. Best of the public hunting is found on Buck Hill SMA, Black Hut SMA, George Washington SMA, Indian Cedar Swamp SMA. There are modest numbers of snowshoes also on: Woody Hill SF; Burlingame SF; Great Swamp WR; Carolina SF; Arcadia SF; Wickaboxet SF; Durfee Hill SMA.

GRAY SQUIRRELS

Squirrels are second to rabbits in popularity and numbers annually taken. The kill averages 5000. Durfee Hill SMA is considered one of the top squirrel tracts for public shooting. So are both Arcadia SF and Carolina SF. Next in line, and about equal in hunting quality for squirrels: Buck Hill SMA; Black Hut SMA; George Washington SMA; Wickaboxet SF; Great Swamp WR; Indian Cedar Swamp SMA; Burlingame SF; and Woody Hill SF. There is of course squirrel hunting in privately owned woodlands, if permission can be arranged.

DEER

It is a most interesting commentary on the success of the whitetail deer in adapting to modern civilization that deer hunting is still possible in a state so heavily populated. Compared to the amount of suitable range, deer are fairly plentiful. In fact, they are abundant enough so that hunting is for either sex.

There is usually a split season—early and late—and either bow or shotgun (but no rifles) may be used. During an average season the deer kill is around fifty animals for the shotgun hunters and twenty for archers.

On the public lands, the ones considered best are: Durfee Hill SMA; Wickaboxet SF; Arcadia SF; Carolina SF; Great Swamp WR; Indian Cedar Swamp SMA; Burlingame SF. Rated as offering somewhat less chances of success but still with fair hunting: Buck Hill SMA; Black Hut SMA; George Washington SMA; Woody Hill SF.

OTHER ANIMALS

Raccoons are considered as game and there is a season and bag limit. They are quite plentiful. All public areas except Newtown Swamp have modest to high populations. The best raccoon hunting is offered at Indian Swamp SMA, Great Swamp WR, Carolina SF, and Arcadia SF.

Foxes and woodchucks are not protected. There are fair populations of each, but little hunting for them except as incidentals on public lands. Some woodchuck hunting is available by permission on private lands.

REGULATIONS

Game laws pertaining to seasons, bag and possession limits, areas to be hunted, special hunts, license fees all may have numerous changes from year to year. For current regulations, and for other specific queries, write to: Department of Natural Resources, Veterans' Memorial Building, 83 Park Street, Providence, Rhode Island.

CONNECTICUT

This northeastern state has the variety of terrain encountered in most coastal states. In many ways, Connecticut is more coastal than is generally realized. Over its greatest dimension, roughly 250 miles fronting chiefly on Long Island Sound, there are stretches of marsh, the mouths of numerous small streams, the marshlands surrounding the mouths of several large streams, all of which flow down from the hilly uplands.

Northward the rolling and very scenic and sometimes rugged countryside elevates toward the southern border of Massachusetts. Aside from the cleared farms and estates, there are some surprisingly handsome pockets of forest here and there. These, as related to the hunter, are sections of forest or game lands from which the press of civilization has been stubbornly fended by wise conservationists determined to preserve at least a scattering of approximate wilderness. There is in the state of course no true wilderness. Connecticut is a heavily industrialized state, and its proximity to the millions of Greater New York residents has made it a prominently residential area also.

Good roads are everywhere. There is no corner of the state to which one cannot drive swiftly, on excellent parkways or via intersecting state routes. Air transport is almost as highly developed as at any point in the nation. However, because Connecticut is small, except for visiting sportsmen coming into the state, air transport is not at all necessary for travel from home to hunting ground.

From north to south Connecticut averages, in fact, only about fifty to sixty miles in depth, and from its western border with New York State to its eastern border with Rhode Island it is less than a hundred miles wide. The total in square miles is 5009. Into this relatively small area are packed at latest estimate about three million people. It is obvious that with such concentrated population hunters must expect to find many limitations on their sport. Yet Connecticut does have a surprising amount of good hunting for those who are willing to seek it and to be reasonably tolerant of traffic and crowded conditions.

There are an average of some 63,000 hunting licenses sold annually in Connecticut. Of these, about two-fifths are sold strictly to hunters. The remaining bulk goes mostly to persons who purchase the license that allows both hunting and fishing. Not many nonresident hunters visit Connecticut, and yet the number is surprisingly close to some much larger, less populated inland states—approximately 1500 nonresident hunting licenses are sold annually. Because of crowding, archery hunting is fairly popular, with an average of 1200 licenses sold each year.

For management purposes, the Connecticut Board of Fish and Game lists its game as: "Farm Game," which includes bobwhite quail, pheasant, chukar, cottontails; "Forest Game," meaning ruffed grouse (called "partridge" locally), gray squirrel, snowshoe hare, deer, woodcock; "Waterfowl and Furbearers," the former an extremely varied array listing sea ducks, other ducks, geese, rails, snipe, coot. Also available for hunters are such lesser targets as raccoons, foxes, an occasional bobcat. Game birds and animals that get the most emphasis are ruffed grouse and woodcock, waterfowl, squirrels, and rabbits.

Needless to say, in a state so populous holding public lands is extremely difficult, and thus Connecticut's are limited. Most land is privately owned, and because of crowded conditions many landowners are not as sympathetic to requests from strangers for hunting privileges as they might be in less settled regions. There are no National Forests. There are, however, a number of excellent State Forests, well managed and with a surprising amount of acreage. Some 70,000 acres of such lands are utilized for hunting.

There are a number of other blocks of land, some in the forests, some along the densely populated coastal areas, some on marshes and lake and pond shores, open to public hunting. These are in general areas where game management is extensively practiced. In fact, the game management officials do under difficult conditions an amazing job of helping to produce crops on all these lands. Over the past decade some 30,000 acres of farm-game lands have been improved by the planting of food shrubs and crops and other effective practices. As an example, wild apple trees, of which there are many in the state, have been grafted by hundreds with crab apple, to produce game food. About 40,000 acres of forest-game lands have been improved also over the past ten years, and at least 14,000 acres of new, additional waterfowl habitat has been either added by purchase or gift, or created.

For residents and nonresidents alike who anticipate hunting in Connecticut, the most valuable information possible is contained in a booklet readily available from the Board of Fisheries and Game (address at end of chapter.) It is titled "A Hunting Guide to Game Management Areas." It gives details on practically all public hunting lands in the state, with notations on available game, and access.

Although there are a number of camping spots in Connecticut, chiefly in the State Parks, few hunters in this state camp because other accommodations are at hand everywhere. Motels, hotels, rooms that may be rented in the smaller villages are numberless. In the larger cities and along the thruways, however, it would be wise always to make reservations ahead, because of the normal heavy traffic load.

During hunting seasons, which begin in late October, weather will usually be gently crisp but pleasant. Light wool shirts for upland hunting are recommended. The waterfowler, however, should wisely be equipped both with rain gear and warm clothing, for the coast can be cold and damp at any time. As the season progresses into November and December, weather and storms can be severe, with sudden heavy snows not uncommon.

This is chiefly a state for shotgun hunters and archers. In fact, handguns are not allowed without a municipal permit, nor are rifles larger than .22 rimfire long rifle. Shotgun loads should all be for birds and small animals. There is extremely limited shotgun hunting for deer, none on public lands. Shotgun loads should be based on about No. 7½ for grouse and woodcock and other small game, with perhaps some No. 6's for pheasants and short-range duck shooting. Heavier loads are needed for much coastal duck shooting, such as for sea ducks, and also for geese.

RUFFED GROUSE

This is the most important of the native game birds. While the total number taken annually by no means matches kill figures in larger, less populous New England states, there is fair grouse hunting under quite secluded forest and forest-edge conditions. It is unusual, and a compliment to Connecticut's game management, that a forest bird like the ruffed grouse can still be found in deep-woods oases surrounded by a teeming civilization. A brace of grouse taken here over a long day is perhaps for that reason more satisfying than a half dozen taken more easily in the wilderness.

Unless a hunter has friends who own Connecticut property with small grouse coverts, permission for hunting on private lands is unlikely to be granted. It is therefore all but mandatory that a hunter acquaint himself with the public hunting grounds.

Some of Connecticut's best grouse cover is in the Housatonic State Forest. This is in the northwest corner of the state, in rugged hill country. Like many other Connecticut grouse habitats, this has a few conifers, much mixed hardwood forest perfect for ruffed grouse, and with lower cover of laurel thickets and other brush. There are small rivulets and beaver flowages. On the Game Management Areas, of which there are two, forest openings have been made, aimed at forming edges for forest game such as grouse and deer. Some small marshes have also been man-made, and there is some natural swamp.

One area of 3030 acres is called the Sharon Mountain Block (1). Access is via the village of Sharon, at the intersection of State Routes 4 and 41. Several large highways from the New York City area run north along both New York State (State 22) and Connecticut (U.S. 7) borders and lead, via the routes mentioned, to Sharon. The Cream Hill Block (2) is a 2290-acre tract on the east side of U.S. 7. Access is via Cornwall and Canaan.

A number of other State Forest blocks offer comparable grouse hunting. The Cave Mountain Block of Mattatuck State Forest (3) is a 594-acre tract near Watertown, which is at the intersection of U.S. 202 and State 63, in west-central Connecticut. The terrain here is about like the Housatonic blocks. Centered in Naugatuck State Forest is 2191 acres of pine plantings and hardwoods called the Hunters Mountain Area (4). This is a short distance south of the city of Waterbury, with nearby smaller cities of Naugatuck, Oxford, Beacon Falls.

Near Kent, on U.S. 7 against the New York border, the Spectacle Lake Block of Wyantenock State Forest (5) offers 301 acres of public hunting, and farther south, not far from Danbury and Newtown (U.S. 202) there are 1044 acres of Paugussett State Forest (6) with fair grouse hunting. Some other State Forests either with blocks of open hunting for grouse or entire areas are as follows: Spectacle Meadow Block (7), Cockaponset SF near Durham; and another large block of 2300 acres, Turkey Hill (8) near Haddam; Nassahegon SF (9) near Burlington; Tunxis SF, Howell's Pond Area (10), 2300 acres near West Hartland; Nepaug SF (11), New Hartford; Peoples SF (12) near Barkhamsted, with 2954 acres; Nye Holman SF (13), Tolland; Dickerson Area, Salmon River SF (14), Hebron, and another plot, Larson Lot (15), near Colchester, and still another of 1000 acres, Dickinson Creek and Bull Hill (15), near Marlborough.

The Nehantic SF near Lyme has 1200 in a tract called the Tanney Hill Block (17). Shenipsit SF (18), Stafford, offers two blocks of good size. Nathan Hale SF (19), Andover, has one. The largest areas of all, with a great deal of mixed hardwood, various conifers, much oak to furnish mast, and some swampy

CONNECTICUT

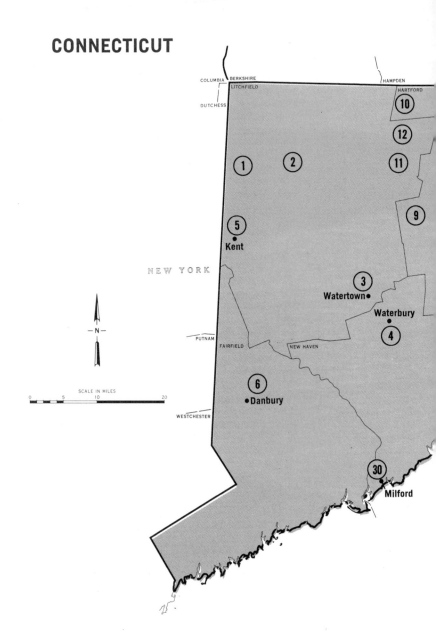

NEW YORK

—N—

SCALE IN MILES
0   5   10   20

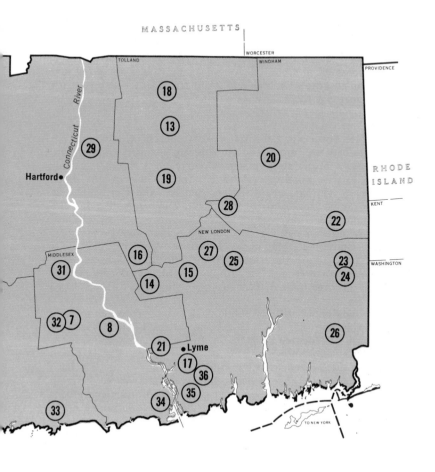

KEY TO HUNTING AREAS

1. Sharon Mountain Block, Housatonic SF
2. Cream Hill Block, Housatonic SF
3. Cave Mountain Block, Mattatuck SF
4. Hunters Mountain Area, Naugatuck SF
5. Spectacle Lake Block, Wyantenock SF
6. Paugussett SF
7. Spectacle Meadow Block, Cockaponset SF
8. Turkey Hill Block, Cockaponset SF
9. Nassahegon SF
10. Howell's Pond Area, Tunxis SF
11. Nepaug SF
12. Peoples SF
13. Nye Holman SF
14. Dickerson Area, Salmon River SF
15. Larson Lot Area, Salmon River SF
16. Dickinson Creek and Bull Hill Area, Salmon River SF
17. Tanney Hill Block, Nehantic SF
18. Shenipsit SF
19. Nathan Hale SF
20. Natchaug SF
21. Nipmuck SF
22. Pachaug SF No. 1
23. Pachaug SF No. 2
24. Pachaug SF No. 3
25. Franklin Swamp
26. Assekonk Swamp
27. Pease Brook
28. Mansfield Shooting Grounds
29. Dr. John E. Flaherty Field Trial Area
30. Charles F. Wheeler Wildlife Area
31. Cromwell Meadows
32. Durham Meadows
33. Great Harbor
34. Ragged Rock
35. Great Island
36. Lord's Cove

and cedar areas are as follows: Natchaug SF (20), 10,827 acres with access through Ashford, Eastford, Chaplin; Nipmuck SF (21), 7862 acres, via Union; Pachaug SF No. 1 (22), 5000 acres near Plainfield, No. 2, 9000 acres via Griswold (23), No. 3, 8500 acres, North Stonington (24).

There are several small and one or two substantial tracts not under the State Forest label. Attempts are being made to add more. Check with the Board for information and maps of these.

WOODCOCK

Woodcock migrate down along the valleys of Connecticut, coming from farther north, and a scattering are raised here during summer. In the State Forests and a few other places there is fair shooting, in a mixed bag with grouse. Hunters should seek woodcock where grass or ground cover is short, never in tall grass. They will be along the edges, and sometimes in coniferous plantings, under old apple trees and in crab apple thickets, and along the courses of streams, but not in truly swampy cover.

Some of the best places are in a number of the public State Forest areas described for grouse: Housatonic, Mattatuck, Naugatuck, Wyantenock, Paugussett, Nye Holman, Larson Lot of the Salmon River, ditto for Dickinson Creek and Bull Hill, Shenipsit (Tower and Bald Mountain Blocks), Nathan Hale, Natchaug, Nipmuck, all three units of Pachaug. Refer to "Ruffed Grouse" for directions.

There are a few additional areas of public lands where woodcock hunting is available. Franklin Swamp (25) is a 452-acre plot of open fields, swale and hardwood swamp north of Norwich on State 32. In the extreme southwest, on the shore, is the village of Stonington. This is almost on the Rhode Island border. Here there is tidal marsh that rises to oak forest, 707 acres (Barn Island) that furnish at times good woodcock shooting. Assekonk Swamp (26) is a bit farther up, at North Stonington. Mixed forest and farmland grades into swamp here, a tract of 694 acres. Pease Brook (27), near Lebanon, offers another third-section of public land. Lebanon is located on State 87 and 16. The Mansfield Shooting Grounds (28) in the vicinity of Mansfield, Chaplin, and Windham has 2500 acres of a mixed cover proper for woodcock. And there is a small area (260 acres) near East Windsor called the Dr. John E. Flaherty Field Trail Area (29) where hunting is allowed except when field trials are being held.

PHEASANT, CHUKAR, QUAIL

Pheasant and chukar partridge were introduced birds, and Connecticut is not the proper habitat for them. Pheasants in particular were stocked for many years, but the state at last decided the birds would not be able to establish themselves. Thus, today pheasant shooting, and a small amount of chukar shooting, is a rather semi-artificial form of hunting. Each year a number are released to supplement the shooting on native and migratory birds. Little is done with chukar. Pheasants are found during hunting season on a number of the suitable public grounds so far described. It is best to check with the Board as to where releases have been made. Following are a few places that usually have them:

Housatonic State Forest (Sharon Mountain Block); Naugatuck, Wyantenock, Paugussett, Salmon River (Larson Lot and Dickinson Creek), Nathan Hale, Natchaug, and Pachaug State Forests. On most of the public grounds mentioned for woodcock that are not in State Forests some releases are made.

There is not much quail shooting. Some bobwhites are found on the Barn Island tract at Stonington, and on the Flaherty Field Trial Area already noted, at East Windsor.

WATERFOWL, RAILS, SNIPE

At the mouth of the Housatonic River there are 750 acres called the Charles F. Wheeler Wildlife Area (30). This is near Milford. The area is made up of tidal marsh and has numerous creeks of a tidal nature. This is a good spot for rail hunting and for waterfowl. At Cromwell, south of Hartford, the Cromwell Meadows (31) offer almost 500 acres of hunting that includes waterfowl and snipe. Cockaponset State Forest (Spectacle Meadow Block) offers a modest amount of waterfowling on an impounded marsh. This is reached via Durham and Haddam. Durham Meadows (32) nearby is another block that has some waterfowl shooting. Several other of the State Forests should be checked for waterfowl possibilities. Development of ponds and small lakes is in progress regularly.

A small plot of 188 acres, tidal marsh, called Great Harbor (33), situated near Guilford, on the coast east of New Haven, is strictly for waterfowl, and the Ragged Rock public grounds fronting on the Connecticut River near Old Saybrook has pothole hunting. A good spot for both rails and waterfowl is Great Island (35), a 500-acre tract of creeks and tidal marsh at Old Lyme. This, plus Lord's Cove at Lyme (36), which furnishes snipe as well as waterfowl and rails, makes a good area to hunt. Barn Island, previously mentioned, also has some waterfowl shooting.

RABBITS, SQUIRRELS, RACCOONS

The gray squirrel is considered an important small-game species. It is found in modest abundance on all of the State Forest lands open to hunting, and in most of the other public lands mentioned here, except of course the tidal waterfowl areas. The same is true of the cottontail. There are some snowshoe hares, but by no means as many as cottontails. The Pachaug State Forest and the Nipmuck SF offer some shooting for these big rabbits. So do Peoples SF and Tunxis SF. Raccoons are in all of the State Forest areas and most of the others.

DEER

Whitetail deer have a peculiar status in Connecticut. The Game Board does not have regulatory authority on deer, and they might almost therefore be considered legally in the "agricultural pest" category. There is no rifle hunting for deer. Shotguns may be used on private lands, but few deer are killed. On the public lands open to deer hunting, only bow and arrow is admitted. Archers should scan the laws carefully. For example, all arrows in possession while hunting must bear the full name and address of the owner. There are other strict rules.

In past seasons the Housatonic State Forest has been the top area for deer, followed by Natchaug, Nehantic, Nipmuck. But as a rule only about twenty-five deer are taken annually by the archers.

NON-GAME ANIMALS AND BIRDS

There is a small amount of shooting for such non-game creatures as foxes, crows, and woodchucks. Of these, woodchucks probably receive the most attention. However, none of this shooting, in such a heavily populated state, is very important.

REGULATIONS

Game laws pertaining to seasons, bag and possession limits, areas to be hunted, special hunts, license fees all may have numerous changes from year to year. For current regulations, and for other specific queries, write to: State Board of Fisheries and Game, State Office Bldg., Hartford, Connecticut 06115.

NEW YORK

From the viewpoint of the hunter, New York is one of our most amazing states. Long the most populous, but now left in second place by California, it has about nineteen million people living in an area less than a third as large as California, 49,576 square miles. Yet here is one of the top deer states in the nation, and an aggregate total of over four million small-game animals and birds fills hunters' game bags each season.

The location of the state is unique. On the west it might actually be considered a Great Lakes state, since almost all of that border is formed by Lakes Erie and Ontario and the Saint Lawrence River. There is in the northeast a short border with Quebec. On the east New York becomes a part of New England, bordering Vermont, Massachusetts, and Connecticut. And then in the southeast it is a seaboard state, with its great port, and with all of Long Island surrounded by the Atlantic and Long Island Sound. Nearby in the same general area New Jersey is a southward neighbor. But the great share of the southern border, and a short section of the southwestern border, is with Pennsylvania.

The terrain also is diverse. The Catskills and Adirondacks, an extension of the Appalachian chain of mountains, ruggedly march up across central New York. Here, rather surprisingly, there is still much well-preserved wilderness forest. Westward toward the Great Lakes rolling farmlands support a varied agriculture that is in some crops first in the nation. Yet this state is also the nation's leading manufacturing region, with an awesomely diverse output.

Quite obviously with such heavy settlement roads reach to everywhere and are excellent. Only in the forest preserves of the Catskills and Adirondacks are there areas where any transport except a passenger car may be needed. In these mountain regions, a pickup or a 4WD vehicle can sometimes be used to advantage to get beyond the pressure of the majority of hunters. With many large cities, and a vast air transport network based in and around New York City, hunters can easily fly to almost any spot in the state.

Hunting is popular in New York, but the population percentage of hunters is lower than in many other states, probably because of the concentration of well over half of the state's people in the New York City vicinity, where great numbers of people have no interest in the sport. License sales in total average around 750,000. It is interesting to note that as many as 50,000 nonresident licenses and various permits are sold each season.

Game species are quite varied. Upland game birds include bobwhite quail, ruffed grouse, pheasant, Hungarian partridge, and wild turkeys. There are also waterfowl, and woodcock. There are squirrels, cottontails, varying hares, plus raccoons, foxes, woodchucks. The whitetail deer is the important big-game animal, but there are also black bears in fair supply.

The public lands in New York State, considering the dense population and pressures, are astonishing. Almost 50 percent of the land area is forested. Of that 14.5 million acres almost 3.5 million are in state ownership. Much of this land is in two huge forest preserves, the Catskill Park in the southeast, the Adirondack Park in the north-central and northeast. These total slightly more than 2.5 million acres.

There are also hundreds of thousands of acres in Reforestation Areas, or State Forests. These are scattered in a great number of tracts, the majority of only modest size. They are far too numerous to deal with individually later on under species, but they are very important to the public hunting picture and therefore some material about them deserves consideration here.

There are at least 400 tracts, differing in size from 500 acres to several thousand. Most are in the southern counties and along the fringes of the two great preserves already mentioned. These State Forests differ from the two Forest Parks in that most of them are multiple-use areas where timber is raised and cropped, whereas the Forest Parks are kept as they are, not given over to such multiple use. The state is divided by various agencies for management purposes; to avoid confusion it is important that hunters understand these. The Forestry Division splits the state up into numbered districts for management of the many State Forests. The Parks Division has named regions. Both of these differ from the Game Division numbered Regions, and it is these Game Division Regions that will be used for all references here, even, in a moment after explanation of the Game Regions, to offer an inkling of the location of the numerous State Forest Lands.

There are nine Game Regions. No. 1 covers the northern half of western New York, No. 2 the southern counties of the western part of the state. No. 3 is south-central, No. 4 north-central. Nos. 5, 6, 7, 8 begin in the northeast and run to the southeast. No. 9 is Long Island. There is a Regional Game Manager for each Region. A Conservation Department folder titled "Popular Public Hunting Grounds" lists their addresses. Although the many State Forests are not listed in the folder, the Regional Managers can be most helpful in assisting hunters with information about specific counties and in locating the State Forests within their Regions.

The Game Region boundaries are drawn along county lines. The counties in each Region are listed below for ready reference.

Region 1—Niagara, Erie, Orleans, Genesee, Wyoming, Monroe, Livingston, Wayne, Ontario, Yates, Seneca. Region 2—Chautauqua, Cattaraugus, Allegany, Steuben, Schuyler, Chemung. Region 3—Cayuga, Tompkins, Tioga, Onondaga, Cortland, Broome, Madison, Chenango. Region 4—Jefferson, Oswego, St. Lawrence, Lewis, Oneida, Herkimer. Region 5—Franklin, Clinton, Essex. Region 6—Hamilton, Fulton, Warren, Saratoga, Washington. Region 7—Montgomery, Otsego, Delaware, Schenectady, Schoharie, Albany, Greene, Rensselaer, Columbia. Region 8—Sullivan, Orange, Rockland, Ulster, Dutchess, Putnam, Westchester. Region 9—Nassau, Suffolk.

Region 1 has 1900 acres of State Forest in Yates Co., 2590 acres in Livingston Co., with deer, grouse, squirrels and rabbits the chief game species available. In Region 2, State Forest county acreages in total are as follows in round numbers: Allegany, 42,000; Cattaraugus, 27,000; Chautauqua, 15,000; Chemung, 600; Schuyler, 16,500; Steuben, 23,000. Species most plentiful are deer, rabbit, squirrel, grouse, wild turkey. In Region 3 species are about the same, with varying hare also important, and county acreages are rounded off as follows: Broome, 9000; Cayuga, 8000; Chenango, 68,000; Cortland, 30,000; Madison, 23,500; Onondaga, 2000; Tioga, 9000; Tompkins, 19,000.

Region 4 has predominantly Forest Park land but much State Forest land, too, with the usual forest game species. Region 5 offers over 22,000 acres in

Franklin Co., about 19,500 in Clinton Co. Much of Region 6 is in the huge Adirondack Park, but there are some Reforestation lands outside the boundaries so that the total in state ownership, including the Park, is almost 1,100,000 acres. Region 7 State Reforestation Lands in round numbered acreage are, by county: Delaware, 15,500; Otsego, 17,000; Schoharie, 30,000; Montgomery, 6500, with the other counties having lesser amounts of from 500 to 2000 acres each. In Region 8 almost all State Forest lands are in Ulster and Sullivan Cos., with acreage respectively approximately 142,000 and 10,000. The usual forest species, including woodcock along edge cover, and some waterfowl, are found on all of these public hunting lands. Region 9 (Long Island) is without Reforestation Lands.

This rather generalized State Forest guide above will offer hunters a quick reference, pointing them to counties with substantial public acreages, and should be used as a reference later as individual species are dealt with. Regional Managers, incidentally, will furnish in most Regions range maps of the prominent game species to assist hunters in orienting themselves toward areas of highest density for each variety.

Added to the above public lands at this writing are some fifty public hunting grounds in Game Management Areas owned by the state, and Cooperator Areas privately owned but state managed, on some of which permits are required. The hunter may acquaint himself with all these lands by obtaining from the Conservation Department, address at chapter end, two publications. One (previously mentioned) is a folder titled "Popular Public Hunting Grounds." This lists, locates, and describes most of the GMAs. There is also an excellent map, "Outdoor Recreation Map of New York," which shows the locations of all public lands in the state, including State Forests. It also describes the GMA and CA tracts, in listings on the back. This same map has three smaller ones printed on it showing the districts or regions into which the state is divided by the various agencies mentioned previously.

Hunters who may wish to use recreational vehicles or tents, and camp out, will find opportunity in the State Parks and the Forest Preserves. Several booklets are available from state sources. "Camping in New York State" lists private and public sites, can be obtained from the State Department of Commerce, 112 State Street, Albany, 12207. "New York State Parks" is available from the Division of State Parks, Albany, 12200. The Conservation Department can furnish "New York State Public Campsites." Other accommodations such as motels, lodges, camps in the mountains, hotels are so numerous that noncamping hunters face no difficulties finding lodging. There is only one caution. On opening day of deer season in some rural areas it may be well to reserve in advance. Some of the better counties have a large influx of hunters.

Seldom do any hunting seasons open in New York until early October, at which time the weather usually is invigorating, crisp, suitable for a light jacket and wool shirt. Hunters should go prepared however for something a bit colder. Fall can be unpredictable, and in the mountains or in northern New York cold snaps may occur. By November the weather is chillier and there is almost certain to be snow in the north at least, and in the mountains. Later on, weather is predictably cold and down or other warm clothing and insulated hunting boots are mandatory.

There is little need in New York hunting for anything more than the standard arms and ammunition used commonly east of the Mississippi. Deer hunters will need a favorite rifle in any caliber from the popular though somewhat outmoded .30/30 to the .30/06, .308, .270 or a comparable caliber. Some

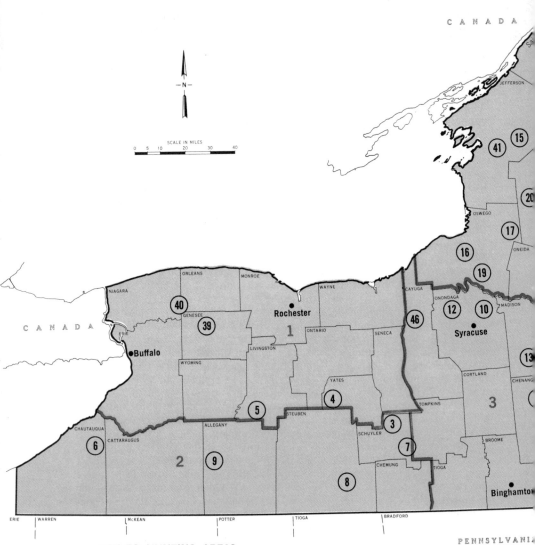

KEY TO HUNTING AREAS

1. Catskill SP
2. Adirondack SP
3. Hector CA
4. High Tor GMA
5. Rattlesnake Hill GMA
6. Canadaway Creek GMA
7. Connecticut Hill GMA
8. Erwin GMA
9. Hanging Bog GMA
10. Cicero Swamp GMA
11. Pharsalia GMA
12. Three Rivers GMA
13. Tioughnioga GMA
14. Big Moose Lake CA
15. Camp Drum CA
16. Happy Valley GMA
17. Littlejohn GMA
18. Stillwater Tree Farm
     CA

19. Three Mile Bay GMA
20. Tug Hill GMA
21. Upper and Lower
     Lakes GMA
22. DeBar Mountain GMA
23. Finch, Pruyn &
     Company CA
24. Lake Alice GMA
25. Split Rock CA
26. Wickham Marsh GMA
27. Speculator Tree Farm
     CA
28. Bear Spring
     Mountain GMA
29. Capital District GMA
30. Crystal Lake CA
31. Milton-Copake CA
32. Partridge Run GMA
33. Dutchess County CA

34. Ellenville CA
35. Hickock Brook GMA
36. Putnam County CA
37. Swan Lake CA
38. Suffolk County CA
     (including Navy
     Section)
39. Oak Orchard GMA
40. Tonawanda GMA
41. Perch River GMA
42. Wilson Hill GMA
43. Vischer Ferry GMA
44. Ausable GMA
45. Rogers Island GMA
46. Howland Island GMA

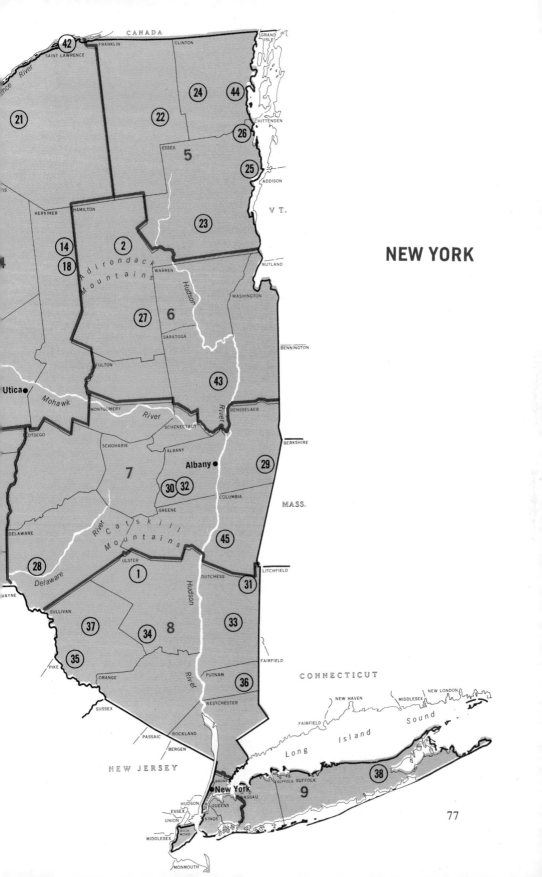

NEW YORK

77

rather large bears are taken in New York, and heavy loads should be used for them. The .30/06 with 180-grain bullet is an example of a serviceable load. Bird hunters in the uplands will use shot sizes No. 7½ and No. 6 most commonly. Quail hunters often use No. 8. Waterfowl gunners will need No. 4s for ducks, No. 2s preferably for geese. Where legal to use it, a .22 rifle is a handy implement for the squirrel hunter.

RUFFED GROUSE

The ruffed grouse is New York's most important and popular game bird. During an average season close to 200,000 hunters are afield after this forest grouse, and the total kill runs from 400,000 to over half a million. The season is long, presently from October through the end of January. The state is divided into northern and southern zones, with the southern-area season beginning a bit later than the north.

The two large Park regions furnish excellent public grouse hunting. The Catskill Park (1) lies chiefly in Regions 7 and 8, in southeastern New York. Greene and Ulster Cos. contain most of it, but other portions lie across county borders in Sullivan and Delaware Cos. The huge Adirondack Park (2) is in the northeast, based mainly on Region 6 but overlapping broadly into Regions 4 and 5. Counties involved are: Lewis, St. Lawrence, Herkimer, Hamilton, Fulton, Warren, Essex, Clinton, Franklin, and a bit of Saratoga and Washington.

A fair picture of grouse possibilities can be gained by looking at the state by Game Regions. Although grouse range throughout New York wherever there are suitable forest-edge habitats, eastern New York with its vast forests and its mountains is far better than the remainder of the state. Region 1, in northwestern New York, is poor grouse territory, with only small acreage of State Forest. Some hunting for grouse is available, but even in a good year the kill is modest.

Region 2, the southwestern counties, rates as good, with a kill in better years of approximately 50,000. There is a fair amount of State Forest here in numerous scattered tracts of modest size where public hunting is offered. As noted in the chapter opening, addresses of Regional Game Managers are printed on the folder, "Popular Public Hunting Grounds," and from these sources pinpoint details on the numerous State Forests and on paper company tracts open to hunting may be obtained. The counties in Region 2 that rate best for grouse are, in order, Allegany, Cattaraugus, Steuben, Chautauqua.

Region 3, which is made up of south-central counties, rates approximately fourth among the nine regions. Kill is estimated in good seasons at around 22,000 birds. The southern tiers of counties here furnish the best hunting and the most acreage of public lands. Tompkins, Cortland, Chenango, especially the latter, have many State Forest and other public tracts. A few more are found in Tioga and Broome.

Region 4, north-central, has a great deal of good grouse hunting for these counties border and some of them lie within the Adirondack Park region. Best of the hunting is the peripheral Adirondacks, and the Tug Hill Plateau area of western Lewis Co.

Region 5, which contains the three northeasternmost counties, does not rate high for grouse, even though a large acreage of the Adirondack Park is here. The kill is low, and the three counties all rate about the same. Grouse hunters here will find their best shooting, however, below the 1500-foot altitude contour.

Region 6, east-central, is in excellent grouse range, and has a vast expanse of public forest lands in the Adirondack Park. The northern and north-central parts of this Region are best, outside the heavily farmed Hudson and Mohawk valleys. In all of this Region hunters should shy away from the densely and continuously wooded areas and hunt such places as abandoned farms, alder and thornapple patches, and all such forest-edge habitats.

Region 7, which includes the southeastern counties immediately below Region 6 is one of the best grouse ranges in the state. In good years upwards of 60,000 or more birds are bagged here. Much of the Catskill Park region is here, and there are also numerous State Forest tracts. Rated in order, the first five counties are listed as follows: Delaware, Otsego, Schoharie, Greene, Columbia. The first three of those counties offer some of the best grouse hunting in the state. The other counties not listed all furnish fair to good shooting.

Region 8, the southeast, though close to the huge metropolitan centers, rates third in the state and furnishes some very good hunting indeed. Large portions of the Catskill Park offer ample public opportunity. The counties rate in order as follows: Sullivan, Ulster, Dutchess, Putnam, Orange, Rockland, Westchester. The northern halves of Sullivan and Ulster are best. The southern half of Dutchess Co., the northeastern part of Putnam Co. are next. Orange, Rockland, Westchester actually are rather poor grouse range.

In Region 9, Long Island, grouse are only locally abundant and the range is quite restricted. This is a Region of heavy human population. Some local residents who know the area will find modest opportunities, but so heavy is the pressure that visitors unacquainted with Long Island will find little chance to hunt, and too much exasperation to make it worthwhile. For all practical purposes there is no upland hunting west of a line drawn from Port Jefferson in the north to Bellport in the south.

There are numerous Game Management Areas and Cooperator Areas for grouse hunting. Hunters should check before hunting to make sure about regulations. Some of these Areas are completely open, some have only a portion open to hunting, and on some there is controlled hunting, with permits required. By Regions, locations of these Areas follow.

Region 1 has the Hector Cooperator Area (3), part of which spills over into Region 2. It is in Seneca and Schuyler Cos., contains over 13,000 acres west of Trumansburg. High Tor GMA (4) is in Yates Co. of Region 1, with 3640 acres east of Naples. Rattlesnake Hill GMA (5), partly in Region 2, Livingston and Allegany Cos., has over 5000 acres near Nunda.

Region 2 has Canadaway Creek GMA (6), 2000-plus acres near Cassadaga, Chautauqua Co. Connecticut Hill GMA (7) is split between Region 2 and Region 3, Schuyler and Tompkins Cos., contains 11,610 acres northeast of Alpine. Erwin GMA (8) is in Steuben Co., west of Painted Post, has 2500 acres. In Allegany Co. is Hanging Bog GMA (9), with 4340 acres near Black Creek Village.

Region 3 Areas are as follows: Cicero Swamp GMA (10), 3720 acres near Cicero, Onondaga Co.; Pharsalia GMA (11), 4500 acres near North Pharsalia, Chenango Co.; Three Rivers GMA (12), 3490 acres near Baldwinsville, Onondaga Co.; Tioughnioga GMA (13), 3600 acres near Erieville, Madison Co.

Region 4: Big Moose Lake Cooperator Area (14), 1800 acres near Eagle Bay, Herkimer Co.; Camp Drum Coop. Area (15), 65,000 acres out of Watertown, Jefferson Co.; Happy Valley GMA (16), 8620 acres northwest of Parish, Oswego Co.; Littlejohn GMA (17), over 8000 acres near Redfield, Oswego Co.;

Stillwater Tree Farm Coop. Area (18), 7500 acres, Herkimer Co., north of Eagle Bay; Three Mile Bay GMA (19), 1640 acres near Central Square, Oswego Co.; Tug Hill GMA (20), 4980 acres near Rector, Lewis Co.; Upper and Lower Lakes GMA (21), 8900 acres west of Canton, St. Lawrence Co.

Region 5: DeBar Mountain GMA (22), Franklin Co., 8390 acres east of Meacham Lake; Finch, Pruyn and Co. Coop. Area (23), Essex Co., 2000 acres near Blue Ridge; Lake Alice GMA (24), Clinton Co., 1450 acres near Chazy; Split Rock Coop. Area (25), Essex Co., 7000 acres east of Whallonsburg; Wickham Marsh GMA (26), Essex Co., a small acreage near Port Kent.

Region 6 has one Area, the Speculator Tree Farm Coop. Area (27), owned by International Paper Company, a 29,400-acre tract near Speculator, Hamilton Co.

In Region 7 there are: Bear Spring Mountain GMA (28), Delaware Co., over 7000 acres near Walton; Capital District GMA (29), Rensselaer Co., 3900 acres near Cherryplain; Crystal Lake Coop. Area (30) in Albany and Schoharie Cos., 7000 acres near Rensselaerville; Milton-Copake Coop. Area (31), Columbia Co. (and Dutchess Co. of Region 8), 6600 acres near Millerton; Partridge Run GMA (32), Albany Co., 4440 acres near Rensselaerville.

Region 8: Dutchess Co. Coop. Area (33), same Co., 7000 acres near Verbank; Ellenville Coop. Area (34), Ulster Co., 8000 acres near Ellenville; Hickock Brook GMA (35), Sullivan Co., 1175 acres near Barryville; Putnam Co. Coop. Area (36), 12,000 acres in same county, near Brewster and Patterson; Swan Lake Coop. Area (37), Sullivan Co., 4000 acres southwest of Liberty.

Region 9: Navy Section of Suffolk Co. Coop. Area (38), Suffolk Co., 2450 acres west of Riverhead.

PHEASANT

The ringneck is the most important farm game bird in New York. Approximately a quarter-million hunters annually bag slightly more than 400,000 pheasants. Ringnecks have been hunted in this state since early in the century. Numerous introductions of several ringneck varieties and hybrids make today's birds of rather uncertain ancestry. The early seasons were in several Genesee Valley counties in 1908. Today (and since about 1920), pheasants are found in suitable farm environment throughout the state. During the early 1940s a decline in the high pheasant population was rather drastic, but over late years the population has apparently leveled off, and is consistent with present land use. The western Lake Plains region of the state forms the best habitat, but even that, by standards in the pheasant states of the interior U.S., is marginal. Nonetheless, hunting as illustrated by the kill is surprisingly good.

Experiments are progressing in the stocking of two other pheasant varieties that may be able to establish themselves in the areas doubtful for or uninhabitable by the ringneck. These are the Korean pheasant, first tried in the southwestern counties, and the Japanese green pheasant, released in the southeast.

Region 1, in the northwest, is far and away the most important pheasant location. It rates as No. 1, with annual bag running anywhere from 250,000 to 350,000. These are self-sustaining birds, although some stocking also is done in second-class range to afford extra hunting. The kill of stocked birds is however inconsequential compared to the bag of self-sustaining pheasants. Best Region 1 counties: Niagara, Orleans, Monroe, Wayne, Genesee, northern half of Erie, Livingston, Ontario, Seneca. Second-class range is in Wyoming and Yates Cos. and the southern half of Erie, Livingston, Ontario, Seneca.

Most of the hunting is on private lands, by permission. There are pheasants also on some of the GMAs and Coop. Areas of Region 1. The Hector CA (partly in Region 2) offers pheasants (see "Grouse"). Oak Orchard GMA, with 2560 acres plus another 4000 in a bordering CA, is in Genesee and Orleans Cos. near Oakfield. Tonawanda GMA, 5500 acres east of Wolcottsville, lying in Niagara and Orleans Cos., also is a pheasant location.

Region 2, in the southwest, is a poor pheasant area with only a few bagged annually, mostly stocked birds. There is very little winter carry-over. The Korean pheasant may in due time change this situation.

Region 3 rates possibly fourth in the state, with a kill of from 15,000 to 20,000 birds. Winter carry-over in the southern counties is poor because of land use, somewhat better in the Lake Plains portions of the Region. Best counties: Cayuga, Onondaga, Madison. The Three Rivers GMA ("Grouse") offers public hunting.

In Region 4, the north is poor but the southern portion fair. Birds sustain themselves to some extent in the south but the northern carry-over in winter is limited and stocking is done. The farming country of the Mohawk Valley, and farmed areas along Lake Ontario and the St. Lawrence, offer the best pheasant habitat here. Camp Drum CA furnishes some hunting, and so does the Upper and Lower Lakes GMA. Both are described under "Grouse." Perch River GMA (41) in Jefferson Co. covers 7150 acres north of Watertown and has fair pheasant shooting. The same is true for Wilson Hill GMA (42) in St. Lawrence Co., with 3410 acres west of Massena.

Region 5 is very poor, with all birds previously stocked but with even this discontinued during 1969. The kill has been possibly 1000 birds a season, mostly in the St. Lawrence and Champlain valleys. Region 6 also is poor for pheasants. There is a modest carry-over but most birds have been stocked. Farming areas are scarce here, only found in portions of Washington, Saratoga and Fulton Cos. One public tract, the Vischer Ferry GMA (43) in Saratoga Co., with 810 acres near town of like name, offers pheasants. Region 7 also is of minor importance. The Hudson and Mohawk Valleys have some wild pheasants sustaining themselves, but stocking is also done, and excepting those valleys hunting is entirely dependent upon stocking. Crystal Lake CA, Millerton-Copake CA (partly in Region 8), detailed under "Grouse," offer some hunting.

Region 8 also is low in pheasants. They have been stocked so far but probably this will have been discontinued as this is read. It is hoped the Japanese green pheasant may take hold here. There is a bit of hunting in northern Putnam, Orange and Ulster Cos., and in eastern Dutchess. Several public tracts do offer pheasants. These are: Dutchess Co. CA, Ellenville CA, Putnam Co. CA, Swan Lake CA, all described under "Grouse." Region 9 has some pheasants, chiefly stocked, but with some self-sustaining east of Shinnecock Bay. That in fact is the best portion of the Region but is virtually closed by various town laws to public hunting. Two public tracts in Region 9 offer pheasants: the Navy Section of the Suffolk Co. CA, and the Suffolk Co. CA, both noted under "Grouse."

QUAIL

Originally the bobwhite was found over much of New York State where suitable habitat occurred. But even before this century it had disappeared from most of its range. Many, and several large, attempts at stocking to reestablish the bobwhite have been made over the years but none has met with success.

Today quail are confined mostly to Long Island and to the lower Hudson and Delaware valleys. At this writing there is an open season of fairly short duration in Putnam, Westchester, and part of Orange Co. with 4 birds a day legal, and a two-month season on Long Island with a bag limit of 6 per day.

Even though the season is open as above, hunting is poor for average gunners. In the Region 8 counties stocking has been terminated and only scattered coveys remain. A very few birds are taken on the Putnam Co. CA ("Grouse"). There is really no good quail range left in these counties. In Region 9, Long Island, the picture is somewhat different. Suffolk Co. has the state's only truly significant quail population. It is self-sustaining and requires no stocking. Hunting here can be rugged, in dense catbriar and other such cover, but very good. Access isn't easy. Some public hunting is available on the two Suffolk Co. CAs noted under "Grouse." There are also three areas open by daily drawing to Suffolk Co. residents only. It is best to check with the Regional Game Manager regarding these.

HUNGARIAN PARTRIDGE

Between 1927 and 1932 over 27,000 Huns were stocked in this state. They disappeared except along the St. Lawrence River in Jefferson, St. Lawrence, and Franklin Cos. Here, in grain crop habitat, they increased until the first season was held in 1952. With small competition from pheasants, they did well. But in later years lands put into the Soil Bank harmed the habitat appreciably. The Hun, it seems, must have grain stubble and other cropland habitat in order to survive in huntable numbers. Today there is open season in Jefferson, St. Lawrence, Franklin, and Clinton Cos., as this is written, with a daily bag limit of 4 birds.

In the Region 4 counties of Jefferson and St. Lawrence, the birds are quite popular. Best hunting is in the lowlands along Lake Ontario, and along the St. Lawrence River shoreline. Hunting is entirely on private lands, by permission. In the two Region 5 counties, all hunting is on privately owned lands. The kill is not high and pressure is low because coveys are widely scattered. Hunting for Huns in both Regions is therefore substantially a sport for the native who knows his own area thoroughly.

WILD TURKEYS

The history of the wild turkey in New York State is much the same as in many others. It was abundantly present over the southern half of the state in pioneer days, wiped out, and during the middle of this century reestablished. In 1959 restocking experiments had been so successful that a fall season was held in a few western counties. In 1968 the first spring season was held, and all of Region 2 was opened excepting Schuyler Co.

At this writing turkey flocks in Region 2 appear to be well established and heading toward a stable population. They are building up in some portions, decreasing in others. The kill during one of the latest seasons was 650 in fall, 150 the following spring. All of Region 2 has now been opened.

The wild turkey is also spreading over much of the southern half of Region 1. A part of Erie Co. has been opened and it is anticipated that more of this Region will be open for both spring and fall hunts as the flocks spread and grow. In both Region 1 and 2 a special permit by application is required.

To the east, in Region 7, turkeys became established some years ago from release of game farm stock. They disappeared everywhere except in southern and eastern Delaware Co. where they managed to survive. Beginning in the early 1960s a season was held and one has been held each year since. The original purpose was to cull out the unwary birds and attempt to make remaining birds wilder. More recently live-trapped birds from western New York have been introduced. They are prospering. Much of the range in this Region is good turkey habitat and it is believed that coming years will see good hunting here, and perhaps elsewhere in New York. For example, wild-trapped birds have been stocked in Region 8, in Sullivan and Ulster Cos., and the future there looks promising. At present the kill in Delaware Co. is low. A special permit is required by application to the Regional Game Manager.

WOODCOCK, SNIPE, RAILS

Though both jacksnipe and rails are present in numerous locations, they get little attention from hunters. Lake Erie and Ontario marshes have both in Region 1. In western Region 2 snipe are fairly popular in scattered marshes. Rail hunting is not important. Although a few of both species are present elsewhere in the interior of the state, there is virtually no hunting for them and opportunities are not broad. On Long Island there are both snipe and rails along shoreline marshes but snipe almost never turn up in hunters' bags. There is some interest in rails, and the best areas are in the town (township) of Hempstead and in the wetlands and offshore islands of the Oyster Bay region. Recently population of rails has been low.

Woodcock are far more important and are available in all suitable habitats and edge cover on the fringes of the large forest preserves and on many of the public tracts where stream courses and thickets offer feeding grounds. The kill averages somewhat over 100,000, with between 40,000 and 50,000 participant hunters. In Region 1 woodcock hunting is very good, with Wayne, Monroe, Orleans and Niagara Cos. best locations. In Region 2 the nesting population is not large and flights are only fair. There is a modest amount of hunting in the western counties. In Region 3 both nesting and flight birds are present in only modest numbers and the kill probably does not exceed 1000 annually. Some shooting on abandoned pasture lands is fair.

In the north-central part of the state, Region 4, the picture is brighter. There is excellent woodcock hunting here, on both native and flight birds. The central and western portions of the Region have the highest woodcock populations, with counties peripheral to the central Adirondacks and central Tug Hill area the best. Large expanses of public lands on the forest edges furnish good sport, and there is more on the several GMAs. Region 5 rates probably next to the above, with a good nesting population and a good flight, given proper weather. Adirondack foothills offer the best possibilities.

Region 6 is just fair, but in Region 7 the kill goes as high as 15,000, with both native and flight birds in good supply. Upland areas of Otsego, Delaware, Schoharie and Greene Cos. are best. Rating for Region 8 is roughly fourth among the Regions. Sullivan and Ulster Cos. are good, and so is northern Westchester. The Coop. Areas in Putnam and Dutchess Cos. furnish fair public shooting. In Region 9 there are a fair number of flight birds but finding places to hunt, as noted earlier, is a great problem.

WATERFOWL

With its Great Lakes shores, numerous large inland lakes, stream valleys and Long Island Sound, New York is a fairly important waterfowl state. The duck kill, including sea ducks, averages about a quarter million annually, with hunter numbers above 40,000. The kill of geese and brant is tabulated as one figure, runs as high as 40,000 in the best seasons. Following is the general picture by Regions. GMAs will be noted afterward.

The rating for Region 1 is good, with shoreline marshes of Lakes Erie and Ontario among the best locations. The Finger Lakes also furnish good shooting, and two National Wildlife Refuges, Iroquois and Montezuma, have some hunting. Both ducks and geese are available in this Region. In Region 2 waterfowling is just fair. There are puddle ducks on inland marshes, occasionally diving ducks along Lake Erie shore and the Finger Lakes. Goose hunting is fair if the season happens to coincide with the flight. It is usually best along Lake Erie, occasionally but erratically so inland. Region 3 is rated as good for both ducks and geese, with the Finger Lakes region best. There are no public goose hunting areas but there are several private fee spots. Check with the Regional Game Manager.

Region 4 is excellent for ducks, fair for geese. The Lake Ontario and St. Lawrence River shoreline marshes are fine locations and there are public opportunities. There are also several GMAs, to be noted later. Region 5 rates rather low, with a kill of possibly 5000 ducks and 50 geese an average. The Champlain Valley is best for both ducks and geese. Region 6 also rates poorly, and public sites are very scarce. Region 7 also is poor. There is a bit of shooting along the Hudson, some on beaver ponds, and some jump-shooting on rivers and creeks. Occasionally goose flocks pause to feed in corn and wheat fields but shooting is poor at best. Region 8 is a repetition, rating not more than fourth or fifth among the nine. Goose hunting is extremely scarce, and probably the best duck area is along the Hudson north of Newburgh.

Region 9 has ample waterfowl habitat but of course many problems of access occur. Black ducks, scaup, golden eyes are found in public-access situations in the Great South Bay and Oyster Bay areas. There are sea ducks available via rental boats or one's own craft out of many locations along the Sound. There is also good shooting on the ocean front. Hunters use Jones Inlet, which is a dangerous water with good shooting available, but it is not recommended for amateurs. Brant are very abundant some years. Most are located in and around the southern bays, and most common along the Nassau Co. and western Suffolk Co. shores. Eastward they are spotty. The north shore bays seldom gather brant. There is not much shooting for other geese. Some pit shooting occurs but it is severely controlled and thus not a public opportunity. In practice waterfowling on Long Island is almost totally restricted so far as access from land is concerned by a network of local laws and ordinances. A hunter must be equipped with boat and decoys and often must travel long distances on the water to get any shooting.

Public waterfowling grounds over the state are in alphabetical order as follows: Ausable GMA (44), Clinton Co., on Lake Champlain out of Plattsburgh, Region 5; Capital District GMA, Cicero Swamp GMA, High Tor GMA ("Grouse"); Oak Orchard GMA, Perch River GMA ("Pheasant"); Partridge Run GMA, Putnam Co. CA, Rattlesnake Hill GMA ("Grouse"); Rogers Island GMA (45), Columbia Co., south of Hudson and accessible only by boat, Region 7; Three Mile Bay GMA, Three Rivers GMA ("Grouse"); Tonawanda GMA ("Pheasant"); Upper and Lower Lakes GMA ("Grouse"); Vischer Ferry GMA ("Pheasant"); Wickham Marsh GMA ("Grouse"); Wilson Hill GMA ("Pheasant").

RABBITS AND HARES

Cottontails are in good supply and are the most popular of small-game animals. The kill averages around 1.5 million a season, with approximately a quarter-million participant hunters. Varying hares, or snowshoe rabbits as they are most often called, are abundant in most forest habitats, especially to the north. From 200,000 to 300,000 are bagged each year. The European hare was introduced years ago and is hunted during open season in most counties of Regions 7 and 8, the southern counties of Region 6, and at this time in part of Herkimer Co., Region 4. The kill is not high.

All of the GMAs and CAs except two or three without any proper habitat furnish fair to excellent rabbit and snowshoe hunting. One not so far mentioned, Howland Island GMA (46), Cayuga Co., Region 3, with 3200 acres northwest of Port Byron, has rabbit hunting (and deer) for archers only. State Forests and the two Parks give hunters plenty of public acreage.

A brief rundown by Regions is as follows. Region 1 has excellent cottontail shooting, with bag of over 200,000, but negligible hunting for snowshoes. Region 2 is fair to good for cottontails, with the northwest sector and river flats best. Snowshoes are popular but not abundant. In Region 3 the cottontail kill probably averages around 45,000, with best hunting in agricultural counties —Cayuga, Onondaga, Madison, Tompkins, Cortland. Some snowshoes are found here. Kill runs between 2000 and 3000, and Chenango, Cortland, and Madison Cos. are best. State Forest lands with dominant spruce planting in the twenty-year age class offer the quality hunting. Region 4 has cottontails in general abundance over all suitable ranges, but this Region is better known for its high snowshoe population, with the northern sector and the Tug Hill Plateau the important portions.

Region 5 has almost no cottontails, but a good population of varying hares. In fact, the Region rates possibly first for that species. Second growth and cutover areas with young spruce and balsam furnish fine shooting. Region 6 is not an especially important area for cottontails, although there are some outside the Park, in the southern portion. Snowshoes are plentiful in the Adirondacks and their fringes.

Region 7 has important populations of both cottontails and varying hares. It also gets heavy hunting pressure. The cottontail kill runs over 100,000 and the snowshoe kill at least 20,000. Most cottontail range of importance is in Columbia, Rensselaer, Montgomery, Albany, Greene, and Schenectady Cos. For snowshoes, Delaware, Greene, Schoharie, and Otsego are the best counties. In Region 8 cottontails are quite plentiful, with Dutchess, Putnam, Orange, Ulster good county locations. Varying hares are not plentiful, but the Fir Brook region of Ulster Co. and the DeBruce region of Sullivan Co. furnish fair hunting. Region 9 has abundant cottontails but restrictions on hunting are perplexing.

SQUIRRELS

Squirrels are popular and quite abundant. The annual bag averages from 750,000 to slightly under a million. The gray squirrel is the dominant species everywhere. A scattering of fox squirrels occurs in western New York, and there are a very few in the central part of the state. Much of the state has only grays. The large Forest Park preserves and the numerous State Forests all offer good squirrel hunting except where the forest is too dense. Woodlots and fringes of the large forests are the best bets. Nearly all the GMAs and CAs furnish fair to excellent chances.

Region 1 rates only fair; Region 2 rates as good, with best hunting ordinarily in the central and eastern portion. Region 3 stands perhaps as fifth in the state, with the Lake Plains counties showing better squirrel populations than the southern tier. In Region 4 there is opportunity for fair to good hunting throughout except in stands of heavy forest. The squirrel population in Region 5 is small. Region 6 offers best hunting outside the Forest Preserve, in the farming sectors where woods are scattered between. Region 7 is probably first in the state, has grays only. First five counties rated in order are: Delaware, Otsego, Schoharie, Greene, Rensselaer, with Albany, Columbia, Montgomery and Schenectady following. In general the western portion of this Region is best. Region 8 has grays only, with Putnam, Dutchess, Ulster, Sullivan Cos. in that order considered best. The CAs in Dutchess and Putnam Cos. are good bets for public hunting. Region 9 has some gray squirrels, but rifles are outlawed. Squirrels here are only incidentals in the bag.

DEER

The whitetail is the great big-game prize in New York. It is little short of amazing that the state has such an abundance of this species, considering the human population. It is estimated that New York has slightly more than 31,000 square miles of possible deer range. The annual bag is from 2 to 3 per square mile, spread over the whole range. Kills in round numbers for four recent consecutive seasons were as follows, including both bucks and antlerless deer: 67,000; 73,600; 78,500; 92,000. Buck kills during those seasons: 43,800; 43,800; 51,000; 54,000.

Although deer hunters are numerous, and some parts of the state crowded, there is really no great difficulty, considering population density, in finding a place to hunt. The two large Forest Park Preserves, the thousands of acres of State Forest, the GMAs and CAs, all but a few of which have deer in fair to top abundance, add up to hundreds of thousands of acres within the deer range that is public domain.

Kill figures are usually set up by three general regions of deer range and abundance: The Catskill Region, the Adirondack Region, the Central and Western Region. Over the four consecutive seasons mentioned above, total take in these three regions is revealing. The Central and Western sector showed the highest kills and the most stable ones: 30,000; 30,400; 30,200; 37,400. The Catskill region was next, though it is much smaller than either C. and W. or Adirondack. It had: 18,800; 24,000; 27,600; 34,300. The large Adirondack area showed an excellent kill but not as high as the others proportionately to its size: 17,800; 19,250; 20,700; 20,250.

The high-kill counties remain startlingly consistent. Over the four seasons the first three in each region were the same: Adirondacks: St. Lawrence, Hamilton, Franklin; Catskills: Delaware, Sullivan, Ulster; C. and W.: Steuben, Allegany, Cattaraugus. Many other counties were not far behind. In the Adirondack area Essex, Herkimer, Lewis, Warren show consistently high harvests. In the Catskills, the same is true for Columbia, Dutchess, Greene, Orange, Otsego and Schoharie. In C. and W., high counties in addition to the top three are Broome, Chautauqua, Chemung, Chenango, Livingston, Madison, Ontario, Orleans, Schuyler, Tioga, Yates.

To give readers perhaps a fuller picture of where the deer are, the kill per square mile of deer range in the top counties is not only revealing but astonishing. In the last season as this is written, the top ten were as follows: Sullivan, 8.9 deer bagged per square mile of deer range; Delaware, 8.3; Allegany, 6.6; Steuben, 6.5; Yates, 6.3; Ontario, 6.1; Schuyler, 5.9; Columbia, 5.4; Chemung, 5.1; Chenango, 5.1. Nine of these counties had substantially the same deer-kill density the previous season.

Some of the very best hunting is in the farm and woodlot areas of the

Central and Western region. Much of this hunting is on private lands, by permission. There has even (1968) been an open season on parts of Long Island, the first in forty-one years. This was shotguns only, by permission of landowner and with special permit, on lands over ten acres in area. Another unique hunt has been held on the Seneca Army Depot in Seneca County. This acreage, fenced with deer-proof fence, contains approximately 7500 acres of deer range, and special hunts have been held to control the herd. White deer, not albinos but a white mutation, started here from what is presumed to have been a single white buck sighted in 1957 and protected. A recent aerial count showed at least ninety-three of these deer, or about one to every four of normal color, and during that season a few were harvested, fifteen in all, under controlled conditions so that a proper sex ratio was observed. Conceivably another hunt for this rare trophy may eventually be held.

Although prospects are excellent for any deer hunter and enough public land exists, astute hunters will beware the high-kill, high-density counties near large cities. For example, in Region 8 Sullivan Co. is first-rank in the state for kill per square mile of deer range. However, large clubs control much land, restrict kills to keep a high deer population, but the result is deer of very poor quality. Also, there is obviously heavy demand for use of the CAs. Without doubt the northern and central and western parts of the state will consistently offer easier access, less crowded conditions, and better deer. Bear in mind that many low-kill areas in wilderness or near-wilderness or else farmland situations usually furnish the largest, heaviest bucks.

BEAR

There is a substantial black bear population. The kill fluctuates widely, due not so much to population ups and downs as to mast and weather conditions during the season. Over four consecutive seasons the kills were as follows: 648, 644, 457, 387. By far the great majority are taken in the Adirondacks. During the season when 644 were bagged, 569 came from there, 65 from the Catskills, only 10 from western and central New York. When the 387 were bagged, 328 were from the Adirondacks, 48 from the Catskills, 11 from C. and W.

The large expanses of forest provide the best hunting. Most bears are taken as incidentals by deer hunters. A few of the GMAs and CAs have bear populations. Among these are Bear Spring Mountain GMA, Delaware Co.; DeBar Mountain GMA, Franklin Co.; Ellenville CA, Ulster Co.; Finch, Pruyn and Co. CA, Essex Co.; High Tor GMA, Yates Co.; Speculator Tree Farm CA, Hamilton Co.; Split Rock CA, Essex Co. All have been covered under foregoing species.

OTHER ANIMALS

Raccoons are plentiful and on the protected game list with prescribed open seasons. It is estimated that upwards of a quarter million are taken some seasons by an enthusiastic group of hunters numbering over 30,000. Most public lands offer hunting for them. There are also animals such as woodchucks and foxes, some coyotes. Not long ago a timber wolf, very rare, was killed in upper New York.

Region 1 has plentiful raccoons, foxes and woodchucks, but no coyotes or bobcats, or at least they are both rare. The same is true of Region 2. In Region 3 both raccoons and foxes are plentiful, but coyotes and bobcats are rare. In Region 4 raccoons and foxes are popular and plentiful but still underhunted. There is some hunting for coyotes, and also for bobcats in the central Adirondacks and Tug Hill Plateau.

In Region 5 raccoons are abundant but fur prices have discouraged hunting. Posting of lands has also cut down hunter interest in training dogs for the purpose. The same is true regarding foxes. Woodchuck hunting is discouraged by landowners. There are a fair number of coyotes but most are bagged as incidentals by deer hunters. Bobcats are present but trained dogs are scarce and the result is little hunting for this species.

In Region 6 both foxes and raccoons are abundant and underhunted. Woodchuck hunting is popular in spring before hay gets high, and after it is cut. There are a few coyotes and coy-dog crosses in mountainous areas but little interest in hunting them. Bobcats are here in huntable numbers but hunters lack good dogs for the purpose.

Region 7 has abundant raccoons, a moderate fox population, but a minor amount of hunter interest. Woodchucks are abundant and popular. There is a bit of bobcat hunting by specialists, particularly in Greene and Delaware Cos.

In Region 8 raccoons are common, lightly hunted. Foxes are seldom hunted except, in several counties, by clubs riding to hounds. Little woodchuck hunting is available because of posting. There are no coyotes and bobcats are scarce. Although Long Island has some foxes and raccoons, restrictions make this hunting precarious for any but residents who know their areas thoroughly.

REGULATIONS

Game laws pertaining to seasons, bag and possession limits, areas to be hunted, special hunts, license fees all may have numerous changes from year to year. For current regulations, and for other specific queries, write to: State of New York Conservation Department, Division of Game and Fish, Albany, New York 12226.

NEW JERSEY

From the hunter's viewpoint, New Jersey is a rather amazing state. It would seem almost impossible that good hunting could remain here, yet it does. New Jersey fronts to the east on the Atlantic Ocean and at its northern extreme along the lower part of the Hudson River. Across the Hudson lies teeming New York City. The state's northern border is with New York State. On the west the Delaware River forms the entire border, with Pennsylvania on its other side all the way south to below Philadelphia, where the river begins to widen to become Delaware Bay, with Delaware the neighbor to the west.

New Jersey is a small state, only 7836 square miles. It is long from north to south. Even so, the extreme north-south straight-line distance is less than 175 miles, and east-west at its slender waist the distance from Trenton to the Atlantic is only roughly forty miles. Yet into this smallest of the Middle Atlantic states is packed the heaviest per-square-mile population of any state in the Union. With population steadily pushing ever higher, it is already well past the seven million mark.

Manufacturing and shipping are important parts of the busy pattern. The state heads all others in production of chemicals. Yet, oddly, it is one of the most important farm states, with about 70 percent of its land area still in farms or in forests. Vegetables, poultry, and dairy cattle produce the highest income per acre of any state in the U.S. It is therefore amazing to discover that New Jersey even has excellent hunting for big game—deer—on which the kill if spread over the state evenly would average each fall better than one per square mile.

The paradox lies in the fact that about half of New Jersey's area is actually rural, and probably 25 percent of its total area is still in forests, chiefly because of poor soils in part of the state that have made the land unsuitable for farming. In the northwest the land is glaciated, rocky farm country, with numerous large lakes and a substantial amount of upland hardwood forest. To the south there is the densely populated corridor that runs between the Newark-New York City complex and Philadelphia. Oceanside resorts range down the coast, but below the waistline corridor there are loamy farmlands broadening, and then in the lower center of the state the curious area known since settlement of the state in the early seventeenth century as the Pine Barrens. It is a curious fact that after over 300 years of civilization there are large expanses of the Barrens that still today have no people, and other portions with only very small towns.

Transport to hunting grounds is no problem. New Jersey has more modern highway mileage per square mile of area than any other state. Besides, any hunting tract is only a short drive from any other point. Airlines and railways are numerous, but hardly needed by sportsmen except possibly by those coming in from outside the state.

Obviously hunting conditions are somewhat crowded. But hunter numbers are not large compared to total population. License sales average presently under 170,000, with slightly more than 3000 nonresidents visiting the state. Upland game includes pheasants, ruffed grouse, and quail. There is excellent duck, goose, and brant hunting, with snipe and rails in addition. Rabbits, squirrels, raccoons, and woodchucks furnish small-game hunting. Deer, as noted, are plentiful, and there are a few black bears.

The big surprise a hunter discovers in New Jersey is the amount of lands open to public hunting. Many local hunters of course have made friends with landowners and hunt by permission on private lands. There are also numerous hunting clubs. But in addition there are over 300,000 acres state-owned and open to public hunting. Further, even in this era of pressure from exploding population, the acreage is slowly growing.

The Division of Game and Fish administers as this is written some forty-three Wildlife Management Areas, and is adding more. These run in size from less than 200 acres to almost 14,000 acres. Total acreage at this time is over 123,000. These tracts were originally called Public Shooting Grounds. To avoid confusion by old signs or in terminology, hunters should be aware of this. The Division of Forestry, Parks, and Recreation administers a number of State Forests totaling almost 175,000 acres, plus approximately 19,000 in State Parks that allow hunting in designated areas. Like the WMAs, the State Forests vary greatly in size, from a few hundred acres up to Wharton SF with over 99,000 acres

The Green Acres Program, in progress in a number of crowded eastern states, is adding land to the above. In a recent period over 31,000 acres of the present total was brought under Game Division administration through the Program. The public tracts are concentrated for the most part below the waist-line corridor south of Trenton, and in the northwest. Yet any resident is never more than an hour's drive from one or more. A map showing locations of all is available from the Game Division, and individual information sheets on each are also available. The Division address will be found at the end of the chapter.

Accommodations are numerous everywhere in motels and resorts. Hunters who may wish to camp do not have as broad a selection of sites as they may find in less populated states. But there are State Park and State Forest campgrounds, and numerous highly rated private ones. A booklet, "New Jersey State Forest and Park Campgrounds," can be obtained from the Department of Conservation and Economic Development, 520 East State Street, Trenton 08609.

New Jersey weather during early seasons, as for rails and woodcock in September and October, is generally warm to mild. When quail, pheasants, and grouse open later on in November it is commonly crisp wool-shirt and jacket weather. Late seasons along the coast or inland can be quite cold. One should be prepared for a variety of weather. Rabbit hunting runs into February and some duck seasons are open through early January. These late dates may be severely cold, blustery, and along the coast exceedingly damp.

Arms and ammunition in New Jersey are simplified because there is no rifle hunting allowed, except for woodchucks at specified seasons and by special rifle permit. Public shooting grounds allow no rifle hunting. Deer hunters must use no gun smaller than 12 gauge, with only buckshot legal. Bow and arrow also are legal. For upland birds, rails, and woodcock, shot sizes of No. 7½ and No. 6, the latter for pheasants, are needed. Waterfowl by consensus require heavier shot, from No. 4 short magnum to heavier loads for geese and for sea ducks. Check varied special regulations carefully. For example, proof of having passed a safety instruction course is mandatory, and Sunday hunting is prohibited.

In the following material under individual species the State Parks will not be specifically located. Boundaries inside which hunting may be allowed should be checked by hunters wishing to try these acreages. And they should contact either the Division of Fish and Game or the Division of Forestry, Parks, and Recreation for State Park hunting information. Some of the Parks presently allowing hunting are as follows: Allamuchy, in Morris and Sussex Cos.; Double Trouble, Ocean Co.; Duck Island, Mercer Co.; Farny, Morris Co.; Great Sound, Cape May Co.; Greenwood Lake, Passaic Co.; Inskip, Gloucester Co.; Millstone, Somerset Co.; Rancocas, Burlington Co.; Ringwood, Passaic, and Bergen Cos.; Swartswood, Sussex Co.; Voorhees, Hunterdon Co.; Wawayanda, Sussex Co.

QUAIL

Bobwhite quail are native to New Jersey, but are confined almost entirely —except for some released birds—to the southern half of the state. Quail range begins in Mercer and Middlesex counties, which are in the heavily populated center corridor of the state from Trenton northeast to South Amboy. Most of the better quail hunting is well below this line. It is practically mandatory to have a good pointing dog working in order to be successful at bobwhite hunting in New Jersey. A major portion of the best shooting is of course on privately owned land, for bobwhites are predominantly birds of cultivated lands with adjacent fencerow or woods cover. However, there is a considerable amount of good quail shooting on the public lands.

Annual harvest is remarkable for a state so heavily populated. The average over recent seasons has held rather stable at 100,000-plus birds, bagged by an average of approximately 45,000 quail enthusiasts. Careful management is reflected in a limit as this is written of seven daily. Added to the wild birds are as many as 30,000 birds annually reared by the state and by youth cooperators in several counties. Most releases are made at the public areas. Stocking of the WMAs is done periodically throughout the season. As a rule the quail season is long, to give hunters an opportunity to harvest stocked birds on the WMAs.

Turkey Swamp WMA (1) in Monmouth Co. contains about 1100 acres in several tracts. This county is at the northeast part of the quail range, east across the state from Trenton. The WMA lies east of Smithburg which is on State 537. Stocked quail are available in season.

Ocean Co., directly south of Monmouth Co. and on the coast, has a number of WMAs with quail. Colliers Mills WMA (2) contains 11,000 acres east of New Egypt and east of State 539. The Manahawkin WMA (3) contains 965 acres, portions of which are tidal marsh, near Barnegat Bay, east of the town of Manahawkin, State 72 and U.S. 9 junction. Butterfly Bog WMA (4) is small, 100 acres, with quail in scrub oak, off State 528 near Van Hiseville. The Manchester WMA (5) contains 2300 wooded acres, with quail hunting considered good. It is directly south of the Colliers Mills tract (above) and bordered on the west by State 539. Whiting WMA (6) has 1000 acres of good quail lands farther south near the town of Whiting and the intersect of Routes 539 and 70. Also reached via State 539 in Ocean Co. is the 2330-acre Pasadena WMA (7). Actually this one is part of the Greenwood Forest-Pasadena Area, with Greenwood WMA (8) containing over 7000 acres for a total of about

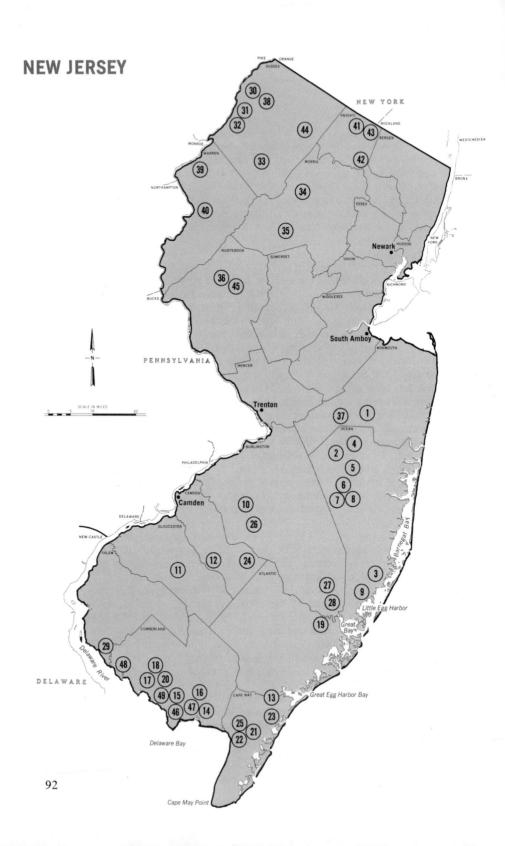

NEW JERSEY

KEY TO HUNTING AREAS

1. Turkey Swamp WMA
2. Colliers Mills WMA
3. Manahawkin WMA
4. Butterfly Bog WMA
5. Manchester WMA
6. Whiting WMA
7. Pasadena WMA
8. Greenwood Forest WMA
9. Stafford Forge WMA
10. Medford WMA
11. Glassboro WMA
12. Winslow WMA
13. Tuckahoe-Corbin WMA
14. Heislerville WMA
15. Millville WMA
16. Peaslee WMA
17. Dix WMA
18. Menantico WMA
19. Port Republic WMA
20. Nantuxent WMA
21. Beaver Swamp WMA
22. Dennis Creek WMA
23. Marmora WMA
24. Wharton SF
25. Belle Plains SF
26. Lebanon SF
27. Penn SF
28. Bass River SF
29. Mad Horse Creek WMA
30. Hainesville WMA
31. Flat Brook WMA
32. Walpack WMA
33. Whittingham WMA
34. Berkshire Valley WMA
35. Black River WMA
36. Clinton WMA
37. Assunpink WMA
38. Stokes SF
39. Worthington SF
40. Jenny Jump SF
41. Abram S. Hewitt SF
42. Norvin Green SF
43. Wanaque WMA
44. Hamburg Mountain WMA
45. Ken Lockwood Gorge WMA
46. Egg Island WMA
47. Berrytown WMA
48. Osborne WMA
49. Fortescue WMA

10,000. Excellent quail hunting is found here. Stafford Forge WMA (9) near West Creek, Ocean Co., is another good bet.

To the west, in Burlington Co., there is Medford WMA (10), a small one, 214 acres, reached via the Medford-Mount Holly Road. Gloucester Co., bordering the Hudson and south of Camden, has one tract, Glassboro WMA (11), 2337 acres, near Glassboro, State 47 and U.S. 322 junction. Camden Co., bordering Gloucester on the north, contains the Winslow WMA tract (12) of 1882 acres south of Sicklerville, State 536.

Others in the extreme southern counties are as follows. Tuckahoe-Corbin WMA (13) has 12,000 acres, much of it tidal marsh, but with inland portions of woods and fields. It is partly in Atlantic, partly in Cape May counties, and reached from the city of Tuckahoe, north and east. Heislerville WMA (14), 2678 acres in Cumberland Co., southwesternmost county, is off State 47 south from Millville. There is also the large Millville WMA (15), 12,000 acres of woods and fields southwest from Millville off State 555.

Peaslee WMA (16), Cumberland Co., has 9538 acres off Route 49; Dix WMA (17) with almost 1000 acres, Cumberland Co., is primarily marsh but has some good quail shooting near Fairton on State 553; Menantico WMA (18), same county, has about 300 acres off Route 49. The Port Republic WMA (19) in nearby Atlantic Co. has 755 acres near its namesake town. And Nantuxent WMA (20), of 787 acres, about half upland and the remainder tidal marsh, offers good quail shooting near the town of Cedarville.

Cape May Co., the southeastern tip of New Jersey, has several WMAs with quail shooting. There is Beaver Swamp WMA (21) with 1400 acres near Dennisville, with State 47 and 83 giving access, and west of Dennisville the Dennis Creek WMA tract (22) of 1162 acres. The Marmora WMA (23) is south of that city, with 1445 acres.

Two State Forests rate well for quail. Huge Wharton SF (24) lies in the triangle formed by U.S. 30 and U.S. 206 south and east from Camden and contains almost 95,000 acres. Belle Plains SF (25) is in Cape May Co., south of Woodbine, with 6792 acres. Not rated quite as high, but still with fair quail hunting, are three other State Forests. Lebanon SF (26) is in Burlington Co., with State 70 giving access. It has 22,216 acres. The Pasadena-Greenwood tracts (previously noted) are immediately to the southeast. Penn SF (27) is also in Burlington Co., with almost 3000 acres, access State 563. And Bass River

SF (28), Burlington Co., is over 9000 acres north of New Gretna, which is on U.S. 9.

There are small amounts of quail hunting on several other WMAs. For example, Mad Horse Creek WMA (29), primarily a waterfowl area, has a fair quail population. This is in the southwest, in Salem Co., west of Bridgeton, which is on State 49, and thence via State 540 to the south. There are over 3000 acres here. Any other WMAs noted later on but which are located in southern New Jersey may be worth trying, for released birds if not for a self-sustaining population.

PHEASANT

Pheasants were brought to New Jersey late in the last century. Much stocking has been done over many years. Currently some green and Korean types are being tried. There is a fair wild breeding population of ringnecks, and many birds are released on the WMAs before and during the season. As many as 60,000 birds are stocked annually. Pheasant hunting is exceedingly popular, and in peak years the kill runs over 275,000, with an average of 100,000 hunters participating.

The primary pheasant range is north of a line drawn from Trenton to the coast. It encompasses parts of Monmouth, Mercer, Middlesex, Somerset, Hunterdon, Morris, and Warren counties. The Hunterdon Co. farm belt has the most consistently high pheasant population, with a continuance into western Somerset, northern and eastern Mercer, and western Monmouth counties. The remainder of the primary range might be classed as having generally a medium bird population.

Below the mid-state line, there are good pheasant populations along parts of the coastal plain. While not many public tracts lie in the prime northern range, released birds furnish good hunting on many of the quail areas already mentioned, in the south. And, in the extreme northwest, in Sussex Co., there are several tracts that offer excellent shooting. These are: Hainesville WMA (30), with 282 acres, U.S. 206; Flat Brook WMA (31), 2235 acres west of U.S. 206 and near Bevans; Walpack WMA (32) with 388 acres south of Bevans; Whittingham WMA (33) 1500 acres, south of Newton, U.S. 206.

In Morris Co. there is the Berkshire Valley WMA (34), 1140 acres, with excellent shooting. It is north of Dover via State 15. Black River WMA (35), also in Morris Co., 2800 acres northeast of Chester, has good shooting.

In Hunterdon Co. the Clinton WMA (36), with 900 acres, north of Clinton and along the northwest shore of Spruce Run Reservoir, is one of the best.

Assunpink WMA (37) near Clarksburg, Monmouth Co., with 359 acres, is fair.

Among the WMAs located under "Quail" that also furnish pheasants are: Colliers Mill; Medford; Manahawkin; Glassboro; Tuckahoe-Corbin; Heislerville; Millville; Dix; Nantuxent. Some other WMA's and even some of the State Forests have a bit of pheasant hunting, particularly for released birds. Check with the Game Division for others not listed here.

RUFFED GROUSE

It is interesting that a state so heavily populated still sustains a husky annual crop of ruffed grouse in its forests. There are grouse in the forested northern counties, and also in the southern counties that have woodlands. Heaviest concentrations are in the north. As many as 40,000 hunters try for grouse each fall, and though the kill, compared to effort by hunters, is not high, it is considerable. Most seasons it averages from 40,000 to 50,000 birds.

State Forests are among the best of the grouse habitats. Stokes SF (38), U.S. 206, Sussex Co., offers over 14,000 acres of good hunting. Worthington SF (39), Warren Co., contains about 6000 acres. Jenny Jump SF (40), also in Warren Co., is small, 967 acres, but worthwhile. Lebanon SF, Penn SF, Bass River SF ("Quail") offer fair opportunity. Wharton SF, and Belle Plain SF, also under "Quail" are excellent. Abram S. Hewitt SF (41), State 511, with almost 2000 acres in one of the best grouse counties, Passaic, and Norvin Green SF (42) in the same county, with 2260 acres, are both good bets.

Many of the WMAs already noted offer fair to excellent grouse hunting. Under "Quail": Turkey Swamp; Butterfly Bog; Colliers Mills; Manchester; Medford; Pasadena-Greenwood Forest; Peaslee; Tuckahoe-Corbin; Millville; Stafford Forge; Menantico; Port Republic. Under "Pheasant": Hainesville; Flat Brook; Berkshire Valley; Clinton; Whittingham; Black River; Assunpink.

Several WMAs not so far located offer fine grouse shooting. Wanaque (43), 1470 acres near Hewitt via State 511, Passaic Co. is one. The 3500-acre Hamburg Mountain WMA (44), Sussex Co., near Newfoundland off State 23, is another. Ken Lockwood Gorge WMA (45) in Hunterdon Co. is small, 213 acres near Clinton, but has fair hunting. Some of the other WMAs not noted here under "Grouse" offer hunting of varying quality. The Game Division can offer up-to-date information about grouse populations on any tract.

CHUKAR PARTRIDGE

This introduced game bird appears in the game laws with an open season. However, they are found almost entirely on posted lands where they have been privately stocked.

WOODCOCK

New Jersey has some of the finest woodcock hunting along the eastern seaboard. This is not very well known, even among resident hunters. The bird is underhunted in the state, with interest shown only by a small group of enthusiasts. Best hunting is when the fall migration flight is on. Usually this occurs at peak in October.

The northern tier of counties furnishes excellent shooting. Flat Brook WMA, Sussex Co. ("Pheasant"), is one of the best spots. Cape May Co. in the extreme south is, a bit later, undoubtedly the best region of all. At times when weather urges migration exactly right this county has unusual concentrations of birds as they gather for the flight across Delaware Bay and along the coast. Other southern counties also have good flights.

All of the public hunting lands (see "Quail," "Pheasant," "Grouse") have woodcock shooting, at proper times when the flight is on, of varying quality. This is a rather specialized endeavor, since birds may be in and gone in a day or two. As mentioned, the northern counties, and those in the far south, Cape May first, plus Atlantic and Cumberland especially, will usually offer the top opportunities.

WATERFOWL

With its long coastline and its "inside" waters such as famed Barnegat Bay, Little Egg Harbor, Great Bay, and Delaware Bay, New Jersey has long been famous for its waterfowling. Although there is fair hunting to be had inland around the lakes and swamps—where many wood ducks and black ducks are annually bagged—the bulk of the shooting is along the vast coastal marshes, a large share of them fortunately in public ownership, from Ocean County on south to and around Cape May and up through Delaware Bay into the lower reaches of the Delaware River to Trenton.

Goose hunting is not especially noteworthy. Many Canada geese rest briefly along the coast or pass over on their way south. Only a few are killed on public marshes. Greater snow geese tarry in numbers, but they are on the fully protected list. A good picture of species representation and importance can be gained from a look at coastal aerial waterfowl surveys made during and after a recent season. In early December some 375,000 waterfowl were present along the coast. Black ducks, the mainstay puddle duck of the East, numbered 66,000. Scaups (bluebills) were most plentiful at 138,000. Brant, for which New Jersey has quality shooting, numbered about 110,000. There were a large number of sea ducks (scoters). These build during migrations to as many as 100,000. Canada geese numbered barely over 4000. Earlier in the season teal are plentiful and important and occasional large flocks of baldpates and canvasbacks are present. Mallards and pintails also often make up a considerable percentage of the total.

Annual duck kill of late has been nearly 80,000, with around 25,000 participant hunters. Brant are next in importance by annual bag, averaging about 25,000 taken by 10,000 hunters. All of the WMAs and even the State Forests mentioned previously under upland birds have from fair to good waterfowl shooting. Among the quality tracts are: Tuckahoe-Corbin, Mana-hawkin, Marmora, Port Republic, Beaver Swamp, Dennis Creek, Heislerville, Mad Horse Creek, Nantuxent, all located under "Quail."

Hainesville WMA ("Pheasant") has a small amount of waterfowl shooting. Clinton, also under "Pheasant," has shooting around and on the Spruce Run Reservoir. Stafford Forge ("Quail") has wood ducks and some Canada geese. Dix WMA ("Quail") has some of the finest tidal marshes in the state.

Egg Island WMA (46) has over 6000 acres of quality tidal marsh along Delaware Bay, Cumberland Co. Some of the state's best waterfowling is here. It is south of Millville via State 555. The 1610-acre Berrytown WMA (47) in Cumberland Co., also south of Millville via State 47, is another excellent spot. The Osborne WMA (48) is exclusively managed for waterfowl, contains three tracts of salt marsh totalling 183 acres. These are in Cumberland Co., along Delaware Bay southwest from Shiloh. The 885-acre Fortescue WMA (49), another Cumberland Co. tract, is tidal marsh south of Cedarville and Newport.

Colliers Mills ("Quail") has numerous ponds with duck shooting on most. Flat Brook ("Pheasant") offers shooting on impoundments on the tract.

Hunters should make special note of the excellent brant hunting along the coast. It is considered the best in the Atlantic flyway. Numerous decoys are needed and the birds are wary. There is good brant hunting almost every-where just offshore or at the marsh edges. The Brigantine National Wildlife Refuge, which has public hunting on certain portions, is one good general area for brant. It is also excellent for other waterfowl. The Refuge Manager can be reached at Oceanville 08231.

Guides for brant hunting and other waterfowling are available in many coastal locations. The Game Division may be able to assist in locating guides but cannot make recommendations. Along with brant, the sea duck shooting off the Jersey coast and on the bays is very good. Among the sea ducks are the scoters, eider, and old squaw. It is the scoters that are most abundant and most hunted. To avoid confusion, hunters should know that coastal New Jersey waterfowlers call them "coots." From Barnegat Inlet south to Cape May Point is the stretch considered best for sea ducks, although they are found elsewhere.

SNIPE AND RAILS

There are snipe to be shot in the inland freshwater marshes, but this bird does not get much attention. However, rails are extremely popular with a small group of enthusiasts. The clapper rail, a bird of good size—twelve to fifteen ounces—is the eagerly sought tidal marsh target of around 4000 hunters, who harvest from 5000 to 8000 annually. From the vicinity of Tuckerton on the coast in lower Ocean County on south to Cape May Point and up the Delaware there is excellent rail shooting and a perennial underharvest of these game birds. Many are reared in these same marshes, with some flight birds coming in. The season is early, generally beginning of September, and therefore offers some of the first shooting of the season.

There are upwards of 30,000 acres of publicly owned tidal marsh in the southern region where rail hunters can have fine shooting. New Jersey rail hunters claim to have perfected the art of "walking up" the clapper rail, although poled skiffs are used in wild rice areas, with a guide, on high tides, for sora rails. Old clothes, an old shotgun, plastic shells, and sneakers are the uniform and equipment for walking after clappers. Jersey rail hunters are certain to get wet and muddy Weather may be extremely hot, and insects out in force. Repellent and suntan lotion are musts. A foam belt such as water skiers wear is a good safety precaution. When hunting with a dog to flush and retrieve, low tides are best. When walking without a dog, high tides push the birds out of ditches and channels.

All of the southern coastal WMAs cited as best for waterfowl will offer excellent rail shooting. The highest population of rails is probably in the strip of marshland north from Cape May Point to Great Egg Harbor Bay. On the other side of the state, in Salem Co., the Mad Horse Creek tract noted earlier has both clapper and king rails. Dennis Creek, Heislerville, Egg Island, Fortescue, Tuckahoe-Corbin, Marmora, all mentioned earlier and for "Waterfowl," are perfect rail habitat.

RABBITS

Cottontails abound throughout New Jersey and are the most popular of all game species, with more hunters interested in them than in any other species and a higher kill than for others. Annual bag runs up to 350,000, with about 100,000 hunters participating. While a great deal of good rabbit hunting is on private lands, there is ample opportunity on the public lands. All of the State Forests, WMAs and the State Park lands open to public hunting have fair to excellent cottontail populations, excepting the few areas that are entirely marsh. There is really very little choice. The closest WMA or Forest will do nicely. Ordinarily those with quail and pheasant cover have the highest rabbit populations. See material on those birds earlier in chapter.

There are a few snowshoe hares in the state, but this is not an important species. Also, the blacktailed jack rabbit was imported from the west some years ago and releases were made at several locations. These big hares stay for the most part in open country. The farming areas of Hunterdon and Monmouth counties, where potato fields spread over many acres, are good places to find jacks.

SQUIRRELS

The gray squirrel ranges throughout almost all of the New Jersey woodlands and forests. Mature stands of such trees as oaks and beeches have the largest squirrel populations, and often the larger tracts of State Forests and WMAs offer the best squirrel hunting. The gray squirrel is not hunted in New Jersey as diligently as it might be. Some 50,000-plus hunters take around 160,000 squirrels each season. Squirrels are present in fair to excellent numbers on all of the wooded public lands which have been described so far.

BEAR

The black bear appears on the game list with an open season, but the number of bears in the state is extremely low. The natural range is in the northwest, in the Kittatiny Mountains. Occasional records of bear have also come from west-central New Jersey. However, during one recent season only three bears were reported killed by hunters.

DEER

For its size and population, New Jersey garners an exemplary deer harvest. For over a decade there have been more than 5000 deer taken annually. During recent seasons figures have been up, in two instances, to 8646 and 9844. Interesting is the fact that even though there are a hunter's choice season, a bow season during which either sex may be taken, and a number of special permits, any-sex, for another hunt, by far the major share of the kill is bucks. Ordinarily the buck kill makes up about two-thirds or more of the total. Hunter numbers average over 100,000. As mentioned early in the chapter, only shotguns with buckshot, or bow and arrow, are legal. During the season when 8646 deer were harvested, 1498 were brought in during the bow season, an excellent record indeed.

A study of figures on firearms kills by counties readily establishes where the most New Jersey deer are. For three consecutive recent seasons Hunterdon Co. was first, with a kill from 850 to over 900. Warren Co. was second. For two of the seasons Sussex in the far north was third, but in the other year it was Burlington, a close runner. Morris Co. was fourth two years, Sussex the other season. Atlantic Co. was in fifth spot all three seasons. Burlington was sixth twice, with Morris in the third year. Even in sixth place, kills ran from 357 to 507. In seventh place, Ocean Co. took all three seasons, Somerset did likewise for eighth, and Cumberland for ninth. Mercer and Passaic both made good records, with Cape May following. Other counties show only modest kills.

The larger acreages of State Forests and WMAs offer some of the better deer hunting. However, many smaller tracts, with farms surrounding, are excellent. Hunterdon Co. is a good example. It is interesting to note that all of the WMAs and State Forests except those almost totally of tidal marshlands sustain deer herds. A comparison of these public lands against the counties listed above will give a hunter an excellent chance of success. See the upland game birds and waterfowl for locations of these lands, and their acreages.

Some of the WMAs and State Forests where deer are listed as primary game species are as follows: Stokes SF, Wanaque WMA, Worthington SF, Jenny Jump SF, under "Grouse"; Flat Brook, Walpack, Clinton, and Berkshire Valley WMAs, under "Pheasant"; Colliers Mills, Manchester, Whiting WMAs, Lebanon SF, Pasadena-Greenwood WMA, Penn SF, and Bass River SF, all under "Quail." Also Wharton SF, Peaslee WMA, Tuckahoe-Corbin WMA,

Belle Plain SF, Millville WMA, Stafford Forge WMA, A. S. Hewitt SF, Norvin Green SF, all under "Quail"; and Whittingham WMA and Black River WMA under "Pheasant."

OTHER ANIMALS

Raccoons are abundant over much of the state, foxes are fairly so. These animals sustain some hunting, and are becoming more popular. There are problems for hound men who may run such animals on small public tracts, for the chase onto private lands cannot be controlled. However, many farmers welcome raccoon hunters. The animals are destructive to crops. On the larger State Forests and WMAs, there is fair hunting for both raccoon and fox. There is also some shooting for woodchucks in the farm, fencerow, and field areas. But rifle hunting can be done only with specific permits, and there is no rifle hunting allowed on the WMAs. This is, therefore, a minor sport.

REGULATIONS

Game laws pertaining to seasons, bag and possession limits, areas to be hunted, special hunts, license fees all may have numerous changes from year to year. For current regulations, and for other specific queries, write to: New Jersey Division of Fish and Game, P.O. Box 1809, Trenton, New Jersey 08625.

Atlantic
Coast
States

DELAWARE

The long peninsula that separates Chesapeake Bay from Delaware Bay is called the Delmarva Peninsula because Delaware takes up a portion of its eastern side, Maryland has the western half and much of the area farther south, and Virginia shares the southern tip. The entire eastern shore of the small state of Delaware fronts on water. At the north end the broad Delaware River separates the state from southwestern New Jersey. Then comes Delaware Bay as the river meets the Atlantic, and finally the far southern beaches may be considered on the Atlantic itself.

This coastal location makes Delaware a rather marshy state. About one-twelfth of its acreage is in fact marshland. There are low, rolling hills in the north, but the state's highest elevation is under 450 feet. Southward the hills sweep down to a coastal plain that is almost at sea level. At the north end of this narrow strip of coastland there is heavy industrialization. Southward, in the central and southern portions, there is a rural quality, and a good bit of the low, swampy south has managed to remain in a reasonably natural state.

Delaware refers to itself as the "First State" because it was first of the original thirteen to ratify the Constitution. To a hunter it is obvious therefore that civilization has been here a long long time. There is no truly wild country, but there is a surprising amount of good hunting. All of it is easily accessible. Good roads streak north to south—U.S. 301, U.S. 13, U.S. 113—carrying one the entire length of the state. Cross routes give access to every corner, and at the southern end State 14 takes one along the outer beaches. Fortunately for waterfowling, much of the marshland on Delaware Bay in the central half of the state, though accessible, is not harried by main routes. Air travel is easy, to such cities as Wilmington and Dover. But in a state this small hunters hardly need to fly to their destinations.

The state is in fact only ninety-six miles from north to south, at its widest point about thirty-five miles, at its narrowest only nine. It is our second smallest state, covering 2057 square miles. There are only three counties. Population is high, over half a million at present. Seen through a hunter's eyes, however, this is a deceiving picture, for license sales are fairly low. They average an annual total of only around 25,000. Not many hunters are from out of state, possibly 500 per season.

Although Delaware has several game species, this is primarily a waterfowling state. It has some excellent shooting for ducks, geese, and rails. There is some pheasant shooting, quite good quail hunting. Doves, woodcock, and snipe are also available. Whitetail deer do surprisingly well, and some very large bucks are taken each season. Rabbits and squirrels are plentiful in some areas. Foxes, raccoons, and woodchucks are hunted by hound men and varmint shooters.

In so small and heavily populated a state it is difficult to keep public lands. The Board of Game and Fish Commissioners has done an admirable job against severe pressures over many years. There are upwards of 20,000 acres of state lands managed for public hunting. Some of these are quite large, the Canal Wildlife Area with some 5000 acres, Woodland Beach with over 3500. But even where only small acreages are available, game men have done their best to keep these productive.

There is also Bombay Hook National Wildlife Refuge near Smyrna. This has an area of about twenty-two square miles, supports concentrations of ducks and geese sometimes in tens of thousands, and also provides deer hunting for several hundred hunters. Prime Hook, another National Refuge farther south, also furnishes fine waterfowling. Maps of these areas, showing portions open to hunting, and maps of other public hunting areas can be had from the Board of Game and Fish Commissioners.

Accommodations for hunters are no problem. Cities and towns along all the main routes have ample facilities, and the state is so small one is quickly at the hunting location. Camping is to some extent restricted. There are several State Parks, and some tent camping in State Forests. Camping is specifically prohibited on the public wildlife areas, except for some supervised group camping by conservation groups or youth groups.

Because Delaware is low and coastal, it is likely to be chilly and damp and sometimes quite cold during hunting seasons. Also, because much hunting is along the marshy shore, one should be well equipped not only with warm clothing but with rain gear also. During the early upland seasons, as for doves and squirrel, weather may be warm—cotton-shirt weather. There may also be mosquitoes whenever it is warm.

This is basically a shotgunner's state. There is in fact very little rifle shooting allowed. Also, the emphasis is heavily on waterfowl, the main attraction for all visitors and most natives. With both geese and ducks available, shotgun loads should be selected in proportion, some No. 2 and No. 4, some No. 6. For the upland hunting, No. 7½ is good, and for squirrels a .22 rifle is a good addition, and allowed.

PHEASANT

There is no established and sustaining pheasant population to speak of in Delaware. Hunting is almost entirely for released birds. In New Castle County, the northernmost of the three counties, the Chesapeake and Delaware Canal cuts the county approximately in half, running from the Maryland line in the west straight across to the Delaware River. Along this Canal lies the Canal Wildlife Area (1), containing 5000 acres of public lands. The eastern end is marshy, but much of the remainder is suitable for pheasants, and this Area is one of the two more important pheasant hunting locations for released birds. It is easily reached north-south via U.S. 301, and by State Routes 896 and 71. Delaware City is a location point at the east end of the Area.

A second pheasant release with consequent hunting is at Little Creek Wildlife Area (2). This lies along the coast on Delaware Bay, about midway down Kent County, the middle county of the state. Little Creek WA contains 3221 acres. It is only three miles east of the city of Dover, easily reached by a side road (No. 8) running out from Dover, and also by north-south Route 9, which runs along the western edge of the Area. Little Creek WA is predominantly a waterfowl habitat, but the western portion is high enough for pheasant hunting.

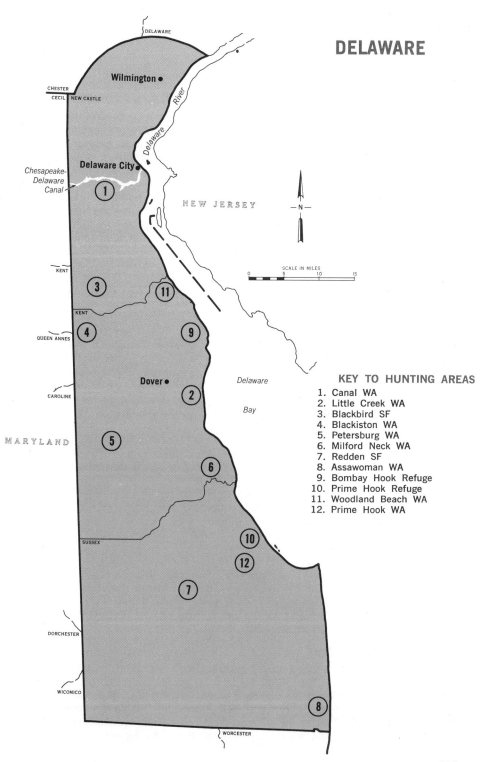

DELAWARE

KEY TO HUNTING AREAS

1. Canal WA
2. Little Creek WA
3. Blackbird SF
4. Blackiston WA
5. Petersburg WA
6. Milford Neck WA
7. Redden SF
8. Assawoman WA
9. Bombay Hook Refuge
10. Prime Hook Refuge
11. Woodland Beach WA
12. Prime Hook WA

QUAIL

Delaware has some rather good bobwhite hunting, both on public and private lands. Private-land hunting is of course by permission only. Best of the private-land shooting is found in two places: southwestern Kent Co. and mid-western Sussex Co. The first general region lies northwest of the town of Harrington and extends to the Maryland line. This is a quite rural region, with small settlements and with numerous side roads crisscrossing it. Farther south, the region in Sussex Co. surrounds for a good distance the village of Seaford, and runs across to the east and south toward and above Laurel. All of it is easily accessible via U.S. 13, and State Routes 24, 28, 20.

Public lands where quail hunting is fair to good are quite well scattered over the state. Beginning in the northern portion of the state, in southern New Castle Co., Blackbird State Forest (3) is open to public hunting. This is a modest-sized tract well down toward the southwest corner of the county. It is reached via a side road running southwest from the village of Blackbird, on U.S. 13. To the south of this State Forest, across the line in Kent Co., is the Blackiston Wildlife Area, 1325 acres, north of the village of Blackiston. This village is at the intersection of State Routes 42 and 6. The WA is in the extreme northwest corner of Kent Co.

The large and excellent Petersburg Wildlife Area (5) lies well down toward the southwestern part of Kent Co. West of U.S. 13, it is easily reached from Camden, Woodside, Felton, all on or near U.S. 13. Several smaller roads cross the Area. It contains 2687 acres of open fields, brush, and woodland. Some of the Area is farmed as a test site for upland game plantings. Food patches are planted and so are shelter belts of evergreens. This WA is in some of the state's best quail habitat.

Eastward across the state and to the south, in the southeastern corner of Kent County, is Milford Neck WA (6). There are 1216 public acres here that furnish quail hunting. At one point the Area borders the Mispillion River on the south. It is east of U.S. 113. Thompsonville is a key village to the north. The city of Milford, on U.S. 113 straddling the Kent-Sussex Co. line, is the main point of access. The WA is a short distance to the northeast.

There are several Forest tracts open to public hunting about in the center of Sussex Co. The Redden State Forest (7) takes in most of the acreage. These tracts lie on either side of north-south-running U.S. 113, a few miles north of the city of Georgetown. These are in a portion of Delaware with some of the state's better quail habitat.

Far down in the extreme southeast corner of the state (Sussex Co.) is the Assawoman Wildlife Area (8). It comprises 1460 acres. While this is primarily a waterfowl management and hunting Area, there is fair quail shooting along the inland fringes. The beach highway State 14 leads to it and so does State 26, which comes in from the west to the beach road (14) at Ocean View and Bethany Beach north of the Area.

MOURNING DOVES

Delaware has some good dove shooting, with the annual kill running around 150,000. Much of the kill, however, is on private lands. All parts of the state except the marshlands have at least some dove hunting. Because of the industrial expansion in the north, the best opportunities for dove hunters are found in the southern half of the state, in the farmland regions. An increase in soybean acreage over past years has helped to reverse a downtrend in both quail and doves. There is no best area specifically for doves, but the western halves of Kent and Sussex counties are in general most likely to offer good shooting. All of the Wildlife Areas except the marshes, and including Canal in the north, offer some dove shooting. See "Quail" and "Pheasants" previous to this portion, and following material that locates other WAs.

WOODCOCK

Although woodcock are not highly pressured by hunters in Delaware, there is some fair shooting in a number of places, dependent of course on how flights of birds from farther north materialize and on the hunter being active during the migration. Scattered birds are found on the Canal WA, Blackbird State Forest, Blackiston WA, Petersburg WA, Little Creek WA, Milford Neck WA, and Assawoman WA, all of which are located in the material pertaining to pheasants and quail. Petersburg WA should be particularly noted for woodcock possibilities.

Other woodcock hunting is available on the upland areas of two National Wildlife Refuges, parts of which are open to public hunting, with varied restrictions. Maps of the refuges showing details of the open areas and listing all special regulations are available from the game commission. The two are: Bombay Hook Refuge (9), and Prime Hook Refuge (10).

Bombay Hook Refuge contains almost 15,000 acres of salt marshes with some fringes of upland cover. It is located on the coast in northern Kent Co., northeast of Dover and southeast of Smyrna. State routes 6, 8, 9, and 42 all lead to the vicinity. These and other side roads branch from or tie into U.S. 13. The portion of Bombay Hook open to upland hunting is the southwest extremity. This places it closest to Dover and the quickest approach is from that city.

Prime Hook Refuge is farther down the coast, in Sussex Co. It borders on Delaware Bay between Slaughter Beach and Broadkill Beach. State Route 14 running southeast from Milford to Rehoboth Beach is the main access road, and the Refuge is reached by several offshoot side roads from 14. The designated upland hunting areas are rather complicated here, some in the north and some at the south end. It is best to acquire a map.

For further detailed hunting information pertaining to either of these Refuges—which are mentioned later in regard to other hunting—one may contact the Refuge Manager. For Bombay Hook, the address is R.D. #1, Box 147, Smyrna, Del. 19977. For Prime Hook, R.D. #1, Milton, Del. 19968.

SNIPE, RAILS, COOTS, GALLINULES

Coots and gallinules are not important game birds here. Snipe get small attention but offer good shooting on open areas of the two National Refuges mentioned under "Woodcock" and on most of the waterfowl shooting grounds mentioned and located later under "Waterfowl." There is also snipe shooting in many Delaware marshes that are not public. Permission is not easily arranged because many private marshlands are leased by waterfowlers or kept for private hunting by their owners.

The coastal tidal marshes have good rail hunting. But it is mandatory that a rail hunter find a spot that does have tidal marsh, so that the high tides move the birds. Otherwise it is virtually impossible to flush them. Rails do not get much hunting pressure in Delaware. The best area for this hunting undoubtedly is the Woodland Beach Wildlife Area (11). This is a 3543-acre public ground in the extreme northeast corner of Kent County, on the mouth of the Delaware River where it becomes Delaware Bay. It lies along the Smyrna

River and southward, is northeast of the city of Smyrna. State Route 6 running to Woodland Beach is the best access. Other small side roads probe the region. Public boat-launching sites are available. This WA is divided into two units—north and south. The two are separated by a water area. It is necessary to acquire detailed maps from the Commission, for all the marsh areas are likely to have privately owned sectors nearby or bordering the public lands, and some also have refuge tracts.

WATERFOWL

As noted in the opening material of this chapter, about one-twelfth of Delaware is marshland, and thus there is much emphasis on waterfowl. Along the coast of southern New Castle Co., all of Kent Co., and the northern half of Sussex Co. there is an almost solid stretch of salt marshes. A great deal is in private hands, but there are several excellent shooting grounds open to the public, although visitors should be warned that these may be crowded.

Most Delaware waterfowl are migratory. The Commission does all it can, and so do private interests, to hold the birds. Many small ponds have been constructed in central Delaware, some surrounded by open farm fields, and these are especially attractive to Canada geese. There are also marshes stretching along the main streams of the state, especially as the streams near the coast, and these hold waterfowl.

The majority of the good public waterfowl grounds have already been located under foregoing game birds. These are: Woodland Beach WA (see "Rails") which offers good shooting for both ducks and geese; Bombay Hook National Refuge (see "Woodcock"), which in its northern sector fairly well inland is an attractive area for geese, and farther south in the Kent Island and Kelly Island portions along the Leipsic River and the Simons River offers both ducks and geese; the Little Creek WA (see "Pheasant") with shooting for both ducks and geese; Prime Hook National Refuge (see "Woodcock") with both; Assawoman WA in the extreme southeast (see "Quail") which has both ducks and geese.

There is another area that could be confusing to those not familiar with the state. This is the Prime Hook Wildlife Area (12), a 635-acre state-owned tract near Milton in northeastern Sussex Co. This is an excellent spot for both ducks and geese. It is reached by a small side road branching from the intersection of State Routes 14 and 16 just east of the village of Milton.

Regulations for all of the waterfowl Areas are rather complicated, and they differ from Area to Area and also at the Refuges. At some places hunters build their own blinds, use them on a first-come basis. At others state or federal blinds are available for a fee, with drawings at a stipulated hour on each hunting day. Only certain weekdays, in some cases, are open to hunting. Some of the areas stipulate what equipment each hunter must have. Thus it is certainly advantageous, if not mandatory, that prospective waterfowlers contact the Commission for maps and regulations of the desired public areas, or write to the Refuge Manager (addresses given under "Woodcock") when planning a hunt.

DEER

Whitetail deer still do surprisingly well in Delaware, notwithstanding the crowding of civilization. Hunting is by shotgun and bow only, and seasons in each of the three counties are brief, from two to five or six days. During a recent season 851 deer were harvested. Some whitetails here are of substantial trophy size, bucks of three and a half years and up weighing field-dressed from 160 to 180 pounds.

Generally speaking, the middle portion of Delaware has the heaviest deer population. This is reflected annually in the kill. For example, over a period of ten years Kent County, the central county of the state's three, invariably showed the highest kill. During a recent good season Kent Co. had 54 percent of the kill, Sussex Co. 27 percent, northern heavily industrial New Castle Co. the remaining 19 percent. Even so, in that year New Castle showed 165 deer taken, a fair record for such density of population. Heaviest kills however appear to be consistently in the northwestern and coastal portions of Kent Co.

The present-day thriving deer herd is the result of an extremely long build-up. Delaware had no deer hunting for over a hundred years. The first season of modern times was in 1954. It lasted two days and only shotguns were legal. Over 500 deer were taken. Now there are annual seasons, in general for either sex, and an average of about 6000 hunters participate. Thus one has approximately a 1 in 7 chance of success.

There is of course plenty of private-land deer hunting, but it is not easily available except to those who have acquaintance contacts with individual landowners. The areas of best deer range on private lands lie in western Kent Co. and southwestern Sussex Co. The ranges given under "Quail" on private lands in those areas are identical. But to the north of those, lying between the Petersburg WA and the Blackiston WA there is good deer range, crossed by State Route 8, along the Maryland border.

The public lands best for deer hunting are among those already located under other species. Blackbird SF, the Blackiston WA, the Petersburg WA (see "Quail") in the western part of the state, the Bombay Hook Refuge (see "Woodcock"), the Milford Neck WA, the Assawoman WA (see "Quail") in the east all furnish top-notch public deer hunting. So does the central-south Redden SF (see "Quail"). The Bombay Hook Refuge has in recent years been opened to hunting because of a deer problem of overbrowsing. It may possibly furnish greater kills in the future as the herd is further controlled.

RABBITS AND SQUIRRELS

Rabbits and squirrels are important small game in Delaware, and they thrive over much of the state where there is suitable habitat for either or both. Private-land hunting is excellent for both, but permission is not easily obtained.

The large (5000-acre) Canal Wildlife Area in Central New Castle Co., noted under "Pheasant," is one of the best of the small-game areas. Six or seven hundred rabbits reach game bags from here each season. Petersburg WA and Little Creek WA, also previously noted, are excellent rabbit hunting areas. There are squirrels, too, and for squirrels the State Forests where hunting is allowed—Blackbird, Redden—are usually good. Milford Neck and Assawoman WAs in the east also furnish quality small-game hunting.

OTHER ANIMALS

Foxes and raccoons are fairly plentiful over much of Delaware. Fox hunting is by "chase" only. The several Wildlife Areas of the western part of the state, and the State Forests, offer good public opportunities for both raccoons and foxes. Private lands in the southwest also have fair populations of these animals, and so does southwestern Kent (the central) Co.

There is some oppossum hunting, but this animal is chiefly taken incidentally by raccon hunters. It is not on the game list. Woodchucks are hunted to some extent in the farmland areas. This animal, and squirrels, are the only ones for which rifles are legal. There is little public-land woodchuck shooting. Most is by permission on private lands.

REGULATIONS

Game laws pertaining to seasons, bag and possession limits, areas to be hunted, special hunts, license fees all may have numerous changes from year to year. For current regulations, and for other specific queries, write to: Board of Game and Fish Commissioners, Dover, Delaware 19901.

MARYLAND

Maryland has a most unique location, seemingly sharing with neighboring states portions of their topography yet tossing in some exclusive features of its own. In the southeast portion it is typically eastern seaboard, with outer beaches on the Atlantic, Chincoteague Bay separating the outer islands from the mainland, and with low coastal plains sweeping inland. In the narrow strip of the northwest, on the fringes of the Appalachians, which has its northern border with Pennsylvania, Maryland is dramatically different, with Backbone Mountain in the Alleghenies, highest point in the state, pushing up to 3360 feet.

West Virginia and Virginia border Maryland to the west and the south, and on the east it shares with Delaware the bulk of the Delmarva Peninsula. It is in the center of Maryland that its most distinctive feature lies. Here Chesapeake Bay broadly slashes the state in two from north to south. It is as if Maryland is chiefly important as the "land that encloses Chesapeake Bay." It is this long, broad thrust of water into the state's interior that shapes the major share of its general atmosphere, activity, and personality.

Maryland's economy is as diverse as its terrain. It is heavily industrialized, with production in metals, chemicals, electronic products, ships, and a host of other manufacturing businesses. It is an important producer of sea foods, of tomatoes, tobacco, vegetables, cement. Yet, even though it was settled in the 1600s, it still today has almost half its land area wooded.

To be sure, there is no wilderness in the real sense. Settlement is too heavy. But between the forested portions westward and the vast tidewater regions, there is still a comparative abundance of recreational lands that serve the hunter well. And there is a substantial percentage of land in agriculture that offers abundant game cover, and occasionally hunting by permission on private lands.

Travel for the sportsman is easy. The state is small. Good roads lead to everywhere. Because of the important port of Baltimore on upper Chesapeake Bay, and the location of Washington, D.C. up the Potomac, transport is highly developed. Interstates and U.S. highways form a veritable grid. Air transport, though hardly needed by hunters in a state this size, reaches to all the larger cities, and rental car trips from any one to anywhere in the state are brief.

Considering its small size and heavy population, Maryland's abundance and variety of game are surprising. Because of total lack of any geometric symmetry in its shape, distances are a bit deceptive. From far east to far west can be upwards of 300 miles in a straight east-west line. Yet at one point in Washington Co. near Hancock the state is only two miles north to south.

Maryland covers only 10,577 square miles, total. Population at present is well past the 3.5 million mark. Almost a million of this number are in

Baltimore, and while there are several fair-sized cities, most of the numerous towns are of modest dimensions and well scattered. A tremendous population is based near Washington, D.C., and thus the countryside, considering general population density, is rather pleasantly rural, with the long, narrow western "panhandle" in the mountain-and-valley section most lightly settled of all.

Hunting interest is high in Maryland, again considering the state's small size. Upwards of 200,000 licenses are annually sold. Counting various special deer and duck blind permits probably another 50,000 are added. Nonresidents make up an average 7500, most of them after the famous waterfowling, but usually most of them shooting on private grounds.

After the primary-place waterfowl, which includes ducks, geese, rails of several varieties, and jacksnipe, Maryland has an interesting variety of upland and migratory non-water birds. These include pheasant, ruffed grouse, bobwhite quail, woodcock, doves, turkey. Rabbits and squirrels are abundant. Deer are in good supply. There are raccoons, opossums, woodchucks, foxes.

The state has an admirable situation in public hunting lands. There are some 175,000 acres of these, in Wildlife Management Areas, State Forests, State Recreation Areas. A list can be obtained from the Department of Game and Inland Fish, address at chapter end. There is also a booklet available from the Department of Forests and Parks, which owns and administers some of the public hunting grounds, titled "Maryland Forests and Parks," which is of value to hunters. It is obtained from the Department, State Office Building, Annapolis, Maryland 21404. There is also an excellent map, prepared by the Maryland State Roads Commission cooperating with the Department of Game and Inland Fish, that lists and shows locations of all public hunting lands. This can be had from either cooperating agency. The Road Commission address: Box 717, Baltimore 21203.

The Maryland Game Department is extremely active in research and field work aimed at providing more and better hunting, with emphasis currently on waterfowl, doves, deer, building up turkey flocks, and attempts to possibly establish new pheasant strains. The forestry people try diligently to keep up with the demand of hunters and others for camping; those hunters who wish to camp on their trips should write to the Department of Forests and Parks for the booklet "Camping in Maryland."

There are a number of excellent State Parks. Maryland also has several camping areas under federal jurisdiction, and there are a growing number of private campgrounds. Other accommodations—motels, hotels—are numerous throughout the state. It is advisable on all the heavily traveled routes, however, to reserve in advance. Normal traffic is heavy, and hunting-season traffic is likely to be heavier because of the movement of northerners to the south for the winter.

Maryland climate in fall is mild and pleasant. As the season progresses, tidewater and Eastern Shore hunters and those in the higher country of the far northwest will find conditions changeable, from crisp to sometimes chill. The coast can be intensely cold in any rainy late-fall weather and clothing should be selected accordingly. For late seasons and midwinter, wool clothing and heavy underclothing will never be amiss, although many a day may be mild.

Arms and ammunition are easy choices here. Deer hunters will not be allowed to use rifles in all counties. Where rifles are permitted, standard whitetail calibers are all that are needed. Shotgunners must use slugs for deer. Buckshot is at this writing illegal. For heavy sea ducks and geese shot-gunners should be ready with No. 2 and No. 4 shot, the latter preferably in at least short-magnum loads. For upland birds, shot sizes from No. 6 down to No. 8 make a proper selection.

Many persons may wish to hunt waterfowl, whether ducks, geese, or rails, with a guide. There are guides available, and there are also private properties along the shore where such hunting can be done for a fee. It is extremely helpful in most cases to contact a Regional or District Wildlife Officer for assistance in locating such guides or shooting facilities. Names, addresses, and telephone numbers can be obtained from the Game De-partment. Or the annual game-law digest, titled "Hunter's Guide for Mary-land," can be utilized.

PHEASANT

Although Maryland has a pheasant season and some fair shooting in a restricted range, this state is not truly within established breeding range for the ringneck. Generally speaking, ringneck range where birds can be con-sidered self-sustaining runs south in this part of the U.S. about to the southern Pennsylvania line above central Maryland. This places the authentically estab-lished range just north of Maryland's Carroll and Baltimore Cos. Those counties are where the best of the pheasant hunting is found in the state. U.S. 140 crosses Carroll Co., with the city of Westminster centrally located, and I 83 runs north-south across Baltimore Co. Both counties border Penn-sylvania. Most of this hunting is on private lands. There are at present no public hunting grounds within these two top-rated pheasant counties.

For some time Maryland, like several other states, experimented with the Japanese Green Pheasant in an attempt to establish a bird that was suitable for much of the state's habitat. Those experiments have to date been unsuccessful and that bird is now considered impractical. However, one of the Iranian pheasants is now considered a possible candidate for estab-lishment south of practical Chinese ringneck range. These birds have at this time been released in some of the north and central counties, and it is hoped that they may build wild, breeding populations.

RUFFED GROUSE

It is an interesting commentary on the tenacity of this fine game bird, and on its ability to adapt to civilization, that it is still available in huntable numbers in Maryland. The kill is not high, but there is fairly good ruffed grouse hunting in the forest sections for those who diligently pursue it. Al-though the season is open statewide, and scattered birds may be found in most well-forested areas where there are hardwoods, the best grouse hunting, in fact almost all of it, is in the western counties.

Reading east to west, these counties, which lie in the narrow strip of northwestern Maryland thrusting in between southern Pennsylvania and por-tions of West Virginia, are as follows: Garrett; Allegany; Washington; Fred-erick. There are several State Forests here and also several Wildlife Man-agement and Recreation Areas where ruffed grouse are considered among the primary game species.

Garrett Co., farthest west and with the most forest acreage, has five such public hunting areas. One of the best, and also the largest public acreage in the state, is Savage River State Forest (1). It contains 52,520 acres, covers in irregular blocks a good portion of the northeastern sector

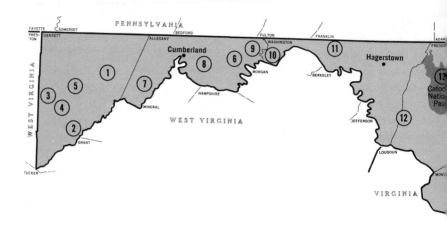

of Garrett Co. Routes U.S. 40 and 219, running together, cross the northern portion east-west. At the key town of Grantsville, State 495 runs south from those routes, with Forest on either side. Farther south, 495 intersects State 135, which runs across the southern end of the Forest. Secondaries reach into the Forest to give good access.

Next in size is 12,050-acre Potomac State Forest (2). This is in the southern part of the triangular county, and on the eastern side of the triangle. Its eastern boundary is the North Branch of the Potomac River, which is also the state boundary with West Virginia. Access can be had from U.S. 219 or State 135, or from U.S. 50 which crosses the southern end of the county. From any of these roads State 560 can be reached, and from 560 secondaries run east into the Forest. The village of Kearney is the key here.

Swallow Falls State Forest (3) is near the western border, about midway north-south. It contains 7400 acres. From U.S. 219 there is a secondary running off to the west just south of Thayerville that reaches it. Farther south on U.S. 219, at Oakland, another secondary runs northwest up into the Forest. The two secondaries mentioned intersect near the village of Browning Mill and then run as one road northwest to give access to the remainder of the Forest. Browning Mill can be reached also from the western side, from Cranesville, West Virginia.

There is one WMA in the county, Mount Nebo (4), with 1751 acres. It is near Oakland and reached via U.S. 219. There is also Deep Creek Recreation Area (administered by Forests and Parks) with 1648 acres open to public hunting where grouse are available. This is roughly centered in the county, near Deep Creek Lake and the town of Thayerville on U.S. 219.

The next county to the east, Allegany, though more heavily settled, has some fair grouse hunting on one State Forest and three different WMAs. Green Ridge SF(6) offers 25,630 acres of land open to hunting. This is in scattered and numerous blocks in the eastern part of the county. U.S. 40 runs east-west across the county. At the village of Piney Grove a secondary goes south through much of the Forest. Other parts can be reached from U.S. 40, or from State 51 at the southern edge of the county.

Among the WMAs, Dan's Mountain (7), with 7861 acres, is the largest. It is in a solid block in the southwest part of the county, southwest from

114

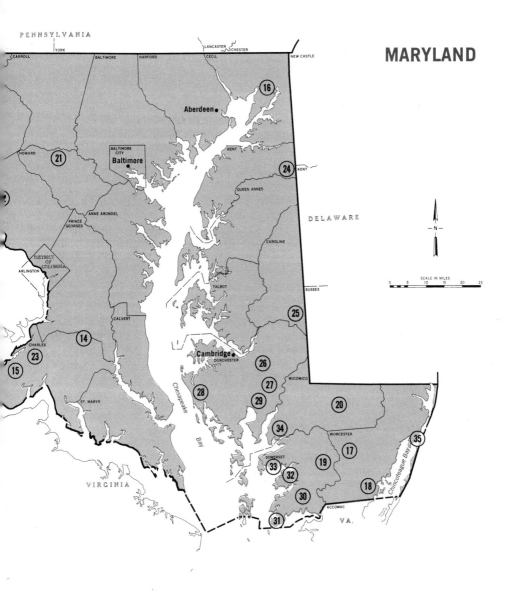

MARYLAND

KEY TO HUNTING AREAS

1. Savage River SF
2. Potomac SF
3. Swallow Falls SF
4. Mount Nebo WMA
5. Deep Creek
   Recreation Area
6. Green Ridge SF
7. Dan's Mountain WMA
8. Warrior Mountain
   WMA
9. Billmeyer WMA
10. Sidling Hill WMA
11. Indian Springs WMA

12. South Mountain
    Watershed Area
13. Cunningham Falls
    Recreation Area
14. Cedarville SF
15. Doncaster SF
16. Elk Neck SF
17. Pocomoke SF
18. Ernest Vaughn WMA
19. Wellington WMA
20. Johnson WMA
21. Hugg-Thomas WMA
22. Strider WMA

23. Myrtle Grove WMA
24. Millington WMA
25. Idylwild WMA
26. Linkwood WMA
27. LeCompte WMA
28. Taylor's Island WMA
29. Fishing Bay WMA
30. Pocomoke Sound WMA
31. Cedar Island WMA
32. Fairmount WMA
33. Deal Island WMA
34. Ellis Bay WMA
35. Sinepuxent WMA

115

the city of Cumberland, via U.S. 220. It lies west of this highway. It can be reached also from the west side, off State 36.

Warrior Mountain WMA (8), has 2376 acres, lies east and a bit south of the City of Cumberland. Between east-west State 51 in the south of the county, and east-west U.S. 40 in the north, there is a secondary that runs from Spring Gap on 51 to Flintstone on 40. This is the main access road. Near the WMA, northwest of it on this secondary, is the settlement of Twiggtown. Another secondary reaches this village from Cumberland.

The third and smallest of the public tracts in the county is Billmeyer WMA (9). It is a bit less than a section of land near the village of Piney Grove on U.S. 40 in the northeast part of the county.

A few miles east of Piney Grove, across the county border to the east, in Washington County, there is Sidling Hill WMA (10), with 2136 public acres. It is near U.S. 40 also.

A much larger unit, Indian Springs WMA (11), contains 4944 acres open to public hunting in several blocks of forest. It is along the northern border of Washington Co. some miles east of the above. It, too, is reached from U.S. 40 (or I 70). A secondary runs north to it from the village of Indian Springs.

On the eastern border of Washington Co., and lying partly in that county and partly in the next (Frederick) county, is the South Mountain Watershed Area (12). This is a plot of 1115 acres in a strip one-half mile wide along South Mountain, which has an elevation of 1100 feet. The Appalachian Trail runs through this exact region on the border between the two counties. The public hunting ground extends from the Potomac River to the Mason-Dixon Line.

Entirely in Frederick Co. is the Cunningham Falls Recreation Area (13). Both this Area and the above are under the Forestry and Parks Department administration. Cunningham Falls offers a public hunting acreage of 3950, although the entire area is larger but hunting is not allowed on all of it. Part of the Area is a State Park. The hunting ground lies in the northwestern portion of the county. State 77 runs east-west across the county, and U.S. 15, running north-south, intersects near the village of Thurmont. The grouse hunting acreage is west of Thurmont, off State 77. Incidentally, Catoctin National Park is in the general region.

The various lands so far described and located blanket all but a minor percentage of Maryland's public grouse hunting. There are of course good spots on private lands, but permission without prior contact is not easy to arrange.

WILD TURKEYS

At the present time Maryland's turkey hunting is restricted to the three westernmost counties: Garrett, Allegany, Washington. The birds are not abundant and the kill is not high. Continuing attempts are in progress as this is written to restore the wild turkey elsewhere. Florida turkeys have been released in Dorchester Co., in the southeast. Earlier releases of Florida stock in Somerset and Worcester Cos. in the extreme southeast have resulted to date in some broods being observed. It is quite possible that turkey hunting on the Eastern Shore in Maryland may soon be a reality.

Meanwhile, turkeys trapped in Allegany Co. have been moved east into Frederick Co. in the Catoctin Mountain region, in an attempt to bring the western turkeys farther east. There is some hope that in due time all suitable areas in Maryland may have at least huntable surpluses of one or the other subspecies.

The public areas now offering turkey hunting are all noted under "Ruffed Grouse." In Garrett Co. these are: Savage River SF; Potomac SF; Swallow Falls SF; Mount Nebo WMA; Deep Creek Recreation Area. In Allegany Co. are: Green Ridge SF; Dan's Mountain WMA; Warrior Mountain WMA; Billmeyer WMA. Washington Co.: Sidling Hill WMA; Indian Springs WMA.

QUAIL

Bobwhites are most abundant in that part of Maryland known as the Eastern Shore, that is, the counties on the east side of Chesapeake Bay. Of these, the lower, or southern, counties undoubtedly offer the best shooting. However, there are also bobwhites in good supply in the southern counties across on the other side of the Bay and along the Potomac. Several State Forests and Wildlife Management Areas offer public quail hunting.

Taking the State Forests first, Cedarville SF(14) overlaps the southern border of Prince George Co., into the northern portion of Charles Co. This is southeast some miles from Washington, D.C. There are 3200 acres here. U.S. 301 is west of the Forest. A secondary out of the village of Townshend (just east of 301) reaches east to Cedarville, then branches south into the Forest. This road runs on south to join State 382, giving access from either side.

Doncaster SF (15) is entirely in Charles Co., over in the southwest part almost directly across the Potomac from Quantico, the U.S. Marine base in Virginia. This Forest, with 1400 acres, is crossed by State 6, on which is the village of Doncaster on the west side of the area.

Elk Neck SF (16) is way up in northeastern Maryland, in central Cecil Co. There are 2742 acres with quail hunting here, reached southwest out of Elkton. The area lies south of U.S. 40. State 7 and State 272 and secondaries from them offer access.

In the southeast, in Worcester Co., is the Pocomoke SF (17). It is in several blocks, covering all told 11,950 acres. This is considered a good quail location. U.S. 113 between Pocomoke City and Snow Hill crosses the area, and other tracts to the north can be reached off this route and from State 12 via secondary roads.

In the same county (Worcester) there is a WMA with 445 acres open to hunting. This is Ernest Vaughn WMA (18). State 12 south from Snow Hill runs to it, or it can be reached from U.S. 13 by taking State 366 east to Stockton and thence north on State 12.

Two WMAs of modest size are in bordering counties. One is Wellington WMA (19), 389 acres, in Somerset Co., which borders Worcester Co. on the west. It is reached via a secondary that runs to the village of Wellington, either from U.S. 13 at Princess Anne or else from State 364 north of Pocomoke City. The other is the 175-acre Johnson WMA (20) in Wicomico Co. to the north. This is a short distance east of the city of Salisbury.

Two other small WMAs with quail are north of Washington, D.C., and southwest of Baltimore: Hugg-Thomas WMA (21) with 250 acres in Howard Co.; Strider WMA (22) with 225 open acres in Montgomery Co. Hugg-Thomas is on the northern border of Howard Co., with access via

State 32. It is not far from Sykesville, a town across the border in southern Carroll Co. Strider WMA is in west-central Montgomery Co., off State 118 near Germantown.

Farther south, in Charles Co., is another small area—300 acres are open to hunting—called Myrtle Grove WMA (23). There is a refuge here also, hunters should note. The WMA location is off State 225, which runs west from its junction with U.S. 301 to the town of Mason Springs.

Across the Bay to the east, in Kent Co., is 655-acre Millington WMA (24). This is in the southeastern corner of the county, almost to the Delaware border, and reached by State 291 out of the town of Millington. Also in the east, in Caroline Co., which borders Delaware, there is Idylwild WMA (25), with 1418 acres open to hunting. This lies in the southeastern corner of the county, northeast of Federalsburg, and is reached via State 306 or by a secondary out of the same town.

There are three other WMAs with quail as a primary species, all of them in the Eastern Shore county of Dorchester, which lies immediately south of Caroline Co. and borders on the west on Chesapeake Bay. Linkwood WMA (26) has 313 acres on the north side of U.S. 50 near the village of Linkwood. LeCompte WMA (27) is a bit larger, with 400 acres open to hunting. It is on the eastern side of the county, south of U.S. 50, reached from the village of Vienna by a secondary that runs south to Henry's Crossroads and thence northwest to Drawbridge. Still larger is Taylor's Island WMA (28), with 973 acres. This is on the west side of the county. It can be best reached by traveling from the city of Cambridge south and west on State 16.

Numerous private lands over the southern counties on both sides of the Bay have good quail hunting, but as noted earlier, unless one is acquainted with landowners permission is not in general easy to arrange.

MOURNING DOVES

Doves are abundant and much hunted in Maryland. The kill may run as high as a million birds annually. Because doves are migratory and exceedingly mobile, as well as dependent upon field crops to a large extent for food, by far the major share of the shooting is on private lands. Generally speaking, the Eastern Shore offers the best shooting, although all the southern counties and farmlands are good. While doves are not considered primary game on the WMAs and Forests, nonetheless there is some shooting on all of the ones that offer suitable habitat and feeding areas. Those noted for "Quail" should not be overlooked, especially in the east and south.

Also, during recent seasons with ever greater interest in dove hunting in Maryland, the Department has begun to develop both cooperative and Department-owned areas especially for dove management. In the cooperative experiment, farmers have been signed up to agree to public hunting on their lands after harvest of crops. Dove hunters should check with the Department for locations of these cooperatives, and also to locate state-owned areas where dove management for hunting purposes is in progress each season.

WOODCOCK

Woodcock do not receive as much hunting in Maryland as they might. Many hunters are unaware that a very substantial percentage of the eastern migratory flights of this bird filters down across Maryland. As on many other woodcock migration routes, a good covert that has no birds today may be filled with them tomorrow. They migrate at night, and particularly when there are hard storms farther north they pour southward in large numbers. Hunters who keep track of weather to the north can often spot a good flight coming.

Although many woodcock can be found in various covers along the Eastern Shore and elsewhere over the state, some of the best shooting is in the west. Here, when migrations are in progress, one should seek valleys that run north-south, and hunt on the sunny sides. Although woodcock can at times be found in a number of the public areas noted under "Quail," most of the better shooting will be found on some of the WMAs and State Forests mentioned under "Ruffed Grouse." Chief among these are: Green Ridge SF, Swallow Falls SF, Potomac SF, Savage River SF; Dan's Mountain WMA, Cunningham Falls WMA, Indian Springs WMA.

SNIPE AND RAILS

Both snipe and rails are in good supply on all of the waterfowl hunting grounds in Maryland, especially on those along Chesapeake Bay and the various rivers. Snipe are in general hunted incidentally to waterfowl. But there is a good bit of interest in rail hunting in the tidewater regions, for birds are plentiful and the higher tides move them, making it possible to flush them and get shooting.

Even though it is true that Maryland is famed for its duck and goose shooting, it must be remembered that for many years more and more of the wetlands and bay locations have been taken up in private ownership. Most private lands with waterfowl potential are held with hunting as one of the prime purposes. Thus, access by permission is highly unlikely. It was mentioned early in this chapter that guides, and fee hunting at camps and lodges, are available. This applies to rails particularly, but can also apply to snipe. Check with the Department or with a District officer concerning availability of these services.

In addition a number of the public lands where waterfowl are the prime game species offer excellent rail and snipe shooting. Among the best are the following WMAs, which will be located under "Waterfowl": Fishing Bay, Dorchester Co.; Cedar Island, Somerset Co.; Deal Island, Somerset Co.; Fairmount, Somerset Co.; Ellis Bay, Wicomico Co.

WATERFOWL

As noted above, while there is excellent waterfowling along Maryland's shores, most of it is privately controlled. Shooting with guides along Chesapeake Bay is often excellent, however, and it is likewise for those who have the opportunity to erect blinds offshore. The laws are rather complicated and should be well studied beforehand. There is a blind fee required. Riparian owners have first rights on obtaining blind license opposite their shores; blinds must be no more than 300 yards off a natural shore; blinds must be 500 straight-line yards apart in most cases. There are other rules. Methods of hunting are controlled—sneak boats, for example, must be licensed, used by residents only, and only on stipulated waters.

Hunters who have opportunity to hunt in the vicinity of the refuges get a good chance at ducks and a better than average chance at Canada geese. For example, Blackwater National Wildlife Refuge in southeastern

Dorchester Co. gathers thousands of Canada geese each year. It is south of the city of Cambridge. Chincoteague Refuge, below Maryland borders on a Virginia barrier island, nonetheless draws large numbers of waterfowl to the general region of southeastern Maryland. Martin National Wildlife Refuge is on Smith Island, offshore in Chesapeake Bay westward from southern Somerset Co. (of which the island is a part). It also holds many waterfowl in the vicinity.

Maryland waterfowling is varied, from snipe and rails (section previous to this) to Canadian geese, numerous species of ducks, plus brant and varied sea ducks. Recently a special sea duck season in lower Chesapeake Bay, Chincoteague Bay, and coastal waters sparked this shooting as a popular Maryland sport, offshore and from points along shore. During a season previous to this writing, aerial flights were made monthly and ground surveys weekly so that sea-duck concentrations might be reported to gunners to assist them. The unique idea has worked very well since.

Midwinter waterfowl surveys in recent seasons tend to show that canvasbacks, scaup, and black ducks are the three most populous species, as well as highly desirable. These are followed in numbers by mallards and redheads about even, widgeon, and pintail. Eiders, scoters, mergansers (the old-time "shelldrake" of the eastern seaboard) are numerous. Brant are few.

Fortunately, Maryland has several very good public areas for waterfowling. Three of these have been noted previously, under "Quail": LeCompte WMA; Taylor's Island WMA; Ernest Vaughn WMA.

Several others not so far mentioned are without question among the best the state has to offer in public waterfowl shooting. All are in the southeast, which is prime wintering ground for migratory water birds of all species. Fishing Bay WMA (29) is in southern Dorchester Co. not far from Blackwater Refuge. It covers 11,233 acres. It is reached south from the city of Cambridge via secondaries leading to the village of Bestpitch. It can also be reached from U.S. 50 by a secondary that leads south and then west from Vienna.

Somerset Co. to the west has four excellent locations. Pocomoke Sound WMA (30) has 922 acres. It is on the sound of like name, south of the village of Marion on State 357. West along the shore to the southernmost point of the county is Cedar Island WMA (31). The location here, with over 3000 acres, is exemplary. State 413 to Crisfield, and then State 380 to Birdtown offer the nearest access point.

Turning north up the shore, there is Fairmount WMA (32), with 2346 acres open to hunting. State 361 from Westover, which is on State 413 just south of the intersect with U.S. 13, takes one to this Area. Still farther north, there is Deal Island WMA (33), with almost 8000 acres open for hunting. (Note that these Areas are mentioned as fine spots for rail and snipe hunting also, under that heading.) Deal Island is on State 363, west from its intersect with U.S. 13 near the village of Princess Anne.

Across the Wicomico River, which forms part of the northern boundary of Somerset Co., is Ellis Bay WMA (34), in southwestern Wicomico Co. There are 1913 acres here. State routes 352 and 349 southwest from Salisbury reach the vicinity. There is also a very small and rather obscure WMA open for waterfowling in a prime spot, on the Atlantic shore south of Ocean City. This part of Worcester Co. lies behind the barrier island of Assateague. This is Sinepuxent WMA (35), composed of small islands in the bay of the same name.

DEER

Interest in deer hunting in Maryland is high. Some 80,000 hunters go deer hunting annually. The whitetail population is astonishing, considering density of human population. The seasonal kill runs from 8000 to 12,000, with an average somewhere in between. This counts both antlered and antlerless deer. Some counties or sections have bucks-only seasons, some others as surpluses dictate, offer any-deer seasons. Hunters should check carefully the areas where rifles may, or may not, be used.

In general the success percentage on the overall—antlered and antlerless combined—probably runs about 1 in 10 or at best 1 in 7 or 8. The pattern of deer abundance as shown by harvest stays consistent: eastern Maryland is first, western Maryland second, the central and southern portion poorest.

Narrowing this down to counties, in a recent season the top counties, in order, were as follows: Dorchester (southeast, 1384 deer total); Worcester (southeast, 974); Allegany (western, 941); Garrett (western, 847); Kent (northeast, 771). Again, this shows that the west and the southeast are best, with the east in general better.

Following the above five counties were several that were about even, with kills of 500 or more but not over 600: Cecil (extreme northeast); Somerset, Wicomico (southeast); Washington (west). This is a rather consistent pattern each season for the state, and hunters should note it well.

Still there are several fair counties in addition, with kills averaging around 200 to 300-plus. These are: Frederick, Baltimore, Charles, Queen Anne's, Talbot. Other counties average consistently lower. It is interesting to note that surveys show the western deer kill mostly by local residents, with few incoming hunters from eastern metropolitan areas, whereas the eastern Maryland kill is heavily the "take" of the city majority in the region.

There are numerous good public tracts that furnish excellent deer hunting. All of the State Forests and the WMAs noted under "Ruffed Grouse" are in the west, and furnish the cream of the deer hunting in this part of the state. All of the same noted under "Quail" also offer deer hunting, and these are chiefly in the eastern regions of fair to good deer populations. In addition to all of the above, two areas noted under "Waterfowl" are also good deer areas. These are the large Fishing Bay WMA in Dorchester Co. and Ellis Bay WMA in Wicomico Co.

There is a most interesting aspect of Maryland deer hunting not well known outside the small area involed. The Japanese sika, a dark deer of modest size with dainty ivory-hued antlers, is well established in Dorchester Co. A private release was made some years ago on 280-acre offshore James Island west of Cambridge in Chesapeake Bay. They became so numerous that there was soon at least a sika per acre, and some swam, apparently to Taylor's Island. They quickly spread to the mainland and now are hunted during the regular firearms deer season.

In addition to this exotic, Maryland has on Mills Island in Chincoteague Bay a scattering of fallow deer. Oddly, at this time the origin of these animals is not known. Game status of these animals must be checked with the Department.

SMALL GAME AND OTHER ANIMALS

Squirrels and rabbits are important small game and there is quite good hunting for them throughout much of the state. Best of the squirrel hunting is in the western hills and valleys. Here the public lands noted under "Ruffed Grouse" all have squirrels in fair to good supply. All of those noted under "Quail" also are considered fair to good squirrel hunting locations. Rabbits are found in all these locations under both "Ruffed Grouse" and "Quail," too. In the western mountain sections there are a few varying hares (snowshoe hares or rabbits). This is almost the southern limit of their range.

Raccoons and opossums are present throughout much of the state, are hunted to some extent. There is a season on both. Virtually all the public lands offer some hunting for these species. There are also red foxes, chiefly in the farm and woodlot areas. There is no state closed season, but some counties protect them. The agricultural lands have woodchucks, and there are scattered populations of these on the public lands. However, there is no avid interest in hunting woodchucks. Hunters who are interested should check legality of using rifles.

REGULATIONS

Game laws pertaining to seasons, bag and possession limits, areas to be hunted, special hunts, license fees all may have numerous changes from year to year. For current regulations, and for other specific queries, write to: Department of Game and Inland Fish, State Office Building, Annapolis, Maryland 21401.

VIRGINIA

Triangle-shaped Virginia, first settled in 1607, has had hunters prowling its forests, mountains, and coastal marshes for over 360 years. It would seem hardly possible that any game could be left. Nonetheless, it is still today an excellent state for sportsmen. It is located almost exactly midway north-south along the East coast and has one of the most uneven eastern and western boundaries of any state. Only the southern border, chiefly with North Carolina but with a small portion of Tennessee in the extreme west, is straight.

The coastal tidewater area and the coastal plain are composed of a series of large peninsulas between which lie bays formed by large rivers—the mouths of the Potomac, the Rappahannock, the York, the James—all of which open upon Chesapeake Bay. Across that bay the tip of the Delmarva Peninsula is also somewhat incongruously a part of Virginia. Thus, all but the southernmost extreme of the coastal section has well protected shore waters, and all are historically famed havens for waterfowl. In the northeast and the north the zigzag border is with Maryland, and on the west with West Virginia except in the narrow far-western section, where the state adjoins a bit of Kentucky.

Virginia's terrain changes rapidly westward from its coastal lowlands, rising to the central piedmont plateau and then on up to the Blue Ridge Mountains of the west. On the western slope of the Blue Ridge the land dips down into the fertile farming region of the Shenandoah Valley, and then rises again steeply into the Alleghenies down which much of the western border runs.

The state is a mixture of teeming activities. Manufacturing, widely diversified agricultural pursuits such as tobacco, peanuts, sweet potatoes, apples, coal production, tourism to the numerous historical places—all play their part. Over 4.5 million people live within Virginia's 40,817 square miles. An estimated 80 percent of its game resources are found on private lands. Nonetheless, there are vast stretches of forests, some of which, in the more rugged mountain sections, can be considered virtually true wilderness, with rugged and often difficult access. Thus Virginia is a land of emphatic contrasts, long settled and heavily populated, yet with numerous back-country sections where the land and its forests are much as they were hundreds of years ago.

Virginia has numerous and excellent, though often winding, highways. Sportsmen have no difficulty getting from place to place except in a few mountain regions where, on back trails, 4-wheel-drive vehicles or even a backpack may be needed. The average hunter, however, can reach by passenger car almost any place he wishes to go.

Distances are not excessive. North-south at its greatest depth the state is less than 200 miles. East-west distances vary greatly because Virginia is

123

shaped like an uneven triangle, with the base and the western border the long lines. Straight-line distance along the southern border, for example, is over 400 miles. But from Arlington (across the Potomac from Washington, D.C.) in the northeast westward to the West Virginia border is no more than seventy-five miles. Air transport is good in the east but sparse in the western mountains, and hardly needed by sportsmen anyway in a state of this modest size.

While scores of small villages are scattered over the entire state, the bulk of the population is in the larger cities of the east. Hunters number less than 10 percent of the population, with license sales currently averaging around 370,000 each season. It is interesting to note, and a commentary on good hunting here, that Virginia attracts by far more nonresident hunters than any of its bordering states. Various nonresident permits account for over 10 percent of the total of paid license holders.

Deer hunting is good, bear hunting fair, turkey hunting excellent. There are quail, ruffed grouse, doves, waterfowl, squirrels, rabbits, plus rails and snipe in the marshlands. Foxes, raccoons, woodchucks are also present, and there are occasional bobcats. Deer, turkeys, rabbits, squirrels, quail, doves, and varied lowland birds get the most attention and furnish the highest harvests.

Although the major share of hunting in such a densely populated state obviously must occur on private lands, Virginia has over three million acres of land in state, federal, and private ownership that are under wildlife management authority of the Game Commission. This is in addition to the Commission's owned lands.

The largest blocks of public lands are in the two National Forests: the George Washington NF (1), with a bit over one million acres, a small part of which is across the line in West Virginia; the Jefferson NF (2) with over 540,000 acres. The George Washington NF is in several main blocks in the northwest and central-west region. The Forest Supervisor can be contacted at Harrisonburg, Virginia, where maps and details may be obtained. The blocks of Forest are not entirely solid, but are broken here and there into numerous smaller portions with other lands intervening. Thus it is important that hunters have good orientation by map.

The Jefferson NF is the same type of situation. Its numerous blocks of land are in the southwest, with the Supervisor's headquarters located at Roanoke, from which maps and details are available. It should be noted, too, that the State Game Commission also has excellent maps that show the general overall locations of the blocks of both NF lands. Because these Forests stretch over the major portion of western Virginia, and are broken into so many tracts, it is not possible to give here routes leading to each one. A much better picture can be had by acquiring one of the maps mentioned.

The Commission owns a number of tracts termed Wildlife Management Areas. These are scattered from the western mountains to the eastern shore. They presently total some 150,000 acres. New tracts are being purchased and managed as fast as Game Commission revenue and availability of lands for sale and suitable for wildlife development will allow. New ones undoubtedly will have been added before this is read. It is therefore a good idea to check with the Commission prior to planning a trip. Some of these WMAs are within the National Forests, large tracts managed cooperatively between the state and the federal Forest Service. A booklet, "Wildlife Management Areas," and a pamphlet, "Virginia Public Hunting Areas," may be obtained from the Game Commission, address at end of chapter. There are also several State Forests, some Corps of Engineers lands surrounding reservoirs, and some military lands open to public hunting.

Those unfamiliar with Virginia laws should be aware that various permits in addition to the hunting license are required for certain public lands. A $1.00 stamp must be purchased before hunting in the National Forests, and another for hunting on State Forest lands. Some counties also require special permits. Free permits must be obtained for waterfowl hunting on some of the state lands and fees paid for blinds on others.

Virginia also has a large acreage of lumber company and other corporation lands open to hunting under various plans. Because these may change from year to year, they will not be dealt with specifically later under the various game species, except in instances where such lands have become established under Commission management as Wildlife Management Areas. Examples of these lands are certain tracts under ownership of Chesapeake Corporation, Lester Lumber Company, Appalachian Power Company, and West Virginia Pulp and Paper Company.

The last named owns about 76,000 acres of Virginia forest lands. This firm has a very active "Westvaco Outdoors" program. It has turned some of its holdings over to the Commission for wildlife management. It also has large blocks of its acreage open to hunting under a $2.00 permit system. Permits may be obtained from the Virginia Woodlands Division of Westvaco, Route 3, Box 135-A, Lynchburg. Hunting license number, and a stamped, self-addressed envelope should be mailed with application. Boundaries are plainly marked. Maps showing tracts in a single county are available. Presently four areas under Commission management are open without permit. For hunters wishing to check game conditions on these, they are: Buffalo River tract, Amherst Co.; Shady Grove tract, Powhatan Co.; Hudson and Adams tract, Prince Edward Co.; Young Estates tract, Spottsylvania Co.

Camping hunters will find a number of the WMAs with camping facilities. The National Forests are also good camping locations. A booklet, "Camping in Virginia," can be had from the Department of Conservation and Economic Development, 911 Broad Street, Richmond, and "Virginia State Parks" from the Division of State Parks, 1108 East Main, Richmond. National Park campgrounds and Corps of Engineers campgrounds are listed in the booklet first named. Other accommodations, such as motels and hotels and lodges, are numerous everywhere.

The weather during hunting seasons can range from hot during dove shooting to balmy in early fall, to very chilly along the coastal marshes during late waterfowl seasons, to snowy in the western mountains during big-game seasons. Hunters should not be fooled by the central-coast location of the state. It has flurries of severe weather as winter wears on. Visitors should go prepared for quick changes any time after the mid-fall period.

Arms and ammunition will depend to some extent upon where the hunting takes place. County laws differ. Some prohibit rifles for deer, some prohibit rifles larger than .22 except for woodchucks, and in some counties shotguns must be used, but with buckshot only. Laws in general should be carefully checked. For example, Sunday hunting is prohibited. And on private, posted lands written permission is required before hunting, although only verbal permission is needed on privately owned lands not posted. Where rifles are permitted, standard deer and bear calibers such as the .30/06,

VIRGINIA

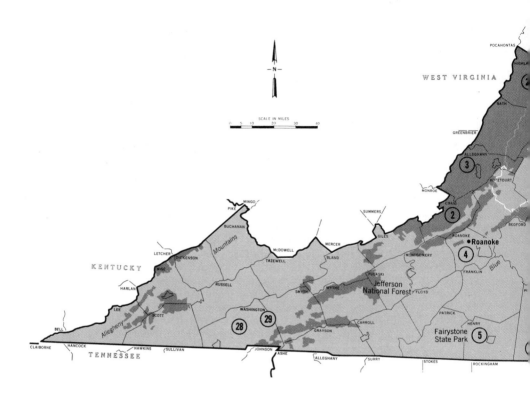

KEY TO HUNTING AREAS

1. George Washington NF; Big Levels WMA
2. Jefferson NF
3. Gathright WMA
4. Havens WMA
5. Fairystone Farms WMA; Philpott Reservoir; Fairystone SP
6. Powhatan WMA
7. Amelia WMA
8. Lee Forest WMA
9. Kerr Reservoir WMA
10. Cumberland SF
11. Appomattox-Buckingham SF
12. Prince Edward SF

13. Seward SF
14. Quantico Marine Reservation
15. Camp Pickett
16. A. P. Hill
17. Union-Bag Camp Co. WMA
18. Lester Lumber Company WMA
19. Appalachian Power Company WMA
20. Smith Mountain WMA
21. Chesapeake #1 WMA
22. Chesapeake #2 WMA
23. Goshen WMA
24. Little North Mountain WMA

25. Wunder WMA
26. Rapidan WMA
27. Highland WMA
28. Hidden Valley WMA
29. Clinch Mountain WMA
30. Elm Hill WMA
31. Pocahontas-Trojan Marsh WMA
32. Saxis Island WMA
33. Game Farm Marsh WMA
34. Mockhorn Island WMA
35. Hog Island Refuge
36. Chincoteague National Wildlife Refuge

126

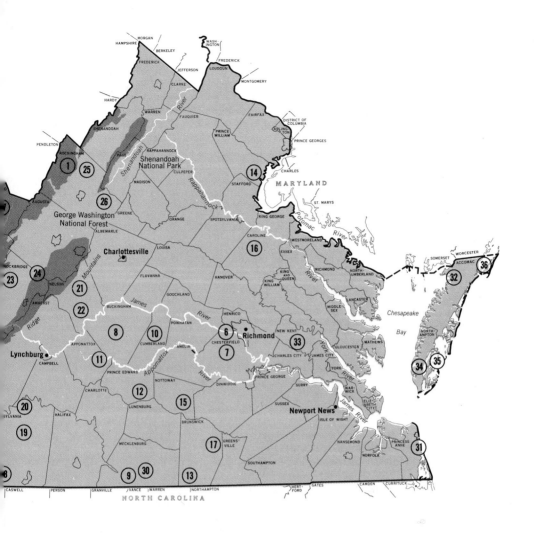

.270, and comparable calibers are adequate. Bird hunters, excepting water-fowlers and turkey hunters, will need shot sizes averaging around No. 8 to No. 6. For turkey hunters using shotguns, No. 6 short-magnum loads or No. 4s do well. The same make good waterfowl loads.

Guides are seldom used in Virginia except for bear, waterfowl, and rail hunting. The Commission can assist hunters in finding guides. A few advertise in national mediums. Duck, goose, and rail hunters along the coast have little difficulty finding guides. The Back Bay area of the extreme south-east is depicted on a map obtainable from the Commission, titled the "Back Bay Sportsman's Guide." Maps covering Chesapeake Bay region and the mouths of the large rivers are also locally available. The Commission, incidentally, publishes names and addresses of Area Game Managers for all Commission-managed lands in its "Roster of Personnel." To make last-minute checks on game conditions on any specific WMAs or other Commission-managed lands, request this list from the Commission and contact the proper Area Manager.

Hunters should be familiar with the terms used in Virginia to divide the state for differing seasons for several game species: "West of the Blueridge" and "East of the Blueridge." The "West" encompasses about a third of the state, with the dividing line running roughly down the crest of the Blue Ridge Mountains. This line runs north-south on a southwesterly slant along the western borders of the following counties. Reading from north to south: Loudoun; Fauquier; Rappahannock; Madison; Greene; Albemarle; Nelson; Amherst; Bedford; Franklin; Patrick. In other words, this group of counties is the first tier, from north to south, in the "East of the Blueridge" division of the state. All counties west of these make up the "West of the Blueridge" region.

QUAIL

Quail hunting has a long tradition in Virginia. The bobwhite is popular, and the annual harvest places it at the top of the game bird list. Only the mourning dove competes. The average quail kill in a normal year is over a million and a quarter birds. About 25 percent of Virginia hunters do at least some quail hunting.

As in many parts of the eastern bobwhite's range, however, good quail habitat has been diminishing, changes in land use have made serious inroads upon the population. In addition, the swiftly growing human population has seriously hampered public quail hunting. Since this is a bird of farm and woodlot edges, probably at least 90 percent of the bobwhite crop each season is found on privately owned lands. Unless a hunter is locally acquainted, permission is rather difficult to obtain.

There are, however, a number of the public tracts that offer from fair to excellent quail hunting. The Gathright WMA (3), over 18,000 acres along the Jackson River in the western part of the state, has a fair number of quail in the agricultural portion lying along the river. It is located fifteen miles north of Covington, which is at the junction of U.S. 60 and 220. To the south is the 6400-acre Havens WMA (4). It lies just west of Salem (and Roanoke). This is a rough region with poor access and one suffering still from a bad fire some years ago. It is marginal for quail. Still farther south, near Philpott Reservoir, which is located northwest of Martinsville, is the Fairystone Farms WMA (5). There are almost 4800 acres here. The area is largely wooded, not prime quail habitat, but does offer fair shooting. About centered in the state, west of Richmond and near the village of Macon on U.S. 60, is the Powhatan WMA (6), with almost 2000 acres. This is partly wooded, partly open country and usually has a fair to good quail crop. A new WMA still under development, 2083-acre Amelia WMA (7), south of the Powhatan WMA, includes three miles of Appomattox River frontage. Although development on the river is aimed for waterfowl, other portions have fair quail shooting.

There is some quail hunting in the west in both of the National Forests. Note in the early part of this chapter the material relating to these Forests. They are so large and in so many scattered blocks that it is necessary to acquire maps and to check with the headquarters or various Ranger Districts to pinpoint quail hunting. The forest areas are of course in general only marginal quail habitat. The Lee Forest WMA (8), owned by the U.S. Forest Service, has 2500 acres near Buckingham and U.S. 60 in Buckingham Co. This is about sixty miles west of Richmond.

Corps of Engineers lands managed in cooperation with the State Game Commission as WMAs also furnish quail hunting. There are 4750 acres along the Philpott Reservoir south of Roanoke and northwest from Martinsville. As at the nearby Fairystone Farms WMA, quail shooting is fair. In the south, lying astride the border with North Carolina, is the large Kerr Reservoir WMA (9), with 38,000 acres of surrounding public lands. Fair quail hunting is obtainable here, too. The key location town is Clarksville, junction U.S. 15 and 58.

The Virginia Division of Forestry and the State Game Commission cooperatively manage three State Forests as WMAs. All three offer quail hunting of varying quality. The Cumberland SF (10), over 15,000 acres, is north of U.S. 60 near the village of Cumberland in central Cumberland Co. The Appomattox-Buckingham SF (11), with about 18,500 acres, is a short distance southwest from the Cumberland Forest. It is along the border between Buckingham and Appomattox Counties, with State 24 and 636 nearby roads. The Prince Edward SF (12) contains over 6000 acres, lies to the southeast of the last-named Forest. Green Bay, on U.S. 360 in southeastern Prince Edward Co., is a key to its location. The Seward SF (13), under ownership of the University of Virginia, is another quail hunting area, with 3600 acres. It is in southern Brunswick Co., which borders North Carolina inland several counties in the southeast.

Military lands in Virginia offer some of the better public quail hunting. Special regulations may be in force, and one should check with the military authorities at these bases for details. Quantico Marine Reservation (14), 57,000 acres under management, is in the northeast, west of U.S. 1 near Quantico, only a short distance south of Washington, D.C. Camp Pickett (15), with 47,000 acres, and A. P. Hill (16), 77,000, are under U.S. 2nd Army authority. Pickett is in southern Virginia, Nottoway Co., southeast of Blackstone. A. P. Hill is crossed by U.S. 301 north of Bowling Green. This large acreage is southeast from the city of Fredericksburg.

WMAs on land privately owned by several business firms also furnish a fair amount of quail shooting. There are 15,000 acres of Union-Bag Camp Company lands (17) in numerous small tracts near Edgerton in the southeast near the village of Edgerton, which is on U.S. 58 in Brunswick Co. Lester Lumber Company lands (18) of 3800 acres are near the southern border, central portion, west of the city of Danville near the village of Axton. Appalachian Power Company holdings (19) of 6000 acres are not far away, on Smith Mountain in Pittsylvania Co. And at the northern tip of the same county on the Roanoke River south of Leesville there are over 2500 acres of Burrus Lumber Company lands known as the Smith Mountain WMA (20). Chesapeake Corporation tracts known as Chesapeake #1 and Chesapeake #2 contain respectively 3000 and 2645 acres. Chesapeake #1 WMA (21) is composed of several blocks in Nelson Co., in the central-west part of the state. Chesapeake #2 WMA (22) is south of Leesville and the Roanoke River on State 631.

Probably the best quail hunting available for visiting hunters is on private lands where fees are charged and various accommodations offered. Several such lodges and hunting preserves, with wild not released quail, are located in Virginia. These advertise in various national outdoor magazines.

Hunters should be aware that Virginia law forbids hunting quail when there is snow on the ground.

PHEASANT

At present it is illegal to shoot any pheasant in Virginia at any time. Various pheasant strains and species have been tried, and further experiments are underway. Some years ago a modestly successful introduction of pheasants was made in Charles City Co. in the east. There may be a few of these birds still producing in the wild. Sections of the eastern shore are considered possible habitat for the Japanese green pheasant. These birds, which have established themselves to some extent in Accomack and Northampton Cos. have learned to roost in pines to fifteen feet high. Some white-crested Kalij pheasants have apparently done fairly well in stocked areas on the Jefferson Forest. This is a grouselike pheasant that utilizes wooded cover. Attempts are in progress to establish it on ranges marginal for the native ruffed grouse. Other pheasants are being stocked elsewhere. Currently at least twenty-eight Virginia counties have token pheasant populations. Whether any will become firmly established is not known at present. Hopes are high that various types may someday offer hunting from the wooded mountains to the farm areas to the eastern shore.

RUFFED GROUSE

Much of the mountainous, forested portion of Virginia is excellent ruffed grouse habitat. But much of it also is rugged country not easy to hunt. The annual grouse kill during normal and up-cycle years is surprisingly high, as many as 85,000 birds. It is estimated that 30,000-plus hunters participate.

Fortunately there is ample opportunity for grouse hunting on public lands. The two chief reservoirs of grouse abundance are the two large National Forests. See front material in chapter relating to these. Maps acquired from the Forest headquarters in each case will be exceedingly helpful to grouse hunters. Paper company lands open to hunting in the mountains also carry good populations of grouse. Notes on these lands are also to be found early in this chapter.

Several of the WMAs and other tracts described under "Quail" furnish grouse hunting. In some instances it is better than for quail, with larger portions of their areas better suited to forest game such as grouse. Gathright and Havens WMAs both have grouse. So do the Kerr Reservoir tract, Cumberland State Forest, Appomattox-Buckingham State Forest, and Quantico Marine Reservation.

Other lands not so far described have some excellent grouse hunting. The Goshen WMA (23) in the mountainous west covers 15,954 acres in Rockbridge Co. near the village of Goshen. It is rugged, access is limited, walking and hunting difficult because of dense laurel. But for determined hunters who like uncrowded hunting this is a good grouse area. Little North Mountain WMA (24) adjoins the Goshen WMA to the north. It contains 16,225 acres, is long and narrow, with its northern end near Staunton, junction U.S. 11 and 250. This also is rugged, with old logging roads and foot trails, but more easily hunted than the former. Wunder WMA (25) is farther north and near the West Virginia border. It is smaller, with slightly more than 1300 acres in three tracts. It is located northwest of Harrisonburg and west of the village of Broadway on State 259. This is a good grouse location.

The 8332-acre Rapidan WMA (26) is east of Harrisonburg, toward Madison. It is made up of four tracts along the borders of Shenandoah National Park. This also is a good grouse area. It is advisable, however, because of the several separated sections, to obtain a map of this WMA from the Commission to assist in locating its various portions. Another one with four separate tracts, all close together and comprising in total 17,753 acres, is Highland WMA (27). This also is in the west, in Highland Co., five miles southeast from the village of Monterey, which is at the junction of U.S. 220 and 250. All of the tracts offer good grouse cover and substantial populations.

Two other WMAs with grouse are in the far southwestern triangle. Hidden Valley WMA (28) contains 6400 acres a dozen miles northwest of Abingdon—U.S. 19 and 58—in Washington Co. Grouse hunting is very popular here. Clinch Mountain WMA (29) has over 18,000 acres with fine grouse hunting. It is located a short distance north of Saltville, which is on State 91 north of the intersect of that route with U.S. 11. This Area is only a short distance east of Hidden Valley.

These are the main public lands for grouse hunting. Again, the vast expanses of the two National Forests in western Virginia should get close attention. To avoid confusion, incidentally, there is a large area (over 30,000 acres) within the George Washington NF in Augusta Co. that is now called the Big Levels WMA, although for many years this was a refuge cooperatively managed by the State Game Commission and the U.S. Forest Service. For all practical purposes this is a part of the Forest, with grouse and other hunting. But special regulations should be checked.

MOURNING DOVES

The mourning dove is an exceedingly important game bird in Virginia, vying with the bobwhite quail for first place in popularity and sometimes placing ahead of quail in the gross annual harvest. Although drastic fluctuations in dove kill occur, good seasons show as many as 1,300,000 bagged. However, that figure may be cut almost in half during a season when weather or food conditions are not conducive to holding this migratory bird.

Virginia is accorded an early and a late season. By far the larger percentage of the kill occurs from September through November. Recently the early season showed a kill of a million and a quarter birds, the late season in December and January only 121,000-plus.

Doves are of course extremely mobile, tied for a few days or weeks at a time to areas where waste grain and other forage is abundant. They are whimsical about both feeding conditions and weather changes. Therefore, a place that has large numbers of doves one season does not necessarily have them every season. The major share of the kill is on private croplands. Probably 90 percent of the doves are bagged on such lands.

Many of Virginia's public tracts are not suitable for attracting large numbers of doves. However, managed dove hunts on some of the public lands, with specially prepared fields, are becoming extremely popular and management attempts to attract and hold doves for this purpose are rapidly developing. As this is written, a number of the WMAs have experimental dove fields open without fee for hunting two days per week during the first half of the split season. It is increasingly likely that more such developments will occur, for the popularity of dove hunting is swiftly growing. The piedmont region has seen the most experimentation.

Here are the public locations at this time. Noted under "Quail": Kerr Reservoir; Cumberland Forest; Camp Pickett; A. P. Hill; Powhatan; Quantico;

Amelia. Elm Hill WMA (30), not so far covered, has 871 acres, is a fairly new tract slanted presently at waterfowl and doves and with some quail cover under development. It is considered a good dove spot, even though smaller than some of the others. It is below the Kerr Dam on the north side of the Roanoke River. This is in the south, along the North Carolina border. Note that the Kerr Reservoir WMA mentioned in this paragraph is nearby, and described under "Quail." Camp Pickett and the Kerr Reservoir fields have over several years had the best shooting. Up in the center of the state, in Orange Co., is another, Hawfield, under co-op agreement with the owner, the Hawfield estate north of Unionville, which is on State 20 near U.S. 522. Usually this tract supports a fine dove population during hunting season.

WILD TURKEYS

The wild turkey has since pioneer times been one of the most important game species in Virginia. Because of the large expanses of forest and unbroken blocks of timber that have remained, it is still comparatively abundant, well managed, and with both fall and spring seasons the flock stays adequate while furnishing a comparatively high kill. The fall kill, when any turkey is legal (exceptions during some recent seasons have limited hunting east of the Blue Ridge to gobblers only) runs from 3000 to 4000 birds in better years. Two-thirds or more of the total come from West of the Blueridge. Approximately half the total kill in both areas are hens. The spring hunt, with gobblers-only legal, accounts for from 600 to over 1300 birds. Sentiment at present is to have more and more counties restricted to gobblers-only both fall and spring.

Some years ago the future for the wild turkey in Virginia looked bleak indeed. But restoration, careful management and a crackdown on illegal practices have brought the flock back to quite stable levels, even though recently the high hen kill has worried both game men and hunters. However, the central piedmont, which was at one time the prime turkey range, is now far surpassed by the mountain region based on the National Forests. The high-kill counties for the fall season give an excellent indication of where the birds are. A kill survey over a period of several years shows the high counties alphabetically as follows: Alleghany, Augusta, Bath, Botetourt, Craig, Frederick, Highland, Rockbridge, Rockingham, Shenandoah. All of these are in the far west and northwest. During a recent spring season Rockbridge in the west was among the high-kill counties, but three of the first four in spring were East of the Blueridge: Fauquier in the north, Amelia and Dinwiddie in the south. Bath Co. in the west is far and away the leader in fall harvest.

There is no difficulty in finding public lands on which to hunt turkeys. The two National Forests (see opening of chapter) hold a large percentage of the total state flock. Hunters should check for special regulations pertaining to the WMAs, State Forests, and military lands. But most have turkeys, and are either open at this time or possibly will be over the next few years.

Described under "Quail" are the following tracts with turkeys: Gathright, Havens, Philpott Reservoir, Kerr Reservoir, Lee SF, Cumberland SF, Appomattox-Buckingham SF, Prince Edward SF, Camp Pickett, A. P. Hill, Seward SF, Union-Bag Camp, Fairystone, Appalachian Power, Burruss Lumber (Smith Mountain), Chesapeake #1 and #2, Powhatan, Quantico, Amelia. Under "Grouse" in addition to the foregoing: Goshen, Little North Mountain, Rapidan, Highland. Big Levels ("Grouse") should also be checked for a season.

Not long ago approximately 2400 acres of Fairystone State Park, which adjoins the Fairystone Farms WMA ("Quail"), was opened, under multiple use concept, to hunting. This was the first parcel of State Park land ever opened. It has a good turkey population. For those with access to private lands, there is excellent turkey hunting over much of the state. During most seasons only the east and the extreme southwest are closed. Over seventy counties offer turkey hunting either in fall, or spring, or both. All turkey kills must be checked in at official stations.

WATERFOWL

Virginia is blessed with a vast amount of tidewater area, with bays and broad rivers in the east, and with the entire southern portion of Chesapeake Bay lying between the mainland and the peninsular counties across the Bay below Maryland. Much of the coastal region forms excellent waterfowl habitat. Yet waterfowling in Virginia is not today especially popular with large numbers of hunters, and the annual bag, by standards elsewhere along the eastern shore, is not high.

In an average year from 15,000 to 18,000 duck hunters take 80,000 to 100,000 ducks. The black duck, and some of the divers such as redheads and scaup, are among the main species. The goose kill, predominantly of Canada geese, is fair. A recent season showed 11,032 geese taken by 7534 hunters. Inland along the rivers the wood duck is common. There is a growing interest currently in waterfowling around the several large reservoirs of southern and western Virginia—Kerr, Smith Mountain, Leesville, Gaston— and in hunting along the larger inland rivers that hold birds along their courses.

At one time the waterfowling clubs along the eastern shore were popular and expensive and at their peak. For example, in the famed Back Bay region south of Norfolk, good club lands could not be purchased at any price. Today many coastal stretches are in private ownership and clubs continue, although on a somewhat reduced scale due to the drastically lowered bag limits and the smaller numbers of birds available.

Nonetheless, there is ample waterfowling available to the public. But the large waters along both Virginia shores of Chesapeake Bay, and the Atlantic shore on the eastern edge of the peninsula, require boats, decoys, and blinds that average hunters do not have or else feel are too expensive and troublesome for the small limits involved. Much of the coastal waterfowling by inland Virginians and by visitors is done with guides. Noted early in the chapter is a Game Commission pamphlet that gives lists of Back Bay guides and accommodations. Chambers of Commerce in the coastal towns can furnish information about guides also. And interested hunters can easily track down such services by acquiring the "Roster of Personnel" from the Commission, and asking assistance from local conservation officers.

Several federal refuges gather and hold large numbers of waterfowl in their vicinities. The Back Bay Refuge is south of Norfolk about twenty-five miles, covers 4600 acres. Chincoteague is perhaps most famous. It is a typical barrier island on the Atlantic shore at the northeastern extreme of the

Virginia portion of the Delmarva Peninsula. This, incidentally, is an important gathering place for brant, and there is fair to excellent brant hunting along the coast here. This refuge covers some 9000 acres. Presquile is an island in the James River south of Richmond and near Hopewell.

Not long ago a small tract of 192 acres was given to the State Game Commission on the Rappahannock River about five miles downstream from the U.S. 301 bridge at Port Royal. This is to be a refuge for waterfowl (but with some small-game hunting probably allowed) and is being managed especially for geese. Estimates are that it can support 5000 to 10,000 wintering geese. The state also owns Hog Island Refuge of about 2500 acres. This is on the James River, Surry Co., six miles northeast of Bacons Castle. It was established as a refuge to encourage waterfowl use of the lower part of the James. As many as 10,000 Canada geese and half again as many ducks often utilize it.

Several WMAs and other lands offer good to excellent waterfowl hunting. One of the most important is the Pocahontas-Trojan Marsh WMA (31). This is strictly a waterfowl ground, with both ducks and geese available. It is in the extreme southeast, in the portion of Virginia Beach formerly called Princess Anne County. There are two tracts here. Pocahontas has 790 acres, Trojan 352. Pocahontas is for the hunter without boat and decoys. There are a number of blinds built to accommodate from one to three hunters. Total fee, per day, is $23. This includes boat, motor, safety equipment, decoys, guide. The fee is divided: $3 for the blind, $20 for the guide. The Trojan tract is operated for hunters with their own equipment. The fee is $3 a day, blinds built to accommodate one to three hunters. Boat-launching facilities are included. Applications are taken between September 1 and October 15 by mail from the Game Division or from the Area Manager (Creeds Station, Virginia Beach). After season opening reservations must be obtained from the Area manager. Drawings are held. If all dates and blinds are not filled, these go on a first-come basis. Details and all regulations can be obtained from the Commission.

Saxis Island WMA (32) is another area strictly for waterfowl. It is located at the extreme northwest corner of Virginia's portion of the Delmarva Peninsula, at the village of Saxis. Total acreage of 5136 is split almost evenly between refuge and hunting ground. There is no fee. But check which days of the week hunting is allowed. This is primarily a black duck marsh.

There is a modest amount of duck hunting on Gathright WMA ("Quail"), which is located in the west on the Jackson River. Some fairly good shooting may be had at 400-acre Game Farm Marsh WMA (33), a flooded swampland along the Chickahominy River. This tract has not been mentioned so far. This is in the east, in New Kent Co., a short distance from Providence Forge. The Kerr Reservoir WMA, Camp Pickett, A. P. Hill, Quantico ("Quail") all offer waterfowling of varying quality. At the Amelia WMA noted under "Quail" intensive waterfowl development is at present under way, chiefly to attract puddle ducks, particularly wood ducks which are found numerously along the Appomattox River where this tract is located. The Elm Hill WMA, noted under "Doves," is a refuge tract primarily for waterfowl near the Kerr Reservoir on the North Carolina border. Its purpose is to attempt to hold waterfowl in the region. See "Rails," below, for another waterfowl location.

RAILS

"Marsh hens," as rails are usually called in Virginia, have a small but avid following. Two or three thousand hunters at most pursue this marsh sport, and they bag upwards of 18,000 birds in good seasons. Many marsh-lands along the coasts have good rail populations. Guides can be hired for rail hunting in numerous coastal and Peninsula locations. For best results tides must be high enough to push the birds out of the lower portions of the marshes and to concentrate them. The species most hunted and most common is the clapper rail.

The Commission owns one of the best rail hunting areas on the Virginia Coast. This is Mockhorn Island WMA (34), over 9000 acres of marsh and lowlands cut by channels and canals, in Northampton Co. on the Atlantic side of the Eastern Shore. It lies offshore almost at the southern end of the Peninsula, opposite the town of Oyster. It is approximately eleven miles long, extending south about to Townsend. It is a protected, or interior, island between the mainland and the barrier islands. No fee or reservation is needed. However, hunters should note that some 3000 acres of "high ground" along the western side is refuge. The remainder is open to hunting. A boat is needed for access, and tides should be checked to make certain they are high enough to push a boat across the flooded marshes. One good launching place is Bull's Landing, near Townsend.

There is fair duck hunting at Mockhorn, too. The most abundant species is the black duck.

WOODCOCK AND SNIPE

Some snipe are killed on the waterfowling grounds but this bird gets little attention in Virginia.

Woodcock are more important, but are to a great extent incidentals killed by quail hunters and by grouse hunters who hunt the stream courses of the valleys. The woodcock kill is estimated to run as high as 40,000 some seasons. This is a rather specialized sport, for the bulk of the birds only migrate through, and are whimsical as to their resting places and length of stay. All of the public lands with damp areas having open overhead cover and loam containing abundant earthworms, the prime food of the woodcock, furnish woodcock hunting. But at best it is unpredictable, unless one is thoroughly acquainted with a specific local plot used season after season by flight birds.

SQUIRRELS

Virginia is traditionally a squirrel hunter's state. Almost half the hunters go after squirrels each year, and the kill ranges up toward two million. The forests with abundant hardwoods that furnish squirrel food form almost limitless room for public hunting. Squirrel seasons differ widely, county to county, and should be checked with care. All of the public lands already noted under "Quail," "Grouse," and "Turkey" furnish fine squirrel hunting. This, of course, includes the enormous acreage of the two National Forests. Overall the region West of the Blueridge is probably the better squirrel ter-ritory. But even that is questioned by numerous resident hunters. Squirrel hunting in any hardwood forest in Virginia is excellent, and there is little choice as to locations on the public lands.

RABBITS

Rabbits are also extremely important game, but interest in rabbit hunting is not as high as in squirrel hunting. The kill is estimated to average slightly over a million annually. As with squirrels, there is no difficulty finding rabbit hunting on the public lands. Most of the tracts noted under "Quail" have good rabbit populations. While there are fair numbers West of the Blueridge, in agricultural valleys and around old homesites and clearings on the public tracts, the bulk of the rabbit hunting is East of the Blueridge.

DEER

The whitetail deer herd in Virginia has seen many difficulties over the years. Once abundant, deer herds were decimated until within this century there were only remnants left in the least accessible places. Even West of the Blueridge, where the bulk of the National Forest land lies, for all practical purposes deer and deer hunting had been destroyed. Then illuminated thinking in conservation circles launched a determined restoration program. Today deer hunting in Virginia can be considered excellent. In the neighborhood of 100,000 deer hunters avidly take to the woods each fall, and for some seasons now the total kill has run from 25,000 to 28,000 animals. Authorities keep close track of the annual harvest, for all deer kills must be checked at official checking stations.

Both sections of the state, West of the Blueridge and East of the Blueridge, have good hunting. While the west has a smaller total bag, its area is smaller. In one recent season the figures were as follows: west, 11,392; east, 13,259. That season the leading eastern counties were Southampton, Caroline, and Sussex. Some counties are bucks-only. That season Buckingham, one of those, was a top-kill area, in fact it was in fourth place in the east. In some others, any deer is legal. Deer in both east and west have in some areas become too numerous and control has been necessary to bring the herd into line with carrying capacity of the range.

While concentrations of hunters may influence kill figures to some extent, counties that consistently have high kills are obviously the counties with the best hunting. Over a period of several consecutive seasons, the following counties had total kills of over 2000 deer, and in some instances the kill was close to 2000: Augusta; Bath; Rockingham; Southampton. These are quite consistently the "big league" deer counties. The first three are closely grouped in the far west, the fourth is in the southeast. Next in line, and very good, with kills consistently between 500 and 1000: Alleghany; Botetourt; Craig; Frederick; Giles; Highland; Rockbridge; Shenandoah, all in the west; and Buckingham; Caroline; Lancaster; Norfolk; Surry; Sussex; York in the east. Numerous other counties come close. Above or slightly below 250 deer over several seasons were: Albemarle; Amherst; Cumberland; Fulvanna; Grayson; Isle of Wight; King George; King William; Nansemond; Northumberland; Page; Patrick; Prince George; Stafford; Warren; Wythe.

Virginia has a most fortunate situation so far as public lands for deer are concerned. Both the National Forests cover much of the best deer counties of the west. To avoid undue repetition, without fail every one of the public tracts described as good for both turkey and grouse furnish fine deer hunting. A number of those WMAs and other lands were first noted under "Quail." Therefore, refer first to "Grouse" and "Turkeys" and then if necessary to "Quail." Although any of the areas will give a hunter a good chance of bagging a deer, if these are checked against the consistently good counties listed above the percentage chance of success will be even better. Success on the overall invariably averages from 25 to 30 percent. This includes the entire kill, bucks-only and any-deer counties.

In addition to regular seasons, there is some deer hunting on refuges. Hog Island, mentioned under waterfowl, is one. There is also some most interesting hunting on the Chincoteague National Wildlife Refuge (36). About 1923 a half-dozen sikas, a handsome, small exotic deer native to Japan and Malaysia, were released on Assateague Island. It is thought this release was made by Boy Scouts who had obtained them as payment for assisting with an island roundup of cattle and ponies. The herd, taking hold on what is now the Chincoteague Refuge, increased until control hunts were necessary. The first hunt was held in 1964. Since then several more have occurred. During one recent season whitetails on the Refuge also were legal game. For information regarding these hunts one may contact the Refuge Manager, Chincoteague NWR, Box 62, Chincoteague, Virginia 23336. The Presquile NWR also has occasional deer hunts, to control whitetails. These are by application and drawing.

ELK

There is a small band of elk in a portion of the southwest. Recently a two-week season was proposed for Giles and Bland Cos., with either-sex legal. As this is written no season has been held. Interested hunters should contact the Commission with queries as to the possibility of such a season in the future.

BEAR

There are black bears in Virginia, most of them on the large forest expanses of the west. The kill is not high, but still is enough to keep interest. Over a period of four recent seasons the totals were as follows: 246, 122, 349, 332. Best counties as a rule are Augusta, Rockingham, and Alleghany. Albemarle has at times had fairly high kills, Botetourt is fair. So is Bath, and occasionally Amherst. The last stronghold of the black bear outside the Blue Ridge country is in Dismal Swamp in the southeast. Union Camp Paper Company, with lands there that have been publicly hunted, has closed these lands to bear hunting as this is written because of a drop in the bear population. It is anticipated that reopening may occur after a few years.

Among Commission lands and others offering bear hunting with a reasonable chance of success are: Gathright; Goshen; Haven; Little North Mountain; Rapidan; Highland Co. WMAs. The National Forests probably hold the largest bear population in the state. All bear kills must be checked at official stations.

OTHER ANIMALS

Red foxes are rather abundant. So are raccoons. There is good, and popular, hunting for both. But laws are exceedingly complicated county to county. Some regions have closed seasons, some do not. It is necessary to check the regulations thoroughly. Traditional hunting method for both species is with hounds. Some 25,000 Virginia hunters annually enjoy fox and raccoon hunting, with a bag of over 100,000 raccoons, and approximately half that number of foxes.

There are a few bobcats scattered throughout the forests and along the stream bottoms, but they are nowhere plentiful. They are not protected. Woodchucks are abundant, particularly along the slopes where valleys bring agriculture and wooded cover in proximity. Woodchuck hunting is popular among a small number of enthusiasts. The woodchuck is also unprotected. But for any unprotected animal a hunting license is still needed.

All of the public lands excepting the waterfowl marshes have fair to excellent populations of raccoons and foxes, and in proper terrain, of woodchucks.

REGULATIONS

Game laws pertaining to seasons, bag and possession limits, areas to be hunted, special hunts, license fees all may have numerous changes from year to year. For current regulations, and for other specific queries, write to: Commission of Game and Inland Fisheries, Box 1642, Richmond, Virginia 23213.

NORTH CAROLINA

North Carolina owns some of the most stunning and varied terrain and scenery to be found anywhere in the U.S. In the west along the rugged border with Tennessee are the Blue Ridge Mountains and the Great Smokies of the Appalachian chain. Here forested mountains with exceedingly steep slopes reach up over 6000 feet, running the length of the border from Virginia on the north down to northeastern Georgia and northwestern South Carolina in the south.

Eastward the mountains level off in the central piedmont plateau. This in turn slants gently down to become a broad sweep of coastal plain, and finally, in the central portion along the eastern coast, there are huge stretches of tidal marshlands. The North Carolina coast is protected almost in entirety by strings of slender offshore islands. In the north and the central part of the coast these take the form of narrow strips of sand, the Outer Banks, lying some distance offshore. Inside the Banks are Albemarle and Pamlico sounds, well-protected waters.

With such varied terrain, from open ocean beach to marsh to lowland to mountains, the economy of the state is varied also. First in tobacco production, with sweet potatoes, peanuts and many grain and fruit crops also important, North Carolina is today heavily industrialized as well. Textiles are the chief products, with furniture a close second. Although a large percentage of the land area is in farms, there is also a substantial amount of forest, a sizable amount of which is still today authentic wilderness.

Good roads and many of them quickly get sportsmen to any point. North Carolina has over twenty-five U.S. highways and Interstates angling across it virtually in every direction. State roads are also excellent and link up the other routes to scores of small villages. Because the state has no extremely large cities but a number of them of medium size, local air transport is unusually good and national lines reach the major centers. Although hunters for most game need no special type of transport, in the National Forest regions of the western mountains the small four-wheel-drive vehicles can be most useful.

Because of a large population in a state of modest size, North Carolina has had over the years a hard fight to keep enough public hunting. But it has done well in the face of its problems. In a land area of 52,712 square miles, there is a population currently of over five million. This population is not concentrated to any extent, but is rather evenly distributed across the state.

Hunting is popular. In a recent season over 433,000 licenses were sold. Many resident hunters have for years belonged to clubs, leasing or owning the land they hunt on. This is a common practice in the South, and North Carolina, climatically neither truly North nor South, has long leaned toward the southern tradition. Fee hunting is also growing, especially near the cities.

No great numbers of nonresident hunters test North Carolina's hunting. License sales to nonresidents average only seven or eight thousand a year.

Variety of game species is intriguing. There are rails in abundance along the coast, and ruffed grouse in the western mountains. Quail, turkeys, doves, some pheasants, woodcock, plentiful waterfowl are on the list. There are deer, black bear, wild boar, as well as rabbits and squirrels, foxes, raccoons, and woodchucks.

The public-land picture in North Carolina is, fortunately, bright. The Wildlife Resources Commission is justly proud of its game management programs and its success in acquiring various lands by ownership or lease. The state is also rich in federal lands held in National Forests. Some locations within these Forests are managed as Wildlife Management Areas by the state, in cooperation with the Forest Service. All told there are 1,125,196 acres of National Forests in North Carolina.

The Croatan National Forest (1) has over 150,000 acres, is located in the pine and swamp-hardwood area of the east coast south of New Bern. Highways in the area are U.S. 17 and 70, State 24 and 58. There are lakes in this Forest, and the game is varied, from migratory birds to bear, deer, turkey, quail. The small Uwharrie National Forest (2), 43,571 acres, is in the center of the state, northeast from the city of Albemarle and southwest from the city of Asheboro. State 49 and 134, U.S. 220 and 64 all run nearby. In the southwest section of the state is 449,281-acre Nantahala National Forest (3), its setting the dense timber of the Appalachians, with thick undergrowth of rhododendron. In this high, rough country are boar, deer, bear, grouse, and turkey. Numerous highways lead here—U.S. 19, 23, 64, 129, State 28, 107. In the west also, farther up the border, with the city of Asheville a focal point, is the Pisgah National Forest (4). Here are 478,297 acres of mountain country with the state's highest point, the highest east of the Mississippi, Mount Mitchell, 6684 feet. There are hunts in the Pisgah for bear and deer as well as for small game. U.S. 19, 23, 64, 70, and numerous other highways all lead to or near it. Maps and details on all of these Forests can be obtained from the Forest Supervisor, Asheville, North Carolina.

In addition to federal lands, the state has eighteen Wildlife Management Areas scattered over the state (several as noted within the Forests) that comprise upwards of 200,000 acres. A map showing the Areas is printed on the regulations governing hunting on them. There is also a very successful program for leasing private lands for dove hunting locations, and for small-game hunts. During a recent season there were twenty-one such areas especially for dove hunting. Details on these, and locations for any current season, can be had from the Wildlife Resources Commission, address at end of chapter.

The vast tidewater area of North Carolina contains thousands of acres of water and marsh open to waterfowlers. The only thing necessary is to have knowledge of where access for boats may be found. There is a booklet (at this writing the cost is 75¢)* titled "Boating Access" available from the Commission. It has maps that give locations, and descriptions of the hunting to be found.

For hunters who may wish to camp while on a hunting trip in North Carolina, the National Forests are one of the best bets. There are also State Parks, campsites along the Blue Ridge Parkway and in Great Smokies National Park. There are numerous Corps of Engineers campgrounds on several reservoirs. And there are an unusually large number of privately operated campgrounds in this state. Other accommodations, in motels, lodges, etc., are numerous, and well distributed over the state. There are in addition a number of hunting camps and lodges that advertise in magazines, offering big-game hunts, hunts for quail, and for waterfowl.

Hunters in North Carolina find a mixture of weather. The early fall, during dove season for example, is warm to hot. But any western mountain hunting in the state, regardless of time of year, will find dawn and dusk crisp, with more severe cold as winter comes on. Snow and low temperatures are not unusual in the mountains. Along the coast waterfowlers will need warm clothing, too, and for all hunters rain gear here is a must. The state has a heavy average rainfall.

Big game hunters after boar or bear need rifles in the general class of the .30/06, .270, .308. These double properly for deer also, although rifles of smaller caliber, such as the 6mm and .243, are qualified for North Carolina whitetails. Shotgunners will need standard loads of about No. 7½ average for quail, doves, rails, with heavier loads for ducks, and No. 2s or the various magnums for geese. A .22 for squirrels is a good addition.

For management purposes North Carolina is split into nine Wildlife Resources Districts. These are drawn along county lines. Because it will be necessary to refer to these districts under individual species, they are listed here by number with the counties contained in each. Reference to this listing from any mention under species will quickly orient the reader.

District 1, northeast: Currituck, Camden, Pasquotank, Perquimans, Chowan, Hertford, Gates, Bertie, Martin, Washington, Tyrrell, Dare, Hyde.

District 2, southeast: Pitt, Beaufort, Pamlico, Greene, Craven, Carteret, Lenoir, Jones, Onslow, Duplin, Pender.

District 3, northern border, west of District 1: Vance, Warren, Halifax, Northampton, Franklin, Nash, Edgecombe, Wake, Wilson, Johnston, Wayne.

District 4, southern border, west of District 2: Harnett, Hoke, Cumberland, Sampson, Scotland, Robeson, Bladen, Columbus, Brunswick, New Hanover.

District 5, north-central: Rockingham, Caswell, Person, Granville, Guilford, Alamance, Orange, Durham, Randolph, Chatham, Lee.

District 6, south-central: Davidson, Rowan, Cabarrus, Stanly, Montgomery, Moore, Mecklenburg, Union, Anson, Richmond.

District 7, northwest: Ashe, Alleghany, Surry, Stokes, Watuga, Wilkes, Yadkin, Forsyth, Alexander, Iredell, Davie.

District 8, southwest of District 7: Yancey, Mitchell, Avery, Caldwell, McDowell, Burke, Catawba, Rutherford, Lincoln, Cleveland, Gaston.

District 9, extreme west: Cherokee, Graham, Swain, Haywood, Madison, Clay, Macon, Jackson, Buncombe, Transylvania, Henderson, Polk.

There are a number of professional guides for bear, deer, boar, turkey, waterfowl in North Carolina. Lists of these may be obtained from the Commission, as well as lists of lodges and camps offering hunting services.

RUFFED GROUSE

Ruffed grouse are surprisingly plentiful in North Carolina. Although the kill is substantial, considering the rugged terrain of the western mountains which form the grouse range, the species is still thought to be underhunted, so far as its potential is concerned. One of the last complete state kill surveys shows well over 60,000 grouse bagged that season.

NORTH CAROLINA

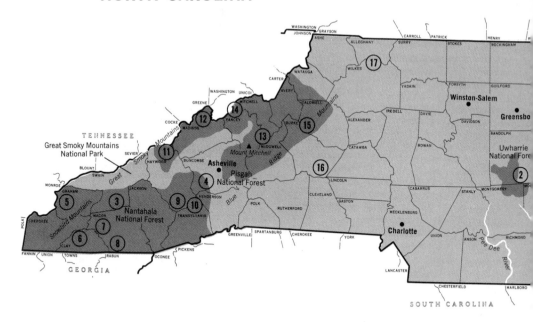

KEY TO HUNTING AREAS

1. Croatan NF; Croatan WMA
2. Uwharrie NF; Uwharrie WMA
3. Nantahala NF
4. Pisgah NF
5. Santeetlah WMA
6. Fires Creek WMA
7. Wayah Bald WMA
8. Standing Indian WMA
9. Sherwood WMA
10. Pisgah Game Preserve WMA
11. Harmon's Den WMA
12. Rich Laurel WMA; Shelton Laurel WMA
13. Mount Mitchell WMA
14. Flat Top WMA
15. Daniel Boone WMA
16. South Mountain WMA
17. Thurmond Chatham WMA
18. Sandhills WMA
19. Caswell WMA
20. Holly Shelter WMA
21. Northwest River Marsh PHA
22. Gull River WMA
23. Pamlico Point WMA
24. Goose Creek WMA
24. White Oak WMA

The entire state kill comes from the three westernmost Districts: 7, 8, 9. The highest kill is in District 8, from which comes about two-thirds of the total state bag, taken by about one-fourth of the hunters. Success here is also far above the other two Districts, usually running three to four times as great. The western border counties in District 8 furnish the best hunting: Avery, Yancey, Mitchell, with Avery the best. McDowell Co., south of Yancey and Mitchell, also is considered good. This District, and these counties, get by far the majority of the grouse hunters, but conditions are never crowded.

District 9 usually gets the greatest number of grouse hunters, but is lowest in success. When mast is abundant, however, grouse are well distributed over the District. The extreme western counties usually offer the better opportunities. These are Cherokee, Graham, Clay, Swain. In District 7 hunter numbers are modest, and the area rates second in success percentage. The northwestern counties of the District are best: Watuga, Ashe, Alleghany, Wilkes.

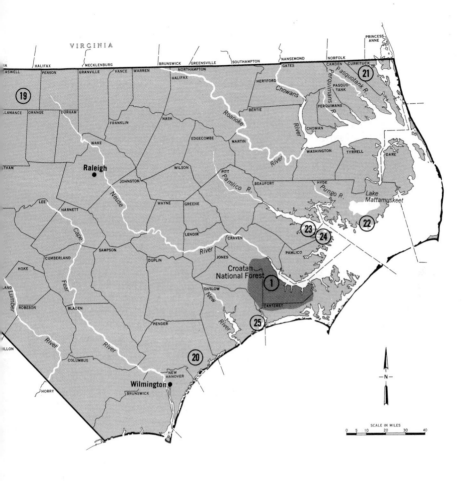

Public hunting grounds abound for grouse hunting. There are close to a million acres of federal lands here in these Districts in the Pisgah and Nantahala National Forests. Hunts are held also on some of the Wildlife Management Areas.

In District 9, Graham Co., there is the 37,000-acre Santeetlah WMA (5) with good grouse hunting. Note this is in one of the best counties. It lies along the western state border, with U.S. 129 the boundary of the northern side. The Fires Creek WMA (6) is also in this District and in one of the best counties, Clay. This one contains 14,000 acres of exceedingly rugged terrain. U.S. 64 is to the south, U.S. 19 and 129 to the north and west. Up until now at least, because of the tough terrain, hunting has been restricted to men only. The 11,000-acre Wayah Bald WMA (7) is to the east, in Macon Co., same District and still in good grouse terrain. It is much less rugged than the foregoing. U.S. 64 at the town of Franklin is a good location point a short distance east. Most of these lands mentioned in this paragraph are within National Forest boundaries.

143

Also in District 9, and in the same county, Macon, is the 28,500-acre Standing Indian WMA (8). This is considered to have some of the best grouse shooting in western North Carolina. It is near the northern border of Georgia. U.S. 23 is to the east, and U.S. 64 north and west. Also in District 9, there is the 31,000-acre Sherwood WMA (9), in Haywood Co. This is National Forest land, a portion of the Pisgah. The WMA is southwest of Asheville. Bordering Sherwood to the east and south is the Pisgah Game Preserve (10), 100,000 acres utilized as a WMA. This also is in the Pisgah NF. U.S. 276 runs across it. At the northern tip of Haywood Co., on the Tennessee border, is Harmon Den WMA (11) of over 10,000 acres. Some hunters consider this area some of the finest grouse shooting in the state. Secondaries reach this region from State 209. It is just outside the northeastern boundaries of Great Smoky Mountains National Park. Also in District 9 and northeast up the border from Harmon's Den is Rich Laurel WMA (12). There are 26,500 acres here, divided into two sections, Rich Laurel and Shelton Laurel. Both lie along the Tennessee border in Madison Co. U.S. 25 and 70 reach the region, State 212 runs along the eastern and southern edge, State 208 passes between the two sections. The terrain is not excessively rugged.

In western District 8, on the border between Yancey and McDowell Cos., is Mount Mitchell, highest mountain in the eastern part of the U.S. On its slope is the 25,000 acre Mount Mitchell WMA (13). Farther north, partly in Yancey and partly in Mitchell Cos., and lying along the Tennessee border, is Flat Top WMA (14), more good grouse terrain, in a 15,000-acre tract. As noted previously much of these lands are within the National Forest boundaries but managed for game by the state. U.S. 19W is a key route to Flat Top. Daniel Boone WMA (15) is a rugged 46,500 acres with the Linville Gorge Wilderness Area inside its boundaries. Portions of this WMA are in three District 8 counties: Avery, Burke, Caldwell. State 181 crosses the tract, and U.S. 221 runs near the western edge. To the south and a bit east, in Burke Co., is the 17,000 acre South Mountains WMA (16). It is directly south of Morgantown.

In District 7, in Wilkes and Alleghany Cos. near the Blue Ridge Parkway, is Thurmond Chatham WMA (17), with 12,000 acres. However, as this is written not all of it is open to hunting. Two tracts are. Hunters should carefully check.

There are a number of tracts in the state, several of them in these western Districts, called Big Game Restoration Areas. These may or may not be open to hunting of small game and are therefore not covered here. Check with the Commission.

PHEASANT

The appearance of pheasants in the hunting regulations, with an open season but with county exceptions, may be misleading to hunters. There is actually no pheasant hunting in North Carolina except for pheasants raised and released by private individuals. During the 1930s a diligent effort was made by the state to establish pheasants. It was unsuccessful, except for an exceedingly modest foothold gained by the birds on Hatteras Island. A very few still remain but there is no open season on the island. Pheasants appear in the regulation only to make it legal for those who raise and release birds to hunt them.

QUAIL

Half a century ago North Carolina was one of the truly great quail states, with bobwhites found throughout the state, even in good supply in the mountain counties, where valley farms formed excellent habitat. Changing land use has drastically affected the bobwhite here as it has almost everywhere across the East and South. The mountain counties, the industrial portions of the piedmont no longer provide more than fair shooting. The agricultural counties of tidewater stretching inland to the lower piedmont still offer excellent hunting. However, virtually all of this is on privately owned lands.

Guides may be found in most areas of quality quail shooting who have access to lands where the birds are abundant. Also, numerous hunting reserves are found in the quail region, not just the type that release birds but private preserves where fee hunting for wild birds may be had. The Commission can assist hunters with a list of such preserves, and in some instances assist in locating guides.

On the western WMAs covered under "Grouse," a few quail are found. But the shooting cannot be considered very good. Kill surveys show only a scattering of birds bagged. However, in eastern District 6, in Moore and Richmond Cos., the Sandhills WMA (18), which has thirty-two separate tracts that range from a few acres to as many as 20,000, offers excellent public quail shooting. U.S. 1 runs across the area, between Rockingham and Southern Pines. In the north, District 5, Caswell Co., the Caswell WMA (19), of 14,000 acres, is also a fair quail location.

Actually a serious quail hunter here will be far better off to get permission, or arrange a guided hunt on private lands. Thus, a look at quail conditions in the various districts will give a good general picture of where the best possibilities are. District 1 in the northeast offers good shooting. Here cut-over pulp lands furnish habitat during their first few years of new growth. The hunting terrain in this district is fairly rugged. Annual quail kill has recently averaged a bit over 100,000. There are club lands here, and some of these can assist visiting hunters in lining up guides. In District 2, quail are well distributed. Beaufort Co. rates high. Permission to hunt private lands is not too difficult to obtain. The quail kill recently has averaged just under 200,000.

District 3 has almost all hunting on private lands. There is very good quail hunting in general, with a kill of over 400,000 birds, by well over 20,000 quail hunters. There are some small Public Hunting Areas for small game only scattered across North Carolina. Because these may be added to, or deleted, from time to time, it is best to check with the Commission about them. Presently there is one near New Hill in southern Wake Co. Permission to hunt quail can often be obtained in this District, even though pressure is fairly high. The situation in District 4 is very much the same, with both quail and hunters rather abundant, and most hunting on private lands, by permission. Again, check for small-game Public Hunting Areas in this District.

District 5 is an excellent bet for quail. Best counties: Alamance, Guilford, Caswell, Randolph, Rockingham, Granville, Person, Orange. Quail kill runs from 400,000 to half a million. District 6 quail hunting is mostly under club control or on posted lands. Farming areas have plentiful birds. District 7 is rather similar. Best quail counties are in the eastern half of the District. There is a 4000-acre Public Hunting Area for small game in Davie Co. In

District 8 the best quail county is Cleveland. In District 9 there is only scattered quail hunting and a low kill.

The Croatan NF, in the southeast, District 2, offers quail hunting in portions of its area. Hunters should note that within this Forest, east of State 58 about where it joins U.S. 17, there is an 18,000-acre WMA. This management area may or may not be open for small-game hunting. Also, the Uwharrie National Forest in Districts 5 and 6 has some quail hunting. There is also a WMA here, of 18,000, usually open for small game hunting. It lies along the Montgomery-Stanly Co. border.

MOURNING DOVES

Dove hunting in North Carolina is excellent. Usually there is a split season, the first during September and part of October, the second beginning in mid-December and running into January. Although mourning doves range throughout the state, the best hunting is along the coastal plain and inland throughout the piedmont to the beginning of the mountains.

The great share of dove hunting is on private lands where crops are raised. The total kill for the state is high, anywhere from two to three million. During a recent season harvests by District were as follows: District 1, 140,000; District 2, 412,000; District 3, 427,000; District 4, 457,000; District 5, 487,000; District 6, 513,000; District 7, 200,000; District 8, 270,000; District 9, 50,000. These figures show precisely where the best shooting can be found.

A WMA in the southeast, in District 2, Pender Co., that has not thus far been noted is Holly Shelter WMA (20). It is a 48,500-acre tract. It may or may not have a special dove hunt, but has had in the past. This is a region of sandy ridges and of peat bogs. Routes surrounding it are as follows: U.S. 17, State 210, U.S. 117, State 53, State 50. It lies northeast of the city of Wilmington.

Wherever doves can be found on the WMAs, most of which have small-game seasons, they may of course be hunted. The Sandhills WMA ("Quail") offers the best hunting. In two recent seasons from 10,000 to over 16,000 doves were shot on this Area. The Croatan WMA has in the past been open for dove hunting at times. The Forest of same name is a dove hunting possibility, along its fringes. So are the Small-Game Public Hunting Areas discussed under "Quail."

However, the best public shooting for doves is found on a series of public tracts set up purposely for this sport by the Commission. For the past decade the state has pushed this project, primarily designed to allow the city sportsman an opportunity to hunt doves on some of the best fields. The average number of Dove Hunting Areas runs around twenty annually. On these shooting is allowed on designated days, afternoons only. Some are open as a rule on Monday and Wednesday, others Wednesday and Saturday, a few on all three days. There is a modest special-permit fee, and of course the regular license is needed. These areas, almost all of which are privately owned, are well distributed across the state. Some may be added, or deleted, annually.

The Commission usually publishes in or before September a list of the dove-hunt tracts, both the Public Hunting Areas for small game that are open, and the special Dove Hunting Areas. To this are added the few WMAs where dove shoots are held. Because of possible changes, it is best for dove hunters to request from the Commission a list for the season in question.

Complete directions for reaching each location are given. Or, one may request dove-field locations in any particular District.

A few notes about dove shooting in the various Districts follow. District 1 has its best hunting during the late half of the split season. Permission is not difficult to obtain after crops are harvested. District 2 is about the same. In District 3 there are at least four Dove Hunting Areas plus the Small Game Area noted under "Quail." District 4 has at least two very good Dove Areas for public hunting where specially managed millet fields are used. District 5 has several special Dove Areas, in Orange, Guilford, and Randolph Cos.

In District 6, one of the best, hunting is excellent on private lands and permission fairly easy to obtain after crop harvest. If crops are in before the end of the first part of the season, shooting is very good. A few of the best locations: western Rowan Co.; south and west Union; southern Stanly; central Cabarrus; south and west Davidson. Small Game and Dove Areas are several in this District, but the Dove Areas are subject to annual change. The eastern half of District 7 offers fair dove shooting in corn and millet fields. District 8 has several Dove Areas. In District 9, opportunities are limited. The corn-growing region of Mills River, Henderson Co., offers fair chances. The area near Hendersonville does also.

WILD TURKEYS

North Carolina has much excellent turkey range. But for some years now the wild turkey has been in a serious decline in this state, while most surrounding states have had just the opposite experience. Strong sentiment for a solid turkey restoration program at last got underway a comprehensive study of the problem beginning in 1967. For years North Carolina had had no spring season for gobblers only, but instead had had a long fall season covering as much as three full months. It was quickly recognized by biologists that paring down the fall season and adding a brief spring season would be the first helpful measures.

Presently there is a spring hunt of about two weeks' duration in the coastal plain, and of one week or less in the piedmont. The fall season has been drastically shortened, and restricted to only the central portion of the state. It is possible that further limitations on fall hunting may occur. At any rate, a firm restoration program, with reestablishment of flocks in places suitable in the west and elsewhere over the state, is now underway.

Because of the new approach, regulations may change from season to season. Hunters are advised to check thoroughly for the season a hunt is planned. At this writing the piedmont counties offer almost two months of fall or winter hunting for bearded turkeys. Hardwood bottoms are the best terrain here. Caswell, Person, Durham, Chatham, Orange, Montgomery, Moore, and Richmond Cos. have the best range, but mostly in private ownership. The spring piedmont season as this is written is for one week only, and for a longer period in the coastal plain counties.

Several WMAs have fair to good turkey flocks and have had brief spring seasons in the past. In May of 1969 more were opened for a spring hunt. These were: Daniel Boone, Wayah Bald, Standing Indian, Santeetlah, South Mountains. See "Grouse." There are both fall and spring seasons now on the Caswell WMA in the piedmont. These WMA hunts require a permit. Presently the fee is $5.25 for the season and includes small-game hunting on areas managed just for small game, and also on the Big Game Restoration Areas.

WOODCOCK, SNIPE, RAILS

There is very little interest in woodcock hunting in this state. In addition, the main migration line for the major share of the continental flight misses the region. Pockets of good woodcock shooting might be located in the western or piedmont valleys and in certain scattered coastal swamp areas. But at this time at least woodcock are shot chiefly as incidentals.

The jacksnipe is another underhunted species. There is a fairly good wintering population and others migrating along the coast to winter in Florida. The main flight pattern, however, is to the west, where most of the continental jacksnipe population wind up in southern Louisiana for the winter. Nonetheless, there is an opportunity for excellent snipe hunting, particularly in marshes of Currituck Co. in the extreme northeast, and on down the coast in numerous wetland and prairie-type marshlands and bogs and along the marshes of the lower coastal stream courses. Some of the waterfowling areas (see "Waterfowl," following) furnish good snipe shooting for the specialists who wish to pursue this exciting sport.

Rail hunting along the North Carolina coast is excellent, yet is practiced by a very small number of hunters. Rails here are usually called "marsh hens." There are sora rails and king rails in the freshwater marshes of Currituck Sound and elsewhere in coastal marshes not invaded by salt water. But it is the clapper rail of the marine marshes that furnishes the favored shooting. Best success requires a tide level of at least five or more feet. Such tides occur at full or new moon, or are due to storms. The high water pushes the birds into concentrations on islands of reeds that remain above water. Shooting is at peak only for a couple of hours while the tide is at its highest. Thus, during a given season—usually most of September, all of October, and throughout early November—only a relatively few hours of prime hunting are available. The practice requires two hunters, or a hunter with guide. The guide poles the boat. A list of rail guides can be obtained from the Commission. There is no problem at all in finding hunting places, since the tidal marshes are in great part public domain. There are enormous stretches of salt marsh especially along the southeast coast, in Carteret, Onslow, Pender, New Hanover, and Brunswick Cos.

WATERFOWL

Coastal North Carolina is one of the continent's most famous waterfowling grounds, and one of the important wintering grounds for both ducks and geese. There are vast marshes, both fresh and salt. The great island sounds cover some two million acres: Currituck, Albemarle, Roanoke, Croatan, Pamlico, Core, Bogue. Farther south there are numerous smaller sounds: Stump, Middle, Masonboro, Topsail, and the mouths of numerous large rivers that empty into the sounds.

Canada geese are abundant. Most locate on Lake Mattamuskeet, which used to gather as many as 100,000 annually but over recent years has been getting no more than half that or less, and on Currituck Sound. Kill figures show for a typical season about 85 percent of the geese bagged in District 1, where both Currituck and Mattamuskeet are located. The duck kill here amounts to more than a third of the total for the state, and District 1 and 2 together furnish about 65 percent of the duck bag.

While there is ample opportunity for public shooting, there are many clubs, and in hot spots like Currituck, for example, it is almost impossible to get a blind. Here blinds are registered and often passed down in the same family for generations. However, guided hunts are easily arranged, and this is the best arrangement for any visitor.

Breaking the waterfowl hunting down by regions, undoubtedly the coastal sounds and lakes come first. The National Wildlife Refuge at Lake Matta-muskeet, in cooperation with the Game Commission, has public hunting for geese and ducks in portions of its acreage. Permits and reservations are required; blinds, decoys, and guides are available. Since the arrangements and regulations are fairly complicated, it is advisable that waterfowlers wishing to try this famous shooting contact either the Refuge Manager or the State Game Commission for details. In addition to the Refuge hunting, there are surrounding farmlands where cornfield shooting and other feeding field shooting is on a fee basis.

In Currituck Sound large flocks of geese congregate, in addition to important concentrations of black ducks, widgeons, some pintails and mallards. Guided hunts from blinds, either on water for ducks or in fields for geese, are readily available here. In Roanoke and Croatan sounds there are guided hunts available for geese and ducks, and some seasons there is very good brant hunting here, too. Bodie Island Marshes offer hunting controlled and administered by the National Park Service. Reservations are necessary. At this writing there is no fee, but hunters furnish decoys and have no guides.

Pamlico Sound at times has the major share of the wintering waterfowl, many scaups, some sea ducks such as scoters, plus geese and brant. Because the water area is vast and most hunting near shore, the region serves as a kind of refuge. Guided hunts are numerous here, with blinds and decoys furnished.

In Core and Bogue sounds redheads and scaups have long been the mainstay. In all of these waterways and shores hunters can find ample opportunity for hunting on their own, but guided hunts will be far more successful. As noted previously, the Commission will furnish a list of guides and accommodations for waterfowlers anywhere along the coast.

The lower reaches of the coastal rivers also offer limitless opportunity for hunting from boat or blind. The Pasquotank, the Perquimans, the Chowans, Pungo (and Pungo Lake and the Terra Ceia area), the Pamlico, Neuse, New, Cape Fear, Lumber, and Roanoke all offer excellent shooting for various species of ducks and some geese. Flooded hardwood bottomlands in several of these rivers have concentrations of wood ducks, black ducks, mallards. Drifting and jump-shooting are common public practices. There are also corn and peanut fields along some of the rivers where owners allow hunting, for a fee or by permission. During winters of heavy rains, streams such as the Neuse flood thousands of acres of hardwoods where mast forms food for black ducks, mallards, and wood ducks. The Cape Fear is a similar situation.

Brant enthusiasts will find the best shooting near Hatteras and Ocracoke along the Outer Banks. Inland goose hunters can locate a good concentration most seasons in Anson Co., in the southern part of District 6 at Gaddy's Pond. There is no hunting at the Pond, but there are field blinds on surrounding farms. Most of the inland impoundments such as those on the Yadkin-Pee Dee River and on the Catawba offer fair duck hunting and occasionally some goose shooting.

There are several public waterfowling locations along the coast not so far noted. Northwest River Marsh (21) is a Small and Migratory Game PHA in the extreme northeast, in Currituck Co. near the village of Moyock just below the Virginia border. Gull Rock WMA (22) is down the coast, immediately south of Lake Mattamuskeet, Hyde Co. This is a 300-acre impoundment on Pamlico Sound reached by the Outfall Canal Road seven miles from U.S. 264. Pamlico Point (23) is an impoundment of 800 acres near the mouth of the Pamlico River. A boat is necessary to run the three miles to it from Oyster Creek landing near the village of Lowland, reached by a spur secondary from State 33. Goose Creek WMA (24) is at the turnoff point from State 33 to Lowland. It is in Beaufort and Pamlico Cos., reached by State 33, 304, and 307. White Oak (25) is on down the coast to the south, and below the southern edge of the Croatan NF and WMA. It is small, a 100-acre impoundment on the White Oak River, north of the village of Swansboro, State 24, and near Stella, which is on a secondary west of State 58.

RABBITS

Cottontails provide good shooting in all counties and excellent in many. There are swamp rabbits in the swampy portions of the tidewater region. Rabbits of one or the other variety provide hunting on portions of all of the public lands. The annual bag runs anywhere from two to three million.

In District 1, Martin, Bertie, Hyde, and Hertford Cos. are considered best. District 2 has rather evenly distributed rabbit populations. Total kills in these districts recently ran about 130,000 for each. District 3 usually has a higher kill, over 300,000, but most hunting is by permission on private lands. The same is true of District 4. In District 5 the counties of Chatham, Lee, Randolph, Rockingham are considered best locations, and a kill of as many as 400,000 is common. District 6 has plentiful rabbits in all farmland portions. The same is true of District 7. In District 8, Cleveland Co. is best. Lincoln, Gaston, Rutherford, Catawba are fair. Rabbits are not very abundant in District 9 but offer fair hunting in the less mountainous portions.

The Sherwood WMA ("Grouse") has a fair amount of open ridge country where rabbit hunting with dogs is productive. Caswell WMA and Sandhills WMA ("Quail") are good rabbit locations. The Small Game Public Hunting Areas noted elsewhere in this chapter all have varying supplies of rabbits.

SQUIRRELS

The gray squirrel is the more common species, and is especially abundant in the hardwoods of the coastal plain, and in portions of the west wherever hardwoods are available to support these forest animals. In the Sandhills area the southern fox squirrel is abundant, especially in scrub oak and scrub pine stands. Total squirrel bags are very large, up to 3.5 million in good seasons. Gray squirrels make up the preponderance of the kill because they have far greater range. Heaviest kills are made in the western districts, although the overall picture, successwise, is almost as good in the eastern half of the state. The National Forests, the WMAs, the Small Game PHAs all offer fine squirrel hunting.

District 1 hunters often float streams for squirrels. Hardwood bottoms in Bertie, Chowan, Martin, Hertford, Gates Cos. are all good bets. District 2 also has good float hunting, and a high squirrel kill. The float hunting is unique, and of course open to the public. Both Districts 3 and 4 have excellent squirrel hunting, chiefly on private lands. District 4 has a good supply of fox squirrels. District 5 squirrel hunting is mostly in farm woodlots where oak and hickory grow. In District 6 the National Forest lands in Montgomery Co., the Uwharrie Refuge, wooded stream bottoms, and wooded areas surrounding the impoundments along the rivers are all good places to hunt squirrels. In the western Districts the NF lands and WMAs furnish an abundance of excellent opportunity.

DEER

At the turn of the century deer were scarce in North Carolina, with the major herd in a small tidewater area. Today deer are widely spread throughout the state, with the total herd estimated at between 300,000 and 400,000 animals, and increasing. Either-sex seasons are held in various portions of the state. Total kill is upwards of 40,000. The picture by Districts is as follows.

District 1, most prime range leased by clubs, but public hunting on large tracts of pulp company lands. One 20,000-acre parcel in Bertie Co. is under lease by the Commission. Another 300,000 in Dare, Tyrrell, and Wash. Cos. is open by company permit. District 2 has good hunting on the Croatan WMA ("Quail") and Holly Shelter WMA ("Doves"). In District 3 most good deer range is leased by clubs. Some private-land hunting is available in the north and west of this region. District 4 is heavily leased. Some guided hunting is at this writing publicly available in Columbus Co. In District 5 there is a managed hunt held at present by the North Carolina National Guard, on state property. Contact the Guard headquarters in Raleigh for details. There is also some day hunting for fees on private lands.

District 6 contains the Uwharrie WMA, which has good hunting. The same is true of the NF lands of Montgomery Co. The Sandhills WMA is also a top spot. Wooded Pee Dee River bottoms in Stanly Co. have plentiful deer. In District 7, Thurmond Chatham WMA is excellent. In District 8 all of the WMAs support good herds. Burke Co., where South Mountain WMA is located, is the best portion of this region. In District 9 the better deer herds are chiefly on the WMAs. Most of this acreage is within National Forests. Hunting outside the WMA boundaries is on NF lands and thus open to the public.

Special managed hunts are held on a number of the WMAs, some of them buck hunts, some either-sex with quotas. It is necessary to check seasonally with the Commission for regulations pertaining to the various WMAs. Some high-kill WMAs to date have been: Pisgah, Daniel Boone, Mount Mitchell, Sherwood, Uwharrie, Flat Top, Wayah Bald, roughly in that order. Santeetlah, Fires Creek, Standing Indian, Rich Laurel, Thurmond Chatham also show up well. As noted earlier Sandhills in the south-central part of the state also is a quality deer hunting location. See "Grouse," "Quail," and "Doves" for locations of these various WMAs.

BEAR

Surprisingly, the bulk of the black bear kill comes from the tidewater swamps rather than from the western mountains. Districts 1 and 2 furnish during some seasons almost the entire kill. As an example, several seasons ago the total state bag was 628 bears. Of these, 238 were taken in District 1, in the northeast, and 380 from District 2, along the coast to the south. In the west the best hunting is during the managed hunts on the WMAs, and in counties which get bears moving out of Great Smoky Mountains National Park.

Hunts on the western WMAs are of two types: bear (and boar) party hunts with dogs, several of which are held on specified dates; bear (and boar) still-hunts. Only certain WMAs are open. During a recent season seven were open for dog hunts, four for still-hunts, two of which were for only a single day. It is thus necessary to check the regulations for a current season in order to plan and apply for a hunt.

In the east, both Holly Shelter and Croatan WMAs have dog hunts for bear. There is of course hunting on National Forest lands, but the WMA portions are usually best. Guided bear hunts have the highest chance of success. The Commission can furnish a list of guides. Also, for hunting with dogs, local wardens are a good source of information regarding guided hunts. They usually know where dog packs are located. Again, package hunts of this sort will have the best success percentage in Districts 1 and 2.

BOAR

North Carolina is one of the few states with boar hunting on public lands. The boars originated from preserve stock held in the early part of the century on a private preserve on Hoopers Bald in Graham Co., on the Tennessee border, District 9. Since then boars have broadened their range, especially into Cherokee and Clay Cos., which border Graham in the extreme west. The Russian or European boars have crossed with feral swine in some portions of the range. Virtually the total kill of boars comes from the Santeetlah WMA. During two recent seasons the managed hunts collected eighty-one and sixty-five. Interested hunters should contact the Commission for rules pertaining to application procedures. Hunts are by drawing. Party hunts, five or fewer persons, resident, $75, nonresident with five or more nonresidents in party, $150.

The Snowbird Mountains in Graham Co. are a good boar-hunt location for other than WMA managed hunts, and so are portions of Cherokee Co. A few are also taken in Macon Co. Some 275 were bagged during a recent season. Guides and lodges in these counties cater to boar hunters, and also to bear hunters.

OTHER ANIMALS

Both raccoons and opossums are abundant throughout the state. Red foxes and gray foxes also are in good supply, with the red the dominant species west of the fall line of the rivers. There is high interest among hundreds of hound men in "racing" foxes and in hunting raccoons. There is also a fair amount of formal fox hunting in this state. For the average hunter, any of the public lands already covered will offer fair to good hunting for any of these animals.

Woodchuck hunting is gaining much popularity in the west. The mountain counties have them in abundance, especially in sections where grazing and farmlands meet on the slopes. Ashe Co. in the northwest is considered one of the best locations. The western WMAs all provide shooting of varying quality.

REGULATIONS

Game laws pertaining to seasons, bag and possession limits, areas to be hunted, special hunts, license fees all may have numerous changes from year to year. For current regulations, write to: North Carolina Wildlife Resources Commission, Raleigh, North Carolina 27602.

SOUTH CAROLINA

Although the partially triangular state of South Carolina, squeezed in below North Carolina to the north and against Georgia on the southwest, can claim a portion of the Blue Ridge Mountains in its northwest apex, the state's highest point, Sassafras Mountain, is only 3560 feet. From the northwest the state drops with lovely mountain scenery down across dense pine forests of the lower piedmont plateau. The rivers flowing southeast to the Atlantic—the Savannah forming the border with Georgia, the Santee and its upper branches, the Pee Dee and many others—all course fertile farmlands as the slope of land reaches toward the coastal plain.

Tobacco, cotton, peaches, peanuts all are important here. But manufacturing has passed agriculture over recent years, and farms have grown fewer and larger. As the coastal lowlands reach toward the semitropic beaches, evidence of the importance of tourism, the resort trade, is everywhere, and the Old South plantations still exist here. In fact, South Carolina is very much South still today, with many of the traditions and much of the way of life still intact. Along with the large coastal plantations, there are nowadays huge tracts inland in timber. Pine "farming" is tremendously important, and while this means large areas of virtually unbroken forest, it has both advantages and disadvantages so far as game is concerned.

Because South Carolina lies on a direct route from all coastal points north of it to all those south and west, it is a veritable grid of good highways. Hunters have no difficulties getting to any corner of the state. Air travel between major cities is wholly adequate, and the state is small enough so that few hunters will wish to fly from one point to another in it anyway. From the extreme northwest to the coast is roughly 200 miles, and the coastline from the North Carolina border to Savannah, Georgia, is little more than 160. Compared to the two bordering states, South Carolina is much smaller, with an area of 31,055 square miles. Present population is over 2,600,000. It is rather evenly distributed. There are no exceptionally large cities, but numerous smaller ones.

Hunting is popular, and an emphatic private-land tradition still remains here with hunt-clubs and the social significance of hunting often noted in the South. Some 200,000 licenses are sold annually. Less than 5 percent of these are to nonresidents. In fact, hunting in South Carolina is not especially easy for those who visit the state without contacts, although invitations or arrangements to hunt on private lands usually result in superb sport. Quail are among the important upland species. There is also shooting for ruffed grouse, turkeys, waterfowl, rails. Doves are extremely popular. Deer are quite plentiful, there are a few bear. Small game—rabbits and squirrels— are abundant, and there are also foxes, raccoons, opossums. There are some snipe, and a scattering of woodcock.

The Wildlife Resources Commission is very frank about public hunting

153

conditions in South Carolina. While it is doing an excellent job of providing managed public lands, and the program has grown from a mere 20,000 acres fifteen years ago to some 900,000 today, and presumably with more to come, the Commission admits that the best of the quail hunting, the water-fowling, and most of the better hunting of other varieties is on private lands, large plantations kept for hunting by and for their owners and friends.

This does not mean public-land hunting is poor. Managed lands are doing extremely well, with restoration of species such as deer and turkeys growing annually. Quail lands, on the other hand, have difficulties. The pine tree, as many southern biologists have said, is an enemy of the bobwhite. The importance of pulp and of pine for other purposes sees lands that might otherwise support good quail populations taken up in tree farms, whereas plantation owners who are avid quail hunters often manage large acreages of private land just for quail and quail hunting.

The Commission-managed lands, many of them in large Game Management Areas, are largely owned by the U.S. Forest Service. These are tracts within National Forests set up as management projects cooperated in by federal and state personnel. Other tracts of Forest generally surround the Management Areas. Hunting can be done on the National Forest at any time of open season, but on the GMA portions of it under specified rules only. The next largest acreage of lands managed by the Commission for public hunting is in private ownership, some owned by power companies, other tracts by paper companies. There are also some Corps of Engineers lands thus managed. The Commission itself, at this writing, owns only a modest amount of land, less than 20,000 acres, but arrangements on the other acreages have worked admirably.

There are two National Forests. The Sumter NF is in three large sections, one in the extreme northwest, one on the border with Georgia about at the midpoint, another approximately in the north-central region. The total acreage is 341,624. Most of the northwestern block is in Oconee County. U.S. 76 crosses it. The town of Walhalla is a key location point a bit to the east. The block on the Georgia border has U.S. 25 skirting along its northern edge and passing through the city of Greenwood. Interstate 26 passes through the mid-state block, and U.S. 176 also crosses it, with the city of Union a location point on the northern edge. The second National Forest is the Francis Marion. It is near the coast, about centered between north and south borders. The city of Charleston is to the south, Georgetown to the north. U.S. 17 and 52 are both access roads, with several state routes crossing. The acreage here is 245,650.

As noted above, these Forests have GMAs within them. These will be detailed later, under species, but the general locations of the Forests are given here for reader convenience. Maps and more details on these two Forests can be obtained from the Forest Supervisor, Columbia, South Carolina. There is a map and brochure offered by the South Carolina Wildlife Resources Commission titled "Game Management Areas of South Carolina." This is annually revamped to show locations of the GMAs and also to give up-to-date regulations and seasons pertaining to each.

Hunters not interested in public lands but who like package hunts on private lands with lodges or other accommodations will find a number of such South Carolina places advertising in various outdoor magazines. These in general offer prime quail and other hunting. Guides also can be located here and there along the coast for rail hunting—local people call these birds "marsh hens." Best contacts for such guides are via Chambers of Commerce.

Hunters headed for the public lands who wish to camp will find facilities in a large number of State Parks. There are even vacation cottages in some of the parks. A booklet called "South Carolina Campgrounds" is published by the Department of Parks, Box 1358, Columbia, South Carolina 29202. There are also campgrounds in the National Forests and along the Corps of Engineers Reservoirs. Motel and other accommodations are found in abundance over the entire state.

Early fall in this state, as for dove hunting, is exceedingly warm. Later in season, with many hunting seasons opening in November, it is entirely pleasant. Grouse or deer hunters in the higher northwest may find some crisp days, but in general mid-fall is a delightful time. Later in the winter, colder weather will make woolen clothing mandatory. Coastal waterfowlers may discover chill breezes, and hunters in the hills will find a jacket comfortable.

No very specialized arms or ammunition are needed in this state. The standard deer rifle and a shotgun with plenty of No. 7½ or comparable loads for average bird hunting (and possibly buckshot for deer) will be basic. For waterfowl heavier shotgun loads are called for, and a .22 is handy for squirrels. The main caution in South Carolina is to be sure one understands the regulations properly. There are general state laws for the various Game Zones, or Districts, of which presently there are eight. There are also regulations pertaining to specified GMAs. To complicate matters, there are a number of county laws in effect here and there. Check the map of the GMAs with care, and if in doubt contact a local warden regarding county regulations.

QUAIL

It is estimated that some two million quail are bagged annually by South Carolina hunters. By far the vast majority of these are killed on private lands. Probably at least half of South Carolina's hunters do at least some quail hunting. The entire state has varying open seasons, dates differing among the eight Zones. In general the heaviest quail populations are in the lower part of the state, inland some distance from the coast.

The counties of Clarendon and Williamsburg in the east-central sector, and those of Allendale and Hampton on the Georgia border toward the southeast are, generally speaking, the best. However, most of the lands of high quality are posted. Quail hunters, to have the proper picture of this sport here, should realize that although almost all of the GMAs have at least some quail hunting, these Areas are managed primarily for timber. This means that deer, and in some cases, turkeys, do well, but for the most part the Areas have cover too thick for good quail shooting, even though they may sustain a fair quail population. The big plantations of the low country have heavy quail concentrations, but for all practical purposes there is no public hunting.

There is also the problem in South Carolina in regard to which GMAs are open to hunting for what is generally lumped together as "small game." The large GMA tracts are managed at this time primarily for deer and turkeys. Restoration programs are chiefly aimed at these species. Thus, no guarantees of quality quail hunting can be made for any of them, what with both the Forest Service and the pulp and paper firms primarily interested in trees rather than quail.

The best therefore that can be done is to note some of the public lands that at least have quail hunting of varying quality, and that are open to

KEY TO HUNTING AREAS

1. Horse Pasture GMA
2. Chauga GMA
3. Sumter National
   Forest; Broad River
   GMA; Carlisle GMA;
   Enoree GMA;
   Wateree GMA;
   Fishing Creek GMA;
   Dutchman Creek
   GMA
4. Clark Hill GMA;
   Forks Key GMA;
   Parsons Mountain
   GMA
5. Gapway Bay GMA;
   Walker Farm GMA
6. Francis Marion
   National Forest:
   Wambaw-Francis
   Marion GMA;
   Waterhorn-Francis
   Marion GMA

7. Barton Tract GMA
8. Angel Tract GMA
9. Early Branch GMA
10. Palachucola GMA
11. Dangerfield GMA;
    Murphy GMA;
    Odom GMA;
    Whitener-Tucker
    GMA; Yaun GMA
12. Bear Island GMA
13. Slater GMA
14. Big Pee Dee GMA
15. Santee Delta GMA
16. Cape Roman Refuge
17. Carolina Sandhills
    Refuge
18. Santee Refuge
19. Buist GMA
20. Milberry GMA
21. Eatmon Tract GMA

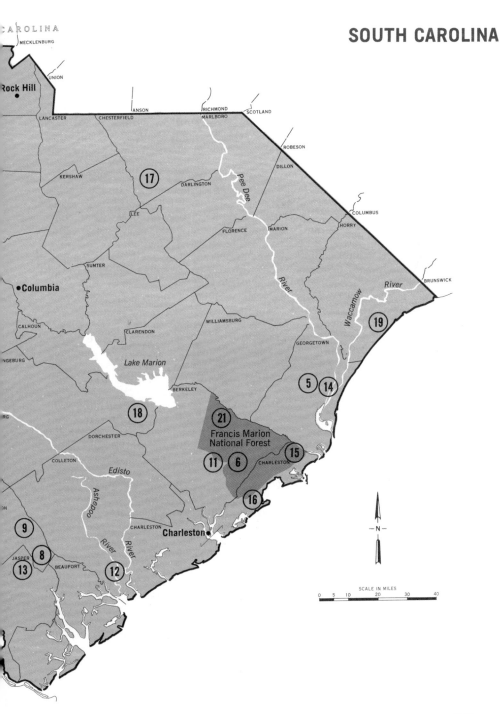

SOUTH CAROLINA

157

hunting. Both National Forests list quail as one of the game species. These two Forests have been described earlier. But in speaking of National Forests it must be emphasized that they should be considered as separate from GMAs, even though some GMAs are within them, and presumably in future most of South Carolina's National Forests may come under state game management.

As this is written, the Horse Pasture GMA (1), of 50,000 acres, is open to quail hunting during the regular season for that Game Zone. This is Zone 1. The GMA is in Pickens Co. in the northwest, east of the town of Pickens. This Area is near the block of Sumter NF in the northwest, but is owned by Duke Power Company. Hunters should not confuse it with the Horse Pasture Restoration Unit to the north, on which at this writing no hunting is allowed.

Also in the Northwest, in Oconee Co. and owned by the USFS is the Chauga GMA (2), of over 72,000 acres. It is located in the extreme southwest corner of the county, in Sumter NF. Hunters for quail on all these lands should very diligently study the regulations. For example, these conform to Zone regulations, but prohibit buckshot or any rifles except .22's during small-game hunts, prohibit shooting of deer, bear, turkey during small-game hunts, and prohibit any small-game hunting until after Thanksgiving Day on Areas that offer hunts for big game. U.S. 76 west from Westminster is a good access for the Chauga GMA.

In the north-central part of the state is a huge region designated presently as Hunt Unit 1, not to be confused with Game Zone 1. There are approximately 800,000 acres in this region, in general in two large blocks. Much of this is Sumter National Forest, but a great deal is in private lands. National Forest lands require no permission but private lands do. A marking system is in effect but hunters must use care and judgment on boundaries. It is necessary to study the Commission map for orientation on this Unit. It is in two main blocks, northwest and northeast of the city of Columbia. The cities of Winnsboro and Chester are key towns lying between the two blocks. The larger block encompasses the Sumter NF lands here (see front of chapter). U.S. 21 skirts the west edge of the other, smaller block. Small-game hunts, including quail, are held here (at this writing) from Thanksgiving Day to the end of the Zone season. Within this Unit are the following GMAs: Broad River, Carlisle, Enoree, Wateree, Fishing Creek, Dutchman Creek (3). Check the GMA map for detailed locations on each, for all are grouped together.

Under the same general setup is Hunt Unit 2. Basically this is the block of Sumter NF on the middle section of the border with Georgia. But a vast share of the lands are in private ownership and the permission rule on these applies, so the signs must be watched. This Unit covers 550,000 acres in total, lying in the counties of Edgefield, Greenwood, McCormick, Abbeville. To somewhat complicate matters for visiting hunters who may be perplexed by the maze of South Carolina laws and property divisions, within the borders of Unit 2 are the following GMAs: Clark Hill, a Corps of Engineers tract of 12,000 acres; NF lands under GMA names Forks-Key Bridge and Parsons Mountain (4). Regulations as for Unit 1 apply—but beware of seasonal changes.

Over near the coast, in the region to the west of Georgetown are a pair of GMAs that as this is written have quail (and other small-game) hunting "with bird dogs only." This season is short, about two weeks. Actually these are privately owned lands but they are not far north of the Francis Marion NF. They are close together. Gapway Bay GMA (4) has almost 10,000 acres. Almost touching it to the southwest is Walker Farm GMA with over 8000 acres. U.S. 17A and 521 run along the south border of Walker Farm; State 51 runs just north of Gapway.

South of these Areas is the Francis Marion NF, already mentioned. Within the Forest are two GMAs. One is the Wambaw-Francis Marion with 43,000 acres, the other the Waterhorn-Francis Marion with 17,000 (6). Quail hunting is legal here during the regular season. State Route 45 roughly separates the two Areas, and U.S. 17 and 701 run near the coast on the east side.

In the southwest are some Commission-managed, privately owned tracts that offer quail hunting, usually after the first of the year. These are in some of the better quail range. The Barton Tract GMA (7) has almost 15,000 acres west of U.S. 321 near the border between Hampton and Allendale Cos. The Angel Tract GMA (8) is smaller, 1741 acres, and is open *only* for small game (quail, etc.). It is west of U.S. 17 near the village of Yemassee. Northwest of this tract is Early Branch GMA (9), 8564 acres in Hampton Co. near the village of like name and to the west of U.S. 21. There is another GMA in Hampton Co. open for quail, 12,512 acres of Continental Can Company lands called the Palachucola GMA (10). This is on the Savannah River in the southwest corner of the county. State 119 and U.S. 321 give access from east and north, with the village of Garnett a key.

In Berkeley Co. north of Charleston and to the west of the Francis Marion NF are a scattering of small tracts of Continental Can Company lands open during regular season. These are named as individual GMAs and range from 140 to over 1,700 acres. The names: Dangerfield, Murphy, Odom, Whitener-Tucker, and Yaun GMAs (11). There are a few other lands comparable to these but it is best to check the map for any given season to ascertain if they are open for quail. Farther to the south, in Colleton Co. between the Edisto and Ashepoo Rivers, is Bear Island GMA (12). This has 7500 acres, is owned by the Commission, and is open to varied game in season, but managed primarily for waterfowl.

Some additional lands may be open to the public for quail in the future, or from time to time as management dictates. Again it must be emphasized that the quality of the quail hunting on any lands noted here is unpredictable. The change in land use, with the pine tree so important, plus the emphasis on quail on the large plantations, in addition to the basic interest of so many hunters in deer and turkeys, have all influenced the diminishing quality of public-land quail hunting in South Carolina.

RUFFED GROUSE

In South Carolina this is a specialist's bird. Ruffed grouse are found only in the extreme northwest, in Game Zone 1, which takes in Oconee, Pickens, and Greenville Cos. Even here, grouse are not found throughout, but the season is now open throughout this Zone. Oddly, for many years the ruffed grouse was not on the game list in South Carolina but was classified as a songbird, or non-game bird. Actually the songbird classification was in force simply because of scarcity and because the bird did not seem to fit in the two other classifications of domestic game or destructive birds. Keeping the grouse off the game list of course did utterly nothing to further the growth of its population. In 1964 a state senator from Oconee Co. put through a bill to place the ruffed grouse on the game list and it has been there since.

The kill runs very low because few hunters will brave the rugged and steep up-country walking in dense cover to kill these birds. In two recent seasons surveys show 250 and 110 grouse bagged. At that, hunters were determined and dedicated. It took 1250 hunters to bag the 250, 610 to bring in the 110. Nonetheless, for the few who admire this dynamic game bird of the forests the hard work and the sport are worthwhile.

The block of Sumter National Forest described earlier, in the north-west, is one of the best grouse possibilities. The Chauga GMA within the Forest, in southwestern Oconee Co., is an excellent choice. The remainder of this block of the Forest also has birds. The Horse Pasture GMA in Pickens Co., owned by the Duke Power Company and covering 50,000 acres, is another good grouse range. This is the extent of public grouse lands pres-ently open to hunting. Greenville Co. has isolated pockets of mountain cover with grouse, but these lands are privately owned and permission is required. All told, this portion of northwestern South Carolina is notable for grouse simply because this region and parts of north Georgia are in the southern extremities of ruffed grouse range. The public lands mentioned are described under "Quail."

WILD TURKEYS

The eastern wild turkey has been an important game bird in South Carolina since the early days of settlement along the southeast coast. At present there are both fall and spring seasons in portions of the state. Kill survey figures are often suspect even among the people who make the final estimates. But if those from South Carolina are to be taken as a fair repre-sentation, the hunting, for the segment of specialist hunters who go after wild turkeys, is excellent. One fairly recent season showed that the total of turkey hunters was 6531, the kill 3687. During a later season, spring found 6506 hunters afield and a kill of 1064 gobblers. The following fall there were 8662 hunters, and they killed 5799 birds. This would appear to indicate that the overall success percentage, counting any year and both seasons, runs somewhere from 40 percent to 50 percent, which is far above the na-tional average.

South Carolina for many years has had its problems with indiscriminate shooting of turkeys by poachers. With protection on the GMAs in the north-west turkeys have thrived. Lately the spring seasons have been immensely successful on some of these areas. Downstate toward the coast there are lots of turkeys on suitable habitats within the big plantations where they get rigid protection. These private lands have their usefulness, even though some hunters may resent them. They serve as a reservoir of good stock. So do areas like the Francis Marion National Forest. The two GMA units de-scribed under "Quail" for this Forest (Waterhorn and Wambaw) have one of the highest densities of pure-strain eastern wild turkeys in the entire South-east. It is even possible that on these units they need more hunt pressure than they get. Both units offer a spring gobbler season.

The illegal kill of turkeys is undoubtedly substantial in the state. The kill on private lands is probably quite high, and surveys are not really ac-curate or even possible here. A diminishing turkey population in numerous sections has been brought back admirably by restoration projects. Basically, the areas of best native populations are : 1) along the mid-coast; 2) in the extreme southeast and reaching up the Savannah River through south Hampton Co.; 3) up the large river bottoms of the coastal and inland area. Occasional small local populations are found over much of the southeast half of the state. In the central and northwest sections, restored turkey populations are doing well mostly in Hunt Units 1 and 2 and in the blocks of Sumter NF in the northwest in Oconee and Pickens Cos., and on the GMAs therein where transplants have been made. See "Quail" for location and description of these areas. The central and northwest GMAs today have good turkey hunting where a decade ago there was none. The total South Carolina flock is estimated currently at somewhere over 25,000 to 30,000 birds.

Because the turkey restoration and management program is currently progressing, it is not possible to predict what GMAs may or may not have open seasons for fall and for spring during any given year. But a look at past seasons can give an idea of possibilities. During the 1968 spring season for gobblers only the following areas were open with a 2-gobbler limit, which indicates a sturdy population: Unit 1, Unit 2, Chauga (which at this time takes in all NF lands in Oconee Co.). Both GMAs of the Francis Marion Forest (Wambaw and Waterhorn) had spring seasons for 1 gobbler. See "Quail" for locations of all of these. And the Slater GMA (13), a 9125-acre tract owned by Continental Can Company near Gillisonville in Jasper Co. in the southwest, with access via U.S. 278, had a 1-gobbler spring season.

Under general regulations much of the northwestern third of the state has been closed to turkey hunting and restoration is in progress. However, most of the GMAs with sizable turkey flocks have hunting in portions of the National Forests. In Hunt Unit 2 (Forks, Key Bridge, Clark Hill, Parsons Mountain GMAs, "Quail") in one recent season 102 turkeys were taken by 937 hunters, about the national average for success. In the various piedmont Areas under Unit 1, success was less and more restoration is needed. At present, Hunt Units 1 and 2, the Francis Marion NF, and the mountainous Chauga GMA furnish most of the public kill. The largest birds come from Chauga, the smallest from Hunt Unit 2.

To sum up, though private-land turkey hunting is excellent in South Carolina, the public-land hunts and the restoration programs are still growing and unsettled. There is fine hunting but the time and place of each fall and spring hunt are at this writing somewhat unpredictable. In general the large tracts of National Forest lands will be best and the GMAs within them probably best of all. Check seasonally with the Commission for open public lands, limits, time of seasons, legal methods.

MOURNING DOVES

The mourning dove is on a par with the bobwhite and often ahead as the most popular, by numbers killed, of all South Carolina game birds. It runs over two million annually. Doves are hunted by almost half of the state's hunters. However, many dove hunters here are dedicated to the sport and hunt no other birds. In much of the south and particularly here, a dove shoot is as much a social affair as a hunt. This has been the tradition for many years on the big plantations. When a large concentration of birds is at hand, invitations go out, there is a gathering sometimes of scores of guests, often with families, a bounteous outdoor meal, not uncommonly with a bar set up too, and the shoot progresses as a kind of enjoyable excuse for the party.

Dove hunting on the average is good across much of the state. The early season finds the birds in the central and upper portions and the last half down across the lower country. This second-half shooting can be extremely good when grain harvests are properly timed and weather is just right to concentrate the flocks.

Public dove shooting is found on a number of GMAs. Any of them so far noted that are open to small-game hunting allow dove shooting. But South Carolina is also experimenting with management of certain properties especially for doves. Hunt Unit 1, in the north-central and northwesterly portion of the state, and the GMAs of the northwest have been the scene of much of this operation. During one season there were twenty-one fields in fourteen counties prepared, planted, and managed for public dove shooting. And in one year there were nineteen fields contracted for on private lands and nine utilized on GMAs. Over 10,000 doves were harvested during the experiment, and numerous hunters participated.

The private-land fields are prepared by the owners, under a contract with the Commission, which pays a lease fee. Attempts are made to locate fields near population centers, where hunting needs are heaviest. There is no charge to hunters. The fields are shot only one day per week, to keep from driving birds away. Usually the shooting days in the past have been either Wednesday or Saturday. Signs are put up along roads directing hunters to the fields, and a warden is present to assist and to gather kill statistics.

This program was launched in an attempt to illustrate to landowners the possibility of profit from fee hunting for doves. It is felt that if enough landowners will set up such shooting grounds on their own, with a reasonable charge, it would be both profitable to them and of great advantage to hunters. Currently the GMA fields will undoubtedly continue but it is not possible to predict what the outcome of the fee-hunt scheme will be. Nor is it possible to list here the location of such dove fields, for they are subject to change, year to year. Emphasis so far has been in the following upstate counties of the north and northwest: Abbeville, Anderson, Cherokee, Chester, Chesterfield, Fairfield, Greenville, Kershaw, Lancaster, Laurens, Lexington, McCormick, Marlboro, Newberry, Oconee, Pickens, Spartanburg, Union, York.

WOODCOCK, SNIPE, RAILS, EXOTICS

Some of the woodcock migration does pass this way, but the bulk of it does not. Woodcock hunting is seldom pursued here, except by quail hunters with dogs who happen to stumble upon a few birds. The kill is inconsequential. Scattered flights are now and then found during small-game hunts on the various GMAs.

Snipe hunting has almost no followers. Undoubtedly it could be enjoyed by more, except that there is little interest. From a public-land viewpoint, there are not many opportunities.

Rails have a following of enthusiasts along the coast. Estimates indicate that from 3000 to 5000 hunters try the rail hunting annually. Coastal rail hunting success is entirely dependent upon high tides to move the birds. A guide to pole the boat is mandatory, except for those natives who know the sport well. Such guides can best be located by contacting the Commission for subsequent contact with local wardens along the coastal area. These in turn, or else Chambers of Commerce in small coastal cities, can put one in touch with opportunities. Public rail hunting as such, however, is quite limited, and one is well advised to make plans as to time, tide, and local contacts meticulously.

Like several other southern states, South Carolina is experimenting with the raising and release of red junglefowl. A few have been released in the piedmont area. It is not known as yet whether they will form huntable populations.

WATERFOWL

There is excellent duck shooting on some of the coastal plantations managed for ducks, south from Georgetown to the Georgia line, and there is more of the same, for landowners, along such rivers as the Edisto, Ashepoo, and Combahee. Public duck hunting is rather limited. Goose hunting is not very important in the state. A few are killed, but the total averages probably not over 1500 annually, and there are about that many hunters who try for geese. Coastal hunting camps and lodges that advertise offer some good duck shooting.

Some good public duck hunting can be had be those who will take the trouble to seek it by floating the large rivers and jump-shooting birds. There is also a limited amount on GMAs. Noted under "Quail" is Bear Island GMA, in the southeast near the coast, between the Edisto and Ashepoo rivers. This Area is managed purposely for waterfowl, with controlled water level in marshes and abandoned rice-growing lands. A winter goose pasture is maintained, and sharecropping of grains leaves duck food, too. As many as 25,000 ducks and 350 geese have been counted during a January survey here. Public hunts have been held at Bear Island for some years. These are set up on an application and public drawing basis, with dates assigned after the drawing. In one past season this Area accommodated over 300 hunters.

In Orangeburg Co., near Eutaw Springs on Lake Marion, there is a tract of public land of about 1000 acres utilized as a GMA and managed for ducks and geese. A good many geese winter here, and a fair number of ducks. Hunting surrounding lands may be possible, but check whether or not the GMA itself is closed at any given season to hunting.

Near the coast, in Georgetown Co., are two GMAs managed for waterfowl. One, Big Pee Dee GMA (14), is on the lower Pee Dee and Waccamaw rivers, north of Georgetown and lying between U.S. 701 and U.S. 17. There are over 1200 acres here, owned by the Commission. This was a gift of an original plantation, plus several hundred acres of abandoned ricelands purchased by the state. Controlled waterfowl hunting is available here, on a drawing basis. To illustrate capacity, recently there were 19 hunts during a season, with 185 hunters accommodated. The kill was quite good; over 500 ducks. South of Georgetown and crossed by U.S. 701 is the Santee Delta GMA (15), 1500 acres in the coastal delta area of the Santee River. This also is open to public waterfowl hunting, and is a good spot.

There are several refuges in South Carolina and some shooting by fee and on private lands surrounding. Cape Romain Refuge (16) is on the coast north of Charleston. The Francis Marion NF GMAs are nearby, west of U.S. 17-701. The Carolina Sandhills Refuge (17) is in the northeast, in Chesterfield Co. near the town of McBee at the intersect of U.S. 1 and State 151. Santee Refuge (18) is the largest, and is located on Lake Marion in Clarendon Co. near Summerton, which is at the junction of U.S. 301 and 15. A great many Canada geese as well as thousands of ducks use this Refuge.

DEER

There is usually a deer hunt for archers only on the Bulls Island unit of the Cape Romain Refuge, above, and also deer hunting allowed on the Carolina Sandhills Refuge, also noted immediately above under "Waterfowl."

For a great many years the traditional deer hunt in South Carolina has been the low-country chase with hounds, and with buckshot used by hunters on stands. Except for check stations on GMAs there is no way of checking individual deer kills. Some South Carolina game men admit that limits are therefore meaningless and that certain hunters may kill as many as several dozen deer annually. The deer kill is variously estimated at from 25,000 to 45,000 animals. At any rate, deer hunting on low-country private lands is excellent and in fact some of the low country may presently have over-populations, even on public lands.

The upstate areas were becoming depleted of deer some years ago and a restocking program was begun in the 1950s. It has proved very successful. Today no county of South Carolina lacks deer. While the traditional hunting methods are still maintained on private lands, the interest in still-hunting and hunting with rifles is growing as these are stipulated or allowed on the GMAs.

The deer harvest on the GMA system is steadily growing. Although success percentage is not high, it too is increasing as hunters learn the still-hunt art.

Regulations may differ from season to season on the GMAs. In general the best bets are as follows: Hunt Unit 1; Hunt Unit 2; the two GMAs of the Francis Marion NF; Walker Farm; Gapway, Early Branch; Chauga; Palachucola; Yaun; Odom; Barton; Dangerfield; Murphy; Whitener-Tucker, Bear Island. All of these are described under "Quail." The Slater GMA ("Turkeys") also offers deer hunting.

Several other tracts not so far noted are among the good deer Areas. Buist GMA (19) is spotted on the Commission map as a 19,000-acre hunting ground in the coastal area of the northeast coast. It is near Conway, with U.S. 17 and 501 nearby. The Milberry GMA (20) has 6494 acres on the Savannah River in Allendale Co., is reached via U.S. 301. There is also the Eatmon Tract GMA (21) in the east, near St. Stephen, junction of U.S. 52 and State 45. The large Horse Pasture GMA ("Quail") will undoubtedly become a good deer hunting area in due time. It had been hunted hard until taken over by the Commission and now restoration is being accomplished.

On all of the public lands hunters must carefully check regulations. Seasons, hunting methods, sex of deer and limit differ from one to another. Some are still-hunts only, some are dog hunts on certain days, on some hunts there is a limit of 2 deer of either sex, and on others only 1 buck deer. There is also a hunt from time to time on the lands of the Savannah River plant of the AEC, where an overpopulation of deer has existed. A small fee is charged and there is a drawing for hunters. The Commission should be contacted regarding this hunt.

The future for the piedmont and mountain portions of the state on the managed lands looks bright. It is significant that for several seasons the largest deer have come from these regions while the smaller deer are from the coastal sector. This indicates good range conditions on the restocked range, and of course a lower but more healthy population.

BEAR

The black bear is all but gone from South Carolina, but it may be able to make a comeback to some extent. Presently there is a season only in Game Zone 1, which is the extreme northwest—Oconee, Pickens, Greenville Cos. This is only a short, token season. There are estimated to be only a few dozen bear left in the state. Some surveys have shown a season kill of over 300 but the Commission is certain the figure is wholly incorrect and doubts there are that many in the entire state. Fortunately, some stray bears drift into the northwest from the mountains in North Carolina. On the huge Horse Pasture GMA in Oconee and Pickens Cos. the black bear, under protection, is slowly building up a better population.

RABBITS AND SQUIRRELS

Rabbits are fairly plentiful except in the heavily populated upper third of the state. Interest in hunting them is not great anywhere, although a sizable kill is made each season. All of the GMAs noted, and the National Forest lands, offer rabbit hunting of varying quality.

Cutting of hardwoods in the state is a major debacle for squirrels. There are still good populations in the river swamps where hardwoods are left. But the pine plantings continue to cut down squirrel concentrations. However, the forested GMAs and the other National Forest lands offer very good squirrel hunting, and presumably will save these small-game species. The Francis Marion Forest and GMAs within turn up good kills of squirrels. So do Hunt Units 1 and 2 upstate, and also the northwestern counties, where the Horse Pasture GMA is located. All of these Areas are described under foregoing species. The federal waterfowl Refuges offer some squirrel hunting. See "Waterfowl."

OTHER ANIMALS

Opossums are plentiful except in pine plantings, but are not hunted to any great extent. Raccoons appear to be increasing, get some hunting with hounds. The GMAs in the piedmont offer the best opportunities. Foxes are fairly abundant throughout the state, are not protected. GMAs with openings, as for quail, offer fair fox hunting, but regulations on use of dogs and fire-arms must be checked.

WILD HOGS

The Francis Marion National Forest and the GMAs based on it have a population of wild hogs. These are legal game during the big-game hunts and are so noted in the regulations. This region apparently has the largest huntable population of hogs on public lands. During one recent season ninety-nine were collected by hunters after other game.

REGULATIONS

Game laws pertaining to seasons, bag and possession limits, areas to be hunted, special hunts, license fees all may have numerous changes from year to year. For current regulations, and for other specific queries, write to: South Carolina Wildlife Resources Commission, P.O. Box 167, Columbia, South Carolina 29202.

GEORGIA

Almost everyone thinks of Georgia as strictly "Deep South," with cotton, peanut, and tobacco farms, never-ending warm sunshine, and lazy ways. But Georgia is much more. The terrain is highly varied. The Appalachian Mountains thrust down into the northern part of the state along almost all of that border, which is with Tennessee and North Carolina. Rough foothill country eases southward along the South Carolina border to the east, and lowers into coastal plain until tidewater is reached on Georgia's own long and intricately indented coastline on the Atlantic.

Airline distance along the Georgia coast is about 100 miles, but river mouths, small bays, and tidal meanderings turn it into at least 1000 miles of salt and brackish frontage. There are indeed seemingly endless expanses of rich farmlands over much of central and southern Georgia. And there are pine forests also, covering large areas of the east, and along the southern border with Florida, and on the west throughout much of Georgia's border with Alabama. Mountains in the north reach up almost to 5000 feet, but far down in the southeast is famed Okefenokee Swamp, one of the largest swamplands in the U.S., covering 660 square miles, most of which are in Georgia.

The state economy is a mixture of industry, intensive agriculture, and lumbering. Marble in the north, textile factories, pulpwood and turpentine, peanuts, tobacco, cotton, clay and limestone mining, furniture making, cattle farming, pecan production—the list of activities in the state accent its variety of terrain and resources. While a great deal of Georgia is in farmlands, there is also a substantial amount of near-wilderness, in National Forests, Okefenokee Swamp, and in the vast pine forests under lumber company ownership. In fact, tree farming is today one of the most thriving of industries, and it has influences both good and bad upon game, destroying what once was good quail habitat but enhancing areas for forest game.

The highway system in Georgia is excellent, allowing hunters swift travel to virtually all areas of the state on numerous U.S. Highways and a host of paved state roads. In addition, I 75 runs from north to south clear from the Tennessee border at Chattanooga to the Florida border just south of Valdosta. The only parts of the state difficult of access are a few small mountain areas of the north, some of the coastal lands and the famed Sea Islands off the coast, and the depths of Okefenokee Swamp. Air transport is good to all main cities, with Atlanta one of the largest air-transport centers in the nation.

Few hunters realize that Georgia is the largest of all the states east of the Mississippi. It encompasses 58,876 square miles. At its widest point just south of Savannah, Georgia is roughly 230 miles across. From north to south it is about 300. Considering its size, Georgia's population is not excessive. It is at present about four and a half million. At least one million of this number are urban, residing in the larger cities such as Atlanta, Savannah, Columbus, and another million reside in cities of smaller size.

Thus there is still plenty of "countryside" left in this state. Nor are hunter numbers excessive. License sales currently average around 325,000. Oddly, only a small percentage—around 5000 or so annually—are nonresident. Most of these are quail hunters who have come to shoot on large private lands. As most outdoorsmen know, Georgia has long been known as the Quail Capital.

Unfortunately, except for private lands of well-to-do owners,—lands kept chiefly for quail hunting—the bobwhite is having many difficulties. There still is good shooting, however, but preponderantly on the privately owned lands. Other game birds available are ruffed grouse in the mountains, doves, woodcock, wild turkey, and waterfowl, including rails and snipe. There is good deer hunting, some hunting for black bear. There are abundant squirrels and rabbits, raccoons, opossums, and foxes.

By far the major share of hunting in Georgia is on deeded lands. This is by permission, which is becoming more and more difficult to obtain, or by lease. A great many local and a few out-of-state sportsmen form groups and lease quail hunting or deer hunting or coastal waterfowl shooting lands. Lease and fee hunting in Georgia is growing. There are vast private lands owned by timber companies, and on much of this acreage hunting is available to the general public. But in most cases it is necessary to obtain a permit—ordinarily free—and to notify the company of number in party, their addresses, how long the hunt will be, and exactly where.

This is not to say that Georgia is without public hunting lands. There are two National Forests. The Chattahoochee NF (1) contains almost 681,000 acres. It is in northern Georgia, north of Atlanta. Nearby key cities and towns: Clayton at junction of U.S. 23 and 76; Blue Ridge on U.S. 76 west of Clayton and about midway across the state just below the northern border; Dalton, south of Chattanooga on U.S. 41. The Oconee NF (2) contains 96,066 acres. It is in two blocks east and south of Atlanta, and north of Macon. U.S. 278 and 129 are main access routes, with vicinity towns Greensboro and Madison on U.S. 278 and Eatonton to the south on 129. Both the Forests may be hunted during open season on any game, with the exceptions that certain areas within them designated as State Game Management Areas are subject to special regulations. Maps and details on both Forests may be obtained from the Forest Supervisor, Gainesville, Georgia 30501.

Three federal refuges offer some hunting for several game species such as deer, turkey, waterfowl. Blackbeard Island Refuge (3) is located north of Darien on U.S. 17 along the coast. Savannah Refuge (4) is on the Georgia-South Carolina border just north of the city of Savannah. Maps and details of hunts on these Refuges can be obtained from the Refuge Manager, Route 1, Hardeeville, South Carolina 29927. The Piedmont Refuge (5) is in central Georgia, covers some 32,700 acres north of Macon, which is at the junction of U.S. 80 and 41. It lies in the area between U.S. 23 and 129. The Refuge Manager can be addressed at Round Oak, Georgia 31080.

One other federal tract offering hunting is the Fort Stewart Military Reservation (6). It is located west of Savannah. Nearby towns are Hinesville on U.S. 82, Glennville and Claxton both on U.S. 25 and 301. Hunting regulations for Fort Stewart may be obtained from the Provost Marshal, Fort Stewart, Georgia 31314.

There are also at this writing twenty-two State Game Management Areas. Most of these are leased lands, or lands within the National Forest boundaries. Georgia is planning outright purchase of more lands. Presently, however, very little of the GMA lands are owned by the Game Commission. In addition to attempts to purchase more land, the Commission is attempting to lease more and more tracts suitable for public hunting areas.

Currently there are about 500,000 acres under lease. It is hoped that within five years this may be brought to two million or more. There are at least four million acres of private timberlands that, Georgia authorities feel, might be brought under game management programs by agreement with the state. Thus, though the present amount of public hunting lands managed by the state is not as great as it probably should be, the future looks reasonably bright. A brochure listing and describing all GMAs in Georgia and giving hunting seasons for the current year on each may be obtained from the Commission, address at end of chapter. Individual maps of the GMAs are also available, and so is a map of the state showing locations of all.

For hunters who may wish to camp out during their trips, there are facilities in the two National Forests described above. There are also numerous camping possibilities on the GMAs. Opportunities differ, and so do regulations as to "where" on any individual GMA. Suggested campsites are shown on individual GMA maps, noted above as available from the Commission. There are also thirty-seven State Parks in Georgia with excellent camping facilities. A booklet, "Georgia State Parks," is available from the Department of State Parks, 7 Hunter Street, S.W., Atlanta, Georgia 30334. Corps of Engineers campgrounds are numerous on most of the large reservoirs in Georgia. Because the state is crisscrossed by so many U.S. highways and is on a direct route to Florida from much of the north, motel and other accommodations are numerous, and well distributed everywhere.

In general a hunter may expect to find Georgia weather warm, or even hot, in the south during early seasons, such as for doves. But even in south Georgia it can also be bitterly chill during inclement times later in season. And the northern mountains may be cold. Therefore visiting hunters should be prepared for at least modestly chill weather, but also for a variety. Coastal weather is at times chilly because it is damp.

No great range of arms and ammunition are required here. Bird hunters will need No. 7½ or No. 8 shot for quail, doves, rails, grouse. Waterfowlers should have heavier loads, averaging around No. 4 for ducks. Rifles for deer can be of nominal caliber, but hunters should carefully check regulations specifying in certain cases which calibers may or may not be used.

QUAIL

For many years Georgia has billed itself as the Quail Capital of the World. This refers of course to the bobwhite quail, the only species present. To some extent the title may still be apt, especially on large private holdings where cover is managed for the birds. The overall quail picture in Georgia, however, especially when viewed long-range, is disturbing.

Generally speaking, southern Georgia, south of an arbitrary line drawn east-west from Savannah to Columbus, offers the prime hunting. And in this region the best of it is found in the southwest quadrant, in the Albany and Thomasville area. The coastal plains also offer good shooting, and this reaches to some extent into the piedmont area of central Georgia. Northward the bobwhite population gradually thins. Farmlands in the northwest offer spotty shooting. But the Blue Ridge Mountain area cannot be considered good quail country.

Basically the present quail problem in Georgia is one of swiftly changing habitat. Only a few seasons ago over four million quail were bagged by about

GEORGIA

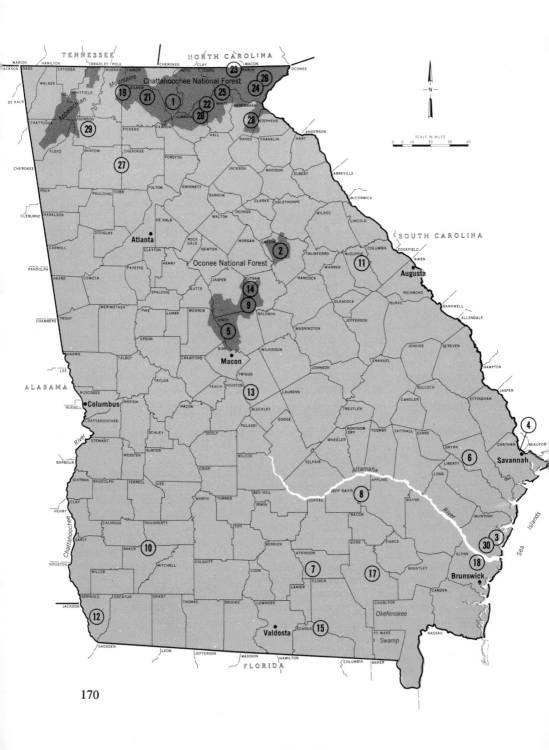

KEY TO HUNTING AREAS

1. Chattahoochee NF
2. Oconee NF
3. Blackbeard Island
   Refuge
4. Savannah Refuge
5. Piedmont Refuge
6. Fort Stewart Military
   Reservation
7. Arabia Bay GMA
8. Bullard Creek GMA
9. Cedar Creek GMA
10. Chickasawhatchee
    GMA

11. Clark Hill GMA
12. Lake Seminole GMA
13. Okay Woods GMA
14. Piedmont Experiment
    Station GMA
15. Suwanoochee GMA
16. Whitesburg GMA
17. Waycross State Forest
    GMA
18. Brunswick Pulp and
    Paper GMA
19. Cohutta GMA
20. Blue Ridge GMA

21. Chattahoochee GMA
22. Chestatee GMA
23. Coleman River GMA
24. Lake Burton GMA
25. Swallow Creek GMA
26. Warwoman GMA
27. Allatoona GMA
28. Lake Russel GMA
29. John's Mountain GMA
30. Altamaha GMA

135,000 hunters. That figure has since dropped rather drastically. Although the total bag still runs as high as 2,800,000, the number of hunters has remained roughly constant. The quail decline is in direct proportion to the growth in timber acreage and cattle lands. Today two-thirds of Georgia's thirty-seven million acres is in timber. For over two decades, an average of 200,000 acres of pine plantings per year has been made in the state. As soon as the seedlings grow to substantial size, quality quail habitat is destroyed. Meanwhile, pasturing of dairy and beef cattle has taken up more quail habitat. Small family farms have dropped tremendously. On these, crops were once raised. Grasslands for cattle grazing are no better than forest lands for quail.

Although the Game Commission tries to solve the quail problem, it is difficult. Leased small-farm lands are not suitable for public hunting. They cannot service many hunters. Also, owners dislike leasing. Only the large timberland tracts appear for the most part available. Some of the more open timberlands do offer fair quail shooting. But hunters should be aware that the quality of once readily available public quail hunting in Georgia probably can never be regained.

Hunters who will diligently seek permission on small farmlands in any of the coastal and southern counties will be well rewarded, if they are successful in gaining entry. As noted in the front of this chapter, groups can also lease good quail shooting. At present the going rate runs around 50 cents per acre. This means a section of land (640 acres) would cost $320 annually. For a group, if the cover is good, this is feasible.

There is a modest amount of quail hunting available in the two National Forests described earlier in the chapter, the Chattahoochee and the Oconee. Of the two, the Oconee, which is farther south, is somewhat better. Neither can be considered top-notch. However, these forests cover varied terrain and a careful search will turn up pockets of fair bobwhite abundance. Hunting is allowed during normal open seasons, except on the GMAs within Forest boundaries. These are clearly marked by yellow posted signs and by yellow paint blazes on trees.

Best opportunities for public quail hunting are on some of the state GMAs. These will be covered here in alphabetical order as a matter of convenience to the reader.

The Arabia Bay GMA (7) offers fair quail hunting. It is a tract of 45,000 acres in the south, about midway across the state. It can be reached north out of Homerville or south out of Pearson, both of which are on U.S. 441. The tract lies west of this highway. This is flat pine and palmetto country cut by swamp creeks.

Another with fair quail hunting is Bullard Creek GMA (8). This is an

18,000-acre tract lying in Appling and Jeff Davis Cos., on the south bank of the Altamaha River, a region of river swamps plus upland hardwoods and pines. Access is via U.S. 221 out of Hazlehurst or Mt. Vernon. The Area is east of the highway.

Far to the north, in central Georgia, is another GMA that can be labeled as fair for quail. This is Cedar Creek GMA (9), encompassing 40,000 acres of private and National Forest lands. It lies north of Macon and west of U.S. 129. Access is via Monticello on State 16 and 212.

Down in the southwest is the Chickasawhatchee GMA (10). This cannot be considered a good quail area, but it has a small amount of quail habitat scattered throughout its 26,000 acres of timberlands southwest of the city of Albany. It can be reached from that city via State Routes 91 and 62.

Somewhat better is Clark Hill GMA (11), up toward the nothwest near the border with South Carolina. This is Corps of Engineers land along the large Clark Hill Reservoir. It covers 10,000 acres, is reached north out of Thomson via U.S. 78.

One of the best public quail tracts is the Lake Seminole GMA (12) down in the extreme southwest in Seminole Co. Although this is primarily a waterfowl Area, there is quality quail cover in portions of it and high quail populations as a rule. There are 3700 acres here, some of it in islands, some along the shore of the Jim Woodruff Reservoir. This is Corps of Engineers land. State 253 out of Bainbridge, which is at the junction of U.S. 27 and 84 gives access.

Another area that currently offers good quail hunting, and will continue to until forest growth becomes tall, is Okay Woods GMA (13). There are 37,000 acres in this one. It lies southeast of Macon, in central Georgia, and to the west of U.S. 23 and 129. Several secondaries lead to it.

North of Macon, and in fact just to the north of the Cedar Creek GMA described above, is the Piedmont Experiment Station GMA (14). There are 15,000 acres here, in Putnam Co. Some of it is open land with fair to good quail populations. State 16 west from Eatonton, which is on U.S. 441 and 129, leads to the Area.

There is also fair quail hunting on 60,000-acre Suwanoochee GMA (15), Georgia's largest. This is in the extreme south, almost directly south of the Arabia GMA described above, and east of the city of Valdosta, which is on I 75. U.S. 84 east from Valdosta, and then U.S. 129 to the south, take one to the Area. It is a vast tract of low-lying timberlands.

Spotty quail hunting in the just-fair class can be found on the Whitesburg GMA (16), of 26,000 acres, southwest of Atlanta. This GMA is in a number of scattered blocks. Alternate U.S. 27 north from the town of Newnan to Whitesburg, or south from Carrollton gives access.

Down in the extreme southeast, out of Waycross, is one of the best GMAs in the state for quail. This is the Waycross State Forest GMA (17), with 37,500 acres of coastal plain covered by pine and palmetto. U.S. 1 south from the city of Waycross reaches the boundary.

As noted earlier the Commission is seeking to add swiftly to its lease holdings. For example, a new GMA of 40,500 acres was recently established near the coastal city of Brunswick, in the southeast. Called the Brunswick Pulp and Paper GMA (18), it is in several separate tracts. Some sections have been cleared and replanted, and now offer good quail hunting. They will continue to until the tree growth destroys quail habitat. Hunters should contact the Commission periodically to apprise themselves of the location and quality of new GMAs that are certain to be set up year by year.

RUFFED GROUSE

The northern mountainous section of Georgia has some surprisingly good ruffed grouse hunting. The terrain is exceedingly steep and rough, hunters have to be in good physical shape, and it is by far best to use a dog. Only a small percentage of Georgia hunters pursue the sport, probably about 5000 each season. The kill of grouse in a good up-cycle year averages around 2500.

All of the good grouse counties are in the north, along and slightly below the border with Tennessee and North Carolina, where the mountains thrust southward. Murray Co. on the Tennessee border, Fannin half on Tennessee and half on North Carolina, Union, Towns, Rabun bordering North Carolina are the top counties. There is, however, good grouse shooting to the south of these counties, in portions of Gilmer, Pickens, Lumpkin, White, Habersham, and Stephens Cos.

Fortunately, virtually all of the land in the ruffed grouse domain is held by the Forest Service, thus providing excellent public hunting for this fine game bird. Much of the Chattahoochee National Forest offers grouse hunting and is open during the regular season. This Forest has been described in the chapter opening. GMAs within the NF boundaries are excellent bets for grouse, but seasons for managed hunts may differ, so hunters must check the Commission rulings.

One of the best of the GMAs is huge Cohutta (19), with 90,000 acres of Forest land in Fannin, Murray, and Gilmer Cos. This old GMA was abandoned a few years ago because of an extremely serious local poaching problem and indiscriminate use of dogs for taking deer. This is one of the largest wilderness regions still remaining in Georgia. It is presently reactivated. Much of this region requires 4-wheel-drive transport. The country is exceedingly rugged. It is also important to get county maps from the State Highway Dept. (25¢ each, address 2 Capitol Square, Atlanta 30334) or else a map of the Chattahoochee NF. The towns of Blue Ridge on U.S. 76 in Fannin Co. and Chatsworth at 76-441 junction in Murray Co. are good reference points.

The Blue Ridge GMA (20) is another top grouse spot. This also is National Forest land, with 40,000 acres in Lumpkin, Fannin, Dawson, and Union Cos. The town of Dahlonega on U.S. 19, Lumpkin Co., is a good reference point. Again, on all the large NF grouse areas, maps are most useful and 4-wheel-drive all but mandatory to get to the truly remote areas.

The Chattahoochee GMA (21), 20,000 acres of NF land on the head-waters of the Chattahoochee River, is also excellent grouse terrain. General access is out of Robertstown via State 17.

In the same general region is Chestatee GMA (22), another fine grouse possibility. It covers 25,000 acres north of the town of Dahlonega in White, Union, and Lumpkin Cos.

Coleman River GMA (23) is on the North Carolina border, west of Clayton which is on U.S. 76. This 13,000-acre tract is in one of the most rugged parts of the state. It is in Rabun Co. It is primitive, steep, and demands 4-wheel drive for its rough trails.

Lake Burton GMA (24) also has excellent grouse hunting, is near Clayton in Rabun Co. and contains 15,000 acres of NF lands. Also in the same area is the Swallow Creek GMA (25), with 9000 NF acres. Access is off U.S. 76 in the vicinity of the Appalachian Trail. The Warwoman GMA (26) comprises 14,000 acres of National Forest east of Clayton in Rabun Co.

Hunters should check to make certain that the GMA selected has a grouse season during any given year. Permits are also required on most GMAs and there are special regulations with which all who hunt these public areas must be familiar. Check stations at the locations, or ask the Commission.

MOURNING DOVES

The mourning dove is the most popular of Georgia's game birds. The kill on the average is greater than for quail. Since doves are exceedingly mobile, and drift from feeding ground to feeding ground and from north to south in fall as weather urges them, it is not possible to pinpoint any exact spots as best. However, it may be said that southern Georgia offers by far the best dove hunting. The state strongly desires—and to date has been unable to get from the federal authorities—a zoning plan so that northern Georgia and southern Georgia would have hunting at staggered times. Currently there is a split season, the first statewide during September and early October, the second also statewide in December and January.

Some seasons the kill runs around three and a half million birds. It averages around three million. In a normal season, the dove concentration in the northern half of the state occurs during the middle two weeks of September. This is the time when crops such as millet, corn, and other feed grains are ready to cut. Ordinarily, most of the birds move south by late September and shooting in the north is spotty to nil.

In southern Georgia, dove hunting is excellent during most of both seasons. About half the total of dove shooters are in the south, but in an average season they take upwards of 70 percent of the early-season birds and as high as 80 percent of the late-season birds. Statewide, approximate averages show about 60 percent of the total kill during the early season, 40 percent during the late season.

By far the major share of dove hunting is on privately owned lands. However, since this is a convivial and group sport in Georgia, it is not especially difficult to strike up a quick acquaintance with local residents in any of the good dove territory and arrange a hunt. There is also some fair to good dove hunting on a few of the GMAs.

North of Atlanta and Marietta and east of U.S. 41 are the scattered blocks of the 28,000-acre Allatoona GMA (27). There is some dove shooting here, particularly during the early season. The Clark Hill GMA (28) offers dove hunting, and so does Lake Seminole GMA (29) in the southwest. Okay Woods and Piedmont Experiment Station GMAs are both fair dove tracts. The same may be said of Whitesburg, Waycross State Forest, and Cedar Creek. All of these have been covered under "Quail."

WOODCOCK

Although woodcock do migrate to some extent down across Georgia, this is not an important game bird here. There are few hunters interested. Estimates show fewer than 4000 annually purposely hunting woodcock. Most of the kill is incidental, by quail and grouse hunters. The kill runs an estimated 7000 birds each season. The northeast, the piedmont, the coastal plain offer most of the hunting, with stream courses, spring-branch heads, and lightly wooded coves good spots to find birds. Most of the GMAs have scattered woodcock in modest numbers when the migration is on. November is a good average month for finding birds. The northern GMAs such as Blue Ridge and Chattahoochee ("Grouse") are good bets. Allatoona ("Doves") also has woodcock. So do

Whitesburg, Clark Hill, Seminole ("Quail"). Interested hunters should check out any of the GMAs where they happen to be hunting other species. Light ground cover with dappled shade above and moist earth full of earthworms are the components of good woodcock resting and feeding grounds.

RAILS AND SNIPE

Rails of the king and clapper varieties, locally called "marsh hens" in Georgia, are important to a small but avid group of coastal hunters. Shooting, when tides are right, is excellent. Annual kill is small, probably around 8000 birds, and it is estimated that no more than 2500 to 3000 hunters pursue the sport. To assure good hunting, there must be extremely high tides, which push the rails out of the marshes and concentrate them. A guide who knows the marshes and how to pole a boat for rail shooting is a must. There is plenty of opportunity for rail hunting along the coastal marshes and especially around the coastal islands. Guides are available. The Commission can be helpful in locating guide services for prospective hunters, but cannot be expected to recommend guides. Chambers of Commerce in coastal towns are also good contacts. See "Waterfowl" later in chapter.

Snipe are found in varying numbers during migration season on most of the waterfowl areas, which see. But they are so seldom purposely hunted, and so scattered, that they are not important lowland birds.

WILD TURKEYS

The annual wild turkey kill in Georgia is substantial. It averages around 3000 birds. There are fall seasons in certain counties for birds of either sex, and spring seasons in several portions of the state for gobblers only. Open counties and/or GMAs may change from season to season, so the current laws should be checked. Generally speaking, however, there are five regions of the state that have open seasons and the preponderance of the birds. These five regions are located around the perimeter of the state.

The far north usually has from eighteen to twenty counties open, but for spring hunting only. The same applies to a section of the piedmont along the South Carolina border. As this is written five counties in this sector are open: Wilkes, Lincoln, Columbia, McDuffie, Warren. These are surrounding and west of the city of Augusta. The counties with spring season only have fewer turkeys than the other areas, which have either fall-only or both spring and fall seasons. Roughly three north-south tiers of counties along the coastal plain are currently open both seasons. The extreme southwest has ten counties open with a two-bird limit, fall only. On the western border, not quite midway up from the south, are several counties open for both seasons. At this writing these are Stewart, Chattahoochee, Muscogee, Marion, Talbot. Again, open counties may change from year to year. But the five general regions noted are presently the good turkey range.

Two of these regions are the best turkey range in the state. One is the group of eastern piedmont counties. The Clark Hill GMA ("Quail") in this region is considered one of the best public-land turkey locations. A sizable amount of paper company land in this piedmont region may be hunted by permission. The other prime region is the extreme southwest, but this is private land and permission must be arranged.

In addition to the Clark Hill GMA, several of the northern GMAs in the mountain region offer managed hunts. During one recent season there were spring gobbler hunts on Chattahoochee, Chestatee, Blue Ridge, Warwoman, all of which are covered under "Grouse." Two other northern GMAs not so far mentioned were included, and are considered excellent turkey tracts. The Lake Russel GMA (28) is one. It contains 17,000 acres of National Forest and private lands near Toccoa, a town in the extreme northeast on U.S. 123 in Stephens Co. The other is John's Mountain GMA (29), a 20,000-acre area containing both National Forest and leased private lands in the northwest. It is northwest of the town of Calhoun, which is located on U.S. 41 (I 75). State 143 northwest out of Calhoun crosses the area.

At this writing several other GMAs have building turkey flocks and will undoubtedly be open to hunting soon. Among these are: Bullard Creek, Chickasawhatchee ("Quail"), Lake Burton ("Grouse"), Piedmont Experiment Station ("Quail"). Others of the northern GMAs noted under "Grouse" probably will eventually present huntable turkey flocks.

Hunters should note also that National Forest lands outside the GMAs and in counties open to turkey hunting provide public opportunity. In addition there are turkey hunts held on the Piedmont Refuge and the Blackbeard Refuge described in chapter opening. Fort Stewart may also have a season. Check with the Provost Marshal, address early in chapter.

WATERFOWL

Georgia is not one of the top waterfowl states. It does offer good duck hunting in several locations, but very little goose hunting. The coastal lowlands and marshes are of course the most important waterfowl locations. There is some shooting along the large coastal rivers and the ponds and swamps along their courses. Of the rivers, the Altamaha is considered best. There is also shooting to be found around the large impoundments, such as Clark Hill, north of Augusta, Sinclair near Milledgeville, and in the extreme southwest around the Jim Woodruff Reservoir. As in most states with coastal marshes, much of the best waterfowling area is under private control. A good measure of duck hunting activity in Georgia is gained by noting that only about 22,000 hunters on the average annually pursue the sport.

There is hunting at the Savannah Refuge, noted in chapter opening. This Refuge is partly in South Carolina. In the vicinity of Blackbeard and Piedmont refuges, also described earlier in chapter, there is more of the same. Around the perimeter of Okefenokee Swamp in the southeast some opportunities are available, and for the hunter well equipped with a sturdy boat, shooting may be had around the offshore coastal islands.

Public waterfowl hunting is undoubtedly best at the coastal Altamaha GMAs (30), a track managed primarily for waterfowl, and in fact usually called the Altamaha Waterfowl Public Hunting Area. It contains 18,000 acres located on the Altamaha delta near Darien, Georgia. This town is on U.S. 17 north of the city of Brunswick. The Area is owned by the state.

Ducks are plentiful, and so are rails and snipe. Some geese use the area but there may or may not be an open season in any given year. This is a permit area and permit must be applied for by mail. Interested hunters should check with the Commission for details and application dates. There is a $5 per person per day charge, covering blind, boat, and decoys. This is for hunting on Butler Island. Presently there are twenty-five blinds. It is interesting to note that there is seldom any crowding. To date of this writing blinds have never been completely filled. There are a number of other island locations on the Area—

Dedundy, Rhetts, Rock, Broughton, Camber and others—not managed. Hunters furnish their own equipment.

The Lake Seminole GMA described under "Quail" is predominantly a waterfowling ground and is generally known as the Lake Seminole Waterfowl Public Hunting Area. Excellent duck shooting can be had here.

EXOTIC BIRDS

A number of experimental stockings of the ringneck-Talisch pheasant have been made and a study is continuing to ascertain if the bird can establish itself. There is to date no hunting.

Showing more hope for the future are stockings of red junglefowl. This bird appears suited to climate and habitat in middle and south Georgia. Birds have been released periodically since 1963. Late releases have been at Lake Seminole and Clark Hill. Biologists are encouraged and it appears that the junglefowl may be able to establish itself eventually to huntable proportions.

More recently, two species of tinamou have been tried. It is impossible to guess at the moment what the result may be.

DEER

There is excellent deer hunting available in Georgia, although deer herds over the years have had many difficulties in the state, especially from poachers and dogs. An average of about 120,000 hunters go deer hunting annually, and the success ratio is roughly 25 percent in the better years—a kill of about 30,000. This includes the bag of both buck and any-deer hunts.

Georgia's deer herd is slowly growing. The largest herd presently is in the central section. Best counties in this region: Putnam, Morgan, Jones, Jasper, Greene, Monroe, McDuffie. To the west, the counties near Columbus —Stewart, Chattahoochee, Muscogee, Marion—have a good herd. In the northeast, based on Augusta as a key city, and the Clark Hill Reservoir, there are abundant deer. Along the Savannah River, the counties of Jenkins, Bulloch, Screven, all north of the city of Savannah, are considered good. The National Forest lands in northern Georgia are excellent. Counties with good deer populations: Rabun, Towns, Union, Lumpkin, White. The northwest sector of the state is rated only fair. Coastal counties rate fair to good.

On the whole the outlook for Georgia deer hunting in coming years is ever brighter. Land use changes (see "Quail") form more and more good deer habitat. It is estimated that within a decade deer will blanket the state and possibly all counties will be open to hunting. The coastal plains have long been hunted by organized drives and with dogs. The piedmont and the northern mountains are strongholds of the still-hunter. Still-hunting is growing in favor throughout Georgia, and this may well assist better herd management by eliminating poacher and dog problems.

There is ample public deer hunting. The National Forests (see front material in chapter) have good herds. And many of the GMAs are diligently managed for deer. While hunter success to date does not average, on the GMAs, as high as the state average, this is probably because of more restrictive regulations on the individual public tracts. Nonetheless, a recent survey showed good scores on a number of the GMAs: Lake Russel ("Turkeys") 23 percent success; Allatoona ("Doves") 16.8 percent; Clark Hill ("Quail") 16.5 percent. A number of others ran from 10 to 13 percent.

Practically all of the GMAs offer deer hunting. There are primitive weapons hunts on a few, special archery hunts on others, bucks-only, either-sex and antlerless-only hunts on some, as herd buildups appear to dictate. A few GMAs not presently open to deer hunting are slowly coming to a point in herd development so that they will be. Most of the GMAs noted under "Quail," "Grouse," "Turkey" have deer hunts. Because regulations may change a great deal from season to season, it is best for prospective deer hunters to write to the Commission for a schedule of managed hunts on the various GMAs. In addition to these public lands, there are periodic hunts on Blackbeard and Piedmont refuges. The Fort Stewart Reservation is also considered a good area. See front material in chapter for locations of all three.

Hunters should also check paper company lands. Many of these are open by permission or permit. The Commission can assist in directing hunters to such lands. Two Georgia counties in particular are currently considered by experienced Georgia deer hunters to be the best in the state. These are Jasper and Jones Cos. Both have ample public lands.

BEAR

Georgia has a total black bear population estimated at about 400. Annual kill estimates (legal kills) range from 25 to 150. Probably the low figure is more nearly correct. Virtually all bear hunting is with dogs. At this writing only five counties, all in the Okefenokee region, allow an open season: Brantley, Charlton, Clinch, Echols, Ware. It is possible to set up a guided bear hunt. In fact, for a visitor this is practically mandatory. Guides are available in Valdosta for Okefenokee camp-out hunts. Check with the Commission for information, or with the Valdosta Chamber of Commerce.

WILD HOGS

Feral hogs, though in many instances completely wild, are not considered game animals in Georgia and actually belong to the landowner. It is therefore illegal to shoot them without permission. Questions may arise, however, on GMAs where wild hogs appear. One such is Lake Seminole ("Quail"), which is Corps of Engineers land managed by the Commission as a GMA. Check with the local warden or with the Commission as to status of wild hogs on public hunting lands in any given season.

SQUIRRELS

Excellent squirrel hunting is available. This is the most hunted small-game animal, and the kill is estimated to run well up toward two million. The species is predominantly the gray squirrel. Happily, public lands offer some of the best squirrel hunting. The two National Forests are excellent. (See early material in chapter.) So are most of the GMAs: Arabia Bay; Blue Ridge; Bullard Creek; Cedar Creek; Chattahoochee; Chestatee; Chickasawhatchee; Clark Hill; Coleman River; Lake Burton; Lake Seminole; Okay Woods; Piedmont Experiment Station; Suwanoochee; Swallow Creek; Whitesburg; Waycross State Forest. All have been described under foregoing species. Note that these are scattered from the high northern mountains to the low country of the south. In other words, fine squirrel hunting can be found almost anywhere in the state.

RABBITS

Rabbits are abundant. Cottontails range through most of the state. Larger swamp rabbits are found in the northwest, and a close kin, the marsh rabbit, inhabits swamps and marshes of the south. The rabbit bag annually vies with that of squirrels. The state is split into north and south zones, with bag limits differing. Thus hunters should carefully check regulations. There is no difficulty in finding places to hunt rabbits. Many landowners will allow rabbit hunting, and practically all of the National Forest and GMA lands offer fair to excellent hunting. Even the Altamaha Waterfowl Area (see "Waterfowl") has quality rabbit hunting; the animals are pushed into concentrations on the dikes after flooding of the duck ponds.

OTHER ANIMALS

Raccoons and opossums are plentiful and so are foxes. The fox is unprotected, but there are regulations pertaining to running them with dogs. Be sure to check. Raccoons are a popular game animal. Upwards of 200,000 are bagged each season. Ordinarily north Georgia has a stipulated season on raccoons but in the southern half they are unprotected. Most of the public lands offer raccoon hunting. Some of the GMAs have special raccoon seasons. Recently both Lake Russel ("Turkey") and Chestatee ("Grouse") had such seasons. During these only tree dogs are allowed, .22 rimfire rifles are the only weapons allowed, and there is a charge of $1 per night. There are regulations about the use of dogs for all the above animals. Check with the Commission before hunting, and read the law digest thoroughly.

REGULATIONS

Game laws pertaining to seasons, bag and possession limits, areas to be hunted, special hunts, license fees all may have numerous changes from year to year. For current regulations, and for other specific queries, write to: State Game and Fish Commission, 401 State Capitol, Atlanta, Georgia 30334.

Appalachian
States

PENNSYLVANIA

It is rather symbolic of Pennsylvania's place in the hunter's world that this state, with a first settlement in 1643, second of the original thirteen to ratify the Constitution, and in a recent census ranked third in the nation in population, should have as its official state bird that wilderness gamester the ruffed grouse. In many ways Pennsylvania is a delightful impossibility. Heavily settled, bordered by at least three states with comparable human population per square mile—Ohio on the west, New York on the north, New Jersey on the east—Pennsylvania still contains areas in the northern mountains that are for all practical purposes authentic wilderness.

Pennsylvania's terrain and its cultures and outlooks are diverse. It is a kind of transition between the quiet, hill-folks country of West Virginia below its southwestern corner, and the bustle of a strip of busy Maryland bordering the remainder of its southern portion. It is transition, too, in that the Pennsylvania-Maryland border is the Mason-Dixon line.

Pennsylvania is partially rugged mountains. It sits astride the Appalachian and Allegheny ranges, with valleys in between. The mountains split the coastal plain portion eastward from the farms and the dense industry of the west. The mountains run down from the northeast to the south-central area. Streams are numerous. Placid pastoral scenes belie the dense woodland of numerous State Forests and the almost half-million-acre Allegheny National Forest on the northern border west of center.

The terrain is, indeed, so varied that good supplies of game of great variety —farm, woodlot, forest species—have been able to survive. And this, notwithstanding the fact that Pennsylvania means coal, steel, and tremendous and diverse manufacturing from a first in shoes to candy to machinery and chemical products. But set apart and interspersed with all this are the woodlots, the mountain forests, the steep wooded hills that seem to a walking hunter much higher than they are. Davis Mountain, in the southwest, is the highest point, at 3213 feet.

Access to everywhere is not difficult. Good roads, though seldom running in straight lines very long, grid the state in every section. Air transport, because of numerous large cities, is excellent. In most portions hunters have no difficulty getting ordinary vehicles to their hunting grounds. In a few of the wilderness or near-wilderness sections a short-couple four-wheel-drive vehicle is certainly not amiss. But such transport is not seen as commonly here as in the West.

Considering how long Pennsylvania has been settled, and its present population of over eleven and one-half million, it is an astonishingly good hunting state and is in many ways exemplary among the eastern states. It is roughly 280 miles wide east-west, by 160 miles north-south. The total area is 45,333 square miles. Fortunately for outdoorsmen, a heavy percentage of the population is concentrated in metropolitan areas like Pittsburgh (over two million), Philadelphia (roughly five million). However, small towns are scattered everywhere across the state.

Hunting here can be crowded, and many residents are used to it. There are plenty of open lands, but there are also over 900,000 hunting licenses sold annually. It is interesting to note, and a commentary on good hunting here, that some 50,000-plus nonresidents prowl Pennsylvania's game fields every season. It is also an excellent commentary on how well the Game Commission has handled its chores that more private lands are open to general hunting here than over a combination of numerous other eastern states. This helps tremendously to spread out the pressure.

Pennsylvania is a fantastic deer state. In a recent season over 144,000 whitetail deer were taken. Deer are the prime big game, but black bear are quite plentiful and much hunted, too. Pennsylvania is among the top turkey states. There are abundant ruffed grouse, a modest quail and pheasant population, good dove hunting, excellent woodcock shooting. Squirrels, both gray and fox squirrels, are popular, cottontails draw mass attention and there are some snowshoe hares. Excellent waterfowling is found in certain sectors. Raccoons are found in nuisance proportions, woodchucks are plentiful.

Public lands, and private lands open to hunting due to carefully nurtured Commission programs, are where Pennsylvania really shines. For one wishing to hunt here, a good picture of possibilities may be had by looking at figures on these lands. There is a total of almost seven million acres open to hunting. That amounts to nearly one quarter of the entire acreage of the state. These lands are made up of Game Lands managed by the state (over one million acres in 235 tracts scattered in almost every part); State Forest and State Park and a few federal lands, plus the nearly half-million-acre Allegheny National Forest (total over two million acres); farm lands signed up and brought into two different Commission programs (over three million acres). An official highway map of Pennsylvania, available from the Game Commission, indicates each of the Game Land tracts by number, and others except private farm program lands by color. A hunter once in his territory in Pennsylvania can easily spot the open farmlands, by black and white signs on them furnished by the Commission. One program is called the Farm Game Cooperative Program, and the other is the Safety Zone Program. Black and white safety-zone signs are posted on the edge of a 150-yard closed hunting area surrounding houses and farm buildings. Cooperators also receive special attention in law enforcement.

Because individual tracts of open hunting lands are so numerous here, not all can be covered in detail later in this chapter under each species. Instead, more attention will be given in some cases to pinpointing best hunting for each species by counties, with the number of acres of each type of open lands indicated for each county. It is therefore advantageous for readers to have a clear picture of how Pennsylvania is divided by the Commission for management and other purposes.

There are six clean-cut divisions of the state: northwest, north central, northeast, southwest, south central, southeast. Because the state is almost a rectangle and county lines run reasonably straight, each of these sections is roughly equal in size to the others.

The northwest contains ten counties. Reading as nearly as possible left to right in tiers beginning at the top, these are: Erie, Warren, Crawford, Venango, Forest, Mercer, Clarion, Jefferson, Lawrence, Butler. The northwest terrain is glacier-effected land in its northwest half, with big-woods ecology in the other half, the line running diagonally northeast to southwest. There are forty-eight Game Lands with over 139,000 acres in these ten counties. There are some 930,000 open farmlands under the programs, 37,000 acres of State Forest, Parks and Military lands, and about half of the huge Allegheny National Forest.

The north-central section also has ten counties: McKean, Potter, Tioga, Elk, Cameron, Clinton, Lycoming, Clearfield, Centre, Union. In general this is the Pennsylvania "big woods" country, with deer, bear, turkey in abundance, and over two million acres of public hunting lands. Some of this will pass for wilderness. There are thirty-eight Game Lands (approx. 270,000 acres), 250,000 acres of open farmlands, almost one and one-half million acres in various forests.

The northeast encompasses thirteen counties: Bradford, Susquehanna, Wayne, Sullivan, Wyoming, Lackawanna, Pike, Northumberland, Montour, Columbia, Luzerne, Carbon, Monroe. Terrain is diverse in the northeast—dairy and grazing areas, deep forest, agriculture. There are about 776,000 acres of open hunting lands. These are divided as follows: forty-five Game Land tracts (292,000 acres); 325,000 farm co-op acres; about 160,000 in varied forest and other lands. Game here is as varied as terrain, with deer, bear, woodcock, snowshoe hares among the most abundant.

The southwest section has ten counties: Armstrong, Indiana, Cambria, Beaver, Allegheny, Westmoreland, Somerset, Washington, Greene, Fayette. This is an area of rolling hills with two major ridges crossing it, and with the highest point in the state (Mount Davis, Somerset Co.). This is chiefly a small-game sector, but with some good deer hunting. There are about 700,000 acres of public hunting lands: 83,000 in some thirty-one Game Land tracts; almost 600,000 in farm co-op; a scattering of forests.

The south-central division is composed of eleven counties. These are: Blair, Huntington, Mifflin, Snyder, Juniata, Perry, Bedford, Fulton, Franklin, Cumberland, Adams. This is a curious combination of the state's most rugged ridge country, plus lowland valleys, and a mixture of game big and small. Very close to one million acres are open to hunting. The thirty-six Game Lands total roughly 126,000 acres, there are at least 475,000 open farm acres, over 360,000 in forests and others.

Even the very heavily populated southeast, based on the vast Philadelphia complex, has an amazing three-fourths million open hunting acres. Thirty-seven Game Land tracts add up over 100,000 acres, farm co-ops equal over 600,000, and there is a modest forest acreage. In general this is farm country, with species to match. The southeast takes in twelve counties: Schuylkill, Lehigh, Northampton, Dauphin, Lebanon, Berks, Montgomery, Bucks, York, Lancaster, Chester, Delaware. There is one other county here, Philadelphia Co., in the extreme southeast, but it is a non-hunting county, the only one in the state.

This, then, is the general picture a hunter needs of this state. It is easy to see from the above that the Game Commission is most active and has been extremely successful in its continuing programs. Details on open lands, as noted, are contained on a map available from the Commission, and pinpoint details regarding the Allegheny National Forest can be obtained from the Forest Supervisor, Warren, Pennsylvania.

Accommodations for hunters are legion. The entire state is well geared to crowds of visitors. However, in the popular deer counties it is well to have a reservation for opening of seasons. Hunters who wish to camp will find numerous accommodations. There are thirty-seven well-scattered State Parks, there are the National Forest campgrounds and some Corps of Engineers sites. Pennsylvania, like many eastern states, also has nowadays hosts of good

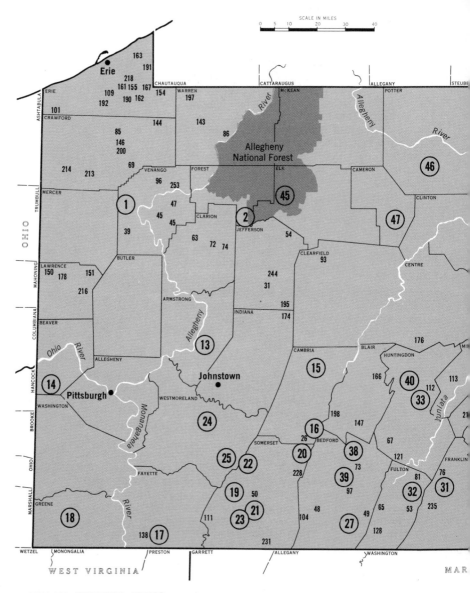

KEY TO HUNTING AREAS

1. Pymatuning SP
2. Kittanning SF
3. Tioga SF
4. Hickory Run SP
5. Lackawanna SF
6. Ricketts Glen SP
7. Delaware SF
8. Tobyhanna-Gouldsboro SP
9. Big Pocono SP
10. Delaware SF
11. Wyoming SF
12. Lackawanna SF
13. Crooked Creek SP
14. Raccoon Creek SP
15. Prince Gallitzen SP
16. Gallitzen SF
17. Braddock SF
18. Ryerson SP
19. Laurel Hill SP
20. Babcock SF
21. Blue Hole SF
22. Linn Run SF (Jennerstown)
23. Negro Mountain SF
24. Keystone SP
25. Linn Run SF (Rector)

186

PENNSYLVANIA

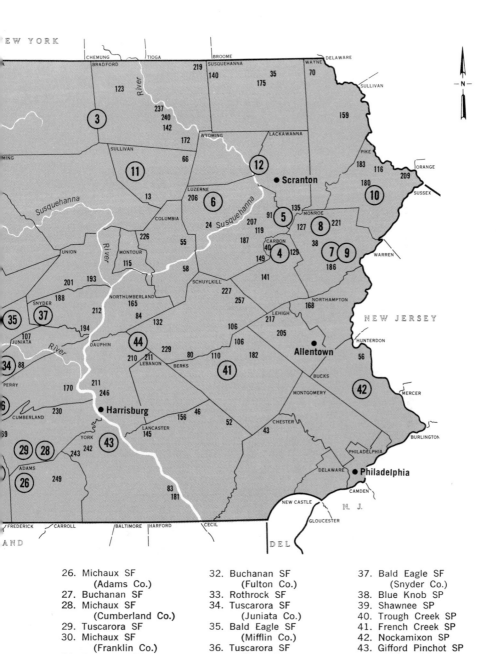

26. Michaux SF
    (Adams Co.)
27. Buchanan SF
28. Michaux SF
    (Cumberland Co.)
29. Tuscarora SF
30. Michaux SF
    (Franklin Co.)
31. Buchanan SF
    (Franklin Co.)

32. Buchanan SF
    (Fulton Co.)
33. Rothrock SF
34. Tuscarora SF
    (Juniata Co.)
35. Bald Eagle SF
    (Mifflin Co.)
36. Tuscarora SF
    (Perry Co.)

37. Bald Eagle SF
    (Snyder Co.)
38. Blue Knob SP
39. Shawnee SP
40. Trough Creek SP
41. French Creek SP
42. Nockamixon SP
43. Gifford Pinchot SP
44. Weiser SF
45. Allegheny NF

private campgrounds. The Department of Forests and Waters, Harrisburg, is a good source of State Park and campground information.

Early fall seasons in Pennsylvania will be warm and pleasant, but evenings especially in the mountains are crisp. Light woolens are called for, and as the season progresses cold-weather clothing is a must for the deer hunter and others. Snow may be expected, sometimes a lot of it.

No special arms are needed. Standard deer rifles such as the .30/06, .270, .308 are good examples of guns for both deer and black bear here. Shotgunners need mostly No. 6, 7½, and 8 for the varied uplanders, and the waterfowler should consider No. 4 for ducks, and for the modest amount of goose shooting available No. 4 in magnums or else No. 2. A scoped .22 for squirrels is an excellent addition.

RUFFED GROUSE

There is fine ruffed grouse hunting in numerous locations in Pennsylvania. Total annual kill crowds half a million. Referring to the foregoing notations on the six divisions of the state, here is how these large areas rate: northwest— excellent in Crawford and Venango Counties; north central—although this big-woods region would suggest abundant grouse, hunting is poor here, but there are some grouse in a few places, notably Clearfield and Centre Cos.; northeast—very good, except for the farming portions of Montour, North-umberland, and Columbia counties; southwest—excellent in all wooded hill and valley sections over all ten counties, with numerous minor operations in timber forming perfect habitat; south central—in all the mountain portions, which are numerous, hunting is good; southeast—some grouse but rated only fair or below.

In the northwest, Crawford Co. has several Game Lands noted for grouse. These are: the 4000-acre tract near the town of Guy Mills, No. 69; the tract No. 144, near Spartansburg, with 422 acres; No. 146 near New Richmond, 495 acres; a small area of 154 acres also near New Richmond, No. 200.

The other top-rated county as noted is Venango. Near Franklin is Game Land No. 39, with 8500 acres, and near Van there are 4836 acres in No. 45. Another good area is No. 96, near Dempseytown, with over 4000 acres, and there is a 655 acre tract near Plummer, No. 253.

Grouse hunters should not overlook the large No. 101 near Springboro in Erie Co., where grouse rate as top game. These are the best of the grouse coverts in this Division, but the official map will indicate a few others that offer fair results.

The northwest also has, in the two best grouse counties, the following additional acreage of public lands: Crawford Co.: 57,000-plus in the Farm Game Cooperative Program; 51,000 in the Farm Safety Zone Program; Pymatuning State Park (17), with hunting allowed on 18,575 acres; Venango Co.: approximately 168,000 acres in the two farm programs. Many of these lands are good spots for the grouse hunter.

While noting public lands here, which will be referred to later under other species, it should be stated that all other counties here have tremendous amounts of land brought into the farm programs. Other species of game in varying numbers are available on these lands. These lands can be checked easily by contacting the Commission. There are also several State Parks in the northwest besides Pymatuning, with modest acreages open to hunting. And, there is the Kittanning State Forest (2) in Forest and Jefferson Cos. with approximately 11,500 acres of hunting lands.

The north-central section, as mentioned, is not good grouse range, except for incidental chances in scattered spots.

In the northeast, of the forty-five Game Land tracts, at least thirty-five furnish grouse hunting. Because these are so numerous, they are listed here as compactly as possible, without acreages. However, several of these are very large, from 3000 to almost 40,000 acres. The number of each and the nearest town is given.

COUNTY	TRACT NO.	NEAREST TOWN
Bradford	123	Gillette
	142	New Albany
	172	Wyalusing
	219	Warren Center
	240	Monroeton
Carbon	40	Whitehaven
	129	Lake Harmony
	141	Jim Thorpe
Columbia	55	Orangeville
	58	Catawissa
Lackawanna	135	Gouldsboro
Luzerne	91	Bear Creek
	119	Mountain Top
	149	White Haven
	206	Sweet Valley
	207	Mountain Top
	224	Hunlock Creek
Monroe	38	Tannersville
	127	Tobyhanna
	186	Bartonsville
	221	Cresco
Montour	115	Danville
Northumberland	84	Trevorton
	165	Trevorton
Pike	116	Lackawaxen
	180	Greeley
	183	Tafton
	209	Shohola
Sullivan	13	Sonestown
	66	Lopez
Susquehanna	35	Hallstead
	140	Friendsville
	175	New Milford
Wayne	70	Susquehanna
	159	Lookout

Other fine grouse opportunities in the northeast are in some of the farm-woodlot country. There are over 165,000 acres in this division in the Farm Game Co-op lands, and some 145,000 in the Safety Zone Program. This is also one of the best divisions for State Forest and State Park lands. Among the largest of these are: Tioga SF (3), north of Canton, Bradford Co.; Hickory Run SP (4), east of White Haven, Carbon Co.; Lackawanna SF (5), west of Thornhurst, Lackawanna Co. and a portion of the same Forest in Luzerne Co., west of Plymouth; Ricketts Glen SP (6), Luzerne Co.; Delaware SF (7), Tannersville, Monroe Co.; Tobyhanna-Gouldsboro SP (8), near Tobyhanna, Monroe Co.; Big Pocono SP (9), Tannersville, Monroe Co.; almost 63,000 acres of the Delaware SF (10) in Pike Co.; the Wyoming SF (11), Forksville and Hillsgrove, Sullivan Co.; Lackawanna SF (12), Wyoming Co., near Eatonville. There are several other State Parks open with acreages of 1000 or more each.

The southwest division as noted earlier is an area of hills and farms and small timber operations, with fine grouse hunting, much of it in pockets of modest acreage, from a few hundred to several thousand acres. The farm co-op lands in each county should not be overlooked. Good coverts are found in their woodlots.

Counties with largest co-op acreages are: Armstrong, 58,000; Cambria, over 40,000; Fayette, 30,000; Indiana, 33,000; Somerset, almost 70,000; Westmoreland, approximately 25,000. All the other counties have substantial amounts of these lands open.

There are the following State Forests and State Parks: Armstrong Co.: Crooked Creek SP (13), southeast of Ford City; Beaver Co.: Raccoon Creek SP (14), near Burgettstown; Cambria Co.: Prince Gallitzin SP (15), near Patton; Gallitzin SF (16), Fayette Co.: Braddock SF (17), south of Uniontown; Greene Co., Ryerson SP (18), west of Waynesboro; Somerset Co.: Laurel Hill SP (19), west of Somerset; Babcock SF (20), east of Windber; Blue Hole SF (21), near Rockwood; Linn Run SF (22), west of Jennerstown; Negro Mountain SF (23), south of Rockwood; Westmoreland Co.: small Keystone SP (24) north of Latrobe; a second unit of Linn Run SF (25), southeast of Rector.

Of the thirty-one Game Land tracts of the southwest, a few are especially noted for grouse, and a few others place grouse as secondary game. The top listing: No. 26, Cambria Co. near Beaverdale, over 9000 acres; No. 138, Fayette Co. near Fairchance, 2834 acres; No. 174, Indiana Co. near McGees Mills, 3000-plus acres; and in Somerset Co.: No. 50, 3168 acres near Somerset; No. 111, 9394 acres near Confluence; No. 228, 900 acres near Central City; No. 231, 429 acres near Salisbury.

The south-central division has so many hills and wooded ridges that grouse hunting is of good quality over most of it. Of the thirty-six Game Land tracts, twenty-one offer ruffed grouse as the main species. Bedford County has five: No. 48 near Buffalo Mills, 7251 acres; No. 49 near Clearville, 5131 acres; No. 73 near Martinsburg, 15,355 acres; No. 97 near Everett, 6012 acres; and No. 104 near Hyndman, 5111 acres.

Blair is another good grouse county, with: No. 147 near Martinsburg, 4400 acres; No. 166 near Canoe Creek, 5217 acres; No. 198 near Newry, 3313.

Fulton Co. has three quality grouse tracts with from 1500 to 4500 acres; No. 53 near McConnellsburg; No. 65 near Warfordsburg; No. 128 near Amaranth.

The best grouse tracts in Huntingdon Co. all run from 1600-plus acres up to over 5000. With nearest towns given, these are: No. 67, Broad Top City; No.

81, Three Springs; No. 112, Huntingdon; No. 121, New Grenada.

In Juniata County there are: No. 107, Mifflintown, over 4000 acres; No. 171, Thompsontown, 941; No. 215, East Waterford.

Mifflin County has one tract, No. 113, relatively small, near Strodes Mills.

Perry Co. has two: No. 170 near Marysville, 839 acres; No. 88 near Ickesburg, 6835 acres.

Other open lands in south central are extensive. All the counties have large acreages in the farmland programs. Bedford, for example, has over 55,000 acres in the Safety Zone Program alone, Huntingdon has almost 60,000 in the same. The Commission can furnish acreage and number of farms for each county.

State Forest lands are massive. Following are listed most of these, with general location by towns, and with round-number acreages given:

STATE FOREST	ACRES	COUNTY	NEAREST TOWN
26. Michaux SF	22,000	Adams	Caledonia
27. Buchanan SF	30,000	Bedford	Chaneysville
28. Michaux SF	35,000	Cumberland	Pine Grove Furnace
29. Tuscarora SF			Doubling Gap
30. Michaux SF	38,000	Franklin	Caledonia
31. Buchanan SF			Upper Strasburg
32. Buchanan SF	30,000	Fulton	Cowans Gap
33. Rothrock SF	66,000	Huntingdon	State College
34. Tuscarora SF	portion	Juniata	Reeds Gap
35. Bald Eagle SF	56,000	Mifflin	
36. Tuscarora SF	38,000	Perry	New Germantown
37. Bald Eagle SF	28,000	Snyder	Beaver Springs

There are some State Park lands also open. Check Blue Knob SP (38) and Shawnee SP (39), Bedford Co.; Trough Creek SP (40), Huntingdon Co.

In the southeast, as noted earlier, ruffed grouse are not found in great numbers. There are, however, several Game Land tracts on which they are in fair supply. These, which can be located on the map if one attempts grouse hunting in the southeast, are by number and county: No. 106, 110, Berks Co.; No. 56, Bucks Co.; No. 43, Chester Co.; No. 210, 211, 246, Dauphin Co.; No. 52, Lancaster Co.; No. 145, Lebanon Co.; No. 217, Lehigh Co.; No. 168, Northampton Co.; No. 80, 106, 110, 132, 229 in Schuylkill Co.; and No. 181, 242, and particularly No. 243 near Franklintown in York Co.

Farmlands open in the southeast are impressive, with York Co., for example, having over 88,000 in the Safety Zone program and over 36,000 in the Farm Game Co-op program. But all these southeast lands are likely to be exceedingly crowded. There are in addition French Creek SP (41) in Berks Co., Nockamixon SP (42) in Bucks Co., and Gifford Pinchot SP (43) in York Co. with fairly large areas open to hunting. The Weiser SF (44) lies in Dauphin and Schuylkill Cos. and offers about 15,000 acres.

PHEASANT

There is good pheasant shooting, cocks only, and pheasant hunting is popular with a kill averaging perhaps a million annually. But Pennsylvania cannot be claimed as a pheasant state with a large self-sustaining pheasant population. The birds are confined chiefly to farming areas, and the state assists in replenishment by raising thousands annually. Hunters should bear in mind that the farm programs lands are where much of the best shooting can be found. Each Division has many thousands of acres of these.

In the northwest, best pheasant hunting on Game Land tracts is in Erie Co. Most tracts here run from 200 up to as much as 1600 acres. Here are some to note, with nearest towns given: No. 109, Waterford; No. 154, Wattsburg; No. 155, Phillipsville; No. 161, Phillipsville; No. 162, Wattsburg; No. 163, Colt Station; No. 167, Wattsburg; No. 190, Waterford; No. 191, Little Hope; No. 192, Waterford; No. 218, Erie.

Lawrence Co. also has some good shooting: No. 150, Pulaski; No. 178, East Brook; No. 216, Harlansburg.

A few other tracts with pheasants are scattered over the northwest. Other open lands and an indication of farmlands possibilities have been noted under "Grouse."

The north-central division is not good pheasant territory. There are some birds, however, mostly in southern Union, Lycoming, Centre and Clearfield Counties, but shooting is only fair.

The northeast has a good many stocked birds, no natural reproduction. Best habitat here: farm portions of Montour, Columbia and Northumberland Cos., and in southern Luzerne and Carbon Cos.

In the southwest there is some farmland shooting, and there are two places where management concentrates to some extent on pheasants. These are: the Conemaugh Flood Control Reservoir lands, some 8000 acres in Indiana Co.; the Loyalhanna Flood Control Area with 4500 acres in West-moreland Co. Both are federally owned.

The rather mountainous south-central division has good pheasant hunting in its farmed valleys. Best of the shooting is found in Adams, Perry, Snyder, Cumberland, Juniata, and Franklin Cos. Some of the Farm Co-op lands are good, and there are several Game Lands where pheasants are top species. Adams Co. has a small one near Biglerville, No. 249. There are two especially noteworthy in Cumberland Co.: No. 169 near Newville, No. 230 near Carlisle Springs. In Snyder Co., No. 188 near Beaverton, No. 194 near Meiserville, No. 212 near Selinsgrove are all good.

The southeast has some of the best pheasant habitat in the state, but again, hunters must be warned that conditions are often crowded. The farm-game lands are on the whole probably the best bet. And, the counties to check out thoroughly are southern portions of York, Delaware, Lancaster, Chester. Parts of Bucks, Lehigh, and Northampton also bear scrutiny. A few Game Land tracts to note are: No. 46 near Hopeland, No. 52 near Bowmansville, and No. 156 near Elstonville, all in Lancaster Co.; No. 154, Mt. Gretna, Lebanon Co.; No. 205, Schnecksville, Lehigh Co.; and in York Co. No. 83, York Furnace, No. 181 Kyleville, No. 242 Rossville.

QUAIL

A low daily and season limit (as this is written, four and twenty) indicates that Pennsylvania has a very modest amount of quail hunting. There are some scattered coveys, mostly on farmlands, in several portions of the state. Most of these are known and hunted only locally. The south-central division has the best quail population. Most of the birds there are in three counties: Franklin, Cumberland, Adams.

Adams Co. has about 26,000 acres in the Farm Game Co-op Program and over 14,000 in the Safety Zone Program. Acreages in Franklin Co.: over 29,000 and 31,000; Cumberland Co.: 23,000 and 14,000. More than 400 farms are in the Safety Zone Program throughout the three counties. This indicates a substantial hunting area.

There are two Game Land tracts, each somewhat less than a thousand acres, that offer quail hunting. Both are in Cumberland Co. These, also mentioned under "Pheasant," which indicates possibility of a mixed-bag hunt, are No. 169 near Newville, and No. 230 near Carlisle Springs.

The southeast also has a modest amount of farmland quail hunting, and it contains several Game Land tracts with quail populations. In Berks Co., No. 182 near Kutztown is a small area. No. 205 near Schnecksville (also noted under "Pheasant") contains 1263, is in Lehigh Co. Two good-sized areas in Schuylkill Co. place quail third in importance among game species: No. 227, near Barnesville, 1200 acres; No. 257, near Tamaqua, 3227 acres.

WILD TURKEYS

Pennsylvania is an excellent turkey state, with a large population of these birds, and a harvest recently reported over 20,000. Early in the century wild turkeys were nearly extinct here. Remnant flocks were confined almost entirely to the south-central section. Today, because of maturing forests there and changes in land use, the turkey population center is farther north. However, of the eleven counties that comprise the south-central division, all but Adams and Cumberland have fair to good turkey populations. The Game Land tracts in Bedford, Blair, Fulton, Huntingdon, and Perry Cos. mentioned under "Grouse" all offer some turkey hunting. In Franklin Co. are two others: No. 76 near Roxbury and No. 235 near Fort Loudon. These are large areas—3800 and 4500 acres. The numerous State Forest lands in south central (see "Grouse") also have turkey flocks.

The northwest is just fair. Four counties furnish the best opportunities: Clarion, Jefferson, Warren, Forest. Two especially noteworthy Game Lands spots here are: Forest Co., near Newmansville, No. 24 with 8000-plus acres; Warren Co., near Warren, No. 29, with 9000-plus. The huge Allegheny NF (45) covers much of southeast Warren Co., most of Forest Co. This is a good place to try for turkey in the northwest.

Pennsylvania's leading turkey area is north central. This ten-county section has turkeys in all counties. The counties considered to have highest populations are: Potter, Tioga, Elk, Cameron. Part of the Allegheny NF is in western Elk Co. The Tioga SF covers nearly 150,000 acres in that County. Potter Co. has 266,000 acres of the Susquehannock SF (46). In Elk Co. is the Elk SF, 36,000-plus, and the Moshannon SF, 37,000-plus. Much more of Elk SF (47) lies in Cameron Co., in fact, over 118,000 acres. There are numerous large State Forests in the other counties, too. These are easily located on the official map.

In fact, so vast and numerous are lands open for turkey here that much more than half of the entire north central can be publicly hunted. Of the thirty-eight Game Land tracts totalling 269,489 acres, there are thirty-one on which turkeys are considered second only to deer in importance. A check of the map will show that it is extremely easy here to find a place to hunt.

Although there is some turkey hunting in the southwest and the southeast, it cannot be considered important except perhaps locally. In the northeast, less than twenty years ago there were no turkeys. Careful nurturing has brought them to fair abundance in seven of the thirteen counties involved. These are: Sullivan, which is considered the primary range here, Pike, Monroe, Lackawanna, Bradford, Luzerne, Wyoming. The large sectors of State Forest and State Parks lands noted under "Grouse" are good bets for turkeys. Some of the Game Lands listed for "Grouse" also furnish turkey hunting. The official map will show a few others.

All told, however, a visitor to Pennsylvania who wishes to try for a gobbler will do best to select the north-central region where the heaviest population is found. The Pennsylvania turkey season has been traditionally in fall only. The first spring season—additional to the fall season—was held with high success and popularity in May of 1968.

MOURNING DOVES

Compared to some of the high-kill dove states of the south and southwest, Pennsylvania's kill is not large. It averages perhaps a quarter-million annually. However, even though the state has a large number of hunters, only a few pursue this fast-paced sport avidly. Thus the kill belies the excellence, in some places, of the shooting.

Most of this hunting is found on the farmlands where one must hunt by permission. But as illustrated throughout this chapter, there are vast acreages open. Thus we will note here only the general areas or counties where dove hunting of fair to good quality is found.

In the northwest, there are stretches of flat croplands in Erie, Crawford, Mercer, and Butler Cos. where in early season the hunting is fair.

In north central there is only a small amount of shooting, furnished by local dove populations early in season, before migration begins. Southern Centre and Clinton Cos., portions of Lycoming and Union Cos. are best.

In the northeast, local dove populations that move early are found chiefly in the "Pheasant" habitat, *which see.*

The south-central section is one of the two best places for dove hunting. The habitat corresponds here exactly to that of "Quail" and "Pheasant." Many of the open farmlands of course have excellent dove populations, where good feeding conditions can be found.

The southeast is the second of the top-quality dove areas. Pressure is heavy and the sport has become very popular here. With the exceptions of nonhunting Philadelphia Co., and Delaware Co., all the rest of southeast is prime habitat. Early season hunting anywhere in the state is likely to be best, however, for cold snaps may send concentrations of birds on south.

WOODCOCK

This is to some extent a specialist's game. There is some top-notch opportunity to enjoy its delights in Pennsylvania. During a recent season the harvest was 75,000 birds. In the northwest, excellent woodcocking is found in two counties: Erie and Crawford. All of the Game Lands noted under "Pheasant" for these counties are woodcock hotspots. So is No. 101, near Springboro, mentioned under "Grouse." Farmlands open in these counties also should be checked out. Those with woodlots where ground cover is light but over-cover gives dappled shade are excellent choices. The large Pymatuning State Park acreage in Crawford Co. also is a select woodcock haven.

Flight woodcock shooting is fair, when one hits it just right, in the north-central region. Good bets: north and east Tioga Co.; southern Clearfield Co.; Centre Co.'s. Bald Eagle Valley; Bennett's Valley in Elk and Cameron Cos.

The very best of woodcock shooting in Pennsylvania is in the northeast. Migrating birds here often swarm into coverts along the many stream courses, the marsh edges and along suitable lake borders. The one county considered above all others is Sullivan. Pike, Monroe, Lackawanna, Luzerne are not far behind. The Game Lands noted under "Grouse" are good bets. So are the State Forests and Parks noted under that species.

South central and southeast also offer some woodcock hunting, in the moist or swampy areas that have proper light low cover and heavier cover above. Check the various lands noted for "Grouse" and hunt the lower portions.

WATERFOWL, SNIPE, RAILS

Neither snipe nor rails are important game in Pennsylvania. A few of each are taken as incidentals each season. Although ducks and geese are hunted by a number of persons, this is by no means a prominent waterfowling state. Nonetheless, it has some excellent shooting, chiefly in the northwest, and some spotty shooting elsewhere. With resident hunters, the northwest is famous for its waterfowl opportunities.

The focal point is the Pymatuning Waterfowl Area in southwestern Crawford Co. Linesville on U.S. 6 is at the north end of the area, and Hartstown on U.S. 322 is at the western edge near the south end. This is on Pymatuning Reservoir. It is separate from the State Park mentioned previously. Not all of the Area is open to hunting, but there are public hunt tracts with plain demarcations ringing a central reservoir and propagation area. Some of the hunting is controlled duck and goose, some is for ducks only. There are blinds and parking areas.

A map showing all details is available from the Commission. Hunters for goose and duck shooting must mail applications in fall (check dates with Commission) and there is a drawing. Several hundred hunters are thus picked for specific dates to occupy the available blinds. Hunters are allowed specified numbers of guests. The duck shooting areas are on a first-come basis. Some thousands of Canada geese, and a few snows, plus chiefly black ducks and mallards are the species here.

Although the Pymatuning area is the famous northwestern waterfowl spot, several Game Lands furnish some shooting. No. 69, near Guy Mills, Crawford Co., is a prime duck area, and in the same county there are: No. 85 near Cambridge Springs, No. 213 near Conneaut Lake, No. 214 near Hartstown. Erie Co. offers a good duck area, No. 109, Waterford, and another with ducks the first choice, No. 218 near Erie. Warren Co.'s No. 197 near Columbus is also a duck shooting tract.

In the north-central area the West Branch of the Susquehanna River offers some waterfowl shooting, and there are scattered beaver ponds and water impoundments in the Allegheny NF that furnish a bit of shooting. There is not much in this area to hold waterfowl for long.

The northeast has quite good shooting. This is on the flyway but migrating birds do not stop long. The Susquehanna River puts both ducks and geese into hunter's bags, and there are some Game Lands that are closed to hunting but designed as rest and feed areas to hold waterfowl in the vicinity. Beaver ponds, smaller streams and lakes furnish catch-as-catch-can shooting over the entire northeast.

In southern Pennsylvania the south-central area offers spotty shooting along the Susquehanna. This is mostly for ducks. A few geese may at times show up. Ducks gather in creeks tributary to the big river. These turn up surprisingly good hunting for prowling jump-shooters and none should be by-passed by serious waterfowl enthusiasts.

The southeast has some creek and farm-pond shooting. It also contains, in Lebanon and Lancaster Cos., the recently developed Middle Creek Waterfowl Project, a Commission development aimed at controlled shooting.

RABBITS AND SNOWSHOE HARES

Cottontails range over most of the state. Snowshoe hares are not abundant, but build up good populations over most of the northeast, where the Commission carefully manages them and experiments with restocking. The northeast furnishes almost all of Pennsylvania's snowshoe hare hunting. There are some snowshoes also in the north-central sector, mostly in Lycoming, Tioga, and Clinton Cos. Upwards of three million cottontails are taken each season, and perhaps 6000 hares.

The vast amounts of farmlands in the hunting programs are all told the best bets for cottontails throughout the state. But there are certain Game Lands managed specifically for rabbits. And there are a few counties that usually have the best cottontail populations. In the northwest, Crawford Co. is considered best. Game Land areas No. 146, Crawford Co., and 151, Lawrence Co. are where the Commission concentrates on cottontails here. Erie Co. has numerous good rabbit hunting spots in its Game Lands—see all those for "Pheasant."

In the north-central area, cottontails are not abundant. Game Lands managed for them are: No. 93, Clearfield Co., No. 176, Centre Co., and Nos. 193 and 201 in Union Co.

The northeast management spots are No. 219, Bradford Co., No. 187, Luzerne Co., No. 226, Columbia Co. Cottontails are extremely popular and very abundant in the northeast. Most public lands previously mentioned have good populations but the farm program lands are best as a general rule.

The southwest also offers good rabbit hunting. The flood control projects noted under "Pheasants" are also managed extensively for rabbits as well. Most of the Game Lands offer good cottontail hunting, with those in Allegheny, Armstrong, Beaver, and Washington Cos. among the top.

Best counties of the south-central area are those under "Pheasants."

In the southeast farmlands, rabbit populations are generally high. In Lebanon Co. (No. 145) and in Lehigh Co. (No. 205) the Commission manages lands especially for rabbits.

SQUIRRELS

Pennsylvania has both gray and fox squirrels. The gray squirrels are found chiefly in the various forest tracts, the fox squirrels on many farmland woodlots and along the fringes of deep woods where gray squirrels range. Squirrels are abundant, popular, and important, and range throughout the state. The kill is over two and a half million.

In the northwest fox squirrels are fairly plentiful in Venango Co. and also in Mercer and Butler Cos. Gray squirrels are well distributed throughout the forested lands here.

The north-central division is the prime range of the gray squirrel, the deep-woods species. Occasionally melanistic (black) phases show up in the bag. The northernmost tier of counties here is the best, but this near-wilderness portion of Pennsylvania has good squirrel hunting, for grays, almost everywhere.

The northeast does not evidence a very high squirrel population. Hunting is rated poor to only fair.

In the southwest, there is excellent squirrel hunting. Most are grays, but there are also numerous fox squirrels. The Game Lands and other lands noted for "Grouse" are overall the best squirrel spots here. The south-central area rates fair to good. Check the "Grouse" spots for best shooting, and farm woodlots for fox squirrels. The southeast is not considered especially good squirrel range. The ridge portions are best, and again, under "Grouse" the better possibilities are listed.

DEER

Pennsylvania's continuing record as a high-kill deer state is in proportions little short of amazing. During a recent season, as noted early in this chapter, 144,415 deer were taken. Furthermore, 78,268 of these were bucks, 66,147 were antlerless. This indicates a tremendous basic herd. There is consistent annual high success among both gunners and archers. Of the total kill noted above, archers bagged 3251 deer. Surprising as it seems, deer range in abundance over every county of the state.

Happily, in so populous a state, there is no problem for deer hunters in finding good places to hunt. Obviously the large wooded sections in the State Forests, the National Forest, and the very large State Parks generally offer the best hunting (see "Grouse"). But the farm program lands should not be overlooked. Many large bucks hole up in woodlots of modest size on such lands. However, to pinpoint good farm hunting spots requires some detailed scouting prior to season. For visitors, particularly nonresidents, it is advantageous to hunt the areas with the highest deer populations and highest consistent kill.

Checking off the sections of the state to give an indication of deer abundance, the very best portion is the north-central area. This ten-county region invariably turns up the heaviest kill. It is the Pennsylvania "big woods" and supports more big game than any other part of the state. Potter Co., the center county of the northern tier here, lying against the New York border, is consistently the highest deer-producing county of the entire state. During the season noted with 144,415 kill, Potter Co. alone furnished 8170, and of those, a whopping 4899 were bucks. Second in kill is generally Centre Co., with Clearfield third. However, all counties of the north-central area offer high-quality deer hunting. As an indication, of the thirty-eight Game Land tracts here, every one lists the whitetail as the main attraction.

The northwest has surprisingly good deer hunting, too. The two top counties here are Venango and Warren, which each harvested over 4000 deer during the same season mentioned previously. These are followed by Forest and Jefferson.

Warren, Forest, Jefferson all contain portions of the Allegheny National Forest. While the Forests will offer the great share of the best hunting, several Game Lands should be noted. There are three of these rated high for deer in Clarion Co., which incidentally often furnishes high deer kills. They are: No. 63, near Shippenville, almost 3000 acres; No. 72, Clarion, with about 2000; No. 74, Strattanville with over 6000.

Jefferson Co. has several that are excellent. Near Brockway, No. 54 contains 21,820 acres; No. 31, Punxsutawney, has over 4000; No. 195 near Big Run and No. 244 near Emrickville each comprise over 1000.

In Warren Co. there are three where deer rate first: No. 86, Tidioute, approximately 14,000; No. 143, Garland, almost 8000; No. 197, about 1000 near Columbus. Venango, as noted one of the very best counties in the northwest, also has several good-sized Game Lands where deer are first: No. 39, Franklin;

No. 45, Van; No. 47, Oil City; No. 253, Plummer.

The northeast is second only to the north-central area in deer abundance, good deer habitat, and kill. Of the forty-five Game Lands, thirty-three rate deer at the top. Many of these, as well as the large Forest and Park lands, are located under "Grouse." The top county here as a rule is Bradford, the north-western corner of this division. During the season mentioned, Bradford furnished over 4000 of the total kill. Next in line usually is Wayne Co., then Luzerne, Pike, Monroe, Sullivan, Carbon in approximately that order. Hunters in the northeast would do well, when seeking trophy heads, to check surveys the Commission has made of kills by county. The lands where timber has been cut and dairy lands in Bradford, Wyoming, and Susquehanna Cos., the three in the northwest, north-central and central part of the region, usually turn up the best racks.

The southwest is not rated high for deer hunting. But the fact is that some large deer, with heavy racks, come from here, principally from wooded parts of Indiana, Somerset, and Cambria Cos. Hunting, though challenging, is more difficult and most hunters go north.

The south-central region has fair hunting because of the numerous ridges slanting from northeast to southwest across this region and the consequent good deer habitat. Top county is Huntingdon. Perry is also very good, followed by Blair, Bedford, Mifflin, Juniata, Franklin in about that order season to season. The other counties have fair kills, but much of the hunting is by local people who know the country.

In many ways the southeast is an enigma in deer hunting. It gets low deer-hunt presure, yet numerous portions of the southeast have too many deer. Most hunters go to the big "north woods," to get away from dense human population, and consequently they leave behind many large deer with larger racks than they may bring back. Thus the modest kill in the southeast is not much of an indication. Certainly hunting here is more difficult, but it can be very good. All of the Game Land tracts in Berks, Bucks, Chester, Dauphin Cos., most of those in Lancaster, Northampton, Schuylkill, York list deer as the top species.

BEAR

Black bear hunting everywhere is a rather specialized sport if one pursues it purposely. Most black bear, in Pennsylvania as in most other states, are incidental kills by deer hunters. However, in the north-central counties many a native makes a real issue of bear hunting. The annual kill here is fairly good, considering the need of bears for large wilderness tracts. It runs from 500 to 600 annually.

The north-central area is always by far the best bear area, with Potter Co., the big deer producer, generally well out ahead in bears, too. Spreading to east and west of the north-central counties, there is good bear hunting too. The best and most concise picture of Pennsylvania bear hunting can be given simply by listing kills by county during a recent and quite typical season.

Potter, 66; Elk, 64; Clearfield, 50; Tioga, 43; Cameron, 39; Lycoming, 35; McKean, 29; Clinton, 26; Centre, 19; Sullivan, 17. In the northwest, Warren, Forest, and Jefferson Cos. average a few bears—10 to 15—annually, and the same is true in the northeast of several counties. However, on the eastern border in the northeast, Pike and Monroe show fair kills at times. During the year noted by figures above, Pike had 35, Monroe 20.

Bear kills across all of southern Pennsylvania are low. A few animals are taken each year in the northern portion of the south-central region.

OTHER ANIMALS

Raccoons are extremely plentiful throughout all of Pennsylvania. They are underharvested, and in many sections are abundant to nuisance proportions. There is no closed season and they need harder hunting. No special areas are significantly better than others, although mixed farm and woodlands offer the best hunting.

Foxes range the state, too, and are hunted to some extent, with hounds and by use of calls and by still-hunting and tracking in snow. In the southeast, riding to hounds by organized fox-hunt clubs is traditional.

Woodchuck hunting is quite an important and popular pastime. Much of the state's terrain, with its slopes and valleys, farm fields and woodlots, is perfect 'chuck habitat. In the north-central section, the counties of Potter, Tioga, McKean are good woodchuck areas. Other north-central counties here have some. The dairy and grazing lands of the northeast are excellent 'chuck hunting. Bradford Co., and Wayne and Susquehanna have much good habitat, and the farm fields of Montour, Columbia, and Northumberland Cos. also produce plenty of this sport.

All of the farm-woodlot portions of the southwest are woodchuck habitat. The remainder of the state furnishes fair to good shooting, with the southeast a good bet although rather heavily settled in parts for long-range rifle shooting. The Game Land tracts of both the southwest and southeast offer some 'chuck hunting.

A NOTE ON ELK

In the north-central counties of Elk, Clearfield, and Cameron, there are a few elk. Native Pennsylvania elk have been gone for a century, but some were brought in from the west many years ago. There was even an open season during the twenties and early thirties. Now, however, the herd is only a remnant, probably less than fifty animals. Elk warning signs are posted in the areas where the animals are most likely to be seen. But occasionally a deer hunter kills one, which is of course illegal. Deer hunters in these counties should be aware of the elk and take great care not to mistake a target.

REGULATIONS

Game laws pertaining to seasons, bag and possession limits, areas to be hunted, special hunts, license fees all may have numerous changes from year to year. For current regulations, and for other specific queries, write to: Game Commission, P.O. Box 1567, Harrisburg, Pennsylvania 17120.

WEST VIRGINIA

West Virginia calls itself the "Mountain State," an apt and authentically descriptive nickname. It is almost entirely a series of ridges and valleys, the slopes steep and the valleys mostly narrow. The eastern and central portions of the state are formed by the zigzagging spines of the Appalachians, and in the west the mountains ease downward in rugged stairstep fashion until they meet the valley of the Ohio River, which forms much of the undulating western border.

Streams careen through most of the snug valleys, and forests, often dense, clothe the slopes and the mountain tops. The state is most scenic and appealing, and in fall when leaves turn it is a riot of color that in itself warms the blood and hastens the heartbeat of any hunter. West Virginia's borders are as anguished in their turnings as the limitless angles of its mountains. The only straight lines are on the eastern side of the narrow northern panhandle that juts up along part of western Pennsylvania, the strong stretch of border in the north with southern Pennsylvania, and a brief line along the western edge of Maryland.

Here a clot of eight helter-skelter counties are wedged without seeming reason in between portions of Maryland and Virginia. In the main portion of the east, and the south, the ragged border is with Virginia, in the southwest with Kentucky, where the Big Sandy River and Tug Fork form the border. Near Huntington in the upper southwest the Big Sandy has its confluence with the Ohio, and that big river, upstream, snakes along to separate West Virginia from Ohio.

If the borders are crooked, they are mimicked tenfold by the highways. Roads are good, and reach into all sectors, but hardly a mile runs straight in this mountainous terrain. Numerous secondaries take hunters into the small settlements and the sparsely inhabited ridges, but if one intends to get off the solid roads, a 4WD vehicle is a most welcome item of equipment. Air service is adequate to the larger cities, but thinly spread overall.

Coal is king here. West Virginia leads the nation in coal production and allied industries. There is some agriculture, but the terrain is suitable mainly for small farms, and the charm of the state for sportsmen is the nostalgic feeling of early America and hills unchanged, seemingly, since first the white man came. To some extent this is deceiving, for there are about 1.8 million people here, in a state that seems large only because so much of it is up and down. The actual area is only 24,181 square miles.

Interesting is the fact that of approximately 15.5 million acres total in this state, some 14 million furnish hunting of one or another variety, and approximately 6 percent of the state's total acreage, or roughly 1.3 million acres, are in public ownership. Finding a place to hunt—except for the strictly farm-game species—is therefore not especially difficult.

Compared to total population, hunters however are numerous and the

201

sport exceedingly popular. License sales total close to 200,000, and there are some thousands of residents who under the law need not purchase a license. Nonresident visitors find Mountain State hunting appealing, and their numbers grow season after season. Currently more than 17,000 enter the state each fall.

Game is of both farm and forest variety. Ruffed grouse are found in all fifty-five counties, there are quail in the farming areas, and a limited number of pheasants. Wild turkeys furnish good hunting, and there are doves, woodcock, a scattering of snipe and rails, and in a few locations fair waterfowl shooting. Squirrels and rabbits are everywhere, and popular. There are varying hares in the mountains. Whitetail deer are abundant, and some extremely large bucks are bagged each season. Black bears are present in modest numbers. Woodchucks, raccoons, foxes, and bobcats also furnish much sport.

Most prominent and largest of the public lands is the Monongahela National Forest (1), which contains 808,898 acres. This Forest lies along the eastern border from just north of the U.S. 60-219 junction at its southern end on north all the way to the border with Maryland. It also juts into the western part of the eastern panhandle. Numerous good highways parallel or cross it—U.S. 219, 250, 33, 220, State 28, 39, 72. Several secondaries also are within this Forest, but there is a great deal of wilderness back-country where only trails lead. Headquarters of the Forest Supervisor, from which details and maps may be obtained, is at Elkins.

Not as well known, and sometimes overlooked by visitors in particular, is the portion of the George Washington National Forest (2) headquarters at Harrisonburg, Virginia, that spills across the border of the eastern panhandle from Virginia into West Virginia. This million-plus-acre Forest is mostly in Virginia, but approximately 110,000 acres are on the western slopes of the Shenandoah Mountains, in West Virginia. This acreage begins near Capon Springs, Hampshire Co., in the north, and reaches south for approximately seventy-five miles, with one break in the middle so there are actually two blocks of it, to the point south of Sugar Grove where the West Virginia border turns abruptly west.

The Department of Natural Resources, address at chapter end, assists in game management on the National Forests lands. It also owns nearly 161,000 acres of land in sixteen public hunting tracts well distributed throughout the state. There are also approximately 77,000 acres in nine State Forests. In addition to the state and federal lands, there are some paper company holdings that are open to hunting under varying rules. It is best for interested hunters to check with the Department regarding these privately owned tracts.

The state is divided into six Districts, for management purposes. There is a headquarters for each, and addresses of these can be obtained from the DNR. Much valuable pinpoint information can be had for any given season from the biologist in charge of any District. Later in this chapter the information under the species headings will be handled by these Districts and by counties within them. These are therefore listed below. Also, because kill figures and success percentages are not readily available for the several public tracts in state ownership, those tracts—PHAs and State Forests—will be noted below under the Districts and counties in which they are located. Thus the reader may refer back to this section from any species heading. Some of course will be mentioned under species as particularly good.

District 1 is in the north and includes the northwestern panhandle. It contains the panhandle counties of Hancock, Brooke, Ohio, Marshall, and the northwest and north-central counties of Wetzel, Monongalia, Preston,

Marion, Harrison, Taylor, Barbour, Tucker. The Lewis Wetzel PHA (3), in southeastern Wetzel Co. southeast from Jacksonburg, contains almost 10,000 acres. Pleasants Creek PHA (4) is a 1000-acre tract in southeastern Taylor Co., below Grafton. Coopers Rock State Forest (5) has over 13,000 acres, on the border between Monongalia and Preston Cos.

District 2 contains the counties of the eastern panhandle. These are, reading from west to east: Grant, Pendleton, Mineral, Hampshire, Hardy, Morgan, Berkeley, Jefferson. Hampshire Co. has two PHAs, both located in the southern part of the county. Nathaniel Mountain PHA (6) has almost 9000 acres south of Romney and Augusta. Short Mountain PHA (7) contains over 8000 acres a few miles to the east of Nathaniel Mountain PHA. On the border between Berkeley and Morgan Cos. is Sleepy Creek PHA (8), with more than 22,000 acres. It is northwest from Martinsburg.

District 3 is east-central. Counties are: Lewis, Braxton, Clay, Upshur, Webster, Nicholas, Randolph, Pocahontas. In this District are three State Forests and two PHAs. Kumbrabow SF (9) is in southwestern Randolph Co., has almost 9500 acres with a secondary running through it west from Elk-water on U.S. 219. Seneca SF (10), east-central Pocahontas Co., contains 11,685 acres with a secondary crossing it south from Dunmore on State 28. The Calvin Price SF (11) is in the southern part of the same county, has almost 9500 acres south of the above, with the same secondary crossing it south from Huntersville. The Elk River PHA (12) is in eastern Braxton Co., has 13,740 acres east of U.S. 19 and south of Sutton Reservoir. Williams River PHA (13) is in southwestern Pocahontas Co., with 784 acres reached by secondary west from Edray, U.S. 219.

District 4 is in the southeast, contains Fayette, Raleigh, Wyoming, Mc-Dowell, Summers, Mercer, Greenbrier, and Monroe Cos. There are three State Forests and two PHAs in this District. Panther Creek SF (14) is in western McDowell Co., has 7810 acres reached west from Roderfield, U.S. 52. Camp Creek SF (15) contains nearly 5900 acres in northwestern Mercer Co., reached via Camp Creek on U.S. 19 and 21. Greenbrier SF (16), in southeast Greenbrier Co., has 5000 acres south of I 64 and White Sulphur Springs. Plum Orchard Lake PHA (17), of about 3000 acres, is west of Mount Hope in southwestern Fayette Co. Bluestone PHA (18) has almost 20,000 acres, partly in three counties: Mercer, Monroe, Summers. Most of it is in Summers Co., along Bluestone Reservoir.

District 5 encompasses the southwestern counties of Mason, Cabell, Wayne, Putnam, Lincoln, Mingo, Kanawah, Boone, Logan. Here there are six PHAs and two State Forests. McClintic Wildlife Station PHA (19) in northwestern Mason Co. lies north of Point Pleasant, contains almost 2500 acres. Chief Cornstalk PHA (20) is in central Mason Co., has over 10,000 acres lying between routes State 2 and 17 south from Point Pleasant. Mill Creek PHA (21) is east from Wayne (U.S. 52) in northeastern Cabell Co. Big Ugly PHA (22) has 5700 acres, is in southern Lincoln Co. east of State 10 and the villages of Ranger and Harts. Laurel Creek PHA (23), 12,850 acres, is in northern Mingo Co., east from the junction of U.S. 52 and State 65. Fork Creek PHA (24), in northern Boone Co., has 9000 acres a few miles south of Charleston. The Kanawha SF (25) is a short distance northeast, across the line in Kanawha Co. Cabwaylingo SF (26) is in southern Wayne Co. east of U.S. 52. It contains 8125 acres.

District 6 is in the northwest below that panhandle. The counties: Tyler, Pleasants, Wood, Jackson, Ritchie, Wirt, Roane, Doddridge, Gilmer, Calhoun.

The Hughes River PHA (27) is here, along the border of Ritchie and Wirt Cos., with 10,000 acres. This lies along the Hughes River between State 47 and 53 near where those routes intersect.

Accommodations for hunters are ample everywhere except in the back-country. A delightful arrangement for the hills is to make plans to stay on a farm somewhere in a remote valley. The DNR has available a folder brought up to date each season titled "Food and Lodging for Sportsmen on West Virginia Farms." Camping hunters have a wide choice of sites in the National Forests, the numerous State Parks, State Forests, and even on the PHAs. Facilities on the latter are rough or nonexistent but most allow camping. There is a folder published by the DNR titled "Tent and Trailer Camping in West Virginia State Parks and Forests."

Weather in early fall is delightful in the mountains. During mid-fall it is invigorating and crisp, and like mountan hunting anywhere will require a light wool shirt, and a jacket for early and late in the day. During late fall and into the winter the weather can be quite cold, and one should go prepared for it. Good boots are mandatory in any season for the steep walking that prevails.

No very specialized arms or ammunition are required. Bird hunters will be best served with No. 7½ shot size as an all-round load, though for the modest amount of waterfowling heavier loads, such as No. 4s, will be needed. A .22 for squirrels is a fine extra arm, and for deer or bear the standard deer-rifle calibers such as the .30/06 and comparable ones are certainly adequate. Timber hunting can be dense in many places and numerous local hunters prefer the so-called "brush" calibers such as .30/30 or .35 Remington. However, more modern ones in the class with .243 or .270 are fine also.

RUFFED GROUSE

Because of its mountainous terrain with many brushy creeks and small farm edges, West Virginia is a rather good ruffed grouse state. It may surprise many hunters to know that the ruffed grouse is in fact by far the most important game bird. Grouse are found in every county in the state.

During an average good year, the kill runs about 95,000. The two Districts with the highest kill are usually 1 and 4 Nearly half the total kill often comes from these. District 4, the southeastern counties, is considered first. All counties here offer fair to excellent hunting. In order, the best counties are: Greenbrier, Raleigh, Mercer, Summers, Wyoming, Monroe. Some consistently good hunting has been sustained for many years on the watersheds of the Greenbrier and New Rivers. All public lands in the District have grouse, and fair to good hunting. Camp Creek SF, Mercer Co., is considered especially productive.

In District 1, in the northwest, the actual kill sometimes exceeds that for District 4, but hunting pressure differs also. Best counties in order of importance here are Marshall, Hancock, Harrison, Preston, Barbour, Ohio.

District 6, the western counties south of the northwest panhandle, rates third, with a kill of around 15,000 birds. Public lands are not in large supply here. Wood Co. is probably the best, followed by Doddridge, Roane, Jackson, Wirt. In Districts 2 and 3, which take in all of the northeast and east-central portions of the state, grouse hunting is fair, with the two Districts tied roughly for fourth place. First three counties in each, by recent kill, are as follows: District 2—Hardy, Hampshire, Grant; District 3—Pocahontas, Braxton, Nicholas.

Some of the best hunting on public lands is available in these Districts, even though the state rating of the Districts is not at the top. There are large areas of National Forests. In District 2 the Nathaniel Mountain PHA rates as one of the best grouse tracts in the state. Short Mountain PHA also is excellent, and so is Sleepy Creek PHA. In District 3, all the PHAs and State Forests furnish good grouse hunting. Kumbrabow SF, Seneca SF, Calvin Price SF, Elk River PHA all rate as quality opportunity for grouse hunters.

Although District 5, the southwest, rates fifth, it may be because grouse are by no means heavily hunted here. During a recent season, Mason Co. had the highest kill. Hunters who will seek grouse on the State Forests and PHAs can discover some excellent sport. All of these (see opening portion of chapter for locations) are fair to good. Best grouse populations probably occur on Chief Cornstalk and Big Ugly PHAs.

QUAIL

Although the bobwhite is second in importance to the ruffed grouse by numbers of annual kill, actually West Virginia cannot be considered at best as more than a mediocre quail state. Even though the season is long, and the bag limit at this writing seven a day, the total kill during a recent season was only slightly more than 50,000 birds. Best quail populations are generally found in the major river valleys and in the eastern farmlands. To be sure, there is some good local shooting, on private lands, but public opportunities are neither abundant nor excellent.

Widely separated areas furnish the best of what quail shooting there is. District 2 has the highest kill. These are the northeastern counties. District 5, in the southwest, is second.

In District 2, which is far and away the best quail hunting in the state, Berkeley and Jefferson Cos. are considered the top two. There are farming areas here and these consistently produce some very good hunting, but it is on private lands. There are few quail on public lands, and many private lands are not anxious to give hunting permission. Prior arrangements should be made.

In District 5 the public hunting situation is somewhat better. Among the best counties are Mason, Putnam, Kanawha, Wayne. The McClintic Wildlife Station PHA and Chief Cornstalk PHA offer quail hunting. McClintic PHA is in fact considered the best public quail location in the state. (See chapter opening for location.) Actually more quail might be harvested in District 5. They are lightly hunted here.

Although District 4 rates as third for quail, the rating is misleading. The kill is low. The little farming here has changed to mostly grassland and meadow, and much of the best quail habitat has been lost. There are a few birds on the Bluestone PHA. In District 6 there are modest quail kills in Wood, Jackson, and Roane Cos. In Districts 1 and 3 kills are only incidental.

PHEASANT

Although the pheasant season is long—almost eight weeks at present— and either sex may be shot, this is not an indication of abundant ringnecks.

WEST VIRGINIA

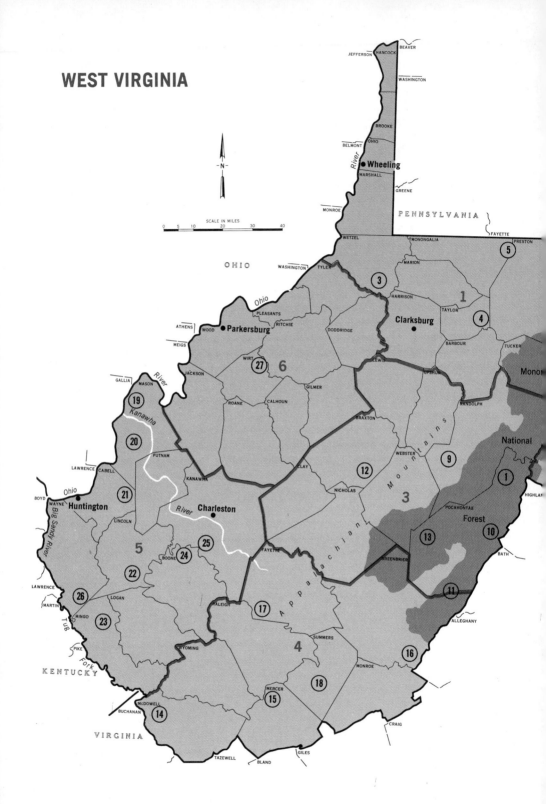

SCALE IN MILES

PENNSYLVANIA

OHIO

KENTUCKY

VIRGINIA

Wheeling

Clarksburg

Parkersburg

Huntington

Charleston

KEY TO HUNTING AREAS

1. Monongahela NF
2. George Washington NF
3. Lewis Wetzel PHA
4. Pleasants Creek PHA
5. Coopers Rock SF
6. Nathaniel Mountain PHA
7. Short Mountain PHA
8. Sleepy Creek PHA
9. Kumbrabow SF
10. Seneca SF
11. Calvin Price SF
12. Elk River PHA
13. Williams River PHA
14. Panther Creek SF
15. Camp Creek SF
16. Greenbrier SF
17. Plum Orchard Lake PHA
18. Bluestone PHA
19. McClintic Wildlife Station PHA
20. Chief Cornstalk PHA
21. Mill Creek PHA
22. Big Ugly PHA
23. Laurel Creek PHA
24. Fork Creek PHA
25. Kanawha SF
26. Cabwaylingo SF
27. Hughes River PHA

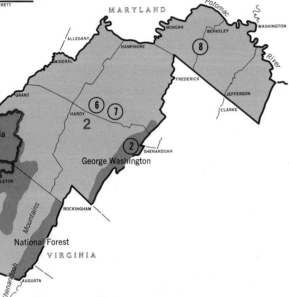

The season limit, two birds, is the more important listing. There are a few pheasants in portions of the Ohio River Valley but hardly in huntable numbers. The few pheasants killed in West Virginia are found in the counties of the northern panhandle and the few northern counties immediately below it. An average season kill for the state is from fifty to a hundred birds. There is no pheasant hunting on the public lands. As this is written no experimentation is being carried out with other pheasant species or strains, but such experiments are contemplated.

MOURNING DOVES

While there is some good dove shooting in West Virginia, it is extremely localized. This state does not have the abundant farm croplands so necessary to holding doves during migration. There are shootable numbers of doves chiefly in the valley of the Ohio River and in the Potomac drainage, and along river valleys where row crops are still grown.

As this is written West Virginia has an interesting season arrangement covering the best possible chances for all parts of the state. The season is split into three parts, the first segment beginning September 1 through most of that month, the second segment during October, the third during late December and the first half of January.

Although the annual kill has fluctuations, it is doubtful that it averages, over a period of years, even 20,000 birds. During a recent season it was slightly less than 15,000. Thus the mourning dove is not a very important game bird here.

Districts 2, 5, and 6 are best. Tabulations for the most recent season at this writing show District 3 with no reported kill, Districts 1 and 4 with negligible kill. In District 5, Mason Co. was best, with the state's highest harvest. In District 2, Jefferson Co. led. In District 6, Wood Co. was best.

District 2, which has the highest kill, actually does not have high hunting pressure and could stand more. Dove hunting here is just beginning to draw hunter attention. This is almost entirely private land hunting, but so far permission is not prohibitively difficult to obtain. In District 5 the McClintic Wildlife Station PHA offers some dove hunting. The same is true for the Bluestone PHA, Summers Co., District 4.

WOODCOCK

The woodcock is more important by annual harvest in West Virginia than the mourning dove. There is a fairly substantial breeding population, with birds nesting in suitable habitat in every county. A survey of several years ago showed estimates as follows, on birds nesting in the state: 26,000 males, 35,000 females, with a fall progeny count of 64,000. An intensive woodcock study has recently been under way here. The present average annual bag is about 20,000 birds. Undoubtedly it could be more, and probably will be, for currently there is an early opening, in September, with a split season, the second segment in October. This gives hunters a good opportunity before the birds migrate. There are not too many woodcock "specialists" among West Virginia hunters. As more sportsmen turn their attention to this grand species, the annual bag will probably rise. Nonetheless, there is limited suitable habitat in the state.

Unfortunately, the public lands such as PHAs and State Forests have very few woodcock. District 1, in the north and the northwest panhandle, shows the highest harvest. The Canaan Valley is the hot spot here, in Tucker Co. District 6, below it in the west, is next. Here the Ohio River bottom offers best hunting. A recent survey shows Preston, Tucker, Marshall as high counties in District 1, and Gilmer, Calhoun, Jackson in District 6.

River courses in District 2 draw flight woodcock, but the kill is low. In District 5 a few birds are bagged, mostly as incidentals, on the McClintic PHA. In District 3 there is some hunting of fair rating south of Elkins. While some birds are taken in District 4, it is not considered one of the better areas.

SNIPE AND RAILS

There are seasons for both snipe and rails. But there is very little interest, and very little hunting, and in fact the habitat for both is exceedingly limited. Surveys show that probably less than 500 snipe and 50 rails are bagged annually by hunters. There might be a somewhat higher harvest, if hunters avidly sought these birds.

For example, the Canaan Valley, District 1, furnishes good snipe shooting especially when rains have left wet bottomlands. A few rails are found here, too. In District 6, when there is flooding along the Ohio, a few snipe and rails are killed, but generally as incidentals by grouse and woodcock hunters.

WATERFOWL

West Virginia's mountainous terrain does not lend itself to production of waterfowl to any appreciable extent, nor does it catch and hold many birds during waterfowl migrations. This is evident in the annual bag. During the most recent season at this writing less than 8000 ducks were harvested over the entire state. The goose kill, widely scattered and rather incidental to other hunting, is thought to average not over 300 birds annually.

Districts 5, 6, and 2 in that order represent the areas of highest duck kills, but this means less than 3000 in any District. Counties within these Districts with highest bags are as follows: District 5, over half the total for the entire District from Mason Co.; District 6, more than two-thirds of the total kill from Wood Co.; District 2, almost all from Berkeley Co.

Best waterfowling in general is along the Ohio and Potomac river systems. By Districts, here are some individual comments and spots: District 1, Tygart Lake Reservoir, Upper Deckers Creek Impoundment, Cheat Lake, jump-shooting on floatable streams. District 2, jump-shooting along the Potomac and tributaries, ducks only. District 3, so little opportunity as to be negligible, a bit of hunting at Elk River PHA. District 4, early shooting for wood ducks along Greenbrier and New rivers, late season shooting on same streams for mallards and blacks, some public waterfowling on Bluestone PHA, Summers Co. District 5, McClintic Wildlife Station PHA is the best waterfowl area in state, with thirty-eight man-made ponds offering wood ducks early, teal, mallards, blacks later. There is a resident Canada goose flock established, and more geese pause during migration, but the PHA is closed to date for goose hunting until a substantial flock builds up. Shooting along the Ohio is good at times late in season for diving ducks. District 6, hunting along the Ohio River and tributaries, but dependent mostly on weather conditions; a few geese killed in Wood and Jackson Cos.

To get a focus on waterfowling in this state, one must realize that total water expanse is not more than 150,000 acres, and that, unhappily, much is polluted. There appears to be little chance of increasing the potential waterfowl habitat in this state. The wood duck has long been the most important species, makes up at least half the total bag. A new regulation, incidentally, gives hunters reciprocal rights on water on either side of the Ohio River border between West Virginia and Ohio.

WILD TURKEYS

During pioneer times the wild turkey was present over much of what is now West Virginia, with river valleys such as the Ohio, Potomac, and Kanawha probably furnishing some of the better habitat. But indiscriminate killing of them for food—sometimes large numbers were trapped in baited enclosures—had cut down their superb abundance as early as Civil War days. Later in the century the assault on the forests by lumbering interests further depleted the turkey habitat, and flocks. From there on, during the first decades of the 1900s, the wild turkey disappeared swiftly from county after county.

Although the bird was never extinct in the state, the only remaining remnants when serious restoration was begun were discovered in two locations in the southwest. Live trapping and release of wild stock on the various PHAs and State Forests, and management on the National Forests, have brought the wild turkey back to reasonable and huntable abundance in portions of the state. Kill figures over five recent and consecutive seasons total as follows: 1209, 1587, 1334, 957, 1692.

By no means all of the state is open during any given season. Most recently most of the northern counties, excepting the northwest panhandle, and most of the eastern counties, have been open. There is a fall season, but dates differ in groups of counties. In 1966 a spring season was also initiated, and has continued up to time of this writing and probably will. Spring seasons have varied as to areas open. The first one allowed hunting only on state-owned lands, the second included federal lands (the National Forests), but later state-wide seasons have been held. A recent total spring kill, gobblers only, was 140. Fall seasons allow either sex.

District 2, the eastern panhandle counties, currently furnishes the preponderance of the kill. A late tabulation: of a total kill of 1692; 1030 came from District 2; 451 from District 3; 157 from District 4. Best counties in same survey: District 1, Tucker, with 34 birds killed; District 2, Hampshire (271), Hardy, Pendleton, Grant; District 3, Pocahontas (222), Randolph; District 4, Greenbrier, Monroe. Other Districts, not open or else negligible kill.

Virtually all of the National Forest lands are within the better turkey counties and the open ones. They offer excellent opportunities. Some of the state lands, by District, that have turkey hunting or that will have eventually, are as follows. District 1: Cooper's Rock SF; Lewis Wetzel PHA. District 2: Nathaniel Mountain PHA; Short Mountain PHA; Sleepy Creek PHA. District 3: Seneca SF; Kumbrabow SF; Calvin Price SF; Elk River PHA, this last one only fair at best. District 4: Greenbrier SF; Camp Creek SF. District 5: no fall hunts at this writing, spring poor, see "Ruffed Grouse" for public opportunities, excepting McClintic PHA. District 6: Hughes River PHA. This District has had transplants in numerous counties, but presently only a portion of the District is open in fall and only Doddridge Co. has shown birds harvested, along Arnolds Creek and Maxwell Ridge.

SQUIRRELS

The gray squirrel is the number one game species in West Virginia. Gray squirrels are distributed throughout the state. There are also some fox squirrels, chiefly in the counties bordering the Ohio River and in Monroe, Greenbrier, Hardy, and Hampshire Cos., a few elsewhere. But the ratio overall is considered to be at least ten gray squirrels in the bag to one fox squirrel. The average seasonal squirrel kill approaches 1.5 million. By Districts the distribution is so well spread that there is no truly provocative choice. Recently the total, broken down by Districts, showed the following harvest, in round numbers: District 1, 213,000; District 2, 264,000; District 3, 160,000; District 4, 318,000; District 5, 313,000; District 6, 204,000.

The National Forest lands offer good squirrel hunting almost everywhere. Prime counties in District 1 are Harrison, Monongalia, Preston. The lowlands of Cooper's Rock SF, the Lewis Wetzel PHA, and the Pleasants Creek PHA are excellent bets here on public lands. There are some fox squirrels. In District 2, top counties are Hampshire, Hardy, Berkeley, Mineral, but others are close. There are some fox squirrels here, too, along with the dominant grays. Both of the National Forests and the three PHAs here (see chapter opening) offer good hunting. The three easternmost counties of this eastern panhandle are not rated as high as the remaining five counties.

Highest kills in District 3 are in Braxton, Nicholas, Clay, and Pocahontas Cos., but all others offer good hunting. Fox squirrels are fairly numerous. The best state lands here are Seneca SF and Elk River PHA. District 4 has all counties witth excellent kills during seasons of plentiful food. Recently Fayette, Greenbrier, Raleigh, McDowell, Wyoming, Summers were the top half dozen. Greenbrier SF, Camp Creek SF, Bluestone PHA all furnish fine hunting. In all counties, the lower elevations have the best squirrel populations.

In District 5, tabulations for a late season place Kanawah Co. first, followed by Wayne, Boone, Lincoln, Logan, Mingo. Other counties are not bad, also had large harvests. The public lands furnishing ruffed grouse shooting here (which see) are all good for squirrels. In District 6, top counties are: Roane, Wood, Jackson, followed by Ritchie, Doddridge. Other counties furnish harvests at least half as large. The Hughes River PHA is a good bet here.

RABBITS AND HARES

The cottontail is second only to the gray squirrel in popularity. Annual harvest is in good seasons about 600,000. The animals are well distributed over the state. However, by far the best hunting is on private lands. Kill figures by Districts give a good clue to abundance. For the latest available season they are as follows, with the top three counties in each District also listed.

District 1, 160,000; Preston, Harrison, Marshall. District 2, 102,000; Berkeley, Jefferson, Mineral. District 3, 49,000; Upshur, Braxton, Nicholas. District 4, 97,000; Raleigh, Greenbrier, Fayette. District 5, 97,000; Kanawha, Putnam, Mason. District 6, 107,000; Wood, Jackson, Roane. All other counties of the state have fair kills of cottontails. However, as noted by the above figures, Districts 1, 6, 2 in that order show highest kills, while 4 and 5 are tied, and 3 is the lowest.

On public lands, the Pleasants Creek PHA is considered best in District 1, although Lewis Wetzel PHA and Cooper's Rock SF furnish fair sport. In District 2 the same public lands as for "Squirrel" offer rabbit hunting, but not of the quality of private lands. It is felt that cottontails could sustain more hunting here. In District 3 the Elk River PHA bottomlands have plentiful cottontails. Bluestone PHA in District 4 is another good bet. In District 5, Chief Cornstalk and McClintic PHAs are the spots for public hunting, and in District 6 the Hughes River PHA offers this hunting. Cottontails in West Virginia, incidentally, should be hunted well below the 3000-foot elevaton level.

The varying hare, or snowshoe, is also found in the state, up on the high spruce ridges and in the high laurel thickets. Though the cottontail is one of the state's best-known game animals, the snowshoe is hardly known at all. Probably fewer than 2500 are bagged annually, yet this species could furnish a great deal of sport to hunters hardy enough to go after it in the dense and snowy high terrain where it holds forth. Curiously, not a great deal is known about the snowshoe even by game men in West Virginia, but it is possible studies may be conducted.

High areas in Tucker, Randolph, Pendleton, Pocahontas Cos. are the outstanding places. The National Forest lands undoubtedly offer some of the best hunting. The mountains surrounding Canaan Valley in Tucker Co. have a substantial hare population. Other known spots: Kennison Mountain; upper Cranberry River and Black Mountain; head of Shavers Fork; Cheat

Mountain; Otter Creek and McGowan Mountain; Roaring Plains on Allegheny Mountain. There have been suggestions that the varying hare be introduced to other portions of West Virginia above about the 3600-foot elevation where it is not now known.

DEER

The whitetail, originally abundant, had all but disappeared from West Virginia by the first decade of this century. It was then estimated that the total deer population was no more than 1000 animals. Restocking was begun as early as 1923 on a small scale, and there also appears to have been an influx into the state of deer from southwestern Pennsylvania. Later a law was passed outlawing deer hunting with dogs, and as better management practices occurred the deer began making a comeback

By 1946 some antlerless hunting was allowed and by 1951 the first hunter's choice deer season was held, with a record kill of nearly 22,000 animals. It is believed that today the state deer herd numbers over 100,000 animals. A two-week season in 1966 with two days during which either sex might be taken resulted in a kill almost up to the 1951 record.

More recently there has been a return to bucks-only hunting, under revised management plans, with a resultant kill slightly over 10,000. Deer are present in all counties. In the southern counties, however, herds at this time remain small. Highest population densities are in Hampshire, Hardy, Grant, Preston, Tucker, Randolph, Pocahontas, and Greenbrier Cos. All of these, it will be noted, are in the northeast and east-central parts of the state. Presently some southern counties are closed, others have a one-week season. All the remainder of the state is open. However, because whitetails are under close management any deer hunter should carefully check prior to season to make certain of regulations, and open counties.

The latest seasonal kill figures show District 2 producing very nearly half the entire deer kill. District 3 was next, with about 25 percent, and District 1 was third, with roughly 18 percent. These three Districts thus were responsible for 8437 deer out of a state total kill of 10,364. The National Forests, the State Forests, and most of the PHAs furnish good deer hunting. In counties with lower deer populations it is believed these are increasing. The future for whitetail hunting in this state is bright.

Counties recently showing kills, bucks only, of over 1000 are Hampshire and Hardy. Of over 600: Grant, Pendleton, Pocahontas, Randolph. From 400 to above 500: Preston, Tucker, Mineral. From 200 to above 300: Morgan, Braxton, Webster, Greenbrier, Ritchie.

BEAR

The black bear, once quite plentiful here, has had difficult times for many years. Even though this is the state animal of the Mountain State, bears have been consistently hunted out of season, bountied in some counties, and without game status shot on sight commonly. For one rather recent season seventeen bears were bagged legally in the state and forty-four were known bagged illegally, in only two counties. Because of this distasteful situation, the DNR has begun a severe crackdown on illegal bear hunting, and has set aside an area called the "Back Country" as a bear haven in portions of Pocahontas, Greenbrier, and Webster Cos. where no hunting is allowed.

Latest kill figures show: District 1 with a kill of nine, all in Tucker Co.; District 2 with nine, from Pendleton, Grant, Hampshire, and Hardy Cos.;

District 3 with forty-four, from Randolph and Pocahontas Cos. chiefly but with three from Webster Co.; District 4 with a kill of fifteen, of which thirteen came from Greenbrier Co., and two from Monroe Co. Total kill for that season: seventy-seven. As this is written, only a few eastern and east-panhandle counties are open, with a split season in November and December.

Plainly, bear hunting in West Virginia is an exceedingly specialized, and localized, endeavor.

OTHER ANIMALS

Raccoon hunting is popular in West Virginia. The animals are distributed throughout the state, are on the game list, and a total of some 80,000 on the average are annually collected, mostly by hunters with hounds. There are numerous 'coon hunting clubs in the state. The State and National Forests and PHAs offer plenty of chances on public lands, and permission for this hunting on private lands is not too difficult to obtain.

Fox hunting is also popular. Both red and gray foxes are present. All counties have fair populations. Some of the best where fox hunting is most popular: Wayne, Kanawah, Lincoln. Although foxes are not protected, hunters should be aware of regulations relating on a county basis, and to other laws concerning methods and areas during closed seasons on game.

There are a fair number of bobcats, mostly in the mountain counties. They furnish some hound sport. The public forests have bobcats in scattered areas of lowland and dense thickets. Along edges of the agricultural areas in foothill and valley country there is modest opportunity also for woodchuck hunters.

REGULATIONS

Game laws pertaining to seasons, bag and possession limits, areas to be hunted, special hunts, license fees all may have numerous changes from year to year. For current regulations, and for other specific queries, write to: West Virginia Department of Natural Resources, State Capitol, Charleston, West Virginia 25305.

KENTUCKY

Kentucky immediately conjures visions of Daniel Boone, squirrel rifles, and days of the early pioneers. The state was, in fact, the earliest pioneer settlement west of the Alleghenies. On the east its border with West Virginia and Virginia is formed by rugged portions of the Appalachians. Some of the eastern mountains rise to over 4000 feet, especially in the Cumberlands. Here, and in over almost half the state, the undulating terrain is forested. Lumbering of hardwoods is still an important industry.

The entire northern and almost all of the western border with Ohio, Indiana, and Illinois is formed by the gentle meandering of the Ohio River, which joins the Mississippi at Cairo, Illinois, and thus gives Kentucky a brief border in the extreme southwest with Missouri. The southern border is with Tennessee. Within the central area of the state the land begins to slope down toward the west. At the Mississippi River the elevation is about 300 feet. In the flatter, rich western lands, and in the central and bluegrass regions, agriculture is important, with tobacco and livestock the principal crops. Thus, between the farmlands and the eastern forests, Kentucky offers habitat for game species of both field and woodland.

This is a state of only modest size, slightly more than 40,000 square miles. But it covers an east-west distance of nearly 500 miles. From north to south in its deepest center portion, from Covington in the north down to the Tennessee line, the distance is about 150 miles. Yet in the far west, due to the meandering of the Ohio River border, north-south distance is less than forty miles.

Roads everywhere are good, but in the east many wind through the rugged ridges and there are not the number of highways the remainder of the state boasts. While hunters can get to almost any spot they select by using a passenger car or a pickup truck, there are some remote parts of the east, back in the mountains, where a 4-wheel-drive vehicle can be used to good advantage. This is especially noteworthy because while Kentucky is in general fairly heavily hunted, a few sections of National Forest and other forested lands get little pressure because of their lack of easy access. Plane transport to the large cities is readily available. However, except for visitors flying in from long distances, hunters have little need for air transport here.

Population in Kentucky is rather dense, having moved well past the three million mark. The eastern third of the state has the least density. While hunting is popular, license sales run less than 10 percent of the population. An average year sees a total of about 250,000 hunters afield. Nonresidents are few, averaging only 5000 or 6000. Over the 200 years of its settlement, Kentucky hunting has seen many ups and downs in game populations. It is interesting to note that the gray squirrel, famed in Kentucky's hills since Daniel Boone appeared there, is still the most important and popular game species. There is good hunting for deer, quail, rabbits, doves, plus plentiful opportunity for grouse, waterfowl and such species as raccoon, groundhog, and fox. Turkeys are slowly making a tentative comeback.

Hunting in Kentucky has been heavily organized over many years by local clubs. And, as in all regions of heavy population, there is much private-land hunting, with most such lands posted and permission not always easily obtainable. Nonetheless, there are adequate opportunities for hunting on public lands.

Without question the most important blocks of public lands are in the Daniel Boone National Forest. Until 1966 this Forest was called the Cumberland NF. The main section of the Forest begins at the Tennessee border in the southeast, in McCreary and Whitley counties, and runs northeastward up across the state to touch the southern border of Lewis Co. Thus it almost traverses the eastern part of the state. Interstate 64 crosses the north end, the Mountain Parkway cuts across the center, and over much of the lower part Interstate 75 and U.S. 27 give ready access. Southeast of the center of this long, narrow main section of the Forest there is another large block, originally known as the Redbird Purchase Unit but now an official part of the Daniel Boone. U.S. 421 is the main artery across it. Total NF acreage is 538,777 acres. Details about the Daniel Boone NF, and a map, can be obtained from the Forest Supervisor, Box 727, Winchester, Kentucky 40391.

There is another minor block of National Forest land in Kentucky. The Jefferson NF (see "Virginia" chapter) spills across the line in the southeast. There are about 116 acres of it inside the Kentucky border. This Forest is administered from the office of the Forest Supervisor in Roanoke, Virginia.

In addition to the National Forest lands, there are numerous tracts, from a few hundred to over 100,000 acres, in public lands under varied ownership and administration. Some of these are in State Wildlife Management Areas. Others are owned by the State Division of Forestry, the Department of Highways, the Atomic Energy Commission, the Tennessee Valley Authority, the Corps of Engineers, or are military lands. All told, and counting the National Forest, there are at least forty tracts containing close to a million acres of public lands. These are spread over fifty-seven of the state's 120 counties. A pamphlet titled "Places To Hunt" can be had from the Department of Fish and Wildlife Resources, address at chapter end. It lists the public lands and locates them on a small map. Individual detail maps of some of these are also available from the Department. Most of these public lands have special regulations with which hunters must familiarize themselves.

Later in this chapter reference will be made to four general divisions of the state. These are Weather Bureau Divisions, and are called: Western; Central; Bluegrass; Eastern. By reference to the map, and attention to the following county lines, readers can easily orient themselves. "Western" Kentucky is that part of the state west of a line that runs, from north to south, along the eastern borders of the following counties: Hancock, Ohio, Muhlenberg, Logan. "Central" Kentucky lies between this line and one running down the eastern side of these counties: Jefferson, Bullitt, Nelson, Marion, Casey, Russell, Clinton. The "Bluegrass" division is in the north-central part of the state, the eastern boundary line running along the eastern edge of Mason, Fleming, Bath, Montgomery, Clark, Madison, Garrard, and Lincoln Cos., where it joins the previous (Central demarcation) line. The "Eastern" division encompasses all counties east of "Bluegrass" and the lower portion of "Central."

Accommodations for hunters are no problem in Kentucky. Lodging is plentiful along all the main highways. Campers also find many sites. There are numerous State Parks and State Recreation Areas. The National Forest, Mammoth Cave National Park, Corps of Engineers lands, TVA lands all offer camping grounds. Two booklets, "Kentucky Tent and Trailer Camping" and "Kentucky Vacation Parks," can be obtained from the Department of Public Information, Capitol Annex Building, Frankfort 40601.

Weather during hunting seasons can be of great variety. Early fall is certain to be warm. But as the season wears on the days may be balmy or crisp. Much depends on whether the hunter is along the rivers in the west, or in the eastern mountains. Late seasons are certain to be chilly almost anywhere across the state, and in some cases with a moderate amount of snow. Thus one should go prepared for the time of the year, and to some extent for the area where he will operate.

Needs in arms and ammunition are not complicated. For deer any of the standard deer calibers will do, from the old-time .30/30 to the .243, .30/06 and others that are comparable. A .22 is an excellent choice for squirrels. Shotgunners will need shot sizes running from No. 8 and 7½ for quail and grouse to No. 2 or No. 4 for geese and ducks.

It should be noted that Kentucky has a special tract within the Daniel Boone NF that is called the Pioneer Weapons Hunting Area. It contains over 7000 acres. There are deer, grouse, squirrels, and turkeys are being restored, with a vigorous flock currently in residence. This land has been set aside for use of old-time weapons only—the flintlock and percussion-cap rifles, muzzle-loading shotguns and pistols, longbows and crossbows. A pamphlet and map of the Area are obtainable from either the Department of Wildlife or the Forest Service, addresses elsewhere in this chapter. The unique PWHA is located partly in Bath and partly in Menifee Cos., not far from Frenchburg, U.S. 460.

QUAIL

The bobwhite is traditionally Kentucky's favorite game bird, and has competition only from the mourning dove in annual harvest. Depending on the quail crop for a given year, anywhere from 60,000 to 100,000 hunters harvest around a million birds. The best quail habitat is found in the Western Division, much of the Central Division, and in a few counties near Covington in the northern part of the Bluegrass Division. These—Kenton, Boone, Gallatin, Carroll, Trimble, and portions of the counties bordering them to the south— lie inside the big northward loop of the Ohio River. The remainder of Bluegrass, all of the Eastern Division, and much of east-Central are poor in quail.

Kentucky's quail habitat has its troubles, and is apparently shifting to some extent. Many marginal farms are being abandoned to brush and trees, and some others cleaned for more intensive farming. Both practices are bad for bobwhites. However, urban dwellers meanwhile buy up more small farms for recreation, and in many instances better quail conditions result. Thus, over some years the bobwhite population here has remained fairly stable. The Department sells some hatchery-raised quail to landowners willing to provide food and cover.

While by far the major share of quail shooting is on privately owned lands, there is hunting of varying quality on a number of the public blocks. Probably one of the best is the West Kentucky WMA (1), jointly administered by the state, the AEC and TVA. There are 6896 acres here, in the far west, near Paducah in McCracken Co. Among TVA lands, the Kentucky Lake Area (2), of over 3000 acres in several parcels, is fair. These are in the west, along the

KENTUCKY

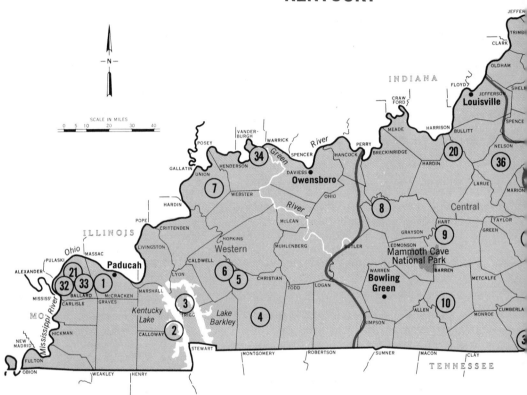

KEY TO HUNTING AREAS

1. West Kentucky WMA
2. Kentucky Lake WMA
3. Land Between The Lakes
4. Fort Campbell Military Reservation
5. Pennyrile SF
6. Jones-Keeney WMA
7. Higginson-Henry WMA
8. Rough River Tract
9. Nolin Reservoir
10. Barren Reservoir
11. Green River Tract
12. Mullins WMA
13. Twin Eagle WMA
14. John A. Kleber WMA
15. Lake Cumberland Reservoir
16. Grayson Reservoir
17. Buckhorn Reservoir
18. Dewey Reservoir
19. Fishtrap Reservoir
20. Fort Knox
21. Ballard WMA
22. Curtis Gates Lloyd WMA
23. Central Kentucky WMA
24. Daniel Boone NF
25. Robinson SF
26. Olympia SF
27. Kentucky Ridge SF
28. Kentenia SF
29. Cranks Creek WMA
30. Pine Mountain WMA
31. Jefferson NF
32. Mitchell Tract WMA
33. Peal Tract WMA
34. Henderson Sloughs WMA
35. Bluegrass Army Depot
36. Knob SF
37. Dale Hollow Lake Tract
38. Tygarts SF

218

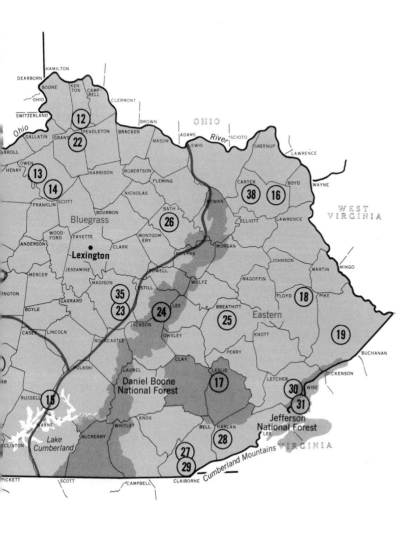

western shore of huge Kentucky Lake, in Marshall and Calloway Cos.

On the other (eastern) side of Kentucky Lake, and between it and Lake Barkley, is the huge TVA recreation area called The Land Between the Lakes (3), part of which is in Kentucky and part in Tennessee. There are approximately 100,000 acres in Kentucky. Quail hunting is from fair to good. This vast expanse is formed from land left surrounded by the two long impoundments. The dams are at the northern end of the area, on the Tennessee and the Cumberland rivers. This land is mainly in western Trigg and Lyon Cos. State 80 crosses it east-west, and State 453 runs down through the center of it. Not all may be hunted, and there are special regulations. Details can be obtained by writing to LBL Headquarters, Golden Pond, Kentucky 42231.

Also in the west, down in the southeastern corner of Trigg Co., the southwestern corner of Christian Co., and spilling far over into Tennessee is the large Fort Campbell Military Reservation (4). There are 34,000 acres here, with quail hunting. Special regulations are in force. The Reservation is easily reached south from Hopkinsville. Northwest from Hopkinsville some twenty miles via State 109 is the Pennyrile State Forest (5). It contains over 15,000 acres, with Dawson Springs the key town nearby. Just west of Dawson Springs, in Caldwell Co., is the Jones-Keeney WMA (6), with 1350 acres offering quail.

Still in the west, but up toward the northern border, is the Higginson-Henry WMA (7). Quail hunting is usually good on its 5400 acres, located in eastern Union Co., east of the city of Morganfield, which is at the junction of U.S. 60-641 and State 56. Rough River (8) is a 3000-acre tract of Corps of Engineers land at the western edge of the Central Division. It is located in northwestern Grayson Co., at Falls-of-the-Rough on the Rough River near Rough River Reservoir. State 79 crosses nearby.

To the southeast, and not far above Mammoth Cave National Park, is Nolin Reservoir (9), with 6500 acres of Corps of Engineers lands along the impoundment. Nearest town of consequence is Leitchfield, north of the Reservoir. Still farther south is another Corps of Engineers public tract, with 5200 acres along Barren Reservoir (10). A good orientation point is the city of Glasgow to the northeast, at the junction of U.S. 31E and 68. A third Corps of Engineers tract of undefined acreage is farther to the east, in the southeast part of Taylor Co. It is called the Green River Tract (11) and is on the Green River and reached out of Campbellsville.

A small WMA administered by the Wildlife Department and the Highway Department is Mullins WMA (12), with 317 acres. It has a fair quail population, is located up in the northern Bluegrass Division of the state, where as previously mentioned quail habitat is good. It is in southwestern Kenton Co. near U.S. 25. The villages of Bracht and Crittenden are in the vicinity. Twin Eagle WMA (13), also small—166 acres—is in this same north-Bluegrass region. It is in northwestern Owen Co., near Worthville, U.S. 277. The John A. Kleber WMA (14), of 678 acres, is in the same county, but in the southwestern part, near the village of Monterey, U.S. 127.

In the south, but still within the Central Division's fair to good quail range, is large Lake Cumberland Reservoir (15). There are 23,000 acres of Corps of Engineers lands open to the public here along the Reservoir. A good key to area access is via the city of Jamestown, on U.S. 127 in Russell Co. While the remaining public lands that offer quail are outside the better range, they are all on Corps of Engineers lands along impoundments, and thus are such in terrain that they are able to sustain some birds. These are as follows: the 9500-acre Grayson Reservoir area (16) near the town of Grayson, in the northeast, Carter Co.; 2500 acres at Buckhorn Reservoir (17) down in the southeast, near the village of Buckhorn, Leslie Co.; in the east-central extreme, 8650 acres along Dewey Reservoir (18), northern Floyd Co. near Prestonburg on U.S. 23-460; the 15,000 acres along Fishtrap Reservoir (19) in the southeast, out of Pikeville, U.S. 119, 23, 460, in Pike Co.

One other large and quite famous area offers quail shooting in the northern edge of the better quail habitat. This is 80,000-acre Fort Knox (20), which is located south and west of Louisville. This is under U.S. Army jurisdiction, and high game populations are well managed. There are special regulations.

Quail hunters in Kentucky can gain insight into average quail populations in the several Divisions described early in the chapter by noting the harvest by Division. Over several seasons recently the kill in the Western Division ran between 411,000 and 540,000, with approximately 18,000 to 21,000 hunters participating. The Central Division showed about 224,000 quail bagged by

19,000 to 28,000 hunters. In the Bluegrass Division 14,000 (average) hunters took between 150,000 and 200,000 birds. And in Eastern, 7000 to 11,000 hunters bagged 100,000 to 130,000. The west was by far the best.

MOURNING DOVES

The mourning dove is a most important game species in Kentucky. The annual harvest averages around one million birds. This is the more remarkable because, in a state where the mountainous eastern section has few doves, only about one-fifth of the total number of hunters shoots doves. Ordinarily about 45,000 pursue the sport. The Western and Central Divisions are about equal in kill and number of hunters. At least two-thirds of the total bag comes from this half of the state. Bluegrass is fair, and in some portions excellent. The East shows low kills and few hunters.

Certain sections within these regions show the heaviest concentrations. In a normal season in the far west there is a broad corridor taking in much of Ballard and McCracken Cos. and running southeast to the Tennessee border through most of Graves and Calloway Cos. that holds many birds. Moving east, there is a huge U-shaped corridor with dove concentrations. It is located roughly as follows. Beginning at the Ohio River and taking in most of Crittenden Co., it sweeps south along the east side of Barkley Lake and dips into Tennessee. But it now swings east, broadly covering the Hopkinsville and Bowling Green regions and thence north up across toward Louisville. The region spreading out from Louisville west, south, and east is another heavy concentration area. Still another spreads over a large expanse around Lexington, and there are pockets of abundance above Lake Cumberland. This is the basic picture of dove populations in Kentucky.

These extremely mobile birds stick to the farmlands where food is plentiful. Thus the major share of the hunting is automatically based on privately owned lands. For some time the state tried cooperative hunts on private lands, but these did not prove very successful and were discontinued. Many of the public lands have doves, but hunters must bear in mind that all are not necessarily open each season to dove shooting. One must check the hunts for a given season to make sure.

West Kentucky WMA, Kentucky Lake, Higginson-Henry, Mullins WMA, Twin Eagle WMA, Lake Cumberland, all mentioned under "Quail" have offered dove shooting recently. Others where doves have been hunted previously are: Barkley Reservoir, Barren Reservoir, Cumberland Reservoir, Fort Campbell, Fort Knox, Jones-Keeney WMA, Land Between the Lakes, Nolin Reservoir, Pennyrile SF, all of these also mentioned above under "Quail."

In addition to these, there are three other good locations not so far located. Ballard WMA (21) contains over 7000 acres in the northwesternmost county of like name. It is on the Ohio River, and is primarily a waterfowl area, reached north and then east from the village of Bandana via State 1105 and then 473. The Curtis Gates Lloyd WMA (22) covers over 1100 acres in Grant Co., far up in the northern sector south of Covington, not far from the village of Crittenden. Central Kentucky WMA (23) is the third. There are 1673 acres here, in Madison Co., which lies southeast out of Lexington. The city of Berea just east of I 75 in southern Madison Co. is near the WMA.

RUFFED GROUSE

At one time the ruffed grouse, a bird of the forests and at this latitude chiefly of the mountain forests, was all but extinct in Kentucky. Today, through careful management and protection it has become one of the important game species. The annual kill runs up to 30,000 or 35,000 birds, with good interest among sportsmen and as many as 20,000 following the sport.

The eastern quarter of the state is the prime grouse country, beginning about at the western side of the long block of Daniel Boone National Forest boundary and continuing from the south in a northeasterly direction up to the Ohio, through Lewis County. In fact, the thirty-four counties of the Eastern Weather Division contain almost all of the state's ruffed grouse, excepting a few scattered in the interior, and some that have been stocked elsewhere.

It is interesting that the state has live-trapped and transplanted wild ruffed grouse to (at present) four other locations: Pennyrile State Forest, Fort Knox ("Quail") plus Mammoth Cave National Park, and the Bernheim State Forest south of Louisville. There is no hunting as yet in transplant areas and of course there cannot be in the National Park. But it is believed that Fort Knox, where birds are apparently doing well, will offer grouse hunting shortly.

The best grouse counties are rather widely separated. Lewis in the northeast is one. But there is a slow decline in numbers of grouse as one moves southwestward down through the National Forest. The three counties considered in top-quality category with Lewis are in the extreme southeast: Letcher, Harlan, Bell. It is presumed that their high elevation may be an influence. The Black Mountain and Pine Mountain chains in these southeastern counties furnish the best hunting. However, outside the four counties mentioned there is fair to good grouse shooting in numerous places in the east.

Some of the public lands already noted are good grouse locations. The Corps of Engineers lands at Lake Cumberland, Buckhorn Reservoir, Dewey Reservoir, Fishtrap Reservoir are all worth hunting. These are listed under "Quail." The Daniel Boone National Forest (24), which is described early in the chapter, is undoubtedly the largest area of public land suitable as grouse habitat and for grouse hunting. Birds are scattered over much of it, and it is so large that hunters will be well advised to make up-to-date checks with the Forest Supervisor or with Kentucky Wildlife personnel as to best areas at any given season. By and large, the Redbird block (Purchase Unit) described early in this chapter will be best. It lies just on the western edge of the best counties in the southeast. In addition, there are many old fields here, and there is a past history of burning on this Unit, which has formed prime grouse situations. As mentioned earlier, there are grouse on the Pioneer Weapons area of the Forest.

Three State Forests, and one belonging to the University of Kentucky, the Robinson SF (25), offer grouse hunting. The small, 780-acre Olympia SF (26), is in eastern Bath Co., in the vicinity of Owingsville. Kentucky Ridge SF (27), has 11,600 acres in the prime grouse habitat of Bell Co. in the extreme southeast and is reached via Pineville, which is on U.S. 25E. State 190 enters this Forest. The Kentenia SF (28) contains 3624 acres in northern Harlan Co., also in the midst of the good grouse terrain. The town of Harlan is the orientation point. The Robinson Forest, above, is of 10,000 acres, in eastern Breathitt Co. in the central-east, with the village of Quicksand on State 15 nearby.

Two state-owned WMAs complete the public lands picture for ruffed grouse. These are as follows: Cranks Creek WMA (29) has 1288 acres near Cawood, Harlan Co., in the extreme southeast. The village location is on U.S. 421 almost to the Virginia border and the WMA is south of that route and closer still to the border. Pine Mountain WMA (30) encompasses slightly more than 5000 acres in another top grouse county, Letcher, bordering Harlan Co. on the north. This is near Whitesburg, which is on U.S. 119. This location also is on the edge of the small acreage of Jefferson National Forest (31, see chapter opening) that spills over the Virginia border into Kentucky. The Jefferson NF land in Kentucky should be well noted by grouse hunters.

WOODCOCK

Some woodcock pause in various parts of Kentucky on their southward migration. But the bird, though regularly listed in the game laws, is not an important species in the state. Some are killed, but invariably as incidentals by hunters after other game. No heavy concentrations are officially known in the state and it is doubtful that this bird is abundant enough at any time to provide more than token hunting.

WILD TURKEYS

Many years ago wild turkeys were abundant throughout Kentucky. Market hunting, cutting of forests and other habitat destruction all but wiped them out. By 1925 only scattered remnants remained. By 1946, which marked the beginning of the Department's attempt at restoration, the only known turkey range was in what had long been called the "Land Between the Rivers" in western Kentucky, in Lyon and Trigg Cos. This expanse, between the Tennessee and Cumberland rivers, became the "Land Between the Lakes." Turkeys had survived there in sparse numbers because of the isolation of the region, and because the habitat was suitable. A part of this region shortly became the Kentucky Woodlands National Wildlife Refuge.

Transplants were begun. Pen-reared birds also were tried, but as they have been everywhere these were a failure. Over a number of years about a fourth of Kentucky's counties have received transplanted live-trapped wild birds. Meanwhile the Refuge from which the first birds came has been changed to a huge recreation area, and carefully regulated turkey hunts are in progress there. It is estimated that possibly 500 turkeys may be on the LBL region now, and that the state flock is somewhere between 2000 and 3000. A very slow increase in turkey hunting area is anticipated. The supply of birds is small and not rapidly increasing.

During a recent spring hunt for gobblers only, 659 hunters on the LBL bagged 27. This same season 5 gobblers were taken in a 16-county area of the east that was also open. The wild turkey on the Daniel Boone National Forest is in fair supply, but there so far appears to be but minor interest in hunting, due chiefly it is thought to lack of skill on the part of the hunter. In coming years Kentucky may well be a prime turkey state. Large tracts—Fort Knox is one—have had birds transplanted and in most instances populations are slowly gaining.

WATERFOWL

Kentucky is by no means a top waterfowl state, but it does have some quality shooting for a small number of enthusiasts. From 9000 to 12,000 hunters bag 20,000 to 40,000 ducks annually. The goose kill runs from 1500 to 2500, with roughly 4000 participant hunters. By far the major share of the kill comes from the Western Division, with a scattering of success in the Central Division.

Probably the single most important public area for waterfowl, with emphasis on geese, is the Ballard Co. WMA ("Mourning Doves"). Kill figures here for two recent seasons on geese, all of which were Canadas: 1301, 2004. There are a very few snows and blues taken elsewhere in the state, but the

Canada goose is the predominant species.

Best general areas for geese are along the western stretch of the Ohio River, along Kentucky Lake and Lake Barkley, where the Land Between the Lakes public lands ("Quail") are located. A few geese will be found in the extreme southwest, along the Mississippi, and also between Covington and Louisville on the Ohio. For both ducks and geese there are ample opportunities, free public hunting or fee hunting with or without guides, on Lake Barkley, Kentucky Lake, and the Ohio River below Paducah. In general these spots may be considered the best the state has to offer, with the Mississippi River region second.

Ballard Co. WMA, which has already been mentioned under "Doves," is located about thirty-five miles southwest of Paducah. Reservations must be made prior to hunt, by writing or phoning the WMA, address Box 100, LaCenter, Kentucky. Presently the fee is $3 per day. Regulations may be had in pamphlet form from the Department. Other public areas with waterfowl previously mentioned are West Kentucky and Kentucky Lake, "Quail."

Others not so far mentioned are as follows: The 245-acre Mitchell Tract WMA (32) is in Ballard Co., south of the Ballard Co. WMA and near Wickliffe, on U.S. 62-51-60 where State 286 meets. The Peal Tract WMA (33) contains 1746 acres, also in Ballard Co., with the village of Barlow a nearby location point. Henderson Sloughs WMA (34) has 1300 acres, near town of like name in Henderson Co. This is on the Ohio River, on U.S. 41, just south across the river a short distance from Evansville, Indiana.

Small amounts of scattered waterfowling may be had via boat on public waters of the large reservoirs, or with guides, or from shore on Corps of Engineers and other public lands. Most of these reservoirs have already been mentioned: Rough River, Nolin, Barren River, Lake Cumberland, the portion of Dale Hollow Lake just south of Lake Cumberland that lies on the Kentucky side of the border, Dewey Lake, Fishtrap Lake, the last two in the east. Although floating the numerous rivers for ducks is not done to any extent, it could be, and can prove enjoyable and productive.

EXOTIC GAME BIRDS

Numerous imported game birds have been under study and experimentation. Several of the various pheasants, the chukar, the coturnix quail, the black francolin, the red junglefowl are among them. Some are still being studied but to date there has been no success with any species.

DEER

Whitetail deer, once plentiful in Kentucky, were all but exterminated during the early part of the century and continuing until World War II. The one best reservoir of deer population left was at Mammoth Cave National Park. After the war a vigorous program of restoration was begun. By the mid-fifties hunts were held. Most transplanted deer came from the National Park and a few refuges such as the Kentucky Woodlands, which is now the Land Between the Lakes. Some 300-plus deer were also purchased from Wisconsin for transplanting. Fort Knox and Fort Campbell began importing stock of their own. To date the great share of Kentucky counties with suitable habitat have been stocked.

Presently the average annual kill, though not high by standards in many other deer states, is moving upward and is substantial in light of the history of the species in the state. It averages around 8000 animals, sometimes a bit higher. Some 25,000 hunters compete. This indicates a rather good success percentage of about 1 in 3. The best herds appear currently to be in the upper and middle portions of the Central Division. In fact, the counties rated as the first five are here. These are, in order, Hardin, Bullitt, Meade, Edmonson, Hart. No. 6 is Owen Co., in the upper Bluegrass Division. Other top counties are in the Western Division: Ohio rates 7th, Livingston 8th, Christian 9th.

Locations of these counties show almost exactly where the best deer range is today in Kentucky. The far west is poor, and oddly, so is the far eastern mountain area. Portions of the National Forest have excellent herds. But the kill at this time does not always reflect this. Hunters concentrate in large Forest blocks, miss some that have deer populations approaching or at carrying capacity. Lack of accessibility is one reason these good spots are bypassed. Also, after many years without deer hunting, many hunters have yet to acquire the needed skill to reap a proper and possible harvest.

Certainly there is ample opportunity for deer hunting on public lands. The military lands are some of the best to date in kill percentages. Fort Knox and Fort Campbell were noted under "Quail." There is deer hunting also on the 14,600-acre Bluegrass Army Depot (35) near Richmond on U.S. 25-421, Madison Co. The West Kentucky Area, Land Between the Lakes, Pennyrile State Forest, Jones-Keeney WMA, Barren Reservoir, Green River, Lake Cumberland, Grayson Reservoir, Buckhorn Reservoir, Dewey Reservoir, Fishtrap Reservoir, all noted under "Quail," also have deer in varying numbers. Olympia State Forest, Kentucky Ridge State Forest, Cranks Creek WMA, Kentenia State Forest, Pine Mountain WMA, Robinson Forest, all located under "Grouse," also are good deer areas.

The 4000-acre Knob State Forest (36) has not so far been noted. It is a good deer tract. It is in Nelson Co. in the vicinity of Bardtown, U.S. 62 and 31E junction. Also, a 3000-acre area on Dale Hollow Lake (37), Corps of Engineers land, has deer hunting. This is in the Tennessee border region, in Cumberland Co., near Albany, U.S. 127. The relatively small Tygarts State Forest (38)— 800 acres—in Carter Co. up in the northeast, near Olive Hill, U.S. 60, is another fair possibility.

Kentucky has a small amount of hunting for fallow deer. These exotic deer have for a number of years run wild on what is now the Land Between the Lakes. Estimates place their numbers there at approximately 300. During one recent bow hunt on LBL 22 fallow deer were taken. There is also a small population on Fort Campbell. Hunters should check with the Department for seasons and any special regulations.

BLACK BEAR

There is some evidence of bears in Greenup, Carter, Harlan, and Marion Cos., but without proof to date. There is presently no legal bear hunting in Kentucky.

RABBITS

Cottontails are important game animals in Kentucky but land use has over recent years had a serious effect upon habitat and consequently upon rabbit populations. Nonetheless, the kill still averages close to a million annually, although there are some signs of a slow decline in the bag. At present the western half of the state is the best habitat. Formerly, and in fact over recent years, the Bluegrass Division was best. Intensive agriculture has apparently passed the state of forming optimum conditions there, while in the west grazing and cover balance are now better suited to raising larger rabbit populations. All of the WMAs, the Corps of Engineers lands around the reservoirs, most of the TVA lands and also Fort Knox offer fair to excellent cottontail hunting. These lands have been covered under other species. See especially "Quail."

There are a scattering of swamp rabbits in Kentucky, but they are a rather rare species, confined to bottomland timbered reaches along the Mississippi, and along the Ohio and a few tributaries from Henderson Co. westward. A few are also found along the Green River. Recent attempts have been made to transplant these large rabbits eastward. Small transplant populations appear to be maintaining themselves in Casey and Pulaski Cos. and it is felt that eventually they may become firmly established.

SQUIRRELS

Kentucky is by tradition a squirrel hunting state, and by popular vote the squirrel leads all other game. The kill is higher as a rule than for any other species, running to a million and a half in good years, with half the total of hunters participating. There are some fox squirrels, along the river bottoms of the west, and up in the Bluegrass Division. But it is the gray squirrel that provides the bulk of the hunting and of the kill. With the exception of the Bluegrass region, the entire state offers excellent gray squirrel hunting.

In Daniel Boone National Forest squirrel hunting is far out front as the leading sport. This is an excellent public-lands location. All of the State Forests, the WMAs, and other public lands covered previously under "Quail," "Grouse," "Doves," "Deer," and even "Waterfowl" furnish plentiful squirrel hunting opportunities. There are occasionally brief seasons with special regulations at the Reelfoot Lake Wildlife Refuge located in the extreme southwest near Hickman. In selecting a location, obviously large expanses of hardwoods are best, and particularly during a year when acorns are abundant.

OTHER ANIMALS

Both red and gray foxes are abundant, with the reds favoring the more open farming areas. Fox hunting is chiefly with hounds, and therefore rather specialized. Only a modest percentage of the total of hunters pursue this sport.

Raccoons are extremely plentiful, and they are also popular game with hunters, with 75,000 to 100,000 taken each year. Best general area is in the West, with the Central and Bluegrass areas fair, the East rated as good. Opportunities for hunting both foxes and raccoons on the public lands covered under other species are virtually limitless.

By annual kill the woodchuck, or groundhog, stacks up as far and away the most popular of the so-called non-game species. The estimated kill runs well over 200,000 annually. While woodchucks are well distributed throughout the state, the region of greatest abundance is in the Bluegrass Division. Because woodchucks do best in farming areas not too intensively cultivated, much of the best shooting is to be found on privately owned lands. However, the public lands covered in detail under foregoing species offer ample opportunity. Avoidance of the heavier forests and concentration on habitats good for such game as quail and rabbits will generally locate the best hunting.

REGULATIONS

Game laws pertaining to seasons, bag and possession limits, areas to be hunted, special hunts, license fees all may have numerous changes from year to year. For current regulations, and for other specific queries, write to: Department of Fish and Wildlife Resources, State Office Building Annex, Frankfort, Kentucky 40601.

TENNESSEE

Tennessee has long been famed as "hill country." Its hills are more than that; they are rugged mountains. Along the eastern border, that portion of the Appalachians renowned as the Great Smokies thrusts steeply up to 6000 feet and is densely forested. This is beautiful, rugged country. Immediately to the west the Great Valley of the Tennessee River with its numerous large man-made impoundments runs, like the eastern mountain, on a sharp slant from northeast to southwest, and beyond this valley are the Cumberland Mountains and Plateau.

The Tennessee River dips far southward into neighboring Alabama and back up in a broad U to form that state's border for a short distance with Mississippi. Then it winds in long curves northward clear across the west-central portion of Tennessee. In between its crossings of the state, and west of the Cumberlands, is the Central Basin, with much of the famed Bluegrass country. Kentucky Dam, far downstream (north) on the Tennessee River, in northern Kentucky, backs the river up until it is in its more westerly crossing of Tennessee almost entirely lake—huge Kentucky Lake. West of this dividing line the country slants gently down to the bottomlands of the Mississippi River, which forms the snake-tracking border with Missouri and Arkansas.

Kentucky is the neighbor to the north, except for a span in the east where the border is with Virginia. Across the Smokies eastward lies North Carolina, and in the extreme southeast Georgia makes contact on the south. Midway up the eastern border, and astride it, is Great Smokies National Park.

Tennessee fits a unique spot in the jigsaw of the mid-south states, as if binding a number of them together over its narrow strip. It covers a modest 42,244 square miles, yet it reaches east to west almost 500 miles, encompassing extremes in habitat that give it game of both mountain and bottomland variety, yet nowhere is the state much over a hundred miles from north to south. At least half of Tennessee is well forested. Over half a million acres of water in twenty-two large impoundments have changed the state drastically from its original appearance, and influences of these have changed the economy also. Though tobacco, cotton, other farming, and lumbering are important, manufacturing is swiftly turning the state more and more urban.

Population is up near the four million mark, but roughly a fourth of it is based on the four largest cities. There is still a vast amount of rural country, small towns, back roads, and mountain trails. Highways everywhere are excellent. Almost any hunter can reach his proposed hunting ground with an ordinary passenger car. For those who like it more remote, 4-wheel-drive is not amiss, particularly in the rough eastern portion. Air transport to the larger cities and towns is well organized. The largest of these—Knoxville, Chattanooga, Nashville, Memphis—are located almost perfectly for the flying hunter who wishes to get quickly from one part of the state to another.

227

On the average, hunter numbers are about 10 percent of the total population. During a recent season there were slightly less than 400,000 license holders. Nonresidents are few, averaging around 8000 annually. Doves, quail, squirrels, rabbits are the most popular species. There are also ruffed grouse, waterfowl, wild turkeys, deer, some black bear, and good hunting for wild boar. Raccoons, woodchucks, and foxes are also present in good numbers.

In a state of modest size and as densely populated as Tennessee, obviously most hunting must be on privately owned lands. However, the Game and Fish Commission has been extremely active over a number of years in acquiring public-use lands in Commission ownership, and in managing lands in cooperation with the State Forestry Division, TVA, the Corps of Engineers and others. At this time there are forty-odd tracts ranging in size from as little as a hundred acres to over 80,000 acres, scattered over the entire state and totaling approximately 650,000 acres open to public hunting. Hunters should be aware that not all game species may be hunted on any given tracts, that species hunted one season may be closed the next, and that special regulations apply. On some of these public lands there are special fees. A recent ruling has made it possible for a hunter to purchase a $12 permit that allows him to hunt waterfowl on the daily-fee areas designated for waterfowl, and small game on any of the others. A booklet is available from the Commission titled "Tennessee Hunting Guide" which gives the regulations and seasons for each public unit updated for the current year. It also contains a small map locating them.

The largest expanse of public land in Tennessee is in the east. Here the 600,437 acres Cherokee National Forest stretches in a comparatively narrow strip along almost the entire border, broken only in the center by the interspersion of Great Smokies National Park. It should be noted that several of the State Wildlife Management Areas that will be dealt with later are actually sections of this Forest, with cooperative management. Numerous highways reach into and across this National Forest. The cities of Bristol, Elizabethtown, Johnson City, Erwin, Greeneville, Maryville, Athens, Cleveland are all nearby access points. A map and details of this Forest can be obtained from the Forest Supervisor, Cleveland, Tennessee 37311.

Most details on the state-managed lands are easily obtainable from the Commission, but two other addresses are of note. One is for the Land Between the Lakes Wildlife Management Area. This large tract is in the northwestern part of the state, in northwest Stewart Co. It is the Tennessee portion of lands lying between Kentucky Lake, impounded on the Tennessee River, and Barkley Lake, impounded on the Cumberland River by the Tennessee Valley Authority. More of these LBL lands lie to the north, in Kentucky. Since they are TVA lands, many details may be obtained from: TVA, Land Between the Lakes, Box 27, Golden Pond, Kentucky 42231. The second address to be noted is Fort Campbell, Kentucky 42223. Fort Campbell furnishes some excellent hunting, is on the Kentucky-Tennessee line just east of Land Between the Lakes, and with Clarksville, Tennessee, the nearest city. Details may be obtained from the office of the commanding officer. The Tennessee Game Commission can also furnish information about these hunts.

Hunters have no difficulties finding lodging and other accommodations in Tennessee. Along all the main highways motels and hotels are numerous, and there are a number of hunting lodges that advertise in various outdoor publications. For campers, a booklet titled "Camping in Tennessee" can be obtained by writing the Division of State Parks, Tennessee Department of Conservation, 2611 West End Avenue, Nashville, 37203. In addition to State Parks and State

Forests, there are campsites in many areas of the National Forest, in Great Smokies National Park, on the all but limitless Corps of Engineers and TVA lands along the reservoirs.

Tennessee weather is of infinite variety. Early fall is hot in the west, balmy in the eastern mountains. Mid-fall is thrilling shirtsleeve weather in most parts of the state, but as winter advances, the waterfowler in the west or along the lakes will need warm clothing and later on there may be snow in the mountains. One should go prepared for the time of season and the portion of the state in which the hunt is planned.

No special arms are needed here, but there are certain restrictions as to types of weapons in specified counties at specified times, so hunters should peruse game laws thoroughly. Standard deer-rifle calibers, a .22 for squirrels, shotguns with No. 8, 7½, or 6 shot sizes for upland birds and small game, plus heavier loads for waterfowl, are all one needs. On boar hunts one is well advised to use a rifle of caliber at least comparable to the .30/06 and to be prepared for shots often at short range and in heavy cover.

QUAIL

The bobwhite has long been a great favorite with Tennessee hunters. Though the annual kill still averages probably close to a million quail, the bobwhite is facing more and more difficulties of habitat in the state. Clean cultivation, heavy grazing, and the planting of pines in what were once weedy, abandoned fields have drastically cut into what was until a decade or so ago some of the best quail habitat in the southeast. On the large privately owned plantations quail are often well managed. But with approximately half of the state forested, and the Game Commission managing not more than 2 percent of the total acreage, quail hunters have less and less opportunity. Also, emphasis on the public lands is on deer, turkeys, waterfowl because most of these lands are not quality quail habitat. Notwithstanding all the problems and a declining quail population, there is still some fair to good public quail shooting available. And occasionally hunters are able to get permission to hunt on private lands. Quail are found on all of the agricultural lands within the state.

On public tracts, one recently acquired is of unique interest. This covers 1700 acres bordering the J. Percy Priest Reservoir near Nashville. It is called the Percy Priest Wildlife Management Area (1) and is set aside as a special-use area, with certain season dates only for hunters under sixteen to hunt quail (and rabbits), and with other dates for bird dog (and beagle) field trials.

One of the top quail tracts for public use is the AEDC Wildlife Management Area (2). It covers 40,000 acres, 4000 of which are under water in the Woods Reservoir but the rest in fields, mixed hardwood, and pine. Bobwhite hunting here is excellent. It is located in the southern central part of the state, in southern Coffee Co., southeast of the city of Tullahoma and near Estill Springs, which is on U.S. 41 Alt.

The Barkley WMA (3) is primarily a waterfowl area, but offers fair to good quail hunting. It contains 3600 acres up in the northeast, in Stewart Co., near the Land Between the Lakes. It is on the east side of Barkley Reservoir, north of Dover, where U.S. 79 and State 139 meet.

Another spot considered among the best for quail is the 80,000-acre Catoosa WMA (4). Some of this large area is forested but there are 179 fields distributed throughout the entire tract. It is in Cumberland and Morgan Cos., in the central area and a bit east. U.S. 70, 27, and 127, plus State 62 all but surround it. Nearby cities are Crossville, Monterey, Harriman. The 17,000-acre

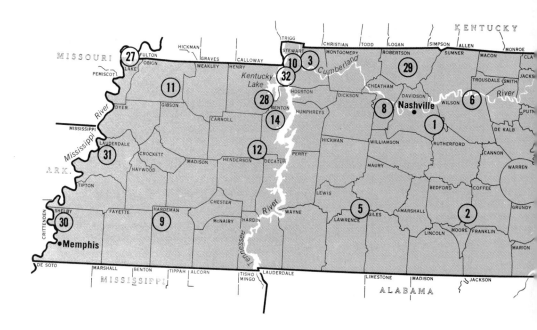

KEY TO HUNTING AREAS

1. Percy Priest WMA
2. AEDC WMA
3. Barkley WMA
4. Catoosa WMA
5. Laurel Hill WMA
6. Old Hickory Reservoir WMA
7. Central Peninsula WMA
8. Cheatham Reservoir WMA; Cheatham WMA
9. Chickasaw WMA
10. Land Between the Lakes WMA
11. Gooch WMA
12. Natchez Trace WMA
13. Blythe Ferry WMA
14. Camden Waterfowl Area
15. Cherokee National Forest
16. Kettlefoot WMA
17. Laurel Fork WMA
18. Unicoi WMA
19. Andrew Johnson WMA
20. Tellico WMA
21. Ocoee WMA
22. Tackett Creek WMA
23. Cove Creek WMA
24. Pickett WMA
25. Standing Stone WMA
26. Fall Creek Falls WMA
27. Reelfoot Lake Refuge
28. Big Sandy WMA
29. Springville Bottoms
30. Shelby WMA
31. Anderson-Tully WMA
32. Nickey Brothers WMA
33. Prentice-Cooper WMA
34. Fort Campbell Military Reservation

Laurel Hill WMA (5) has been open to hunting only for a short time. Plans are being made to enlarge it to 20,000 as this is written. While early hunts make predictions difficult, it is thought this expanse of fields and mixed hardwoods will be an excellent quail hunting location. It is in Lawrence Co., which borders Alabama and is west of I 65, not far from the town of Lawrenceburg, where U.S. 43 and 64 intersect. Old Hickory Reservoir WMA (6), with 3600 acres, is also considered a good quail tract, even though ducks are the main attraction here. It is on Old Hickory Reservoir, north of Lebanon via I 40 and then State 109. The general location is northeast out of Nashville.

Most other public tracts that offer quail hunting can be considered only fair.

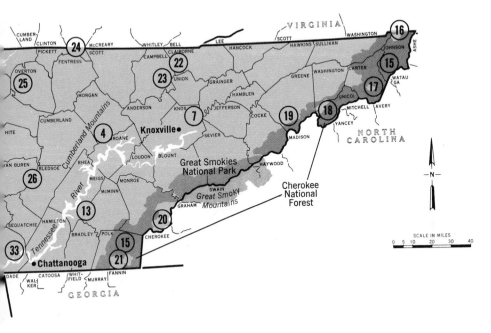

Central Peninsula WMA (7) is one. Located in Union Co., it contains 25,000 acres of rolling to hilly terrain with some fields. This country is fairly well up toward the northeast, and the unit is managed in cooperation with the Division of Forestry. The land lies along part of Norris Lake. Maynardville on State 33 is a key location point. Cheatham Reservoir WMA (8), another area managed predominantly for waterfowl, has fair quail hunting on its 2800 acres. It is west of Ashland City, in Cheatham Co., which is northwest of Nashville. State 49 is the nearby access route to the WMA.

The Chickasaw WMA (9), with 11,125 acres, also has a modest quail population, although it is mostly rolling upland timber. It is in Hardeman and Chester Cos., in the southwest part of the state, with State 100 out of Henderson giving access to the west. The Land Between the Lakes (10), discussed in opening of chapter, also offers fair quail shooting. There are 70,000 acres here, in the northeast part of Stewart Co. between Kentucky Lake and Lake Barkley. Up in the northwest, in Obion Co. and lying east of U.S. 51 between Trimble and Obion, is the Gooch Waterfowl WMA (11). While predominantly a waterfowling location it has some quail shooting.

The Natchez Trace WMA (12), with 43,000 acres chiefly of mixed pine and hardwoods, lies astride the border of two east-central counties, Carroll and Henderson. I 40 bisects the Area and the town of Lexington on State 22 is to the south. Hunting on the area is just fair, but quail hunting in surrounding counties, on private lands, is excellent. On the whole the Tennessee quail hunter who can make contacts for private-land hunts, and especially in the western half of the state, will do best.

MOURNING DOVES

By numbers annually harvested the mourning dove is ahead of the bobwhite in popularity. Ordinarily the bag is well over a million birds. Doves nest in, and migrate across, all agricultural portions of Tennessee. The western half of the state has by far the larger number, with the far west and the counties near the Mississippi River best of all. The regions surrounding many of the reservoirs also get good flights.

Most of the best dove hunting is on privately owned lands. Hunters will discover that it is not as difficult to get permission for dove hunting as for quail hunting. One reason is that dove shooting is a more stationary sport, with less chance for damage of crops by walking hunters and most of the best hunting done on harvested croplands, where doves feed on waste grains.

There is a substantial amount of good dove shooting on the public lands. In fact, most areas considered only fair for quail offer good dove possibilities. In addition, it has been discovered over recent seasons that dove hunters utilize most of the areas managed predominantly for waterfowl much more than do waterfowl hunters, and with a greater kill.

All of the public lands covered in the foregoing section under "Quail" offer dove hunting of varying quality. The plots rate about as follows: AEDC, good; Barkley, fair; Catoosa, poor to fair; Laurel Hill, good; Central Peninsula, fair; Cheatham Reservoir, fair and in fact much better than for quail; Chickasaw, fair; Land Between the Lakes, good; Gooch, fair; Natchez Trace, poor to fair, but as with quail, excellent in surrounding counties; Old Hickory Reservoir, good, with many more doves taken than quail, and more also than ducks.

The Blythe Ferry WMA (13), a tract of modest size with 625 acres in rolling uplands, is one of the waterfowl areas that offers good dove shooting. In fact, so far managed hunts have been held for only two species, doves and geese. The dove hunts were brief, three days only, but some 1300 birds were bagged. This is on Chickamauga Lake in Meigs Co. northeast of Chattanooga, the location southeast of Dayton, which is at the junction of U.S. 27 and State 60 and 30.

The Camden Waterfowl Area (14) also has fair to good dove shooting It is up in the northwest, on the west side of Kentucky Lake, near U.S. 70 in Benton Co. The small city for which it is named is on U.S. 70 where State 69 crosses.

The Cheatham WMA, with 20,000 acres, and not to be confused with smaller Cheatham Reservoir WMA, is another tract that offers fair dove hunting. There are some fields here among hardwood hills. It is near the smaller Area, in Cheatham Co. near Ashland City.

There are a scattering of small public tracts where dove hunting has been good recently. These run from 40 to possibly 250 acres. Since management of these may possibly change, it will be best to check with the Commission regarding their locations and whether or not dove (or other) seasons are being held. Most of them were set aside primarily as waterfowl areas, or access points for waterfowl hunting, but in several cases doves have become the principal target. Names of these are as follows: Candies Creek WMA; Rogers Creek WMA; Cottonport WMA; Riley Creek WMA; Goodfield Creek WMA; Soddy Creek WMA; Sale Creek WMA; Long Island WMA.

This discussion of dove hunting is quite general. The fact is, most of the public lands dealt with have specifically dated and managed hunts. In a number of instances, prepared dove fields are made ready purposely for dove shooters only, with staked shooting positions and drawings for them at least for the first days. Recently hunts have been held as follows: Old Hickory Reservoir, on fields near Barton's Creek, Cairo access, Marsay's Boat Dock, MacMillan Bottoms. On Cheatham Reservoir a field on Johnson's Creek has been opened prior to the opening of the remainder of the WMA. On Percy Priest, noted for having a hunt for youngsters for quail, a harvested millet field has been hunted on certain days. Other hunts of a special nature for doves only have been held in both east and west Tennessee. Since these may change from year to year, some are mentioned here only as examples. Hunters should check with the Game Commission well before season to learn where prepared fields or special dove shoots may be planned.

RUFFED GROUSE

Range of the ruffed grouse, often thought of as a bird of northern wood-lands, extends much farther south than many hunters realize. In Tennessee the ruffed grouse is found in portions of the midstate Cumberland Plateau, and from there eastward to the top of the Appalachians along the eastern boundary. The highest populations are found as a rule along the eastern border, with the northern Plateau region second. Ruffed grouse hunting, though pursued by a nominal number of enthusiasts who do not mind hunting the steep slopes, accounts for about 15,000 birds each season.

There is plentiful opportunity for ruffed grouse hunting on public lands, since this is a species of the forests and the stream courses of the forest terrain. The 600,000-plus acres of the Cherokee National Forest (15) offer all but unlimited grouse hunting, and much of the area in more remote sections never sees a hunter from one season to the next. This Forest, which stretches along the entire eastern border except where broken by the boundaries of Great Smoky Mountains National Park, is described in more detail in the early part of this chapter.

Three of the areas located under "Quail" have diverse terrain which makes them suitable for grouse. Huge Catoosa WMA is one, and it could probably produce more grouse than it does, if diligently hunted. Another is Central Peninsula, and the third is Chickasaw.

Earlier it was mentioned that some of the renowned WMAs are actually blocks within the boundaries of the National Forests. There are several of these that furnish good grouse hunting. In the far northeast, in northwestern Johnson Co. touching the Virginia border, is 39,000-acre Kettlefoot WMA (16). This is a sweep of mixed hardwoods in elevations up to 4000 feet. State 133 runs through the center of it. Some distance south in the Forest is Laurel Fork WMA (17). There are 10,000 acres of mixed hardwoods here, with elevations similar to Kettlefoot and numerous steep slopes. This is in east-central Carter Co., with U.S. 19E crossing to the south of it through the village of Roan Mountain. In the next county to the south, Unicoi, but also spilling westward across the line into Washington and Greene Cos., is the Unicoi WMA (18), a huge chunk of Forest land with the village of Erwin nearby on the east side and U.S. 23 and 19W passing along the eastern edge.

Southwest a short distance is the Andrew Johnson WMA (19). It lies in southeastern Greene Co. south of the Bald Mountains region. State 70 south from the village of Greeneville gives access. The Tellico region and Tellico WMA (20), of 80,000 acres, has long been known for its boar hunts (see "Boar" later in chapter), but it is also a good bet for grouse. It is below the National

Park, has all of its eastern boundary as the border of North Carolina. It is in Monroe Co., and is a very rough area of hardwood and pine mixed. Best orientation point is the village of Tellico Plains on State 68 southwest of the bulk of the area. A short distance to the northwest this route joins U.S. 411 at Madisonville. Down in the southeast corner of the state, and still in Forest land, is the Ocoee WMA (21). There are 40,000 acres here, mountainous, and with hardwood and pine intermixed. U.S. 64 crosses the upper part of the expanse. This is in Polk Co. The village of Ocoee is to the west at the intersection of that route and U.S. 411.

Several other areas outside the forest offer grouse hunting. In the northern Plateau region Tackett Creek WMA (22) is one. It contains 20,000 acres. This is rough, mountainous terrain with few roads. Recently small-game hunts were not scheduled because of lack of participation. Whether they will be reinstituted cannot be predicted, but hunters should check with the Commission. For the grouse hunter who wants to get "back in," this should be a good spot to hunt. It is in western Claiborne Co., near Clairfield, State 90.

To the south, in Campbell Co., is a small unit, the 2120-acre Cove Creek WMA (23), with fair grouse hunting. Jacksboro is a key location town. Another in the northern Plateau region is the 11,000-acre Pickett WMA (24). This also is mountainous country. It is in Pickett Co. near the Kentucky line north of Jamestown.

West and a bit south and beginning to get into the western limits of good grouse range is Standing Stone WMA (25) with almost 9000 acres. It is hilly, forested. It is north of Livingston, State 52, in Overton Co. and lies just south of the dam and south arm region of Dale Hollow lake.

Straight south and down into the central area of the state is one other good grouse spot. This is Fall Creek Falls WMA (26), with 16,000 acres of mixed hardwood, some of it rough terrain. It lies astride the county line between Van Buren and Bledsoe Cos. State 30 crosses to the north and a secondary leads from it into the Area.

WOODCOCK, JACKSNIPE, RAILS

These cannot be considered important game birds in Tennessee. A few woodcock and jacksnipe are killed each season, but most woodcock are taken as incidentals by quail hunters, and most jacksnipe by waterfowlers. It is doubtful if the total woodcock kill is more than a token few thousand, and estimates place the snipe bag at possibly 3000 average. Ratings for the hunting on a few of the public lands already covered are about as follows: Those under "Quail"—AEDC, poor for both birds; Laurel Hill, the same; Land Between the Lakes, likewise; Gooch, a few snipe; Catoosa, poor for woodcock, no snipe; Chickasaw, poor for both. Under "Doves"—Camden, a few snipe. Under "Grouse"—Tackett Creek, a few woodcock (possibly no further small-game seasons); Cove Creek, poor for both species; Pickett, poor for woodcock, no snipe; Standing Stone, a few woodcock; Fall Creek Falls, poor for both. Note that even though most are rated "poor," this should be interpreted to mean some birds are found, and thus to an avid woodcock or snipe hunter the area may be worthwhile.

Rails, in Tennessee, are only a name on the list of open seasons. There is for all practical purposes no hunting for them.

WATERFOWL

The state has some excellent duck and goose hunting, with the duck kill up around 180,000 and geese around 10,000, most of them Canadas. The goose kill is impressive. Not many years ago geese hardly paused in migration across Tennessee. The building of the large impoundments made excellent resting and wintering places for them. Kentucky Lake, and Chickamauga where the first waterfowl refuge in the state was established in 1948, are two of the best. However, most of the lakes and large rivers in central and western Tennessee carry substantial flights of ducks and geese. In addition, the Reelfoot Lake Refuge (27) up in the extreme northwest near the Mississippi River holds many ducks, and the Mississippi itself is one of the famed migration routes for both ducks and geese. There is also a federal goose refuge on Kentucky Lake where large concentrations of geese have stayed in recent years and where some hunting has been allowed to assist in breaking up the flocks. There are several other refuges on the lakes and rivers.

Regulations for Tennessee's Public Waterfowl Areas are fairly complicated. On most there are fees for waterfowl hunting, and on some reservations must be made by application and a drawing. Because such regulations change from season to season duck and goose hunters should contact the Game Commission for specific-season details about any of the areas mentioned here.

Look first at tracts described under "Quail." The AEDC WMA has some water area, and is rated as "fair" for both ducks and geese. It is estimated that kills may average around 2500 ducks, 200 geese each season. Barkley WMA is a top-notch duck spot, with river valley terrain. Duck kill on this modest-sized area may run to 1000 birds. A few geese are killed. Cheatham Reservoir WMA is another river-valley duck spot rated fair to good, and with a kill matching the one above. Geese are only incidentals. Land Between the Lakes has numerous waterfowling possibilities probably not entirely realized by hunters. Duck hunting is good, geese are killed occasionally but the area rates as poor. The Gooch Waterfowl WMA is noted under "Quail" as predominantly for waterfowl. (There is good raccoon hunting here and fair small game shooting.) Old Hickory Reservoir WMA is a good duck spot, but goose hunting is hardly worthwhile.

Under "Doves" a group of small tracts were listed with suggestion that their locations and regulations be checked with the Commission. Some of these, though small, have good waterfowl possibilities, and most in fact were set up predominantly as waterfowl areas. Here are the best: Candies Creek, ducks fair; Yellow Creek, ducks good; Rogers Creek, ducks good; Cottonport, both ducks and geese fair to good; Long Island, ducks fair, geese good.

Two others described under "Doves" are extremely important. These are the Blythe Ferry WMA, where only doves and geese are currently hunted. The goose season (recent) lasts thirty days. As many as 350 geese are taken at this 625-acre plot in a season. The Camden Waterfowl Area was also dealt with under "Doves." This is another of the important public tracts for waterfowlers. It is excellent for ducks. A few geese show in hunters' bags. Fair small-game shooting is available there, too.

There is also the Big Sandy WMA (28) near the town of Big Sandy on the west arm of Kentucky Lake. This is chiefly a waterfowl area, excellent for ducks. (Found here also, good dove, squirrel, and rabbit hunting.) Big Sandy is on State 69 between Paris and Camden. Just to the west is the West Sandy unit, called Springville Bottoms (29), near the village of Springville. Duck kill here averages almost 4500. Doves and small game are also available.

Waterfowl management in Tennessee is becoming more and more important. Undoubtedly new public areas will be opened. Periodic checks with the Game Commission concerning such should be made. In addition, duck hunters will find many of the rivers of Tennessee productive by float hunts, something not often attempted.

WILD TURKEYS

Tennessee has a moderately adequate wild turkey population, and at this time only a spring season, split into an early and late segment, gobblers only. Not all counties are open. And open counties may change. It is therefore important to check with the Commission before planning a hunt. Some seasons the kill may run as high as 600 birds. Statistics for one recent season show that on the statewide open hunt about a third of the total was bagged, while on the managed WMA hunts the other two-thirds were accounted for. In the extreme southwest, in Shelby and Tipton Cos. along the Mississippi, some high kills have been recorded. Cumberland and Morgan Cos. in the east-central area were next.

The Cherokee National Forest is a good reservoir of wild turkeys, but by and large a great deal of the best hunting appears to be on the lands managed by the Game Commission. On tracts noted under "Quail" a number of turkeys are bagged. Here are the ratings: Central Peninsula WMA is rated as fair to good. On one recent hunt forty gobblers were taken. Catoosa WMA rates about the same. On Natchez Trace WMA the first hunt was held in 1968 and results, considered against the turkey flock, were rated as fair, with three gobblers taken. Land Between the Lakes has a few turkeys, but is not highly rated. Laurel Hill WMA was recently stocked. Hunters should check as to possible upcoming hunts. On the AEDC turkey hunting is rated as good, although not a great number of birds are averaged.

On the "Grouse" lands some turkeys are found. Kettlefoot WMA is rated fair. So is Tellico, where recently five two-day hunts, with a total of 190 hunters for all, turned up fifteen gobblers. Ocoee is also considered fair, but may sometimes rate higher, with up to thirty-five gobblers collected. Fall Creek Falls also rates fair, with about one in fifteen hunters scoring. It must be remembered, however, that several WMAs not listed here may have good hunting but happen at this time to be closed to turkey hunting. Management rules are flexible, and hunters should make seasonal inquiries.

One of the very best turkey tracts is the Shelby WMA (30), not previously described. This is in the far southwest, in one of the best turkey counties in the state. It covers 12,500 acres, has had as many as fifty gobblers per season taken from it. The terrain is in mixed hardwoods and fields, with about two-thirds of the acreage in bottomland. It is in northwestern Shelby Co. north of Memphis. Another not mentioned so far is Anderson-Tully WMA (31), with 30,000 acres of bottoms and mixed hardwood. This area is just getting started with turkey hunting but will probably average as many as fifty gobblers per season. This is north of the Shelby WMA, above. The upper section is accessible west from Ripley via State 19 and the lower section via State 87 west from Henning.

SQUIRRELS

Squirrel hunting is excellent. There are both gray and fox squirrels, with the gray predominant over most timbered areas of the state and fox squirrels in lesser numbers along the river bottoms and near agricultural areas. Total kill runs around 1,300,000. This places squirrels as the most popular game animals in the state.

Squirrel hunting on the National Forest is excellent, especially in years when the mast crop is heavy. All of the WMAs listed under "Grouse" rate from fair to excellent for squirrel hunting. Grouse habitat as a rule is identical to that for good gray squirrel production.

Most of the areas under "Quail" also have fine squirrel hunting. Among the best are these: Cheatham Reservoir WMA; AEDC, where 3000 were taken, mixed between fox and gray squirrels, one recent season; Laurel Hill WMA, which opened recently and is predicted to be excellent; Land Between the Lakes, where as many as 5000 squirrels are bagged in a season; Natchez Trace; Catoosa, which annually produces several thousand; Central Peninsula, one of the best, with a recent record of 7000 squirrels one season; Chickasaw.

The Cheatham WMA (not Reservoir; "Doves") is a good bet for squirrels, and Reelfoot Lake ("Waterfowl") turns up a substantial annual bag. Two of the hottest spots for squirrels are those noted under "Turkey"—Shelby WMA, with a kill around 6000, and Anderson-Tully WMA with as high as 10,000 to 15,000.

The Nickey Brothers WMA (32), with 12,000 acres, forested and hilly, in Benton Co. near the town of Big Sandy, State 69, is one not so far listed that has good squirrel hunting. This is in the region where the Big Sandy River enters Kentucky Lake. One other, 22,000-acre Prentice Cooper WMA (33), a mountain expanse of mixed pine and hardwoods in Marion Co. down in the southeast near Chattanooga and Jasper, is also a good squirrel tract. Many of the large public blocks of land have squirrel populations away from the easy-access portions that are never properly harvested and anyone in Tennessee can find good squirrel hunting if he is willing to put out a bit of research effort and then a bit more physical effort.

RABBITS

Rabbits are abundant over all the agricultural parts of the state. The kill near equals that of squirrels, averaging over one million. The public lands— virtually all of them except the high mountain portions—have some rabbits. However, the fact that management is aimed chiefly at deer, turkey, and waterfowl, and that such vast areas of public lands are not really suitable habitat or at least not optimum habitat for rabbits, means that most of the best hunting is on private lands.

Ratings on the betters WMAs are as follows: under "Turkey," Anderson-Tully, good; under "Quail," Chickasaw, Laurel Hill, good, Catoosa, AEDC, Old Hickory Reservoir, Barkley, fair; under "Grouse," Tackett Creek, Pickett, Standing Stone, fair.

EXOTICS

Tennessee has tried a number of imported game birds. None has so far been successful, with the exception of a small self-sustaining population of ring-necked pheasants, not large enough to provide hunting, that has hung on along Old Hickory Lake for over a decade. Japanese green pheasants and one or two other strains appear to be doing well in several stocked areas but nothing can be predicted at this time. Several other exotic game birds are under study.

DEER

Originally deer were plentiful in Tennessee. But market hunting and lack of regulations decimated the herds. By the 1930s it is doubtful that a thousand deer were left in the entire state. Establishment of the first WMAs undoubtedly was responsible for the slow comeback of the whitetail in Tennessee. Meanwhile there was concentrated activity in stocking private lands and closing them to hunting until the deer could get a foothold. Today some 50,000 hunters annually look forward to deer hunting. An average kill of 7000 is tallied, and a great part of the entire state is open to hunting.

It is interesting to note that of the total kill, excluding recent any-deer hunts at Fort Campbell Military Reservation, nearly as many deer are harvested from the managed WMA hunts as from the state-wide hunts. As an example, during a very recent season the statewide hunt accounted for 2291, the managed hunts for 8892. That season the Fort Campbell kill was 2018. While there have been several heavy kills at Fort Campbell, the harvest is likely to decrease as the herd is brought under control and a return to bucks-only hunting is made.

Because deer were transplanted or stocked or protected in various suitable habitats, the places of greatest abundance are well scattered over the state. In general, however, they are about as follows. Highest populations are in the region along the Mississippi River, the valley of the Tennessee River, the Cumberland Plateau Region, along the eastern border over National Forest lands. A check of kills by county shows that this abundance pattern is followed quite closely.

The Cherokee National Forest, although with a good herd, does not always turn up high kills. Part of the reason may be that hunts are made on the WMAs—some of the best of which in the east of course are actually on NF lands. At any rate, with about a third of the kill presently coming from the WMAs and another third from Fort Campbell, most of the remainder is certain to come from private lands. And this gives solid evidence that a deer hunter's best opportunity is on the public domain.

Location of Fort Campbell (34) will be found early in this chapter. Following are some details on the other public lands. It should be noted that regulations may change from season to season. There may be closures, or new openings. In addition, special regulations are usually in effect on various WMAs. Check with the Commission when planning a hunt.

The AEDC offers good deer hunting. So does Catoosa WMA, where some 400 were recently bagged during a hunt. Laurel Hill is considered only fair. A few deer are killed on Cheatham Reservoir. For a large area, Land Between the Lakes is disappointing. On its 70,000 acres an average of twenty-five deer are taken. Natchez Trace rates excellent. So does Central Peninsula. In fact, by kill average it is one of the best spots. See "Quail" for details on all these.

Cheatham WMA is fair ("Doves"). A few are taken at Reelfoot ("Waterfowl"). Shelby WMA ("Turkeys") is very good. The same is true for Prentice-Cooper ("Squirrels"). All of the lands under "Grouse" rate from fair to good. On Tellico, for example, there was recently a 12 percent success with 350 deer taken. Anderson-Tully, noted under "Turkey," is a fair bet. Over several seasons the success percentage stayed highest on Central Peninsula, Catoosa, Tellico, Shelby. Regulations for any given season of course influence success; in some seasons with land at carrying capacity a few any-deer days may be opened.

Deer hunting in Tennessee has been steadily improving for over two decades. In 1942, only nine were legally killed in the state. Management concentrates on the WMAs that have deer. Thus hunting is certain to keep on improving.

There is a most unique deer experiment under way in Tennessee. Several years ago blacktail deer from Oregon were brought into the state and releases made. The coastal blacktail utilizes somewhat the same type of habitat as does the whitetail. No prediction can yet be made but it is possible that this heavy-cover relative of the mule deer eventually may be added to the huntable species in Tennessee.

BLACK BEAR

The black bear is not plentiful. There are a few in forest portions of the state, and a number in the Smokies. They are of course protected in the National Park, and they also receive protection on much of the National Forest. Very few counties are open. Recently only five counties of the mountain east had a one-month season. These were: Greene, Cocke, Sevier, Blount, Monroe. The bear kill is officially estimated as averaging about seventy annually. It is probably much less.

Figures for one recent season show only six taken during the open hunts, five of them in Blount Co., one in Monroe. During the managed (WMA) hunts the total was fifteen. These were bagged during varying hunts under specified regulations: still-hunting, wilderness hunting, party hunting with dogs. All were taken on Tellico WMA ("Grouse"). The next season thirty-two bears were brought in on managed hunts, thirty-one from Tellico, one from Unicoi ("Grouse"). Ordinarily only these two WMAs are open. Check with the Game Commission.

WILD BOAR

Tennessee gained fame some years ago with its managed hunts for Russian boar. These European or Russian boars came originally from stock imported by a private hunting lodge and placed in an enclosure barely across the line in North Carolina. In the early 1920s these boars escaped, and eventually extended their range across the mountains into what is now the Tellico WMA located in the Cherokee National Forest south of Great Smoky Mountains National Park. It is possible, in fact probable, that the original pure strain has interbred with feral swine to some extent even in the wilderness areas and certain that they have outside it. Nonetheless, even crosses are exceedingly wild, and can be dangerous.

Presently there is an open boar season during the month of October in Blount, Sevier, and Monroe Cos. In addition to this open hunt, there are five types of managed hunts on the Tellico WMA. These are two- and three-day hunts for which application must be made, and all include deer, bear, boar. One is for archers only, a single two-day hunt without hunter quota. Another has three two-day hunts, with quota, either sex, no dogs. A third is a single two-day group-hunter hunt, number of parties on quota (8) and no dogs. The fourth is a pair of two-day hunts, parties, with quota, dogs allowed. The fifth is called a wilderness hunt, no quota, no dogs. Applications for boar hunts must be made to the Commission on forms provided by them. Hunters interested in any of these managed hunts should first obtain from the Commission the current-year booklet, "Hunting Wild Boar in Tennessee." From 100 to 250 boars are taken annually in the state.

OTHER ANIMALS

Raccoons are exceedingly plentiful over most of the agricultural and stream-bottom portions of the state. They are avidly hunted by hound men. There is a season on them, and special seasons for many of the public lands, which have good hunting. Probably some 75,000 are bagged each year. All of the WMAs that offer open raccoon seasons have hunting that can be rated from fair to excellent.

Opossums are also plentiful, and are hunted, often incidentally, by raccoon hunters with hounds. There is a season on the opossum, too, and good hunting on any of the open-season WMAs.

Foxes are fairly abundant and of two species, gray and red. The gray is far more common than the red. Gray foxes are unprotected, but red foxes with certain exceptions have full protection. Laws should be carefully checked.

Bobcats are not common, although perhaps more so than most hunters realize, since these are secretive, chiefly nocturnal animals of wilderness areas. They are not protected, nor important as a sport species.

Woodchucks are rather abundant in much of the farming and foothill country. They are also fairly popular with varmint hunters. They are unprotected.

REGULATIONS

Game laws pertaining to seasons, bag and possession limits, areas to be hunted, special hunts, license fees all may have numerous changes from year to year. For current regulations, and for other specific queries, write to: Tennessee Game and Fish Commission, 706 Church Street, Nashville, Tennessee 37203.

Great
Lakes
States

MICHIGAN

Some years ago Michigan coined a state slogan, calling itself the "Water Wonderland." The description is apt. As the hub of the so-called Great Lakes States, Michigan is almost surrounded by the waters of four of the five Great Lakes: Lake Superior separates its Upper Peninsula from the province of Ontario; Lake Huron plays the same role for the eastern shore of the Lower Peninsula. Lake Erie touches the southeast part of the Lower Peninsula between Detroit and Toledo, Ohio; on the west Lake Michigan lies between all of the Lower and much of the Upper Peninsulas and Wisconsin.

Across far western Lake Superior is a portion of Minnesota. The only land borders Michigan has are in the western Upper Peninsula, with northern Wisconsin, and the southern border of the Lower Peninsula, which is shared with both Ohio and Indiana. In addition to the vast areas of Great Lakes waters surrounding the state, both Peninsulas, of gently undulating terrain, are cut to ribbons by streams, and dotted with thousands of lakes large and small. The state is oddly shaped, almost as if it were two, and indeed in many ways it is almost that, with the Upper Peninsula in some respects more closely allied to northern Wisconsin. The Lower Peninsula is like a huge right-hand mitten lying palm up, with the Thumb region thrusting into Lake Huron to form Saginaw Bay. Across the Straits of Mackinac, which separate the two Peninsulas, the Upper drifts off incongruously to the west, as if unrelated, and from it the smaller, rocky Keweenaw Peninsula thrusts sharply north into frigid Lake Superior.

Michigan is a study in contrasts. It is the world's largest auto-producing region. Based on this vast industrial complex flung across the southern part of the state are a myriad other related industries. Over the past several decades, an unbelievably teeming population has burgeoned here. Yet when one drives north, it is not far until the forests are evident. From here on, encompassing all of the northern Lower and much of the Upper Peninsulas, tourism, fishing, and hunting are the big businesses. Situated as it is to the north of several states less fortunate in having natural outdoor "playgrounds," Michigan for many years has absorbed a tremendous influx. Farther on, in parts of the Upper Peninsula, iron and copper have been and in some instances still are important industries, feeding the southern factories.

Sandwiched between the heavily industrialized south and the touristed lake and forest country there is a great deal of farming and fruit growing. Thus the contrasts are many, and the problems, with population swiftly growing, are many, too. Until a few years ago, Michigan was able to absorb, in its north country, seemingly endless hordes of hunters and vacationers. Today, with a population of about nine million, the great bulk of it packed into the southern third of the Lower Peninsula, and a high percentage buying weekend places in the north and racing via excellent highways into the north each weekend for recreation, Michigan is beset by many perplexities.

Yet, with an area of over 58,000 square miles, and blessed with some seven million or more acres of public lands, Michigan still manages to keep its proud reputation as a superb hunting state. Hunting here is indeed traditional. So much so that over 10 percent of the total population are hunters. Counting both deer hunters, which nowadays total almost 600,000 annually, and small-game hunters, which are about the same, license sales soar to about 1,200,000 each season. Well over 20,000 nonresident hunters visit Michigan each fall. The majority are deer hunters.

Certainly the fine highways are capable of getting hunters into the woods in a hurry. From the Ohio border to the Straits is approximately 350 miles. By traveling Interstates, it can be driven today almost without a stop. Other Interstates take one east-west across the southern Lower Peninsula, which is a distance of over 200 miles. The northern part of the Lower also has quality roads everywhere. The Upper Peninsula, some 350 or more miles east-west, has fewer large highways, but excellent access to everywhere. Even huge portions of the National and State Forests offer good gravel and sand trails on which ordinary passenger cars can maneuver. Except for a few obscure locations, special transport is not needed—except in time of deep snow—to negotiate the hunting country. The snowmobile has become so popular throughout all of the north country, however—even to problem proportions—that even deep snow does not deter hunters. Air transport for those in a hurry also is excellent. One may fly from the southern cities to most of the larger towns anywhere in the north.

Although some game species are feeling the problems of swiftly changing land use, game is plentiful. Whitetail deer are abundant, black bears are fairly so. There is a small elk population and seasons have been held. Ruffed grouse, pheasants, sharptail grouse, quail, woodcock, reintroduced wild turkey, ducks, and geese offer fine bird hunting. There are foxes and gray squirrels, cottontails, snowshoe hares, bobcats, coyotes, raccoons, and woodchucks.

Except in the heavily populated southern Lower Peninsula, there is little difficulty finding a place to hunt, even with the large number of hunters. Among the most important of the public lands are the four National Forests, totaling over 2,600,000 acres. Two of these Forests are in the Upper Peninsula, two in the Lower. In the far western Upper Peninsula is the Ottawa National Forest (1), with over 886,000 acres. It covers much of Gogebic and Ontonagon counties, the two westernmost, plus southern Houghton and western Iron counties. Main access highways: U.S. 2 and 45, State 28 and 64. Not all of this expanse is solid National Forest land. Private holdings are intermixed. Maps and information about this Forest may be obtained from the headquarters of the Supervisor, Ironwood, Michigan.

To the east in the Upper Peninsula is the Hiawatha National Forest (2), with over 839,000 acres. This is in two main blocks, but like the former, there are private holdings interspersed. The western block is about in the center of the Upper Peninsula, covering much of Delta Co., central Alger and western Schoolcraft Cos. U.S. 2 and 41, State 94 and 28 are access routes. The eastern block of this Forest was once known as the Marquette National Forest. It lies directly north of the Straits of Mackinac, in parts of Mackinac and Chippewa Cos. U.S. 2, State 123 and 28 offer access. Forest Supervisor headquarters, where details and maps may be obtained, are at Escanaba, Michigan.

In the Lower Peninsula, the Huron National Forest (3) lies east of the city of Grayling (I 75), on the east side of the state in the upper half of the Peninsula. It encompasses over 415,000 acres, in parts of Crawford, Oscoda, Alcona, and Iosco Cos. Numerous highways give easy access: U.S. 23 on the east, State 65, 72, 33, 144 all crossing.

Across the state and farther south is the Manistee National Forest (4), of 465,000-plus acres. Reading from north to south, it lies within Manistee, Wexford, Mason, Lake, Oceana, Newaygo, Muskegon and Montcalm Cos. U.S. 131, 31 and 10, State 37, 115, 55, 20, 82 and other routes offer ready access. The Supervisor for both these National Forests can be contacted for maps and details at Cadillac, Michigan.

In addition to the National Forests, Michigan is perhaps richer in State Forest lands than any other state in the Union. To avoid confusion for those acquainted with these lands, they have recently been to some extent consolidated so that by numbers there are less than in previous years. The Upper Peninsula contains fifteen State Forests, total acreage 1,861,092. The northern half of the Lower Peninsula, that is, the portion north of Saginaw Bay (Bay City) and a line drawn west across the state, contains another fifteen State Forests, with combined acreage of 1,890,902. These Forests will be located and dealt with under species involved.

Even this is by no means all of the public lands. There are at least sixty-three tracts ranging from several hundred to over 43,000 acres, state owned, that are either all or in part open to hunting. The bulk of these are distributed throughout the more heavily populated south, and in fact almost all are within the Lower Peninsula. These fall under several categories, and will be mentioned later: State Game Areas, State Wildlife Areas, State Wildlife Research Centers. A map is available from the Department of Natural Resources (until recently the Department of Conservation) showing the locations of all of the above. The address is given at chapter end.

As this is written, the Cropland Adjustment Program, which has diverted many farmland acreages into conservation uses and to public hunting grounds, is having difficulties. Whether or not the over a quarter-million acres in the program at this time in Michigan will continue so is not predictable. However, much of it has been in the populated sections and hunters are well advised to check. Agricultural Stabilization and Soil Conservation Services can locate such tracts and advise about the current situation. There are also numerous commercial forests on which public hunting may be had. The DNR can assist in locating these.

Over the past season there has been a program for organizing farmers into cooperative public-hunt-club groups. This program, urged by the DNR, has had some success and is most important in the southern part of the state. Adjoining farmers meet and decide which of their holdings they will pool as a cooperative hunting club. These lands they enroll with the DNR, which gives them signs so that the boundaries may be properly posted. The farmers then issue free tickets to hunters, but can limit number of hunters to whatever they decide will not overcrowd the lands. The scheme in one recent season brought almost 100,000 acres of farmland in the densely populated south into public shooting. Interested hunters should check the status of this co-op plan. By and large, however, with the vast amounts of National and State lands there is little need to search further. Most hunters have fewer problems that way. On private farmlands, even in the north where population is less dense, gaining permission to hunt is not easy.

Accommodations for hunters are numerous. The entire state is geared to tourism. Hotels, motels, camps, lodges are everywhere, and of course after the summer tourist season there is in general during hunting seasons an almost

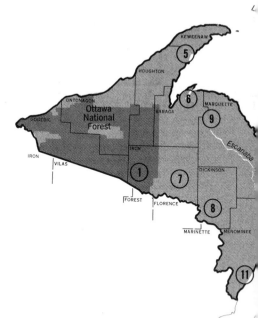

SCALE IN MILES
0 5 10 20 30 40 50 60

KEY TO HUNTING AREAS

1. Ottawa NF
2. Hiawatha NF
3. Huron NF
4. Manistee NF
5. Mishwabic SF
6. Baraga SF
7. Iron Range SF
8. Sturgeon River SF;
   Ford River SF
9. Michigamme SF;
   Escanaba River SF
10. Bay de Noc SF
11. Menominee SF
12. Manistique River SF
13. Grand Sable SF
14. Lake Superior SF;
    Tahquamenon
    River SF
15. Mackinac SF;
    Munuscong SF
16. Black Lake SF
17. Hardwood SF
18. Jordan River SF
19. Pigeon River SF
20. Thunder Bay River SF
21. Betsie River SF
22. Fife Lake SF
23. Pere Marquette SF
24. AuSable SF
25. Houghton Lake SF
26. Kalkaska SF
27. Oscoda SF
28. Ogemau SF

29. Chippewa River SF
30. Tittabawassee SF
31. Rogue River SGA
32. Stanton SGA
33. Tuscola SGA;
    Vassar SGA
34. Vestaburg SGA
35. Allegan SGA
36. Barry SGA
37. Small Cass City SGA
38. Dansville SGA
39. Deford SGA
40. Edmore SGA
41. Flat River SGA
42. Gratiot-Saginaw SGA
43. Gregory SGA
44. Langston SGA
45. Little Beaver Islands
    SGA
46. Unadilla SWA
47. Cusino SWRC
48. Houghton Lake SWRC
49. Gourdneck SGA
50. Lapeer SGA
51. Oak Grove SGA
52. Pointe Mouille SGA
53. Port Huron SGA
54. Sharonville SGA
55. Fish Point SWA
56. St. Clair Flats SWA
57. Wildfowl Bay SWA
58. Rose Lake SWRC
59. Petersburg SGA

60. Shiawassee River
    SGA
61. Backus Creek SGA
62. Betsie River SGA
63. Crane Pond SGA
64. Erie SGA
65. Grand Haven SGA
66. Haymarsh Lake SGA
67. Lowell SGA
68. Manistee River SGA
69. Maple River SGA
70. Martiny Lake SGA
71. Minden City SGA
72. Muskegon SGA
73. Pentwater River SGA
74. Petobego SGA
75. Lost Nation SGA
76. Portland SGA
77. Rush Lake SGA
78. Three Rivers SGA
79. Tobico Marsh SGA
80. Nayanquing Point SWA
81. Quanicassee SWA
82. Wigwam Bay SWA
83. Sanilac SGA
84. Pere Marquette SGA
85. Cannonsburg SGA
86. Chelsea SGA
87. Fulton SGA
88. Middleville SGA
89. Murphy Lake SGA

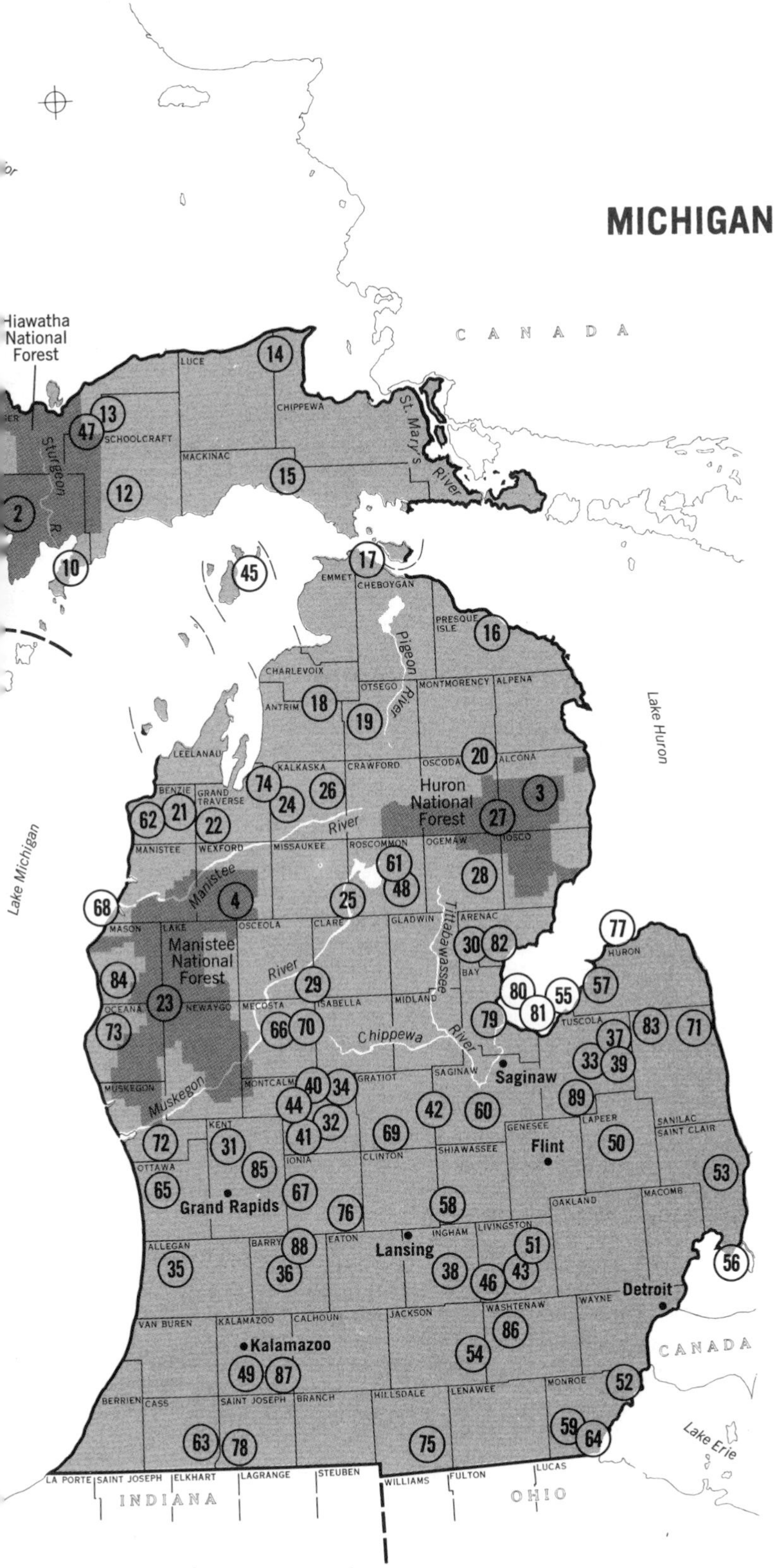
MICHIGAN
CANADA
Hiawatha National Forest
LUCE
CHIPPEWA
SCHOOLCRAFT
MACKINAC
Sturgeon R.
St. Mary's River
EMMET
CHEBOYGAN
PRESQUE ISLE
CHARLEVOIX
OTSEGO
MONTMORENCY
ALPENA
ANTRIM
Pigeon River
Lake Huron
LEELANAU
KALKASKA
CRAWFORD
OSCODA
ALCONA
BENZIE
GRAND TRAVERSE
Huron National Forest
MANISTEE
WEXFORD
MISSAUKEE
ROSCOMMON
OGEMAW
IOSCO
Manistee River
Lake Michigan
MASON
LAKE
OSCEOLA
CLARE
GLADWIN
ARENAC
Tittabawassee River
Manistee National Forest
HURON
BAY
OCEANA
NEWAYGO
MECOSTA
ISABELLA
MIDLAND
TUSCOLA
Chippewa River
MUSKEGON
Muskegon
MONTCALM
GRATIOT
SAGINAW
Saginaw
SANILAC
SAINT CLAIR
KENT
GENESEE
LAPEER
OTTAWA
IONIA
CLINTON
SHIAWASSEE
Flint
Grand Rapids
OAKLAND
MACOMB
ALLEGAN
BARRY
EATON
INGHAM
LIVINGSTON
Lansing
Detroit
WAYNE
WASHTENAW
VAN BUREN
KALAMAZOO
CALHOUN
JACKSON
Kalamazoo
CANADA
BERRIEN
CASS
SAINT JOSEPH
BRANCH
HILLSDALE
LENAWEE
MONROE
Lake Erie
LA PORTE
SAINT JOSEPH
ELKHART
LAGRANGE
STEUBEN
WILLIAMS
FULTON
LUCAS
INDIANA
OHIO
2 3 4 10 12 13 14 15 16 17 18 19 20 21 22 23 24 25 26 27 28 29 30 31 32 33 34 35 36 37 38 39 40 41 42 43 44 45 46 47 48 49 50 51 52 53 54 55 56 57 58 59 60 61 62 63 64 65 66 67 68 69 70 71 72 73 74 75 76 77 78 79 80 81 82 83 84 85 86 87 88 89

endless choice. It is wise, however, to make reservations ahead for openings such as deer season. In the more popular areas there is always a large influx. For those who may wish to camp, and this is exceedingly popular in Michigan, there are hundreds of possibilities. A "Michigan Campground Directory" can be obtained from the Department of Natural Resources. State Parks are numerous and well equipped, there are scores of sites in State and National Forests, and at Public Fishing Access Sites.

Weather throughout the hunting season runs the gamut. Nights will invariably be crisp, with light frosts, even in mid-September. But during that month and October days are as a rule lovely, with a light wool shirt and a hunting vest all that is needed except for dawn and dusk, when a jacket must be added. Later, however, during deer season, there is usually snow and occasionally the cold is severe. Clothing should be on hand to fit the occasion, and footwear should be insulated and waterproof. Late in the season, as for bobcat hunting or hunting for snowshoe hares in the north, it is often impossible to get around in the woods without snowshoes, if one intends to leave the now-popular snowmobile trails.

Guides are not much used in Michigan. There are a few who cater to bear hunters, or to winter bobcat and coyote hunters. In general, however, none is needed. In all of the north, in both Peninsulas, a hunter should carry a compass and know how to use it. The woods are dense, and there are few long-view vantage points of terrain. Guns and ammunition required are quite standard. Any of the popular calibers such as .30/06, .243, .270 are perfectly adequate for deer and the occasional bear. Bird hunters will need shot size No. 7½ as a standard for all uplanders, with smaller or larger shot as desired for ruffed grouse, woodcock, and pheasant. While bird shot is fine for cottontails, most hunters favor heavier shot such as No. 4 for snowshoe hares. These also do well on ducks, but for geese short-magnum 2s are better. The .22 rifle is a handy arm, too, for small game.

Before going on to individual species, it should be explained that for season and harvest purposes Michigan has for many years been divided into three Zones. There is some possibility that there may be changes in divisions for management purposes, but for ease of reference here we will use the Zones established as this is written. Zone 1 contains the entire Upper Peninsula. Zone 2 is the northern half, roughly, of the Lower Peninsula, bounded on the south by a line that runs from the Lake Michigan shore near Muskegon east across to a bit north of Bay City on Saginaw Bay. This is not an exact description but used only for chapter purposes. Hunters should check regulations precisely. Zone 3 is the remainder of the Lower Peninsula below this line. These Zones are split into Districts, which are not important here, and then for certain purposes, such as antlerless deer seasons and permits, there are numbered Areas. These should be checked on a DNR map furnished as part of the regulations for such seasons.

RUFFED GROUSE

The ruffed grouse is the most important native upland game bird in Michigan. Cutting of the original virgin forests during the last century did much to assist the species, because it thrives on edge cover. The introduced pheasant eventually caught the interest of more hunters, but even though ruffed grouse everywhere are highly cyclic, having drastic ups and downs of population, the grouse has remained with a firm foothold while the pheasant, once tremendously abundant in the south, has declined. Today, though less than half as many sportsmen hunt ruffed grouse as hunt pheasants, the grouse kill exceeds that of the pheasant.

Ruffed grouse are forest and woodland birds, and are far more abundant in the two northern Zones therefore than in the south. Nonetheless, there are a fair number in Zone 3. Over recent years, estimated kills there have averaged from 80,000 to 100,000 birds. Zone 1, the Upper Peninsula, and Zone 2, the northern half of the Lower Peninsula, show annual harvest almost identical. Each, over a period of years, has tallied from slightly below to somewhat above 200,000 grouse. Because of the vast amount of public land in these Zones, it really makes little difference where one hunts. Areas along the stream courses, where alders and underbrush grow and food is abundant, are favorite grouse haunts. It is noteworthy that the total grouse kill of an average one-half million annually places Michigan as perhaps the best ruffed grouse state in the Union.

The four National Forests, which have already been located in the front of this chapter, all offer excellent grouse shooting. Of the four, the three farthest north usually furnish the higher kills. Quite often the Huron NF is exceptional, and the Great Lakes shore portions of the Hiawatha NF in the Upper Peninsula likewise. Inland lake shores, openings and stream courses of the far-west Ottawa NF are also excellent.

Because grouse populations fluctuate widely, hunters should be aware that a low cycle in the western Upper Peninsula does not necessarily mean the same situation will occur in the Lower Peninsula. Thus it is an excellent idea, in this state with far-flung grouse opportunities, to make a last-minute fall check with the Department, or local conservation officers, to establish the grouse population of the selected hunting territory. This applies of course to the State Forests as emphatically as to the National Forests. The State Forests are, in fact, among the finest grouse covers in the state, and just possibly in the entire nation.

Because these Forests are so numerous, they will be noted here by Zones, by the county or counties which contain the individual Forests, and by acreage. All State Forests in Michigan offer good grouse hunting.

Beginning in the western Upper Peninsula, Zone 1, the Mishwabic SF (5) has a total of 61,000-plus acres, spread over three counties: Keweenaw, which is the wild tip of the far-north Keweenaw Peninsula, Ontonagon, and Houghton. About two-thirds of this Forest is in Houghton Co. Just to the east, the Baraga SF (6) contains 67,588 acres in Baraga Co., a beautifully wild and sparsely settled region on the south shore of Lake Superior. Iron Range SF (7) is for all practical purposes in Iron Co. to the south. Only a few acres overlap into a neighboring county. There are over 78,000 acres in this one, in a wilderness area of many lakes and streams. To the southeast, in Dickinson Co., which like Iron borders Wisconsin, there are two State Forests. These are Sturgeon River SF with 64,000-plus acres and Ford River SF (8) with almost 153,000. This is an excellent grouse county, although some of it is dense and virtually roadless, as are portions of areas previously mentioned.

Marquette Co., a very large county north of the above, fronting on the south Lake Superior shore and with the city of Ishpeming as a central point, has two large State Forests: Michigamme, with over 116,000 acres in a handsome wilderness setting, and Escanaba River (9), almost 142,000 acres of the same. These are excellent bets for grouse, but hunters should expect vast stretches of roadless wilderness area. Farther east, in the narrowed center of the Upper Peninsula north of Big Bay de Noc in northern Lake Michigan, there is the Bay de Noc SF (10), with about 55,000 acres in Delta Co., and another 24,000 north across the line in Alger Co. South, in Menominee Co., which borders Wisconsin and fronts on Green Bay of northwestern Lake Michigan, there is the almost 90,000-acre Menominee SF (11). Then, back to the north and east, past the first block of Hiawatha NF and in Schoolcraft Co., there is the Manistique River SF (12) with slightly under 142,000 acres. All of the stream courses here offer good grouse shooting.

In this same general region, partly in Alger but chiefly in Schoolcraft Co., is the 204,000-plus-acre Grand Sable SF (13). Still farther east, and taking in frontage on Lake Superior, are two Forests, each lying partly in two counties: Chippewa and Luce. These are the 175,749-acre Lake Superior SF and the 187,355-acre Tahquamenon River SF (14). Both are fine bets for ruffed grouse. So, also, are two others south of these, fronting on northern Lake Michigan and Lake Huron, the nearly 180,000-acre Mackinac SF in county of same name and the 120,000-plus Munuscong SF (15) lying in Chippewa and Mackinac Cos. This is one of the best grouse locations in the Upper Peninsula.

Now moving down into Zone 2, the northern half of the Lower Peninsula, there are five State Forests here that are considered among the finest grouse covers extant. These are: Black Lake SF (16), in Cheboygan, Mackinac, and Presque Isle Cos., with over 146,000 acres total; Hardwood SF (17), in Cheboygan and Emmet Cos. with approximately 188,000 acres; Jordan River SF (18), Antrim and Charlevoix Cos. totaling over 85,000 acres; Pigeon River SF (19), probably the cream of the grouse cover in Michigan, with better than 90,000 acres replete with excellent stream courses, in Otsego Co.; Thunder Bay River SF (20), over 176,000 acres in Montmorency and Alpena Cos.

On the west side of the state, below Traverse City and Grand Traverse Bay, three Forests are located. The Betsie River SF (21), 86,272 acres, is chiefly in Benzie Co., but overlaps broadly also into Leelanau and Manistee Cos. Fife Lake SF (22) lies in Grand Traverse and Wexford Cos., contains over 103,000 acres. And the Pere Marquette SF (23) has tracts totaling better than 60,000 in Lake and Oceana Cos. While there is good grouse hunting here, this is beginning to get south far enough so that bird populations are usually thinner than farther north. A very arbitrary rule of thumb places the cream of the grouse hunting north of State 55, which crosses east-west from Tawas City on the east to Houghton Lake, central, and Manistee on Lake Michigan.

The AuSable SF (24) is in the above good grouse region, north of Houghton Lake and surrounding Grayling, with 152,000-plus acres in Crawford Co. Houghton Lake SF (25) has over 282,000 acres in Missaukee and Roscommon Cos., and the Kalkaska SF (26) lies to the immediate northwest, with better than 138,000 acres in Kalkaska Co. Back across the state to the east, there is the nearly 78,000-acre Oscoda SF (27), in Alcona, Iosco, and Oscoda Cos., and below it and east of Houghton Lake the 80,491-acre Ogemau SF (28), lies mostly in Ogemau Co., but with about 9000 acres in Iosco Co.

Once again below the State 55 line, there are two more State Forests. The Chippewa River SF (29) comprises 71,538 acres in four counties: Clare, Isabella, Mecosta, Osceola. These tracts are west of the center of the state. I 75 runs north-south down the approximate center and is a good orientation route. It used to be U.S. 27. The Tittabawassee SF (30) is the last one of the Forests, lies east of center, in Arenac, Bay, Gladwin, and Midland Cos., with over 151,000 acres.

The picture one should form, from all the foregoing, including the descriptions of the National Forests, is that Zones 1 and 2 in Michigan contain almost as much public as private land. There is no reason in these Zones to ask permission on private lands. The hunting is usually better on the public acreages.

There are a number of State Game Areas and others that offer ruffed grouse hunting. These are worth noting, for most are in Zone 3, the southern Zone, and thus closer to the region of dense population. Some of these furnish surprisingly good shooting. Rogue River SGA (31), 5260 acres, is north of Grand Rapids, in northwestern Kent Co. near Kent City. Stanton SGA (32), almost 4000 acres, is to the east, near Stanton, State 66. Tuscola SGA (33), over 8000, is in the Thumb region, southeast of Bay City, near Caro, State 81. Beside it is Vassar SGA, outside town of like name, with over 3000 acres. Vestaburg SGA (34), about 1500 acres, is back to the west, and northeast of the Stanton SGA, at village of Vestaburg near State 46.

Allegan SGA (35) used to be listed as a State Forest, contains over 43,000 acres and is partly refuge. It is on the lower west side of the state, central Allegan Co., near city of like name, with State 40 and 89 access. Next county east is Barry, with the 14,741-acre Barry SGA (36), west of Hastings, with State 37 and 43 access. Small Cass City SGA (37) with 723 acres is in the Thumb, in northeast Tuscola Co., near town of like name, State 81. Dansville SGA (38), with over 4000 acres, is southeast of Lansing and Mason, Ingham Co. and south of Dansville, State 36. Deford SGA (39), almost 10,000, is back up in the Thumb, and near the several others already mentioned; it is east of Caro, south of Cass City, near village of Deford. Edmore SGA (40), 2319 acres, is back in the center of the state in this Zone, near town of like name, State 46, and briefly north of the aforementioned Stanton SGA. South of Stanton and Edmore, near the cities of Belding and Greenville, State 57 and 91, is the 10,000-acre Flat River SGA (41).

To the east, on the border between Gratiot and Saginaw Cos. and lying southwest of the city of Saginaw, is the nearly 13,000-acre Gratiot-Saginaw SGA (42). Several counties south, near Plainfield, southwest Livingston Co. and State 36, is 2440-acre Gregory SGA (43). Again back in the central area and near the cluster of SGAs around Stanton, is the Langston SGA (44), 2862 acres near village of same name, State 91, Montcalm Co. Last among the SGAs with ruffed grouse shooting is one of the best, and most remote. This is the Little Beaver Islands SGA (45). It comprises several islands in northern Lake Michigan, lying in the vicinity of large Beaver Island. The SGA islands are High, Garden, Hog, South Fox. Access is by charter plane from the mainland to Big Beaver and thence via guide and boat, or via ferry from Charlevoix on the mainland to St. James on Beaver Island and thence via guide and boat. This is rough, big water and not for small craft, and distances are long. Hunting here is of the wilderness variety, but exceedingly interesting.

One of the State Wildlife Areas offers grouse shooting. This is Unadilla SWA (46), with about 900 acres, in the southwestern corner of Livingston Co., down in Zone 3. It is near the Gregory SGA noted above, and near the village of Unadilla. There are also two State Wildlife Research Centers with ruffed grouse. One is Cusino SWRC (47), in the central Upper Peninsula near the village of Shingleton, intersect of State 28 and 94. It has approximately 1600 acres. Not all of it is open to hunting. The second is the nearly 12,000-acre Houghton Lake SWRC (48), also closed in part, near lake of same name, Zone 2, Roscommon Co.

SPRUCE GROUSE

There are a few spruce grouse in Michigan. Most are in northern portions of the Upper Peninsula, in dense spruce stands. Some, however, are in Oscoda and Crawford Cos., in the Lower Peninsula. This bird is not legal game and is fully protected. Because ruffed grouse hunters may see an occasional spruce grouse, they should be aware of them and learn to identify them. They are comparable in size to the ruffed grouse, but generally appear darker in overall color and are much tamer.

PHEASANT

Ringnecks were brought into Michigan many years ago. They began to be common in the Thumb region and across southern Michigan in the 1920s, and from then until after World War II Michigan's Zone 3 pheasant hunting was excellent. Farms were small, fencerows and swales numerous. Habitat was ideal. The pheasant quickly became the most important game bird in the state, even though heavy concentrations were restricted to the southern half, approximately, of the Lower Peninsula. The kill remained high even during postwar years when clean farming practices and zooming human population levels were working against the pheasant. Primarily this was because hunter numbers also skyrocketed. Presently, however, it is obvious that Michigan pheasants are in trouble. Popular belief is that foxes are decimating the flocks. Predation has been the excuse for pheasant decline in many states. However, changing land use is responsible for pheasant problems almost everywhere, and unquestionably is in Michigan.

As late as the early 1960s pheasant kill ran around a million birds. The all-time high was in 1944, with 1,400,000. Although there have been spurts of hope during years of good nesting since, the overall picture is one of steady decline. During one recent season, the kill was around 400,000. Up until then, hunter numbers had held fairly stable. Now, however, because of poor hunting, hunter numbers also have slipped. That season in question, there were about 376,000 hunters.

Presently experiments are under way to introduce Korean pheasants, which it is believed may do better under today's conditions in Michigan than the ringneck. There is also experimentation on a modest scale with the Hungarian partridge, which could possibly help to fill in empty spots in the pheasant range.

Even with the general picture rather bleak, there is still some good pheasant shooting in Michigan. While private lands are difficult, the co-op system noted early in the chapter is some relief. However, today some of the best shooting is on public lands, since these are managed for game. The Dansville SGA ("Grouse") is a good spot. Just south of Kalamazoo in the southwest part of the state is Gourdneck SGA (49), with about 2000 acres offering pheasant hunting. Lapeer SGA (50), north of city of like name, State 24, Lapeer Co., has 6736 acres. Oak Grove SGA (51), with about 1800, is to the southwest, near like-named village in Livingston Co. Pointe Mouille SGA (52), with over 2700 acres, is primarily a waterfowl operation, and is partly refuge, but does have good pheasant hunting. It is located on the Lake Erie shore in southeastern Michigan, between Detroit and Monroe. The 6000-plus-acre Port Huron SGA (53) is in excellent pheasant range on up the shore, inland from the city of Port Huron, eastern St. Clair Co., with access via U.S. 25 and State 51. Sharonville SGA (54) has well over 2000 acres between Ann Arbor and Jackson, on the line between Jackson and Washtenaw Cos.

Three of the State Wildlife Areas devoted chiefly to waterfowl have pheasants also. Fish Point SWA (55), 3035 acres, partly refuge, on the southeast shore of Saginaw Bay near Sebewaing, State 25, is one. The 6597-acre St. Clair Flats SWA (56), partly refuge, is another, located along the northeast shore of Lake St. Clair between Detroit and Port Huron. Last is Wildfowl Bay SWA (57), also partly refuge, with about 1500 acres. This is north along the Saginaw Bay shore a short distance above Fish Point. Of the State Wildlife Research Centers, one, Rose Lake SWRC (58), offers pheasants. It contains 3261 acres northeast of Lansing.

To get an overall picture of pheasant range, kill figures for the Zones are enlightening. During the high-kill years of an average million birds total, all but about 75,000 on the average came from Zone 3. The remainder were from the lower fringes of Zone 2. During a recent season when total kill was 404,720, 31,710 came from Zone 2—almost entirely the lower portion of it—and 371,830 came from Zone 3. For many years the Thumb region has been the prime pheasant range. There is a small self-sustaining pheasant population in the Upper Peninsula along the west side of northern Lake Michigan. Recent regulations have limited hunting to southern Menominee Co. and southwestern Delta Co. below the Escanaba River. Pheasants were first stocked here in 1940, with later additions. The kill is not high.

QUAIL

Until a few years ago the bobwhite quail was on the songbird list in Michigan and fully protected. Since 1965 there have been seasons, but these are presently restricted to a few counties—currently ten—in the southeast, the area covering territory from Lansing and Fenton south to the Ohio border, plus a couple of counties to the west bordering Indiana. Quail are not very plentiful, and season limits are as low as 12 birds, with a daily bag of 4. The theory behind these token quail seasons is that the birds are marginal here. They do not become more abundant, whether hunted or not. Thus a small harvest does no harm.

Most quail hunting is on privately owned farmlands, by invitation. Hunters who are acquainted with landowners in the open area who have quail on their lands occasionally obtain permission. But this is not easy otherwise. Only two public tracts offer huntable quail populations at the present time. These are the 435-acre Petersburg SGA (59) near village of like name in the southeasternmost county, Monroe, and the Sharonville SGA southeast of the city of Jackson, Jackson Co., which was noted under "Pheasant."

SHARPTAIL GROUSE AND PRAIRIE CHICKEN

At one time both of these birds had substantial populations in several regions of Michigan. The future, at least for the sharptail, looked bright. Today the prairie chicken, which appeared in modest and huntable numbers in parts of the Upper Peninsula some years ago, is considered entirely gone there. And in the Lower Peninsula they are known to exist only in four of the northern counties, with fewer than fifty cocks recently checked during spring dancing-ground counts, in ten small counties. Prairie chickens here are probably on their way to extinction and are fully protected.

Sharptail grouse in the Lower Peninsula are in much the same situation, with only five known colonies in four counties. There has been no open season in the Lower Peninsula since 1963 and there is no present prospect that there ever will be. In the Upper Peninsula sharptails, though not as abundant as they were some years ago, have remained fairly stable in population for the past decade. Portions of the eastern Upper Peninsula, the eastern islands such as Drummond, Neebish, Sugar in northern Lake Huron have fair populations, and for many years the Seney area and west to Shingleton, State 28 and Schoolcraft Co., has had a good number of birds. Other colonies of good size are in the westernmost counties.

However, game men have established that the balance is somewhat precarious, that open seasons appear to affect sharptail populations, and that with closed seasons they make a good comeback. As this is written, Drummond Island, one of the best sharptail spots, is closed. So are the other nearby islands, and a number of the western Upper Peninsula counties. Any of these may be reopened as bird populations dictate. But planning a Michigan sharptail hunt requires a careful check of the regulations for the season in question. There are not enough birds to allow a high kill, regardless. Recently 2 a day and 8 in season have been the rule. An average, estimated season kill is around 1000 birds. Current best sharptail populations are in Alger, Marquette, and Ontonagon Cos. in the Upper Peninsula.

WOODCOCK

Michigan offers some of the finest woodcock hunting to be found on the continent. The woodcock is also growing in popularity, with at least 85,000 or more hunters now taking from 175,000 up toward 200,000 birds annually. Zone 2 accounts for over half of the kill. There are several reasons for this. Zone 1 has plenty of woodcock, but fewer woodcock hunters. The Upper Peninsula bag runs an average of 20,000 to 25,000 with possibly as many as 10,000 hunters participating. However, in the northern portion of Zone 2, that is, the upper part of the Lower Peninsula, there is not only a large nesting population of woodcock, but the arrangement of the Great Lakes is such that virtually all woodcock from the eastern Upper Peninsula and a large expanse of Ontario are funneled south into the northern Lower Peninsula counties when the migration is on. After a severe fall frost or storm north of the Straits, birds by thousands move south and tumble into coverts along such streams as the Pigeon, Black, and Sturgeon rivers where habitat is virtually perfect.

There is so much good woodcock hunting in the state that in proper cover success can be had in almost any section. Even Zone 3 turns up a kill of about 50,000 birds on the average each season. However, most of these come from the northern portion of this Zone. The best hunting in the Lower Peninsula, that is, with the largest concentration of both nesting and flight birds, is found in three counties: Emmet and Cheboygan, which are the first counties the flights hit as they come across the Straits, and Montmorency immediately to the southeast. In the Upper Peninsula, although there is good shooting in numerous places, Marquette and Dickinson Cos. are considered best.

Finding a place to hunt woodcock is not difficult. As many hunters know, ruffed grouse and woodcock are commonly found in combination. All of the State Forests, located under "Grouse," furnish woodcock hunting. The same is true of the National Forests, which are covered in the chapter opening. Check these against the top counties. Hunting stream courses is the quickest way to locate birds. While there are scattered woodcock, during flights, on the SGAs only one is noted for its woodcock hunting. That is the group of islands in northern Lake Michigan called the Little Beaver Islands SGA, described under "Grouse."

WILD TURKEYS

The wild turkey was originally native to Michigan, and plentiful especially in southern hardwood regions. Late in the last century the birds were brought to extinction. For some years now experimentation has been in progress to re-establish the turkey. It appears now to have succeeded, with the eastern subspecies doing well. There have been restricted seasons both fall and spring, with permits allotted in certain areas. One of the first years with two seasons showed a fall kill of 135 birds, spring kill of twenty-five gobblers. It is anticipated that both seasons will continue, with numbers of permits tailored to expansion or decline of flocks in varied areas.

As this is written, turkeys are considered to be established in Menominee Co. in the Upper Peninsula, on Beaver Island, in the Baldwin Area, which is centered on the City of Baldwin in Lake Co., with turkeys spreading out over portions of Newaygo, Mecosta, Osceola, Wexford, Manistee, and Mason Cos., and in the Mio Area, which is centered on the village of Mio in Oscoda Co. and with birds fanning out over parts of Ogemaw, Iosco, Alcona, Alpena, Montmorency, Otsego, Crawford, and Roscommon Cos. This takes in a vast expanse of public forest lands. Thus, locating a hunting place is not difficult, but drawing a permit—and locating turkeys—may be. There is also an established turkey population in Allegan Co., where some of the first experiments were done.

The Department of Natural Resources plans to establish turkeys in all suitable forest blocks. Roughly thirty more areas show potential. These are chiefly in the northern Lower Peninsula. Hopes are that all counties of Zone 2 may eventually have turkeys established. A few Upper Peninsula tracts may be feasible, too, and a very few Zone 3 in the south. Interested hunters should check with the Department regarding permits and where they are allocated. Deadline for application is presently in late September.

WATERFOWL

Michigan has good waterfowl hunting, but considering the vast amount of water surrounding the state and in its interior it is not exceptional. Much of the reason is that large marshes are not abundant, and that too much open shoreline, and forest, prohibit the possibility of any vast feeding grounds for migrating birds. Nonetheless, the annual duck kill has been slowly rising over some years, and now averages above 400,000. One late season showed a tally of 461,000. The goose kill is surprisingly high, and remains reasonably stable, fluctuating from 10,000 to 15,000. Sometimes it is substantially higher.

Kill figures indicate over a period of years that kills in the various Zones bear a stable relationship. In a recent season when 14,210 geese were bagged, 2430 came from Zone 1, 2710 from Zone 2, 9070 from Zone 3. However, the duck picture is different. The Upper Peninsula (Zone 1) supplies far less in comparison, probably because of fewer hunters. With a kill of 461,040, there were 39,770 from Zone 1, 103,650 from Zone 2, 317,620 from Zone 3.

Most of the geese killed in Michigan are Canadas. Some years the kill of blues is also quite high. Two of the spots considered best for geese are the Allegan SGA ("Ruffed Grouse"), and the Saginaw Co. Goose Management Area. The latter includes the Shiawassee River SGA (60) and the Shiawassee National Wildlife Refuge. There is controlled hunting (some seasons) in parts of this region. The SGA is located southwest of the city of Saginaw between State 13 and 47, and contains 7660 acres. In the Upper Peninsula, there is often excellent goose hunting by fee or invitation on private lands in the vicinity of the huge Seney National Wildlife Refuge. This covers almost 100,000 acres of marsh and wild lands in Schoolcraft Co., west of State 77 and south of State 28. The town of Seney is at the junction of those highways.

There is a good deal of excellent jump-shooting for ducks by floating or canoeing the backwoods streams. There is also good duck shooting on and around most of the larger inland lakes. Along the marshy stretches of the Great Lakes shores there is shooting for both ducks and geese. While the State Forests' may not be thought of as waterfowl havens, many of them offer rather good hunting, on secluded lakes, beaver ponds, and streams. All State Forests are covered under "Grouse." In the Upper Peninsula the Bay de Noc SF area near Lake Michigan is noted for waterfowl. On the Lake Huron end of the Upper Peninsula, the Munuscong SF is also. Down across the Straits, the same is true of Thunder Bay River SF.

A large number of the SGAs furnish good waterfowling. Under "Grouse": Allegan, Flat River, Gratiot-Saginaw, Gregory, Little Beaver Islands, Tuscola. Under "Pheasant": Lapeer, Oak Grove, Pointe Mouillee (chiefly waterfowl). Under "Pheasant," the following State Wildlife Areas are predominantly waterfowl locations: Fish Point, St. Clair Flats, Wildfowl Bay. The Rose Lake Wildlife Research Center ("Pheasant") also offers waterfowl.

A number of other SGAs not so far dealt with are good waterfowling tracts. Backus Creek SGA (61) contains over 3000 acres in central Roscommon Co., near State 18 and Houghton Lake. Betsie River SGA (62) is 698 acres in an excellent location: the Lake Michigan shore, Benzie Co., near Frankfort and Beulah. Crane Pond SGA (63) has over 3000 acres down in the southwest corner of the state near the junction of State 119 and 60. The 1795-acre Erie SGA (64) is in the extreme southeast corner, a short distance north of Toledo, Ohio, near the town of Erie and U.S. 25. Grand Haven SGA (65) contains slightly under 1000 acres near town of like name on the Lake Michigan shore, Ottawa Co., between State 50 and 104. Haymarsh Lake SGA (66), over 6000 acres, is in Mecosta Co., northeast of Big Rapids, U.S. 131. Lowell SGA (67), 1850 acres, is near town of like name, junction State 21 and 91, east of Grand Rapids.

The Manistee River SGA (68) has 3625 acres. It is near Manistee, in Manistee Co. The Maple River SGA (69) is almost 6000 acres. It is on the line between Clinton and Gratiot Cos., between State 31 and 57 and west of I 75. Martiny Lake SGA (70), 3467 acres, is in northeastern Mecosta Co., near the Haymarsh Lake SGA. Minden City SGA (71) is 6431 acres, located in the Thumb, in northern Sanilac Co., near Minden and State 51 and 19. The Muskegon SGA (72), primarily for waterfowl, contains over 6000 acres, near city of like name on the Lake Michigan shore. The small Onstead SGA, 500-plus acres, is in the southeast, south of Jackson and near U.S. 112 and State 50 intersect. Pentwater River SGA (73) is primarily for waterfowl, a small one, 506 acres, near the town of Pentwater and U.S. 31 and the Lake Michigan shore. Another small one, with waterfowl the only game, is 442-acre Petobego SGA (74). This is near U.S. 31, between Elk Lake and the East Arm of Grand Traverse Bay, northeastern Grand Traverse Co.

While primarily for small-game animals, the Lost Nation SGA (75), with 2374 acres, has waterfowl hunting. It is in the south, Hillsdale Co., near Pittsford and State 34. Portland SGA (76), with almost 2000 acres, is about the same situation. It is in southeastern Ionia Co., near Portland. Rush Lake

SGA (77) is small, 471 acres, but waterfowl only, and is important because of its location near the tip of the Thumb, in Huron Co. between Caseville and Port Austin. The 2000-acre Three Rivers SGA (78) has some waterfowling, is in the southwest, in southwestern St. Joseph Co. west of U.S. 131. And, last of the SGAs with waterfowl, the 1694-acre Tobico Marsh SGA (79), partly refuge, is waterfowl only. It is on Saginaw Bay north of Bay City.

There are three State Wildlife Areas not so far mentioned that are waterfowl-only habitat. Nayanquing Point SWA (80), partly refuge, contains over 800 acres. It is immediately north of the Tobico Marsh SGA, named above. The 218-acre Quanicassee SWA (81) is important because of its location, near village of like name, on Saginaw Bay east of Bay City. Wigwam Bay (82) has a tract of only 137 acres. It is an access to bay of same name, north up the Saginaw Bay shore from Nayanquing Point, above.

Here are waterfowl spots considered among the most important in the state, even though there are hundreds of others that, when well known, offer comparable shooting. Saginaw Bay region: Wildfowl Bay, Middle Grounds, Sebewaing Bay, Fish Point, Quanicassee, Tobico Marsh, Nayanquing Point, Wigwam Bay.

Lake St. Clair near Detroit: Harsens and Dickenson Islands, Anchor Bay, Muscamoot Bay.

Lower Detroit River: Stoney Island, Hickory Island.

Lake Erie: mouth of Detroit River, Pt. Mouillee, Erie SGA.

Upper Lake Huron: Tawas Bay, Thunder Bay, St. Martin Bay in Upper Peninsula, and Les Cheneaux Islands, St. Mary's River (connecting Huron and Superior), Munuscong Bay, Drummond Island waters, Potagannissing Bay.

Lake Superior: Whitefish Bay, Portage Marshes in Houghton Co. Lake Michigan: in Upper Peninsula, Big & Little Bay de Noc; in Lower Peninsula, Wilderness Park west of Mackinaw City, Grand Traverse Bay, Beaver Island.

In the interior of the state there are the following important spots:

Upper Peninsula: Indian Lake, Hayward Lakes, Manistique Lakes.

Northern Lower Peninsula: Skegemow Lake, Fletcher Pond, Lake Leelanau, Crystal Lake, Platte Lake, Grass Lake (Benzie Co.), Houghton Lake, Martiny and Haymarsh SGAs, Hamlin Lake, Tawas Lake, and the Manistee, Muskegon, Chippewa, and Titabawassee rivers.

Southern Lower Peninsula: Shiawassee River SGA, Muskegon Lake and marshes, Maple River SGA, Waterloo Recreation Area (Jackson and Washtenaw Cos.), Lapeer SGA.

SNIPE AND RAILS

A few of each of these are killed generally as incidentals by waterfowlers. Although sora rails are common in the marshes along the Great Lakes, they are exceedingly difficult to flush and therefore are not hunted purposely. A few hundred may be bagged annually. Snipe hunting is spotty. There are enough birds, but they are scattered, seldom found in concentration. Possibly 5000 are bagged by duck hunters. To plan a jacksnipe hunt with any chance of success would be difficult.

DEER

For many years Michigan has been one of the leading whitetail deer hunting states. Whitetails, native to original Michigan forests, were not abundant until after the vast lumbering operations of the last century opened great expanses to second growth. During the last several decades, deer herds expanded until in numerous sections of the state they occurred in problem proportions. The general Zone 3 region, which was virtually without deer thirty years ago, has had a steadily increasing spread and abundance. Today as many as 10,000 bucks are taken in the south each season.

For the past decade the total kill of deer has averaged around 100,000 each season. There have been a number of antlerless seasons, with a survey-related number of permits offered by hunter application. Antlerless harvest has been planned to keep the deer herd tailored to its range and food supply. Because hunter numbers have steadily increased, so that today up to 600,000 deer hunters annually participate, much controversy has resulted from the antlerless deer hunting. Total harvest remains fairly stable, but as hunter numbers increase success percentages have fallen. Nonetheless, the average is still about 12 percent, or 1 in 8.

While the harvest fluctuates somewhat in makeup, the following figures from a recent season give a fairly accurate picture of where the deer come from, and where the favorite hunting regions are. Upper Peninsula: 12,400 bucks, 11,100 antlerless. Northern Lower Peninsula: 33,700 bucks, 21,300 antlerless. Southern Lower Peninsula: 10,000 bucks, 1900 antlerless. Hunter numbers affect the kills to some extent. However, as a general rule the north-central counties of the Lower Peninsula are first choice, the western and southwestern Upper Peninsula next. Southern Michigan produces many big, and usually fat, deer and is excellent for those who know the area. An annual check on where the high allotments of antlerless permits go will give hunters a clue to deer concentrations. This does not necessarily mean a clue to large bucks, but simply to a better chance of success.

For antlerless permits, the state is divided into numbered Areas, the numbers beginning in the western Upper Peninsula and working progressively across to the east and thence down through the Lower Peninsula. Each Area is then assigned a specified number of permits for that season. Application cards are issued with the hunting license, and bear the same number as the license. Hunters should check carefully the regulations regarding these antlerless permits. If the number of applications for any Area exceeds the number of permits for that Area, a drawing is held.

Michigan deer are so well distributed over the public lands, and in such general abundance, that there is little possibility of pinpointing any specific localities as best. Remote parts of the Upper Peninsula will get the person who likes uncrowded wilderness hunting farther from the disturbance of other hunters. Conversely, the heavily hunted northern Lower Peninsula insures that deer will be moved by others, thus often offering opportunity for those who are not skilled stalkers.

There is no difficulty whatever in finding places to hunt. The National Forests covered in chapter opening furnish fine hunting. All of the State Forests offer more of the same. These have been covered under "Grouse." Among the State Game Areas, most of them in the south, there are a number with deer. These should not be passed up. Hunting on farms surrounding some of these pushes deer into them. Also, even though some of the Areas may be a bit crowded with hunters, success chances are very good. Noted under "Grouse" are the following that also offer deer: Allegan, Barry, Danville, Deford, Edmore, Flat River, Gratiot-Saginaw, Gregory, Langston, Little Beaver Islands (much wilderness hunting here), Rogue River, Stanton, Tuscola,

Vestaburg. Mentioned under "Pheasant": Oak Grove. Under "Waterfowl": Backus Creek, Betsie River, Haymarsh Lake, Manistee River, Maple River, Portland, Shiawassee River. There is also deer hunting on two State Wildlife Areas: St. Clair Flats ("Pheasant") and Unadilla ("Ruffed Grouse"). All three State Wildlife Research Centers have deer: Cusino, Houghton Lake ("Ruffed Grouse"), Rose Lake ("Pheasant").

The Sanilac SGA (83), not mentioned thus far, offers 1100 acres with fair deer hunting. It is in Zone 3, in the Thumb, in the northwest corner of Sanilac County. State 19 and 53 are nearby access routes. There is also a small deer hunting Area in Mason Co. near the Lake Michigan shore and the city of Ludington. It is Pere Marquette SGA (84).

ELK AND MOOSE

Centuries ago elk were native to Michigan. They disappeared long ago. A small band was brought in to the northern Lower Peninsula about forty years ago. From this beginning a herd of modest size was established, chiefly in the region of the Pigeon River State Forest. Elk eventually were spread from about Gaylord on up toward the Straits and quite broadly on either side of U.S. 27. Concentration area was east of the villages of Vanderbilt and Wolverine. These elk became a tremendous tourist attraction for summer visitors to the north.

For some years there was sentiment in some quarters for a controlled hunt. After a bitter battle, a hunt was held in 1964, with 300 permits offered. The kill was 269. Apparently herd size estimates by officials had been in error on the high side and the elk situation after the hunt became precarious. Elk still remain on this range, in low numbers. It is doubtful that a season will be held soon again. Deer hunters in the elk range should therefore identify targets with extreme care. A few elk are annually killed. The fine is severe.

There are a very few moose in the Upper Peninsula. There is no open season. Deer hunters should be aware of the possibility, slight though it is, of seeing a moose and shooting it in error.

BEAR

The black bear has been over many years fairly common in the northern Lower Peninsula and throughout the Upper. Annual kills at one time ran up toward 1000. With no spring season, bears in Michigan are killed incidentally by deer hunters, or hunted with hounds. Over recent years bears have become very scarce in the Lower Peninsula. As this is written there is no open season here. If bear populations build high enough again, there may be a season at some future time. There is an open season presently in the Upper Peninsula. Prospective bear hunters should carefully check the regulations dealing with type of license held and whether or not dogs are permitted under the license held. Most successful hunts are with dogs. However, the total kill is not high, possibly averaging 200 or less. The counties of the western Upper Peninsula furnish a large percentage of the total kill.

RABBITS

Michigan has both cottontails and snowshoe rabbits, the latter properly called hares. Both species are exceedingly popular. Total cottontail kill runs from 600,000 to over a million. Bulk of this kill comes from Zone 3, southern Michigan, where farmlands provide excellent cottontail habitat. In Zone 2, the northern Lower Peninsula, cottontails are in fair supply, especially in the lower part of the Zone, but diminish in abundance rapidly as one moves up toward the Straits. In the northern counties there is little hunting specifically for cottontails. There is a minor amount of cottontail hunting in the Upper Peninsula. But these rabbits are never plentiful there except in small local concentrations. During a season when over a million were bagged in southern Michigan, Zone 3, less than 40,000 were taken in the Upper Peninsula.

The snowshoe rabbit is extremely popular and during high cycles supremely abundant in the two northern Zones. Annual kill averages from 200,000 to 350,000 or more. As a rule well over half of the snowshoe bag is in the Upper Peninsula. Almost all of the remainder is in Zone 2. Southern Michigan has very few of these hares, and the kill is negligible. Snowshoes concentrate in evergreen swamps during the deep-snow period of winter and are generally hunted then, with or without dogs. Since snowshoes do not hole up when chased, as cottontails often do, hunting them with dogs is a grand sport. Also during a winter thaw when snow may be scarce, the hares, which have turned white, stand out plainly in the woods, and many are hunted without dogs and with a .22 rifle. The National Forests covered early in this chapter, and the State Forests described under "Ruffed Grouse," all offer excellent snowshoe rabbit hunting. Among the SGAs, Backus Creek ("Waterfowl") and Little Beaver Islands ("Ruffed Grouse") are additional snowshoe locations. Two Wildlife Research Centers may be added to these: Cusino and Houghton Lake, both under "Ruffed Grouse."

In the prime cottontail habitat of the south, most of the hunting is on privately owned lands. However, there is excellent cottontail shooting on the public lands, too. All of the SGAs listed under "Ruffed Grouse," "Pheasant," and "Waterfowl," excepting only the ones noted above that are in the north and have snowshoes, and the ones where waterfowl-only is indicated, offer excellent cottontail hunting. In addition, the Unadilla Wildlife Area ("Ruffed Grouse") and the Rose Lake Research Center ("Pheasant") furnish more of the same.

There are several SGAs not so far listed where cottontails are the primary game species. Cannonsburg SGA (85) has 1336 acres a short distance northeast of the city of Grand Rapids. Chelsea SGA (86) has 654 acres near its namesake village on State 92 northwest of Ann Arbor. Fulton SGA (87), with 672 acres, is near the village of Fulton, in the extreme southeastern corner of Kalamazoo Co. There are 3225 acres in the Middleville SGA (88), in northern Barry Co. northwest of the city of Hastings between State 37 and 50. Murphy Lake SGA (89) contains over 2500 acres, is located a few miles from the village of Fostoria in Tuscola Co. and from Millington on State 15.

SQUIRRELS

Squirrel hunting has never been excessively popular in Michigan except among a modest number of enthusiasts chiefly in the southern part of the state. However, as hunters have increased, so has interest in squirrel hunting. Nowadays the total bag averages from about 600,000 up to slightly less than one million. There are two species, fox squirrels and gray squirrels. Two-thirds of the kill are fox squirrels.

The gray squirrels are almost all in Zones 1 and 2. The Zone 3 farm woodlots and public lands are often very productive of fox squirrels. The kill of squirrels in this southern Zone is about double what it is over the remainder of the state. While there is good gray squirrel hunting in the north, the vast expanses of forest often make the locating of prominent gray squirrel populations somewhat difficult. Much of the timber is in conifers, poplar, birch, maple. Stands of mature nut-bearing trees upon which squirrels rely in forest habitats are not abundant.

The northern Lower Peninsula accounts for the bulk of the gray squirrel bag, with the Upper total kill averaging only from 20,000 to 30,000. The National Forests and the State Forests already covered, in front of chapter and under "Ruffed Grouse," furnish unlimited opportunity for gray squirrel hunting. Fox squirrels, and in a few instances grays, abound on practically all the state lands in the southern sector (Zone 3) already covered, excepting those for waterfowl only. For locations of these, see "Ruffed Grouse," "Pheasant," "Waterfowl," "Rabbit."

OTHER ANIMALS

Michigan has hunting for bobcats, coyotes, foxes, raccoons, woodchuck. There are some opossums and badgers, the latter with a specified season.

Bobcat hunting with hounds became very popular over past years. Some hunters allow the cats to go free after being treed. But bobcats became so scarce in the northern Lower Peninsula that they were placed on the game list. Zone 3 and certain areas of Zone 2 are at this time completely closed. In the Upper Peninsula there is no closed season. Stream courses and evergreen swamps in the State and National Forests where snowshoe hares, a favorite forage of the bobcat, consort abundantly in winter are excellent places for this hunting. The bobcat kill presently is not high, possibly an average of 400 annually.

Coyotes, some of unusual size, are quite common in northern Michigan. Coyotes are bountied in Michigan, although the DNR is opposed to continuation of any bounties, which are not effective. Almost all coyote hunting is done by specialists with hounds, in winter, and often when deep snow makes wearing snowshoes mandatory. The animals are fairly well distributed over much of the northern Lower Peninsula and all of the Upper. The Gaylord-Indian River region in the northern counties of the Lower Peninsula offer some of the best hunting. The Mio region is also good. The western Upper Peninsula is excellent over much of its territory and especially along the south Lake Superior shore. Hunters seeking guided hunts for either bobcats or coyotes should contact local Chambers of Commerce in specific areas for assistance. The Department may also be helpful in suggesting guides with hound packs but obviously cannot make recommendations. During a recent year 3683 coyotes were bountied.

There is quite good fox hunting, mostly for red foxes, in southern Michigan. Fox calling here is becoming quite popular. The public lands offer good opportunities. About 30,000 foxes are taken each year.

Raccoons are exceedingly plentiful and much hunted with dogs. They are found throughout the state, and as many as 275,000 are bagged each season. Hunters should note that raccoons are considered game animals and given protection, although there is no bag limit during open season. Southern Michigan has by far the most raccoons. However, hunting is quite good on the State and National Forests of the northern Lower Peninsula. Only a small number of raccoons are bagged in the Upper.

As noted above, there are some badgers, mostly in the south, and they are on the game list, with open and closed seasons. Woodchucks also are quite plentiful in the south, with a scattering across the northern Zones. There is no closed season in the Upper Peninsula, but there are specified seasons in the Lower. Michigan also has a small amount of an unusual sport, hunting mink with hounds. It is a highly specialized endeavor and dogs must be trained to the task. There are stipulated seasons. Mink range over the entire state.

REGULATIONS

Game laws pertaining to seasons, bag and possession limits, areas to be hunted, special hunts, license fees all may have numerous changes from year to year. For current regulations, and for other specific queries, write to: Department of Natural Resources, Steven T. Mason Building, Lansing, Michigan 48926.

WISCONSIN

It is fitting that Wisconsin should be named for a water-way, the major river of the state, the Wisconsin, that meanders erratically down through much of the interior. Wisconsin is a land of many waters. Almost the entire border on the east is formed by the Lake Michigan shore. Much of the north is bounded by the western reaches of Lake Superior. In between those two Great Lakes the western Upper Peninsula of Michigan furnishes the remaining northern and eastern borders, with most of these demarked by rivers, the Montreal in the north, the Menominee in the south.

Most of the western boundary is drawn by the flow of the St. Croix and the Mississippi, separating Wisconsin from Minnesota and northeastern Iowa. Illinois lies to the south. Within the interior of Wisconsin there is a veritable welter of lakes, over 8000 of them large and small, and there are thousands of miles of streams.

This middle one of the three Great Lakes States is in many ways like two. It is popularly known as "America's Dairyland." True enough, most of southern Wisconsin is a paradise of farms. This is the famed milk and cheese country. But in the north there are vast forests, where forest industries are important. Here the game species of the forest lands abound, while over the thousands of acres of rolling pasturelands farther south, where the nation's largest dairy herds graze, farm game varieties complement the northern species.

Wisconsin's road system is excellent. Even in the forested north the net-work leads to almost everywhere. Hunters have no need for special vehicles, except that a pickup or 4WD may often come in handy for getting far back into the northern forests on unpaved and little-used trails. There is also exceptionally good rail transport here. And, for those coming into the state from across Lake Michigan, there are several ferry lines. Air transport to all of the major cities is abundant. While most of the large cities are in the south, cities of between 30,000 and 40,000 population such as Eau Claire and Wausau north of center in the state connect well by air with Duluth at the head of Lake Superior. However a hunter arrives here, he has little difficulty getting to the scene of the hunting, regardless of variety.

Wisconsin is by a small margin the smallest of the Great Lakes States. It contains 56,154 square miles, slightly less than Michigan. At the southern border it is rather narrow, roughly 135 miles east to west. But across the broad north the distance is close to 300 miles, and the north-south expanse is roughly 320. The present population has climbed well above four million and is increasing. About a fourth of this population is in the Milwaukee area, and another half million is concentrated in several of the larger cities. The remainder of the population is well distributed in numerous small settlements, but the preponderance of these is in the south. Northern Wisconsin is still only lightly populated, and there is plenty of wilderness remaining there.

Hunting is exceedingly popular. Well above 10 percent of the population enjoy some variety of the sport each season. License sales in total are up near 600,000 annually. Wisconsin is popular with nonresidents also, with most of them coming into the state for deer. An average at present of about 20,000 nonresidents are included in the total license sale.

Whitetail deer are the chief big-game attraction. There is also hunting for black bear. Game birds include pheasant, ruffed grouse, Hungarian partridge, sharptailed grouse, plus migratory woodcock and the various waterfowl. There are gray and fox squirrels, cottontails and snowshoe hares, foxes, coyotes, some bobcats, and raccoons.

Fortunately for the great numbers of Wisconsin hunters, finding public lands on which to hunt is no problem. The state has approximately six and one-half million acres of recreational lands, and most of it is open to hunting. There are two large National Forests in the north. The Chequamegon NF is the largest, with 831,000 acres. It is in three blocks, in the northwest and north-central part of the state. The largest block is in the northwest, in Bayfield, Ashland, and Sawyer Cos. U.S. 2, 63, and State 13, 70, and 27 all give access. The town of Ashland is near the northern part of this block. A second block lies in northeastern Price Co. State 70 and 182 both cross it. The town of Park Falls on State 13 is just to the west. The third block lies to the south and west, in northern Taylor Co. State 13, 73, and 64 run near it on three different sides. Medford is a nearby town to the southeast. The Supervisor for this Forest may be contacted for maps and details at Park Falls, Wisconsin.

The second National Forest is the Nicolet, with 643,875 acres. It is in the northeast, with portions taking up some of eastern Vilas Co., most of Forest Co., some of western Florence Co., northern Oconto and eastern Langlade Cos. U.S. 8 and 45, State 70, 64, 32, 52, all offer access. Eagle River, Rhinelander, Marinette are key cities. For details and maps, contact the Supervisor at Rhinelander.

There are several State Forests, most of them in the north, that total approximately 413,000 acres. County Forests in Wisconsin are even more important in total acreage than the National and State Forests. There are presently almost two and a quarter million acres of these, with the major portion in the north and the west-central part of the state. There are several hundred thousand acres of forest industry and hydropower company lands on most of which hunting is permitted. But perhaps most important overall to the hunter, because of the statewide distribution of them, are the owned and leased lands of the Department of Natural Resources. Some years ago the state began buying lands for recreational purposes and for game and fish management. Presently there are roughly 322,000 acres in state ownership. Added to these, often in bordering tracts, are leased lands that total a quarter million acres. These tracts, anywhere from a few acres to several thousand, are scattered over the entire state. There are over 250 of them.

Brochures covering the County Forests, and the State Forests, are available from the Department of Natural Resources, address at chapter end. In addition, a map showing locations of all the State Wildlife Areas, stating size of each and game of primary importance on each, may be obtained from the same source. Locations of State, County, and National Forests are also shown on this map but these are not named. This map is invaluable to visiting hunters.

In fact, because of the great number of public tracts it will not be possible here to name and locate all. Therefore, under the various species the best portions of the range of each will be given, and where possible the best counties. Some of the larger tracts of public land will be dealt with, but the remainder, where necessary, noted only by the number of tracts in any given county.

The camping hunter has bright prospects in Wisconsin. The various forests all have camping sites, and there are numerous State Parks. From the DNR a booklet, "Wisconsin Campground Directory," may be obtained. Another, "Enjoy Wisconsin State Parks and State Forests," can be had from the same source. Other accommodations in Wisconsin are legion. Motels and hotels are numerous throughout the south in all towns and along major highways. Northern Wisconsin has scores of fine lodges and restaurants in the forest hunting country. Weather in the north will be crisp and invigorating in early fall, wool-shirt weather in October during good years, but with a warm jacket needed for dawn and dusk. Deer season usually means snow, and some severe storms and cold can occur. Hunters at any time of the seasons should go prepared to face either lovely fall weather or weather demanding down jackets and insulated boots.

Arms and ammunition required here depend entirely on what is to be hunted. The deer and bear hunter will need a good solid though standard caliber. The .30/06, .270, and comparable calibers are examples, although the old .30/30 is still locally popular and the newer .243 does very well. Bird hunters will need shot sizes No. 7½ and No. 6 for most upland birds and small game. Because ducks and geese are important in this state, No. 4 for ducks and No. 2 for geese should be on hand. A .22 is a handy rifle also but hunters should carefully check laws as to where it may be used. Deer hunters should also read carefully the laws pertaining to shotguns-only in certain hunting Units.

For management purposes Wisconsin is divided into five general districts or regions, and these will be used in the following material to help orient the reader. These areas are: the Northwest, which takes in twelve counties; the Northeast, also with twelve; the West-Central, with fifteen counties; the East-Central, with seventeen; the south, with sixteen. It should be noted that open seasons for any given species do not necessarily follow the lines of these districts. In fact, the Game Law Digest for any season is usually illustrated with small maps for each species, showing demarkation lines for open or closed seasons. Deer management, and seasons, and in some cases quotas, are all handled in a different manner. There are Unit divisions, and these at present number over seventy. It is necessary for a hunter to acquire the regulations, with its map, for any given season in order to know which Units are open, and what the quotas, if any, are. This same Unit system also applies to bear.

The state-owned and state leased tracts, incidentally, are spoken of on the previously mentioned map as Public Hunting Grounds but are termed in some individual brochures Wildlife Areas. As a compromise, in following material the term Public Hunting Areas will be used.

PHEASANT

The ringneck was introduced to Wisconsin in 1916. Peak populations were reached in the 1940s, and about 800,000 were bagged in 1942. Since that time the birds have declined, due chiefly to intensification of agriculture. However, a fairly stable level has been reached and the state has excellent

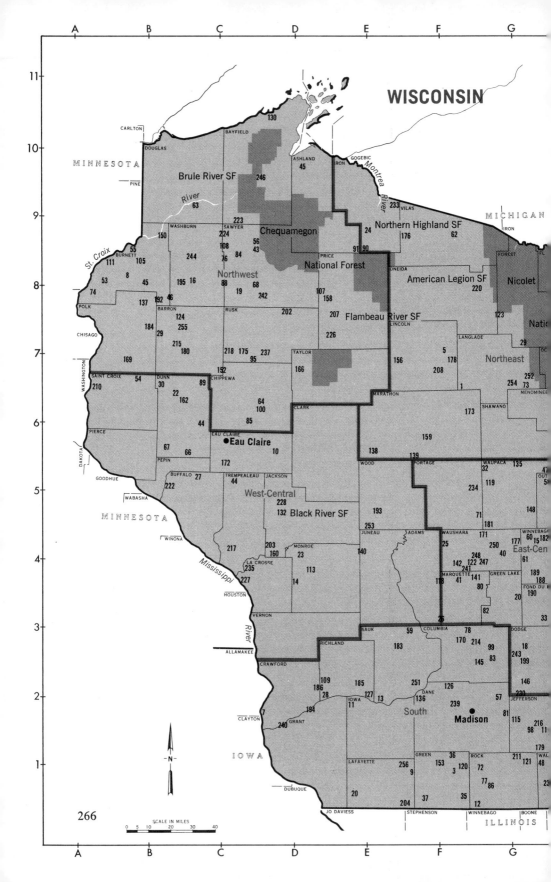

KEY TO HUNTING AREAS

1. Ackley   F6
2. Adell   I 3
3. Albany   F1
4. Allenton   H2
5. Alta Springs   F7
6. Amberg   H7
7. Ambrough Boat
   Landing   C2
8. Amsterdam Sloughs
   B8
9. Argyle   F1
10. Augusta   D5
11. Avoca   E2
12. Avon Bottoms   F1
13. Bakken's Pond   E2
14. Bangor   D4
15. Bay Boom   G4
16. Beaver Brook   C8
17. Beaver Creek
    (N. Branch)   H6
18. Beaver Dam Lake
    R-O-W   G3
19. Benson Creek   C8
20. Benton   E1
21. Beulah Station   H1
22. Big Beaver Creek
    B6
23. Big Creek   D4
24. Big Island   E9
25. Big Roche a Cri   F4
26. Big Spring   F3
27. Big Swamp   C5
28. Blue River   D2
29. Bog Brook   G7
30. Bolen Creek   B7
31. Bong   H1
32. Bradley Creek   G5
33. Brandon   G-3
34. Brillion   H4
35. Brodhead   F1
36. Brooklyn   F1
37. Browntown   F1
38. Caves Creek   F4
39. Cedarburg Bog   H2
40. Cedar Springs   G4
41. Chaffee Creek   F4
42. Charles Pond   H6
43. Chief River   D8
44. Chimney Rock   C5
45. Clam Lake   B8
46. Clam River   B8
47. Clintonville   H5
48. Clover Valley   G1
49. Colburn   F4
50. Coleman   H6
51. Colgate   H2
52. Collins Marsh   I 4
53. Crex Meadows   A8
54. Cylon   B7
55. Danbury   B8
56. Dead Creek
    Springs   D9
57. Deansville   G2
58. Deer Creek   H5

59. Dell Creek   E3
60. Deltox Marsh   G4
61. Deppe Marsh   G4
62. Dorothy Dunn   F9
63. Douglas County   C9
64. Drywood Creek   D6
65. Dunbar   H8
66. Dunnville   B6
67. Eau Galle River   C5
68. Eddy Creek   C8
69. Eden   H3
70. Eldorado   G4
71. Emmons Creek   G5
72. Evansville   F1
73. Evergreen River   G7
74. Fish Lake   A8
75. Flag River   D10
76. Flat Creek   C8
77. Footville   G1
78. French Creek   F3
79. Gardner Swamp   I 6
80. Germania Marsh   G4
81. Goose Lake   G2
82. Grand River
    Marsh   G3
83. Grassy Lake   G3
84. Grindstone Springs
    D8
85. Hallie   C6
86. Hanover   G1
87. Hartford   H2
88. Hauer Springs   D8
89. Hay Creek   C6
90. Hay Creek   E8
91. Hoffman Lake   E8
92. Holland   H5
93. Honey Creek   H1
94. Horicon Marsh   G3
95. Island Lake   C7
96. Jackson Marsh   H2
97. Jaeger's Island   H4
98. Jefferson Marsh   G1
99. Jennings Creek   G3
100. Jim Falls   C6
101. Karcher Marsh   H1
102. Kewaskum   H3
103. Kewaunee Marsh   I5
104. Kiel Marsh   H4
105. Kiezer Lake   B8
106. Killsnake Creek   H4
107. Kimberly-Clark   D8
108. Kissick Swamp   C8
109. Knapp Creek   D2
110. Knob Hill   G2
111. Kohler-Peet   A8
112. LaBudde Creek   H4
113. La Crosse River   D4
114. Laing Creek   F3
115. Lake Mills   G2
116. Lake Noquebay   H7
117. Lakewood
     Hatchery   H7
118. Lawrence Creek   F4
119. Leer Creek   G5

(continued)

267

120. Liberty Creek F1
121. Lima Marsh G1
122. Little Pine Creek
       F4
123. Little Rice G7
124. Little Silver
       Lake B7
125. Little Scarboro I 5
126. Lodi Marsh F2
127. Lone Rock E2
128. Long Tail Point H5
129. Loon Lake B7
130. Lost Creek D10
131. Lost Lake J6
132. Lowe Creek D5
133. Mack H5
134. Maine H5
135. Marion G5
136. Mazomanie F2
137. McKenzie Creek B7
138. McMillan Marsh E6
139. Mead F6
140. Meadow Valley E4
141. Mecan F4
142. Mecan F4
143. Miscauno I 7
144. Muddy Creek C6
145. Mud Lake G3
146. Mud Lake G2
147. Mud Lake J6
148. Mukwa G5
149. Mullet Creek H3
150. Namekagon
       Barrens B9
151. Navarino Marsh H5
152. New Auburn C7
153. New Glarus F1
154. New Holstein H4
155. New Munster H1
156. New Wood E7
157. Nichols Creek H3
158. Niebauer
       Springs E8
159. Nine Mile
       Swamp F6
160. North Bend D4
161. Oconto River
       (S. Branch) H6
162. Otter Creek C6
163. Outagamie
       County H5
164. Paris I 1
165. Pensaukee
       Marsh I 6

166. Pershing D7
167. Peshtigo Brook H7
168. Peshtigo
       Harbor I 6
169. Peterson Creek B7
170. Pine Island F3
171. Pine River G4
172. Pleasant Valley C5
173. Plover River F6
174. Popple River H8
175. Potato Creek C7
176. Powell Marsh F9
177. Poygan Marsh G4
178. Prairie River F7
179. Princess Point H1
180. Quaderer Creek B7
181. Radley Creek G4
182. Rat River H4
183. Reedsburg E3
184. Rice Beds Creek B7
185. Richland E2
186. Richwood D2
187. Rome Pond H1
188. Rush Lake G4
189. Rush Lake R-O-W
       (North) G4
190. Rush Lake R-O-W
       (South) G4
191. Salem H1
192. Sand Creek B8
193. Sandhill E4
194. Saunders Creek D2
195. Sawyer Creek B8
196. Scuppernong H1
197. Seagull Bar I 6
198. Sensiba H5
199. Shaw Marsh G3
200. Sheboygan Marsh
       H4
201. Silver Creek G3
202. Silvernail D7
203. South Beaver
       Creek D4
204. Spafford Creek E1
205. Spoehr's Marsh H5
206. Spread Eagle H8
207. Spring Creek E8
208. Spring Lake F7
209. St. Cloud H4
210. St. Croix
       Islands A7
211. Storr's Lake G1
212. Suamico H5
213. Supple Marsh H4

214. Swan Lake F3
215. Sweeny Pond
       Creek B7
216. Tamarack G2
217. Tamarack River C4
218. Ten Mile Creek C7
219. Theresa H3
220. Thunder Lake F8
221. Tichigan H1
222. Tiffany B5
223. Totogatic Lake C9
224. Totogatic River C8
225. Town Corner H7
226. Township Corners
       D7
227. Trempealeau
       Lakes C4
228. Trempealeau River
       (N. Branch) D5
229. Troy H1
230. Turtle Creek G1
231. Two Rivers I 4
232. Ulao I 2
233. Underwood E9
234. Upper Tomorrow
       River F5
235. Van Loon C4
236. Vernon Marsh H1
237. Washington
       Creek D7
238. Waterloo G2
239. Waunakee F2
240. Wauzeka D2
241. Wedde Creek
       (S. Branch) F4
242. Weirgor Springs D8
243. Westford G3
244. Whalen Creek B8
245. White River D10
246. White River C9
247. White River F4
248. White River
       (W. Branch) F4
249. Wildcat Marsh H3
250. Willow Creek G4
251. Witwen F2
252. Wolf River G7
253. Wood County E4
254. Woods Flowage G7
255. Yellow River B7
256. Yellowstone E1

hunting, with the annual kill for some years now averaging somewhere between 350,000 and 500,000.

Pheasants range over much of the state, with the exception of the forested portions of the north, and a part of the West-Central area that is also forested. However, the South has by far the most birds, and furnishes about 50 percent and sometimes more of the total kill. These southern counties are: Columbia, Crawford, Dane, Grant, Green, Iowa, Jefferson, Kenosha, Lafayette, Milwaukee, Racine, Richland, Rock, Sauk, Walworth, Waukesha. The concentration of pheasants in the South is in the eastern and central portions. A recent season showed Racine and Kenosha counties of the extreme southeast among the leading five counties of the state. Dane and Jefferson counties also were leading ones.

The East-Central region is next in pheasant importance, and furnishes on the average 30 to 40 percent of the total state kill. These counties are: Brown, Calumet, Dodge, Door, Fond du Lac, Green Lake, Kewaunee, Manitowoc, Marquette, Outagamie, Ozaukee, Portage, Sheboygan, Washington, Waupaca, Waushara, Winnebago. Recently Manitowoc Co. has been among the first five.

While the remainder of the state has spottily adequate hunting, it is not very important except locally. The Northeast and West-Central districts each furnish around 5 to 7 percent of the kill, with the West-Central area the better of the two. Only 1 or 2 percent of Wisconsin's pheasant kill comes from the Northwest.

There are numerous Public Hunting Areas in the quality range, the South. Columbia Co. has two tracts noted for pheasants, French Creek and Jennings Creek, and four other tracts on which at least some pheasants are found. Dane Co. has five tracts of good size noted for pheasants, and as mentioned above, this is one of the high-kill counties. These tracts are: Deansville, Goose Lake, Lodi Marsh, Mazomanie, Waunakee. In Green Co. six PHAs are primarily pheasant hunting grounds: Albany, Brodhead, Brooklyn, Browntown, New Glarus, Liberty Creek. Jefferson, another high-kill county of the South, has seven good tracts: Jefferson Marsh, Knob Hill, Lake Mills, Princess Point, Rome Pond, Tamarack, Waterloo.

Kenosha, another top county, has four PHAs: Bong, New Munster, Paris, Salem. In Lafayette Co., Argyle, Benton, and Spafford Creek PHAs are noted for pheasants, and Yellowstone has some. Racine, another top county, has four tracts: Beulah Station, Honey Creek, Karcher Marsh, Tichigan. There are six good PHAs for pheasants in Rock Co., two in Sauk where pheasants are primarily, Reedsburg, Witwen. Walworth Co. has three tracts, and Waukesha has two.

In the East-Central district the top county, Manitowoc, has two PHAs noted for pheasants: Killsnake Creek and Two Rivers. Brown Co. has some pheasants on four different PHAs, Calumet Co. has good hunting on two. Dodge Co. has five PHAs with pheasants primary, and in Fond du Lac Co. three (of seven) PHAs are the same. Other counties that have at least some PHAs, out of several, that are noted for pheasants are: Green Lake Co., 1; Kewaunee Co., 1; Outagamie, 3 that are fair; Ozaukee, 1; Sheboygan, 3; Washington, 5; Waupaca, 1; Winnebago, 3.

While the other districts, as mentioned, are not quality pheasant range, there are a few PHAs in two of them where pheasants are the primary games species. In West-Central: Adams Co., Big Spring PHA; Buffalo Co., Big Swamp PHA; Dunn Co., Bolen Creek, Muddy Creek, Hay Creek; Eau Claire Co., Pleasant Valley; Jackson Co., Lowe Creek, South Beaver Creek, Trempealeau River; Monroe Co., Bangor; St. Croix Co., Cylon; Trempealeau Co., Chimney Rock, Tamarack River. In the Northwest, there are the following: Chippewa Co., Drywood Creek, Hallie, Jim Falls PHAs.

RUFFED GROUSE

Wisconsin is one of the best ruffed grouse states in the nation. During peak years over half a million grouse are bagged. Even when the cycle is low, about half that many are harvested. Because these are forest and forest-edge birds, the greater share of the kill comes from the northern half of the state, where most of the woodlands are located. The Northeast, which has the Nicolet National Forest, an excellent place for grouse hunting, plus a great deal of County Forest lands, plus two State Forests furnishes on the average a bit less than half the state kill. Occasionally the East-Central district is in second place. There are many PHAs here with wooded cover suitable for grouse. The Northwest, where the Chequamegon NF is located, also contains numerous County Forests and two State Forests. It vies with the West-Central region, each furnishing around 15 percent of the kill. This West-Central district contains large County Forests in Jackson and Clark Cos., plus one State Forest. Even the South has some rather good grouse hunting, with 5 to 10 percent of the kill originating here. During one recent season when the birds were not at peak, four of the first five counties were in the Northeast, which is a good indication that at high cycle the region is even better. These four counties were: Lincoln, Marathon, Marinette, Vilas. Another of the first five was in the East-Central district. This is Manitowoc Co.

The two State Forests in the Northeast are the American Legion SF of almost 43,000 acres in northern Oneida Co., and the 138,874-acre Northern Highland State Forest immediately to the north in Iron Co. In Iron, Oneida, Lincoln, Langlade, Marinette and Florence Cos. there are large acreages of County Forest.

Some very good hunting for grouse is found also on PHAs in the Northeast. Here are some of the better tracts: in Florence Co., Popple River and Spread Eagle; in Iron Co., Big Island, Hay Creek, Underwood; Langlade Co., Ackley, Evergreen River, Wolf River; Lincoln Co., Alta Springs, New Wood, Prairie River; Marathon Co., Nine Mile Swamp, Plover River; Marinette Co., Beaver Creek, Coleman, Dunbar, Miscauno, Town Corner; Oconto Co., Lakewood Hatchery, Oconto River, Peshtigo Brooks; Shawano Co., Navarino Marsh. Some other PHAs have grouse as a secondary species.

In the Northwest, in addition to the National Forest there are large County Forests in Douglas, Bayfield, Washburn, Sawyer, Price and Rusk Cos. and several others of lesser expanse in the remaining counties. The Brule River State Forest, with over 30,000 acres, lies in northeastern Douglas Co. and the Flambeau River SF, with nearly 80,000 acres, is in eastern Sawyer and northwestern Price Cos.

The PHAs with grouse the primary game are numerous here, too. In Ashland Co. there are Hoffman Lake and White River. Barron Co. has Yellow River PHA, Burnett Co. has Danbury PHA. The Douglas Co. PHA is in Douglas Co., and Price Co. has Niebauer Springs. Sawyer Co. has Hauer Springs, Kissick Swamp, and Weirgor Springs, and Washburn Co. has Sawyer Creek. Again, many other PHAs in the district furnish fair ruffed grouse hunting, with grouse as a secondary species.

Following are some of the better tracts in the West-Central region: Adams Co., Colburn PHA; Eau Claire Co., Augusta PHA; Juneau Co., Meadow Valley PHA. In addition to the County Forests already mentioned above for this region, there is the 63,000-acre Black River State Forest located in Jackson Co.

In the East-Central district there are: Mud Lake PHA in Door Co.; Bradley Creek, Emmons Creek, Upper Tomorrow River PHAs in Portage Co. with fair hunting; six PHAs in Waupaca Co. with fair hunting; seven in Waushara Co. Some grouse are found in this district on several of the tracts noted under "Pheasant." In the South, Grant Co. has good shooting on

Saunders Creek PHA and Richland Co. has two good tracts, Richland and Richwood.

SHARPTAIL GROUSE

This handsome grouse requires much open grass country with scattered thickets and early-stage forests. Following the heavy logging operations of the last century, sharptails became abundant in portions of northern and central Wisconsin. Maturing of the forests in this century, plus changes in land use, have drastically reduced sharptail numbers. An open season has not been an annual occurrence during the past few years. One was held in 1965, and another, north of Highways 64, 12, and 29, during 1968. For any given season hunters should check to ascertain whether or not a season is expected.

The kill is only a few thousand birds. And the areas of concentration are spotty. As a rule the best hunting is likely to be found in parts of the northwest, on some of the managed areas and farm edges in Douglas, Bayfield, Price, Rusk, Sawyer and Taylor Cos. Following are a few PHAs known for sharptail coveys: Burnett Co., Namekagon Barrens; Price Co., Kimberly-Clark; Taylor Co., Pershing. Brush and grass edges of the National State, and County Forests at times furnish fair shooting. However, hunters are advised to check during any pre-season with the DNR to ascertain where the current sharptail population appears to be highest.

PRAIRIE CHICKEN AND SPRUCE GROUSE

These species are mentioned simply to caution hunters that both are protected. Sharptail hunters may possibly see an occasional prairie chicken, and ruffed grouse hunters in the dense northern conifers may see spruce grouse.

HUNGARIAN PARTRIDGE

Huns were introduced from Europe in 1908. They are partial to cultivated farmlands. They reached a population peak in the 1930s, then leveled off to some extent. However, there is quite good shooting and the annual kill now averages, with some severe fluctuations, between 30,000 and 50,000 annually. The range of the Hun in Wisconsin is in the east, with the heaviest density in a strip along the border south of Green Bay. The birds are spread thinly westward, with the bulk of the range in the south.

Presently, over thirty counties are open each fall to hunting, south and east of the Wisconsin River. The open agricultural area of East-Central Wisconsin furnishes the best shooting, with the lakeshore counties of Brown, Calumet, Kewaunee, Manitowoc, Sheboygan among the best. Outagamie, Dodge, Jefferson, and Dane Cos. also have shown up in high-kill figures over recent seasons. For two consecutive seasons lately the first five counties were: Brown, Manitowoc, Outagamie, Sheboygan, Dodge, all in the East-Central district. The season prior to those two the first five were Brown, Manitowoc, Outagamie in East-Central, plus Jefferson and Dane in the South. Around 70 percent of the state kill comes from East-Central and the remainder from the south.

PHAs that furnish shooting for Huns, either as a primary or secondary species, are quite numerous, although much hunting of high quality is in the stubble and corn fields of private farmlands. In the East-Central region, Calumet Co. has Brillion and New Holstein PHAs with Huns resident. Dodge Co. has Wildcat Marsh, Fond du Lac Co. has Eden. In Kewaunee Co.,

Kewaunee Marsh PHA is a good bet, and in Manitowoc Co. there are Collins Marsh and Two Rivers. In Ozaukee Co. there is the Ulao PHA, in Sheboygan Co., Adell PHA, in Washington Co. there are Allenton and Theresa PHAs.

Following are South district PHAs that offer Huns: Dane Co., Deansville; Jefferson Co., Knob Hill, Princess Point, Waterloo; Kenosha Co., New Munster, Salem; Racine Co., Beulah Station; Rock Co., Evansville, Footville, Hanover, Lima Marsh; Walworth Co., Clover Valley, Troy; Waukesha Co., Vernon Marsh.

QUAIL

Bobwhites moved into southern and western Wisconsin as farmlands increased some years ago. At one time they were a fairly important game bird, with an average annual kill of about 20,000 birds. Clean farming and hard winters have brought them difficult times. As this is written there is no open season, but field reports of quail populations sound some note of hope for possible future seasons. Iowa, Sauk, Richland, Columbia are among the best counties.

MOURNING DOVES

The dove has long been classed as a songbird in this state. Over the past several years there has been agitation for a hunting season. Proposals have been brought before the legislature but up to the time of this writing have been defeated. It is quite possible that a dove season may materialize in the near future.

WILD TURKEYS

During pioneer days turkeys were common over much of southern Wisconsin. They were exterminated by the turn of the century. In recent years reintroduction into the West-Central area began, and met with some success. There were limited spring seasons in 1966, '67, and '68. In 1968, 1300 hunters were drawn for the hunt, and twenty gobblers were taken. A severe winter in '68–'69 badly harmed the turkey flocks and no 1969 season was possible. However, it is believed that Wisconsin will be able to have limited hunting during years of high nesting success. As this is written, most of the turkeys are located at the point where Juneau, Jackson, and Wood Cos. join. Live-trapped birds have been stocked in Clark, Eau Claire, Grant, Marinette, Crawford and Buffalo Cos., and there have been reports of a few broods from these transplants.

WOODCOCK

Woodcock are very plentiful in Wisconsin. There is a substantial nesting in the northern counties, and a good flight from the north during migration. Woodcock are found throughout the state wherever there is suitable cover. The average annual bag runs from 60,000 to 100,000, is usually less than the high figure. Most are killed as incidentals by grouse hunters but woodcock hunting is becoming more popular here, and there is quality hunting available for anyone who wishes to seek it.

The Northeast and East-Central areas furnish the highest percentages of the kill. The West-Central region is also quite good, and a fair number of birds are bagged in the South. Ordinarily the Northwest is lower than the other areas. However, the high-density portion of the state is a mixture of all four districts above the South. It can be described as bounded by

State 8 on the north, by State 27 on the west, and State 21 in the south, and running east to the Lake Michigan shore. Some of the top counties in these districts are: in the Northwest, Price; in the Northeast, Langlade, Marathon, Marinette, Oconto; in the West-Central, Adams and Clark; East-Central, Portage. Manitowoc Co. also shows up well and during one late season the first five were: Clark, Marathon, Manitowoc, Marinette, Oconto. The following season the first five were: Marinette, Wood, Marathon, Langlade, Price.

Actually it is easy to locate good woodcock shooting almost anywhere along tagalder-bordered streams and in comparable cover in the National, State, and County Forests, and on a number of the PHAs. While woodcock are not considered the primary species on any of the PHAs, mostly because they are migratory and a bit unpredictable, following is a list by counties of some of the tracts that usually have them in fair to abundant supply. The counties are listed here alphabetically, not by districts in which they are located.

COUNTY	PHA
Ashland	Hoffman Lake, White River
Barron	Loon Lake, New Auburn
Columbia	Jennings Creek
Dane	Deansville
Eau Claire	Pleasant Valley
Fond du Lac	St. Cloud
Green	Albany, Brooklyn, Browntown
Iowa	Avoca
Iron	Hay Creek, Underwood
Jackson	North Bend
Jefferson	Princess Point
Kenosha	New Munster, Salem
Lafayette	Spafford Creek
Langlade	Ackley
Lincoln	Alta Springs, New Wood, Prairie River
Marathon	McMillan Marsh, Mead, Nine Mile Swamp, Plover River
Marinette	Beaver Creek
Polk	McKenzie Creek, Rice Beds Creek
Price	Kimberly Clark, Spring Creek
Racine	Beulah Station, Karcher Marsh
Rock	Evansville
Rusk	Potato Creek, Silvernail, Tenmile Creek, Washington Creek
Sawyer	Eddy Creek, Flat Creek, Hauer Springs, Weirgor Springs
Shawano	Navarino Marsh
Washburn	Beaver Brook
Waukesha	Scuppernong
Waupaca	Mukwa

In addition to the above, almost all of the tracts noted under "Ruffed Grouse" will offer incidental woodcock shooting.

SNIPE AND RAILS

There is very good snipe hunting most seasons. The numerous wetlands are perfectly tailored to use by this bird during migration. Mud flats and semiflooded pasturelands are the spots that draw the birds. Most of the marshes used by waterfowl will have flights of snipe. There is no high interest in hunting jacksnipe, but the birds are available for those who wish to pursue this interesting shooting. Although there is a season on rails, the hunting is difficult and gets virtually no attention.

WATERFOWL

Wisconsin has an abundance of water for both ducks and geese, high interest among hunters and quality shooting in both categories. The duck bag fluctuates, but runs from half to three-quarters of a million or more. Perhaps most exciting in the waterfowl picture is the fortunate location of Horicon Marsh, a famed resting place for Canada geese during their migration. From 100,000 to almost 150,000 geese have used this area in a season. The goose kill has run over 15,000 Canadas in a season and at least 80 percent of the kill has come from what is known as the Horicon Marsh Zone.

Horicon Marsh lies in Dodge and Fond du Lac Cos. north of the city of Horicon. The southern portion, of 10,794 acres, is state owned. The northern part, of 20,924 acres, is federally owned and comprises the Horicon National Wildlife Refuge. Much of the state portion is open to small-game hunting and roughly 8000 acres are open for waterfowl hunting. There is good duck hunting as well as goose hunting, but the marsh is more famous for its concentrations of geese. There is some managed hunting under strict regulation on the federal portion.

Hunters desiring to hunt Horicon need to post themselves meticulously on regulations for the season of their hunt. There have been numerous problems here both with the geese and the shooting and consequently some fairly complicated rules are in force. Horicon gathered so many geese, which are field feeders, that the area could not support them for food. Vast flocks ranged out into surrounding farm country and caused extensive crop damage. Meanwhile the competition for food was so severe that the birds were rather easy to kill.

In 1960 very short seasons were begun for this reason. The 1967 season is a good example of the situation. Federal quotas were set up in stipulating how many Canada geese might be killed in Wisconsin. The quota was 20,000. Of these 15,000 could be taken in what was called the Horicon Marsh Zone, an eleven-county area with boundaries also stipulated. The remaining 5000 could be taken elsewhere in the state. The quota system means that if the quota is collected before the end of the season, then the season automatically ends.

That year 15,305 Canada geese were bagged over 69 of the state's 72 counties. But the 11-county Horicon Marsh Zone accounted for 12,332 of these. As this is written, no one may hunt Canada geese anywhere in the state without a permit. The permits, on a quota system for Horicon, are offered by drawing. Those who do not draw permits are automatically issued one for outside the Horicon Zone. Or, those who wish an outside permit and do not enter the Horicon drawing will get one. Successful Zone applicants are (presently) allowed to take one Canada goose, but four permits are issued for outside. There are tags with the permits and geese must be tagged. The permits are federally issued. There are three hunting periods for the Zone, and permits are valid for only one. The Zone has also been made smaller than originally. It should be noted that this is the system only as of this writing. Regulations may change at any time. Landowners are requested by the DNR to list with them available rental blinds. Thus the DNR can assist hunters in lining up a goose hunt on private lands.

The goose kill elsewhere corresponds closely to refuge areas. Juneau Co., where the 39,600-acre Necedah Wildlife Refuge is located, has a high goose kill. Neighboring Wood Co. also gets geese from the Refuge flights. There is also usually a good kill in Columbia Co., where Pine Island Refuge is located. Although there are twelve counties bordering the Mississippi River, the goose kills here are not high but there is fair hunting.

Many of the PHAs offer waterfowl as secondary species, and these should not be overlooked. However, a number of them are primarily for waterfowl. These are listed below, with the counties in alphabetical order. Hunters can be well oriented by keeping in mind that for both ducks and geese the south-eastern quarter of the state is the density section. With the welter of lakes and marshes there is of course much good shooting elsewhere, but the south-east funnels in the heaviest flights.

COUNTY	PHA
Barron	Loon Lake, New Auburn, Quaderer Creek, Sweeny Pond Creek
Bayfield	Lost Creek, Totogatic Lake
Brown	Long Tail Point, Sensiba
Buffalo	Tiffany
Burnett	Amsterdam Sloughs, Clam Lake, Crex Meadows, Fish Lake, Keizer Lake
Columbia	Grassy Lake, Mud Lake, Pine Island, Swan Lake
Crawford	Ambrough Boat Landing, Wauzeka
Dodge	Beaver Dam Lake, Horicon Marsh
Door	Gardner Swamp, Lost Lake, Mud Lake
Dunn	Big Beaver Creek, Dunnville, Eau Galle River
Fond du Lac	El Dorado, Mullet Creek, Rush Lake, Supple Marsh
Forest	Bog Brook, Little Rice
Grant	Blue River
Iowa	Avoca
Jackson	North Bend
Jefferson	Lake Mills, Rome Pond
Kenosha	Bong
La Crosse	Van Loon
Langlade	Woods Flowage
Manitowoc	Collins Marsh, Kiel Marsh
Marathon	McMillan Marsh, Mead
Marinette	Lake Noquebay, Peshtigo Harbor, Sea-gull Bar
Marquette	Germania Marsh
Oconto	Charles Pond, Pensaukee Marsh
Oneida	Thunder Lake
Outagamie	Outagamie

Ozaukee	Cedarburg Bog
Polk	Peterson Creek
Price	Spring Creek, Township Corners
Racine	Tichigan
Richland	Knapp Creek, Lone Rock
Rusk	Island Lake, Potato Creek, Tenmile Creek, Washington Creek
Sauk	Bakkens Pond
Sawyer	Benson Creek, Dead Springs Creek, Eddy Creek, Brownstone Springs, Totagatic River
Shawamo	Navarino Marsh
Sheboygan	Sheboygan Marsh
St. Croix	St. Croix Islands
Trempealeau	Trempealeau Lakes
Vilas	Powell Marsh
Washington	Theresa
Waukesha	Vernon Marsh
Waupaca	Muckwa
Waushara	Poygan Marsh
Winnebago	Jaeger's Island, Rush Lake
Wood	Wood

RABBITS

The state has cottontails ranging throughout but with low population in the forested north, and with the heavier concentrations in the southern half. The annual bag fluctuates from half a million to about a million. The South district and East-Central account for roughly 80 percent of the kill. The Northeast is next, then West-Central, then Northwest, the latter with only about 3 percent. During two recent seasons the five high counties were as follows: first season, Manitowoc, Waukesha, Dane, Jefferson, Marathon; second season, Dane, Manitowoc, Racine, Brown, Kenosha. A great many of the PHAs offer fine cottontail hunting.

The whitetailed jack is also on the game list. It is not abundant, but it is a sporty animal that turns white in winter and grows to large size. The animal ranges over the southern two-thirds of the state, with highest population in the southwest.

Snowshoe hares are also found in Wisconsin, in the northern half of the state but with greatest numbers in a broad forest swath along the northern border. Oddly, there is no great interest among hunters in this sporty hare, as there is in many other states. However, there are a few enthusiasts. The National and State Forests of the north, already mentioned, are good locations. A few PHAs also offer good snowshoe hunting. Among these are White River in Ashland Co., Flag River and White River in Bayfield Co. In Burnett Co. there are Danbury, Kohler-Peet, Namekagon Barrens, in Iron Co. there are Big Island and Underwood. Lincoln Co. has Spring Lake, Marinette Co. has Amberg. In Price Co.: Kimberly-Clark, Spring Creek; Rusk Co.: Silvernail; Sawyer Co.: Chief River, Flat Creek, Kissick Swamp.

SQUIRRELS

There are both gray and fox squirrels. The grays inhabit large stands of mixed and hardwood timber, the fox squirrels are more abundant in farm woodlots. Together they are very important to hunters, with a kill averaging around 1,250,000, but sometimes much higher. The major share of the bag is in the southern half of the state, and grays predominate. As a rule the leading counties are Sauk, Dane, Marathon, Grant, Juneau. All of the public lands with woodlots, or with good stands of hardwood forest or with hardwood intermingled with conifers offer squirrel hunting.

DEER

Wisconsin is one of the top whitetail deer states in the nation. With all its forests and other suitable habitat, the state estimates roughly 29,000 square miles of deer range over its 72 counties. There are presently some 450,000 gun hunters and 100,000 bow hunters following this sport annually. The deer herd is estimated to number about 700,000. A few years ago the state had set a goal of harvesting from 75,000 to 100,000 deer each season. But for several years now the kill has exceeded that. For three consecutive seasons of late the total kills have run in round numbers 103,000, 116,000, 136,000. Of the last figure, 128,597 were gun kills, 7523 were bow kills.

The state is divided for regulations purposes first into five general Zones for which the general gun seasons are set. Hunts in these differ by dates, and some may be bucks only, some either sex, as the level of the herd dictates. The archery season, which is usually a split season, covers all counties. Then in addition to these general seasons there are Quota Areas. The state is divided into (at present) seventy-nine Units for each of which a specified number of permits is offered, or, in some cases, only for a certain number of the Units, while the others remain closed. Most of these are either-sex hunts. Obviously, boundaries and quotas may change for any given season. It is thus mandatory that Wisconsin deer hunters obtain from the DNR, address at chapter end, the Big-Game Hunting Regulations for that year, which contain a map showing Zones and Units and giving numbers of permits for each Unit.

An interesting caution for hunters to note well is that it is not legal in Wisconsin to kill any white deer. A number of albino deer have shown up here, and in several instances a small number of them have been observed in the same areas. Some years ago one of the most famous of wildlife photos was taken by a Department official, of several white deer feeding together in winter. The white deer subsequently received much publicity and full protection.

The National Forests, State Forests, and County Forests already described earlier in the chapter furnish excellent deer hunting, and the bulk of it. Sixty-three of the PHAs also have deer as a primary game species, and many of the others offer fair hunting. It is therefore not difficult to locate a hunting spot.

To give deer hunters a fair basic picture of chances of success and where they may be best, the following facts should be studied. During a recent high-kill season, the buck kill was over 73,000. The quota permits totaled 64,200, and 47,785 deer were taken on these. Thirty-one of the seventy-two counties were open entirely or in part to either-sex hunting. Forty-one of the 72 counties had kills of 100 or more, from Iowa Co. in the South with 1027 to Bayfield in the far Northwest with 4144.

A few counties were still higher. The top-ranked 10 were, in order, Waupaca, Jackson, Marinette, all with over 5000 deer taken; Oneida, Bayfield, Wood, with each over 4000; Waushara, Shawano, Marathon, Price, each over 3000. Interesting indeed is the fact that top-ranked Waupaca was limited to shotguns only. This county also led in the bow kill.

There is actually not much choice among the various districts, except that the South, with its numerous farms, has a lower kill than the others. One recent season the five districts were rated in order of numbers of deer taken as follows: Northeast, West-Central, Northwest, East-Central, South. The previous season they stacked up: Northwest, Northeast, West-Central, East-Central, South. However, the four districts above the South all were within a few thousand of each other.

To help orient hunters further in selecting their place to hunt, the ten top-ranked counties have for several seasons accounted for from 30 to 33 percent of the total state kill. These same ten counties also have for several seasons accounted for about 35 percent of the buck harvest.

Looking at buck harvests by districts and counties within them, the listing is as follows for first five in each for high buck kills. Northwest: Bayfield, Douglas, Price, Burnett, Sawyer. Northeast: Marinette, Oneida, Shawano, Marathon, Lincoln. West-Central: Eau Claire, Wood, Adams, Clark, Juneau. East-Central: Waupaca, Portage, Waushara, Marquette, Outagamie. South: Columbia, Sauk, Jefferson, Richland, Green. Excepting the last four counties of the South, all of the above had kills of over 1500 deer each and a number of them between 2000 and 3000. This shows quite well where the bucks are most likely to be bagged.

BEAR

There is fairly good black bear hunting. The better range is in the north along the border counties, but bear also range over most of the northern third of the state, and reach in smaller areas into the interior. Only specified Units are open each season. There are special early bear seasons when dogs may be used. Archers may participate in these. Quite a number of bear are taken by archers. Over a three-year period the archery kill was 56, 54, 92. The total kill for the same three seasons: 308, 475, 541.

Almost all of the kill comes from the Northwest and Northeast. When some Units are open in the East-Central area only a few animals are bagged, from one to three or four per county. There is little choice between Northwest and Northeast. During the same three seasons mentioned above, the kills in the Northwest were 144, 229, 265, and in the Northeast they were 163, 243, 276. The National and State Forests of these districts, plus some County Forests, furnish the bulk of the hunting.

Most counties of the northern two tiers have good bear populations. Among the best bear counties: Bayfield, Ashland, Washburn, Sawyer, Forest, Marinette.

OTHER ANIMALS

Hunters should be aware that moose, elk, timber wolves, badgers, lynx have full protection. It is also illegal in Wisconsin to shoot woodchucks, except as provided under laws pertaining to animals doing damage.

Raccoons are quite plentiful, are considered a game animal, but much of the state is open all year to hunting them. Check the regulations and map therein showing seasons in various parts of the state. The northern counties have light populations. The areas of abundance are in the extreme southeast and the counties along the major rivers.

Red foxes also are plentiful, and offer good hunting especially after the game seasons. They are not protected. There are a few gray foxes, mostly in the southwest. They also are unprotected. Bobcats are not abundant, are found in the northern fringe of forested counties, and have so far no protection. Coyotes, while far from abundant, are found in the north and the interior.

They elicit interest from hound men and animal callers, and some organized winter hunts are held for them. One such large hunt, in winters, is held in the vicinity of Phillips. There is a registration fee. The coyote, like the foxes, has no protection.

There are some guides with dog packs who will book hunts for such animals as coyotes, foxes, bobcats, and bear. Contact the DNR for assistance in locating them.

REGULATIONS

Game laws pertaining to seasons, bag and possession limits, areas to be hunted, special hunts, license fees all may have numerous changes from year to year. For current regulations, and for other specific queries, write to: Wisconsin Department of Natural Resources, Division of Conservation, Box 450, Madison, Wisconsin 53701.

MINNESOTA

Minnesota can be pictured as a kind of transition zone between the densely forested region of the Great Lakes and the wide-open plains of the Dakotas. It has distinct attributes of each, and its economy is based upon the diversity of its terrain. About two-thirds of Minnesota is rolling prairie. This encompasses much of the west and the south, and here croplands and dairy farming are the chief activities. But in the north-central region and the northeast, and also in the southeast, there are huge expanses of forest. The northeast especially furnishes vast amounts of pulpwood and other forest products, and from here, too, comes iron ore used by numerous U.S. manufacturers.

The diversity of terrain and vegetative cover has made Minnesota a grand state for the hunter. So have the thousands—over 14,000—of lakes large and small that are distributed almost everywhere over its surface. Here are some of the most important wetlands for waterfowl production on the entire continent.

Minnesota, with over 84,000 square miles, is larger than any of the states surrounding it. To the west are both Dakotas. Iowa is to the south. On the east is Wisconsin, with much of the boundary formed by the Mississippi and St. Croix rivers. In the northeast the boundary is the western shore of Lake Superior. To the north Minnesota touches southwestern Ontario and southeastern Manitoba. For hunters driving from the south to far northern Minnesota the distance is almost 400 miles, straight-line, and east-west along the northern border it is about the same. The narrow middle, however, west from Minneapolis, is not quite half that, and along the southern border the straight-line width is roughly 275 miles.

The highway network throughout all of the state is excellent, but there are two areas where roads are few or nonexistent. One of these is the wonderful wilderness region of the extreme northeast, the Quetico-Superior Boundary Waters Canoe Area. The other is a portion of the north to the west of International Falls. However, hunters operating almost anywhere in the state get along nicely with standard passenger car transport, although a pickup or 4WD is an excellent type of vehicle for the forest trails of the north. Air travel is easy within the state. The hub is at Minneapolis, but there are over 200 airports well distributed to put a hunter into almost any sector.

The population presently has passed 3.5 million. About a third of this total, however, is centered in the Minneapolis-Saint Paul complex, and most of the remainder in numerous small cities and towns. Thus there is still ample room for the hunter, and in the deer country of the north population is sparse and true wilderness available as soon as one moves off the forest roads.

Hunting is extremely popular, with well over 10 percent of the population pursuing either small or big game or both each season. More than 300,000 hunt deer each year, and there are at least 350,000 small-game hunters. Total hunter numbers average around 470,000. Oddly, even with the excellent hunting available, nonresident visitors are few, and at this time seldom more than 3000 a season.

Game is varied. Pheasants and ruffed grouse are the most abundant upland game birds, but there are also sharptail grouse and Hungarian partridge. Small-game species are gray and fox squirrels, cottontails, snowshoe hares, jackrabbits. There are woodcock and snipe, and abundant waterfowl. The whitetail deer is the prime big-game species, but black bear are also present. A few wolves, numerous foxes, raccoons, some bobcats and lynx offer other hunting possibilities.

Finding a place to hunt in Minnesota is easy. This state has been foresighted in keeping public lands and constantly adding to them. Approximately 26 percent of the state is public land. While most of that is located in the north, there are literally hundreds of small tracts elsewhere, and even though many of these are small, their value is great because they sustain the popular species such as ducks and pheasants. Often excellent shooting can be had for these on only a few acres.

The north has two large National Forests. The Chippewa NF (1) contains over 640,000 acres. It is located in north-central Minnesota, with U.S. 2, 71, and 371 all giving access, and with numerous state highways also entering the region. The headwaters of the Mississippi River are here, and some large lakes such as Leech, Winnibigoshish and Cass. The towns of Grand Rapids, Cass Lake, Bemidji, Blackduck, Walker are key locations. The Superior National Forest (2) covers a huge portion of the northeast, over two million acres. The Boundary Waters Canoe Area is here, one of the Wilderness Areas of the National Forest System. U.S. 53 and 61, State 169, 35, 73, and 1 are access routes, with Duluth, International Falls, Ely, Grand Marais some of the key cities and towns. Maps and details pertaining to these Forests can be obtained from the Forest Supervisor, as follows. Chippewa NF, Cass Lake, Minnesota; Superior NF, Duluth, Minnesota.

There are nearly three million public acres in fifty-four State Forests. Most of these are in the north central and northeast but a number are in the east, and one very large one, the Minnesota Memorial Hardwood SF (3) takes in much of the extreme southeast. There is a booklet, brought annually up to date, titled "Recreational Areas," which lists and locates all of the State Forests and pinpoints camping sites and other facilities within them. It also lists district offices from which specific details for any of the Forests may be obtained. The booklet can be had from the Division of Lands and Forests, Minnesota Conservation Department, address at end of chapter. There are also listed in this same booklet a number of other recreational areas outside the State Forests. Hunters should check as to whether or not individual tracts are open to hunting.

Counties in Minnesota also own in total a vast public acreage. This amounts to some 3.5 million acres. For locations of these tracts it is best for visiting hunters to query either regional supervisors of the Department of Conservation, or else to go directly to county seats to study county maps.

The number of State Wildlife Management Areas in Minnesota is amazing. At the present time there are about 630 individual tracts and more are constantly being added. These vary greatly in size. The Red Lake WMA, for example, contains 488,509 acres. The Roseau River WMA has 53,376. Yet many of the wetland WMAs are as small as 40 acres and some have as little as 5 acres. These wetlands tracts are for the most part in the west and southwest, but there are many across the interior and the south and southeast. There is a large map available, "Minnesota Wetlands—Location of State Wildlife Management Areas," which is brought up to date periodically. It shows all the tracts on the map, lists them on the back with exact location by county, nearest town, and number of miles from it. All of these public tracts are fenced where necessary and posted with signs that show their boundaries. The map can be obtained from the Conservation Department.

Another group of public tracts of importance are the federal Waterfowl Production Areas. These were purchased by the federal government for the purpose of assisting nesting waterfowl in the Prairie Pothole Country of Minnesota and the Dakotas. Most of them are in the central part of western Minnesota. They are open in fall to public hunting, and while they are primarily waterfowl grounds, they furnish a great deal of hunting for pheasants and other small game. At this writing there are 384 of these WPAs. They range in size from a few acres to over 600 acres. A map that lists all and gives directions to each plus the size of each can be had from the Regional Director, Bureau of Sport Fisheries and Wildlife, 1006 West Lake Street, Minneapolis 55408. Title of this map: "Your Guide to Federal Waterfowl Production Areas of Minnesota."

Thus, with 2 National Forests, 54 State Forests, and over 1000 tracts in State WMAs and Federal WPAs, Minnesota is peppered with public hunting grounds. In addition to all of these, there are several hundred thousand acres of forest lands owned by paper companies that allow hunting. Boise-Cascade, Kimberly-Clark, Saint Regis, Baldwin, and Northwest Paper companies all have such lands. Because many of these are interspersed with other lands it is impossible to locate them here. However, the Department of Conservation and especially the regional supervisors and/or conservation officers can be of great assistance in helping hunters locate specific tracts. Almost all of these are in the north and northeast.

Because of the huge number of public hunting grounds in Minnesota, they will not be individually described and located in the following material dealing with individual species. Instead, the range of greatest abundance of each species will be described, where possible by counties, and the number of public tracts in those counties noted. Hunters visiting those counties can thus at a glance pinpoint select spots to hunt and will never be more than a few miles from several. Those who write to the Department of Conservation for the booklets and maps already mentioned will by reference to ranges of species have a complete picture.

For hunters who wish to camp, the "Recreational Areas" booklet noted is an excellent guide to State Forest and other recreational area campgrounds. There are also the National Forests, and State Parks. A booklet, "Let's Go Camping in Minnesota," can be had from the Division of State Parks, Centennial Building, Saint Paul 55101. For non-campers, motel and lodge accommodations are abundant. It might be wise, however, on some season openings such as pheasant and deer to make reservations in a selected area ahead of time.

Weather during the September openings of several fall game seasons is likely to be gently crisp and lovely. As October nears, although a light wool shirt will do nicely during the day, mornings and evenings may be frosty, especially in the north, and a jacket mandatory. From then on storms may arrive at any time. Deer season can be cold, with snow, and heavy clothing should be on hand. In fact, during any hunting season it is not a bad idea here to be outfitted for either mild or cold weather.

Shotgun hunters should consider No. 6 shotshells for pheasants, No. 7½ for ruffed grouse, but fall back to something larger, such as highbase No. 6 or else No. 4 for ducks, and No. 2 for geese. Deer hunters can use any of a number of standard calibers as representative—the .30/06, .308, .270, .243 or something comparable.

PHEASANT

The ringneck was introduced to Minnesota in 1905, and the first season was held in 1924 in two counties near Minneapolis, with approximately 300 roosters bagged. By 1931 pheasants had colonized so swiftly from game farm stocking and natural breeding that 49 counties were open and a million cocks were harvested. The pheasant had quickly become the most important upland game bird in the state, and has remained so ever since.

However, it has had many ups and downs. Total pheasant population ranges from as high as five million to lows of one million. Over recent years changes in land use, with farms too cleanly stripped of cover, has brought decline to the pheasants. Without adequate winter cover especially, severe storms have drastically reduced populations. As recently as 1967 the pheasant kill had dropped to about 141,000. Presently a concentrated effort to get landowners to assist the birds, and to provide better management for them, is slowly gaining results. The goal for present-day Minnesota is a peak population of about 3.5 million birds each fall, so that the harvest can be a million. Biologists feel that this goal can be attained.

Minnesota has some 45,000 square miles of pheasant range, or a bit more than half of the state. This range is in the south and west, excepting the northwest. It begins in the east in southern Pine County and the northern limits of adequate range follows a line toward the northwest that touches the western border in southern Polk County. Not all of the broad range has high pheasant density. The counties of the south-central, west-central, and southwestern sectors are best, in the regions of concentrated agriculture.

The very best concentrations are in the southern counties: Martin, on the southern border about centrally located, eastern Jackson which borders it on the west, parts of Cottonwood and Watonwan to the north of these, and Brown and Nicollet bordering those on the north. Spreading out from this area

284

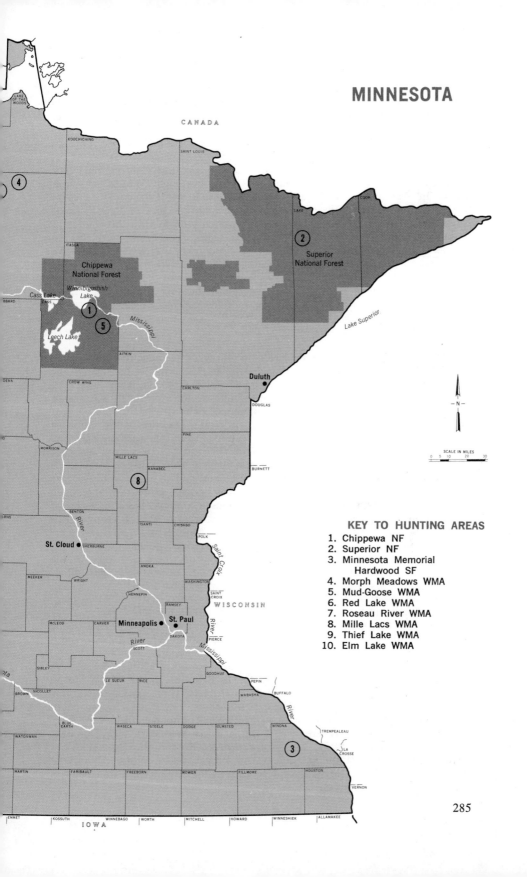

MINNESOTA

CANADA

Chippewa
National Forest

Superior
National Forest

Lake Superior

Duluth

St. Cloud

WISCONSIN

Minneapolis St. Paul

IOWA

KEY TO HUNTING AREAS
1. Chippewa NF
2. Superior NF
3. Minnesota Memorial
   Hardwood SF
4. Morph Meadows WMA
5. Mud-Goose WMA
6. Red Lake WMA
7. Roseau River WMA
8. Mille Lacs WMA
9. Thief Lake WMA
10. Elm Lake WMA

SCALE IN MILES
0 5 10   20   30

285

over a wide portion of the southwest is what may be considered "good" range. A line drawn roughly from Albert Lea in Freeborn Co. on the southern border northwest to Moorhead in Clay Co. on the North Dakota border takes in all of the "good" and "best" pheasant range below it. A narrow strip in the extreme southwest running along the western border across Lincoln, Pipestone, and Rock Cos. is considered just "fair."

Martin Co. contains four WMAs. Jackson Co. has eighteen plus nine Waterfowl Production Areas. Cottonwood Co. has eight WMAs and four WPAs. In Watonwan Co. there are nine WMAs. Brown Co. has four. All of these are thus within limits of the quality pheasant range. The "good" range spreading out from this nucleus is literally dotted with WMAs throughout its southwestern and northwestern portions especially. There are over 100. In addition, the concentration of Waterfowl Production Areas lies within the northwestern part of this range, with about 200 tracts inside its borders. No hunter within all of the better pheasant hunting quarter of the state is thus ever more than a few miles from a well-marked public hunting ground. Many more of the public blocks are within the range of fair abundance to the north of the line.

RUFFED GROUSE

Originally the top uplander prior to pheasant introduction, the native ruffed grouse has long been exceedingly popular. Minnesota is considered one of the top grouse states, and the kill has in a few peak years run from 1¼ to 1½ million birds. It averages closer to half a million. Because the ruffed grouse is strictly a forest and forest-edge bird, its range is almost exactly opposite that of the pheasant. The bird is found from the border counties of the southeast throughout the east, central, and north excepting the extreme northwest.

The southeastern population is just fair. The heaviest concentrations occur in the southern half of the northern forest region. This is because there are more openings, more second growth, forest cutting, burns and trails. Dense stands of evergreen forest never hold as many grouse as do the more open mixed second growth portions. In some sections Minnesota has a program of seeding forest trails and old log roads with clover to attract grouse. This makes them easily available to hunters walking the trails.

Beginning in the north, on the western edge of the quality grouse range, and reading south and around to the eastern border, here are some of the better grouse counties: eastern Roseau and all of Lake of the Woods; all of Beltrami and Clearwater south of those; all of Hubbard and Cass; eastern Wadena and Todd; all of Crow Wing; northern Morrison; northern Mille Lacs; all of Kanabec and Pine. All of the remaining counties north and east of these are within the best grouse range but, as mentioned, the southern forests in the range generally have the highest populations. Counties immediately south and west of those named have fair grouse populations.

There are numerous WMAs within the top range: 3 of modest size in Lake of the Woods Co.; 3 in Roseau; 8 in Beltrami, including the Morph Meadows WMA (4) of over 5000 acres; 5 in Hubbard Co.; 7 in Cass, with one of them, Mud-Goose WMA (5), almost 11,000 acres; 3 in Wadena; 17 in Todd; 6 in Crow Wing; 7 in Morrison; 3 in Mille Lacs; 7 in Kanabec; 9 in Pine. In addition to these, there are several much larger WMAs in these counties. Red Lake WMA (6) lies in Lake of the Woods, Roseau and Beltrami Cos., contains almost half a million acres. The Roseau River WMA (7) in that county has 53,376. The Mille Lacs WMA (8) in that county and Kanabec Co. contains nearly 38,000 acres.

Both of the National Forests, the Chippewa and Superior, lie within the grouse range and furnish excellent hunting. They are noted early in the chapter. In addition, all but a few of the fifty-four State Forests are in the grouse territory of the north and east, and the remainder are along the western fringe, and in the southeast where fair grouse shooting can be had. Taking all these lands in total, they add up to the fact that over half of the entire range of the ruffed grouse is in public ownership, and thus finding a good hunting spot for this species presents no problems.

SHARPTAIL GROUSE

This handsome grouse once ranged over much more territory in Minnesota than it does today. Fundamentally a bird of the prairie brushlands, its habitat has decreased in the face of farming, reforestation, and the maturing of forests logged during the last century. Although just recently there has been some improvement in sharptail numbers, this may be only a cyclic peak; it is probable that the continued deterioration of habitat may mean further decline.

Hunting pressure is not severe, however, and there is still fairly good shooting, presently with a limit of 3 birds per day. Ten to fifteen years ago the average annual sharptail kill ran anywhere from 50,000 to over 100,000 bidrs. In the mid-sixties it hit a drastic low of 5000, but during a recent season climbed to over 15,000.

Almost all of Minnesota's sharptails are in the northwest. The best counties are: eastern Kittson; all of Roseau; all of Lake of the Woods; the eastern half of Marshall; the northern half of Beltrami. To the east, south, and west of this region there is habitat of lesser importance in a modest fringe. There is another pocket of fair sharptail habitat on the other side of the state roughly along the line of U.S. 2 west of Duluth. However, the boundaries within which hunting is currently allowed are carefully drawn each season, and hunters should read the laws carefully to make certain of the open area. Recently there has been a closed portion of the northwest in the vicinity of Williams and Warroad, south of Lake of the Woods Reservoir. And, in the east, U.S. 2 has been a demarcation line, with no hunting south of it.

The large amount of public lands in Lake of the Woods, Beltrami and Roseau Cos. has already been noted under "Ruffed Grouse." Kittson Co., which is all within sharptail range but with the eastern half the best, has two large WMAs of some thousands of acres, and Marshall Co., also all within the range but with the eastern half best, has 8 WMAs, one of which, Thief Lake (9), is over 33,000 acres and another Elm Lake (10) over 15,000. There are several large State Forests in the region, too, and their fringes, and the mixed grass and second growth of these, often offer good shooting.

Although there is ample public land in sharptail territory, the fact that the northwest is a mixed pattern of farms, forests, burns, and bogs has drawn the sharptail predominantly to farmlands and their fringes, where grain is available. Thus the best of the hunting is on private farmlands. Permission is often granted, but the wise hunter will try to line up his hunting spot previous to opening day.

HUNGARIAN PARTRIDGE

The Hun, introduced many years ago, is not truly abundant, but is nonetheless well established over a fairly large range. This covers much of the agricultural area of the state. A line drawn south, beginning in western Roseau Co. up in the northwest and continued down through Mahnomen Co., then gently curved on south and east across Becker, mid-Otter Tail and continuing on an increasingly acute curve down to mid-Fillmore Co. in the southeast encloses most of the Hun range to the west of it. Over almost all of this area Huns are in scattered coveys and only locally abundant. The area of greatest density is along the Red River (the North Dakota border) in western Polk Co., the western half of Norman Co., all of Clay Co., northeastern Wilkin and northwestern Otter Tail Cos.

Much of this density region is within the northwestern limits of fair pheasant range, and almost all of the remainder of the Hun territory lies within the better pheasant range. Thus, Huns are as a rule hunted as incidentals by pheasant hunters. They lie well to a dog and a scattering of Hun specialists concentrates on them, but the number of such hunters is not large. Some years ago the kill ran as high as 50,000 birds annually. The 1960s saw a drastic drop, but at this writing an upward trend is under way. A recent seasonal kill was almost 15,000.

Although most coveys will be found on private lands because this bird clings to grain fields and their edges, many can also be located on the public shooting grounds. The several hundred tracts in this part of the state in WMAs and WPAs give ample opportunity for Hun hunting.

In the counties of highest density public tracts are numerous. Polk Co. contains 27 WMAs running from 25 acres up to 1280 acres. Eastern Polk Co., which has a fair Hun population, also contains 13 Waterfowl Production Areas. Norman Co. has 11 WMAs from 80 to 1300 acres. These are mainly in the central and east, but still in fair Hun range. Clay Co. has 17 WMAs and 13 WPAs, all in good Hun territory. Wilkin Co. has 4 WMAs, the largest, Rothsay, of nearly 3000 acres. There are also 2 small WPAs in Clay Co. Otter Tail Co. contains 20 WMAs and 55 WPAs.

SPRUCE GROUSE, PRAIRIE CHICKEN, CHUKAR, QUAIL, MOURNING DOVES

These species are mentioned to make certain hunters are aware that there are no open seasons on them. Spruce grouse may be encountered in dense forest areas of the north and east by ruffed grouse hunters. Prairie chickens, once abundant but now almost certainly headed toward extinction here unless changes in land use to save them can be instigated, are found in the west-central part of the state and in the northwest, may be flushed on occasion by pheasant or sharptail hunters. There are probably no more than 10,000 prairie chickens in the state. Bobwhites occur as remnant populations in the southeast.

WILD TURKEYS

The wild turkey has been stocked in Whitewater State Park. It is known that broods have been reared. However, there is at this time no open season and indications are that hunters are not likely to find this bird on the game list even on a limited basis in the near future.

WOODCOCK, SNIPE, RAILS

None of these birds is hunted to any extent in Minnesota. It is doubtful that the state has more than a thousand woodcock hunters. Biologists estimate that the kill of woodcock and snipe probably is in the aggregate under 10,000 and the rail kill is infinitesimal. Although rails are exceedingly difficult to hunt around inland waters because they seldom can be flushed, the possibilities for both woodcock and snipe hunting here are excellent.

As this is written a thorough woodcock investigation is underway. Presently most woodcock hunting is done in the east-central part of the state. The greatest breeding population of birds is thought to be located along the many stream courses of the north Lake Superior shore. Flight birds funnel south along the St. Croix and the Mississippi. Pine Co. and adjacent counties get good numbers of birds. Virtually all of the northeast and north, except the far northwest, is woodcock territory, and so is the border country of the east. This hunting needs to be thoroughly investigated by more sportsmen.

The same is true of jacksnipe shooting. Almost all of the hundreds of WMAs and WPAs of the west, southwest, and south offer snipe shooting of varying quality, and so do the hundreds of lake shores and marshes lying within State and National Forest boundaries.

WATERFOWL

Minnesota is an excellent waterfowl state. It is one of the prime nesting states for ducks, and it gets a good migration flight also, plus large flights of geese. In addition to migrating geese, Minnesota has been experimenting with establishment of resident flocks of Canadas. There is also a large flock of giant Canadas, at Rochester. Waterfowl hunting is extremely popular here. Recently as many as 158,000 waterfowl hunters have been afield in a season.

The duck kill runs as high as 1,300,000. As a rule the mallard makes up about a third of the bag, bluewing teal a fourth, the ringnecked duck another fourth. There are also wood ducks, some redheads, scaups, pintails, canvasbacks and other species. In good years at least a fourth of the ducks taken in the fourteen-state Mississippi Flyway are harvested in Minnesota.

The goose kill is also high. Recently a total of 31,500 were bagged in a season. The average is somewhat lower. At least half of the geese bagged are Canadas. Snows and blues, about evenly divided, make up almost all of the other half. A very few white-fronted geese (specklebellies) are killed along the western border. Their main migration route is farther west. Usually only a few hundred turn up in a season's bag.

There are so many places for public waterfowl hunting that they cannot possibly be lised here. As mentioned early in the chapter, the federal Waterfowl Production Areas number 384 and are open to hunting. Their numbers within counties, listed by counties alphabetically, are as follows: Becker, 26; Big Stone, 42; Clay, 13; Cottonwood, 4; Douglas, 39; Grant, 29; Jackson, 9; Kandiyohi, 30; Lac qui Parle, 9; Mahnomen, 15; Otter Tail, 15; Polk, 13; Pope, 34; Stearns, 10; Stevens, 29; Swift, 17; Traverse, 7; Wilkin, 2; Yellow Medicine, 1. A study of the map will show that the major share of these is in the central part of the west. This is the state's great waterfowl-producing region.

As was mentioned early in the chapter, Minnesota's WMAs, which number at present about 630, are predominantly wetlands. These are also concentrated in the west and south, with at least 500 of them within this region where duck hunting is at its best and where geese pause to feed in grain fields on their way south. Thus, finding a place to hunt waterfowl in Minnesota is simply a matter of selecting a site. Aside from these hundreds of wetlands tracts, there are hundreds of beaver ponds and lakes of varying size within State Forest and National Forest boundaries where duck shooting is excellent. And stream floats can also be enjoyed. Also, goose flights follow the large rivers to some extent—the St. Croix, the Mississippi, the Red River of the North, the Sioux, the Minnesota.

There are several waterfowl refuges in the state that are important for their concentrations of waterfowl. These are: Agassiz in Marshall Co. in the northwest; 35,000-acre Tamarac in Becker Co. in the lower northwest; Rice Lake in Aitkin Co. in central Minnesota with over 18,000 acres; the Upper Mississippi Refuge, a portion of which lies in southeastern Minnesota along the Mississippi River.

RABBITS

There are three species of rabbits and hares in Minnesota; the cottontail, the whitetailed jackrabbit, the snowshoe hare. Oddly, although these animals are quite plentiful, they have never been so very popular among Minnesota hunters. Among the three they almost blanket the state in range, but an average annual kill is about as follows: cottontail, 100,000; jack, 20,000; snowshoe, 13,500.

The cottontail inhabits all the southern half of the state and ranges on up the west and west-central portion to southern Polk Co. The region of highest density is in the southwestern quarter of the state. The hundreds of WMAs and WPAs here and in the remainder of cottontail range offer limitless opportunities for public hunting.

The range of the big whitetailed jack covers most of the cottontail territory, but does not run down into the southeast in any of the border area. And the jacks range in the west clear up a county-wide strip of western border to the Canadian border. The area of greatest abundance is about like that for the cottontail. These large hares, which turn white in winter, are often hunted for their pelts. They grow very large, from six to nine pounds and sometimes even larger, and offer good winter sport in open farm country. The jack is considered a game animal and thus given protection except during the stipulated season.

The snowshoe hare is plentiful in forests of the northeast, even though it does not get much attention. The National Forests, and the State Forests that are concentrated in the northeastern third of the state, furnish excellent opportunities.

SQUIRRELS

There are both fox squirrels and gray squirrels in Minnesota. Because it is dependent upon hardwood forests for food, the gray squirrel is found in greatest abundance over much of central and southeastern Minnesota. The predominantly coniferous forests of the north and northeast do not offer proper habitat. The Memorial Hardwood Forest of the southeast, the State Forests along and south of U.S. 2 running west from Duluth are in gray squirrel territory. As is the case with rabbits, squirrel hunting is not especially popular in the state. The gray squirrel kill is the higher of the two species, averaging around 150,000. Fox squirrels are found in the woodlots of the southern farming region. The kill runs from 100,000 to 145,000. Almost all of the many public tracts of the south have woodlots that offer fair to good fox squirrel hunting.

DEER

The whitetail deer is Minnesota's important big-game animal, and this state is one of the best whitetail states in the U.S. Deer range over the entire state. The total herd is variously estimated today at from 600,000 to 750,000 animals. For the past decade the kill has been near or over 100,000 annually. It has run as high as 127,000-plus. And total hunter success in a single season has run over 50 percent. During the past few seasons, with 300,000 or more deer hunters, it has run from about 35 to 40 percent. This is much higher than average whitetail success in most states. Interestingly enough, records kept since 1918 show that even though hunter numbers were less than 24,000 that year and are now pegged at over 300,000, success has remained curiously consistent so far as low range is concerned. It has never run below 28 percent; most seasons have run in the 30s or 40s. Some exceptional ones have skyrocketed into the 70s and 80s. Nowadays a bit less than half the deer killed are bucks. It is therefore almost certain that anyone hunting deer in Minnesota has at least one chance in three of scoring, and usually better than that, even with hunter numbers ever growing.

For season purposes the state is divided into Zones. At this writing there are eight open Zones. The southwest, south, and west of U.S. 212 and State 15 has been closed, except for a bow season. The Zones are set up not for issuance of a certain number of permits, but for length of seasons and firearms specified.

The best deer range is in northeastern, eastern, central, and northern Minnesota, excepting the extreme northwest. In this vast region are the two National Forests, and all of the fifty-four State Forests, plus several of the very large WMAs such as Red Lake in Beltrami, Lake-of-the-Woods and Roseau Cos., Thief Lake in Marshall Co., Roseau River in Roseau Co. Thus there is no problem whatever in finding a place to hunt deer. A number of the smaller WMAs also offer some deer hunting. But the large forest tracts are usually best.

In fact, surveys show that the northern forest region that is heavily weighted to public lands has the greatest number of successful hunters. However, it takes a bit longer, according to these surveys, for the forest hunters to bag a deer. Agricultural area hunters are much less successful, percentagewise, but those who get a deer do so more quickly. This is because the farm-country hunters are much more likely to have deer spotted before season and to quickly bag their quarry, after which remaining deer become exceedingly wary. The forest hunter must hunt a greater area, but given enough time is reasonably sure of bringing home a deer.

Louis Co. in the northeast (the city of Virginia is a key point) usually has the highest harvest. Atasca, Cass, Aitkin to the west and south come next in order. Koochiching, northwest of Saint Louis and bordering Canada (International Falls) is next. Then comes Beltrami to the west, followed by Pine, which is south of Duluth and along the eastern border. This indicates that the bulk of the harvest is in the north, northeast, and east forest region. However, success percentages by counties show the following, which is the same general north-forest pattern but with counties somewhat different, and a few surprises outside the north-forest district. In order they are: Cook in the extreme northeast; Mahnomen in the lower northwest; Big Stone in the upper southwest on the South Dakota border; Koochiching and Lake in the north and northeast; Clearwater, Red Lake; Kittson, Beltrami in the northwest; and Traverse Co., which borders Big Stone (upper southwest) on the north.

In a recent season that may be considered representative, the following counties had success percentage of over 50 percent: Beltrami; Big Stone; Carlton; Chippewa; Clearwater; Cook; Cottonwood; Kittson; Koochiching; Lake; Mahnomen; Marshall; Otter Tail; Pipestone; Red Lake; Roseau; St. Louis; Traverse; Waseca; Wilkin. Of these, however, a few had such small kills that they are not really relevant: Cottonwood; Pipestone; Waseca. However, the same season fifty-four of Minnesota's counties showed hunter success of above 40 percent. That indicates excellent deer hunting indeed.

There are usually several hunts on military installations and bow hunts in specified State Parks to remove surplus deer. Contact the Department of Conservation for information about these.

BEAR

The status of the black bear in Minnesota is at this time undoubtedly in transition. Traditionally it has not received protection and has in general been considered a nuisance animal. However, some measure of protection has been given it over recent years and it is quite probable that the black bear will in due course receive better treatment here than it has so far been accorded. It is in fact surprising that in today's world of need for recreational hunting and in a state practicing enlightened game management the black bear has so far been so shoddily, or ineptly, treated.

Range of the black bear is today in the northeastern third of the state, north and east of a line roughly drawn from Roseau to Pine City. This is only a meager portion of the original range in the state, and corresponds in general to the heavily forested wilderness area. Between 1945 and 1965 bears were bountied. Bounties paid in 1946 were on 1495 bears, in 1960 only on 12. The bounty law was killed in 1965 but attempts have since been made to revive it.

As this is written bears have seasonal protection in Cook, most of Lake and northern St. Louis Cos. in the northeast, in most of Itasca Co., and in a portion of Cass Co. Throughout the rest of their range they are not protected, may be taken at any time. No license is required of residents to take bear anywhere. Nonresidents must have either a small game or deer license. The kill is never high. It averages around a hundred a year. Hunters can therefore hardly consider Minnesota a good bear hunting state, but may look for possible improved conservation of this species in future. There is no difficulty in finding public lands on which to hunt. The vast acreages of National and State Forests of the northeast are within the best bear range, and have the highest bear populations.

OTHER BIG-GAME ANIMALS

There are a surprising number of moose in northern Minnesota, with the range stretching across all of the northern border country and for at least a second tier of counties below it. Estimates have placed the moose herd at as many as 7000 animals. Moose have been protected in Minnesota since 1922. Some biologists feel that there should be limited moose seasons, by permits, to remove surplus animals. Aerial surveys have shown as many as sixty moose on fifteen square miles in the best range. Lake, Cook, Marshall, Beltrami, and Kittson Cos. are the high-density counties. The Department has urged a limited season. As this is written the legislature has not let such a bill pass. It is fairly predictable, however, that in the interest of proper game management a limited season on moose will eventually materialize in Minnesota.

Elk have been stocked in Minnesota in modern times on several occasions. Poaching decimated much of the potential. At this time it is not known if all are gone or if remnants remain. There is no season, and probably never will be.

At one time woodland caribou were fairly abundant in the north-Minnesota forests. The last known band to brave settlement was in the Red Lake region over thirty years ago. Later, a few were transplanted from Saskatchewan to the Red Lake region. Occasional reports of a lone caribou are still checked, but it is presumed the species is extinct in the state.

OTHER ANIMALS

There are numerous predator and fur species hunted by varying numbers of enthusiasts in Minnesota. The red fox is the most plentiful and most popular. It ranges throughout the state. While most are taken by trappers—about 25,000 annually—a good number are hunted with dogs and the art of calling is annually accounting for more and more. Gray foxes are far less numerous, are found in greatest abundance in the southeast and in the interior but not in the north. Raccoons are second in importance to the red fox in the fur take, but are not as popular with hound men as they are farther east and south.

There are some coyotes. Several hundred are bagged each year. Bobcats are not numerous, but appear in fair numbers in the forest regions. A scattering of lynx are caught in the north, mostly by trappers, an occasional one by sportsmen using dogs. Western Minnesota varmint hunters occasionally hunt the badger.

Perhaps the most interesting of Minnesota's predators is the timber wolf. Its major range is in the extreme northeast, in Cook, Lake and St. Louis Cos., but it also ranges on across the heavily forested north. In some recent seasons well over 400 have been taken. The average may be half that. As this is written there is a wolf bounty in those counties mentioned, even though the wolf is on the Endangered Species list of federal authorities. Probably the highest density of wolf population is in the Superior National Forest. Koochiching and Lake of the Woods Cos. also have a few.

REGULATIONS

Game laws pertaining to seasons, bag and possession limits, areas to be hunted, special hunts, license fees all may have numerous changes from year to year. For current regulations, and for other specific queries, write to: Minnesota Department of Conservation, Centennial Building, 628 Cedar Street, St. Paul, Minnesota 55101.

Central
States

OHIO

Although Ohio lies far to the northeast of the center of America, no other state could possibly be considered more typically "central U.S.A." It is in part one of the Great Lakes states, with Lake Erie forming most of its northern border. It is also nearly eastern, touching Pennsylvania and almost cornering with New York. Yet to the south, where it borders both West Virginia and Kentucky, it becomes one of the "hill-country" states. And again, westward, butting up against Indiana, it is strictly Midwest farmland.

Northern Ohio reflects in its flat rolling expanses the effects of Lake Erie. The northern third of the state lies in the watershed of the Great Lakes and the St. Lawrence. Southward, however, two-thirds of Ohio drains down in quickening streams to the broad Ohio River and thus into the Mississippi system. All of Ohio's southern border and a great share of its eastern border are marked out boldly in the meanderings of the Ohio River. Reaching up from this river, particularly in the east, southeast, and south, are forested hills, many of them surprisingly rugged. But on the western border with Indiana the land is gently rolling to flat. Thus Ohio offers an interesting variety of terrain, from Great Lakes marshes to rural fields to hilly forest.

The state is in many ways an odd intermixture of agriculture and industry, of teeming large cities and quiet pastoral vistas. It is third in the nation in industrial output, with a fantastic variety of products, yet it is also one of the wealthiest states in crop and livestock production. With all this activity there is little wilderness left in Ohio, none in the western mountain sense, but there is an amazing amount of woodland, forest, and game cover nonetheless.

Fine highways crisscross the state. Good side roads take a hunter to every possible game location. Several of the main arteries are Interstates and toll roads. Thus, auto transport is no problem, and visiting hunters coming virtually from any direction can reach an Ohio destination in a matter of hours from distant points. Air transport is excellent. Ohio has a greater number of cities over 50,000 than any state of comparable size in the nation, and almost all are reached by one airline or another.

It would almost seem that Ohio with its welter of activity could not possibly have any hunting left, yet it turns up a rather enviable record of game harvests, particularly in view of its limited size and its large population. It is roughly 225 miles east-west by 210 miles north-south. It contains a modest 41,222 square miles, an astonishing human population of approximately 10,500,000. To be sure, much of this population is concentrated in the large cities, but there are also hundreds of smaller towns and villages scattered across the state.

Even so, Ohio has managed bravely and admirably with its hunting. An indication that game is available is seen in the average annual license sale of about 600,000. Almost all of these hunters are residents. An average of less than 2500 nonresident hunters visit the state each season. This does not necessarily mean that Ohio has little to offer visitors. It simply indicates that surrounding states are in good shape for game, too, and probably that most central-U.S. hunters who travel after hunting go completely away from their home regions.

Small-game animals and upland birds make up the bulk of the shooting. Rabbits and squirrels are plentiful, with an aggregate kill among these animals of well over three million in good seasons. A substantial number of pheasants (running to several hundred thousand) are harvested annually, and bobwhite quail are abundant in numerous areas. Ruffed grouse hunting is surprisingly good in the hills. A growing turkey population is currently furnishing some hunting, will furnish more. Deer occur in all eighty-eight counties. There is good waterfowl shooting in several portions of the state. And there are foxes, raccoons, woodchucks.

Considering its heavy population, Ohio has an amazing amount of public hunting lands. The Department of Natural Resources constantly battles to acquire more. There are presently over 500,000 acres of free public lands. Over fifty Wildlife Areas are scattered so that some are available in every sector. These run in size from only a few acres to several thousand acres, and cover a broad variety of terrains and huntable species managed on them. There are a number of State Forests, with from several thousand acres to as much as 58,000 acres. Hunting is allowed in portions of some of the thirty-three large State Parks. Most of the reservoirs and reclamation projects have public hunting on adjoining lands. The Wayne National Forest, in several segments, located in the southeastern quadrant of the state, comprises in total 106,129 acres. A folder may be requested from the Division of Wildlife that lists all of these public areas by name, gives their acreages, and locates them on an accompanying map. This publication lists the Wayne National Forest, but further details on it may be had from the ranger stations at either Ironton or Athens.

In addition to all the above, Ohio has a unique plan whereby quail may be hunted, by permission, on some one and a half million acres of private lands throughout the state. The Department has been diligent in pursuing this program, and is ever active in research, stocking, and land purchase or other public-land agreements to keep hunters of all inclinations well supplied with opportunity.

Accommodations for hunters are no problem here. Motels, hotels, and lake cottages are available in great quantity everywhere one may elect to stop. Along Interstates and toll roads, however, it is best to reserve accommodations well ahead for the heavy traffic keeps motels full. For those who wish to camp, sites are plentiful in the State Parks (contact the Division of Parks, Department of Natural Resources, Columbus), National Forests, and in the Muskingum Conservancy District (the Department of Natural Resources can offer information). There are also a few city, county, and civic campgrounds. In addition Ohio has a great many privately owned campgrounds, the popular new trend in camping in the more heavily populated states.

Hunting season weather in Ohio can change drastically as the fall wears on. In September it is very pleasant and may be quite warm. October and November are crisp, and grow ever more so as the season advances. Waterfowling along the big marshes at this time can be a cold, wet endeavor. Wool clothing and rain gear are needed. Late seasons, of which there are several running in December and past the first of the year, are invariably cold and generally snowy. Waterproof footwear is needed then.

The hunter who visits Ohio will need nothing extraordinary in firearms or ammunition. Excepting muzzle-loading rifles for some deer hunts, rifles are not used. Ohio is therefore basically a shotgunner's state. Archery is of course popular. The .22 is handy for small game. Shotgun loads needed will be in general No. 8 or No. 7½ for quail, No. 6 for pheasants, No. 4 and No. 2 for ducks and geese.

PHEASANT

Although Ohio is not one of the top pheasant states, it has some very good hunting in certain locations. Some of its quality pheasant range produces in good years as many as eighty cock birds to the square mile. Annual pheasant kill, with some sections allowing hens in the bag, runs as high as 300,000. The game department has a co-op pheasant plan whereby six-week-old chicks are farmed out for raising and releasing, to add to the established pheasant population in thin areas.

Best of the pheasant range is in the lake plain region of northwest Ohio, in the intensively farmed limestone region of the central counties, and in some of the upper-southwest prairie counties. The Toledo area and south through Wood Co. is high-density range. So is much of Paulding Co., third county south in the northwest corner of the state. The three extreme northwest counties are low density range, but spreading south and east from those three corner counties (Defiance, Williams, Fulton) there is a fairly broad swath of fair density pheasant population. This can best be described as running from Toledo in a southwest slant about two counties broad, and ending with Mercer Co. on the Indiana line, about at the city of Celina.

There are only light pheasant populations over much of the interior of the state. However, Fayette Co., approximately south-central location, with the county seat of Washington intersecting U.S. Highways 35 and 62, is a center of pheasant abundance. Fair density spreads broadly over several counties surrounding this area, mainly to the northeast, northwest, and southwest. Miami Co. (cities of Troy, Piqua, I 75 and U.S. 36) is also a fair area.

Up in the northeast there are two medium pheasant concentrations. These are based on: southern Trumbull and most of Mahoning Co. in the Warren and Youngstown district; a narrow strip running across several counties from about Cleveland southeast through Akron and beyond. Southern and southeastern Ohio are outside the pheasant range.

Some of the best public lands for pheasant hunting are as follows: the Willard Marsh Wildlife Area (1), 1669 acres, west of intersection U.S. 224 and State 61, Huron Co.; Kelleys Island WA (2), 491 acres off the coast in Lake Erie north of Sandusky, reached by ferry from Sandusky; Killdeer Plains WA (3), south-central Wyandot Co. off State 67, over 6000 acres. Pheasants are also important game on several other WAs and other public lands: Little Portage WA (4) southwest of Port Clinton on Lake Erie; Clark Lake WA (5), Clark Co., out of Springfield; Darke Co. WA (6), county of same name on Indiana border, northeast of Greenville (U.S. 127); Delaware Reservoir, north of Columbus and on past Delaware, on U.S. 23; Wyandot WA (8), same county, northwest corner off U.S. 23; Auburn Marsh WA (9), northeastern Ohio, south-central Geauga Co. off State 44; Mohican Memorial Forest (10), vicinity of Loudonville (southeast from Mansfield); Nimisila Reservoir (11), south of Akron; Resthaven WA (12), southwest of Sandusky off U.S. 6; Shreve Lake (13), southwestern Wayne Co., reached via State 3 or 226 south from Wooster; Spencer Lake WA (14), western Medina Co., reached by

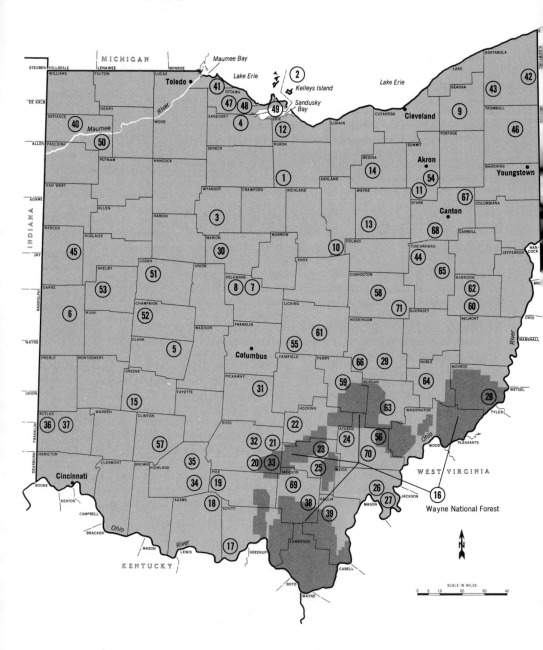

OHIO

KEY TO HUNTING AREAS

1. Willard Marsh WA
2. Kelleys Island WA
3. Killdeer Plains WA
4. Little Portage WA
5. Clark Lake WA
6. Darke Co. WA
7. Delaware Reservoir
8. Wyandot WA
9. Auburn Marsh WA
10. Mohegan Memorial Forest
11. Nimisilia Reservoir
12. Resthaven WA
13. Shreve Lake
14. Spencer Lake WA
15. Spring Valley WA
16. Wayne NF
17. Shawnee-Roosevelt SF
18. Brush Creek SF
19. Pike Lake SF
20. Scioto Trail SF
21. Tar Hollow SF
22. Hocking SF
23. Zaleski SF
24. Waterloo SF
25. Richland Furnace SF
26. Raccoon SF
27. Forked Run Lake SF
28. Sunfish Creek SF
29. Blue Rock Lake SF
30. Big Island WA
31. Hargus Lake
32. Pleasant Valley WA
33. Ross Lake
34. Brush Creek SF
35. Rocky Fork Lake SP
36. Rush Run WA
37. Pater Lake WA
38. Tycoon Lake WA
39. Cooper Hollow WA
40. Oxbow Lake WA
41. Metzger Marsh WA
42. Pymantuning SP
43. Orwell WA
44. Beach City Reservoir
45. Grand Lake
46. Mosquito Creek Reservoir
47. Magee Marsh WA
48. Toussaint WA
49. East Harbor SP
50. Auglaize River Power Dam
51. Indian Lake
52. Kiser Lake SP
53. Lake Loramie
54. Portage Lakes
55. Buckeye Lake
56. Burr Oak Lake SP
57. Cowan Lake SP
58. Mohawk Dry Dam
59. Perry Co. Reclamation Area
60. Piedmont Reservoir
61. Powelson WA
62. Tappan Reservoir
63. Wolf Creek WA
64. Wolf Run Lake
65. Atwood Reservoir
66. Avondale WA
67. Berlin Reservoir
68. Bolivar Dry Dam

side roads west of Medina or via State 301 running north from U.S. 224; Spring Valley WA (15), southwest sector, between Xenia and Lebanon on U.S. 42.

A few other State Forest and WA lands offer at least some pheasant hunting but the above are the best. It will be noted that most of these public lands are not centered in the highest density pheasant population areas. Most of those prime lands are under private ownership and require permission. Check the Division of Wildlife public-lands map for further locations. The Division also can furnish a small map showing high, medium, and low pheasant densities throughout the state. This is a handy reference.

RUFFED GROUSE

This grand forest grouse, once almost extinct in Ohio as the forests were removed, has made a most interesting resurgence. During the past century husky portions of eastern and southeastern Ohio have reverted in some part to forest and brush. This has provided habitat that allowed the ruffed grouse to enlarge its population and to become solidly reestablished.

As on all ruffed grouse range, these birds evidence drastic high and low population cycles. In good years, Ohio hunters take an estimated 100,000 birds. This is an amazing record for a state so densely populated. The season is long as a rule, running most of the fall and on through January and February. Grouse hunting is slowly becoming more and more popular in Ohio, yet there are many forest areas that receive very little hunting pressure. Numerous hunters are not aware of the fine sport. Others find it too difficult.

The entire ruffed grouse population of Ohio is contained in an area lying east of a line drawn from Cleveland southwest across the state to the Ohio River at the western edge of Adams Co. This takes in a little less than half the state. Grouse are by no means abundant over this entire region.

The counties of the extreme northeast—Ashtabula, Lake, Geauga, Trumbull—have one of the high populations. Moving south and west, the next two tiers of counties are only fair. There is another high population area to the south of these. It covers, along the eastern border, southern Columbiana Co., all of Jefferson Co. to the south, then, moving west, southern Carroll Co., all of Harrison Co., all of Tuscarawas Co., northern Guernsey Co., and still farther west most of Coshocton Co. and much of Holmes Co.

Below these counties lies another east-west swath of only fair grouse abundance. Higher populations begin again with southern Monroe Co. (eastern border) and most of Washington Co. just south of it. Then to the west and northwest populations are good in southwestern Morgan Co., most of Perry Co., and in the eastern half of Fairfield Co. Below these counties, and within the line drawn above, the entire southeast (nearly one quarter of the state) is good grouse country.

There is no problem in finding public lands on which to hunt grouse. All of the blocks of the more than 106,000-acre Wayne National Forest (16) lie in the southeastern quarter. There are also several State Forests, among them the Shawnee-Roosevelt (17), of 58,000 acres, lying along the border between Adams and Scioto counties along the Ohio River; the Brush Creek State Forest (18), just to the north, with 11,694 acres; Pike Lake State Forest (19), above this in northwest Pike Co., 11,085 acres. Ross Co., north of the above, has the Scioto Trail SF (20) of 9400 acres, and the Tar Hollow State Forest (21) of 16,600 acres. East of these lie: Hocking SF (22), Hocking Co., 8538 acres; Zaleski SF (23), Vinton Co., 18,215 acres; Waterloo SF (24), same general area; Richland Furnace SF (25); Raccoon SF (26), in Meigs Co. on the Ohio River; and 3100-acre Forked Run Lake SF (27) in the same sector. The small Sunfish Creek SF (28), eastern Monroe Co. near the West Virginia line, is a good grouse spot. Likewise for 4900-acre Blue Rock Lake SF (29) southeast of Zanesville.

Several of the larger State Parks in the northeast have public hunting for grouse, and there are WA lands scattered here and there over the entire grouse range. The best of the hunting is invariably found in the large blocks of Forest lands, and here, for those who get "back in," crowding of hunters is usually at a minimum.

HUNGARIAN PARTRIDGE

This introduced bird has been stocked in many states and in some has done very well. It is carried on the game list in Ohio, with an open season. But it is not an important or abundant species here, and is rather obscure so far as consistent hunting success is concerned. Original stockings established coveys in the northwestern counties and in all but the southern counties along the Indiana border. Populations also were found eastward into what is the prime central pheasant range. The Hun is found in several northern agricultural states in crop-field situations. Most of the better Hun area in Ohio has long been in private lands. There are Wildlife Area lands here, too, but Hun populations are not of importance on them. Hunters interested in this bird should check with the Division of Wildlife for assistance in pinpointing possible remnant flocks.

QUAIL

Bobwhite quail are found in all counties of Ohio. However, Ohio is almost at the northern extreme of bobwhite range (the bird ranges in lessening populations on up into parts of Michigan), and thus there is never the abundance of bobwhites in Ohio that are found farther south. There are pockets of relative abundance in every quarter of the state—small ones in the northeast in Trumbull and Columbiana Cos., in the extreme northwest in

Williams, Fulton, and Defiance Cos., some others southwest of Cleveland and south of Lorain and Sandusky, plus some excellent areas of modest size far down in the southeast, particularly in Athens and Meigs Cos. and in Gallia and Jackson Cos. But by far the best quail hunting is found in the central and southwestern parts of the state.

Hunters familiar with bobwhites in heavy populations consider one quail per acre as about maximum over most of the bobwhite range. A comparative figure gives a clue to Ohio quail hunting, for here in the best ranges a quail per four acres—or a ten-bird covey to each forty-acre tract—is considered a very good average.

Undoubtedly the bobwhite is Ohio's most populous upland game bird. Nonetheless, relatively few Ohio hunters seek it. Surveys show that less than 20 percent of license buyers hunt quail. The kill is far lower than on pheasants, and curiously about even with ruffed grouse. A Division of Wildlife estimate gives a harvest figure of 100,000, although some years it runs no more than half that. For forty years there was no open season on quail in Ohio, and it may be that hunters are still not used to having the quail as a game bird.

Quail hunters have ample opportunity to find places to hunt. Some 50,000 acres of public lands are available, much of it in prime quail range. In addition, Ohio has conceived and has been operating since 1959 a unique system of opening private lands to quail hunting by permission. Under this system land-owners sign up with the Division of Wildlife to legalize quail hunting on their lands. Over past seasons some 9000 landowners have signed agreements that have put one and a half million acres of private lands in line for quail hunting. This does not mean the lands are automatically open to the public. The discretion of the landowner dictates how much or how little hunting is done. Check with the Division of Wildlife for location of these lands.

The high population area for quail in central Ohio covers the following counties: most of Wyandot and western Crawford bordering it, thence spreading south over western Marion and eastern Hardin Cos., and on farther south to cover all of Union Co., western Delaware Co. and northern Madison Co. U.S. 23 and State 4 are arteries into this whole area and key cities are Bucyrus, Marion, Marysville. Directly west of the lower end of this abundance area lies another. The city of Troy, in Miami Co., is about centered in it. The area spreads over much of Miami Co., western Champaign Co. (Urbana), and northwestern Clark Co. (Springfield). The other large area of best bobwhite hunting lies in the southwest: Butler, Warren, Clinton Cos. are in its northern-most tier, followed to the south by Clermont, Highland, Brown, western Adams. The extreme southwest corner, around Cincinnati, is outside the best range.

Happily a number of public shooting grounds are located in or on the fringe of these better sections. Big Island WA (30) offers over 1000 acres west of Marion. Hargus Lake (31), near Circleville (south of Columbus), is a small area just outside the top range but still good. Pleasant Valley WA (32) comprises 1400 acres northwest of Chillicothe (U.S. 23-35 intersect) and Ross Lake WA (33) has almost a thousand acres to the southeast of Chillicothe. Brush Creek State Forest (34) is almost 12,000 acres, lies to the southeast of Hillsboro, and can be reached via State 73 and other crossing roads. Just outside Hillsboro (U.S. 62 and 50 intersect) is Rocky Fork Lake State Park (35), with a land area of almost 1400 acres and quail hunting—but check special State Park regulations. Near the western border, northwest of Cincinnati and on past Hamilton there are two public areas with quail: Rush Run WA (36); and small Pater Lake WA (37).

In the southeastern abundance pockets mentioned earlier are two good areas: Tycoon Lake WA (38), and 3465-acre Cooper Hollow WA (39). Both of these are northwest of Gallipolis, between that southern border city and Jackson, with U.S. 35 and State 93 key highways. Up in the northwest corner of the state, in an area of fair abundance, is Oxbow Lake WA (40), a small area (about 300 acres), near Defiance. There are a number of other public lands where quail hunting is of lesser importance. Check the Division of Wildlife map for these. The private lands are often best of all, and under Ohio's system permission is not too difficult to obtain.

WILD TURKEYS

Turkeys were long ago abundant in Ohio, but forest removal and the push of civilization wiped them out. Over recent years a slow reestablishment has been in progress. Turkeys will probably never be very abundant in Ohio, but they are now furnishing a small amount of hunting and a great amount of excitement. The first season in modern history was held in 1965, in the spring, with 500 permits offered. Twelve gobblers were killed. Similar seasons have followed annually, with a high kill to date of eighteen.

The turkey population is presently estimated at possibly a thousand birds. It is based on the State and National Forest Lands in the southern and southeastern part of the state. To date the open counties have been, reading from west to east: Adams, Ross, Pike, Scioto, Hocking, Vinton, Athens, Washington, Monroe. The Forests are of course open to public hunting. See "Ruffed Grouse" for their locations.

WOODCOCK, SNIPE, RAILS

Although there are scattered flights of rails along the Lake Erie marshes and around the larger reservoirs, there is virtually no activity in rail hunting. The birds are neither plentiful enough nor easily enough located to make hunting them worthwhile.

Snipe hunting is only an incidental here to waterfowling. Flights are scattered, and get meager attention. Also, fall appearance at any given point for snipe flights is unpredictable. However, one particular public area consistently furnishes good snipe shooting. This is Little Portage WA southwest of Port Clinton on Lake Erie, mentioned under "Pheasant." Other waterfowl Areas (see "Waterfowl") often have a few snipe.

The woodcock picture is a bit brighter. The kill is low and only a scattering of hunters gives the woodcock attention, but for one who carefully checks the flights there is fair shooting at several public areas. One of these is on the Lake Erie shore east of Toledo, small Metzger Marsh WA (41), near Crane Creek, reached by State 2. Clear across the state to the east, along the shore of Pymatuning Reservoir on the Pennsylvania border, is Pymatuning State Park (42), with well over a thousand acres land area and woodcock hunting when flights are on. Nimisila Reservoir (see "Pheasant") also furnishes fair woodcock shooting. Back up in the northeast, and to the west of Pymatuning Reservoir, there is Orwell WA (43), small but with woodcock. The village of Orwell is at the intersection of U.S. 322 and State 45. A larger area for woodcock (840 land acres) is located at Beach City Reservoir (44). This is south of Massillon at Beach City, where U.S. 21, 250, and 62 form a triangle. Little Portage (see "Snipe") also offers woodcock. Many other public lands have coverts where hunters after other game occasionally stumble upon a bit of woodcock shooting.

WATERFOWL

Like many heavily populated states with a long waterfrontage, Ohio has seen many of its best waterfowling grounds come under private ownership or lease. Nonetheless, the state has managed to keep some fair public shooting. Even goose hunters after the prize Canada fare rather well at times. The goose kill is never high, an average of around 3000 birds, but the Division of Wildlife has a good goose management program going and the future for goose hunting at least appears stable. There are three state-owned areas operated primarily for geese. About half the annual harvest now comes from these spots. They are: Grand Lake (45), a 12,500-acre lake with over 2000 acres of public lands surrounding, near Celina, Mercer Co., southwest part of state; Mosquito Creek Reservoir WA (46), in the northeast, a short distance from Warren; and Killdeer WA (previously located). A fair number of geese are also killed along Lake Erie. All the areas noted for geese are good duck locations, too. Metzger Marsh WA and Little Portage (see "Snipe-Woodcock") are good Lake Erie choices. Magee Marsh WA (47) is only a short distance southeast of Metzger, offers 2050 acres of prime waterfowling grounds. Toussaint WA (48) is a smaller public ground south of Magee. In the same general region East Harbor State Park (49) offers some waterfowl shooting. This is on the peninsula that juts into Lake Erie at Port Clinton to form the north side of Sandusky Bay.

In the western portion of Ohio are several good waterfowl spots open to the public. Just south of Defiance in the northwest sector is the Auglaize River Power Dam (50). Indian Lake (51) is an important waterfowl location. It is in northwest Logan Co., out of Bellefontaine on U.S. 33. At Kiser Lake State Park (52), northwest of Urbana, Champaign Co., there is a small waterfowl area. Lake Loramie (53) is larger, and located northwest of Sidney, at Minster.

Elsewhere in the state, a few good bets are the following: Portage Lakes (54), just south of Akron; Beach City Reservoir (see "Woodcock"); Buckeye Lake (55), south of Newark and I 70; Burr Oak Lake SP (56), north of Athens on State 13; Cowan Lake SP (57), south of Wilmington on U.S. 68.

SQUIRRELS

Both fox squirrels and gray squirrels are on the Ohio game list. The fox squirrel is found in most abundance in woodlots bordering farm fields; the gray squirrel is the squirrel of hardwood forests with brushy ground cover. Although fox squirrels range over the entire state, their primary range of abundance covers that portion lying north of a line drawn roughly from the southwest corner of the state in a general northeasterly direction to touch the Pennsylvania border about at the northeast corner of Columbiana Co. Below this line is the prime domain of the gray squirrel.

Squirrels are very popular with Ohio hunters, and in good mast years the squirrel population is high. Squirrel kill runs second only to cottontails. The average annual harvest is at least one million. Visitors, and resident Ohio hunters who may not have concentrated on squirrels, will find the best hunting and the most public grounds with quality hunting throughout the gray squirrel range. This is because most of the State Forests and the Wayne National Forest are located here.

All of the public lands noted under "Grouse" and "Turkey" will produce the best of Ohio's squirrel hunting. Most of the State Parks and Wildlife Areas noted for quail, pheasants, and even some of the larger ones for waterfowl, have squirrels of one or the other variety. See also "Rabbits" for some additional excellent choices.

RABBITS

The cottontail is Ohio's chief game species. Annual harvest reaches over two million. A great number of Ohio hunters are avid beaglers. But one can find much good rabbit hunting by "walking them up," too. Cottontails occur throughout the state, although the hilly country of southeastern Ohio has a greater number than the flat to rolling lands north and northwest. Some of the best cottontail range has as high as two or more rabbits per acre, in up-cycle years.

Except for noting the general area of greater abundance above, there are no "best places" to hunt rabbits in Ohio. All of the public lands noted for all foregoing species have their share of cottontails. The quail and pheasant lands often have high populations. There are a number of large tracts of public lands not noted previously, however, where the rabbit is the most important game. These are listed below.

Mohawk Dry Dam (58), 4572 acres, lies just to the northwest of Coshocton. (This is a good squirrel hunting tract, too.) The Perry Co. Reclamation Area (59), comprising 4400 acres, is another good squirrel location, although cottontails are the important species. This is near New Lexington in Perry Co. Piedmont Reservoir (60) has a public area of surrounding lands of over 4000 acres, located off U.S. 22 southwest of Cadiz in eastern Ohio. The Powelson WA (61), 2691 acres west of Newark, and Tappan Reservoir (62), with over 4000 surrounding public acres northwest of Cadiz on U.S. 36 and 250 are both excellent. (Both of these also offer good squirrel hunting.) Also in the southwest are two large areas fairly close together where cottontails are the main attraction (with squirrels second). These are 3598-acre Wolf Creek WA (63) and Wolf Run Lake (64) with 1182 land acres. The first is south of McConnelsville (State 60) and the second is near Caldwell (I 77).

Atwood Reservoir has a large hunting area east of New Philadelphia. Avondale WA (66) has 3590 acres between Zanesville and New Lexington. Berlin Reservoir WA (67) is comparable, just north of Alliance. Bolivar Dry Dam (68) covers 1450 acres between Canton and New Philadelphia. Most of Ohio's WAs and other public-access lands have rabbit hunting from good to fair. Check the suggested Division of Wildlife map for further selections.

DEER

Whitetail deer, abundant as settlement in the Ohio region began, were practically exterminated by 1900. Some restocking, plus a rejuvenation of much land now held by the public to fair deer habitat, has brought the whitetail back to huntable numbers. Eastern Ohio, and several counties of the extreme northwest, are the best ranges. From north to south through the center of the state there are some deer. Most of central and western Ohio, however, have only a scattered population.

The kill is not high, but some excellent heads have come out of several counties. Compulsory check-in of deer killed by hunters gives an exact picture of success. During a recent season the total kill was 1903. Deer permit sales are above 24,000. Thus about 1 in 12 hunters may expect to bag a deer. The herd appears to be growing.

Numerous public lands are open to deer hunting, and some of these turn up the best kills. Perry Co. Reclamation Area, Pike Lake SF, Raccoon SF, Scioto Trail SF, Sunfish Creek SF, Tar Hollow SF, Wayne NF, Waterloo SF, Zaleski SF, Avondale WA, Blue Rock Lake SF, Bolivar Dry Dam, Burr Oak Lake SP, Cooper Hollow WA, Forked Run Lake SF, Hocking SF—all of these have been previously noted and located under other species. They are among the best of the deer areas open to public hunting, and furnish many thousands of acres.

Several other choices: Mead WA (69), 2500 acres in the southern part of the state, near Jackson; Strouds Run SP (70), another 2500 acres also in the south, east of Athens; Wills Creek Reservoir (71), with 3500 acres, between Coshocton and Cambridge. All the areas so far given add up to the best chances for hunters on public domain. There are some others, and new ones appear as the deer herd grows. Check with the Division of Wildlife.

OTHER ANIMALS

Many Ohio hunters are avid coon-dog men. Others chase foxes (mostly red fox) with hounds. Opossums are in fair supply and are taken by the raccoon hunters. Raccoon hunting is an especially popular Buckeye sport. The animals are plentiful throughout the state. In fact, hunting for all of these animals (note there is a season on raccoons and opossums) is very good on all of the public lands located under foregoing sections. Woodlots along stream courses are best for raccoons, the more open and brushy field and woodlot habitat for foxes.

There is a fair amount of woodchuck (goundhog) shooting in Ohio, too. Much of this is on private farmlands, by permission. However, several public tracts may be noted as especially good. These are: Atwood Reservoir (see "Rabbits"); Bolivar Dry Dam (see "Rabbits"); Brush Creek WA (see "Deer").

REGULATIONS

Game laws pertaining to seasons, bag and possession limits, areas to be hunted, special hunts, license fees all may have numerous changes from year to year. For current regulations, and for other specific queries, write to: Department of Natural Resources, Division of Wildlife, 1500 Dublin Road, Columbus, Ohio 43212.

INDIANA

The varied features of the vast interior country of the U.S. between the eastern mountains and the Mississippi Valley are perfectly exemplified by Indiana. In the north where it borders southern Michigan there are numerous lakes, and in the northwest there are stretches of sand dunes along the shore of southern Lake Michigan. Southward most of the central area is a rich, level plain. But in the south, where the meandering Ohio River denotes the entire border with Kentucky, there are broken, steep hills, none very high. The state's highest point is 1257 feet, in Wayne County.

The north of Indiana is a teeming, bustling industrial complex based on the steel-producing cities streaming east from Chicago. Indiana is third in the nation in steel. But as one moves south Indiana becomes pleasantly rural, a farm country producing hogs and corn, in which it also ranks third in the U.S. In the far south it is still more genuinely rural, with small, quiet villages and rolling countryside where small-game cover is copiously scattered.

Good roads are everywhere throughout the entire state. Travel to any corner is no problem and no hunting ground can possibly be considered remote. Only the hills of the south have a few truly secluded sections. Air transport is excellent between the largest cities, such as from Chicago and South Bend to Indianapolis, Fort Wayne, and Louisville, Kentucky, on the southern border. There is no need anywhere in Indiana to seek guides or special transport in the field.

While Indiana cannot be considered one of the top hunting states today, because of heavy settlement and concentrated land use, it nonetheless offers a very substantial amount and variety of sport. The state is of only modest size, 36,291 square miles, yet packed into it are some five million people. Because of the agricultural activity, and modern clean-farming practices, room for game has drastically declined over the years. Nonetheless, there is an avid interest in hunting. License sales equal roughly 10 percent of the population —around 500,000 annually. Most of these hunters are residents. Only a very few visitors, less than 3000 annually, try Indiana hunting.

By numbers taken, squirrels and rabbits are the most popular game targets, and these two are also most abundant and most widely distributed. There are also quail, pheasants, Hungarian partridge, ruffed grouse. Waterfowl hunting is surprisingly good, and woodcock and jacksnipe migrate through. One of the big surprises in a state with only a modest amount of woodlands is the number of deer. Hunters harvest as many as 6000 annually, 500 are poached illegally, another 500 killed by cars. Hound game such as raccoons, opossums, foxes is plentiful.

The Department of Natural Resources, Division of Fish and Game, does its best under a close budget to manage wildlife and to make public hunting available. By far the great share of the land is privately owned, with hunting by permission. Needless to say, in so heavily populated a state permission, unless one is acquainted, is difficult to arrange. Many residents in rural areas are landowners and hunt on their own lands. For others, there is a substantial acreage of public lands.

The Game Department at this writing either owns or leases in total some 60,000 acres of State Fish and Game Areas, in sixteen separate tracts. There are also thirteen State Forests of varying size open to hunting, with a total area of 125,000 acres. The Game Areas and State Forests are well distributed across the northern and southern thirds of Indiana. Central Indiana has very little public hunting.

Added to state lands are some federal areas open to hunting. Three of these are military: The Crane U.S. Naval Ammunition Depot, Camp Atterbury, and Jefferson Proving Ground. These lands are exceedingly important to deer hunters. In some seasons approximately half of Indiana's deer kill has come from these military lands. The largest tract of public land in the state is the Hoosier National Forest. This is in two large units in the southern-central part of the state. It contains 117,906 acres. Maps and detailed information on this Forest may be obtained from the Forest Supervisor, Bedford, Indiana. A large additional acreage connected with the Forest is in Land Utilization Projects.

The game department has over past years encouraged groups of farmers to cooperate in allowing public, but regulated, hunting. On these lands signs are posted indicating membership in the program. A hunter must report to farm headquarters when entering and leaving, and sign an agreement outlining conditions under which he may hunt. The plan appears to be working well. Some fee-hunt arrangements are already in operation, and undoubtedly more will be. This appears to be a coming trend in heavily settled areas. It has the advantage of influencing landowners to practice better game management while assuring hunters of places to hunt and more abundant targets, at nominal costs. Indiana also has been operating a unique pheasant hunting plan on a fee-hunt basis on some of its Game Areas. This is described in detail under "Pheasant."

For hunters who may wish to camp, there are numerous facilities. Most of the Game Areas and the State Forests offer campgrounds. There are over twenty excellent State Parks. Some of these, incidentally, have lodges. These make fine places for hunters to reserve lodging and meals. The Hoosier National Forest offers camping, and there are numerous city, county, and civic campgrounds, as well as other private ones. A booklet, "Camping in Indiana," can be obtained from the Tourist Division, Department of Commerce, State House, Indianapolis 46204, and also from the Department of Natural Resources (address end of chapter). Also available from the Department is a booklet, "Indiana State Parks and Memorials." Other accommodations are no problem: motels and hotels are numerous along the many highways.

Weather here during early and mid-fall is ordinarily delightful. Light wool shirts are the ticket for October. Rain gear is needed. As the season wears on, waterfowlers especially need heavier clothing. Even without snow, the weather can be chill. Again, rain gear is good insurance, and waterproof footwear also. By and large, no special clothing is needed for Indiana hunting. Canvas-faced bird-hunting pants are a good idea for the briar thickets of the south.

In guns and ammunition, bird hunters need shot sizes No. 6 and No. 7½ as an average, with heavier loads for waterfowl. A .22 is a good arm for squirrels. Hunters after deer should check regulations carefully. Hunts are for bow and arrow, shotguns, and specified muzzle-loading rifles.

PHEASANT

The pheasant kill is not large, considering the number of hunters. It is estimated to run slightly over 100,000 annually.

Indiana practices on some of the Game Areas a unique pheasant hunting system. In addition to wild-reared birds, a number of pen-reared birds are released, generally late in the season. As a rule the hunting prior to releases is on a 2-cocks-per-day basis. After releases are made, hunters may then take 2 birds of either sex, but they pay a $3 fee to hunt on the release area. Each hunter is permitted as many as three hunts on such a release area, must check in and out, leaving his license and picking up a badge to wear while hunting. Rules and a map are issued and if the GA is busy on any particular day hunters are assigned to specified portions. At one of these, for example, there are sixteen designated plots where such hunting is available. The Division of Fish and Game can supply hunters with details about these hunts.

Pheasant range in Indiana is almost entirely in the upper half of the state. Heaviest concentrations of birds are in general in the northwest. There are three counties south of the ones that border southern Lake Michigan that are considered the top producers. These are Benton, Newton, and Jasper. Newton and Benton lie along the border with Illinois. Jasper is immediately east of Newton. Still farther south, and again along the western border, there are good populations in both Warren and Vermillion counties.

Along the northern border, in St. Joseph Co. where South Bend is located, there is a pocket of fair abundance in the northwestern portion of the county. To the south, skipping a couple of counties, other pockets of abundance are found in Pulaski and Cass Cos. And to the southeast of these in the center of the state, most of Tipton Co. is quite good. Surrounding all these areas are swaths of range that can be considered fair, so that most all of the northwestern fourth of the state is fair to good.

Eight counties of the northeast also are fair, with small areas within them rated "good." These counties are: Elkhart, LaGrange, Steuben, Kosciusko, Noble, DeKalb, Whitley, and Allen. For orientation, Fort Wayne is in Allen Co. Farther south, along this eastern portion of the state, pheasants are found in scattered pockets of fair to good hunting. Southern Wells Co., and a part of southern Jay Co. are rated "good."

Although none of the Game Areas is considered exceptional for pheasants, on seven of them pheasant hunting is rated as "fair." The Pigeon River GA (1) has 5571 acres northeast of the city of LaGrange in LaGrange Co. This county is on the northern border, in the northeast. The Area lies north of U.S. 20, and is reached easily via State 3 and 120. Tri-County GA (2) offers 3030 acres. This is a typical one on which the release system described above has recently been operating. It is in northeastern Kosciusko Co. This is to the southwest of LaGrange Co. (above). The Area lies south of Lake Wawasee, is reached via State 13, 5, and 8.

Across the state to the west, and lying on the line between Jasper and Pulaski Cos. (northeast Jasper, northwest Pulaski) is the Jasper-Pulaski GA (3), with 7280 acres. U.S. 421 runs north-south along the eastern border and State 10 crosses east-west above it. This is in some of the better pheasant range.

INDIANA

MICHIGAN

COOK
LAKE
PORTER
WILL
KANKAKEE
JASPER
NEWTON
IROQUOIS

BERRIEN
LA PORTE
SAINT JOSEPH
CASS
ELKHART
SAINT JOSEPH
LAGRANGE
BRANCH
HILLSDALE
WILLIAMS

LaPorte •
South Bend •

(1)

STEUBEN

(4)

MARSHALL

NOBLE
DE KALB
DEFIANCE

(28)

STARKE
KOSCIUSKO

(2)

WHITLEY
ALLEN
PAULDING

(6)

PULASKI
FULTON

Fort Wayne •

(3)
(7)

WABASH
HUNTINGTON
VAN WERT

(5)

WHITE
CASS
MIAMI

WELLS
ADAMS

River
Salamonie Reservoir

(15)

BENTON
CARROLL
(16)
Mississinewa Reservoir
GRANT

BLACKFORD
JAY
MERCER

VERMILION
WARREN
TIPPECANOE
HOWARD

OHIO

CLINTON
TIPTON
MADISON
DELAWARE
DARKE

Wabash
RANDOLPH

MONTGOMERY
BOONE
HAMILTON
HENRY
WAYNE

FOUNTAIN

VER-
MILLION
PARKE
HENDRICKS
MARION
HANCOCK
PREBLE

EDGAR
PUTNAM

Indianapolis •

RUSH
FAYETTE
UNION

ILLINOIS

SHELBY
FRANKLIN
BUTLER

VIGO
CLAY
MORGAN
JOHNSON

CLARK
OWEN
DECATUR

(17)
MONROE
BROWN
(29)
BARTHOLOMEW
DEARBORN
HAMILTON

(18)
(9)

SULLIVAN
GREENE
RIPLEY
BOONE

CRAWFORD
(11)
(19)
JENNINGS

Monroe Reservoir
JACKSON

(14)
LAWRENCE
(8)(32)
(30)

(25)
(24)
JEFFERSON
OHIO
SWITZERLAND

KNOX
DAVIESS
MARTIN
(31)
SCOTT
GALLATIN

LAWRENCE
WASHINGTON
River
TRIMBLE
CARROLL

(21)
ORANGE
(20)

WABASH
(13)
CLARK
KENTUCKY

PIKE
DUBOIS
(12)
(22)
OLDHAM

GIBSON
(23)
CRAWFORD
HARRISON
FLOYD

(10)
(33)
JEFFERSON

WHITE
POSEY
SPENCER
PERRY

VANDERBURGH
WARRICK
(26)

MEADE

(27)
HENDERSON
Hoosier National Forest Land

GALLATIN
UNION
Hovey Lake
HANCOCK
KENTUCKY
HARDIN

DAVIESS
BRECKINRIDGE

Ohio

SCALE IN MILES
0 5 10 20 30 40

-N-

KEY TO HUNTING AREAS

1. Pigeon River GA
2. Tri-County GA
3. Jasper-Pulaski GA
4. Kingsbury GA
5. Willow Slough GA
6. LaSalle GA
7. Winamac GA
8. Brush Creek GA
9. Atterbury GA
10. Patoka GA
11. Monroe GA
12. Springs Valley GA
13. Glendale GA
14. Greene-Sullivan SF
15. Salamonie River SF
16. Frances Slocum SF
17. Owen-Putnam SF
18. Monroe-Morgan SF
19. Yellowwood SF
20. Jackson-Washington SF
21. Martin SF
22. Clark SF
23. Pike SF
24. Crosley GA
25. Hoosier National Forest Land
26. Harrison-Crawford SF
27. Hovey Lake GA
28. Kankakee GA
29. Camp Atterbury
30. Jefferson Proving Ground
31. Crane Naval Ammunition Depot
32. Selmier SF
33. Ferdinand SF

The reason the rating is only "fair" for all the GAs noted is that in general this is about how the pheasant rates at best in Indiana. North of this Area and a bit east, in southeastern LaPorte Co., is the Kingsbury GA (4). This one has 4522 acres, is southeast from the city of LaPorte, and reached via U.S. 35 or State 104 and 4.

Over on the western border west of U.S. 41 at the town of Enos and in Newton Co., in the better pheasant range, is Willow Slough GA (5). There are 8360 acres here. Straight north, lying along the Kankakee River, which forms the northern border of Newton Co. with Lake Co. is the LaSalle GA (6), with 3064 acres. East of Jasper-Pulaski and surrounding Beardstown in northern Pulaski Co. is the Winamac GA. It is on U.S. 35 and contains 4113 acres.

Most of the remaining pheasant hunting is on private lands. Locations of co-op lands described early in the chapter can be traced via the signs when one is seeking a spot to hunt, or the game department can be queried for locations of any of these for any given season. They may differ year to year. The GAs mentioned all have release hunting as described. A few others may. These can be checked with the Department. Hunters should also note that some Indiana counties are closed to pheasant hunting. Check the seasonal regulations.

QUAIL

There is some very good bobwhite quail hunting in Indiana. In fact, the bobwhite is the most important of the upland game birds. An annual kill of between 600,000 and 700,000 is about average. Although quail are distributed statewide, the best quail hunting is found in the southern half of the state. An east-west line drawn through Indianapolis will place the major share of top quail range to the south. The northern half has some pockets of good hunting. The prairie counties have low populations. In the north, quail are for the most part restricted to the stream courses and drainage areas and to sandy ridges. The two very best ranges are found in the southeast and the southwest.

A number of the state GAs and also State Forests offer quail hunting from fair to good. Of the GAs located under "Pheasant," Winamac and Willow Slough are rated "good," and Pigeon River, Tri-County, Jasper-Pulaski, Kingsbury, and LaSalle are "fair."

Following are descriptions and locations of several other GAs which are rated as "good." Brush Creek GA (8) with 1135 acres is in the southeast, in central Jennings Co. near Vernon, which is at the junction of U.S. 50 with State 3 and 7. Atterbury GA (9) is a lease agreement on lands within Camp

Atterbury. This is south of Indianapolis, the Camp acreage chiefly in the northwest corner of Bartholomew Co., northwest of the city of Columbus. U.S. 31 is a key route. Patoka GA (10) covers 4280 acres in the southwest part of the state. It is in south-central Pike Co., with the towns of Winslow and Arthur nearby and with access via State 56 and 64.

Monroe GA (11) is in the south-central area, south of Indianapolis. It is composed of lands within the upper portion of those surrounding Monroe Reservoir, a Corps of Engineers development but with acreage leased to the Game Department. This large reservoir is in the southeast portion of Monroe Co., southeast from the city of Bloomington. State 37, 46, and 446 are key routes. Springs Valley GA (12) has 1205 acres. It is in southwest Orange Co., a county farther down in the southern-central part of the state. The Area lies to the southeast of the famous town of French Lick, with U.S. 150, State 145 and 37 nearby access routes. Glendale GA (13) totals 6382 acres, located in the general southwest quadrant. It is in southeastern Daviess Co., southeast of the city of Washington, which is on U.S. 50 and 150. A secondary road leading from State 257 reaches the Area.

Several of the Indiana State Forests also have quail. One of these that is rated as "good" is the Greene-Sullivan SF (14). There are 5180 acres in it, located in southeastern Sullivan Co. and spreading east across the line into Green Co. Sullivan Co. is in the west, well below midway of the state. U.S. 41 and 150 cross the county north-south, and the Forest can be reached from those routes via State 54 to the east, thence south on State 159.

Several Areas and Forests are rated as "fair" for quail. The Salamonie River SF (15), a small one with 800-plus acres, is located in the northern half of the state, in Wabash Co., east of the city of Wabash and near the Salamonie Reservoir. U.S. 24 is the key access route. The small Frances Slocum SF (16) is also in the northern half of the state, in southeast-central Miami Co., reached out of Peru via State 124. It is on the shore of Mississinewa Reservoir.

The 6124-acre Owen-Putnam SF (17) is southwest from Indianapolis, in the north-central part of Owen Co. A side road from U.S. 231 west via the village of Carp gives access. The Monroe-Morgan SF (18) is a large one, of 22,697 acres. It is east and a bit south of the above, most of it in the northeast corner of Monroe Co. but overlapping northward into Morgan Co. State 37 north out of Bloomington is the key access route. Yellowwood SF (19), almost as large, with 21,583 acres, also has fair quail hunting. It is south and a bit east of Monroe-Morgan SF, in several blocks, in western Brown Co. The city of Nashville is to the east, and State Routes 45 and 46 run on either side of the Forest.

Next comes Jackson-Washington SF (20), located in the southern area, in blocks in those counties. There are almost 14,000 acres. U.S. 135 is a key route crossing the two counties. Martin SF (21) has 3541 acres. It is in the southwest quarter, in the east-central part of Martin Co., southeast from the huge Crane Naval Ammunition Depot. U.S. 50 runs along its southern border.

Clark SF (22) is in the southwest, in northwestern Clark Co., with I 65 running north-south to the east of it and State 160 crossing it east-west between Henryville and New Liberty. This is a large tract, 20,431 acres. And the last State Forest with fair quail hunting, Pike SF (23), with 2986 acres, is also in the southeast, roughly centered in Pike Co., with State 364 reaching its southern border.

One other State Game Area is rated as "fair" for quail. That is Crosley GA

(24), with 3300 acres in the southeast, in central Jennings Co. directly south of the city of Vernon and reached by State 3 and 7. This is near the Brush Creek GA. Other Forests and GAs noted under other species should be checked out for quail but for the most part quail populations on them are poor. Private lands, particularly in the southern half of the state and especially southeast and southwest, should be considered. Those owners with lands joined up with the co-op plan are open to hunters and ordinarily offer good shooting.

HUNGARIAN PARTRIDGE

Huns were introduced to Indiana years ago, established themselves and managed to continue modest populations. However, only a small number are bagged annually by hunters and the good range is not large. An average kill of four or five thousand, mostly as incidentals while hunting other species such as quail and pheasants, is about the extent of this hunting. For numerous season purposes, this bird included, the state is divided into the North Zone and the South Zone. The east-west line is drawn from Richmond westward along U.S. 40, through Indianapolis, and thence westward to the western border along U.S. 36. Although all of the state is open on Huns, usually seasons differ slightly between northern and southern Zones.

The major range—and it is thinly populated with birds—is in the east-central part of the state. There are also portions of the north-central area about comparable. The south has few. The best counties for Huns are: Grant, Blackford, Jay, Tipton, and Delaware. These are all down in the center of the state, running from center eastward. Other counties with major ranges are, in the same general grouping, Clinton, Boone, Hamilton, Madison, Henry, Rush, Hancock, Shelby, and Randolph. Farther north, Marshall, Fulton, eastern Cass, central Kosciusko, and western Whitley all will bear checking.

None of the State GAs nor the State Forests have enough Huns to furnish worthwhile shooting. Check with the Department for private lands under the co-op system in the counties noted for possible action with this bird. Again, it is largely an incidental and cannot be considered an important Indiana species at present.

RUFFED GROUSE

It is indeed a fine commentary on the art of modern conservation that the ruffed grouse, a bird originally of the deep forests, is today still huntable in Indiana. In pioneer times it was abundant in this state of hardwood forests and stream bottom habitat. But concentrated settlement brought it to the verge of extinction. The last open season was held in 1937—until a resurgence due partly to changes in land use and partly to wise management made the ruffed grouse once more available to hunters in 1965.

A century ago at least fifty-eight of Indiana's ninety-eight counties had this bird in abundance. Cutting of forests doomed it. In the 1930s, however, many hill farms in the south were purchased by federal and state sources for forests. In the steep hills and deep hollows pine and hardwood began to reappear and greenbriar thickets closed open areas. Oddly, over recent years some of these natural barriers have kept ruffed grouse from spreading their range, as growth reverted to thickets that were too dense. More recently, biologists have trapped and released ruffed grouse in suitable areas, hoping to enlarge their range.

As this is written there have now been several consecutive open seasons. The kill has not been high, probably averaging 1000 to 1500 birds annually. But this is a bird new to modern Indiana hunters, the terrain is difficult, and this influences the low kill. More birds might be harvested as hunters become more adept at this sport.

During the season that this is written the following counties were open to ruffed grouse hunting: Bartholomew, Brown, Jackson, Lawrence, Monroe, Morgan, and part of Johnson. These counties are in a block south of Indianapolis. Within these counties lies a substantial amount of Hoosier National Forest Land (25). There are two Ranger Districts in the Forest, one at Brownstown, the county seat of Jackson Co., the other at Tell City on the southern border and presently outside the open area. The National Forest is among the important ruffed grouse public hunting lands.

Several of the State Game Areas and State Forests hold up well as good ruffed grouse choices. Those already mentioned are: Monroe GA, Morgan-Monroe SF, Yellowwood SF, Jackson-Washington SF (see "Quail"). Check as "fair" the following: Atterbury GA, Owen-Putnam SF, Martin SF, all also under "Quail." The Clark SF mentioned under quail has a few grouse, but it is not an important grouse area. The Harrison SF (26), not so far mentioned, is rated as "fair." This large Forest (listed usually as the Harrison-Crawford SF, 20,642 acres) is located in the southeast, in the southwestern part of Harrison Co., west of the town of Corydon, which is on U.S. 460. This forest on its southwestern boundary borders the Ohio River, the boundary between Indiana and Kentucky.

At present it is too early to tell what the transplant program may mean to Indiana grouse hunting, but reports are that the picture, aimed at increased range and more birds, is encouraging.

OTHER UPLAND BIRDS AND EXOTICS

There has been some experimentation with Korean, Japanese green, and Iranian-cross pheasants, in attempts to find strains better suited to present land uses. To date no conclusions have been drawn.

Doves are fairly plentiful but so far Indiana is not a dove hunting state, and the season is closed.

Hunters who happen to see prairie chickens should be reminded that it is illegal to shoot them. Once abundant in portions of the state, prairie chickens are now almost gone. It is believed there will never again be an open season and indeed the bird appears close to extinction in Indiana.

Chukar partridge have had some attention as an introduced species. But these also are on the illegal list and this should be known to bird hunters.

Although the wild turkey is not presently on the game list, there is hope that it may be brought to huntable surplus in due time. Currently several management areas have been established and results of periodic releases appear promising. Two important areas are: 1) within the Harrison-Crawford State Forest; 2) at Morgan Ridge within the Hoosier National Forest in Perry Co. and Tell City Ranger Station. Both of these Forest locations are near the southern border, in large blocks of Forest lands. Undoubtedly, if and when turkeys become legal game, Perry and Harrison Cos. will be the center of the basic range.

RAILS, WOODCOCK, JACKSNIPE

Rails are hardly hunted at all in Indiana. A few are killed as incidentals by waterfowl hunters. Possibly some shooting might be developed on sora rails in marsh areas but flushing the birds is so difficult it is doubtful if hunters would find it worthwhile.

There is hunting available for both woodcock and jacksnipe. Indiana hunters, however, give these birds small attention. It was estimated in one recent season that only 1000 snipe were bagged. More can be, if hunters pursue the sport on marshy areas. Woodcock are somewhat more popular, and there are good flights here and there in the fall. A kill estimate on woodcock recently was placed at 11,000 for the season.

Rated as "good" for both woodcock and jacksnipe are the following public lands: LaSalle, Kingsbury, Pigeon River GAs, all noted under "Pheasant." Considered "fair" for both: Atterbury, Monroe, Salamonie, Brush Creek, Glendale, all under "Quail," and Jasper-Pulaski, Tri-County, Willow Slough, Winamac under "Pheasant."

The Crosley GA, Patoka GA, Frances Slocum SF, Salamonie River SF, all noted under "Quail," have some woodcock, but are either poor for snipe or have none. Coverts along stream courses on private lands, where there is open ground cover but shade above, are good bets for Indiana woodcock hunting, too. And comparable cover in the Hoosier National Forest and along its fringes should not be overlooked.

WATERFOWL

Although Indiana is not one of the prime waterfowling states, it has some fair shooting. The numerous lakes in the northeast, the large reservoirs of the central area, and the many streams that meander through often wooded courses furnish resting places for migrating waterfowl. There is also a modest amount of goose hunting on farm grain croplands, although this state is without the large federal refuges to hold geese that some others have.

The average annual duck kill runs by estimate around 65,000, and in one recent season survey a bag of 7000 geese was the tally. Coots also are hunted to some extent, or at least bagged as incidentals by duck hunters.

The several large reservoirs make possible public hunting for both ducks and geese. Floating the rivers and jump-shooting is also productive, and public. Hunters should check regulations, however, for certain portions of the state are closed to waterfowling. Waterfowling on some of the reservoirs is operated on a permit basis. For example, at Monroe Reservoir, southeast of Bloomington in Monroe Co., permits may be obtained each day at the Reservoir office (Smithville Road), and also at the Cutright launching ramp.

A good indication of waterfowl concentrations can be gained from winter surveys made after the season closes, usually in January. One recent survey showed most of the Canada geese in the Hovey Lake region, in Posey Co. Largest duck concentrations were at Hovey Lake and at the Kankakee GA. There is a GA at Hovey Lake, too. The locations of these two good shooting grounds are as follows. Hovey Lake GA (27), considered good hunting for both ducks and geese, is an 885-acre tract managed for waterfowl in the extreme southwest. It is in the southwest corner of Posey Co., near the confluence of the Ohio and Wabash rivers that form the borders here with Kentucky and Illinois. State 69 runs to it. The Kankakee GA (28) covers 2302 acres. It is in the northwest sector of the state, in southern LaPorte and western Starke Cos., lying along both sides of the Kankakee River. State 39 and 8 intersect near the northeastern end of the Area. This GA is good for ducks, fair for geese.

A number of other GAs rate as good or fair for ducks or geese or both. Located under "Pheasant" are the following, with their ratings: LaSalle, ducks good, geese fair; Willow Slough, both good; Tri-County, ducks fair, geese poor; Pigeon River, both fair; Kingsbury, ducks fair, no geese. Noted under "Quail": Atterbury, ducks fair, no geese; Monroe, ducks good, very few geese; Glendale, ducks good, geese fair; Brush Creek, both fair; Salamonie, both fair; Patoka, ducks fair, no geese.

DEER

Considering dense human population and farming practices, Indiana has surprisingly good deer hunting. All counties of the state have at least a few deer, and all are open during season, which is limited to bow and arrow, shotguns of specified bore, and certain muzzle-loaders. The annual deer kill runs from 4000 to 6000 animals. Deer populations are thinnest across the middle of the state. They are heaviest in the northern third, particularly in the eight counties of the northeast corner, and westward in a swath across portions of Marshall, Starke, and Pulaski Cos. In the southern region, the southeast is the prime range, with another good concentration south-central, in Monroe, Brown, Bartholomew, and Jackson Cos. Directly west of these counties is another heavy concentration area, with counties reading north to south in a straight line: Montgomery, Putnam, Owen, Greene, Martin. The southernmost central counties, along the Ohio River, also have good populations, particularly Spencer, Perry, Crawford, and Harrison.

Many of the counties above show up well in seasonal kill surveys. However, over the entire state, counting public and private lands, roughly half of the annual deer kill usually comes from three locations, all military: Camp Atterbury, Jefferson Proving Ground, and Crane Naval Ammunition Depot. During one recent season, for example, the kill was as follows: Camp Atterbury, 932; Jefferson Proving Ground, 1186; Crane N.A.D., 928. The highest county kill during the same season was 124, in Brown Co. Next highest was Perry, with 107, and third Owen, with 90. Average county kills run from a dozen to fifty.

The military installation hunts are by permit. Hunters should check with the game department for details on these special hunts. Camp Atterbury (29) is located south-central, southeast of Indianapolis, in the northwestern corner of Bartholomew Co. and with a portion to the north in Johnson Co. Jefferson Proving Ground (30) is in the southeast, in Jefferson, Ripley, and Jennings Cos. Crane N.A.D. (31) is across the state toward the west, in northeastern Daviess Co.

The Hoosier National Forest, which spreads over a number of the southern counties already mentioned, offers good deer hunting. So do some of the State Game Areas and the State Forests. Two of the State Forests, both listed under "Quail," are rated as "good." These are Pike SF and Owen-Putnam SF. A number of GAs are listed likewise: under "Pheasant"—Winamac; Jasper-Pulaski; LaSalle; Willow Slough; Kingsbury. And under "Quail"— Atterbury; Monroe; Patoka.

Indicated as "fair" are the following GAs under "Quail": Salamonie; Brush Creek; Glendale; Crosley. Kankakee ("Waterfowl") and Pigeon River ("Pheasant") also rate as "fair." State Forests rating a "fair" label, and noted under "Quail" are: Clark; Martin; Jackson-Washington; Yellowwood; Morgan-Monroe; Greene-Sullivan; Salamonie River; Frances Slocum. And, under "Ruffed Grouse," Harrison SF is considered a fair deer area.

Two State Forests not so far located are in this same category for deer hunting. One is Selmier SF (32), a small tract of 352 acres in the southeast, north of Vernon in Jennings Co. The other is Ferdinand SF (33), a 7378-acre forest in the south-central region, in the southeast corner of Dubois Co., southeast of the city of Jasper and reached via State routes 162 and 264.

RABBITS

Cottontails are abundant and extremely important game in Indiana. The kill runs well over a million annually. They are hunted almost everywhere in the state, on private and public lands. The landowners who have joined in co-op hunting should be checked by rabbit hunters, for much good hunting is to be had on these privately owned farms.

All of the State Forests furnish at least some rabbit hunting, although these lands must be considered only fair. All have already been noted under other species. All of the GAs excepting Hovey Lake and Kankakee ("Waterfowl") offer fair to good cottontail hunting. Among the best: Tri-County and Pigeon River ("Pheasant"); Monroe and Atterbury ("Quail"). All the rest can be considered worthwhile but somewhat less attractive than these. The southern half of the state has the heaviest rabbit population.

SQUIRRELS

Indiana has fox squirrels in farmland and stream bottom woodlots and gray squirrels in the forests. Squirrels are, by annual kill, Indiana's most popular and important game species. In good years one and a half million squirrels are bagged. The season generally opens in mid-August. Gray squirrels are a favorite target over the southern half of the state, in the forest areas. The Hoosier National Forest is an excellent bet for squirrel hunting. See opening material of chapter for location and details.

All of the State Forests furnish squirrel hunting and all can be rated as "good to excellent," except the following three, which are classed as only fair: Frances Slocum; Salamonie River; Greene-Sullivan. All of the GAs offer squirrel hunting. The best is found on: Jasper-Pulaski; Atterbury; Monroe; Glendale; Springs Valley; Brush Creek; Crosley; Tri-County. All of the others have modest squirrel populations. All of the State Forests and Game Areas are described under foregoing species.

OTHER ANIMALS

Major non-game animals are foxes and raccoons. Over 40,000 foxes are taken annually and the raccoon kill runs above 200,000. These animals are hunted chiefly with hounds. This is a traditional sport over much of Indiana, in both the farm-country woodlots and along the river bottoms, and in the hills and forests of the south. Distribution is quite general. All of the State Game Areas have fair to heavy populations of both animals. So do the State Forests and the National Forest. Opossums are also hunted along with raccoons and the kill runs upwards of 20,000 a year. They are most abundant in the southern part of the state. There are specified seasons for dog running. Hunters should check the regulations. Permits are obtainable for what are known as "Organized Hunts," such as fox hunts.

REGULATIONS

Game laws pertaining to seasons, bag and possession limits, areas to be hunted, special hunts, license fees all may have numerous changes from year to year. For current regulations, and for other specific queries, write to: Department of Natural Resources, Indianapolis, Indiana 46209.

ILLINOIS

Although it is seldom thought of as such, Illinois is actually a plains state. Lying at the southwestern foot of the Great Lakes region, it borders Lake Michigan in the Chicago area and has its northern border with Wisconsin. Here also is the state's highest point, a bit over 1200 feet. From the north, and from the eastern border which is chiefly matched to the prairie portion of Indiana, there is an almost imperceptible slope of flat lands to the south and west, down and across to the Mississippi River, which forms the entire western border.

The river is the emphatic topographical feature of the state. It separates Illinois in the northwest from Iowa and along the west-central and south-western portions from Missouri. Several large streams of the interior—the Rock in the north, the Illinois slanting down across the center—move south-westward across the farmlands to join the Mississippi. At Cairo in the extreme south the Ohio forms the border with Kentucky, and upstream its tributary the Wabash demarks a section of border with southwestern Indiana. The confluences of these rivers, their long funnelings, and the gentle southward meandering of the ponderous Mississippi have since ancient times brought waterfowl by millions magnetically down through this sweep of verdant low-lands.

Today Illinois is a teeming state, intensely farmed and settled. Some years it has ranked second in the entire U.S. in farm crops, third in products from livestock and no farther down the list than third in entire agricultural output. It is also rich in coal and oil, and busy throughout with manufacturing. Needless to say, there is no longer any wilderness here. Highways grid the state. Air transport takes one to practically every county. Hunters have no difficulties getting where they wish to go. And, surprising as it may seem in a state so heavily settled, there are many hunters and there is a fair abundance of game.

Illinois covers 56,400 square miles. At its greatest north-south distance it is almost 400 miles. At the widest bulge across the center it is approximately half that. Packed into its many large cities and its welter of small towns are very nearly eleven million people. Although the large cities account for a substantial percentage, Illinois is everywhere busy and populous. Thus, the game picture is basically one of species adaptable to croplands. There are pheasants, quail, a few Hungarian partridge, abundant rabbits and squirrels. Raccoons and foxes prowl woodlots and croprows. Woodchucks are common. There are a surprising number of deer, some of them unusually large, all of them fat and well fed. But the fame of Illinois has long rested upon its waterfowling, particularly its goose shooting. While curtailed to some extent today by restrictive laws, it is still excellent.

Perhaps because of dense population and the fact that by far the major percentage of land is in private ownership, hunters are fewer than in many states with comparable population. They number slightly more than 4 percent of the population, with license sales running between 400,000 and 500,000 annually. Less than 7000 are nonresidents. Most of these go to Illinois for goose hunting.

Crowded conditions and the tradition of waterfowling have led more and more over the years to the formation of private hunting clubs. They are numerous. So are commercial bird-shooting preserves, which depend for their trade on the dense urban populations. Nonetheless, public lands are available in modest supply. State Parks and State Conservation Areas make up approximately 100,000 acres. Of this, most of the Conservation Areas and portions of several State Parks are open to public hunting. There are lands along the Mississippi and several Corps of Engineers impoundments that furnish public waterfowl and other hunting. Waterfowl refuges along the river have sections open to hunting. Fortunately, too, there are a number of farmlands in the waterfowl flyways that double in grain crops and ducks and geese, renting pits by the day or by season lease. Several State Forests of modest size supply hunting, and in the south there is the 211,000-acre Shawnee National Forest (1), in numerous scattered blocks large and small.

Because this Forest has intrusions of other varied lands, including some refuges, and is also developed for full recreational values, hunters should obtain an official map. The source is from the Forest Supervisor, Harrisburg. Very generally, the location of the Shawnee Forest is along the southwestern border through Jackson, Union, and Pulaski counties, and along the southeastern border in Saline, Gallatin, Pope and Hardin counties. Other Forest tracts stretch across at the top to more or less join the main sections. Highways into the area are numerous.

For information and maps on hunting areas open on the waterfowl refuges, hunters should contact the Illinois Department of Conservation, address at end of chapter. A map of Crab Orchard National Wildlife Refuge can be obtained from the U.S. Government Printing Office, Washington, D.C., or from the Refuge Manager (see "Quail"). The Conservation Department also publishes a booklet listing and locating numerous public hunting lands in the state. Chambers of Commerce in towns along the rivers where goose hunting guides or pits are available can be helpful with addresses to be contacted, and the Conservation Department can also furnish information, although not recommendations. The Official Highway Map of Illinois, which may be had from the Highway Department, State Office Building, Springfield 62706, lists and locates all the State Parks and Conservation Areas.

Accommodations for hunters throughout the state are numerous. Along main highways, however, and the Interstates, hunters are well advised to make motel reservations ahead, for general travel on such routes ordinarily keeps them heavily booked. For those who wish to camp, there are the State Parks, the Conservation Areas, some of which have campsites, and the National Forest. A booklet can be had from the Department entitled "Tent and Trailer Camping in Illinois State Parks and Conservation Areas." There are campgrounds also on some of the Wildlife Refuges, and on Corps of Engineers lands.

Early fall weather in Illinois is warm. By the time waterfowl seasons open, however, it may be very chilly and damp. Woolen clothing is necessary for blind sitting or in the goose pits. Late fall hunting afield may also be cold. Selection of arms and ammunition is a simple matter here. For geese No. 2 or Magnum 4 are mandatory. Ducks should be hunted with No. 4 or

Magnum 6. Upland birds will require shot sizes in No. 6, No. 7½, perhaps No. 8 for quail. A .22 is good for squirrels, but there is virtually no need for a big-game rifle. Deer are hunted with shotguns shooting slugs, or with muzzle-loaders.

PHEASANT

The ringneck is a most important game bird in Illinois. It is surprisingly populous, but by far the major share of the hunting is done on private crop-lands. Kill estimates run from around 600,000 birds some seasons—cocks only—to as high as a million during peak years. Probably the lower figure or a bit less will strike a seasonal average.

The Illinois pheasant range covers the northern and east-central portions of the state. It takes in all the territory north and east of a line drawn approximately as follows: from Rock Island on the upper western border south roughly to Beardstown in Cass County, thence south and gently eastward to Carlinville in Macoupin Co., severely southeast by east now to Vandalia in Fayette Co. and then east to the border at about the middle of Crawford Co. Inside this line along its western perimeter there is a swath roughly one county wide where the pheasant population is very light and spotty. All of the remaining area has modest to good to heavy concentrations.

However, inside this large area are a few east-central counties that can be rated as having heavy populations. These counties, beginning at the north and reading east in tiers: Lasalle, Kendall, the southwest half of Will, all of Grundy south of Kendall; most of Putnam, Marshall, all of Livingston, Kankakee, and Iroquois; northeast Woodford, northeastern half of McLean, all of Ford; northeastern DeWitt, all of Champaign and Vermilion; small portions of counties immediately south of the last named. This is all told the quality pheasant range in Illinois. In its very center, in southeast Livingston, northeast McLean, northern and western Ford counties is the hub, with the highest Illinois concentration.

Obviously this places most of the pheasants near the largest urban areas. Competition for places to hunt is therefore severe. During opening days landowners invariably keep the hunting for themselves and their friends. Later in season it may be possible to obtain permission. Birds are then wild, difficult to find, but the hunting, for diligent gunners, is good. For those who plan to hunt private lands it is almost mandatory to seek a place and permission, perhaps for specified dates, well before the season opens. Hunters should be warned against trespass without permission. It is never legal, of course, anywhere, but with competition for hunting space at a premium it is certain to be disastrous here.

In addition to permission hunting, the Department operates seven special-permit areas for pheasants. On these, the birds are released. Permit applications are accepted at the Permit Office of the Department beginning September 1. Details on filing applications may be had from the Department. The charge to a hunter, when he checks in at the area for which his permit calls, is $5. In some cases (generally excepting the Chain-O-Lakes and Des Plaines special areas) a hunter has a fair chance, weekdays, of getting on to hunt simply by showing up. They are often not completely filled. However, on weekends, and on all days on the two areas mentioned, all permits are usually filled by application.

Certain special regulations pertain to the Special Pheasant Areas. Three of the Areas—Shelby County, Clinton County, Richland County—are on

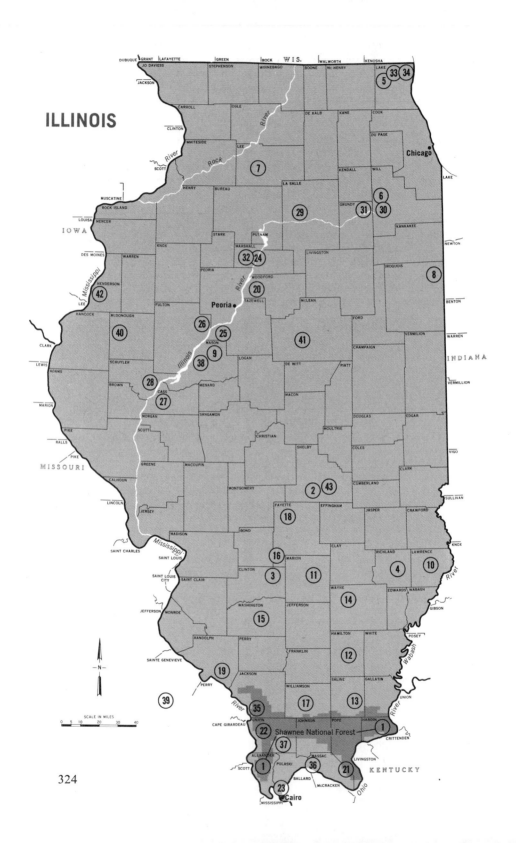

ILLINOIS

324

KEY TO HUNTING AREAS

1. Shawnee NF
2. Shelby Co. SPA
3. Clinton Co. SPA
4. Richland Co. SPA
5. Chain-O-Lakes SPA
6. Des Plaines SPA
7. Green River SPA
8. Iroquois Co. SPA
9. Mason SF
10. Red Hills PHA
11. Stephen A. Forbes PHA
12. L. P. Dolan PHA
13. Saline Co. PHA
14. Sam Dale PHA
15. Washington Co. PHA
16. Carlyle Lake PHA
17. Crab Orchard National Wildlife Refuge
18. Ramsey Lake PHA
19. Randolph Co. PHA
20. Woodford Co. PHA
21. Pope-Massac PHA
22. Union SF
23. Horseshoe Lake Refuge
24. Marshall Co. PHA
25. Spring Lake PHA
26. Rice Lake PHA
27. Sanganois PHA
28. Anderson Lake PHA
29. Starved Rock PHA
30. Will Co. PHA
31. Grundy Co. PHA
32. Sparland PHA
33. Grass Lake PHA
34. Fox Lake PHA
35. Oakwood Bottoms
36. Mermet Lake PHA
37. Union Co. PHA
38. Chautauqua Refuge
39. Mark Twain Refuge
40. Argyle Lake PHA
41. McLean Co. PHA
42. Henderson SF
43. Shelby SF

lands leased from farmer landowners. On these three, no game except pheasants may be shot. And after the permit season for pheasants has ended the lease also ends and no public hunting is allowed. The other four Special Pheasant Areas—Chain-O-Lakes, Des Plaines, Green River, Iroquois County—are located on public lands. On all but Chain-O-Lakes, other game in season may be hunted before and after the permit season for pheasants.

These seven Special Pheasant Areas are located as follows: Shelby Co. SPA (2) is in extreme south-central Shelby Co. near the village of Cowden on State 128. This places it some miles south of the city of Decatur and northwest of the city of Effingham. Clinton Co. SPA (3) is to the southwest of the above, in the northeast corner of Clinton Co. near the east shore of Carlyle Reservoir. It can be reached by secondaries north from U.S. 50. Richland Co. SPA (4) is to the east, southeast of the city of Olney in Richland Co., reached via secondaries either from U.S. 50 or State 130. These three, as noted earlier, are on privately owned leased lands.

Here are the locations of the public-land SPAs: Chain-O-Lakes SPA (5) is in the extreme northeast, in northwestern Lake Co., off U.S. 12 near the town of Fox Lake. This SPA, as noted, is for pheasant hunting only. Des Plaines SPA (6) is a large area of over 3000 acres, in southwestern Will Co., southwest of Joliet, reached off I 55. Green River SPA (7) is in the north-central region, in southwestern Lee Co., contains 2330 acres, is reached west from State 26 which is a few miles north of the village of Ohio. Iroquois Co. SPA (8) is near the eastern border, in the northeast corner of Iroquois Co., and is reached east from State 1 via a secondary through Beaverville. It contains almost 2000 acres.

There is one other spot with fair public pheasant hunting. This is the 5525-acre Mason State Forest (9) southwest of Peoria, near the village of Forest City, which is reached by secondary running north from U.S. 136.

QUAIL

Bobwhite hunting in Illinois attracts approximately a third of Illinois' hunters, and the kill is excellent for so populous a state. It runs, according to state estimates, anywhere from one to two million birds annually, depending on the seasonal crop. Best of the quail range is in the western and southern counties. The region below U.S. 40, which runs from Terre Haute, Indiana, southwest to St. Louis, Missouri, is the best of the quail territory. This southern quarter of the state is less urban than much of the rest. Finding a place to hunt by permission, though not always easy, is by no means impossible, and quail hunters in general have more luck at it than do pheasant hunters. There is also some fair quail hunting along the Mississippi counties of the west, but quail are less numerous there than in the south.

As with other game, the major share of the best hunting is on private lands. However, Illinois has several fair to good public tracts that furnish quail shooting. One of these is the Shawnee National Forest. Department personnel feel that the Forest (described early in this chapter) is not hunted as much as it might be. Quail hunting there rates as "good."

On the Special Pheasant Areas ("Pheasant") there is fair quail hunting on the Green River tract and on the Iroquois Co. tract. The same is true of the Mason SF also noted under "Pheasant."

A number of the public areas noted earlier—which we will term Public Hunting Areas from here on—offer quail. Those PHAs which may be rated as best are located and described herewith. Red Hills PHA (10) is a 948-acre tract in the southeast, in Lawrence Co. ten miles west of Lawrenceville Route 50. Stephen A. Forbes PHA (11) is in Marion Co., to the west of the above, contains 2784 acres northeast of the town of Salem, which is at the junction of U.S. 50 and State 37. The two above are portions of State Parks.

The 500-acre L. P. Dolan PHA (12) is also in the southeast, in Hamilton Co. south of McLeansboro on State 142. Saline Co. PHA (13) has 524 acres southeast of Harrisburg in Saline Co. This county is directly south of Hamilton Co. North of Hamilton Co. is Wayne Co., with the Sam Dale PHA (14) of 1300 acres, reached west from U.S. 45 by secondary out of Cisne. To the southwest is Washington Co., with 1363-acre Washington Co. PHA (15) located near the town of Nashville which is at the intersect of U.S. 460 and State 127. To the north, in the southwest corner of Fayette Co. and at the northern tip of Carlyle Reservoir is the Carlyle Lake PHA (16), with 6000 acres. It is southwest from the city of Vandalia and west of U.S. 51.

In addition to all of the above, almost half (20,000 acres) of the 43,000-acre Crab Orchard National Wildlife Refuge (17) is open to varied hunting and offers good quail shooting. A map and all details can be obtained (as well as from address noted early in chapter) from Crab Orchard National Wildlife Refuge, P.O. Box J, Carterville, Illinois 62918. The Refuge is in southwestern Illinois, in the southwest part of Williamson Co., south and west of the city of Marion and off I 57 and south of State 13.

Four other PHAs and one State Forest not so far mentioned have quail hunting rated as "fair." Ramsey Lake PHA (18), with 815 acres, is south-central, in the northwest corner of Fayette Co., north of Vandalia and west of U.S. 51 from the village of Ramsey. Randolph Co. PHA (19) has 763 acres in the southwest, near the Mississippi River in southern Randolph Co., near the town of Chester on State 3. Woodford Co. PHA (20) with almost 2900 acres is in the like-named county, northeast of Peoria and between State Routes 87 and 88. Pope Massac PHA (21) has 820 acres, lies in the extreme southeast, inside the Shawnee NF. It is on the border between Pope and Massac Cos., west of the village of Bay City. Union State Forest (22) contains 3753 acres, is in the southwest, in Union Co. It is surrounded by Shawnee NF lands, lies just west of State 127 and northwest from the town of Anna on U.S. 51.

HUNGARIAN PARTRIDGE

The Hun is something of a mystery bird in Illinois. There is no record of stocking by the Department. Some private stocking may have been done, or birds may have drifted in from Wisconsin. Hun range is predominantly in a few of the counties of the north. These are, along the northern border: Stephenson, Winnebago, Boone, and, just to the south, Ogle, DeKalb, Kane. South of these, Lee Co., which contains the Special Pheasant Area noted under "Pheasant," the only public hunting acreage of note where Huns are quite abundant and the hunting rated as "good." The birds are known to range very spottily as far south as Peoria Co. but the counties listed are the only ones within the best range. Lee Co., where the Green River SPA is located, has the highest Hun population of all.

Few Illinois hunters purposely go after Huns. Most are incidentals in the bag of pheasant hunters. Estimates place hunter numbers around 1.5 percent. The seasonal kill runs from an estimated 5000 to 16,000.

MOURNING DOVES

As the only state in its general area to have an open dove season, Illinois well proves that the dove is an important game bird. Doves run a close second to quail in numbers annually bagged. Estimates range up toward almost two million in some good seasons. Approximately 20 percent of Illinois hunters are dove addicts.

The birds range over most of the state, and with their mobility may be found almost anywhere at various times of the season in shootable numbers. Harvested grain croplands adjacent to woodlots and brushy roosting areas are prime places to find flocks, and pass shooting at flights. All but a modest amount of dove hunting is on private lands, by permission.

Some dove shooting may be found sporadically on almost any of the public lands where suitable feeding, roosting, and watering sites are available. At least three of the public tracts are noteworthy for doves: Red Hills PHA ("Quail") and Green River SPA ("Pheasant") rate as "good"; Iroquois Co. SPA ("Pheasant") as "fair."

OTHER UPLAND BIRDS

Many years ago Illinois was one of the great ranges of the prairie chicken. The decline of the chicken with the push of settlement was one of the true debacles of wildlife within the interior U.S. An all but extinct remnant of prairie chickens still exists, but without question the bird will never again be hunted in Illinois and it is currently illegal to kill one at any time.

In pioneer days, before the demise of most of the forests in Illinois, ruffed grouse were common throughout the entire state. Today there is no ruffed grouse hunting. Transplants of northern grouse were made some time ago in southern Illinois forest regions but the experiments were not successful. During 1967 ruffed grouse trapped in Ohio were introduced to the Shawnee National Forest. Broods were authenticated in the spring of 1968. Whether or not this particular experiment will succeed is currently questionable. But there is optimism that in due time there will be at least token ruffed grouse seasons in the southern forest area.

The wild turkey also once roamed all of Illinois. Those birds were deleted long ago by civilization. However, turkeys were in recent years introduced to the Shawnee NF in the south. Wild-trapped birds from several states have been added periodically, and today turkeys appear to be on the way to permanent establishment there. As this is written there is no open season. But guesses by Department personnel place a possible season in the early 1970s.

Unlike many other states, Illinois is not programming numerous experiments with exotic uplanders. A substantial release of Reeves pheasants several years ago failed to show any establishment. At present the only birds released are some quail and ringneck pheasants.

RAILS, WOODCOCK, JACKSNIPE

There is no open season on rails. This is noted here because most other surrounding states do have a season.

Although jacksnipe are legal, they get little attention from Illinois hunters. However, there is good shooting for those who will seek it. Most of the bottomlands, the courses of small creeks, the fringes of flooded fields get snipe during migration. Most of the waterfowling grounds attract snipe during their migration. Interested hunters should check the public lands under "Waterfowl."

Woodcock migrate across Illinois, and a good many pause in moist coverts, especially in the south. There is almost no purposeful hunting for woodcock. A few are shot, mostly by quail hunters who happen upon them in damp black-dirt lowlands where there is overhead cover and thin ground cover. Woodcock can be found by determined specialists on a number of public tracts. The only one particularly noted for fair woodcock shooting, however, is the Green River SPA ("Pheasant").

WATERFOWL

The enviable location of Illinois along the Mississippi, flight route over the centuries for millions of waterfowl, has long made the state famous, especially for that great prize the Canada goose. Duck hunting, too, is excellent, but it is the goose shooting that has attracted thousands of hunters over the years. Duck hunters account nowadays for between 200,000 and 250,000 birds annually when seasons and bag limits are as satisfactory as they can be made under restrictive regulations. Goose hunters during recent seasons, and still continuing, are restricted by a state quota of Canada geese. This is the most abundant species. When 20,000 Canadas have been killed, the season is automatically ended. Hunters should be aware of this quota system, for it can shorten the season appreciably. For example, during one very recent season the closing date was set originally as December 24 on geese. But the quota was reached, the proper legal notice given, and the season stopped at 3:00 P.M. on December 13.

Four counties of the extreme south and southwest account for almost the entire goose kill in Illinois. In fact, it is estimated by Department personnel that more than 90 percent of the geese are bagged in the four counties of Jackson, Union, Alexander, and Williamson. The first three named border the Mississippi and are the southernmost three counties that do. The famed Horseshoe Lake Refuge (23) and its PHA of some 8681 acres is located in southern Alexander Co., north of Cairo. And in Williamson Co., which lies immediately east of Jackson Co., is the famous Crab Orchard Refuge and shooting area, already noted under "Quail."

There is a vast amount of club hunting in Illinois. These waterfowl clubs are private, licensed by the Department. Most of them are on or near the Illinois River. Membership fees are high, and waiting lists are long.

Some of the good duck hunting areas to be noted in a general way are as follows. The Illinois River from Spring Valley in extreme southeast Bureau Co. downstream to about Meredosia and the Lake of same name in northwest Morgan Co. Mallards are the chief target, and although the hunting has been harmed both by pollution and drainage, it is still excellent at times, providing one can find a place to hunt. The Marshall Co. PHA (24) is along this stretch of river and offers fair duck hunting. It contains 2615 acres up the Illinois River from Peoria some miles via State 87. South of it is the Woodford Co. PHA ("Quail") also with fair duck shooting. Downstream from Peoria, near Manito, is the 1583-acre Spring Lake PHA (25), rated as above, fair for ducks. Rated somewhat better for ducks is another PHA right across the river and near the town of Banner. This is Rice Lake PHA (26), with 2617 acres. Also rated as "good," and much farther downstream north of Beardstown and on the east side of the river is Sanganois PHA (27) with almost 7000 acres. Upstream a short distance and across the river is Anderson Lake PHA (28) with 2067 acres, rated "fair."

There is an Area of 1451 acres slightly above the stretch of river under discussion. This is Starved Rock PHA (29), a portion of a State Park of like name, upstream from Spring Valley and between LaSalle and Ottawa. Still farther upstream near the town of Channahon southwest from Joliet are two small areas with fair duck shooting, the Will Co. (30) and Grundy Co. (31) PHAs. A newer area downstream and on the west side of the River is below Spring Valley, at Sparland, at the junction of State 17 and 29. This is the Sparland PHA (32), with 2300 acres and fair duck hunting.

Up in the extreme northeast, in upper Lake Co., near the Wisconsin border are Grass Lake and Fox Lake Areas with approximately 1000 acres and fair duck shooting.

Down in the south-central sector there is an excellent spot, slated to become still better with further planned development. This is Carlyle Lake (Reservoir), already noted under "Quail." A series of levees are in construction which will flood pin oaks in fall. Duck hunting, however, has already been good on this area.

Farther south and west, in southwestern Jackson Co. near the village of Grand Tower, is a federal project called the Oakwood Bottoms (35). This is on the Big Muddy River almost at its confluence with the Mississippi. The project is what is becoming known as a "greentree reservoir." This is a hardwood area flooded during the period the timber is dormant, then drained during growing time. The timber is not harmed by this procedure; in fact, it does better during each growing season, and the flooded timber forms excellent waterfowl hunting, especially for ducks. There are 2000 acres of public duck hunting here that rates as "good."

Also in the south, almost on the border near U.S. 45 at the village of Mermet, is Mermet Lake PHA (36) with good duck shooting and nearly 2500 acres. To the west and a bit north, in Union Co. and not far from Jonesboro, is the 6202-acre Union Co. PHA (37). This is a goose hunting Area and rated as "good."

Along the northwest border, which is formed by the Mississippi, there is a portion of the Upper Mississippi Refuge. There is a good bit of shooting here, primarily for ducks. The Savanna region should be noted. Other good spots can be found near the River in Whiteside and Rock Island Cos., and along Mercer and Henderson Cos.

Along the lower Illinois and Mississippi Rivers there are large acreages of Corps of Engineers and Bureau of Sport Fisheries and Wildlife lands. The Illinois Department does much of the waterfowl management on these lands, and there are many thousands of acres of refuge also, under federal control. These lands, and the so-called "navigation pools" on the Mississippi, have rather complicated waterfowl hunting regulations. A navigation pool is the stretch of water between dams, or navigation locks. Thus Pool 26 is the water above that lock and up to the next, No. 25. Regulations for the various pools are set forth in detail each season by the Illinois Department. These may be obtained from the Department and it is advisable for interested waterfowlers to do so, and to inform themselves carefully as to where and how blinds may be built, how registered, etc. Pool 26, which reaches from Alton almost to Batchtown, the area surrounding Pool 19, a private one, plus Pools 13, 12, and 11 in the north are recommended.

Goose hunters especially should note that there are numerous farms surrounding the famed southern goose concentrations where pits are rented for daily fees. Chambers of Commerce in the region, or the Department, can give information about these.

There are two federal refuges not so far mentioned, around which waterfowl hunting may at times be located on private lands. One is the 4500-acre Chautauqua Refuge (38) near Havana, which gathers great numbers of ducks. The other is Mark Twain Refuge (39), with over 12,000 acres stretching for many miles along the Mississippi. These lands are noted casually several paragraphs previously where it was mentioned that thousands of acres of federal refuge lie along the river.

DEER

Illinois is proof that whitetail deer do an amazing job of adapting to civilization. Once tremendously abundant during pioneer days, deer were brought almost to extinction. As early as 1853 it was necessary to place a season on them, although the open season lasted almost six months. By the turn of the century there was no open season and deer steadily declined until it was thought they were extinct. The season stayed closed over half a century, until 1957. But in the later years, under careful and enlightened management and some transplanting, whitetails prospered and adapted until it was deemed necessary to keep them in check. Today whitetails are hunted within an hour's drive of Chicago and are present in all counties of the state.

Hunting is restricted to bow and arrow, shotguns, muzzle-loaders. It is on a permit system. Some 50,000 permit holders take an average of 6000 to 7000 deer annually. Some extremely large whitetails are killed. A recent survey showed only four counties listing the largest deer at less than 200 pounds. A great many were over 250, several over 300, and the largest 323. That same season some of the high-kill counties were as follows: Carroll, 296; Jo Daviess, 420 (both in extreme northwest); Johnson, 315; Hardin, 234; Pope, 1051; Union, 260; Williamson, 222 (all in extreme south and southeast.)

Those figures give a hint as to where there are many deer, but they also show where concentrations of hunters are. Success ratios paint a somewhat different picture. Hunters flock to Pope Co., for example, where the kill is usually highest in the state, but the ratio is about one deer to eight hunters. During the season for which the above county kills are quoted, best success-ratio counties with one deer to every four, or 25 percent kill success, were: Adams, on the Mississippi River, west-central; Hancock, immediately north of Adams and on river; Carroll, already noted, in northwest on river. Counties with 20 percent success were: Jo Daviess, extreme northwest on river; McDonough, immediately east of Hancock named above; Rock Island, northwest on river; Warren, to the south and bordering on McDonough. The Department can furnish county-by-county kills and ratios for any current season. These can be valuable to a hunter.

To date deer seasons have in general been for any deer, bag limit one. An excellent bet on public lands is the Shawnee National Forest (see material early in chapter). Within the Forest are several state-managed public areas. Details on these can be obtained from the Department. The Shawnee is exceedingly important to the deer-hunt picture. One recent season almost 2500 deer came from the Forest counties and it was estimated that at least two-thirds were taken on NF lands. This places Forest lands as furnishing perhaps one-third of the total kill for the entire state.

PHAs already covered that offer deer hunting are rated as follows: Marshall Co. ("Waterfowl"), fair; Saline Co. ("Quail"), good; Pope Massac ("Quail"), good—this one is within the NF; Union State Forest ("Quail"), fair; Mason SF ("Pheasant"), fair; Carlyle Lake ("Quail"), fair; Crab Orchard NWR ("Quail"), good.

Deer hunters should consider that though Pope County for some reason gets the greatest number of hunters, surrounding counties in the National Forest area may well offer better hunting. There are, in fact, parts of the Forest, in out-of-the-way tracts hard to get to, that feel little pressure. Hunters who will seek these can find, even in this heavily populated state, some near-wilderness deer hunting. Also, there have been special hunts on Crab Orchard—the Refuge portion—to control deer. These are set only when deemed necessary and cannot be predicted. On the long Mark Twain Refuge paralleling the Mississippi, occasional bow hunts are offered on specified units.

SQUIRRELS

Squirrels are abundant in Illinois. There are both fox and gray squirrels. Fox squirrels range over the entire state, in open timber, in woodlots and hedgerows. Gray squirrels are found in the forest lands of the south, and along the more heavily timbered river bottoms of the west, even up into the northwest. At least half of Illinois hunters hunt squirrels, and the kill is estimated to run from two to three million annually.

In the game laws black squirrels are mentioned. The black squirrel is actually only a melanistic color phase of either the gray or fox squirrel. In some areas dark color phases are more common among the grays than among fox squirrels. Partial melanism is still more common, and numerous Illinois squirrels partly black are taken each season. There is also a famous colony of pure white squirrels in the state, at Olney, Illinois. These are vigorously protected.

Most of the squirrel hunting in Illinois is done on private lands. However, nearly all of the public lands offer excellent opportunities. The Shawnee NF is prime habitat for gray squirrels. Other tracts and their rating are as follows: Under "Pheasant," the Iroquois Area, good. Under "Quail," Red Hills, fair; Ramsey Lake, good; Stephen A. Forbes, good; L. P. Dolan, good; Randolph Co., fair; Saline Co., Sam Dale, Washington Co., Carlyle Lake, Crab Orchard, Pope Massac, good; Woodford Co., fair; Union SF, Mason SF, good. Under "Waterfowl," Horseshoe Lake, good; Marshall Co., fair.

Several other PHAs not so far described offer squirrel hunting. The 1052-acre Argyle Lake PHA (40) has good squirrel hunting, is located west of McComb in western Illinois, McDonough Co. It is off U.S. 136 and is a portion of a state park. McLean Co. PHA (41) has good shooting on its 760 acres southeast of Bloomington off U.S. 150. The Henderson SF (42), over a thousand acres, rates "fair," is on the western border along the Mississippi, in northwest Henderson Co. Shelby SF (43) has about the same acreage and rating. It is near the Shelby Co. PHA noted under "Pheasant," northwest of Effingham and west of State 32.

RABBITS

Cottontails range over the entire state, are very important, with an annual kill averaging in highest cycles up to four million and in lower years over a million. As with other species, most of this kill comes from privately owned lands. However, almost all of the public lands offer rabbit hunting from fair to excellent. Virtually all of the hunting lands noted above under "Squirrels" furnish sport with cottontails also, and that section is a guide to this hunting as well. The Des Plaines and Green River Areas under "Pheasant" also have rabbits available.

OTHER ANIMALS AND BIRDS

Crows are numerous, and there are some excellent winter roost concentrations. One roost of several thousand has recently been located out of Chester, on the Mississippi. Crows have also been using an area southeast of Dixon, in Lee Co. Roosts have been checked from time to time in Clark, Clay, Gallatin, Livingston, Logan, Marion, Mason, Rock Island, and Tazewell Cos. Permission can often be gained for crow shooting on private lands.

Woodchucks are plentiful, especially in the west and south. They may be hunted on the Shawnee NF, but not on state lands. Most are hunted by landowners on their own property.

Hunting raccoons with hounds is a long tradition in southern and western Illinois and the animals are plentiful. Public lands have numerous raccoons but most are hunted on other lands. Both red and gray foxes are also plentiful. The gray is dominant in the south, the red farther north. Red foxes appeal most to the hound men, and there are many in the state, for it gives the best chase. Gray foxes climb trees readily and thus give up sooner. Traditionally many Illinois fox hunters do not hunt to kill the fox but simply for the chase. Calling is beginning to be more and more popular, too. There is some snow hunting, tracking without hounds, which is a high quality sport. Numerous fox and 'coon hunting clubs exist. Public-land hunting for foxes is not important in this state, but callers in particular may find some action in it.

REGULATIONS

Game laws pertaining to seasons, bag and possession limits, areas to be hunted, special hunts, license fees all may have numerous changes from year to year. For current regulations, and for other specific queries, write to: Department of Conservation, 102 State Office Building, Springfield, Illinois 62706.

IOWA

Iowa is a kind of kingpin state of the Midwest, the true heartland of the rich-soil farm belt. On the east its entire border, with Wisconsin and Illinois, is formed by the Mississippi River. On the west the border with Nebraska is the Missouri, and the remaining, northern portion bordering South Dakota is marked off by that large tributary of the Missouri, the Sioux. Boxed in on both sides by large rivers of our most important system, and with the Cedar and Des Moines rivers among others slanting southeastward to join the Mississippi, Iowa soils have been enriched for millions of years.

It is estimated, in fact, that 25 percent of the Grade A land of the entire nation is located in Iowa. Based on this rich resource, and without the massive forests of Minnesota to the north, or the hills of Missouri to the south, Iowa has long been one of the leading agricultural states. Basically this is a gently rolling plains state, with elevations from a bit less than 500 feet to a high point of 1649. Many years it is first in the nation in corn, near the top in several other grains and hay. Often Iowa leads the whole nation in livestock, hogs particularly, although some years it has been second only to Texas in cattle production.

Lately manufacturing has dominated the farm picture in total income importance, but it is the intensive agriculture of the state that affects the hunter. So valuable is Iowa land that percent-wise very little is publicly owned. There is no true wilderness, but there are in several State Forests some sections surprisingly close to it.

Roads are excellent and lead to every portion of the state. At least ten main routes, spaced handily, run north-south, and a like number east-west. Because Iowa has numerous cities of substantial size, air transport to practically every part of the state puts sportsmen within easy drives of any hunting area.

This picture of heavy settlement may give a false notion of a dearth of wildlife and of opportunity for hunters. Oddly, this is not the case at all. Iowa has amazingly good and varied sport. First of all, the size of the state is quite adequate compared to its population. It is roughly 320 miles east-west by 220 north-south, encompasses 56,290 square miles, has approximately 2,750,000 people. With at least a million of this population grouped in the dozen largest cities, which are well distributed over the state, it becomes evident that Iowa still has room for hunters to operate, even though for the most part on privately owned farmlands.

Hunters number a shade above 10 percent of the population. Annual average license sale is 300,000 to residents, about 10,000 to nonresidents. Many of the nonresidents come for pheasants. Though Iowa seldom is so credited, it is actually among the top three or four pheasant states in the U.S. It also offers excellent hunting for bobwhite quail, cottontails, squirrels. There are Hungarian partridge, plentiful waterfowl, a few ruffed grouse. Deer are surprisingly abundant. So are foxes, raccoons, jack rabbits, crows for the non-game hunter, and there is a scattering of coyotes.

333

Possibly because of the intensive agricultural use of Iowa's land, its Conservation Commission has made all the more diligent and quite successful efforts to acquire public lands for the sportsman. There are presently over 115,000 acres state owned or leased. The Commission has an admirable record of concentrated game management on all of it. Further, the modest acreage is split up into over a hundred Public Hunting Areas, sizes ranging from only an acre or two up to several thousand.

These are so well distributed throughout the state that virtually all residents are within only a short distance of one or more, and in some counties where these public tracts are concentrated hunters have numerous close-in choices. Although there are no National Forests in Iowa, there are several State Forests, each containing a few thousand acres where hunting is allowed. An excellent booklet, "Iowa's Public Hunting and Hunting Access Areas," is available from the Commission, address at end of chapter. It is kept up to date, pinpoints, describes, and lists game species for each PHA.

In addition to the state-owned and state-leased public hunting grounds there are over a hundred plots that are county owned. Iowa has a state system set up with what are called County Conservation Boards. Each is in great part autonomous. Many counties, realizing need for more public lands, have grasped opportunities to purchase small acreages and to develop them to whatever extent finances allow for recreational purposes. At this writing twenty-two of Iowa's ninety-nine counties have County Hunting Areas. Some may be farm-game habitats of as little as half an acre. Others contain a hundred to several hundred. A few are over 1000. The twenty-two counties noted at present have over 7800 acres of public hunting lands. While these are of most value to the local resident, visitors will find them very much worthwhile. Besides these CHAs some of the counties allow hunting on their undeveloped or forest lands. Any county seat can furnish information about these lands in its domain.

Hunters should be aware, however, that numerous county regulations are in force on such lands. Any county may adopt the same laws as the State Commission. But this is not mandatory. A county may set its own policy in regard to such lands. Therefore one plot may open only for a certain species during the state season, or it might be open, for example, only for rabbit hunting during December. At this time almost all of Iowa's counties have Conservation Boards. Most are trying to develop public lands. Thus it is important for a hunter seeking such opportunities to contact county board members or the county courthouse in a county where he elects to hunt.

One of the most unique refuges, chiefly for waterfowl, on the continent, lies along Iowa's eastern border. This is a long portion of the Upper Mississippi Wildlife and Fish Refuge. This, and 2077-acre Union Slough National Wildlife Refuge in north-central Iowa, greatly enhance public opportunities for nearby waterfowl hunting, and these will be dealt with in detail under "Waterfowl."

While there is excellent public hunting available on the numerous PHAs (in Iowa various terms are used for the areas, but the foregoing will be used here for consistency), it is obvious that by far the major share of hunting is on private lands. In most of the farm country it is not difficult to obtain permission, if one will use courtesy and mind his manners afield. Farmer-sportsman relations are on the whole quite good.

Lodging and other accommodations are no problem. For campers there are innumerable sites, both public and private. The best source of campground information available for the state is in a most detailed booklet prepared by the Iowa Development Commission, 250 Jewett Building, Des Moines 50309, and available either from that address or from the Conservation Commission. It is titled "Camping In Iowa," lists all sites, with full details on facilities, and with a map showing locations. Other accommodations· such as motels are extremely abundant throughout the state. However, it may be a good idea, for such dates as the opening of pheasant season, to make reservations ahead, especially if one intends to stay in a small city.

Iowa hunting weather covers a broad spectrum of changes. In September when rabbit and squirrel seasons open it is delightful. Early in that month it may even be hot. October quail opening brings crisp weather, perhaps with frosts and some chill. Later on, in November, wool clothing and warm jackets are called for. Many Iowans are avid for hunting during the later seasons, in December and January. This is snow time, and days can be very cold, although enjoyable for properly equipped sportsmen. Waterfowlers should have rain gear always, and bird and small-game hunters should be able to change from leather hunting boots to rubber-bottomed pacs or other waterproof footgear for snowtime.

No hunter needs a big-game rifle in Iowa, except perhaps for fox, coyote, or woodchuck hunting at long range. Only shotguns, muzzle-loaders, and bow and arrow are allowed for deer. A .22 is fine for squirrels and rabbits. Bird hunters will need shot sizes about as follows: No. 6 for pheasants; No. 7½ for quail; No. 4 for ducks; No. 4 Magnum or No. 2 for geese.

PHEASANT

Nationally Iowa seldom gets pheasant-hunt publicity equal to the excellence of its hunting. The state is among the three or four top pheasant states in the nation. Although pheasant populations are anywhere subject to wide fluctuation from season to season, an average annual kill for Iowa, cock birds only, is about 1,500,000 during a season of approximately six weeks' duration. This harvest is accomplished by an average of roughly 250,000 pheasant hunters.

Ringnecks have been established in Iowa since introduction early in the century. They have been hunted since the mid-twenties. Some problems arise from severe winter blizzards, but Iowa's climate has never harmed pheasant populations more than temporarily. Currently the greatest hazard comes from changes in land use. Scores of shelter belts are giving way to cleaner farming practices and the concentration upon crop utilization of all available space. It is possible that Iowa pheasant hunting may face severe problems if the trend is not altered, or enough landowners enlisted to think more of their game as a crop.

At present, however, hunting remains excellent. Pheasants range over almost the entire state. However, prime ranges are on the better soils. Along the entire eastern border populations are poor to only fair. A large swath surrounding Des Moines and reaching southeast to the border around Burlington is poor. The extreme southwest may be considered just fair. Most of the north, and the center interior of the state, rates good to fair. Along the western border a rating of fair is proper. But there are two general areas where the quality range offers the largest concentrations of birds. These are in the east-central part of the state, with this large prime-range region leaning more north than south, and in the southwest—not the extreme southwest but northeastward some distance from Council Bluffs.

These regions will in most seasons be best. Winter storms, poor nesting

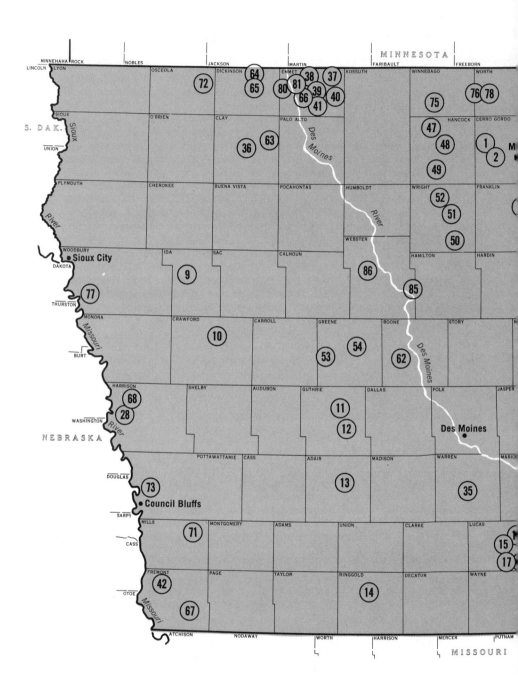

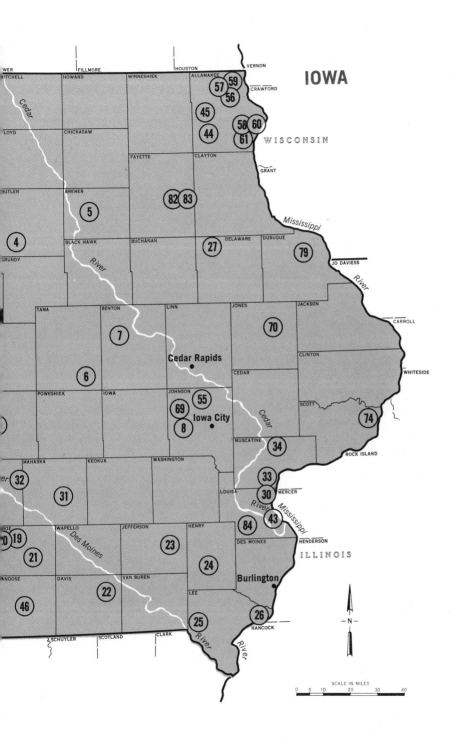

KEY TO HUNTING AREAS

1. Clear Lake Pond PHA
2. Ventura Marsh PHA
3. West Fork Access PHA
4. Big Marsh PHA
5. Sweet Marsh PHA
6. Otter Creek Marsh PHA
7. Dudgeon Lake PHA
8. Swan Lake PHA
9. Washta Access PHA
10. Abandoned Railroad PHA
11. Bays Branch PHA
12. Lakin Slough PHA
13. Meadow Lake PHA
14. Mount Ayr PHA
15. Stephens Forest PHA
16. Browns Slough PHA
17. Colyn Area PHA
18. Williamson Pond PHA
19. Miami Lake PHA
20. La Hart PHA
21. Cottonwood Pits PHA
22. Eldon PHA
23. MacCoon PHA
24. Oakland Mills PHA
25. Shimek SF
26. Green Bay PHA
27. Backbone SF
28. Nobles Lake PHA
29. Kellog PHA
30. Muscatine Slough PHA
31. Hull Strip Mine PHA
32. Pella PHA
33. Keokuk Lake PHA
34. Weise Slough PHA
35. Hooper PHA
36. Mud Lake PHA
37. Birge Lake PHA
38. Grass Lake PHA
39. Ryan Lake PHA
40. East Swan Lake PHA
41. Ingham Lake PHA
42. Forney Lake
43. Lake Odessa
44. Upper Mississippi Wildlife and Fish Refuge
45. Union Slough Refuge
46. Rathbun Dam
47. Crystal Lake PHA
48. Eagle Lake PHA
49. East Twin Lake PHA
50. Big Wall Lake PHA
51. Elm Lake PHA
52. Morse Lake PHA
53. Dunbar Slough PHA
54. Goose Lake PHA
55. Hawkeye PHA
56. French Creek PHA
57. Cains Lake PHA
58. Little Paint Creek PHA
59. New Albin Big Lake PHA
60. Yellow River SF
61. Waukon Junction PHA
62. Holst Forest PHA
63. Smith Slough PHA
64. Diamond Lake PHA
65. Kettleson Hogback PHA
66. West Swan Lake PHA
67. Riverton PHA
68. Deer Island PHA
69. Hawkeye Wildlife Area
70. Picture Rock PHA
71. Willow Slough PHA
72. Rush Lake PHA
73. Wilson Island PHA
74. Princeton PHA
75. Myra Slough PHA
76. Rice Lake PHA
77. Browns Lake PHA
78. Elk Creek Marsh PHA
79. White Pine Hollow PHA
80. Cheever Lake PHA
81. Four Mile Lake PHA
82. Big Rock Access PHA
83. Grannis Creek PHA
84. Klum Lake PHA
85. Deception Hollow PHA
86. Lizard Creek PHA

conditions, land-use changes all affect Iowa pheasants, but because the birds range almost throughout the state seldom do all three have drastic effects at any one time. In general, the northern half of the state may be considered better than the southern half. In fact, determined and intricate experiments are presently under way to ascertain if a ringneck strain may be bred locally that will be as well suited to the south as birds now are to the north.

To pinpoint more closely the two broad corridors of top range, some counties centered in them and cities marking them out are listed here. The east-central portion begins in the vicinity of Mason City in Cerro Gordo County. Parts of Mitchell and Howard Cos. to the north are included. East of Cerro Gordo are top-range Floyd and Chickasaw Cos. This establishes the northern portion. A line drawn on a long ellipse from just west of Mason City gently southeastward to Hampton, Marshalltown, Montezuma, then circling eastward slightly below Interstate 80 and curving around northeastward toward and west of Iowa City and Cedar Rapids, and thence on a generally north tack to Independence, West Union, and on around north and west to Mason City again will encompass this entire range.

The southwest quality range is another somewhat elliptical one. It can be marked out as follows. The line begins about halfway between Sioux City and Holstein on U.S. 20. It runs south roughly to Smithland, Woodbine, then more to the southeast clear down to the vicinity of Red Oak. From here it curves east and then northward in a long loop about through Creston, Guthrie Center, Jefferson, and gently back around to the beginning point.

It must again be emphasized that the major share of hunting will be found on private lands. One reason is that these are croplands and thus serve as feeding grounds for pheasants. However, many of the PHAs furnish excellent shooting, and especially so on blustery days when pheasants seek the heavier cover that is generally found on these.

Because Iowa PHAs are so numerous and some quite small, it is not possible to list in detail all of them here. The booklet noted early in the chapter lists and locates all of them. However, here are some of the ones lying within the two prime pheasant ranges, listed by counties. In the east-central range, Cerro Gordo Co. has two offering pheasants: Clear Lake Pond PHA (1) and Ventura Marsh PHA (2). Franklin Co. has West Fork Access PHA (3); Butler Co., Big Marsh PHA (4), a 2835-acre tract; Bremer Co., Sweet Marsh PHA (5), over 1500 acres; Tama Co., 2000-plus-acre Otter Creek Marsh PHA (6); Benton Co., Dudgeon Lake PHA (7), over 1000 acres, small Swan Lake PHA (8), Johnson Co.

In the southwest primary range there are: small Washta Access PHA (8) in Ida Co.; smaller Abandoned Railroad PHA (9), two plots in Crawford Co.; in Guthrie Co. two, Bays Branch PHA (10) of 797 acres, Lakin Slough PHA (11) of 300; Adair Co., 240-acre Meadow Lake PHA (13) plus upland.

A few counties that have numerous state-owned PHAs in good pheasant range are: Clay in the general northwest sector; Palo Alto immediately east of Clay; Dickinson, one of the very best bets because of at least fifteen public areas of fair size offering pheasants, and lying on the northern border directly north of Clay; Emmet Co., directly east of Dickinson with 12 PHAs and in range, as the foregoing, rated as good; Kossuth Co., east of these with four PHAs; Pocahontas Co., south of Palo Alto Co. with four PHAs running from 160 to almost 400 acres; Winnebago Co., on the northern border east of Kossuth with three PHAs of good size, from over 400 to over 1800 acres; Wright Co., one county south of Winnebago with three Areas running from 172 to 978 acres.

Numerous other counties have state- or county-owned public lands with pheasants. Check these with sources noted, but just as important, seek permission on private lands in the prime zones, or anywhere across the northern half of the state except the eastern and western border areas.

QUAIL

Bobwhite quail come very close in importance, by numbers annually harvested, to pheasants. An average in peak years of over a million are taken. Other seasons at least half that number are bagged. However, quail hunters are fewer, seldom over 65,000. The Iowa season is usually long, running toward the end of January. The daily bag limit is a bit lower, however, than in quail states farther south. Currently it is eight.

Iowa quail populations fluctuate widely. Severe winters occasionally decimate high cycles. Much of the best hunting comes in December and January, when the birds have established their winter cover and feeding ranges. Much of this is hunting in the snow. It can be cold, but rewarding.

Peak populations of bobwhites at the top of explosive up-cycles are estimated as high as ten million birds. This, and the annual kill, places Iowa as a quail state far ahead of the position in which most hunters picture it. The birds range throughout the state, but the northern half of the state—slightly more than half—is rated as poor. Iowa's best quail ranges are on the lower-grade soils of the south. This is due in part to the fact that much cover is available in brush and weed tracts adjacent to grain fields.

In general the bottom two tiers of counties encompass this prime quail range. But the extreme southwest is not quite as good as the remainder. Thus, the region south of U.S. 34 and east of U.S. 71 blocks off the best. The counties involved, reading west to east and taking the bottom tier first: Taylor, Ringgold, Decatur, Wayne, Appanoose, Davis, Van Buren, Lee; second tier, Adams, Union, Clarke, Lucas, Monroe, Wapello, Jefferson, Henry, Des Moines.

To the north of this quality range is one in a broad swath that can be considered "good." This takes in the extreme southwest, runs up the western border narrowly about to Onawa. But the broad west-to-east corridor demarcation line cuts east about from Council Bluffs to Interstate 35, thence north almost to U.S. 30, then east again and a bit northeast to Cedar Rapids, and northeastward to the border about at Bellevue, which is south of Dubuque. Above this line there is a lesser cross-state corridor rated as "fair." The remainder of the state, as noted, is marginal, but there are pockets of fair populations scattered over it.

Most quail hunting is on deeded lands, by permission. Some of the PHAs, however, offer fair sport. In the best range, there is the Mount Ayr PHA (14) of 1158 acres in Ringgold Co., near the village of Mount Ayr. Lucas Co., middle of second tier, has four PHAs with good quail populations: Stephens Forest PHA (15), 4302 acres; Browns Slough PHA (16), 847 acres; Colyn Area PHA (17), 770 acres; Williamson Pond PHA (18), 126 acres. Immediately east, in Monroe Co., are three PHAs—Miami Lake PHA (19), La Hart PHA (20), Cottonwood Pits PHA (21)—with quail. Davis Co. has the Eldon PHA (22) with over 600 acres; Jefferson Co. has the small MacCoon PHA (23); Henry Co. has tiny (27-acre) Oakland Mills PHA (24). Lee Co. in the extreme southeast has the 3975-acre Shimek State Forest (25), and 228-acre Green Bay PHA (26).

Outside the prime range, Dudgeon Lake in Benton Co. ("Pheasant") offers quail. So does small Backbone SF (27) in east-central Delaware Co. Harrison Co., north of Council Bluffs on the western border, has quail at Nobles Lake PHA (28). Jasper Co., immediately northeast of Des Moines, has a small Area with quail, Kellog PHA (29). Louisa Co., on the eastern border immediately north of Des Moines Co., has 1813-acre Muscatine Slough PHA (30). Mahaska Co., southeast from the city of Des Moines, offers Hull Strip Mine PHA (31) of 378 acres, and Marion Co., bordering Mahaska on the west, has 274-acre Pella PHA (32). Muscatine Co., on the eastern border north of Louisa Co., offers two Areas with quail: Keokuk Lake PHA (33) and 1180-acre Weise Slough PHA (34). Warren Co., south of the city of Des Moines, has the Hooper PHA (35) of over 300 acres.

A few of the other PHAs listed in the booklet noted earlier have some quail shooting. But again, the major share of the quality hunting will be found on private lands.

HUNGARIAN PARTRIDGE

The Hun has been in Iowa, as an introduced exotic, since very shortly after this century began. It is a bird chiefly of open prairie country where grain is grown. It does quite well in regions of severe winters, and in its Iowa range, which is in the northwest quarter of the state, it sustains itself throughout many such. Oddly, and as in many other states where Huns are established, they are not hunted with any concentration, and are generally taken as incidentals by pheasant hunters. Probably this is because the pheasant is a larger reward for the hunter, and because Huns are on the whole not as plentiful and certainly are more difficult to locate and hunt. Only a small percentage of Iowa's hunters diligently pursue the Hun, and the annual kill averages only around 12,000 birds.

The season coincides with pheasant hunting. Perhaps if it were possible to hunt Huns only, interest would be greater. At any rate, Iowa does have a substantial population of these birds. In fall they are found mostly in hay and stubble fields, and later in winter in cornfields or plowed fields, with coveys retiring to weed patches or brushy coverts in bad weather and at evening.

Basically the range of good shootable populations begins on the east about at north-south U.S. 65, which runs through Mason City, and covers the region west to the border and south to U.S. 30 and State 141. At this writing, these are also the boundaries for legal shooting. This includes very roughly the northwest quarter of the state. But check current laws for season boundaries. Present seasons are over more counties than previously. The Hun appears to be spreading its range slowly south.

As with other game, most of the better shooting is on private lands. But several PHAs have fair to good Hun populations. In Clay Co., Mud Lake PHA (36) with 252 acres has Huns. This is roughly centered in Hun-season range. Emmet Co., northeast of Clay, has five PHAs where Huns are considered prominent. These are: Birge Lake PHA (37) and Grass Lake PHA (38), each with less than 200 acres; Ryan Lake PHA (39) with over 300; East Swan Lake PHA (40) with almost 800; Ingham Lake PHA (41) with nearly 1000.

RUFFED GROUSE

The ruffed grouse is native to northeastern Iowa. This region, particularly the extreme northeast, and predominantly in Allamakee County, is made up of steep wooded hillsides and more open farmed valleys. Grouse are not abundant. Neither are they rare. There was no open season for many years. But a study project was begun in 1966 to ascertain the status and stable population of this fine game bird. The 500-acre plot set aside for the research was within the Yellow River State Forest in Allamakee County, a forest of 5250 acres. As the study progressed it was obvious that ruffed grouse populations were remaining fairly stable. Since this bird is highly cyclic, this appeared to be a sign of a good basic population.

In 1968 a season of approximately two weeks was announced, presumably as an experiment, with a two-bird bag limit and four-bird possession limit. The boundaries were U.S. 63 north-south and State 3 east-west. This enclosed several counties and portions of counties in the northeast. Ruffed grouse are also being reintroduced into forest areas of the southeast. At this writing it is too early to draw conclusions as to what the future may hold for ruffed grouse hunting in Iowa. It is thought that a small huntable surplus birds may be available for specialists for some years to come.

WILD TURKEYS

Written records from over a century ago indicate that wild turkeys were at that time abundant in northeastern Iowa. There were a few elsewhere in the state, but by early in this century wild turkeys had become extinct in Iowa. During the winter of 1960-61, thirty-nine Texas turkeys of the Rio Grande subspecies were brought to Iowa and released in the Yellow River State Forest in the northeast. They were placed here because it is one of the few large blocks (over 5000 acres) of forest in the state. Although this stocking made a bit of progress, several years later an estimate of no more than 100 turkeys was made and the population has appeared to remain stable but without spreading or indication of ability to increase.

Originally the eastern subspecies was the native bird. In 1965 small plantings of this bird were made in the Shimek State Forest in Lee Co. in the southeast. These birds appear to have made encouraging progress toward establishment, as they have in Missouri to the south. Missouri has also stocked birds near the border and it is felt there may eventually be free ranging of the eastern strain across the border. In 1966 the western mountain turkey, the Merriam's subspecies, was stocked in a small planting in the Stephens State Forest in northeastern Lucas Co. Broods have been sighted, but results appear less encouraging than with the eastern strain. More recently other transplants of Merriam's have been made, and more also of the eastern subspecies. These last were brought to the Stephens SF during 1968. To date it appears that Iowa has had a good opportunity to evaluate three subspecies of wild turkeys for its terrain, and the eastern turkey appears to have so far the best chance of establishment. State wildlife biologists are hopeful that within the next few years Iowa will be able to have at least token seasons for wild turkeys again after more than a century with none.

EXOTIC BIRDS

As this is written the Iowa Conservation Commission is disturbed about the consequences of further usurpation of wildlife habitat by agriculture. It is felt that the face of Iowa's land is swiftly changing, that the hedgerows are disappearing all too fast, that too many small farms are being turned into grassland ranches. This prompts a search for new game birds to fill voids that may be opened by the disappearance of such staple uplanders as quail and pheasants due to habitat changes. It is felt that the Hun may be part of the answer. Meanwhile, however, Iowa is trying, as have many other states, the Reeves pheasant. This is a bird at home in forest areas. As farmlands are swept too clean of agricultural practices, perhaps such birds may save hunting in critical situations. To date Iowa makes no predictions, but hunters may be well advised to watch developments with this handsome bird.

DOVES, WOODCOCK, SNIPE

Doves and woodcock are mentioned here because Iowa is on the fringe of states with seasons on these birds. However, Iowa has no open season on either.

It does have an open season on snipe, and more good hunting than Iowa hunters and visitors realize. Not more than one-half of one percent of Iowa hunters attempt snipe hunting. This means that probably fewer than 1500 hunters annually hunt this excellent game bird, and most take it as an incidental while waterfowl hunting. The annual bag is estimated at less than 5000 jacksnipe. Many of Iowa's marshes, creek banks, and river bottoms offer good snipe hunting, if gunners will only avail themselves of the opportunity. See the following section on waterfowl for basic information on good areas to try.

WATERFOWL

As with its other good hunting, Iowa's waterfowling is far better than its small publicity would indicate. This state is in fact an excellent duck state and one of the best goose hunting locations in the nation. The Mississippi and Missouri river valleys have for many centuries been the most important midcontinent migration routes for waterfowl. Boxed in between these two, and with hundreds of thousands of acres of grain fields, plus many hundreds of farm ponds and small marshes, Iowa is a virtually perfect resting area for the millions of waterfowl moving south in fall.

The duck kill runs from 400,000 to 600,000, taken by 50,000 to 60,000 hunters. The goose kill is high, from 50,000 up to as high as 65,000. Wood ducks and teal make up a substantial portion of the duck bag, but the mallard is the supreme bird here. Large numbers of snow and blue geese are harvested because they follow the Missouri valley on their way from their far-north nesting grounds to their wintering grounds in Texas and Louisiana.

While waterfowling is excellent, the famous locations are likely to be crowded. Attempts are being made toward more and more controlled hunting to alleviate the hazards of crowding. Forney Lake (42) is a good example. This lake was formed many years ago as a cutoff from the Missouri River. Located in southwestern Iowa, in Fremont Co., it is reached off U.S. 275 between Glenwood and Sidney. Forney Lake, partly a refuge, is a rest and feeding stop for many thousands of blue and snow geese. It is presently, and has long been, the major harvest point for these species in the state.

So popular was Forney Lake, and so successful the hunting, that elbow-to-elbow shooting became the rule. To correct the mounting problems of safety and bad hunting manners due to this overcrowding, the Commission closed the north and west sides of the lake to public hunting, installed twenty-five blinds spaced at safe distances from each other and from the refuge. While there is resistance among some hunters to this control, it has offered quality goose hunting and those who have hunted the control area are enthused. Applicants can send for blind reservations to the Commission in Des Moines until mid-September, from then on should address the Commission at Forney Lake, Thurman, Iowa. A $1 reservation fee is required with the request, and an additional $1 is charged at the time of drawing for blinds. Applicants should list three choices of dates. During one fairly recent season almost eight hundred geese were shot from the twenty-five blinds.

Another excellent area with semicontrol is Lake Odessa (43), one of the best spots in Iowa for mallard shooting. This lake, or river cutoff, is adjacent to the Mississippi River in the southeastern part of the state, in Louisa Co., east of Wapello, which is on U.S. 61. There are some 6000 acres here, 2500 of which are federal refuge. The remaining 3500 are maintained and managed by the Commission as a public hunting ground. Water level is manipulated to drain down to mud flats in summer. Duck foods such as smartweed and wild millet then spring up. In suitable dryer areas some food crops are planted, particularly on the refuge portion. All these lands are then flooded to shallow depth in fall. As many as a quarter-million ducks, 90 percent of them mallards, gather at Lake Odessa each fall. On a portion of the public lands known as The Flats, crowding of hunters forced the Commission to stake out hunting sites. Hunting parties must hunt from these staked-out stations, which are safely spaced. Since the area is large, as many as 250 hunting parties can utilize it daily with no serious crowding.

An excellent bet for duck hunters is in the northeast, near Lansing, which is on the Mississippi in Allamakee Co. on State 9. This region is not as heavily hunted as many others. Noted early in the chapter were the Upper

Mississippi Wildlife and Fish Refuge (44), and Union Slough Refuge (45). The Upper Mississippi is unique among refuges. It runs from Clinton, Iowa, all the way up the river and far into Wisconsin. About 20 percent of the total area is closed to hunting, in plots ranging from a few hundred to over 7000 acres. Most waterfowl rest in the closed areas once shooting starts, but good pass shooting is available as the flocks fly out, or up and down the river. Union Slough Refuge is a rest-stop for waterfowl. There is no hunting on the refuge but surrounding lands offer good hunting by permission or for fees. It is located in north-central Iowa, near Titonka in Kossuth Co., reached off U.S. 18 via State 226.

All along the western border there is good waterfowl shooting along the Missouri and the Sioux, but much of the best is taken up by clubs and private organizations. In the interior of the state, several locations are especially noteworthy. Rathbun Dam (46) near Centerville in south-central Iowa, Appanoose Co., provides good duck hunting. A short distance northwest, near Chariton on U.S. 34, are Brown Slough and the Colyn PHA, both of several hundred acres and both with fine duck shooting.

The last-named areas are but two among dozens of PHAs that offer fair to excellent public waterfowling. Some of the best is to be found in Hancock Co., north-central, with Crystal Lake PHA (47), Eagle Lake PHA (48), and East Twin Lake PHA (49), all not far from the junction of U.S. 18 and U.S. 69. Immediately to the south, in Wright Co., are three more: Big Wall Lake PHA (50), Elm Lake PHA (51), Morse Lake PHA (52), all near Clarion, which is on State 3 near the junction with U.S. 69. Greene Co. in the central-west region has Dunbar Slough PHA (53) and Goose Lake PHA (54), well known for waterfowl, with a general location point near Jefferson at intersect of U.S. 30 and State 17. A large PHA consisting of flooded river bottom in Johnson Co. is also excellent for ducks. This is the Hawkeye PHA (55), upstream from Lake McBride, an impoundment near Iowa City in east-central Iowa.

Of Iowa's hundred-odd Public Hunting Areas, over ninety offer waterfowl shooting of varying quality. The booklet mentioned earlier as obtainable from the Commission lists and locates all of these. Among the counties with the most and best units are, in alphabetical order: Buena Vista; Calhoun; Clay; Dickinson (with two dozen, the county located in the northwest, with Spirit Lake on U.S. 71 a focal point); Emmet (east of Dickinson, with ten units); Guthrie; Kossuth; Louisa; Lucas; Palo Alto; Winnebago; Worth.

Goose hunters should be aware, as many apparently are not, that the Canadas migrate early, as soon as goose season opens, but are not inclined to stay, although they utilize as rest stops hundreds of farm ponds and many of the PHAs. Snows and blues come somewhat later and hang on longer at spots like Forney Lake. Experiments are under way in Iowa attempting to build up and develop rest areas that will attract and hold Canadas, and perhaps encourage formation of native flocks. Big Marsh in Butler Co. is one such area. Another, with a captive flock presumed to be the giant Canada strain, is in Emmet Co. Goose hunting, for Canadas, incidentally is currently closed in portions of counties near the goose experiment points, to avoid the killing of free-flying progeny of these birds.

As a final note for hunters interested in Iowa waterfowl, the state's numerous streams, most of them slow and meandering, furnish excellent jump-shooting and float-shooting, especially for ducks. Snipe hunters, as mentioned under that heading, should check out public marshes and stream banks mentioned here under waterfowl. Fine hunting is available for those who will pursue this wetland sport. It should be noted also that coots are abundant in Iowa waterfowl areas, and make up a surprisingly large part of the total waterfowl bag. It is estimated that 25,000 to 30,000 are taken each season

DEER

Iowa deer hunting is for residents only, and only by the use of bow and arrow, shotgun, and muzzle-loader. Hunting is for any deer, with a bag limit of one. Archery seasons are approximately two months long, but gun seasons are two or three days, with changes from year to year. No bow quotas are set, but gun permits are limited. They average around 20,000 annually at present. These are paid licensees. In addition to these, landowner-tenant permits are given free. These make up a substantial percentage of total hunters. During one recent season these non-fee permitees hunting on their own property numbered almost 15,000. An average total deer kill currently runs from 10,000 to 12,000 animals. Hunter success hangs around 30 to 33 percent.

Iowa has not always had such good whitetail hunting. Some years ago deer had reached a low ebb, and there were no open seasons. But since 1955 there have been consecutive seasons, and deer have increased phenomenally. The 1955 kill was less than 2500.

For permit purposes the state is divided into zones. Some years there have been six. As this is written there are four, and permits offered in these reflect to a great extent the herd status in different portions of the state. Zone 1 is in the west and southwest. It encompasses the area west and south of U.S. 71 and State 3. Comparatively, this is a small Zone, but had—at this writing—5500 permits. Zone 2 is across southern Iowa and extends up into west-central Iowa. It is east of U.S. 71, bounded on the north by U.S. 175, then on the east by U.S. 69 down to State 163 and 92 running east. Permits: 9500. Zone 3 is central, east-central, and northeast. It lies east and north of the routes just mentioned—U.S. 69, State 163, and 92, and has as its western boundary U.S. 63 down to U.S. 20, west to U.S. 65 and south to U.S. 175. There were 4000 permits here. Zone Four is north-central and northwest, the remaining portion of the state, with only 1500 permits.

Thus it becomes obvious that the south and west-central areas, plus parts of the east and central sections, offer the best hunting. To further narrow the locations of best ranges, a corridor along the western border from Council Bluffs north to the border, narrowing at its northern end, is one of the best. A second corridor reaching from a bit west and north of Des Moines south to the border and taking in all the area east of U.S. 169 and south of U.S. 34, and also north of that route roughly from Ottumwa to Des Moines, is in the quality range. Another excellent area can be enclosed to the east of a line beginning on the eastern border about at Clinton and running north and west to the northern border about where U.S. 63 crosses it.

Kill figures for some of the counties are revealing. Of course, certain counties in the high-permit areas get heavier hunting than others. But consistent high kills nonetheless occur in a few. Although the season is statewide and every county contributes to the total harvest, some are very low (Grundy Co. had three kills in a recent season) but others are outstanding. Guthrie Co., two counties west of Des Moines, contributed that same season 423 deer. Other counties with over 300 were: Decatur, on the south-central border; Lucas, one tier up and to the northeast; Monroe, immediately east of Lucas; Harrison, on the western border north of Council Bluffs; Monona, immediately north of Harrison; Allamakee, in the extreme northeast. This presents a fairly precise pattern of populations. Counties surrounding those mentioned are good to fair.

Hunters should bear in mind that whitetails love cover, and in Iowa this means for the most part the river bottoms. In any section these will produce the best hunting. It is also interesting to note that in the wide-open farm country deer have adapted to the few brushy draws and the cornfields. Some very large, fat deer are killed in such terrain. Incidentally, deer hunters, excepting archers, must wear an article of iridescent orange clothing.

A large number of the PHAs offer deer hunting. The largest of these are listed here alphabetically by counties, whether within or outside the prime range.

Allamakee Co.: French Creek PHA (56), Cains Lake PHA (57), Little Paint Creek PHA (58), New Albin Big Lake PHA (59), Yellow River SF (60), Waukon Junction PHA (61).

Boone Co.: Holst Forest PHA (62).

Bremer Co.: Sweet Marsh PHA (63).

Butler Co.: Big Marsh PHA (64).

Clay Co.: Smith Slough PHA (63).

Davis Co.: Eldon PHA (22).

Dickinson Co.: Diamond Lake PHA (64), Kettleson Hogback PHA (65).

Emmet Co.: East Swan Lake PHA (40), Ingham Lake PHA (41), West Swan Lake PHA (66).

Fremont Co.: Riverton PHA (67).

Hancock Co.: East Twin Lake PHA (49).

Harrison Co.: Deer Island PHA (68).

Johnson Co.: Hawkeye Wildlife Area (69).

Jones Co.: Picture Rock PHA (70).

Lee Co.: Shimek SF (25).

Louisa Co.: Lake Odessa (43), Muscatine Slough PHA (30).

Lucas Co.: Stephens SF (15).

Mills Co.: Willow Slough PHA (71).

Muscatine Co.: Keokuk Lake PHA (33), Weise Slough PHA (34).

Osceola Co.: Rush Lake PHA (72).

Pottawatamie Co.: Wilson Island PHA (73).

Ringgold Co.: Mount Ayr PHA (14).

Scott Co.: Princeton PHA (74).

Warren Co.: Hooper PHA (35).

Winnebago Co.: Myre Slough PHA (75), Rice Lake PHA (76).

Woodbury Co.: Browns Lake PHA (77).

Worth Co.: Elk Creek Marsh PHA (78).

A number of these have over 1000 acres and some have several thousand. All offer fair to good hunting. Much quality deer hunting, however, is still found on privately owned lands.

SQUIRRELS

Squirrels are important small game in Iowa, abound in woodlots and river bottoms throughout the state, especially where there are oaks and hickories. The southern half of the state has the highest population, yet there are good opportunities here and there over the entire state. The annual bag runs somewhere over a million. Both fox and gray squirrels are native, but in general the fox squirrel is predominant in the small woodlots, the gray squirrel in the larger forest blocks.

At least half of Iowa's hunters go squirrel hunting. Most do their hunting on private lands. However, the State Forests and the numerous PHAs furnish excellent opportunities. Hunters should carefully check the booklet listing public lands. Some of the counties and PHAs with the best hunting are however listed here.

Allamakee Co. has French Creek PHA (56) and Yellow River SF (60) with good hunting. This is in the northeast. In Boone Co. northwest of Des Moines, the Holst Forest PHA (62) is of modest size but offers excellent hunting. Dubuque Co. on the eastern border, central location, has White Pine Hollow PHA (79) near Luxemburg, a forest tract. Emmet Co. in the general northwest part of the state has a number of fair squirrel areas—Cheever Lake PHA (80), Eagle Lake PHA (48), Four Mile Lake PHA (81), Ingham Lake PHA (41), Ryan Lake PHA (39), West Swan Lake PHA (66).

In the northeast, Fayette Co., southwest of Allamakee Co., has two PHAs of modest size: Big Rock Access PHA (82); Grannis Creek PHA (83). In the extreme southeast, Lee Co. contains the Shimek SF (25) with excellent squirrel shooting, and to the north Louisa Co. has Klum Lake PHA (84), Lake Odessa PHA (43), and Muscatine Slough PHA (30), all of large acreage. Lucas Co., south of Des Moines in south-central Iowa, offers fine opportunities, with 4302-acre Stephen Forest PHA (15), Browns Slough PHA (16), the Colyn PHA (17). Monroe Co., immediately east, has squirrels at Miami Lake PHA (19). Weise Slough PHA (34) in Muscatine Co. in the east is a good bet. And Webster Co., west-central, northwest of Des Moines, has two small but good PHAs—Deception Hollow PHA (85), Lizard Creek PHA (86).

RABBITS

Cottontail rabbits are abundant and much hunted in Iowa. An average of approximately two million are annually bagged. About half of Iowa's hunters follow this sport. By far the major share of the kill is during the snow months of the season, in December and January. The southern one-third of Iowa has the highest cottontail populations. Western Iowa is second in importance, northern Iowa third, and the east of lesser importance. In the south there are considerable expanses of low-grade lands where brush cover is abundant. Presumably this is responsible for the high cottontail populations there.

Jack rabbit distribution—predominantly the large whitetailed jack that turns white in winter—differs from that of the cottontail. These rabbits are abundant chiefly in the northwest, west-central, and central part of the state, are much hunted locally, especially by landowners in winter, after a fresh snowfall. They of course utilize more open range than smaller cottontail. An average good season sees about 100,000 taken by 20,000 hunters. Practically all of Iowa's PHAs offer rabbit hunting. There is therefore no problem whatever for hunters who seek public-land hunting. Permission hunting for rabbits of either species on private lands is also seldom difficult to arrange.

OTHER ANIMALS AND BIRDS

Raccoons and foxes are abundant. Coyotes are in fair supply. It is estimated that some 40,000-plus hunters collect over 100,000 foxes and about 2000 coyotes annually. Iowa still bounties these animals, a situation not particularly pleasing to professional wildlife personnel. Raccoon hunting, a sport avidly followed by Iowa farmers who own 'coon dogs, accounts for at least 300,000 animals each season. Foxes range throughout the state, coyotes chiefly along the Missouri River in the west and in portions of the south. Raccoons are plentiful almost everywhere, especially where river bottoms, woodlots and croplands adjoin. Practically all of the public lands offer hunting for one or more of these animals. Foxes, incidentally, are of two species—red and gray.

Woodchucks are numerous in Iowa, but there are few hunters, chiefly because rifles are not used for deer and therefore few rifle hunters follow this pest-hunt endeavor. Bobcats are scarce. There are a few along the wilder river bottoms and in the forest regions but they cannot be considered of importance.

Numerous Iowa hunters are avid for crows, and these birds are abundant. The kill is estimated to run around 200,000 each season. Crows nest in Iowa, and others migrate through. Some winter in the state. Roosts of several thousand birds are not uncommon, but most shooting is done for small groups of local or migrating birds. The public lands offer good crow shooting to the enthusiast who will put out decoys and who knows how to use a call.

REGULATIONS

Game laws pertaining to seasons, bag and possession limits, areas to be hunted, special hunts, license fees all may have numerous changes from year to year. For current regulations, and for other specific queries, write to: State Conservation Commission, East 7th and Court Avenue, Des Moines, Iowa 50308.

MISSOURI

The "Show-Me" state, Missouri, is loaded with the romance of the Ozarks, and with the history of the pioneers who by thousands launched from here the many expeditions that eventually conquered the West. Its location was perfect for that. The Mississippi River forms the entire eastern boundary of the state, which is chiefly with Illinois but touches brief portions of Kentucky and Tennessee in the southeast. Flowing across the state from west to east is the Missouri, which formed the main water route into the West.

The southern boundary of Missouri is with Arkansas. On the west there are brief contacts with Nebraska and Oklahoma, but Kansas embraces most of that border. Iowa lies to the north. In many ways the terrain of the state is a mixture of all the states that surround it. There are rolling hills in the north, heavily farmed. In the southeast is the "bootheel" or "delta" country where cotton and melons are grown. Portions of the northwest and the west are prairie country, and throughout the south the steep, forested Ozarks hide in their valleys rushing streams that pour southward.

For game management purposes Missouri may be divided into eight distinct natural regions. There is the Northwest Prairie lying along the Missouri River north of Kansas City, the Western Prairie below Kansas City and along the central western border, the Western Ozark Border Area of the southwest. Portions of the north are termed the Northern Riverbreaks. In the northeast are the Northeast Riverbreaks, along the Mississippi. Spreading out from St. Louis is the region of the North and East Ozark Border Area. In the southeast are the Mississippi Lowlands, and in the south is the Ozark Plateau.

Although Missouri, once a frontier wilderness teeming with game, became an agricultural state, today its greatest income derives from manufacturing. Agriculture is in second place. Missouri is also an important tourist state. Although public lands are adequate, approximately 90 percent of the state is in private ownership. In the southern Ozarks some counties have as high as 85 percent of their area in forest, with large expanses of solid timber. In the central counties woodlands and farmlands are about evenly split. In the West, the prairie areas are chiefly devoted to agriculture, with scattered woodlots and game cover along the stream bottoms.

There is no difficulty here in reaching hunting grounds. Good roads probe all parts of the state. In the Ozarks, however, 4WD vehicles are useful for back trails and sideroads, and it is important to remember that in wet weather Missouri mud is famous for its sticking qualities. Air transport contacts all major cities. Secondary flights take one to numerous smaller population centers.

Total area of the state is 69,686 square miles. Presently the population is close to five million. At least two million residents, however, live in or near St. Louis and Kansas City. Remainder of the population is rather evenly distributed over small towns and rural communities. Thus there is still ample room for the average of about 500,000 hunters, even though most must hunt on private lands. Permission is still not too difficult to obtain in outlying areas, but fee hunting—payment of a trespass fee—is becoming more and more popular. By far the majority of hunters are residents. Nonresidents number around 15,000. Perhaps a third of these are deer hunters, the remainder small-game hunters.

Rabbits and squirrels are the most important small-game species, and the bobwhite quail is the top game bird. There are mourning doves, pheasants, waterfowl, woodcock, snipe, and rails. The whitetail deer is the only big-game animal. Wild turkey, avidly hunted, are making a swift comeback. Foxes, raccoons, opossums, coyotes, bobcats occur in varying abundance.

The largest blocks of public hunting lands in Missouri are in two National Forests. Both Forests are located in the southern half of the state, and predominantly in the southeastern quarter. The Clark National Forest (1) contains 768,254 acres with headquarters at Rolla. The Supervisor may be contacted there for maps and details. The Clark NF is actually in four large separate tracts. One is based on Rolla, lying southwest from that city. To the east, with the town of Bixby about centered in it at the junction of State 32 and 49, is a second, and larger, tract. Still farther east, mostly in Madison Co., and crossed by U.S. 67, is a third tract. The fourth is directly south, chiefly in Wayne and Butler Cos., north of the city of Poplar Bluff.

The Mark Twain NF (2) contains 608,719 acres, is also split into four separate tracts, all of them along or near the southern border. Headquarters of the Supervisor is at Springfield. Table Rock Lake in the southwest lies mostly within one tract. To the east, in Christian, Taney, and Ozark Cos., is a second tract. Mostly in eastern Douglas Co. and western Howell Co. is the third, lying northwest from West Plains. The fourth and largest tract is still farther east, divided among Shannon, Carter, Oregon, and Ripley Cos.

There are over 200,000 acres of State Forests in Missouri. The majority of these are difficult to pinpoint. Many are in scattered small tracts and are designated simply as "tracts" without a special Forest name. Some of these contain only a few acres, and also there are some named as State Forests with very small acreage. For detailed information on all state-owned forests, one may contact the State Forester at the Department of Conservation (address at chapter end). In the following material under individual game species only the larger State Forests that exist in continuous blocks will be noted.

In addition to foregoing public lands, there are over 100,000 acres in Wildlife Areas owned and managed by the Department of Conservation. The more important ones will be noted under individual species. Missouri continues to add both State Forests and Wildlife Areas. Thus as this is read there may be several new ones. The Department publishes a brochure, "Conservation Areas—Public Lands Managed by the Missouri Department of Conservation." This is annually updated. It lists the various WAs and the larger State Forests and other state lands, giving size, location and principal use of each. It is advisable to acquire this publication to keep updated on new opportunities. Individual maps are available from the Department for most of the WAs and Forests.

Hunters find virtually limitless accommodations well distributed throughout the state, for Missouri is highly geared to tourists. Motels, hotels, and cottage camps are available along all main highways and around the major lakes. For camping hunters, there is a booklet, "Camping in Missouri," which may be obtained from the Division of Commerce and Industrial Development,

803 Jefferson Building, Jefferson City, Missouri 65101. A map of State Recreation Areas can be had from the Conservation Department.

Missouri weather is ordinarily lovely in early and mid-fall. September is generally hot, October a season for light wool shirts and jackets. Later on there may be snow and much colder weather during November and December when deer season is open. There are also spring seasons, as for turkeys, and these may be chilly but not severe. Missouri hunts small game in late spring and during summer, and of course clothing for these periods should be regular warm-weather attire.

Arms and ammunition for Missouri hunting require no very specialized consideration. Popular deer rifles for the timbered sections run all the way from the .30/30 to the .30/06, .270, and .243. Many squirrel hunters are avid .22 rifle fans. Shotgunners require No. 8 or No. 7½ shot for quail and small game, short-magnum No. 6 or No. 4 for turkeys, the same for ducks, and No. 2 or else short-magnum 4s for geese.

QUAIL

Most seasons more bobwhite quail are bagged by hunters in Missouri than any other game bird or animal. Over three recent seasons the kill has fluctuated from slightly less than three million to almost 3.8 million. Hunter numbers run, depending on the season, from about 130,000 to 170,000. Although it is believed that quail habitat destruction by increase of cropland and cutting of brush is slowly downgrading the future of the bobwhite, hunting is still very good today.

Quail are distributed throughout the state. The best hunting is generally found in the sections of agricultural land not too intensively farmed. In the north, the Western Ozark border country, and the counties near the Arkansas line, hunting is usually good. The bag per day is not as high as a rule in the heavily farmed Mississippi Lowlands or in the timbered Ozarks. Largest percentages of the total kill ordinarily come from the Ozark Plateau, the Northeast Riverbreaks, the Western Prairie and the West Ozark Border Regions. However, the kills are not necessarily in that order and may fluctuate widely from season to season. These four Regions are also the scenes of the heaviest hunting pressure. Nonetheless, over a period of several seasons statistics on the number of coveys flushed per hour and the number of birds bagged per hunter per day tend to show that good quail hunting can be had in any of the eight Regions (see front of chapter).

Although most quail hunting of quality is found on privately owned lands, there is a substantial amount available on the WAs. Some of the tracts offering quail hunting are listed alphabetically below, and located.

The Atlanta WA (3) contains 1845 acres in Macon Co. near Atlanta. Near Kingston in Caldwell Co. is the Bonanza WA (4) with 1024 acres. The Brickyard Hill WA (5) is near Watson, Atchison Co., contains 1476 acres. The Danville WA (6) is near town of same name, Montgomery Co., has 1055 acres. Deer Ridge WA (7) has 4259 acres near Monticello, Lewis Co.

Deer Run State Forest has some quail in edge cover; it contains over 120,000 acres, is the largest of the State Forests. Nearby towns are Eminence and Ellington; the Forest is in Reynolds, Shannon, Carter, and Dent Cos. The Gainesville WA (9) is near town of same name in Ozark Co., covers 1077 acres. There are also Haysler A. Poague WA (10), 879 acres near Clinton, Henry Co., and Henry Sever WA (11), 748 acres near Newark, Knox Co.

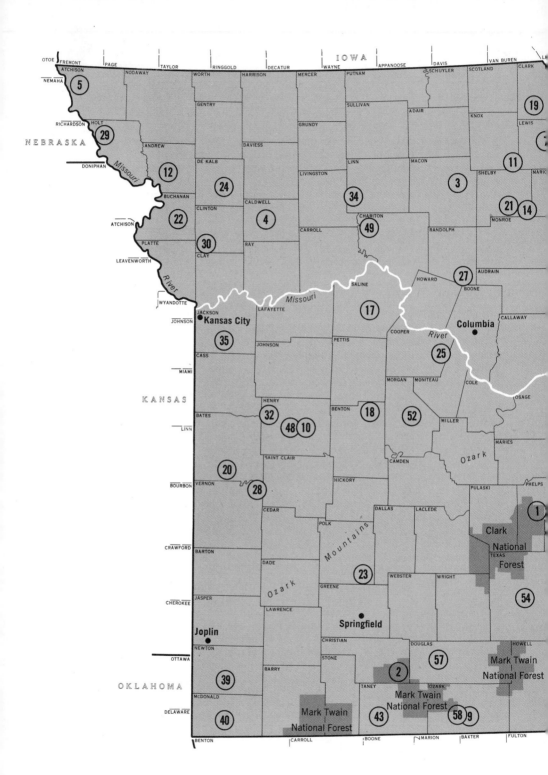

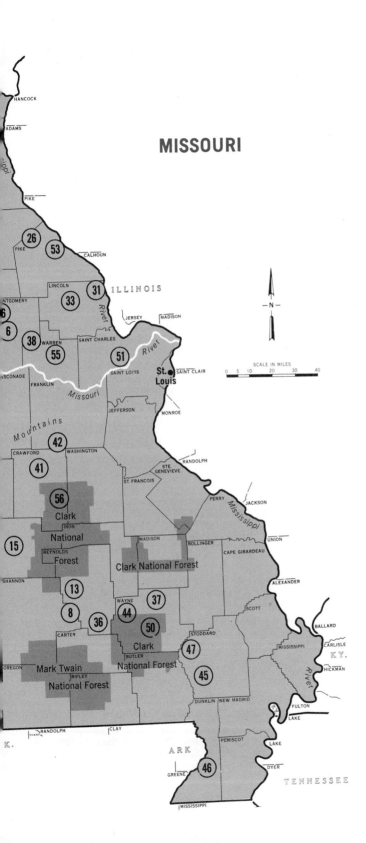

MISSOURI

ILLINOIS

−N−

SCALE IN MILES
0 5 10   20   30   40

St.
Louis

KEY TO HUNTING AREAS

1. Clark NF
2. Mark Twain NF
3. Atlanta WA
4. Bonanza WA
5. Brickyard Hill WA
6. Danville WA
7. Deer Ridge WA
8. Deer Run SF
9. Gainesville WA
10. Haysler A. Poague WA
11. Henry Sever WA
12. Honey Creek WA
13. Hungry Mother WA
14. Hunnewell WA
15. Indian Trail SF
16. Marshall I. Diggs WA
17. Marshall Junction WA
18. Mora Prairie WA
19. Neeper WA
20. Peabody WA
21. Pin Oak WA

22. Pigeon Hill WA
23. Pleasant Hope WA
24. Pony Express WA
25. Prairie Home WA
26. Ranacker WA
27. Rudolf Bennitt WA
28. Schell-Osage WA
29. Thurnau WA
30. Trimble WA
31. Upper Mississippi WA
32. Urich WA
33. William R. Logan WA
34. Fountain Grove WA
35. James A. Reed
    Memorial WA
36. Bozarth SF
37. Coldwater SF
38. Daniel Boone MF
39. Fort Crowder WA
40. Huckleberry Ridge SF
41. Huzzah SF

42. Meramec SF
43. Mincy WA
44. Sam A. Baker SF
45. Bradyville WA
46. Drag-Over WA
47. Duck Creek WA
48. Montrose WA
49. Swan Lake WA
50. Wappapello Reservoir
51. August A. Busch
    Memorial WA
52. Big Buffalo Creek WA
53. DuPont Reservation
54. Pairlee Freeman
    Narnes WA
55. Reifsnider SF
56. Richter WA
57. Rippee WA
58. Caney Mountain WA

Honey Creek WA (12) has 1448 acres near Savannah, Andrew Co. Hungry Mother WA (13) is in Reynolds Co. near Bunker, with 274 acres. Hunnewell WA (14) contains 1200 acres near Hunnewell, Shelby Co. Indian Trail State Forest (15) has 13,255 acres, is near Salem, Dent Co. The Marshall I. Diggs WA (16) contains 850 acres in two counties, Montgomery and Audrain, can be located out of Wellsville. Marshall Junction WA (17) is near like named town in Saline Co. Mora Prairie WA (18), Benton Co., has 320 acres near Cole Camp.

Neeper WA (19), 227 acres, is near Neeper, Clark Co. Peabody WA (20), 300 acres, is near Rich Hill, Bates Co. Pin Oak WA (21) is very small, only 65 acres, is near Shelbina in Shelby Co. Pigeon Hill WA (22), Buchanan Co. near Agency contains 221 acres. Pleasant Hope WA (23) has 1105 acres near town of same name, Polk Co. Pony Express WA (24), 1597 acres, is near Maysville, DeKalb Co. Prairie Home WA (25) near town of same name in Cooper Co. has 496 acres. Ranacker WA (26) is in Pike Co. near Frankford, with 717 acres. Rudolf Bennitt WA (27) contains 3324 acres in three counties, Howard, Boone, and Randolph, and is easily located out of Higbee.

Schell-Osage WA (28) is a large one, of 8633 acres, with Schell City a good location point; it spreads over portions of Vernon and St. Clair Cos. Thurnau WA (29), 366 acres, is near Craig, Holt Co. Trimble WA (30), 1197 acres is in two counties, Clinton and Clay, is located out of Trimble. The large Upper Mississippi WA (31) spreads over 12,093 acres with portions in St. Charles, Lincoln, Pike, Ralls, Marion, Lewis Cos.; a good location point is Elsberry. Urich WA (32) is near like named town, Henry Co., has 480 acres. Wm. R. Logan WA (33) has 1787 acres near Silex, Lincoln Co.

MOURNING DOVES

Doves range throughout the state but are most abundant during hunting season in the farm areas and the flatter country such as the Western Prairie and the Miss. Lowlands. The number of hunters participating has been steadily increasing for the past two decades, from less than 8000 to a current average of nearly 60,000. Over the same years dove success has remained remarkably consistent, but of course the total bag has increased. Several seasons it has passed one million. One year it was above 1.5 million, but more recently dipped below one million.

Regional surveys show that the highest kill and the highest success per hour of hunting is in the Mississippi Lowlands. The Northeast Riverbreaks get the most hunting pressure, show fair success, and a high kill. The Western Prairie is on a par with the above, in general. All of the eight Regions evidence success from fair to good. If weather holds, the end of the season is likely to be excellent, with incoming birds from the north plus local birds ready to migrate. Stubble fields where wheat straw has been baled, millet and soybean and weed fields all furnish good locations.

Some of the public lands with quail offer good opportunities for dove hunters. Atlanta WA, Bonanza WA, Brickyard Hill WA, Gainesville WA, Indian Trail SF, Marshall I. Diggs WA, Marshall Junction WA, Mora Prairie WA, Neeper WA, Peabody WA, Pigeon Hill WA, Pony Express WA, Prairie Home WA, Rudolf Bennitt WA, Schell-Osage WA, Thurnau WA—all these noted under "Quail" also furnish dove shooting. In addition, there is some dove shooting to be found on the Fountain Grove WA (34), primarily a waterfowl area, with 5166 acres in Linn and Livingston Cos., with Meadville a location point. The James A. Reed Memorial WA (35) near Lee's Summit, Jackson Co., with 2150 acres also has doves.

PHEASANT

The ringneck pheasant has never been an important game bird in Missouri. The kill, chiefly incidental by quail hunters and with only a few specialist pheasant hunters, averages perhaps 10,000 birds. The species simply does not do well in the state, either in survival or reproduction, except in the northwest corner. For some years biologists have been attempting to find a pheasant species better tailored to the environment. The Reeves, Iranian blackneck, and Korean varieties have been tried. The Korean currently appears to have the best chance. It has done fairly well to date in the "bootheel" country, but it is still too early to tell if it will be a continued success. Other plants have also been made.

The northwest, for reasons not fully understood, has seen a recent rise in ringneck population. So has southwestern Iowa. Missouri appears to be reaping some of the benefit from that state. Counties that presently have ringnecks in portions of their terrain are as follows: Atchison, Holt, Andrew, Worth, Gentry, DeKalb, Livingston, Nodaday, Harrison, Daviess, Mercer, Grundy, Adair, Putnam, Schuyler, Sullivan, St. Charles.

RUFFED GROUSE, PRAIRIE CHICKEN

Historically ruffed grouse were present in portions of Missouri, but none have been present in recent times. Reintroduction efforts were begun a decade or more ago. Wild-trapped birds from Ohio, Indiana, and Iowa were released on several sites. Recent investigations appear to prove that reintroduction has been successful in central Missouri. There is known reproduction and extension of range. There is still no hunting as this is written and it is presumed that success may be extremely limited because of lack of optimum habitat.

The prairie chicken was once abundant in Missouri. Today only a few hundred square miles of possible habitat remain, mostly in the southwest. The small population of birds is carefully inventoried and managed in an attempt to preserve it. There is no hunting.

WOODCOCK, SNIPE, RAILS

Woodcock are present in scattered numbers over most wooded areas and stream bottoms of Missouri during their migration. But they are almost ignored by hunters. A few are shot as incidentals by quail hunters. Woodcock are not actually abundant anyway. The main migration route places Missouri on its western fringe.

Snipe are present in modest numbers on waterfowling grounds and in wet pastures, along the Mississippi River especially. But as with woodcock, there is virtually no purposeful hunting for them.

There are two quite good rail hunting spots. One is the Fountain Grove WA. The other is the Schell-Osage WA. Both of these are primarily waterfowling grounds, and both are noted under "Quail." Very few hunters concentrate on these birds. There is an open season on sora, Virginia, and yellow rails.

WILD TURKEYS

During early settlement of Missouri wild turkeys were abundant. They were in fact so easy to collect for food that no one considered raising domestic turkeys. By the beginning of the 1900s, however, it was estimated that no more than 3000 birds remained. These were in remote portions of the Ozarks. Cutting of timber, the growth of farming, and heavy hunting all contributed to the swift decline. Many thousands of game-farm turkeys were released, but the project was not successful. By 1937 the season was closed.

After World War II research had shown that wild-trapped birds were the only answer to reestablishment. The Game Department purchased a large tract where some birds remained, and intensive management was begun. Soon transplants were accomplished. By 1960 a short spring hunt was possible in fourteen Ozark counties, for residents only. There have been seasons ever since, with the range ever growing, the annual bag increasing, and nonresidents allowed to hunt in 1967.

As this is written, the past season has seen 38 counties open, and a kill, gobblers only, of 1270 birds. It is believed that the wild turkey will in due time be restored to possibly as much as two-thirds of the state. For several seasons, the three top counties by number of birds bagged have been Iron, Madison, and Ste. Genevieve, each with over 100 birds taken. The order of success has differed among the three, however. These also are heavily hunted counties. Total number of turkey hunters in the state has been averaging from 7000 to 8000-plus. Average success runs from 12 to 17 percent. Other counties with high total kills in addition to the three have been: Crawford, Dent, Douglas, Phelps, St. Francois, Texas, Washington, Wayne. Slightly lower but still fair: Adair, Howell, Jefferson, Montgomery, Ozark, Pulaski, Reynolds, Shannon, Warren.

The National Forests in open counties offer good public opportunity. Bozarth State Forest (36), 9000 acres near Garwood, Reynolds Co. is also a good bet. So are the 7000-acre Coldwater SF (37) near Coldwater, Wayne Co., and the Daniel Boone Memorial Forest (38), 2940 acres in Warren Co. near Jonesburg. The Danville WA, Deer Run SF, Gainesville WA, Indian Trail SF, all noted under "Quail," also furnish turkey hunting.

Other public tracts not so far mentioned are as follows: Fort Crowder WA (39) has 1920 acres near Neosho, Newton Co. Huckleberry Ridge SF (40) contains 1866 acres located near Pineville in McDonald Co. The 6078-acre Huzzah SF (41) is in Crawford Co. near Leasburg. The Meramec SF (42), 3437 acres, is near Sullivan, Washington Co. In Taney Co. near

Kirbyville is the 3580-acre Mincy WA (43). Lying in Bollinger, Wayne and Iron Cos. is the 16,140 acre Sam A. Baker SF (44), with Piedmont a good locating point.

WATERFOWL

Waterfowl hunting in Missouri is unique. In a state where the heavily forested Ozarks are such a prominent part of the terrain, there is still some of the finest lowland hunting in the U.S., with both ducks and geese funneling by thousands down the Mississippi and along the Missouri. Mallards are perhaps the most important duck species, but pintails and teal and wood ducks are also popular. Total duck kill averages around 150,000. Most dramatic of Missouri's waterfowling is the kill of as many as 40,000 geese in peak years. Canadas swarm to the Swan Lake National Wildlife Refuge in the northcentral part of the state, and as many as a quarter-million blues and snows have been tallied at Squaw Creek NWR in the northwest.

Special hunting zones occur around both refuges. A quota system has been in effect during recent seasons on Canadas at Swan Lake. A season is set but is automatically closed if the kill quota (20,000 or 25,000 birds on the average) is reached before closing date. At the several public waterfowling areas in the state there are varied rules. In some instances drawings are held for blinds and there are fees. Others are on a first-come basis. Because regulations may change from season to season it is best for hunters to check with the Department for complete briefing on all waterfowl areas. In some places hunters are allowed to build blinds, but under strict specifications.

Here are the chief waterfowl areas open to the public under varying regulations. Bradyville WA (45), 268 acres, is near town of like name, in Stoddard Co. Drag-Over WA (46), Dunklin Co. near Kennett, has 956 acres. The Duck Creek WA (47) is one of the more important waterfowling locations. There are 5968 acres here, with over 1700 acres of water. The towns of Westover and Puxico are locating points; the area overlaps into several counties: Crawford, Bollinger, Stoddard, Wayne.

The Foundation Grove WA is also an important waterfowling tract. It has already been noted under "Doves." Water acreage here is over 2000, with total for the tract of above 5000. The Montrose WA (48) is also an important waterfowling ground. It contains 3600 acres near Clinton in Henry Co. The large Schell-Osage WA noted under "Quail" is also predominantly a waterfowl location. Swan Lake, already mentioned, has a WA (49) of 2500 acres where hunting is for geese only. The WA location is near Sumner, Chariton Co.

Trimble WA, noted under "Quail," is chiefly a waterfowl area. There are 170 acres of water here, out of about 1200 total. One of the state's most important waterfowl locations is the long, 12,000-acre Upper Mississippi WA. It has also been noted under "Quail." This is actually federal land but is state managed. The varied regulations here should be carefully checked. Wappapello Reservoir (50) is also a most important waterfowl location. Total acreage here is 44,500, with 5700 of it water. A good locating point is Greenville in Wayne Co.

Hunters not familiar with procedures in Missouri should be aware that some drawings, as for sites on the Upper Mississippi WA, are held as early as July.

Duck hunters who enjoy jump-shooting are well advised not to overlook the excellent opportunities available by floating Missouri streams. The Big Piney, the Current, Jacks Fork, Gasconade, Meramec, Osage, Bryant, Niangua,

Black, St. Francis, and Elk rivers are all good examples of streams where much duck shooting is often passed up by persons who do not realize the existent opportunities.

SQUIRRELS

Squirrel hunting is exceedingly popular in Missouri and the animals are superbly abundant. There are both fox and gray squirrels. Fox squirrels ordinarily are more numerous and more easily hunted than grays. They are found in woodlots, open woods, fencerows and timberland that is pastured, are most abundant north of the Missouri River and in the Western Prairie region. Gray squirrels are found in the dense timber of the Ozarks, and in wooded parts of the Mississippi Lowlands. Probably close to 200,000 Missouri hunters annually go out after squirrels. The total bag fluctuates with seasonal food supply, but has run for many years well over a million when forage is adequate, and during recent peak years past 2.5 million. This state has an exceptionally long squirrel season. For some years traditional opening has been at the end of May, and the season has remained open all summer and through until the end of December.

All 114 counties of the state offer squirrel hunting. The oak and hickory forests are the standard best locations for both species. The heaviest kills of squirrels of both species for recent seasons have been in the Mississippi Lowlands and the Ozark Plateau. The Northeast Riverbreaks and the Western Prairie Regions have been next. However, there is good hunting in all of the eight regions.

Public lands with good squirrel hunting are numerous. The National Forests are among the best. Listed alphabetically below are other tracts that furnish opportunity.

The August A. Busch Memorial WA (51), 7000 acres near Weldon Springs, St. Charles Co., has fox squirrels. The 1434-acre Big Buffalo Creek WA (52), in Morgan and Benton Cos., and with Versailles a locating point, offers gray squirrels. So does the Bozarth SF ("Turkeys"). Brickyard Hill WA ("Quail") has fox squirrels. Coldwater SF and Daniel Boone Forest ("Turkeys") have gray squirrels. There are some fox squirrels also on the last named. The Danville WA has both species, and the Deer Ridge WA has fox squirrels; both are under "Quail."

Deer Run SF ("Quail") has good hunting for gray squirrels. The DuPont Reservation (53), a public tract of 1322 acres near the town of Louisiana, Pike Co., offers fox squirrels. Gray squirrels are on Fort Crowder WA ("Turkeys") and on Gainesville WA ("Quail"). Henry Sever WA, Honey Creek WA, Hungry Mother WA, Hunnewell WA all have fox squirrels and are listed under "Quail." Gray squirrels are found in Huckleberry Ridge SF, Huzzah SF ("Turkeys") and on Indian Trail SF ("Quail").

James Reed WA ("Doves"), Marshall Diggs and Marshall Junction WAs ("Quail") offer fox squirrel hunting. The Meramec SF and Mincy WA ("Turkeys") have grays. The Neeper WA under "Quail" has fox squirrels. The 120-acre Pairlee Freeman Narnes WA (54) near Houston in Texas Co. has gray squirrels. Pigeon Hill WA, Pleasant Hope WA, Prairie Home WA, Ranacker WA, all noted under "Quail," are fox squirrel locations. Both species are found on the 1352-acre Reifsnider SF (55), Warren Co. near Warrenton. The small (80-acre) Richter WA (56), Crawford Co. near Huzzah, and the still smaller Rippee WA (57) near Ava, Douglas Co., are both locations for gray squirrels. Rudolf Bennitt WA, Schell-Osage WA, Thurnau WA, Upper Mississippi WA, Wm. Logan WA, all noted under

"Quail," have fox squirrel hunting. There are grays on Sam A. Baker SF ("Turkeys") and around Wappapello Reservoir ("Waterfowl").

RABBITS

For many years Missouri has touted itself, quite justly, as the hottest cottontail state in the U.S. The annual kill runs to several million. Cottontails are found everywhere, but the Ozarks and the Mississippi Lowlands are the least productive regions. In general the best hunting is north of the Missouri River. The Western Prairie is also good. Hunting with beagles is immensely popular. At least half of Missouri's hunters hunt cottontails each year.

A vast amount of the best cottontail hunting is on private farmlands where intensive cropping is not practiced and where there are woodlots, brush patches, and fencerow cover. However, virtually all of the public lands mentioned under other species have fair to excellent cottontail hunting. The National Forests and State Forests, except in edge cover, are the poorest of the lot. By and large, however, any hunter can find sport with cottontails in any county of the state.

In a few southern counties, along swamp stream bottoms, there are scattered, modest populations of swamp rabbits. They are not abundant.

DEER

When the first white man came into what is now Missouri they found the whitetail deer abundant. Plowing of the prairies, cutting and burning of forests, market and indiscriminate hunting did not take long to bring the deer close to extinction. By 1925 the whitetail was all but gone. Hunting was closed. Trial seasons were held in the 1930s but then hunting was again prohibited.

Transplants to suitable areas began to have some positive effect within the next few years, and apparently the whitetail also began to fit itself to the new environment. In 1944 there was a two-day buck season. Some 7500 hunters turned out, but bagged less than 600 deer. Reestablishment was nonetheless underway. Twenty years later some 120,000 hunters took almost 20,000 deer in a season. Recently the entire state has been open to hunting. Some counties have regulations for bucks with forked antler only, others do not.

Some of the better Ozark deer range is now thought to have as many as 20 deer per square mile. Over recent seasons the annual bag has run from 22,000 to about 28,000 deer, and there have been an estimated 175,000 hunters participating. Bucks make up approximately two-thirds of the kill in most seasons. There are, incidentally, several special hunts held each year, including a primitive weapons hunt. Deer hunters should contact the Department for information about the various specials and their locations.

Because 90 percent of the state is in private ownership, obviously most deer hunting is on private lands. On the overall, the Ozark counties generally furnish the best hunting. For several seasons recently top kill counties by numbers of animals taken have been Texas, Ozark, Benton, in varying order. Other high-kill counties: Howell, Ste. Genevieve, Pulaski, Wayne, Taney, Carter. The bulk of the state kill comes from south of the Missouri River, but not including the Mississippi Lowlands. In some counties no deer at all are taken.

Because of the variance in regulation by county from season to season success also fluctuates, and so does the kill per square mile. However, in one rather recent season the following counties showed kills of over one deer per square mile: Benton, Camden, Carter, Hickory, McDonald, Ozark' (over two per square mile), Pulaski, Ste. Genevieve, Taney, Texas, Wayne.

The two National Forests, situated as they are in the south, are excellent areas for deer hunters. Other public opportunities are available on the following tracts already noted under foregoing species: August Busch WA; Big Buffalo Creek WA; Bozarth SF; Coldwater SF; Daniel Boone Forest; Danville WA; Deer Ridge WA; Deer Run SF; Duck Creek WA; DuPont Reservation; Fort Crowder WA; Gainesville WA; Huckleberry Ridge SF; Huzzah SF; Indian Trail SF; Meramec SF; Mincy WA; Reifsnider SF; Rudolf Bennitt WA; Sam A. Baker SF; Trimble WA; Wappapello Reservoir; Wm. R. Logan WA. There is a special hunt for deer on Caney Mountain WA (58), a 5489-acre tract near Gainesville in Ozark Co.

BLACK BEAR

Although bears are not common nowadays in Missouri, they are not truly rare. They are fully protected, and appear to be increasing. There are differences of opinion as to whether the black bear was extinct in Missouri and has come back due to infiltration of bears from Arkansas, or whether some were left and have increased. The game department has no policy toward increasing the bear population to huntable numbers, but does keep the animals on the game list, with closed season.

OTHER ANIMALS

There are a surprising number of coyotes found in the northern and western prairie regions and a few in the Ozarks. They have been uselessly bountied by many counties for years, yet are even more plentiful than formerly. A recent season showed bounties paid on over 12,000. There is a modest amount of coyote coursing with greyhounds in western Missouri. Calling might be more successful and popular than it is.

There are both red and gray foxes, and bobcats. These, too, have been bountied, but recently a season has been established on both foxes and bobcats. The bobcat was placed on the game list because it is becoming rare, and foxes because of the amount of hound sport they furnish to enthusiasts.

Woodchucks are quite plentiful everywhere in the state except in the Mississippi Lowlands. Hunting them is a popular sport. Raccoons and opossums are also popular with hound enthusiasts, and are plentiful in the river bottoms and woodlands throughout the state. There is fair to good hunting for all of the animals so far listed on most of the public lands.

Missouri is a favorite wintering ground for crows. Because crow shooting has gained swiftly in popularity, department personnel have begun locating winter roosts and listing them. Some of these are along the Mississippi, the Missouri and other stream bottoms, and some are quite large. One recent season over 120 such roosts had been located and listed, with the list available to interested sportsmen.

REGULATIONS

Game laws pertaining to seasons, bag and possession limits, areas to be hunted, special hunts, license fees all may have numerous changes from year to year. For current regulations, and for other specific queries, write to: Missouri Department of Conservation, P.O. Box 180, Jefferson City, Missouri 65101.

ARKANSAS

In atmosphere and appeal Arkansas is a mixture of the South, the Midwest, the romance of the big-river and bayou country, all with an overlay of mountain flavor. In the west its rough, rugged, and forested hills spill over into Oklahoma. To the north along the Missouri border there is more of the same for much of the expanse. But in the east, where Arkansas meets a bit of Tennessee and has the remainder of its eastern border with Mississippi, flat-country stands of pine and low country along the Mississippi River take over more and more until in the southeast there are the effects of the big river and its tributaries, with flooded pin-oak flats and brakes where waterfowl are abundant and deer hide in dense river-bend coverts.

The Ozark plateau dominates much of the western two-thirds of the state, behind a line drawn from the northeast to the southwest corner. The Ozark mountains are not very high. The highest point is Magazine Mountain at 2753 feet. But the Ozarks are steep, rocky, dense with timber. In fact, at least 60 percent of Arkansas is forested, with oak, hickory, pine, and with gum and cypress in some of the southern bottoms. There are over twenty million acres of forest.

Lumbering is important in Arkansas. But there are innumerable farms, too. Cotton and rice, grown mostly in the east and southeast, are among the chief crops. Chicken farms are also big business here, and oil production is high. Arkansas is growing swiftly in manufacturing, too, but so far, though population is advancing and concentrating in many once-small cities that have grown large, there is no feeling of crowding or overpopulation. At present there are a bit less than two million people, in an area covering 53,104 square miles.

Because of its position in relation to many other large centers of population and commerce, Arkansas has numerous excellent highways. Interstate 55 comes down along the west side of the Mississippi to opposite Memphis, then slants off southwest to Little Rock and thence to Texarkana in the southwest corner. From Little Rock Interstate 40 leads to Fort Smith and on westward. U.S. 67 cuts from northeast to southwest across the state and numerous other U.S. highways gather in from every direction. Side roads are good, but many are winding as they meander through the hills. Back-country side roads of dirt in either the Ozarks or the river lowlands can be sticky and difficult during bad weather. A 4-wheel-drive vehicle, though not mandatory, is handy for any hunter. Air transport for those coming in from long distances reaches all of the major points, but from these, including Fort Smith, the more remote hill-country villages require ground transport.

Although Arkansas is of fair size, driving distances from any given spot within its borders are not excessive for hunters. From Little Rock to

Fort Smith or to the Memphis area is a straight-line distance not much over 120 miles. North to south, 225 miles is roughly the span, and from northeast to southwest less than 300.

Roaming the hills or the river bottoms with a gun is a long tradition in Arkansas. Quite a few more than 10 percent of the population are hunters. License sales average around 260,000 annually, and only a modest number of visitors is among them. Average nonresident licenses: roughly 12,000. There is good reason for the popularity of hunting. The mixture of hills and bottomlands, with ample cover, offers abundance and variety of game. There are whitetail deer in every county. The eastern wild turkey is native. Fox squirrels and gray squirrels have since pioneer days been a favorite species; so have bobwhite quail. Both cottontails and swamp rabbits are plentiful, doves are a favorite target in the flat croplands, and some of the finest and most famous waterfowling in the U.S. is here. There are woodcock and snipe, and also abundant hound game such as foxes, raccoons, and opossums.

It is not difficult to find a place to hunt in Arkansas. The Game Commission at this time owns over 200,000 acres, split into twenty-five areas all but one or two of which are Public Hunting Areas. Individual maps of these can be obtained from the Commission (address at chapter end). There is also a brochure, "Fishing and Hunting in Arkansas," available from either the Commission or from the Arkansas Publicity and Parks Commission (State Capitol, Little Rock), that contains a map showing location of all these areas. Some other lands not owned outright are leased. The PHAs are well scattered over the state and all native game species are found among them.

Arkansas has no State Forests but it is most fortunate in having three excellent National Forests. These total within Arkansas borders over three million acres open to public hunting. Although these Forests will be mentioned under individual game species later, they are for general convenience described here.

The Ouachita NF (1) contains over one and a half million acres, but part of this is in Oklahoma. This Forest is directly west of Little Rock, and cover a vast area of the west-central part of the state. The city of Hot Springs is at the southeastern Forest border. From this city both State 7 and U.S. 270 offer easy access. At the southwest border of the Forest is the city of Mena, with U.S. 59 and 71 giving Forest access. Across the north is State 10, running west from Little Rock to Booneville and the junction with U.S. 71. Details and maps of this Forest can be had from the Forest Supervisor, Hot Springs.

The Ozark National Forest (2) lies north of the above and is in several blocks. One block of modest size is just to the northeast of Booneville, or can be reached southwest from Russelville, which is on U.S. 64 and State 7. Straight north is the main block. State 7, 23, and U.S. 71 are access roads. Fort Smith on the western state border is to the southwest. Numerous other cities are nearby. Then, to the west of the main block, above Fort Smith, and to the northwest near Springdale (U.S. 71) and to the northeast at the confluence of the Buffalo and White Rivers are other blocks. The largest one can be reached northeast from Marshall on U.S. 65, or southeast from Cotter and Mountain Home, which are both on U.S. 62. In entirety the Ozark National Forest encompasses 1,046,309 acres, and is a most important hunting ground, as is the Ouachita Forest described previously. The Ozark Forest Supervisor can be reached at Russelville.

Across the state, on the eastern border roughly midway down, and touching at one point the Mississippi River, is the small Saint Francis National Forest (3). Although it covers by National Forest standards a very nominal acreage—16,000—it is a quality stand for all of the forest species: deer, turkey, squirrel.

In addition to the PHAs and the National Forests, there is some hunting on refuges, which will be noted under the species involved. Private lands are also an excellent bet for hunters in this state. Except in the immediate vicinity of large cities, where crowding may be severe, all one need do in most cases is ask for permission to hunt such game as doves and quail. The Game Commission is exceedingly active in attempts to acquire more land either by purchase or lease, and in improving for game those lands at its command. There are restoration programs, particularly at this time one for black bears. All told, the game people are progressive, optimistic, forward-looking, and the future of hunting here for the native species traditional in the Ozarks and the Mississippi bottoms is bright.

Accommodations for hunters are numerous throughout the state. There are motels and lodges almost everywhere along the main routes. Also, because there have been so many large impoundments built on Arkansas' rivers, and the entire state has been geared more and more toward tourism both summer and winter for numerous years, camps and cottages of great variety are scattered throughout the state.

Nor do campers face any problems. State Parks, the Hot Springs National Park, the National Forests offer numerous sites. The Corps of Engineers campgrounds on at least ten reservoirs number in the dozens. From the Arkansas Publicity and Parks Commission, Capitol Bldg., Little Rock, a "Campers' Guide" may be obtained, and also a "Guide to the State Parks."

For the most part the hunting weather in Arkansas is mild. Early seasons —doves in September, for example—will be hot. But as fall progresses the hills are gently cool and enjoyable, with light wool shirts in order, and the river bottoms are still warm and somewhat humid. On into late fall, weather is likely to be crisp, and can be very humid also, which adds to its bite. But most of this period requires clothing of only modest weight. Canvas-faced pants for bird hunting in brush are handy, and rain gear should be in every duffel bag. Late seasons, after the New Year, can at times be severely cold and damp.

Nothing very special in arms and ammo are needed. Squirrels are traditionally game for a .22 here. Deer hunters can use any standard deer caliber, but should bear in mind that most, although not all, shots are offered in heavy cover at modest range. No. 7½ shot or something a bit lighter or heavier as one desires does well for the smaller game birds. Duck hunters should rely on nothing less than No. 4, preferably in short or standard magnums. And goose hunters can step up to No. 2. Turkey hunters often rely on No. 6, but the No. 4 short-magnum is a better choice.

QUAIL

Arkansas is an excellent bobwhite state. But as in many other states across the South, quail have fared badly here of late because of farming practices. A recent report from the Commission stated flatly that if Arkansas

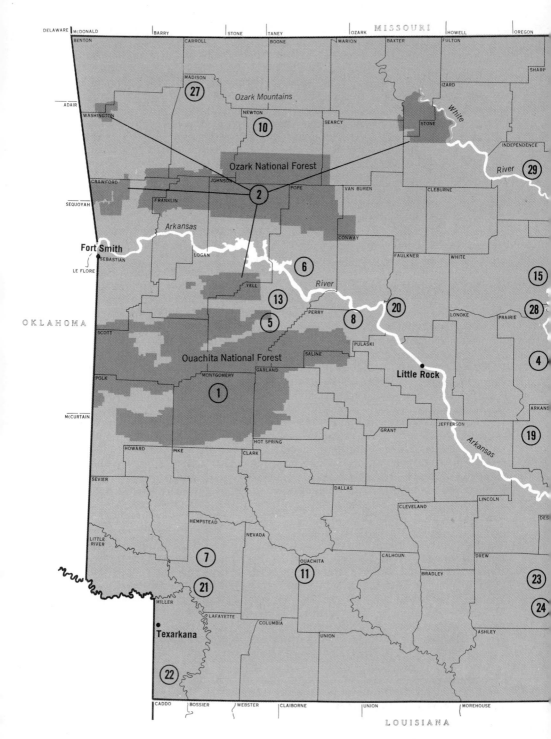

DELAWARE | McDONALD | BARRY | STONE | TANEY | OZARK | MISSOURI | HOWELL | OREGON

BENTON | CARROLL | BOONE | MARION | BAXTER | FULTON

MADISON | ㉗ | SHARP

ADAIR | Ozark Mountains | IZARD

WASHINGTON | NEWTON | SEARCY | STONE | White | INDEPENDENCE

⑩ | River | ㉙

Ozark National Forest

CRAWFORD | JOHNSON | ② | POPE | VAN BUREN | CLEBURNE

SEQUOYAH | FRANKLIN

Arkansas | CONWAY | FAULKNER | WHITE

Fort Smith | LOGAN | ⑥ | ⑮

SEBASTIAN | YELL | River

LE FLORE | ⑬ | PERRY | ⑧ | ⑳ | LONOKE | PRAIRIE | ㉘

OKLAHOMA | ⑤ | SCOTT | PULASKI | ④

Ouachita National Forest | SALINE

POLK | MONTGOMERY | GARLAND | Little Rock | ARKANSAS

MCCURTAIN | ① | GRANT | JEFFERSON | ⑲

HOWARD | PIKE | HOT SPRING | Arkansas

CLARK | DALLAS

SEVIER | LINCOLN

CLEVELAND | DES

HEMPSTEAD | NEVADA | CALHOUN | DREW

LITTLE RIVER | ⑦ | OUACHITA | BRADLEY | ㉓

⑪ | ㉔

㉑ | MILLER

LAFAYETTE | COLUMBIA | UNION | ASHLEY

Texarkana

㉒

CADDO | BOSSIER | WEBSTER | CLAIBORNE | UNION | MOREHOUSE

LOUISIANA

364

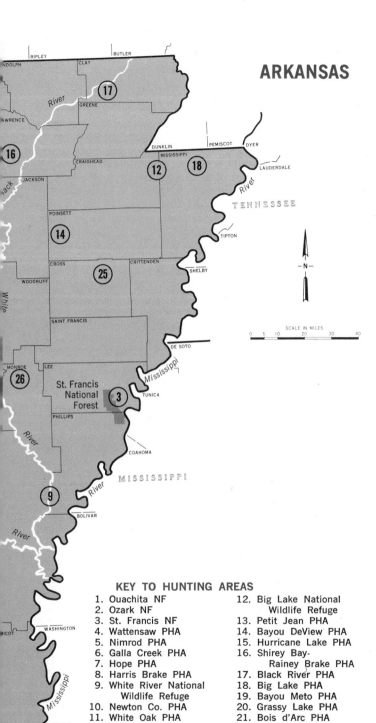

ARKANSAS

−N−

SCALE IN MILES
0 5 10   20   30   40

St. Francis
National
Forest

KEY TO HUNTING AREAS

1. Ouachita NF
2. Ozark NF
3. St. Francis NF
4. Wattensaw PHA
5. Nimrod PHA
6. Galla Creek PHA
7. Hope PHA
8. Harris Brake PHA
9. White River National
   Wildlife Refuge
10. Newton Co. PHA
11. White Oak PHA

12. Big Lake National
    Wildlife Refuge
13. Petit Jean PHA
14. Bayou DeView PHA
15. Hurricane Lake PHA
16. Shirey Bay-
    Rainey Brake PHA
17. Black River PHA
18. Big Lake PHA
19. Bayou Meto PHA
20. Grassy Lake PHA
21. Bois d'Arc PHA

22. Sulphur River
    Bottoms PHA
23. Seven Devils
    Swamp PHA
24. Cut-Off Creek PHA
25. St. Francis Sunken
    Lands PHA
26. Dagmar PHA
27. Madison Co. PHA
28. Des Arc PHA
29. Independence Co.
    PHA

continues to have good quail hunting landowners will have to devote more habitat to quail. This is not to say that quail hunting is poor at present. But it has slipped from what it once was. Southern and eastern Arkansas were once among the greatest of U.S. bobwhite hunting grounds. The vast area between the higher mountains of the west and northwest, and the intensively cultivated stretches of the delta, together form the top quail range. Within this region of hills and valleys, farms, edges, stream bottoms, and pine lands, the greatest share of good quail hunting is on private lands. But, as noted, permission on most is not too difficult to obtain. A line drawn along U.S. 70 on the southwestern border near DeQueen, north and east across the state to Little Rock, and thence on northeast along U.S. 67 will take in most of the better quail territory to the south and east.

Hunters should be aware that a great many hunting-fishing camps and lodges offer quail hunting with guides at daily fees. Many of these places advertise in outdoor oriented magazines. The state also does some stocking, but most of it is on private lands or club lands. As this is written the state has been raising at a hatchery about 25,000 quail annually, which are sold at cost (about 30 cents each) to groups for release. The reason for this is that all such quail are banded. Band returns are used in survival study and to evaluate the future trend of quail management in Arkansas.

There is a fair amount of quail hunting in the National Forests, described early in this chapter, although quail are not in general among the chief game species on these public lands. There are also several PHAs that offer quail among the three or four most important and abundant species. Other PHAs should be checked out for modest opportunities.

The Wattensaw PHA (4) is a large tract, 16,474 acres, in Prairie County. Quail hunting here is fair to excellent, depending on the season. This tract is within the better quail range. It lies east of Little Rock. U.S. 70 (I 40) runs east-west to the south of it. The small town of Hazen is a key location near the southwest corner of the tract. State 11 turns north along the PHA at Hazen.

The Nimrod PHA (5) covers 7000 acres in Yell County. This is in the west-central portion of the state, west of Little Rock. The PHA lies on the north border of the Ouachita NF. It surrounds the western end of Nimrod Reservoir, an impoundment on the Fourche le Fave River, a tributary of the Arkansas. State 28 and State 7 join near it at the village of Ola. To the northeast, across the Arkansas River which forms the Yell Co. border, is Pope Co. This county has the Galla Creek PHA (6), a quail hunting ground with 2634 acres. This is southeast of Russelville, on the north side of the Arkansas River. U.S. 64 (I 40) is north of the Area and the villages of Galla Rock and Atkins are near it.

Down in the southwest is Hempstead Co. Near its eastern border is the city of Hope. The Hope PHA (7) lies to the northwest. It contains 2115 acres, and bobwhites are one of the most important species. U.S. 67 (I 30) is the key route just to the south.

Another good quail spot is Harris Brake PHA (8), 2844 acres in Perry Co. This one is back up near Little Rock, a bit northwest of that city. It is west of the Arkansas River and State 10 skirts it on the west border, near the village of Perryville. This PHA is near the edge of the Ouachita NF, at its northeasternmost corner.

The five PHAs so far noted, plus the National Forest lands, are the best of the public quail lands. There is, however, one other public tract of interest to quail hunters who hunt with dogs. This is the Camp Robinson Quail Area. There is no hunting allowed here. It is managed strictly as a place for hunters to train dogs. There are over 4000 acres in the tract. It is located twenty miles northwest of Little Rock on the east side of Lake Conway. Many food plots are planted for quail, and there is generally a high quail population. The Area also has rabbits, red foxes, and raccoons. In addition to quail dog training and field trials, the Area serves for fox hunts, beagle trials, 'coon dog trials.

MOURNING DOVES

The agricultural areas of Arkansas offer excellent dove shooting. The south and southwest and a broad swath along the Mississippi River furnish the best of the shooting. The Arkansas River valley has many birds, with sandbars and good watering places. Almost all shooting is on private lands, for the large dove flights are over croplands where feed is good. Asking permission gains fairly ready access to dove shooting, after crops are harvested.

There is fair dove shooting on the PHAs and the Forest fringes. But none of these lands is especially noted for doves, except for the Hope PHA described under "Quail." Other PHAs that offer quail shooting have scattered dove shooting, because of fairly similar types of cover where both feed. However, dove flights are erratic and the flocks extremely mobile. Thus, since Arkansas has at this time no cooperative programs for furnishing public dove shooting on specifically managed plots, it is impossible to pinpoint where shooting may be had. Hunters who seek concentrations of birds, especially in the east and south, and then ask landowner permission, will have the best shooting. Generally speaking, there are more birds during the first part of the season, before many drift on south.

WILD TURKEYS

The eastern wild turkey, native to Arkansas, originally had virtually perfect habitat over much of the state. Indiscriminate killing and other influences had brought it to such low population by 1950 that it was thought to be headed for possible extinction. In the early 1950s a determined restoration program was launched, with turkeys trapped and transplanted. The original large-scale trapping operations were in Ouachita Co. By 1960 hundreds had been moved to suitable areas, and such areas were not opened to hunting until it was known that a huntable surplus existed. Even then, spring hunting was the only hunting in Arkansas, at least by firearms, until 1966. In October of that year the first fall firearms season was held. There was a brief fall hunt and two spring hunts. A total of 1634 turkeys was taken. This was a tremendous year for the state and marks for all practical purposes the unqualified success and return of the wild turkey in numbers over a large portion of Arkansas.

As this is written the fall season is brief for gun hunters—less than a week—but archers get a month or more. Spring seasons in the past have been split in April for several days to a week each. Figures to date indicate a higher spring kill, possibly because of shorter fall seasons and because most native hunters are used to spring hunting techniques. A kill of 1200 turkeys per year at present is considered about average, and thus this state takes its place as one of the quality turkey hunting states in the U.S.

During one recent year, considering all seasons, the following counties had by a long margin the highest kill: Arkansas, near the eastern border in the southeast fourth of the state; Desha, immediately south of the above county and bordering the Mississippi River; Lee, also bordering the river and north of the above about midway up the border. Next were: Chicot Co., extreme southeast and also on the river; Phillips, on the river and bordering Arkansas Co. This indicates that the southeast, along and near the river is the top general region. Next is a group of counties west and south of Little Rock, based on and bordering on the Ouachita NF. These are Yell, Garland, and Grant.

The National Forests offer fine turkey hunting. They furnish, it is estimated, at least 10 percent of the entire turkey kill. Considering the fact that probably the majority of hunters have favorite privately owned hunting grounds, this is a high harvest for Forest lands. The small Saint Francis Forest (see front material in chapter) is considered an excellent turkey hunting location. It is near the Mississippi River. Both the Ouachita and the Ozark Forests are considered "good" for turkeys, with the Ouachita placing the wild turkey as its top species and the Ozark placing it third, behind deer and squirrels.

A large area with controlled and limited hunting that offers good chances for turkeys is the White River National Wildlife Refuge (9). This 116,300-acre Refuge, primarily a duck refuge, lies along both sides of the White River for some distance prior to its confluence with the Mississippi. State Route 1 and various secondaries lead to it. DeWitt, a town famed for its duck hunting, is on this route west of the refuge. Hunters interested in regulations and other information pertaining to this refuge should write to its supervisor at Saint Charles, Arkansas 72140.

The foregoing lands all told offer several million acres of prime territory readily available to turkey hunters, and it is well known that large blocks of forests offer the best opportunities in turkey hunting anywhere. Several of the PHAs have at least fair turkey hunting, and at least two are quite well noted for this bird.

One of these is the Newton Co. PHA (10), a 9800-acre tract located in the county of the same name. This is up in the general northwest sector. The main block of the Ozark NF blankets much of the general region. The town of Jasper, on State 7, and the junction to the south of this road with State 16 are keys to locating the Area. The other noteworthy PHA is White Oak (11), 7879 acres lying on the border between Ouachita and Nevada Cos. These counties are in the southwest quarter of the state. The Area is northwest of the city of Camden. White Oak Lake is here. State 24 runs across the Area, from Camden to Prescott, which is on U.S. 67.

WOODCOCK, SNIPE, RAILS, EXOTICS

It is probably unfortunate that virtually no interest in hunting woodcock, snipe, and rails is apparent in Arkansas. There are fair supplies of all three. However, it is doubtful if more than a paltry scattering in the aggregate is killed annually by hunters, and most of these are as incidentals. The fact is that very little is actually known, officially, about the high spots for these birds within the state, although Arkansas, particularly in the east and all across the south, helps to funnel all three down the Mississippi River Valley to their wintering grounds along the Louisiana bottomlands and coast.

Hunters interested in woodcock should have a close look at southwestern Arkansas, and at all of the PHAs that are listed as lowland areas for waterfowl later in this chapter. Moist areas, not flooded, on the fringes of the wooded duck areas, are perfect woodcock cover.

All of the waterfowl areas which offer mud flats and pond edges have from fair to good snipe shooting. Arkansas hunters evidence no interest whatever in snipe, but along the Mississippi and in the lowland parts of the state there are good flights. None of the PHAs is especially noteworthy, by official indication, for either woodcock or snipe.

Without any question there is at least fair rail hunting awaiting those hunters who will research the rice-growing areas of the state in the south and east, and also the fish farms, of which this portion of Arkansas has a number. Local hunters do not hunt these birds. There a few, unhunted, on the waterfowl areas, which see. Stocking programs for exotics in Arkansas are at present on a limited basis. Some black francolins and Iranian pheasants have been released. At this writing there is no quotable opinion as to the success, or lack of it, of these releases.

WATERFOWL

For many years Arkansas has been nationally famous for its duck hunting. Much of this fame has accrued from the hunting in timber in the flooded pin-oak flats of the river bottoms, where mallards by thousands come sideslipping down through tall trees to present shots unmatched anywhere else. At one time Arkansas also had excellent goose shooting. It still has some, but at the present time the goose picture is rather unsettled. All states have discovered that they can hold birds on large refuges and even build pseudo-native flocks. With so many geese currently wintering farther north, Arkansas goose hunting is nowadays only fair. Duck hunting, however, remains excellent.

Years ago most eastern Arkansas was swampy country. Drainage has changed that, but there is still much lowland flood country, some of it purposely flooded for incoming mallards, the most abundant duck species. Others are pintails, wood ducks, gadwalls, baldpates. There are numerous fee-hunt camps and lodges along the Mississippi and in other areas of eastern and southeastern Arkansas. Stuttgart and DeWitt in the south-central region are famed names in waterfowling, worldwide.

The Commission, recognizing that duck hunting is one of the prime attractions, has emphasized wetlands in its purchase program and in addition certain managed lands are purposely flooded each year to attract waterfowl. At least 40,000 acres of the Commission's owned 200,000 are in flooded lands.

There is a great deal of jump-shooting available along all of the rivers, and on sandbars of the larger rivers, also around the myriad bayous and chutes of the Mississippi backwater country. Adding to this and also to the acreage involved in fee hunts out of various camps and clubs that advertise are the fee spots in territory surrounding the refuges. The White River Refuge (see "Turkeys") attracts large numbers of waterfowl to its vicinity. There are also the following refuges, locations of which should be known to waterfowl hunters.

Big Lake Refuge (12) covers some 9900 acres near Manila, Arkansas, which is on Route 18 in the northeast. Smaller Holla Bend, 4000 acres, is southeast of Russelville and near the Galla Creek PHA (see "Quail"). Wapanocca is 3800 acres, near Turrell. This is near the Mississippi River north of West Memphis and a bit to the east of I 55. Again, waterfowl hunting is not allowed on these refuges, including White River, but they attract many birds to their vicinities.

At the present time none of the PHAs is noted for geese, although spotty goose hunting turns up here and there. But several are noteworthy for ducks, and chiefly managed for them. The Harris Brake PHA mentioned under "Quail" is in fact primarily a duck Area. So are Nimrod and Galla Creek, also under "Quail."

Following are a number of others so far not described. In west-central Arkansas, Petit Jean PHA (13), west and slightly north of Little Rock, on the Petit Jean River, was the Commission's first purchase some years ago. It has been added to until there are now over 9000 acres. Near the Holla Bend National Waterfowl Refuge and Lake Nimrod, it can be reached from the south from Route 10, and via Route 154 from the north. State 7 between Ola and Russelville crosses one end.

In the general northeast quadrant is Bayou DeView PHA (14), in one of the better duck areas, with rice and other farm crops and storage reservoirs in the area. There are 3893 acres, west of Harrisburg on State 14. Southwest some distance is Hurricane Lake PHA (15), one of the largest and best in the state, with 15,497 acres in lakes and timber. It lies along the west bank of the White River, a bit southwest of Augusta on U.S. 64. Low areas on this and the above are flooded for duck hunting. The interior of this tract is difficult to reach by passenger car but can be reached with a 4-wheel-drive vehicle or a boat.

Northwest of Bayou DeView, on the west side of the Black River, which joins the White to the south, is another excellent duck spot of 10,042 acres: the Shirley Bay-Rainey Brake PHA (16). This is made up primarily of bottomland hardwoods. There is a refuge area in its center. This one is reached south from Hoxie on U.S. 67 and then west. The small State Route 25 passing through the town of Lynn is the nearest approach and it is to the east of Lynn.

Still farther north, and lying along both sides of the Black River above Pocahontas where the Current River joins it, is 18,090-acre Black River PHA (17), with some of the finest duck habitat in the state. It is also right on a major flyway down the Black. This Area is in the extreme northeast. U.S. 62 intersects U.S. 67 just north of it at Corning. The entire Area is highly developed for waterfowl shooting.

To the southeast, and lying right along the border of Big Lake National Wildlife Refuge, is the Big Lake PHA (18), another prime duck shooting ground of the northeast. Thirteen miles west of the city of Blytheville, it has 12,160 acres. It can be reached from State 181, or by boat by using a floodway ditch off State 18 from Blytheville. This also is highly developed for duck hunting.

One of the largest state-purchased duck hunting grounds probably in the whole U.S. is Bayou Meto PHA (19), in Jefferson and Arkansas Cos. of the southeast sector, with 34,331 acres. This is on a major flyway route and has long been a wintering ground for ducks. Almost all shooting grounds are in timber, and the Area is so large and wild that a compass is recommended. The tract is north of the Arkansas River. U.S. 79 running through Pine Bluff and to Stutgart is west of it, and State 1 through DeWitt is to the east. The White River National Refuge is east of DeWitt. Thus, all told this PHA is in one of the most famous duck hunting spots in the nation.

There is a small PHA, Grassy Lake (20), north of Little Rock, in Faulkner County, not far from the main intersect of U.S. 64 and 65 at Conway. It contains 1480 acres and is primarily a duck hunting spot.

There are several more in the southern part of the state. In the southwest, not far from Texarkana, there are two important ones. Bois d'Arc PHA (21) has approximately 7500 acres, is located along the creek of the same name, near the town of Spring Hill and about twelve miles south of Hope, which is on U.S. 67. South of it, and in the southwestern corner of the state, below Texarkana, is Sulphur River Bottoms PHA (22). This is near the Sulphur River, contains 9940 river-bottom acres and is primarily a duck Area. U.S. 71 skirts it on the east.

Across in the southeast corner of the state are two more excellent duck spots. The Seven Devils Swamp PHA (23) has 2510 acres in Drew Co. It is to the north of State 35. This road joins north-south running U.S. 65 and 165 near McGehee and U.S. 81 near Monticello. Access is from State 35. Nearby, on the south side of State 35, and near Lake Wallace and U.S. 165 is the Cut-Off Creek PHA (24), with 8153 acres. Dams have been constructed here to hold slough water.

Back up in the northeast is a 6033-acre tract called the Saint Francis Sunken Lands PHA (25), an excellent duck location. This is in Cross Co. near the St. Francis River. A key town in the vicinity is Wynne, near the junction of U.S. 64 and State 1. Southwest of this PHA is another that is considered one of the state's best duck locations. This is the Dagmar PHA (26), a 6472-acre tract in Monroe Co. It is southwest some distance from Forrest City via U.S. 70, on the east side of the Cache River. A nearby town is Brinkley, from which access is possible.

From all the foregoing, it is obvious that Arkansas has concentrated for many years on duck hunting. On most of these public lands there are also an abundance of other species (see following material), but duck hunting is the main tradition in all this river-bottom country along the Mississippi flyway. Hunters should carefully check rules pertaining to each individual PHA. They differ considerably. The Commission, as noted earlier, can furnish individual maps and information.

RABBITS

There are both cottontails and the larger swamp rabbits in Arkansas. The cottontail is quite liberally distributed over the state. There is a good deal of hunter interest in rabbits, and beagling for them gains an ever increasing following. The National Forests and almost all of the PHAs have rabbit hunting. Some notably good choices for cottontails are: Petit Jean ("Ducks"); Wattensaw ("Quail"); Hope ("Quail"); Cut-Off Creek, St. Francis Sunken Lands, Seven Devils Swamp ("Ducks"); Harris Brake, Galla Creek, Nimrod ("Quail").

The big swamp rabbits are found along the stream bottoms. Some counties in the middle of the state with good possibilities are Conway, Faulkner, and Jefferson, all of them along the Arkansas River. In fact, the Arkansas River Valley has probably the largest population of these rabbits. The southwest also is a good location, for example along the Sulphur River. This is a major species on the Sulphur River Bottoms PHA. Another is the huge Bayou Meto PHA on the east side of the state near the Arkansas River. Both of these are located under "Waterfowl."

SQUIRRELS

Arkansas is one of the best squirrel states. Squirrels are the most important species here by numbers killed. The vast amount of woodlands, in hardwoods, both in the hills and the river-bottom swamps, furnish perfect squirrel habitat. There are both fox squirrels and gray squirrels. The gray squirrel, a forest species as contrasted to the fox squirrel that prefers edges, small woodlots and farmland edges, is by far the most abundant and popular.

The several National Forests, described in the opening of this chapter, are among the best of the squirrel hunting territory. It is estimated that they furnish at least 25 percent of the kill, which undoubtedly is in total several million annually. Both the Ozark and Ouachita NF rate squirrel hunting as "good" and in the smaller St. Francis NF on the eastern border, at the confluence of the St. Francis and Mississippi Rivers, the lowlands are rated as excellent.

Squirrel hunters also get a chance to hunt this favorite species on two of the National Refuges: Big Lake in the northeast; White River toward the southeast. Both are excellent. The Refuge hunting is carefully controlled, should be checked with either the Commission or the Refuge managers. Exact locations of these refuges have been given earlier under "Turkey" and "Waterfowl."

A great many of the PHAs have fine squirrel hunting, especially because of their locations among hardwoods of the bottoms. Noted under "Waterfowl" are the following, with squirrels rated among the primary species: Petit Jean; Bayou DeView; Hurricane Lake; Grassy Lake; Black River; Bois d'Arc; Shirey-Rainey; Sulphur River; Cut-Off Creek; Seven Devils Swamp; Dagmar; Big Lake; Bayou Meto. Mentioned and described under "Quail": Wattensaw; Harris Brake; Galla Creek; Nimrod. Under "Turkeys": Newton Co.; White Oak.

There is a fine squirrel location in Madison County, the 9126-acre Madison Co. PHA (27). This is in the northwest, and lies near and east of State 23, between Eureka Springs and Huntsville. This is a rough, hilly, well-forested region. U.S. and State 68 are main routes nearby. There is also a small tract of 880 acres over in the east-central area, near the White River and only a short distance north of Wattensaw PHA ("Quail"). This small one is called Des Arc PHA (28). The village of like name is the key location point, and crossing routes are State 11 and 38. One other, Independence Co. PHA, of 1173 acres, is located farther north, in Independence Co. Batesville, on U.S. 67 where the White River crosses, is a key point.

DEER

Several decades ago deer were almost gone from this state which should have had, with its excellent habitat, thousands of them. It was estimated that there were at the lowest ebb possibly less than a thousand in the entire state. An aroused public, urged by the Commission, backed a dedicated trapping and transplant and study program. During the 1950s the deer kill began to expand tremendously. By the early 1960s one record harvest totalled almost 28,000. Today the herd appears quite stable, with an estimate of from 250,000 to 300,000 deer in the state herd. There is quality deer hunting, and the future of the Arkansas whitetail looks secure. An average of 20,000 animals or better is the yearly harvest.

Figures from a recent fall show that numerous counties had kills of well over or just under 500. These were Arkansas, Ashley, Bradley, Calhoun, Chicot, Clark, Cleveland, Dallas, Desha, Drew, Nevada, Ouachita, Union, and Sebastian. All of these except the last are in the south and southeast. Sebastian is west-central, near Fort Smith. Although deer are liberally spread over all of the state, the above pattern of heavy kills in the south and southeast appears valid season to season. Arkansas ordinarily has a three-way-split season for gunners. It also has one of the longest bow seasons, perhaps the longest (four months), in the U.S., and has become extremely popular with archers.

Good public deer hunting areas are numerous. All three of the National Forests (described early in chapter) offer hunting rated as "good." The Forests in fact account for an estimated 17 percent of the annual deer kill. There is also a highly popular deer hunt on the White River National Wildlife Refuge (("Turkeys")). This is in the DeWitt-Stuttgart region of the lower White River near its meeting with the Mississippi and is in some of the best deer habitat in the state.

Numerous PHAs furnish fine deer opportunities. Here are some of the best, with the species under which they have already been described. Under "Turkeys": Newton Co.; White Oak. Under "Quail": Wattensaw; Hope. Under "Waterfowl": Petit Jean; Bayou DeView; Black River; Shirey-Rainey; Cut-Off Creek; Dagmar; Big Lake; Bayou Meto. Uuder "Squirrels": Madison Co.; Independence Co.

BLACK BEAR

As this is written there is no bear hunting in Arkansas. But this state has the distinction of carrying on the largest bear restoration endeavor so far attempted. The black bear was originally native and plentiful. But it was hunted hard and killed indiscriminately. By the early 1950s estimates placed the total number at not over fifty and probably less. In 1959 the Commission arranged with Minnesota and with Manitoba to trap and ship in bears for restocking. Up until the present over 200 animals have been brought in. Releases have mostly been made in remote portions of the Ozark and Ouachita Mountains. The bears are increasing rapidly under full protection and with a heavy fine for illegal kills. It is now believed that there are upwards of a thousand in the state, and predictions are for a controlled hunt, by permit, in about four or five years.

WILD HOGS

There are a number of feral swine in the bottoms and forests of Arkansas. They are hunted to some extent. However, hunters should be aware that the Commission has no jurisdiction. There is neither an open nor a closed season, and all such swine are presumed to be the private property of someone. Hunters therefore should know and have permission from a landowner before hunting or killing feral hogs.

OTHER ANIMALS

Raccoons, foxes, and opossums are very plentiful throughout the state. Arkansas has a reputation as a "hound state" where hundreds of enthusiasts are avid for the chase after all three species. All of the public lands offer hunting of varying quality for these animals. Regulations relative to dogs and night hunting should be carefully checked.

REGULATIONS

Game laws pertaining to seasons, bag and possession limits, areas to be hunted, special hunts, license fees all may have numerous changes from year to year. For current regulations, and for other specific queries, write to: Arkansas Game and Fish Commission, Game and Fish Bldg., Little Rock, Arkansas 72201.

NORTH DAKOTA

North Dakota is a kind of transition state. Mostly of rather gentle terrain, it separates the glacial region of the Great Lakes represented by Minnesota on the east from the rough country of eastern Montana on the west that eventually becomes the towering Rockies. It is for the most part flat to rolling prairie, with a continuance of the same terrain north above U.S. borders into its neighboring Canadian Provinces, Manitoba and Saskatchewan, and to the south much of the same in its sister state, South Dakota.

North Dakota might be termed the Prairie Pothole State. It is heavily dotted with thousands of small wetlands, small ponds or potholes in the grass country, which in total form one of the most important areas of wetlands within contiguous U.S. borders. It is perhaps the foremost "duck factory" in the United States. On the east the Red River of the North and its tributaries form the border with Minnesota. Westward from the river, plains undulate away. In the northeast there is a small timbered area called the Pembina Hills.

West from the Red River the country rises easily and gains a bit in roughness. Along the northern border, about center of the state, are the Turtle Mountains, another timbered hill area of modest size but mountains actually in name only. The chief feature of terrain farther west is the Missouri River, which enters from the west a bit above midway on the Montana border and flows southeast to leave the state roughly midway along the southern border. Huge dams on the Missouri have drastically changed the terrain and wildlife picture of western North Dakota. Oahe Reservoir backs up from far down in South Dakota to reach almost to the capital at Bismarck, and to broaden the river on up to the northwest until Garrison Dam forms another enormous reservoir, one of the world's largest, which continues upstream as a huge lake almost to the western border.

In the southwest is another distinctive and important feature of terrain. Here the Little Missouri, flowing generally north, comes into the state at the extreme southwestern corner and proceeds up through the southwestern quarter. Along it are the rugged, broken, scenic North Dakota Badlands. Below the confluence of the Little Missouri with its arm of Garrison Reservoir are the Killdeer Mountains, another rough area of hills. However, none of this terrain is very high. The highest point in the state is near Amidon in the southwest—White Butte, 3506 feet.

There is not much true wilderness in North Dakota in the sense of the same in the western mountains. North Dakota is a grain and cattle state, with some mining. Approximately 95 percent of its acreage is in farms and ranches. Main roads are good. There are four north-south U.S. highways and at least a half dozen state routes of comparable quality. Two main east-west roads cross the state—U.S. 2 and I 94—and numerous state roads of good quality take hunters to all the main cities and towns. There are, however, in this sparsely populated state many side roads that in wet weather or snow require caution. Air transport between main cities is good. Reaching outlying towns in general requires ground transport. Hunters can utilize 4-wheel-drive vehicles to good advantage, but guides and horseback hunts are seldom necessary, except that some Badlands hunting can best be accomplished on horseback.

North Dakota's hunting is varied and excellent, yet has had little publicity. The state is large, at widest nearly 400 miles across, by roughly 225 north-south. It covers 70,665 square miles, and is far from crowded. The present population is less than 640,000. License sales illustrate just how wide-open the spaces are. They total, for large and small game and including all various permits, only around 100,000, but the actual hunter total is probably closer to 75,000. Visitors from out of state are consistently scarce—around 2500 annually. Much of the reason for this is that with a small population budgets for publicity are necessarily curtailed.

Game species are varied and in up-cycle years extremely plentiful. North Dakota might be termed primarily a "bird" state. There are pheasants, sharptail grouse, Hungarian partridge, ruffed grouse, sage grouse. There are wild turkeys, hordes of waterfowl, both ducks and geese. Squirrels are spottily abundant, rabbits—cottontails, big whitetailed jacks and snowshoe hares—together blanket the state. There is very good deer hunting, with extremely high success, chiefly for whitetails but with some mule deer. There are also antelope. Bighorn sheep have been reintroduced after disappearing many years ago.

An important game-crop influence here, which must be well understood by hunters, is weather. North Dakota has some extremely severe winters, with long-drawn-out blizzards at times. Bad winters can decimate game crops, especially in plains country. In recent years, for example, pheasants —ordinarily the most popular and abundant of upland birds—were brought to such low levels by winter kills that the season had to be closed entirely one year. The harvest dropped, from one season to the next, 79 percent. Hungarian partridge, also abundant, may show a kill one season of 50 to 70 percent less than the previous one. Good management, and good years, rather quickly bring bird flocks back up. But visiting hunters should check any year to establish whether it is a feast or famine prospect. A serious decline can change, of course, with even a single perfect nesting year, to a bonanza season. Even big game, particular antelope, are susceptible to debacles of winter weather, but the herds come back more slowly than bird crops. A single bad winter, of '64-'65, took an estimated 60 percent of North Dakota's antelope. Waterfowling, conversely, is rather consistently among the best in the United States.

Certainly there is no problem in finding places to hunt. In western North Dakota alone there are over a million acres of federal lands open to hunting. These are in the Little Missouri National Grasslands, administered as part of the Custer National Forest. A detailed map of these is available from the Forest Service Headquarters, Northern Region, Missoula, Montana. Scattered over all of the state except the Badlands are almost 300 Waterfowl Production Areas administered by the Bureau of Sport Fisheries and Wildlife. All are open to public hunting, not just for waterfowl but for other game as well. There are no fees. Duck stamp money supports these.

A detailed map locating all of these areas is available from the Department of Interior in Washington, D.C., or from the Regional Director, BSF&W, 1006 W. Lake Street, Minneapolis, Minnesota 55408. The North Dakota State Game and Fish Department at Bismarck also has copies.

There are Bureau of Land Management lands and Corps of Engineers lands, the latter mainly along the reservoirs of the Missouri. Many of these are managed in cooperation with the state. And that is only the beginning of State Game Management Areas. There are at this writing a total of 97 locations, some small, some large, from an 80-acre spot for pass shooting at ducks to the almost 24,000-acre Oahe GMA with varied game. A list of these, with exact locations, can be had from the Game Department. The Department, incidentally, does an exemplary job under most difficult circumstances. Operating on one of the smallest incomes from license sales of any state its size, it strives diligently and with small personnel to manage each species and to provide ever increasing acreage for public hunting. Severe winters, as has been noted, add to the problems.

For hunters who wish to camp while hunting in North Dakota, prospects could hardly be better. Sites of various kinds from State Parks and Theodore Roosevelt National Park (two sections) in the west to National Grasslands, city parks, and private campgrounds are scattered over the entire state. An excellent map listing all of these and their facilities, plus all Water Recreation Areas with camping and other facilities, can be had from the North Dakota Travel Department, State Highway Division, Capitol Building, Bismarck. It is titled: "Guide to Outdoor Recreation in North Dakota." Other accommodations such as motels are numerous along all main routes and there is seldom need during hunting seasons to reserve ahead. All but the very smallest villages offer lodging and food.

Early fall weather in North Dakota is generally perfect hunting weather, with mornings and late afternoons crisp and enjoyable, midday warm. As fall wears on, the weather becomes cold. Early blizzards can occur. After September one should go prepared with clothing for any occasion, and late in hunting seasons it is certain to be cold and usually snowy, with low temperatures. Waterfowlers should think in terms of down clothing and insulated boots at almost any time.

Guns and ammunition require nothing specialized. Deer hunters will want rifles in calibers comparable to the .270, .30/06, .243. They commonly experience open shots. Bird hunters after grouse and pheasants will need No. 6 or No. 7½ shot at least. Duck hunters should use an average of No. 4s. Because there is a great deal of goose hunting here, hunters after these birds should be prepared with choked barrels in 12 gauge or magnums, and with standard goose loads.

PHEASANT

The ringneck has had drastic ups and downs over recent years in North Dakota. It is by no means in serious danger. But land use changes are to some extent diminishing good habitat, and hard winters tend toward unstable populations. In good average years the kill runs upward of 300,000, cocks only. A sharp decline due to winter kill closed the season entirely in 1966. After that, however, the Department reopened it briefly and with low bag limit for it was established that small-game license sales—slightly over 50,000—were about the same regardless, and at least a token season might as well be utilized. Currently the pheasant population is building up again

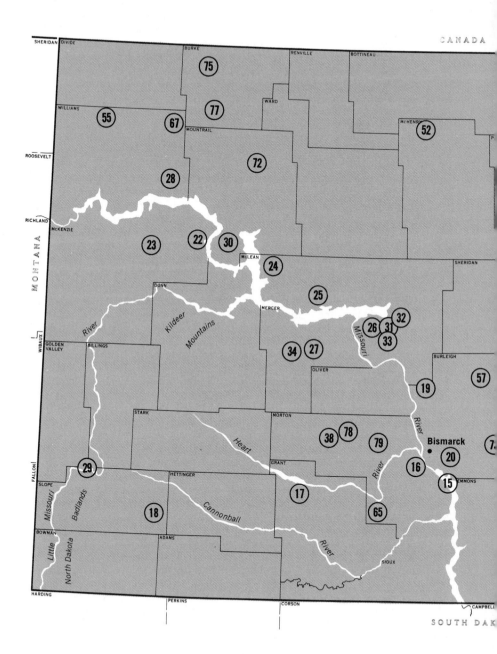

NORTH DAKOTA

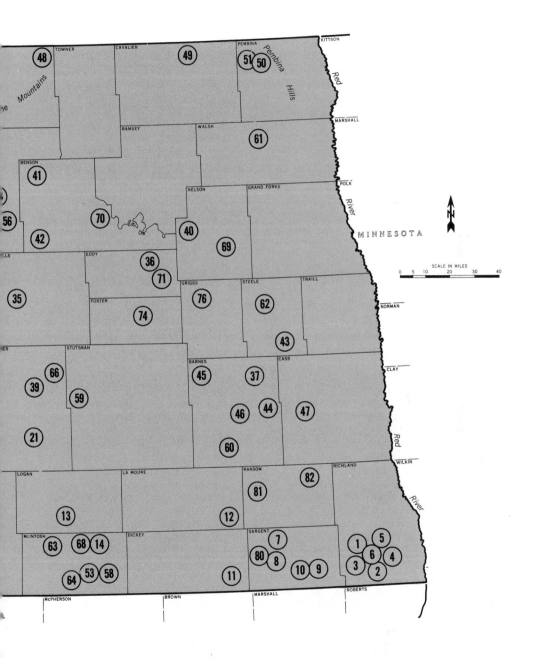

KEY TO HUNTING AREAS

1. Krieser Lake GMA
2. Mud Lake GMA
3. Park Lake GMA
4. Swan Lake GMA
5. Stack Slough GMA
6. Wild Rice GMA
7. Crete Slough GMA
8. Meszaros Slough GMA
9. Schudar GMA
10. Tewaukon GMA
11. Hyatt Slough GMA
12. Seth Gordon Marsh GMA
13. Logan Co. GMA
14. Lehr GMA
15. Oahe GMA
16. Morton Co. GMA
17. Heart Butte GMA
18. Cedar Lake GMA
19. Wilton Mine GMA
20. McKenzie Slough GMA
21. Dawson GMA
22. Antelope Creek GMA
23. Tobacco Garden GMA
24. Deep Water GMA
25. Douglas Creek GMA
26. Riverdale GMA
27. Hille GMA
28. Hofflund GMA
29. Little Missouri National Grasslands
30. Van Hook GMA
31. Wolf Creek GMA
32. Snake Creek GMA
33. deTrobriand GMA
34. Beaver Creek GMA
35. Wells Co. GMA
36. Lake Washington GMA
37. Bald Hill Reservoir GMA
38. Fish Creek Dam Site GMA
39. Horsehead Lake GMA
40. Black Swan GMA
41. Knox Slough GMA
42. Lake Legried GMA
43. Fuller Lake GMA
44. Koldok GMA
45. Ray Holland GMA
46. Valley City GMA
47. Magnolia GMA
48. Wakopa GMA
49. Pembina Hills GMA
50. Clifford GMA
51. Tongue River GMA
52. Upham GMA
53. Ashley GMA
54. Balta GMA
55. Blue Ridge GMA
56. Buffalo Lake GMA
57. Bunker Lake GMA
58. Camp Lake GMA
59. Chase Lake GMA
60. Clausen Springs GMA
61. Charles C. Cook GMA
62. Golden Lake GMA
63. Green Lake GMA
64. Kisselberry Lake GMA
65. Lake Patricia GMA
66. Lake Williams GMA
67. McGregor Dam GMA
68. McIntosh Co. GMA
69. McVille GMA
70. Minnewaukan GMA
71. Overbeck Slough GMA
72. Palermo GMA
73. Rice Lake GMA
74. Rusten Slough GMA
75. Short Creek GMA
76. Sibley Lake GMA
77. Smishek Lake GMA
78. Storm Creek GMA
79. Sweetbriar Lake GMA
80. Taayer Lake GMA
81. Fort Ransom GMA
82. Mirror Pool GMA

and when it levels off even at general average the state can be considered excellent for hunting this bird.

Although pheasants range throughout the state, and seasons are state-wide, the northern half of the state is marginal pheasant range. The quality pheasant range lies in the two southernmost tiers of counties and in the southern portions of the third tier. The top counties are, reading west to east and beginning with the bottom tier: Bowman, Adams, Sioux, Emmons, McIntosh, Dickey, Sargent, Richland; then in the second tier, Slope, Hettinger, Grant, (Emmons), Logan, La Moure, Ransom, (Richland). The southern halves of the third tier up from the south are in: Golden Valley, Billings, Stark (entire county), Morton (almost entire), Burleigh, Kidder, Stutsman, Barnes, Cass.

Very generally the next two tiers of counties to the north across the state are secondary, but in up-cycles still very good, pheasant range. Also in general, southeastern and south-central North Dakota offer the cream of the pheasant hunting, as compared to hunting farther west.

In the extreme southeast, Richland County, one of the best, has a number of GMAs where pheasants are important game. All are in the southern half of the county. Krieser Lake GMA (1), 480 acres, is north and west of Lidgerwood (State 18 and 11 intersect). Mud Lake GMA (2), 350-plus acres, is southwest of Hankinson (State 11). Park Lake GMA (3), 160 acres, is a few miles southwest of Lidgerwood (above). Also near Lidgerwood, east of it, is 290-acre Swan Lake GMA (4), and near Hankinson (four miles northwest) is 316-acre Stack Slough (5). A somewhat larger Area in the Lidgerwood vicinity is Wild Rice GMA (6), with 640 acres.

West of southern Richland Co. is Sargent Co. Here Crete Slough GMA (7) offers pheasants on 150 acres north and east of the village of Crete, in the northwest part of the county, near State 13. Meszaros Slough GMA (8), 238 acres, is reached from Cogswell (State 11), and 103-acre Schudar GMA (9) is south and west of Cayuga, also on State 11. In the southwest part of this county also near Cayuga there is a larger Area, Tewaukon GMA (10), with 1125 acres.

Still moving west, the southeast corner of Dickey Co. has Hyatt Slough GMA (11), with 1212 acres west and south of Ludden, near the intersect of State 11 and 1. North of Dickey Co. in southeast La Moure Co. is Seth Gordon Marsh GMA (12), with 482 acres near Verona (intersect of State 13 and 1).

In the next counties to the west in these bottom tiers of prime pheasant range there is 480-acre Logan Co. GMA (13) in the south-central part of that county, west and north of Lehr (State 30), and across the line to the south in McIntosh Co., but still reached from the village of Lehr is 610-acre Lehr GMA (14).

There is a very large Area (almost 24,000 acres), Oahe GMA (15), leased from the Corps of Engineers, lying in tracts along the river partly in Burleigh, Emmons, and Morton Cos. still farther west. This GMA is prime pheasant country. It is reached eight miles south of either Bismarck or Mandan on state routes. Three miles farther south from Mandan is Morton Co. GMA (16), about a section of land. To the southwest, in western Grant Co., is large Heart Butte GMA (17) with over 7000 acres, about halfway between Glen Ullin and Elgin on State 49. And still farther west, in southeastern Slope Co., is Cedar Lake GMA (18), 817 acres, reached by going sixteen miles south and five miles west from New England (State 22 in Hettinger Co.).

In the southeast quarter of the state, but in counties north of those so far touched, there are some good pheasant Areas. Wilton Mine GMA (19) is one of about 250 acres in northwest Burleigh Co. and spreading northwest into McLean Co. It is near Wilton (U.S. 83). And in south-central Burleigh Co. is McKenzie Slough GMA (20) with 614 acres, near the town of McKenzie west of Bismarck on I 94. To the east in Kidder Co. and still in good pheasant country is 2958-acre Dawson GMA (21), a few miles south of Dawson, which is on I 94 where State 3 intersects from the south.

There is some pheasant hunting in the west, on the National Grasslands, and there are several GMA tracts outside the prime range that still offer fair shooting on up cycles. Names and locations of these are as follows: Antelope Creek GMA (22), 1880 acres northwest of New Town in McKenzie Co.: Tobacco Garden GMA (23), 1664 acres twenty-five miles northeast of Watford City, McKenzie Co.; Deep Water GMA (24), over 6000 acres south of Parshall, McLean Co.; Douglas Creek GMA (25), 1080 acres in McLean Co. in two tracts near Emmet; Riverdale GMA (26) with over 2000 acres in McLean Co. southwest of the town of Riverdale; Hille GMA (27), 3000-plus acres in Mercer Co. twenty miles north of Beulah; and up in the northwest, in Williams Co. southeast from the town of Ray, 2500-acre Hofflund GMA (28).

There are some pheasants on many other GMAs but the foregoing locates the best hunting. However, hunters should not overlook the Waterfowl Production Areas noted early in the chapter. There are nearly 300 of them. Their locations are easily pinpointed from the map suggested as available for them. There is also of course good pheasant hunting on private lands and many owners will allow it if one asks politely and observes all the rules of good sportsmanship.

SHARPTAIL GROUSE

Some of the best—possibly the very best—sharptail grouse hunting remaining in the U.S. today is located in North Dakota. There is a great deal of very good sharptail grouse habitat here. These handsome, sporty prairie grouse, dark-meated and delicious and weighing from 1½ to 2½ pounds, are birds of the grasslands, but with a penchant also for brushy pockets and edges as well. They are hardy, northern grouse, tempered by centuries to difficult and severe winters. Unlike the pinnated grouse, or prairie chicken, which most hunters assume was native here but which actually came into the state with early settlement, the sharptail is a centuries-long native.

Sharptails are less subject to fluctuations because of winter hardships than are the imports such as pheasants and Hungarian partridge. While North Dakota hunters have for some years leaned toward pheasant hunting because the birds have been abundant and more easily hunted, it is interesting to note that during pheasant declines (as currently) the sharptail takes its place as a standby game species of great importance. Part of this, of course, is that in many areas sharptail and pheasant ranges overlap.

As many as 150,000-plus sharptails are harvested each season in North Dakota. Even during pheasant difficulties, hunters took around 100,000 sharptails. Thus it may be that viewed practically and without sentiment the sharptail may in the long run turn out to be North Dakota's most important upland species. Certainly few other states if any can compete.

The sharptail grouse is the only native nonmigratory, upland game bird with a range that blankets the entire state. However, the primary hunting area and best habitat covers the western half, with a large eastward bulge in the middle of the state. A line drawn from north to south about as follows will enclose the best hunting on its western side. It begins at the northern border in western Bottineau Co., runs on a general southeastern slant across the middle of McHenry Co., southern Pierce Co., the southwest corner of Benson and Eddy Cos., and finds its most easterly point about in the middle of Foster Co. Here the line turns on a long curve back toward the southwest, taking in the northwestern half of Stutsman Co., all but the southeast corner of Kidder Co. It slants southwest across the middle of Emmons Co., and touches the southern North Dakota border there. In other words, everything west of this line is prime sharptail hunting ground. To the east, over all of that part of the state, it is labeled "fair."

Under "Pheasant" numerous GMAs have been cited that offer as good or better hunting for sharptails. They are: Hofflund, Tobacco Garden, Antelope Creek, Deep Water, and Douglas Creek in the northwest quarter of the state. Then in the southwestern quarter there are Hille, Morton Co., Wilton Mine, Heart Butte. In the southeast quarter there are Dawson in Kidder Co., and Oahe divided among Burleigh, Emmons, and Morton Cos.

There is some excellent sharptail hunting on the Little Missouri National Grasslands (29) in the west. These varied and vast tracts lie in Slope, Golden Valley, Billings and McKenzie Cos. in the far west. Although these Grasslands were mentioned early in the chapter, and briefly under "Pheasant," because they are in the quality sharptail range (and important for much other hunting) they are more carefully defined here.

East-west U.S. 2 crosses just above the Grasslands on the north, with the city of Williston near the western North Dakota border a key point. U.S. 85, north-south, intersects U.S. 2 at Williston and runs south into the

Grasslands. Watford City is a key town at the north edge of the Grasslands on U.S. 85. A bit below midway of the area, southward, is the town of Medora, on east-west U.S. 10 (I 90). U.S. 85 crosses U.S. 10 just east of the main Grasslands swath, and intersects east-west U.S. 12 at Bowman, a town at the southern edge.

The North Unit of Theodore Roosevelt National Memorial Park is in and surrounded by tracts of Grasslands in the northern edge. The South Unit of the Park is in the south-central Grasslands area. Hunters should understand that the Grasslands are not continuous, but are made up of many tracts, some only a half-mile across, others stretching ten miles or more. Interspersed are blocks of private lands. Yellow signs mark the Grassland tract boundaries.

There is sharptail hunting on the Waterfowl Production Areas (check suggested map), and on private lands by thousands of acres by permission. There are also several good GMAs not located under "Pheasant." Van Hook GMA (30), located five miles southeast of New Town with a huge 14,000-plus acres in Mountrail Co., is one. Then there are almost 5000 acres to the southeast, in east-central McLean Co., in Wolf Creek GMA (31). This area is near Coleharbor, a town on the south side of Garrison Bay (of the impoundment) on U.S. 83. Snake Creek GMA (32), 11,000-plus acres nearby, a bit farther northwest of Coleharbor, also has sharptails. And a short distance west, deTrobriand GMA (33) with nearly 3000 acres has a few. This GMA is four miles south of Garrison, in McLean Co. The 540-acre Beaver Creek GMA (34) some miles north of Zap in Mercer Co., a bit to the southwest, also offers sharptail shooting.

To the east there is Wells Co. GMA (35), a section of land north of Hurdsfield in Wells Co., in the middle of the state, and Lake Washington GMA (36) still eastward in Eddy Co., six miles south of Warwick, with almost 1000 acres. This is about the limit of the best range. But in the southeast quarter, in Barnes Co. the 1197-acre Bald Hill Reservoir GMA (37), twelve miles northwest of Valley City, at times has a good sharptail population. There is a small GMA, Fish Creek Dam Site (38), a potential dam site, back to the southwest in Morton Co.—160 acres—near Judson that currently has some sharptails. And to the east in Kidder Co. there is Horsehead Lake GMA (39), 437 acres southwest from the town of Robinson with a fair supply of sharptail grouse.

Sharptails can be found elsewhere in North Dakota, for as noted they range over the whole state. These guides give pointers to the best of the public-land shooting.

HUNGARIAN PARTRIDGE

These imported birds were established in North Dakota many years ago and the state has proved to be a proper habitat for them. Although their range is somewhat different from that of the sharptail, they too blanket the state and offer excellent to fair shooting.

They are somewhat cyclic, having quite drastic ups and downs. In top years hunters take substantial numbers—one fairly recent season 233,000. This kill, considering the comparatively modest number of hunters, indicates a large partridge population at peak. During the two following seasons, however, the kill dropped to 70,000 and 90,000. Following that, the birds started an upward trend again.

The Hun is becoming more popular and important in North Dakota. At the present time many Soil Bank land contracts are ending. More land is being turned to agricultural use instead of lying fallow. The Hun is quite compatible with intensive land use, and thus is considered able to adapt to the changes, perhaps· far better than other prairie habitat uplanders. It is a covey bird, whimsically inclined both to flush wild and to sit inordinately tight when an efficient dog is used. It is a swift, uneven flyer, smaller than the prairie grouses but larger than the quail, and an excellent table bird.

The eastern third of the state, the extreme south-central, and the far southwest are the "secondary" areas of Hun population. All of the northwest and the interior of the state are the primary ranges. A line drawn as follows will box in behind it to the north and west most of the quality Hungarian partridge range. It begins in the northeast area, in the northwestern corner of Cavalier Co., proceeds south along the Towner Co. line, and on to take in the western two-thirds of Benson and then Wells Cos., all but the far southeast corner of Kidder Co. Below Kidder Co. it cuts southwest to include the northwestern corner of Logan Co. Now the bulge turns sharply to the west and curves a bit south, taking in half of Emmons Co., the northern tip of Sioux, northern Grant. It now bends back to the northwest, along the southern boundary of Dunn Co. and to include a northern strip of both Billings and Golden Valley Cos.

Thus hunters after Huns can plan on fair shooting in the east, extreme south, and southwest, but for a chance of finding the most birds might well try the south-central, central, north-central, northwest, and west. All of the Grasslands, described in detail under "Sharptail Grouse," are in Hun range, with the northern portion in the range of concentration.

Many GMAs already noted offer good Hun shooting. Here, in alphabetical order, are those located under "Pheasant": Antelope Creek; Dawson; Deep Water Creek; Douglas Creek; Heart Butte; Hille; Hofflund; Lehr; Morton Co.; Wilton Mine. Under "Sharptail": Bald Hill; Beaver Creek; Snake Creek; deTrobriand; Van Hook; Wells Co.; Wolf Creek.

Other GMAs not dealt with so far where Huns are found are as follows. Some are within the primary range, some outside it. Black Swan GMA (40) is in the east-central part of the state, in Nelson Co., has 854 acres, six miles south of Bartlett, which is on U.S. 2. Knox Slough GMA (41) is in northwest Benson Co. near the village of Knox on U.S. 2. Lake Legried GMA (42) is also in Benson Co., in the southern part, near the town of Maddox on State 30. In southern Steele Co. in the eastern part of the state is 720-acre Fuller Lake GMA (43) with fair Hun shooting, seven miles southeast of Hope, which is on State 38. To the south in Barnes Co. is small (214 acres) Koldok GMA (44), east of Oriska at I 94-State 32 intersect. The 200-acre Ray Holland GMA (45), also in Barnes Co., near Leal in the northwest on State 9, usually has a few Huns. And a third Barnes Co. location, somewhat larger, 759-acre Valley City GMA (46), near the city of like name just north of I 94, is a fair bet. The same is true of 109-acre Magnolia GMA (47) to the east in Cass Co., near Buffalo, State 38.

As was mentioned previously under the other upland bird species, hunters should not overlook the wealth of opportunities on the Waterfowl Production Areas. See "Waterfowl" for some further mention of these, which are extremely numerous and open to hunting of all game found on them.

RUFFED GROUSE

This grouse is native to North Dakota but enjoys an extremely limited range. Practically all the birds are found in two restricted areas along the northern border: the Turtle Mountains about midway on the border, in Bottineau and Rolette Cos.; the Pembina Hills in Cavalier and Pembina Cos. in the northeast. The kill is never large. Ruffed grouse are prone to low and high cycles and interest diminishes between highs. Also, the restricted range draws few hunters. However, during peak populations there is some quite good ruffed grouse hunting here.

An excellent spot is the Wakopa GMA (48) in northwestern Rolette Co., 5178 acres west of the town of St. John, which is on a secondary running west from State 30 just below the Canadian border. Cavalier Co. also has a good Area, 748-acre Pembina Hills GMA (49). This is located in the northern central part of the county, northwest of the village of Vang. This settlement may not show on all maps. It is on a small secondary running west out of Walhalla, which is on State 32.

Pembina Co., the northeasternmost county, has two GMAs with ruffed grouse. A small one of eighty acres is Clifford GMA (50), near Leyden, a settlement southeast from Walhalla. The other has far more room, 1310 acres. This is Tongue River GMA (51), eight miles south and two east of Walhalla.

Hunters should also check the Waterfowl Production Areas for possible grouse pockets. There are some in Bottineau, Rolette, and Cavalier Cos.

SAGE GROUSE

Sage grouse are found only in the extreme southwest, in Bowman and Slope Cos., western Adams, Hettinger, Stark, southern Billings, and Golden Valley. There is a lot of National Grassland in portions of Slope, Billings, and Golden Valley Cos. The area open by proclamation to hunting has lately been only that south of U.S. 10 and west of U.S. 85. This takes in the southern parts of Golden Valley and Billings Cos., western Slope and Bowman Cos. There have been sage grouse seasons only for the past several years, and they are exceedingly brief—usually three days—with a one-a-day limit and two birds in possession. Pressure, and kill, is invariably light. Seldom more than 200 birds are taken. There are no GMAs located within the open area if it remains as above. The Grassland tracts furnish the public lands.

WILD TURKEYS

Wild Turkeys were introduced to North Dakota a few years ago, and a modest population has built up, in general along the Missouri River—Garrison and Oahe reservoirs. There have been very limited hunting seasons since 1960, but seasons are not necessarily approved every year. From 200 to 330 permits have in the past been offered, via application, public drawing, and a $3 permit fee, to residents only. The kill has run so far about 38 percent, which is quite good. Counties that have so far been open, although not necessarily all during the same seasons are: McKenzie, Dunn, McLean, Mercer, Oliver, Burleigh, Morton, Grant, Emmons, Slope. The last county is in the southwest, away from the others, in the Grasslands region, and has the Little Missouri running across it.

So far the great problem for turkey hunters has been finding a place to hunt. The birds stick closely to river-bottom habitat, which receives the heaviest posting of any lands in the state. It is advisable to select a hunting ground and secure permission to hunt before applying for a permit. There is however one excellent public location. This is the 23,901-acre Oahe GMA ("Pheasant").

OTHER UPLAND BIRDS

There are a few chukars in North Dakota but they are not hunted at present. There are also prairie chickens in remnant flocks. They are in such serious circumstances that they are not hunted, and it is thought that unless drastic measures are taken to acquire permanent suitable range for them they will soon disappear from the state.

While the mourning dove is in a strict sense a migratory bird, it is mentioned under this heading because it is not at present hunted in North Dakota. Mourning doves are plentiful, nesting throughout the state and staying late enough so that an annual season might easily furnish fine sport to many hunters. There is strong hunter sentiment for an open season. There were two successful seasons, 1963 and 1964. But as this is written, other factions have succeeded in taking and keeping the mourning dove off the game list. This may well change during the next few seasons. If it does, any of the public lands in grain country and along stream courses will without question offer excellent shooting.

WATERFOWL

Thousands of ducks are raised on the pothole nesting grounds and the federally owned Waterfowl Production Areas of North Dakota. Thousands more migrate down across the state each fall. Mallards, pintails, and teal are among the major species nesting in the state. The annual duck kill fluctuates to some degree, depending on weather and on nesting conditions of the season, but it runs anywhere from 200,000 to 360,000 or more, and that is indicative of fine shooting, for hunter numbers are seldom much over 40,000.

A few geese are raised in the state, mostly on federal refuges, but their numbers are small. However, North Dakota gets tremendous migratory flights, and with its vast grain fields added to abundant water it becomes one of the finest goose hunting locations on the continent. It is in fact amazing that so few visiting hunters sample it. The kill averages some 75,000 geese annually, with highs up around 100,000 and one fairly recent low of 56,500. The geese are of several species, Canadas, snows, and blues. Of the Canadas, the "small" Canada geese make up very close to one-half of the total annual kill in North Dakota.

Because of an uncommon amount of confusion in scientific and sportsman circles about identification and ranges of the Lesser Canada, which was originally called Hutchins's goose, and the Richardson's goose, both small species of white-cheeked geese, the "small" Canadas in North Dakota are locally called both Richardson's and Hutch's or simply small Canadas. For biological study purposes these geese are now known as the Tall Prairie Grass Geese. An intensive banding program is in progress on their Arctic nesting ground to see how they may be better managed, because of their importance.

The North Dakota laws over recent seasons have been conducive to holding waterfowl. Goose hunting on a half-day schedule, for example, has had favorable results for hunters. Also, for both ducks and geese there are many refuges in the state, a total of over sixty, including the famed Upper and Lower Souris. Needless to say, hunting in the vicinity of the refuges is usually good. But all told there is little difficulty in finding places to hunt. Some ranchers and farmers allow hunting, and there are goose pits for rent here and there. But the public waterfowling spots are so numerous that residents or nonresidents can easily locate birds.

Hunters should, however, have a broad picture of concentration regions. While ducks are found over the entire state, there are two portions with only fair possibilities. One is in the southwest. A curving line from northwest to southeast drawn from the western border, starting at the northwest corner of McKenzie Co. and passing midway across Dunn, Mercer, Morton, and Sioux Cos. to touch the southern border will approximately cut off to the south and west the poorest duck populations. In the northeast, and the east, the border counties also have less ducks. Thus, an extremely broad swath encompassing all of the northern border except the extreme northeast and flowing down across the state to the south and southeast takes in the bulk of the prime duck shooting.

Goose concentrations and flights are much narrower. In general the eastern half of the state gets the bulk of the migration. But within this wide sweep from north to south there is a more confined corridor where most of the birds pass. On the northern border, as geese come into the state, the three counties of Rolette, Towner, and Cavalier are roughly centered under the heavy flights. This swath narrows a bit southward, and is drawn on a slightly southeastward line. Where it leaves the state it is centered over all of Dickey and the western half of Sargent Cos. From the eastern border of this heavily used flyway to the state's eastern border goose hunting is good but not quite as good as inside the corridor. On the western side of the corridor the situation is the same over several counties bordering the flight lane.

Because public waterfowling opportunities are so numerous they cannot possibly all be listed here. However, a basic idea can be given. The many federal Waterfowl Production Areas have been mentioned earlier. These are managed by the Bureau of Sport Fisheries and Wildlife chiefly as duck nesting grounds. All are open—280 of them as this is written—to hunting in the fall. Earlier an address was given where a map showing all of them is available. To give hunters a fundamental picture here of the extent of this hunting, the accompanying table lists counties, with the number of Waterfowl Production Areas in each and the total acreage in each county.

COUNTY	NO. OF WP AREAS	TOTAL ACRES
Benson	12	1855
Bottineau	3	696
Burke	2	382
Burleigh	4	472
Cavalier	6	1013
Dickey	16	3306
Divide	29	5306
Eddy	3	386
Emmons	4	1638
Foster	3	543
Grand Forks	1	885
Griggs	4	1000
Kidder	8	2245
LaMoure	11	2360
Logan	7	1968
McHenry	2	440
McIntosh	17	2885
McLean	9	1513

COUNTY	NO. OF WP AREAS	TOTAL ACRES
Mountrail	15	2277
Nelson	11	1630
Pierce	5	415
Ramsey	6	1104
Ransom	1	161
Richland	2	466
Rolette	6	611
Sargent	4	825
Sheridan	18	4862
Steele	2	795
Stutsman	35	9878
Towner	3	481
Walsh	5	993
Ward	9	1474
Wells	9	1890
Williams	8	2719

By checking the waterfowl concentration corridors and the number and sizes of the WPAs in any county, a prospective hunter can easily see where his best opportunity may lie, depending on how far he can travel, how much time he has, and where he is traveling from. As noted earlier under other species, many of these WPAs also have hunting for other game such as sharptail grouse, Huns, etc. The WPAs are open to all this other hunting too.

In addition to the tremendous opportunities on the above lands and waters, numerous GMAs offer fine waterfowl hunting. Of those already dealt with under foregoing upland species, the following, listed alphabetically, are important: Antelope Creek; Bald Hill; Beaver Creek; Black Swan; Cedar Lake; Crete Slough; Deep Water Creek; deTrobriand; Douglas Creek; Fullers Lake; Heart Butte; Hille; Hofflund; Horsehead; Hyatt Slough; Knox Slough (except during low water); Koldok; Krieser Lake; Lake Legreid; Lake Washington; Lehr; Logan Co.; Magnolia; McKenzie Slough; Meszaros Slough; Mud Lake; Oahe; Ray Holland Marsh; Seth Gordon Marsh; Schudar; Snake Creek; Stack Slough; Swan Lake; Tewaukon; Valley City; Van Hook; Wakopa; Wild Rice; Wolf Creek.

There are some other GMAs not so far mentioned that are particularly important for waterfowl. Small (seventy-eight-acre) Upham GMA (52) is a goose pass located in McHenry Co., northeast of Upham near the northern county border on State 14. Many small lakes and sloughs set up as GMAs offer duck shooting and some goose shooting. These are in size anywhere from a few acres to a couple hundred.

Briefly they are: Ashley GMA (53), McIntosh Co. near Ashley (a duck pass); Balta GMA (54), Pierce Co. south of Balta; Blue Ridge GMA (55), Williams Co. northeast of Appam; Buffalo Lake GMA (56), over 400 acres, Pierce Co. west of Esmond; Bunker Lake GMA (57), Burleigh Co. northwest of Wing; Camp Lake GMA (58), McIntosh Co. out of Ashley; Chase Lake GMA (59), Stutsman Co. southwest of Woodworth; Clausen Springs GMA (60), Barnes Co. near Hastings; Charles C. Cook GMA (61), Walsh Co. near Edinburg; Golden Lake GMA (62), Steele Co. northeast of Finley; Green Lake GMA (63), McIntosh Co. near Wishek; Kisselberry Lake GMA (64), McIntosh Co. near Ashley; Lake Patricia GMA (65),

Morton Co. near Flasher; Lake Williams GMA (66), Kidder Co. near Lake Williams; McGregor Dam GMA (67), Williams Co. near McGregor; McIntosh Co. GMA (68), McIntosh Co. southeast of Lehr; McVille GMA (69), Nelson Co. near McVille; Minnewaukan GMA (70), Benson Co. out of Flora; Overbeck Slough GMA (71), Eddy Co. northwest of McHenry; Palermo GMA (72), Mountrail Co. near Palermo; Rice Lake GMA (73), Burleigh Co. north of Sterling; Rusten Slough GMA (74), Foster Co. southwest of Grace City; Short Creek GMA (75), Burke Co. near Columbus; Sibley Lake GMA (76), Griggs Co. near Binford; Smishek Lake GMA (77) Burke Co. north of Powers Lake; Storm Creek GMA (78), Morton Co. northwest of New Salem; Sweetbriar Lake GMA (79) (888 acres), Morton Co. near Judson; Taayer Lake GMA (80), Sargent Co. east of Oakes.

COOTS, SNIPE, RAILS, WOODCOCK

Coots are very abundant on all of the sloughs and the reedy lakes listed above for other waterfowl. They are modestly popular with hunters. Some seasons it is estimated that 20,000 or more are shot.

Jacksnipe get little attention but all of the pond and marsh and mud-flat locations on the WPAs and GMAs offer fair to good snipe hunting. Hunters who will concentrate on this sport can find plenty of it on these public lands. There is no open season on woodcock or rails.

DEER

Whitetail deer range over the entire state. Mule deer are found in the southwest. The state is divided into a number of Units with various seasonal regulations. In some any deer is legal, in others only whitetails are legal, or a specified number of permits is offered by drawing, or only antlered bucks may be taken. Thus one needs to read the laws carefully when planning a hunt. Mule deer permits are usually limited, to control the harvest of this species. During a recent season, for example, 7950 were offered by public drawing.

Annual deer kill in the aggregate averages around 25,000 animals, with modest variation up and down, depending on permits available and on weather. Hunter success percentage is excellent. On the overall picture it often runs as high as 60 to 70 percent. In any-deer Units 75 percent is a fairly standard figure for success. In bucks-only hunting 50 percent is average. The prairie and river-bottom hunters usually score a bit higher than those in spots like the wooded Turtle Mountains.

Many habitat changes have greatly altered the deer picture in North Dakota over a period of years, and they are just now becoming more emphatically apparent. The huge impoundments on the Missouri wiped out, as they slowly filled, thousands of acres of the best deer habitat. Soil Bank lands once with numerous deer are now mostly back into agricultural production. Timber clearing in wooded areas such as the Turtle Mountains and Pembina Hills has decimated much habitat. While deer, whitetails particularly, are not in real danger, their stable populations have shifted and are shifting more and more to permanent habitats of woodland, brushy areas, and marshes. Such areas, rather than the Soil Bank lands that have held many deer over past seasons, are the spots for hunters to seek.

In general the public lands have quality deer hunting. The National Grasslands in the west ("Pheasants") should not be overlooked. Sharp hunters will keep tabs, too, on some of the National Refuges, such as those for waterfowl. On some of the large ones deer hunts are held periodically when populations need cropping, and these hunts offer high success. The Waterfowl Production Areas have some good deer hunting. While many of these are of small size, quite a few are in tracts of 400, 600, 800, 1200 to 1750 acres. These larger ones are the best bet and can be spotted on the map mentioned previously in the front part of this chapter.

Many of the GMAs have good deer populations. The larger and medium-sized tracts will of course have advantages. Of those so far mentioned under other species, here, alphabetically and by species where first mentioned, are the ones offering best opportunities: Antelope Creek; Dawson; Heart Butte; Hille; Hofflund, Hyatt Slough; Lehr; Logan Co.; McKenzie Slough; Morton Co.; Oahe; Riverdale; Tobacco Garden under "Pheasants." Bald Hill; Beaver Creek; Lake Washington; Snake Creek; Wells Co.; Wolf Creek under "Sharptail Grouse." Clifford; Pembina Hills; Tongue River; Wakopa under "Ruffed Grouse." Fullers Lake under "Hungarian Partridge" and Rice Lake under "Waterfowl."

There are two GMAs of modest size in Ransom Co. not so far noted that offer some deer hunting. One is Fort Ransom GMA (81) west of Fort Ransom. The other is Mirror Pool GMA (82), seven miles southwest of Leonard.

ANTELOPE

North Dakota antelope range is throughout the western half of the state, with the most animals by far found in the far west and southwest, from McKenzie Co. and western Dunn Co., south to the border through Bowman and west Adams Cos. Although antelope hunting regulations are subject to annual change, for some time now gun hunting has been restricted to residents, although nonresidents might hunt with a bow. Landowners in an open area may apply each year for a permit. Only those nonlandowner residents who have not had a permit for the last five years are eligible.

During a fairly recent severe winter many antelope were lost but the herd is slowly building up again. The first season in half a century was allowed in 1951. There were at that time less than 4000 antelope in the state. By 1964, even with fairly liberal numbers of permits each season, the herd had built up to an estimated 14,000. That winter a devastating loss occurred, with only approximately 6000 animals left. Nonetheless, carefully controlled hunting has continued, with 1200 animals harvested in 1965. The fall of 1967 saw 1901 permits issued and since then slow recovery is being made. It is doubtful that North Dakota can ever be one of the top pronghorn states, but undoubtedly limited hunting can continue.

Some of the best of the range is in the National Grasslands region of the southwest. The major share of the hunting, however, is on private lands and each hunter must make his own contacts, if he is fortunate enough to get a permit.

SQUIRRELS

Squirrels are not very important game in North Dakota. It is estimated that less than 3000 hunters annually hunt them, and only 6000 to 10,000 are harvested. Almost all are taken in the east. Cass Co. on the southeastern border accounts for almost half the kill, and Richland Co. below it (the southeasternmost county) turns up nearly a fourth of the harvest. The GMAs in these counties should be checked out by squirrel hunters. However, on public lands the most prominent squirrel hunting is farther west, on huge Oahe GMA ("Pheasant"). The Turtle Mountains also have squirrels, and varying numbers occur along most wooded stream bottoms of the state.

RABBITS

There are three varieties: cottontails, whitetailed jacks, snowshoe hares. Rabbits are not protected in North Dakota. Though plentiful, hunting interest varies. The outsized whitetailed jacks turn white in winter and are much sought as fur animals. There has long been a good market for their skins, when pelted in the cold months after they have changed coat to white. Early settlers considered them good eating. A few residents still do. They range statewide in prairie situations, are not seen to any extent in wooded regions. There are a few blacktailed jacks in the southwest.

Cottontails range widely, are found in fair abundance on numerous of the public tracts already noted under various species. Heart Butte GMA, Oahe GMA, and Riverdale GMA, all described under "Pheasant," are good locations for cottontails.

The snowshoe hare requires wooded habitat. It is not especially plentiful because of the modest amount of requisite terrain. The ruffed grouse country is in general snowshoe country. This means the Turtle Mountains and the Pembina Hills. Clifford GMA, Tongue River GMA, and Wakopa GMA are the best spots.

OTHER ANIMALS

Coyotes range statewide, are most abundant in the southwest, with a fair population also east of the Missouri and along it, and another in the northern counties in the Turtle Mountains and Pembina Hills. But coyotes are not, by standards elsewhere, especially plentiful in the state. The Grasslands and GMAs in the regions mentioned offer some hunting.

Red foxes are abundant, gray foxes have more recently come into the state and are confined chiefly at present to the southeast. Many thousands of foxes are taken annually, the bulk of them red foxes. They are found throughout the state, and on almost all of the public lands. Calling, or hunting with hounds, or tracking on snow are favorite sports of many residents.

Bobcats are not generally plentiful, or of importance. However, calling enthusiasts can find a fair number of bobcats in the southwest along the Little Missouri, also along the Heart, Missouri, and Cannonball rivers, and now and then a few along the Red River, which is the eastern border.

Raccoons were not originally present over all of the state, but now are. The prairie pothole areas and the wooded stream bottoms of the east and central portions of the state have the largest number. Raccoon hunting has never become very popular here.

Hunting the red fox is far and away the most important predator sport, and is growing in popularity. So far, anything goes regarding hunting methods. Foxes are hunted from planes, and currently there are numerous snowsled enthusiasts chasing them. They are chased on prairies with old hunting cars and shot from the cars. Whether or not these methods should be considered sporting, they are popular in North Dakota and to date not illegal.

A NOTE ON BIGHORN SHEEP

Original bighorns have been gone from North Dakota for many years. In 1956, eighteen were obtained from British Columbia and held for some time in a large pasture. They increased and some were moved to other holding pastures. A few have escaped from these pastures. At present there are upwards of a hundred bighorns in the state. It is hoped they may spark a population that in time will be of huntable proportions. Interested hunters should closely watch this experiment.

REGULATIONS

Game laws pertaining to seasons, bag and possession limits, areas to be hunted, special hunts, license fees all may have numerous changes from year to year. For current regulations, and for other specific queries, write to: North Dakota Game & Fish Department, Bismarck, North Dakota 58501.

SOUTH DAKOTA

Like its sister state to the north, South Dakota is a rectangle of transition from the rich plains of the Midwest to the rough country leading to the Rockies. But it differs in terrain from North Dakota by becoming exceedingly rough in portions of the west, where the oldest mountains of the U.S., the pine-forested Black Hills, are located, with 7242-foot Harney Peak the highest point east of the Rockies.

South Dakota borders Minnesota and Iowa on the east, Nebraska on the south, both Montana and Wyoming on the west. Its topographic features are distinct. The eastern half of the state, spoken of as the East River area by natives, is rich plains soil famed for its grain crops—wheat, oats, rye, flax. The western half, the West River area, is rolling to rugged and broken, and it is cattle and sheep country. The dividing line that splits the state down the center is the Missouri River. But this big, lazy river is no longer just that in South Dakota. Huge dams—for example Randall at the southern border, Oahe near the capitol city of Pierre—have made South Dakota's long stretch of the Missouri vast lakes that reach north to south from border to border.

Along the eastern border there are numerous small lakes and potholes. West of the Missouri there are few. Here numerous slow tributaries of the Missouri cut the rough land, and in the southwest, where the Black Hills lie, the streams are swift and there are now a number of reservoirs of fair size. The Black Hills are heavily forested with pine, in contrast to most of the rest of the state, excepting small portions of the northwest. Portions of the Black Hills can be considered very close to wilderness, even though the region is heavily touristed. Parts of the nearby Badlands are also wilderness in their barren way, and there are areas of broken country on privately owned West River lands that are also remote.

The state is over 90 percent in farm and ranch lands. Roads are good, but not in such an abundance of excellence as in more heavily populated states. In the east, where the major share of population centers, they are plentiful, and main arteries—at least five U.S. highways running north-south and five more east-west—cross the entire state. But west of the river main roads are few. Side roads are quite good throughout the state, but hunters are well advised that during wet times unpaved secondaries can be troublesome. Air transport is good to the main cities, such as Sioux Falls, Pierre, Rapid City. Most small cities have airports. But there is a lot of wide-open space in this state and it is not easy to fly commercial lines to just anywhere.

This is in its way refreshing. And the reason of course is that South Dakota's population is extremely low. At this writing there are only an estimated 675,000 people here, spread thinly except for the few cities over a large land area, 77,047 square miles. Distances are long, roughly 350 straight-line miles across the state east-west and 200 north-south. Hunting is far from crowded. License sales of late have averaged around 120,000.

Of these, about 15,000 or less are nonresidents, the majority of them pheasant hunters.

Hunting is excellent and varied, notwithstanding the drastic pheasant decline that has worried the Plains states for several seasons and that will probably continue now indefinitely to be troublesome. Among game species there are the pheasants for which South Dakota has long been famous; sharptail grouse, prairie chickens, bobwhite quail, Hungarian partridge are all on the list. So are doves and jacksnipe. Waterfowl, both ducks and geese, are abundant, but nonresidents should be aware that they are excluded from this shooting. Wild turkeys roam restricted ranges. Deer, both whitetails and mule deer, are plentiful, antelope modestly so. Some elk and mountain goats are in the Black Hills. Rabbits are plentiful, and there are foxes, raccoons, coyotes, and bobcats.

Even though most of the land is privately owned, finding a place to hunt in South Dakota is not difficult. The Game Department has for many years had an active purchase and development program on lands acquired. Approximately 240,000 acres of dry lands and 160,000 of meandered lakes are in the state ownership managed for hunters. There are some 300 tracts of such lands open to public hunting. Most are small, from 40 to 300 acres. A few are over 1000 and several over 3000. They are well distributed over the state. A folder and map titled "South Dakota Guide to Public Shooting Areas" can be obtained from the Department of Game, Fish and Parks, address at chapter end. As this is written, some extensive updating is being done and a series of maps are in preparation that will show the combined state and federal public lands. Much Bureau of Land Management land is open to hunting, particularly in the West River area. The maps above will show these lands.

In the eastern half of South Dakota there are well over a hundred plots of federal Waterfowl Production Areas. These are open to hunting, and many have game other than waterfowl, even though management is aimed at producing waterfowl. A map and brochure, "Guide to Federal Waterfowl Production Areas, South Dakota," is available either from the Game Department, or from the Regional Director, Bureau of Sport Fisheries and Wildlife, 1006 West Lake Street, Minneapolis, Minnesota 55408.

In the southwest is the huge Black Hills National Forest (1) with well over a million acres of public hunting land. Rapid City, Custer, Deadwood, Lead, Spearfish are all key towns here, and a number of U.S. highways— 18, 385, 16, 14, 212, 85, Interstate 90—all lead to the area. This is one of the most important hunting grounds in the state and the largest public one. Details and maps of this Forest can be obtained from the Forest Supervisor, Custer, South Dakota.

Up in the northwest, in Harding Co., there are six blocks, most of them small but one of fair size, of the Custer National Forest (2). This Forest contains over a million acres, but is, excepting these minor blocks, in Montana. The Supervisor of the Custer NF can be reached for details and maps of the South Dakota tracts by writing him at Billings, Montana. U.S. 85 is a main north-south access through Harding Co., and State 20 east-west crosses a main block of the Forest.

In addition to the Forests, there are 864,268 acres in National Grasslands. One large block, the Grand River NG (3), is located in Perkins Co. in the northwest with main access via U.S. 12 and State 73. Another is in the extreme southwest, below the towns of Edgemont and Hot Springs, with

U.S. 18 and 385 the main routes. But this huge block runs on north and east, too, and comprises the Buffalo Gap NG (4). A third Grasslands tract is Fort Pierre (5), south of the capital city, with U.S. 83 crossing it. For information and maps, use the following addresses: Grand River NG, Federal Building, Missoula, Montana 59801; Buffalo Gap and Fort Pierre, Federal Center Building 85, Denver, Colorado 80225. Detailed maps of the Grasslands are important to hunters, for many parcels of private lands are interspersed. Although the federal lands are marked with yellow and black signs, these could in some instances be missed.

Over one-tenth of South Dakota's total area—some 8400 square miles— is in Indian Reservations. These lands are open to public hunting, but one must have a Reservation license in addition to a South Dakota license. The state has little control over Indian lands and the Tribal Councils may close such areas as they desire. Since Indians are permitted to hunt year-round, the quality of hunting on Indian lands may not always be high.

There is a long tradition of private-land hunting by permission in South Dakota and ordinarily it is not difficult, particularly away from crowded areas, to obtain permission. There are also a number of farmers and ranchers who take pheasant hunters on a daily fee basis, furnishing board and room and sometimes guide and transport. Chambers of Commerce in various towns in the best pheasant areas are good contacts for locating such accommodations. A few ranchers also guide deer hunters and antelope hunters.

Accommodations in motels, hotels, etc., while not as abundant as in states with larger populations, are nonetheless not too difficult to obtain. All of the towns and villages along main highways offer ample opportunities. Pheasant hunters in particular, however, should attempt to make reservations ahead, especially for opening of season. Antelope hunters should do likewise, because of the spare human population in much of the antelope range.

Campers find few problems. There are a number of State Parks and Recreation Areas. A guide to these may be obtained from the Game, Fish and Parks Department. Camping is allowed in many Roadside Parks in South Dakota. There are numerous campgrounds in the National Forests, others along the Corps of Engineers reservoirs, and there are a number of city and county parks. The Grasslands, while not developed for camping, can be utilized by those who need no hook-ups or other facilities.

Weather in South Dakota may be extremely varied during hunting seasons. In September it is hot. During pheasant season it may be light-wool-shirt weather but it may also be rainy and chill, even at times with snow. As fall wears on the weather is cold, often severely so, and winds across the open areas can be bitter. Down jackets and warm headgear are mandatory.

The most used ammunition in South Dakota is that needed for pheasants (No. 6 or No. 7½) and waterfowl (No. 4 for ducks, No. 2 or 4 for geese). Pheasant loads can be utilized for grouse and Huns, the lighter ones even for quail. Turkeys of course require heavy shot and a highbase loading. Standard deer rifles are needed, with attention to flat trajectory for the open country. This is true for antelope, too. Rifles such as the .270, .243, .30/06 are good examples.

PHEASANT

Although the introduced ringnecked pheasant has done well over a large portion of the U.S., it found its most perfect habitat years ago in

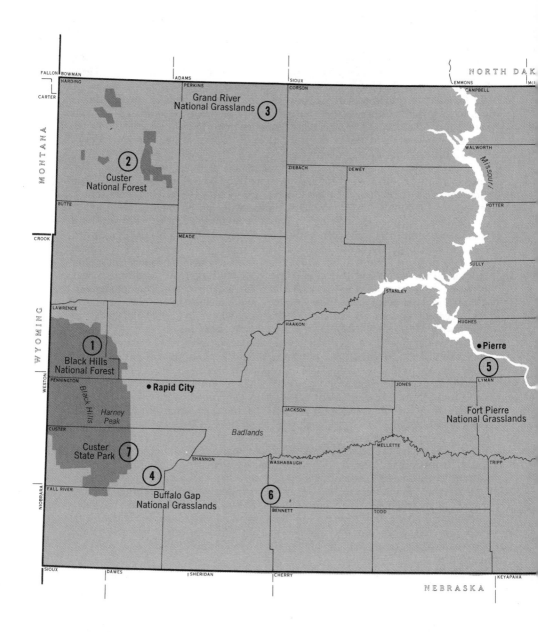

KEY TO HUNTING AREAS

1. Black Hills NF
2. Custer NF
3. Grand River National Grasslands
4. Buffalo Gap National Grasslands
5. Fort Pierre National Grasslands
6. Pine Ridge Indian Reservation
7. Custer SP

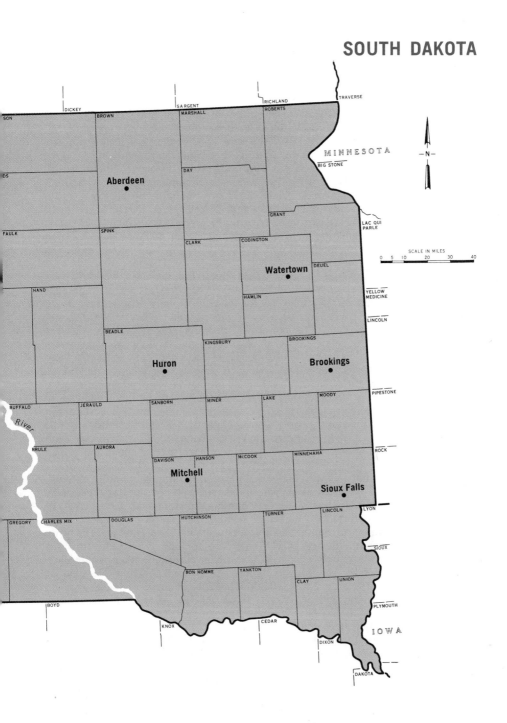

SOUTH DAKOTA

MINNESOTA

- N -

SCALE IN MILES
0 5 10   20   30   40

DICKEY SARGENT RICHLAND TRAVERSE
SON BROWN MARSHALL ROBERTS

DS DAY BIG STONE

Aberdeen

FAULK SPINK CLARK CODINGTON GRANT LAC QUI PARLE

Watertown DEUEL

HAND HAMLIN YELLOW MEDICINE

BEADLE LINCOLN

KINGSBURY BROOKINGS

Huron **Brookings**

BUFFALO JERAULD SANBORN MINER LAKE MOODY PIPESTONE

River

BRULE AURORA ROCK

DAVISON HANSON McCOOK MINNEHAHA

Mitchell

Sioux Falls

GREGORY CHARLES MIX DOUGLAS HUTCHINSON TURNER LINCOLN LYON

SIOUX

BON HOMME YANKTON

CLAY UNION PLYMOUTH

BOYD

KNOX CEDAR I O W A

DIXON

DAKOTA

South Dakota and prospered phenomenally. South Dakota became and remained the Pheasant Capital of the World, just as it billed itself. During early pheasant days the change in land use, with agriculture making crops available and plowing up grasslands, was disastrous to prairie grouse but created a perfect pheasant habitat. No one knows how many pheasants South Dakota had, but they were actually sometimes in nuisance proportions. Some estimates place the peak flocks at upwards of fifty million birds!

This was in the early 1940s. The face of the state was being progressively changed by intensified agriculture, but Soil Bank lands now added quality habitat as other portions were cultivated. However, there was a steady decline in birds until by 1947, due to a combination of adversities, but pheasant population was, South Dakotans thought, at "bottom," with an estimated seven million. Over the next fifteen years the birds followed what had come to be known as a normal three-year cycle—two good years and a poor one. Population went up to around eleven million. Then it began dropping again, and kept on dropping, finally hitting somewhere around a drastic low of two million in 1966.

They have recovered to some extent since, but the drop was a serious matter, even for the economy of the state. Where once tens of thousands of nonresident hunters swarmed in for pheasants, only a relatively small number now came. There have been many surveys and studies of the pheasant debacle in South Dakota. The consensus among topnotch biologists is that change in land use is the truly important factor. Soil Bank lands have now been put back at work. Probably, with U.S. population growing, there will never again be as much land resting. Clean farming adds to difficulties. Pheasants require grassy habitat as well as croplands. This is diminishing in South Dakota. It is believed that if landowners will plan their practices to allow a 7 or 8 percent increase in permanent nesting cover, the state can maintain a basic pheasant population of eight or ten million birds. But if the agricultural face of the state continues to change at its present rate with no consideration for pheasants, peak populations will not be much more than half that.

All of this is not to imply that good pheasant hunting is done for in South Dakota. Actually it is excellent still today. It will continue so for many years. There will undoubtedly be less hunting pressure and thus plenty of birds to satisfy the curtailed number of hunters. But the days of unbelievable pheasant populations in South Dakota are probably gone forever. The pressure is automatically adjusted by the bird crop for any given year. In 1966, for example, there were only about 66,000 resident pheasant hunters in the state, and 6000 nonresidents. The kill was slightly above 400,000. Three years earlier there had been a total of over 200,000 pheasant hunters, 68,000 of them nonresidents, and the kill was over three million! A recent season saw what may become a general average, some 80,000 residents, 15,000 nonresidents, and a kill of 700,000.

Pheasants are found throughout almost all of the state. But the West River region is by no means as good as the East River range. There are spotty concentrations west of the Missouri but always the peak populations have been east of the river. In this eastern half of the state, the prime range is in the southern three-fourths. In peak years there are a good many birds north of U.S. 12, which runs east-west through Aberdeen. But by and large the heaviest concentrations are found some distance below that arbitrary line. The region along U.S. 212—with key cities Watertown and Redfield—is excellent. So is the one along U.S. 14 through Brookings and Huron, and farther south along U.S. 16, Sioux Falls, Mitchell. Also, very generally speaking, the eastern half of the East River region has heavier concentrations of birds than the western half. The cities and routes named above have for years been famous ones among pheasant hunters, and the cream of the pheasant range. With the bird population now seemingly fairly stable at a much lower level, these key spots are still good bets for visitors.

Public Shooting Areas are so numerous that each cannot be individually located. However, selecting some key towns and cities, and then placing these by the counties in which they are located, followed by the number of PSAs in that county, can give a prospective pheasant hunter a good picture. Keep in mind, too, that most landowners will give permission if properly approached, providing they are not leasing out hunting rights on their lands.

Faulk Co. is in the west-central part of the East River country. The town of Faulkton is on U.S. 212 about centered in the county. This county has long had an excellent population of birds, but may be classed as on the western and northern edge of the best range. There is one PSA in this county, in the northeastern corner near the Scatterwood Lakes. To the east is Spink Co., with the key city Redfield at the junction of U.S. 212 and 281. There are a half dozen PSAs in this county, with nearest towns Tulare (2), Redfield, Northville (2), Conde.

Next county to the east is Clark. U.S. 212 bisects it, with the town of Clark about halfway across. There are over twenty PSAs in this county. In the next county east, Codington, where the city of Watertown, long pheasant-famous, is located, there are eighteen PSAs. Deuel Co. east of Watertown, and on the Minnesota border, has eleven PSAs.

Moving back to the west again and taking the next swath of counties from west to east, Hand Co., south of Faulkton Co., has eight PSA tracts. U.S. 14 crosses this county, and the town of Miller is centered, at the intersect of U.S. 14 and State 45. Next eastward is Beadle Co., with Huron on U.S. 14 the key city. There are seven PSAs here. Kingsbury Co., still moving eastward along U.S. 14, with DeSmet a key town has a dozen PSAs. Hamlin Co., north of it and just south of the city of Watertown, has at least eighteen; U.S. 81 crosses this county north-south. And east of Kingsbury Co. on U.S. 14 and bordering Minnesota is Brookings Co., with the city of Brookings a key location. There are seven PSAs here.

The next tier of counties to the south lie along east-west State 34. Reading west to east again, Jerauld Co. has a half-dozen Areas, Sanborn Co. has two, Miner County has two, Lake Co. has over a dozen. Moody has two. Along U.S. 16 in the next tier south, Aurora Co. has seven, Davison has one, Hanson has two, McCook eight, Minnehaha ten.

While this is by no means all of the good pheasant territory, it is the center of the highest population area. One planning a trip can easily find in the counties mentioned the numerous public lands. It is an excellent idea, however, to acquire the "Guide to Public Shooting Areas" mentioned earlier in the chapter. Almost all of the PSAs over the state have their quota of pheasants. Also, up in the northeast there are a great many PSAs managed primarily for waterfowl, which see. But these also offer good to excellent pheasant hunting. Brown, Marshall, Roberts, and Day Cos. have among them approximately a hundred public tracts. In addition, there are many federal Waterfowl Production Areas, noted earlier. These will be reviewed under waterfowl. There is good pheasant hunting on many of them.

SAGE GROUSE

The big sage grouse, native to South Dakota, is found on the sage flats of the far western part of the state. At one time very plentiful, this grouse has declined here as it has over much of its range. Nowadays when seasons are held they are only token affairs. For example, the current one at this writing lasts from August 26 through September 1, with 2 birds per day allowed and 4 in possession. Only the best of remaining range is open. This open portion is all of Harding Co., the northwesternmost county, and to the south of it, that part of Butte Co. north of Highway U.S. 212. This takes in all of Butte Co. except the extreme south and a triangle of the southeast.

A check of BLM lands should be made in this range for possible public hunting opportunities. There are also two PSAs shown on the guide map One is in Harding Co., near Buffalo which is on U.S. 85. The other is in Butte Co., north of Newell, which is at the junction of U.S. 212 and State 79. Check with the Game Department for other possibilities on their new maps of public lands of the West River area, which will be issued as they are completed. Permission on private lands in this region is not difficult to obtain, and the sage grouse gets so little attention that hunting is not crowded.

SHARPTAIL GROUSE AND PRAIRIE CHICKEN

The sharptail grouse was native to South Dakota but the prairie chicken was not. The chicken moved in with settlers in the eastern part of the state, and soon became extremely abundant. But the chicken, which did best in prairie grasslands somewhat broken by the plow, moved westward as hunting for market decimated the flocks and as the grasslands disappeared under cultivation. The sharptail is a bird that needs grasslands that are at best lightly grazed. Today both birds are found west of the Missouri and except for a narrow strip on the east side of the river in both north and south, are hunted entirely in West River country.

The sharptail is the most abundant. When natives in this state speak of "grouse" this is invariably the bird they mean. Conceivably the prairie chicken, which is only in fair supply, might deserve full or almost full protection. The problem arises because both birds are found in the same range to some extent and hunting would be difficult if one were not on the game list, for as they flush they are not always instantly easy to distinguish.

Because the two species are hunted together, separate records on kill are not available. An average aggregate kill runs from 70,000 to slightly over 100,000 annually. The best of the prairie chicken range is in the south-central part of the state. The main sharptail range is described as the eastern two-thirds of the West River country.

Grouse seasons are opened by zones, and there are at present three. Limits are usually the same in all, but seasons of differing length apply. By and large the best grouse range is in Zone 1, which has the longest season. It takes in a small amount of territory east of the river, but covers the eastern two-thirds of the West River country mostly north of the Cheyenne River. The counties are as follows: Perkins, Corson, Ziebach and Dewey on the west side of the Missouri, the western half of Campbell, Walworth, Potter on the east side of the Missouri. The Grand River National Grassland (see early part of chapter) is in Perkins and Corson Cos. This is an excellent grouse hunting ground. Perkins Co. has four PSAs, near the towns of Sorum, Bison, and Lemmon. Dewey Co. has three, near Isabel, Firesteel, Timber Lake. Across the river, Walworth Co. has two in the open area, near Glenham. Landowners are fairly receptive to requests by grouse hunters in this lightly settled area.

Zone 2, which is almost on a par with Zone 1, covers the region west of the Missouri, south of the Cheyenne, and east of the Black Hills. As noted, much of the better chicken range is here. The counties, beginning at the upper left and scanning as one reads a printed page, are: Haakon, Stanley, then Jackson, Jones, Lyman; third tier, Washabaugh, Mellette; bottom tier, Shannon, Bennett, Todd, Tripp, Gregory. Of these, Shannon, Washabaugh, and Todd are entirely Indian Reservation—the Pine Ridge Reservoir and the Rose Bud Reservoir. To the north and along the river in Lyman Co. there is also some Indian Reservation, the Lower Brule. The Reservations, as noted, require extra licenses and may or may not be opened by the tribes. On the east side of the river most of Buffalo Co. is open (it is Reservation in the western half), and parts of Brule and Charles Mix Co. are open.

The Fort Pierre National Grassland is west of the Lower Brule Indian Reservation (see front material in chapter) and is a good grouse spot. Lyman Co. has half a dozen PSAs; Bennett Co. has one near Martin; Tripp Co. has seven, with key towns Milboro, Clearfield, Winner, and Hamill; and Gregory Co. has three, near Burke, Herrick, and Gregory. On the east side of the river there is a PSA in the open portion of Brule Co., and several near the river in Charles Mix.

Grouse Zone 3 has the shortest season and the fewest birds, although there are spots that are very good here. It covers everything west of the two Zones described above. Hunters will do well to check out BLM lands in this area. Other public lands worthwhile for prairie grouse are not abundant, but permission is not difficult to obtain on private lands.

QUAIL

There is a modest amount of hunting for bobwhite quail in the southeastern part of the state. There are spots of fair abundance along the Missouri in that region, in fact on both sides of the river. The kill is not high, and clean farming practices are swiftly depleting bobwhite range. At the present time the open counties west of the river are Tripp and Gregory. U.S. 18 and 183 are key routes here. PSAs in these two counties are noted immediately above under "Grouse."

East of the river a substantial area is open. The counties are: Charles Mix (see "Grouse" above re public lands), Bon Homme, Yankton, Clay, Union. These four counties all lie along the southern border to the southeast corner of the state, and all border the Missouri along the Lewis and Clark impoundment. Bon Homme Co. has two PSAs, near Scotland and Tyndall. Yankton Co. has three with key towns Irene, Utica, Volin. Here again, in all the quail counties, hunters who ask politely will usually find private lands with good shooting.

There has been some stocking of western quail, the valley quail species, in the southwestern part of the state near the Nebraska line. This was begun in 1961, with the hope that these quail would establish themselves and spread possibly over a good portion of western South Dakota. They are not presently hunted, and their future is still questionable.

HUNGARIAN PARTRIDGE

The Hun was stocked many years ago in South Dakota, in the hope that it would to some extent replace in agricultural areas the sharptail and prairie chicken, which were so to speak in retreat before the plow. The first season was held in 1937. The birds have been hunted ever since. They are not truly abundant and the kill is low. A few are taken incidentally by pheasant hunters and other bird hunters. It is doubtful if more than a couple of thousand hunters on the average purposely hunt Huns each season, and a kill of 5000 is considered average, although trustworthy kill figures are difficult to obtain.

The open counties are all east of the Missouri and in the first two tiers along the northern border. They are at present reading left to right: first tier, Campbell, McPherson, Brown, Marshall, Roberts; second tier, Walworth, Edmunds, Day. There is a PSA in Campbell Co. near Mound City. McPherson Co. has over a dozen, with locations around Hillview, Long Lake, Eureka, Leola. Brown Co. has nineteen with the towns of Hecla, Columbia, Claremont, Westport some of the keys. Marshall Co. has upwards of thirty, Roberts has at least twenty. As mentioned under "Pheasant," these are primarily waterfowl areas, but Huns are found here and there on them. Walworth Co. has several PSAs near Hoven, Java, Glenham; Edmunds Co. has some in the vicinity of Bowdle and Ipswich; Day Co. has almost thirty, again managed chiefly for waterfowl but worth checking for Huns. The Waterfowl Production Areas (see "Waterfowl") should also be tried in the northeast. There are many, and they often provide other game in addition to waterfowl.

CHUKAR PARTRIDGE

Chukars were stocked beginning in 1960 and 1961 with heavy plantings in Harding Co., the northwesternmost county. The bird appears to have precariously established itself there, and to some extent in Washabaugh Co. also. In 1965 a season with a very few permits was held in the latter county. Three birds were killed. In 1968 a thirty-permit test season was allowed in the northwest quarter of Harding Co. There may be further test seasons but the future for chukars here does not look encouraging.

RUFFED GROUSE

The ruffed grouse is found in the Black Hills, but only in very limited numbers. The last season held on the bird was in 1965. At this time the department hopes to introduce blue grouse to the same area. There is no prediction on success of this venture.

MOURNING DOVES

Doves range over most of South Dakota. The eastern half of the state, because grain farming is centered here, has the greatest dove population. However, much of the West River country also has good numbers of doves. Shelter belts, and small stands of brush or trees, particularly those on cattle ranges where there are windmills, offer excellent spots for doves west of the river. In the east the watering places and shelter belts in grain areas get dove concentrations.

South Dakota has only begun, as this is written, to experiment with dove hunting. There has long been strong sentiment in the state against dove hunting, and the dove has been considered a song bird and hardly sporting as a target. The federal authorities have continued to offer South Dakota a season of sixty days or longer, but until recently it had always been turned down. At last a brief season of five days was accepted by the state as a trial. Hunters were few but those who did hunt were enthused. More recently a season of September 1 through 8 was approved. Whether or not South Dakota will in due time accept long dove seasons, or revert to ignoring the dove as a game bird, is at present questionable. Surveys have shown that there are an ample number of birds for good shooting and that no harm to the nesting surplus results. Most hunters in the state, as well as the Game Department, consider the mourning dove a wasted resource when the season remains closed.

WILD TURKEYS

Originally the eastern wild turkey ranged along portions of the Missouri River and its tributaries in South Dakota. With settlement and hard hunting, often for market, the turkeys disappeared. Over twenty years ago the Merriam's subspecies, the one native to western mountains, was introduced to the Black Hills. So far as is known, turkeys had never inhabited the Hills.

The Merriam's did very well. Some plants were made elsewhere in suitable West River habitats. During the late 1950s the turkey population reached what is now considered its full possibilities in the available range. More recently, in attempts to add to the range, plants of the Rio Grande subspecies have been made in the river bottoms of central and eastern South Dakota. The first plants of these were made in 1963.

The first trial season was held in 1954. Then in 1957 there was another open season and this has continued each fall. South Dakota was the first of the northern midwest states to offer a spring gobbler season additionally to its fall hunt. Lately fall kills have run as high as 1000-plus and as low as 400. In one recent spring season there were a few more than 1000 hunters and the kill was 230 gobblers. That is close to 25 percent success, which is very good. Some fall hunts have had success almost as high. In general the fall hunts run 15 percent to 20 percent, which is above national average. Interest is high. Some 5000 hunters try turkey hunting each season.

The Black Hills area is the major turkey range. This offers opportunity for hunting on the lands of the Black Hills National Forest, so there is little problem for hunters about finding a place to hunt. Seasons are set by counties. Presently the longest fall season is roughly six weeks, and covers Fall River and Custer Cos. in the extreme southwest, plus portions of Pennington, Lawrence and Meade Cos. immediately to the north of them. The rest of Lawrence and Meade Cos. has a shorter season. All but a small portion of the area covered by the above counties is within the National Forest.

Spring seasons vary as to open territory, but a recent one indicates an attempt to open more area to hunting. Generally the Black Hills Management Unit offers an unlimited number of licenses. This Unit is composed of all of Fall River, Custer and Lawrence Cos., and portions of Meade, Pennington and Butte Cos. Note that Butte Co. is north of the Black Hills in some of the rough West River country. Most of this land is privately owned. To the east of the Hills and the Badlands, a few licenses (thirty during the last season as this is written) are allowed in Unit 2, composed of Jackson and Washabaugh Cos. Hunters should note that all of the latter county is in the Pine Ridge Indian Reservation (6).

The eastern parts of Meade and Pennington Cos., plus parts of central-West River Ziebach and Haakon Cos. are in Unit 3 and have a modest number of spring licenses. There is a substantial amount of Indian Reservation in Ziebach Co. Other counties in other Management Units that have been offering modest numbers of spring permits are all located west of the Missouri but lying along or near it. These are, reading from north to south: Stanley (west of Pierre); Jones, Mellette; Tripp; Todd (Indian Res.); Gregory on the southern border.

To avoid any confusion for nonresidents, they are now allowed to apply for spring turkey permits, and also to hunt during the fall season when in the open area permits are not limited. Through 1966 turkey hunting was limited to residents, but with the 1967 season that restriction was removed.

WATERFOWL

South Dakota has some of the finest duck and goose hunting on the continent. For some years, however, all waterfowling in the state has been for residents only. The duck kill averages upwards of 300,000 and the goose kill approximately 50,000 annually. For resident hunters there is no problem in finding public areas on which to hunt. Principle locations are along the Missouri River and its impoundments clear across the state from north to south; the northeast quarter of the state where many scores of small lakes and potholes, as well as a number of larger lakes, are found. The southeastern quarter also has good shooting, and there are many spots west of the Missouri where wetlands are numerous. All of the river bottoms of the major streams offer from fair to excellent shooting.

Among the best counties of the northeast are, reading in tiers west to east: Brown, Marshall, Roberts; Day, Grant; Clark, Codington, Hamlin, Deuel. As noted earlier, PSAs are so numerous they cannot be individually located here. However, reference to the map ("PSA Guide") easily pinpoints them. For quick reference, here is a listing of the above counties with cues to PSA abundance. Brown Co. has 19, with principle key town located nearby as follows: Verdon, Ferney, Columbia, Claremont, Hecla, Westport. Marshall Co. has 27, based on the towns of Britton, Eden, Lake City. Roberts Co. has 23, near White Rock, Rosholt, Ortley, Wilmot, Peever, Sisseton, New Effington, Victor. Day Co. in the next tier to the south: 28, with Waubay, Lily, Webster, Roslyn, Holmquist the nearby towns. Grant Co.: Summit Lake PSA near Marvin. In the counties to the south, Clark Co. offers 31 locations near Willow Lake, Clark, Vienna, Crocker, Bradley, Naples. Codington Co.: 23 PSAs, key towns in Watertown, Florence, Wallace, Henry, South Shore. Hamlin Co.: 18, near Estelline, Hayti, Lake Norden, Bryant, Vienna, Hazel. Deuel Co.: 15 Areas, near Bemis, Astoria, Altamont, Goodwin, Brandt, Clear Lake, Tunerville, Gary.

Shooting lands along the Missouri are available on Corps of Engineers lands and on the PSAs, most of which are located along the lower portion of the river. For others, see "Pheasant," for most of the PSAs in the southeast offer waterfowl shooting too.

As important as the public lands so far mentioned are the Federal Waterfowl Production Areas. These are all open to hunting in the fall. Source of a map showing these has already been given in the introductory material in this chapter. All at present are east of the Missouri, with the concentration in the northeast and east-central part of the state. There are presently 127 of these FWPAs. They range in size from as little as 9 acres up to around 600. Most are from 50 to 200 acres.

Largest concentrations of these Areas is in Day County, which has 27, with key towns Bristol, Grenville, Holmquist, Roslyn, Waubay, Webster. Brookings Co. (east-central, with city of Brookings the key) has 12, based on Arlington, Arlington Beach, Sinai. McPherson Co. on the northern border northwest of the city of Aberdeen, has 11, surrounding Leola and Long Lake. Other counties with one to several: Aurora, Brown, Campbell, Charles Mix, Clark, Codington, Davison, Deuel, Douglas, Edmunds, Faulk, Grant, Hand, Jerauld, Lake, McCook, Marshall, Miner, Moody, Roberts, Sanborn, Spink, Walworth.

Very generally, goose shooting is best along the Missouri, and on private lands where grain is grown and where the flocks go out to feed. There is, incidentally, a growing flock of the giant Canada goose in South Dakota. These huge geese, once thought extinct and then rediscovered, are being raised at the Sand Lake National Wildlife Refuge in Brown Co. Some have been transferred to other refuges. Some counties—and hunters should note this—have recently been closed to goose hunting to protect flocks of free-flying giant Canadas. The state has high hopes of establishing a flock of these geese with a huntable surplus.

There are several National Refuges in the state devoted chiefly to water-fowl. The most important is Sand Lake, near Columbia, northeast of Aberdeen in Brown Co. This is a favorite resting spot for geese, has as many as 100,000 at a time during the fall. Surrounding private lands offer quality shooting. The public lands, federal and state, in this area also are good choices because of the nearby Refuge.

DEER

South Dakota has abundant deer and excellent hunting. Deer, mainly whitetails, range throughout the state, from the cornfields of the east to the western prairies and the forests of the Black Hills. Most of the mule deer are west of the Missouri, but even there whitetails predominate. In the East River region mule deer are scarce but not unknown. The current total deer kill averages close to 25,000 annually. Very generally the state may be divided into three sections for deer hunting: the Black Hills, the West River Prairie, the East River. In the East River area, which takes in all of the state east of the Missouri, only residents may hunt deer.

The East River area has the smallest herd and the least hunters, but the highest success percentage. It is a limited-permit area. For example, during a recent season there were 8510 permits (for rifle hunting) available, and success ran roughly 90 percent. Of the available permits each season in the East River region 50 percent are offered first to bonafide landowners and tenants, under specifications of the Game Department. Only one member of a family may apply. The other 50 percent of permits is available to other South Dakota residents. Permit allotments are on a county basis. Of the total permits, as many as 150 are for the Sand Lake National Wildlife Refuge, to keep the herd there under control.

The West River Prairie Hunt is also by permit and drawing. Some 15,000-plus permits have been up for application annually over recent seasons. Nonresidents may apply for West River Prairie Hunts. The harvest here runs as high as 11,000 deer, and the success averages around 80 percent. Much of the area is open, usually, to taking of deer of either sex. Mule deer are fairly plentiful, although whitetails, as mentioned above, are the dominant species. Permits, as in the east, are on a county basis, so many allotted for each county.

In the Black Hills area permits are not limited, and both resident and nonresident may hunt. Generally the season here is bucks-only. Because of this, and the forest cover, success is lower, around 55 percent. During one recent season 15,550 hunters took 8500 deer. Again, these are mostly white-tails. Of late, in restricted portions of the Black Hills some antlerless deer permits have been allowed.

Archery seasons differ to some extent from rifle seasons, and so do the regulations as to what deer may be taken. Archers should check the regulations, which are quite lenient.

There is little problem for deer hunters in finding a place to hunt. The Black Hills Unit includes the National Forest. The West Prairie Hunt includes the large area of National Grasslands noted early in the chapter, as well as the blocks of Custer NF in the northwest. The various PSAs already located under other species are of course open to deer hunting and most have fair to excellent opportunity. In addition, hunter-landowner relationships are good and most landowners will allow hunting when properly approached. Many West Prairie ranchers now take deer hunters on a board-and-room arrangement plus a guided hunt, and many that do not furnish accommodations will guide hunters for a fee. In some places here there are several hundred square miles set up by cooperating ranchers to protect the game and thus offer trophy hunting, guided, at established fees. Check with the Game Department for exact locations of such co-ops, and also for information on guides and ranchers who furnish board and room. By and large, in the West Prairie region, the river bottom breaks furnish the best hunting. Streams such as the Bad, White, and Cheyenne are typical, and excellent.

Some of the best trophy counties of the West Prairie are Stanley, Haakon, Jackson, and eastern Pennington. These are all east of the Black Hills in the area reaching toward and bordering the River. In Perkins Co. of the north-western area there have been attempts recently to increase mule deer and reduce whitetails. There have even been local "Big Doe" contests during the any-sex hunting to assist this program.

East of the Missouri River, where only residents may hunt, the scores of state and federal lands already noted under other species—the PSAs and the FWPAs—have fair deer populations. Private-land hunting is, however, best. Because the number of permits for non-landowners is not large, there is very little difficulty in arranging a hunt. As a rule the counties of the extreme northeast offer the greatest number of permits.

ELK

The Black Hills has a small elk herd, estimated at possibly 500. Intermittently a season is opened to crop the surplus. The 72,000 acres of Custer State Park (7) also has an elk herd and an occasional season is opened within the Park itself. Wind Cave National Park in the southern Black Hills uses a unique method to avoid hunting within the Park but still to get rid of surplus elk. Shortly before elk season in the National Forest area, a drive is made and a stipulated number of elk—100 during a recent fall—are driven into the Forest. Number of permits allowed is then judged by the cropping that needs to be done in the Forest, plus the extra elk. For example, in 1967 only 130 permits were allowed, but in 1968 a drive from Wind Cave NP made 350 permits possible.

These token elk hunts are for residents only. Success varies. Over three seasons, tabulations were as follows: 120 permits, 72 elk killed; 300 permits, 92 elk; 130 permits, 70 elk. Residents interested in drawing for elk should contact the Game Department for information as to when the applications will be accepted. The season is usually in mid-September for approximately two weeks.

ANTELOPE

In early days there were hundreds of thousands of antelope in South Dakota but market hunting and other influences cut them down to near zero. Careful management has brought the pronghorn back almost from extinction in South Dakota. Today there is a substantial huntable surplus. Only residents are allowed to hunt during the gun hunt, although nonresidents may hunt during archery season. Almost all of the hunting is west of the Missouri, and the season is fairly brief, nine or ten days in late September and early October. Because of careful surveys and management, number of permits may differ quite drastically from season to season. For example, over a recent six-year period, numbers of permits were: 8465; 7470; 8750; 4965; 6310; 3230. Severe winter blizzards can be extremely damaging to the antelope bands. The stable population of antelope in South Dakota in average good years is probably around 30,000.

There has to date been only a negligible amount of antelope hunting east of the Missouri. The first season occurred there in 1966 with only twenty permits. Currently it is seldom over 200.

West River antelope hunting has a high success ratio, from 75 to 95 percent. During the archery season, which is usually split, an early and a late season of almost a month each, animals of either sex are legal. This makes the late (December) season possible, for by then the bucks have shed their horn sheaths.

Occasionally there is a hunt for surplus antelope in Custer State Park in the southern Black Hills, to crop the herd. This also is a permit hunt and only a few permits are offered. Check with the Game Department.

South Dakota has a method for distribution of hunters so that the herd is properly cropped. But this means also that a statement of pinpoint "best spots" is impossible. It all depends on where one applies for a permit, and what the management divisions happen to be that season. The management plan is known as the "flexible unit plan." The antelope range west of the river is divided into Management Units. But these Units can be changed from season to season as herd numbers dictate, just as numbers of permits can be changed. Thus, a Unit that had, as a simple illustration, 200 square miles and 200 permits one year might contain 500 square miles and 300 permits the next. The whole idea is to keep antelope numbers within landowner tolerance, since almost all of the range is privately owned, and at the same time distribute hunters to avoid overcrowding and insure proper harvest.

Landowner and hunter relationships to date have been excellent. Most hunters return year after year—whenever they draw a permit—to the same ranches. The Public Shooting Areas of the West River region are not really large enough or numerous enough to be important as antelope hunting grounds, and the chance of drawing a permit where one is located is small. The best antelope range is west of the Missouri and north and east of the Black Hills and the Badlands. This takes in roughly the northwestern one-fourth of the state. There are some BLM lands open to the public here, with antelope ranging them. Maps must be carefully checked for these (see opening of chapter). The other important public area is the Grand River National Grasslands in the northwest, in Perkins County. Ranch hunting, however, is the basis of South Dakota antelope hunting.

The original "last stand" of the antelope in South Dakota, from which the present large herd stemmed, was an inviolate preserve area of some years ago in Harding Co., in the northwest corner. This county, plus Perkins and Corson to the east, Butte and Meade to the south, are among the best in the antelope range.

MOUNTAIN GOAT

Many years ago Canadian mountain goats were placed in Custer State Park in the Black Hills. In the 1920s six of them escaped. Since then goats have multiplied in the Hills. Surveys indicate they range over some 32,000 acres. But the primary range is only slightly over 2000. The goats have never spread from two portions of the Hills: The Needles area and Harney Peak. Recent studies indicate that the population, now at an estimated 300, which has remained static for some years, has reached a point past which it cannot increase. There appears to be no more suitable goat habitat in the Hills, and annual mortality balances reproduction. Further, there are signs of deterioration of the habitat by overbrowsing and studies of trapped animals appear to indicate a declining health pattern in the herd.

If browse plants are not allowed to reestablish themselves, undoubtedly a sharp decline in the herd will follow. And if that were to occur it would still require many years before a build-up of browse could induce a herd buildup. From these study conclusions it became obvious that a herd reduction on a controlled basis should be accomplished by hunting. As this is written the first season has been held, with twenty-five permits offered, to residents only. All were successful. Whether or not there will be annual seasons or staggered ones cannot be predicted. Much depends on production in the herd from year to year. Almost certainly, however, permits offered will be for South Dakota residents only.

MOUNTAIN SHEEP

Long ago there was a subspecies of the bighorn called Audubon's bighorn native in parts of South Dakota. It has been extinct for almost half a century. The Rocky Mountain bighorn has been introduced into locations in the Black Hills, in Badlands National Monument and to the Slim Buttes of southeastern Harding Co. in the extreme northwest. Bighorns that were hanging on after introduction in Custer State Park have declined. Some of the Slim Buttes sheep were killed by hunters, either purposely or by error. Currently the bighorn is not present in huntable numbers, the population remains about the same year after year and no season is at this time anticipated.

RABBITS

Cottontails are abundant almost everywhere in South Dakota. Shelter belts and brushy draws and stream bottoms near crop fields are the prime habitats. Practically all of the public lands except the Forests offer good cottontail hunting. The eastern third of the state and the extreme west have the heaviest populations. There are also good populations along all of the large rivers where cover is available. Cottontail hunting is, however, pursued very little by South Dakota hunters. This might be termed one of the state's neglected species. Cottontails may be hunted at any time, without restrictions. It is not difficult to find places to hunt. Most landowners, in this state where trees are scarce over such large sweeps of country, welcome rabbit hunters, for rabbits gnaw planted trees and they like to have them controlled.

The rabbit—more properly hare—that gets the big share of the hunting in South Dakota is the whitetailed jack. These big jackrabbits turn white in winter, at which time the fur has a modest value. As many as a million whitetailed jacks are killed annually for the fur market and the carcasses sold for food in some cases to mink farms. There is no closed season nor bag limit. This is snow-time hunting, and is an interesting off-season sport for cold weather. Permission may be had almost anywhere to hunt jacks on private lands, and they are plentiful almost everywhere.

SQUIRRELS

Fox squirrels are fairly well scattered over the state, but because the fox squirrel is not a forest animal, it is found chiefly in the southeastern quarter of South Dakota, in shelter belts, old orchards, small woodlots and river valleys where trees grow and food is available. Oddly, the fox squirrel, though it grows large here, is an almost unused resource. It is hunted little. There is no closed season and no bag limit, and thus for all practical purposes the fox squirrel is not considered a game animal. Possibly lack of attention is in some degree related. Hunting is quite good, particularly after upland bird seasons when leaves are off. But the spotty locations of squirrel abundance are not always easy to find. The Public Shooting Areas of the southeastern counties and timbered bottom lands along the lower Missouri River are the best locations.

OTHER ANIMALS

Foxes are extremely plentiful throughout the state, and are bountied by several thousands annually. Bobcats are moderately abundant, particularly along the Missouri River and throughout the rougher parts of the West River country. Coyotes are plentiful in the West River region and along the Missouri River, but range in the east as well. Coyotes and bobcats are also bountied. Some excellent hunting for all three species can be had, by calling or other hunting methods, west of the Missouri. Calling is becoming more and more popular here and the open country is well adapted to it. The National Grasslands and the PSAs offer good opportunities. Private lands are readily opened to this hunting if one politely requests permission. Popular also in South Dakota are mass fox hunts. Scores of neighbors and friends get together on a weekend and organize walking hunts to drive foxes. Many are killed in this manner on these hunts that are partially social events, and rather unique to this area.

There is excellent specialized hunting on the grasslands and prairies for badgers. South Dakota is in fact one of the best locations for this unusual varmint hunting. A number of hunters nowadays try to collect a badger or two as real trophy animals. The Grasslands are good places for this hunting.

Raccoons are fairly plentiful, particularly east of the river, but are in general considered fur animals here and trapped rather than hunted. Although prairie dogs, found mostly west of the river, have been severely controlled, there is some shooting left, on private lands, and on the Grasslands.

REGULATIONS

Game laws pertaining to seasons, bag and possession limits, areas to be hunted, special hunts, license fees all may have numerous changes from year to year. For current regulations, and for other specific queries, write to: Department of Game, Fish and Parks, Pierre, South Dakota 57501.

NEBRASKA

Nebraska is generally considered one of the central plains states, but it is more than that, with terrain far more varied than is at once apparent. At the eastern border, which is formed entirely by the broad Missouri River, the land is a transition from Iowa and a portion of Missouri, which lie across the stream. South and for some distance west the land flattens to join the Kansas plains. In the northeast the Missouri River comes out of South Dakota to sweep along in a slow curve forming more of the border there, and this area is rather flat, too. But westward the land slopes up and up and presently becomes broken. There are immense expanses of sandhills, and there are pockets of rugged country.

Much of the far west portion of the state is broken table lands, actually the beginning of the foothills of the Rockies. In the northwest the terrain changes in places rather abruptly from grassy sandhills to steep hills with stands of pine. These are the spillover of the Black Hills of southwestern South Dakota. All along the western border with Wyoming and Colorado, the land is reminiscent of the rolling, wide-open cattle country of those states, with the highest point over 5000 feet. The dominant physical feature of Nebraska is the Platte River, which snakes its way in long, gentle curves west to east across the entire state.

Nebraska is predominantly agricultural. In the east and south there are millions of acres of grain—wheat, corn, rye, sorghum. Westward it is cattle country. There is little true wilderness. But there are vast areas of treeless sandhills virtually roadless, and these, though predominantly in private ownership, are in their way a variety of wilderness.

Roads are good. In the eastern third of the state they are also abundant. But westward they are not. Main arteries take hunters to any section of the state, but visitors should be aware that immense sweeps of country here and there are all but roadless. Sand trails do lead across many of these. However, in the Sand Hills region these can be difficult for the tyro whether wet or dry, and a 4-wheel-drive vehicle is often most useful. Air transport is perfectly adequate, with airports at all major cities. There are also, in this big country, dozens of smaller airports and air strips for sportsmen who may fly their own planes in.

Nebraska offers excellent and quite varied hunting. It also offers plenty of room. At its broadest it is over 400 miles east-west, and from north to south over 200. Area totals 77,227 square miles. In this expanse there are presently less than one and one-half million people. The eastern third of the state is the most heavily settled, with many small towns and villages, and with the large cities of Omaha and Lincoln. These two cities contain almost one-third of the state's entire population. Thus it is obvious that, in the west particularly, human population is thinly spread. There is ample room for game, and for hunters.

411

Hunters, too, are in most parts of the state spread thinly. An average of 200,000 licenses are sold annually. Late years a substantial number of these—at least 25 percent—are nonresidents, for Nebraska has done an excellent job of publicizing its hunting, and of keeping popular species available in numbers that insure high success. Big game includes deer, both whitetails and mule deer, antelope, and wild turkeys. Pheasants, bobwhite quail, and prairie grouse—both sharptail and prairie chicken—are in excellent supply. There is quality hunting for waterfowl. Rabbits are everywhere, squirrels abundant in some parts of the state. Hunting for predators such as coyotes and bobcats is very good. During recent seasons pheasants, deer, turkeys, and waterfowl have been the species most avidly sought and with which success percentage has been highest.

Hunters in Nebraska experience very little difficulty in finding places to hunt. Although most of the land area is in private ownership, landowner-sportsman relations are on the whole excellent. Most farmers and ranchers will allow hunting if politely approached. There is also good progress currently in Nebraska with farmlands under the Cropland Adjustment Program. These CAP lands, marked by signs indicating that they are open to public access for hunting and other activities, presently number well over 100,000 acres. There are varying acreages in all but a few counties of the state. The state Game Commission can furnish details on such lands in any county.

In addition to such private lands open to hunting, wholly public lands are in good supply and well distributed throughout the state. There are almost a quarter-million acres of the Nebraska National Forest (1). This is in three tracts. One, the Pine Ridge tract, is in the northwest. It lies south of U.S. 20 in Dawes County, between the towns of Crawford and Chadron. State 2 south from Crawford and U.S. 385 south from Chadron both cross this block. The Niobrara block of the Forest is to the east, in Cherry County, southwest from the town of Valentine, which is at the junction of U.S. 20 and 83. To the south, in Thomas and Blaine counties, is the Bessey block. It lies along State 2 and near U.S. 83, which intersect nearby at Thedford. The Forest Supervisor can be contacted at Lincoln for details on this National Forest.

Another important tract of federal lands is the Oglala National Grasslands (2). These are located in the extreme northwest corner of the state, in northern Sioux Co. and northwestern Dawes Co. There are 94,307 acres of National Grasslands in Nebraska. Map and details can be obtained from the Nebraska National Forest Supervisor in Lincoln.

Nebraska is among the states of the central U.S. where the Federal Waterfowl Production program is in operation. Like the Dakotas and Minnesota, Nebraska has a number of Waterfowl Production Areas that are open to public hunting for all game present on them. The portion of the state where these are concentrated is called the Rainwater Basin. It lies south of the Platte River, in the south-central area. There are over twenty plots of these WPAs, the majority of them grouped southeast, south, and southwest from Grand Island. Most are of modest size, from 60 to about 800 acres, but some good hunting is available on them. A map of this Rainwater Basin showing locations of these lands can be obtained from the Regional Director, Bureau of Sport Fisheries and Wildlife, 1006 West Lake Street, Minneapolis, Minnesota 55408.

State lands for hunting are numerous. There are two classes of these. One is called State Special-Use Areas. These, unless otherwise posted, are open to hunting year-round for whatever is legal at any season. The other class of state lands are State Recreation Areas. These are open in season from October 1 to April 1 unless otherwise posted or designated. As this is written there are 44 SUAs and 18 SRAs. There are in addition to all the above public lands several other federal tracts under Corps of Engineers and National Wildlife Refuges where special hunts are allowed. Lists and locations of all state and federal lands are available from the Commission. Most of them will be located later in this chapter under various game species found on them.

Accommodations for hunters are numerous in Nebraska. The Commission has been extremely active not only in its game programs but in people-to-people programs that assist hunters to find places to stay. Those who may wish to camp will find ample opportunity. There are campgrounds on many of the SRAs and SUAs, others in the National Forest, in State Parks, and even in some State Waysides. Booklets available from the Game, Forestation and Parks Commission (address at chapter end) list and describe state and federal campgrounds and also private and municipal ones.

Most appealing in Nebraska, however, are the dozens of farms and ranches that offer accommodations, at extremely economical prices. Some offer camping opportunities, others board and room. Many will guide hunters, even furnishing dogs if needed. Some will dress and freeze game. The Commission has encouraged landowners in these activities, and can furnish lists with details on services offered. Motel and hotel accommodations are numerous along the main highways, but are few on less traveled routes particularly in the western two-thirds of the state. However, the private lodgings noted here are plentiful in most of the off-highway locations. *Nebraskaland* magazine, published by the Commission, carries advertising from many of these places, and also advertising of guides. Annually the Commission also publishes a booklet, "Nebraskaland Afield," which contains detailed hunting information and is available free.

Nebraska weather runs the gamut from hot to very cold. Early seasons, such as for squirrels and grouse in September, may be warm or even hot. But by October and November when most general seasons open many of the days will require a light wool shirt at least, and many will be chilly enough so a jacket is called for. As the season progresses the wind can be bitter, and nights very cold. Heavy clothing should always be taken on a Nebraska hunting trip. Even spring turkey hunting in April can sometimes be frosty and chill.

Arms and ammunition for Nebraska's game need not be specialized. For deer and antelope, calibers such as the .30/30, .30/06, .243, .270, or comparable weapons are all one needs. Pheasant and grouse hunters will use No. 6 and No. 7½ shot sizes, and the latter will do well for quail. Turkeys and waterfowl will of course require heavier shot, in No. 4 and No. 2, with the short-magnum loads very popular.

PHEASANTS

For many years Nebraska has been a top pheasant state, but within the past decade especially it has emereged as one of the most important pheasant "capitals," and with much state emphasis on its extremely long (recently ninety-three days) season and liberal bag limits. Generally the entire state is open for most of November, December and January with a 4-cock a day limit, 16 in possession. However, in the northeast, the west, and the southwest

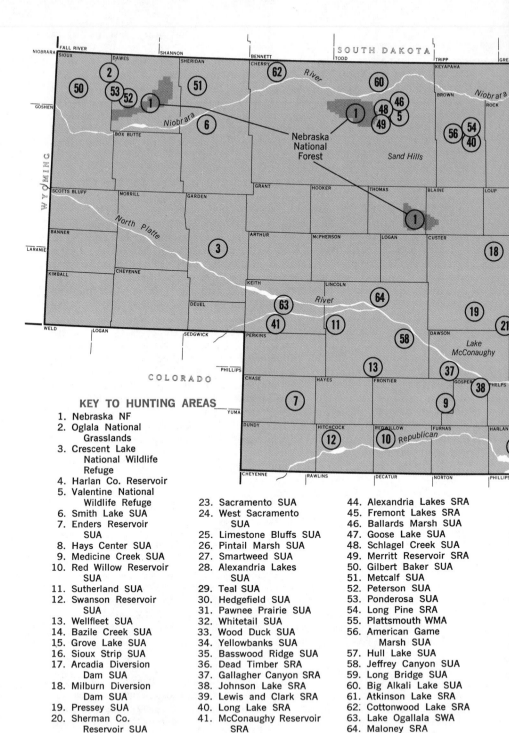

KEY TO HUNTING AREAS

1. Nebraska NF
2. Oglala National Grasslands
3. Crescent Lake National Wildlife Refuge
4. Harlan Co. Reservoir
5. Valentine National Wildlife Refuge
6. Smith Lake SUA
7. Enders Reservoir SUA
8. Hays Center SUA
9. Medicine Creek SUA
10. Red Willow Reservoir SUA
11. Sutherland SUA
12. Swanson Reservoir SUA
13. Wellfleet SUA
14. Bazile Creek SUA
15. Grove Lake SUA
16. Sioux Strip SUA
17. Arcadia Diversion Dam SUA
18. Milburn Diversion Dam SUA
19. Pressey SUA
20. Sherman Co. Reservoir SUA
21. Platte Valley SUA
22. Cornhusker SUA

23. Sacramento SUA
24. West Sacramento SUA
25. Limestone Bluffs SUA
26. Pintail Marsh SUA
27. Smartweed SUA
28. Alexandria Lakes SUA
29. Teal SUA
30. Hedgefield SUA
31. Pawnee Prairie SUA
32. Whitetail SUA
33. Wood Duck SUA
34. Yellowbanks SUA
35. Basswood Ridge SUA
36. Dead Timber SRA
37. Gallagher Canyon SRA
38. Johnson Lake SRA
39. Lewis and Clark SRA
40. Long Lake SRA
41. McConaughy Reservoir SRA
42. Ravenna SRA
43. Salt Valley SRA

44. Alexandria Lakes SRA
45. Fremont Lakes SRA
46. Ballards Marsh SUA
47. Goose Lake SUA
48. Schlagel Creek SUA
49. Merritt Reservoir SRA
50. Gilbert Baker SUA
51. Metcalf SUA
52. Peterson SUA
53. Ponderosa SUA
54. Long Pine SRA
55. Plattsmouth WMA
56. American Game Marsh SUA
57. Hull Lake SUA
58. Jeffrey Canyon SUA
59. Long Bridge SUA
60. Big Alkali Lake SUA
61. Atkinson Lake SRA
62. Cottonwood Lake SRA
63. Lake Ogallala SWA
64. Maloney SRA
65. Memphis Lake SRA
66. Two Rivers SRA

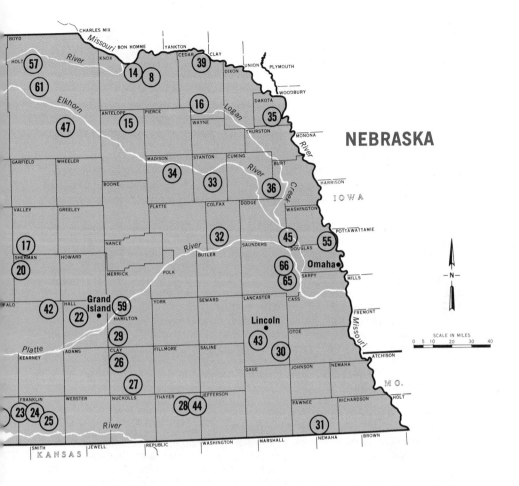

there have recently been "hen areas," where, during the late part of the season, 1 hen may be in the bag each day, and 4 are allowed in the possession limit. Hen areas are of course subject to change from season to season. All told the pheasant is the most popular and most publicized game species in the state. Estimates some seasons have placed the kill at around one and a quarter million birds.

Pheasants range throughout Nebraska. There are however portions of the state where they are more abundant than in others. The strip of counties along the eastern border—the Missouri River—is in secondary range. West of this strip the pheasant population is good north-south from border to border until at roughly the point where the Missouri River portion of the border with South Dakota ends. From here on west across the northern half of the state the pheasant range is, with exceptions, secondary. The southern half of the state continues with primary range clear to the western border. The exceptions noted in the north are in the northwest. Here, in most of Box Butte Co. (Alliance is a key city), and northeastward sweeping across southeast Dawes Co. and most of northwest and central Sheridan Co. is a broad swath of excellent pheasant population. Northern Dawes Co. also has an area

415

of concentration. Thus, in the better range the following cities and towns can serve as keys: Alliance, Rushville in the northwest; Sidney in the southwest; North Platte, McCook, Broken Bow, Grand Island across the central and southern region; Norfolk, Columbus, Fremont, Lincoln in the east.

Unquestionably the very best of the pheasant hunting is on private farmlands. These, as noted earlier in chapter, can be hunted by permission in almost all cases. Excellent hunting can be located by getting from the Commission the list of farms and ranches noted earlier that accommodate hunters for board and/or lodging. In addition, by far the great share of CAP farmlands mentioned in the chapter opening are within the best pheasant ranges. Many primary-range counties have from 1000 to 6000 or more acres. The Commission can furnish lists. Also, many USDA offices in towns and cities in Nebraska have in their front windows maps showing exact locations of such lands.

On the federal public lands, all of the Waterfowl Production Areas are located in some of the state's best pheasant habitat and all offer pheasant hunting. See "Waterfowl" later in chapter for details. Crescent Lake National Wildlife Refuge (3) offers hunting for pheasants on specially posted areas during the regular season. This refuge is a bit north of the primary range. It is in the west, in central Garden Co., north of the North Platte River and U.S. 26, which parallels the river. The town of Oshkosh is on that route some miles south of the Refuge. Several secondaries lead north to it.

In quality range about centered on the southern state border is Harlan County Reservoir (4), where there is public pheasant hunting on Corps of Engineers land. The town of Alma, at junction of U.S. 136 and U.S. 183–383, is the location. There is also some pheasant hunting on specially posted areas of the Valentine National Wildlife Refuge (5) in the north. This is outside the prime pheasant range but offers fair shooting. The location is twenty-two miles south of Valentine on U.S. 83.

At least thirty-one of the forty-four State Special-Use Areas, and eight of the State Recreation Areas, have pheasant hunting. It is best to review these in relation to the prime pheasant shooting portions of the state. Considered by Commission personnel as top locations by counties are the following: northwest—northern half of Sheridan Co.; panhandle (that part of state jutting west between South Dakota and Colorado)—Box Butte Co.; southwest—Perkins, Chase, Dundy, Lincoln, Hayes, Frontier; northeast—Cedar, Dixon, Knox, Wayne.

The following SUAs are either within the counties or portions of counties listed above, or so close to these county locations that they can be considered of prime importance as pheasant hunting locations. In the northwest, Sheridan Co., there is one, Smith Lake SUA (6), twenty-three miles south of Rushville via State 250.

The southwest has seven. Enders Reservoir SUA (7) is eight miles southeast of Imperial in Chase Co. via U.S. 6 and State 61. Hays Center SUA (8) is twelve miles northeast of village of same name via State 17. Medicine Creek Reservoir SUA (9) is in southern Frontier Co. It is north of Cambridge, which is located on U.S. 6 and 34. In southwest Frontier Co. is Red Willow Reservoir SUA (10), eleven miles north of McCook, a city at the junction of U.S. 83 and 6–34. In western Lincoln Co. near Interstate 80 and the Platte River is Sutherland SUA (11), six miles southwest of Sutherland. Swanson Reservoir SUA (12) is in Hitchcock Co. west of McCook, three miles west of Trenton via U.S. 34. Wellfleet SUA (13) is near village of same name, southern Lincoln Co. on U.S. 83.

In the northeast there are three Areas. Bazile Creek SUA (14) is near the town of Niobrara in northern Knox Co. on State 12. Grove Lake SUA (15) is straight south of the above and across the line in Antelope Co., two miles north of Royal, which is on U.S. 20. Sioux Strip SUA (16) is near Randolph in the southwest corner of Cedar Co., on U.S. 20.

A number of SUAs are outside the counties considered as top quality, but still well within the primary pheasant range. In the central part of the state, surrounding at some distance the town of Broken Bow are the following: Arcadia Diversion Dam SUA (17), to the northeast a few miles out of Arcadia; Milburn Diversion Dam SUA (18), twenty miles north of Broken Bow near Milburn; Pressey SUA (19), to the south near Oconto; Sherman Co. Reservoir SUA (20), southeast of Broken Bow near Loup City. There are the Platte Valley SUAs (21) in a series posted along and adjacent to I 80 between North Platte and Grand Island. There is also the Cornhusker SUA (22) four and a half miles west of Grand Island.

South of the river and I 80 and in the south-central and southeastern primary range are more of these SUAs. South and east of Holdrege (U.S. 183) are two: Sacramento SUA (23); West Sacramento SUA (24). Limestone Bluffs SUA (25) is farther south and east, near Franklin, junction U.S. 136 and State 10. To the east, in the general southeastern quarter of the state are several more. Pintail Marsh SUA (26) is west of Harvard (U.S. 6); Smartweed SUA (27) is near Edgar (State 4 and 14); Alexandria Lakes SUA (28) is east of Alexandria (U.S. 81 and 136); Teal SUA (29) is near Kramer (State 33); Hedgefield SUA (30) is southeast of Lincoln, near Holland (U.S. 77); Pawnee Prairie (31) is near the border southwest from Pawnee City (State 4 and 99).

The northeastern quarter has four others. Whitetail SUA (32) is north of the Platte, near Schuyler (U.S. 30); Wood Duck SUA (33) is near Stanton, county of like name (State 24); Yellowbanks SUA (34) is near Battlecreek and Norfolk (U.S. 275); Basswood Ridge SUA (35) is in the far northeast near Homer (U.S. 77). Hunters might check locations of other SUAs in secondary range (list and locations elsewhere or available from the Commission) but those given so far will ordinarily be the best.

State Recreation Areas with pheasant hunting are noted below. Since the best pheasant areas have already been explained, the SRAs will be noted without special reference to those counties. Dead Timber SRA (36) is in the northeast quarter, near Crowell at junction of U.S. 275 and State 91. Gallagher Canyon SRA (37) is south-central, near but south of the Platte River and I 80, nine miles south of Cozad. Johnson Lake SRA (38) is nearby to the southeast, seven miles south of Lexington. Lewis and Clark SRA (39) is far up in the northeast, almost on the South Dakota border, fifteen miles north of Crofton and near Gavins Point Dam on the Missouri, with routes U.S. 81 and State 98 giving access.

Long Lake SRA (40) is north-central, thiry-four miles southwest of Ainsworth, which is on U.S. 20. This is in secondary range. McConaughy Reservoir SRA (41) is far across the state in the southwest, out of Ogallala. State 61 leads to it. Ravenna SRA (42) is south-central, west of Grand Island, near Ravenna on State 2. And the Salt Valley SRAs (43) are in tracts as posted, around Lincoln.

QUAIL

Bobwhite quail are found to some extent throughout most of Nebraska. The state is near the western and northern limit of range, however, and quail are not populous except in somewhat restricted ranges. However, the bird is an important game species, with 50,000 to 60,000 hunters annually interested in it, and with an average annual kill of between 400,000 and 500,000 birds. The heaviest bobwhite concentrations are in the southeastern counties, which furnish approximately 40 percent of the entire quail kill.

A picture of the best quail range is about as follows. In the southeast, reading in tiers north to south, primary range covers these counties: Saunders, Lancaster, Gage; Douglas, Sarpy, Cass, Otoe, Johnson, Pawnee; Nemaha, Richardson. To the west of these, and south of U.S. 30 and the Platte River, is considered good range, but the quality portions of it is in a swath along the southern border narrowing down as it reaches toward the Colorado line. North of McCook there is a northward bulge in this swath, to include most of Frontier Co. In addition to the quality range described, quail are also fairly abundant in the northeast along the river courses: Logan Creek, the Elkhorn River, and also along the Missouri clear up to its entrance into South Dakota and at that point westward for a short distance along the Niobrara River. Then, across the east-central area quail populations follow in good supply up the river courses—the Cedar and the various forks of the Loup. This population culminates in particularly good supply between the branches of the Loup and in a fairly large area to the southeast of Broken Bow, which is in Custer Co. There is also a fairly thin line of quail population running clear up the Platte River and continuing to the borders along both North and South branches of the Platte. Thus, the best areas briefly can be set up as southeast, southern border, river courses of east-central and northeast.

Without special regard to this range but listing them alphabetically, the following SUAs and SRAs located under "Pheasant" offer quail shooting. The Special-Use Areas: Alexandria Lakes; Basswood Ridge; Bazile Creek; Cornhusker; Grove Lake; Hayes Center; Hedgefield; Limestone Bluffs; Medicine Creek Res.; Pawnee Prairie; Platte Valley; Pressey; Red Willow Res.; Sherman Co. Res.; Sioux Strip; Sutherland; Teal; Wellfleet; Wood Duck; Yellowbanks. The State Recreation Areas: Dead Timber; Lewis and Clark; McConaughy Res.; Ravenna; Salt Valley.

There are two SRAs not so far located that have quail. The Alexandria Lakes SRA (44) is five miles east of the town of like name, with U.S. 81, 136 and State 4 offering access. The Fremont Lakes SRA (45) is three miles west of Fremont via U.S. 30. There is also fair quail hunting on the Corps of Engineers land at Harland Co. Reservoir (see "Pheasant").

Much of the best quail shooting is, as with pheasants, on private lands. Permission as earlier mentioned is usually not difficult to obtain. The CAP lands are especially productive, in the better quail counties, and permission is not needed on these. Hunters should be aware that it is illegal to shoot quail in Nebraska except when they are in flight.

GROUSE

In Nebraska the term "grouse" refers to two species that range for the most part in the same region: the sharptail grouse and the prairie chicken. Approximately 10 percent of Nebraska hunters hunt grouse. The aggregate kill averages between 40,000 and 50,000 birds. The sharptail is present on the whole in greater numbers. In recent surveys prairie chickens made up from 22 to 39 percent of the bag. Both are birds of the open country. The primary range is in the Sand Hills area of the north-central and interior region north of the Platte. Prairie chickens appear to be more abundant on the east and south of the range, but sharptails blanket it. The birds are generally found in meadows early in the morning. Stubble fields, alfalfa attract them. Later they retire to wild plum thickets, shelter belts, or the rough portions of the heavy-grass hills. Rose hips are a favorite food, and birds are often found in wild rose thickets during feeding hours.

Very roughly, the basic range of these birds is marked off on the east by north-south U.S. 281, from the northern border down to about State 91. Here the demarcation line turns west and runs straight across along the southern border of Blaine Co., then south to the Platte and west up the river to U.S. 385 and then north through Alliance to the northern border. Within this range, the top counties are: Cherry, Brown, Rock, Holt, Thomas, Blaine, and Garfield.

Ranchlands hunted by permission in the Sand Hills region based on Cherry and surrounding counties are good. Some birds are also found on CAP lands in the range. A few Special Use Areas offer grouse. Ballards Marsh SUA (46), twenty miles south of Valentine, in Cherry Co. via U.S. 83, is one. Goose Lake SUA (47) is another. It is located twenty-five miles south of O'Neil, in southern Holt Co., and is reached via U.S. 281. Schlagel Creek SUA (48), another with limited grouse hunting, is in the Valentine region, fourteen miles southwest via U.S. 83 and State 483. Two SUAs listed under "Pheasant" also offer some grouse: Milburn Diversion Dam and Smith Lake.

Among the State Recreation Areas are two with grouse hunting. Long Lake SRA has been noted under "Pheasant." Merritt Reservoir SRA (49) is approximately twenty-six miles southwest of Valentine via U.S. 83. Crescent Lake National Wildlife Refuge ("Pheasant"), the two blocks of Nebraska National Forest in the north-central area—Niobrara, Bessey—(both described in opening of chapter), and the Valentine National Wildlife Refuge ("Pheasant") all furnish some grouse shooting.

WILD TURKEYS

Turkey hunting success in Nebraska, with rather liberal regulations, is phenomenal. Originally there were only a few turkeys in the state, along the river bottoms of the east. They were completely gone many years ago. In recent years the Merriam's turkey, a subspecies of the western mountain country, was stocked in a number of sites, chiefly in the north and west. Later, introductions of the Rio Grande subspecies were attempted. Most releases of these were made in the central and southern parts of the state. The Rio Grande turkey has not proved itself to date capable of more than minimal establishment, but the Merriam's turkey has done exceedingly well, particularly in the so-called Pine Ridge country of the northwest, where the Black Hills spill over from South Dakota into a part of Nebraska.

Currently there are spring and fall seasons, both by special permit. Under specified regulations hunters may hunt both. The spring season, for gobblers only—hunters must carry a call while hunting—shows up an average harvest of as many as 300 birds, out of an average of upwards of 1500 permits. A recent success percentage was 23.9. During the fall season either sex may be taken. From 2000 to 2500 or more permits are usually allowed, and success runs at times over 50 percent.

Not all of the state is open. Management Units have been set up in various parts of the state, and after annual surveys permits are allotted as deemed advisable for each Unit. These Units are of course subject to addition or substraction as the fluctuation of turkey population dictates. More territory

may be opened in the future. As this is written, however, the Units that
have had seasons and may have are located as follows. Round Top is in the
northwest, bounded on the south by the Niobrara River and on the east
by the Cherry Co. line. This is considered the top Unit, usually offers the
greatest number of permits and has the highest kill and in general the highest
success percentage. Wild Cat is in the southwestern area, bounded northward by U.S. 26 and on the east by State 27. Permit numbers are small
but success is excellent.

In the north-central area, taking in Cherry, Brown, and Rock counties is
the Niobrara Unit. This large Unit has ordinarily the second largest number
of permits, and success runs very close to the Round Top Unit. Immediately
south (Thomas Co.) is a small Unit named Halsey. It has had spring
seasons with very limited permits. Still farther south and crossed by the Platte
River is the Lincoln Unit, bounded on the west by State 61, on the north by
State 92, on the east by U.S. 183 and on the south by State 23. Only a
modest number of permits are usually available and success is in the middle
bracket. Below this Unit, taking in all the area south of it to the Kansas
border, is Red Willow Unit. Permits and success are both a bit below
Lincoln.

In the eastern third of the state, reading north to south, are three
small Units: Verdigre, Silver Creek, Nuckolls. Permits so far in all have
been few and success rather low. It should be understood that not all of the
Units have both spring and fall seasons. Hunters applying for permits will
have the best chances, both of getting a permit and of success in bagging birds,
in either Round Top or Niobrara. The smaller Units and Units with few
permits are most successfully hunted by local sportsmen who intimately
know the country.

Much hunting is on private lands. Farms in the Pine Ridge country that
are partly tilled and partly in pine-forested hills are an excellent bet. In the
northwest, the Oglala National Grasslands offer turkey hunting on public
lands. So does the Pine Ridge block of the Nebraska National Forest. Both
have been described early in the chapter.

Several State Special-Use Areas not so far mentioned have turkeys.
Gilbert Baker SUA (50) is four and a half miles north of Harrison and
U.S. 20, in the extreme northwest. Metcalf SUA (51) is fourteen miles north
of Hay Springs, which is also on U.S. 20 east of the Pine Ridge block of
National Forest. Peterson SUA (52) is back to the west, reached out of
Crawford (U.S. 20) ten miles south via State 2. Ponderosa SUA (53) is
seven miles southeast of Crawford. A State Recreation Area not noted thus
far which offers turkey hunting is Long Pine SRA (54), near town of same
name off U.S. 20 near the junction with U.S. 183, in east-central Brown Co.

The Game Commission should be contacted for details on application
for permit and for regulations concerning permits pertaining to both seasons.

CHUKAR PARTRIDGE

During 1966 several thousand chukars were released along the Platte
Valley, in Garden, Keith, Morrill, and Phelps Cos. Some broods have been
seen. So far it is too early to tell if the species is capable of permanently
establishing itself in the state.

WATERFOWL, SNIPE, RAILS

Nebraska offers some of the best waterfowling in the Central Flyway.
Currently waterfowlers are estimated to number around 30,000 each season.

Although the annual harvest fluctuates broadly over several seasons, a recent kill indicated approximately a quarter million ducks taken. Geese numbered 15,000-plus, bagged by around 5000 hunters. A scattering of coots are killed, but the bird makes up no significant portion of the total bag. Virtually no interest is shown in rails, and though jacksnipe probably could be hunted with fair success on most marshes, only a few incidentals—estimated at not over a couple of thousand—are tallied in the wetlands bag.

Species which predominate in kill surveys and in flock counts are, for geese, Canadas first, blues and snows second, with only a few whitefronted geese in the bag, and, for ducks, mallards by far in the majority (three-fifths of the total) with greenwing teal next, bluewing teal third, pintails fourth, scaup fifth. A fair number of redheads and canvasbacks, gadwalls, and bald-pates are also collected.

During the early season one of the best areas for ducks is found in the Sand Hills. This may sound odd to nonresidents, but Nebraska's Sand Hills are a welter of small lakes, sloughs, and ponds, and a great number of waterfowl nest here and also rest here during migration. The counties concerned: Cherry, Brown, Rock, Grant, Sheridan, Garden. The other early-season duck location considered best is the so-called Rainwater Basin (see chapter opening and also "Pheasant"). In general this covers Clay, Fillmore, York, and Hamilton Counties, south and east of Grand Island and thus south of the Platte.

The Rainwater Basin, in the counties mentioned and in some counties to the west of those, has numerous public Waterfowl Production Areas, federal tracts that are open to fall hunting. As noted earlier a map showing locations of all these is available. Some excellent waterfowling is furnished by these public lands.

One group of these tracts lies along U.S. 6 east of the city of Hastings. Most are south of the highway, at least two north of it. They are all located chiefly in Clay and Fillmore Cos. All are grouped within a few miles. The names are as follows: Theese Lagoon; Smith Lagoon; Alberding Lagoon; Massie Lagoon; Moger Lagoon; Eckhardt Lagoon; Harms Lagoon; Hansen Lagoon; Mallard Haven; Rancher Lagoon; Rolland Lagoon; Weis Lagoon; Wilkins Lagoon; Sinninger; County Line Lagoon. These, and some others to follow, were suggested under "Pheasant" for hunting that species. They are, however, primarily waterfowl areas but do have other game.

West and south of Hastings, south of U.S. 6-34, and between Hastings and Holdrege, are more of these tracts. This group, also all within a few miles of each other: Jensen Lagoon; Lange Lagoon; Lindau Lagoon; Richardson Lagoon; Youngson Lagoon. There is also Harlan Co. Reservoir near Alma (see "Pheasant"). West of Holdrege, lying along State 23 are: Atlanta Lagoon; Elley Lagoon; Peterson Basin; Victor Lake Basin. All of these WPAs are, as noted, excellent for early-season duck shooting.

Later in the season the smaller lakes and ponds freeze. Then the good hunting changes to the large reservoirs and rivers. Among the best, with plenty of public-hunt opportunities and numerous guides available also (query Game Commission) are: the North Platte River from Scottsbluff to Lake McConaughy and including it; Lewis & Clark Reservoir on the northeast border, and the Missouri River from Gavins Point downstream to Ponca; the Republican River, from Swanson Lake to and including Harlan Reservoir. There is in addition a vast amount of good jump-shooting along all of the lesser streams.

During the early part of the season goose hunting, predominantly for snows and blues, is excellent along the Missouri from Gavins Point to Platts-mouth south of Omaha. There is a Plattsmouth Waterfowl Management Area (55) here, with limited hunting. Five blinds on the perimeter of the 1500-acre area are utilized daily. Each will accommodate up to four hunters. Applications are made in late summer to the Commission, and a drawing de-cides which hunters win use of blinds on stipulated dates. Later in the season much of the best goose shooting is for Canadas along the North Platte from Scottsbluff to and including Lake McConaughy. As mentioned previously there are numerous commercial operations in this and the Missouri River regions, where guides and other services may be obtained. The Game Com-mission will furnish lists. Chambers of Commerce in all the towns along the rivers are also excellent contacts for locating guides and related services.

Some of the other public lands also have good or limited waterfowling. The American Game Marsh SUA (56) is south and east of Johnstown, which is on U.S. 20 in Brown Co. Hull Lake SUA (57) is southwest of Butte, with access via U.S. 281 or State 11. This is near where the Nebraska border begins on the Missouri River. Jeffrey Canyon SUA (58) is southwest of Brady on U.S. 30, which parallels the Platte. Long Bridge SUA (59) lies south of Chapman, which is on the same route as above. Big Alkali Lake SUA (60) is seventeen miles south, four miles west of Valentine on U.S. 20, in Cherry Co.

Other Special-Use Areas already covered that furnish waterfowling: Arcadia Diversion Dam ("Pheasant"); Ballards Marsh ("Grouse"); Bazile Creek, Enders Res. (both under "Pheasant"); Goose Lake ("Grouse"); Grove Lake, Hayes Center, Hedgefield, Medicine Creek Res., Milburn Division Dam, Pintail Marsh, Platte Valley, Red Willow Res., Sacramento, Sherman Co. Res., Smartweed, Smith Lake, Sutherland, Swanson Res., Teal, Wellfleet, West Sacramento, Whitetail, Wood Duck, Yellowbanks (all under "Pheasant"); Schlagel Creek ("Grouse").

Of the State Recreation Areas, those offering waterfowling and described under "Pheasant" are: Gallagher Canyon, Johnson Lake, Long Lake, Mc-Conaughy Res. Under "Quail": Alexandria Lakes, Fremont Lakes, Lewis & Clark. Under "Grouse": Merritt Res.

Several other SRAs not so far covered should be noted. Atkinson Lake SRA (61) is near the town of like name on U.S. 20. Cottonwood Lake SRA (62) is near Merriman on U.S. 20. Lake Ogallala SWA (63) is a Special Waterfowl Area nine miles northeast of that city. Maloney SRA (64) has limited shooting, is located near North Platte on U.S. 83. Memphis Lake SRA (65) is near the town in the Lincoln area. The Two Rivers SRA (66) offers controlled waterfowl shooting near Venice, via State 92 or U.S. 30A.

Lands surrounding the National Refuges—Crescent Lake, Valentine, both described earlier—often hold abundant waterfowl.

DEER

Nebraska has some excellent deer hunting for both mule deer and whitetails. There are also a few introduced fallow deer. These are legal game during regular deer season and a few (recently thirty-four) are killed each season. It is not felt that the fallow deer will ever produce more than a remnant population. Of the two native species, whitetails predominate in the east, mule deer in the west, but there is much overlapping of species. Gen-erally speaking, the best deer concentrations are along the river systems, and in the southeastern counties and along the southern border. However, a high kill—often the highest—comes from the Pine Ridge country of the northwest.

Deer hunting is on a permit basis. Number of firearms permits averages between 20,000 and 25,000. During two recent seasons when permit numbers (firearms) ran just under 25,000, the kills were 17,073 and 13,695. Thus, success percentages average very good, from over 50 percent to upwards of 70 percent. The hunting and the issuance of permits is on a Management Unit basis and some Units often show a success percentage of around 80 percent. Between the two species, mule deer are usually taken in greatest numbers. Recently the species composition of the kill was 10,101 mule deer to 6920 whitetails. Some Units restrict hunters to antlered deer only, some offer either-sex hunting, and some have bucks-only hunting until the last one or two days, when either sex is legal. Recently archery permits have not been limited, the entire state has been open, and any deer could be taken by an archer. Bow hunter success has hung around 20 percent.

By and large the number of permits issued for each Unit is comparable. That is, the size of a Unit with 2000 permits offered is usually on about an equal scale with a smaller one with only 300 permits. Harvest figures for a recent season show that all but two Units of the extreme southeast, Nemaha and Omaha, showed both whitetails and mule deer in the kill. Those two were entirely whitetails. Areas of heaviest kills were, in order, as follows: Pine Ridge in the northwest, with 2528 mule deer, 269 whitetails, and a total of 3496 permits issued; Sand Hills, Cherry Co. and parts of counties south of it, 1208 mule deer, 440 whitetails with 2496 permits; the Keya Paha Unit, east of Sand Hills and along the northern border, 941 mule deer, 881 whitetails with 2298 permits.

Other good Units showing in surveys: Buffalo, central-south, lying along either side of the Platte, with about half and half mule and whitetail deer; Loup, just north of Buffalo, and Calamus, lying still farther north between Loup and Keya Paha, also approximately half and half. All three of these show high success. The Missouri Unit is in the northeast, is predominantly a whitetail area, and runs over 50 percent success. Platte and Upper Platte Units, both along the river in the west, show high success and mule deer in the lead, more so in the Upper Unit which is farther west.

This briefing, therefore, should give prospective applicants for permits a fair indication of what to expect. The Game Commission will furnish details on applying for permits and also have available survey figures showing kills and success percentages in each Unit. A map shows the specific locations of all Units.

It will be obvious that by far the great share of deer hunting is done on private lands. Checking areas ahead of time, after a permit is obtained, helps assure a place to hunt. Or, hunters may avail themselves of the numerous guides noted earlier. As mentioned, lists of these and services offered can be obtained from the Commission. Public lands for deer hunting are also in fair supply. The Oglala National Grasslands of the northwest ("Turkeys"), the Pine Ridge tract of the Nebraska NF ("Turkeys") and the other two NF tracts ("Grouse") all furnish good deer hunting. Both Valentine and Cresent Lake National Wildlife Refuges have special deer hunts.

Of the State Recreation Areas, all described previously under other species, Long Pine, Merritt Reservoir, Salt Valley have some deer hunting. Among the Special-Use Areas there are deer on: Arcadia Diversion Dam, Basswood Ridge, Bazile Creek, Gilbert Baker, Grove Lake, Limestone Bluffs, Metcalf,

Pawnee Prairie, Peterson, Pressey, Red Willow Res., Schlagel Creek, Swanson Res., Whitetail, Teal, Yellowbanks. On some of these hunting is quite limited. Although most of the Waterfowl Production Areas are of modest size, deer hunting can be had on most of them. Hunters would be well advised also to check the CAP lands. Most deer hunting, however, it must be emphasized, is on private lands and either acquiring permission from an owner, or hiring a guide, or paying for farm and ranch accommodations will do most to insure success.

ANTELOPE

Although antelope hunting is limited, success is quite good. An average season sees 1500 to 1750 firearms permits for antelope, these distributed over eight or nine Management Units. The Units are all in the western half of the state and north of the Platte River. Hunter success runs from 70 to over 90 percent from Unit to Unit. Recently archery permits have been unlimited, and success has run around 20 percent. Hunters interested in Nebraska antelope should contact the Commission for a Unit map and details on how and when to apply for any given season. The firearms season is usually brief—three days. Bow hunters have a month or more. Because success runs so high, there is little choice among Units.

Almost all of the antelope hunting is on private lands, by permission. Again, hunters who will check lists of guides and accommodations (list from Commission) in the Unit where they are drawn can often arrange a hunt most easily. There is some hunting on the public lands. The Oglala National Grasslands are a good bet in the northwest. Crescent Lake Refuge southwest of Alliance has designated hunting.

SMALL GAME

Cottontails are abundant. They are most plentiful in the eastern one-third of the state, although wherever cover is available there are cottontails throughout the state. Rabbit hunters who will look first for suitable cover will find ample targets. The average cottontail kill runs from 300,000 to over 500,000, with some 60,000 hunters pursuing this sport. Virtually all of the public lands—SUAs, SRAs, WPAs, plus CAP farmlands offer good cottontail shooting.

The squirrel kill averages around 200,000 by some 30,000-plus hunters. The eastern and central parts of the state have the most squirrels but populations are limited only by availability of wooded areas and food. Most stream courses offer fair to good shooting. Southeastern Nebraska can be rated as excellent. A few of the public areas are particularly noted for squirrel hunting. Among these: Grove Lake, Pawnee Prairie, Pressey among the Special-Use Areas, and Fremont Lakes, Lewis and Clark, Salt Valley, Two Rivers among the Recreation Areas. The Waterfowl Production Areas, where timbered, should not be overlooked. Private land hunting by permission, and the CAP opportunities, are all told best for this endeavor.

OTHER ANIMALS AND BIRDS

There is a good population of coyotes throughout the state. Top concentrations are in the Sand Hills, the southern half of the panhandle, and along the Missouri River in the northeast. The southeast has some. Bobcats are quite common in the northwestern Pine Ridge area of Sioux and Dawes counties and in the drainage of the Niobrara River in Cherry, Brown, Rock and Keya Paha counties.

Raccoons are fairly plentiful but are for the most part considered fur animals here. Foxes are reasonably abundant, get some attention, along with plentiful coyotes and bobcats, from callers and chase hunters. There are good populations of jack rabbits, especially in the south-central region and the Sand Hills. A bit of prairie dog shooting is to be found on private lands of the west. Red Willow Reservoir SUA, noted under "Pheasant" and located north of McCook, is an example of a public area where prairie dogs are found.

Crows are abundant. Roosts in the south-central area near Holdrege and vicinity have numbered an estimated 50,000 birds. During October and November many crows migrate through, and pass back through again during March and April. Best winter months are January and February.

REGULATIONS

Game laws pertaining to seasons, bag and possession limits, areas to be hunted, special hunts, license fees all may have numerous changes from year to year. For current regulations, and for other specific queries, write to: Nebraska Game, Forestation & Parks Commission, State Capitol, Lincoln, Nebraska 68509.

KANSAS

Kansas lies almost in the exact center of the United States. Although known generally as a plains state, Kansas has a varied terrain. In some sections of the east it is hilly, with broad valleys, rolling grasslands, and some wooded areas. Westward the country slopes up from a few hundred feet above sea level to 4000 feet in places at the Colorado border. Most of the western two-thirds of Kansas is gently rolling to exceedingly flat prairie and plains. In the south-central region there is a fairly rugged break in the plains.

This is an agricultural state, with vast stretches of croplands. Farms cover some fifty million acres, or approximately 95 percent of the state. Many are in wheat. At least one-sixth of the nation's wheat production is here. However, throughout all of the state there are slow, meandering rivers and creeks along the courses of which brush and cottonwoods and other good game cover is abundant. Because there is no true wilderness, good roads lead everywhere. At least ten north-south U.S. highways and six or seven east-west main routes slice across the state. There are scores of side roads. Thus, getting to any point by car is fast and easy. Air transport is good in the eastern third, where the larger cities—Kansas City, Topeka, Wichita—are located. But westward the numerous towns are mostly small.

Although Kansas hunting has had meager publicity, the state has a great deal to offer and is generally far underrated. It is a large state, roughly 400 miles east to west, and 200 miles north to south. It encompasses a whopping 82,264 square miles. Scattered over this vast area there is at this time a population of only about 2,275,000. The bulk of this modest population is in the eastern half of the state. Thus there is plenty of room for hunters, a most important aspect of any hunting terrain. Further, this state that calls itself "Mid-Way U.S.A." is a friendly region of down-to-earth rural people. It is usually not too difficult to get permission to hunt at least some area of private lands.

There are no great crowds of hunters. The state at this time sells a few less than 200,000 hunting licenses annually. Whereas some states swarm during open seasons with a tremendous influx of visiting nonresident hunters, to date Kansas gets at the most about 15,000. These are almost entirely bird hunters. The state boasts a fine and growing deer herd, so far limited to hunting by residents only. But pheasants, prairie chickens, bobwhite and some blue or scaled quail, and waterfowl are the main attractions for the majority. Small game (rabbits and squirrels), pests (crows), and predators (coyotes) are also abundant.

Although Kansas is heavily farmed, and thus most of its area is in private lands, there are ample public hunting grounds also—over forty well-scattered areas at this time. All state-owned or state-managed lands are plainly marked with yellow and black signs proclaiming "Public Hunting Area,

Kansas Forestry, Fish and Game Comm." The Commission acquired by act of Congress some years ago certain lands located adjacent to federally built reservoirs, to be used as Game Management Areas. Most of this land, presently almost 100,000 acres, lies along the twelve major reservoirs in the state— Cedar Bluff, Cheney, Council Grove, Elk City, Fall River, Lovewell, Milford, Norton, Toronto, Tuttle Creek, Webster, and Wilson. More such public hunting land is becoming available as new reservoirs are completed. Major roads leading to these lands are well marked by black and white signs proclaiming "Game Management Area." Interior boundaries and trails are also well marked. So are the Refuge Areas within, where no hunting is allowed. These lands are managed for the species deemed to have the best habitat on each, or for combinations, such as pheasants and waterfowl, or doves, bobwhites, and deer. There is no charge to hunters on these lands, and all furnish excellent shooting for a variety of species. Information maps and bulletins concerning all these public-access areas are available from the Commission.

At present there are at least 125,000 acres of state-owned or state-managed lands open to public hunting in Kansas. In addition there is a growing amount of land open under the federal Cropland Adjustment Program. These CAP lands are farmlands taken out of production under the Soil Conservation Service program, but if the owners allow hunting on them they receive added payments. Owners may limit number of hunters at any one time, and ask them to check in and check out. CAP lands will undoubtedly become more abundant. As this is written Kansas has some 10,000 acres under the program. Such lands are marked with blue lettered signs. Maps are prepared and updated periodically showing all CAP tracts, and are available from the Commission.

In the southeast corner of the state there are extensive strip-mining operations. Several thousand acres of these rehabilitated lands are managed now as recreational areas. Though they have been publicized chiefly for the fishing they offer, there is also excellent hunting here, for waterfowl and for upland game. Maps and information on these areas are also available from the Commission, as well as locally from Chambers of Commerce in the surrounding towns, such as Pittsburg and Oswego.

Although federal lands in Kansas are not as large as in many other states, there is a sizable amount of excellent public hunting land. The Cimarron National Grassland, in the southwest corner of the state, is an expanse of 106,000 acres, all open to public hunting. National Grassland boundaries are marked. Elsewhere there are several reservoirs—Corps of Engineers and Bureau of Reclamation—along and around which public hunting is available. There are also some acreages open to hunting on such National Wildlife Refuges as Quivira and Flint Hills.

Kansas has an excellent program of game management. Numerous research programs are constantly in progress. Unquestionably the state will grow in importance as an area of interest especially to shotgunners, for the Commission has shown that it can by sensible management sustain and add to its game crops.

The state is also incessantly active in development of more and more areas where sportsmen may camp. There are at present seventeen excellent State Parks. A guide to these may be had by writing the Commission. Almost all of the public hunting lands have at least some facilities, such as those available at federal reservoirs. There are also some thirty-eight state lakes scattered across the state, small waters created by the Commission. These have camping facilities. There are numerous county parks, and a number of city campgrounds where visitors may park campers, trailers, or tents.

Almost all towns along the Interstate routes, such as 70 and 35, have abundant, large motels, as do most villages of 1000 to 3000 population along the U.S. highways. Accommodations in small rural villages are not as readily available, but it is doubtful that any hunter will have difficulty finding good places to stay. There is one exception. On opening day of any important season, such as that for pheasants, certain towns in sparsely populated areas may be sold out several weeks in advance, and it would be wise to reserve well ahead.

Hunters new to Kansas may plan on warm, pleasant weather during any early season, such as in September. In fact, that month is often hot. But October and November are whimsical. Bad storms and cold, snowy weather must be expected. Wool clothing is part of the upland hunter's basic equipment, and certainly the waterfowler should be well backed up with rain gear, as well as with wool or down beneath.

Although there is some rifle hunting for visitors, for example for jack rabbits and coyotes, with the exception of resident deer hunters who may use a bow or a rifle, Kansas is a shotgunner's state. In wide-open pheasant range, No. 6 shot in long-range loads is excellent, with gauges 20 to 12. Visitors hoping for combination hunts, as for both upland birds and waterfowl, should have loads ranging from No. 8 and No. 7½ for quail to No. 4 for ducks and No. 2 for geese.

PHEASANT

Kansas has quality hunting for this species, one of the state's top game birds. Pheasants were first established in western Kansas, have spread steadily east. They have now reached what is undoubtedly the end of their expansion potential. The best hunting is still in the west. Quality diminishes slowly but progressively eastward. The southeast portion of Kansas has very few. All the rest of the state has them in varying abundance. Even the marginal eastern range is fair. Although the general statement may thus be made that three-fourths of Kansas furnishes pheasant hunting, the high plains of the west are the prime range.

Pheasant populations vary anywhere from year to year. The total kill in Kansas averages from roughly 400,000 to 650,000 annually. With cocks-only hunting, and less than one-third of the state the range of greatest abundance, this is an indication of excellent hunting.

A block of counties in the northwest furnishes what is generally considered the very best. These, just below the Nebraska line and bordering on Colorado on the west, are plains with much grain farming. Reading west to east, in tiers, these counties of the northwest are as follows:

Tier One: Cheyenne, Rawlings, Decatur, Norton, plus the northwestern half of Phillips. U.S. 36 runs east-west straight through the center of this tier. Along this route are the small cities of Phillipsburg, Norton, Oberlin, Atwood, St. Francis. Hunting out of any of these places is excellent, with plenty of accommodations available. Much of the land is privately owned, but there are three public areas in these counties. Kirwin Reservoir (1) is a Bureau of Reclamation project near Kirwin, Kansas, where the Resident Engineer can be contacted. This is an 1890-acre tract open for hunting. Norton Game Management Area (2) is state-leased. It is a 5656-acre public hunting ground five miles west and two miles south of Norton. Decatur County

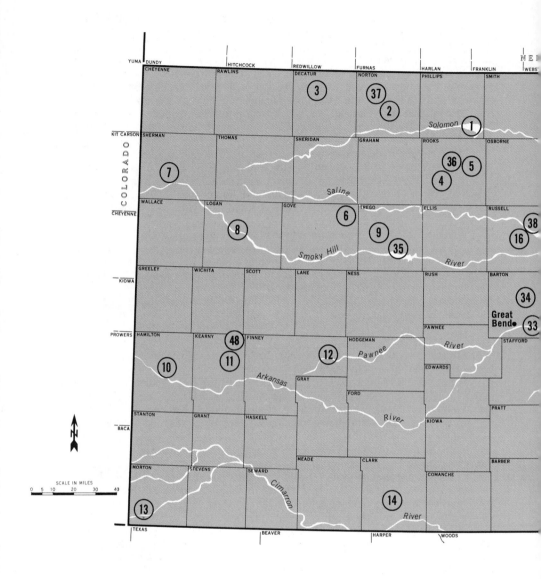

KEY TO HUNTING AREAS

1. Kirwin Reservoir	9. Cedar Bluff GMA	17. Lovewell GMA
2. Norton GMA	10. Hamilton Co. GMA	18. Milford GMA
3. Decatur Co. GMA	11. Kearney Co. GMA	19. Ottawa Co. GMA
4. Webster GMA	12. Finney Co. GMA	20. Cheney GMA
5. Woodston Diversion	13. Cimarron National	21. Washington Co. GMA
Dam	Grasslands	22. Nemaha Co. GMA
6. Sheridan Co. GMA	14. Clark Co. GMA	23. Tuttle Creek GMA
7. Sherman Co. GMA	15. Kingman Co. GMA	24. Council Grove GMA
8. Logan Co. GMA	16. Wilson GMA	

KANSAS

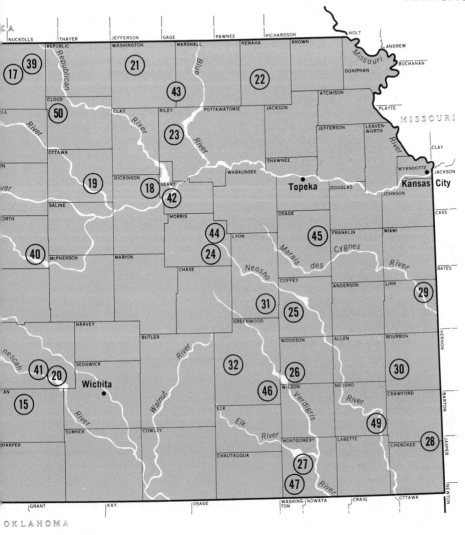

25. Flint Hills National
    Wildlife Refuge
26. Toronto Reservoir
27. Elk City GMA
28. Strip Pits WMA
29. Marais des Cygnes
    WMA
30. Bourbon Co. GMA
31. Lyon Co. WMA
32. Fall River GMA

33. Quivira National
    Wildlife Refuge
34. Cheyenne Bottoms
35. Cedar Bluff Reservoir
36. Webster Reservoir
37. Norton Reservoir
38. Wilson Reservoir
39. Lovewell Reservoir
40. Kanapolis Reservoir
41. Cheney Reservoir
42. Milford Reservoir

43. Tuttle Creek
    Reservoir
44. Council Grove
    Reservoir
45. Pomona Reservoir
46. Fall River Reservoir
47. Elk City Reservoir
48. Lake McKinney
49. Neosho WMA
50. Jamestown WMA

431

Game Management Area (3) is a 351-acre state owned plot one mile east and one mile north of Oberlin.

Tier Two: Sherman, Thomas, Sheridan, Graham Cos. U.S. Highway 24 and I 70 traverse the area east-west, with Hill City, Hoxie, Colby, Goodland, and the larger locations to use as bases. There are of course numerous small towns and cross roads. Again, much of the land is in farms, but there are some excellent public lands open. Webster Game Management Area (4), 6098 acres, is a short distance east of the Graham Co. line, located eight miles west of Stockton. There is a good pheasant population here. The Woodston Diversion Dam (5) is eight miles east of Stockton, offers 210 acres with pheasant hunting. Both these are state-leased. Sheridan Co. GMA (6), 436 acres, four miles north and two miles east of Quinter, is owned by the state. So is Sherman Co. GMA, 1295 acres, ten miles south and two miles west of Goodland.

In the next tier of counties to the south, all of Wallace on the Colorado border is considered prime pheasant range. Next to it, the northwest portion of Logan Co., in the McAllaster vicinity of U.S. 40, is good. Public hunting is available at the Logan County GMA (8), a 271-acre tract north of the Smoky Hill River, near Russell Springs. Northeastern Grove Co. is also in the quality pheasant range. All of Trego Co. to the east is, too. State-leased Cedar Bluff GMA, sixteen miles south of Wakeeney, is here, with over 12,000 acres under management and with heavy emphasis on pheasants.

To the south of these counties for some distance there is still good hunting but not quite on a par with the foregoing. Fanning out from the town of Leoti, however, at the intersection of Routes 96 and 25, there is usually a good bird population. The next tier of counties to the south—Hamilton, Kearney, Finney—are all top-notch range. Centered in Hamilton Co., near Syracuse, is a 432-acre public unit, state owned. At Lake McKinney near Lakin is the 3000-acre state-leased Kearney Co. GMA, and in northeast Finney Co. is a state-owned unit of 852 acres, the Finney Co. GMA (12), near Kalvesta on U.S. 156. The Garden City area is also a fine pheasant range of privately owned land.

All counties of the far southwest are in the quality range also. Stanton, Grant, Morton, Stevens furnish some of the best. Morton Co., in the southwest corner of the state, contains 106,000 acres of the Cimarron National Grasslands (13), all open to public hunting. Contact the Resident Manager, U.S. Forest Service, Elkhart, Kansas, for details. This town, just off U.S. 56, is, incidentally, a gateway to the Grasslands.

East of all the pheasant range so far noted, there is a broad and irregular swath running from southwest to northeast up across the state that is classified as "good" as against "best" for the former. A number of public hunting areas are in this large section. Locations of all these are shown on a map, available from the Commission, in a brochure titled, "Public Hunting in Kansas." Individual maps of each area are also available. A few public areas to be especially noted: Clark Co. GMA (14), 1043 acres near Kingsdown; Kingman Co. GMA (15), 4020 acres, near Kingman; Wilson GMA (16), 6539 acres near Bunker Hill; Lovewell GMA (17), 4905 acres near Mankato; Milford GMA (18), 11,130 acres near Wakefield. These last two are in the north east-central part of the state but still in some of the major "good" pheasant range.

There are several other public areas, and any hunter who asks politely can by diligence usually find at least some hunting on farmlands. A small map available from the Commission indicating relative pheasant population densities over the entire state is invaluable in planning a hunt.

QUAIL

Quail and pheasant are tied for most popular game in Kansas. Bobwhite range in virtually every corner of every county. There are some scaled, or blue, quail in the southwest. Kansas has, in fact, become over the past few years one of the most important quail states in the U.S., season after season usually among at least the top five. Kill figures range anywhere from two million a year up to an officially estimated four million-plus in one recent season.

Bobwhite hunting in Kansas is along the woodlot and fencerow edges, the planted windbreaks, along ditch and creek banks, in brush clumps and weed patches and stubble fields of the endless farmlands and the managed public lands. But the bobwhite range, looked at from a viewpoint of population density, is exactly the reverse of pheasant densities. The eastern one-third of Kansas, with the exception of most of three counties in the extreme southeastern corner, holds the quality hunting. Throughout this entire area there are more birds than westward, and hunting is termed "best." The southeast corner can be labeled "good," but slightly below the quality of the remainder of this third of the state.

The top habitat lies east of a north-south line about as follows: State Route 15 south from the Kansas-Nebraska border to Abilene and Newton, thence on south through Wichita via I 35 to the Oklahoma border. West of this line, the bobwhite hunting labeled as "good" lies in an irregular corridor between the above-mentioned line and one drawn as follows north to south: from north of Norton where U.S 283 enters Kansas southeast to about Salina, then southwest on a long slant to Dodge City and on south on U.S. 283 again to the Oklahoma border. West of this line, in the large eastward bulge into the central part of the state thus created, and on throughout all of western Kansas, bobwhite hunting is in general labeled only "fair." In both the "fair" and "good" sections, of course, there are oases of abundance that are true "hot spots."

One of these is the only area where scaled (blue) quail are found in any quantity. This is in the extreme southwestern corner of the state, taking in the four corner counties. Morton, the corner county, is particularly attractive. Here, on the Cimarron National Grassland, a public-land area of 106,000 acres north of Elkhart, and with U.S. 56 an easy approach, there is excellent shooting for blues and also for bobwhites. For blues, hunting windbreaks on abandoned farms in the Garden City region is usually productive, too. There is a minor amount of shooting for blues some distance up the western border. But it is the bobwhite that holds the quail spotlight throughout all the rest of the state.

For locations of good public-hunt areas in much of this "fair" western range, read the foregoing section on pheasants. All of the areas noted for pheasants also have good quail hunting. In the mid-state swath termed "good," here are some public areas that offer hunting to match: Lovewell GMA, twelve miles northeast of Mankato (U.S. 36); Ottawa Co. GMA (19), near Bennington (U.S. 81 intersection with State 18); Cheney GMA (20), fourteen miles southeast of Hutchinson (U.S. 50 intersection with State 61). There are several other public areas. A list and maps of these (for the entire state) may be had from the Commission. In addition, thousands of acres of private lands in this region rated "good" can be opened by a proper approach to their owners and courteous hunting manners while afield.

In the prime bobwhite ranges of rolling farmlands, woodlots, fields, and hedgerows of the east, unfortunately the bulk of Kansas' human population also exists. But, happily, so do the greatest number of public hunting lands. In the northeastern counties bordering Nebraska, there are two: the 408-acre Washington Co. GMA (21), seven miles north and three miles west of the county seat of Washington; Nemaha Co. GMA (22), 200 acres near Seneca on U.S. 36. A short distance to the south, in the next tier of counties, two very important public areas are Milford GMA, already located under "Pheasant," over 11,000 acres of excellent quail shooting near Wakefield; and Tuttle Creek GMA (23), 12,500 acres near Randolph. These are, respectively, south and north of U.S. 24, in the general area northwest of the city of Manhattan.

Other notable public areas are as follows: 2650-acre Council Grove GMA (24), five miles northwest of Council Grove, a town at intersection of U.S. 56 and State 177; John Redmond Reservoir, Flint Hills National Wildlife Refuge (25), 5000 acres of hunting lands near Burlington on U.S. 75 (contact manager of the Refuge); 4266 acres at Toronto Reservoir (26), one mile south of Toronto, off U.S. 54 on State 105; Elk City GMA (27), 11,680 acres near Independence, intersection of U.S. 75 and 160.

There are a number of other smaller units easily located from the available Commission map of public hunting grounds. In the extreme southeast, although as noted the hunting is slightly poorer, it is growing steadily better and an interesting and good bet is at the Strip Pits Wildlife Management Area (28). This is a group of scattered tracts totaling over 6000 acres, in Crawford and Cherokee Cos. One should make local inquiry in area towns—Pittsburg, Oswego, Columbus, Parsons, etc.—to determine precise locations of these tracts.

PRAIRIE CHICKEN

Once fabulously abundant on the unplowed prairies, prairie chickens are found in huntable numbers today only in a few states. Kansas has one of the best-sustained flocks in the nation, and good hunting, although bag limits are fairly restricted. The state continues much research to keep its prairie chicken population and possibly enlarge it. There are a few of the lesser prairie chicken species in the southwest, but no open season. The greater prairie chicken is the bird hunted. Its range is in the eastern one-third of the state. Annual kill averages from a low of 30,000 to a high of 70,000.

Eight northeastern and north-central counties are closed to hunting, and so are the four corner counties of the southeast. The two center counties bordering Missouri—Linn and Bourbon—are open, and considered "fair." There is a public area in each. Marais des Cygnes WMA (29), near Trading Post in Linn Co., is primarily a waterfowl area, but there is some hunting around it. Bourbon County GMA (30), 380 acres near Elsmore, is worth trying. Crowley and Chautauqua Cos. on the southern border are rated "fair." Likewise the northern border counties of Marshall and Nemaha. Southeastward from these there is a belt of counties also fair.

Inside this belt of counties is the range termed "good." Here, in Pottawatomie Co., and southeast of Junction City in Geary Co., there are stable populations. Tuttle Creek GMA and Milford GMA (see "Quail") are good public grounds. Marion Co. to the southwest is good chicken range, but without public lands. The prime habitat and range lies inside the blocks of counties so far noted.

Here are the counties considered "best": Morris, Wabaunsee, Chase, Lyon, Coffey, Anderson, Butler, Greenwood, Woodson, Elk, and the northwest corner of Wilson. Of these, counties in the center of the range are usually the top spots. Greenwood is a good example. A few cities and towns that may be used as bases, and to help in locating the best ranges, are as follows: Council Grove, Alma, Emporia, Eldorado, Eureka, Yates Center, and Burlington.

By counties, here are the public areas in this "best" range: Morris Co., Council Grove GMA (see "Quail"); Lyon Co., Lyon Co. GMA (31); Coffey Co., Flint Hills National Wildlife Refuge (see "Quail"); Greenwood Co., Fall River GMA (32), 10,892 acres near Eureka; Woodson Co., Toronto Reservoir (see "Quail").

Not much dog hunting or "walking up" is done in Kansas for prairie chickens. Feeding fields are spotted, and hunters take stands there at dawn and evening, well hidden, waiting for birds to fly in.

WATERFOWL

Kansas has some very good waterfowl hunting, most of it centered on the numerous large reservoirs in the state, some of it along rivers, and over the strip-mining pits of the southeast. The refuge or sanctuary, plus a public hunting area nearby, form the basis of waterfowl management for hunting in Kansas. Without the rest and feeding areas, it is doubtful that ducks and geese would stay. Much effort is expended to keep the waterfowl areas attractive to the birds during migration and on through the winter.

The Flint Hills National Wildlife Refuge (see "Quail") established around the John Redmond Reservoir near Burlington, Kansas, attracts as many as 50,000 snow and blue geese, 20,000 Canada Geese, and 100,000 mallards. The mallard is one of the most important ducks in the Kansas flyway. There are presently two hunting units at the refuge: Eagle Creek and Hartford. The refuge manager can be contacted at Burlington for rules, directions, etc.

The broad area around Great Bend, Kansas (intersection of U.S. Highways 56, 156, 281), is one of the great waterfowling spots of the entire central plains. Here are located the Quivira National Wildlife Refuge (33) to the southeast, with public hunting, and Cheyenne Bottoms (34), an excellent free public area, to the northeast. Marais des Cygnes Waterfowl Management Area (see "Prairie Chicken"), another top location, lies along the Missouri border north of Fort Scott and Pleasanton, Kansas, beside U.S. 69. As many as 50,000 ducks winter here. Mallards, baldpate, scaup are common, with teal, pintails, etc., migrating through. This is considered one of the best waterfowling locations in the state.

Cedar Bluff Res. (35), U.S. 283, Trego Co.; Webster Res. (36), U.S. 24, Rooks Co.; Kirwin Res. (see "Pheasant"), U.S. 183, Phillips Co.; Norton Res. (37), U.S. 36, Norton Co.; Wilson Res. (38), I 70, Russell Co.; Lovewell Res. (39), north of U.S. 36, Jewell Co.; Kanapolis Res. (40), south of U.S. 40, Ellsworth Co.; Cheney Res. (41), north of U.S. 54 in Reno Co.; Milford Res. (42), Tuttle Creek Res. (43), Council Grove Res. (see "Quail"); Pomona Res. (45), U.S. 75, Osage Co.—all these offer fine waterfowling. In addition, in the general southeast portion of the state there are Fall River Res. (45), Toronto Res. (see "Quail"), Elk City Res. (47), plus all of the strip-pit waters.

Regulations vary a great deal from reservoir to reservoir, dependent upon its management and size. Thus, the Commission should be contacted, or else contact made with resident managers, to be certain all the hunting rules are followed. There are in addition to the above numerous other waterfowl projects scattered across the state. Several of the best of these: Lake McKinney (48) near Lakin, on U.S. 50 in the southwest; the Neosho Waterfowl Management Area (49) in the southeast, near Parsons; the Jamestown Waterfowl Management Area (50) two miles west of Jamestown in north-central Kansas. New impoundments and waterfowl projects are constantly in progress. The new Glen Elder Dam west of Beloit is one to watch.

Recent post-season winter surveys of Kansas waterfowl showed an estimated 700,000 ducks and 23,500 geese on the state waters. This is a good indication of the quality of hunting one may expect.

OTHER GAME BIRDS

Although there is open season annually for rails, snipe, and woodcock, little hunting is done for these birds in Kansas. The specialist will find a few spots where snipe limits can be shot, on the moist meadow and mud-flat edges of the waterfowling grounds. But this shooting is spotty and unpredictable. Woodcock, located invariably in brushy coverts with moist earth beneath, are scarce. A few are found near the waterways of eastern Kansas. A scattering of rails hide in the marshes in fall, but the hunting is so unproductive that it is hardly worthwhile.

Mourning dove hunting, on the other hand, is usually excellent. The kill averages from a million to a million and a half annually. Because doves are highly mobile, flocks concentrate during the season in the areas where feed is best that year. It is impossible to give specific areas where dove shooting will be best. However, all of the public hunting lands invariably offer fair to excellent dove hunting. Almost all are now managed so that food strips are planted, and much attention is paid to making each area that has suitable dove-feeding plots attractive to the birds. Locations where hedgerows border grain fields are especially good and may be found all over the state. Often private lands may be hunted, by permission, because hunters shooting doves are likely to select one stand and stay put.

Wild turkeys are not hunted at present, but almost certainly there will soon be a season. They have been widely stocked. Prior to trapping and transplant, there were some 500 turkeys along the Kansas-Oklahoma line. Stocking has now been done all the way from Morton Co. in the extreme southwest to Tuttle Creek Reservoir in the northeast. It is hoped that turkeys will in due time be a stable population with a huntable surplus over a major share of the state, especially in the western half. Many of the new flocks are being started on the public GMA lands. However, a number have purposely been placed on private lands, for careful protection. But agreement has been made with all landowners in these instances that when a season is open they must allow public hunting. There are as this is written an estimated 1000 wild turkeys in Kansas.

DEER

There is a steadily building deer herd of substantial proportions. To date deer hunting, which was begun only a few seasons ago, is for residents only. It is likely to stay that way for some years. Hunting is quite good, with

some very large bucks taken, probably because of the farm country where
they live, and little hunting over many years. Deer were thought extinct in
Kansas up until about 1930. Since then they have slowly made a comeback.
There are now an estimated 50,000. Most are whitetails. The bulk of them
are in the eastern area, along wooded streams and in upland timber. In the
high plains of the northwest there are a few mule deer. Success runs high
on them, around 46 percent in a recent season. But the bulk of the kill, about
75 percent, is whitetails. Total deer kill averages from 1500 to 2000 annually
at present.

Permits are offered to residents on a first-come basis. Firearms permits
usually number around 6500 currently. Archery permits are unlimited. The
state is divided into deer management areas for this hunting. Prospective
hunters should check carefully, and seasonally, what areas are open. A deer
unit map is available each fall from the Commission. So far hunter-landowner
relationships for deer hunting have been exceptionally good. However, in
addition to private lands, almost all of the larger public areas (detailed under
the foregoing various game birds) have top-notch deer hunting.

Almost without fail, the deer population density patterns follow the
stream courses. In the southeast quarter, the Neosho, Verdigris, Elk, Walnut,
and Ninnescah bottoms have good whitetail populations. Northeast, all of the
area along the Missouri River and westward over the first three counties in
four tiers is the same. The Marais des Cygnes River throughout its length is
a top strip for whitetails. Centrally, north to south, the Blue River, Republican,
and Solomon all are good bets throughout their lengths. Likewise, a bit
to the west, the Saline, Smoky Hill, Pawnee, and Arkansas rivers. The Arkansas
in the Great Bend region and on downstream provides quality hunting. In
the southwest, the Cimarron has good spots, particularly in Seward Co. In
the mule deer country of the far northwest, the forks of the Republican,
Sappa Creek, Prairie Dog Creek, and the forks of the Solomon, all are fair to
good. There are some whitetails here, too.

OTHER GAME ANIMALS

Antelope are not presently hunted, but a season is expected within a
few years. The extreme northwest has a fair herd. Releases have been made
to start herds along the upper reaches of the Smoky Hill River in the west,
southwest of Medicine Lodge in south-central Kansas, in McPherson Co.
in the center of the state, near Kanapolis Reservoir in Ellsworth Co., and
along the Arkansas River near Kinsley.

Squirrels provide a substantial amount of hunting, the bulk of it in the
east, and along the western stream courses. All of the public areas covered
under upland birds, and most under waterfowl, offer squirrel hunting from
fair to excellent. Estimates of the annual kill average from 200,000 to
330,000.

Rabbits are found over the entire state, the cottontail abundant in all
counties, and jacks abundant in the west. The cottontail kill fluctuates from
around 350,000 to upwards of one million. All the public areas offer good
rabbit hunting, but some have restrictions about use of dogs. Hunters should
check each public area for its rules. Jack rabbits are considered a pest and
furnish off-season shooting throughout the entire western half of the state.

PREDATORS AND PESTS

Coyotes are plentiful, particularly over the western half of the state. They
are still bountied, the only Kansas predator that is. Coyote hunting in Kansas

is practiced to some extent with coursing greyhounds. Plains hunting with a rifle is also pursued to some extent, as is calling. Of the public lands available, the Cimarron National Grasslands in the extreme southwest offer the best coyote hunting.

Bobcats and foxes are hunted only incidentally. There is a modest amount of this hunting by use of a call to be had on the management areas open to public hunting.

Raccoons are plentiful along all stream courses of the state, are mostly hunted with hounds by local residents.

Crows are abundant in winter, with large concentrations forming particularly down through the central part of the state. The larger public areas located in this broad corridor offer good winter crow shooting. Some other large roosts form from time to time along stream courses to the west.

There is a fair amount of pest shooting for prairie dogs in the west, especially the southwest and northwest extremes, and for woodchucks on farms in the east. These animals, however, are not especially abundant on public lands, excepting possibly some prairie dogs in the Cimarron National Grasslands, and thus permission is generally required for hunting. Small prairie dog towns and woodchuck colonies are scattered widely. There are no concentrations worth pinpointing.

REGULATIONS

Game laws pertaining to seasons, bag and possession limits, areas to be hunted, special hunts, license fees all may have numerous changes from year to year. For current regulations, and for other specific queries, write to: Forestry, Fish and Game Commission, P.O. Box 1028, Pratt, Kansas 67124.

OKLAHOMA

Oklahoma might be termed an "in-between" state, neither truly northern or southern, eastern or western. It is also different in physical attributes from the way most non-natives visualize it. The terrain is highly varied, from an extreme low elevation in the far southeastern corner of only 400 feet, to above 4000 feet at the far northwest. Nor is this any longer a "dust bowl." Man-made impoundments of large size, plus changes in farming and ranching, have brought Oklahoma excellent and highly varied game covers, and almost two million surface acres of water in lakes and streams.

In the northeast the Ozarks spill westward across the Oklahoma line. Here is a chain of impoundments as well as many streams large and small. In the southeast the Kiamichi and Ouachita mountains, cut by swift, sparkling small rivers are in certain places close to true wilderness. West of the Ozarks there are the Prairie Plains, and sweeping the southern border river-bottom lands stretch along the Red River, which separates Oklahoma from Texas. There are two other small mountain ranges, both curious formations: the Arbuckles in the south-central part of the state; the surprising Wichita Range in the southwest.

Cutting north to south in a wide central swath are the flatter Redbed Plains, then the Gypsum Hills to the west, and finally in the far northwest the so-called High Plains. All of the west is a low rainfall area, and there are therefore no forests. In the east, however, there are extensive pine and hardwood forests, perfect for forest game of several varieties. Most of the large lakes are in the eastern third of the state, right on a heavily traveled waterfowl flyway of the Mississippi Basin, toward the Gulf Coast.

An excellent highway system crisscrosses the state. Interstate 44 plus I 40 run from northeast to southwest, bisecting north-south I 35 at Oklahoma City. Half a dozen east-west U.S. highways and at least eight running north-south grid the state. Smaller roads split up the in-between sections. Air transport is excellent to all areas except the far west and the narrow strip of northwestern panhandle, where towns are mostly small.

Nationally Oklahoma hunting has had very little publicity. Nonetheless, it is excellent. The state is quite large, 200 miles north to south at its widest point, roughly 275 miles east to west in the major portion, but with the narrow Panhandle thrusting westward, up in the northwest, another 150 miles. Population is substantial, almost 2.5 million. But there are just under 70,000 square miles to contain it. The bulk of this population is situated from the state's center up toward the northeast. Primarily Oklahoma is a wheat, oil, and cattle country. Roughly 95 percent of its area is privately owned. Near the large cities hunting permission may be somewhat difficult, but in general Oklahomans are a friendly, rural folk who will allow hunting if properly approached.

Hunting is seldom crowded. License sales run around 250,000 total. But this includes a double-up of several thousand because of extra deer license. Surprisingly, nonresidents have barely discovered what is here. Only about 3000 to 3500 visitor licenses are sold. Most hunters, both resident and nonresident, are bird hunters. Although it is little known, Oklahoma ranks roughly third in the nation in its quail harvest. Most are bobwhites. There are some blue, or scaled, quail. In the Panhandle and eastward there is good pheasant hunting. Turkeys are numerous over the western half of the state, deer are in every county. These are whitetails, with exception of the far northwest, where some mule deer are also found.

Very good prairie-chicken hunting is still available in widely separated areas, northeast and far west. Doves and waterfowl are excellent. Some famous waterfowling, in fact, exists. Squirrels and rabbits are abundant, the latter in two varieties, cottontails and swamp rabbits. A fair antelope herd is building, a very few elk are available. Varmint populations are high, particularly coyotes across the west. Millions of crows swarm roosts in winter.

Although much of the land is owned, there are some half million acres managed for wildlife and hunting by the Department of Wildlife Conservation. These areas are well scattered over the state. There are twenty-plus Public Hunting Areas, some large, some small. These offer a variety of game, from upland birds to deer. Some are major waterfowl areas. The Department will furnish excellent maps of any or all of these, showing access and game varieties available. On the designated Public Hunting Areas there is no fee.

There are also some excellent federal lands open to hunting. In the far southwest corner of the Panhandle the Rita Blanca National Grassland spills over the line from Texas. Black Kettle National Grass Land, lying along the north-south border with the Texas Panhandle offers some 30,000 acres chiefly for birds. In the southeast there are a quarter-million acres of the Ouachita National Forest, excellent deer and forest-game cover. The McAlester Naval Ammunition Depot also has specified hunts, with quality deer hunting. And in private lands, commercial forests have some 500,000 open acres in the southeast.

In addition to all the above, there are some thirty-five tracts of land not under Department management where public hunting is available. On some of these permits are required, on some there are fees. They include city lakes, county lakes and land surrounding them, plus some odds and ends of others. Although these lands will not be detailed in this chapter, since they are of minor importance compared to the others, hunters can get lists of them from the Department, with their size, exact location, and regulations given. It is best to inquire about these by specified county where one's hunt is planned.

The Oklahoma Department of Wildlife Conservation has become over the past decade or so a crack organization with excellent management people. Game such as deer, turkeys, and prairie chickens are constantly being trapped and transplanted to new areas. Waterfowl management is on the upswing, and numerous research projects are constantly progressing to give sportsmen more and more.

Places for hunters to stay are no problem. All the U.S. highways offer motels and hotels in large number in the vicinity of cities and towns. It is wise, however, when attending an opening of a season in the far west or northwest to reserve ahead. For example, when pheasant season opens, everybody goes. Such places as Guymon and Boise City often have all motel-hotel accommodations taken.

For hunters who like to camp, there is no problem. Oklahoma has an exemplary State Park System. These are spaced conveniently across the state, from Ten-Killer Lake in the east to Quartz Mountain in the southwest and Black Mesa in the far northwest Panhandle. Several of these parks have lodges, and some have excellent rental cottages. There is also camping on all of the federal lands—numerous locations around the Corps of Engineers reservoirs, in the National Forest and Grasslands, near the National Refuges such as the Wichita Mountains Wildlife Refuge, and in Platt National Park.

During early seasons Oklahoma can be hot, dry in the west, humid in the east. But quick northers can materialize. It is a good idea to go equipped with clothing for either warm or chilly weather. Late seasons, and waterfowling, can be very cold when storms strike.

Arms and ammunition here should be varied, from No. 7½ and No. 8 shot for quail, No. 6 and No. 7½ for prairie chickens and pheasants, to heavy loads for turkeys, ducks, geese. Deer hunting in the forests will be in heavy cover, but westward in more open and stream-bottom terrain. Rifles should be selected accordingly, and so should power of scope. For antelope, a flat-shooting, long-range rifle is needed.

QUAIL

Oklahoma is an excellent quail state. By numbers annually taken—as many as three million—quail are in fact the chief game crop. Most are bobwhites. There are some scaled, or blue, quail in the west. The greatest abundance of all quail is in the western half of the state. Nonetheless, eastern Oklahoma has many areas of good quail hunting. All brushy regions, preferably adjacent to croplands, offer quail hunting, especially along and spreading out from the rivers and their many tributaries. Oklahoma's several large river systems run in a general direction from northwest to southeast. This places them across the longest dimension of the state and thus makes an enormous amount of quality quail habitat available. The main river systems with numerous tributary streams, are, reading from north to south: The Arkansas, Cimarron, North Canadian, South Canadian, Washita, Red. Quail hunters should plan hunts as much as possible based on the river systems.

As noted earlier, much hunting is by permission on private lands. Public lands, however, offer a tremendous amount of prime quail hunting. For scaled (blue) quail, the top Public Hunting Area is Rita Blanca (1). To avoid confusion, this is actually the Rita Blanca National Grassland, under U.S. Forest Service administration. But the state cooperates in game management. This PHA is located in southern Cimarron Co., the westernmost county of the Panhandle. Boise City, and U.S. Routes 287, 385, 64, 56, offer Area access. The Grassland is split into numerous plots, all plainly marked with yellow Forest Service signs. There are 16,000 public acres here, chiefly short-grass country, with water furnished by windmills. There are some bobwhites, but blues predominate.

On some of the PHAs, quail (usually bobwhites) are the primary game species. These spots—and in the west—will be noted first. Altus-Lugert PHA (2) covers 3600 acres. This is in the southwest, along the border between Greer and Kiowa Cos. It surrounds the upper part of Altus Res-

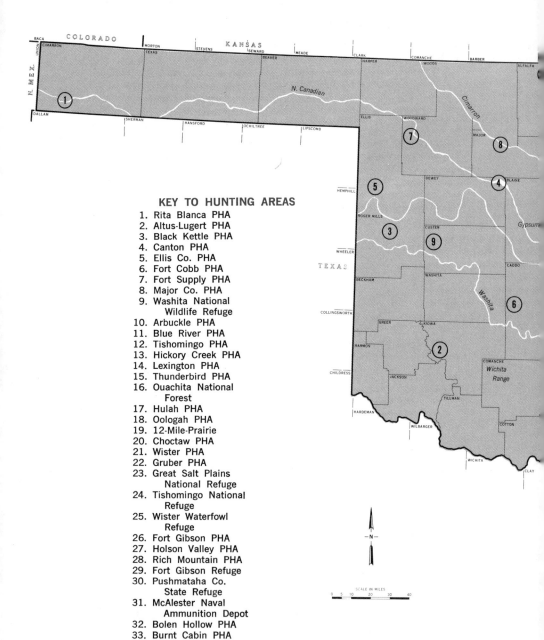

KEY TO HUNTING AREAS

1. Rita Blanca PHA
2. Altus-Lugert PHA
3. Black Kettle PHA
4. Canton PHA
5. Ellis Co. PHA
6. Fort Cobb PHA
7. Fort Supply PHA
8. Major Co. PHA
9. Washita National
   Wildlife Refuge
10. Arbuckle PHA
11. Blue River PHA
12. Tishomingo PHA
13. Hickory Creek PHA
14. Lexington PHA
15. Thunderbird PHA
16. Ouachita National
    Forest
17. Hulah PHA
18. Oologah PHA
19. 12-Mile-Prairie
20. Choctaw PHA
21. Wister PHA
22. Gruber PHA
23. Great Salt Plains
    National Refuge
24. Tishomingo National
    Refuge
25. Wister Waterfowl
    Refuge
26. Fort Gibson PHA
27. Holson Valley PHA
28. Rich Mountain PHA
29. Fort Gibson Refuge
30. Pushmataha Co.
    State Refuge
31. McAlester Naval
    Ammunition Depot
32. Bolen Hollow PHA
33. Burnt Cabin PHA
34. Okmulgee PHA
35. Stringtown PHA

442

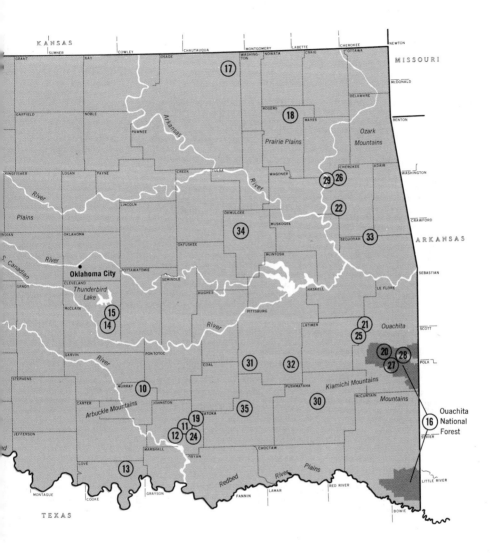

OKLAHOMA

ervoir. The city of Altus is a few miles south on U.S. 283. Numerous food plots are planted here. Black Kettle PHA (3) covers 31,000 acres, in 111 units, is one of the best quail-producing areas in the state. This, like Rita Blanca, is a National Grassland. It is administered by the U.S. Forest Service, but managed in cooperation with the state. This huge area is in Roger Mills Co., which lies along Oklahoma's north-south border with the Texas panhandle. The PHA units are scattered chiefly to the north and northwest of the town of Cheyenne on U.S. 283. This is in the upper reaches of the Washita River watershed.

Another excellent western tract is Canton PHA (4), 16,775 acres of grass with some oak, cottonwood, and hackberry. Numerous cover crops are grown here, and many miles of roads give good access. The Area is based on Canton Lake, a reservoir on the North Canadian. The public land lies partly in Blaine, Dewey, and Major Cos. U.S. 183, 270, 60 all lead to the region. The largest nearby city is Watonga, to the south.

Back to the far west, again on the border with the Texas Panhandle, is Ellis Co. and Ellis Co. PHA (5). This 3936-acre tract is near the border, west and south of the town of Arnett, through which runs U.S. 60. There is much grass cover here, with some scrub oak, sumac, and a large planted shelter belt of locust.

Fort Cobb PHA (6) is also in the western best-quail-habitat part of the state. The entire PHA, almost half of which is water (an arm of Fort Cobb Reservoir) covers 3315 acres. It is located in midwestern Caddo Co., on a tributary of the Washita River. State routes 58, 152, 146, and 9 form a square around the reservoir region; the town of Albert is three miles east, on 146.

Fort Supply PHA (7) is another reservoir-based tract. It covers 5500 acres in western Woodward Co., up in the northwest almost to the Oklahoma Panhandle. The city of Woodward is sixteen miles to the southeast, on U.S. 270, which goes on past Fort Supply Reservoir on the North Canadian River.

Another excellent choice not far from the above is Major County PHA (8), in northwest Major Co. U.S. 281 and State 15 are the key routes. There are three units in this PHA. All are of modest size—205, 240, 280 acres. The units lie along or near State 15, one of them near the U.S. 281 junction, the others some distance east toward the village of Orienta.

Farther to the southwest is the Washita National Wildlife Refuge (9). This is owned by the federal government but the state cooperates in management. The area is in Custer Co., six miles west of Butler. Butler is on U.S. 183. State 33 to the west goes to the Refuge area. The Washita River, with its bottomland timber, runs through the 1500 open acres. Some 1400 of these acres are in farmland, raising grain crops. This is near Foss Reservoir on the Washita.

All of the above are the best of the public lands in western Oklahoma's top quail habitat. A word must be said here about regulations. On some PHA lands hunting is allowed seven days a week, but on some only on certain staggered days. Also, on some open lands such as Washita only certain game (in this instance quail and rabbit) may be hunted. Check all regulations thoroughly relating to individual tracts. They may differ.

Moving eastward to about the center of the state, there are several PHAs where quail are still among the primary species hunted. One of these is Arbuckle PHA (10), almost 1200 acres based on Arbuckle Reservoir in

Murray Co. This is good mixed cover. The junction of U.S. 177 and State 7, and the town of Sulphur, are location keys. The PHA is to the west. Platt National Park, incidentally, is nearby. Blue River PHA (11) is in the next county to the east, Johnston. Its 923 acres lie along the Blue River east of the city of Tishomingo, through which run State Routes 99 and 78. Also near Tishomingo, on State 99 a few miles south of that city and adjoining the Tishomingo National Wildlife Refuge, is Tishomingo PHA (12). There are 3170 acres here, managed in good part for waterfowl but with fine quail hunting also. In the same general part of the state, but south and west, in northeastern Love Co.—a Texas border county on the Red River—is 8000-acre Hickory Creek PHA (13). Native bluestem grass, with mixed oak, hickory, and other timber form good habitat here. It is northeast of Marietta, at which town U.S. 77 intersects State 32.

To the north, still about in the middle part of the state, there are two more quality quail spots. Both are in Cleveland Co. Lexington PHA (14) contains 7980 acres. It is southeast of Noble, which is on U.S. 77 a short distance south of Oklahoma City. The other is Thunderbird PHA (15), a two-tract Area on arms of Thunderbird Lake, practically within sight of the capital. Each contains approximately 3500 acres.

As noted previously, while eastern Oklahoma is not the quail concentration half of the state, it still offers very good shooting. The two large blocks of the Ouachita National Forest (16), both in the southeast, one along the Arkansas border in LeFlore Co., the other in the extreme southeast corner of the state, in southeast McCurtain Co., offer in places some fair quail hunting. There is also good hunting on a number of PHAs in the east. These will be located under other species, but names to keep in mind for reference to those where quail are among the primary species will be given here. They are: Bolen Hollow PHA: Choctaw PHA; Fort Gibson PHA; Gruber PHA; Hulah PHA; Oologah PHA; Stringtown PHA; Wister PHA. A few others have bobwhites in lesser numbers as a secondary species. Quail enthusiasts can assume that almost any of the Oklahoma Public Hunting Areas where it is legal to hunt quail will have a fair supply.

PRAIRIE CHICKEN

At this time Oklahoma is the only state with huntable surpluses of both the greater and lesser prairie chicken. The greater chicken is by far the most numerous. Its area of concentration is in the general northeast part of the state. The lesser chicken is found in the west, along the Texas border. In up-cycle seasons Oklahoma has very good hunting for these birds, with a total kill of as many as 10,000. Once abundant throughout much of the interior of the U.S., the prairie chicken population rapidly diminished with the breaking of virgin sod and the disappearance of the grasslands. Today it is in serious danger over most of its original range, with only remnant populations still existing. Oklahoma is carefully managing the two varieties and has high hopes of keeping them in fair supply and even of extending their range within the state.

The greater prairie chicken is most abundant in Osage Co. This large and rather sparsely settled county lies north of the Arkansas River, which is its southern boundary, and has its northern border with Kansas. U.S. 60 crosses it east-west; so does State 20. State Routes 18 and 99 are the main north-south roads. The town of Pawhuska is roughly in the center of the county. There is quite a bit of virgin unplowed range grass in this county and elsewhere in the northeast in surrounding counties. One of the prime areas is the ranchlands north and west of Pawhuska, near the settlements of Foraker and Grainola, and also farther northwest across the line in Kay Co., in the vicinity of Hardy.

As this is written, the prairie chicken season is brief—three days—and the area open for greater prairie chickens is described as follows: that part of northeastern Oklahoma bounded on the north and east by the state line, on the west by the Arkansas River from the Kansas line to the crossing of State Route 51 near Tulsa, thence eastward along State 51 to the Arkansas line. This takes in a portion of Kay Co. on the northwest corner, all of Osage, part of Tulsa, all of Washington, Nowata (one of the concentration counties), Craig, Ottawa, Rogers, Mayes, Delaware, parts of Wagoner, Cherokee, and Adair.

Hunters interested in these birds should keep track of transplant operations in which the Department is active. As many as 300 greater chickens are trapped in a year in Osage Co. and elsewhere in the northeast, and attempts are being made to establish flocks in all suitable grassland areas down through the center and west-of-center of the state and into the south. Eight counties are slated for experiment, and some have at this time already been stocked. These are: Caddo, Grady, Garvin, Murray, Pontotoc, Johnston, Bryan, Marshall. In general these counties lie along the Washita River. Southern Caddo Co. has already been stocked as this is written, and other transplants have been made in the vicinity of Pauls Valley in Garvin Co.

There are not many PHAs within the open-season area of the greater prairie chicken. Two, mentioned but not located under "Quail," are the following: Hulah PHA (17) is an 1800-acre tract in northeastern Osage Co. It is tall-grass prairie but with a large amount of varied timber also. The tract is based on the Birch Creek and Cotton Creek arms of Hulah Reservoir, an impoundment on Caney Creek. State 99 north from Pawhuska leads to the vicinity. This PHA is primarily a quail and waterfowl tract, somewhat east of the better chicken range. The second area is the Oologah PHA (18) located along Oologah Reservoir in southern Nowata and northern Rogers Co. This 33,000-acre Area is reached via U.S. 60 east of the town of Nowata. While prairie chickens are of secondary importance here, they are present.

The lesser prairie chicken is hunted at present in the following western counties: in the Panhandle reading west to east, Texas and Beaver; from the Kansas line south along the north-south border with the Texas Panhandle, Harper, Ellis, Roger Mills, Beckham, and on the eastern border of Ellis Co., Woodward. The best concentrations are usually found in Ellis and Roger Mills Cos. The Ellis Co. PHA ("Quail") offers fair hunting. Also within the open range: Black Kettle; Fort Supply. These also are located under "Quail." There is usually a special one-day season in mid-December on the lesser chicken in the counties listed above, in addition to the regular season.

It is presently estimated that there are at least 120,000 prairie chickens, aggregate of both species, in Oklahoma. By standards elsewhere this is substantial, and hunters seeking at least token experience with this handsome and delicious prairie grouse will do well to consider an Oklahoma hunt for it.

PHEASANT

Oklahoma pheasant range is somewhat restricted, but an average of 10,000 avid hunters manage to bag 20,000 to 25,000 birds annually. The three counties of the Panhandle—Cimarron, Texas, Beaver—furnish the best hunting. And the best of this is found in grainfields and bottoms along the North Canadian River, which courses across all three counties. The expansion of irrigation is at this time assisting the pheasant to spread its range eastward over the high plains along the Kansas border. All told, pheasant hunting in Oklahoma is steadily improving, but the Panhandle continues to be the quality range, and in general the farther west one goes, the more birds there are. The Panhandle counties get a heavy play from opening-day hunters and most of the accommodations in the towns—Guymon, Boise City—are booked up far ahead.

Outside the Panhandle, currently the following counties are open: Harper, Woodward, Woods, Alfalfa, Grant, Kay. As in the Panhandle, the grain fields adjacent to the rivers offer the most birds. Daily limits differ in these counties from those in the Panhandle as a rule.

The major portion of the pheasant crop is taken on private lands. However, there are two public areas where pheasants are present even though of secondary importance. These are the Rita Blanca Grasslands in southern Cimarron Co., and the Fort Supply PHA in western Woodward Co. Both these are described and located under "Quail."

WILD TURKEYS

Only twenty years ago there were no turkeys in Oklahoma, or if any at all were present they were indeed rare. There was no hunting. Stocking of the Rio Grande subspecies of turkey from Texas was begun, and today the state flock is estimated at somewhere between 30,000 and 50,000 birds. It is steadily growing. The western half of the state has the preponderance of the birds. But yearly the range is being pushed farther east, by transplants of as high as 400 to 600 live-trapped wild birds each winter. The Department hopes eventually to have the Rio Grande wild turkey established throughout all suitable areas of the entire state.

Hunting seasons were begun with fall shooting. In 1965 a spring season was added. It is necessary to buy a special turkey permit in addition to the regular hunting license. A permit not filled in fall is still good for the following spring hunt. As this is written permits have been averaging about 6000-plus annually. With an either-sex law in fall and gobblers only in spring, hunters have run up an astonishing success score. During a recent season over 3200 birds were bagged, for a success percentage of 57.6. That is extremely high.

Areas of turkey concentration are presently almost entirely west of U.S. 77 (I 35), which runs north-south border to border, passing through Oklahoma City and dividing the state about in half. The concentrations are based for the most part on and spreading out from the large-river courses. For example, there is an isolated concentration in the far northwest, in northwest and north-central Cimarron Co. where the Cimarron River cuts across and leaves the state to enter Colorado. In Texas and Beaver Cos. of the Panhandle, the turkey flocks are along the North Canadian. They continue along it almost into the central part of the state, to west of Oklahoma City in northwestern Canadian Co.

In the north, where the Cimarron River reenters the state, there is another heavy concentration beginning in Woods Co., and following along the river to north of Oklahoma City in Kingfisher Co. On the western border, along the Texas Panhandle, southern Ellis Co., all of Roger Mills Co., most of Greer, some of northern Harmon and Jackson Cos. are well blanketed with birds. This concentration continues along the South Canadian eastward clear into Blaine Co. South and west of Oklahoma City there is another large area of concentration. This covers almost all of Caddo Co., spills eastward along the streams well past the city of Chickasha in Grady Co., and reaches westward into southeast Washita Co. and south from Caddo Co. into northwestern Comanche Co.

There is another good concentration area up along the northern border. It begins well west of Great Salt Plains National Wildlife Refuge in Alfalfa Co., follows the Arkansas River system (Salt Fork) across southern Grant Co., on across southern Kay Co. along the Salt Fork, and then reaches on south some distance into Osage Co. along the main Arkansas, and north also up this branch around Lake Ponca, the Kaw Reservoir to the Kansas line. Scattered flocks are of course found elsewhere over the entire western half of the state, and others are east of U.S. 77, but the regions described hold the most birds. Hunters should carefully check open counties for any given season. For example, during a recent fall season all or parts of twenty-nine counties were open, but the following spring forty-two counties plus a portion of Osage were open. Some of these counties were east of I 35, in the area southeast from Oklahoma City.

Much turkey hunting is on private lands. So far cooperation of landowners has been very good whenever permission has been politely requested. There is also some excellent turkey hunting on the public lands. Among the best bets are: Fort Supply and Canton PHAs, and the Black Kettle Grasslands (and PHA). Ellis Co., Lexington, and Hickory Creek PHAs also offer good hunting. Most of the other PHAs in turkey range have fair to good hunting. Altus-Lugert, Arbuckle, and Fort Cobb are examples. All of the above are described and located under "Quail."

MOURNING DOVES

The dove kill averages around a million birds annually. Birds are plentiful. Undoubtedly more could be harvested if more hunters concentrated on them. Doves range over the entire state, but the heaviest concentrations are usually in the south and southwest. However, some parts of the southeast are also excellent.

A favorite dove shooting region, with probably the heaviest flights found in the state, is north of Lake Texoma. This is in Johnston Co. in the Tishomingo vicinity. The 12-Mile-Prairie (19) east of Tishomingo is the hottest spot. Another good region is in the southwest, particularly near Frederick in Tillman Co. This is near the Texas border, with U.S. 183 passing through the city of Frederick.

There is excellent dove hunting on some of the PHAs. Altus-Lugert in the southwest is good. Arbuckle, south-central, offers the dove as a primary species. So does south-centrally located Blue River. These are all noted under "Quail." In the east, near the Arkansas border, there is surprisingly good dove shooting in portions of the Ouachita National Forest lands. The Choctaw PHA (20) is actually composed of 181,000 acres of this Forest, in southeast LeFlore Co. Doves are among the important species here. U.S. 259, 270, 271 all reach the huge area, which is south of the town of Poteau. In this same vicinity is 17,996-acre Wister PHA (21). It is partly in LeFlore, partly in Latimer counties, and is located southwest of the town of Wister, which is on U.S. 270. Wister PHA is considered a hotspot for doves. These two Areas were mentioned, but not described, under "Quail."

Ellis Co. PHA, Fort Cobb, Fort Gibson, Fort Supply, Hickory Creek,

Lexington, Rita Blanca, Thunderbird, Tishomingo (all noted under "Quail") offer dove shooting of varying quality. Hulah PHA furnishes some dove hunting up in the northeast, and at Oologah PHA, also in the northeast, the dove is a primary target. (See "Prairie Chicken" for both of these.)

One other spot to be noted in the northeast part of the state is Gruber PHA (22). This 42,540-acre Area is jointly managed, under license from the U.S. Army, by the Oklahoma National Guard and the Department of Wildlife Conservation. It is partly in southwestern Cherokee Co., and partly in northeastern Muskogee Co. U.S. 62 is the key route, and signs directing to the Area can be located approximately ten miles east of the town of Fort Gibson. Almost half of the Area is in open fields and abandoned farms, the remainder in varied timber. There are creeks and ponds, food plots planted in the portion lying in Muskogee Co. Many miles of access roads lead through the Area.

WOODCOCK, RAILS, SNIPE

These species have almost no importance in Oklahoma. They could have some, however, if hunters would actively seek them, although none are very plentiful. Oklahoma has over two-dozen impoundments, some extremely large, some of medium size, and these, plus the vast river system, gather a number of jacksnipe, some rails, and a few woodcock during fall migrations. Few of the birds stay long, however, for the main flights of all three wind up wintering farther south, chiefly in Louisiana. Waterfowlers who will concentrate on snipe hunting in marshy areas around the impoundments can get some shooting, nonetheless, and there are spotty concentrations of both woodcock and rails. The latter are difficult to hunt because it is almost impossible under inland conditions without tide effects to get them to flush. Woodcock hunters who will diligently hunt the stream bottoms where moist earth is available with thin ground cover but dappled shade above will find some shooting. The Hulah PHA in the northeast, with flat flood plain along the Caney River, a marsh, and a number of small ponds, is of some modest note as a rail hunting location. Oologah PHA, also in the northeast, with many plum thickets, bottomland timber, and a lake of almost 6000 acres, at times offers fair woodcock shooting. Both these areas have been located under "Prairie Chicken."

WATERFOWL

Few hunters realize what an excellent waterfowl state Oklahoma is. The state has hundreds of miles of rivers and creeks with good jump-shooting and decoy shooting along them. There are a third of a million farm ponds that draw waterfowl flocks and hold them in scattered locations over the state. The large impoundments at the present contain over half a million acres and more impoundments are constantly under construction or planned. Farther south Gulf Coast waterfowl habitat has been slowly deteriorating, but meanwhile Oklahoma's wintering areas have been steadily improving. The Central flyway funnels vast numbers of ducks and geese down through the state. There is great variety: ducks of numerous species, with heavy emphasis on mallards and pintails; blue, snow, white-fronted (specklebelly) and Canada geese. It is estimated that half a million mallards migrate through, and at least 150,000 winter on the refuges. The total duck kill is probably between 75,000 and 100,000. Well over 10,000 geese are taken annually.

The large impoundments offer excellent duck and some goose hunting for the hunter equipped for big water. Those such as Eufaula, Grand, and Texoma require a large and sturdy boat, large numbers of decoys—as many as 100—and a blind that can stand rough weather. Of the diving ducks, redheads and canvasbacks are most sought. Eufaula has recently been a hotspot for redheads. Late in the season large rafts of puddle ducks also show up on the huge impoundments—baldpates, mallards, pintails. The smaller tree-lined streams almost anywhere will have good jump-shooting for teal, wood ducks, and mallards. Many hunters also shoot pintails, teal, etc., from quickly built blinds along the larger streams, with a few decoys out front.

Shooting along the Red River, the border with Texas, can be excellent almost anywhere on cold, overcast days. There may even be large goose flights here. Red River shooting for ducks and geese can be hard work, though. It requires much walking through dense scrub, or else the use of large stools of decoys. Floating the smaller streams in a canoe or small boat is an excellent method for getting wood ducks and mallards. One of the better larger streams, the Deep Fork that cuts across Oklahoma, Lincoln and Creek Cos. east of Oklahoma City, is considered a good example of a stream where a few decoys and a hastily built blind will pay off.

In western Oklahoma there is a wealth of good waterfowling all but untouched by hunters, on such reservoirs as Altus (Kiowa-Greer Cos.), Ellsworth, Fort Cobb (Caddo Co.), Foss (Custer Co.), Canton (Dewey Co.), Fort Supply (Woodward Co.), Lake Lloyd Vincent (Ellis Co.). These and all other lakes in the west get little pressure. Ellis Co., for example, has good river and lake shooting, but in one recent season there were not even a dozen waterfowl stamps sold in the entire county. Thus, much Oklahoma waterfowling is still to be ferreted out by hunters, and there are all sorts of opportunities on the big reservoirs and along the streams for public hunting.

The two most popular, and undoubtedly best, goose hunting locations in the state are in the country surrounding the two most important National Refuges: Great Salt Plains (23), and Tishomingo (24). Great Salt Plains is located near the northern border, west of center, in Alfalfa Co. U.S. 64 is the key major access route. This highway, plus State Routes 8, 11, and 132 box in the 32,400-acre Refuge. Tishomingo Refuge, over 16,000 acres, is far to the south, just a short distance north of the Texas border near the town of Tishomingo, and is located on an arm of Lake Texoma. State Routes 99 and 78 intersect at Tishomingo. Well over half of the geese shot in Oklahoma each season are taken in the countryside surrounding these Refuges. Many ducks are shot in the same areas, too.

The small village of Jet, on U.S. 64 just south of Great Salt Plains Refuge, is a goose hunting headquarters. There are a small motel and a cafe here, and residents who will pluck geese. Surrounding wheat farms rent pits and decoys for from $5 to $10 per day, and the goose shooting is generally excellent. At Tishomingo there is some fee shooting. But here also is located the 3170-acre Tishomingo PHA ("Quail"). This is an excellent waterfowl Area. There are at present thirty three-man cement-block goose blinds, utilized on a first-come basis. There are also nineteen one-acre potholes to provide duck shooting. This PHA adjoins the western edge of the Refuge, borders both sides of the Washita River, and has both timber and marshy bottomland.

Another fine Refuge situation is near the Wister Waterfowl Refuge (25), in the southeast, in LeFlore Co. This is the only Refuge of its kind in the east. There are 5000 acres, with around 500 planted as feed to hold waterfowl as a kind of rest stop. This Refuge is west of Lake Wister and east of U.S. 271. It is a part of the almost 18,000-acre Wister PHA ("Doves"), although of course there is no hunting on the refuge portion. Diked areas have been constructed to form waterfowl marshes. One of these, and numerous food plots, are on the hunting portion. Willows form natural duck blinds.

Other public acreage that offers fine duck hunting are Fort Cobb ("Quail") and Fort Gibson PHAs (26), the latter for geese as well as ducks. Fort Gibson, mentioned but not described under "Quail," contains 14,000 acres, is located on Fort Gibson Reservoir, in the northeast, and lies partly in three counties: Mayes, Wagoner, and Cherokee. It is north of Muskogee on U.S. 69. The intensively managed portion is east of the village of Wagoner (U.S. 69) on State 51. Other parts of the Area are reached via U.S. 69 north of Wagoner. There is a Refuge here also. The Area is still under development. Currently there are nine marsh plots, an acreage of wheat to attract geese. Some goose pits are built and more will be.

Other PHAs that offer waterfowl hunting: Altus-Lugert, Canton, Hickory Creek, Lexington, Thunderbird (all under "Quail"), Hulah and Oologah ("Prairie Chicken").

EXOTIC BIRDS

Like many other states, Oklahoma is experimenting with various imported game-bird species in attempts to fill thin spots in their game picture. Black-necked pheasants have been tried at Fort Gibson, and the Afghan white-winged pheasant, which has done well elsewhere in arid terrain, is also being tried in the west. Both tinamou and jungle fowl are also under experiment. In addition, sixty of the giant geese of the long-lost Canadian variety were purchased in an attempt to start a nesting flock. It is hoped that in coming years some of these birds may be available for hunting.

DEER

Some years ago deer were all but gone from Oklahoma. Expert management plus land-use changes have sparked an excellent modern herd. There are at present an estimated 50,000 or more deer in the state, ranging in all seventy-seven counties. During a recent season all but a few counties showed at least some kills, one county had almost 500, several others were close behind. In the past decade the herd is believed to have doubled. It is predicted that by the early 1970s it will have doubled again. At present there are several deer management areas within an hour's drive of the major eastern cities that have from twenty to forty deer per square mile. An average of 50,000 deer hunters bag over 5000 deer annually, and the kill is steadily rising.

Whitetails range throughout the state, from the cypress swamps and pine forests of the southeast throughout the oaks, the prairies, the sagebrush clear to the juniper and pinyon of the northwest mesas. Many are large. A number dress out each year over 200 pounds. Cimarron Co., the far-west county of the Panhandle, has mule deer along with whitetails, in the northern portion along the Cimarron River. Not many mule deer are killed. Most are on public school land leased to individuals and thus not available for public hunting. Mule deer have been released, however, as much as 200 miles east of their normal range and it is hoped they may become established.

Best deer hunting is in the southeast, followed by portions of the east-central and northeast. During a recent season the ten highest-kill counties in order were as follows: McCurtain, Cherokee, Pittsburg, Delaware, Pushmataha, Sequoyah, LeFlore, Osage, Muskogee, Atoka. This is the general pattern from year to year. Next in line, and still in the east, were Latimer, Mayes,

Creek, Okmulgee. Central Nowata Co. in the northeast also has a good deer concentration. So does Washington Co. immediately to the west. There is another good pocket of abundance running across Lincoln Co., east of Oklahoma City. Numerous other smaller areas of special abundance are scattered over the eastern half of the state.

Moving west, and reading from the north down, there is a good area lying on the border between Alfalfa and Grant Cos. and extending well into each. Below these, southeastern Major Co. and northwestern Kingfisher Co. contain another. In the eastern portion of the southwest, three counties are outstanding: Canadian, Caddo, Comanche. Then, farther west along the Texas Panhandle border and near it, north to south, Woodward, Ellis, and Roger Mills Cos. have the bulk of the deer.

This gives a broad picture of general abundance. Hunters must bear in mind that as the herd grows, areas surrounding the counties noted will probably get better. Each fall a number of refuges are open for deer hunting under special regulations and usually with a limited number of permits. Some of these refuges are within PHAs. For example, Choctaw, which is actually Ouachita National Forest ("Doves"), contains two management areas within its boundaries, Holson Valley PHA (27) and Rich Mountain PHA (28) that are open only to deer hunting. Fort Gibson ("Waterfowl") adjoins the Fort Gibson Refuge (29), which is open for special deer hunts. There is Pushmataha Co. State Refuge (30) in the southeast, near which U.S. 271 runs below the town of Tuskahoma, which has a special deer season. Several others should be checked with the Department for possible seasons: Spavinaw Hills; Cookson Hills; Cherokee; Atoka; Wister; Hulah. Great Salt Plains N.W. Refuge also has a deer season.

One of the high-kill special seasons is at the McAlester Naval Ammunition Depot (31). This federal property is in southwestern Pittsburg Co., southwest of the city of McAlester. U.S. 69 runs along the eastern edge. An interesting item here is that some white fallow deer are on the property and a few are occasionally taken.

Although a substantial amount of deer hunting is done on private lands by permission, the public lands offer top-notch hunting. Both blocks of the large Ouachita NF, in LeFlore and southeast McCurtain Cos. are among the best. The PHAs actually offer in many instances better deer hunting than privately owned lands. Following are noted the PHAs where deer are considered a primary species.

Bolen Hollow PHA (32) is one. This PHA was mentioned, but not described, under "Quail." It lies in southeastern Pittsburg Co., one of the high-kill deer counties of the southeast. There are 1385 acres of oak and some pine. This is in the portion of the county where the Jack Fork Mountains are located. The Area is some miles down a gravel road south of the village of Hartshorne, which is at the junction of U.S. 270 and State 63. Burnt Cabin PHA (33) in southern Cherokee and northwest Sequoyah Cos., both also high-kill counties, is another good spot. It contains 1950 acres of oak and hickory, borders on Tenkiller Reservoir on the Illinois River. Routes 10 and then 10A southeast out of Muskogee lead near the Area.

Canton PHA, Ellis Co. PHA, Fort Supply PHA, Hickory Creek PHA, Tishomingo PHA ("Quail") all have abundant deer. So do Choctaw ("Doves"), Gruber ("Waterfowl"), and Oologah ("Prairie Chicken").

Two other PHAs not so far described are quality deer range. One is Okmulgee PHA (34). This contains almost 8500 acres in midwestern Okmulgee Co. It is reached from the city of Okmulgee on State 56. This is oak country along the Deep Fork River. Some cropland is farmed to produce deer food. The second tract is Stringtown PHA (35), briefly noted under "Quail." There are 2260 acres here, partly hardwood timber, partly prairie grass. It is in midwestern Atoka Co., a few miles off U.S. 69 out of the village of Stringtown.

Other PHAs with fair deer hunting: Arbuckle, Black Kettle, Fort Gibson, Hulah, Lexington, Thunderbird, Wister. All have been described elsewhere in this chapter.

ANTELOPE

Oklahoma had its first antelope season in 1966. There have been seasons since. Only two counties are open at present, both in the Panhandle: Cimarron and Texas. Permits have averaged about 100 annually. The animals are all on private lands. Before a hunter can get a permit he must procure an application for permission to hunt, have it signed by a landowner where he will hunt. Although hunting so far is extremely limited, some big bucks are taken, probably because there has so far been so little hunting. During one of the first seasons a Boone & Crockett record head was collected. The state hopes to enlarge its antelope herd, currently estimated at about 500 animals.

ELK

There are elk on the Wichita Mountains National Wildlife Refuge, in the southwest, in Comanche Co. near Lawton. Some spill over onto private ranches north and northwest of the Refuge as escapees, in both Kiowa and Comanche Cos. A season is occasionally opened. There is at present no elk license as such. Elk are taken in the two specified counties on a deer license. Very few are killed—twenty-six one season—but there are some large heads. Obtaining permission from ranchers for this hunt is difficult, and of course competition for opportunity is severe.

RABBITS

Cottontails range statewide and hunting is good, especially along the rivers and in brushy areas. There are many jackrabbits in the west. The small Merriam's cottontail is found in the extreme northwest. In the southeast, along the stream bottoms, there are good numbers of the large swamp rabbits and they are popular with hunters. However, all told rabbits are by no means as avidly sought here as most other species. Approximately 40,000 hunters are interested, and the kill is estimated at less than 400,000. Rabbits were not even recognized in Oklahoma as game animals, with any protection, until 1966.

Almost all of the public lands have good rabbit hunting. There is little choice, and no problem finding a place to hunt on these lands. One location that should be mentioned in particular is the Washita National Wildlife Refuge ("Quail"), in the west, in Custer Co. Only quail and rabbits are hunted here. PHAs where rabbits are considered one of the primary species are as follows: Arbuckle, Choctaw, Fort Cobb, Lexington, Oologah, Stringtown, Thunderbird. All these are described elsewhere in this chapter.

Visitors as well as natives may wish to try for swamp rabbits because they are not as common as the others, and they are large. McCurtain Co., extreme southeast, is one of the best locations. Little River out of Broken Bow is a good bet. Choctaw Co. to the west, and LeFlore to the north also have fair swamp rabbit populations. There are some throughout much of the east, even north to the Kansas line in Nowata Co. Hunters should stick to the stream bottoms for this animal. Here are some good streams, all in the southeast and east-central: Kiamichi, Poteau, Arkansas, Glover, Red, Mountain Fork, Muddy Boggy.

SQUIRRELS

There are gray and fox squirrels in Oklahoma. Large numbers—between one and two million—are bagged each season. The grays are found almost entirely in the east, in the big forests and the oak and hickory timber. The Ouachita NF is excellent squirrel territory. The fox squirrel ranges statewide, is present along the rivers and timbered ravines of the west. Most of the PHAs furnish very good squirrel hunting, and the remainder that have timber and suitable squirrel habitat offer at least fair shooting. Here are the ones on which squirrels are among the top species: Blue River, Burnt Cabin, Choctaw, Lexington, Oologah, Stringtown, Thunderbird, Tishomingo. All are described earlier in this chapter.

PREDATORS, PESTS, OTHERS

Some of the best large-predator hunting in the U.S. is found here. Surveys show some 50,000 coyotes and around 7500 bobcats taken annually. Calling of these animals is popular, and there is some coursing. The heavy cover along the Red River, and all of the western half of the state, have the largest populations of these animals. Most of the PHAs have good predator hunting, and often ranchers will give permission.

As for the smaller predators, there is a minor amount of prairie dog shooting, mostly on private lands. There are also some gray foxes, in the eastern third of the state, chiefly in the brushy lowlands and swamps.

With the growing interest in hunting for large predators, coyote and bobcat hunters may wisely select Oklahoma as a hunting ground. Coyotes in some areas are so plentiful—even in the south-central area north of Lake Texoma—that ranchers have set up their own bounty system. Thus, finding a hunting ground is not difficult. In the rough juniper and rock of the northwest there is excellent opportunity, and also on the plains. The broad areas of dense brush along the rivers, such as the Red, are among the most productive locations for calling.

In addition to the animals noted above, there are raccoons, especially in the east and along the river bottoms. Many Oklahoma hound men are dedicated raccoon hunters. All of the PHAs with timber and water have plentiful raccoons.

Perhaps Oklahoma's most famous pest hunting is for crows, and the prime location is Fort Cobb PHA in midwestern Caddo Co. Here is located a winter crow roost thought to be perhaps the largest on the continent. Estimates of crows using it run as high as ten million. This has been a permanent winter roost for some seasons. There are others, some of which may shift location seasonally. The Department can assist interested hunters in locating these.

REGULATIONS

Game laws pertaining to seasons, bag, and possession limits, areas to be hunted, special hunts, license fees all may have numerous changes from year to year. For current regulations, and for other specific queries, write to: Department of Wildlife Conservation, 1801 North Lincoln, Oklahoma City, Oklahoma 73105.

Gulf
Coast
States

FLORIDA

The State of Florida is a completely unique portion of the United States. Excepting the panhandle of the northwest that lies along the southern borders of Georgia and Alabama, it is a subtropical peninsula thrusting far southward over 400 miles, with the Atlantic on the east and the Gulf of Mexico on the west. This large peninsula and the 160-mile string of islands, or keys running westward off its southern tip form a portion of the barrier that partly encloses the Gulf of Mexico.

The terrain, climate, and vegetation are all influenced by the hundreds of miles of far-south ocean and Gulf on either side. Florida is very nearly flat, sloping from a minor highest point of a bit over 300 feet in the panhandle to barely above sea level over much of the southern third. Although many beaches are of white sand, there are also endless miles of salt marshes, mangrove swamps, and mazes of tiny keys or near-shore mangrove islands. As one moves inland, in the northern portion and along the "ridge country" of the center of the state, there are heavy stands of pine, plus much live oak decorated by long strands of moss. Along the numerous rivers, many of them tidal, and the innumerable inland lakes and swamps, there are dense stands of cypress.

About midway down the interior, the pine lands begin to fade and are replaced by ever greater expanses of palmettos, cypress, and finally the sawgrass flats and swamplands with tangled shrubs of numerous semitropical varieties. This is the deep, mysterious wilderness of the Everglades and Big Cypress Swamp, one of the last areas of authentic southern wilderness left in the U.S., and the largest of its kind. Here and there in the great swamplands there are small oases a few feet higher than the half-submerged sawgrass lands. These, called hammocks, permit stands of trees and form islands of refuge for various game species.

Florida's greatest industry is in tourism and retirees. This has increased the population over the past twenty-five years, so much so that encroachment upon wild lands has been severe. The tremendous citrus industry, some 80 percent of the U.S. total, and the truck-farming vegetable business, second only to California, have removed hundreds of thousands of acres from the original lowland wilderness. There is also a large amount of manufacturing, production of phosphates and minerals, and the massive test centers for missiles.

Florida, indeed, is a busy, diverse, and thriving state. Yet it is in some ways an enigma, for there is still a large amount and variety of good hunting. Numerous sweeps of this lowland remain unsuitable for modern settlement. From huge (700-square-mile) Lake Okeechobee on south until the Keys begin, there are only three major highway systems—the complex along the east coast from West Palm Beach to Coral Gables, with U.S. 1 and I 95 the prime routes; U.S. 27, the center-of-Florida main route coursing south from below Okeechobee; and U.S. 41 along the western side. Smaller roads cut into the Everglades region, but much travel there to secluded sectors is necessarily by airboat or swamp buggy. While some native hunters know the area, visitors are well advised in this south-Florida region to be guided. Any of the local Chamber of Commerce groups, as well as the Game Commission, will assist in locating guides, who must be licensed.

Above Lake Okeechobee, the pattern is far different. Roads crisscross everywhere, with fast interstates running along the east coast and down the center, and with numerous U.S. highways. Excepting swampy areas, many of which are owned in large tracts by cattle ranchers and others, there is no transport problem to any point. Air travel is fast and easy, and useful in a state of such length. All major cities have terminals and service, and charters are available for short flights.

Florida in its narrower portions is little more than a hundred miles east-west. But from Homestead in the far south to points in the northwestern panhandle, depending on the route followed, a trip may be well over 600 miles. The state covers a total of 58,560 square miles. A husky percentage of it is water—lakes, swamps, streams. Population at present is crowding six million and is growing swiftly. Much of the total is concentrated in the larger cities and along the beach retirement developments. But all of central and northern Florida also have a myriad of smaller towns.

The number of hunters, compared to many states of comparable population, is surprisingly low. License sales average about 215,000 annually at present. Part of the reason may well be that a vast number of persons who have settled in Florida over late years were attracted by the climate, the beaches, and the fishing, and had little interest in hunting. This is fortunate for avid hunters, because it alleviates what could be severe crowding. It is interesting to note that nonresident hunters are few. License sales are only around 2500 a year.

Certainly the game list in Florida is attractive, the species quite abundant. Big game includes deer, in some areas in problem herds, plus black bear and wild hogs. Rabbits and gray squirrels are extremely abundant, with a few fox squirrels also resident. Turkeys are numerous almost throughout the state. Quail and doves are harvested by millions. There is good hunting for the lowland birds—ducks, jacksnipe, rails and gallinules, and there is some goose shooting. Raccoons are overabundant, foxes and bobcats fairly plentiful.

With the startling influx of new residents over past years, and the consequent buying up of lands, there is of course a vast acreage in private holdings, where hunting is by permission only and not in general easy to arrange. However, Florida has done an excellent job, under difficult conditions, of keeping, and continuing to buy or lease, lands for public hunting. Many of the lands managed by the state for public hunting are actually owned in large tracts by various paper companies and other businesses.

These lands are designated as Wildlife Management Areas. There are at this writing thirty-four of them, scattered from the western panhandle to the southern tip of the state. Most of these are large. The Nassau WMA up in the far northeast, for example, covers approximately 80,000 acres; Fort McCoy WMA in central Florida comprises 30,000 acres. The Edward Ball WMA more recently established and at present closed to hunting, is on the coast of the eastern part of the panhandle and has 70,000 acres. Well over a million acres are held in these Wildlife Management Areas.

A most fortunate situation obtains in Florida regarding federal lands. There are three National Forests. The Apalachicola NF, 556,480 acres, lies in the eastern part of the panhandle. The Osceola NF is in the northeast, west of Jacksonville, with 361,029 acres. Ocala NF is in the north-central area, with 157,233 acres. Maps and details on all three may be acquired from the forest supervisor, Tallahassee.

The Management Areas and the National Forests furnish almost all of the public lands. However, Florida also has recognized the importance in the state of the mourning dove—over three and a half million are annually taken— and has set up in recent seasons a Dove Fields Program. There are over seventy of these uints well distributed in all the good dove territory, and for a daily fee (see "Doves" later in chapter) plus a regular hunting license the public may indulge in this grand sport. Listings of Dove Fields, and a Regulations Booklet for the current year titled "Florida's Wildlife and Fish Management Areas," are available from the Game Commission and invaluable to one planning a hunt.

The Areas booklet is particularly important because the annual regulations for the WMAs differ a great deal from the statewide game regulations, and each WMA may have regulations for a given season quite different from any of the others. For hunting on the WMAs a stamp costing at present $5 for adults and $2.50 for juveniles under fifteen is needed, in addition to a regular Florida hunting license. It entitles the holder to hunt on most of them. On some there are special hunts, with dates varying broadly from the statewide season. Dogs may be prohibited on some, or only bird dogs may be allowed. On some camping is prohibited, and hunting is allowed for specified game species only, and only on certain days of the week. The booklet for any year gives all details on all WMAs open to hunting. Individual maps of the WMAs with current regulations are obtainable from a list of Commission offices given with addresses in the booklet, or may be obtained at the Area during open seasons. (See "Doves" for Regional addresses.)

Because reference will be made often later in this chapter to areas of the state as officially designated by the Game Commission, it is necessary here for readers to have them explained. The state is divided into five "Regions." The Northwest Region takes in all of the panhandle. Jefferson County is the last county in it to the east. The boundary runs from north to south along the eastern border of Jefferson Co., which is actually the Aucilla River. Reading eastward, the next Region is the Northeast. The boundary line runs on a southwestern slant across the state, beginning on the east coast just below Jacksonville, following the eastern and southern borders of these counties: Duval, Clay, a short stretch of Bradford, all of Alachua, and Levy, ending at Yankeetown where the Withlacoochee River enters the Gulf. The Central Region lies below this line south to the following one: the southern boundary of Brevard Co., which begins at about Sebastian on the Atlantic and runs from there around the southern and western boundaries of Osceola, Lake, Sumter, and Citrus Cos. The South Florida Region lies below most of this line, but west of Lake Okeechobee. The boundary line butts into the one above at the southwest corner of Osceola Co., runs south along the western edge of Okeechobee Co., around the west edge of the Lake (east border of Glades Co.), goes along the eastern and southern edges of Hendry Co. and the south edge of Lee Co., to meet the Gulf just west of Bonita Springs, at Hickory Pass. To the south and east of this line is the fifth, or Everglades Region.

To illustrate how well the Management Areas are distributed over these Regions, there are ten in the Northwest (one closed at present to hunting),

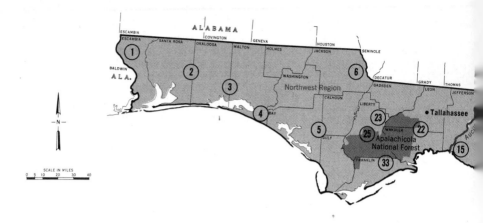

ten in the Northeast, seven in the Central, four in South Florida, three in the Everglades.

Hunters who wish to camp in Florida will find ample accommodations, but should be aware that with fall tourists and winter visitors pouring in at hunting-season time, campsites may be crowded. There are over twenty State Parks. (The Florida Board of State Parks is at 101 West Gaines Street, Tallahassee.) There are also campsites in the National Forests, in Everglades National Park, numerous county and civic parks, and scores of private campgrounds. The Florida State Advertising Commission, Tallahassee, is an excellent source of information, and the Game Commission will lend assistance, too. Motel and other accommodations, in this state so dedicated to tourism, are legion.

Early-fall dove shooting or other hunting will invariably be done in rather hot weather. Midfall is usually warm and enjoyable, with only cotton shirts necessary and perhaps a light jacket for mornings and evenings. In north Florida during winter the climate can be surprisingly chill, because of humidity. The panhandle in particular at such season is whimsical. Light wool shirts and a hunting coat may be required at least until middle of the day.

There are no special problems here in arms and ammunition. Shotgunners will need shot sizes No. 7½ for smaller birds, and No. 6 and No. 4 highbase loads for turkeys and ducks. A .22 is a handy arm for rabbits and squirrels, for those who prefer it to a shotgun. Deer, bear, and hogs are hunted with any of the popular calibers in the deer category, and in some instances with shotguns and buckshot. There are of course archery seasons.

QUAIL

Florida's quail are bobwhites, in two subspecies. The eastern bobwhite of northern Florida is slightly larger, weighing perhaps an ounce more than the Florida bobwhite of the south. The ranges overlap. Mexican bobwhites, stocked some years ago, have apparently disappeared. Although Florida has good quail hunting, the bobwhite has not been without its difficulties here in late years, as in many other southern locations, because of changing land uses. The best hunting is in the north and south. Central Florida has had varied trouble with poor influences upon quail habitat.

460

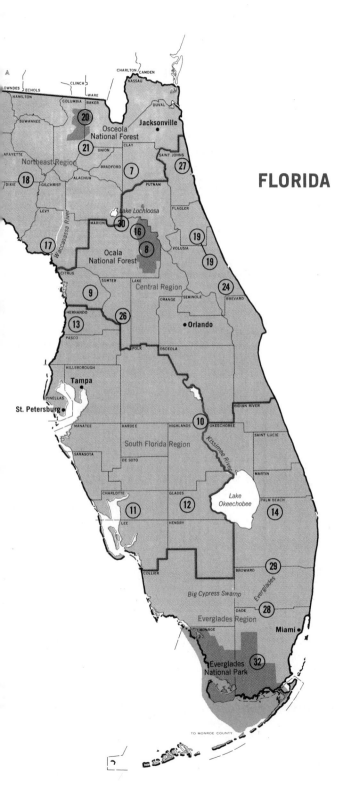

FLORIDA

KEY TO HUNTING AREAS

1. St. Regis WMA
2. Blackwater WMA
3. Elgin Field WMA
4. Point Washington WMA
5. Gaskin WMA
6. Apalachee WMA
7. Camp Blanding WMA
8. Ocala NF
9. Citrus WMA
10. Avon Park WMA
11. C. M. Webb WMA
12. Fisheating Creek WMA
13. Croom WMA
14. J. W. Corbett WMA
15. Aucilla WMA
16. Fort McCoy WMA
17. Gulf Hammock WMA
18. Steinhatchee WMA
19. Tomoka WMA
20. Osceola WMA
21. Lake Butler WMA
22. Leon-Wakulla WMA
23. Telogia Creek WMA
24. Farmton WMA
25. Liberty WMA
26. Richloam WMA
27. Guano River WMA
28. Everglades WMA
29. Loxahatchee Waterfowl Refuge
30. Lochloosa WMA
31. Tide Swamp WMA
32. Aerojet WMA
33. Apalachicola NF

461

Much private-land quail hunting is excellent, for numerous landowners carefully manage their birds. Although some hunters "walk up" their birds, Florida's quail hunting is done traditionally with well-trained dogs and with the use of specially equipped trucks on which the gunners ride as the dogs cast about, and from which they alight when the dogs are on point.

Because the Wildlife Management Areas are purposely managed for greatest output of game, the best public quail hunting is found on them. Although all but a few of the WMAs furnish at least some quail hunting, a number are outstanding, while the rest have quail only as an incidental species of low population. In the Northwest Region, a prime quail hunting area, one on which quail are the top species, is the St. Regis WMA (1). It is located in the north-central part of Escambia Co., Florida's westernmost county. U.S. 29 and State 97 give near access. Moving into the next county to the east, Santa Rosa, there is another excellent quail Area, Blackwater WMA (2). It lies about midway up on the eastern border of the county, and overlaps into the next county to the east, Okaloosa. East-west State 4 crosses the county border here, with the village of Munson just below it on State 191 in Santa Rosa Co. Several thousand quail are taken from each of the above Areas during good years.

At Elgin Field WMA (3), which spreads over most of the southern half of Okaloosa Co. and much of southwestern Walton Co., there is good quail hunting, but because of the interest here in big-game hunting (deer, hogs) quail get very little play. The Point Washington WMA (4), southeast of Elgin, also furnishes fair hunting. This Area is along the Gulf in Bay Co., reached via U.S. 98 at Point Washington and west out of Panama City. Another fair Area is Gaskin WMA (5) to the East. It is a large unit on the eastern border of Bay Co. and the southwest corner of Calhoun Co. U.S. 231 and secondary route 388 lead to it. One of the best of the Northwest quail Areas is Apalachee WMA (6). This is in eastern Jackson Co., with U.S. 90, State 71, and the city of Marianna keys to its location.

In the Northeast Region quail hunting is only fair. Camp Blanding WMA (7), located in western Clay Co., is one of the best areas, but is heavily hunted for big game with quail getting small attention. In some years, however, kills are fairly good. U.S. 301 and State 16 lead to the vicinity. The Central Region has some fair shooting in the Ocala NF (8) and the WMA connected with it in western Marion Co. In central Citrus Co. near the Gulf Coast the Citrus WMA (9) is also fair. This Area is west of Inverness. However, in general the Central is not the best of the quail hunting territory.

The southern half of the South Florida Region (see introductory portions this chapter) furnishes the best public quail shooting in the state. Three WMAs are notable here. One of them, with quail near the top in game kill, is Avon Park WMA (10). This large tract lies in the northeast corner of Highlands County and the southeast corner of Polk Co. It is along the Kissimmee River on the west side, and can be reached from Avon Park via secondary Route 64. The second tract of note: C. M. Webb WMA (11), with quail top game and some seasons the highest kill per hunter-day of any of the WMAs. This is in Charlotte Co. to the west of Punta Gorda. State 31 and secondary 74 intersect in the vicinity at the village of Bermont.

Straight east, in the next county (Glades), or reached from the other side straight west from Lake Okeechobee, is Fisheating Creek WMA (12). This also is large, and consistently offers quality quail hunting. The town of Palmdale on U.S. 27 is a good key to its location. One other WMA, in the north part of this Region, offers fair shooting. This is Croom WMA (13), in western Hernando Co., west of U.S. 41 and Brookville.

The Everglades Region offers only a minor amount of quail hunting. One tract, J. W. Corbett WMA (14), east of Lake Okeechobee in the north-central part of Palm Beach Co., is fair. The others sustain few if any quail.

MOURNING DOVES

Florida is one of the top dove states. Many birds are raised there. Many thousands more migrate into Florida. The kill during a recent season was estimated at 3,558,000. Florida had in the past a problem with its dove flocks because of their movements, and because of federal insistence that zoned hunting not be allowed. Studies revealed that large dove concentrations were in western Florida during October but they did not stay. They moved quickly to south Florida and when the regular season opened many of the northwest counties had few. To cure this ill of distribution, which inhibited proper harvest, a split season was instigated. Nowadays it is in three parts, and all Florida hunters thus get a chance at the flocks.

The great majority of dove shooting is done on private lands by permission, or by the owners. All of Florida except the swamps have good winter dove populations. While there are a good many birds at times on portions of the WMAs, the mobility of the dove requires rather special management and shooting is not in general more than just fair on the Areas. One Northwest Area, Apalachee, located under "Quail," is outstanding. Several thousand doves are shot here annually during good flights.

There is a bit of shooting in the Northeast. Aucilla WMA (15) furnishes a few doves. This Area is just over the border into the Northeast Region, and on the upper Gulf in southwestern Taylor Co. It lies along the Aucilla River, with U.S. 98, and U.S. 27 and 19, which fork at Perry to the east, giving access. A small secondary route (14) is useful, too.

In the Central Region one tract worth mention, although surveys show the dove kill is light, is Ft. McCoy WMA (16). This is in northern Marion Co., just west of the Ocala Forest. The town of Ft. McCoy is at the junction of State 315 and secondary 316.

The South Florida Region is somewhat better. Croom WMA (see "Quail") has some few birds; Avon Park ("Quail") also furnishes a small amount of shooting. C. M. Webb is at times quite good, and so is Fisheating Creek WMA, both of which are located under "Quail." The Everglades WMAs offer little dove shooting.

The Dove Fields Program mentioned in the opening portion of this chapter is responsible for the basis of most of the good public dove hunting. The Commission constantly attempts to expand this program. During a recent season public dove shoots had been arranged on seventy-eight different fields, located in twenty-one counties. Each of the five regions had some. Most of these fields are planted with crops of millet, or with sorghum or corn. These are natural dove foods, and the crop-planting system is not considered baiting. The fields may be as small as thirty-five acres and run on up to 1500 or more, with an average around 300 to 400.

To avoid driving birds away, the fields are shot only on specified days. Each hunter must have his regular hunting license, and in addition there is a Dove Field Permit fee of $2 per day. Certain fields are open during all three phases of the split season, some are not. The first phase is invariably the best, with the most birds and the highest kills. Fields are not necessarily the same each year, and thus no listing is given here. The Commission will furnish lists of dove fields for any Region for the current season. Maps and detailed regulations pertaining to individual fields are furnished by the Regional Offices. A list of addresses is in the WMA's booklet. But for reader convenience the Regional Office addresses are also given here. They are useful, of course, not only for Dove Field information but for any other regional queries.

Northwest: 226 Airport Drive, Panama City
Northeast: Box 908, Lake City
Central: 2520 Silver Springs Blvd., Ocala
South Florida: 2202 Lakeland Hills Blvd., Lakeland
Everglades: 551 N. Military Trail, West Palm Beach

Some of the Dove Fields are actually located on WMAs. An example is at Apalachee and C. M. Webb. Most are not. Because of the rapid movement of dove flocks and other influences that concentrate them, the October (first) season phase generally will turn up a high kill in the northwest and at the same period also far to the south, in Dade, Broward and Monroe Cos.

WILD TURKEYS

The Florida turkey (so named) is a distinct subspecies. It is not quite as large as the eastern wild turkey and the western Merriam's, and it is darker in coloration. In northern Florida there is some overlap of range and intermixing between the eastern and the Florida subspecies. While attempts are made to avoid interbreeding with domestic turkeys, over many years some of this has occurred in Florida as elsewhere in settled areas. The purest strain of the Florida turkey left today is found far back in Big Cypress Swamp, in south Florida. However, elimination of restocking from pen reared birds, and the continued transplants of wild trapped birds has kept the Florida turkey quite pure and in good condition.

Some years ago many Florida counties had lost all or nearly all their turkey flocks. Over many years poaching was a serious problem. Happily, management and transplants have revitalized the turkey flocks and expanded populations until the birds range almost everywhere in the state. The state is considered to have one of the largest turkey populations east of the Mississippi, the annual harvest running into several thousand birds There are seasons both fall and spring, with a current season bag limit of three birds in fall and two in spring. This is an indication of population size. Furthermore, in fall turkeys of either sex are legal. The total flock is currently estimated at above 75,000. Skyrocketing human population in Florida will almost certainly limit more and more the possibility of further turkey expansion, but presently the outlook is far from pessimistic.

The largest turkey population, and consistently the highest kills on public lands, are on the Fisheating Creek WMA, South Florida Region, Glades Co., west of Lake Okeechobee. This WMA is located under "Quail." Over a number of past seasons this Area has had a consistent take of from 300 to 350 birds annually. The three National Forests provide good turkey hunting locations, but by and large the lower central and southern portions of the state are best.

Some of the better WMAs are as follows: Aucilla (see "Doves"), Avon Park, Blackwater, Camp Blanding (see "Quail"). All four of these Areas usually have annual kills of from 50 to 175 birds. Usually somewhat higher kills are established at several others. Gulf Hammock WMA (17) in the

Northeast Region gets heavy hunting but is a good bet. It is located in southwestern Levy Co. near the Waccasassa River, with U.S. 19 and 98 a key route and the towns of Otter Creek and Lebanon Station location points. Steinhatchee WMA (18) turns in an annual kill of 100 to 200 birds. This large Area is northwest of the Gulf Hammock Area, is partly in Lafayette Co. and partly in Dixie Co. to the south. There is a large, low, swampy area here, north of Cross City (U.S. 19, 98). Several other highways —among them U.S. 27 north of the Area—and secondaries give access.

Many other WMAs offer fair hunting, with kills below 100 birds on the average. J. W. Corbett, Croom, Gaskin, Point Washington (see "Quail") are among them. Others so far not located are as follows: Tomoka WMA (19) is in the Central Region, in two tracts, one in southern Flagler Co., the other, much bigger, covering a large portion of Volusia Co., to the south. This is in the DeLand area. Osceola WMA (20) is in the Northeast Region, in Baker and Columbia Cos., just below the Georgia line, northeast of Lake City. Immediately to the south of this Area is the Lake Butler WMA (21), mostly in Union Co., but spilling northward across the Baker and Columbia Co. lines. The Leon-Wakulla WMA (22) is also fair. It is in the eastern part of the Northwest Region, lying along the border between Leon Co. and its southern neighbor Wakulla Co. This is easily reached south from Tallahassee. Telogia Creek WMA (23) is also fair. This is to the northwest of Leon-Wakulla, in northern Liberty and southern Gadsden Cos. The village of Telogia is on State 65 near its junction with State 20 at Hosford.

Farmton WMA (24) is in the Central Region, near the east coast, in southern Volusia Co. This places it northeast of Orlando. The village of Farmton is on a secondary reached off State 415 out of Sanford. This Area gets many hunters, had a recent season kill of seventy-seven turkeys. Liberty WMA (25) is in the Northwest, in central Liberty Co. to the south of the Telogia Creek Area. It is fair. Recently the kill here has been low, but hunters are not especially numerous. Richloam WMA (26) has stacked up rather consistent kills of around fifty birds per season. It lies across the border of the Central and South Florida Regions chiefly in southern Sumter Co. The village of Richloam is on State 50, a short distance east of its intersection with U.S. 301.

There is some turkey hunting on the other Areas. Check the booklet or with the Game Commission. Guided trips into the Everglades or Big Cypress make interesting and productive turkey hunts, too, and there is much excellent hunting on private holdings for those who can arrange permission.

WOODCOCK, SNIPE, RAILS, GALLINULES

Woodcock are not important game birds in Florida. The main winter concentration migrates to points much farther west. Undoubtedly careful search would uncover more woodcock shooting possibilities in Florida than are so far known. However, the woodcock kill on all of the public lands is almost nil. A few were shot during a recent season at Apalachee WMA (see "Quail").

These birds are chiefly confined to the moist northern woodlands and to fields bordering forests and shady thickets with thin ground cover. A very few woodcock nest in north Florida. These also migrate farther south, but woodcock in Florida seldom go farther than necessary to escape areas where the ground may freeze. They are rare below Orlando.

Snipe, or jacksnipe as they are commonly called, furnish a good bit of shooting and could furnish much more if only more hunters became enthused about them and sought them out. They are fairly abundant on marshy bogs and mud flats. Although it is generally conceded that snipe are most common in the northern part of the state, they are hunted more in the south and some good kills are made there. Without doubt all suitable habitats in the state have quotas of wintering snipe and could offer excellent shooting.

Several of the Wildlife Management Areas are especially good snipe shooting grounds. Avon Park WMA northwest of Lake Okeechobee is excellent. So is J. W. Corbett WMA east of the same lake. Fisheating Creek WMA is undoubtedly the best of all, with a consistent record of some hundreds of snipe taken annually. A few are shot also at Croom WMA. The C. M. Webb Area is quite good. Apalachee furnishes some birds. All of these locations are pinpointed under "Quail." The Guano River WMA (27), should be checked out for snipe, too. Not previously mentioned, it is at the extreme northeast edge of the Central Region, on the east coast at the northeast tip of St. John's County. This places it below Jacksonville Beach and north of St. Augustine.

It should be understood that along with the places mentioned a great deal of good snipe shooting can be found in most waterfowl habitat, and in boggy areas with fairly sparse grass or other cover where jacksnipe can feed by probing with their long bills. The good kills on the Areas noted are simply because hunters are attracted to snipe shooting there. Attention to snipe in many other locations will pay off in good sport.

Rails and gallinules are abundant in numerous Florida locations. Many hunters inexperienced with gallinules do not know for sure what these birds are. They are relatives of the rails, but more closely related to the common coot with which duck hunters throughout the U.S. are familiar. There are, including the coot, three species. The coot appears slaty black and has a white bill. The common, or Florida, gallinule is a bit smaller, slaty gray and dusky brown with some white under the tail, and with a red bill that has a yellow tip. The purple gallinule is the third member of the group, another coot-like bird fond of walking with its wide-splayed toes on lily pads and other floating vegetation. Gaudily colored, it sports a yellow-tipped red bill, an aqua forehead, blue and purplish breast with iridescent greens on the back and wings. It seldom ranges north above Tennessee.

Both these gallinules, as well as the coot, are common in Florida. They and the several rails could stand far more hunting pressure than they get. The large king rail and the next-in-size clapper rail are the two most sought. The clapper inhabits tidal marshes and creeks, the king rail is predominantly a freshwater marsh bird. The smaller sora is also hunted to some extent here, around freshwater marshes. The clapper rail is the most important target of all in Florida.

Two main methods of rail hunting are employed in Florida: on the Atlantic coast, tides are high enough to move the birds, and they are hunted from a poled skiff at high tide; on the Gulf side, tides are seldom that high, and hunters slog through the mud and marshes. In the east the best "rail tides" occur in the extreme northeast, along Nassau, Duval, and St. Johns Cos. Access to the marshes here is in general not difficult and birds are plentiful. On the Gulf side, Bay, Franklin and Gulf counties provide the majority of the tidal flats best suited to walking, and with the best footing.

Rails—and sometimes gallinules, too—are commonly called "marsh hens" in Florida and other parts of the South. In addition to the counties named, there is very good shooting to be had along the east coast in Flagler and Volusia Cos., and in the far-southwest counties of Collier and Monroe. The only deterrent to more of this shooting is that many good marsh areas are limited as to access.

The gallinules are birds of fresh water. Usually the canals through the Everglades and all comparable locations where some open water and heavy vegetation are in combination have many of these birds. They are considered quite good sport and eating here. The Everglades WMA (28), a huge expanse lying in northwestern Dade Co. and covering a vast region of western Broward Co., is an excellent spot for this hunting—and in combination with other waterfowl hunting (which see). U.S. 41 and U.S. 27 are access highways, but much of the best hunting here is via airboat or swamp buggy. The Guano River WMA noted under "Snipe" in this section is one of the very best for coots and gallinules, with a consistently high kill.

WATERFOWL

With its great wealth in shorelines, marshes, lakes, and rivers, Florida has some very good duck shooting. But the state also has a most disturbing situation concerning goose hunting. Some few years ago goose hunting was spotty but good. A wintering population of approximately 25,000 Canada geese visited Florida annually, and the kill averaged around 1000 birds. A few snows and blues also migrated here, but not in any substantial numbers. Over recent years the goose flights have dwindled until only a few thousand geese now arrive and the kill is down to one hundred or below. Research tends to prove that the "Florida" geese are being killed early in the Chesapeake Bay region, and that management practices to attract and hold geese at other more northerly points along the migration routes have robbed Florida of its birds. The giant Canada subspecies, recently discovered still to be in existence, and with birds weighing as much as twenty pounds, generally nest farther south than any of the others. Florida is now attempting to stock some of these birds, hoping to get them to adopt this southern environment as a permanent home. Whether or not Florida goose hunting will be revived is not possible to predict at present.

There are several waterfowl refuges in Florida. Chassahowitzka in Hernando and Citrus Cos.; Loxahatchee in Broward and Palm Beach Cos.; St. Marks in Wakulla, Taylor, and Jefferson Cos. are the more important ones for ducks. Some shooting is available surrounding these sanctuaries, and Loxahatchee WFR (29) has a large sector open to duck hunting. There is much good duck shooting on privately owned marshes, a good deal more spottily scattered over hundreds of lakes. Jump-shooting is productive along accessible streams where it is legal.

For average hunters, however, the WMAs are the best and surest bet. Apalachee is fair. So are Aucilla, Corbett, Fisheating Creek, Ft. McCoy, Ocala, all pinpointed elsewhere in this chapter. Everglades (see "Gallinules") is consistently excellent. Guano River (see "Snipe") is predominantly a duck shooting Area, and very good. Gulf Hammock also is good, noted under "Turkey." Point Washington up in the Northwest Region and noted under "Quail" is another good bet, and at Richloam and Steinhatchee ("Turkeys") there is a bit of scattered shooting.

Two other WMAs not so far mentioned offer at least fair shooting. Lochloosa WMA (30) is one. This is on the south-central border of the Northeast

Region, in southeastern Alachua County. Lake Lochloosa south of Gainesville is here. Another is Tide Swamp WMA (31). This is a hunting ground of moderate size lying on the Gulf at the southeastern corner of Taylor County. State 51 crosses U.S. 19, 98, and Alt. 27 near here and runs south to the village of Steinhatchee to take one into the region. Many others of the public Areas offer at least some shooting for those who avidly seek it.

EXOTIC BIRD INTRODUCTIONS

Florida experimented for some time with black-necked pheasants. The birds proved unable to establish themselves and experiments have been discontinued.

There is however at this time enthusiasm for trying several species of non-native ducks. Migratory ducks are not coming into the state in sufficient numbers and it is thought that subtropical species may have merit. The *pato real,* or "royal duck," from Venezuela is one, the greater Bahama pintail another. Ringed teal, the rosy-billed pochard, and the southern pochard, birds of South and Central America, are others. It is at this time much too early to predict what results may be, but it is not impossible that some of these species will eventually establish themselves.

Florida is also doing some trial stocking of Asiatic jungle fowl. The species under experiment is of bantam size. Releases have been made in the Everglades Region.

DEER

The whitetail deer in Florida has had many ups and downs. Poaching over many years was a serious problem. Market hunting was common. Disease was rampant. New stock was brought in from several northern states to see if other bloodlines would help. Under careful management Florida deer have expanded their range and become abundant. In some places, in fact, over-population has now become a serious matter. Recently a bad die-off occurred for this reason in Collier County. Some of the overpopulation is a result of the eradication a few years ago of the screwworm fly. Thousands of fawns perished immediately after birth from screwworms in wounds or in their navels. Thus, today Florida has very good deer hunting and will undoubtedly attempt to harvest more and more deer over coming seasons.

To illustrate how swiftly the herds have built up, it is now estimated that at least 200,000 deer are in Florida. On the Fisheating Creek WMA, which contains 275,000 acres, a decade ago fewer than 100 deer were in residence. Now at least ten times that many roam the areas. Changes in land use over much of Florida have in many ways favored deer, by offering openings and areas cleared of dense brush. It is estimated that a saturation point will be reached if and when Florida's herd approaches 400,000. But severe cropping of antlerless deer will be necessary on a continuing basis to keep the herd in balance with its range and food supply.

More and more Florida deer hunters are beginning to still-hunt. However, much of the terrain is not really suited to this method, and besides numerous hunters here have traditionally used dogs for many years. In the big swamps, special equipment is needed in vehicles even to get the hunter into the range of his quarry. The largest deer live in the central and north and northwest portions of the state because there they have better feeding conditions. These lands, also, in pine and pine-oak combinations, are much easier for average hunters to get around in.

The National Forests offer excellent chances at deer. So do the Management Areas. Regulations must be carefully checked for each WMA. They differ radically. Hours may be stipulated. On some rifles are not allowed, and buckshot sizes are specified. Dogs may, or may not, be legal. Fires and camping may be prohibited. Season dates differ and numerous special hunts are held. Although laws may sound complicated, they actually are not when one simply checks the ones relating to the Area where his hunt is planned.

The hunting is excellent on many of the Areas. Some of the best Areas, all of which are located previously under other species, are as follows: Aucilla; Camp Blanding; Elgin (much hunted but plenty of territory and a very high kill); Farmton; Everglades; Gulf Hammock; Lake Butler; Ocala (again a heavily hunted area but massive and kill high); Osceola; Steinhatchee; Tomoka. Every one of the WMAs except Croom showed during a seasonal survey recently at least a fair kill of deer. An interesting one not so far mentioned is the Aerojet WMA (32). The kill is low, but there is little hunting. This Area is far down in southern Dade County, in the swampy region out of Homestead and nearby small towns.

For those who like to hunt the very large areas, the Apalachicola National Forest (33) is excellent. The Ocala National Forest (see "Quail") matches it, and has one of the heaviest deer populations in the state. All told, it makes little difference which one of the public lands is selected. The overall chance of success is very nearly comparable, per man-days of hunting, on all of them. Hunters harvest from 15,000 to 20,000 deer annually.

BEAR

Although Florida black bear are eagerly sought, and usually hunted with dogs because few kills are possible otherwise, neither the bear population nor the annual kill is impressive. There are estimated to be possibly 1000 bears in the state. The legal kill seldom reaches more than 100. The illegal kill is thought to be equal. One reason is that many bees are kept in back-country areas and bears raiding the hives are indiscriminately shot. Not more than 200 to 300 hunters annually hunt bear as a main quarry. A few kills are made incidentally by deer hunters. Several special hunts are held on the National Forests and the WMAs. During the season prior to this writing, however, a total of only six bears was taken on the entire list of Management Areas. A guided bear hunt in Florida, with a capable guide and a good hound pack, is an interesting experience and has a fair chance of success. Otherwise the odds are long. Liberty, Osceola, and Tomoka WMAs, previously mentioned, are considered fair for bear hunting. It is illegal to kill a bear "under 100 pounds." The law is to protect cubs, but it puts great responsibility on the hunter.

WILD HOGS

Feral hogs, many of them large and ferocious and as wild as any never-domesticated animal, have roamed and bred free in the Florida river bottoms, pine woods, and swamps for so many years that for all practical purposes most of them truly are wild. They are important big game here.

Certain cautions about hunting them, however, must be noted. There is a Florida saying that "Not all that grunts is fair game." Thousands of hogs range free but are private property and the offense of killing one can be a serious matter. Each season the Game Commission stipulates very plainly what portions of the state are open. During a recent season, for example, three Florida counties—Levy, Alachua, and Palm Beach—were open in entirety, and 16 WMAs were also. Elsewhere over the entire state the Game Commission had no jurisdiction whatever over wild hogs and hunters were on their own.

A surprising number of wild hogs are bagged annually on the several WMAs with open season. Following is a list of the best ones, with indications of a kill during the season prior to this writing. These same Areas show in surveys consistent good kills year after year. Aucilla, 250; Avon Park, 403; J. W. Corbett, 252; Elgin, 170 (but often much higher—in 1966, 1000); Gulf Hammock, 450; Point Washington, 159. Others with substantial kills that have ups and downs: Camp Blanding; Everglades (stocking being done here by various clubs to up the hog population); Farmton; Fisheating Creek, Lochloosa; Richloam; Telogia Creek; C. M. Webb. All the above areas have been noted for location under others species in this chapter.

SQUIRRELS

Florida has both fox and gray squirrels, but fox squirrels are so few that they make up only a minor proportion of the bag and cannot be considered consequential game. The gray squirrel, conversely, is one of the most abundant, most sought, and popular of all Florida's game animals. Yearly kill runs from half a million up to close to a million.

Gray squirrels are primarily animals of the deep woods. Thus the three National Forests furnish excellent squirrel hunting. Wherever oaks grow the populations are consistently highest. Florida gray squirrel populations of one to the acre are considered average, with two per acre during peak seasons. All of the WMAs except the ones in the far south offer fair to excellent gray squirrel hunting. Thus, the poor or squirrel-less Areas are Aerojet, J. W. Corbett, Everglades, C. M. Webb.

The high-kill Areas are as follows in alphabetical order: Aucilla; Camp Blanding; Croom; Elgin; Farmton; Fisheating Creek; Ft. McCoy; Guano River; Gulf Hammock; Ocala; Point Washington; Richloam; Steinhatchee; Tide Swamp; Tomoka. Of these, some of the highest kills per man-days of hunting occur in Croom, Richloam, and Tide Swamp. The top kill for an Area has gone for some seasons to Gulf Hammock, but it gets a lot of hunters, too. Several other fair to good Areas: Avon Park; Blackwater; Lake Butler; Leon-Wakulla; Liberty; Lochloosa; Osceola; St. Regis; Telogia Creek. All of these Areas have been dealt with under foregoing species.

Some excellent squirrel hunting is missed in numerous places in Florida, in oak hammocks that are difficult to reach. One who seeks these and finds ways to get to them can unearth fantastic shooting.

RABBITS

There are three varieties of rabbits in Florida—the eastern cottontail, the marsh rabbit, and the swamp rabbit. Swamp and marsh rabbits are much larger than cottontails, live generally in wet places or actual marshes, swim well when necessary. Rabbits are exceedingly plentiful throughout the state, but hunting pressure is low. They are considered game animals, and one must have a license to hunt, but there is no closed season and no bag limit. Traditionally Florida hunters passed up rabbits because the animals were so commonplace, and they had other game in abundance. Today some interest is growing in hunting all varieties. Hunting is good almost everywhere. There are no especially noteworthy areas.

OTHER ANIMALS

Raccoons are so plentiful they are in nuisance proportions in numerous parts of the state. There are both red and gray foxes, opossums, some bobcats. None of these is considered a game animal and all are unprotected. Hound hunting for all can be good, but is not followed to any extent. The often dense or swampy cover, and the likelihood of running into snakes at night, dampens much enthusiasm for the nocturnal hound sports. All these animals might furnish more recreation if hunters became interested in them, in calling, for example, or hunting in other ways.

REGULATIONS

Game laws pertaining to seasons, bag and possession limits, areas to be hunted, special hunts, license fees all may have numerous changes from year to year. For current regulations, and for other specific queries, write to: Game and Freshwater Fish Commission, Tallahassee, Florida 32304.

ALABAMA

Although Alabama is one of the Gulf Coast states of the Deep South, its actual coastline along the Gulf, measured in a straight line east-west, is the shortest of any of the Gulf States, about sixty miles. However, the broad, deep indentation of Mobile Bay gives the state far more saltwater shoreline than is apparent. There is a sizable amount of marshland here as well as several long barrier islands off the coast. This marine region, plus the numerous lowland bayous that are offshoots of the Tensaw and Mobile Rivers pouring down into the Gulf, give Alabama scores of miles of brackish cypress swamps that form excellent habitat for wintering waterfowl.

To the north above this jut of land and water that dodges around the Florida panhandle to touch upon the Gulf, the land rises gently from coastal plain to forested hills. Numerous large rivers meander down from the hills, and farther to the north immense man-made reservoirs lie along them. Although Alabama cannot be said to have true mountains, since its highest point is a bit under 2500 feet, nonetheless many of the hills are steep. Over much of the state they are handsomely forested, chiefly with pine.

These hills are actually the southern end of the Appalachian Mountains. They reach down as far as Birmingham. Up in the northwest, along the Tennessee border, and over in the piedmont of the Georgia border, the land begins its slope in general southward. Originally much of it was heavily pine forested, with gum and cypress, hackberry and hardwood in the bottoms.

Alabama passed through many years as a somewhat single-industry "cotton belt" state, with much cleared land. Now various industries—hydroelectric power from the huge dams, coal in the north, agriculture of varied kinds, cattle raising—balance the state's economy, and happily there are still almost twenty-two million acres of woodland left. Much of this is in timber company lands. There is also a large acreage of grasslands, and all in all Alabama has managed, in a swiftly changing world and with population growing as swiftly, to remain a state with plentiful game and hunting opportunities.

There is no difficulty for hunters in getting from place to place. The Alabama road system is excellent. Interstate Highways slant clear across the state from northeast to southwest through both Birmingham and Montgomery. Others run full length north to south. State highways are good, reach into every corner of every county. Air transport touches several major cities in each quadrant—from Huntsville and Decatur in the north of Gadsden, Birmingham, on to Montgomery in the center, Dothan in the southeast and Mobile southwest.

In size Alabama might be classed as roughly average for states east of the Mississippi. In the north its width is roughly 160 miles. At its wider girth the distance averages about 220. North to south its longest reach, from the Gulf to the Tennessee border, is about 360 miles. Total square miles are 51,609. The population at present is fairly large but not as dense as in Alabama's neighbors to the east and south. It stands at roughly 3,540,000 people. Happily for hunters, however, because of swift industrial growth much of this population is concentrated in the larger cities.

Average hunting license sale is approximately 350,000 annually. This indicates lack of severe crowding, compared to the area available. Also, for many years Alabama, like some other southern states, has been traditionally a hunting-club state. Groups of friends band together and lease hunting lands, with their own clubhouses and facilities. Thousands of such club-member hunters thus place no pressure, or very little at least, on the public lands.

Quail and doves are the two chief game birds of smaller size. Although the bobwhite quail has suffered everywhere in the South of late from modern agricultural practices, still there is some fine Alabama quail shooting. Doves are extremely plentiful. Wild turkeys have long been abundant, and are still increasing. The same is true of the deer herd. Small game such as squirrels, an Alabama favorite, and rabbits are abundant. There is a sizable amount of waterfowl shooting in the vicinity of several National Waterfowl Refuges and along the large river swamps and the impoundment shorelines. For those who know where to seek them, there are some woodcock, snipe, and rails. Foxes, raccoons, and opossums are plentiful. Bobcats still live in the deeper covers.

Alabama, with an active and exceedingly professional game department, is doing an excellent job of managing public game lands. There are currently over twenty Wildlife Management Areas covering many thousands of acres and well scattered throughout the state, where game of every native variety is available. Deer and turkey hunting on these, and hunting for all small game and game birds, is as good as and sometimes better than the hunting one may find on private lands. Individual maps of these WMAs may be had by request from the Department of Conservation. These maps, annually revised where necessary, have printed on the back the detailed regulations for hunting on the specific Area.

There is some good hunting on Federal military lands, such as at Fort McClellan, near Anniston in the northeast. This reservation encompasses over 45,000 acres. Hunters must purchase a post license for the managed hunts. Small game, deer, and turkeys are plentiful.

Some timber company lands are open also in large acreages to the public. The Department of Conservation can furnish information on these, which are subject to season change.

Alabama is also most fortunate to have within its boundaries several National Forests. The Bankhead National Forest in the north contains nearly 179,000 acres. The Talladega NF, in two large sections, one in the east-central and the other in the west-central portion of the state, contains all told over 357,000 acres. There are two others: the small Tuskegee NF, 10,777 acres east of Montgomery; and the 83,790-acre Conecuh NF on the southern border with Florida. While hunting by permission on private lands is also available, due to the long tradition of hunting clubs and leasing, it is not especially easy for a visitor from out of state to find it. Making local contacts ahead of time, however, opens up unlimited good hunting of this sort, for the country people and landowners of Alabama are genuinely friendly and hospitable.

For nonresidents, or residents who travel from one part of the state to another and who may wish to camp, there are ample opportunities. The National Forests are a good example. Excellent campgrounds are offered. Information on the forests and their facilities and game may be had, and maps also, from the Forest Supervisor's Headquarters, National Forest Service, Montgomery, Alabama. On some Wildlife Management Areas camping is allowed. Alabama's State Parks also offer camping, and so do the Corps of Engineers use areas on some of the reservoirs. The Alabama Bureau of Publicity, State Capitol, Montgomery 36104 is a good information source on both.

Along all the main highways there is an abundance of motel and hotel accommodations. Because of a great amount of winter tourist travel from the north, almost all the towns even of modest size offer good facilities. But these are on the main roads. The small back-country roads of Alabama have few. However, there are good lodgings and meals to be had within easy distance of any of the public lands.

Visitors should be aware that Alabama's climate is humid. Early in fall, for example, when one is dove hunting, the weather may be very hot and damp. As fall progresses, it becomes cool and damp and it can be exceedingly and deceptively chill for the late fall and winter hunter who unwarily approaches. Again, in spring during turkey season, when dogwood, wild honeysuckle, and redbud make the countryside a riot of exciting color, mornings can be extremely chill. Thus, a hunter should dress in accordance, never going without a heavy jacket handy in late fall, and during early fall making sure to wear light clothing and in open areas at least a broad hat to ward off the sun. Low areas can be very wet going both spring and fall. Short and long rubber boots, as well as rain gear, are worth taking.

Deer hunters should carry a rifle adapted not just to short-range shots. Some large whitetails are taken in Alabama at substantial open ranges, as well as in cover. About the only other rifle need is a .22 for squirrels. While there is a modest amount of goose hunting, it is very specifically located. Thus the shotgunners, unless after geese in particular, will need loads from No. 8 to No. 6 for smaller birds. Highbase No. 6 is a traditional turkey load in Alabama, although the newer short-magnum No. 4 is even better.

QUAIL

There is good bobwhite quail hunting in Alabama, but it is nowadays likely to be spottily scattered and local. Quail range throughout the state. Agricultural practices have drastically lowered the quail population over all of the South. Many clubs stock and attempt to manage their quail, by plantings, controlled burning, and careful harvest. Invitations to hunt on such club lands are of course made only through personal acquaintance. There is also a fair amount of quail hunting by permission on private lands. And, the fringes of some of the lumber company lands open to public hunting offer at least some quail shooting. These lands may change from season to season. The Department of Conservation, as noted earlier, and especially through its district offices, can assist in locating open lumber lands. The National Forests, while better known for deer, turkey, and squirrels, have a bit of edge-area quail hunting.

The annual quail harvest in Alabama is estimated to run between one and a half and two million birds. Again, the major share of these are taken on private lands. At one time the bobwhite was undoubtedly the most popular game bird in Alabama, but to illustrate the change in land use as it pertains to hunting, presently the number of hunters who hunt quail here is in fifth place on the list, with squirrels, doves, deer, and rabbits more popular.

The best opportunities for quail hunting open to the public are undoubtedly on the Wildlife Management Areas. Most of these areas are diligently managed by the planting and harvesting of various crops, so that quail are kept reasonably abundant. As noted earlier, seasons and numerous regulations pertain individually to each WMA. For example, shot size is stipulated (for quail No. 6 or smaller). Only specified portions of a WMA may be open to quail, or all may be. On some no small game or bird hunting is allowed on deer-hunt days. On others the quail (and other small-game) hunting is on staggered or specified days of the week only. Dogs are allowed at specified times and places and prohibited at others. Thus it is important when planning a hunt to obtain the individual map of the WMA where the hunt will take place and to carefully study the instructions printed on the back.

All of the WMAs have at least some quail hunting. One of the best areas is in Jackson County. This county covers the extreme northeastern corner of the state, with its northern border along the Tennessee line and a short stretch of its eastern border in common with Georgia. There are actually three Areas close together here, and they are mapped and listed as the Crow Creek (1), Mud Creek (2), and Raccoon Creek (3) Waterfowl Management Areas. All three are along the Tennessee River, in a marshy and sometimes creek-flooded stretch in the vicinity of the towns of Stevenson, Fabius, and Bridgeport. The Raccoon Creek area covers over 7000 acres and lies on the south side of the river. The other two—Crow Creek, 2161 acres, and Mud Creek, 8393 acres —are on the north side of the river. U.S. 72 runs parallel to the river here on the north side, and State 117 crosses through Stevenson on the north side and Fabius on the south side. The entire Areas of course do not offer good quail habitat, but a substantial kill is usually made each season and the season as a rule is quite long.

In the same county (Jackson) there is a large WMA called Skyline (4). State 79 runs north-south along the western edge of the Area, which lies immediately below the Tennessee-Alabama line. The villages of Skyline and Hytop are on this route in the vicinity. This is a 23,000-acre tract of broken terrain, with some dense woods and some open. There are some bottomlands, a number of creeks and small valleys. Although the quail kill is not large here as a rule, and the seasons may be shorter than on the ones mentioned above, there are few quail hunters and more quail shooting is possible.

In the southwestern part of the state, the Scotch WMA (5) generally gets a modest number of quail hunters but turns up a good kill record. This is a region of rolling to fairly level lands, with much wooded area, some of it dense. It covers over 20,000 acres. It lies west of the stretch of U.S. 43 running between Thomasville and Grove Hill, in Clarke County. Only designated portions are open to quail.

Following U.S. 43 north to the city of Demopolis, there is another WMA also lightly hunted for quail but with a good kill record. This is the Demopolis WMA (6). There is also a section here known as the Demopolis Waterfowl Management Area, marked off from the rest by signs that state "Hunting by Permit Only." The remainder is marked by signs that indicate "Public Hunting

KEY TO HUNTING AREAS

1. Crow Creek WMA
2. Mud Creek WMA
3. Raccoon Creek WMA
4. Skyline WMA
5. Scotch WMA
6. Demopolis WMA
7. Lauderdale WMA
8. Black Warrior WMA
9. Choccolocco WMA
10. Fort McClellan Military Reservation
11. Swan Creek WMA
12. Mallard-Fox Creek WMA
13. Seven Mile Island WMA
14. Hollins WMA
15. Coosa WMA
16. Barbour County WMA
17. Wolf Creek WMA
18. William B. Bankhead NF
19. Talladega NF
20. Conecuh NF
21. Blue Spring WMA
22. Covington WMA
23. Butler County WMA
24. Rob Boykin WMA
25. Oakmulgee WMA
26. Wheeler National Wildlife Refuge
27. Dam Site WMA
28. Thomas WMA

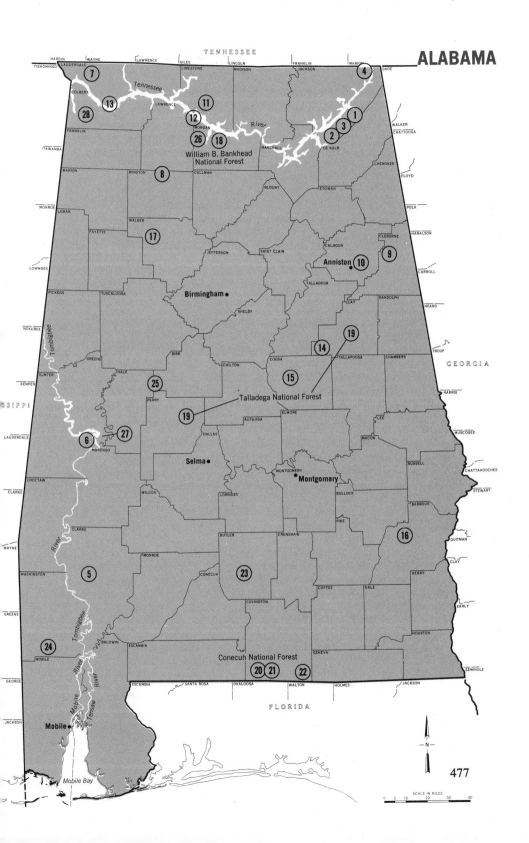

ALABAMA

TENNESSEE

William B. Bankhead
National Forest

Anniston

Birmingham

Talladega National Forest

Selma

Montgomery

GEORGIA

MISSISSIPPI

Conecuh National Forest

FLORIDA

Mobile

Mobile Bay

N

477

SCALE IN MILES
0 5 10   20   30   40

Area." The Demopolis WMA covers over 7000 acres. It lies in a bend of the Tombigbee River, where river-bottom land and some swamp is overlooked by bluffs.

Up in the extreme northwest, in Lauderdale Co., is 25,000-acre Lauderdale WMA (7). Also lightly used by quail hunters, it has a good kill record, with a fairly late season recently and dogs allowed. This Area is in the triangle formed by the Tennessee border to the north and the curve to the south of part of huge Pickwick Lake impoundment, formed by Pickwick Dam across the border in Tennessee. The city of Florence is to the southeast. County roads 14 and 1 lead to the Area.

Several other WMAs offer fair to good quail hunting. Many of these public Areas, it should be emphasized, could undoubtedly furnish more shooting for quail if hunters concentrated on the birds. Black Warrior WMA (8) is actually within the William B. Bankhead National Forest. It is extremely large, covering some 96,000 acres. This terrain is hilly, broken, in general heavily forested. There are some bottomlands. The unit is predominantly a deer-turkey-squirrel area, but quail hunting is surprisingly good for those who seek out pockets of proper habitat. Quail hunters are not numerous here. The kill ratio is fairly good. This Area is located in the northwest, in Winston Co., a few miles east of Haleyville, and near the village of Grayson. U.S. 278 runs east-west below it. The quail season may be short here. Dogs are currently allowed.

Choccolocco WMA (9) is another unit comparable to the above. It is also within a National Forest, the northern portion of the Talladega NF. The tract is slightly less than 40,000 acres, forested and hilly. Not many quail hunters are here, but the kill is fair. This also is chiefly a deer Area. The quail season currently comes late, after the first of the year. This unit is on the east side of the state. It lies along the border between Cleburne and Calhoun Cos. This places it northeast out of the city of Anniston and near the village for which the Unit is named. U.S. 78 runs near the Area and the town of Heflin is just off the southern boundary. State route 9 running north-south in Calhoun Co. also gives access.

Just west of this WMA is another location where good quail hunting may be had. This is at Fort McClellan Military Reservation (10). There are over 45,000 acres here, and in some portions of the Reservation good quail habitat is well managed. Estimates of a population of perhaps 10,000 quail have been made here, and they are common on all the open areas. Hunters must purchase a post license. Passes are on a first-come basis, and hunters check in until hunter density is deemed sufficient. Then no further permits for that day are given. Game kills must be checked also, and a specified area is closed when authorities presume it to have been harvested enough for that season. The Reservation is located at the northeast edge of Anniston, with U.S. 431 and State 21 running along the western boundaries.

In later portions of this chapter, under other species, several other WMAs will be noted. A few names to keep in mind as fair for quail: Rob Boykin; Swan Creek; Mallard-Fox Creek; Seven Mile Island; Thomas; Covington; Wolf Creek. Several of these are covered under "Doves," below.

MOURNING DOVES

Doves are one of the most important game species in Alabama by number of hunters interested in them. About one-third of Alabama's hunters avidly pursue the sport, and the kill is established at upwards of two and a half million annually. In all areas of the state where there are farming operations that allow doves to feed, the shooting is excellent. However, by far the greater share of it is on private lands, by invitation or permission.

There is some fair to good shooting on several of the WMAs also, where management and hunts purposely for doves are in operation. Notable among them are the following: The Jackson Co. group noted under "Quail"—Crow, Mud, Raccoon Creek—showed a kill during a recent season of 5390 doves, with a good ratio per hunter per day. West of the Jackson Co. group of units, in Lawrence, Morgan, and Limestone Cos., are two other WMAs of note for doves. One is the Swan Creek Waterfowl Management Area (11) along the north bank of the Tennessee River (Wheeler Lake Impoundment at this point). Interstate 65, Alt. U.S. 72, and U.S. 31 are access highways to the region, and the city of Decatur is on the south side of the river. The second of the two units is on the south side of the river and a short distance west. The Lawrence-Morgan Co. north-south line bisects it and U.S. 72 Alt. and State 20 run east-west below it, with the village of Hillsboro nearby. This is called the Mallard-Fox Creek Waterfowl Management Area (12). The combined kill on these twin units runs about like the foregoing.

Seven Mile Island WMA (13) is another good location for doves, with hunting dates specifically set and with a kill-success ratio about like. the others. This is still farther west. The tract is actually an island in the Tennessee River, with almost 5000 acres of river-bottom terrain, fertile and wooded to some extent. This is an interesting and excellent location. It gets a modest number of dove hunters and has had a good success pattern in the past. It is west of the city of Florence, where the river forms the north border of Colbert Co. Access is from either side. The main route along the south side of the River is U.S. 72.

Dove seasons are set on some other specified WMAs. But one must be sure to check what days of the week may be hunted, and to check all other rules. Hollins WMA (14) is an area of approximately 25,000 acres within the southwestern boundaries of the eastern unit of the Talladega National Forest. It is located in the southwest corner of Clay Co., east of the city of Sylacauga. Coosa WMA (15) contains 39,000 acres and is southwest of the Hollins WMA, in Coosa Co. Mitchell Dam, forming Lake Mitchell, is at the southwestern corner of the Area. State 22 skirts the southern boundary and U.S. 231 runs north-south through the town of Rockford on the east. This terrain has a number of abandoned farms, in a generally hilly, wooded region lying along the shores of the impoundment. It is a good bet for doves.

Down in the southeast, in western Barbour Co., is the 15,848-acre Barbour Co. WMA (16), where a dove season is offered annually. This Area also has abandoned farms set against a background of rolling, wooded hills and some sandy and rocky terrain. U.S. 82 runs north of it east-west from Eufaula to Union Springs, and State 51 skirts the western edge from the village of Midway on U.S. 82 south through the settlement of Mt. Andrew.

Last among the units with dove seasons is Wolf Creek WMA (17). This is well up in the northeastern part of the state, in western Walker Co. Several secondary routes run near it, one of which is State 124 just north of it. The main highway is U.S. 78 to the north, between Jasper and Carbon Hill. This is a fairly steep, wooded region of over 25,000 acres, with a number of openings formed by small, abandoned farms.

There is some dove shooting also at Ft. McClellan, which is noted under "Quail."

WOODCOCK, RAILS, SNIPE

These are not important game birds in Alabama. Without question there are moderate to good winter populations of all three in various portions of the state—in the vast bayou country along the Tensaw and Mobile rivers north of Mobile, along the borders of the numerous large impoundments and in the waterfowl areas. Conditions here are not conducive to rail hunting, however, because of lack of saltwater marshlands along the Gulf and lack of proper footing in other areas where rails may be.

A scattering of both woodcock and snipe are shot, but surveys indicate almost no one concentrates on these game birds. Probably no more than 3500 hunters annually manage to collect any of either species, and the total kill is estimated at probably not over 5000 to 7000 of each. Snipe are found in the waterfowl areas (which see), and some woodcock are located incidentally while hunting quail and doves and waterfowl on the WMAs. The winter migration pattern carries the bulk of both species farther west.

WILD TURKEYS

Alabama is famous for its wild turkey hunting. The state has long had a large population of the eastern wild turkey, and even today that population appears to be increasing. No one is certain of the exact number of turkeys in the state, but the total flock is presently estimated to be well over 100,000 and possibly 150,000 or more. With hunts both in fall and spring, and a limit of five gobblers for the combined season, it is obvious that turkeys are in good supply. There are turkeys in all sixty-seven counties of the state. During a recent season fifty-three counties had seasons.

To illustrate how popular this king of the game birds is, and how plentiful, the kill in spring season alone runs around 6000 toms. Surveys on total kills are never as complete and accurate as game men might desire, but it is believed that at least some 17,000-plus turkeys, and possibly a much higher figure than that, are harvested annually. On a nationwide basis, a hunting-success percentage on turkeys of around 12 percent is considered good. Alabama surveys indicate approximately 50,000 hunters trying each season for a gobbler. Some of course may kill several. Nonetheless, the overall chances of success here appear to be high, around 30 percent if figured against number of hunters and presuming even the lowest estimate of total kill to be reasonably accurate.

Much turkey hunting is done on club lands and private lands and on lumber company lands where hunting is permitted. For the public hunts, the National Forests are fine choices. These have been mentioned previously but will be more specifically located here. The William B. Bankhead NF (18) is in the northwest. Nearby towns are Decatur, Cullman, Haleyville, Jasper, Russellville; highways in the area: U.S. 31, 78, 278, State 5, 74, 195. The total Forest area is almost 179,000 acres. Under "Quail" it is noted that a large WMA, Black Warrior, is within this area. That will be touched separately later in this section.

The Talladega NF (19) is another excellent choice. There are two sections of it. One is in the east stretching from above Anniston southwest to near Sylacauga. U.S. 231 and 78 are main routes. There are two WMAs, already detailed, within these borders: Hollins, and Choccolocco ("Quail" and "Doves"). The other portion of the Forest is across the state between Selma and Tuscaloosa. U.S. 82 and State 5 are access routes. Total acreage of the two, some 350,000.

The Conecuh NF (20), smallest of the three, also has turkey hunting on its almost 84,000 acres. The Conecuh is in southern Alabama, in the Andalusia vicinity. This small city is at the intersection of U.S. 29 and U.S. 84.

The Forests, and the WMAs mentioned, are mostly hilly and heavily wooded, with stream courses and stream bottoms where hardwoods grow. All of these large tracts—the Forests and the WMAs—are especially attractive and well suited to turkeys, because the very purest strains of wild turkeys require tracts of unbroken forest country of at least 3000 or more acres in which to produce at their best.

Some 18 percent of Alabama's turkey hunters utilize the Wildlife Management Units. Comparing total acreage of the WMAs against the entire state, this is a high percentage hunting on the Areas and indicates an abundant turkey crop. Black Warrior, Choccolocco, and Hollins (above, in the Forests) get a high number of hunters. A recent season kill at Black Warrior was highest of the three, at fifty-six birds, and the success percentage was best there, too, although the others were fair.

A number of other WMAs well distributed over the state offer quality hunting for turkeys. Coosa ("Doves") attracts numerous hunters. Interestingly enough, some of the Areas that issue fewer permits turn up some of the very best kills, so far as success percentage is concerned. A good example is Barbour Co. WMA ("Doves"). In a study done on turkey harvest one season, there were 278 permits issued at Barbour, and twenty-six gobblers taken. A check on number of man-days hunted indicated 250—a bit less than a full day per man. Even though success was slightly less than 11 percent, no great effort was expended to collect the birds.

An excellent record is set by Blue Spring WMA (21), an Area not so far mentioned in this chapter. This is in the south, in fact within the Conecuh NF. It encompasses almost 25,000 wooded acres. There are a number of ponds and creeks, with much rolling and some broken country. The Forest has already been located—south of Andalusia, with State 137 crossing the region, south from U.S. 29. This Area gets only a modest number of hunters, and at least one survey indicates they hunt long and diligently. But the kill is excellent. A short distance east of Blue Spring, in the southeast portion of Covington Co., is Covington WMA (22). It is larger than Blue Spring—over 42,000 acres, has many creeks, much wooded and bottomland in a gently rolling to level terrain. Success here is excellent too. The towns of Florala and Opp, both on U.S. 331, are good access points. The Area lies east of this highway.

Butler Co. WMA (23) is another choice location. It lies in south-central Butler Co., which is some distance north of the two Areas just mentioned. U.S. 31 is east of it and State 106 runs across below it. The town of Georgiana is just to the south. The kill in this 24,000-acre tract is excellent compared to the small number of hunters it generally gets.

Two others also evidence modest pressure and high chances of success. Scotch WMA ("Quail"), had a kill during a recent season of thirty-six gobblers for 162 hunters, with a single day of hunting for each. That equals slightly over 22 percent success.

Rob Boykin WMA (24) turns up comparable success some seasons. This Area, not mentioned thus far, is in the southwest, in southern Washington Co. It lies between U.S. 45 and U.S. 43. State 96 runs across below it between Citronelle on U.S. 45 and Mt. Vernon on U.S. 43. It is a heavily wooded, rolling to level tract of 23,345 acres.

Most of the other WMAs furnish fair to good turkey hunting, and there is some also at Fort McClellan, although the population there is not high. One other National Forest location should not be overlooked. This is Oakmulgee WMA (25), in the western section of the Talladega NF, about halfway between Marion on State 5 and Tuscaloosa to the northwest on U.S. 82. Heavily wooded, with some steep hills, it contains 39,000 acres.

WATERFOWL

The TVA waters of northern Alabama are among the chief hunting grounds for ducks and geese. There have been special hunts and there may from time to time be others on the Wheeler National Wildlife Refuge (26). This is located near Decatur, in northwest Alabama, on Wheeler Lake, the Tennessee River impoundment. This Refuge draws large numbers of geese. The special hunts have accounted for goose kills of about a thousand annually. In this same region are two waterfowl management areas, Mallard-Fox Creek WMA and Swan Creek WMA. These are noted under "Doves." Some geese are taken here, and several thousand ducks. A few snipe (see "Snipe") are also shot on these Areas. Many coots also are shot on these Areas, and coot hunting is fairly popular in this part of the South.

Farther west, along the river, there is Seven Mile Island WMA ("Doves"). There is a fair amount of duck hunting here. On the eastern side of the state, still on the TVA system, the Jackson Co. group of WMAs—Crow Creek, Raccoon Creek, Mud Creek ("Quail")—all offer excellent waterfowl hunting, with good kills on both ducks and geese. In this same region, along Guntersville Lake (the Tennessee River), there are two Refuges. One is Crow Creek Refuge. This borders the Management Area of Crow Creek, near Stevenson on U.S. 72. Plantings are made here for winter waterfowl food, and shooting outside the Refuge borders is fairly good. The other refuge is southwest a short distance, near Scottsboro. This is North Sauty Refuge. There are goose pits on private lands surrounding the Refuge and several hundred geese from the "Guntersville flock" are harvested here each season.

At Demopolis the Waterfowl Management Area lies in a bend of the Tombigbee River at about the point where the Black Warrior River joins it. (See "Quail" for explanation.) This is called the Dam Site Area (27). It is bounded on three sides by water, and covers 2600 acres. Yellow and black signs plainly mark its boundaries. Hunting is by permit only, and these can be purchased locally at several stores, or by writing to the Department of Conservation in Montgomery. This is a duck area.

There is scattered waterfowling on other WMAs—Barbour Co. ("Doves") and Oakmulgee ("Turkeys"). There is also waterfowling in the bayou area out of Mobile, where boat access is possible, and along the large rivers and all the impoundments. In fact, for the hunter with a boat there is little difficulty finding spots to set out decoys on the TVA system in the north, or along the lakes of the Coosa River south from Gadsden to Montgomery and vicinity. Lake Walter F. George, on the Georgia line in the southeast at Eufaula, is also a possibility. There is also shooting to be had for one who seeks out secluded spots along the salt water south from Mobile. All of this southern Alabama hunting is almost entirely for ducks and coots (snipe and rails as incidentals).

To point up the better possibilities for goose hunters, it is important to know that few geese winter in Alabama below the Tennessee Valley. It is estimated that 98 percent of all geese in the state winter along that river system and the TVA impoundments there. The "Wheeler Flock" annually furnishes 3000 or more geese to hunter's bags and the "Guntersville Flock" possibly 600 to 800. A total of between 4000 and 6000 geese, depending on seasonal flock changes, is estimated killed in Alabama. Inventories taken during November indicate a total of approximately 45,000 to 50,000 geese in the state.

The same inventories show in an average year a total of around 200,000 ducks in the state. Their whereabouts is a good clue for hunters: upwards of 40,000 at Wheeler Refuge; 18,000-plus at Guntersville Reservoir; 25,000 Mobile Delta; scattered throughout the inland areas, 120,000.

In the north, throughout the TVA area, flocks run predominantly to mallards, with baldpates and pintails next. The Mobile Delta attracts canvasbacks, gadwalls, baldpates (widgeon), scaups, ringnecks. There are a tremendous number of wood ducks scattered throughout the inland areas. Estimates for a season run to as many as 70,000. Statewide total duck kills are not very accurately compiled, but probably run somewhere from 40,000 to 65,000.

EXOTIC BIRDS

Like many other states, Alabama has been experimenting with exotic game birds. Some bamboo partridges have been tried but presently the program has been discontinued. In Dale and Autauga Cos., Iranian pheasants are currently under experiment, with numerous birds released on study areas. Red junglefowl have been released in northern Baldwin Co. Both the pheasants in Autauga Co. and the junglefowl in Baldwin Co. have at this writing been doing quite well and reproducing. Broods have been reported and nests found. It is interesting to note that some of the junglefowl have crossed with domestic chickens, but the crosses apparently show wariness and game possibilities. It is quite possible that both pheasants and junglefowl may establish themselves well enough for experimental seasons to be opened during the next few years.

DEER

Deer hunting is extremely popular in Alabama, with well over 100,000 hunters avidly pursuing the sport. Under good management, deer appear to be increasing. Annual kill estimates run from 25,000 to 30,000. This includes both antlered and antlerless animals.

There is excellent deer hunting in the National Forests. These have been located under "Turkeys." There is also deer hunting from fair to excellent on most of the WMAs, and also at Ft. McClellan ("Quail"). Traditionally much deer hunting in the state is with the use of dogs. Though this method is still exceedingly popular and is practiced on numerous club and private lands, it is replaced to some extent on public lands by regulations that dictate the manner of hunting.

There are, for example, hunts specified in certain WMAs where dogs may be used, and others that are designated as "stalk" hunts. There are special hunts both for archers and gunners. Some of the WMAs set aside season dates for each type of hunting, so that all may be satisfied. Most of the managed lands stipulate that no other hunting—that is, for small game— may be done during the dates of the deer hunts. Thus, the deer hunters have the woods to themselves, and the stalk hunters are not annoyed by dogs, and vice versa. It is a good system.

By far the major share of deer killed in Alabama are taken on private lands, by various clubs which have for many years been organized chiefly for deer and turkey hunting. Nonetheless, the kill on the WMAs and the Forests is substantial. It runs between 10 and 20 percent of the total state kill. Comparing acreages open, this is excellent. While hunter success percentages do not run as high on the WMAs and Forests, they make a good showing when one considers that all types of hunts are totaled. Statewide a hunter has roughly 1 chance in 5 of bagging a deer, according to recent kill and hunter figures. This 20 percent chance is raised greatly by the private-land kills where well-organized clubs with good dog packs and a detailed knowledge of their club lands operate very efficiently. The public-land kill-success percentages run from 4 to 10 percent, on the better Areas, depending on the season, but occasionally some zoom up to match the statewide success.

During a recent season, the Coosa WMA ("Doves") led the harvest with 460 bucks and 223 antlerless deer. This Area invariably is among the high-kill spots. Choccolocco ("Quail") was second with 338 bucks, and Oakmulgee ("Turkeys") was third with 283 and 125. It is worth noting that both Choccolocco and Oakmulgee are in sections of the Talladega NF. All three of these Areas have past records of consistent high kills.

One WMA not so far noted that also sustains high kills of over a hundred bucks annually is Thomas WMA (28). This is up in the northwest corner of the state, in the southwest part of Colbert Co. Thomas WMA comprises 30,000 acres, with broken to rolling terrain, some abandoned farms, creeks, bottomlands. It is well wooded. It is south of Cherokee, which is on U.S. 72, and can also be reached via the village of Maud and by State secondaries 1 or 15.

Other good bets for deer: Barbour Co. WMA ("Doves"); Butler Co. WMA ("Turkeys"); Rob Boykin ("Turkeys"); Covington ("Turkeys"); Scotch ("Quail"). Lauderdale, Blue Spring, and Skyline WMAs noted elsewhere in this chapter also turn up some fair kills. The other Areas have some deer hunting but with lower kills as a rule.

A note must be made here that Alabama is striving to acquire new management Areas. Some of those already established are in cooperation with various lumber companies and private-land owners. Coosa is a good example, where three different lumber firms and several private owners allow use of lands. For deer especially, but for turkey and small game as well, hunters should check as this is read to see if new WMAs have come into existence, or been opened to hunting. Two large tracts, for example, Little River (18,000 acres) and Cahaba (20,753 acres) were set up but not open as this is written. Check with the Department of Conservation in Montgomery regarding these and any others.

RABBITS

There are almost as many rabbit hunters as deer hunters in Alabama. Cottontails are the dominant species, although there are also some swamp rabbits, which are larger and found in the moist bottoms and often in actual swamp situations. Rabbits of both species are hunted mostly with small hounds. Some stalk hunting also is done. The cottontail especially is abundant, and distributed over the entire state. Swamp rabbits are found mainly in the southern area.

While rabbits are by no means as popular with hunters as are squirrels, there is an estimated kill of at least three-fourths of a million annually. All of the WMAs have rabbit hunting. Those with edge areas and abandoned farms, and dry to moist swamps, are among the best, since the heavily forested tracts are not as suitable for rabbit habitat. However, the bottoms and "branch heads" on most of the public lands offer good hunting. There is little choice among them. But laws regarding use of dogs on each should be checked.

To illustrate how well distributed rabbit hunting of good quality is, up in the northeast during a recent season the Jackson Co. group of WMAs ("Quail"), the Thomas WMA in the northeast ("Deer"), and the Rob Boykin WMA ("Turkey") down in the southwest all had comparable kill success. The largest number of rabbits taken on WMAs that season were from the Jackson Co. group, Rob Boykin, and the Swan Creek and Mallard-Fox Creek Areas along the Tennessee River in the north ("Doves").

SQUIRRELS

The gray squirrel is the abundant species here, and in terms of numbers of hunters who concentrate on a single species this one tops the list. Estimates show almost 200,000 hunters annually doing at least some squirrel hunting. The kill runs around two and a half million a season. Because Alabama has a great deal of woodland and bottomland where mast from oaks, hickory, and other nut-bearing trees is abundant in good seasons, there are really no "best" places to hunt. Squirrels are well distributed over the entire state. The National Forests, and the WMAs noted previously as within their borders, are good bets. As an example, Black Warrior ("Quail") in William B. Bankhead NF showed in one survey a total daily average kill per hunter of about three squirrels. One WMA may be slightly better than another during any given season, dependent upon mast conditions that particular season. It is a good idea for squirrel enthusiasts to check with the Department prior to hunt plans. At times north Alabama has a better crop than the south, or vice versa. Hunters should note also that there is a slight difference in season dates above and below U.S. 78. Under proper seasonal conditions, any or all of the WMAs will furnish excellent squirrel hunting.

OTHER ANIMALS

Raccoons and opossums are considered both game and fur animals. They are exceedingly plentiful, and fairly popular with hunters. Estimates show at least 100,000, probably more, of each taken per season. The National Forests and all of the WMAs have good populations. Most of the WMAs have a season. On some these animals may be taken with bow and arrow during deer season. On some night hunting only is permitted. There is little choice of location.

Foxes and bobcats are not on the game list, but foxes are fairly numerous and bobcats are occasional quarry for hound men. The annual fox take is not high. Most fox hunting is done by hard-core enthusiasts of the chase. On some of the WMAs foxes may be run at night (not taken with gun or bow) during closed seasons for other game, and dogs may be used for actual hunting during a stipulated season. Check the WMAs individually for pertaining laws. There is little choice among locations.

EXOTIC BIG GAME

Some years ago a few fallow deer were released or escaped from private owners along the Alabama River. Indications are that a herd of modest size has grown up here, particularly in Wilcox and Dallas Counties in the south-central part of the state. The Alabama River runs southwest with many deep bends across this area, from Selma in Dallas Co. to the southwest corner of Wilcox. The entire region is west and southwest from Montgomery. During regular deer seasons these animals are now legal game and a few of them are generally taken each season.

REGULATIONS

Game laws pertaining to seasons, bag and possession limits, areas to be hunted, special hunts, license fees all may have numerous changes from year to year. For current regulations, and for other specific queries, write to: Alabama Department of Conservation, Game and Fish Division, Montgomery, Alabama 36104.

MISSISSIPPI

Mississippi can lay legitimate claim to being one of the Gulf Coast states, with approximately eighty straight-line miles of frontage on the Gulf along its southern boundary. The eastern jut of neighboring Louisiana on the west came close to crowding Mississippi off the Gulf Coast. In the north Tennessee borders the state, and on the east the entire border is with Alabama. The western boundary is formed by the Mississippi River for most of the distance, then a straight west to east line cuts across to form a section of southern border with Louisiana, thence again south to the Gulf, with the Pearl River the demarcation line.

Mississippi is almost entirely a lowland state. There is an area of low, sandy hills in the northeast, the highest slightly over 800 feet in altitude. From the northeast the land slopes gently west and south, to the Mississippi River and to the Gulf. There are areas of pine, bottomlands of hardwoods, great expanses of moss-hung cypress swamps in the south. Large, lazy and often winding rivers work their way toward the Gulf. A striking physical feature is the Delta country of the northwest and west. Here, in the large triangle formed by the Mississippi River and the tributary Yazoo, is the Delta, a flat alluvial plain. Cotton is king here.

In fact, cotton is the chief crop for the state. Pecans, livestock, sorghum, sweet potatoes are other products of the land. Lumbering is exceedingly important, and indeed upon the forests, which cover more than half of the area of the state, is based the good hunting which is readily available. This is a leading state in the production of hardwood pulp, hardwood lumber, and in slashpine products. Because of superior soil, expanses of bottomlands and hardwoods, the Delta and the Mississippi River counties contain the state's largest wildlife resources.

Roads are excellent and abundantly crisscross the entire state. Several U.S. Highways and Interstates run the entire distance north to south, and half a dozen comparable highways intersect east-west. A grid of other highways takes sportsmen to any location they wish. Air transport to the larger and well-scattered cities is good. Except for the swamps, where rivers often give easy access via small power boats, no special transport is required. Short 4-wheel-drive vehicles are handy anywhere in the state, however, especially during rains, when bogging down on dirt trails is all too easy.

Mississippi encompasses 47,716 square miles. At its widest point it is a bit over 200 miles. From the northern border with Tennessee clear to the Gulf is about 350. Scores of small towns and rural settlements dot the state. The population is currently close to 2.5 million. Basically, however, the state is rural. Only a dozen cities have over 20,000 people, and only two have passed 100,000. In many ways this is an ideal situation for hunters.

Hunting is extremely popular, with a current average of over 230,000 participants. Of these, upwards of 18,000 are nonresidents. Game is in good

487

supply, and management practices are aggressive and professional. It was not always thus. Mississippi was for many years, until at least the early 1930s, one of the least progressive states in management. Then alarmed conservationists, seeing turkeys, deer, and other game brought to the verge of extinction by lack of laws, enforcement and management, brought sound practices and a serious Game Commission into being. Today, while changing land use handicaps to some extent the production of bobwhite quail and cottontails, there is nonetheless good hunting for these species, and for revived herds of whitetail deer, turkey flocks, and for doves, waterfowl, squirrels. There are woodcock, snipe, fur and game species such as foxes, raccoons, and opossums. Highest hunter interest is in quail, squirrels, deer, turkeys, and doves.

The situation regarding public lands is ideal. Foremost among these are the National Forests. Mississippi is extremely fortunate in having six Forests within its border. Beginning in the north and reading southward, these Forests and their locations are as follows:

Holly Springs NF (1) is in two main blocks in the north, the larger one just below the Tennessee border, with the towns of Holly Springs (U.S. 78) and Oxford a short distance south good orientation points. The smaller block is to the south. The entire Forest covers over 143,000 acres.

A short distance southeast of this Forest, but still in the northern half of the state and well toward the eastern border, is the Tombigbee NF (2), also in two main blocks. This Forest is slightly over 65,000 acres, with Tupelo (U.S. 78), Columbus (U.S. 82 and 45), and Ackerman (State 12) nearby.

Near the western border about halfway down the state is the Delta NF (3), with almost 59,000 acres. This is north of Vicksburg. The town of Rolling Fork is near the northwestern corner. U.S. 61, State 16 and 3 offer access.

East of the capital city of Jackson, in the central-south region is Bienville NF (4), with 175,697 acres. It lies between Jackson and Meridian, with the smaller towns of Forest and Raleigh on the fringes. U.S. 80, and State 35, which intersect at Forest, offer access.

Near the Mississippi River in the southwest is the Homochitto NF (5), covering slightly more than 189,000 acres. It lies chiefly between Natchez and Brookhaven, with Meadville on the fringes, and all three cities located on U.S. 84.

Down in and slightly above the southeastern "bootheel" that reaches to the Gulf is the Desoto NF (6). There are two main blocks, one near Laurel, the larger to the south, south of Hattiesburg and with the town of Wiggins near its center. This is the largest of the Forests in Mississippi, with a bit more than half a million acres. All of these Forests are administered from the office of the Supervisor, Jackson. Maps and other details may be obtained there on any or all.

There is a great deal of commercial forest land in Mississippi, in private ownership, but much of it open to hunting under special regulations set up by the owners. For example, International Paper Company has over 860,000 acres in timberlands here, and offers printed material about recreational facilities. Write the firm at Southern Kraft Division, IPA, P.O. Box Drawer A, Mobile, Alabama 36601. St. Regis Paper Company also has Mississippi acreage, and offers printed material as above, from 150 E. 42nd Street, New York, New York 10017. The Mississippi Game Commission, address at end of chapter, can be helpful with other information about timber company lands.

Few hunters will need to search that far for hunting space. The Commission has a series of excellent Wildlife Management Areas well distributed over the state, and totaling over 1.5 million acres. Hunters should be aware that a number of these WMAs are within National Forest boundaries, and are large NF tracts on which game management is administered by the state. Other WMAs belong to individuals or corporations and are under state lease and management.

Besides the WMAs, there are public hunting lands along several large reservoirs. Most of these—Arkabutla, Sardis, Enid, Grenada—are Corps of Engineers projects. One, Ross Barnett, is under authority of the Pearl River Valley Water Supply District. These will be dealt with later, particularly in relation to waterfowl hunting.

Some years ago, when game populations were swiftly on the downgrade, a great number of hunting clubs were formed by groups of Mississippi hunters who banded together, leasing or buying lands on which they practiced their own game management. This procedure became quite traditional. Thus today numerous private club lands offer their members excellent hunting, and take much pressure off public lands. In addition, the rural quality of the state is for the most part unspoiled, and permission to hunt on private farmlands and woodlots for such species as quail, doves, squirrels, rabbits is never very difficult to obtain, if hunters are polite, and mannerly in hunting conduct.

There is no problem for visitors in finding places to stay. Good motels and other accommodations are never far from any given hunting spot. Camping hunters have a wide latitude of choices. The National Forests, the State Parks, the Corps of Engineers campgrounds can handle large numbers, especially since hunting seasons fall after the summer vacation period of family vacation travel is over. Booklets titled "Camping in Outdoor Mississippi" and "Mississippi State Parks" can be obtained respectively from: Travel Department, Mississippi Agricultural and Industrial Board, 1504 State Office Building, Jackson 39201; Mississippi Park System, 1104 Woolfolk State Office Building, Jackson.

In early fall, during such seasons as for doves, and the beginning of squirrels, Mississippi weather is hot and humid. Later on, it may be moderate but is invariably damp. Midwinter seasons, and even spring turkey seasons, can be chill. Often the weather feels colder than the temperature would indicate, because of dampness. Thus hunters active after, say, October, should be prepared with warm clothing.

The quail and dove hunter in Mississippi will need shot sizes of about No. 7½ and No. 8. Waterfowl will require something heavier, from short-magnum No. 6 and No. 4 for ducks, to No. 2 for geese. Most squirrel hunters and a good many rabbit hunters utilize the .22. Shotgun hunters use bird shot for these animals. Traditionally, for turkeys in the Deep South No. 6 shot has long been used. This, in short-magnum loading, or No. 4 likewise, is a lethal dose. Deer hunters will be most of the time in dense cover. Any standard caliber of rifle does nicely, but traditions dictate the older favorites such as .30/30, .35 Rem. and such so-called brush rifles. Shotguns with buckshot, or slugs, are also used.

QUAIL

Bobwhite quail are exceedingly popular game birds in Mississippi. While the Commission has no annual kill figures available, the bag most certainly runs high, and bobwhites, along with the mourning dove, are the important game birds in the state. The quail population is substantial, but it is by no means as high as it was over past decades, and it is slowly declining, in general, due to changes in land use. Much burning and clearing some years ago made good habitat for quail, in new, low growth and around small farms. But with about 50 percent of Mississippi today in forest, and with timber and pasturing ever more important and small farms becoming fewer, quail suffer.

Nonetheless, there is excellent quail hunting. Much of it is on private lands. Some of these are club lands where no public hunting is allowed, but the still existing small farms and fallow areas provide good quail habitat and on most such lands permission to hunt is not difficult to obtain. There is also good quail hunting on many of the public lands.

While the densely forested portions of the National Forests obviously offer little habitat for quail, there are edges and portions of these Forests that have fair to good quail shooting. All have some. The Bienville NF, De Soto NF, Holly Springs NF, Tombigbee NF may be considered the best. These Forests are described and located in the opening portion of this chapter.

Of the WMAs, a number furnish from fair to excellent quail hunting. They are as follows:

Bucatunna Creek WMA (7) is located in Clarke Co., in the upper southeast quarter of the state. This county is on the Alabama border. The nearest town is Quitman on U.S. 45. There are 102,000 acres in this WMA. Up in the north, about centered east-west across the state, in Calhoun Co., is the Calhoun Co. WMA (8), of 15,000 acres. Calhoun City on State 9 offers easy access. The city of Grenada to the southwest on U.S. 51 is also a good orientation point.

To the southeast, and actually within boundaries of the Tombigbee NF in southeastern Choctaw and northwestern Winston Cos. is the Choctaw WMA (9). It encompasses 50,000 acres. Ackerman, at junction of State 9, 12, and 15, is a good location point for access. Over in the southwest, in western Copiah Co. west of the town of Hazlehurst on U.S. 51, is the Copiah Co. WMA (10), of 6000 acres. The Hugh L. White WMA (11), sometimes called the Marion Co. Game Area, is in eastern Marion Co., east of the town of Columbia, State 13 near U.S. 98. This county is on the southern border, and the Pearl River crosses it. The WMA contains 7500 acres.

In the west, along the Mississippi River and centrally located north-south, is the Issaquena Co. WMA (12), of 13,000 acres. The village of Mayersville at the end of State 14 and west of Rolling Fork on U.S. 61 offers access. Far down in the southeast is the huge Red Creek WMA (13), with a total of 340,000 acres lying in four counties: Stone, George, Harrison, Jackson. Some of this acreage is within the DeSoto NF but a great deal lies outside it. Thus, including all of the Forest lands, this corner of the state offers a

KEY TO HUNTING AREAS

1. Holly Springs NF	11. Hugh L. White WMA	19. Homochitto WMA
2. Tombigbee NF	(Marion County GA)	20. Leaf River WMA
3. Delta NF	12. Issaquena County	21. Tallahalla Creek WMA
4. Bienville NF	WMA	22. Noxubee National
5. Homochitto NF	13. Red Creek WMA	Wildlife Refuge
6. De Soto NF	14. Wolf River WMA	23. Sunflower WMA
7. Bucatunna Creek	15. Yazoo National	24. Arkabutla Lake MA
WMA	Wildlife Refuge	25. Pearl River WMA
8. Calhoun County WMA	16. Adams County WMA	26. Grenada WMA
9. Choctaw WMA	17. Bienville WMA	27. Sardis WMA
10. Copiah County WMA	18. Chickasawhay WMA	28. Yellow Creek WMA
		29. Enid Reservoir

MISSISSIPPI

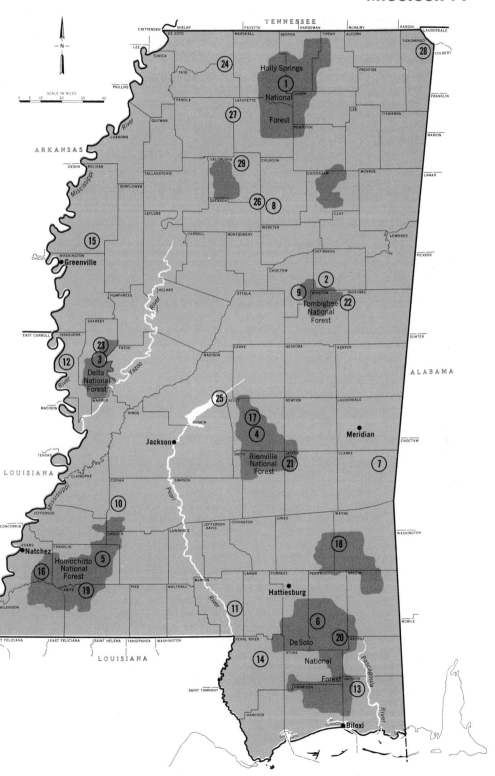

vast space for quail hunters. The town of Wiggins, U.S. 49 and State 26 in Stone Co., may be considered an access point, although any other towns in the region generally to the southeast of the city of Hattiesburg place hunters in good quail territory.

West of this large WMA is the Wolf River WMA (14), another enormous one, of 240,000 acres. It also covers parts of several counties: southeast Marion, southwest Lamar, much of northern and eastern Pearl. Interstate 59 runs through Pearl Co., and the village of Poplarville on U.S. 11 and State 26 is a good orientation point. It is obvious from the above that a large percentage of the entire "bootheel" of southeast Mississippi is in public lands.

All of the WMAs have resident managers. The folder "Hunt In Mississippi," mentioned in opening of chapter, gives their addresses and telephone numbers. They can be helpful when one is planning a hunt, especially for hunters visiting the state who do not know the area.

Some of the Reservoirs mentioned early in the chapter as having public surrounding lands offer fair quail shooting. Since these are managed primarily for waterfowl, refer to that section for information about them.

Although quail are very generally distributed throughout Mississippi in all favorable situations of habitat, the prime range and the best populations are in a few counties of the central portion of the far north. Immediately below the northern border: Marshall, Benton, Tippah, and Alcorn Cos.; below and partly bordering these: Lafayette, Union, Prentiss, Pontotoc. Some landowners in the counties—and elsewhere in Mississippi—cater to visiting hunters at reasonable costs. The local warden in any county can offer valuable help in setting up a hunt.

MOURNING DOVES

Mississippi has excellent dove shooting, and the bird is extremely popular. Exactly opposite of the bobwhite, doves have increased over the years in this state as farming practices have changed. The mechanization of farming leaves more grain on the ground, where mourning doves, which do not feed from the stalk, can easily find it. Pasturing has opened more lands. Thousands of farm ponds have concentrated doves in pasture and farming areas.

The intense farming of the Delta, that portion of the Mississippi in the northwest lying between the Mississippi River and its tributary the Yazoo, has made this section of the state unquestionably the best for dove shooting. However, virtually all of the region is in private ownership. Cotton, corn, sorghum are primary crops. The terrain is flat and fertile, there is ample water for doves, bounteous supplies of food, and roosting locations in strips of trees. Even though public lands are not found here, few landowners object to giving permission for dove shooting on specific, harvested tracts.

There is of course good dove shooting elsewhere in the state. This also is predominantly on private lands. Permission is usually granted. Some dove shooting is available around the reservoirs on public tracts. See "Waterfowl."

Several of the WMAs offer dove hunting. Copiah County WMA, Hugh L. White (Marion Co.), Issaquena County, Red Creek, Wolf River all are noted for their dove shooting. See "Quail" regarding all of these. The Yazoo National Wildlife Refuge (15), a waterfowl refuge primarily, also offers managed dove hunts. There are almost 10,000 acres here, located in the west, in Washington Co., with Hollandale on U.S. 61 and State 12 a focal point. Although the National Forests are not on the whole proper dove habitat, they furnish a scattered bit of shooting. On the whole, arranging permission in the Delta, or shooting one of the above mentioned tracts, will give a hunter the best chance of fast action.

WOODCOCK

Very oddly, not much is known even officially about the woodcock hunting possibilities in Mississippi. The bird has never been purposely hunted to any extent, although a modest number of woodcock are bagged each season as incidentals by quail hunters and others. This is especially puzzling, because without question a substantial number of woodcock migrate across portions of Mississippi. The chief nesting grounds in summer are from northern Wisconsin and Michigan east throughout southern Canada and New England to Nova Scotia. The main wintering ground for the continent's birds is in Louisiana. To reach Louisiana therefore many thousands must pass across Mississippi or funnel down its river bottoms. Without doubt any hunter who cared to make a project of it could find excellent woodcock shooting in Mississippi.

Woodcock are recognized as important game on some of the WMAs, for example Copiah and Hugh L. White ("Quail").

The Commission has recently instituted a thorough woodcock study covering migration, movement, and concentration points. A banding program is in the offing. Migrating birds are thought to arrive in numbers about November and many may stay until northward migration begins during January and February. There is good reason to believe that concentrations of woodcock may occur in late winter in the southwestern counties, and also along the lower bottomlands of the Pearl River, which forms in its lower reaches the border with northeastern and central Louisiana. Another concentration area is thought to be along the Pascagoula River in the southeast, where it crosses George and Jackson Cos.

SNIPE AND RAILS

Although there is an open season on jacksnipe, there appears to be little interest in this hunting. A few are shot on waterfowling areas but finding concentrations is difficult. Some snipe shooting is possible along the coast or near it, but few hunters participate.

Nor is rail hunting practiced to any extent, or very successfully. Tides along the Mississippi Gulf Coast are seldom high enough to produce good rail shooting by concentrating the birds. In addition, the Gulf Coast is rather heavily developed and lacks the extensive marshes and marsh-bordering wetlands and prairies that form such perfect wintering grounds for snipe to the west.

WILD TURKEYS

Originally the wild turkey was awesomely abundant in Mississippi. Intensive logging operations during the late 1800s and the early part of this century decimated a great deal of turkey habitat. By 1932, when the Mississippi Game Commission was established, turkeys were at a low ebb and were found chiefly along the wilder river bottoms. Stocking was soon begun, with pen-reared stock, which was not very successful. Later live-trapped wild birds were used and careful turkey management has been in force ever since.

With the exception of two years during the late '40s, the season has remained open. It is during the spring only, excepting certain high-density areas along the Mississippi River. It is thought that fall any-turkey hunts may become more common as the flock needs control in other high-population sections. The annual bag has steadily increased for the past ten years and now averages somewhere around 4000 per year. This is thought to be about 10 percent of a total flock of 40,000 or more. The goal is a state flock of at least 100,000 birds, and appears attainable.

Heaviest concentration presently is in a narrow strip along the Mississippi from the northern border to the confluence of the Yazoo. Second most populous regions are: in portions of the four southwesternmost counties; the counties of the southeast lying along the Alabama border, beginning with southern Lauderdale and moving south. The central part of the southeastern "bootheel" is included here, too. There are fair turkey populations in the National Forests. The Bienville NF in Scott, Newton, Smith and Jasper Cos. stands highest. Other smaller spots of fair density are scattered over the entire state.

More than half of Mississippi's eighty-two counties are open to turkey hunting as this is written. To illustrate wild turkey expansion, two seasons previously thirty-three counties had open season, as against the present forty-eight. Kill figures over a period of some seasons show the following counties in the high brackets, listed in order according to highest kill: Bolivar on the Mississippi in the Delta; Coahoma, immediately north of Bolivar; Tunica, bordering Coahoma on the north; Perry, in the southeast near Hattiesburg; Amite, southwest; Greene, southeast, bordering Perry; Lauderdale, eastern border and central, with Meridian the chief city; Pearl River, in bootheel.

There is no difficulty finding places to hunt. As noted, the National Forests offer from fair to excellent hunting. They are covered in chapter opening. The majority of the WMAs also offer good turkey hunting. These are usually managed hunts, and the WMAs open may differ from season to season. During a recent season several already noted under "Quail" were open: Bucatunna, Choctaw, Red Creek, Wolf River. Issaquena also has turkeys, may or may not be open any given season.

Some others that were open during a recent season, and not so far described are as follows: Adams Co. WMA (16) is near Natchez in Adams County, in the southwest, contains 16,000 acres. Bienville WMA (17), of 20,000 acres, is within the northern portion of the Bienville NF, in Scott Co., in the vicinity of Morton, U.S. 80 and State 13. The Chickasawhay WMA (18) is a huge one, of 120,000 acres. It also is within a National Forest, covering the northern part of the DeSoto NF in Jones and Wayne Cos. southeast from the city of Laurel. Homochitto WMA (19) is another NF tract, of 51,500 acres within the Forest of like name, in the southwest, in Amite and Franklin Cos. with a key town of Meadville, U.S. 84 and 98.

The Leaf River WMA (20) contains 44,000 acres, in Perry and Greene Cos. in the southeast. This is another NF tract, in the southern block of the DeSoto NF. The village of McLain is one good access point, on U.S. 98. In the southeastern portion of the Bienville NF is another WMA, of 33,000 acres near the town of Montrose, State 15. This is Tallahalla Creek WMA (21), located partly in three counties: Jasper, Scott, Newton. There is also a managed hunt some seasons on the Noxubee National Wildlife Refuge (22). This large Refuge, of almost 50,000 acres, was set up originally to assist both waterfowl and wild turkeys. It is in the east, in Noxubee and Winston Cos., immediately to the east of the Tombigbee NF. The Sunflower WMA (23), with 70,000 acres, also has open turkey seasons and managed hunts. It is within the northern portion of the Delta NF, in Sharkey Co., in the west, and west of Yazoo City. An access point is Holly Bluff.

It is obvious from the above that much of the best turkey range is in public ownership. Over the past few seasons high kills have been established on Chickasawhay and Red Creek. In second place were Wolf River and Bucatunna. Homochitto also has been good. Total bag on the WMAs averages around 12.5 percent of the total state kill, an excellent record indeed.

WATERFOWL

There is some very good waterfowl hunting in the state, especially for ducks. At one time goose hunting, particularly along the Mississippi, was superb. Late years this has drastically declined, but attempts at goose management may revive it, or replace it. Goose hunting, almost entirely for Canadas, was excellent on the river sandbars and in adjacent cornfields until the late 1940s. By the early '50s it had virtually disappeared. Development of goose refuges and wintering grounds farther north is thought to have ruined Mississippi River goose shooting here.

Experiments were quickly begun in goose management, the first project at Sardis Reservoir with a Waterfowl Management Area. This large impoundment is in the northwest, in Panola and Lafayette Cos. The management project is ten miles north of the town of Oxford, Lafayette Co., contains an 1800-acre refuge plus 50,000 acres of public hunting grounds. Launched with a decoy flock and food plantings, it has to date, after about twenty years, been only mildly successful. Recently about 2000 geese wintered there. However, there is a good possibility the flock may slowly enlarge. Uniquely, about 30 percent of the birds are of the giant Canada variety. Attempts are now underway to establish a flock of nonmigratory geese. Similar experiments are in progress in other states and several, including the one in Mississippi, appear promising. These of course are Canadas. Blue and snow geese migrating through in fall make up an inconsequential part of the kill, probably no more than 200 birds annually.

The two National Refuges, Yazoo and Noxubee, have tried with no success to date to establish geese via a transplant program and holding the transplants there by wing clipping. Thus it appears that goose hunting in Mississippi in the coming years will be marginal, with the best hope the Sardis project.

The duck picture is much brighter. There is excellent shooting for mallards and wood ducks, which make up about 90 percent of the total bag. Green-winged teal and ringnecked ducks are the other most abundant species. Probably the best and most concentrated duck shooting in the state is in LeFlore County, which has more than fifty lakes and the Yazoo River south of Greenwood for a portion of its southern border. It is estimated that approximately 25 percent of all ducks killed in the state are bagged in this county. Although much of the hunting is on private lands, public shooting is traditional and permission seldom difficult to obtain. During the past year the Commission established a public controlled duck hunting area in southern LeFlore Co., seven miles south of Swiftown, in the extreme southwest corner. Plans were for a lottery system, about forty hunters allowed per day, morning shooting only, and a fee.

Avid duck hunters who will check the weather can occasionally find sensational hunting in many parts of the Yazoo Delta. When fall and winter rains are heavy large areas are flooded. Ducks swarm into bottomland hardwoods and croplands from the river, and from the northern reservoirs. The Delta, prior to drainage and intensive agricultural use, was the prime duck region of the state.

There is of course scattered duck hunting along the rivers everywhere, around ponds, and some along the Gulf. But the Commission has done much for waterfowlers in setting up six WMAs primarily focused on ducks. Arkabutla Lake Management Area (24) is owned by the Corps of Engineers. This reservoir is located in the northwest corner of the state, in DeSoto and Tate Cos. It is five miles northeast of Coldwater, Interstate 55, contains 2200 refuge acres and 26,000 acres of public hunting grounds. Small-game hunters should note that quail and rabbits are also found here. The Pearl River WMA (25) is in conjunction with the state-owned and developed Ross Barnett Reservoir, near Jackson, in Madison and Rankin Cos. This is in the Pearl River Valley Water Supply District. The hunting ground, and refuge, is about nine miles southeast of Canton in central Madison Co. The entire Reservoir area is open to public hunting. Again, small game hunters should note that quail, doves, and other species are found on portions of the land. The refuge covers only about 800 acres.

Grenada WMA (26) is twelve miles southwest of Calhoun City, lies partly in three counties: Calhoun, Grenada, Yalobusha. It is based on Grenada Reservoir. There is a 2700-acre refuge, 48,000 acres of public hunting lands. This, too, is a fine small-game area. Estimates place the duck kill at about 7 percent of the state total. Sardis WMA (27), noted in connection with geese, has an 1800-acre refuge and 50,000 acres of hunting grounds. Hunting pressure is high here and so is the kill, about 12 percent of the state total. There may be anywhere up to 70,000 ducks on the area during a season. Small-game hunting is, as on the other waterfowl areas, very good.

Sunflower WMA has already been described under "Turkeys." But portions of it are extremely important for duck hunting. The Waterfowl Management Area covers about 1500 acres of bottomland hardwoods. This acreage is annually flooded by pumping in water from the Sunflower River. The tract is about five miles east of the village of Rolling Fork. This is thought to be one of the first areas on which the Forest Service allowed flooding for public hunting. Shooting is mornings only, and there is a $3 permit, plus of course the regular hunting license. Shooting is excellent, and almost entirely for mallards and wood ducks. Another Waterfowl Management Area of about 1000 acres, with a small acreage flooded, is Yellow Creek WMA (28). Pressure is high, the kill small. This is TVA land in Tishomingo Co., up in the extreme northeast. It is seven miles north of Iuka, U.S. 72 and State 25.

As this is written a new Waterfowl Management Area was being prepared in Sharkey Co. southwest of Rolling Fork. This is to be a fee area, with lottery. In addition to all the locations covered so far, the sandbars of the Mississippi are mostly public, and offer good shooting when water is rising on the main stream. The oxbow lakes along the river course also furnish excellent shooting when the weather is bad enough to drive ducks from the main channel. Much of this shooting is public. Several of the WMAs mentioned earlier under other species also furnish some duck shooting. Among these are: Chickasawhay and Noxubee ("Turkeys"), Issaquena, Red Creek, Wolf Creek ("Quail"). There is also some shooting on public Corps of Engineers tracts at Enid Reservoir (29), which is located about halfway between Sardis and Grenada impoundments and lies along the northern border of Yalobusha Co.

RABBITS

Cottontails are distributed in varying abundance in all counties. Swamp rabbits are found in low, wet places. They are common along the Mississippi, mainly between the river and the main levee system. However, most of these lands are in private clubs. In Delta, Coahoma, Issaquena, Quitman, Sharkey, Yalobusha counties many areas have more swamp rabbits than cottontails. The swamp rabbit is larger, but all told makes up no more than a small percentage of the total rabbit kill. All of the public lands so far covered offer rabbit hunting from fair to excellent. The Corps of Engineers lands and Waterfowl Management Areas, the edge cover of the National Forests, the WMAs furnish all but limitless hunting. A few of the WMAs offer good swamp rabbit shooting as well as cottontails. Chief among these are: Sunflower, Issaquena, Tallahalla Creek, Red Creek. Thus there is no problem finding rabbit hunting locations. For that matter, most rural landowners in Mississippi will give permission for rabbit hunting.

SQUIRRELS

Squirrel hunting is very popular in Mississippi in all the hardwood and farmland parts of the state. Squirrels in fact surpass rabbits in small-game popularity.

There are both fox and gray squirrels. Fox squirrels are of two subspecies. The Delta fox squirrel is found in the Yazoo Delta region. The Hill fox squirrel is found in upland timber generally cut up by openings or farms. The Delta fox squirrel inhabits lowland timber much the same as the gray squirrel. There is a black phase quite common in portions of the Delta. The gray, or "cat," squirrel is an animal of the forests and is more generally distributed in Mississippi than the fox squirrel. In all of the hardwood bottomlands where magnolia, beech, gum, hickory, and oak grow these squirrels are abundant.

Squirrels abound on most of the public lands. With such a huge acreage of National Forest lands, the squirrel hunter has no problems locating a place to hunt. Although most of the Delta is privately owned, there is little problem there also in obtaining premission for pursuits such as squirrel hunting. However, the National Forests are the prime reservoir of squirrel populations in the state. Many of the WMAs, as explained under foregoing species, are within the National Forest boundaries. Virtually all the others have squirrel populations. There are managed hunts on these, although not all are necessarily open every season. Check the current game-law digest for the listing of managed hunts and the dates and special regulations for each.

There are also managed squirrel hunts on both the Noxubee and Yazoo National Wildlife Refuges, and on some of the Waterfowl Management Areas described under "Waterfowl." It is necessary to inquire about these for the year in which the hunt is to be made. Dates and regulations are seasonally liable to change.

BLACK BEAR

This animal is mentioned merely to make certain hunters realize that there is no open season. There may still be a few bears in the state, but they enjoy total protection.

DEER

The whitetail is avidly hunted in Mississippi by several methods. Some counties or areas allow hunting with dogs, some do not. While many natives love the traditional chase with large dog packs where it is legal, the art of stalking and still-hunting is growing. So is the whitetail population.

In pioneer times Mississippi deer were teemingly plentiful. By the late

1920s it is estimated that there were no more than 1500 deer in the entire state. Ruthless hunting, both for meat and for market, had brought them near to extinction. The few remaining animals were in the dense hardwood swamps along the large rivers. By 1932, when the Commission was formed, there was only a remnant left, mostly in Washington, Coahoma, Sharkey, and Issaquena Cos. Careful and enlightened management from that point on has brought the whitetail to a high peak, with probably a quarter million deer in the state herd and hunting seasons open in all but a few (presently) of the state's eighty-two counties. During the season of this writing only three counties were closed.

At present the annual kill averages around 10 percent of the herd, or 25,000 animals. However, recent seasons have been much higher, one late one at 31,578, with almost 71 percent bucks. This kill was accomplished by roughly 115,000 hunters, which gives a success quotient of over 1 in 4. Besides, at least two-thirds of the open counties have had over several recent seasons a continuing higher success from the former season. This means the herd is still growing, and that Mississippi deer hunting is getting better and better. The present success percentage is far above the national average. And, the size of Mississippi's whitetails is surprising. Many weigh over 200 pounds field dressed.

To give a picture of where the deer are, although this does not offer a clear idea of pressure or success percentage, over the past several seasons 55.4 percent of the total state deer kill has occurred in ten counties, nine of which border the Mississippi River. Warren Co. was first; Claiborne, second; next, to the south, Jefferson, third; Bolivar, in the Delta, fourth. The others: Wilkinson, extreme southwest; Washington, lower Delta; Adams, southwest; Issaquena, west-central river; Tunica, northwest. The other county, Kemper, is on the Alabama border in the east, centrally located.

Some of these kills may be influenced by the fact that many club lands or leases are along the Mississippi. There is, however, no great difficulty in this state for the average deer hunter in locating a good place to hunt. All National Forest lands have abundant deer. See chapter opening for description of these. Every one of the WMAs—all of them covered previously under various species—offers deer, with managed hunts. These may not all occur during any given season. Opening or closing is a prerogative of management.

Recently, however, during seasons when all have had hunts, here are the ten with highest kills. Bear in mind that these kills must be measured against the size of the tract, and hunter pressure. In order of number of deer taken, the WMAs were: Red Creek; Choctaw; Noxubee Refugee; Sunflower; Chickasawhay; Wolf River; Issaquena; Leaf River; Tallahalla; Hugh L. White.

Even some of the impoundment lands primarily managed for waterfowl have deer herds. The National Refuges also have managed hunts, as note Noxubee above. Many nonresident hunters who travel far for good chances at whitetails overlook Mississippi. This is unfortunate, since opportunities here are excellent and growing better year by year.

OTHER ANIMALS

Raccoons and opossums are plentiful. They occur in all counties and on all public lands, may be run with dogs (chase only) all year. An odd law in this state makes these animals legal "for food" but taken "without a gun" in all counties during a specified season, usually October. They may be taken for food with guns and dogs in all counties during a later season, and with guns and dogs for pelts during a still later, and longer, season.

Foxes are also quite plentiful, are classed as predators and may be hunted at any time and by any method.

REGULATIONS

Game laws pertaining to seasons, bag and possession limits, areas to be hunted, special hunts, license fees all may have numerous changes from year to year. For current regulations, and for other specific queries, write to: State Game and Fish Commission, P.O. Box 451, Jackson, Mississippi 39205.

LOUISIANA

Louisiana, with 600 miles of tortuously indented and island-strewn Gulf Coast, is unique among the states in its topography. Its entire southern boundary is truly indefinable. It simply lowers through tidal marshlands, shallow embayments, low barrier islands until the Gulf of Mexico finally and completely takes over. From the last vestiges of marsh at the edge of open blue water, this vast lowland habitat sweeps inland a full thirty miles or more before "dry land" is much in evidence. Indeed, southern Louisiana is one of the world's greatest tidal marshlands. There are almost five million acres of it, just possibly the most important single wintering ground for waterfowl and water and marsh birds on the continent.

Much of this area is of course at sea level or below. An astonishing total of some 7500 square miles are actually under water. Northward the level rises gently and the land becomes a rich alluvial plain, with a number of broad slow rivers, numerous cypress-studded bayous, and swamps with moss-draped bottomland hardwoods. The Mississippi River forms much of the eastern boundary, then flows on through the southeastern area the rest of the way to its union with the Gulf. There are rolling hills and pinelands in the north, bluffs along the Mississippi, but the elevation is little more than 500 feet at the highest.

Although there is a tremendous amount of industry, oil and chemicals chiefly, lumbering has long been important and thus many large, privately owned forest tracts still exist. Unfortunately, over late years there has been a great amount of timber clearing, especially of the hardwoods in rich bottomlands. These lands, among the best of the habitat for small-game animals and game birds, are being planted in vast acreages of soybeans, with much resultant loss of prime cover. From a hunter's point of view, however, there are nonetheless a wealth of possibilities still existing.

Roads throughout Louisiana are excellent. Especially over the northern two-thirds of the state they crisscross everywhere. Along the Mississippi, and also to the south of Interstate 10, which runs east-west along the top of the southern lowland borders, there are still a number of places fairly difficult to get to except by boat in the canals, or over lumber trails where 4-wheel-drive vehicles may be necessary. Air transport to the larger cities is of course excellent.

Louisiana is not an especially large state. At its western border it extends north from the Gulf about 225 miles. Across its narrow waist from Texas to the Mississippi is only a bit over a hundred miles. The extremely irregular Gulf Coast is the longest dimension. The state covers 48,523 square miles. Packed into this "Lower Mississippi River Country" of timber and lowland, however, is a great variety of excellent and not unduly crowded hunting. Population, though fairly heavy (estimated just now at approximately 3,660,000) fortunately is concentrated in the industrial areas. There is a good deal of near-wilderness still available, especially in the tidal marsh expanse.

Annual average hunting license sales—under 300,000—also indicates little crowding. A surprisingly few nonresidents partake of the hunting opportunities in Louisiana. The total is seldom over 5500 per year. One of the reasons, perhaps, is that Louisiana like many another southern state has long been owned in large blocks of plantations, rice or cane farms, or timber tracts. Private clubs traditionally exist on many such lands, by lease, or organized by the owners themselves. General access for hunting has for years therefore been not easy for visitor or resident who lacked contacts. This has been more and more noticeable in the lowlands, as the marshes were leased by waterfowling groups.

Emphasis everywhere here is on waterfowl. Less known, southern Louisiana is a kind of focal point for flights of rails, snipe, and woodcock from over the entire continent. Quail and doves have since early-settler times been the chief attractions among upland birds. Rabbits and squirrels, especially the latter, teem in many varieties of habitat. Wild turkey and deer are making excellent strides under management.

Management is, in fact, the key nowadays both to good hunting in Louisiana and to the opportunity for the average hunter to partake of it. The Louisiana Wildlife & Fisheries Commission is an extremely progressive, far-sighted department thoroughly dedicated to keeping and developing all game populations, and to making more and more tracts of quality game habitats constantly available, through outright ownership or lease, to all hunters. There are to date thirty-odd Wildlife Management Areas scattered all over the state and open to public hunting. These run from a few hundred acres to as much as 60,000. They blanket the range of game species, from rabbits, rails, and waterfowl to deer, turkeys, quail, and woodcock. Complete lists and locations of these public grounds may be had on request.

One development of extreme importance to hunters is a program of building boat ramps, parking areas, and in some cases campsites, so that access to many waters and marshes may be had where previously this was difficult. The Commission has in the past few seasons built over fifty such ramps. A list of them and their locations is free on request. They are well scattered across the state. In a state where ducks, geese, and lowland birds get so much attention, this is an important service. In addition to the state-owned Wildlife Management Units, the one other best opportunity on public grounds is the 591,726-acre Kisatchie National Forest scattered in several huge blocks generally to the northwest of Alexandria. There are also in the state some sixteen million acres of commercial timberlands. Some of these are posted but many are open to public hunting, or by arrangement under rules of their owners. These open lands are subject to change under company policy from time to time. The Commission can assist with information concerning them. Also, American Forest Products Industries, 1835 K Street, N.W., Washington, D.C. 20006, can furnish addresses of lumber firms operating in Louisiana.

Accommodations for hunters are good throughout Louisiana. Populous centers along main arteries are so well spread over the state that good motels and hotels are everywhere in evidence. It is seldom more than a short drive from such lodging to a public hunting ground, even from a center such as New Orleans. There are also a fair number of opportunities for those who wish to camp. These are in State Parks, of which there are eight (list from

State Park and Recreation Commission, Box 2541, Old State Capitol Building, Baton Rouge), and particularly in the Kisatchie National Forest.

Weather in Louisiana during hunting seasons can be changeable, even during the course of a single day. Generally the early fall will be hot, and weather at all times will be humid. On into the mid-fall the days are pleasant, but by late fall and the late end of waterfowl or other seasons much chilly and often damp weather may be encountered. Often days like this feel much colder than they really are. Wool clothing and warm, wetproof jackets and rain gear are mandatory. But it is a good idea even in chilly weather to plan so that some clothing can easily be shed as the day wears on and warms. Mornings and evenings may be quite different from summer-like middays. For this low country, needless to say all lowland hunting and many times much pineland hunting require boots that can take wet going. Waders or hip boots are a must for the marsh hunter.

Louisiana is primarily a shotgunner's state. Waterfowl get the heavy emphasis and so No. 4 and No. 2 loads are necessary, with short-range duck shooting dropping back to No. 6. The same loads can be used for the small lowlanders—snipe, rails—as for quail and woodcock. No. 8 and No. 7½ are good choices. Turkeys can be hunted with waterfowl loads, and No. 6 and No. 7½ serve well for rabbits and squirrels. Many deer hunters in dense cover here use shotguns with buckshot or slugs. But the general battery of deer rifles is useful, from the traditional .30/30 to heavy-cover guns like the .35 Remington. The .243, .30/06, .270 are other good examples of adequate and useful deer rifles here.

Hunters in Louisiana seeking directions and following those given in all the following material, should be aware that in this state the term "county" is not locally used. Each "county" is called a "parish" and a "county seat" is a "parish seat." The two words will be used interchangeably as a reminder, and thus should cause no confusion.

QUAIL

The bobwhite quail was at one time the top upland game species in Louisiana, as it was all over the South. Late years, however, quail have had serious problems. Most are due to drastic changes in land use. The Louisiana bobwhite used to find its prime habitat on the small farms, along fencerows and hedgerows and edges of woodlots. Today clean farming practices have all but wiped out that habitat. The best of the quail shooting now—and some is very good—is mostly in the "piney woods." In the early part of the season in good years quail will feed on the seeds of longleaf pine, and may be found among mature stands of trees. Shortleaf pine and hardwood mixtures that have been thinned by lumbering also hold coveys and so do immature plantings where other seed crops may be available. Any year-old burned-over areas are also good bets.

Although quail range throughout the state, in the two general types of habitat—farmlands and cutover or other pinelands—virtually all of the farmland hunting is by permission and not always easy to arrange. The two main sources of public quail hunting are in the several blocks of the Kisatchie National Forest and on a number of the state-owned or leased Wildlife Management Areas. While the bobwhite is not today in the high position it once held, there is good hunting on the lands mentioned. All those located below are about even in quality from year to year. Much of the northern half of the state is the best for public quail hunting because

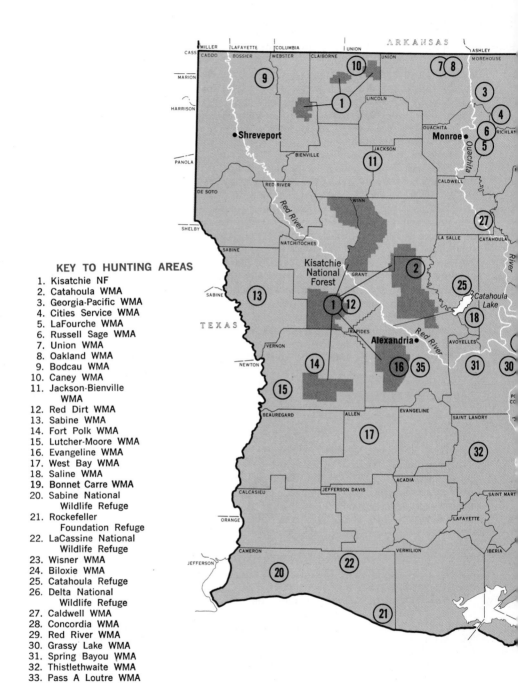

KEY TO HUNTING AREAS
1. Kisatchie NF
2. Catahoula WMA
3. Georgia-Pacific WMA
4. Cities Service WMA
5. LaFourche WMA
6. Russell Sage WMA
7. Union WMA
8. Oakland WMA
9. Bodcau WMA
10. Caney WMA
11. Jackson-Bienville
    WMA
12. Red Dirt WMA
13. Sabine WMA
14. Fort Polk WMA
15. Lutcher-Moore WMA
16. Evangeline WMA
17. West Bay WMA
18. Saline WMA
19. Bonnet Carre WMA
20. Sabine National
    Wildlife Refuge
21. Rockefeller
    Foundation Refuge
22. LaCassine National
    Wildlife Refuge
23. Wisner WMA
24. Biloxie WMA
25. Catahoula Refuge
26. Delta National
    Wildlife Refuge
27. Caldwell WMA
28. Concordia WMA
29. Red River WMA
30. Grassy Lake WMA
31. Spring Bayou WMA
32. Thistlethwaite WMA
33. Pass A Loutre WMA
34. Zemurray Park WMA
35. Alexander State
    Forest WMA

LOUISIANA

MISSISSIPPI

MISSISSIPPI

SCALE IN MILES

0 5 10   20   30   40

N

CHICOT
WASHINGTON
ISSAQUENA
WEST
CARROLL
EAST
CARROLL
MADISON
WARREN
FRANKLIN
TENSAS
CLAIBORNE
JEFFERSON
CONCORDIA
ADAMS
WILKINSON

River

AMITE PIKE WALTHALL MARION
WEST FELICIANA EAST FELICIANA SAINT HELENA TANGIPAHOA WASHINGTON PEARL RIVER

Pearl

EAST BATON ROUGE
LIVINGSTON
SAINT TAMMANY

River

HANCOCK

Mississippi

WEST
BATON ROUGE
IBERVILLE
●Baton Rouge

ASCENSION

River

SAINT JOHN
THE BAPTIST
SAINT JAMES
Lake
Pontchartrain

ASSUMPTION
SAINT CHARLES
ORLEANS
●New Orleans
JEFFERSON
SAINT BERNARD

SAINT MARY
PART OF
ST. MARTIN

LAFOURCHE

PLAQUEMINES

TERREBONNE

River

28

34

19

24

23

26   33

505

more open lands are there. The southwest and southeast, however, often have higher quail populations.

The Forest Supervisor of the Kisatchie National Forest (1) may be addressed at Alexandria. Maps of the Forest are available there, showing the precise locations of the several blocks. The bulk of the almost 600,000 acres lies in the west-central part of the state. A key city is Alexandria, in Rapides Co. Both U.S. 165 and 167 pass through Alexandria and both, along with U.S 71 that also crosses here, are routes to the Forest area. U.S. 84 to the north and the town of Winnfield through which it passes are keys also. So is State Route 28 running west from Alexandria to Leesville, another key town. Farther north, and straight west of Shreveport on I 20 (U.S. 80) is the city of Minden, another location point for Forest access.

On all Wildlife Management Areas (these are sometimes also called Game Management Areas) very close attention must be given to seasons and special regulations for the individual Area. For certain Areas and species, permits either by the day or the season are required. In many cases dogs are allowed for bird hunting, but no quail hunting is allowed during deer seasons. The WMA regulations are set for each Area annually and all are easily obtained from the Commission.

Catahoula WMA (2), a large expanse below the southeast corner of Winn Co., in northeast Grant Co., is considered one of the better quail shooting grounds. This is inside a block of the National Forest, with both U.S. 165 and 167, running north from Alexandria, leading to the vicinity. U.S. 165 goes to Georgetown, an access point. U.S. 167 runs to Winnfield, to the northwest.

Beginning at the northern state border, east of the center of the state and running south, there is a series of four large WMAs fairly close together. All are in good quail territory. Incidentally, it should be noted during any given season that not all WMAs are necessarily open to hunting, or some may not be open to all species. This is a matter of careful management.

In the series mentioned, the farthest north is Georgia-Pacific WMA (3). It lies in western Morehouse Co., along the east bank of the Ouachita River, which is the western county line. The nearby county (parish) seat is the city of Bastrop. U.S. 165 runs north from Monroe to reach Bastrop. Secondaries reaching west and north from Bastrop give access to the hunting ground. Next in line to the south is Cities Service WMA (4). There are some 18,000 acres in this one, in Ouachita Parish. The city of Monroe on I 20 and U.S. 80 is nearby to the southwest. All of this region, incidentally, is flat to rolling, with many pinelands intermixed with cypress bayous, some hardwood areas and many small and large farm operations.

South of Cities Service WMA are two more that run practically together in an arc with its bend to the east. These are Lafourche WMA (5) and Russell Sage WMA (6). Monroe is the key city here also. It is a short distance to the west, and U.S. 80 bisects these tracts. As this is written, Lafourche had no seasons given for the current year. Russell Sage, however, is a top quail tract. There are over 15,000 acres in it.

Hunters familiar with Louisiana, and those who may somehow study outdated regulations, should be aware that the Chicago Mills WMA east of the above and a bit south, in Madison Co. near the city of Tallulah, has been lost to the Commission. This huge area was a great producer of several game species but was leased, not owned land, and is no longer under that agreement.

Two other Areas along or near the northern boundary of the state offer good quail hunting. One of these is Union WMA (7). It is west of Georgia-Pacific, in north-central Union Parish. The town of Marion on State 33 is near the eastern border. Oakland WMA (8) is to the north, just below the Arkansas border. State roads 348, 549, 551 enclose and give easy access to the Area. Farther west, in fact almost into the northwestern corner of the state, there is an Area with fair quail shooting, called Bodcau WMA (9). This is in Bossier County (Parish), west of Bodcau Bayou Flood Control Reservoir. Secondaries running north and northwest of Shreveport and Bossier City reach the vicinity. State 2, 157, 160 are location routes nearby.

In the same general region, and noted briefly earlier, there are three small sections of the Kisatchie National Forest. Because these are outlying tracts from the main Forest they could easily be overlooked. One is immediately north of Minden on U.S. 79, and with State 159 running north-south through it. Another is a few miles to the northeast, out of the village of Homer, also on U.S. 79, and with State 520 reaching it. The third is a few miles farther to the northeast, and just below the Arkansas line. State 9 crosses it and Junction City on the Louisiana-Arkansas border gives access via U.S. 167.

There is a double-tract WMA right here, too, based on the last two Forest sections named above. There are two streams or bayous here, the Middle Fork near the next-to-last named section of Forest and the Corney (with a dam forming Corney Lake) near the last one. The two tracts located in this area are called the Caney WMA (10).

Directly south of this general region, and across on the south side of Interstate 20 and U.S. 80 a few miles south of the city of Ruston, is one of the better quail Areas. This is Jackson-Bienville (11), a huge tract lying along the border between the two counties for which it is named. U.S. 167 south from Ruston skirts the southeastern corner of the Area, with the small towns of Ansley and Quitman at this point.

Moving from here down into the central portion of Louisiana, there is a general middle-belt swath of quail abundance and also of good hunting on several public grounds. Note that this brings us again into the large acreage covered by the National Forest. The largest blocks of it spread across the state here, and several of the Management Areas, as noted with Catahoula WMA, are within Forest boundaries.

Red Dirt WMA (12) is one of these. It is in a section of Forest west of the Red River, in Natchitoches Parish, south of the city of the same name. Easiest access is via State Route 1 south from Natchitoches or north from Alexandria. The small villages of Derry and Montrose are on this road along the eastern border of the WMA. A secondary, No. 493, runs from Montrose into and across the area to join Route 117 to the west. That route bisects the Forest tract north-south.

Almost straight west of Red Dirt, and a bit north, is Sabine WMA (13). This is an area of modest size, on the west side of U.S. 71 and almost to the Texas border. It is in central Sabine Co., near the towns of Many and Swolle on U.S. 71.

South of Red Dirt, in central Vernon Co., immediately east of the city of Leesville on U.S. 171, is the Fort Polk WMA (14), with fair quail hunting. Note that this Area requires military clearance as well as a hunting permit. It should also be noted that Fort Polk lies along the northern border of a section of the Kisatchie NF. The Forest should not be overlooked as a possibility. On the west side of U.S. 171, and south of Leesville, there is a very large tract called Lutcher-Moore WMA (15). This can be reached via side roads off 171, or out of De Ridder west via U.S. 190 and then north on State 111. State 464 runs north-south through the WMA. This is one of the Areas where, under regulations as this is written, no quail hunting is allowed during deer season.

Moving east, there is a public Area of modest size a short distance south of Alexandria and west of U.S. 165 and lying within another block of the Forest, Evangeline WMA (16). A secondary west from Woodworth on 165 crosses it. Still farther south and a bit west is an excellent area, much larger, and sometimes with a longer quail season than the others, although it must be remembered that seasons depend upon yearly game-crop surveys. This is West Bay WMA (17). It is in central Allen Co. The town of Oakdale on U.S. 165 is to the east. State 26 out of Oberlin touches the southern edge of the tract and a secondary runs up the full length of the western boundary to join State 112.

There are several other WMAs with fair to good quail hunting, but the best have been covered so far. However, note the other WMA locations under following species. Some of them are well worth checking out. But be certain there is a quail season during the year you intend to hunt, on the individual Area you wish to try. Timberlands, and other privately owned lands, as has been mentioned earlier, are all good quail prospects but acquiring permission is a matter of individual approach.

WILD TURKEYS

At the present time Louisiana has only a spring turkey season, usually in late March and during several weeks in April. This is for gobblers only, with a 2-bird-per-season limit as this is written, and with use of dogs and baiting prohibited. Hunting areas presently are quite limited, too. This might give an impression that the wild turkey in Louisiana is in severe straits. Quite the opposite is true. The turkey has been in serious difficulties here, but is in the process of building up a substantial state flock, with future prospect of very much more, and better, hunting than now is available. In 1967 the turkey season was the longest in thirty-five years. The potential is only beginning to be realized.

Originally, so far as old records show, forty-one of Louisiana's sixty-four Parishes (Counties) had wild turkeys in large numbers. The coastal marshes, the South Mississippi Delta, the southwestern prairie lands were the only areas that had none. Some estimates indicate perhaps a million turkeys in Louisiana early in the century. But by about 1950 there were probably not more than 1000 to 1500 wild turkeys in the entire state. Louisiana has long had—and still has to some degree—a very serious poaching problem, particularly with big game—that is, deer, and the wild turkey, which is considered as big game here. However, continuing loss of habitat has been the primary cause of turkey demise.

A most serious matter for the turkey population is the clearing of hardwoods. Turkeys need large tracts, especially of hardwoods and bottom-land swamps. Tens of thousands of acres of hardwoods in the state have been cleared over recent years. It is probable that the Commission's foresight in recently acquiring large tracts of land in outright ownership, and others by lease, plus the existence of the National Forest lands and numerous commercial forest lands, are to be in total the salvation of the wild turkey here. Today the wild turkey is in huntable numbers in four areas of the state, and it has been stocked in many places over the state—excepting the southernmost strips of counties in about three tiers—and it is felt that there are still several million acres of forest lands that offer suitable turkey habitat but are still uninhabited by the birds. Given even fair success in the ventures in stocking live-trapped wild birds now under way, there is high hope that Louisiana may in due time become once again one of the important turkey hunting states.

During a recent season the state kill total was 236 gobblers. Following are descriptions of the open areas, by Districts, and by counties (parishes) or parts of counties. For management purposes Louisiana is divided into eight Districts. No. 2 is the North Central. It encompasses the following counties, reading west-east in tiers with the northernmost first: Union, Morehouse, West Carroll, East Carroll; Lincoln, Ouachita, Richland; Jackson. Various entire counties here, and/or portions of counties, have as of this writing been open to hunting. Presumably the total open area here will broaden. This by recent kill is the third-best general region of the state. It is impossible to say at this time which WMAs in this District will or will not have turkey seasons from year to year. As the flock grows, more hunting will be opened. Check the WMAs in this District noted under "Quail" and then check the regulations for the season you may be planning a hunt.

Directly south of District 2 is District 4. The eastern portion of this District, along the Mississippi River in the general region opposite Vicksburg, Mississipi, is another of the good turkey areas which will undoubtedly grow better and better. At the northeast corner of this District is Madison Parish. Below it, west to east are Caldwell, Franklin, Tensas parishes. Then come LaSalle, Catahoula, Concordia. This is the East-Central District. During a recent season portions of Madison, Franklin, Catahoula, Concordia, and Tensas Counties were open. The second highest kill of birds was here. Note well that WMAs in any of these Districts may or may not be open. In due time as the turkey population builds, some of the best hunting will undoubtedly be on the WMAs. But at present they require seasonal check-up, and will for some years to come.

Farther south and east, the parishes below the east-west portions of the Mississippi state line and east of the Mississippi River are known as the "Florida Parishes." In two portions of these are the other two regions of huntable turkey abundance, and the highest kill recently has occurred here. Both these regions lie within what is known as District 7. One of them takes in East Feliciana, East Baton Rouge, Livingston, St. Helena, Tangipahoa, and Ascension parishes. All or parts of these have open season. The other area here covers the two northeasternmost counties of this part of Louisiana, Washington and Saint Tammany, north of Lake Pontchartrain and with Bogalusa and Covington key cities. These two sections in combination of the northeast and southern panhandle have recently accounted for the highest turkey kill.

So that hunters may be able to follow burgeoning turkey flocks, here are some places where releases have been made and where it is believed resident populations may take hold: In the northwest, along the Bossier-Webster county line; the Bienville-Jackson county line. In the northeast, on the Mississippi River in East Carroll County; on the Ouachita-Richland Co. line. To the south in central Caldwell Co. Across the center of the state as follows: central Sabine Co.; southern Winn Co.; southeast LaSalle Co.

Still farther south: central Vernon Co. (it borders Texas); central St. Landry Co. With state purchase of new lands, and with constant attention to trapping and stocking, Louisiana seems destined to become, once again, an important oasis of wild turkey hunting for both resident and visitor.

MOURNING DOVES

Louisiana has some very excellent dove shooting. As in all states, the great share of it is on privately owned lands. Doves are extremely mobile, require feeding fields, and will move in large concentrations to where the best feed is, even if they must fly some distance both to water and to roost. Water of course is no problem in Louisiana, nor are roosting sites. But the most abundant feed is always in the farm areas. Thus it is best to try to get permission to shoot on such lands. However, most of the WMAs in Louisiana offer at least some dove shooting, and, on some, active programs are in progress for planting food patches to attract and hold doves.

Over recent years Louisiana has been given a three-segment split season on doves. The first portion falls during September for about two weeks. The second is longer, during late October and most of November. The third is the last half of December. The early season provides the best shooting. One recent season the estimated total kill was 2,354,000. Of these, 1,120,000 were taken during the early segment. High hunter interest in the early season is partly responsible. But birds also become more scattered and wary as the season wears on. The second segment kill that same year, for comparison, was 842,000. The third segment: 392,000.

Of the numerous WMAs discussed under "Quail," several usually offer quality dove shooting. Among the best are Bodcau, Russell Sage, Fort Polk, Lutcher-Moore. This does not mean that others should be overlooked.

Another one, Saline WMA (18), is a good example of the dove programs now under way. On this public area food plots of ten acres each have been developed in scattered and suitable locations, specifically to draw and hold doves. The Saline WMA is a huge plot, over 60,000 acres. It is in the southeastern corner of LaSalle Co. This county lies northeast of Alexandria. The Area borders large Catahoula Lake on the north, is bounded on the west by Big Saline Bayou, the county line. U.S. 84 crosses above Catahoula Lake. State 28 runs from Alexandria and Pineville northeast, crosses the northern part of the Area and joins U.S. 84 at the small village of Archie. This is the best access.

Certain WMAs consist of lands not owned by the Commission but managed by them, and on some of these there is no permit required nor any check in or check out. One such, near New Orleans, that offers fair dove shooting is Bonnet Carre WMA (19). This is in northwestern St. Charles Parish. Actually the Area is based on the Bonnet Carre Spillway between Lake Pontchartrain and the Mississippi River. The town of Norco is on the south side, and U.S. 61 into New Orleans crosses the Spillway here.

WOODCOCK

For many years woodcock hunting has been thought of as almost wholly an enjoyment to be found in New England, Nova Scotia, and the Great Lakes area. It is surprising that Louisiana has made almost no name as to top woodcock state. The fact is, Louisiana winters probably 80 percent of the total continental woodcock supply. For some reason there has not been traditionally much interest among resident Louisiana hunters in this bird. Currently, however, woodcock popularity is growing here. Undoubtedly the best woodcock hunting in North America is to be had here during winter. Avid woodcockers who may wish to visit Louisiana should note this well.

The best shooting often comes late in the season, in January. During severe winters there is also excellent shooting earlier. But by and large December and January are the best months. Louisiana terrain is virtually perfect for woodcock. The "branches" coursing lightly wooded areas, all stream borders and thickets with open ground cover are excellent spots. Interestingly enough, both hardwood and pine offer good shooting. Woodcock hide and rest at the bases of small trees, beneath holly bushes and small evergreens. Creeks or "branches" in pine country are prime covers. Areas of tall, dense grass should be avoided, but many woodcock are found in winter in Louisiana in rather open situations, as well as in the sparsely wooded spots.

There are several chief woodcock concentration regions in the state. One is in the northeastern parishes. These include the several counties from Union, Quachita, Caldwell, LaSalle eastward to the Mississippi River. The next region of abundance is in the Florida parishes. Roughly this area might be described as east of the Mississippi River, south of the east-west Mississippi State border with Louisiana, and north of Lake Pontchartrain. All of the counties in this region offer excellent opportunities, clear to the Pearl River, which completes the border with Mississippi. The third region, a broad swath beginning in the southwest in the Lake Charles vicinity and sweeping northeast to and a bit north of both Alexandria and Bunkie. The last region takes in the vast bottomland and swamp of the Atchafalaya River. There are often amazing concentrations of birds here during the season. Thus there is plenty of area over the state to hunt. From St. Tammany Parish north across the lake from New Orleans (excellent) to the bottoms of the Calcasieu River north of Lake Charles, to the far northeast corner of the state near Lake Providence, birds are plentiful.

Some of the better hunting on the WMAs is as follows: Bonnet Carre Spillway, Saline ("Doves"), Catahoula, Cities Service, Evangeline, Georgia-Pacific, Jackson-Bienville, Red Dirt, Sabine, Union, West Bay ("Quail"). Most of the other WMAs noted under "Quail" have at least fair to good shooting. The National Forest blocks should not be overlooked. Wherever there are pockets open enough on the ground, birds will generally be found in them.

SNIPE

Louisiana is one of the most important snipe wintering regions of the U.S. Estimates place the seasonal snipe population at several million. Jacksnipe are next in numbers to mourning doves among the smaller migratory birds. Although in years past snipe hunting was only casually enjoyed here, its popularity is swiftly growing.

There are four major sections of the state that attract jacksnipe. One is in the southwest, on the open prairie marshes. Cities such as Crowley, Jennings, Lake Charles are key general locations, with the prairies stretching east-west below and above I 10. Second is the rice belt area lying just above Louisiana's vast coastal marshes. Third is the entire flood plain region of both the Mississippi and the Atchafalaya rivers. The fourth is the delta marshes of the southeast.

Because of leasing of marshlands by waterfowlers, it is not always easy to find places to hunt or to acquire permission. However, here are a few of the southern area spots to keep in mind as best. In the far southwest is the Sabine National Wildlife Refuge (20). This is south of Sulphur (I 10) and reached via State 27. The general area is excellent. To the east along the Gulf, 27 joins for some distance with State 82 and this route crosses near the huge Rockefeller Foundation Refuge (21). All of this vicinity also offers shooting. North of this Refuge and reached from I 10 out of Jennings or other cities on the route is LaCassine National Wildlife Refuge (22). The prairie area around this Refuge is usually excellent for snipe, although access may be difficult. However, researchers doing snipe studies have concluded that the general southwest, and particularly Cameron Parish south of Lake Charles, gets one of the heaviest, possibly the heaviest, concentrations of birds.

There are two WMAs to the east not yet noted that should be known to snipe enthusiasts. One is Wisner WMA (23). This is far south of New Orleans. It can be reached out of Thibodaux, Raceland, or Houma by following State 1 south almost to its end at Grand Isle. All of this intervening area, incidentally, is good snipe habitat. The other WMA is east of New Orleans, covering a large, ragged land area on the south of Lake Borgne. It is Biloxi WMA (24). It is not easily reached except by boat.

All of the waterfowl grounds in Louisiana have from fair to good snipe shooting. Some of these are on WMA tracts. Check them under "Waterfowl." Wet coastal meadows and wet rice fields all the way from the Pearl River on the east to Sabine Pass on the west form good snipe hunting grounds. Hunters seeking good spots should take note of marsh tracts that have been burned over. These usually attract concentrations of snipe.

WATERFOWL

It is paradoxical that while Louisiana has the most immense stretches of marshland—over four million acres—to be found along U.S. borders, and vast habitat for and concentrations of ducks (up to five million) geese, and coots, the visiting hunter, and many local hunters, find themselves with few and sometimes no places to hunt. Any nonresident will be far better off when he comes to Louisiana for waterfowling if he will hire a guide, or else make a most careful study of public areas. In many instances, the guide may be the best answer.

Though there are millions of acres of marshland, and millions of birds, vast portions of the marshes have long been under lease. And the situation annually grows worse as more and more hunting pressure is added. There is one very possible and most imaginative cure that is being considered nowadays, and that may well evolve within a very few seasons. There are in southwest Louisiana over one and a half million acres of rice lands. During any given year, approximately one-third is planted while the other two-thirds remain fallow or are pastured. All of these lands near the marshes can easily be managed for wintering waterfowl, and for hunting by fee. Thinking appears to be moving in that direction. Such arrangements would be most desirable so far as hunters are concerned.

When shooting places can be located near the several Refuges, hunters find excellent opportunities. Sabine and LaCassine Refuges and the Rockefeller Foundation Refuge have been located under "Snipe." Catahoula Refuge (25) is on Catahoula Lake near the Saline WMA, noted under "Doves." Delta National Wildlife Refuge (26) is located far south of New Orleans, at the mouth of the Mississippi.

It should be mentioned that coots are not only extremely abundant, but in Louisiana have long-been popular with hunters of the Cajun country not so much for the sport but for the eating. They are locally called *poule d'eau,* and are made into a stew or gumbo. Around New Orleans and Houma coots are eagerly sought.

The largest concentrations of geese are along the coastal marshes and prairies. Greatest concentrations of blue geese are at the mouth of the Mississippi. Westward the mixture between blues and snows shades toward more and more snows until in the southwest they predominate. There are some whitefronts (specklebellies). The wintering population of Canada geese has dwindled to only a scattering. But the blues and snows are here upwards of half a million in number each year.

Fortunately, a number of the WMAs offer excellent waterfowling, although it is predominantly for ducks. The most important single public waterfowl area is at Catahoula Lake. The Refuge and Saline WMA are noted above. This lake covers about 30,000 acres, is usually very shallow in fall and produces vast quantities of duck food. There may be anywhere from 100,000 to half a million ducks wintering here, plus a few geese and many coots. Most abundant species: mallards, pintails, teal, gadwall, baldpate.

Several WMAs not so far mentioned are managed in part for waterfowl. One is Caldwell WMA (27). This lies between the Ouachita and Boeuf Rivers in the southeast corner of Caldwell Co. This is the north-central part of the state. Columbia, the county seat, is on U.S. 165. Southeast from here State Routes 4 and 559 branch to go on either side of the Area. Another is Concordia WMA (28). This is southeast of the above, in northern Concordia Co. not far west of one of the many bends of the Mississippi. The town of Ferriday on U.S. 84 is a key access point. South of Concordia are Red River WMA (29) and Grassy Lake WMA (30). Red River, to which new purchases of land have recently been added to boost it to approximately 16,000 acres, lies along the Red River in southern Concordia Parish. Grassy Lake is across on the south side of the Red River. The new area purchased and added to the Red River WMA is, incidentally, predominantly forest land suitable for deer and turkeys, with at least 1000 acres to be managed for quail and doves. The entire region here, however, is an excellent waterfowl setting.

Another of the newer tracts is Spring Bayou WMA (31). This lies to the southwest of Red River, covers some 11,000-plus acres, with a rest area for ducks built by the Commission. It is in Avoyelles Parish near the county seat of Marksville. State 1 runs through this town. This is a prime duck hunting spot. Directly south of this Area, in the next county, St. Landry, and north of the city of Opelousas, is Thistlethwaite WMA (32). State 10 runs along the western edge, from the town of Washington. There is waterfowl shooting allowed here during a late portion of the season. Up in the far northwest is Soda Lake. This is primarily a waterfowl area, but with small game hunting also. It is a few miles northwest of Shreveport and just west of U.S. 71.

There is some waterfowl hunting on a few other WMAs noted under "Quail." But one of the most important hunting grounds, with rather specialized regulations, is the public shooting ground at Pass A Loutre WMA (33) off the mouth of the Mississippi. There is a 66,000-acre tract of delta marshland here, surrounded by a myriad of channels and islands. The closest access point by auto is Venice, fifteen miles north. The Commission furnishes water transport to the area. There is a $5 trip fee. There are furnished camps available to accommodate the hunters. Trips are two-day hunts, on specified days. Application must be made and hunters are selected by a drawing. There is excellent hunting here. The Commission will furnish all details on request. There are some 30,000 acres also open for hunting here for those who furnish their own equipment—boats as well as other facilities. Permission must be obtained from the Refuge Division of the Commission.

It must be noted that the early teal seasons of the past few years (they may or may not continue) have been both exceedingly popular and successful in Louisiana. During a recent early season some 33,000 permits were given, and approximately 100,000 teal, chiefly bluewings—which is the reason for the early dates—were taken. The Louisiana kill during the early teal season has made up at least 25 percent of the entire kill for the Mississippi and Central flyways. This is an indication of how excellent the shooting. Best of the success appears in general to be at Catahoula Lake, and in the southwest.

As this is written the Commission is in process of purchasing two tracts —27,000 acres southwest of New Orleans bordering the south bank of Lake Salvador; 28,000 acres southeast of Houma in the Grand Bayou area—both of which will be managed primarily for waterfowl. Some other game—deer and rabbits—probably will be managed, too, but these new areas should soon furnish new and important hunting grounds for waterfowlers.

RAILS

Rails are perhaps more abundant in the Louisiana marshes and rice fields than anywhere else in the U.S. Bag and possession limits are high, and there are four species popular with the modest number of hunters who go after them: the good-sized clapper rail of the salt and brackish marshes; the larger king rail of the rice fields; the smaller sora and Virginia rails that hang out in both fresh and brackish marshes. Some duck hunters finish their waterfowling, then wade, slog the soft marshes, or push a shallow-draft boat after rails.

In Louisiana rails are called marsh hens or prairie hens. Seldom do tides along the marshes get high enough to move rails, as they do on the east coast. Groups of hunters, often with dogs, usually spread out and walk. It is tough going, often hot and often with plentiful mosquitoes. But the birds are extremely abundant and many more could be harvested if interest were higher in the sport. Wherever access can be gained to the marshes across the south, good rail hunting will be found. The two best locations for public grounds where rails are extremely abundant are two noted under "Snipe": Wisner and Biloxi WMAs.

If a hunter can locate a rice field that is being harvested, and get permission to shoot there, a successful method, particularly for king rails, is to watch the combine and as it cuts down to a small remaining area, follow along behind or to the side. Rails prefer to run rather than fly, and the big king rails will keep moving into still-standing rice until finally the hiding places are too cramped. Then they take flight and present a target.

EXOTIC BIRDS

Like many another state, Louisiana has been experimenting over past seasons with several imported game birds. These include several varieties of pheasant possibly suitable to the climate and terrain, plus red jungle fowl, bamboo partridges, tinamous, and black francolin. To date there is no hunting.

Hunters should be aware that these birds may have been stocked on certain of the WMAs and take pains not to shoot them. For example, black francolin were stocked on Bodcau WMA ("Quail").

DEER

The whitetail deer in Louisiana has had many difficulties over numerous years. Poaching has long been a serious menace to the herds. Officers nowadays diligently prosecute poachers. Deer hunting, until the development of WMAs, had for many years been almost entirely private. One either owned the land, was invited, or joined a club that leased land. Large clubs are traditional in much southern deer hunting.

Due to many influences, including changes in land use and lack of proper management, deer diminished until twenty years ago there was deer hunting in no more than 20 percent of the state. Today the figure is almost exactly reversed. Deer are now hunted over approximately 80 percent of the state. Over 110,000 hunters now annually hunt deer. During a recent season the kill was 32,000-plus, with almost 30,000 of the animals bucks. That is an excellent success percentage.

District 4, which encompasses Madison, Caldwell, Franklin, Tensas, LaSalle, Catahoula, and Concordia parishes in the east-central part of the state and with Madison, Tensas, and Concordia bordering the Mississippi River, currently has the highest deer population. A great deal of stocking of trapped animals, plus careful harvest and management planning long-range, is spreading deer over vast areas, and the northwest also is becoming an excellent hunting area. There is good public deer hunting within the several blocks of National Forest. Although southern Louisiana has numerous deer, and in some places overpopulation problems in relation to available food, the northern half of the state turns up the major kill.

One recent survey showed District 4 (described previously) first with a total kill of 10,856. Second was District 2 (the north-central district described under "Turkeys") with 6083. District 3, which is the west-central part of the state opposite District 4, was third with 4421. And the northwest (District 1) was fourth with 3852. The counties southeast from Alexandria, along U.S. 71 were next, with 2220. This is a rather precise picture year to year of the present deer population.

Narrowing down to parishes for the same season kill survey, the following show "where the deer are." To be sure, hunter numbers will influence the figures, but forest acres checked against kill show the acres per deer killed fairly consistent. The high counties, in order: Tensas, Madison, Concordia, East Carroll, Union, Morehouse, Natchitoches. All these were over 1000 and the highest over 4000. Some others just below 1000: Allen (southwest quadrant), Bossier (extreme northwest), Vernon (west-central), Winn (central). Other counties with good kills (400 to 600-plus): Ouachita, Rapides, Richland, Saint Landry.

The WMAs offer excellent public deer hunting. The success percentage is lower than for the state as a whole. But this is obviously because club kills, with use of dogs quite often, and the hunters intimately knowing their territory, assist in success. A help to hunting chances on the WMAs is the fact that management dictates harvest in numerous instances of antlerless as well as antlered deer. Most of the WMAs offer deer hunting. Top Areas recently have been: West Bay; Georgia-Pacific; Catahoula; Fort Polk. All these are located under "Quail." Vying with these are: Caldwell ("Waterfowl"); Evangeline;

Jackson-Bienville; Red Dirt; Russell Sage; Sabine; Union (all under "Quail");
Saline ("Doves"); Thistlethwaite ("Waterfowl").

Most other WMAs so far mentioned offer at least fair deer hunting.
Bodcau, Caney (both tracts), and Cities Service offer seasons. Concordia has
a short season. Lutcher-Moore is fair, and so is Red River. The newer WMAs
such as Spring Bayou also have deer.

There are several WMAs where deer hunting may be had that have not
been noted so far. One is in the lower section of the state, in its northeast
area. This is Zemurray Park WMA (34) in Tangipahoa Parish. State 40,
running east from its intersect with U.S. 51 gives access. Another rather good
area is Alexander State Forest WMA (35). This is a few miles south of
Alexandria, just outside the eastern border of one of the National Forest
blocks, and between north-south running U.S. 165 and U.S. 71-167.

Hunters should keep track of the opening on new WMAs as they are
developed. Most will be managed for deer as well as for suitable small game.

RABBITS

There is fine rabbit hunting in Louisiana and it is fairly popular. Though
rabbits range throughout most of the state, the greater share of the hunting
is done in the south. Cottontails predominate. There are also the larger swamp
rabbits. Often both are hunted in the same general cover, along the bottoms.
Small hounds—beagles—are ordinarily used. The swamp rabbit, once more
plentiful than today, has been harmed greatly by the clearing of brush and
hardwoods in the bottoms and by the planting of soybeans. This trend of
destroying hardwoods in Louisiana is a growing problem. Cane belt areas
are excellent for swamp rabbits (called colloquially "cane cutters"), but
cottontails do well almost everywhere. Most of the public lands offer good
rabbit hunting. But hunters should check laws for individual WMAs (located
under foregoing species) to make certain if dogs are allowed for rabbit
hunting. There is little choice as to where to hunt, for the quality of rabbit
hunting is approximately even from Area to Area.

SQUIRRELS

Squirrels are abundant, important, popular, and in a wide and interesting
variety in Louisiana. There are both fox and gray squirrels. There are three
subspecies of fox squirrel: big-headed, delta, Bachman's. There are two subspecies of grays: southern and bayou. Among the five races they blanket the
state in all forested places, and the interesting color variations among them
are numerous. There are believed to be more, in fact, than anywhere else in
the U.S. A booklet available from the Commission shows pictures of the
various races, with descriptions and ranges.

All the WMAs offer excellent squirrel hunting except those made up of
marshlands. (See all previous species for locations.) The Areas with large
expanses of hardwoods are in general best for squirrels. A good example is
Thistlethwaite WMA. Here (St. Landry Parish) there are some 10,000 acres
of hardwoods, with one of the best squirrel populations in the state. On this
one stand of timber, hunters in a recent season bagged approximately 6000
squirrels. The National Forest blocks offer good squirrel hunting also. But
all the Areas from the northwest and far northeast to the Florida parishes
and portions of the central and southwest offer little choice. Squirrels are
everywhere abundant.

OTHER ANIMALS

There are raccoons, regulated under fur animals, plus unprotected foxes and some bobcats. None of these is especially important to hunters in Louisiana, but their populations are well scattered over the forested regions of the state. They can be hunted on the WMAs with fair success. Individual tract regulations must be checked.

REGULATIONS

Game laws pertaining to seasons, bag and possession limits, areas to be hunted, special hunts, license fees all may have numerous changes from year to year. For current regulations, and for other specific queries, write to: Louisiana Wild Life and Fisheries Commission, Wild Life and Fisheries Building, 400 Royal Street, New Orleans, Louisiana 70130.

TEXAS

From a hunter's as well as a geographer's viewpoint, Texas is an exceedingly complex state, ranging from the terrain of tidal marshes, to pine woods, to plains, desert, and mountains. More than half of the U.S. international boundary with Mexico is measured along the Texas border, which for the entire distance is the Rio Grande River. Counting only the major bends, this border is 889 miles. The arc of Gulf Coast line, counting no inlets or bays, is almost 400 miles.

The northeast is the pine woods section, with some areas of cypress swamps, others of rolling forests and farmlands. Southward along the Gulf are the coastal prairies, flat, heavily farmed in rice and other products. In the lower Rio Grande Valley intensive truck farming wipes out much original game cover except for birds. But northwestward up the river, centering on Laredo and stretching approximately 150 miles over a large half circle fanning out from that city, is the so-called Brush Country, a seemingly endless arid expanse of rolling terrain covered with cactus and thornbush, unprepossessing in appearance but a top game country for deer, birds, and predators.

Above the brush country, west and north of San Antonio, is the Edwards Plateau, or Hill Country, rough, forested, approximately 150 miles across in each direction. This is prime turkey and whitetail deer range. Northward the vast North Central Plains stretch to the Oklahoma border. From here northwestward is the Panhandle, generally rolling plains but in some places extremely rugged, such as the Palo Duro Canyon area south of Amarillo. In the southwest lies the so-called Trans-Pecos region—west of the Pecos. This is high, mountainous desert, its southern portion the sparsely settled Big Bend Country, with Big Bend National Park included in it.

Over this vast area—the state's entire borders are almost 3000 miles—altitudes range from sea level on the Gulf to extremes of 6000 and 8000 feet in the Trans-Pecos. Crisscrossing the entire state is an exemplary highway system, over fifteen U.S. and Interstate highways north-south, and a dozen or more east-west. All state roads and farm roads are just as good, virtually all of them paved. Distances are long, and thus air travel is extremely well developed, via commercial lines and via charter to practically any point in the state, even to hundreds of private ranch airstrips. Oil, cattle, sheep, cotton, rice are all big-land operations in Texas.

North to south, the greatest dimension of Texas is about 800 miles, and east-west approximately 775. Largest of the contiguous states, and second now in the Union only to Alaska, Texas has 265,986 square miles. The population is now reaching toward the 11,000,000 mark, but of course the spaces are vast. The great bulk of population is in the large cities of the eastern third of the state.

Spacewise, hunters have an awesome amount of room. License sales at present average only slightly over 600,000 annually. Of these, only a negligible percentage—less than 1 percent—are nonresident visitors. On this statistic hangs the truly complex situation in regard to Texas hunting. Few visitors come into this excellent hunting state because for practical purposes there is only a meager amount of public hunting. All but an extremely modest acreage of Texas is privately owned. Over many years, because of pressures involved, a strict fee-hunt system has been built up on private lands. Thus, there are three chief arrangements by which one may hunt in Texas: by invitation or permission through friends who are landowners; by annual lease of hunting rights on private lands; by paying a fee per day or per stipulated bag for hunting on private lands.

There are to be sure a few Wildlife Management Areas. These are: Gene Howe WMA, six miles east of Canadian; Matador WMA, eleven miles north of Paducah; Sierra Diablo WMA, thirty-two miles northwest of Van Horn; Black Gap WMA, fifty-five miles south of Marathon; Kerr WMA, twenty-eight miles west of Kerrville; Gus Engling WMA, twenty miles northwest of Palestine; J. D. Murphree WMA, Port Acres; Angelina WMA, in three units as follows: Cherokee, ten miles southeast of Alto; Moore, three miles east of Pineland; Devil's Pocket, twelve miles east of Buna.

These WMAs cannot, however, be considered as permanently open public hunting lands. They are chiefly study areas. Seasons on various game species are declared on them as surpluses may dictate. Most offer hunting each year, some of it excellent, as for example for squirrels and deer. Permits are offered by drawing. Actually only a small scattering of hunters, however, can possibly be served by these Management Areas. One wishing to participate in a WMA hunt should contact the Texas Parks & Wildlife Department, find out which will be open that season and for what species, then apply for a permit and await the outcome of the drawing. In a few instances, permits may be unlimited for small game.

The truly public lands in Texas are only in several National Forests, and in several tracts of National Grasslands. There are four National Forests, all in east Texas. They are located as follows.

The Sabine National Forest (1) is on the west side of the Sabine River, which at that point is the border with Louisiana. It contains 183,842 acres. The town of Logansport is at the northern tip, on U.S. 84. San Augustine is about midway down, on the western border, on State 96. State 87 runs through the Forest north-south, and State 21 crosses east-west.

Immediately west of the Sabine NF is Angelina National Forest (2). It contains 154,392 acres. U.S. 69 and State 147 enter it. The city of Lufkin is a few miles west. The Angelina River flows through this Forest.

West of Lufkin is the Davy Crockett National Forest (3), 161,556 acres. The town of Alto is just north of it, and Groveton is at the southern border. U.S. 287, State 94, 7, 103 all give access.

South and slightly west of this Forest is Sam Houston National Forest (4). It contains 158,204 acres. The city of Huntsville is at the northwest corner, Conroe is near the southern border, and Cleveland is at the southeast boundary. U.S. 75, 59, and 190 all offer access, and State routes 105 and 150 do also.

For maps and detailed information on all four Forests, contact the Forest Supervisor at Lufkin, Texas.

The National Grasslands are in scattered blocks in north Texas and the Texas Panhandle. There are 117,269 acres. The Caddo National Grasslands (5) are small tracts near the Oklahoma border in northeast Texas.

Cross Timbers (6) is in the central part of north Texas. Black Kettle (7) and Rita Blanca (8) are in the northern Panhandle. Because Grasslands are in general split up into small parcels interspersed among private holdings, it is best to contact the regional Forest Service office to acquire maps and specific locations. The National Grasslands in Texas are administered from: 517 Gold Avenue, SW, Albuquerque, New Mexico 87101. Write to the U.S. Forest Service, Regional Supervisor.

This is the extent of the public lands in Texas where one may hunt. Although the fee-hunt system on private lands may at first glance appear to be exasperating as well as expensive, it does have certain advantages for those who hunt under it. Privacy and uncrowded hunting conditions are the chief ones. Lease hunting is a way of life to Texans, who can hardly conceive of public hunting. Also, because landowners make a substantial amount of money from the game on their lands, they are inclined to manage it carefully. Bag limits are virtually assured, in many cases guaranteed or no pay. An old Texas saying is that ranchers "count their deer right with their cattle."

Whether or not one agrees with the fee system and lease system, these are firmly established in Texas and there is no chance whatever that the system can now be changed. Hunters planning to visit Texas, or those in one part of the state who wish to visit another, simply must be fully aware of the situation. Texas is unique among the states in its hunting system. It is all but impossible to approach a landowner—often even though he is a friend—and be granted hunting privileges. In most instances the owner cannot allow permission hunting because he has already leased his full hunting rights, often on long-term leases.

Costwise, considering the excellent hunting, most landowners give good value. Deer hunting is seldom more expensive than guided hunts on federal lands elsewhere, and a kill is invariably assured. Quail or doves, hunted by a daily fee, may cost a group $1 or $2 each for an afternoon of dove shooting in a good field, or $5 to $10 for quail. Waterfowl hunting is about as it is in other states where landowners near the refuges charge—from $10 to $20 per day, but here generally with decoys, blinds, guide, transport furnished.

Because of the competition for good—and often large—hunting areas, a visitor must know that a great amount of good game covers are leased for from one- to ten-year periods by individuals or groups. However, because of this competition, all Chamber of Commerce organizations in even small towns in the better game areas—for deer, turkeys, quail, waterfowl—run during the fall what might be termed "clearing houses" to assist persons in finding day hunting or leases, and conversely to assist the landowner in finding hunters. Contacts should, however, be made well ahead.

While some of the foregoing may sound discouraging, the bright side is that Texas is an excellent game state, both in variety and in game populations. During high cycles, quail, both bobwhite and scaled quail, explode in unbelievable numbers. In specific areas turkeys are extremely abundant. One of the nation's largest whitetail deer herds is here. There are plentiful mule deer in west Texas.

There is a small amount of hunting for prairie chicken and pheasant. Mourning doves swarm over the state, and whitewinged doves in their restricted range are seasonally abundant. Coastal waterfowl hunting is excellent, including snipe and rail. Sandhill cranes and chachalaca are legal in small areas.

KEY TO HUNTING AREAS

1. Sabine NF
2. Angelina NF
3. Davy Crockett NF
4. Sam Houston NF

5. Caddo National
   Grasslands
6. Cross Timbers National
   Grasslands

7. Black Kettle National
   Grasslands
8. Rita Blanca National
   Grasslands

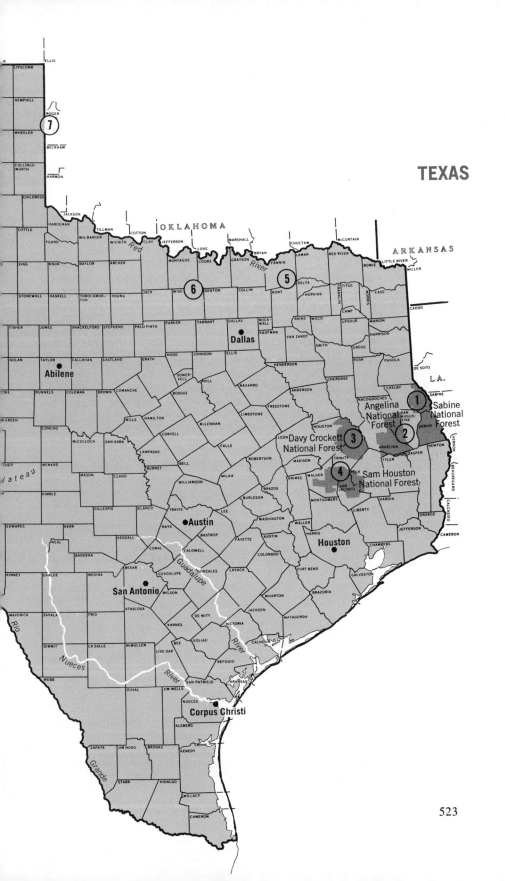

TEXAS

Angelina
National
Forest

Sabine
National
Forest

Davy Crockett
National Forest

Sam Houston
National Forest

Javelina are abundant south and west. Antelope are modestly so in the west.

There is a small amount of hunting for aoudad (barbary sheep), an exotic import from North Africa, and there is a great deal of fee hunting for numerous exotic horned and antlered game animals, imports from Africa and India, etc., with large populations of these animals scattered over much of the state. Small game—rabbits and squirrels—is plentiful. Predators such as coyotes, foxes, bobcats are also. There is some lion hunting, and some for Russian boar and feral swine.

Hunter accommodations are everywhere in Texas. Because of much cross-state travel motels and hotels are numerous. A great many lease-hunt and fee-hunt lands offer camp houses for hunters, built for that purpose. Some offer specific arrangements for board and lodging. For those who wish to camp, there is a large system of State Parks, fifty-eight at present, plus Corps of Engineers locations on the numerous reservoirs. There are also Big Bend National Park and the Padre Island National Seashore, plus certain local campgrounds here and there. A great number of fee-hunters are permitted to camp on the ranchlands where they hunt. In addition, there are the four National Forests and the National Grasslands. Hunters can camp in all of these.

Texas hunting weather is hot during early seasons. In September for example, the coolest clothing should be worn. In much of the terrain rugged boots are a must, because of rocks and thorny vegetation. In these early seasons one should keep an eye out for rattlesnakes. Wearing snake boots or leggings is a wise precaution if one is walking far. Later, during the mid-fall seasons, weather may be gently crisp, but on into the winter it can be cold and damp. However, it is a good idea always to carry both warm- and cold-weather clothing. November and December may have 80-degree days, or a freezing norther may blow in.

No especially heavy rifles are needed, such as the large magnums. The .243, .270, .30/06 are good basic calibers for Texas big game. For birds, heavy shotgun loads are needed for turkeys and geese, preferably No. 2 or No. 4, highbase. For quail and doves, No. 8, 7½, and 6 are used. Residents hunt small game to a great extent with .22s.

Because of the peculiar hunting conditions, the following material under individual species will attempt only to show general areas of range and abundance. Aside from the public lands noted, which will be indicated under the various species, quite obviously it is impossible to state that a hunter may be able to hunt in any given area. It is entirely up to the individual hunter to make his own arrangements. Again, Chambers of Commerce can be most helpful. Sometimes, also, newspapers carry ads offering day or season leases. Certain special arrangements are feasible of course with waterfowl, for exmple, where hunts can be booked by reservation. These instances will be fully documented in the following material wherever possible.

QUAIL

Four species of quail are reported in Texas: bobwhite, blue or scaled quail; Gambel's quail; Mearn's quail. The Mearn's is found in remnants in Big Bend National Park and spottily in high ranges surrounding the Park, but is not hunted. Gambel's quail are very occasionally reported from far west Texas but their existence is at best questionable.

It is the bobwhite and the blue that furnish Texas quail hunting, and in good seasons they are fantastically abundant in the aggregate over practically the entire state. The bobwhite is most abundant in the eastern two-thirds of the state. But it also ranges throughout almost all of the Panhandle, and is absent only from most of the Trans-Pecos area of far west Texas. The blue quail blankets the western two-thirds of the state. It is extremely abundant in the Big Bend and Trans-Pecos. It swarms also in the so-called Brush Country of South Texas, particularly south of the Nueces River on to the border.

Over most of these lower counties to the west, southeast, and north of Laredo the subspecies of blue quail is the chestnut-bellied variety. This is a stunningly handsome bird, the males with a large area of dark chestnut on the belly and the females lightly tinged likewise. This is the only region of the U.S. where this subspecies is found. It fans out across the Mexican border for some distance.

An interesting feature of Texas quail hunting is that bobwhites and blues overlap in range in so many places that the two are commonly found in the same cover. One of the best quail hunting regions, for example, is along and near the Red River, the northern boundary with Oklahoma. In the general Wichita Falls area, and stretching out over a large range here, bobwhites are predominant, but there are a good many blue quail.

Public quail hunting is quite good on the National Forest lands in east Texas. This is for bobwhites, and much of it is in terrain where dogs can be used advantageously. Dogs are not used to any extent down in south Texas because of the dense cactus and thornbrush. There is always, of course, danger of dogs being snakebitten, also.

The other lands open to the public for quail are the Grasslands in the west and north. On almost all of these both bobwhites and blues are found. In general the bobwhites predominate except in far northwest Texas. The National Grasslands are good areas for using dogs. Both the National Forests and the National Grasslands have been described and located earlier in this chapter.

For hunters who wish to use dogs, the bobwhite range in the pinewoods country of east and northeast Texas is probably best. Rather often there is a good quail population, with the terrain much more like the Deep South than one usually envisions Texas. However, quail populations in east Texas by no means come up to those found, in good years, in other parts of the state.

The Edwards Plateau or Hill Country described earlier in this chapter, a hilly region north and west of San Antonio, is one of the few areas of Texas that has few quail. Some parts of it have none. The remainder has so few they are not much hunted. South and west of San Antonio a short distance, for instance in the vicinity of Hondo, Devine, and Uvalde, there is in good seasons an excellent quail population, mostly bobwhites. Some day-lease hunting is often available here. South of this general region the blue quail begin to take over. However, while bobwhites are considered predominantly birds of farmlands, there are pockets of brush country that teem with both bobs and blues.

One of these, for example, is east of Pearsall and another in the vicinity of Artesia Wells, both towns on I 35. From here on south to around the village of Encinal, both bobwhites and blues are occasionally found in typical Brush Country—cactus and thornbrush cover. In the hard (drought) years in this arid land, the blues predominate because they are tougher and sustain themselves better. But in good nesting (wetter) years when the drab brushlands spring up in green and bloom in profusion, bobwhites are as abundant as the blues. Farther south, around Laredo, most of the quail are blues. Some pockets of bobs are found. As one travels southeast down the Rio Grande into the irrigated valley, where much truck farming is done, blues thin out and bobwhites begin to take over.

This entire vast region enclosed roughly by U.S. 90 running from San Antonio west to Uvalde, and by U.S. 181 running southeast from San Antonio to Corpus Christi, is one of the prime quail areas of Texas. While most of the region is leased by hunter for deer and quail, there are some day-hunt spots that are exemplary. These are chiefly huge ranch holdings, and there are not many of them offering this type of hunting. A good example is the George Light Ranch, addressed at Artesia Wells. This ranch has excellent accommodations for hunters, furnishes guides and transport, and in good seasons the quail, of both species, swarm.

Aside from the Brush Country, the east-Texas pine-woods bobwhite hunting (which is typified by the public NF lands) and the north-Texas Red River district already mentioned, the other high points in quail are in the west. Reading from the north down, a line drawn along the western Oklahoma border with the Texas Panhandle on south through the cities of Childress, Abilene, San Angelo, to Del Rio on the border places the best of west-Texas quail hunting from there west to the western border. In general the hunting is far better the farther west one goes. However, most of the northern Panhandle is excellent, and the entire region west of U.S. 285 is likewise. This last offers only blue quail, or with only minor exceptions at least, and the Big Bend region has in general the largest populations.

This region is all in large private ranches. A common arrangement here for quail hunting is made with deer hunters. The deer here are predominantly mule deer and the hunting season is short. Therefore most ranchers do not lease, but offer "one-deer" or "three-day" hunts for from $100 to $300. Almost all of them allow their hunters to do some blue quail hunting "for free" during their deer hunt. This country is quite open and the blues consequently are great runners. Dogs are almost never used.

The most important aspect of Texas quail hunting is that one not accustomed to hunting here could hardly envision the fantastic abundance of quail when moist years with good nesting conditions occur. Many pairs bring off several broods and the Brush Country, north Texas, and west Texas literally are overrun. It is not uncommon during such seasons to find 200 to 300 quail, in proper places sometimes mixed between the two species, within a circle of 300 yards or so. At such times a hunter simply "walking up" his birds can, if he is even a fair shot, kill a twelve-bird limit in less than an hour. These tremendous population explosions as a rule are short lived. By late in the long season or else following the season and through late winter die-offs generally occur. The hunting is fabulous, however, while it lasts, and quite well worth all the difficulty one may encounter in lining up a place to hunt.

WILD TURKEYS

Texas has one of the largest populations of wild turkeys in the U.S. In the pine woods of the far northeast there are probably a number of the eastern subspecies. But the chief variety of turkey that ranges over all but far west Texas is the Rio Grande turkey. It is a slender, tall bird with a buff edging on the tail, the gobblers weighing at maturity an average of fourteen to seventeen pounds.

No one knows even with fair accuracy what the annual turkey kill is in Texas, because of the private-land fee hunting and the difficulty under these circumstances of taking surveys. It is undoubtedly at least 15,000 or more. A hunter intending to hunt turkeys here—as well as other game—should get the mapped regulations from the Department. But interpretation of these, so far as turkey abundance is concerned, is difficult. For many years Texas, with 254 counties, has been a hodgepodge of highly varied regulations from county to county. Some counties are under regulatory authority and some are not. Some have traditional regulations and bag limits that have been in effect many years and are confusing and perhaps should be changed. Thus, in certain counties of northeast Texas there is a season limit of 3 gobblers, but in some other counties where turkeys are more numerous the season limit is 2 gobblers. There is utterly no way by which these limits are enforceable, because no tags are issued for turkeys, and private-land hunting makes a check extremely difficult.

Northeast Texas has a fair turkey population. Certain counties here, however, are closed. It is mandatory that a hunter check the regulations map for the year of his hunt. There are a few turkeys in far west Texas, with open season in Hudspeth and Culberson Counties. These birds are found in the Guadalupe and other mountain ranges in this region. They are not especially abundant, and the land is all in large ranch holdings.

The first six tiers of Panhandle counties, reading from the north down, have at present a brief turkey season. There are quite a good number of birds here, and as this is written an either-sex season is held. There are good acreages of public lands here in the National Grasslands, and a substantial number of birds on these lands. There are also turkeys in fair supply in the east on the National Forest lands, but these should be carefully checked in relation to the counties in which they lie. Some (currently Sabine, Houston, Trinity) are closed. Central and north Texas have a fair turkey population. Particularly along the Red River counties there are flocks along the creek bottoms.

The prime turkey range, however, is the Hill Country and the area just west of it called the "Divide." In the Hill Country proper (Edwards Plateau), the town of Kerrville can be considered approximately in the center of the best turkey range. This county, Kerr, is northwest of San Antonio. Surrounding counties—Real, Bandera, Uvalde, Medina, parts of Bexar, all of Comal, Blanco, Burnet, Llano, Mason, Gillespie, Kimble take in most of the quality range. Much of this region is rocky, wooded hills covered by live oak and Spanish oak and Texas cedar, with cypress and sycamore along the stream bottoms. It is excellent turkey habitat.

The so-called "Divide" area is in the western part of the above. U.S. 83 runs north-south through it, and State 41 from Mountain Home west to its intersect with U.S. 377 to Rock Springs cuts the opposite direction. This is the area where the eastern drainage goes into the Guadalupe River and the western drainage to the Rio Grande. It is at the western edge of the Hill Country, is higher, less scenic, with much scrub live oak and shin oak with some of the largest turkey populations.

Although a great deal of the Hill Country turkey range and the Divide is in leases, there is still available a lot of day-hunting for turkeys. Chambers of Commerce in the small cities are the best contact for getting lined up. There is also some hunting by reservation on large ranches. On most of these the system has evolved of no kill, no pay. A hunter writes or phones a ranch that advertises its turkey hunting, books a date to hunt. Paradoxically, although baiting is hardly legal, high, specially built blinds, or blinds placed high in trees, or blinds with small shooting windows placed on the ground, and with grain scattered to entice the birds in, are traditional, and condoned. Many hunters enjoy this hunting, and oddly, it is not always as surefire as it may sound.

In general, however, a hunter gets in a vehicle with a guide and rides the rough, rocky ranch trails trying to spot flocks of gobblers, then goes after one. A typical and very famous ranch where a main business is hunting in conjunction with raising cattle, sheep, and mohair goats, is the renowned 70,000-acre YO Ranch, address Mountain Home, Texas. A gobbler here, with guide and transport furnished, costs the hunter $50. A few other ranches charge as a rule around $25.

There are a surprising number of turkeys farther south in Texas, along river courses such as the Nueces. But it is difficult, since this is big-ranch country mostly under hunting lease, to arrange a hunt there. The Hill Country and the Divide area in combination are best geared to visiting hunters and get a swarm of them every season. Chances of a kill on a booked hunt as described above are almost 100 percent. On day-lease or other hunting they are also excellent.

PHEASANT

Texas cannot truly be termed a pheasant state, but it does have a small amount of pheasant hunting. There are a few birds, and as this is written a one-week season in the Panhandle Regulatory District allows two cocks daily and four in possession. The kill is low. This District takes in the first six tiers of Panhandle counties They should be read from north to south and left to right, five counties each in the first four tiers, six counties each in the last two. This is a kind of token hunt. Most of the area is privately held. However, the Rita Blanca National Grassland is up in the extreme northwest corner of the Panhandle, chiefly in Dallam and Sherman Cos., and other Grasslands tracts are near the Oklahoma border on the east side of the Panhandle, in Hemphill Co. east of the town of Canadian.

Texas is also experimenting, as are numerous states, with various strains and species of pheasants, trying to find one that may establish itself. At present it is too early to predict what success these may have.

PRAIRIE CHICKEN

There are small numbers of prairie chickens, of the lesser variety, in the Panhandle along the north-south Oklahoma border. There is currently (at this writing) a token season of two days only, with two birds daily, four in possession (season total). All birds must be checked and tagged at check station. The open counties are the three in the extreme northeastern Panhandle: from north to south along the Oklahoma border, Lipscomb, Hemphill, Wheeler. While most of this is privately owned land, with hunting by permission only, the Grasslands areas east of Canadian, Hemphill Co., are here and open to the public.

CHACHALACA

Texas is the only state with an open season on this bird. It is extremely doubtful, however, if any are killed, or if anyone hunts them. The chachalaca is primarily a Mexican species, a slender, long-tailed, rather drab relative of the pheasants. It lives in the most dense thickets of thornbrush and cactus, runs on the ground or through the tangled trees and brush, flies only when forced and for short distances. The chachalaca makes a noisy chatter that sounds like its name repeated over and over. It is an odd creature, with the windpipe running in a long U just under the skin down and back up the entire breast before it enters the body cavity. This long resonator enables the bird to make its curious call. When it hides silently in a thicket, air escaping from the pipe can be heard to fizzle.

The chachalaca is excellent eating, but few, even of Texas hunters, have ever tasted it. It is abundant in Mexico throughout the jungles along and inland from the east coast. Extreme southeast Texas is the only known range of the birds in the state today, with Starr, Cameron, and Hidalgo counties open. Curious hunters who may wish to see but not hunt this bird can find it on the 2000-acre Santa Ana National Wildlife Refuge near San Benito, Texas, between Harlingen and Brownsville in the extreme southeast.

There are a few ranches in southeast Texas that have discovered small colonies of these birds on their densest brushlands, but most if not all of these ranchers give them complete protection. It is undoubtedly unfortunate that the bird still remains on the Texas game list. The listing is misleading, and besides, the remnant flocks on this side of the border deserve careful protection. Clearing of the heavier cover of the border brushlands is responsible for the near extinction of the bird north of the border.

MOURNING DOVES

Because of its position in the extreme southern and near-central border location of the U.S., Texas funnels in millions of doves from a vast area to the north. It is one of the best dove states, with a kill running into several millions. It is one of the very few states that, because of its size and depth from north to south, is allowed by the federal government to have a zoned season. There are the North Zone and South Zone, splitting the state, each with a season running approximately two months. There is good to excellent dove shooting throughout the entire state. Although it is almost entirely on private lands, and by leasing or day-hunt arrangement, there is a good bit of public shooting on the National Forest lands of east Texas and the National Grasslands of the north and the Panhandle. (See descriptive material in chapter opening.) Hunters will do well to check these locations. A few ranchers here and there are not opposed to giving permission for dove hunting, mostly because dove shooters don't wander much but generally take a stand and stay put. However, the no-trespass tradition is so strong in Texas that any visiting hunter is well advised to ask, and if no permission is forthcoming to go his way. Trespass laws are rigidly enforced.

While it is difficult to find areas of Texas that fail to offer fair to excellent dove shooting, without any doubt the most sensational shooting in general is in south Texas, well along in the season, when vast flights have gathered. The border area and some distance to the north, all the way from Eagle Pass to Brownsville, offers flights of tens of thousands of doves. The best type of shooting ground is where grain fields are in proximity to large tracts of brushland, and with watering places—such as the numerous bulldozed cattle "tanks" of the region nearby. By making friends with local hunters in the towns quite often invitations can be had for a shoot.

Actually, dove leases can be obtained quite economically. They are useful mainly, of course, to Texas residents, or to visitors who will be in the state over some weeks of the season. Most hunting leases everywhere are basically for deer and turkeys, and on most the dove shooting (and other hunting) is "thrown in." However, many large ranches give leases only for specified seasons, or for deer only or quail only. On these, one may for a modest fee lease dove-shooting-only, for a group. Good examples of this occur especially in the Hill Country vicinity. Here dove hunters look for small grain fields, or for fields where grain is harvested and croton has sprung up. The seeds of this weed are an especially attractive dove food. A group may lease a hundred-acre field that is attracting hordes of doves for perhaps as little as $1 per gun per shoot (afternoon). They shoot it two or three afternoons per week until the birds leave, and have some excellent sport for modest cost, and with no competition.

WHITEWINGED DOVES

Some years ago the border region of south Texas had vast numbers of whitewinged doves. Predominantly a species from farther south, the northern fringe of whitewing nesting range has always been spread across southern Texas, and on to the Pacific Coast. One of the great ancestral nesting grounds was in the lower Rio Grande Valley. Clearing of brush for truck farming destroyed much of the best habitat. Planting of citrus groves restored nesting sites to some extent. However, the numbers of whitewings that now use the Texas side of the border are limited. There is little hope that any great improvements can be made.

For some seasons now Texas gets as a rule four days of whitewing shooting—two different two-day shoots—in a number of southern counties on or near the Mexican border. Reading from west to east, and beginning in far west Texas, these are: El Paso, Hudspeth, Culberson, Jeff Davis, Presidio, Brewster, Terrel, Val Verde, Kinney, Maverick, Dimmit, LaSalle, Webb, Zapata, Jim Hogg, Brooks, Kenedy, Starr, Hidalgo, Willacy, Cameron. The best of the shooting begins in southern Webb Co. and proceeds on south and east through the counties of extreme southeast Texas listed following Webb. Birds are usually plentiful. These shoots are generally crowded, and finding a place to hunt is difficult.

It should be mentioned here that the best whitewing shooting on the continent is found across the border in Mexico. Here the birds nest by millions in heavy mesquite and thornbrush, and feed in maize and other grain fields. The whitewing is colonial in habit, somewhat similar to the extinct passenger pigeon. Flights containing tens of thousands of birds are common in certain places south of the border—for example, south of Reynosa. Hunting licenses are not difficult to get in Mexico, but getting gun permits is rather complicated. The laws can be checked with any Mexican consulate.

WATERFOWL

Duck and goose hunting is of prime quality along the Texas coast. There is also excellent waterfowl hunting in west Texas, and in parts of north Texas on large ranches where grain is raised, but it is all but impossible for the average hunter without contacts to partake of the latter. Across south Texas, in the Brush Country, ranch tanks (dug tanks, or ponds, for watering cattle) swarm with ducks. Lease hunters who have deer and quail leases get much of this shooting, but oddly few natives pay much attention to it, and this shooting, too, is not open to the public except through a personal acquaintance.

The truly excellent waterfowling in Texas is in the coastal rice country and the wet prairies along the coast, and to a lesser extent on the saltwater bays and lagoons. Vast flocks of snow geese, many lesser Canada geese, a good many specklebellies (whitefronted geese) gather here, and thousands of ducks, predominantly pintails, widgeons, gadwalls, teal, with some canvasbacks and redheads, are present. In general the best of the duck and goose shooting for the non-lease hunter can be booked on a daily basis with guides, at from $10 to $20 per day depending on services and equipment offered.

A system has developed in the rice country whereby guides lease waterfowl hunting rights on huge acreages, from a number of owners. The chief operator, and the several guides who work for him, then shoot certain areas on specified days of the week, as a rule only in the mornings, resting the entire country every afternoon, to keep the birds in the vicinity. Most of these people have good equipment and blinds, have the hunting for both ducks and geese down to a science, and produce excellent success for their hunters. Thus, even though this amounts to fee hunting, like the rental of goose pits on farms surrounding refuges elsewhere, nonetheless the hunting is of top quality and so is the service. Reservations with guides should be made well ahead, for they are often heavily booked.

Here are the chief places where well-known guides operate and where the hunting is considered best. Eagle Lake on Alt. U.S. 90, west of Houston in Colorado Co., is one of the top locations for both geese and ducks. The Lissie and Garwood Prairies are located near Eagle Lake. A number of qualified guides with long experience operate here. Contact the Eagle Lake Chamber of Commerce for a list and rates. Nearer to Houston, on I 10, is the small village of Katy. This is another famed area for both ducks and geese, with rice stubble and some pond shooting. A number of good guides operate here also. Write the Chamber of Commerce, or phone or write one of the outdoor editors on one of the Houston newspapers for names.

East of Houston at the head of Trinity Bay are two towns with well-known guides: Anahuac and Wallisville. South of these, on Galveston Bay, is Baytown, another guide location. This entire bay areas is renowned for its goose and duck shooting. Farther south, and east across the bay from Port Lavaca where U.S. 87 ends, is the town of Palacios. There are guides here also. South of Port Lavaca, the small town of Austwell has shooting in its vicinity, and still farther south all around Rockport, Port Aransas, and Corpus Christi there are blinds to be rented and guides for hire. Some of the good motels—there is one at Rockport—offer package waterfowl hunts.

Throughout Texas, around the several large impoundments, there is scattered waterfowl shooting of varying quality. But the coastal hunts booked by the day offer the prime shooting in this state.

There are several important waterfowl refuges in Texas that gather some millions of geese and ducks in the aggregate. Although there is no refuge hunting, the surrounding countryside in each case offers opportunity, in some instances on a fee basis, and hunters who can make contacts in the refuge area will have excellent hunting. These are: Buffalo Lakes, in northwest Texas, Randall Co., southwest from Amarillo via State 60; Muleshoe Refuge, in Bailey Co., some distance southwest of the above, near the New Mexico border south of the city of Muleshoe (U.S. 70 & 84) via State 214; Hagerman Refuge and Tishomingo Refuge, both near Sherman, Texas, in the northeast, along or near Lake Texoma, which is north of Dallas on U.S. 75 just below the Oklahoma border; Laguna Atascosa and Santa Ana, both near San Benito in extreme southeast Texas north of Brownsville and the Mexican border; Aransas (winter home of the whooping cranes) on the Gulf Coast north of Rockport.

CRANES

A few years ago an annual season was instituted on lesser sandhill cranes in Texas and New Mexico and later in parts of Colorado. Oddly, though the Texas shooting is the best, with the greatest number of birds, it gets little attention. Sandhill cranes are grand game birds, as wary as geese, excellent eating. They deserve more notice from hunters, and offer a thrill unique in wing shooting.

Lesser sandhill cranes migrate across much of Texas. Some of them winter along the coast, many go on into Mexico. However, west Texas is the area of abundance and the open area is the portion of the state lying west of the following line. Beginning in the northwestern part of the Panhandle where U.S. 287 comes out of Oklahoma into Dallam Co., follow U.S. 287 and then U.S. 87 south and east to San Angelo, thence via U.S. 277 to Del Rio. While gatherings of cranes, which feed on grain such as redtop and maize, may be located almost anywhere inside the open territory where this grain farming is practiced on a large scale, the concentrations of the birds by thousands are in a rectangle formed by drawing a line south from Amarillo to Lubbock, then west to the New Mexico border, up the border to opposite Amarillo and back east to it.

Cranes, unlike ducks and geese, have no real down. They do not, therefore, sit on water to roost, but roost in large flocks standing in shallow lakes. The two refuges previously located under "Waterfowl"—Buffalo Lakes and Muleshoe—are concentration points for cranes. Also, shallow Coyote Lake, west of State 214 in Bailey Co. and southwest from Muleshoe near the New Mexico border, is one of the most important roosting grounds.

The birds are hunted by taking a well-camouflaged stand along flight routes from roost site to feeding fields or return. Local hunters are now using huge crane replicas five feet tall as decoys. The birds decoy quite readily. Heavy loads—magnums or short magnums in 4's or 2's—must be used, preferably in a full-choke gun. Shots may be long, and cranes, with wingspread up to six feet, are difficult to bring down.

WOODCOCK, SNIPE, RAILS

There is a minor amount of woodcock shooting in east Texas along the Louisiana border. It gets little attention and the bird is not very important in the state.

There is good jacksnipe hunting on the wet rice-field stubble, on the prairies, and along coastal marshes. This also gets little attention, chiefly because access and permission are difficult to acquire. Goose and duck hunters on day-hunt bookings could undoubtedly get more good jacksnipe hunting if they were to become interested in it. The birds are numerous along the lowlands of the east. A scattering of snipe is found also during the winter around cattle tanks in the Brush Country. Lease hunters there can shoot snipe but seldom do.

Rails, particularly the large king rail, are fairly abundant in the rice country of east Texas. They get little attention because the sport is highly specialized and finding a hunting spot is not easy. The common method of hunting is to make contact with a rice farmer and be on hand when a field is cut. Hunters follow the combine as it reduces the field to a few standing swaths. Rails keep running into the still-standing rice until the cover becomes too scant. Then they flush and are shot ahead of or beside the moving combine.

DEER

Texas just may be the greatest deer state in the U.S. Kill figures are not easily gathered here with accuracy but without question at least a quarter-million deer are annually harvested. All but a negligible part of the state is open to deer hunting and there are fair populations almost everywhere, and problem populations in some places. There is a bit of public-land deer hunting on the National Forest Lands (see chapter-opening material) and permit drawings almost every fall for some of the WMA's. By and large, however, deer hunting in Texas is by season lease, or by day-hunt fee, or by booking a "package hunt" on a ranch. As noted earlier, Chambers of Commerce are the best contacts to help in finding leases or ranches where package or day hunts are available.

While east Texas and north Texas have fair deer hunting, and the Panhandle has a modest population of good-sized whitetails, there are three main deer concentrations in Texas and these are where the bulk of the hunting is based. Any hunter contemplating a Texas deer hunt will be best advised to attempt to book a hunt in one of these areas.

Foremost is the Hill Country and Divide Country of south-central Texas. (See "Turkey" for description of area.) The deer here are whitetails. By average whitetail size standards, they are small. Those on the Divide are larger than those in the Hill Country proper. But deer swarm throughout this region. It is not unusual to see in fall sixty to a hundred deer feeding toward evening on a winter oat planting (often purposely planted for them) of fifty to a hundred acres. Most Hill Country and Divide ranches that are not under private lease offer day hunting at around $10 per day, or else a deer hunt, no kill no pay, at from $75 to $150 for a buck, as little as $25 for a doe. Most counties have regulations allowing two bucks and one antler-less deer in this area. The nationally famous YO Ranch mentioned under "Turkeys" is typical of the package hunt with an all but guaranteed kill and no pay if you don't. This Divide ranch allows—as do some others—shooting for bucks only of eight or more points.

The second most popular area for whitetail hunting is in the southern Brush Country. This is probably the most unusual and difficult and certainly among the most interesting whitetail hunting in the U.S. The whitetails are extremely large, typically with heavy mahogany-colored racks. They live in the dense prickly-pear cactus and thornbrush, are extremely hard to see, and because of the low cover exceedingly wary. It is in this Brush Country, incidentally, that the method of hunting known as "rattling up a buck" was invented. This consists of splitting a pair of antlers from a buck skull, hiding during the rut and rattling this pair of antlers together to represent the fighting of two bucks over a doe. Often large bucks come on the run, hackles up and eyes wild, and all but run over the hunter.

Over recent seasons it has been discovered that the method works elsewhere as well, although for many years it was considered effective only in the Brush Country. It is commonly used, with excellent success nowadays, in the Hill Country, and there are more and more records annually of success in other states.

The Brush Country deer hunting is almost entirely by lease or by invitation. A few ranches offer day hunting. The Dolores Ranch near Laredo is one. Some few others have package hunts. The George Light Ranch (see "Quail") has excellent deer hunting in this category and is mentioned here because places of this sort are so few. Regardless of how a hunter arranges his hunt, a Brush Country whitetail hunt is an unforgettable experience, and one who holds out for a real trophy just may make the record book.

The third area emphasized for deer hunting is the Trans-Pecos region which includes the Big Bend Country. The deer here are almost entirely desert mule deer. They are extremely abundant, and the rough open mountains and desert make sighting them easy. Almost every hunter from elsewhere in Texas tries his best to make a trip after what he erroneously calls "a blacktail" each fall.

Interestingly enough, in a few places in this region there are whitetail deer. These are pockets of higher country where timber grows. The deer is the Texas whitetail subspecies in most cases. But of greater interest, a few high areas where piñon and oak grow rather incongruously above the desert have small populations of a tiny whitetail almost unknown to hunters. This is the Carmen Mountains whitetail, a subspecies locally called a "flag" or "flag-tail" and often confused with the Arizona whitetail, or Coues deer. A mature Carmen Mountains buck may weigh as little as fifty pounds. In a few spots all three varieties—desert mule deer, Texas whitetail, and the small whitetail —may be found living in proximity.

Ranches in this region are for the most part very large, anywhere from 50,000 to over 250,000 acres. Aside from the Black Gap WMA which offers some public hunting by permit drawing, there is no public hunting. The ranches charge from $100 to $300 for a hunt, usually for a single buck mule deer. Prices and services differ. The season here is shorter (about two weeks) than in the two areas previously described (where it is about six weeks) and thus ranchers try to get hunters "killed out" so they can take as many as possible. On the better ranches it is not difficult to collect a good mule deer any morning or afternoon. The whitetails are far more difficult.

Typical of ranches in the region offering quality hunts are the Gage Holland Ranch at Marathon, Texas ($300 for a three-day one-mule-deer buck hunt, with quality services), and the huge Catto Ranch, Marathon, where prices vary with services desired but run around $250 per hunter for a mule deer buck. On this ranch, for example, both the subspecies of whitetail are found. Presently Texas regulations are so arranged that a hunter can take four deer in this region, if he can find a rancher who will allow it and can locate some whitetails. Again, Chambers of Commerce in regional towns are of great help in locating places to hunt.

JAVELINA

The javelina is plentiful in the Brush Country and in the Big Bend Country (see "Quail" and "Deer"). There are small fringe populations elsewhere but the prime hunting is as above. Deer hunters commonly see droves of javelina in these two areas. The easiest hunting, and the greatest abundance, is found in the Big Bend region. The pigs are more easily seen here than in the dense brush of the south. However, a number of border-area counties in south Texas have no closed season, and thus an off-season hunt can be arranged. A few of the Big Bend ranches allow deer hunters to take javelina as a kind of bonus. Some few others are beginning to offer javelina hunts at usually about $100 for two javelinas.

The Brush Country hunting is almost entirely by lease deer hunters, although visitors may be successful in lining up a rancher who will allow an off-season javelina hunt. Few if any are approachable during deer season. The fact is, the javelina has to date not been held in high regard as a game species in Texas and has not had the attention it deserves. It is predictable that future seasons will see more and more ranches offering packaged hunts for this animal.

PRONGHORN ANTELOPE

Antelope are not abundant in Texas. At one time they were, and then after a long decline restorative attempts were made in the Panhandle, the Trans-Pecos and the Permian Basin (west Texas) with fair results. There has been a huntable surplus for some years, but the population has its ups and downs and remains far from stable. Over recent seasons there has been a serious decline, yet there are enough for some hunting.

There is no public hunting. The way the permit system is operated makes booking a hunt rather difficult and uncertain, unless one has personal contacts. The Department does a survey and then decides how many permits will be offered in each of the western areas, and how many will pertain to each ranch. These permits are then turned over to the individual ranchers. They book their own hunters, and at prices they decide upon. The Department has no actual control over the price of the hunt or the "antelope." Going rates are from $100 to $150 for a hunt. Some ranchers furnish guide and transport. Some hunters bring their own off-road vehicles. Many ranches are booked more or less permanently year after year by the same groups of hunters. Others are not, and operate on a first-come basis, at their quoted price. Chambers of Commerce in towns throughout the west-Texas hunting country handle to a large extent the bookings of these ranchers. Prospective hunters without any orientation should begin by contacting the Parks and Wildlife Department for suggestions as to what ranches may be open.

AOUDAD

A few years ago the state stocked aoudad, or Barbary sheep, originally native to North Africa, in the Palo Duro Canyon region of the Panhandle. This is southeast of Amarillo. The aoudad is a large (to over 300 pounds) sheep with a chest mane, and leggings on the front legs, and with massive back-curving horns to over thirty-one inches at maximum. It is a stunning trophy. Currently there is a short annual season in January in the following counties: Armstrong, Briscoe, Donley, Floyd, Hall, Motley, Randall, Swisher.

The Department makes a survey of the population and then decides the number of permits to be issued. These, as with antelope, are given out to the individual ranchers who have cooperated in the program. The rancher then sets his price—$200 is currently average—and hunters book directly with him. Needless to say, there are always many more prospective hunters than permits and hunters acquainted with individual ranchers of the area have an edge. Permits are extremely limited, but success percentage is quite high.

SQUIRRELS

Texas has two species, the eastern gray and the fox squirrel. The gray squirrel's range is in the forested portion of east Texas, with its main populations based on the general region that contains the National Forests. The gray squirrel here tends to be most abundant in dense live oak, water oak, cypress, magnolia and black gum bordering streams. It is an important game species in east Texas, and fortunately there is very good hunting on the public Forest lands. (See front material of chapter for description.) Hunting by permission on private lands of the same area and in counties surrounding the Forests may sometimes be arranged.

The range of the fox squirrel is in more open uplands and mixed woodlands. It is broader than that of the gray. It blankets much of the east-Texas gray-squirrel range, but also extends west about to Del Rio, San Angelo, and Vernon. There are some fox squirrels on the fringe of the Forests in the east, and there are some also in the northeast Panhandle, on the National Grasslands there. Otherwise hunting for fox squirrels is confined mostly to the pecan bottoms of central Texas and the Hill Country and is on private lands by permission only.

Both gray squirrels in the Forests and fox squirrels in privately owned pecan bottoms can furnish excellent hunting in Texas. Seasons and bag limits from county to county are complicated, so the squirrel-season map published by the Department should be studied. Note well that there are many areas open here during May, June, and July, a favorite squirrel hunting time for Texans.

RABBITS

Rabbits are not protected in Texas and can thus be hunted at any time of year. They are extremely abundant in many sections of the state. In north and east Texas, cottontails have tremendously high cycles. The same is true of the small Brush Country cottontails of the south, which incidentally are excellent eating. In west Texas jack rabbits are abundant. The Edwards Plateau region (Hill Country) has fewer rabbits than most other portions of the state. There is not much rabbit hunting with dogs in Texas. Most is done with a .22, simply walking them up or cruising ranch trails at dusk and dawn watching for the numerous cottontails to hop away. The Panhandle Grasslands, and the edges of the Forests in the east, offer some public rabbit hunting. There is all told not a great deal of local interest anywhere in Texas in rabbit hunting, but landowners will occasionally allow rabbit hunting to cut down rabbit populations of nuisance proportions.

RUSSIAN BOAR, FERAL SWINE

In the Hill Country (Edwards Plateau) there are quite a number of Russian boars, descendants of hogs escaped from early preserves. They are exceedingly destructive to young lambs and Angora goat kids, a mainstay of ranching in the region. Much of this region is extremely rough country, with steep, well-forested rocky canyons. Huge boars of several hundred pounds are taken here, generally with trained dog packs. They are not protected, and there is no season, nor any public hunting. However, interested hunters can often arrange a guided hunt on private land.

A good way to trace down a boar hunt is to contact taxidermists in the area. Invariably when a big boar is killed, they get the head to mount, know what ranch it came from, and who had the dogs, etc. The Parks and Wildlife Department can also be of some assistance in steering hunters to the best places to try to set up a hunt, and occasionally in helping them find guides and dogs.

A number of sections of Texas have abundant feral swine. The Houston area has a number in nearby swamps. The Brush Country has many, but they are spottily scattered. There is very little purposeful hunting for them. But the potential is there for anyone who wishes to try to arrange a hunt. Local game wardens make good contacts in this case. They usually know places in their bailiwicks where wild hogs range.

OTHER ANIMALS

Fox hunting is popular with groups of hound men in east Texas. In a few counties red foxes have been introduced for the purpose. The gray fox is abundant natively through much of east Texas and the Edwards Plateau. It is a favorite with the growing number of animal callers, for it comes readily to a call.

Coyotes are abundant over much of the Brush Country, all of west Texas and the Panhandle, and the animals range to some extent almost statewide. They, too, are a favorite with callers. But government poisoning has decimated coyote populations unnecessarily in some areas. Bobcats also range statewide, with heavy populations in south and west Texas and fair populations in the east. They come well to a call and are popular.

There are a few lions in the Big Bend region and occasionally down along the south-Texas border. It is possible also that a jaguar may roam now and then into Texas from Mexico. Two were hunted near Marfa a few years ago and caused a flurry of publicity, but it is rather well authenticated that the animals were purposely imported and released as a hoax. There are a few records of ocelots from extreme southern Texas. It is doubtful if any—or at least not more than a meager remnant—remain.

Very occasionally a gray wolf is reported in west Texas. A few may cross from Mexico, or the reports may be erroneous. Red wolves, however, are fairly often taken in eastern and central Texas, and there are pockets here and there of fair abundance. Most hunters confuse the red wolf and the coyote. There is no true public hunting for any of the above animals. With contacts a hunter can get some shooting or calling, but most Texas landowners are reluctant to give permission for any unsupervised shooting on their lands. The state, however, is one of the best for predator hunting if one can get permission.

The black bear continues to appear on the complex game laws of Texas with various seasons or lack of them. The fact is that with the possible exception of a remnant population in the high mountains of west Texas—the Guadalupes—the black bear is probably gone from Texas.

Raccoons, opossums, armadillos are abundant in a number of locations. A few hound men run raccoons, but all told none of these animals is very important in this state.

EXOTIC BIG GAME

Quite a number of years ago Texas launched the big-game hunting preserve with exotic animals such as blackbuck antelope from India, axis deer from India, sika from Japan, mouflon from Corsica and Sardinia, sambar deer from India, aoudad from North Africa. Many wealthy ranchers with large holdings began acquiring surplus zoo stock (animals cannot be imported and released, but progeny from U.S. zoo animals can) and raising exotics as a hobby. Then hunters clamored to shoot some and the big-game preserve was launched.

Today this is a most important aspect of Texas hunting, for the state still continues to lead in rearing in a wild state many of these introduced species. Many have escaped to other lands. At present there are at least

30,000 head of big-game exotics in Texas. Other species now being tried: nilgai, oryx, ibex, zebra, Asian red sheep, kudu.

While the hunting for these animals is actually preserve hunting, since all of Texas is already under a fee-hunt system, and because hundreds of hunters book hunts in Texas annually to collect one or more of the exotics, it is important to note them here. There are, to be sure, a few such preserves on small acreages in other states. But in Texas most of the hunt preserves for big game are actually working ranches on which the exotics are hunted right along with native deer. However, they are not at present under state regulations and so hunts can be arranged at any time, with no license to purchase.

Prices range broadly, all on a no-kill no-pay basis. Axis or sika deer, fallow deer, blackbuck average from $250 to $400 for a package hunt. Mouflon are in general somewhat cheaper—an example, at the Double Horn Ranch, Marble Falls, mature mouflon rams can be hunted for around $150. The YO Ranch at Mountain Home, mentioned previously, world famous and the largest operator in the U.S. in exotics hunting for free-ranging animals, lists most species at from $300 to $400 and up. When oryx and the rarer species become available as herds build up, they will probably cost well over $1000.

The Parks and Wildlife Department has made numerous surveys on exotic big game in the state, can give information to assist in lining up a hunt. Hunts can be booked by letter or phone and there are a large number of ranchers now in this sideline business.

REGULATIONS

Game laws pertaining to seasons, bag and possession limits, areas to be hunted, special hunts, license fees all may have numerous changes from year to year. For current regulations, and for other specific queries, write to: Texas Parks and Wildlife Department, Reagan Building, Austin, Texas 78701.

Rocky
Mountain
States

NEW MEXICO

New Mexico, bounded on the west by Arizona, on the east by the Texas Panhandle plains, on the north by towering Colorado mountains, and to the south by the deserts of Mexico and west Texas, is to some degree a mixture of all its neighbors. Although it is typically a state of the Rocky Mountains, with the Continental Divide snaking down across its western portion, the major acreage of the state, though high and rather arid, is by no means totally studded with mountain peaks.

Altitudes in New Mexico begin at slightly below 3000 feet. The south and southwest is typically desert country, with small groups of mountains ever distantly looming. The entire east is a high plain, a continuation of the central plains of the U.S. Lower altitudes, from 3000 to 4500 feet, comprise only an eighth of the surface. Two-thirds of New Mexico lies between 4500 and 7500 feet. A small amount, in the ponderosa pine belt, lies above this, and a still smaller portion rises in peaks thrusting up 12,000 feet and beyond. Most of the high country is in the center portion of the north, with other patches in the west, southwest and south-central regions.

Minerals, both oil and mining, are a substantial industry. There is some lumbering, a vast acreage in large ranches and in irrigated and dry farming. Some of the largest remaining ranches in the U.S. are located in New Mexico. Approximately thirty-five million acres, or roughly 45 percent of the state, is in private ownership. This leaves more than half under various public control. There is a vast amount of true wilderness still here, much of it accessible by vehicle but fortunately many large areas where the horse and the backpack are the only means of entrance. There are several Wilderness and Primitive Areas in the National Forests here where no vehicular travel is allowed.

The highway system is excellent. Running north-south from border to border down the center, U.S. 85 and 285 course the state. Several other U.S. main arteries lead generally north-south to get one to almost any main point. Interstate 40 crosses east-west to bisect these. Four other main routes in the west and seven in the east run generally east-west. There are numerous smaller roads to scores of rural and foothill and mountain settlements. Most are good. In the wilderness regions, however, travelers should bear in mind that though today New Mexico is a booming state, parts of it still lie to some extent on the fringe of a frontier.

Because the larger cities are well spaced out, air transport is fast and excellent to most portions. Albuquerque, and El Paso, Texas, on the south-central border, are the two focal points for mainline air travel.

In today's hunting picture, New Mexico is in many ways unique. During the early years of this century, its big game had been all but wiped out. Antelope were only a remnant, deer were scarce, elk were practically extinct, bear and turkey were few. Today, after many years of determined labor by game men, New Mexico stands in an enviable position, with a great variety of game animals and birds, virtually all of them present in huntable surpluses.

The state is large, our fifth largest. Over 300 miles across in each direction, it contains 121,666 square miles. In this huge area there is at present an estimated population of barely over a million. Over a quarter-million of this population is within the city limits of Albuquerque. There are a scattering of smaller cities, and numerous tiny villages. Thus there is little crowding of hunters.

License sales, in fact, average only about 100,000 annually at present. Of these, although nonresident license sales are growing, the vast majority are resident hunters. There is, therefore, limitless room for visitors, for at present seldom more than a total of 3000 nonresidents annually hunt birds and big game combined. The variety of game is most appealing. Among the big-game animals, mule deer are the main attraction. There are also whitetail deer, elk, antelope, mountain sheep, black bear, javelina, and the exotic aoudad or Barbary sheep. New Mexico is a pioneering state in experimenting with other exotic big-game animals. Though none are so far huntable excepting the aoudad, it appears likely that oryx, kudu, ibex, and numerous other foreign introductions undoubtedly one day will be.

There are three varieties of wild turkey, plus scaled quail, Gambel's quail and bobwhites. The lesser prairie chicken, dusky grouse, ringneck and Afghan whitewinged pheasant offer limited hunting. Mourning doves are abundant, whitewinged doves are also available. There is a limited amount of waterfowl shooting, and New Mexico is one of the few states where sandhill cranes, extremely abundant in winter, may be hunted. Abert or tassel-eared squirrels, and the small red squirrel or chickaree, plus rabbits, and predators such as coyotes, bobcats, mountain lions round out the varied list.

Hunters have little difficulty finding places to hunt. The situation in regard to public lands is most fortunate. Chief among these are the National Forests. There are five. Maps and details on each can be obtained from the forest supervisor as follows: Carson NF, Taos; Cibola NF, Albuquerque; Gila NF, Silver City; Lincoln NF, Alamogordo; Santa Fe NF, Santa Fe. These forests cover some nine million acres. It is estimated that over 50 percent of New Mexico's big-game kill comes from these forests.

The Bureau of Land Management administers approximately fourteen million acres, much of which is open to hunting. Most Bureau of Reclamation lands, around reservoirs for example, are also open. Over nine million acres of land are state-owned, and almost all of this is leased for hunting easement by the State Game Commission. Indian lands comprise 6.5 million acres. These, too, in some part—such as the Jicarilla Apache Reservation in the northwest—offer public hunting by special fee. The Game Department owns outright almost 100,000 acres, on some 90 percent of which hunting is allowed. Recently numerous State Parks have been opened to hunting. There is a modest acreage of National Grasslands in the northeast.

Private lands are traditionally open by permission. Nowadays some of them charge fees, which makes them even more readily available for those who wish to pay. Thus, the overall public hunting picture in New Mexico is most inviting.

The New Mexico Department of Game and Fish is a hard-working, farsighted organization, dedicated heartily to finding more lands for public use and keeping ever more game available, with careful, scientific management. It is most helpful to hunters, too, with numerous pamphlets and hunting maps annually suggesting the best spots to try for each species. All such material, plus lists of guides available, may be had from the department, address at chapter end. Field men, both supervisors and wardens, are extremely helpful to visitors.

For management purposes, the state is divided into four large general areas by which seasons are (with some variations) set. The areas: northwest, northeast, southwest, southeast. The north-south line begins just west of Chama and zigzags down across the state to end at the southern border at the western edge of Eddy Co. The east-west line runs from Clovis in the east to bisect the other line at Mountainair, approximately in the center of the state, thence on generally westward to the border where U.S. 60 exits. It is important for a visitor, in discussing plans, to know these general divisions. The state is further divided for various management and season-setting purposes into several dozen small, numbered Management Units. Game maps from the Department show these, for species for which they are necessary.

There is no problem about accommodations for hunters in motels as long as cities or towns of fair size are selected. These are located within easy driving of all portions of the state. Even settlements of modest size along the main highways have some accommodations. New Mexico is also a fine state for camping. There are a number of State Parks. The State Park Commission, Santa Fe, will furnish information on these. The National Forests have dozens of campgrounds. There are the National Parks and several National Monuments with camping facilities, also National Grasslands. A number of State Game and Fish areas offer camping, with details readily available from the Department. Corps of Engineers, Bureau of Land Management, and Indian Reservations also offer some campsites. The New Mexico State Tourist Bureau at Santa Fe is a good contact for such information, as well as regarding other accommodations.

Visitors should be aware that with New Mexico's variable altitudes, weather may be changeable. The south and southwest will be hot and dry in early fall, but December even in the southwestern deserts can be very crisp, though pleasant. New Mexico's winter weather is made up in the northwest and the first snows appear in October and November. One should be prepared over much of the hunting season both for bright, sunny days and for severe storms, although the storms usually last no more than two or three days, with snow melting again.

Arms and ammunition for New Mexico fall into the average pattern. Big elk are tough to put down, and consequently rifles of substantial caliber are needed. The .270 and .30/06 will do, but many nowadays use the several heavy magnums for elk. Deer here require the average rifles, from .243 to .308, .270, and '06, or similar calibers. Heavy shotgun gauges and loads are needed only for turkeys, for sandhill cranes, and for the fortunate few who find geese to hunt. Otherwise, average shotgun loads, such as No. 8, No. 7½, No. 6 are perfectly adequate for the varied game birds.

QUAIL

New Mexico quail on the hunting list are of three species: scaled or blue, Gambel's, bobwhite. There are also some Mearn's quail but they are at

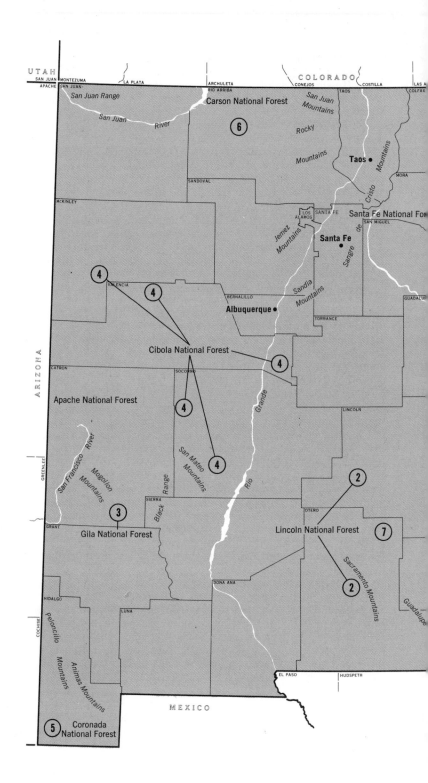

NEW MEXICO

KEY TO HUNTING AREAS

1. Bitter Lakes Refuge
2. Lincoln NF
3. Gila NF
4. Cibola NF
5. Coronado NF
6. Jicarilla Apache Indian
   Reservation
7. Mescalero Indian
   Reservation

SCALE IN MILES
0 5 10 20 30 40

present protected. With the exception of the higher mountains of northern New Mexico, one or more huntable quail species are found almost everywhere in the state. Quail in the aggregate of species are in fact the most important nonmigratory game birds here. At the present time, New Mexico has possibly the highest bag and possession limit on quail of any state: 20 and 40. This of course can change from season to season as quail population cycles move up or down. Annual quail harvests have run from as high as 350,000 to a low of slightly over 100,000. Average yearly kill during years of modest abundance runs around 125,000.

The scaled quail (blue) is the most widely distributed species and also the most numerous. It ranges in varying numbers almost everywhere in the state below the 7000-foot altitude. The eastern half of the state, and all of the south and southwest excepting the north-central portion of Otero Co. and the south-central portion of Lincoln Co., are the most heavily populated blue quail regions. There is also a fair population in much of San Juan Co., in the extreme northwestern corner of the state. This area is high desert, with stream courses of the San Juan River system. However, the desert grasslands of the southwest, the southeast, and east-central sections are without question the optimum habitat for blues.

Reading from left to right across the bottom of the state, Hidalgo, Luna, Dona Ana, Otero, Eddy, and Lea Cos. all furnish good hunting. So do counties in a line north along the Texas border—Chaves, Roosevelt, Curry, DeBaca, Quay. In fact, during normal years the region around Tucumcari (on U.S. 54, east-central), Portales to the south in Roosevelt Co. almost on the Texas border, and the small village of Milnesand south of Portales furnish some of the best shooting for blues. In the southwest, the areas around the towns of Silver City (U.S. 180, Grant Co.), Lordsburg (U.S. 70-80, I 10, Hidalgo Co.), Deming, east of Lordsburg in Luna Co., and the Las Cruces area north of El Paso, Texas, all are prime spots. Blues may also be found in fair abundance all the way up the Rio Grande from El Paso to Albuquerque. Main highways parallel the river.

The handsome, plumed Gambel's quail, a slightly smaller bird, is next in abundance. But its range is somewhat restricted. It follows in general the watercourses of the central and southwestern portions of the state, with an isolated population more recently having invaded the northwest. Although some Gambel's quail are found commonly far from apparent water sources, the stream courses support the best populations.

Some such areas, with dense brush, harbor numerous coveys. These quail are seldom too far from cover, whereas blues may be out in open grasslands. Some of the best of the hunting for Gambel's begins at the Mexican border and follows up the Rio Grande Valley about to the city of Socorro, which is in the center of Socorro Co. As noted in reference to blues, main highways give access to all of this area. All Rio Grande tributaries in this region have populations of Gambel's along them. Thus, the following counties should be carefully checked: Dona Ana; eastern and western (but not central) Sierra; central Socorro. Other major areas: the southwestern counties of Luna, Hidalgo, Grant (especially along the Gila River), and the San Francisco River region of Catron Co., north of Grant Co. U.S. 180 and side roads take one to both the Gila and the San Francisco. The country south of Lordsburg along and near the Mexico and Arizona borders also is well supplied. In the far northwest, the San Juan and Animas Valleys hold a substantial

Gambel's population. Base points are Shiprock, Farmington, Aztec, along U.S. 550.

Least populous and most range restricted but nonetheless offering fine shooting in their small area are the bobwhites. These are confined (often in company with blues) to a few of the eastern counties in the sandy belt bordering Texas. The best hunting is from about Clovis (southern Curry Co., U.S. 60-84-70) south to just north of Hobbs (Lea Co., U.S. 62-180). There are a few bobwhites, and a good many blues, near Logan to the north of the above range, about where the Canadian River crosses into Texas, and there is a small population in the extreme northeast corner of Union Co. still farther north. Certain specified areas are sometimes closed. Check with laws current for the season you hunt.

WHITEWINGED DOVES, MOURNING DOVES, BANDTAILED PIGEONS

The whitewinged dove nests to a minor extent in the southern tier of counties. However, it is scattered except in the southwest, with its most abundant populations in the extreme southwest. It is an early migrant to Mexico. Because New Mexico has a split dove season, the early segment beginning usually September 1, some good whitewing hunting can be had, particularly in the cultivated portions of the southwest. Deming and Lordsburg are good location points. The whitewing, however, to date receives little hunting pressure.

Mourning doves are an important game bird in the state. The annual kill runs over 200,000. Although doves nest throughout New Mexico, the prime hunting is in the eastern tier of counties. Beginning at Tucumcari and moving south through Clovis, Portales, Lovington, Hobbs, the dry-farming belt furnishes excellent shooting. In the late season also there are scattered flocks through numerous grazing lands areas, from Logan on south. (See "Quail" for location points.) The Pecos River Valley is another excellent bet. Begin at Fort Sumner (DeBaca Co., U.S. 60-84 and State 20) and from here south to Carlsbad there is quality shooting. From Albuquerque to Las Cruces along the Rio Grande is also good. The mourning dove is also abundant in the whitewing range mentioned above, and stays later.

New Mexico has a modest population of bandtailed pigeons. These birds stay most of the time in the high mountains, but occasionally come to lower elevations where they do some damage to fruit crops. Prior to 1950 bandtails were hunted in this state. The season was then closed because it was feared the bandtail population was too low to sustain hunting. In the mid-60s biologists began to push for a study of the bandtail in New Mexico, Arizona, Colorado, and Utah. Trapping operations were launched in New Mexico and Arizona, and during 1967 and 1968 numerous birds were banded. In order to further the study, it was decided, with federal permission since the bandtail is migratory, to open a brief season. This would enhance band returns, and offer opportunity for further study.

A nine-day season was allowed in the fall of 1968 in three counties of the southwest: Catron, Grant, Hidalgo. A special, free bandtail permit was required, in addition to proper hunting license, so later survey of success might be made. Approximately 500 pigeons were bagged by a modest number of interested hunters. It is not certain that seasons will be opened every year, but it appears likely that a small amount of bandtail hunting in New

Mexico may be at least periodically available. Springs in the big-pine and oak country of the mountains, particularly where salt may be had, are good places to look for flocks of these grand game birds.

GROUSE

There are actually five grouse species in New Mexico. These are the dusky (or blue) grouse of the higher, forested mountains, the prairie chicken of the plains (in this case the lesser prairie chicken species), the sharptailed grouse, the sage grouse, and the ptarmigan.

There is a remnant population of ptarmigan atop the highest mountain peaks of the Sangre de Cristos in the extreme north. They are not hunted at present. Sharptailed grouse, one of the prairie species, reach the southern limit of their range in northern New Mexico, on the Johnson Mesa, but this is not a huntable population. The big sage grouse of the open sagebrush lands was once extinct in New Mexico, has now been restocked west of Taos and near Tres Piedras, Cebolla, and Burford Lake, but this species also is not able at this time to sustain hunting pressure.

Dusky, or blue, grouse and lesser prairie chickens are not important by numbers annually taken, but because they are sustaining and huntable populations of interesting species. There are very brief seasons on both. Hunters should note that by careful planning they can hunt one or both of these, plus quail, doves, waterfowl, and possibly other small game and game birds all on one trip.

Blue grouse kill averages somewhere between 500 and 1500 per year. These birds are confined to the high mountains. Good spots for them: the Mogollon Mountains of the southwest on the border of Catron and Grant Cos., reached out of Reserve or north from Silver City via U.S. 180; the San Mateo Mountains, southwest Socorro Co. west of U.S. 85 and south of U.S. 60; the high country of the Sangre de Cristos from Sante Fe on north to the Colorado border; the Jemez Mountains west of Santa Fe in the Los Alamos region; the San Juan Mountains west of U.S. 285 on the western border of Taos Co. and just below the Colorado line. In this last-named area, the Lagunitas Lakes region out of Tres Piedras is a good place to hunt.

The lesser prairie chicken has received a great deal of attention in New Mexico. The state bought a range of over 20,000 acres to assist this once-abundant but now troubled species. The New Mexico population is fairly stable. Annual kill nowadays during a two- or three-day season averages from 500 to 1500 birds. The flocks are confined to several counties of the extreme eastern tier, chiefly Roosevelt, portions of Curry, DeBaca, Chaves, Eddy, and Lea. The best hunting portion—and one should check carefully to see what segments are open—is generally in Roosevelt Co., south of Portales, around the small settlements of Milnesand, and of Crossroads just below the Roosevelt Co. line. State 18 passes through these villages. This is shooting early and late in the day in feeding fields where the birds fly in. At times there is some walk-up and pointing-dog shooting in the dwarf shin oak and sand north of Tatum, on the same route.

PHEASANT

There are two varieties of pheasants currently huntable. The ringneck has had a precarious foothold for some years. Although it is hunted during a brief season, it is not especially important numerically. The principal hunting area is along the Rio Grande between Belen and Bernardo. This is a short stretch at the northern edge of Socorro Co., along the route of U.S. 85 (I 25). There are a few ringnecks south of Roswell also, along the Pecos.

Although the pheasant kill is only one or two thousand annually, and often perhaps less, the truly important bird here is the Afghan whitewinged pheasant. This is a bird of arid country. New Mexico was the first state to hold an open season on full-blood (not crossbred) whitewinged pheasants. This was in 1964, an experimental hunt near Red Rock, on the Gila in the southwest, in southern Grant Co. The whitewinged pheasant is an exceedingly wild, hardy bird and appears well established in New Mexico. Other states are swiftly experimenting. New Mexico now has an annual limited season. The species holds great promise for southwestern pheasant hunting. Currently the best hunting area during the brief New Mexico season is along the Gila River from the town of Cliff on U.S. 180 cross-country to the Arizona line. Some shooting is offered to the south, in Hidalgo Co. south of Lordsburg. Other releases in widely scattered suitable areas of the state have been made. The whitewinged Afghan pheasant is presently spreading its range, giving evidence of breeding well in the wild and will almost certainly become an important game bird here and elsewhere in arid areas.

OTHER EXOTIC UPLAND BIRDS

New Mexico has done extensive experimentation with two species of francolin, partridge-like or grouse-like birds. At this time they are suspected to be incapable of establishing themselves. There is no hunting for them.

Both chukars and Hungarian partridge have been tried. The Huns failed. Chukars, with massive releases over some years, are still not known to have established themselves permanently. Some have been sighted in the Pyramid Peaks south of Lordsburg. These conceivably may have come from offspring of distant releases in the Peloncillo Mountains some years ago. Possibly chukars may establish themselves eventually. Currently it is questionable.

WATERFOWL AND OTHER LOWLAND BIRDS

This is not a high-kill waterfowl state. Shooting is limited, and spotty, but at times quite good for the few who pursue it. The annual kill of ducks is seldom much over 30,000 and of geese perhaps a tenth of that. New reservoirs that appear from time to time—such as Ute, full within recent years, and Navajo in the northwest—all help to bring and hold some waterfowl.

The Rio Grande Valley from Belen south to the Texas border offers a good bit of duck shooting. So does the Pecos River Valley from Fort Sumner south. (These areas are located under "Quail" and "Pheasant.") Geese are hunted in this same region, and also in the northeast, near Las Vegas and Springer, both on U.S. 85.

Occasionally the upper end of Elephant Butte Lake, in lower Socorro Co. on U.S. 85, has a good many mallards, and the same is now true on Ute Lake, a fairly new impoundment near Logan, up in the northeast on U.S. 54. The Bitter Lakes Refuge (1) near Roswell on the Pecos River has some public land open and offers rather good duck hunting for a limited number of shooters. The Pecos and the Rio Grande in its lower reaches both offer fair jump-shooting. The Pecos is probably best from Carlsbad south to the state line, and the Rio Grande in the vicinity of Elephant Butte and Caballo reservoirs, twin impoundments only a few miles apart. Conchas Lake northwest of Tucumcari also furnishes some shooting. The most popular goose hunting area is usually along the Rio Grande Valley from Bernardo south to the Bosque Refuge below San Antonio, south of the city of Socorro. By and large waterfowl hunters must know their hunting grounds rather intimately here.

There are open seasons in New Mexico on both jacksnipe and rails but there is virtually no hunting at all for these species. A few are present, but seldom in huntable numbers large enough to draw shooters to any one place.

The most interesting of the state's water-situated birds is the lesser (little brown) sandhill crane. For many years the season on these cranes was closed. Grainfield depredations on their summering grounds in Canadian prairie provinces, and their massive concentrations along the New Mexico-Texas border in winter, sparked an open, limited season on them in the early 1960s. The kill has never been large in New Mexico, possibly 1000 birds each fall. These are large (seven to twelve pounds), exceedingly wary birds, grain feeders that roost standing in shallow lakes and ponds, birds of six-foot wing-spread that decoy rather readily and are delicious eating.

Since the open seasons began, local hunters have learned to make huge decoys four or five feet tall. Flocks fly out from their lake roost at dawn and back at evening. One can shoot the flights, or locate a favorite feeding field and use decoys. Heavy shotgun loads are needed. While this shooting so far has not had a great deal of attention, it is most deserving and dramatic. Probably 200,000 birds winter along the border of east-central New Mexico (and across in Texas). There are two main hotspots in New Mexico for crane shooting. One is in the Roswell vicinity, where many roost in Bitter Lakes Refuge. The other is the plains country with its ponds and grain fields surrounding Portales, northwest of Roswell on U.S. 70 and near the Texas border.

WILD TURKEYS

The wild turkey is an important species in New Mexico. It is classed as big game. There are three varieties, or subspecies. Of greatest importance and most abundant is the Merriam's. This is a large turkey of the mountains, found throughout most of New Mexico's mountain ranges. A clue for hunters is the fact that Merriam's turkeys are closely associated with ponderosa pine. They may range in summer higher than the pine zone, and in winter lower down in the juniper and pinyon belt. But their chief range and association is always with ponderosa. The Merriam's has an ash-colored or bone-cream tail edging and rump.

The Rio Grande turkey, predominantly a Texas subspecies, is slightly smaller, has a buff tail edging and rump, ranges along a few stream courses of northeastern New Mexico. Rarest of turkeys is the Mexican (Gould's) turkey. A very few are found in the extreme southwest. They are fairly abundant across the border farther south in Mexico. Hunting is not allowed for the Mexican variety in New Mexico.

Annual turkey kill averages 2000 to 2500 birds. Total flock is estimated around 25,000 to 30,000. There are both fall and spring seasons, and hunter success averages around 10 or 12 percent.

Good hunting is found in several areas. Some of the best: Johnson Mesa east of Raton, in upper Colfax Co., extreme northeast; the Ocate area west of Wagonmound on U.S. 85, in the northeast; the Sacramento Mountains, Lincoln National Forest (2) near Weed, Cloudcroft, and Ruidoso, Otero Co., south-central; in the southwest, vicinity of Mogollon, State 78, Catron Co. and Silver City, U.S. 180, Grant Co.

Much of the Gila National Forest (3) in the last-named area above is excellent, with the Black Range in the eastern part of the Forest a good bet. Just to the northeast, in the Cibola National Forest (4), the San Mateo Mountains also offer prime turkey range. In the north, west of the Rio Grande in Sandoval and Rio Arriba Cos., the high ranges have turkeys. And for the Rio Grande variety there are pockets of fair abundance in the extreme northeast along the Canadian River, Ute Creek, Carrizo Creek, and the Cimarron River. U.S. 54, State 18, and U.S. 56 and 64 give access to all this northeast region.

DEER

Mule deer are the most important big game in New Mexico. There are two subspecies: Rocky Mountain mule deer in the northern part of the state, desert mule deer in the south. The total mule deer herd is estimated at possibly 300,000. Annual kill averages currently around 30,000 (of all deer varieties) and success is substantial, from 35 to 40 percent. On special hunts it may top 50 percent.

Whitetail deer occur in New Mexico in two subspecies: the western (Texas) whitetail, and the Coues or Arizona or Sonoran whitetail, often called a "fantail." Estimated total whitetails in New Mexico: 10,000. A few western whitetails are found in the Sangre de Cristos west of Raton, a slightly better population in the Sacramento and White Mountains of the Lincoln National Forest, in the southwest. A scarce whitetail population considered to be a race by itself is found in the sandhills and the brushy draws of the extreme southeast, in Chaves, Roosevelt, and Lea Cos.

The most abundant whitetail is the "fantail" or Coues subspecies. This is a handsome, diminutive deer with a small but tight rack, ranging predominantly below the border in Sonora, Mexico, and across the border in Arizona. Some good hunting for it is found in New Mexico in the Black Range and the Mogollon Mountains of the southwest, both located in the Gila Forest, in Catron and Grant Cos. Heaviest population is still farther south, in the Animas and Peloncillo Mountains and the small section of Coronado National Forest (5) in lower Hidalgo Co. This is a rough area serviced by few roads. State 81 and 338 take one into the general region.

It is exceedingly important that deer hunters acquire the state "Proclamation of Big Game Seasons" for the year current to their hunt before making specific plans. Varying areas are open or closed with annual differences. Certain ones are for bucks only, some for either sex. There are a number of special hunts with stipulated quotas. Because the mule deer is the most important and abundant big-game animal of New Mexico, and has the largest range, hunt planning by the current map is mandatory. Here however are given the areas where chances are best, with no guarantee that all will be open during any given season.

Mule deer so nearly blanket the state that it is best to note first where they do *not* range. The eastern counties of Curry, Roosevelt, Lea, most of Chaves, the southern half of DeBaca can be for practical purposes eliminated. Much of central Torrance Co. in the center of the state is without mule deer, too, and in the northwest one may count out much of western San Juan Co. and all but southeast and northwest portions of McKinley Co. to the south of San Juan. Eliminating these small areas, all the rest of the state with only spotty exceptions may be considered mule deer country.

Trophy hunters will do best in the north, simply because the Rocky Mountain subspecies in general is a larger deer with larger antlers. However, all of the Wilderness or Primitive Areas of the National Forests are likely to produce more trophy heads than elsewhere, because they receive less hunting. When making a hunt into one of these, it is best to check conditions first with the Forest Service (addresses given earlier in chapter). Here are the remote areas: Wheeler Peak in the Carson NF; San Pedro Parks, Santa Fe NF; Pecos, Santa Fe NF; White Mts., Lincoln NF; Black Range, Gila NF; Gila, Gila NF; a part of the Blue Range, Apache NF jutting across the border from Arizona. Pack-in hunts in these wilderness regions offer good chances for record heads.

The Jicarilla Apache Indian Reservation (6), a 758,000 acre tract within the environs of the Carson National Forest in northwestern New Mexico, is one of the prime regions for good mule deer hunting. Late-season hunts produce the most trophies. Tribal headquarters may be contacted at Dulce (State Route 17). Special licenses in addition to the state license are necessary. Much of the Carson Forest outside the reservation is also excellent. The mountains and foothills near Chama (U.S. 84 just below Colorado border), the Cuba region west of Los Alamos in the Santa Fe Forest, the Questa, Red River and Eagle Nest regions north of Taos on State 3 and 38 are all quality range.

Hunters seeking abundant deer but not necessarily trophy heads will do exceedingly well in the Lincoln Forest. This large Forest is in several sections in the south-central and southeast. Part of it lies north of the Mescalero Indian Reservation (7) and part to the south of the Reservation. These huge areas center on Ruidoso. U.S. 70, 82, 380, 54 all offer access. The Mescalero Reservation is open some seasons. Tribal permits are required. Headquarters can be contacted at the village of Mescalero (on U.S. 70), zip code 88340. The remaining segment of the Lincoln NF, with excellent hunting, lies to the southeast of all the above and is separate from it. There is an enormous near-roadless region here. It is reached most easily out of Carlsbad (U.S. 285, 62, 180 in central Eddy Co., southeast section of state) by taking State Route 137. The Guadalupe Mountains are here in this Forest section and are excellent mule deer range.

In fact, the northwest area (Carson NF) and the southeast mountains (Lincoln NF) are in general considered the best of New Mexico's mule deer hunting. This does not rule out the southwest. Many good hunts are possible in the section covered by Catron, Grant, Luna and Hidalgo Cos. Some out-of-the-way spots carefully sought out in the southwest pay off well. One of the best: the small south-thrusting portion of the Gila NF on the Arizona border near the village of Mule Creek. This is reached north of Cliff (Grant Co.) on U.S. 180, thence via State 78. Much of the mountain country broadly surrounding this location is a fine choice.

ELK

Originally two varieties of elk were found in New Mexico, the Merriam's, which is now extinct, and the Rocky Mountain. Early in the century elk were almost wiped out here. Slow restoration has now built good herds in all areas of New Mexico with suitable habitat. This habitat is limited. Although attempts are being made to stretch the range into small mountain ranges here and there, most of it is in the large northern ranges, and in the southwest.

While the annual kill is not large, some very good bulls are taken, and chances are quite good. Some portions of the range offer unlimited public licenses, some Management Units are limited to quotas, by drawing. These hunts may be mature bulls only (good trophy bet), antlerless only, either sex. Overall kill ranges from 800 to 1500, with success averaging between 15 and 25 percent. Some specific areas, however, have shown phenomenal success, up to almost 60 percent on certain hunts. There are some private-land hunts, with quota licenses, as well as National Forest hunts. Check with the Department regarding these.

Main elk ranges can be easily pinpointed. Most of northern and central Rio Arriba Co. and east into Taos Co. to just west of the Rio Grande River is one. These counties lie on the northern border, west of center. Chama is a key village. South of it, in the northeastern portion of Sandoval Co., Los Alamos area, is another excellent range. The first range mentioned is in the Carson National Forest, the latter in the western portion of the Santa Fe. East of these ranges, and east of the upper Rio Grande, stretching from Santa Fe northeast in a wide swath to the Colorado border, runs another portion of the Santa Fe and Carson NF, along the Sangre de Cristo Mountains. This is all quality elk range.

South and west of all the above, in portions of Sandoval, Valencia, and McKinley Cos., lies the eastern portion of the Cibola NF. This is a smaller area, but good. It is almost due west of Albuquerque. San Mateo is a key village, off U.S. 66 to the north on State 53. Remainder of the best hunting is in the Apache and Gila National Forests in the southwest, against the Arizona border in Catron and Grant Cos. U.S. 180 leads in here, with numerous state routes probing the wilderness.

A small portion of the Guadalupe Mountains and the southern segment of the Lincoln National Forest also has elk, and a season. This is in the southeast, out of Carlsbad on State 137, along the Texas border and the borders of Otero and Eddy Cos. Permits here are likely to be quite limited. Hunters should be aware, too, that the Gila drainage (southwest, Catron and Grant Cos.) usually has quite a limited license quota.

Without question the best elk hunting in New Mexico is in the Carson and Santa Fe National Forests of the north. Top spots in these are usually the area surrounding Chama (U.S. 84, Rio Arriba Co.); Tres Piedras (western edge of the Carson NF, the village of Tres Piedras on U.S. 285, western Taos Co.); Questa and Red River (east of Tres Piedras, in Carson NF, State 38); Costilla (just below Colorado border north of Questa on State 3); Pecos (south end Santa Fe NF east of city of Santa Fe); the Taos and Eagle Nest region to the north.

ANTELOPE

There are antelope in most of the open areas of the state, but the herd is not large. Annual kill on carefully managed, very brief (two or three day) hunts runs from 1000 to 2000. Permits are by drawing. Hunts may be held in each of the four quadrants, with an average of 3000 permits or less, and success about 65 percent. Although a large area of New Mexico is considered antelope range, and has at least scattered bands, the entire state population, with fluctuations considered during good and poor years, probably never exceeds 25,000 and normally is about 15,000. Some good heads are taken, but with short seasons, drawings, limited permits, these hunts are rather difficult for visitors. Also, the areas of fairly dense pronghorn populations are scattered and compact.

The northeast is usually the best area. Clayton, Capulin, and Raton, all on U.S. 64-87, extreme northeast, are an excellent bet. So is the Wagonmound region to the south on U.S. 85. The plains surrounding Tucumcari, farther south in Quay Co. on U.S. 54, have a good herd. So does the Roswell region, southeast, in central Chaves Co. In the southwest, the Plains of Saint Augustine sweep from the town of Magdalena on U.S. 60 (west of Socorro) southwest into the fringe of the Gila National Forest, around behind and west of the Black Range. This is considered the best antelope area in this portion of the state.

BIGHORN SHEEP

Both Rocky Mountain and desert bighorns exist in New Mexico in small populations. The Rocky Mountain bighorn, once exterminated, was restocked in the Sandia Mountains just out of Albuquerque to the northeast. It has also been transplanted experimentally to portions of the Pecos Wilderness and also the Gila. A few desert bighorns hang on in the San Andres Mountains west of White Sands National Monument in the south-central area, and in the extreme southwest in the Hatchet Mountains.

New Mexico cannot be considered to offer sheep hunting at this time. Three hunts have been held in the Sandia Mountains during the past ten years, with meager permit allotments. Fifteen rams were taken. The Sandia herd is considered the only well-established one and it is possible token hunts may be offered at some future time. Fifteen surplus Canadian bighorns from Banff National Park were placed on Frazer Mountain, Carson National Forest, in 1968 in an attempt to launch a population there.

BARBARY SHEEP (Aoudad) AND OTHER EXOTICS

This large exotic with chest mane and hairy leggings, from North Africa, with mature rams weighing over 300 pounds, was stocked in the Canadian River canyon of northeastern New Mexico (Mora Harding and San Miguel Cos.) in 1950, and later on the Rio Hondo, tributary to the lower Pecos, in Lincoln and Chaves Cos. Token stockings were also made in the northwest, along the San Juan. A number of hunts have since been held. These are by permit and drawing, and some but not all seasons are for residents only. Those who draw a permit for one hunt are ineligible for the next one.

Presently aoudad are considered established: west of the village of Roy (State 39, Mora Harding Co.) in the Canadian River canyon; in the Rio Penasco area west of Artesia (southeast, U.S. 285, Eddy Co.); the Rio Hondo southwest of Roswell. During a recent season there were two hunts, with 100 permits. Fifty-nine sheep were taken, an excellent success figure. This is exceedingly rough hunting. Trophy rams with horns up to thirty-one inches have been taken. Such rams are about maximum. This is an interesting trophy hunt, although chances of drawing are extremely limited, and nonresident license fee continues high.

New Mexico is extensively experimenting with a number of big-game exotics, hoping eventually to establish some of these on ranges empty of native big game. At the experimental farm near Red Rock in the southwest, oryx, kudu, ibex, red sheep, foreign wild goats, and other animals are ranged. There appears at this time some fair hope that several of these may be released on open game ranges experimentally. Hunting hardly can be hoped for during the next few years but it is possible token hunts for oryx or ibex may occur within the next ten to fifteen years.

BEAR

The grizzly is extinct, but a modest black bear population exists, scattered well over the mountain forests, almost entirely in the several National Forests. Quite a few hunters try for bears. A few bears are killed as incidentals by hunters after other big game. Bear hunting with dogs, allowed in certain seasons and sections, is the only successful way to attempt a serious bear hunt here. Even then, success is very modest. On dog hunts with guides (list available from the Department) there is about a 50 percent chance of success. Other hunters score around 5 percent. Annual kill runs from 200 to 600, the smaller figure probably the most accurate average.

The northern mountains have the best bear populations. The Costilla region (see elk), the mountains between Santa Fe and Taos are stable range. The San Juan and Jemez Mountains west of Los Alamos, the Sacramento Mountains of the Lincoln NF near Cloudcroft (south-central) and the Gila drainage region north of Silver City should all produce good results.

JAVELINA

The first javelina season for many years was opened in New Mexico in 1963. Since that time there have been annual seasons in February and March. Currently permits, by drawing, are generally limited to about 250 annually. Permits may or may not be for residents only. Those who draw one season are ineligible the next. Hunters must check in and out for this hunt, at designated check points. Success is fairly good, averaging from 35 to 50 percent. The country is rough and the hunting therefore rather difficult.

The range is confined entirely to the southwestern counties: the southwest corner of Catron, western and southern Grant, the southwest corner of Luna, all of Hidalgo. Best areas: the Peloncillo Mountains and the Animas Mountains of southern Hidalgo Co. (see whitetail deer), the Pyramid Peaks south of Lordsburg (I 10), the Steins Pass region west of Lordsburg.

SMALL GAME

Squirrels of two species, the Abert or tassel-eared, and the red or chickaree, are hunted in New Mexico during brief seasons. Dusky (blue) grouse and squirrels have concurrent seasons and in general the squirrels are hunted in the same areas. While squirrels are not especially popular nor important in New Mexico, still there is some good hunting. The Apache Forest (southwest) in the Apache-Creek-Jewett Gap area, and the San Francisco River south of Reserve and in the Gila Forest are best places for the big tassel-eared squirrels. The chickaree is small and gets little attention, but is plentiful in the northern mountains, particularly in the mountains near Taos, and in the Jemez Mountains west of Santa Fe. There is a third squirrel native to New Mexico, the Arizona gray sqiurrel. It is protected.

Although rabbits, both jacks and cottontails, are found in New Mexico abundantly, especially in the south and east, they are not on the game list and get virtually no attention from hunters. Residents require no license to hunt rabbits. Nonresidents must have one of the several licenses offered— bird, big game, non-game.

PREDATORS

Coyotes are found in fair abundance from the high mountains to the desert floor. Bobcats are in good supply in the broken cliff country throughout the state. The mountain lion is the prize. Lions are fairly numerous in the rugged, broken areas of the southwest. They are no longer bountied in New Mexico. Lion hunting can hardly be successful without a guide. The Department will furnish a list. Guides are currently available at both Cliff and Reserve, villages in the Apache-Gila Forest country of the southwest, some of the best lion country. A special non-game license is required of non-residents for hunting all of the predators or pests.

REGULATIONS

Game laws pertaining to seasons, bag and possession limits, areas to be hunted, special hunts, license fees all may have numerous changes from year to year. For current regulations, and for other specific queries, write to: New Mexico Department of Game and Fish, State Capitol, Santa Fe, New Mexico 87501.

ARIZONA

Arizona is in general thought of as our most classical desert state. It is much more than that. Lying only a short distance north of the Gulf of California and the vast Sonoran deserts of Mexico, it does have typical rolling desert and arid foothill country in its southern portion, with the well-known saguaro and other cactus growth lending a most unique and scenic atmosphere. But even here in the south there are mountain peaks always looming, and many of these, especially in the southeast quadrant, rise swiftly to a zone of oak and juniper and grass and finally to become pine-forested slopes.

Northward the Mogollon Rim curves across a portion of the state, with both high prairie and timberland lying back from and along this rugged mesa. In the north the Kaibab Plateau stands along both sides of the deep gorge of the Colorado—a densely forested, ruggedly mountainous country. The Colorado River winds a tortuous path westward and then turns south to form a portion of Arizona's border with Nevada, and all of it with California. This river, and the Salt in east-central Arizona, are the two main systems. Several large impoundments have been built along them, and along smaller, less consequential streams. Thus this "desert" state is actually one of many contrasts.

Known as one of the chief sunshine states, Arizona has seen tourism become one of its greatest industries. Copper, mining, irrigation farming, and ranching, plus numerous expanding manufacturing businesses, have in some sections robbed portions of the state of its wilderness aspect. Fortunately, however, these areas are simply the ones with easy access—around Phoenix, Tucson, Yuma, and Flagstaff. Huge portions of the state still are true wilderness.

Roads to the population centers are excellent. Interstate 40 runs east-west through Flagstaff across the north-central portion. Interstate 10 and 8 likewise cross the south, via Tucson, and Interstate 19 and 17 begin at Nogales on the Mexican border and run north to join all the larger cities. Smaller state roads are good, too. Air travel, particularly to Phoenix and Tucson, is excellent from anywhere in the U.S. But for much of the best of the big-game hunting in Arizona, and some of the cream of the bird hunting, 4-wheel-drive vehicles or horses are still needed.

Arizona is indeed a most excellent hunting state. It has not had as much publicity for hunting as for tourism, for the simple reason that the game department has long had a policy of concentrating on quality hunting for residents, rather than advertising for nonresidents. This does not mean nonresidents are unwelcome; it is a matter of budget. And certainly there is ample room. Arizona is our sixth largest state, roughly 300 miles wide by 350 north to south, with a total area of over 113,000 square miles. The population at present is estimated at 1,635,000. Phoenix and Tucson, and their environs, account for well over half. Thus it is easy to see that adequate hunting room for both residents and nonresidents is everywhere.

557

Average annual hunting license sales are not high by standards elsewhere. The total is less than 150,000. Variety of game is as broad as the variety of the state's scenic terrain. Desert mule deer, Rocky Mountain mule deer, the diminutive Arizona whitetail (Coues deer) are all popular and abundant. Though elk hunting is limited, it is good. There are antelope, bear, javelina, occasionally a very limited buffalo hunt, and a scanty few permits for that great prize, the desert bighorn. Wild turkey, mourning and whitewinged doves, three varieties of quail, a scattering of blue grouse and chukars, plus waterfowl give bird hunters plentiful action. There are Abert, or tassel-eared, squirrels in northern pine forests, plus rabbits, and a good predator population, including the mountain lion. Among visitors and many residents the javelina, and the great flights of whitewinged doves, are among the main attractions.

There is virtually no difficulty in finding public lands in Arizona on which to hunt. Arizona is in fact unique in this respect. For example, there are within its borders seven National Forests—the Apache, Coconino, Coronado, Kaibab, Prescott, Sitgreaves, and Tonto. These, chiefly in the central, north-central, southeastern, and eastern parts of the state, comprise roughly twelve million acres. Total federal land ownership in Arizona makes up a startling 42 percent of the state's area. The state owns an additional 14 percent. Of this total 56 percent, most is open to public hunting. In addition, there are Indian Reservations totalling 27 percent of state area, and much of this is open under special tribal permits.

Two huge game range refuges, Kofa of 660,000 acres, and Cabeza Prieta of 860,000 were established years ago to give protection on a grand scale to the endangered desert bighorn. There are also several waterfowl refuges—Cibola, Havasu Lake, Imperial—that help bring and hold ducks and geese. A scattering of Wildlife Management Areas, chiefly set up for waterfowl, and with parts of their areas closed during season but the remainder open to hunting, round out the picture.

In general the National Forests, comprising the largest blocks of public land, will be of most interest to the hunter. Maps and details on each may be had by writing the Headquarters of the Supervisor, as follows: Apache NF, Springerville; Coconino NF, Flagstaff; Coronado NF, Tucson; Kaibab NF, Williams; Prescott NF, Prescott; Sitgreaves NF, Holbrook; Tonto NF, Phoenix. Other excellent maps are available showing Bureau of Land Management lands and game resources. At present one of these, of the Kingman Resources Area covering one and a half million acres, is available from the BLM Kingman Resource Area, Kingman, Arizona 86401. Others are planned for other Arizona BLM areas.

The Arizona Game Department, which is active in managing its game resources, is consistently successful in keeping a level of quality hunting in all categories. Hunters should know, for best planning, how the Department has the state divided. For seasons there is a general division into a North Zone and South Zone. The dividing line begins near Clifton on the eastern border and runs gently northwest through Phoenix to about Parker Dam on the Colorado River. There are seven Regional Divisions for management purposes. Regional supervisors are often excellent sources of last-minute, on-the-ground information. The regional headquarters are located as follows: 1—Pinetop; 2—Flagstaff; 3—Kingman; 4—Yuma; 5—Phoenix; 6—Tucson; 7—Pima.

Seasons and game quotas and permit numbers are set by smaller divisions, in Game Management Units. These are numerous—forty-odd—and some are further subdivided. Game maps setting seasons, which are available from the

Department, have these Units marked in so that one may see precisely what area is open and in many instances specifically to what area a permit is valid.

Accommodations for hunters are abundant all along the major highways, and in the larger cities and towns. However, numerous very small settlements showing on a highway map may have no places for hunters to stay. This is still in many sectors a pioneer country. It is best even along main roads to reserve ahead, since there is much tourist traffic during hunting seasons and also because the main arteries carry a great deal of cross-country traffic. For those who wish to camp, there is no problem. Arizona has over 300 listed campgrounds in the National Forests, the State Parks, National Parks, Indian Reservations, BLM Lands, National Wildlife Refuges, and in city and county parks. Lists of campgrounds and other visitor facilities are available from the Arizona State Development Board, State Capitol, Phoenix.

Weather is exceptionally variable. Early-season gunners after whitewings, for example, will find September extremely hot and dry, with middays in the southern part of the state where this shooting is done often well over 100 degrees. Later in fall, in the quail country, days will be balmy and comfortable. But any of the higher country to the north, or the mountains in the southeast, may be chilly and severe storms are not uncommon once fall is well underway. Depending of course on what one intends to hunt, and in which part of the state and at what altitude, it is best to go prepared any time after September for both mild and severe weather. The high north region for both deer and elk hunters can be deep in snow during part of the season, and weather can change rapidly here in the mountains.

For several varieties of Arizona hunting, it is best for visitors to hire a guide. Most resident hunters know their state well enough so they do not need to be guided. And, since there are less than 10,000 nonresident licenses sold annually, with many of these hunting birds only and a surprising number —about a fourth—after javelina, there are not as many guides available as in some of the northern mountain states. However, javelina guides are available in both Phoenix and Tucson, deer guides are fairly numerous in those areas, or booking out of those areas, and in the Kaibab. Although the Game Department cannot recommend any guide, it is a ready source of information, as are regional supervisors, as to availability of guides.

The deer and elk hunter will need rifles (there are archery seasons also of course) in the calibers of .30/06, .270, .308, with the .243 and comparable calibers perfectly adequate for deer. This last caliber, and even short-range ones such as the renowned .30/30, are heavy enough for javelina. Thus no particularly specialized arms are needed for Arizona big game. Bird hunters will hunt doves and quail mostly, with No. 7½ shot a good compromise. Waterfowl hunters should be sure to have No. 4 and No. 2 loads in addition. For the sporty tassel-eared squirrels that live in tall pines, a scoped .22 is the best arm.

QUAIL

Arizona has a wealth of fine quail hunting. To an eastern or southern bobwhite hunter, however, it could prove puzzling. For all of the quail species here—there are three—are desert, or as many hunters say, "running" varieties. These are the scaled or blue quail, the Gambel's quail, and the Mearn's quail. The southern half of Arizona is by far the best portion for quail, and these birds are the prime target of a great share of Arizona's bird hunters.

Because the limit, fifteen quail per day, pertains to the aggregate of all

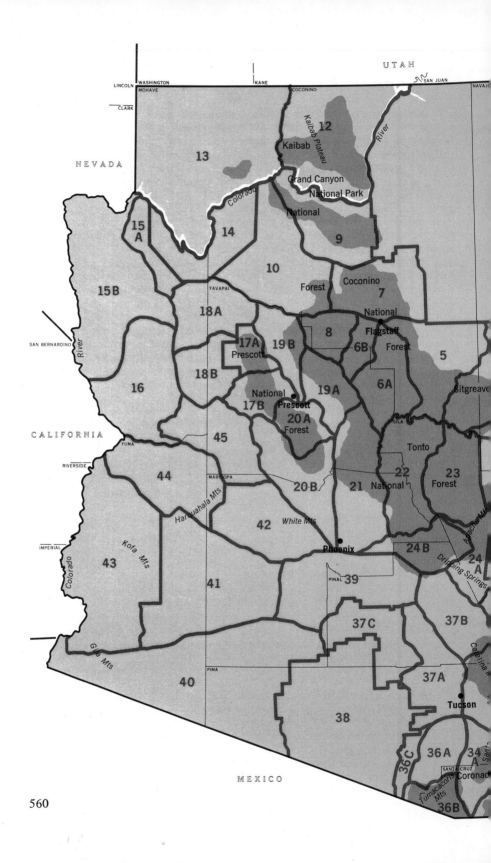

560

COLO.
MONTEZUMA
SAN JUAN

APACHE

ARIZONA

McKINLEY

—N—

SCALE IN MILES
0 5 10   20   30   40

11

VALENCIA

2

CATRON

3

ational

Forest

NEW

MEXICO

1B

Apache

25

GREENLEE 1A

National

San Carlos

GRAHAM

26   Indian Res.

27

Forest

GRANT

Gila Mts

Santa Teresa Mts

Graham Mts

HIDALGO

28

31

Coronado

Galiuro Mts

32

COCHISE

National   Forest

Mts

Chiricahua Mts

29

34B

National 30B Forest

35A   30A

561

three or any two, no separate kill figures are kept on Arizona quail, by species. The Mearn's is the rarest of the three. Although it ranges into New Mexico and west Texas, Arizona is the only state where it may be hunted. Both scaled and Gambel's quail are often found on the same ranges in Arizona. Because quail populations fluctuate violently due to weather conditions, it is difficult to strike an average annual total kill for a state as arid as Arizona. During good years, with enough moisture, bumper crops of quail virtually explode in the desert. In general, some 50,000 hunters take from three-quarters of a million to upwards of a million and a half quail in the aggregate annually here. During a recent good season, hunters in the better ranges averaged from five to eight quail per trip. This gives an indication of how good the shooting can be.

Mearn's quail, sometimes called Harlequin or "fool" quail, are concentrated almost entirely in portions of the southeastern corner of the state. Their range is not down on the desert floor, but up in the oak and grass zone, in the rolling foothills of the mountain ranges, a short distance below where the pine zone begins. Here they feed quite differently from other quail. Their mainstays of diet are small tubers of oxylic and various sedges, scratched up with their peculiarly long toenails. The Mearn's, as has been discovered in recent seasons, is an excellent game bird, lying tight to a dog and exceedingly difficult to locate without dogs. It is in this respect quite unlike the desert quails of the lower elevations.

Best areas for Mearn's quail are the southeastern corner of Pinal County, below Tucson, pockets of proper habitat as described above in Cochise Co., in the extreme southeast, likewise for Graham Co. above it, in the foothills of the Galiuro Mountains, and also oak-zone habitat in Santa Cruz Co., north of Nogales. One of the most accessible areas, and one of the best, is in the Santa Rita Range southeast of Tucson. Much of this region can be hunted by following State 83 south from Interstate 10, toward Patagonia. A small side road leads to an old mining area called Greaterville. Federal lands here have an excellent Mearn's quail population. This is an area of steep ridges and the walking is long and hard, but rewarding.

Scaled quail range over all of eastern Arizona except the far northeast, and continue about halfway across the state, with the heaviest concentration in the southeastern quarter. Gambel's quail range the desert and foothills over most of the state, again excepting much of the northeast. Because of the huge areas that offer rather uniformly good quail hunting for one or both of these species, it is best to look at the quality of several of the better counties.

One of the best counties is Yuma, in the far southwest. This is a land of roadless desert. Consequently it gets only a modest number of hunters, but they average a high kill per trip. Hunting from any of the main highways, Interstate 8, U.S. 95, 60, and 70 should get good results in Gambel's quail. The country just east of the river bed of the Colorado, near Parker and also near Yuma carries good populations.

For hunters who must drive out from headquarters in the larger cities, all of Maricopa and Pima Counties, where Phoenix and Tuscon are respectively located, will offer excellent hunting, although it can be somewhat crowded at times. This can be avoided by getting off the main arteries and using a 4-wheel-drive vehicle. More accessible are the areas along the Black Canyon Highway north of Phoenix, and the region of Roosevelt lake on the border of Gila and Maricopa counties northeast of Phoenix. All of the desert grasslands and cactus country of the southeast, covering Cochise, Graham, and Santa Cruz counties will have both Gambel's and scaled or blue quail in overlapping range. Ordinarily much of this hunting will be best in October, when early-morning temperatures are cool. But many Arizona quail hunters do the bulk of their hunting much later, after the first of the year, when big-game seasons are closed. Quail are then more active, but they are also much wiser and more difficult.

Mohave County in the northwest, with a hunter based in Kingman on Interstate 40, U.S. 66 and 93, is an excellent bet for Gambel's. Here a scattering of good side roads places one in almost limitless quality quail habitat, and the kill average is very high—in fact, one of the highest in the state. Prescott in Yavapai County, in west-central Arizona is also an excellent bet, with a modest number of hunters but in good seasons as many quail as farther south. The Verde River country is often excellent, hunting out of Cottonwood or Clarkdale on U.S. 89 Alt.

The masked bobwhite, once found in Arizona but extinct there since 1900, is seeing an exciting restorative attempt. This quail is slightly smaller than the bobwhite. The male has a brick-red breast and a black head and throat. Two brothers living in Tucson, Jim and Seymour Levy, gathered remnant masked bobwhites from deep in Mexico, raised some in their yard, and are almost solely responsible for the current attempt to launch the species again. Birds from their flock are now parenting flocks being raised at the U.S. Wildlife Research Center, Patuxent, Maryland, and some are being released in their old Arizona range as fast as they are available. It will be a number of years before hunting is possible, if at all.

For visiting quail hunters not familiar with the state, undoubtedly the Department's Region 7, which takes in all of the extreme southeast, and reaches up along the eastern boundary to the limit of the South Zone and into the interior to Roosevelt Lake, is in its entirety one of the best general locations. Here all three species are present. The Mearn's populations in the foothills of the Chiricahua, Santa Teresa, Gila, Graham, and Galiuro mountains are hardly touched by hunters. The Gambel's is the most numerous species and is broadly present throughout, in the lower elevations. Scaled quail overlap, with much good hunting for this species in the grassland foothills bordering Sulphur Springs Valley. Ample public lands are everywhere in Region 7, and accommodations may be had in any of numerous cities—Tucson, Globe, Benson, Safford, Douglas, Bisbee. There are also numerous roads passable by passenger cars to get one to the hunting.

DOVES AND PIGEONS

The mourning dove ranges statewide in Arizona, but the bulk of the shooting, for which the state is among the best, is across the entire South Zone. The whitewinged dove, on which Arizona has the highest limit of any of the several southern-border states that offer this shooting, is more selective. The whitewing is basically a Mexican and Central American species with the northern fringe of its range north of our borders. It nests in large concentrations across southern Arizona, but the bulk of the huge flocks drift south into Mexico even as early as late August. Traditional season opening for both whitewings and mourning doves is September 1. As long as the whitewings are in evidence, both are shot over much of the best dove range simultaneously. The whitewings, however, are inclined to appear in vast flights passing to and from feeding areas, whereas mourning doves fly as a rule in smaller, looser groups.

Some of the best of the whitewing flights are in the Yuma area, in the extreme southwest, and along the Gila River near Buckeye, which is west of

Phoenix on U.S. 80. A short distance south of Phoenix near Maricopa are other good flights. Some other top spots for whitewing concentrations: Arlington, just west of Buckeye; Laveen, almost on the southwestern city limits of Phoenix; Gila Bend, south of Buckeye; farther north at Salome on U.S. 60 and 70; all along the Gila River from Dateland on I 8 westward; the lower Centennial Wash southwest of the Harquahala Mountains, reached via U.S. 60-70 out of Salome; Cibola, just off the Colorado River north of Yuma, reached by side road off U.S. 95; any of the several valleys below Tucson.

Mourning doves are abundant in all these areas, and over virtually all of the south except in the mountains. They will stay regardless of weather, in good concentrations throughout the split seasons. An interesting sidelight on dove shooting is that in the higher country of the White Mountain area of north-central Arizona there are good dove populations during the early season.

The Game Department estimates there are at least ten million doves concentrated in Arizona when the season opens. The best of the dove nesting habitat in the state is along the Gila River, all the way from near Phoenix to Yuma. Good highways parallel all of the river. Most grain fields in this region, where doves concentrate, are open to shooters and so of course is a vast amount of BLM land. There is seldom any difficulty finding a place to hunt. Dove shooting is spoken of here as "best in the world." An average annual kill runs, for mourning doves, one and a half million or more, for whitewings upwards of three-quarters of a million. Compared to hunter numbers, this is tremendous.

By counties, the high-kill-per-trip ones for whitewings are those close to the border: Yuma in the extreme southwest; Santa Cruz toward the east on the border with Nogales, the focal city. These are also high-kill counties for mourning doves. Others are Graham in the east, Maricopa (Phoenix), Mohave in the northwest.

As this is written Arizona is looking forward to its first season in many years on bandtail pigeons. These large pigeons of the west coast and portions of the interior Rockies were for some years hunted in Arizona. Then the season was federally closed. They are migratory birds. Now it appears there may be some hunting again for this species. These are birds of the high country in general, nesting in pine forests and flying the high passes. Trapping and banding studies still under way in Arizona indicate that good populations exist particularly in the White Mountains. Hunters who have an opportunity to try bandtail hunting should check the laws from season to season. The Lakeside and Rye Creek areas accessible from U.S. 60 out of Show Low in east-central Arizona show promise. Other bird concentrations are around Prescott (U.S. 89), and northeast of Phoenix in the scattered groups of mountains west of the San Carlos Indian Reservation.

CHUKAR

The chukar partridge is relatively new to Arizona in open hunting seasons, has to date a limited range, and is still somewhat in the experimental stage. However, it appears to be holding its own and spreading its range. While areas suitable for it may always be limited here, still it furnishes some unusual but exceedingly rugged hunting. The birds range on the steepest hillsides in their adopted range, and it requires physical fitness to keep up with them. Invariably, they run up, not down.

Game Management Unit 12 is the area where they appear to be spreading their range most. This Unit is approximately in the center of the state along its northern border with Utah. It is roughly bounded by the Colorado River canyon on the east and south, and by Kanab Creek on the west. U.S. 89 and State 67 give access to it, with the settlements of Jacob Lake, Fredonia, and Marble Canyon location points. This entire area is rough and with few passenger car roads. The region of Snake Gulch has been the scene of good chukar kills recently, but scattered flocks require that a stranger check with Department personnel to help locate them.

The only other open area at this time is Unit 19A. This is the portion of Unit 19 lying east of U.S. 89. Refer to the state game-unit map for the precise area. Prescott or the Clarkdale-Cottonwood region are good base points. Alt. 89 bisects the area and Oak Creek Canyon is here. There are good camping spots, but bear in mind the chukar country is rugged and a 4-wheel-drive vehicle may be needed.

BLUE GROUSE AND PHEASANT

The blue grouse is not an important game bird here, for it has relatively little range and a brief (three or four day) season in only one place, Unit 1. This Unit is on the eastern border midway north-south. U.S. 666 runs from north to south through it, with Springerville, Alpine, Hannagan, the towns and settlements for location. Since only an average of fifty or sixty birds are annually taken, this is an incidental to an Arizona bag. Escudilla Mountain and Green's Peak are good spots to remember.

The whitewinged Afghan pheasant is under experiment in Arizona and appears to show great promise for future hunting. It has been introduced to agricultural areas west of Phoenix, and to the Arlington and Robbins Butte Wildlife Areas, which are state-operated lands. The Painted Rock Area near Gila Bend has also been stocked, and other releases have been made in Safford Valley, centered in Graham County in the southeast. As this is written a brief experimental hunt appears almost certain. Whitewinged pheasants are exceedingly wild, the only pheasant so far to do well and reproduce in arid areas of the southwestern U.S.

WILD TURKEYS

Arizona considers the wild turkey big game. Turkeys inhabit in varying populations almost all of the timbered country from the north Kaibab to the Mexican border. This is the Merriam's subspecies, a large turkey (weights of twenty to twenty-five pounds are fairly common) with a bone-white edging of the tail and more of the same high on the rump. There are currently two seasons, one in fall during which either sex may be taken, the other a spring gobblers-only season.

The areas open to spring hunting are a good criterion of turkey concentrations. As a rule this season falls in April, and applications for limited permits (around 1500 to 1600 currently) must be in by about mid-March, with the drawing shortly after. Only a few units—from a half dozen to nine or ten, depending on flock surveys—are open in spring. These, as with other game seasons in Arizona, are set by Management Units. Following are some of the best potentials for turkeys, either spring or fall.

Unit 1-A, which is the southern half of Unit 1. This is on the eastern border, midway, with Alpine the town below which most of it lies. An average of 300 permits is generally offered here, and chances of success hang around 15 to 20 percent. Unit 3 or a portion of it lies to the northwest, in Navajo and Apache Cos., south of Holbrook on U.S. 66, with Snowflake a center town. Unit 4 just west of the above, chiefly in Navajo Co., lies in between Routes

65 and 77, with Holbrook and Winslow base towns. Part of this Unit, as in Unit 3, is in the Sitgreaves National Forest. Number of permits for each of the areas so far usually runs about equal. Unit 9 is in the south Kaibab region, below the Colorado gorge in northern Arizona. This, and the north Kaibab area, Unit 12, generally have good turkey populations, although the north may not be open in spring. U.S. 180 runs north-south through the middle of Unit 9. This is in Coconino Co. and sizeable towns are scarce. Success has in the past run above 20 percent here, which is excellent as turkey hunting goes.

To the southwest of the above, in a portion of the Kaibab National Forest, Unit 8 is a rather small Unit to the south of Williams. This is excellent pine-forest habitat, typical of what Merriam's turkey likes. In the region to the northeast of Phoenix, above Roosevelt Lake, lie Units 22 and 23. These are fairly large areas, offer slightly fewer spring permits, but have a good turkey population. These are in general quite heavily hunted, although never crowded, and kill success runs somewhat less. State routes 87 and 288 run through these. This is a big forest country with not many main roads.

Although numerous other locations are available for turkey hunting, the above areas are best overall. There is good hunting for careful, expert hunters in some of the scattered mountain ranges east of Tucson. The Mogollon Rim country and northward are the prime ranges, however. For residents, well-known areas with few hunters and a low kill are good bets, but visitors will do best in the Units with the largest concentrations of birds.

Quite different from eastern and southern turkey hunting, the Merriam's is a bird of big timber and the high slopes and ridges. Total annual kill for Arizona averages around 1500 to 2000. Interestingly enough, the figure has been slowly climbing for some years. Part of this is because of new interest in this challenging hunting, with consequently more hunters. Overall success averages about 12 to 15 percent, down a bit from earlier years because of competition but still a good standard figure for turkey hunting almost anywhere.

WATERFOWL

Arizona is by no means one of the prime waterfowl states. Nonetheless it has at times some extremely good duck and goose shooting, under extremely pleasant weather conditions. Much here depends on weather farther north. If severe storms strike there, then waterfowl pour southward to find new waters that are not habitual wintering spots. This means as a general rule that Arizona waterfowling is likely to be at its very best right at the end of the season. Even so, shooting is spotty. Throughout the southern half of the state, if permission can be arranged to shoot ranch tanks, some great duck hunting is possible. These, however, are private.

To give an idea of Arizona's wintering waterfowl, the January waterfowl survey, a survey taken throughout the U.S., showed about 20,000 ducks and less than 4000 geese in a recent average year. Like many other states, Arizona is attempting to establish breeding populations of Canada geese. This is a trend in many states across the nation. Such birds, once a flock is established, become localized and furnish surplus shooting. Arizona is presently attempting to establish a flock on a lake location in the White Mountains. Prospects appear good.

In general waterfowl hunting in Arizona is along the Salt River and the Colorado and their impoundments. There is also a minor amount of jump- and sneak-shooting along the Gila River in the southwest, the Verde that flows through Cottonwood and near Jerome in the central portion, the Agua Fria west and north of Phoenix. The Topock marshes southwest of Kingman, in the northwest quadrant, sometimes offer excellent shooting. When storms strike farther north, Picacho Lake south of Coolidge and about halfway between Phoenix and Tucson is a good spot. San Carlos Lake, below Globe on U.S. 70, formed by Coolidge Dam, and Roosevelt Lake northeast of Phoenix are also good bets.

The system of impoundments along the Colorado River, the western boundary, is probably best of all. Here, along the river in Yuma and Mohave Counties, are located several Refuges—Imperial and Cibola on the river north of Yuma, Havasu Lake just north of the confluence of the Bill Williams River and the Colorado. The vicinities of these Refuges offer good waterfowling.

There are also several good Wildlife Management Areas, parts of which or all of which may be closed during season but which hold waterfowl in their areas. These are: Arlington, near Buckeye, west of Phoenix on U.S. 80; Chevelon Creek, near Winslow in the northeast off U.S. 66; Luna Lake, near Alpine (see "Turkeys") in the east; Parker Canyon, near Nogales in the south; Robbins Butte, near Buckeye.

DEER

Arizona offers three distinctively different types of deer hunting. Most popular and productive is hunting Rocky Mountain mule deer. This big mule deer ranges over much of the North Zone of the state, in the forested mountains. The desert mule deer, a subspecies, has as its chief range the southeastern quadrant. There is another mule deer subspecies, called the "burro deer," ranging in scattered abundance in the southwest, chiefly in Pima and Yuma Counties, in a variety of below-1500-foot elevations, in the willow and mesquite regions along the Colorado River, and in the dry washes farther to the east. Much of its range is seldom open to deer hunting, but that of the true desert mule deer is. The third type of hunting is for the small, sprightly Arizona whitetail or Coues deer, a whitetail subspecies with a range covering most of the South Zone but with concentration emphasis in the southeast, blanketing to a large extent the general top ranges of the desert mule deer.

Total harvest of deer annually in Arizona runs from about 17,000 to 20,000. High yields a few years ago shot the figure up well past 30,000 but during recent years deer herds have had various difficulties. They are in no danger, but for some years now will undoubtedly not yield as high a harvest as previously. To give a basic picture of Arizona deer hunting, during a recent season the total kill was 17,344, and overall hunter success stood at almost 20 percent. Of the total kill, 11,492 were Rocky Mountain mule deer, 2815 were desert mule deer, and 3037 were whitetails. Again looking at total kill, 12,313 deer came out of the North Zone, and 5031 came from the South Zone.

This quite obviously indicates that the North Zone offers the best deer hunting, so far as numbers of deer are concerned. Of the North Zone kill, only 821 were whitetails. But in the South Zone 2216 were whitetails. Since almost all desert mule deer are found in the South Zone, the figures indicate that for one wishing to hunt either whitetails or desert mule deer, chances are roughly even in the South Zone, but hunting will be more difficult. In fact, the modest kills on these deer do not so much indicate a lack of deer as far more challenging hunting.

The little Arizona whitetail—it takes an exceptional buck to weigh 100 pounds dressed—lives chiefly in the middle zone in altitude, up off the desert floor but not predominantly atop the high peaks so much as in the belt of oak, juniper, brush, and grass of the high foothills. These deer are exceedingly wary. They hide in the brushy draws and the thickets, lie low and dart out behind a hunter, or run all-out from a distant glimpse of danger. Their tight, uniform rack makes them one of the most handsome of deer trophies.

Best places to hunt the whitetails are as follows: the mountain ranges of the general southeast area, the Santa Ritas, crossed by State 83 southeast of Tucson; the Catalinas north of Tucson and to the east of U.S. 80 and 89; the Huachucas south of Benson, reached via route 90 or west of U.S. 80 out of Bisbee; the Grahams, the Galiuros, the Santa Teresa Mountains, all in southwestern Graham County and reached off U.S. 666, 70, and state 77; the Tumacacoris north of Nogales on the Mexican border; the Chiricahuas north of Douglas and west of U.S. 80 along the eastern border.

Any of the small ranges of desert mountains will have whitetails in this region. Relating some of the best areas to the Department game map, high South Zone kills generally come out of Unit 31 (west of Safford); Unit 34A south of Tucson and lying east on U.S. 89 (see Mearn's quail and Greaterville —this is the same country); Unit 35A taking in the Huachuca Mountains; Units 36A and 36B, both south of Tucson and west of U.S. 89.

Interestingly enough, the desert mule deer kills in these same Units and the same mountain ranges given above often approximately match the whitetail harvest. The desert mule deer will be found lower down in the foothills, mostly in typical desert situations, while the whitetails will be up in the oaks or on up in the larger timber at high elevations. However, the desert mule deer also appears in numbers in certain areas that are not especially good whitetail spots. Units 30A (south of Wilcox off I 10) and 30B (Tombstone, Bisbee region), Units 32 and 33, immediately east and northeast of Tucson, Unit 37B east of Florence and U.S. 80-89 all show good annual success. The high ranges in these Units also have good whitetail hunting. The whitetail kill often shows up small because hunters don't get back into the roadless areas after them, and when they do the going is tough. There undoubtedly are desert mule deer and whitetails in such places as the Galiuro Wilderness Area of southwestern Graham County that have never seen a human.

In the western portion of the South Zone, two of the best areas, although actual hunter success percentage is low, are Units 41 and 42. These large areas lie on either side of Centennial Wash below U.S. 60-70 and well east of U.S. 95. The Harquahala Mountains, the Eagle Tail, Big Horn, Vulture, and scattered other ranges are here.

For those wishing to hunt an area where both whitetail and mule deer range in the North Zone, Unit 22 northeast of Phoenix and crossed north-south by State 87 is excellent. Likewise, immediately east of it and directly north of Roosevelt Lake, Unit 23. Unit 24A is also a good bet. Globe, on U.S. 60-70 and State 77 centers this Unit, with the Apache Mountains on the north and the Dripping Springs Mountains to the south.

Though by far the greater share of deer are killed in the North Zone and are predominantly Rocky Mountain mule deer, the South Zone is covered in detail here because of the great interest, challenge, and lack of crowding in the hunting there. In the North, Unit 12, which takes in the north Kaibab, is far and away the most popular region for hunting mule deer in Arizona and annually furnishes the greatest harvest. This Unit lies to the north of Grand Canyon National Park, between it and the Utah border, with Fredonia and Jacob Lake the chief supply points and State 67 and Alt. U.S. 89 the chief access routes. One reason for a high kill here is that the herd constantly needs cropping and almost as many antlerless deer as bucks are taken each year.

Overall success runs as a rule better than 50 percent. For those who hire guides and pack to the most remote portions of the north Kaibab, real trophies may be found.

Other good North Zone regions: the forest area around Williams, south of the Colorado River and west of Flagstaff on U.S. 66; the mountains near Kingman and Seligman in the northwest, both reached from U.S. 66. In the extreme northwest, in the so-called "strip country" (Unit 13) some real trophies can be had. This is a country of few roads and rough but rewarding hunting. Far to the east, the Springerville-Alpine region of the Apache National Forest is a good producer. Also, one of the least known to date is below this point and north of Clifton off U.S. 666. This is the Blue Range, with the Blue Primitive Area located here. Pack-ins should be productive. Whitetails and mule deer both are found here.

ELK

For some few years elk have been increasing in Arizona. This is not a high-kill elk state. Total harvest averages from 1100 to 1600. Hunter success is quite good, stabilized usually around 25 percent. From 5000 to 6000 permits are offered. Rules for some time have restricted hunters to a permit (and an elk) only every three years.

Although some Units well known by residents get only a few permits and turn up high success for the knowledgeable, overall chances are best in the high-density areas of elk concentration. These are very definitely and consistently as follows: Unit 1, based on Springerville and Alpine on the eastern border, and crossed by U.S. 666, a portion of the White Mountains; Unit 25, immediately west, which takes in the entire Fort Apache Indian Reservation and where fees in addition to the regular permit are required; the Mogollon Rim country well south of U.S. 66, that is, below Holbrook, in the Sitgreaves NF, likewise for Winslow in the Coconino NF, and also south of Flagstaff. This whole area covers Units 4, 5, 6A, 6B.

PRONGHORN ANTELOPE

Some good heads come out of Arizona but hunting is quite limited. Permits average about 1200 annually, excepting poor herd years, and success runs around 50 to 55 percent. No person may purchase more than one antelope permit or take more than one antelope every three years. Best areas: Unit 10, north of Seligman on U.S. 66; the entire region surrounding Prescott to the northeast, north, and west, encompassing Units 17, 18, 19 in general; the habitat around and north of Springerville in the east, running up through the high plains toward St. Johns, Holbrook, Winslow.

BUFFALO

Buffalo range on certain ranches and public lands. Occasional hunts are offered for surplus animals. Permits seldom number more than 100 to 150, and are not necessarily offered annually. Only residents may apply. A hunter who has taken a buffalo in Arizona may not ever apply again. Check directly with the Game Department regarding possible season and location.

DESERT BIGHORN

This great and rare prize is doing well in limited numbers in Arizona under rigid protection. A small number of surplus rams with three-quarter curl or at least 26-inch horns are offered by permit drawing nearly every year. Recently permits have averaged eighty to ninety annually. Nonresident quota is not more than 10 percent of the total permits. Thus, drawing a permit is difficult and chancy. Hunting success has run surprisingly high over recent seasons for the few lucky applicants, averaging about 50 percent. These sheep range in several areas but yearly surveys dictate where hunts will be held. Most are in the extreme west and southwest, from the Kingman region to the Kofa Mountains north of Yuma. A few permits are offered for areas southwest of Phoenix and in mountain areas surrounding Tucson. Some transplants have been made to eastern Arizona, in the north Galiuros near Klondyke, and a new band may persevere here for future hunting. Check with the Game Department regarding the special hunts.

BEAR

The total state bear population (black bears—grizzlies are extinct here) is estimated at not over 1500. Annual kill is low, not far over 100 annually. Bear habitat in Arizona is not broad enough for a large population. Most of it is in the mountain areas of timber. A few are killed incidentally by hunters after other big game. Most are taken by hunters hiring guides with dog packs. Several guides are available. Check with the Game Department for names and addresses. Check carefully the regulations pertaining to use of dogs during other big-game seasons.

JAVELINA

This is one of the most popular Arizona big-game animals, especially with nonresident visitors. Upwards of 30,000 tags are now sold annually, with an average kill of over 5000 javelinas. Chances of success in general averages around 20 percent. These desert pigs range from the brushy desert floor up into the foothills and even in some areas to the oak zone. In general, however, the largest bands are located in desert foothill country, some of it very rough. The bulk of the javelina population is in the southeastern quarter of the state.

The large general region northeast of Phoenix and encompassing Units 22, 23, 24A, and 24B offer excellent hunting. So does Unit 26, farther east, which takes in the San Carlos Indian Reservation. The remainder of the best hunting is to the south. Some of this country, between Phoenix and Tucson (Unit 37 surrounding Florence), is as good as the north. But the best hunting of all is usually found in the foothills of all the small ranges and the desert sweeping out from them to the south and southeast of Tucson. These areas are located and described in the "Deer" material for the South Zone. They cover in general Units 30, 31, 32, 33, 34, 35, 36. This is the region of eastern Pima Co., all of Santa Cruz Co., most of Cochise Co. in the extreme southeast, and portions of Graham Co.

A few good pinpoint locations are as follows: the Klondyke-Aravaipa region of southwest Graham Co.; the south slope of the Graham Mountains in the same general location; foothills of the Chiricahuas in the extreme southeast, in Cochise Co.; the Santa Ritas south of Tucson; the Galiuros in Graham Co.; the Santa Teresa Mountains also located there. However, any desert foothill portion of southeast Arizona is a good possibility and it does not need to be far from settlements.

SQUIRRELS

This is the one state where hunters have a thoroughly excellent opportunity for top success hunting the unusual Abert, or tassel-eared, squirrel. This big, handsome squirrel with tufted ears, white belly, and frosted tail is a resident of the Ponderosa pine forests, where the trees are large and tall. Its close relative, the Kaibab squirrel found in the north Kaibab, is fully protected. A .22 is the best arm for the Abert. Some stay up a hundred feet from the ground in huge pines. They occur throughout the North Zone wherever their required habitat is available. Coconino Co. has the highest harvest, upwards of 20,000 annually. This is in the north-central area. The region from Flagstaff to Williams and surrounding forest is a prime hunting ground, with limited opportunities westward a short distance and south around Prescott. Arizona also has a minor amount of hunting for the Arizona gray squirrel, and for the red or spruce squirrel. Gila, Navajo, and Yavapai Cos. are next choice after Coconino. Mohave Co. also offers fair chances.

RABBITS

Cottontails are quite generally distributed over much of the state, with a preponderant population in the southern half. They receive little attention from hunters in general, although over 300,000 are taken annually. In the vicinity of the larger cities they sustain the most hunting. A general distribution means there are no special locations for hunting, but the high-kill counties are, in order: Maricopa (Phoenix); Yuma (Yuma); Pima (Tucson); Yavapai (Prescott); Coconino (Flagstaff); Pinal (between Phoenix and Tucson); Mohave (Kingman); Navajo (north of Winslow).

Jack rabbits of two varieties range abundantly over south Arizona and are shot as pests. The southwest area, and the desert regions of the southeast, are best.

PREDATORS

Arizona, as the last state to keep a bounty on the mountain lion, has moved one step closer to making it a full-fledged game animal. A bill has now been passed that allows the hunter to take a lion and either to keep head and hide or collect the bounty. It is predictable that soon this last hold-out state will place the lion on the protected list, with open seasons and quotas specified. Guided hunts are available. Check with the Game Department for outfitters.

Coyotes are in good supply, especially in southern Arizona, and bobcats are reasonably so. Calling is the method usually employed by varmint hunters here. Ringtails, raccoons, and an occasional badger are available for pest hunters. Also, this is the one state where, in the extreme south, the coatimundi is fairly plentiful and unprotected.

REGULATIONS

Game laws pertaining to seasons, bag and possession limits, areas to be hunted, special hunts, license fees all may have numerous changes from year to year. For current regulations, and for other specific queries, write to: Arizona Game and Fish Department, 120 Arizona State Building, 1688 W. Adams, Phoenix, Arizona 85007.

UTAH

Utah is a state of many and stunningly scenic faces. Awesome mountains, densely forested and in many places with snowy crests march down through the center of the state, covering approximately half of its entire area. To the west of these ranges, highest peak of which is 13,528 feet, lies world-famous Great Salt Lake. Although the lake, covering over 1500 square miles, has no outlet, it is at an altitude of above 4000 feet.

Surrounding it and spreading far to the south and covering approximately a third of the state's area is desert terrain, some of it so flat one can see for many miles, some of it with minor and arid ranges thrusting up in altitudes varying to almost 10,000 feet. East of the forested mountains there is more exceedingly rugged arid and semi-arid country, some of it total desert and much of it with breathcatching red-rock scenery, typified by Canyonland National Park and Arches National Monument. Here, in the southeastern quarter, are the Green and the Colorado rivers, joining south of Moab and soon becoming a huge impoundment some 186 miles long, most of it in Utah and formed by Glen Canyon Dam on the Colorado just south of the border, in Arizona.

The western border of the state is with Nevada. To the north are both Idaho and Wyoming, the latter jutting in the northeast into what would otherwise have been almost a perfect rectangle shape for the state, and cutting out a corner. To the east is Colorado, and to the south Arizona.

This large state, encompassing almost 85,000 square miles, was claimed from total wilderness by the Mormons over a hundred years ago. Today, curiously, it has become chiefly an industrial state, although mining, grazing, and some agriculture in irrigated valleys are also important. Although north-central Utah, along the valley where Ogden, Salt Lake City, Provo, and other cities are situated, is rather densely populated, over much of the remainder of the state the population is thinly spread. The total presently is slightly over one million. Approximately half of this total resides in and within a hundred miles of Salt Lake City. Thus, obviously, there is ample room for hunters.

Main highways are excellent, but there are not a great many of them. They run north-south down the center of the state, reach into the northeast and on a long slant to the southeast. Several also cross the desert west. Lesser roads in Utah are not always of the best quality because of the rugged terrain they must traverse. Although bird hunters after such species as pheasants and doves get along easily with a passenger car, big-game hunters, and hunters after forest and desert and mountain game birds find 4WD or at least a good pickup truck mandatory. A great deal of Utah high country and back-country can be reached best only by backpack or horse.

Air connections via several national and regional lines reach most of the largest cities. Railroad travel is also still available here with good service. Lesser airfields are numerous—there are well over 200—for those who wish to fly in to their hunting. A statewide aeronautical map may be obtained from the Utah State Aeronautics Commission, Salt Lake City Airport, that city.

Utah is an excellent hunting state and the sport is very popular. Close to 20 percent of the total population pursue some variety of shooting each fall, a high percentage when compared to the population. License sales have been averaging over 200,000 annually, and of those 15,000 to 20,000 are non-residents, chiefly deer hunters.

Game species are highly varied. In big game there are mule deer, elk, antelope, moose, buffalo, black bear, mountain lion. Waterfowl hunting is excellent. Upland birds include several species of grouse, chukar and Hungarian partridge, pheasants, doves, wild turkey, quail. There are also rabbits, and numerous predator and non-game species such as bobcats and coyotes. Deer, pheasants, and waterfowl are among the most popular species here, and for deer especially Utah has a national reputation.

Except in the densely populated cropland valleys where pheasant hunters may sometimes be numerous and thus create access problems on private lands, there is no difficulty in finding a place to hunt. Nearly 70 percent of the state is in public ownership. Almost all of this is BLM and National Forest land. Vast expanses of BLM lands lie both east and west of the backbone of the Rockies. A good source of information about these lands may be had from the U.S. Department of Interior, Washington, D.C., "BLM Developed Recreation Sites, Utah." The booklet, "Room to Roam," also a U.S. Government BLM publication, can be ordered, for fifty cents, from the Government Printing Office, Washington, D.C. It has maps that show very generally the extent of BLM lands here and in other western states.

The National Forests are without question the most important hunting lands in the state. There are seven either wholly within Utah or with only small acreage overlapping into a neighboring state, and there are two small sections of other National Forests that reach from the north into Utah. These Forests total over 8.25 million acres. A good reference to the Utah Forests is "A Guide to Utah's National Forests," which can be obtained from the Utah Travel Council, Council Hall, Capitol Hill, Salt Lake City 84114. Incidentally, numerous publications from this same source can be of value to hunters: "Utah's National Recreation Areas"; "Utah's Great Salt Lake"; "Discover Utah's Mountainland"; "Utah Fact Book."

The Ashley NF (1) comprises over 1,270,000 acres, is in the northeast, in the eastern half of the Uinta Mountain Range. The key city here is Vernal, at junction of U.S. 40 and State 44. It is the site of the headquarters of the Forest Supervisor, from whom maps and details of the Forest may be had. Cache NF (2) is north-central, and part of it overlaps into Idaho. Ogden, Brigham City, Logan are key points, with the last-named the headquarters. This Forest contains over 670,000 acres.

The Dixie NF (3), famed for its deer hunting, is in four tracts in the southwest. They total 1,883,688 acres. Headquarters is at Cedar City. U.S. 91 and 89 are the main routes. Fishlake NF (4) is north of the Dixie, is in four main blocks totaling almost 1.5 million acres. Headquarters is at Richfield, and U.S. 91, 89, 50 and 6 lead to the various blocks. The Manti-La Sal NF (5) is over 1.25 million acres mostly in central Utah north of Fishlake NF. But there are two tracts in the southeast, one near Monticello on U.S. 160, the other, overlapping into Colorado, out of La Sal Junction, U.S. 160. The central and larger part of this Forest is west of Price, the headquarters, and lies between routes State 10 and U.S. 89, with U.S. 50 and 6 crossing to the north.

The Uinta NF (6) is 794,686 acres in extent, most of it east of Provo, the headquarters. Smaller blocks are south of that city. U.S. 89, 91, 40, 50, 189 all reach the region. The Wasatch NF (7), a portion of which is in Wyoming, is administered from Salt Lake City, where details may be obtained from the office of the Supervisor. It is east of Salt Lake City and along the Wyoming border. U.S. 30S, 40, 89, 91, 189 are all access routes. Up in the northwest a tract of the Sawtooth NF (8), headquarters Twin Falls, Idaho, lies within Utah's borders. Nearby main routes are U.S. 30S and State 70. A small portion of the Caribou NF (9), also chiefly in Idaho and with the Supervisor's head-quarters at Pocatello, reaches into Utah just east of U.S. 191 on the northern border north of Brigham City.

Added to the BLM and NF lands are several Waterfowl Management Areas owned by the state. These will be described under "Waterfowl." On private lands, where some of the upland bird hunting must be done, permission is not too difficult to obtain, except in the most crowded areas. Recently new laws and arrangements with landowners have been established for pheasant hunting. These will be noted in more detail under that heading. There are some state-owned tracts on which various game species may be hunted, and attempts are constantly being made to purchase more. It is best to check with the Game Division, address at chapter end, regarding these and which may or may not be open during any given season.

Two booklets available from the Department will be excellent aids to any visiting sportsman and often just as valuable to residents. These are: "Utah Fishing and Hunting Guide" and "Utah Upland Game Birds."

Accommodations for hunters are numerous, and even most small towns have at least one motel and restaurant. Up-to-date information for any location can be obtained from the Utah Travel Council, address previously given. Hunters who camp have many opportunities. BLM and NF lands just described offer scores of developed camping sites and of course one may set up a camp without such facilities practically anywhere on these lands. The National Parks and National Monuments also have campgrounds. There are in addition State Parks, and a booklet about them furnished by the Division of Parks and Recreation, Department of Natural Resources, 132 South 2nd Street West, Salt Lake City 84101.

So far as weather is concerned, Utah hunters should go prepared for all kinds, and in any area removed from nearby settlement they should have shovels, tire chains, and other emergency gear. The high altitudes will be crisp to cold even in early seasons and are certain to have snow and cold weather later on. Desert hunting may be hot during the early fall, but the nights get crisp to chill. In any season the hunter is well advised to have a compromise wardrobe to fit any condition. Guns and ammunition for bird hunting will necessitate having shot sizes for pheasants of No. 7½ or No. 6, and these can do nicely for chukar and mountain grouse. No. 7½ is a good dove load, too. Waterfowl hunters will need No. 6 short magnums, or else No. 4s, and for geese No. 2 is undoubtedly most effective. For those fortunate enough to hunt turkeys, magnum sixes or fours are the ticket. For deer, any caliber comparable to the well-known .30/06 and .270 does nicely. Elk and moose can be hunted effectively with these also, but some hunters will prefer one of the heavier magnums for these endeavors.

There is no requirement that nonresidents must be accompanied by guides. However, the Department compiles each year a list of guides and packers, and it can be had on request. This does not constitute any recommendation.

KEY TO HUNTING AREAS

1. Ashley NF
2. Cache NF
3. Dixie NF
4. Fishlake NF
5. Manti-LaSal NF
6. Uinta NF
7. Wasatch NF
8. Sawtooth NF
9. Caribou NF
10. Bear MBR
11. Fish Springs MBR
12. Ouray MBR
13. Locomotive Springs WMA
14. Salt Creek WMA
15. Public Shooting Grounds WMA
16. Harold S. Crane WMA
17. Ogden Bay WMA; Howard Slough
18. Farmington Bay WMA
19. Timpie Springs WMA
20. Clear Lake WMA
21. Powell Slough WMA
22. Stewart Lake WMA

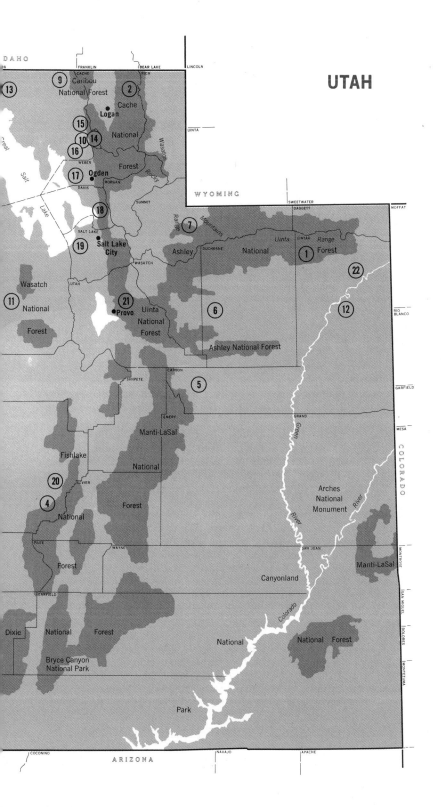

UTAH

PHEASANT

Utah does not have any vast amount of suitable pheasant range, but this bird is nonetheless the most popular of upland game birds with hunters. An average of 80,000 hunters each season bag approximately a quarter-million birds. One recent peak season nearly 300,000 were taken.

Pheasants were introduced to Utah about 1890. Transplanting and natural spread of the birds have resulted in pheasant populations now and for many years in all suitable habitat within the state. It is interesting to note that the pheasant kill, and the number of hunters participating, have both been unusually consistent over the past twenty years.

The pheasant is found in Utah only in agricultural areas, and almost entirely in irrigated situations. Currently there is alarm at destruction of pheasant habitat through clean farming and by crowding of urban areas. Virtually all of the pheasant habitat follows the mountain valleys down through the central part of the state, and in the northeast generally along the line followed by U.S. 40 across Duchesne Co. and toward Vernal.

Some counties are allowed only short hunts of five to seven days. Others get from two to three weeks. Hunts on federal and state lands have special seasons set. Some of the Waterfowl Management Areas offer pheasant hunting. (See "Waterfowl.")

Recent rulings have been in effect setting up plans for pheasant hunting on private lands. Under these rules, landowners band together and put their holdings into units, some of which may be posted "Open to Pheasant Hunting," and some "Open to Pheasant Hunting by Permission." Landowner permits are free and public permits are sold for $3. At least 75 percent of lands in any unit must be open to hunting. Fees pay valid claims for hunter damage. Interested hunters should check with the Department regarding full briefing on this system.

For a number of seasons three counties: Box Elder and Cache immediately below the border in the northwest, and Utah to the south, surrounding the city of Provo, have furnished roughly half of the total pheasant kill. However, these counties also get a large number of hunters. Salt Lake Co., surrounding that city, also is heavily hunted, and accounts for from 6 to 10 percent of the total kill.

Other counties with somewhat fewer hunters and consistently good kill percentages are: Weber Co. in the Ogden area; Davis Co. just to the south. Emery Co. is a good location. So is Millard Co. Both Sanpete and Sevier Cos. in central Utah offer fair to good shooting. Duchesne and Uintah Cos. in the northeast furnish together about 8 percent of the total kill, with hunting along the river valleys. As a rule the counties mentioned show the highest success percentage, or kill per day per hunter. The other open counties show somewhat lower success, and of course many have only small areas of pheasant habitat.

MOURNING DOVES

The dove is second in importance among Utah's upland game birds. There have been seasons here since 1951. The bird ranges statewide but is of course predominantly a bird of the croplands and pasture lands, and is also found in desert locations wherever food is available. As a rule some 20,000 to 25,000 dove enthusiasts bag anywhere from 100,000 to a quarter-million doves annually.

Because of their migratory habits, and changes in food and water distribution year to year, it is not possible to predict where the best dove shooting will be during any given season. Open rangelands where waterholes and windmill seeps furnish a place for doves to drink often provide the best shooting, better than cultivated lands. Morning and evening flights to the rangeland waterholes give most hunters their best chances. Much of the best dove shooting is of course on private lands, and permission is necessary.

The mourning dove kill follows to some extent the same county trends as do pheasants. Usually Box Elder, Salt Lake, and Utah Cos. get the major hunting pressure and also furnish the majority of the kill, from 40 to 50 percent of the total. During a recent season Utah, Salt Lake, Box Elder, Tooele, Juab Cos. in that order yielded the greatest dove harvests, and in slightly different order sustained the most hunting pressure. However, the highest per-day hunter success occurred in Juab Co.

A tabulation for five consecutive seasons shows, nonetheless, that for all practical purposes dove-hunter success is likely to be good in almost any county. It is simply a matter of locating the proper food conditions, getting a proper break in the weather, and of being there during the time of heaviest migration. A list of counties showing the highest consistent success is as follows, in alphabetical order: Beaver, Box Elder, Cache, Duchesne, Iron, Juab, Kane, Millard, Morgan, Rich, San Juan, Sanpete, Summit, Tooele, Uintah, Utah, Washington, Wayne. This is about the same as saying, when one locates these counties on the map, that the mourning dove is well distributed over all of the state.

BANDTAILED PIGEON

This large forest pigeon is native to the West coast and to the spine of the Rockies. It is migratory, and only a modest nesting population exists in Utah. There has not been an open season in many years. Recently, however, studies of the Rocky Mountain nesting and migratory bandtails were begun. The result was a series of trial seasons, two of which at this writing have been held in portions of eastern Arizona and western New Mexico, with good results. Presently Utah, along with Colorado and the states mentioned, has been involved in a banding program. The first successful banding was done in southeastern Utah, along the fringes of one block of the Manti-La Sal NF out of Monticello, in 1969. These birds, which nest in Utah, winter farther south. Whether or not Utah will be allowed a token open season is problematical as this is written. Hunters who are interested in this wonderful high-country forest game species should check with the Department for latest developments.

CHUKAR PARTRIDGE

The chukar was first introduced into Utah in the 1930's, but it was not until 1951 that intensive efforts were begun to establish this arid-country bird. Over the early decades some 128,000 chukars had been set free throughout the state in 140 locations. Soon the bird was well established and in 1958 the first season was held. Today the chukar is found in proper habitats statewide, and is the third most important uplander.

There is far more good chukar habitat in Utah than there is for pheasants, and it is felt that this bird will do better and better over coming years. Although the kill fluctuates widely year to year because of nesting conditions, an upward trend seems to indicate that the future for this species may be very bright here and that just possibly it may eventually surpass the pheasant in popularity and importance. The annual bag over a term of a decade shows an average of about 14,000 hunters and a kill of approximately 32,000 birds. But there have recently been years where the chukar kill rose to over 73,000. Both the number of interested hunters, and the total kill, appear to be steadily on the upswing.

There is a very substantial amount of chukar hunting on the public lands, especially rough BLM lands and along the fringes of the National Forests. In most recent seasons Box Elder Co. has furnished the largest percentage of birds, far higher than any other county. As high as 38 percent of the total state kill has come from here. Other high countries: Uintah, Tooele, Salt Lake, Carbon. Hunting pressure also is high in these, and in Cache Co. But ordinarily Carbon Co. looks good for kill compared to number of hunters. One late season it furnished 6.9 percent of the birds, got only 2.72 percent of the hunters. Over recent seasons the most consistently high success with chukars has been in Uintah and Grand Cos., with Box Elder and San Juan following. However, throughout the state the hunting can be excellent if one simply takes time to locate the concentrations of birds, and then has the stamina to chase them on the ridges. Chukar hunters who will learn to use a call, for locating coveys, and who will then circle the coveys and hunt from the top of a ridge downward will have the best success. Hunting uphill simply allows the birds to outrun the hunter and get over the crest, whereas an approach from the uphill side generally will flush them.

HUNGARIAN PARTRIDGE

The Hun is basically a covey bird of grain stubble and its fringes. In the western mountain states, in any location where this fine game bird has access to croplands with brushy hillsides or gullies or stream-course cover nearby, it appears to do well. But it also appears unable to colonize the more rugged terrain suitable for the chukar. Thus, in Utah it is doubtful that the Hun will ever be generally abundant. Nonetheless, it is locally important and an exciting find when a hunter stumbles upon a group while after other uplanders.

There were several attempts to establish the Hun in Utah some years ago. None was successful. However, in the north and west a modest Hun population has become rooted here, it is thought from birds established in Idaho and Utah. Seasons have been held since 1958, concurrent with the chukar season, and statewide so far, although this is misleading to many hunters, because the Hun is by no means distributed statewide.

Almost all of the Hun population is along the northern border in northern Box Elder, Cache and Rich Cos., and down the western border in a rather thin strip of western Box Elder, Tooele, Juab, and extreme northwestern Millard Cos. Some birds are found in valleys reaching down from the north along Great Salt Lake, and there are pockets here and there that hold a few birds. Wasatch Co. has a fair population. Hunters should seek grainfields with sagebrush borders for best habitat.

Official statistics show, late years, as many as 17,000-plus Huns taken in a year. This may be an optimistic view. A long-term average report shows an average of slightly more than 3500 hunters bagging about 9000 birds per season. But since so many Huns are shot as incidentals by other upland hunters statistics of this sort are virtually meaningless. Regardless, Box Elder and Cache Cos. along the northern border show over 90 percent of the total Hun harvest. Over a period of several seasons Box Elder Co. has reported the largest kill, and Cache has been second. However, some fair hunting for this species is available in several other counties. Because local populations may not be well known even to hunters within the state, hunters interested in this bird should check for any current season with Department personnel.

GROUSE

Several species of grouse are native to Utah. Although they were all perhaps important in early days, none is especially popular with sportsmen today, but at least three are birds deserving of attention and legal to shoot. These are the blue, ruffed, and sage grouse. The sharptail was once abundant in northern Utah, in valleys and in foothills. But man's encroachment decimated the flocks by market hunting while farmers destroyed the habitat. Commercial hunting was also a major factor in the reduction of the sage grouse to a precarious and endangered population.

In 1925 hunting for both open-country grouse species was suspended. In more recent times there has been no open season on sharptails, and probably never can be, but sage grouse have seen some hunting, and undoubtedly will, by careful management, for some time to come. Blue and ruffed grouse, lumped together today in this state and termed "forest grouse," which is unfortunate because they are not at all similar in habits or in habitat preference, still are open to hunting and because of their "back-in" habitats presumably long will be.

The total grouse bag in Utah is not large, but for specialists and enthusiasts there is good hunting. For sage grouse the same counties are not necessarily open each season, and the kill as well as hunter participation thus fluctuates. The average bag is probably about three or four thousand birds, with two thousand or more hunters involved. Occasionally the kill runs up to 11,000 or more. There are sage grouse populations widely scattered over the state. One is in the northwest. Others are in pockets distributed down through the center of the state, and one line of population runs east from the mountains roughly along U.S. 40 toward Vernal and up into the far northeast. At least one other pocket of fair abundance is located along the eastern border, in the southeast, not far from Moab. The sage grouse continually requires careful management in order to survive. Because of yearly fluctuations in bird numbers, and changes in counties that are open, it is best for hunters to check with the Department before any given season, to ascertain where the best shooting may be

Because blue and ruffed grouse are not covey birds but are scattered, and in mountain forest habitat, they never seem to be as numerous as they probably are. The blue grouse ranges throughout the Rockies down across central Utah, with the best population in the northern Wasatch Range. Ruffed grouse range is somewhat more restricted, the best of it in the Cache NF in the north, and eastward across the Wasatch and Ashley National Forests. Total harvest per season of the two species combined is not more than ten or twelve thousand, about evenly divided.

There is no problem in finding public hunting for the various grouse species. BLM and NF foothill lands have sage grouse, and the best of the forest-grouse hunting is on the NF lands. If it is ever possible to have a token season on the sharptail, it will be in the northern area north of Great Salt Lake. This is the only remaining sharptail range in the state.

QUAIL

There is some rather good quail hunting in Utah, but it is restricted to small and widely separated areas. The Gambel's quail is native to southern Utah but this is the northern fringe of its native range. It is found in bottomland desert situations, usually in Utah in sagebrush country near cultivated areas. Probably the best habitat, and greatest average abundance, is in the southwest, in Washington Co. There are scattered pockets of fair abundance in bordering counties to the north, and there are others following a general line along the Colorado River and its tributaries in the southeastern quarter of the state. Because these desert quail are dependent upon rainfall to produce the desert vegetation they require, their numbers fluctuate from season to season.

Kill statistics over several years show Washington Co. by far the best producer for this species. As high as 22 percent of the total quail kill (Gambel's and California quail are lumped together) is taken in Washington Co. The total aggregate kill has run over the past decade from about 14,000 to 28,000 birds. No other counties within Gambel's quail range show a substantial percentage of the total bag.

The California quail was not native to Utah. It is a bird of the Pacific coast rather similar in appearance to the Gambel's. It was introduced to Utah over a hundred years ago, has established itself in good numbers in several parts of the state. A very few are found in specific locations in the southwest and central area. The major range is in the north-central region, in brushy areas along streams or open water in the valleys. Open woodlands and grassy valleys intermingled often hold good numbers. This quail is more populous than the Gambel's.

County kill figures are of course influenced by hunter pressure in the regions of the greatest human population. But by and large the following counties show the best success with California quail over past years: Box Elder, Carbon, Davis, Morgan, Salt Lake, Summit, Uintah, Utah, Weber. Although these birds are found along the stream courses on NF lands, much of the hunting is on private lands, by permission.

Recently a new quail species has been introduced to Utah. This is the mountain quail, largest of the quail native to the United States. The transplant was made with birds trapped in California. They were released in Davis Co., which is north of Salt Lake City, and in the La Sal Mountains near Moab. It is hoped that they will be able to establish themselves and offer future hunting.

EXOTICS

Like many other states, Utah has experimented with numerous exotic upland game birds. Among these are the whitewinged Afghan pheasant, several species of francolin, see-see partridge, several of the tinamous. Whether or not any of these birds will establish themselves in huntable numbers is not known at this time.

WILD TURKEYS

There is no proof that the wild turkey was ever native to Utah. Attempts were made early in this century to launch the species here, but the stock was of the eastern variety and it did not take hold. In 1952 the Merriam's turkey of the western mountains was stocked in the La Sal Mountains, Grand Co., the birds obtained from Colorado. Later on releases were made in a number of other counties: Daggett in the northeast, Garfield, Kane, San Juan, Sevier, and Washington in the south. The first Utah turkey hunt was held in 1963. With three areas open during the next four years for a fall season, the kill was, per season, as follows: 75, 81, 50, 43. A special permit was required.

More recently there have been spring seasons, during late April and early May. A small game license plus a $3 turkey permit allows one to hunt. In the spring of the most recent season, all of Iron, Kane, Garfield, Sevier, Wayne, Grand Cos. were open, plus portions of Washington and San Juan. During some seasons so far there has been a 2-gobbler bag limit, and success has run as high as 22 percent.

Turkey hunting in Utah is therefore just now getting under way and it is likely to get much better and more widespread season by season. Since the Merriam's is a forest bird, most of the hunting occurs on National Forest lands, open to the public.

WATERFOWL

There is excellent duck and goose hunting in Utah. There are some 400,000 acres of wild marshlands much of which are available to the public. There are also over 60,000 acres in eleven state-owned and developed Waterfowl Management Areas. There are also three important federal refuges in the state. The most important of these is the famous Bear River Migratory Bird Refuge (10), with nearly 65,000 acres. The headquarters where one may obtain details are at Brigham City. The Refuge is fifteen miles west. As many as a million ducks consort here during fall migration. Ordinarily pintails are in the majority but there are also teal, mallards, and other species. A portion of the Refuge is open to hunting each season. The other two Refuges, which gather many ducks and geese to their vicinities, are Fish Springs (11) at Dugway, Ouray (12) at Vernal. Both have areas for hunting.

Some 35,000 hunters on the average hunt waterfowl in Utah. The duck kill over a period of years ran about a quarter-million birds but has recently jumped in some seasons to almost half a million. The goose kill also is substantial, although it fluctuates rather widely. Over a twenty-year period it has run as low as 7500 and as high as 18,500. From 12,000 to 14,000 geese may be considered the average. By far the major share of the goose kill is Canadas. The remainder are snows, with one or two thousand bagged each season.

Most of the state-owned WMAs are situated around Great Salt Lake, which has much excellent marshland habitat along certain portions of shoreline. Locomotive Springs WMA (13) contains 12,000 acres, is situated at the northern tip of Great Salt Lake, can be reached from Snowville, U.S. 30. Salt Creek WMA (14) is north of the Bear River Refuge, can be reached from the town of Corinne on State 83 and thence on secondary roads. Public Shooting Grounds WMA (15) is in the same area, lies along the north border of the Bear River Refuge and is crossed by State 83 out of Corinne. There are approximately 12,000 acres here. The Harold S. Crane WMA (16) also is in this general region. It is a fairly new WMA, can be reached by going west from Route 84 at Smith and Edwards.

Ogden Bay WMA (17) is farther south, on the east shore of Great Salt Lake along the Weber River delta. There are 13,700 acres here. It is located west from Roy, near U.S. 91, and on through Hooper. Immediately to the south of this WMA is Howard Slough with 2300 acres, managed as a part of Ogden Bay. It is reached south and west from Hooper. Farmington Bay WMA (18) is still farther south but also on the Great Salt Lake shore northwest from Salt Lake City. There are 10,000 acres here near the Jordan River delta. Entrances can be reached from either Bountiful or Farmington. Timpie Springs WMA (19) is on west around the lower end of Great Salt Lake. The turn off north to the area is on U.S. 40 at Timpie Junction. Approximately 1440 acres are in this WMA.

Clear Lake WMA (20) is in west-central Utah. It is a 4700-acre marsh northwest from Fillmore, U.S. 91, is on the edge of the west desert, at Clear Lake, Millard Co. This is a stopover for migrating waterfowl. Powell Slough

WMA (21) is in central Utah Co., on the shore of Utah Lake, a short drive north from Provo on Route 114. Stewart Lake WMA (22), a small unit, of 635 acres, is in northeastern Utah, in the northeast corner of Uintah Co. It is just off U.S. 40 at Jensen.

A unique aspect of waterfowling in Utah concerns the recent permits for whistling swans. The population of these large birds had grown to such proportions that it was felt some cropping might be desirable. The first season was held in 1963, and seasons have continued annually since, as this is written. It is not predictable, however, whether there will be a season each year. As a rule there have been 1000 or more permits issued. The permits are free, but application must be accompanied by a valid Utah hunting license. When applications exceed permits, a drawing is held. This is a most unusual hunting experience. In one recent season success was about 25 percent. Interested hunters should contact the Department for current details.

SMALL GAME

The only small-game animal is the cottontail. It was given game animal status in the mid-1960s. The season is long, ordinarily running from late September to March. Cottontails range throughout the state in all suitable habitats. San Juan Co. in the southeast, Duchesne, Uintah and Daggett Cos. in the northeast are considered especially good locations. However, fair to good hunting can be found anywhere that forage conditions allow substantial rabbit populations to build up. Presently Utah is embarked upon a management program for this small and popular animal.

There are some Abert, or tassel-eared, squirrels in Utah, in the big-pine areas of the forests. It is illegal to shoot them.

NON-GAME ANIMALS AND BIRDS

Blacktailed jackrabbits are plentiful in the desert and foothill country. Whitetailed jacks are found in lesser numbers. Often heavy winter snows concentrate them in lower valleys along mountain foothills where this terrain adjoins the desert.

Coyotes, bobcats, and some foxes are found throughout the desert and foothill regions. Though these predators have not so far received much attention in Utah, there is excellent sport for callers, or hound enthusiasts, who will seek them out.

Crow shooting is good in Utah in the winter. Probably the heaviest concentrations of birds are found surrounding Utah Lake in Utah Co., and to the south in Sevier and Washington Cos.

Among small varmints and pests, there are rockchucks and ground squirrels. Oddly, the snowshoe hare or rabbit, found in the mountains, is so far without protection. There are a few in the aspen and conifer zones throughout most of the state.

BEAR AND MOUNTAIN LION

The black bear is not abundant in Utah and has for many years been eliminated whenever possible by stockmen. However, it is now on the game list and offered substantial protection, although the open season is extremely long. Presently the season is closed only from July 1 through most of October, and when opened is open only to residents, who must obtain a $1 tag plus a valid hunting license, deer, combination, or small game. The tag method has been adopted as a means to determine the bear harvest. About the only means to a successful bear hunt in Utah is to hire a guide who specializes in this sport.

The mountain lion, or cougar, has been placed on the game list in most western states. In Utah it is still hunted year-round. However, a $1 tag now must be purchased. The purpose is to determine the annual kill. Lions may be hunted by either resident or nonresident. Residents may hunt on any of the several types of licenses, plus the tag, but the nonresident cougar license is presently $50. Interested hunters should acquire the guide list from the Department and book with one who has a well-trained hound pack.

DEER

Utah is an excellent mule deer state. The kill has for some years averaged about 100,000 animals per year, and the overall success ratio goes as high as 50 percent, but often in certain areas reaches to 80 percent or more. In some high-kill years a harvest of over 130,000 animals has occurred. In recent seasons it has been just under 100,000. Some 140,000 resident, and up to 15,000 nonresident hunters participate. Deer management is handled by numbered, and named, Units. The Proclamation map must be obtained each season. It shows the Units, and notes quotas on antlerless deer, also the bucks-only Units, and the varying Unit seasons.

With over seventy Units, and in an average season all but two or three showing hunter success percentages above 25 percent, it is virtually impossible to spot the top deer areas. The entire state, outside the heavily settled portions, furnishes excellent hunting, and quite commonly one need not go far from any city to bag a buck. During one typical season the following Units showed success of above 50 percent and up to 70 percent.

In the far northwest, the western portion of Box Elder Co., the Grouse Creek portion of Unit 1. Lost Creek, Unit 6, most of which is in northeastern Morgan Co. The area partly bordering Unit 6 to the southeast, Coalville, Unit 19. Duchesne, Unit 22, in upper Duchesne Co. The various parts of the Daggett herd area, Unit 25, mostly in Daggett Co. in the extreme northeast. The Range Creek portion of Unit 27, in eastern Carbon and northeastern Emery Cos. The Book Cliffs, long famed for mule deer here, Unit 28 along the eastern border. The Hill Creek area is also a part of Unit 28, and a high-success location. The Moab region, Unit 30, and the southwestern part of the state in the several sections of Unit 31, Blue Mountain, Elk Ridge, Indian Creek. The season from which statistics are quoted here saw Moab and Blue Mountain each with almost 70 percent success.

Fish Lake, Unit 44, and Last Chance, Unit 45, in central-south, partly in eastern Sevier Co. and partly in western Emery. Monroe Mountains, Unit 48, to the west of those just named, in Sevier and Piute Cos. Both sections of the Boulder area, Unit 51, in portions of Wayne and Garfield Cos. Unit 55, Kanosh herd, mostly in eastern Millard Co. The Beaver sectors (north) of Unit 56, south of Unit 55 and mostly in eastern Beaver Co. The Parowan region, well known to deer hunters, Unit 57, in Iron and Garfield Cos., the area mostly lying between the towns of Parowan and Panguitch, in the Dixie NF. The West Zion herd, Unit 58, south of the last named.

This of course is only a sketch of where the good hunting is. Many Units bordering those named turn up almost as high a percentage, and in some seasons higher.

An excellent region with good access and a tremendous number of deer is in the southwest, from St. George to Richfield, and from Bryce Canyon National Park to the western border. This is a scenic area and seldom gets snow during the October hunt. It does get a good influx of California hunters as a rule. For the average hunter the east, central, and southern Units will be best, because they are farthest removed from the centers of heaviest human population. La Sal, east of Moab, as well as the city of Moab, is a good headquarters. The Price region has some huge bucks, in rough country. Monticello, on the eastern border of the Manti-La Sal NF, and just west of the renowned Dove Creek deer herd in Colorado, is an excellent bet. Already mentioned are the Book Cliffs and Daggett Co. in the northeast, both excellent. And, in the southwest, the high cliffs to the northwest of Kanab, called the Pink, White, and Vermillion Cliffs, south of Bryce Canyon, turn up excellent heads.

ELK

Utah elk herds are not large. Hunting to date has been for residents only. And currently one may not apply again for a permit until the fifth season after having held one. Recently as many as 5580 hunters have hunted during the open-bull season on specified Units, and there are also some special permits in limited-harvest areas. During one late season the kill was 1178 bulls, and 174 animals on the limited areas. Because it is not possible to predict in what areas elk will be open, hunters are best advised to contact the Game Department for any given season regarding details. Usually the regulations are set by early July.

MOOSE

There are a limited number of moose in northern Utah, most of them on the north slope of the Uinta Mountains. The herd consistently stays in good shape and is slowly increasing. Hunting, however, is restricted to residents only, and permits are few. The first hunt was held in 1958 on the north slope of the Uintas. Each season since then an average of ten permits have been issued and about half the hunters have been successful. In recent seasons there have been as many as twenty permits for the Uintas, and five for the Ogden River Unit. Those who draw a permit are not allowed to apply again. Hunters should request details from the Department.

ANTELOPE

Originally Utah had large herds of antelope, but the animals were brought close to extinction by settlement and indiscriminate hunting and changes in use of the land. Today there are only small herds. From 100 to 150-plus permits are usually offered each season, with these split into quotas for the several Units where antelope may be safely cropped. The Units are widely scattered over the state, where habitat is suitable to sustain the small bands. Only residents may apply, and permits are given out after a public drawing. Check with the Game Department for location of open Units, time of application, and other details.

BUFFALO

Establishment of a wild, unfenced buffalo herd was begun in 1941 in the Henry Mountains of Eastern Garfield Co. with a few animals brought from Yellowstone National Park. This is steep, rugged terrain up to 10,000 feet and the buffalo, now numbering upwards of 100 head, have adapted to the rocky slopes and to the forest portions also. As a control on the herd, the first hunt was held in 1950. Since the early 1960s a few permits have been given each year, by drawing, on a residents-only, one-in-a-lifetime basis. Ordinarily about ten are issued a season. The kill most seasons is 100 percent. This is a most interesting and unusual hunt. The Game Department will furnish details.

SHEEP

Bighorns once roamed Utah's high country. The Rocky Mountain bighorn was brought to extinction by meat hunting and other influences. A remnant population of desert bighorns remained in the southeast. Plans were made some years ago to reintroduce the Rocky Mountain bighorn, but it was not until 1966 that stock became available. The first were brought in from Wyoming and placed in a fenced area near Brigham City, in March of 1966. The same year more were brought from Canada and placed in the same holding area. Progeny from these animals have been transplanted elsewhere in the state.

Very limited hunts for desert bighorns are held in San Juan Co. in the southeast. Developments are underway in this same part of the state to make water available from seeps, so sheep may utilize it around the year and thus spread their range. Although modern-day sheep hunting is on precarious footing at this time for Utah, the future appears promising for at least a token number of mature ram permits annually, eventually for both varieties.

GOATS

Mountain goats are not native to Utah. However, in 1967 a total of eight goats were obtained from Washington for an attempt at stocking. Two died before reaching their destination. The remaining half dozen were taken by helicopter into the rugged mountain region east of Salt Lake City between Big and Little Cottonwood Canyons. They were lowered by net sling and released. Sightings have been made periodically and apparently the goats are doing well. It is presumed that they will establish themselves, but no hunting is anticipated until such time as a modest surplus is available.

REGULATIONS

Game laws pertaining to seasons, bag and possession limits, areas to be hunted, special hunts, license fees all may have numerous changes from year to year. For current regulations, and for other specific queries, write to: Department of Natural Resources, Division of Fish and Game, 1596 W. North Temple, Salt Lake City, Utah 84116.

NEVADA

Nevada is a unique state, legalized gambling capital of the U.S., tourist entertainment mecca, a vast stretch of desert broken by chains of rough mountains running mostly north to south. It is a rugged plateau, much of it in the Great Basin and hemmed in by mountains to the west and north and partly by the lonely, shimmering, and seemingly endless stretches of the Great Salt Desert of Utah to the east. To the north it touches both Idaho and Oregon, to the west has its entire border with California, the lower half slanting southeastward deeply toward the deserts of the river valley of the Colorado. In the southeast the Colorado River forms a portion of Nevada's brief border with Arizona and here Hoover Dam backs up huge Lake Mead.

Nevada is something of a puzzle in its economy. Once a great silver state, it is still a producer of copper and other minerals in large quantity, a grazing state, an agricultural state in several sectors with irrigated farming, a proving ground for atomic devices, foremost builder of gaming equipment, a state of opposites, ski resorts and desert gambling palaces attended by swarms of tourists. Notwithstanding this apparent teeming activity, Nevada has some of the largest stretches of all but uninhabited desert and mountain wildernesses on the continent.

Main highways are excellent, and get one to most sectors of the state. But they are by no means abundant. Interstate 80 slants upward across the state from Reno in the west headed for Salt Lake City. U.S. 95 and 93, widely spaced, come down from the north and continue, on either side of the state, to zigzag to exits in the south. U.S. 6 and 50 are the main east-west highways in addition to I 80. There are numerous state routes, but there are also huge plots of roadless country, where only 4-wheel-drive trails or horse trails lead. Air transport is fast and excellent to Las Vegas in the southeast corner, and to Reno in the west. Otherwise charter planes take one to almost all the smaller cities. Most other settlements have less than a thousand population.

Nevada is an excellent hunting state but has had little hunt publicity. The big nightclub shows, the divorce mills, and the gambling have grabbed the spotlight. Certainly there is ample room for hunters. East to west in a straight line Nevada is about 350 miles across, before it starts on the west the fast slant to its southeastward triangle corner. North to south along the eastern border it stretches over 425 miles. Although it ranks seventh in size, it still encompasses 110,540 square miles, over twice as much, for example, as New York and Pennsylvania combined. Second smallest of the states in population, it presently has less than 450,000 people spread very thinly over the huge area. People of the small villages are friendly, rugged, direct. Outside the bright-light centers, Nevada is still quite frontier.

Hunters are almost as scarce as the scanty rainfall. An average of around 55,000 to 65,000 licenses are sold annually, not counting extra tags. Nevada has some rather unusual laws concerning nonresidents, and these to some extent keep visitor numbers low. There is a quota system on deer, with a limited number of nonresident licenses allowed, and these only in specified Management Areas. Nonresident bird hunters may hunt only certain game birds, in certain counties only. Total of nonresidents entering the state to hunt each year seldom exceeds 6000 to 10,000. Of those, almost all are for deer hunting and as many as 5000 of them for Elko Co. alone, where the Humboldt National Forest is located and most quota permits given.

Hunting can be astonishingly good. Deer success runs on the overall up toward 50 percent in the average good years, and in some areas way up to 75 percent or more. These are mule deer. The state also has limited numbers of antelope, elk, desert bighorn sheep. Birds are varied—turkeys in very small numbers, chukar and Hungarian partridge in good supply, sage grouse, blue grouse, pheasants, Gambel's quail, valley quail, mountain quail, scaled quail, doves, ducks, geese. There are two kinds of cottontails, one of them the diminutive pygmy or "brush" rabbit, plus jackrabbits. Mountain lions, bobcats, coyotes are quite plentiful.

Public lands in Nevada are so vast that there is hardly any problem of access. The state has one of the nation's highest percentages of public domain —approximately 85 percent. There are two immense National Forests, each in several blocks that are scattered from the extreme north and east to the central and southwest sectors of the state. Maps of these, and detailed information, may be had from their Supervisor Headquarters: Humboldt NF, Elko; Toiyabe NF (partly in California), Reno. The former has over 2.5 million acres, the latter three million plus. There are large BLM lands and Reclamation Bureau lands also.

There are in addition several large waterfowl refuges, a Desert Game Range of over two million acres down in the southern triangle, one of the chief U.S. stands of the desert bighorn. There are ten well-scattered Wildlife Management Areas, most of these managed chiefly for waterfowl in an otherwise predominantly arid sweep of country.

The Game Commission divides the state for management purposes into the following Districts: Owyhee, northeastern; Black Rock, north-central; Charleston, southern; Toiyabe, central; Wheeler, east-central; Sierra, western. Numbered Management Areas (or Units) further subdivide these Districts for season purposes on various game. The game maps showing these divisions are available from the Commission. Also, maps may be had showing, for example, the location of springs and quail-watering devices, to assist bird hunters and others.

Although mule deer can easily be hunted without special equipment by the average hunter who is willing to work hard, visitors are well advised to book hunts with a guide who offers either horses or 4-wheel-drive transport. Many of the best trophy areas require one or the other transport means, and of course horses are best in many ways, for the far-back, roughest country. In at least one area, the Jarbridge Wilderness Area of the Humboldt Forest in the northeast, no motorized travel is allowed. The address of the Nevada Guides and Packers Association: Mountain View Guest Ranch, Wells, Nevada. The Game Commission also will furnish information regarding guides.

Vast areas of Nevada are arid desert just as rugged as the snowy peaks that often loom distantly. Hunters off the main track, and after such prizes as desert sheep, will find maps a must, and water in good supply mandatory. Check with the Game Commission in regard to sources of detailed maps for any specified area. There is a great deal of primitive, roadless country.

The Game Commission is doing an excellent job in Nevada, under difficult circumstances: small human population, modest income from license sale, exceedingly harsh range conditions, and the necessity of keeping a large variety of species available. Active and expert management participation is commendable. There are experiments in progress with exotic birds, such as the several francolins, the Himalayan snow partridge, the Imperial sand grouse. Of most intense interest, and greatest success, are the careful nurturing and expanding of the desert sheep bands.

Accommodations for hunters in Nevada are somewhat limited because of the small population. Happily, however, the great influx of tourists to the nightspot cities, and the few main routes and long drives between towns, have placed an unusual number of motels in small villages that ordinarily might not have such accommodations. Most waystops on any of the main routes therefore have lodging and food, but it is never amiss here to reserve ahead.

For campers, the situation is quite good. Campgrounds are well scattered over the state. There are several State Parks, National Recreation Areas and Monuments, numerous campsites in the National Forests, which are a main center of visiting-hunter activity. Bureau of Land Management and Bureau of Reclamation campgrounds are also available. For self-contained campers who need no facilities, thousands of desert acres are wide open. The Department of Highways, Carson City, is a good source of information on camping and other travel matters.

Weather in Nevada depends entirely on time of a hunt, and the game. Early seasons are hot in all of the high plateau desert, yet there may still be snow in the high mountain country. Mid-fall bird hunters in most altitudes will experience enjoyable, mild weather. Deer hunters during the best times of later seasons, when mule deer are in migration to wintering grounds, should be prepared for snowstorms as well as for bright, crisp weather. The high altitudes will be cold throughout late seasons and usually with much snow.

Rifles for mule deer should be in the general category of .270, .308, .243, .30/06, with good scopes for long ranges, although shots are not all at long range. There is little hunting for the other big game because of limited herds. One lucky enough to draw a sheep permit will need a spotting scope. Bird hunters will need mostly modest loads, No. 8, 7½, 6, with highbase No. 4 preferable for ducks, and a few No. 2s for geese.

CHUKAR

It is an interesting fact that the chukar, an exotic introduced into the U.S. some years ago but not widely huntable until the past few years, is the most popular and numerous of Nevada's several upland game birds. This arid-country bird seems perfectly adapted to the Sagebrush State. Over twenty years ago Nevada had its first unlimited hunt for chukars, the first such hunt held in the U.S. Although populations fluctuate drastically in the severe ecology of the desert, Nevada hunters have harvested as many as 175,000 chukars at peak periods. More recently 131,000 were taken in a season. Drought conditions recently cut the population so that the kill during one season was less than one-sixth that of the former. Yet as soon as a moist year arrives the population zooms.

In Nevada chukars inhabit the rocky, barren ridges where cheatgrass grows, anywhere from 4000 to above 9000 feet. Open hills and mountain slopes without agricultural development are preferred by this hardy, handsome bird. Springs or water seeps hold the coveys. During the better years there are huntable chukar populations in all counties except Clark and Lincoln, in the extreme southeast. However, some stocking has been done there and the birds may take hold. To the north, in mideast counties, the Diamond and White Pine Ranges have scattered coveys.

Western and northwestern counties, and Elko Co. in the northeast, plus some of the central area, are the best rangest to date. Resident hunters may hunt chukar in any open country. Nonresidents are restricted to specified counties, which must be checked by visitors previous to any given season. Ordinarily the high-kill counties are: Elko, extreme northeast; Eureka and Lander southwest of Elko County and in the general north-center of the state; Humboldt, one of the best, in the northwest below the Oregon line; Pershing, immediately south of Humboldt, with a fairly good average population; Churchill, to the south of Pershing, with a somewhat lower but still good population. Washoe, in the far northwest, a narrow county north-south along the California line, occasionally has good shooting, and so do the other smaller western counties.

In Pershing Co., I 80 takes one near some good chukar hunting, in the lower ranges and foothills to the east of the highway, out of Lovelock, Humboldt, Mill City, and on the west side along the Trinity Range. Side roads lead to more, but no accommodations are near. Humboldt Co., north of Pershing, has abundant birds in all foothill areas. U.S. 95 and State 8A lead to many good spots. So do the few side roads. Foothills of the Santa Rosa Range, along U.S. 95, the Pine Forest Range in the northwest sector and south of State 8A, the Jackson Mountains south of Quinn River Crossing on 8A are places to try.

In western Nevada, the Sierra District takes in Washoe, Ormsby, Storey, Douglas, Lyon, Mineral, and Churchill Cos. Chukars are in good supply here. The Desatoya Range and the Clan Alpine Mountains in southern Churchill Co., reached north of U.S. 50 out of Carroll Station and East Gate, are good areas. So are the Virginia Mountains south of Pyramid Lake, Storey Co., State 33; and the Stillwater Range, State 59 north of U.S. 50 at Salt Wells, Churchill Co. All the other small ranges in this western district will offer chukars in the foothills and middle, barren elevations.

QUAIL

There are four varieties of quail in Nevada. Three—the valley quail, Gambel's quail, mountain quail—are native. Scaled (blue) quail were introduced from New Mexico. Quail numbers fluctuate widely year to year in this dry region. Also, quail are by no means spread evenly over the state. During most seasons all counties are open, however, although shooting may be sparse in many local spots.

At the present time scaled quail furnish very little hunting. They appear

KEY TO HUNTING AREAS

1. Key Pittman WMA	5. Railroad Valley WMA	10. Sunnyside WMA
2. Pahranaget Federal Refuge	6. Fernley WMA	11. Ruby Marshes
3. Overton WMA	7. Humboldt WMA	12. Humboldt NF
4. Stillwater WMA	8. Mason Valley WMA	
	9. Scripps WMA	

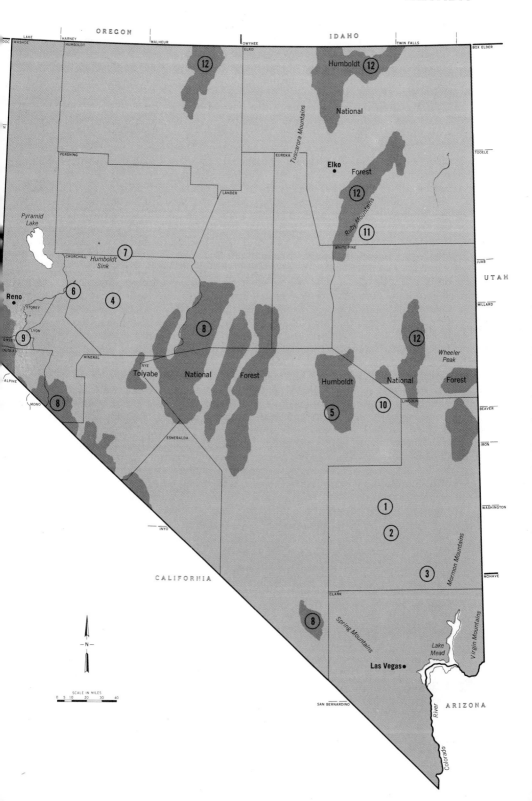

NEVADA

to be established however in the vicinity of the Sunnyside WMA, in eastern Nye Co., south of Lund. This is almost on the eastern County border, reached via State 38. The Sunnyside WMA is a 14,817-acre plot. The settlement of Sunnyside is just east of the White River. Scaled quail have spread along this river valley since their introduction on the Management Area. Other transplants may be made elsewhere in due time.

Mountain quail, large, handsome quail of the foothills and medium altitudes, also are found only in very limited numbers and are something of a specialty. Very few are killed, but more could be if hunters diligently sought them. This is a grand, little-known game bird. Here are a few ranges where mountain quail may be found: the Pine Forest Range, northwest Humboldt Co. south of Denio on route 8A; Virginia Mountains, southern Washoe Co. southwest of Pyramid Lake, state 33 from Reno and Sparks; any of the Sierra foothills and middle altitudes along the western border of Nevada; the Wassuk Range of western Mineral Co., west of Walker Lake and U.S. 95; the White Mountains of Esmeralda Co. along the slanted southern border with California off route 3A out of Dyer. There are also a few mountain quail scattered in the ranges of Churchill and Lander Cos.

The Gambel's quail is chiefly of the southern region, a true desert dweller of the yucca flats. Although it is found in agricultural situations, it does not necessarily depend on such habitat, and does well under the most severe conditions. Clark Co., in the extreme southeast triangle, is the prime Gambel's range. The annual kill here in good years will reach 40,000 or more, but drops during dryer years to as low as 12,000 or less. Southern Lincoln Co., immediately north of Clark Co. on the eastern border, also is good Gambel's habitat. Likewise portions of Nye Co. to the west. In the agricultural valley areas of Clark Co. the population fluctuations of Gambel's quail are not as radical as in their desert habitat. This is private land, and permission must be asked, but usually is forthcoming, and the hunting is likely to be excellent. The Mormon Range, southeast corner of Lincoln Co., reached off I 15 out of Las Vegas, is in general a very good area for Gambel's quail.

The valley, or California valley, quail is the most widely distributed quail of Nevada and makes up the largest segment of the kill. It must be remembered that Nevada does not have masses of hunters, and that among Nevada bird hunters the larger chukar gets the bulk of attention. Thus an annual kill of only several thousand quail in a county does not necessarily reflect scarcity, but simply lack of pressure.

Among the better counties for valley quail: Churchill, key town Fallon, U.S. 50-95; Douglas. Gardnerville, U.S. 395; Humboldt, Winnemucca, U.S. 95 and I 80; Lyon, Yerington on U.S. 95 Alt.; Ormsby, west of Lyon Co., with Carson City the key city; Pershing, Lovelock on I 80; Storey, based on Virginia City; Washoe, the western border county north of Reno. These are the counties with consistently higher kills than some others. Part of this is because of access from fairly large population centers.

Eastern Nevada, in the country around Ely (U.S. 93-50 junction), has good valley-quail hunting in farmland habitat. Key villages: Preston and Lund south of Ely, state 38; Baker on the Utah border off U.S. 50 and 6 on State 73. Northwest of Baker these quail are now found (by introduction) in Spring Valley, between the Shell Creek Range on the west and the Snake Range to the east. Wheeler Peak, rising over 13,000 feet, is a landmark to the south of Spring Valley. In all of the valley-quail areas, it is best to hunt the stream courses and, just as the bird's name says, the valleys.

PHEASANT

Pheasants are not plentiful in Nevada, but have been established in areas of large-scale agriculture, which are few, and in those few places during good years there is a modest amount of shooting, some of it quite good. Harvest figures for over a dozen years show that hunters average per season from less than one bird to slightly more than two. The entire kill seldom runs more than 20,000.

Because cultivated lands, the only feasible Nevada habitat, are invariably privately owned, the Game Commission has stocked pheasants only where owners agree to open portions to hunting. Best counties are: Lyon, Douglas, Churchill, Pershing, Humboldt. Washoe and Ormsby also at times have good populations, and in Lander, Clark, Lincoln there are seasons some years. Current annual conditions and likelihood of seasons should be checked with the Commission. There is some put-and-take shooting on Wildlife Management Areas. The Key Pittman WMA (1) near Hiko, Pahranaget Valley, Lincoln Co. (State 38), shows good numbers taken at times, as does the area of the Pahranaget Federal Refuge (2) near Alamo to the south on U.S. 93.

The Afghan whitewinged pheasant is being tried in Nevada. There has been some shooting for it in the Virgin River Valley at the northern end of Lake Mead, Clark Co., extreme southeast, and near Overton in the same area on the 9805-acre Overton WMA (3). Currently most of this is put and take.

HUNGARIAN PARTRIDGE

This bird was introduced to Nevada over forty years ago but has never become really abundant. Habitat is marginal. Harvest counts are also often lumped in with chukar, which makes a true picture of abundance difficult. However, unlike the chukar, the Hun stays chiefly along stream courses and near agricultural developments. Scattered coveys are found mostly in the northern counties in such areas. Elko Co. is considered best. Some are also found in Humboldt and in the northern portion of Washoe, a few in White Pine Co., near Fallon in Churchill Co., and near Lovelock in Pershing Co. Invariably these are all adjacent to farmlands.

SAGE GROUSE

This large grouse was once the most plentiful of all Nevada's upland game birds. Fifteen years ago it began a general decline over most of the west where it had once been abundant. Recovery has been slow, but with fair results. The sage grouse is found in general throughout Nevada, excepting probably Clark Co. in the southeast triangle. The best counties are across the northern tier: northern Washoe, Humboldt, and Elko. The kill here averages from 2000 to 4000 birds annually for each county in good seasons. Central counties—Eureka, Pershing, Lander, White Pine—also offer fair populations. Most of the other counties do not have important kills. The statewide kill in good seasons averages 10,000 to 15,000 birds. The sage grouse is a bird of the open sage areas, feeding to a large extent upon this plant. Where alfalfa fields or comparable irrigated crop fields are surrounded by sage, the populations generally stay rather consistently high. The open, sage-covered foothills of the various mountain ranges mentioned for the above counties under chukar and quail will usually have sage grouse.

Nonresidents should check before planning a hunt for sage grouse—or in fact for any upland birds in Nevada other than chukar, Huns, and quail. Nonresidents are usually excluded, and on the birds they are allowed to hunt there may be as few as five or six counties open to them.

OTHER GROUSE

The ruffed grouse, though not native, has been stocked experimentally on Soldier Creek in the Ruby Mountains of Elko Co. in the northeast. The nearest ruffed grouse are found in Idaho, and it is hoped they may take hold in northern Nevada. To date the plant appears quite promising, but there is at time of this writing no hunting.

The blue, or dusky, grouse, large grouse of the high elevations and forests, is found in Nevada generally in the upper altitudes among conifers, although aspens and various fruit-bearing shrubs such as chokecherry may hold birds. It is seldom abundant, and in addition is usually in areas where few hunters care to work hard enough to find birds. The kill rarely runs over 300 to 700 birds annually. Scattered small groups are found in suitable habitats of the cool altitudes in the various mountain ranges, particularly in White Pine, Lincoln, Elko, Eureka, Nye, Ormsby, Douglas, Esmeralda, Mineral, and Lander Cos.

WILD TURKEYS

Merriam's turkeys from Arizona were tried in small numbers in Nevada, the first stocking done in 1962. As this is written one token hunt has been held during which two birds were taken. This was in Clark Co. There are also a few turkeys in Washoe Co. It is possible that turkey hunting may evolve at some future time, but at present the tenuous population will not sustain hunting pressure.

MOURNING DOVES

The migratory mourning dove is an important game bird in Nevada, the kill generally exceeding that of any of the upland game birds. It runs on the average from 90,000 to 120,000 annually. The season is usually statewide. Nonresidents, properly licensed, may hunt. The shooting is likely to be excellent around any grain fields, and along river bottoms and near desert waterholes. The several WMAs, which are in general managed primarily for waterfowl, usually furnish good dove shooting also. Refer to "Waterfowl" for a listing and locations of these.

The counties that average the highest dove kills are Clark and Nye in the southeast and Lyon in the southwest. Other good counties: Churchill, Elko, Eureka, Washoe, White Pine. Much good dove shooting might be had in other counties, but doves are simply not sought to any great extent outside the regions of the larger towns and cities.

In the extreme southeast, a scattering of whitewinged doves is found some seasons in the southern tip of Clark Co.

WATERFOWL

Hunting for ducks, with mallards most popular, and for several varieties of geese including Canadas, is surprisingly good in Nevada, and locations are more numerous than one might suppose. Nonresidents may hunt. For ducks the high-kill counties: Churchill, Lyon, Pershing, in that order, followed by Clark, Washoe, Elko, Douglas, Lincoln, Mineral, Nye, White Pine. Good kills of geese are common in: Churchill, with the species split about 50-50 between "dark" and "white" geese; Lyon, Clark, Washoe, where mostly dark geese are taken; Mineral for white geese.

As in other states, many marsh areas are on private lands or under lease. The several WMAs where good public waterfowling may be found are as follows: Stillwater WMA (4), northeast of Fallon (U.S. 95-50), Churchill Co., 143,866 acres, some of which is refuge and over 27,000 acres in marsh; Railroad Valley WMA (5), south of Currant in northeast Nye Co., U.S. 6-State 20, 57,200 acres; Fernley WMA (6), northeast of town of same name, Lyon Co., U.S. 95-Alt. 40, 13,645 acres; Overton WMA ("Pheasant"), near town of Overton, Clark Co., north end of Lake Mead; Humboldt WMA (7), south of Lovelock, I 80, over 36,000 acres in Pershing and Churchill Cos.; Mason Valley WMA (8), north of Yerington, U.S. 95 Alt., Lyon Co.; Scripps WMA (9), Washoe Valley north of Carson City, 2659 acres emphasizing goose production; Sunnyside WMA (10), south of Lund (off U.S. 6 on State 38) in eastern Nye Co., almost 15,000 acres; Key Pittman WMA ("Pheasant"), in the Pahranaget Valley near Hiko, Lincoln Co. The Ruby Marshes (11) in southern Elko Co. are considered excellent. Areas surrounding all of the large lakes of the west and the several reservoirs are also good. There are resident goose populations at several lakes and marshes, among them Pyramid Lake in the west, Humboldt Sink south of Lovelock, Pershing Co., and at the Ruby Marshes. Check the WMAs carefully as to special regulations for all hunting.

RABBITS

There are cottontails of two varieties, the common species and the pygmy or brush rabbit. There are also abundant jackrabbits, the blacktailed jack ranging over most of the state, the larger whitetailed jack in smaller numbers in the northern counties. Nonresidents may hunt all rabbits.

Rabbit populations fluctuate drastically in Nevada from season to season. The cottontail kill runs anywhere from a few thousand to as high as 70,000 but will average generally about 30,000 annually. Any brushy stream or wash course, and all districts where there is agricultural activity have cottontails in varying supply.

PREDATORS

Bobcats and coyotes are fairly plentiful. No bounty is paid on either and either may be hunted at any time. Almost anywhere in good rabbit (their chief food) country both these species are quite plentiful, the bobcat mainly in the rough, broken foothills and the coyote in the vast open areas. No great amount of hunting pressure is applied to either. Predator calling could be an excellent sport throughout the state.

The mountain lion is fairly plentiful and is not bountied. There is currently no closed season nor limit. A hunting license is required. Lions may not be trapped, or hunted with a handgun. The only successful method of hunting lions is with a guide and a good pack of dogs. Lion guides are available. Check with the Game Commission, or with the Guides Association, address in opening portion of this chapter.

DEER

The only deer in Nevada are mule deer, all of them of the Rocky Mountain subspecies with the possible exceptions of straggling specimens of California and Inyo mule deer in the Sierra region of western Nevada. The state deer herd is estimated at around 200,000. All seventeen counties have mule deer. Bulk of the deer population, however, is in the following counties: Elko, Washoe, Humboldt, White Pine, Lincoln, Nye, Eureka, Lander. Elko has by far the greatest deer population. Almost all Nevada mule deer make a migration from summer and fall to winter ranges. Some of these migrations are quite early. Check with the Game Commission to make certain of migration time in any specific area.

For some seasons the deer harvest in Nevada has been on a down trend. This is not presumed to be a permanent situation. The kill has in some instances been smaller over recent seasons only because of less pressure, fewer permits offered. Much of the state is open to either-sex hunting. The buck kill averages twice that of the antlerless kill. Total kill runs from as low as 14,000 to as high as 50,000. Success is often quite high, around 40 to 50 percent, but many hunters have to work hard for a deer. There are a number of trophy heads to be had in Nevada for the serious hunter willing to backpack into the more remote areas.

The southern counties are on the whole the least productive. Some areas with fair herds and good hunting are given below. Southern Lander Co. is one. Here, south of Austin on U.S. 50 and west of the Reese River, is the Shoshone Range, with quality hunting. The Fish Creek Range in the same area produces some trophy heads. At the north end of Lander Co., the Tuscarora Mountains north of Battle Mountain and up toward Midas in Elko Co. are excellent when snow makes the deer move. State 18 leads to Midas and there are side roads. In Pershing Co., to the west, the Humboldt and Tobin Ranges, both with limited access and light hunting because of it, produce trophy deer. I 80 is the key to getting to the general region. In the same county, the Selenite Range, and the East Range east of Humboldt and northeast from Lovelock on I 80, are excellent bets. This is a region of few roads. Pershing Co. is not for hunters who wish an easy kill.

In Humboldt Co., in the northern tier, U.S. 95 cuts across the Santa Rosa Range. This is a favorite area and a good producer. Most hunters concentrate on the east side. The opposite slope will produce better and less crowded hunting, but pack-ins are necessary here for best chances. Horse Creek, Pole Creek, Flat Creek are good pinpoint spots. High country to the west of the Pine Forest Range in northwest Humboldt Co., reached from State 8A, has trophy bucks. The Quinn River region near U.S. 95 and just below the Oregon border also furnishes big bucks.

In the east-central portion of the state, eastern White Pine Co. and northern Lincoln Co. produce good hunting. The Shell Creek range is a prime location. In the west the Sierra foothills and the Pinenut Range, both heavily hunted because of the population centers around Reno, Virginia City, and Carson City, still offer excellent hunting. Lighter pressure and fair hunting is encountered some distance to the east, in the Clan Alpine and Desatoya Ranges of Churchill Co. lying north of U.S. 50. As noted earlier, the southern part of the state is not overall the best, but two good bets here are the Spring Mountains northwest of Las Vegas and south of U.S. 95, and the Virgin Mountains in the extreme east of Clark Co., between Lake Mead and the Arizona border. This last-named range is capable of furnishing trophy deer late in season.

Best of the deer hunting, as noted, is in the northeast. Some access here, in large Elko County, is good, via I 80 (U.S. 40) and U.S. 93, plus several state routes and a number of lesser roads. But there is also a great deal of wild and roadless country. For one who studies the game map available from the Commission, this area is divided into three management Units —No. 6 is western Elko Co., No. 7 the eastern portion, No. 10 the southeastern portion. The deer kill in each of these Units is high, averages about the same in each, and the three are usually the highest in the state, excepting at times the hard-hunted western area based on Reno.

The Humboldt National Forest (12) is one of the finest spots in the northeast. Settlements in the region are small. Jarbridge can be reached from north or south on a long haul over a minor road or via State 51 from Wild Horse Reservoir and via a side trail. The Jarbridge Wilderness Area is here, in the middle of the Humboldt NF. There are Forest Service roads around the periphery but hunts in the interior must be pack-ins. Chances for trophy bucks are good.

The Independence Mountains reached from Elko north on State 11 or from Carlin west of Elko and thence north on a side road along Maggie Creek, often turn up fantastic success. South from Elko into the Ruby Mountains via State 46 is more good hunting. The entire Ruby Mountain area, although not easy of access throughout, is generally excellent.

ANTELOPE

Antelope hunting is limited to residents and only a modest number of permits are offered, generally from 200 to 275, with a correspondingly small harvest, although success is good, around 75 percent. Washoe Co. and western Humboldt Co. get the major share of the permits. There is also a small amount of antelope hunting most seasons in eastern White Pine Co., on the east-central border, and in the south in southern Lander and Eureka and northern Nye Cos. Permits are given for specified management Areas or Units as shown on the game map.

ELK

There are two very small elk herds in Nevada. One is in the Shell Creek Range east of Ely in eastern White Pine Co. The other is in the south, in the Spring Mountain Range of southern Clark Co. All Nevada elk came from transplants. Only residents may hunt. Permits for each area seldom number over fifteen during a season when hunting is allowed to keep the herd tailored to its range.

BIGHORN SHEEP

There are somewhere in the neighborhood of 2000 desert bighorns on the huge Desert Game Range of southern Nevada, near Las Vegas. Some other small sheep populations are being nurtured in the White and Silver Peak Ranges of Esmeralda Co., the southern Toiyabe Mountains, the Grant Range of Nye Co., and a few other ranges. In addition there is currently an attempt to stock the California bighorn. It is quite possible that in future years with careful management sheep may be hunted in Nevada in areas where none have been found for over a century.

At present limited hunting is offered, some years, as herd surveys dictate. Typically less than a hundred permits are the quota, via drawing. Nonresidents are allowed a few. In one recent hunt, there were eighty-five permits, with seven of them for nonresidents. A total of twenty-five sheep was killed.

Almost all these permits were for the Desert Game Range. The sheep hunt is rigidly run, with check in and out, and a hunter must take a short course of two hours before hunting, to be sure he knows how to judge a legal ram.

Recent top trophies have come from the Mormon Mountains in the extreme southeast near I 15. The Red Rock and Potosi portion of the Spring Range (Management Area 26) also should be a good bet for the next hunt, if permits are available here.

REGULATIONS

Game laws pertaining to seasons, bag and possession limits, areas to be hunted, special hunts, license fees all may have numerous changes from year to year. For current regulations, and for other specific queries, write to: Fish and Game Commission, P.O. Box 10678, Reno, Nevada 89510.

COLORADO

For many years Colorado has caught the eye of the big-game hunter as a kind of center of western mountain hunting. The state sits astride the Continental Divide roughly halfway between the Canadian and Mexican borders. Bounded on the south by New Mexico, and the Oklahoma Panhandle, on the west by Utah, the north by Wyoming and a bit of Nebraska, and on the east by Nebraska and Kansas, its terrain is in many ways a mosaic of all those states. In the east there are high, nearly treeless plains, but as one moves westward the country soon becomes broken. Suddenly the foothills appear and from there on to the top of the Divide, which zigzags down across the state to cut off the western third, the mountains soar.

Colorado is in fact the highest of the contiguous states. Fifty-two of the highest peaks are here. Peaks that rise above 10,000 feet number at least 1500. Several are over 14,000 feet. The average low elevation in the state is about 3400, and a state-wide average is roughly 6800. There are of course vast forested areas, and there is much true wilderness. Oddly, however, though Colorado was once known for mining and cattle, today its largest revenue is from manufacturing, with agriculture second and mining third. This hardly detracts from the forested vision hunters have of it. In fact there are over 13,000,000 acres in National Forests alone.

Main highways are excellent, taking hunters to any sector of the state. But in almost every part there are large expanses that are roadless, or that are accessible only by mountain trails or mediocre side roads. And, there are a number of Wilderness Areas in the National Forests where no vehicular travel is allowed. One must backpack, or ride a horse.

A great many hunters who visit Colorado, especially for big-game hunting, take along their own back-country transport, usually a short-wheelbase 4WD vehicle. Others trailer horses to the hunting area. Resident hunters invariably utilize at the least a pickup truck, and often one with 4WD. Thus, while most bird hunters get along nicely with a passenger car only, there is much Colorado territory where tougher transport is needed for big game. Air travel to all of the cities, even to most of the smaller ones, is excellent, and from there on the average big-game hunter is guided.

Colorado is larger than any of its border states except New Mexico. It covers 104,247 square miles. Boundary lines make it almost exactly rectangular, with the long dimension east-west, about 375 miles, and the north-south straight-line distance roughly 275. However, hunters should not take these distances as meaning much, for except in the eastern plains roads must be cut where terrain allows, and many a mountain highway runs, as it's said, "all directions at once."

Present population is over two million, but there is certainly ample room for hunters. Upwards of 300,000 persons hunt here each season. Colorado has long been extremely popular with nonresident hunters after deer and elk. In a recent season over 80,000 nonresident licenses and tags were sold.

Game is abundant, and varied. There are deer, elk, bear, mountain sheep, mountain goat, antelope, mountain lion, and a few buffalo. Game birds include wild turkey, pheasant, three varieties of quail, sage grouse and sharptail grouse, chukar, blue grouse, ptarmigan, mourning doves, plus ducks, geese, and sandhill cranes. There are also snowshoe and cottontail rabbits, plus lesser animals such as raccoons, bobcats, coyotes, and foxes. Although hunting for the birds and small game is very good in various locations, it is the mule deer and the elk that attract the major interest.

Public lands in Colorado amount to over a third of the total area of the state. Most important of these are the National Forests. There are eleven. For reader convenience they are listed below, and located, so that one may refer from the species subheadings to check the Forests all in one place.

The Arapaho NF (1) is slightly more than a million acres. It is located in the north-central region, west of Denver, with general access via U.S. 6 and 40, and with nearby towns Dillon, Golden, Hot Sulphur Springs, Granby. Maps may be obtained from the Forest Supervisor in Golden. The Grand Mesa NF (2) is generally combined in mention with the Uncompahgre NF, as two forests in one that contain over 1,300,000 acres. These Forests are west-central and edging into the southwest. Towns for orientation are Grand Junction, Montrose, Delta, Ouray, Telluride. U.S. 50, 550, and 6 reach the region. Supervisor headquarters are in Delta. The Gunnison NF (3) is nearby, to the east, and covers over 1,600,000 acres. The Supervisor is located at Gunnison, which is a good point for orientation. U.S. 50 crosses here, and State 135 and 149 run to the north and south. In all of the Forests so far mentioned there are Primitive or Wilderness Areas. Many hunters find these regions appealing because by packing far back into them one can get away from any crowding.

Pike NF (4) is in central Colorado, and encompasses slightly over 1,100,000 acres. General access is via U.S. 285, 24, 85, 87, and nearby cities and towns are Denver, Cripple Creek, Colorado Springs, with Supervisor headquarters in the latter. The Rio Grande NF (5) is in the south. The Continental Divide runs along its backbone and separates it from the San Juan NF (6). The Rio Grande NF is on the eastern slope, the San Juan on the west. The Rio Grande contains almost 1,800,000 acres. Monte Vista, Del Norte, South Fork, Creede are all nearby, and U.S. 160 and 285 the general approach routes. Headquarters is at Monte Vista. Across the Divide, the San Juan contains over 1,850,000 acres, is approached from Durango, which is the headquarters for the Supervisor, or from Bayfield, Pagosa Springs, and Silverton. Both the Rio Grande and the San Juan contain Wilderness and Primitive Areas.

Roosevelt NF (7) is in the north-central region, with a bit more than three-fourths of a million acres. Headquarters where maps may be obtained is at Fort Collins. Boulder, Estes Park, Loveland, Longmont are other nearby locations, and routes of approach are U.S. 34 and 287, Colo. 14 and 160.

Routt NF (8) is to the northwest, with over 1,125,000 acres. Headquarters is at Steamboat Springs. U.S. 40, Colo. 131 and 84 reach the region, and other towns here are Yampa, Craig, and Walden. Forests in this paragraph also offer Wilderness and Primitive Areas.

The San Isabel NF (9), about 1,100,000 acres, is headquartered at Pueblo, with Salida, Leadville, Canon City, Walsenberg other nearby towns, and with U.S. 50, 24, 85, 87 and several Colorado routes leading to it.

White River NF (10) is the largest, with almost two million acres, and several Primitive and Wilderness Areas within it. Headquarters is at Glenwood Springs. Meeker, Rifle, Craig, Aspen, all well known to deer hunters especially, are nearby, and highways leading here are U.S. 24 and 6, and Colo. 82 and 132.

A map showing all of the Wilderness and Primitive Areas of the Rocky Mountain Forest Region can be obtained from the Denver Federal Center, Building 85, Denver 80225.

Added to these federal lands are about a quarter-million acres owned in part and all controlled by the Colorado Department of Game, Fish and Parks, address at chapter end. There are some 157 individual tracts, in size from a few to several thousand acres, devoted primarily to wildlife management and known as State Hunting and Fishing Areas, or more briefly as Wildlife Areas. Some offer fishing only, but the major share have hunting either for big or small game. A list of these Areas, giving locations, size, etc., is obtainable from the Game Department. Mention will be made of many of these Areas later on under species headings. There are in addition to these some thirty-three tracts known as State Recreation Areas or Parks. Hunting is allowed on some of these. Detailed information on each may be had from the Game Division.

Yet this is by no means all of the public lands. The federal Bureau of Land Management administers some 8.3 million acres of lands in Colorado. These are important for much game, particularly mule deer. There are numerous access roads and more are being built nowadays especially for hunter access. BLM maps are available from the Game Department of the state, or from the BLM State Office, Room 14023, Federal Office Building, 1961 Stout Street, Denver 80202. As this is written not all BLM maps for the state were completed. Each covers a specific area, and shows hunter access points. Eventually maps will be available and perhaps may be as this is read, for all of the BLM lands in Colorado.

There have also been large expanses of CAP lands in Colorado but in 1968 federal funds were withdrawn from this program. These are privately owned lands on which owners gave hunter access in return for certain federal per-acre payments. There was in print a booklet showing all these lands, and available from the Game Department, but at this writing it has not been reprinted. It may be, however, if the federal program is restored.

For management purposes and for setting quota regulations, the Game Department uses Management Units. The Units used for big game, which number almost one hundred, are not the same as those now used for game birds. Because of the Unit System, it is mandatory that for any given season a hunter acquire the regulations map for that year. Guides are not required for big-game hunting, but certainly any hunter not familiar with the mountain region where he will hunt is well advised to hire one. Guides in Colorado must be licensed, and as a rule a list of them is published each year about midsummer, and may be obtained from the Division.

Several other items of which hunters should be aware are as follows. Unposted land does not mean it is open to hunting. No owner is required to post, or even to fence, his property so far as trespass laws are concerned. Recently, also, Colorado became one of the states where all rifle, or shotgun slug, hunters are required by law to wear a minimum of 300 square inches of blaze-orange material in outer garments. Of immense advantage to visiting hunters especially is the Colorado system—adopted now by several other western states—of permanent opening dates for seasons. These are set either at the first of a month, or for a specified Saturday—second, fourth, etc.—in a specified month. These permanent dates for all seasons are available from the Department, so one may conveniently plan ahead.

Accommodations for hunters are everywhere in Colorado. The state is so well geared to summer, and hunting, visitors that motels, dude ranches, lodges are well distributed. In addition, camping hunters will find hundreds of campgrounds, in the National Forests and elsewhere. There is a booklet, "Campground Guide for Colorado," published by the Game, Fish and Parks Department. It is very detailed. One may acquire it by writing to the Game Department address, end of chapter.

Colorado hunting season weather is variable. It all depends on how early one begins a hunt, and how high up in the mountains he goes. By and large temperatures will be under 60 degrees regardless of early seasons, and it will range anywhere down to below zero. Early storms are common in the high country. Hunters, regardless of species they are after, should go prepared not just for enjoyable wool-shirt-and-jacket weather but for blizzards. Down clothing, rain gear, and insulated boots are never amiss. Nor is equipment such as tire chains, shovels, survival rations, and of course a compass.

Guns and ammunition need to be fitted to the game. Bird hunters will need a variety if they hunt a variety. For doves and quail No. 8 will do, but many use No. 7½. In fact, No. 7 and No. 6 shot sizes are good compromises to cover most of the uplanders. For ducks No. 4s are good, and for geese, turkeys, cranes, either No. 4 short magnum or No. 2s are best. Deer hunters can utilize a wide range of calibers. It is well to remember, however, that Rocky Mountain mule deer are large, and that many hunters will be hunting elk at the same time. The 7mm magnum, the .30/06 with 180-grain bullet are good basic calibers. Some hunters like the heavy magnums for elk, but those are not needed for deer. For antelope the .243 is excellent. Sheep and goat hunters will be best equipped to use a fairly heavy caliber, for shots may be long. Again, the 7mm magnum or the '06 are good examples.

PHEASANT

Although Colorado has no nationwide reputation as a pheasant state, by annual harvest the ringneck shows up as the most important uplander. It even sometimes beats the migratory birds—ducks and doves—in total bag. Hunter interest is high. Over 80,000 hunters usually participate. During the past several seasons the kill has averaged slightly less than 160,000 birds. Compared to the true pheasant states, that of course is by no means impressive. Although there is good hunting in Colorado, the state's hunters are far more oriented to big game. In addition, the ranges of most of the upland game birds, including the pheasant, are rather restricted.

As noted early in the chapter, Colorado has set up Management Units for small game. There are twenty-six of these. Pheasant seasons are set by Units. Usually there is a statewide season, plus other seasons in specified Units later. These sometimes run through until the end of the year. Some years a good number of pheasants are raised by 4-H Clubs for release in the better counties, to assist the wild stock.

The top pheasant populations are widely scattered. On the west slope there is quite a stable population along the Gunnison River Valley along a line through the cities of Grand Junction, Delta, Montrose. Ordinarily the corn and alfalfa fields and irrigation ditches west of the towns of Delta and Olathe have the higher density. This Gunnison River area corresponds to Units 16, 17, 19 and the season there may differ from elsewhere.

In south-central Colorado there is a pocket of fair pheasant production west of Alamosa in the vicinity of the town of Monte Vista. Here there is cropland stubble and irrigation ditch cover. This pheasant population is about centrally located in Unit 22. In the extreme southeast there is another fair pheasant population, in Baca Co. There is some National Grassland here, the Comanche National Grassland (11) and some pheasants may be found on these public lands. To the north, the Arkansas River Valley also has some pheasants, east from La Junta to the Kansas border.

However, the best pheasant range in Colorado is in the northeast. Much of Kit Carson Co. north of the town of Burlington is good. This corresponds to Unit 14. The other northeastern counties of Yuma, Phillips, Sedgwick, southern Logan and northern Washington, and east-central Morgan cover most of the remainder of the best range. This area is in Units 1 and 2. The remainder of the eastern slope has fair hunting in places. But it must be remembered that much of the Colorado pheasant range is fringe, and severe winters often are hard on the flocks. Studies over several years tend to show that Units 1 (northeast), 14 (east-central), and 19 (west-central) maintain the highest densities.

Although most pheasant hunting is on private lands, listed below alphabetically are some public tracts that furnish shooting. Banner Lakes WA (12) is in Weld Co., western fringe of the northeast pheasant range. Bonny State Recreation Area (13) is a large tract in southeast Yuma Co. in prime range. Holyoke Property WA (14) is near like-named town, Phillips Co., in the northeast. Jumbo Reservoir WA (15) is in Logan Co. in the northeast. Means WA (16) is in Phillips Co., northeast, near Holyoke. Murphy WA (17) is small, in Weld Co. near Berthoud. North Sterling Reservoir WA (18) is in Logan Co. Prewitt Reservoir WA (19) is in Washington Co. There are also: Sand Draw WA (20), Sedgwick Co.; South Republican WA (21), Yuma Co.; Tamarack WA (22), Logan Co.; Wellington WA (23), Larimer Co. in north-central Colorado, at the western fringe of the northeastern pheasant range.

QUAIL

Colorado has three species of quail, and is in the process of attempting to establish a fourth. The three native species are the Gambel's blue (scaled) and bobwhite.

The Gambel's quail follows almost exactly the range of the pheasant in the west, along a line roughly following U.S. 50 but beginning about at Loma in the west and running from Grand Junction through Delta and Montrose. This handsomely plumed little quail likes the dense brush of ditch banks and gullies, but fairly close to water. They are not especially abundant. In general the bottomlands bordered by semi-arid brushlands in Units 16, 17, 19 will contain virtually all of this species within the state.

Bobwhites also are limited in numbers, are found chiefly along the river valleys of the eastern pheasant range. The South Platte northeast of Denver, the Arkansas River of the southeast, and the Cimarron are the main strongholds. Big Sandy Creek, the Republican River, Two Buttes Creek also have isolated coveys. The South Platte is considered best.

The scaled quail is the most abundant of the Colorado species. Its area of highest density is in the southeast, in southern Las Animas and Baca counties. However, this species is also fairly numerous over much of the east slope in arid country throughout most of the southeastern quarter of the state.

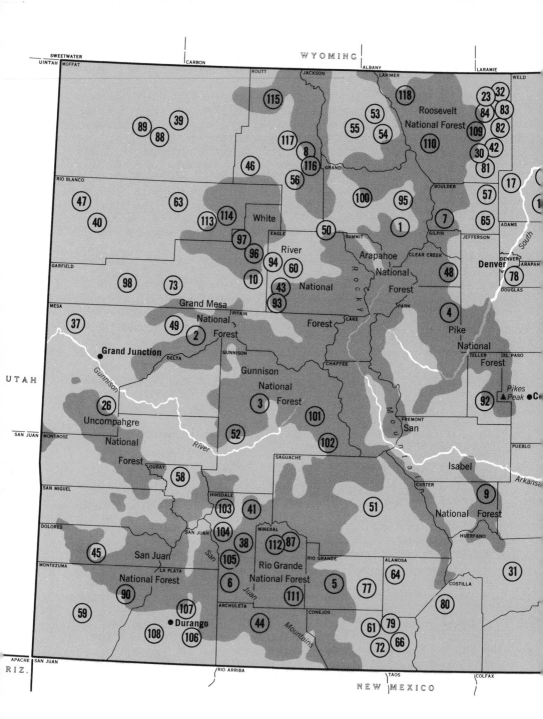

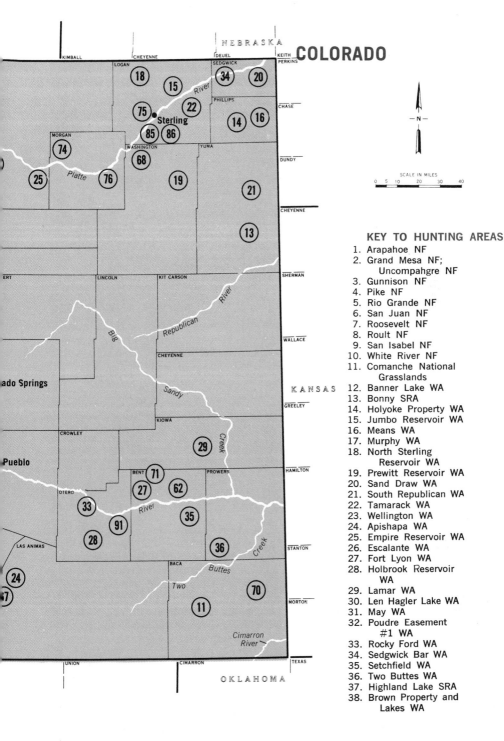

COLORADO

SCALE IN MILES
0 5 10 20 30 40

KEY TO HUNTING AREAS

1. Arapahoe NF
2. Grand Mesa NF;
   Uncompahgre NF
3. Gunnison NF
4. Pike NF
5. Rio Grande NF
6. San Juan NF
7. Roosevelt NF
8. Roult NF
9. San Isabel NF
10. White River NF
11. Comanche National
    Grasslands
12. Banner Lake WA
13. Bonny SRA
14. Holyoke Property WA
15. Jumbo Reservoir WA
16. Means WA
17. Murphy WA
18. North Sterling
    Reservoir WA
19. Prewitt Reservoir WA
20. Sand Draw WA
21. South Republican WA
22. Tamarack WA
23. Wellington WA
24. Apishapa WA
25. Empire Reservoir WA
26. Escalante WA
27. Fort Lyon WA
28. Holbrook Reservoir
    WA
29. Lamar WA
30. Len Hagler Lake WA
31. May WA
32. Poudre Easement
    #1 WA
33. Rocky Ford WA
34. Sedgwick Bar WA
35. Setchfield WA
36. Two Buttes WA
37. Highland Lake SRA
38. Brown Property and
    Lakes WA

39. Brown's Park WA
40. Cathedral Creek WA
41. Cebolla Creek WA
42. Cherokee Park WA
43. Christine WA
44. Devil Creek WA
45. Fish Creek WA
46. Indian Run WA
47. Missouri Creek WA
48. Mount Evans WA
49. Plateau Creek WA
50. Radium WA
51. Saguache Park WA
52. Sapinero WA
53. Delaney Butte Lakes WA
54. Lake John WA
55. Walden Reservoir WA
56. Service Creek WA
57. Baller WA
58. Billy Creek WA
59. Denny Lake WA
60. Dotsero WA
61. Hot Creek WA
62. John Martin Reservoir WA
63. Little Hills WA
64. San Luis Lakes WA
65. Sawhill Ponds WA
66. Sego Springs WA
67. Spanish Peaks WA
68. Washington County Hunting Easement #2 (Higgason); Washington County Hunting Easement #2 (Skaags)
69. Weld County Hunting Easement #4a (Webster); Weld County Hunting Easement #4b
70. Burchfield Lake WA
71. Adobe Creek Reservoir WA
72. Conejos WA
73. Barbour Lakes SRA
74. Leffler Hunting Easement
75. Logan County Hunting Easement #1 (Knudsen)
76. Morgan County Hunting Easement #1 (Beery); #1 (Boyd); #2 (Chartier)
77. Rio Grande WA
78. Cherry Creek SRA
79. La Jara Reservoir WA
80. Smith Reservoir WA
81. Boedecker Reservoir; Equalizer Reservoir; Hoffman Reservoir; Heinrecy Reservoir; Horseshoe Reservoir
82. Cobb Lake
83. Smith Lake
84. South Platte Easement (Frank)
85. Jones Tract
86. Lennartz Tract
87. Road Canyon Reservoirs
88. Lilly Park Road and Bridge
89. Little Snake WA
90. Summit Reservoir Complex
91. Horse Creek Reservoir
92. Pikes Peak WA
93. Basalt WA
94. Eagle WA
95. Hot Sulphur Springs WA
96. Heart Lake
97. Marvine Lakes
98. Piney Road
99. Trappers Lake
100. Rock Creek
101. Beaver Lake
102. Spring Creek Reservoir
103. Middle Fork Piedra River Road
104. Happy Valley
105. Williams Creek Reservoir
106. Henderson Lake
107. Lower Hermosa Reservoir
108. Thompson Property
109. Bliss Tract
110. Bull Montain Road
111. Alberta Park Reservoir
112. Rito Honde Reservoir
113. Bailey Lake
114. Swede Lake
115. Swamp Park Trail
116. Dumont Lake
117. Hahn's Peak Reservoir
118. Hohnholtz Lakes and Road

Mountain quail, not native, have been brought in from both California and Oregon recently and stocked on the Uncompahgre Plateau south of Grand Junction. It is too early at this writing to determine if they have established themselves.

Total quail kill in Colorado fluctuates widely. In some past years the season has been closed because of scarcity. In one peak year the kill was 117,000. Several years ago, however, it was only 17,000. The average lies somewhere between 25,000 and 50,000. Weather dictates these cycles.

Much quail hunting is on private lands. However, the two large blocks of Comanche National Grasslands, in Otero Co. and in Las Animas and Baca Cos., all in the southeast, offer good public opportunities for blues or scaled quail. There are also a number of Wildlife Areas that have fair to excellent quail hunting. They are listed below, in alphabetical order.

Those already noted under "Pheasant" are: Holyoke Property WA; Jumbo Reservoir WA; Murphy WA; North Sterling Reservoir WA; Prewitt Reservoir WA; Sand Draw WA; South Republican WA; Tamarack WA.

Others are as follows: Apishapa WA (24), Las Animas Co., in the southeast, out of Walsenburg; Empire Reservoir WA (25), Weld and Morgan

Co. line; Escalante WA (26), a large one in the west, in Mesa, Delta, and Montrose Cos.; Fort Lyon WA (27), Bent Co., in the southeast; Holbrook Reservoir WA (28), Otero Co., in the southeast; Lamar WA (29), Kiowa Co., in the southeast; Len Hagler Lake WA (30), Larimer Co., north-central region; May WA (31), Huerfano Co., south-central; Poudre Easement #1 WA (32), Larimer and Weld Cos.; Rocky Ford WA (33), Otero Co., in the southeast; Sedgwick Bar WA (34), Sedgwick Co., in the northeast; Setchfield WA (35), Bent Co., in the southeast; Two Buttes WA (36), a large one along the Baca and Prowers Co. line, in the southeast.

In addition to the above there is the Highline Lake State Recreation Area (37) in Mesa Co. in the west, near Loma.

BLUE GROUSE

Because of the great masses of forested mountain country, Colorado has a high incidence of blue grouse. These large mountain grouse live at high altitudes in the timber, usually make an upward, rather than downward, winter migration. Although they are scattered and cannot be considered abundant in any state when compared to many other upland species, Colorado does have a high kill for this species and a good bit of hunter interest in it. As with most grouse species, there are high and low cycles so no true picture of an average annual bag can be gained. It fluctuates from a totally closed season to a low bag of about 3000 to highs of over 25,000. Over several recent seasons, with good crops of birds, the kill has run in three consecutive years 23,000-plus, 16,000-plus, 27,000-plus.

There is really no such place as the "best spot" in the state. Blue grouse range throughout all of the Colorado timbered country from roughly 6500 feet to timberline. Most years all Units are open excepting those in the plains region where no blue grouse are found. There are also post, or late, seasons some years. The regular season falls in September when it is pleasant to be in the mountains, and when the birds can be found in their lower elevations, in aspen and shrub cover. The post season, when it occurs, is in October. After cold weather arrives—if it has by then—the birds will move up into the stands of spruce and fir, where they feed on buds of those trees during winter.

All of the vast acreages of the National Forests offer excellent opportunities for this bird. There is little choice, but local conservation officers can be of great assistance in pointing one toward known concentrations. There are in addition a good many high-country areas in the Forests that have for years been virtually isolated from the public, because no roads went in, or else because private property barred access. A number of roads have been built purposely to open up some of these lands. Many good blue grouse regions have been opened by them. Check with the Game Division concerning these. Incidentally, these are all extremely important to big-game hunters, too.

Quite a number of the Wildlife Areas offer good blue grouse hunting. They are listed here. The Brown Property and Lakes WA (38), in Hinsdale Co., is reached from Creede. Brown's Park WA (39) is in the northwest, Moffat Co. Cathedral Bluffs WA (40) is in Rio Blanco Co., northwest, and Cebolla Creek WA (41) is in Hinsdale Co. and reached from Lake City. Cherokee Park WA (42) is out of Fort Collins, Larimer Co.; Christine WA (43), Eagle Co., is reached out of Basalt in the southwest corner of the county.

Devil Creek WA (44) is reached out of Pagosa Springs in the southwest, in Archuleta Co.; Escalante WA has been located under "Quail." Fish Creek WA (45), Dolores Co., is reached some miles from town of like name. Indian Run WA (46) is in the northwest, Routt Co., out of Hamilton. Missouri Creek WA (47) is in Rio Blanco Co., from Rangely; Mount Evans WA (48) is in Clear Creek Co. west of Denver and reached from Evergreen. Plateau Creek WA (49) is in the west, Mesa Co.'s northeast portion, out of Colbran. Radium WA (50) is a large one lying in Grand and Eagle Cos., north-central, around the town of Radium. Saguache Park WA (51) is near town of like name, in county of like name, southwestern portion of state; and the Sapinero WA (52) is reached out of Gunnison, in Gunnison Co.

SAGE GROUSE

This largest of U.S. grouses is today nowhere abundant, although at one time there were many tens of thousands on the arid sagebrush plains of the interior and western U.S. However, Colorado does have still today some of the best of the hunting for this declining species. Over recent seasons 12,000 to 13,000 sage grouse have been harvested. Much decimation of habitat has occurred, for this species must have large areas of sagebrush plains for survival. The destruction of proper habitat still continues.

The dry sagebrush plains of the north and west are the range of this grouse in Colorado. Many blocks of BLM lands in this part of the state offer good sage grouse shooting. Very often one can find private ranchlands where irrigated alfalfa crops are grown surrounded by sage plains. These oases are perfect for sage grouse. Although numerous small-game Units have open season, hunting is probably best in the northwest. Here, some years, there are extended seasons after the close of the regular season.

Several Wildlife Areas have fair to good sage grouse shooting. Brown's Park, and Cathedral Bluffs, covered under "Blue Grouse" are two. Delaney Butte Lakes (53), out of Walden, Jackson Co., in the northwest quarter of the state, is another good bet. Lake John WA (54), also in Jackson Co., reached out of Walden, is another. Missouri Creek, "Blue Grouse," also offers this species. So does Walden Reservoir (55), another Jackson Co. WA reached from Walden.

SHARPTAIL GROUSE AND PRAIRIE CHICKEN

Sharptails were once exceedingly abundant, and so were prairie chickens. Today there is no hunting for prairie chickens. And the sharptail, though found in at least eleven counties and reported from an additional eleven, is nowhere abundant. Although the open season is the same as for the sage grouse, and thus covers numerous Units, the sharptail kill is low. One of the highest recent harvests was slightly more than 2000 birds.

The counties where existence is certain are: Dolores, Douglas, Elbert, Gunnison, Mesa, Moffat, Montezuma, Montrose, Park, Rio Blanco, Routt. The highest populations presently occur in Moffat and Routt counties, in the northwest. BLM lands and NF lower slopes offer opportunity. There is at least one WA with some sharptails available. This is Service Creek WA (56), Routt Co., near Oak Creek. Although the WA is not large, about 300 acres, it opens up several thousand acres of other public lands. Incidentally, many small WAs are for this purpose primarily, to serve as access so hunters can get to public lands otherwise cut off. Hunters interested in sharptails will be well advised to try the two counties mentioned, and to inquire of local conservation officers where chances may be best.

CHUKAR

The chukar was stocked in western Colorado during the late 1930s. The first season was held in 1958. There have been annual seasons since. The kill is not high. It also fluctuates widely. Highest to date has been 9332 birds. More recent seasons showed a drastic drop, to 2853, then back up to 4469. Nonetheless, the bird seems to be fairly well established, with its firmest foothold probably in the west-central counties, but with scattered populations over most of the western slope.

An early success was in Escalante Canyon, Delta Co. Many birds were live trapped here for transplant elsewhere. This is still a good area. The Gunnison River Canyon is another example of good chukar range. Several WAs furnish good opportunity: Brown's Park and Cathedral Bluffs, both noted under "Blue Grouse"; Escalante WA, covered under "Quail."

A check with Game Department personnel to locate precisely where transplants have been made is helpful. The counties in which most birds have been released over the years, and where the greatest number of continuing releases have been made are as follows, in order: Mesa; Rio Blanco; Delta; Moffat; Fremont; Garfield; Montrose; Montezuma.

PTARMIGAN

The whitetailed ptarmigan is a resident in scattered locations of much of the above-timberline country in Colorado. This is the only one of the contiguous states in which ptarmigan are presently hunted, although they are under experimentation in the northwest. Oddly, though the kill is low due to the difficult terrain in which they live, the ptarmigan is undoubtedly more populous in Colorado than any other grouse except the blue. Hunters are beginning to be more and more interested in it, too. The season just past showed 1798 hunters and a total bag of 3382 birds.

During winter the birds may stay above timberline, feeding on buds of willow and other plants. Or, they may move down into willow patches in adjacent valleys. In some locations in southwestern Colorado they move to lower valleys each winter, regardless of snow conditions in the alpine region. The season lasts for about two weeks, the last half of September. At that time there is not likely to be heavy snow at timberline and above. The hunting is quite specialized, since few hunters have much knowledge of the habits of these handsome little grouse that change from mottled brown and white to pure white in winter.

Usually hunting season finds them feeding on dwarf plants, the alpine willow and mountain dryad. These plants are no more than two inches high, and confined to rocky steeps or flats where little other vegetation grows. Although there is a vast amount of ptarmigan range, about 7000 square miles, in the state, much of it is exceedingly difficult to get into. However, there are places where one can actually drive to good ptarmigan territory.

Mount Evans ptarmigan range can be reached by an improved highway. Most hunters go here, but they are only moderately successful. Exploration of timber roads, or mining roads, using a 4WD vehicle, can get one to better hunting. Here are some passes suggested by Game Commission researchers as worth trying, although one will have to do some walking after arriving on top: Alpine, Argentine, Boreas, Bottle, Buffalo, Cameron, Carleton, Cinnamon, Cottonwood, Cumberland, Engineer, Hancock, Jones, Lizard Head, Mosquito, Ophir, Pearl, Shrine, Taylor, Weston. Again, in specialized hunting such as this, a check with Department personnel to locate known concentrations of birds is most helpful. Because a study of these birds has been underway for some time in Colorado, researchers are anxious to assist hunters. Numerous birds have been banded and return of bands is needed.

The National Forest high country furnishes endless public domain on which to hunt. There is at least one Game Division controlled road leading to ptarmigan hunting. This is Corona Pass Road, in Gilpin Co., out of Rollinsville. It takes one over the Divide, on a drive of about twenty-seven miles to the west side near Winter Park. Many thousands of acres of public lands are there.

MOURNING DOVES

Compared to states in the plains and the south, the dove kill in Colorado is not impressive. However, for the modest number of enthusiasts who pursue this sport, there is fair to excellent shooting. An average good season sees from 125,000 to 150,000 birds bagged. Occasionally it may be double that. The entire state is open. Birds are most plentiful of course in the farming areas where grain is available, and thus much good shooting is on privately owned lands. However, a number of the WAs furnish dove hunting.

Covered under "Pheasant": Banner Lakes WA; Holyoke Property WA; Jumbo Reservoir WA; Murphy WA; North Sterling Reservoir WA; Prewitt Reservoir WA; Sand Draw WA; South Republican WA; Tamarack WA; Wellington WA. Covered under "Quail": Apishapa; Empire Reservoir; Escalante; Fort Lyon; Holbrook Reservoir; Lamar; Len Hagler Lake; May; Poudre Easement; Rocky Ford; Sedgwick Bar; Setchfield. Covered under "Blue Grouse": Brown's Park; Cathedral Bluffs; Missouri Creek.

Wildlife Areas not so far mentioned where dove hunting is found are as follows: Baller WA (57), near Berthoud, Boulder Co.; Billy Creek WA (58), Ouray Co., out of Montrose; Denny Creek WA (59), near Cortez, Montezuma Co.; Dotsero WA (60), out of like-named town, Eagle Co.; Hot Creek WA (61), Conejos Co., near Capulin; John Martin Reservoir WA (62), near Hasty, Bent Co.; Little Hills WA (63), out of Meeker, Rio Blanco Co.; San Luis Lakes WA (64), Alamosa Co., near Mosca; Sawhill Ponds WA (65), Boulder Co., near Boulder; Sego Springs WA (66), near Manassa, Conejos Co.; Spanish Peaks WA (67), Las Animas Co., out of Aguilar; Washington Co. Hunting Easement #2 (68) Higgason, near Merino; Washington Co. Hunting Easement #2 (Skaggs), Logan and Wash. Cos., out of Snyder; Weld Co. Hunting Easement #4a (69) Webster, near Evans, and #4b near Platteville.

A few other tracts or accesses are as follows: In Baca Co., Burchfield Lake WA (70), near Walsh; in Bent Co., Adobe Creek Reservoir WA (71), near Arlington; in Conejos Co., the Conejos WA (72), near Manassa; in Garfield Co., Square S Road, leading to large area of public domain (this is also a good access for both sage and blue grouse). There are also two previously mentioned State Recreation Areas ("Pheasants") that offer dove hunting: Barbour Lakes SRA; Bonny SRA.

WILD TURKEYS

The Merriam's, or mountain variety, of wild turkey is reasonably abundant in Colorado. Currently there are seasons both spring and fall. The spring season was launched in 1965. Many years ago turkeys were superbly abundant over most of the southern half of the state, in foothills and mountains. Uncontrolled hunting and destruction of habitat brought the turkey near to extinction. In 1914 a trapping program was instigated, and transplants made to suitable habitat. Careful management and control of hunting has restored the bird to huntable numbers.

Generally during fall much of the state is open. A recent season saw eighteen of the twenty-six Small Game Units with a week of season in October. The spring season is more restricted. Hunters should check to make certain what Units, or portions of the state, allow a spring hunt in any given year. The total turkey kill has averaged over recent years from 500 to more than 700 birds.

The National Forests described early in the chapter are prime turkey range. But because they are so large, it is a good idea to check with the Supervisor, or with a local conservation officer, regarding specific locations for best hunting.

There are also numerous Wildlife Areas that have turkeys. One of the most important of these is the Spanish Peaks WA ("Doves"). There are special regulations here at present. Hunters must check in and out. No more than seventy-five are allowed on the Area at one time, first come basis. This is a large acreage and it is in some of the original prime turkey habitat.

Here are other WAs with turkeys: Apishapa, Escalante, May noted under "Quail"; South Republican under "Pheasant," Devil Creek and Indian Run under "Blue Grouse."

LESSER SANDHILL CRANE

Only over the past several years has Colorado been allowed a season on the lesser sandhill crane. These birds select shallow ponds or lakes for roosting, where they stand in the water. They are grain feeders and fly out at dawn to harvested maize or other grain fields to feed. They are wary and very sporty, and excellent eating.

The flight from northern summering grounds passes down across eastern Colorado and the bulk of the flight winters in eastern New Mexico and portions of the west-Texas Panhandle. However, a substantial number of birds drop off in the grain country of Colorado where suitable roost sites are available. As this is written Alamosa, Conejos, Costilla, Rio Grande, Hinsdale, Mineral, and Saguache Cos. are closed, but the remainder of the state east of the Continental Divide is open to hunting during October. To date the crane kill has been infinitesimal. Some good sport can be had with these large birds for those who will take the trouble to learn how and where to hunt them.

BANDTAILED PIGEON

This forest pigeon is found in limited numbers in the mountains. For many years the season has been closed. In 1968 experimental seasons were held in Arizona and New Mexico, and they continued through 1969 and 1970. Colorado and Utah are assisting in a bandtail study being conducted in the Rockies. Although at this writing there is no open season predicted for Colorado, it is possible that limited hunting may again be opened for this grand game bird.

EXOTICS

Colorado has been trying a species of tinamou which appears able to thrive in heavily farmed areas that are difficult for pheasants. No conclusion has so far been drawn.

WATERFOWL

It is surprising to discover in this high mountain state such excellent waterfowl hunting, especially for geese. The annual duck bag averages anywhere from 75,000 to 150,000 during recent years, although a decade and more ago it was much higher. The mallard is the major species. Some December counts have shown 99 percent of ducks in the prime eastern shooting grounds to be mallards. Over the past several years the goose kill has been from 20,000 to 30,000.

The state lies in two flyways, Central, and Pacific. Hunters should note therefore that regulations differ depending upon which slope of the Divide is hunted. Also, there are a number of locations, listed annually in the regulations, where closures are in effect. Some indicate hunting for both ducks and geese closed. In some only geese may be taken, in others ducks only. There are in addition certain portions of the state where goose permits must be obtained and where a quota system is in effect.

There are ample opportunities for public waterfowling. Baller WA ("Doves") has shooting for both ducks and geese. Banner Lakes ("Pheasant") has ducks; Brown's Park ("Sage Grouse") offers both. Delaney Butte Lakes ("Sage Grouse") offers duck shooting, as do Denny Lake and Dotsero ("Doves"). Empire Reservoir under "Quail" has both ducks and geese. So do John Martin Reservoir ("Doves") and Jumbo Reservoir ("Pheasant"), Lamar WA ("Quail") and Len Hagler Lake ("Quail"). Two with ducks only are Hot Creek ("Doves"), Lake John ("Sage Grouse"). North Sterling Reservoir and Prewitt Reservoir ("Pheasant") both offer ducks and geese. Ducks only are found at Poudre Easement ("Quail"), and at San Luis Lakes, Sawhill Ponds, Sego Springs, the two Washington Co. Hunting Easements, and the two Weld Co. Hunting Easements, all under "Doves." Sedgwick Bar, Setchfield ("Quail"), Tamarack ("Pheasant"), Walden Reservoir ("Sage Grouse") also offer ducks only. Wellington ("Pheasant") has geese also.

Numerous WAs not yet covered furnish more waterfowling. The Leffler Easement (74), near Goodrich, Morgan Co., has ducks. The same is true for Logan Co. Hunting Easement #1, Knudson (75), near Sterling. Four Morgan Co. Hunting Easements (76) also have ducks only. They are located as follows: #1 (Beery), near Brush; #1 (Boyd), near Fort Morgan; #2 in two tracts under "Chartier," also near Brush. The Rio Grande WA (77) near Monte Vista in Rio Grande Co. is also a duck hunting location. Two Buttes WA ("Quail") is one of the better goose-hunt spots. It is in Baca and Powers Cos., reached from Springfield.

The Cherry Creek State Recreation Area (78) south of Denver has both ducks and geese. The same is true for Burchfield Lake, Adobe Creek Reservoir, and Conejos WAs ("Doves"). La Jara Reservoir (79), near same town, Conejos Co.; and Smith Reservoir (80), near Blanca, Costilla Co., both furnish duck shooting. Boedecker Reservoir (81), at Loveland, Equalizer Reservoir, also near Loveland, the Hoffman Reservoirs in same area, and the Heinrecy and Horseshoe reservoirs in the same vicinity all have both ducks and geese. These are in Larimer Co. Cobb Lake (82), some miles out of Ft. Collins, Larimer Co., is a goose hunting location. Smith Lake (83), same Co., near Wellington, has both ducks and geese, and the South Platte (Frank) Easement (84) offers ducks.

Logan Co. has two duck locations not so far covered. These are the Jones Tract (85) near Atwood; the Lennartz Tract (86) out of Sterling. In

Mineral Co. there are the Road Canyon Reservoirs (87) west of Creede, for ducks. In Moffat Co., Lilly Park Road and Bridge (88), thirty-seven miles from Maybell, has both ducks and geese, and the same is true for Little Snake WA (89) out of Maybell. Montezuma Co. has the Summit Reservoir Complex (90) for ducks, near Mancos. Horse Creek Reservoir (91) near La Junta, Otero Co., has both ducks and geese. Two State Recreation Areas noted under "Doves" and "Pheasants" respectively have duck shooting: Barbour Lakes, Bonny.

The San Luis Valley, in the general Monte Vista-Alamosa region of south-central Colorado, is one of the excellent areas for mallard shooting. The establishment of the Monte Vista National Wildlife Refuge there in 1952, primarily as a duck refuge to attract the birds from crop depredations in surrounding country, has been a great boon for waterfowlers. A large part of the Refuge is open to hunting. There is, incidentally, pheasant shooting here, too. Later, in 1963, the Alamosa National Wildlife Refuge was established. This is northeast of Alamosa along the Rio Grande. It also is partly open to hunting. A resident goose flock has been established at the Monte Vista Refuge. Others are being attempted elsewhere in Colorado.

SMALL GAME

There are four varieties of rabbits and hares in the state. They are abundant but underhunted. The two that are considered game species are the cottontail, of which 250,000 to 350,000 are annually harvested, and the snowshoe or varying hare of the forest country, with a kill of 15,000 to 20,000. The other two are the whitetailed jack and the blacktailed jack.

Cottontails and snowshoes are protected by a specified season. It is long, beginning in October and running to end of February. But hunters pay small attention to rabbit hunting and there is no attempt at management. A great deal of good sport goes begging because of lack of interest in these animals, and it is probable that the future will see them utilized to a much greater extent.

Most of the public tracts so far mentioned have fair to excellent cottontail populations. A few that should be noted especially for snowshoe hares are as follows: Christine WA, Fish Creek WA, Mount Evans WA ("Blue Grouse"). Pikes Peak WA (92), Teller Co., also has snowshoes, but access may be difficult. It is entered through a locked gate at Bison Reservoir, and permission must be obtained at Victor. The Basalt WA (93), with good cottontail hunting, is near Basalt, Eagle Co., and Eagle WA (94), ditto, is located near Gypsum, Eagle Co.

There are some fox squirrels in eastern Colorado. The first open season ever held was in 1968. Only specified Units are open. This is not a very consequential game species.

The Abert or tassel-eared squirrel is found here and there in the western mountains. It is fully protected, and probably always will be.

DEER

Colorado has long been one of the truly great mule deer hunting states. Here the animals grow large. Numerous trophies have come out of the mountains, and deer remain extremely abundant. For over 20 years there has not been a season with a total kill of less than 70,000 animals. Eight of these years tallied kills of over 100,000 and three of the eight topped 140,000! Hunter success has run as high as 89 percent, has often been well over 60 percent. During the past several seasons the kill has averaged around 80,000 animals and the success percentage has hung close to 50 percent.

Deer seasons and regulations are rather complicated. It is suggested that anyone planning a Colorado deer hunt should get the Unit map as soon as it is released, generally about mid-July, and study it thoroughly. There are some early timberline seasons when bucks are still in velvet, which attempt to harvest deer in remote areas. There are regular seasons, for bucks only, and a single deer, others for two deer, either sex. Each year also sees post seasons, late seasons after deer have come down from the high country, to give hunters an opportunity to thin out these animals that otherwise might never be hunted. Locations for these seasons vary considerably from year to year. In certain Units each season there are also usually quota systems, with only a specified number allowed.

There is such a vast expanse of territory where deer hunting is excellent that it is impossible to pinpoint any particular locations as best. The game management personnel attempt to keep the herds tailored to their range. During individual seasons there are usually areas where deer are too numerous, and these of course give a hunter a better than average chance. But he must check on those for the season in question.

The enormous expanses of National Forest abound with mule deer almost everywhere. The bulk of the hunting is on these lands. Many of the Wilderness and Primitive Areas offer, for pack-in hunters, chances at real trophies. There is also plenty of deer hunting on the WAs and on some of the State Recreation Areas. For general orientation, it can be said that by far the best hunting lies west of Interstate 25, that is, west of a line snaked down from north to south about through Fort Collins, Denver, Colorado Springs, Pueblo, Walsenburg, Trinidad. Although some large deer are killed in the eastern part of the state east of this line, deer are not present here in the numbers they are westward.

To give a general idea of where heavy concentrations of deer—and often of hunters, too—are located on a fairly stable basis, here are the Units that in two recent seasons had kills over 2000. In several of these, kills exceeded 3000, in several others topped 4000, and in one instance (Unit 22) went to 5512. First season noted: Units 22, 31, 32, 33, 40, 42, 44, 62. Second season noted: Units 3, 4, 11, 21, 22, 31, 32, 42, 70. Note that several appear two years in a row. These are famous areas for Colorado mule deer.

During the same seasons, here are the Units that showed kills between 1000 and 2000. First season noted: Units 3, 4, 11, 13, 14, 21, 23, 26, 27, 35, 36, 43, 52, 58, 65, 70, 71, 75, 78. Second season noted: Units 5, 13, 23, 33, 40, 43, 44, 58, 60, 62, 63, 65, 71, 75, 78. Note how many Units show up both years, and how many show either in the under or over 2000 paragraphs. Numerous other Units fall just below 1000 consistently. But aside from popularity of a Unit with hunters, these Units are in some of the famed mule deer migration areas, and in areas where vitality of herds is excellent and production high.

Checking success percentages for one season just concluded proves the point by showing that a number of the same Units are extremely high on the list. Units showing from 80 to 100 percent success were: Units 4, 11, 21, 22, 31, 32, 33, 42, 53, 60, 63, 64, 70. Looking now at Units that ran between 60 and 80 percent, there are: Units 2, 3, 5, 10, 23, 25, 34, 35, 43,

52, 61, 77, 78. Two very low-kill Units in the east also were in this category, but kills were inconsequential and undoubtedly hunters few. At any rate, the consistent show-up of various Units in the above statistics should furnish hunters with a fair measure of where the deer are, over rather general ranges. To illustrate, however, just how excellent hunting is almost anywhere, during the average season well over half of the Units show success of above 50 percent.

Although as noted the Forests are the mainstay of deer hunting, the WA tracts should by no means be overlooked, particularly those within the high-success Units. Here are some of the WAs with deer hunting. Mentioned under "Quail": Apishapa; Escalante; May. Under "Doves": Billy Creek; Dotsero; Hot Creek; Little Hills; Spanish Peaks. Under "Blue Grouse": Brown Property and Lakes; Brown's Park; Cathedral Bluffs; Cebolla Creek; Cherokee Park; Christine; Fish Creek; Missouri Creek; Mount Evans; Plateau Creek; Radium; Saguache Park; Sapinero. Under "Rabbits": Basalt; Eagle; Pike's Peak (snowshoe hare).

Hot Sulphur Springs WA (95), not mentioned as yet, is near town of same name, Grand Co. It is valuable also to check other tracts listed under "Blue Grouse" and "Turkey" and not noted above for most also have deer hunting. In addition, see "Elk." Most elk hunting locations also have abundant mule deer. One other valuable tip to hunters, mentioned to some extent, earlier, is to obtain from the Game Department a list of roads in the Unit where one will hunt that have been opened up under control of the Department to furnish access to large public acreages. There are many of these, with hunting along their right of way and thousands of acres of public domain to which they lead.

It is interesting to note that there are a few whitetail deer in Colorado. They began moving westward into the northeast from Kansas some half-dozen years ago. This natural influx was supplemented by a transplant of 200 more from Oklahoma. They are established in the northeast plains. The concentrations are along the streams, chiefly along the Republican and the South Platte.

ELK

Colorado is one of the nation's best elk states. The kill has grown progressively larger over the years until now it averages at a fairly stable range between 13,000 and 15,000. To give a fair picture of the kill composition, over two seasons just passed, statistics were as follows: first season, bulls killed, 7913, cows 4484, calves 791; total kill by residents, 9806, by nonresidents, 3382; second season, bulls 8676, cows 5324, calves 1088; total kill by residents, 10,695, by nonresidents, 4393. Overall hunter success average is about 25 percent, which is excellent.

Elk seasons are varied, and all hunting is west of Interstate 25. There is a regular season, bulls only, in numerous Units, and there are a number of quota hunts for bulls and cows or for cows in certain Units. Each year a few Units have post elk seasons. Hunters must obtain the regulations map for the year they expect to hunt.

Although the top Units in total kill are not the same each season of course, for a recent one the top ten, which accounted for approximately 44 percent of the kill were, in order: Units 24, 23, 78, 74, 76, 12, 14, 75, 77, 13. Unit 24 has a kill of 1161, and Unit 13 a kill of 442. For two previous consecutive seasons, the top Units were as follows: first season, Units 24,

23, 74, 78, 14, 76, 77, 55, 13, 12; second season, Units 23, 24, 78, 74, 76, 14, 75, 12, 77, 55. Note that eight out of ten high Units appear on the list for all three consecutive seasons, and two appear in two seasons. Since the elk herd is fairly stable, this gives a good indication of where the most elk are, although hunting pressure may be high, too, and success percentages may differ.

Another good measure of elk density is by county kills. For two seasons the first ten in order were: first season, Rio Blanco, Routt, Gunnison, La Plata, Archuleta, Larimer, Mineral, Eagle, Grand, Hinsdale; second season, Rio Blanco, Routt, Gunnison, La Plata, Garfield, Archuleta, Mineral, Eagle, Hinsdale, Grand. Note that the first four were in the same position both years. Note also that nine counties appear in both lists.

Other statistics to substantiate where the good hunting is are the success percentages. They are as follows for the eight out of the ten high-kill Units (second paragraph above) for the last one of the three consecutive seasons in which all eight appeared. In numerical order the hunter success in each was: Unit 12, 32%; Unit 14, 30%; Unit 23, 41%; Unit 24, 63%; Unit 74, 35%; Unit 76, 31%; Unit 77, 33%; Unit 78, 33%. Most Units with lower kills had much lower success. A study of all the above statistics will allow a hunter to formulate a good picture of where the elk are and where his chances are likely to be best during any season. It is also worthwhile to note that in the Units where kills per square mile ran from better than one to two-plus elk, the hunters per square mile also ran highest, from about three to five, although of course they were not necessarily all there at the same time.

The National Forests are the great reservoirs for elk hunting. Readers should check the Units and Counties against the locations of these Forests. For further study, a good item is the official highway map of Colorado, which can be obtained either from the Game Department or from the Highway Department, located at 4201 E. Arkansas Avenue, Denver 80222. It is an invaluable aid, since it shows all of the Forests. The Forest maps (see front of chapter) also are invaluable for both elk and deer hunters.

Some of the state-owned or controlled tracts which offer elk hunting are also very much worthwhile checking out. Among the WAs listed under other species are: "Blue Grouse," Brown Property and Lakes, Brown's Park, Cebolla Creek, Cherokee Park, Christine, Devil Creek, Fish Creek, Indian Run, Missouri Creek, Mount Evans, Plateau Creek, Radium, Sapinero, Saguache.

There are numerous others, some of which are land tracts (WAs) and some access roads. These will be listed here by counties. When a hunt is planned, a check with the Game personnel for the county in question will elicit full directions, which in some cases are fairly complicated and over mountain roads.

Garfield Co.: Heart Lake (96); Marvine Lakes (97); Piney Road (98); Trappers Lake (99).

Grand Co.: Rock Creek (100).

Gunnison Co.: Beaver Lake (101); Spring Creek Reservoir (102).

Hinsdale Co.: Middle Fork Piedra River Road (103); Happy Valley (104); Williams Creek Reservoir (105).

La Plata Co.: Henderson Lake (106); Lower Hermosa Road (107); Thompson Property (108).

Larimer Co.: Bliss Tract (109); Bull Mt. Road (110).

Mineral Co.: Alberta Park Res. (111); Rito Hondo Reservoir (112).

Rio Blanco Co.: Bailey Lake (113); Swede Lake (114).

Routt Co.: Swamp Park Trail (115); Dumont Lake (116); Hahn's Peak Reservoir (117).

ANTELOPE

The Colorado antelope population is fairly stable but modest numerically. Most animals are on private ranchlands. The concentrations are scattered. Most are in the east. The Limon and Hugo region is one of the best. The Chico Basin east of Colorado Springs is another good area. Others are northeast of Fort Collins. There are also antelope bands in the northwest, in Moffat Co. and spreading out from it.

Hunting is by permit, by application and drawing for specific Units. Permit numbers usually average from 5000 to 7000. Applicants average 10,000 or more. The kill averages between 4000 and 6000, depending on number of permits. As is usual in antelope hunting, success is high, above 80 percent. Hunters are advised to obtain permission well before the season, because so little hunting is on public lands.

There is really little choice among areas, for success runs so high in all, and the herds are carefully counted and cropped. During a recent season the first ten counties in kill were as follows: Lincoln, 715; Weld, 597; Moffat, 550; Elbert, 485; Las Animas, 330; El Paso, 309; Cheyenne, 258; Kiowa, 243; Park, 202; Larimer, 184. These statistics prove only where the most antelope are, in general terms. Hunter success was just as high in areas with lower kills.

There is at least one public tract where antelope are found. This is Hohnholtz Lakes and Road (118), Larimer Co., out of Glendevey.

BIGHORN SHEEP

Colorado has a fair sheep population in its high country. The species is managed with exceeding care. For over a quarter-century there have been hunts, by application and drawing for a limited number of permits set by areas, or Units. Permits issued have run in numbers from 131 to 285. Annual kill is from 30 to 60 sheep. Success over the years has averaged about 25 percent. In one recent season there were 462 applicants, 131 permits were issued, and 32 sheep were bagged. Colorado sheep hunting is for residents only.

It is not possible to state which permit areas are best. These vary radically from season to season, for sheep hunting is an extremely specialized endeavor. During the 1968 season, as an example, there were some areas where a legal ram was one with three-quarters curl, and some where a half curl was all that was needed. In four areas success ran over 50 percent. These were: Poudre River and Pikes Peak (three-quarters curl) and Sheep Creek and Cimarron Peak (half curl). Yet, there were four other areas open— Collegiate Peaks, Glenwood, Battlement Mesa, Blanco River—where no sheep were killed and no adult rams were seen.

The bighorn in Colorado has had many difficulties. Disease almost wiped them out entirely during the 1920s. Transplanting and full protection built the population up to over 5000 by the early 1950s. Then disease due to winter concentration drastically reduced them again. However, at this time the herd appears fairly stable.

The high peaks in the National Forests hold many sheep. The locations of sheep bands are well checked by the Department field men and hunters intending to apply should make a thorough check with this personnel to ascertain where the best chances appear to be for that year. There are also a number of public tracts under state control that are known for their bighorn hunting. Mount Evans WA ("Blue Grouse") is one. Boiler Creek out of New Castle, Garfield Co., is an access that opens over 17,000 acres of sheep country. The Saguache WA ("Blue Grouse"), and the Pikes Peak WA ("Deer") are also sheep areas.

MOUNTAIN GOAT

Goats were not native to Colorado. The first transplant was made in 1948, with goats from Montana. These were released on Mount Shavano, at the south end of the Collegiate Range. The next release, in 1952, was on Cottonwood Creek, near Sheep Mountain, west of Buena Vista. This site is about fifteen miles north of Mount Shavano. Two other transplants were made, with animals from Idaho and South Dakota. One release was made in 1961 on Mount Evans, near Evergreen. The last, in 1964, was near Lake City, in the San Juan Mountains on the Lake Fork of the Gunnison River. Recently it was discovered this last plant, which was thought to have disappeared, had migrated some distance to Chicago Basin in the Needles Mountains and is becoming established there.

Several hundred animals now roam Colorado's peaks. The first hunt was allowed in 1964. Six permits were issued, four goats were bagged. The following year there were six permits, and three goats were taken. As this is written, the season just passed saw nineteen permits and fifteen goats killed. In the Mount Evans area all hunters were successful. Nine of thirteen hunters succeeded in the Collegiate Range.

This hunting is restricted to residents only. It appears likely that limited hunting will continue and that chances in any area opened will be excellent.

BUFFALO

The Game Department manages four herds that total about fifty animals. The herds are located at Cherry Creek Reservoir State Recreation Area near Denver, Lathrop State Park near Walsenburg, Golden Gate State Park near Blackhawk and Cherokee WA out of Fort Collins. In recent years a few troublesome animals have been eliminated by hunting. From four to six licenses have been issued, to residents only, for each of the past several years, by drawing, and at a fee of $200 each. A buffalo hunt may or may not occur in any given year. Check with the Game Department.

BEAR

The black bear is fairly numerous in Colorado. There is a fall season concurrent with deer and elk seasons, and a spring and summer season beginning in April.

There are thought to be a few grizzlies in a remote region of the San Juan Mountains. A management area has been established there for them. The grizzly is fully protected.

The black bear kill averages from 400 to 700 animals annually. There is presently a special license needed for bear. Previously bear were included in the elk and deer licenses. In one recent season the bear kill of 662 represented a success ratio of about 8.5 percent. About half of the kill was in each season—fall, and spring-summer.

There are no bear concentrations in the state. Best counties in general are: Delta, Mesa, Larimer, Archuleta, Gunnison, Jackson, Montrose, Routt, Grand, Moffat. Some others show up well some seasons. For example, for the season just passed as this is written, the top ten were, in order: Montrose, Mesa, Archuleta, Larimer, Huerfano, La Plata, Grand, Gunnison, Garfield, Las Animas.

Dogs may be used during the spring season. If more than one dog is used, one member of the hunt must be a licensed guide.

MOUNTAIN LION

The mountain lion, after being bountied for thirty-six years, was classed as a game animal in Colorado in 1965. The season runs from September 1 through March, and there have been some special seasons, in April and May, in specified areas. Dogs may be used for lion hunting, except during any deer or elk season. During the past several seasons the kill average has been between fifty and sixty animals. Any lion killed must be offered for inspection by an officer within forty-eight hours.

Very little is known about lion abundance. In the season just concluded, ten were bagged in Unit 58, ten in Unit 69, six in Unit 21, four in Unit 8, four in Unit 49. Other Units showed kills of only one each. Hunters who desire to make a lion hunt should contact a guide with dogs who is experienced at this hunting.

MOOSE

Occasionally moose wander south out of Wyoming into the region above Steamboat Springs. They are not legal game.

OTHER ANIMALS

There are varying populations of red and gray foxes, coyotes, badgers, bobcats, an occasional but very rare lynx. Raccoons also are present along eastern stream courses. Some prairie dog towns still exist. Crows and magpies offer off-season shooting. Magpies, though seldom hunted, offer extremely sporty pest shooting. They are wary birds. Not much attention is paid to the various predators and pests. Coyote calling is followed to some extent in eastern Colorado.

REGULATIONS

Game laws pertaining to seasons, bag and possession limits, areas to be hunted, special hunts, license fees all may have numerous changes from year to year. For current regulations, and for other specific queries, write to: Colorado Department of Game, Fish and Parks, 6060 Broadway, Denver, Colorado 80216.

WYOMING

For many years strikingly scenic Wyoming has held its place firmly among the top big-game hunting states in the nation. The rolling grass and sagebrush plains of the east and interior, set against the massive forests that clothe the mountains of the Continental Divide in the west offer variety of terrain and altitude amenable to almost all big-game species present on the continent. Bounded by Montana on the north, Idaho and Utah on the west, Utah and Colorado on the south, and by Nebraska and South Dakota on the east, Wyoming is situated practically in the center of the big-game country of the Rockies lying within the contiguous states.

Mining, oil, and grazing are the pursuits of most importance here. These are all industries synonymous with vast open spaces. Those Wyoming has in plenty. Rectangular in shape, the state is roughly 330 to 375 straight-line miles east-west, by about 260 north-south. It encompasses 97,914 square miles, and within those borders dwell not many more than 300,000 persons. It is estimated that the state has even lost some residents over the past decade. This places Wyoming as having the smallest population of any state, excepting as this is written possibly Alaska. At least a third of the population centers on the two cities of Casper and Cheyenne. This spreads the remainder extremely thin.

Main highways are excellent. But there is not a wide choice. However, the main routes are so distributed that hunters can easily get to any section of the state. Lesser routes are in no great abundance, and of varying quality. Wyoming is country for the pack-in via horseback, and for utilization by virtually all hunters who wish to get away from the pavement at all of either a pickup or a short-wheelbase 4WD. The 4WD pickup truck is a popular and practical vehicle here. And hunters who drive the back trails, in mountains or plains, even bird hunters, and especially strangers to the area, are well advised to be fully equipped, with such items as chains, shovel, tire-repair equipment, basic tools, extra water, food, and gasoline. It is a huge sweep of sparsely inhabited country.

Air travel to the larger centers is good. There are even numerous flights to many small towns. Charter craft are also available. However, most resident hunters are equipped for vehicular travel within the state, and visitors who fly in are invariably guided. Thus, transport is no real problem.

It is obvious that in a state with so few people there is a great deal of wilderness. Most of the state may be so classed, depending on one's view of the term. Ranches are large, and intermingled with the owned lands are large amounts of BLM holdings. Thus, the treeless or near-treeless areas are as much wilderness as some of the remote stretches of mountains. Even with large amounts of public lands, hunters should bear in mind that they must be certain whether or not they are entering public domain. Trespass in frontier areas such as this is not taken lightly, and both the law and the owner frown upon it severely.

Hunting is exceedingly popular here, and growing ever more so. An average at present of about 135,000 individuals purchase licenses. Probably at least 10,000 of these annually are nonresidents. Many hunters follow only a single favorite sport so far as species are concerned, and there is startling variety. Both mule and whitetail deer abound; there are large elk herds, plus antelope, moose, mountain sheep, mountain goats. Bears are plentiful. Game birds include pheasants, chukar, Hungarian partridge, four varieties of grouse— blue, ruffed, sharptail, sage grouse; there are wild turkeys and waterfowl. Rabbits are plentiful, and predators such as coyotes and bobcats are numerous. Mountain lions are present, though not abundant. Deer, elk, and antelope are the highly popular big game. Though Wyoming hunters are as a group not avid bird hunters, bird hunting is excellent and the pheasant, sage grouse, and chukar the most sought species.

Public lands here are in millions of acres. In fact, there are some thirty million acres of federal lands, or approximately 48 percent of the state's total acreage. There is a great deal of Bureau of Land Management acreage chiefly in the two-thirds of the state outside the forested mountains. The BLM has been in process of drawing up and publishing maps for each section of the western U.S. As this is written, not all are completed, but may be as it is read. There is a publication, "Wildlife and Recreation on Public Lands in Wyoming," available from the Bureau of Land Management, Department of the Interior, 2002 Capitol Ave., Cheyenne, Wyoming 82001. From this office also maps as published may be obtained for various sections of Wyoming.

Without question the most important public lands in the state are those administered by the U.S. Forest Service. There are over nine million acres of these. A rather overlooked category of Forest Service lands are the National Grasslands. These are usually interspersed with privately owned tracts and thus it is advisable to obtain a map. Wyoming has one large National Grassland, Thunder Basin (1). It is in the northeast, beginning a modest distance west of the South Dakota border in the general area of parts of Weston, Niobrara, Campbell, and Converse counties. There are a total of almost 600,000 acres in this Grassland. It is administered from the Headquarters of the Supervisor of the Medicine Bow National Forest, Laramie (which see in following paragraphs) and maps and information may be obtained from that address. There is a relatively small block of this Grassland, incidentally, to the north of the main portion, and much nearer to the Montana border. Such tracts are easily overlooked and in this region of Wyoming these lands have a high potential for hunters.

The National Forests are of course the prime big-game areas of Wyoming. To launch a discussion of them, again it should be noted that one block easily overlooked is in the extreme northeast, in Crook Co., directly west of Belle Fourche, South Dakota. This is a part of the Black Hills NF (2), the major share of which is in South Dakota. Headquarters of the Supervisor, where maps and information may be obtained, is at Custer, South Dakota. The Wyoming town of Sundance is a good orientation point for this Forest tract.

The main Forests of Wyoming are five in number.

The Bighorn NF (3) contains over 1,113,000 acres, has headquarters where one may write for maps and details at Sheridan. This Forest is in north-central Wyoming, reaching down from the Montana border. U.S. 14, 16, and

87 are the main routes, with Buffalo, Greybull, Lovell, Sheridan supply-point towns in the area.

Medicine Bow NF (4) is in the southeast and south-central area of the state, has just under 1,100,000 acres. Headquarters is at Laramie. That city, and Medicine Bow, Saratoga, Encampment, and Cheyenne are good check points. U.S. 30-287 is the main route, with Wyoming 130 and 230 crossing some of the high country.

The Bridger NF (5), 1,700,000 acres, is across the state to the west, slightly south of center. Headquarters is at the town of Kemmerer. Several U.S. Highways reach the region: 30N, 187, 189, 26, 89. Supply-point towns in addition to Kemmerer are Pinedale and Afton.

North of this Forest is the Teton NF (6), 1,700,820 acres. Headquarters is at Jackson. Highways for access are U.S. 89, 187, 26, 287. The town of Dubois is on the east slope.

North and east lies the huge Shoshone NF (7), encompassing nearly 2.5 million acres. Cody is the headquarters town. Others in the region are Dubois, Lander, and Cooke City, Montana.

Sizable portions of several other Forests overlap into western Wyoming from neighboring states. A large section of Idaho's Targhee NF (8) lies along the western Wyoming border north and west of the town of Jackson. Forest headquarters is in St. Anthony, Idaho. There is a small block, also falling across the Idaho border, of that state's Caribou NF (9), with headquarters in Pocatello, Idaho. In the southwest, along the southern border, there is a section of Utah's Wasatch NF (10) overlapping. Headquarters is in Salt Lake City.

State-owned or cooperatively administered lands are also quite numerous. There are at present thirty tracts of varied sizes and well distributed over the state where hunting of wide variety is available, for both large and small game. These individual blocks will be dealt with under species headings later. Some of the tracts are called Wildlife Units, and some are designated as Public Hunting and Fishing Areas. To avoid confusion here, the general term PHA will be used in most instances. The Game Commission published in 1969 its first booklet giving details and locations of all these PHAs. It is titled "Public Hunting and Fishing on Wyoming Game and Fish Commission Areas." This excellent publication, which presumably will be updated as need arises, may be obtained from the Commission, address at chapter end.

Big-game management, and hunting regulations and quotas, utilize numbered Areas. Thus, hunters must obtain what are termed in this state the Hunting Orders, that is, the regulations and accompanying map for the season in question. Also, these orders must be obtained for each species one plans to hunt. The Areas are not the same, nor numbered identically, among the various species. In numerous instances there are quotas on certain big-game animals, and there are limits in some cases on the number of certain types of licenses issued in any one season. Applications for permits must be in by designated dates. The big-game regulations are, in fact, fairly complicated and may change radically from season to season. Hunters should acquire the regulations as early as possible and thoroughly study them. Ordinarily the orders are ready in May. Bird season information is not available until August, but opening dates usually fall in the same general period from year to year.

Nonresidents must be accompanied by a guide when hunting deer, moose, sheep, goat, elk, bear in any National Forest or National Refuge or Park. Landowners may legally insist that hunters on their lands use guides. Any Wyoming resident may act as guide in this instance, but he is not allowed to

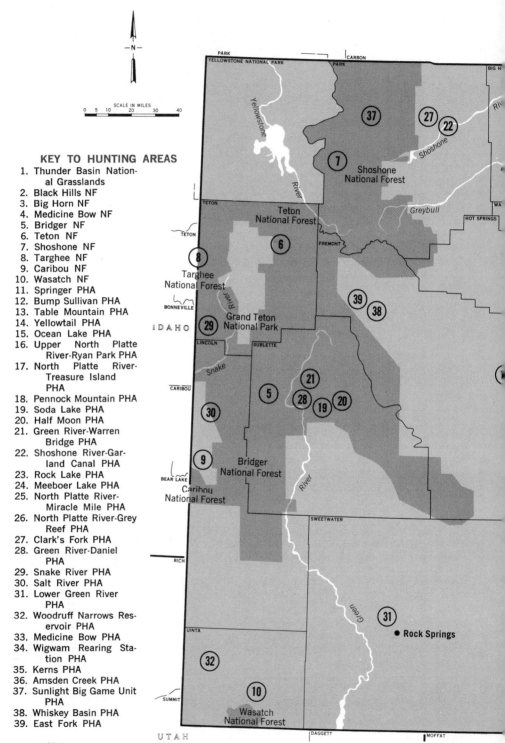

KEY TO HUNTING AREAS

1. Thunder Basin National Grasslands
2. Black Hills NF
3. Big Horn NF
4. Medicine Bow NF
5. Bridger NF
6. Teton NF
7. Shoshone NF
8. Targhee NF
9. Caribou NF
10. Wasatch NF
11. Springer PHA
12. Bump Sullivan PHA
13. Table Mountain PHA
14. Yellowtail PHA
15. Ocean Lake PHA
16. Upper North Platte River-Ryan Park PHA
17. North Platte River-Treasure Island PHA
18. Pennock Mountain PHA
19. Soda Lake PHA
20. Half Moon PHA
21. Green River-Warren Bridge PHA
22. Shoshone River-Garland Canal PHA
23. Rock Lake PHA
24. Meeboer Lake PHA
25. North Platte River-Miracle Mile PHA
26. North Platte River-Grey Reef PHA
27. Clark's Fork PHA
28. Green River-Daniel PHA
29. Snake River PHA
30. Salt River PHA
31. Lower Green River PHA
32. Woodruff Narrows Reservoir PHA
33. Medicine Bow PHA
34. Wigwam Rearing Station PHA
35. Kerns PHA
36. Amsden Creek PHA
37. Sunlight Big Game Unit PHA
38. Whiskey Basin PHA
39. East Fork PHA

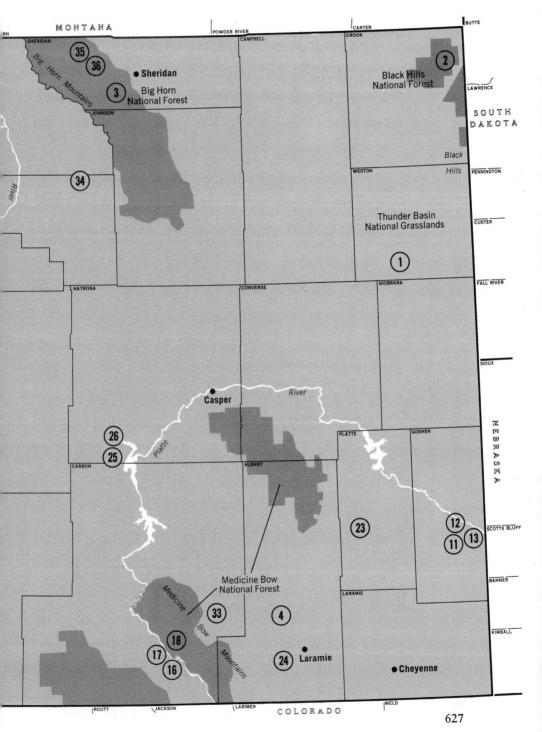

WYOMING

MONTANA

POWDER RIVER

CAMPBELL

CARTER

BUTTE

CROOK

SHERIDAN

35 36

● Sheridan

3 Big Horn
National Forest

Big Horn Mountains

River

34

JOHNSON

Black Hills
National Forest

2

LAWRENCE

SOUTH
DAKOTA

Black

Hills

PENNINGTON

WESTON

CUSTER

Thunder Basin
National Grasslands

1

NATRONA

CONVERSE

NIOBRARA

FALL RIVER

SIOUX

● Casper

River

Platte

26

25

CARBON

PLATTE

ALBANY

GOSHEN

NEBRASKA

23

12

11 13

SCOTTS BLUFF

Medicine Bow
National Forest

Medicine Bow Mountains

33

18

17

16

4

24 ● Laramie

LARAMIE

● Cheyenne

BANNER

KIMBALL

ROUTT

JACKSON

LARIMER

COLORADO

WELD

627

accept pay, must have a guide permit and a big-game hunting license. There are many professional licensed guides and outfitters in Wyoming. The Commission can furnish a list but cannot of course offer recommendations. Hunters should check laws relative to the wearing of visible bright-colored outer garments.

There is little problem in finding places to stay. Even though towns are mostly small, Wyoming is well geared to tourism and for the annual influx of hunters. There are many lodges catering to hunters, and of course nonresidents will ordinarily be guided and their accommodations arranged by the outfitter. For campers there is wide opportunity. The National Forests have almost unlimited campsites. The booklet mentioned previously covering PHAs notes which of these state-administered tracts permits camping. Two useful publications obtainable from the Wyoming Travel Commission, 2320 Capitol Avenue, Cheyenne 82001 are: "Camping Big Wyoming" and "Wyoming Accommodations," the latter a listing of motels, hotels, dude ranches, outfitters.

Weather during Wyoming hunting seasons varies from light wool shirt weather in early fall to severe cold and snow in the high country, often as early as October. The state is high, all of it above 3000 feet, and with peaks reaching close to 14,000. Average altitude at which most hunters will operate lies around six to nine thousand feet. Though the sun may seem hot on some fall days, the moment one steps into shade the air feels chill. This is typical of all high altitude regions where humidity is low. Hunters should be outfitted with a full range of clothing and boots for anything from warm fall days to blizzard conditions.

Arms and ammunition here must cover wide latitude, too. Bird hunters are offered a variety, but probably can compromise best by settling on No. 6 and No. 7½ loads for most endeavors, excepting waterfowl, where No. 4 for ducks and No. 2 for geese are standard. Rifle hunters can use such calibers as the 6mm and .243 for antelope and deer. But something heavier for deer may be better for the average hunters strange to the state. Good compromise calibers for deer-elk hunters are those comparable to the .30/06, .270, and .308, using heavy bullets. These are adequate also for moose, sheep, and goat, but many hunters prefer the magnums, such as the 7mm, .300, etc., for elk, moose, sheep. The first-time bear hunter, or one with only limited experience, should use calibers comparable to the .308 or 7mm.

PHEASANT

The ringneck sustains the highest hunting pressure and annual bag of any of Wyoming's game birds. However, pheasant habitat is limited. The birds sustain themselves only in the irrigated cropland valleys.

Management and setting of seasons and limits is by groups of counties or single counties. The Big Horn Basin is comprised of Big Horn, Hot Springs, Park, and Washakie counties in the northwest, east of Yellowstone Park. Directly south is the Fremont Co. area, where the season and/or limit may differ. East of Big Horn Basin is the Sheridan-Johnson Co. area, made up of those counties. The remainder of the pheasant habitat is in counties slanting from here down to the southeast: Converse Co., then Platte, Goshen, and Laramie in the southeastern corner of the state. Again, seasons and limits may differ in each of those counties.

Although self-sustaining pheasant populations are present in all suitable parts of the range, some stocking is done to assist the continuance of the flock and to boost hunting success. All released birds, however, are banded so that hunters can tell these from wild-reared stock. In one late season approximately

5000 birds were released in the three counties of the southeastern corner of the state.

Pheasant hunters currently total above 18,000. The annual harvest, though it suffers some drastic fluctuations, may be averaged at around 70,000 birds. Goshen Co. in the southeast is the high-kill county. Some seasons it has furnished close to half of the total state bag. Park Co. shows up well, has been recently in second place, with Big Horn and Sheridan about tied for third. Washakie Co. makes a good showing in hunter success, but more birds are taken in Laramie and Fremont Cos.

Most pheasant hunting is on private lands because the birds stick closely to irrigated cropland valleys. Nonetheless, there is opportunity on the PHA lands. In Goshen Co. in the southeast, best of the pheasant counties, there are three tracts within a few miles of each other. Springer PHA (11) is twelve miles south of Torrington, just west of U.S. 85, on Spring Reservoir. Within two miles is the Bump Sullivan PHA and Reservoir (12). To the east of U.S. 85, and near the village of Huntley, is Table Mountain PHA (13).

The public area of which Wyoming is perhaps proudest so far as bird hunting is concerned is the large Yellowtail PHA (14). This is in the north, in northwestern Big Horn Co., on the southwestern shore of Yellowtail Reservoir. It is seven miles east of the town of Lovell. The state administers some thousands of acres here, and a variety of game birds (see others following in chapter), including pheasants, are resident. To the south, in central Fremont Co., Ocean Lake (15) lies to the north of U.S. 26, approximately twenty-five miles west from Riverton. There is a PHA tract here that offers pheasant shooting.

SAGE GROUSE

The big sage grouse is thoroughly identified with Wyoming, where in pioneer times it was teemingly abundant. Even today, when this largest of our native grouse, with old males sometimes weighing as much as eight pounds, is suffering severe difficulties due to progressive destruction of habitat, Wyoming still has excellent hunting for it. Over the past decade the seasonal harvest has never been below 40,000 birds; it has climbed as high as 70,000. At this writing the season immediately past showed a total kill of over 55,000 birds.

Sage grouse are distributed rather generally over the state wherever sage brush plains occur. Recently fourteen of the state's twenty-three counties have had open season. Sweetwater and Carbon Cos. in the south have the highest kills. The Farson area in northwestern Sweetwater Co. is considered one of the best. Fremont and Sublette Cos. north of Sweetwater Co. are about on a par with the others, and Lincoln Co., bordering Sublette and Sweetwater on the west, is next. Natrona Co. in central Wyoming, Albany Co. in the southeast, and Park Co. in the northwest all get fewer hunters but show good hunting success. Other open counties get little hunting and the kill is low.

Large expanses of BLM lands offer excellent opportunity for public sage grouse hunting. Several PHAs also have this species. The Upper North Platte River-Ryan Park PHA (16) is one of these, located in southeastern Carbon Co. It is reached via a road running south from State 130 to French Creek campground, thence via access road about 6.5 miles. There is another tract on the North Platte River in the same general area, North Platte River-Treasure Island PHA (17). It is a few miles south from Saratoga. A third unit is Pennock Mountain (18), northeast of Saratoga near the boundary of the Medicine Bow NF.

The Soda Lake PHA (19) is primarily for big game, giving access to the

Bridger NF, but offers good chances for sage grouse also. It is seven miles north of Pinedale, Sublette Co. Another tract, Half Moon PHA (20), is nine miles northeast from Pinedale. On U.S. 187 some twenty-four miles northwest from Pinedale is the Green River-Warren Bridge PHA (21). There are campsites here and the land is BLM.

CHUKAR

The introduced chukar stands third in importance among upland game birds in Wyoming. The annual harvest fluctuates from some 12,000 birds to 27,000. During a season just concluded, an estimated 5000 hunters participated. Chukar populations are established in several locations. Heaviest density is found in a group of northwestern and north-central counties: Park, Hot Springs, Washakie, Big Horn. There is also fair opportunity in Natrona Co. in central Wyoming, and there are small pockets of chukar population in Sheridan, Johnson, and Sweetwater Cos. Seasons may be opened elsewhere as buildup of this species dictates.

BLM lands where there are arid, rocky hills are good locations. The Yellowtail PHA noted under "Pheasant" is considered one of the better chukar locations. The Shoshone River-Garland Canal PHA (22) is another good tract. It is on the Shoshone River between Cody and Powell, Alt. U.S. 14.

HUNGARIAN PARTRIDGE

Huns are not abundant, but are present in fair numbers in the same counties where the chukar is found. Park, Big Horn, Sheridan, Washakie, and Hot Springs Cos., in that order, recently showed highest kills. Other counties that are fair: Natrona, Johnson, Fremont. Some seasons the bag has been less than 1000 but it has gone as high as 7500. Huns and chukars are often hunted together, but the Hun prefers croplands or their borders rather than the rocky slopes. Some good public hunting is found at Yellowtail ("Pheasant").

BLUE, RUFFED, SHARPTAIL GROUSE

Blue grouse are found in the big timber of the high country. They are in fair supply but get little attention. An average of less than 3000 birds is bagged annually by slightly more than a thousand hunters. During one recent season Lincoln Co. was first, Teton second, Carbon third. A number of counties are open and National Forest lands offer endless opportunity for this bird.

The situation with the ruffed grouse is much the same. A kill of about 3000 grouse by a few hundred hunters is average. Recent harvest statistics show Lincoln Co. with most hunters and over two-thirds of the total bag. Teton Co. was next. Again, the National Forests offer all but limitless opportunity for the diligent bird hunter.

There are a few sharptail grouse in the open country of Sheridan and Johnson Cos. east of the Big Horn Mountains. Sheridan Co. has the most, but the total kill recently has been only about 800 birds.

There are a few prairie chickens, fully protected, in Goshen Co., and there are whitetailed ptarmigan above timberline in some mountain ranges. There is presently no open season.

QUAIL

A few bobwhites are found along the Platte River in the east. There are not enough for hunting. A decade ago pen-raised birds were stocked experimentally along the Shoshone River east of Lovell, Big Horn Co. Other releases, of quail from Washington, were made on the Big Horn and Greybull rivers. There has been a bit of hunting in Big Horn Co. It is believed the winters may be too severe and habitat not conducive to any very solid establishment of this species. A few bobwhites are present, and hunted, on the Yellowtail public hunting area ("Pheasant").

WILD TURKEYS

Since 1955 Wyoming has had a season for the Merriam's turkey in specified areas in fall. There are three turkey hunting Areas at present, and a specified number of permits is offered for each. Largest number of permits is for the Black Hills Area, in the northeast, in Crook and Weston Cos. One recent season there were 2500 permits for this Area. Next is the Sheridan-Johnson County Area, within designated boundaries in these north-central counties. Permits number 500 or more. Third Area is Laramie Peaks, in Niobrara, Albany, Converse, Goshen, and Platte Cos. in the southeast. Permits here have been averaging around 250.

Total turkey kill over some seasons has run from 800 to as high as 1500. In one recent season 464 birds were bagged in the Black Hills Area, 33 in Sheridan-Johnson, 87 in Laramie Peaks. Permits are on an application and drawing basis.

In the spring of 1969 Wyoming had its first spring turkey hunt. Permits numbered 500, on a first-come basis, and were all for the Black Hills Area.

Most turkey hunting is on privately owned lands. One should attempt to obtain permission well before the hunt. Turkeys have been released in thirteen Wyoming counties. They were introduced on the big Yellowtail PHA in 1966. It is possible that in years to come there will be turkey hunting in several more Wyoming locations.

WATERFOWL

Wyoming is not one of the top waterfowl states but it does have some good shooting nonetheless. It is in two flyways, Central and Pacific, and thus regulations for the east slope and the west slope differ. Although the total seasonal bag has varied quite drastically over past years, a recent season that may be considered a good one showed a kill of 36,000-plus for ducks, with over 5000 hunters participating, and a goose harvest of 2591, for 2796 hunters.

Duck hunting opportunity is well distributed in all counties of the state. During the season mentioned above, the high counties in order were: Goshen, Park, Lincoln, Teton, Natrona, Fremont, Carbon, Big Horn, Sheridan, Platte. Most geese were killed in Goshen and Lincoln Cos. Large reservoirs such as Boysen near Shoshoni concentrated large numbers of ducks, chiefly mallards. There is also good hunting along the larger rivers.

There is a great deal of good waterfowling on the PHAs. Springer, Table Mountain, Bump Sullivan, Yellowtail, Ocean Lake ("Pheasant") are among the best locations. Shoshone River-Garland Canal ("Chukar"), Green River ("Sage Grouse") both have good possibilities.

Others not noted thus far are as follows: Rock Lake PHA (23), Platte Co., near Wheatland; Meeboer Lake (24), Albany Co., near Laramie; North Platte River-Miracle Mile (25), between Kortes and Pathfinder Reservoirs south of Alcova which is in southern Natrona Co.; North Platte River-Grey Reef PHA (26), two miles northeast of Alcova; Clark's Fork PHA (27) of the Yellowstone River, north of Cody; Green River-Daniel PHA (28) on the Green River, Sublette Co., near Daniel which is west of Pinedale; Snake River PHA (29), between Jackson and Wilson, Teton Co.; Salt River PHA (30), several tracts north of Afton, Lincoln Co., excellent late in season for geese; Lower Green River PHA (31), near town of Green River, Sweetwater Co.; Woodruff Narrows Reservoir PHA (32), northwest of Evanston, west-central Uinta Co.

Although there is an open season for snipe and rails, almost no attention is paid to these birds.

RABBITS

Cottontails are found over most portions of Wyoming except the mountains. Snowshoe hares in modest numbers live in the timbered higher country. Jackrabbits are exceedingly abundant throughout the plains.

Only the cottontail appears on the game list, and it gets small attention. There are usually two separate seasons but they actually amount to one long one, from late August through until April of the following year. Most cottontail hunting is done on ranchlands, but owners usually give permission. There is also good cottontail hunting on most of the public tracts already noted, where the various game birds are hunted. A great sport potential is presently wasted due to lack of interest in rabbit hunting here, but presumably this activity will become more and more popular as hunting pressures on other species grow.

DEER

Wyoming is one of our best western deer states, especially popular with nonresidents. Mule deer are abundant almost everywhere. The mountain hunting is excellent. Much of the rough open plains country is just as good, a fact not always recognized by first-time visiting hunters. There are also whitetail deer in the state. By far the majority of the whitetails are in the northeast, in the Black Hills region. A few are found elsewhere. Total deer kill over more than a decade has never been less than 60,000 and in some seasons rises above 80,000.

During the season just past as this is written, 80,458 deer were taken. There is hunting for both antlered and antlerless deer, set by management areas. The following statistics referring to the season mentioned give a good picture of the composition of the kill for any average season. Buck mule deer, 49,801, antlerless mule deer 16,766, buck whitetails 8595, antlerless whitetails 5296. It is indicative of the abundance of whitetails in the northeastern corner of the state (and chiefly in Crook Co.) that in the Black Hills Management Areas 12,038 were bagged, out of a total for the state of 13,891.

In fact, this region is usually most popular with nonresidents, and one of the most popular with residents. Total kill, mule and whitetail deer, during the season above, was 27,334 in the group of six Management Units that make up the Black Hills Region of the northeast. That amounts to almost three-eighths of the total kill for the state. Crook Co. alone drew over 5000 resident deer hunters and over 12,000 nonresidents.

Consistently second, and an excellent region, is the Medicine Bow area which includes management units in the Rawlins, Platte River, Laramie Peaks region, south-central and southeast. The total kill here, almost entirely mule deer, was for the above season 16,710. Consistently third is the Big Horn area, which covers the north-central region of the Tongue, Goose, Shell, South Bighorn rivers and Tensleep Canyon and surrounding territory. The kill here: 14,971. This means that approximately three-fourths of the deer killed in

Wyoming come from these three general sections of the state. The western mountains do not sustain herds anywhere near as large.

It is interesting and valuable information for a hunter to know that approximately 60 percent of the total state kill is of buck mule deer. Also, that during the season above, which may be considered a good but average season, there were slightly more than 100,000 hunters. This means that approximately four-fifths of the hunters were successful. A few Areas had two-deer special hunts, but this does not materially affect the high success percentage. Actually, nonresident success was officially figured at a whopping 87.70 percent and resident at 74.50 percent.

Hundreds of thousands of acres of public domain are available to deer hunters. In the northeast there are the blocks of Black Hills NF and the Thunder Basin Grasslands. In the south-central and southeast area, which is second in kill, there is all of the Medicine Bow NF plus large areas of BLM lands. In the Big Horn region there is all of the Big Horn NF plus other BLM lands. And of course there are the vast western Forests and BLM expanses, too. There are many guides to assist visiting deer hunters, and almost all ranchers are congenial about assisting or guiding visiting hunters. Any small town where one stops and asks questions will turn up numerous residents who are friendly and ready to point a nonresident toward a good deer area.

The PHAs also furnish some prime deer hunting. The two North Platte areas, the Pennock Mountain unit, Half Moon, Soda Lake, Green River, all noted under "Sage Grouse," have deer. Others not thus far described are as follows: Medicine Bow PHA (33) is in Carbon Co. in the south, southeast of the village of Elk Mountain. It adjoins the Medicine Bow NF, and the access roads to the unit also give access to good deer country in the Forest. Up in the Big Horn region, there is Wigwam Rearing Station (34), with a deer hunting tract to the north. This is reached off U.S. 16 from east of the village of Tensleep, in northeastern Washakie Co. The Kerns PHA (35) is in northwestern Sheridan Co., northwest from Parkman. There is access here to the Big Horn NF also. Nearby is the Amsden Creek PHA (36) on the Tongue River near Dayton.

The Sunlight Big Game Unit (37), a PHA, adjoins the Shoshone NF and there are access roads leading to it. This is a very scenic expanse in the Sunlight Peak area approximately forty-five miles west of Cody, in Park Co. The Whiskey Basin Big Game Unit (38), and the East Fork Big Game Unit (39) are both in northwestern Fremont Co., near Dubois. The former is a few miles southeast, the latter eighteen miles northeast. The Shoshone NF borders both tracts. There is a six-mile stretch of the Snake River open to hunting, downstream from the State 22 bridge between Jackson and Wilson, in southwest Teton Co. that also has possibilities. This section of the River is often floated. This gets a hunter to good foothill deer range.

ELK

The Wyoming elk herd is one of the largest in the U.S. For some years the annual kill has run from 12,000 to above 14,000. Major elk populations are in the northwest and north-central parts of the state. Areas around Jackson, especially in the Gros Ventre River vicinity, the Cody region, and the region of the Bighorn Mountains are generally the heavy producers.

Elk are hunted on a quota system, except in certain specified Areas. Numbered Areas are set up by specified boundaries, and each Area is assigned a kill quota. These, added, make up the total special-permit kill quota for the state for any given year. Some Areas offer either-sex hunting. But this is for residents only. Nonresidents must hunt bulls only. Also, nonresident elk licenses are limited in number. For some years they have all been taken very early in the year. Recently 32,295 residents and 4526 nonresidents hunted during one season. About 35 percent of the total kill in an average season is of mature bulls. The remainder is made up of spikes, cows, calves. Guided nonresidents show high success, above 50 percent. Success of residents is a bit lower.

Due to overpopulation of elk in Yellowstone Park and a resultant slaughter by Rangers that was highly protested by sportsmen, a number of surplus elk are now being moved out of the Park to other parts of Wyoming. There has recently been some special permit hunting, residents only, in Grand Teton National Park.

The National Forests are the great reservoirs of elk population. Kill statistics show the Teton generally rating first, the Bridger and Big Horn roughly tied for second, the Shoshone and Medicine Bow tied for third. The Gros Ventre and Hoback drainages and general region out of Jackson, Teton Co., accounts on the average for approximately a third of the total elk kill.

With such vast public areas in which to hunt, it is certainly best for any elk hunter to be guided, unless he is native to the region where he will hunt and knows the country intimately. There is some good elk hunting on some of the PHAs that should not be overlooked. The Kerns and the Amsden Creek units, the Sunlight Big Game Unit, Whiskey Basin, East Fork, Soda Lake, all described under "Deer" are the ones to try.

Elk-hunting numbered Areas, incidentally, are not the same as the deer Areas. Hunters should be aware of this when making application. It is necessary to have a copy of the elk Hunting Orders map for the season in question.

ANTELOPE

Wyoming has the largest antelope herd on the continent, of probably at least 100,000 animals, and with an annual harvest of from 23,000 to as high as 37,000-plus. This great antelope population is a kind of monument to conservation and to the cooperation of ranchers and game biologists. Originally antelope raced the Wyoming (and other) western plains by millions. Settlement, fencing, uncontrolled kill of them for food, and other influences soon brought the antelope literally to the verge of extinction. Early in the century alarmed conservationists made desperate attempts to protect remnants of this species and to bring it back to substantial numbers. It is interesting that in 1916 the State Game Warden in Wyoming said that it would be a long time, if indeed ever, when an open season might be allowed on antelope. Since that statement nearly three quarters of a million have been taken, and the antelope, or more properly "pronghorn," appears safe for many years to come, even though continued fencing and destruction of range present continuing problems.

Hunter success in Wyoming is extremely high. Nonresidents chalk up close to 100 percent, and residents are not far behind. Antelope are hunted on a quota system. An annual survey is made, numbered Areas are established (these Areas differ from those for deer and those for elk), and a specified number of permits is allowed for each Area. A percentage of these is allotted for nonresidents, who must have their applications, on proper forms supplied upon request to the Game Department, in the Cheyenne office not later than June 10. After this a drawing is held. Nowadays as many as 10,000 more hunters apply than there are permits available. Applicants may apply for one Area only. Resident permits go on sale in early August on a first-come basis.

Antelope range virtually everywhere in the state except in the timbered mountain portions. It is not possible to state which locations are best. Heaviest concentrations are throughout most of the eastern half of the state. The northeast corner of the state, covering Campbell, Crook, and Weston Cos. has abundant antelope and the Areas covering these counties, in a region based in a general way on Gillette, Sundance, and Newcastle, get as many as 5000 to 6000 permits most seasons. The region north of Douglas and Glenrock has large herds; the same is true of the area east of Douglas, on to Lusk and south to Torrington. All of the region surrounding Casper, south to the border, and southwest into the Sweetwater River country is excellent. The country south of Buffalo to Kaycee and Edgerton is the same. The Lander vicinity, Fremont Co., has superb hunting. Generally speaking the Areas in the southwest and the northwest get fewer permits. But an antelope hunter who holds a permit anywhere in Wyoming and who has several days to hunt is almost certain to bag his game.

Most antelope hunting is on privately owned lands, or on grazing lands leased by ranchers. Permission must be requested, but this presents few problems. There is some antelope hunting on the PHAs. Pennock Mountain PHA ("Sage Grouse"), Medicine Bow ("Deer"), Half Moon, and Green River ("Sage Grouse") are the tracts.

MOOSE

Wyoming has a substantial moose population in the western mountains. Oddly, moose were never reported in what is now Wyoming during the days of the early trappers and explorers. It was not until the late 1800s and early 1900s that mention began to be made of this species. They were so few at that time that a ten-year closed season was established, from 1903 to 1912. By 1916 it was estimated that there were at least 2000 moose in the mountains of western Wyoming, from Montana to the southern border with Utah. In 1942 resident permits for cow moose were issued for the first time. Some attempts were made, later, to transplant moose to the Big Horns, and these resulted in establishment of the animals there.

Presently from 1000 to 1300 permits are issued annually for 26 to 29 numbered Areas in the western mountains. Success is excellent. In two recent seasons it ran 91 and 89 percent. Numerous Areas showed 100 percent success. Applications must be in by June 30. Nonresidents are allowed to take mature bulls only. In some areas residents must take antlered animlas only, but in others either sex is legal. Applicants may receive only one permit in any three-year period.

Since almost all hunting is done on National Forest lands, and nonresidents must be guided there, virtually all will engage outfitters. They are well advised to do so. Residents who do not know the moose country will be better off to be guided also. There is little choice of Area when one applies. The Upper Green River region north of Pinedale is a good choice. What is known as the Pinedale Off-Forest area along the western edge of the Bridger NF, the Upper and the Lower Gros Ventre River areas east of Jackson all have excellent moose populations. These four get the largest number of permits as a rule, and show high success. However, a hunter who books with a good outfitter and draws a permit in almost any moose Area stands an excellent chance of bagging his game. As a general guide to applicants, the following counties are estimated to have the highest moose populations: Teton, Sublette, Fremont, northern Lincoln.

It is wise to apply early in the year. Some years all permits are taken by March or earlier. Only 25 percent are offered to nonresidents.

SHEEP

There is a fairly substantial bighorn population in Wyoming's western mountain ranges, and in the Big Horn Mountains, and in the Laramie Peak area of the Medicine Bow NF in the southeast. Sheep appear to be on the increase in the state. Permit numbers may vary broadly, but lately have remained quite consistent. In one recent season 384 were issued. The next season there were 390. Only rams with three-quarters-inch curl are legal for nonresidents, but in specified Areas occasionally residents are allowed to take half-curl rams. Of the permits issued, 25 percent are for nonresidents. Applications for all sheep hunters must be in by June 30.

Success, considering the rugged terrain where these hunts take place, is quite high. Over recent years it has averaged about 40 percent. Permit holders cannot apply again for a three-year period. Although chances are as good in one Area as another in this specialized hunting, a knowledgeable outfitter certainly gives any hunter an edge. Some of the regions with high kills, good sheep populations, and high success are Jakey's Fork of the Green in the lower part of the Shoshone NF, the Crescent Mountain region of the Divide north and west of Dubois, the mountain country east of Jackson in the Gros Ventre drainage.

MOUNTAIN GOAT

There are only a few goats in Wyoming, and hunting for them is not offered each year. Recently there was an open season, with four permits issued, one of them for nonresidents. The open territory was the relatively small but exceedingly rugged country on the northwestern border north of Clark's Fork River. This area is the Beartooth Pass region reached out of Cooke City, Montana, via U.S. 212. Applications must be in by June 30. One who draws a permit may not apply again for three years. Interested hunters should check with the Department each year to ascertain if issuance of permits is planned.

BEAR

There are a few grizzlies left in Wyoming, mostly in Yellowstone Park. But grizzly hunting was stopped in 1967. Black bears are numerous in the mountains. Largest numbers are found in the northwest. There are some also in the Big Horns and the Medicine Bow mountains. There is a fall season, concurrent with deer and elk, and a spring season during April, May, and June. The black bear is far underhunted. Baiting is legal and many outfitters who book spring bear hunts utilize this method. Fall kills are mostly incidental, but spring hunting gives hunters an excellent chance, on multiple-kill licenses. The total harvest is not high, seldom over 400. Mountain areas out of Jackson, Cody, Afton, Pinedale, Dubois, Saratoga all offer good hunting. Booking with a good outfitter is advisable.

MOUNTAIN LION

As this is written, most states where mountain lions occur have placed the animal on the game list, but it is still classed as a predator in Wyoming. Cattlemen presumably are adamant about keeping it in that category. Actually Wyoming is not very good lion range and the animals are scarce. Wyoming outfitters who book lion hunters usually do their hunting in Colorado or Utah.

There is a curious law in force at this time of which nonresidents should be aware. Residents are required to obtain a trapping license to take predators on National Forest lands. Nonresidents are not allowed this privilege, and thus are restricted from hunting lions on NF lands in Wyoming. Because of objection from cattlemen, there is little chance that the lion will be placed on the game list.

OTHER ANIMALS

Coyotes, red fox, bobcats, an occasional lynx, badgers, raccoons are all present in varying numbers. Some prairie dog towns still exist but poisoning has decimated most of them. There are rockchucks for pest shooting in the rough, high, open country. Not much attention is paid to any of these animals by residents. Nonresidents, as noted under "Lion," are not allowed to hunt any of these animals on the National Forests but may hunt them elsewhere. Some excellent predator hunting, by use of a call or otherwise, is available almost everywhere for those who wish to pursue it.

REGULATIONS

Game laws pertaining to seasons, bag and possession limits, areas to be hunted, special hunts, license fees all may have numerous changes from year to year. For current regulations, and for other specific queries, write to: Wyoming Fish and Game Commission, Box 1589, Cheyenne, Wyoming 82001.

IDAHO

The rugged grandeur of Idaho's mountains, and the quality of its potatoes, are famed throughout the nation. Along much of the eastern border, which is with Montana and Wyoming, the towering and handsome Bitterroots march majestically, and when they end and one moves down through southeastern Idaho, much of which is valley farming landing, still the snow-covered Tetons across in Wyoming are always in view.

Mountains are in fact in view almost everywhere in Idaho, and down through the green valleys scores of swift streams course. The slopes are well fostered. Almost 40 percent of Idaho's 83,557 square miles are in forest. In the south one looks across the border into Utah and Nevada, and in the west the long border is with Oregon and Washington. Idaho is oddly shaped, the southern half forming almost a rectangle from which an ever narrowing northern half reaches up to finally touch a short portion of the southern British Columbia border.

Potatoes, wheat, apples are nationally important agricultural products. There is much grazing, the state is still first in the nation in silver mining, and lumbering is a leading industry. Compared to its size, Idaho's population is low, a fortunate situation so far as hunters are concerned. There are less than three-fourths of a million people.

Main highways are good, but they are not numerous. In a belt across the south where larger cities are located—Boise, Twin Falls, Pocatello, Idaho Falls—the highway network is quite extensive. U.S. 93 runs up through a part of the state east of center, and is joined part way up by U.S. 26. In the west, U.S. 95 and roads extending from it cover all of the border country. But much of central Idaho, and most of the central and eastern parts of the northern Panhandle, and also the extreme southwestern corner of the state are virtually roadless so far as main routes are concerned.

While bird hunters in Idaho get along well enough with ordinary transport near the major routes, by far the greater share of Idaho, for the hunter, is 4WD and pack-in or fly-in country. Airlines contact the main cities. There are numerous small airfields where private planes can let down. The great percentage of big-game hunters in Idaho pack in, by horse or 4WD. There are numerous outfitters and guides in the state. The Game Department, address at chapter end, can assist in locating, but cannot recommend, guides and outfitters. The Idaho Guides and Outfitters Association can be contacted at Box 95, Boise.

Idaho hunting is extremely varied, and popular. There are at this time approximately 200,000 paid license holders each season. But the sale of varied permits totals over 400,000. About 50,000 such permits are taken by nonresidents. The list of game birds and animals reads almost like a list of U.S. species. Pheasants, Hungarian partridge, chukar, bobwhite quail, mountain quail, valley quail and Gambel's quail, plus grouse of five species—blue, ruffed, spruce, sage and sharptail—form an astonishing upland list. There are doves, and limited

639

wild turkeys, and of course ducks, geese, and snipe are available for water-fowlers. There are cottontails, snowshoes, and jackrabbits. Big game includes deer, elk, mountain sheep, mountain goats, moose, antelope, and black bear. Coyotes, lions, bobcats, raccoons, badgers, and numerous small pest animals and birds are present.

Idaho has such vast expanses of public lands that locating a place for al-most any variety of hunt is seldom a problem. It is estimated that approximately 73 percent of Idaho's lands are in public ownership. Almost all of the south-western corner of the state south of the Snake River, which corresponds roughly to the boundaries of large Owyhee Co., is in BLM lands. There are large BLM expanses also in the region north of Twin Falls and northwest from Pocatello. Other smaller patches of BLM lands are scattered throughout the state. An "Idaho Recreation Map" can be obtained from the Bureau of Land Manage-ment, Federal Building, Box 2237, Boise 83701.

The National Forests are the largest of the public lands, and Idaho's allot-ment of them is enormous. There are fifteen National Forests entirely or partly in Idaho, with a total acreage of over twenty million acres, the largest amount of any of the contiguous states. These Forests are detailed below not in geo-graphical order but, because there are so many, by placing alphabetically all with headquarters in Idaho so reference may be more easily made. Further information and maps for any one may be obtained from the Forest Supervisor at the headquarters city, which is given.

The Boise NF (1), with over 2.6 million acres is in the west-central part of the state, with Boise as headquarters. U.S. 20, 30, and 95 are main approach routes and State 15 runs along the western edge. The Caribou NF (2) is slightly less than a million acres, spills over into both Wyoming and Utah. It is in sev-eral blocks, in the southeast, with headquarters at Pocatello, U.S. 91, 191, 30N are key routes. Challis NF (3) is in central Idaho, headquarters at Challis, and with almost 2.5 million acres. U.S. 93 is the most important main highway.

Farther north, with headquarters at Orofino, is the 1.7 million-acre Clear-water NF (4), within which is the famed Selway-Bitterroot Wilderness Area. State routes 9 and 11 are the important ones. The Coeur d'Alene NF (5) is still farther north in the Panhandle, contains over 723,000 acres, with headquarters at its namesake city and with U.S. 10, 10A, and 95A the main access.

The Kaniksu NF (6) is partly in Montana and Washington, contains 1.6-plus million acres far up in the northeast Panhandle. Sandpoint is the head-quarters, and U.S. 95, 195, 10A, and 2 the routes.

The Nezperce NF (7) is to the south, just below the Clearwater. There are 2.2 million acres approximately, with Grangeville on U.S. 93 the headquarters. Payette NF (8) lies immediately south of the Nezperce, has 2.3 million acres headquartered at McCall, on Idaho 15, near U.S. 95. The Salmon River NF (9), with the Idaho Primitive Area, has headquarters at Salmon, is east of the Payette NF. There are nearly 1.8 million acres here, with U.S. 93 and state 28 the routes. The St. Joe NF (10) is up in the lower part of the northern Pan-handle, with 862,000 acres headquartered at St. Maries, U.S. 95A.

Down in the far south are the several blocks of the 1.8 million-acre Saw-tooth NF (11), a portion of which overlaps south into Utah. U.S. 30 N and S, and U.S. 93 are access routes. The Targhee NF (12) is west and south of Yel-lowstone Park, along the Wyoming border, with part of this Forest in Wyo-ming. Total acreage is over 1.6 million, headquarters is in St. Anthony, Idaho, and U.S. highways 20, 26, 191, 91 are all in the area.

Headquartered in Hamilton, Montana, a part of the 1.6 million-acre

Bitterroot NF (13) is in Idaho. There are no main highways in the region except U.S. 93 on the Montana side of the border. Up at the tip of the Panhandle, a part of the Kootenai NF, which in total has over 1.8 million acres, spills over into Idaho, although headquarters are at Libby, Montana. U.S. 2 and 93 are access routes. The Lolo NF (15), totaling over two million acres, also is partly in Idaho, but with headquarters at Missoula, Montana, which is on the part of U.S. 93 within that state.

An interesting large tract of federal land in Idaho that is virtually unknown to all except local hunters is the single National Grassland within this state. It is located near the Utah border, in the southeast. This is the Curlew National Grassland (16), and it contains more than 47,000 acres. Administration is through the U.S. Forest Service, and the Supervisor of the Caribou NF should be contacted regarding maps and other details. The National Grasslands, often overlooked especially by bird hunters because they so seldom are publicized, usually offer above average opportunities.

There are several State Forests in Idaho. These are located near Coeur d'Alene, McCall, Sandpoint, Orofino, and Priest Lake. There are also several Public Hunting Areas, Wildlife Management Areas, and Big Game Winter Ranges, the latter usually designated as WMAs. Added to these are nearly 150 Public Access Areas. Most of these are small, not intended so much for hunting as to allow access to other public lands that previously had been for one reason or another inaccessible to the public. These are so numerous that they cannot be noted later on under the various species. A few of the WMAs will be, but for details on the Public Access Areas one should obtain from the Game Department the excellent map and list, "Public Access Areas." Numbered locations on a map are tied to the listing on the reverse, which gives acreage and precise location. Incidentally, there is another folder, "Hunting and Fishing in Idaho," obtainable from the Department, that will be useful to anyone hunting here.

Camp-out hunters have virtually limitless choices on the public lands described in foregoing paragraphs. A useful booklet, "Idaho Campgrounds," can also be obtained from the Department of Commerce and Development, Capitol Building, Boise 83701. There are good accommodations along all main highways. Many hunters will be booked with outfitters and their food and lodging therefore taken care of.

Weather during early bird seasons is usually mild and enjoyable. But mountain hunting will require, during almost any fall season, a selection of clothing for severe cold as well. Light wool shirts and a hunting vest are fine for birds at lower altitudes in early and mid-fall. But down clothing certainly will be needed even during October at higher altitudes.

With such variety of game, guns and ammunition must come in variety, too. However, there are reasonable compromises. Shotgunners can do well enough for quail, partridge, and grouse if they have a selection of No. 8, No. 7½, and No. 6 shot sizes. If necessary the No. 7½ will serve a rather wide range of shooting. For birds such as the big sage grouse, No. 6 is better. Ducks, geese, turkey, require No. 4 and No. 2 shot, although some turkey hunters like short-magnum No. 6 best. For deer, any caliber from the .243 to .308 is fine. Elk should be hunted with heavy loads and certainly with nothing lighter than the .308 or .270. Moose, sheep, goats require such calibers, too, although some hunters prefer the magnums, such as the 7mm.

Game management in Idaho is handled by Units for all big game, and there are some special bird seasons, as for forest grouse, set by Units. There are many controlled hunts for deer and elk, and certain restrictions via Units as regards nonresidents. In other words, the regulations are fairly complicated, since there are at this writing some 78 Units, with several split into A and B portions. Further, though deer and elk may be set according to these Units, moose, antelope, sheep, and goat are handled by special Unit designation, with differing numbers, and these Units may be only portions of the standard deer Units. It is thus extremely important that any hunter acquire for any given season the full regulations and Unit maps for that year.

Because of the number of Units and the various complications, the material under each species will not regularly refer to Units, but will instead in most instances indicate best hunting according to Region, and county. There are in Idaho eight Regional Offices of the Game Department and the forty-four counties are split up among them. There are Regional Supervisors in each Region, and their addresses are printed as a rule on the big-game regulations for the year. These Supervisors can be invaluable sources for pinpoint information in their areas. Below are listed the Regions by name, and the counties in each.

The Panhandle Region is in the far north, contains Benewah, Bonner, Boundary, Kootenai, Shoshone counties. Immediately below is the Clearwater Region, with Clearwater, Idaho, Latah, Lewis, Nez Perce counties. The McCall Region contains only Adams and Valley counties. The Western Region: Ada, Boise, Canyon, Elmore, Gem, Owyhee, Payette, Washington counties. Actually this is the southwestern quarter of the state. Magic Valley Region: Blaine, Camas, Cassia, Gooding, Jerome, Lincoln, Minidoka, Twin Falls counties, all in the central south. Eastern Region: Bannock, Bear Lake, Bingham, Caribou, Franklin, Oneida, Power counties, in practical terms the southeast. Upper Snake River Region: Bonneville, Butte, Clark, Fremont, Jefferson, Madison, Teton, the group of counties immediately west of the Yellowstone Park Region. Salmon Region: Custer and Lemhi counties in the Salmon River area of the east-central part of the state.

PHEASANT

So far as annual harvest is concerned, the introduced ringneck has long been the most important upland game bird in Idaho. For a number of years the harvest, a portion of which is made up of hens, has run from slightly below half a million to over 600,000 birds. The ringneck is tied in this state as elsewhere to agricultural lands and their fringes. Idaho's pheasants are seeing a difficult struggle nowadays as changing farm practices reduce suitable habitat. The trend is more noticeable in northern than in southern Idaho, but the future in both portions of the state looks more and more precarious.

Almost all pheasant hunting is on private lands. However, for those who know where to locate them, there are some lands along the rivers and the fringes of the public lands, especially BLM lands, that offer pheasants. In Canyon Co. the Fort Boise WMA (17) three miles northwest of Parma, has pheasants on an 801-acre tract along the east banks of the Boise and Snake rivers. Hunters should acquire the map mentioned earlier and check in the better counties for Public Access Areas that open up pheasant hunting lands.

Following are the Regions, and the counties within them, that furnish fair to good pheasant hunting. In the Panhandle Region, the far northern and western counties have fair pheasant shooting. These are Boundary, Bonner, Kootenai, Benewah. In the Clearwater Region to the south the hunting is also just fair. Nez Perce, Latah, Lewis and Idaho counties are the best range. The

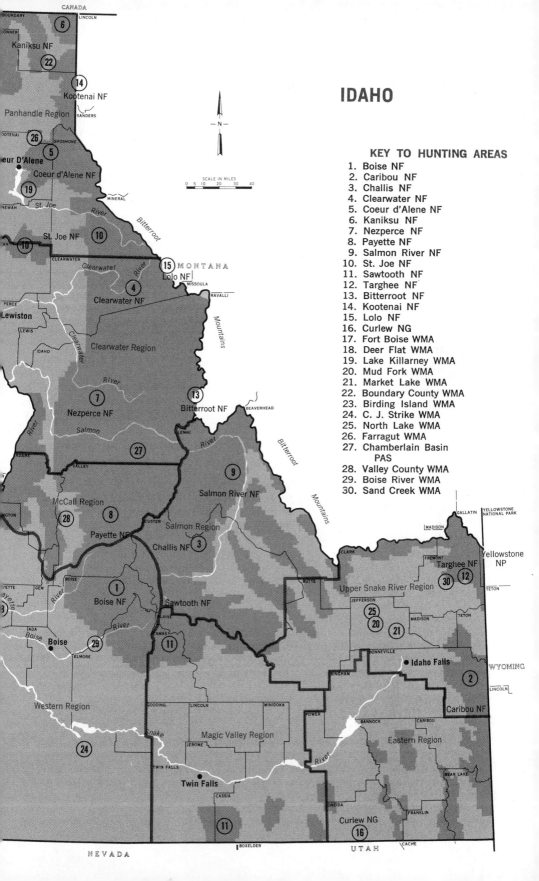

IDAHO

KEY TO HUNTING AREAS

1. Boise NF
2. Caribou NF
3. Challis NF
4. Clearwater NF
5. Coeur d'Alene NF
6. Kaniksu NF
7. Nezperce NF
8. Payette NF
9. Salmon River NF
10. St. Joe NF
11. Sawtooth NF
12. Targhee NF
13. Bitterroot NF
14. Kootenai NF
15. Lolo NF
16. Curlew NG
17. Fort Boise WMA
18. Deer Flat WMA
19. Lake Killarney WMA
20. Mud Fork WMA
21. Market Lake WMA
22. Boundary County WMA
23. Birding Island WMA
24. C. J. Strike WMA
25. North Lake WMA
26. Farragut WMA
27. Chamberlain Basin PAS
28. Valley County WMA
29. Boise River WMA
30. Sand Creek WMA

McCall Region, with only two counties, Magic and Valley, has fair hunting in both.

Pheasant hunting improves farther south. In the Western Region it is rated as good, with Payette, Washington, Canyon, Ada, and Gem the top counties. The Magic Valley Region also rates as good. The best counties here: Twin Falls, Minidoka, Gooding, Lincoln. Good hunting continues into the Eastern Region, with three counties, Bingham, Bannock, and Power the top choices.

In the Upper Snake River Region, good hunting continues in Jefferson, Franklin, and Bonneville counties. The Salmon Region is just fair, with some shooting in Lemhi county.

Northern Idaho pheasant shooting has reached the point where most birds shot in the Panhandle and Clearwater Regions are released birds. In one recent season 72 percent of birds checked in the Clearwater were game-farm reared and almost all of the Panhandle kill had been pen raised. Idaho has been experimenting with the Japanese green pheasant, hoping it may be able to utilize range not useful to the ringneck. As this is written it has been the practice to release surplus green pheasant cocks along with ringnecks in the five northern-most counties. Currently the best pheasant hunting in northern Idaho is in the lower Clearwater drainage. Areas along Tammany and Lapwai creeks are considered top choices here. But by far the best opportunities are in the south.

HUNGARIAN PARTRIDGE

These birds are predominantly dependent upon agricultural lands and their fringes. The Clearwater Region has fair shooting in the better pheasant counties, listed above. The two counties of McCall Region also are fair. Best Hun hunting is in the Western and Magic Valley Regions, where it rates as good in the same counties as for pheasants, which see. There are fair numbers of Huns in pheasant counties of the Eastern Region, and in both counties of the Salmon Region. However, the best Region is usually Western. As high as 55 percent of the kill often comes from here.

Although the Hun rates approximately fourth in importance among upland birds, nonetheless it is important and seems to remain fairly plentiful. Over a period of years the kill has ranged from 55,000 to 95,000 birds. However, as with the pheasant, the adverse influences of decreasing habitat are affecting its potential.

CHUKAR PARTRIDGE

Because the chukar sustains itself admirably in rocky foothills and steep river canyons, with little or no dependence upon agriculture, its future looks bright here. Although there are fluctuations in the average annual bag, the overall figure has been steadily climbing. Between 1954 and 1958 an average kill was 18,000 birds per season. During the most recent season the kill was a remarkable 177,000.

Some of the high chukar populations are found on the lower Clearwater and Salmon rivers, and in Hells Canyon of the Snake, especially between Lewiston and Weiser. An interesting special season has been set recently beginning in early August on a specified portion of the Middle Fork of the Salmon River. The hunt area is within a half mile of the river. The season has been used in an attempt to get a harvest of birds by sportsmen who float this wild river during late summer and early fall. Some of the open area has no access except via float. Any firearm is legal during this season at this writing—shotgun, rifle, pistol, and even air rifles and air pistols. In addition to this early season, there is often a late season well on toward the end of January. Hunters willing to make the effort to get into Hells Canyon on the Snake or the Salmon River drainage in Idaho Co. ordinarily find excellent hunting then.

By Regions chukar hunting stacks up about as follows: Clearwater, fair to good in Idaho and Nez Perce Cos.; McCall, good in both Valley and Adams Cos.; Western, good in Payette, Washington, Canyon, Ada, Gem; Magic Valley, good in Twin Falls, Minidoka, Gooding, Lincoln; Eastern, fair in Bingham, Bannock, Power; Salmon, fair to good both Custer and Lemhi.

Over some seasons up to two-thirds of the chukar harvest as well as hunting pressure has been along the breaks of the Snake, Boise, and Payette rivers in the west.

QUAIL

Idaho has four varieties: bobwhite, Gambel's, California, and mountain quail. The aggregate annual kill runs anywhere from 60,000 to over 100,000. Quail range in Idaho is not very broad. Some seasons more than 75 percent of the total quail harvest has come from the Western Region, along the breaks and fringes of the Snake, Boise, and Payette rivers. Although quail shooting can be excellent locally, one must be rather well acquainted with the hunting area.

By Region and counties quail hunting rates as follows: Clearwater, fair in Nez Perce and Latah, except for Gambel's; Western, fair in Canyon, Payette, Washington, Ada for all species, but best for valley and mountain; McCall, fair for valley and mountain in both Adams and Valley; Magic Valley, fair for all species in Twin Falls, Gooding, Lincoln.

All but a small portion of the quail found in hunters' bags are valley quail. Hunters especially interested in any of the other varieties will be well advised to check carefully with Game Department personnel. For example, knowing where to find the best populations of mountain quail, a bird not much hunted and likely to be scattered in isolated pockets of fair abundance, can save much disappointment and hard work.

FOREST GROUSE

There are three species of so-called forest grouse open to hunting in Idaho. These are the big blue grouse of the high forests and open grassy slopes and parks, the ruffed grouse found in more brushy locations especially along stream courses in the foothills and mountains, the spruce grouse, which likes dense stands of conifers, often in boggy or moist locations.

A vast amount of hunting for these birds goes begging simply because of their steep habitats. However, Idaho hunters do show more interest in these species than hunters in many other states. No statistics are available for kill by species, but the aggregate annual harvest runs somewhere between 100,000 and 150,000 birds.

It is not possible to note specific locations where the best hunting may be found. The enormous expanses of National Forests have great numbers of these birds, and without question only a few here and there ever see a hunter. Some of the best hunting for all three varieties is in all of the five Panhandle counties. The five Clearwater Region counties are probably just as good. In the Western Region, Washington, Gem, Boise, Elmore rate as good choices for all three. There are ample populations also in Adams and Valley counties, and in Twin Falls, Minidoka, and Blaine. In the Eastern Region, Bannock and Power counties rate fair; the same is true for Bonneville, Fremont, Clark in the Upper Snake River Region, and also for Custer and Lemhi in the Salmon Region.

As noted above under "Quail," hunters can get many good local pointers from the Game Department or via Department reference to specific officers in the field. For example, the state's game bird supervisor invariably has much pinpoint information on all these species. The Salmon River slopes near timberline and in south-facing grassy openings inside timbered areas are suggested for some of the state's best blue grouse shooting during mid-fall.

SAGE GROUSE

These large grouse of arid, sage-covered flats and hills are an important upland game bird in Idaho, but, as elsewhere, fighting a difficult battle for survival because of decreasing habitat. The average seasonal harvest is substantial, ordinarily between 20,000 and 30,000. However, in one recent season over 50,000 sage grouse went into hunters' bags.

Sage grouse are found in several parts of Idaho. Records of checking stations that have inventoried opening-weekend kills for several consecutive years show that the greatest number of birds are taken in the Upper Snake Region, with Magic Valley second and Western third. However, hunter success shows up as best in the Western Region, followed by the Upper Snake. There are ample public lands in much of the sage grouse range, in both lower elevation sage areas of National Forests, and on BLM lands.

In the Western Region, Owyhee county is best, with Washington next. Magic Valley counties with best hunting are Camas, Gooding, Twin Falls. Eastern Region: Caribou and Bingham. Upper Snake River: Jefferson, Fremont, Franklin, Clark, Bonneville. Salmon: Lemhi, Custer fair. Hunters should check carefully during any given season, for it is possible some counties listed may be closed, if populations show drastic declines. Idaho is concentrating on a sage grouse study to attempt to assure a future for this once supremely abundant species.

SHARPTAIL GROUSE

The range of the sharptail, and its numbers, are exceedingly limited in Idaho. There have been open seasons in recent years in some counties of both the Eastern and Upper Snake Regions. The open season is brief, and bag and possession limit 2 in the aggregate between sharptail and sage grouse. Presently Fremont, Jefferson, and Clark counties are considered best.

Hunters should be sure to check carefully which counties are open for any given season and if indeed any are. If the southeastern counties in which the Curlew National Grasslands lie happen to be open, both sage and sharptail grouse may be found there.

MOURNING DOVES

Dove hunting is gaining in interest in Idaho, with from 16,000 to 20,000 hunters bagging around 200,000 birds in a good season. The problem for dove hunters here is one of weather, and timing of the season. The season cannot be opened prior to September 1, and most years a large share of the doves reared in Idaho have by then already started migrating south. Presently the season is approximately three weeks in duration, but frost sometimes closes down hunting by the end of the first week because most birds have departed.

There is fair but scattered dove hunting in the Panhandle. In the Clearwater Region all five counties have areas of fairly good shooting. The McCall Region is fair in scattered locations. The Western Region rates good in the better pheasant counties, which see. The same is true for Magic Valley. Eastern, Upper Snake, and Salmon are fair in the better pheasant counties and locations.

WILD TURKEYS

The Merriam's, or western mountain, turkey originally ranged in the yellow pine and oak forests at from 6000 to 10,000 foot altitudes from central Colorado south into Mexico. It was not native to Idaho, but attempts at establishing turkeys on the Middle Fork of the Salmon River were made in the 1930s. They failed. In 1961 a group of seventeen Merriam's turkeys trapped in Colorado was released in Idaho Co., along the breaks of the Salmon. Other releases were made in the same general area in the following two years. By 1965 the birds had done well enough so some were trapped and transplanted within the state, in Nez Perce Co. Transplants are continuing, with the hope that eventually all parts of the state with suitable range will have this grand game bird.

Idaho's first turkey hunt in history took place in the fall of 1967. There were 150 permits, 104 hunters actually hunted, and 17 turkeys were bagged. That success, slightly over 16 percent, compares favorably with success in other turkey hunting states. The following year a general hunt was held for two days in the lower Salmon River region. This was an either-sex hunt. Seasons are continuing, with a limited number of management Units open. Interested hunters must check with the Department regarding Units open and regulations for any given season.

EXOTIC GAME BIRDS

Experimental releases of Japanese green pheasants were mentioned under "Pheasant." These are birds of forest edges and brushy cover removed from cultivated areas. They are tough, fast, difficult to flush, and a dog for hunting them is most important. Some of these birds are already being shot by Idaho hunters in the Panhandle counties where hope is greatest for them at present. Release sites in the past have been near Worley, Bonners Ferry, Priest River, Harrison, St. Maries. More releases are being made. This pheasant is slightly smaller than the ringneck, has no white neck band, has a bright-green sheen on head, neck, and breast.

Japanese bamboo partridges are also under study and experiment in Idaho. In size and color they are somewhat similar to the Hun, and are said to hold well to a pointing dog. Whether or not they will be successful is not yet known.

WATERFOWL

Some excellent waterfowling is available in Idaho. The duck kill is close to half a million per season. Canada geese, which are the major goose species, are taken at a seasonal rate running from 18,000 to about 23,000. Some snow geese also appear in the bag, possibly a thousand each fall. There is an open season on snipe, and some are present, but they get little attention.

Times of best shooting differ in different parts of the state. In eastern Idaho the best waterfowling usually occurs in October. Although fair hunting is found over much of the state during the early weeks, it gets better as cold weather arrives, except that some spots are frozen then. The lower Boise and Payette rivers are excellent into December if there is cold and stormy weather. In the northern part of the state, peak of the migrations in November ordinarily is timed for the best opportunity.

The large rivers in Idaho offer excellent mallard and other duck shooting, and in some stretches goose shooting also, over decoys. A good many geese nest in southern Idaho. One great concentration point for both ducks and geese during migration is American Falls Reservoir near Pocatello. As many as half a million ducks and 16,000 Canada geese have been tallied there at one time during the season. The Game Department selects a number of tally areas throughout the state, concentration points for waterfowl, and a count is made every two weeks to check the waterfowl traffic. Knowledge of these concentration areas is useful for hunters. Currently some of them are as follows: Lower Coeur d'Alene River to Killarney Lake; Benewah-Chatcolet area; Round Lake and Pend O'Reille River below Sandpoint—all in the north—and in the southeast, south-central and southwest, North Lake; Market Lake; Camas, American Falls Reservoir; Minidoka; Hagerman; C. J. Strike Reservoir; Deer Flat WMA (18).

A check of good waterfowl hunting locations by Region follows: PAN-HANDLE: Kootenai River; Bonners Ferry; McArthur Refuge; Lake Killarney WMA (19); St. Joe River, all for both ducks and geese.

CLEARWATER: the lower section of the Clearwater River; Snake River, both ducks and geese.

McCALL: Cascade Reservoir for both; Payette Lake, ducks. Western: for both ducks and geese, Lower Boise and Payette rivers; Snake River; Fort Boise WMA ("Pheasant"); Brownlee Reservoir; C. J. Strike Reservoir.

MAGIC VALLEY: Snake River (Hagerman Valley); Wilson Reservoir; Carey Lake all for both ducks and geese; Big Wood River, Bellevue section, ducks. Eastern Region: American Falls Reservoir; Wolcott Reservoir; Snake River; Blackfoot Reservoir, both ducks and geese for all.

UPPER SNAKE RIVER: Henry's Fork of the Snake; Mud Fork WMA (20); Market Lake WMA (21), all for both ducks and geese.

SALMON: Lemhi River; Salmon River, ducks.

Waterfowl hunters should carefully check the map and list of Public Access Areas. Many lead to places on lakes or rivers feasible for waterfowl hunting. Among the prominent state-owned tracts, some of which have been mentioned above, are the following: The Boundary Co. WMA (22) has over 1000 acres near Naples, east shore of McArthur Reservoir. In Kootenai Co., the Game Access Shooting Area is near Rose Lake, on a marsh south of Killarney Lake. The Birding Island WMA (23), Payette Co., near New Plymouth, is on the Payette River. Fort Boise WMA, located under "Pheasant," also has good waterfowl hunting. C. J. Strike WMA (24) contains 1850 acres, Elmore and Owyhee Cos. It is near village of Bruneau, on the Reservoir. North Lake WMA (25), Jefferson Co., is an area of several thousand acres near Terreton.

RABBITS AND SQUIRRELS

Idaho has both cottontail and pygmy rabbits, plus snowshoe hares and jacks. Best cottontail populations are found in the river bottoms and ranging out into nearby sagebrush country. The tiny pygmy rabbit, close cousin of the cottontail, is an animal of the sagebrush and grass ranges. Cottontails are found in most suitable habitat in the state but chiefly in the south. The pygmy rabbit range is only in a few southern counties. The season on both lasts six months, September through February. Presently the bag limit is five in the aggregate or of either. Average annual bag runs around 50,000. The harvest fluctuates broadly with the seasonal rabbit crop. Considering the number of Idaho hunters, interest in these animals is very modest.

Snowshoe hares are found in the high forested areas. Numerous portions of the National Forests offer good opportunity for this hunting, but it goes begging almost entirely. The snowshoe hare is in fact lumped with the lowly jack-rabbit on the unprotected list.

Squirrels are protected at all times and thus there is no hunting here for them. This does not apply of course to ground squirrels, which are on the pest list.

DEER

Idaho has both mule deer and whitetail deer. Mule deer predominate. The whitetails are found almost entirely in the northern counties, the Panhandle. They make up about 15 percent on the average of the annual kill. Because they are more wary than the mule deer, and ordinarily stay in cover that is dense, most hunters who like to hunt them wait until the first tracking snow is on the ground.

Deer hunting in Idaho is excellent. Roughly 135,000 to 150,000 deer hunters harvest from 65,000 to 70,000 deer. Hunting is by Management Units, of which there are presently seventy-eight. Seasons differ radically among them. There are also controlled hunts with limited permits. Regulations are quite complicated and therefore hunters should acquire the Unit maps with full regulations for the season in question well before planning a hunt.

The management of deer in Idaho has been well handled for a number of years, and the kill remains surprisingly stable. For the past ten seasons the total has ranged from a low of 56,000-plus to 78,000-plus, with most seasons falling around the mean figure. There are three main blocks of Units, or general regions, that offer the best of the mule deer hunting. These are Units where success ranges as high as 60 to 90 percent. These general areas are as follows: One large block of quality mule deer Units lies just south of Lewiston, follows the Snake River south to Cuprum, then angles east and north to Warren and Mackay Bar on the Salmon River and on to Elk City, the Lower Selway and Weippe. A second block begins near Shoup, spreads south on the main Salmon River to Challis, Copper Basin, Soldier Mountain, east to Lava, Crooked Creek, and to the Montana border. The other area is in southern Idaho, from Bruneau and Blackfoot and Swan Valley to the Montana line. Again, the preponderance of deer taken in these regions are mule deer. Virtually all whitetails are found north of the Salmon River. They are abundant but not as avidly hunted as the mule deer.

There is no problem in finding public lands on which to hunt deer. The massive expanses of the National Forests offer all but limitless opportunity. There is also some deer hunting on the several WMAs. For example, Farragut WMA (26), Kootenai Co. south of Bayview, contains about 1500 acres, has some deer hunting for archers. Chamberlain Basin Public Access Site (27), Idaho Co., on Chamberlain Creek, has a modest acreage with deer. The 1500-acre Valley Co. WMA (28) near Donnelly, Valley Co., is another possibility. The Boise River WMA (29) covers in owned and leased lands nearly 20,000 acres with deer hunting. It is in Elmore and Boise Cos., east of Boise. Sand Creek WMA (30) is another good bet. It is reached from Anthony, Fremont Co., has almost 16,000 acres. However, on the whole the Forests and BLM lands furnish the major share of deer hunting.

It is true that weather may complicate hunting in any given year on certain Units, and lower the success. Also, with such vast amounts of forest lands and mountains, there are many Units where access is difficult. On these, hunting might be of superior quality, if only more hunters were able to sample it. By and large, however, the Units that show consistent high kills based on their size in square miles furnish prospective hunters with the best clues as to where the deer are. Some of these are therefore noted below.

In the Panhandle Region, Units 1, 2, 3, 5 take in much of Boundary, Bonner, Kootenai, and Benewah Cos., which means the northern and western portions of the Panhandle. In these for several consecutive seasons the average has run from just below to just above one deer bagged per square mile. In the Clearwater Region, Units 8, 10A and 11, which cover most of the northwest part of the Region in Latah, Nez Perce, Lewis, and part of Clearwater Cos., show from one to one-plus deer killed per square mile. Units 13 and 18 in the southwest corner of this Region, in southwestern Idaho Co. between the Snake and the Salmon Rivers, however, show kills of from three to five deer per square mile. These are among the few Units in the state with such a high average.

Immediately south of the above, mostly in the McCall Region in Adams and northern Washington Cos., but partly across the Region line to the north, are Units 22 and 23. Unit 22 has consistently averaged from one-plus to three deer killed per square mile, and Unit 23 shows a one-plus rating. Across the state in the far northern part of the Salmon Region, northern Lemhi Co., are Units 21 and 21A. These average from above one deer per square mile bagged to as high as four-plus some seasons. Immediately below those Units, and lying along the eastern border of Lemhi Co., are Units 30 and 30A with one to two deer averages.

Across the state, on the western border, northwest corner of the Western Region, in Washington Co., is Unit 31, slightly below one deer per square mile average. East of it, partly in Boise Co., is Unit 33 with one-plus, and to the east of this Unit is Unit 35 with a one-deer average. Still farther east is Unit 36A, across in Custer Co. in the Salmon Region, with one-plus, and 36B just to the north, with nearly one. Unit 37A in southern Lemhi Co. east of the Pashimeroi River has kills of up to three deer per square mile.

Other good Units strung across the south rate as follows: Unit 39, central Western Region east and north from Boise, two-plus; Unit 42, southwestern Owyhee Co., erratic but usually one-plus; Unit 47, southwestern Twin Falls Co., Magic Valley Region, one-plus; Unit 48, Blaine Co. in northern Magic Valley Region, one-plus; along the southern border, Magic Valley Region, and immediately east of Unit 47, Unit 54, one-plus; Unit 66, southeastern Upper Snake Region, Bonneville Co., up to 1.5-plus; Unit 67, immediately north in Swan Valley area, from two to five, one of the best areas of the state; Unit 71, Eastern Region, Pocatello area, one-plus; Units 73 and 73A, mostly in Power and Oneida Cos., southwestern part of Eastern Region, from one to two-plus; Units 76 and 78 in the southeast corner of the state and the Eastern Region, from one to three.

There are many other good deer hunting Units and many that rate almost even with these, averaging slightly less than one deer killed per square mile. However, basing a choice of location on the Units noted will guide hunters to the general areas of the state with the highest deer population densities.

ELK

Idaho is one of the top elk states in the U.S. For the past decade annual kills have run from 14,000 to 17,000. The average is roughly 15,000, with from 60,000 to 70,000 hunters participating. Success thus averages from 20 to 25 percent.

The several Primitive Areas of the National Forests in the better elk range furnish some of the best hunting. The Chamberlain Basin, the Clearwater River drainage including the Selway, Lochsa and north Fork watersheds are prime elk territories. The Salmon and the St. Joe river areas are also important. There are elk in forty of Idaho's forty-four counties. The three areas considered as best of all are the Lochsa, Selway, and Chamberlain Basin. The Lochsa River country is Unit 12, which lies in the eastern part of the Clearwater Region, northeastern Idaho Co. The Selway is immediately south, in eastern Idaho Co., Unit 17. Chamberlain Basin corresponds to Unit 20A, south-eastern Idaho Co. along Chamberlain Creek east of Mackay Bar.

There is good elk hunting elsewhere, over a wide range. Units 6, 9, 10, and 10A, in southern Shoshone and northern and western Clearwater Cos., rate well. A good many Units throughout the forested parts of the state show skills averaging one animal for every two or three square miles. A few elk are killed in several open-season Units scattered across the south, but hunters strange to the state or to certain portions of it will make the wisest decision to hunt somewhere within the northern half, considering the division point as halfway up the western border. This encompasses the Panhandle Region, the Clearwater Region, the northernmost Units of the Salmon Region.

SHEEP

Bighorn sheep are found in greatest numbers in the Salmon River drainage, specifically along the Middle Fork. The East Fork has some bands, and drainages leading into the Salmon from the north also have sheep. Some favorite locations are: the Camas Creek-Loon Creek region of the Middle Fork; the Big Creek area farther north, west of the Middle Fork. Some sheep are found in the Targhee NF, in the mountains west of Yellowstone NP. There is also a band in southwestern Owyhee Co. The first hunt in this region was held in 1969, with five permits available. This herd has evolved from a transplant of thirty-eight bighorns of the California subspecies that were live trapped in British Columbia and brought in beginning in 1963. Bighorns once roamed this Owyhee River area but became extinct long ago. The California bighorn, much like the desert sheep, appears well suited to the region.

Ordinarily sheep hunting is open to anyone, resident or nonresident, with a valid hunting license plus a sheep tag. A few special permits are issued on controlled hunts some seasons. The sheep kill is not large. Recently the totals have been less than fifty animals. For two consecutive seasons: thirty-two, forty-seven. Over 500 tags have been issued for recent seasons. Only a few Units are open, and no prediction can be made as to which ones may be closed, or opened, for any given season. Hunters should contact the Game Department for specific information.

MOUNTAIN GOAT

Goats are fairly plentiful throughout much of the high region of the Salmon River drainage. Other bands are in the St. Joe and Clearwater drainages. They are also found in southwestern Idaho in the upper Payette and Boise river drainages. Chances of bagging a goat are quite good for the determined hunter.

Goats are hunted under a permit system, controlled hunts with limited permits for specific areas. Thus application must be made. Regulations pertaining to dates of drawings and procedure are usually ready by early June. Interested hunters should obtain them immediately after publication to be certain of having the application in on time. Precise descriptions of portions of Management Units open are furnished, and number of permits for each is listed. In a group application, not more than two hunters may apply. There are restrictions also in some Units regarding application by persons who have drawn a permit the previous year.

The total goat kill has run for some years from slightly less than 100 to as high as 160 animals per season. Permits over the same span have numbered from just below 200 to as high as 285. During one recent season there were 285 permits, and 124 goats bagged. The average success is from slightly below 50 percent to as high as 60 percent. Because it is not possible to predict what areas may be open, details should be obtained from the Department.

ANTELOPE

The pronghorn is not abundant in Idaho but a reasonably stable population is present. For the past decade the kill, by controlled hunts and limited permits acquired via application and drawing, has averaged 890 per season. Lowest kill during that time was 549, highest 1294.

Top antelope counties are Lemhi, Clark, Butte, Custer, Jefferson, Bingham, Lincoln, Owyhee. Select among these are Lemhi, Custer, Clark, Butte. Persons who have had an antelope permit for either of the two previous years may not apply for the current season. Group applications for as many as four hunters will be accepted. Check with the Department for details and the published regulations relative controlled hunts.

MOOSE

Moose are not abundant. They are hunted under controlled conditions, by issuance of permits and a drawing. They are found in scattered locations throughout the state: Fremont Co. has a substantial number; the upper Clearwater country between the Lochsa and Selway drainages also is good moose territory; the expanse between the North Fork of the Clearwater and the St. Joe River in the Panhandle is fair.

Chances of collecting a moose when one draws a permit are excellent. Over the past decade permit numbers have run from seventy-five to slightly less than a hundred. The kill has averaged fifty-one per season. Check with the Department for seasonal details and to obtain application forms.

BEAR

The black bear is plentiful in Idaho. A ten-year kill average shows almost 3000 bagged per season. Counties of southern Idaho have year-round bear hunting. Most of the remainder of the state has seasons set by Units. There are fall seasons, but there are also spring seasons in some Units, mostly in the north. It is advisable to obtain the regulations and check them carefully. There is no open season on grizzlies. Favorite hunting spots for black bear are blueberry patches, and streams where spawned-out salmon furnish forage.

Bear are well scattered throughout the forest portions of the state. There are no special concentration points. Best chance of success in bear hunting is by booking with a guide who knows his territory thoroughly. Spring hunting is by far the most successful.

MOUNTAIN LION

Lions are fairly numerous. For some years the average kill has been around 125. Hunting specifically for lion accounted for most of these. Long bountied, this big cat was removed from the bounty list a decade ago. However, as this is written it is still not on the game animal list. Residents may take it on their regular hunting license at any time. There is a special $5 nonresident license for taking of predatory animals and pets. Only on certain preserves are there specified seasons on the lion (and other predators). Hunters should be sure to check these stipulations.

The only feasible manner of making a lion hunt is by hiring the services of a guide with trained hounds who specializes in this sport. There are several in Idaho.

Presently there is a most important long-range lion study in progress in the Big Creek drainage region. The area is closed to killing of lions by any means. Lion hunters must check these boundaries with the Department. This study, in which resident lions of the study area are repeatedly trapped, tracked to check kills, and their home territories plotted, is probably the most thorough and important project of its kind ever launched. It has been in progress several years and much has already been learned. Without question the mountain lion, or cougar, will become more and more important as a trophy game animal, but if it is to avoid extinction studies of this type must be supported vigorously by hunters as well as scientists.

OTHER ANIMALS

Coyotes and bobcats are plentiful in suitable habitats throughout the state. Rockchucks, ground squirrels, and jackrabbits furnish a wide opportunity for varmint shooters. There are some foxes, raccoons, and as mentioned under "Rabbits," the snowshoe hare may be hunted around the year. Crows are abundant locally, and magpies also furnish sporty pest shooting, for they are exceedingly wary. As noted under "Lion," a license is required by all hunters for predator and pest shooting. The regular resident license is valid. Nonresidents must have a $5 special permit.

REGULATIONS

Game laws pertaining to seasons, bag and possession limits, areas to be hunted, special hunts, license fees all may have numerous changes from year to year. For current regulations, and for other specific queries, write to: Idaho Fish and Game Department, 600 S. Walnut, Boise, Idaho 83707.

MONTANA

Montana is a stunningly scenic state with drastic variations in terrain. In the east there are high, rolling plains, often treeless, but here and there with ruggedly broken country where chains of hills dotted by scattered pine and other trees form good open game cover. There is much farming and ranching here, with wheat and other grains interspersed by uncultivated country making excellent game bird situations. Approximately 40 percent of the state lying westward from these high plains is in the great north-south belt of the high Rockies.

Here broad valleys may be in farms and cattle ranches, or offer wide expanses of sagebrush flats between mountain ranges. But forested foothills, dense upper forests and snow-covered peaks above timberline dominate almost the entire western half of Montana. Some of the finest true wilderness, roadless and still unspoiled, on the continent is here. A great deal of this country thrusts up into the 9000 to 12,000 foot altitudes, and even most of the valleys lie at from 4000 to 7000 feet.

This is tremendously rugged country. To be sure, one can get into the valleys and foothills easily, but the awesome high ranges are often difficult of access, and several of the areas, designated Primitive or Wilderness, are roadless, and closed to any motorized travel whatever. The state highway system on the whole is excellent. But unlike states in a less rugged area, the roads do not go to every area where a hunter may wish to operate.

U.S. 10, I 94, and I 90, with tributary routes from the south and east, lead in zigzag fashion east-west across the lower portion of the state. U.S. 2 crosses the northern part, just below the Canadian border. U.S. 87, 89, 91 (I 15) and 93 are the chief north-south roads. There are of course many other good highways and numerous side roads. But hunters strange to Montana should know that though all roads here lead into excellent game country of one kind or another, the difficult terrain, even in portions of the eastern half of the state, plus a modest-sized population, make this state quite unlike the east and the mid-continent U.S. A great deal of Montana is still horseback, or 4-wheel-drive, or backpack country. This is especially true for big-game hunting. Air service is good, but is generally confined, except for private charter and small lines, to the few large cities, and it can be a long way from some of these to a desired hunting location.

Montana has had much publicity as a big-game hunting location, and deserves every bit. Its bird hunting is seldom publicized to any extent, yet is excellent and extremely varied, some of it for the average hunter with targets quite unusual. All of this hunting stretches over a vast area. Montana is fourth in size of the states, is over 500 miles east-west at its widest point and from 250 to about 300 miles wide at various points north to south. All told this equals over 147,000 square miles. In this tremendous sweep of country there are at present only about 700,000 people. At least half of this population is located in a few cities, the largest of which average 20,000 to 55,000 residents.

Hunting, therefore, is a long way from crowded. To further illustrate just how wide-open are the spaces, annual license sales average presently less than 200,000, not counting extra tags. Fewer than 500 nonresidents annually buy birds-only licenses. Full nonresident big-game licenses average well below 10,000. Deer-only hunters who visit Montana annually are in the same numbers, and nonresident antelope hunters seldom number up to 3000. Because of large big-game herds and bird populations, and practically unlimited hunting room, success percentages for both residents and nonresidents usually run very high, some of them among the highest in the U.S.

Big game gets the emphasis here. The elk herd is one of the country's largest. It is chiefly concentrated down through the mountain region. Mule deer are almost everywhere abundant, from the western mountains to the broken plains of the far southeast. Whitetail deer are also abundant. They range the river bottoms throughout all the eastern portion of Montana, and offer excellent hunting up in the northwest, seldom receiving as much hunting pressure as they should.

Antelope are abundant in the eastern prairies and in foothills of the east slope of the Divide. They have also been transplanted elsewhere into pockets of suitable habitat. Both mountain goats and mountain sheep (Rocky Mountain bighorn) are in good supply, in specific high areas. These have also been transplanted until practically all suitable portions of the mountain country have resident groups. The moose population is substantial, with hunting in the southwest and northwest. There are many black bear. There is at this writing some of the last—and very limited—grizzly hunting remaining within the contiguous U.S.

Although Montana has substantial numbers of small-game animals and varmints, these—rabbits, coyotes, prairie dogs, etc.—do not draw much attention. There is too much else.

By the same token, some of the game birds do not receive as much hunting as they could stand. The list is highly varied. Some good pheasant hunting is found in the valleys along fringes of croplands. On the prairie and light-cover areas eastward, sharptail grouse are abundant. Sage grouse are in good supply in several places. Hungarian partridge and chukars are modestly present in proper cover, and the mountain grouses—blue, ruffed, spruce—are found in numerous locations. There is reasonably good turkey hunting, and in certain places surprisingly good waterfowling.

Hunters have no serious problems regarding access. Only in the immediate vicinities of the larger cities does minor crowding make finding a place to hunt difficult. Throughout most of the state the bird hunters, and antelope hunters, and some deer hunters, the three groups that have any need at all to hunt on privately owned lands, find ranchers in general amenable when presented with polite requests to trespass. However, there is such a vast amount of public land that the major share of activity occurs on it. At least one-fifth of all the land in Montana is federally and state owned.

BLM lands spread over hundreds of thousands of acres. The largest expanses of these lands are in the southeast and the north-central parts of the state, but there are others in the west and still more in the southwest. Two BLM publications available from the Department of Interior, Washington, D.C. 20240 are: "Montana Recreation Access Maps" (Bureau of Land Management); and "Your BLM Administered Lands in Montana." The BLM regional office in Billings, Montana, also has printed maps showing public domain over much of the state.

Of first importance to hunters are the National Forests. All or parts of eleven National Forests are in Montana. They total some sixteen million acres. Within these Forests there are five Primitive and four Wilderness Areas. Most of the big-game hunting and a fair share of the bird hunting is on the Forests. Details and locations of them follow.

The Beaverhead NF (1) contains over 2.1 million acres. It is located in the southwest, with Dillon the headquarters from which maps and details may be obtained by contacting the Forest Supervisor. Part of the Anaconda-Pintlar Wilderness Area is within this Forest. Ennis, Virginia City, Wisdom are other area towns, and routes U.S. 91 and State 287, 43, 41, 34 all cross the region.

To the west and north is the Bitterroot NF (2) with over 1.5 million acres. A part of this Forest extends into Idaho. The headquarters is at Hamilton, Montana, on U.S. 93. Missoula, to the north of Hamilton on this route, is another key location.

Deerlodge NF (3) is in this same general sector of the state, with headquarters at Butte. There are nearly 1.2 million acres in this Forest. Anaconda, Butte, Deer Lodge are area cities. U.S. 10 and 91 are key routes.

The Lolo NF (4), also partly in Idaho, lies along the border to the north, with U.S. 10, 10A, and 93 key routes and with Missoula the headquarters of the Forest Supervisor. This Forest contains over two million acres.

Still farther up toward and throughout the extreme northwest is the Kootenai NF (5) with slightly more than 1.8 million acres, part of which are in Idaho. The headquarters are at Libby, and U.S. 2 and 93 are main access routes.

The Flathead NF (6) lies to the east, has over 2.3 million acres and contains the famed Bob Marshall Wilderness and the Mission Mountains Primitive Area. Kalispell is the headquarters city, and U.S. 2 and 93 are also access routes here.

South, and east, of the Flathead NF and in several blocks is the Lewis and Clark NF (7), with approximately 1.8 million acres. Great Falls is the location of the Forest Supervisor, U.S. 12, 87, 89, 91 some main vicinity routes. Sandwiched between portions of this Forest and Deer Lodge to the west is the Helena NF (8) with slightly less than a million acres. Headquarters is at Helena, and U.S. 12 and 91 main routes.

Along and above the southern border, west of center, and just to the north and west of Yellowstone National Park is the Gallatin NF (9) with 1.7 million acres. Headquarters are at Bozeman. Big Timber, Gardiner, Livingston are area towns, and U.S. 191, 10, 89 some of the chief access routes.

These Forests so far noted cover the major portion of the mountains of the western third or more of Montana. Up in the northwest a part of the Kaniksu NF (10), listed as an Idaho Forest and with headquarters at Sandpoint, Idaho, overlaps into Montana. And in southern Montana along the central and southeastern border are several blocks of the Custer NF (11). This Forest, with approximately 1.2 million acres, is partly in South Dakota, but the headquarters is at Billings, Montana. Maps showing the locations of the several tracts can be obtained there from the Supervisor. One of the western parts of this Forest contains the awesomely scenic Beartooth Primitive Area, above Red Lodge. U.S. 10, 12, 312 are key routes.

Because of the tremendous amount of big-game hunting available by

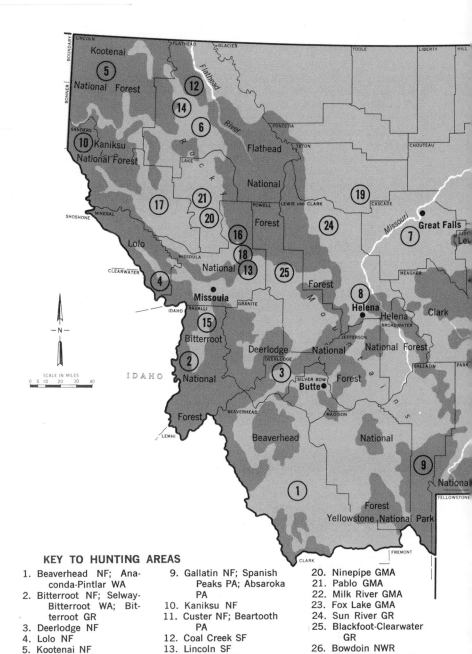

KEY TO HUNTING AREAS

1. Beaverhead NF; Anaconda-Pintlar WA
2. Bitterroot NF; Selway-Bitterroot WA; Bitterroot GR
3. Deerlodge NF
4. Lolo NF
5. Kootenai NF
6. Flathead NF; Bob Marshall WA; Mission Mountains PA
7. Lewis & Clark NF
8. Helena NF; Gates of the Mountains WA

9. Gallatin NF; Spanish Peaks PA; Absaroka PA
10. Kaniksu NF
11. Custer NF; Beartooth PA
12. Coal Creek SF
13. Lincoln SF
14. Stillwater SF
15. Sula SF
16. Swan River SF
17. Thompson River SF
18. Clearwater SF
19. Freezeout GMA

20. Ninepipe GMA
21. Pablo GMA
22. Milk River GMA
23. Fox Lake GMA
24. Sun River GR
25. Blackfoot-Clearwater GR
26. Bowdoin NWR
27. Charles M. Russell NWR

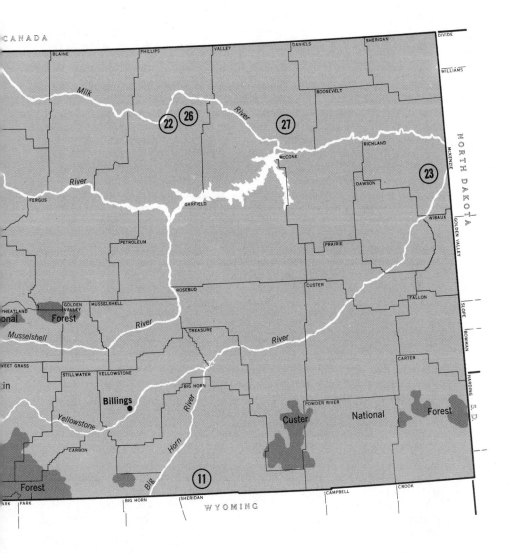

pack-in, in the Primitive and Wilderness Areas, they are listed briefly here. The Bob Marshall WA contains 950,000 acres, in the Flathead and Lewis and Clark Forests. The Anaconda-Pintlar WA has over 157,000 acres spread among the Beaverhead, Deerlodge and Bitterroot NFs. The Beartooth PA contains 230,000 acres, in the Custer and Gallatin Forests. Selway-Bitterroot WA: Montana acreage almost 252,000, Bitterroot and Lolo Forests. Mission Mountains PA, 73,000-plus acres, Flathead NF; Spanish Peaks PA, 49,800, Gallatin NF; Absaroka PA, 64,000 acres, Gallatin NF; Gates of the Mountains WA, 28,562 acres, Helena NF.

There are in addition to the National Forests several important State Forests. Coal Creek SF (12), headquarters at Kalispell; Lincoln SF (13), headquarters at Missoula; Stillwater SF (14), headquarters west of Whitefish near Olney; Sula SF (15), headquarters on Goat Creek, south of Swan Lake; Swan River SF (16), located in that area but headquarters at Missoula; Thompson River SF (17), on river of like name but headquarters at Missoula; Clearwater SF (18), near Seeley Lake but headquarters in Missoula.

Because of the enormous acreage in the public lands noted so far, there is not the need for Game Management Areas and other public shooting grounds available in many states of heavier population. However, Montana does have a few that fall into two categories: Game Management Areas and Game Ranges. The Game Department is a very active and management-minded organization and is constantly attempting to purchase or gain control of more land. It is interesting to note that at the turn of the century big game in this state was left in such small numbers that many conservationists believed it could never recoup. It has been brought literally from the edge of extinction by meat and hide hunting to great abundance through transplant efforts and other management techniques. Also, many portions of Montana that had never had certain of the big-game species even when Lewis and Clark first saw this region now have thriving herds due to live trapping and transplant efforts. A publication of the Department, address at chapter end, that will be most helpful to visitors coming here to hunt is "Outdoors in Montana—Hunting, Fishing, Sightseeing."

With only a few exceptions, guides or licensed residents must accompany visitors for big-game hunting. There are many ranches, lodges, and outfitters who take hunters. Many advertise. Most can be contacted via Chambers of Commerce. Motels and such accommodations are available in all the larger cities and towns, but most big-game hunts by nonresidents are booked with outfitters. A list of licensed guides is available from the Game Department. Outfitter prices run from $35 to $75 per day, depending on services offered. Bird hunters do not need guides. The Montana Outfitters and Guides Association, Billings, Montana, may be contacted for lists and advice. Also, for those flying in to a specific area, the Montana Aeronautics Commission, Box 1698, Helena, Montana 59601, will give detailed information.

For hunters who wish to camp, there are practically unlimited opportunities. National Parks, National Forests, Corps of Engineers Reservoir sites, State Forests, State Parks, State Highway Commission campgrounds, Municipal and Civic campgrounds add up to almost 500 camping places, with several thousand individual sites. Lists of campgrounds, of all varieties, can be had from the Montana State Chamber of Commerce, Helena. The Department publication mentioned a moment ago lists the State Parks, and gives details about each.

Early fall hunting during September and October usually offers pleasant weather. But nights will be frosty and daytimes may be very crisp. Wool shirts and a jacket are in order. For big-game hunting heavy clothing and good boots are mandatory. Cold weather is the rule. Snow may be on the ground, or heavy storms may occur at any time.

Deer and antelope hunters will want flat-shooting rifles in the .243 to .270 category, or for general hunting the .30/06 is a good example of a standard arm. For elk, moose, bear, heavy rifles such as the several magnums in solid caliber are recommended. Because of the variety of bird hunting, shotgunners should be prepared to use various loads, from No. 7½ for Huns to No. 2 for geese. Because most Montana game birds are of good size— pheasants, the various grouses—and several such as sharptail, sage grouse, and pheasants may offer open shooting with sometimes long ranges, a good standard load is the No. 6 highbase in 12 gauge.

PHEASANT

The ringneck was introduced to Montana about 1895. It did not do well until late in the 1930s when farming practices and general land use in suitable habitat allowed it to prominently establish itself. Although there is some excellent pheasant hunting in the state, at this time the ringneck, as in many other states, is showing a decline, undoubtedly attributable to further land-use changes, clean farming and a loss of proper habitat. Feedlot livestock feeding, rather than field feeding, for example, has harmed pheasants in winter in parts of Montana. The trend is definitely downward.

Generally the season is statewide, but with varying dates in several different sectors. Also, some seasons cocks only may be taken in some counties, one hen in a daily limit in others, either sex indiscriminately in still others. Even though the season is statewide, this by no means indicates a good pheasant population everywhere. Pheasants are almost wholly dependent upon croplands and their brushy fringes. Stream bottoms and lands below 4500 feet altitude, especially irrigated valleys where agriculture is important, areas where ditch banks and marsh growth such as cattails offer cover in proximity to farms are the important pheasant areas.

Most of the better pheasant habitat is in eastern Montana, and in the central agricultural area and along the Yellowstone River and the Musselshell River. The vicinities around Lewiston, Stanford, and Billings often have good populations. By and large, the longest seasons and seasons for both cocks and hens are in the southeast quarter of Montana. The northeast and the central third of the state are next, and the west is just fair. However, there are in the west several valleys with plenty of agricultural use and good pheasant populations.

In the southeast probably the best hunting is along the Yellowstone River and some of its tributaries, where thickets adjoin fields. The Forsyth and Hysham areas often offer good shooting. Although the northeast has seen difficulty with its birds, the various river valleys still furnish good shooting. The Milk River is excellent, and the Yellowstone and the Musselshell as noted. There is some shooting in south-central Montana, in the valley of the Big Horn, but this part of the state, and the southwest, are not very good habitat. In the northwest the valley of the Flathead River south from Polson is one of the state's best areas. There is also some hunting just west around Hot Springs. And to the east, in the region northwest from Great Falls where the towns of Choteau, Fairfield, and Conrad are located, birds are usually fairly plentiful.

Although in most pheasant areas there is not much difficulty in obtaining permission to hunt, there are several state-owned tracts where pheasants are found. One is the Freezeout GMA (19) near Fairfield. Two others offer good chances in the Flathead valley. These are Ninepipe GMA (20) near Ronan, and Pablo GMA (21) near town of like name, both towns on U.S. 93. The Milk River GMA (22) is near Malta, U.S. 2 in north-central Montana, and the Fox Lake GMA (23) is near Sidney, in the northeast, on the border, junction State 16 and 20.

There are some pheasants on the Bitterroot Game Range out of Hamilton, U.S. 93 in the southwest. At times there is a bit of pheasant hunting to be had on open portions of the National Wildlife Refuges used chiefly by water-fowl. One should check with the Refuge Manager. See "Waterfowl" for locations of Refuges.

SHARPTAILED GROUSE

Often improperly called "prairie chicken" by natives, the sharptail is the common and quite abundant grouse of central and eastern Montana. Some are found farther west, but this is a bird primarily of the prairies. The wheatlands of eastern Montana where low brush patches are interspersed furnishes some of the best habitat. In some areas vast expanses of wheat without other cover hold sharptails, such as in the extreme northeast. The rough prairie country where grass and brush grow in mixed stands also is excellent.

As a rule the season is open throughout all of the state except the far west and northwest. But sharptails are very spottily distributed in the south-west and along the east slope. North-central Montana offers fair opportunity. Best of the hunting, however, is in three main locations. One is in the foothill country of Judith Basin County between Great Falls and Lewiston. A second is in the dry-farmed wheat fields of the south. And the third is along the so-called breaks, or rough country all along the course of the Missouri River.

There is such a vast range for this grouse over roughly two-thirds of the state that no further or special pinpoint locations can be given. A very good plan for visiting hunters in sharptail territory is to contact the local conservation officer and ask about important concentrations of birds that season in his area. As with most prairie and arid-country game birds, seasonal population fluctuations are often wide. Both farmlands and BLM lands have abundant birds.

SAGE GROUSE

The sage grouse is the second of Montana's two prairie grouses. Its range is patterned very much like that of the sharptail, but the large sage grouse is almost wholly dependent upon sage for both food and shelter, and thus it is tied a bit more closely, within its range, to the specific portions where this plant grows, than is the sharptail. Although some sage grouse are found in the southwest and in the sage-covered mountain valleys and slopes north of Yellowstone Park, the region of greatest abundance is in and east of the following counties: beginning at the northern border and reading south-ward, Liberty, eastern Choteau, Fergus, Wheatland, Sweetgrass, Carbon. All of Montana from these to the eastern border, with the exception of the northeastern counties of Daniels, Sheridan, Roosevelt, and Richland, which at this writing are not open to hunting, contain fair to good sage grouse popu-lations wherever sage is abundant.

Quite often it is possible to find locations on the rolling plains where both sharptails and sage grouse can be hunted at the same time. BLM lands are especially good for sage grouse because they have not been planted as a rule to any crop. Though the sage grouse is not as abundant as the sharp-tail in most of its range, nonetheless 4-a-day limits have been the rule in most of the eastern part of Montana outlined above.

HUNGARIAN PARTRIDGE

The Hun has been established in Montana for many years and is just possibly the most widely spread of all the state's upland game birds.

However, it is never extremely abundant except locally and its numbers fluctuate widely season to season. While the kill is not high, nonetheless it is possible to hunt this species while after several of the others and it adds many a surprise and satisfaction to a mixed bag.

The seasons set for sharptails, and the region over which they apply, are usually the same as for Huns, but of course bag limits differ, and at times, due to low levels of population in some counties, other regulations are set. Best Hun hunting is on the plains where a great deal of wheatlands are interspersed with grass. In good years the better densities are in the Harlowton, Lewiston, Great Falls triangle, in Judith Basin Co., and much of the country farther north following the general course of U.S. 2 and the Milk River drainage. The GMAs near Fairfield and Malta mentioned under "Pheasant" may furnish some shooting. Most of the best, however, will be on privately owned farmlands.

CHUKAR

The chukar has been stocked in numerous places in Montana, and many releases have been made. To date, however, it has not become very generally well established. There are a few in localized spots within the Hun and sharptail range. This bird utilizes the rugged, steep, rocky cheatgrass slopes and is not dependent upon agriculture. Although the season is generally concurrent with that for the sharptail and Hun, and throughout the same territory, and there have been seasons now since 1959, this is by no means an abundant species. It is also quite cyclic. Bag limits are generally set for an aggregate bag between chukar and Hun. Best bet for hunters in Montana chukar country is to make a check with the Game Department and follow this by one to the local officer in the better range for the given season.

FOREST GROUSE

There are three species of so-called "forest grouse" in Montana. These are the large blue grouse of the high country forests, the ruffed grouse of the tangled stream courses at somewhat lower elevations, and the Franklin's or spruce grouse, or "fool hen," of the deep, dark, and often damp evergreen forests.

The kill on none of these birds is high, but the potential for mountain-forest sport is great. In Montana the seasons all run as a rule as for one species. Virtually all of the western one-half of Montana is open, with the season usually beginning during a delightful time of year, September, and running into November. Sometimes and in some areas big-game hunters are allowed to hunt these birds later, and up to this writing all three are legally taken if one desires by rifle or handgun. The blue and the spruce grouse often sit rather calmly in trees at the approach of a hunter and thus a small-caliber rifle can be quite sporting. Ruffed grouse are as a rule more difficult.

The National Forests and State Forests offer practically limitless opportunities for this specialized forest-grouse sport. No one spot can be named as better than another. The plain fact is, no one knows from season to season where these wilderness birds are in best supply. It is truly a hunter's game to find them. The big blues, which may weigh three pounds or more, are generally found at the edges of openings in high-country forests. Ruffed grouse, in lesser numbers in most locations, favor the tangled willows and alders along stream courses at moderate altitudes. Spruce or Franklin's grouse are not very common anywhere but appear to have the greatest density in the northwestern mountains.

A drive during season into any western forest area on lumber trails in a 4WD vehicle is almost certain to turn up opportunities for one or another of these birds. Hunters should consider a grand mixed-bag hunt on the eastern fringe of mountain grouse range for numerous upland birds as well. For example, a well-planned excursion on the east slope of the Rockies is capable of turning up mountain grouse, plus the prairie species and pheasants at lower elevation within easy distance to the east.

WILD TURKEYS

The wild turkey was not native to Montana. Some private releases of turkeys were made over the years but none was successful. The Merriam's turkey of southwestern forests was brought into the state in early 1955, the stock coming from Wyoming. There were eighteen birds, and these were released in a block of the Custer Forest in Carter Co. in the southeast. From establishment there, live-trapped transplants were taken to other parts of the state. The process is continuing, but meanwhile there have been a number of hunting seasons.

Presently the main turkey population is still in the southeast, and each season much of the southeastern quarter of Montana is open. Central Montana also has turkeys established, and they are gaining in the north-central region also. There have been seasons, for example, in Lewis and Clark, Cascade, Judith Basin, Fergus, and Meagher Cos., and also in Phillips Co. In the far west turkeys are established in the forests in Sanders, Mineral, Missoula, and Ravalli Cos.

During the latest fall season as this is written, there were no hunts allowed west of the Divide, presumably indicating a low turkey population there. Lewis and Clark, Jefferson, and Broadwater were open. There was then a closed region in central Montana, but Fergus and Phillips Cos. were open. All of these counties had hunts the previous year, indicating a substantial turkey population. Immediately south of Fergus Co., portions of Musselshell, Yellowstone, Bighorn, and Golden Valley Cos. were open, with fair turkey numbers mainly along the river courses. And, as usual, most of the southeast was open. Ordinarily the open counties here are Garfield, Rosebud, Treasure, Powder River, Carter, Custer, Fallon, Prairie, Wibaux, and southern portions of McCone, Dawson, Richland.

It is not possible to predict from season to season which areas will be open. In recent years there have been some spring as well as fall seasons. A hunter who purchases a turkey license for the spring hunt and fails to get a gobbler is allowed to hunt on the same license the following fall. At the present time the best turkey hunting is located as follows: in the southeast, in the several blocks of Custer NF, one known as the Ashland Division, Rosebud and Powder River Cos., and another the Sioux Division or Long Pines Area, the location where turkeys were first stocked, Carter Co.; the Missouri River Breaks near upper Fort Peck Reservoir and along the Missouri River here, in Fergus and Phillips Cos. Hunters should be very certain of the boundaries of open areas.

WATERFOWL

Montana has some rather good waterfowl shooting. The state is in two flyways, Central and Pacific, and regulations differ in each so hunters should be careful to observe the rules. The wheatlands of the east draw many feeding geese. In fact, a good many geese nest in what is known as the "high-line" area of Montana, along the Milk River drainage across Hill, Blaine, and Phillips Cos. This same high-line region furnishes probably the best duck hunting in the state. Other production areas, and regions of good shooting, are in the west, along the Flathead Valley below Flathead Lake, in the Madison Valley, and around the numerous lakes scattered along the east slope of the Divide. Farther east and south, the Big Horn Valley offers excellent opportunity, and all of the long, broad Yellowstone Valley is excellent all the way from the Billings region to Sidney in the northeast. The enormous Fort Peck Reservoir and its branching bays, and also the extreme northeast in the Plentywood area offer unlimited opportunities.

Chief species in Montana are mallards and Canada geese. There are of course numerous other ducks. Snow geese are plentiful during migration, in central Montana. One excellent area is at Freezeout Lake, near Fairfield. White-fronted geese, or specklebellies, pass through the Plentywood area in northeastern Montana, Sheridan Co.

There are numerous lakes and streams within the massive National Forests that offer good duck hunting. Wise hunters will not overlook these. Along many streams excellent jump-shooting is available. Several of the GMAs noted under "Pheasant" offer waterfowl shooting. Among these are Freezeout, Milk River, Ninepipe, Pablo. Another not mentioned is Fox Lake, near Sidney in the northeast. There is also a moderate amount of duck shooting on waters of the Sun River Game Range (24) near Augusta, which is west of Great Falls, and on the Blackfoot-Clearwater Game Range (25) near Ovando, on State 20 northeast from Missoula.

Although hunting may not be allowed on all of the National Refuges, these do draw and hold waterfowl and there is usually good hunting in the surrounding country. Benton Lake NWR northeast of Great Falls covers 12,400 acres. Bowdoin (26), east of Malta, has 15,500 acres and holds many Canada geese as well as ducks. Ordinarily a large acreage is open to hunting. The Charles M. Russell NWR (27) is an enormous one, containing very nearly a million acres along Fort Peck Reservoir and the Missouri. Both ducks and geese are found here and there is hunting allowed. There are some waterfowl on the National Bison Range, a refuge of over 18,000 acres near Moiese, Montana. Medicine Lake, near town of like name up in the northeast, south from Plentywood, contains 31,500 acres and holds both ducks and geese.

There are also waterfowl refuges in the following counties, all of which offer hunting of varying quality in the surrounding area: Blaine, Hill, Stillwater, Phillips, Musselshell, Wibaux, Teton, Ravalli, Lewis and Clark, Petroleum.

There is some snipe hunting in Montana, but it gets little attention.

DEER

Deer hunting is so excellent over such a vast portion of Montana that a hunter can just about select the type of country in which he wishes to hunt, and be fairly well assured of success. The percentage of hunter success is astonishing. During one five-year period in the 1960s lowest overall success for the entire state was 94 percent and the highest 103 percent, the latter figure because in numerous Hunting Districts (management units) more than one deer could be taken. During most recent seasons success has dropped a bit, but is still fantastically high. In three seasons prior to this writing it ran, for the total state: 92, 77, 79 percent. The harvest figures for those seasons:

98,100; 89,000; 99,000. Highest annual kill over the past decade was 129,000. However, in most seasons under present management there should be a kill of about 100,000 deer by approximately 125,000 deer hunters.

Montana has both mule deer and whitetails. Though many natives and visitors prefer to hunt mule deer because they are larger, are often found in more open country, and are not as difficult to hunt, the whitetail has slowly been climbing in popularity and in numbers, and in importance so far as proportion of the bag is concerned. Usually the proportion of whitetails to mule deer is about 75 percent mule deer, 25 percent whitetails. For example, during the season noted above when 98,100 deer were bagged, the split was 73,000 mule deer, 25,100 whitetails. Incidentally, during an average season about 70 percent of the deer killed are bucks.

There is no problem whatever about finding a place to hunt. The National and State Forests described early in the chapter offer virtually unlimited opportunity. There is also hunting on the Game Ranges, and a great deal of easily obtained hunting on private lands. Deer hunters should be well versed, however, on the fairly complicated regulations.

The state is split into over 150 numbered Hunting Districts or management units. A regulations map is printed each year showing the Districts, giving their exact boundaries in written description, and listing the seasons in each. There are several types of licenses. Residents may hunt on a general license, or on a license good for deer only, of which there are two varieties, one good in any District, one valid only in specified districts. In some Districts only a whitetail may be taken, in others either whitetail or mule deer is legal.

Nonresidents with the expensive general game license may hunt about as residents, except that in most Districts (as listed) they must be accompanied by a resident or resident guide licensed to hunt game. However, a nonresident can purchase a deer-only license and hunt without being accompanied, but this license applies only in specified Districts, is valid only for the District specified on the license, and for whitetail only or for either species, as the District orders show. It is thus easy to see that close study of the regulations before purchase of license is extremely important.

Northwestern Montana is considered the best whitetail hunting, with Lincoln, Sanders, Mineral, Flathead, and Powell Cos. the top locations. Here the deer are likely to be found in situations where forest and stream bottoms are dense with undergrowth, and the hunting seldom easy. East of the Continental Divide whitetails cling to the river-bottom terrain almost entirely, and along the large rivers they are abundant from across the north down to the breaks of the Little Missouri in the extreme southeast. Two forest areas east of the divide, however, are outstanding. One is in the Snowy Mountains near Lewiston, the Little Snow and Big Snowy Ranges in the Lewis and Clark Forest. Here whitetails have steadily increased until they are the dominant species. In the early 1960s, for example, the kill was about 35 percent whitetails, but by the late 1960s it was close to 75 percent. The other excellent whitetail area in forest habitat east of the Divide is in the extreme southeast, in a block of the Custer NF called the Longpine Hills, near the settlement of Ekalaka.

Ordinarily most of the nonresident deer-only licenses are for the southeast. And these, incidentally, are by quota—a specified number for each District. Mule deer are numerous in the southeast, too. The Broadus region in Powder River Co. is a good bet for both species and so are the Little Missouri breaks. Farther north, the Bear Paw Mountains near Havre are a good whitetail location. So is the Milk River and its numerous tributaries.

Many mule deer are also found throughout all of this country. The Missouri River breaks in northern Garfield are excellent, and seemingly endless stretches of steep but low hills dotted with scattered pine, all over the east, are excellent mule deer country.

Some of the finest mule deer hunting to the west is along the lower ranges and the eastern slopes of the Divide. The Little Belt Mountains, the Moccasins, the Judith Mountains, the Highwood Mountains, are all examples of individual ranges with fine hunting. On the east slope of the Divide itself there are numerous trails and lesser roads where by pickup or 4WD hunters can work back into good foothill areas. Much of the high country of course requires packing in, and it is not necessarily any better hunting than the lower altitudes. The east slope has more open forest than the northwest, and the deer are mostly mule deer. The later the season the better chance one has of claiming a real trophy.

West of the Divide, and south from the dense northwestern whitetail country, more open timber appears. There are meadows and grassy, open parks. Both mule deer and whitetails are here, but mule deer are dominant in much of the region. Most foothills are accessible via log roads, but one must pack in to reach the back country. Of course all of the mountain region on both sides of the Divide has limitless public domain, in the Forests.

ELK

Montana is one of our most important elk states. Over three recent seasons kills and success percentages were as follows: 13,400 for a 22.6 percent success; 14,500 for 21.2 percent; 16,000 for 21 percent. Usually the kill is a bit more than 50 percent bulls, possibly 35 percent cows, and the remainder calves, depending of course upon how many antlerless permits are offered. Regulations are in many ways similar to those for deer and thus elk hunters should read the "Deer" section and be aware that a study of laws for any given season is extremely important. There is no elk-only license for nonresidents.

Elk range very generally over all of the western mountains, on both sides of the Divide. East of the Divide the range extends eastward roughly to a line running from Liberty Co. in the north on a southeast slant down past the town of Fort Benton, through Judith Basin, Wheatland, Sweetgrass, and Stillwater Cos. to the city of Red Lodge and thence to the border. From Judith Basin Co. there is an elk range extending toward Lewiston, and Fergus Co. and a small but stable herd up in the Missouri breaks near Fort Peck Reservoir. Almost all of the entire elk range is open during any given season, except game preserves, Glacier Park and the Flathead Indian Reservation.

Hunting grounds may be selected more by type of terrain than by elk population, because of the thorough distribution of the animals. The northwest is difficult hunting because it is dense in vegetation and the elk are usually in small herds. There is much country accessible only by packing in, and snow may come early. The border country, with Idaho, to the south is rugged but moderately accessible in foothill country and good hunting is offered here. Toward the southwest there are areas somewhat more open than the dense northwest. Elk populations are high. The same is true of the east slope. Access into foothills is fairly easy and there are numerous open parks and meadows in the timber. If the weather is favorable, which means severe in the high ranges, elk are driven down to winter range and can be found on the east slope in large herds.

Nonresidents must be guided, and residents who are strange to the country in which they propose to hunt will be well advised to hire a guide or outfitter also. The National Forests are of course the main home of almost all Montana elk and therefore finding a hunting ground is no worry. Broad distribution, again, makes selection of an area something of a toss-up. A good guide who knows the country and where the animals in a particular range are likely to be is without question more important to success than the District selected.

ANTELOPE

The pronghorn ranges in Montana throughout all of the east and the central portion of the state, and clear into the foothills of the east slope of the Divide, which means that there are antelope as far west as southwestern Montana. The central part of eastern Montana usually gets the greatest number of permits. Central Montana also gets a high number. And the extreme southwest, south of Dillon and below Clark Canyon Reservoir, also gets a good number.

By and large, the southeast and east-central areas have the largest number of antelope. As with deer and elk, which see, the antelope hunter should get the map showing open Districts and carefully study the laws for a current season before making application. Antelope are on a quota system in all open Districts, for careful management. The odds on drawing a permit are often high. In the season just past, there were 18,330 licenses to be issued, and almost 25,000 applications. However, some of the Districts most distant from the large cities often have more licenses than applicants. During that same year District 731, which is in the sparsely populated central east, had only 321 applicants for 550 licenses. In general the southeast is a good bet for an applicant. Human population is low and antelope population high, and the region is rather far from most large population centers. Many hunters do not wish to go that far, and thus the diligent sportsman has a fair chance of "drawing lucky."

It does not make a great deal of difference, so far as success percentage is concerned, which District one selects. On the average at least 70 percent or more of Montana antelope hunters bag their game. The average annual harvest runs from 11,000 to 14,000 animals. In the early 1960s it was much higher, up to almost 27,000 one season.

Nonresidents applying for an antelope-only license are allowed to use it only in a few specified Districts, ordinarily in the east-central and southeast.

MOOSE

Heaviest moose population in Montana is across the southwest, from the border counties of Missoula, Ravalli, and Beaverhead eastward to the region north of Yellowstone Park and into portions of Sweetgrass, Stillwater, and Carbon Cos. The other solid moose population is in the northwest, west of Glacier Park and south of it along the Divide and the South Fork of the Flathead.

In an average season over 600 permits are issued, by drawing, with quotas allotted for each of the various open Districts. The kill averages between 400 and 500, and success percentage has for some years ranged from about 70 to 85 percent. Nonresidents must have the $150 (currently) general license and pay an extra $50 for a moose permit. Any hunter who fails to make a kill may apply the next year by returning his unused license and the new fee, but those who make a kill may not apply again (in any quota District) for seven years.

In the days of Lewis and Clark apparently moose were not common in what is now Montana but a few were seen. As early as 1862, it is interesting to note, they received some protection, with a closed season February into August. By 1897, however, the season was totally closed and moose were estimated to number by 1910 not more than 300 in all of the state. It was not until 1942 that any plans for moose management were made and a survey taken, and in 1945 the state had its first season in almost half a century. There were, that year, ninety bulls-only permits, spread in three areas, the Absaroka, the Gallatin, the Bighole drainage.

These same general regions are still among the best. But studies show that though a high percentage of the moose kill is in accessible spots to which hunters can drive, most of the bulls are no more than two-year-olds. Trophy moose come from the hard to get to, pack-in spots. Districts have now been broken into smaller units and quotas set to spread hunters more evenly and thus get a kill over a larger area. Any hunter who draws a permit and is well guided by an experienced outfitter in Montana's moose country is almost certain to score.

MOUNTAIN GOATS AND MOUNTAIN SHEEP

Montana has for some years been especially active in live trapping and transplanting both goats and sheep. Both species are well established in a number of mountain ranges and hunting seasons have been held for a number of years. Permits are of course rather limited.

The goat kill has run over the past decade from 200 to 500 annually. In some open Districts there are no quotas and in others there are quotas. Nonresidents are allowed no more than 10 percent of the total licenses for limited areas. Success percentages vary greatly between limited and unlimited areas and from season to season. Averaged out among both types, success probably runs from 30 to 50 percent. Goats are found in the high mountains north of Yellowstone Park, in others northwest from the Park, in much of the rugged country of the border in the southwest, and throughout most of the higher ranges of the northwest. They have been placed in a number of other locations.

Sheep hunting is far more restricted. Seventy or eighty are taken each season, with success running from 60 to 75 percent. Licenses are of course by drawing. The main sheep bands are in the area north of Yellowstone, the south end of Ravalli Co., the Clark Fork region in Granite Co., the Sun River region in Teton and Lewis and Clark Cos., and up in the northwest in Sanders and Lincoln and a part of Flathead Cos.

BEARS

The black bear is fairly numerous. Only remnants of the once large grizzly population remain. Over two recent seasons the black bear kills were 1950 and 2100, the grizzly kill 45 and 30.

Black bear are hunted from mid-March until December. Spring hunting is more successful than fall, although in fall many are taken incidentally by deer and elk hunters. All of western Montana and the east slope have black bear. Some of the better regions are the Swan River Valley, the South and Middle Forks of the Flathead, the Whitefish Range, the Saint Regis River, Thompson Falls west, the Libby country. Montana game men advise bear hunters to hunt the side drainages because they are invariably steep and allow a good view of the slopes. Bear hunters in Montana must earn their trophies, for use of dogs, and baiting, are both prohibited.

The grizzlies in Montana are almost all in the northwest, around Glacier Park, which forms a kind of protected reservoir for remnants of the species. A few have been taken west of Glacier in recent seasons, in the Districts numbered on the regulations map 101 and 11. Others have been bagged south of Glacier in District 14 and on either side of the Sun River Game Preserve in Districts 42 and 15, and west of 15 in Districts 131 and 28 near the Flathead Indian Reservation. Several have also come from south of the Sun River Game Preserve, in Districts 280 and 281. The only other area inhabited by a notable number of these wilderness bears is immediately north of Yellowstone Park, where a few have been taken. Yellowstone, like Glacier, gives haven to a few grizzlies. The grizzly season begins with deer and elk season, closes as a rule by December. This is a most specialized undertaking, and only a well guided hunt by an outfitter acquainted with grizzly range and habits has much of a chance of success. It is even quite possible that in due time the grizzly will be placed under full protection.

OTHER ANIMALS

There is a great deal of off-season shooting for pests and much of the same for predators. Bobcats are fairly plentiful. Coyotes are found both on the plains and in the high and forested mountains. There are badgers and foxes. Small pests such as ground squirrels are in hordes in much of the sagebrush and plains and cultivated country. Some prairie dog towns are left here and there where ranchers have refused federal poisoning. In some of the farming valleys magpies are extremely plentiful and offer good shooting. They are exceedingly wary. Crows are fairly common.

Rabbits, not on the game list, are plentiful and of several varieties in various portions of the state. There are pygmy rabbits in some brushy and sagebrush locations, and cottontails where cover and forage are suitable. Both whitetailed and blacktailed jacks are present. And snowshoe hares are found in modest numbers in the mountains.

No license is at this time required for any of this shooting, for either residents or nonresidents.

REGULATIONS

Game laws pertaining to seasons, bag and possession limits, areas to be hunted, special hunts, license fees all may have numerous changes from year to year. For current regulations, and for other specific queries, write to: Department of Fish and Game, Helena, Montana 59601.

Pacific
Coast
States

CALIFORNIA

California is virtually everything its enthusiasts claim, an unbelievable land of swarming people and at the same time all but limitless wilderness, of desert and snow-capped mountains, of marine vistas and glacial high-country lakes, of endlessly stretching farmlands and teeming cities A land of never-ceasing contrasts, it contains the highest mountain peak in the contiguous U.S., 14,495-foot Mount Whitney, and the lowest point, only a few miles distant, in Death Valley, 280 feet below sea level.

Fronting approximately 1200 miles on the Pacific, California's northern neighbor is Oregon, its southern neighbor the Baja California Peninsula of Mexico. On the eastern boundary it briefly touches Arizona in the south, and for the remainder butts up against Nevada.

North to south, California is a series of rugged mountain ranges between which lie irrigated and desert valleys. The coast over much of its length is rugged and rocky, except in the south. Jutting upward from the beaches are the Coast Ranges. Then come the vast interior valleys, among the world's most fertile. In the east, rising from the central valley section, lie the mighty Cascade and Sierra Nevada Ranges. There are many less consequential ranges within the state. Because of diversity in both latitude and altitude, climate and game species are highly varied from north to south and from desert to mountain.

California cannot be called either an industrial state or an agricultural state. It is an amalgam of both. Currently, in fact, it leads the U.S. in agriculture, its products chiefly fruit, vegetables, livestock, and poultry. It is also a focal point for the aerospace industry, is rich in oil, in tourism, and in marine fisheries. California is indeed a paradox of sorts. Third largest of the states, with an area of 158,693 square miles, it is now first in population, reaching toward twenty million. Yet this teeming population has as its playground vast amounts of authentic wilderness that vie with any of the contiguous states for greatest number of acres of publicly administered lands.

Good highways and plane transport reach from one end of the state to the other. Thus, sportsmen can go to any destination they wish with ease. Nonetheless, over thousands of square miles of public domain the hunter must resort to pack horse or four-wheel-drive vehicle to get to his final hunting site. Even with such a teeming population, hunting is still excellent. But trips within the state can be long. Airline distance north-south is as much as 825 miles. East-west California is comparatively narrow—from 200 to 300 miles—but the distance is stretched because of mountain ranges.

With its large population, California has a substantial but not unusually large number of hunters. Total annual license sales are reaching toward 750,000. Only a smattering are nonresident, less than 2000. This seems odd, what with the vast public acreages accessible, and the variety and amount of game available. Some of the nation's best waterfowling is here. Upland birds include pheasant, three species of quail, chukar and Hungarian partridge, sage grouse, ruffed and blue grouse, wild turkey, a variety of wild doves and pigeons. There are several kinds of rabbits and squirrels. There are coyotes, foxes, bobcats, lions, badgers, and raccoons. Big game is plentiful, mainly mule deer, of which there are at least six subspecies within the state. There are also three varieties of elk, in small herds, a modest supply of antelope, a substantial number of black bears, plus numerous wild boars and a start toward re-establishment of the mountain sheep. In small game, doves, waterfowl, quail, and pheasants, in that order, are most important by annual average kill. Deer are far and away the most numerous and popular big game.

Particularly because of its huge and swiftly growing population, California is most fortunate to have such wealth in public lands. There are over twenty million acres in National Forests alone. There are nineteen of these, ranging in size from a few hundred thousand acres to over two million. Because these National Forests are so numerous, they are listed and located here as briefly as possible. The general area of the state where each is situated is given, the names of the Forests in that region, the name of the city where that Forest headquarters is located, and the countries in which it is chiefly contained. One may write the Forest Supervisor there for detailed information and maps. The address for the Regional Forest Service Office which administers all these Forests is: U.S. Forest Service, 630 Sansome St., San Francisco, California.

FOREST	HEADQUARTERS	COUNTIES
NORTHWEST		
1. Six Rivers NF	Eureka	Del Norte, Humboldt, Trinity
2. Klamath NF	Yreka	Siskiyou
3. Trinity NF	Redding	Trinity, Shasta
4. Mendocino NF	Willows	Mendocino, Tehama, Glenn, Lake, Colusa
NORTH CENTRAL		
5. Shasta NF	Redding	Shasta, Siskiyou
NORTHEAST		
6. Modoc NF	Alturas	Modoc, Siskiyou, Lassen
7. Lassen NF	Susanville	Lassen, Shasta, Tehama, Butte, Plumas
EAST CENTRAL		
8. Plumas NF	Quincy	Plumas, Butte, Sierra
9. Tahoe NF	Nevada City	Placer, Nevada, Sierra, Yuba
10. El Dorado NF	Placerville	Eldorado, Placer, Amador, Alpine
11. Stanislaus NF	Sonora	Tuolumne, Caloveras, Alpine
12. Toiyabe NF	Reno, Nev.	Mono (partly in Nev.)
13. Inyo NF	Bishop	Inyo, Mono, Madera
14. Sierra NF	Fresno	Madera, Fresno
SOUTH CENTRAL		
15. Sequoia NF	Porterville	Tulare, Kern, Fresno
SOUTH COAST		
16. Los Padres NF	Santa Barbara	Monterey, San Luis Obispo, Santa Barbara, Ventura

SOUTH
17. Angeles NF   Pasadena   Los Angeles
18. San Bernardino NF   San Bernardino   San Bernardino, Riverside
19. Cleveland NF   San Diego   Orange, Riverside, San Diego

These Forests will be referred to later under the various species. Hunters should note that any of the Forests may be closed to public use during a season of high fire hazard. Fire prevention rules should also be checked. Note also that a number of Wild Areas and Wilderness or Primitive Areas, where vehicular travel is not allowed, are contained within some of these National Forests. It is advisable when planning a trip to get a map and full details on any Forest one intends to hunt.

Next in acreage among public lands are those under Bureau of Land Management control. These are exceedingly important, amount to some twelve million acres, chiefly—so far as large solid blocks are concerned—in eastern and southeastern California. There are, however, other blocks scattered throughout the state, often interspersed with private holdings. Because boundaries may be complicated, it is best for hunters to check regarding maps and details either with the main office in California (Bureau of Land Management, 650 Capitol Mall, Sacramento), or else, via the main office, with one of the district offices, which are located in Bakersfield, Susanville, Redding, Folsom, Ukiah, Riverside, and in Carson City, Nevada. Under various species headings some of the District BLM lands important for that species are listed.

There are presently fourteen tracts of BLM lands, the smallest of 4600 acres, the largest of 300,000, that are administered cooperatively with the California Fish and Game Department. These are areas was especially high wildlife potential and will be described individually under the headings of various game species.

Other public lands are numerous. There are several State Forests on which hunting is allowed. There are approximately a dozen National Wildlife Refuges where some hunting, mainly for waterfowl, is offered. The Fish and Game Department has over a dozen management areas, or hunting areas, that offer quality shooting. In addition there are a half-dozen military installations where public hunting is available. And there are, at nominal fees, several hundred thousand acres of Community Pheasant (and other upland game) Hunting Areas open under a program fostered and guided by the Department. These will all be located later in this chapter.

A vast acreage is also open to public hunting on lands owned by a number of paper companies. Scott Lumber Co., Inc., Burney, California 96013, offers a booklet, "A Tree Farm Recreation Program," with details of developments on their holdings. Because paper company holdings are often scattered and interspersed by private tracts, it is best for hunters who wish details to make direct contacts with the firms involved. The California Game Department may be helpful in making such contacts. For example, International Paper Co. has over 100,000 acres in California. The following firms have some printed material about recreation facilities on their holdings: California Redwood Assn.; International Paper Co.; Pacific Gas and Electric; Southern California Edison; U.S. Plywood Corp. Addresses for these firms may be obtained from: American Forest Products Industries, 1835 K St., NW, Washington, D.C. 20006.

Hunters who may wish to camp have few problems in California. Though summer may see numerous campgrounds full, the fall hunting seasons offer a myriad of opportunities. The National Forests are prime spots. The lumber (paper) companies have a good number of camping sites. There are seventy-odd State Parks, plus National Parks and numerous National Monuments. There are, in fact, hundreds of camping places on these alone, plus more on BLM and Corps of Engineers lands. Any good camping guide will list at least 700 locations, with thousands of individual camping sites. Obviously, in a state so heavily populated and so geared to travel and vacationing, there is no problem whatever in locating motels, hotels, lodges, hunting camps and guides in any part of the state. The Department may be able to help with locating guides, but obviously cannot recommend them.

Climate, and weather in general, can be real puzzlers in California. There may be a vicious blizzard in the high-country north, while bird hunters near the Mexican border are shooting in shirt sleeves. Hunters in California thus must gauge their apparel by the latitude, and the altitude, as well as the time of year. One who visits the state planning to participate in several hunting endeavors is well advised to go prepared for weather from desert-hot to high-country zero to chilly-damp coastal. By and large, if one hunts the southern half of the state there is no need for heavy clothing except in the highest altitudes. In the northern half, both warm-weather and cold-weather garments are advisable in the duffel.

Shotgunners will need for doves and quail No. 6 or No. 7½ as basic loads. Pheasants, grouse, ducks will step one up to No. 6 at least and for ducks possibly No. 4. Magnums in 4's and 2's will be best for geese. Any of the standard calibers such as .270, .30/06, .243, and .308 will do nicely for deer. Boar hunters should check with their guides as to what is acceptable to them. Most of the deer-caliber rifles will be. In other words, California hunting requires nothing specialized in arms and ammunition, but the broad variety of game makes it imperative that a hunter know what he is after, and plan accordingly.

PHEASANT

Pheasants were introduced to California about eighty · years ago. The first season was held in 1925. Over the years introductions were made in every county. Success was had eventually only in the more fertile valleys. The chief peasant range today is in the Sacramento and San Joaquin Valleys. The best in the latter valley is in the northern San Joaquin. Other good locations: the far-northern Tule Lake and Lower Klamath Basin areas, the Shasta River Valley. While there are pheasant populations in the southern San Joaquin, the Owens and the Imperial valleys, natural reproduction is not high and often the populations need assistance by stocking. California has experimented with arid-terrain pheasant species, such as the Afghan whitewinged pheasant, in both pure strain and hybrid types. Eventually southern California may discover in these birds a type to match that habitat well.

The Sacramento Valley has long been termed the "pheasant bowl." Top counties lie around and north of the city of Sacramento: Butte, Colusa, Sutter, Yolo, Glenn, Sacramento, San Joaquin, Stanislaus, Solano, Merced. These, plus the scattered and more compact northern spots in Siskiyou, Modoc, Shasta, and Lassen counties form the bulk of the most important pheasant hunting. Recently, however, Fresno Co. has rated high. An average of 240,000-plus hunters bag around 750,000 to 800,000 pheasants annually. In some areas one hen is allowed in the bag. During a recent season the total kill was 623,400 cocks, 134,700 hens.

Because the pheasant inhabits farm country, by far the major share of hunting is on private lands, where permission must be arranged. However, there is a substantial amount of public shooting. Several of the National Wildlife Refuges offer controlled hunting in cooperation with the state. There are fees, hunter quotas, and reservations must be made. These Refuges are: Colusa (20), in southeast Colusa Co., near Williams on U.S. 99W; Sutter (21), in eastern Sutter Co., near Yuba City, U.S. 99E; Delevan (22), Colusa Co., east of Maxwell, U.S. 99W; Sacramento (23), southeastern Glenn Co., south of Willows, U.S. 99W; Merced (24), in Merced Co., southwest of city of same name; San Luis (25), near Los Banos, west of the last named, Merced Co. During a recent season Merced was best, Sutter second. Three other Refuges have portions of their areas open for pheasant hunting. Two are in the extreme north. One of these is Lower Klamath NWR (26), a few miles north of the village of Tule Lake, along the Oregon border on a side road called the State Line Highway. The second is Tule Lake NWR (27), west of the village to the same name which is on State 139. A third, far to the south, in northwestern Kern Co. near Delano (U.S. 99), is Kern NWR (28). Hunters should check special regulations and what days hunting is allowed by contacting the Refuge Manager at any of these.

At one time the California Game Department operated a number of cooperative units for pheasant hunting. This has slowly been phased out over a period of several years, with the Department encouraging instead the formation of Community Areas, with fees. As this is written there are still three State Cooperative Pheasant Hunting Areas. Open acreage and hunter quotas are subject to last-minutes change. Fees by day or season may be charged. The three Areas: Grimes (29), Colusa Co., near town of Grimes; Tyler Island (30), Sacramento Co., near village of Walnut Grove; Staten Island (31), San Joaquin Co., also near Walnut Grove. Recently the hunting was best in the following order: Grimes, Staten, Tyler. Check status of these SCPHAs with the Department before planning a hunt.

The community plan is going well. It is impossible to list the Community Pheasant Hunting Areas for they may change from year to year. At this writing, however, there are fourteen such CPHAs. They range in acreage from 5000 to 145,000 acres, with several in the 20,000- and 30,000-acre class. Membership or season fees are charged. These run from $5 to $15 per person. Some have hunter quotas, some do not. They are run by communities and a current list, with full addresses, is available from the California Fish and Game Department.

Of the State Wildlife (Hunting) Areas, several offer good pheasant shooting. There are fees and quotas, various special regulations. Honey Lake HA (32) is in southeastern Lassen Co., near Honey Lake off U.S. 395. It contains 3700 acres. Gray Lodge HA (33) is to the southwest, in Butte Co., with 4500 acres near the town of Gridley on U.S. 99E. Grizzly Island HA (34) has 5000 open acres in Solano Co., south of Fairfield, State 12 at U.S. 40. Two others are farther south. Los Banos HA (35) is in the southern Merced Co., 2700 acres near the town of Los Banos. Mendota HA (36) is in northwestern Fresno Co., offers 8000 acres near the town of Mendota on State 33 near State 180 junction. These HAs are managed primarily as waterfowl areas, thus hunters should check what days are open. Some limit pheasant shooting to the open days for waterfowl. During one recent season Gray Lodge led in success percentage, Honey Lake was second, Mendota third, followed by Los Banos and Grizzly Island.

CALIFORNIA

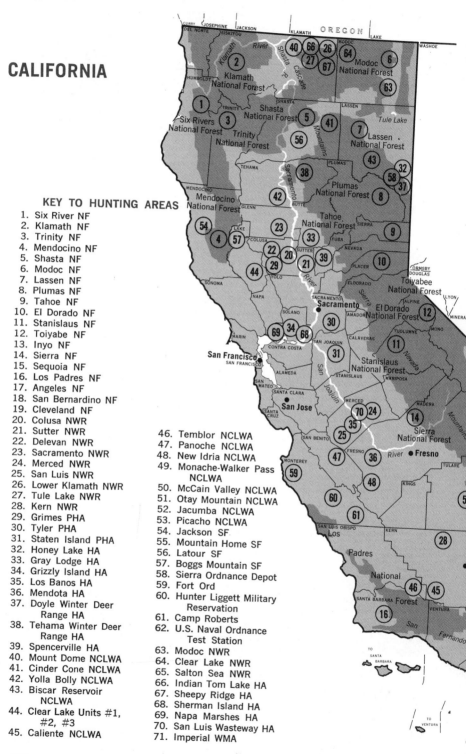

KEY TO HUNTING AREAS

1. Six River NF
2. Klamath NF
3. Trinity NF
4. Mendocino NF
5. Shasta NF
6. Modoc NF
7. Lassen NF
8. Plumas NF
9. Tahoe NF
10. El Dorado NF
11. Stanislaus NF
12. Toiyabe NF
13. Inyo NF
14. Sierra NF
15. Sequoia NF
16. Los Padres NF
17. Angeles NF
18. San Bernardino NF
19. Cleveland NF
20. Colusa NWR
21. Sutter NWR
22. Delevan NWR
23. Sacramento NWR
24. Merced NWR
25. San Luis NWR
26. Lower Klamath NWR
27. Tule Lake NWR
28. Kern NWR
29. Grimes PHA
30. Tyler PHA
31. Staten Island PHA
32. Honey Lake HA
33. Gray Lodge HA
34. Grizzly Island HA
35. Los Banos HA
36. Mendota HA
37. Doyle Winter Deer Range HA
38. Tehama Winter Deer Range HA
39. Spencerville HA
40. Mount Dome NCLWA
41. Cinder Cone NCLWA
42. Yolla Bolly NCLWA
43. Biscar Reservoir NCLWA
44. Clear Lake Units #1, #2, #3
45. Caliente NCLWA
46. Temblor NCLWA
47. Panoche NCLWA
48. New Idria NCLWA
49. Monache-Walker Pass NCLWA
50. McCain Valley NCLWA
51. Otay Mountain NCLWA
52. Jacumba NCLWA
53. Picacho NCLWA
54. Jackson SF
55. Mountain Home SF
56. Latour SF
57. Boggs Mountain SF
58. Sierra Ordnance Depot
59. Fort Ord
60. Hunter Liggett Military Reservation
61. Camp Roberts
62. U.S. Naval Ordnance Test Station
63. Modoc NWR
64. Clear Lake NWR
65. Salton Sea NWR
66. Indian Tom Lake HA
67. Sheepy Ridge HA
68. Sherman Island HA
69. Napa Marshes HA
70. San Luis Wasteway HA
71. Imperial WMA

QUAIL

Quail hunting in California is excellent. The annual kill averages from two to two and a half million or more birds, bagged by an average 200,000 hunters. Listing of the prime quail counties by kill percent may be affected in some cases by the proximity of large population centers. However, recently the top counties were, in order: Riverside, San Diego, Fresno, Kern, San Bernardino, Los Angeles, Ventura, Tulare, Santa Barbara, San Luis Obispo, and Monterey. These counties furnished nonetheless only a bit over half the total kill. Quail of three species are found in California, and among them their ranges practically blanket the state. Thus fair to excellent quail hunting for one or another variety is available almost everywhere.

The California, or valley, quail is the most abundant species, most widespread, and shows up in greatest numbers in hunter bags. In several subspecies it ranges over almost all of the state except the extreme east and southeast. It is lacking from the driest deserts of the southeast and east-central area and from the highest regions of the eastern mountains. The coastal foothills are excellent for valley quail. So are the foothills of the interior, in the valley counties of the Sacramento and San Joaquin. The extreme northeast, in Modoc Co., has a good population and so does the northwest coast. Many of the coastal counties of the south, regardless of human population, are excellent.

In the southeast, the Gambel's, or desert, quail fills an area not suitable for the valley species. It covers practically all of huge San Bernardino Co., the eastern two-thirds of Riverside Co., and all of Imperial Co., plus a spillover into eastern San Diego Co. This species, which looks superficially quite a bit like

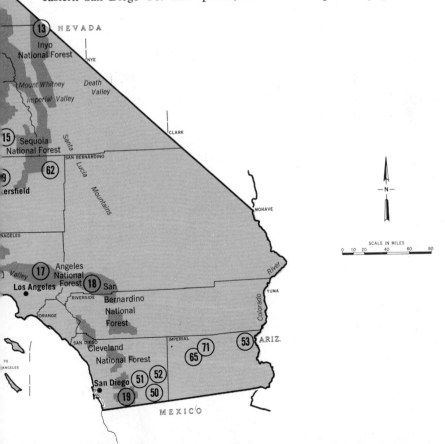

the valley variety, is a bird of more arid washes and foothills and the mesquite expanses along the Colorado River.

The handsome mountain quail, largest of the lot and with a long straight plume atop its head, occupies most of the range of the higher country unacceptable to the valley quail. It is found from the extreme north to the extreme south, along all of the mountain ranges, both coastal and inland. It overlaps to some extent in its lower range elevations with both other species, makes vertical migrations, after nesting, from higher to lower altitudes. These are made on foot. Concentrations may thus often be found in upper foothills during fall. However, mountain quail are seldom as abundant as their relatives.

Some of the better areas for this bird are located on the western slope of the Sierras all the way from Kern Co. in the south-central region through Shasta Co. in the north. The Santa Lucia Mountains of Monterey Co. on southward are considered good range, and likewise the east slope of the coastal mountains from some distance north and east of San Francisco on to the Oregon border.

Quite obviously much quail hunting is on private lands. However, because of the habitat favored by each of these birds, a great deal of excellent shooting is found on public lands. Since the general ranges of each bird have already been noted, they are treated henceforth as one, without species designation. It will be obvious from the locations of the public lands that furnish good quail hunting what varieties one is likely to encounter.

The National Forests (see front of chapter) have a great deal of excellent quail hunting. Here is a list of those with best opportunities: northwest—Mendocino NF; northeast—Modoc NF, Lassen NF; east central—Stanislaus NF, Toiyabe NF, Inyo NF, Sierra NF; south central—Sequoia NF; south coast—Los Padres NF; south—Angeles NF, San Bernardino NF, Cleveland NF.

Bureau of Land Management lands furnish vast acreages of good quail hunting in almost every part of the state. Quail are listed as important game in at least thirty-eight counties where such lands occur. The BLM main address in California, plus locations of District Headquarters offices, have been given early in this chapter. Hunters should refer to these, and check with the one appropriate to a planned hunt. Two BLM Special Recreation Areas, Cow Mountain and Kings Range, are in Lake, Mendocino, and Humboldt Cos. Details can be had from the Ukiah office.

Some of the State Hunting Areas offer quail. Honey Lake, Gray Lodge ("Pheasant") should be noted. Others are: the Doyle Winter Deer Range HA (37), southeastern Lassen Co., near town of Doyle, U.S. 395; the Tehama Winter Deer Range HA (38), Tehama Co., off State 36 near Paynes Creek; Spenceville HA (39), Yuba Co., near Marysville, U.S. 99E.

It was stated early in the chapter that certain BLM lands with high game potential are managed cooperatively with the California Fish and Game Department. Presently there are sixteen of these large units, and all offer quail hunting. These tracts are officially called National Cooperative Land and Wildlife Areas. Following are their locations.

In the northern counties there are several. The Mount Dome NCLWA (40) is in Siskiyou Co., near McDoel, U.S. 97. Cinder Cone NCLWA (41) is in northeastern Shasta Co., in the vicinity of Fall River Mills, U.S. 299. To the south, in Tehama Co., is the Yolla Bolly tract (42). It is in the south-central part of the county, west of Corning (U.S. 99W) on a secondary, with the village of Paskenta a location point. Lassen Co. in the northeast has Biscar Reservoir (43), this Area located north of Susanville and near Karlo, with U.S. 395 the main nearby route.

Farther south, and lying to the east of Clear Lake, which is in central Lake Co., there are three tracts, named Clear Lake Units #1, #2, #3 (44). South and west, in San Luis Obispo and Kern Cos., there are two more tracts. The Caliente NCLWA (45) is west of Maricopa, which is at the junction of U.S. 399, State 33 and 166. The Temblor Area (46) is near Taft, State 33 and U.S. 399. To the north, along the border between Fresno and San Benito Cos. is the Panoche Area (47), named for the Panoche Hills. A secondary west from Mendota (State 33) or east from Hollister (State 156) via village of Paicines reaches it. To the south of this one, and reaching to the northwest out of Coalinga, junction State 33 and 198, is the New Idria Area (48).

Still farther into the south and central region, there is Monache-Walker Pass Area (49). Location is northeast out of Bakersfield, via State 178, with focal point the village of Bodfish. In the extreme southwest, San Diego Co. has three of these Areas: McCain Valley (50), out of Jacumba on the Mexican border (U.S. 80); Otay Mountain (51), east of the village of Dulzura, State 94; Jacumba (52), northeast of that border village. In Imperial Co., the extreme southeastern county, there is the Picacho Area (53), south of the village of Palo Verde. This is on a secondary south from U.S. 60-70 immediately west of Blythe and north from the Mexican border highway, U.S. 80.

California has some State Forest land that furnishes quail (and other) hunting. Actually there are seven State Forests, but most are too small to offer hunting. Two of the larger ones, however, are fairly important quail locations. Jackson SF (54) contains over 50,000 acres, in Mendocino Co. State 20, between Willits (U.S. 101) and Fort Bragg (coast route 1) reach it. Mountain Home SF (55) is much smaller, less than 5000 acres, located near Springville in Tulare Co., State 190. Maps of these Forests are available from the Fish and Game Department. There are two other small State Forests with quail, Latour SF (56) in Shasta Co. and Boggs Mountain SF (57) in Lake Co. These are of secondary importance.

In addition to the tremendous quail hunting opportunities already covered, there are five military installations that offer fair to excellent shooting. In the north, in Lassen Co. near Herlong and U.S. 395, is the Sierra Ordnance Depot (58). In the central coast region there is Fort Ord (59), near Monterey, and also in Monterey Co. the Hunter Liggett Military Reservation (60), west of King City. Camp Roberts (61), between San Miguel and Bradley on U.S. 101, is to the south. One of the most important quail (and other bird) hunting military locations is the U.S. Naval Ordnance Test Station at China Lake (62). Here there are 260 square miles of good hunting. This is in the south-central region, west of U.S. 395 and north of the town of Ridgecrest, which is on a secondary. Mountain and valley quail are both found here. All of the military installations have special regulations. The Fish and Game Department can furnish a list of addresses where the Commanding Officers can be reached for details.

CHUKAR PARTRIDGE

The first chukars, a strain from India, were tried in California in 1932. The first limited hunting season occurred in 1954. Though tried in numerous areas, it was in the high deserts of eastern and south-central California that the bird became firmly established. An average annual kill has run over recent years around 44,000, but has been as high, in peak years, as 88,500. Over a recent season some 33,000 hunters bagged 74,200 birds. This may be presumed to be an exceptional year, although the chukar has been extending its range to some extent. There may also, in the future, be much more hunting area with good chukar populations. Birds of several different strains—French, Spanish, Greek, Turkish—are now being carefully tried in areas where they cannot possibly compete with native birds.

Because of scattered introduction in numerous places, from far north to extreme south, spots where the chukar now is established form no easily described pattern. Also, some places where there are birds are not at present open to hunting. Best counties at present are: Fresno, Kern, Inyo, San Bernardino, Lassen. By and large it may be said that most of the southern third of the state is fair to excellent, all of the eastern border country except the extreme northeast is also, and that the interior from Shasta Co. south through the valley to Kern Co. offers good hunting.

BLM lands furnish much quality chukar hunting. District offices in Bakersfield, Susanville, Folsom, Ukiah, Riverside, and in Carson City, Nevada, list lands in their jurisdictions as having the chukar as a prominent game species. See front of chapter for BLM address.

The Cooperative Lands offer good chukar possibilities at Mount Dome, Caliente, Temblor, Panoche, Monache-Walker Pass, McCain Valley, and Jacumba Areas. See "Quail" for locations of all of these. Among the State Hunting Areas, the Doyle Winter Deer Range ("Quail") is considered a good location. And among the Military installations, the Sierra Ordnance Depot and the U.S. Naval Ordnance Test Station are likewise listed. The latter, at China Lake, is a top spot.

A few special regions for hunters to try are as follows: First, the Providence Mountains and the New York Mountains west of the Nevada border about where it joins Arizona and much of the arid foothill country here between I 15 and I 40. The region to the west, near Barstow; Apple Valley south of it; Lucerne Valley southeast of Apple Valley. "Guzzlers"—watering devices —have been built in many arid places by the Department. The vicinities of these are prime places to find chukars (and quail). Farther north, one should try along the Nevada border, the area east of U.S. 6 and 395 out of Independence, and still farther up, the region around Deep Springs Lake, and north of it out of Bishop and Benton (U.S. 6) in the White Mountains.

SAGE GROUSE AND SHARPTAIL GROUSE

The sage grouse, largest of native grouses, has a small range in California. It clings to the extreme northeast, in Modoc Co., a bit of northeastern Siskiyou, and much of Lassen. There is a narrow corridor of range southward along the Nevada border into northern Inyo Co. Most stable populations are in Lassen and Mono Cos. At this writing there is no open season. There have been seasons during the 1960s. In 1966 some 2700 were bagged. It is possible token seasons may be held periodically.

The Columbian sharptail grouse was once found in a narrow strip of the northeast. It is now thought to be extinct in the state.

OTHER GROUSE

The Hungarian partridge, an introduced species, is listed as a game species in California but recently no open season has appeared. It has an extremely limited range along the Nevada border in the northeast, in eastern Modoc, Lassen, and several border counties south of these.

The ruffed grouse has a small range in the extreme northwest, in Del Norte, Humboldt, western Trinity and western Siskiyou counties. There is a brief open season but the ruffed grouse is not much hunted.

The blue, or sooty grouse, large grouse of the high timber, is more often in California called the Sierra grouse. This is because there are three subspecies in the state, the Sierra subspecies having the largest range. Among the sub-species they cover much of the northwestern high country, eastward into and down the Cascade and Sierra ranges. There are a few isolated populations else-where in small ranges. There is an open season, generally concurrent with that on the ruffed grouse, and most of the range is open. Limits are low. Recently only two birds—aggregate of ruffed and blue—were allowed during a season. The aggregate kill runs on the average from under 2000 to slightly over 3000.

Good opportunities are offered in the National Forests of the northwest and north-central regions: Six Rivers, Klamath, Trinity, Mendocino, Shasta. BLM lands with district headquarters at Redding and Folsom furnish more hunting. See early portion of chapter for details. In this rather specialized sport, undoubtedly the National Forests offer the best chances. The terrain is rugged and access to much of it is difficult. Also, hunting may be done at 8000 to 10,000 feet or more altitude.

WILD TURKEYS

The wild turkey was not native to California in this age, although fossil prehistoric remains have been found. The first stockings were made almost a hundred years ago, to no avail. Modern introductions began on a serious scale in the thirties. Over recent years both Merriam's and Rio Grande turkeys have been tried, with wild stock from Arizona, Texas, Wyoming, Colorado. It ap-pears possible that both Merriam's and Rio Grande subspecies may become established eventually in differing habitats. Most success recently has occurred by live-trapping birds already established in California and using these for seed stock.

A number of counties now have substantial flocks. It is estimated that sev-eral thousand birds, possibly as many as 4000, make up the total. During the fall of 1968 the first California turkey hunt was held, a one-day season, either sex, in San Luis Obispo Co. only. The result was twenty-nine birds taken by 213 hunters. Much of the hunting was done on private lands. In fact, most Cali-fornia turkeys are presently on privately owned ranchlands. It is considered probable that this first trial season will introduce turkey hunting on a progres-sively broader scale over coming years.

DOVES AND PIGEONS

More species of doves and pigeons are hunted in California than in any other state. The mourning dove, the whitewinged dove, the band-tailed pigeon are all native. At least two exotics, the ringed turtle dove and the Chinese spotted dove, both in original stock presumably escapees from birds kept in captivity as pets, have now formed local wild populations of modest size. Both are considered legal during mourning dove season, and must if shot be counted as part of the bag. This was necessary because it was too difficult to distinguish these birds in flight from mourning doves. The ringed turtle dove has spread from the Los Angeles area some distance eastward and through the San Fer-nando Valley. The Chinese spotted dove has managed a much wider coloniza-tion and is now found as far away as Bakersfield to the north and Indio to the southeast. It is considered a good game bird.

The mourning dove is the most important of the family, and indeed by numbers annually bagged the most important game bird in the state. The yearly total kill averages around four and a half million. The vast interior val-leys, and the southern third of the state make up the bulk of the best hunting.

Best counties by kill success are influenced to some extent by the proximity of large cities, therefore by heavy hunt pressure. Nonetheless, approximately 60 percent of the total kill comes from the following: Riverside, San Diego, Imperial Cos. in the south; Fresno, Madera, Tulare, Kern somewhat farther north; San Joaquin, Merced, Stanislaus above these. Counties such as San Luis Obispo and Los Angeles also stack up high kill figures.

Much of the shooting is of course on private farming lands. Other spots are on public lands in the foothills and the desert fringes. National Forests furnish some shooting. Mendocino in the northwest, Modoc in the northeast, Sierra in the east-central region, Sequoia in the south-central are all considered fair. BLM lands with district headquarters in Bakersfield, Susanville, Redding, Folsom, Ukiah, Riverside, and in Carson City, Nevada, all have good shooting. Front of chapter material gives information on all the above. BLM-DFG cooperative lands located under "Quail" all have doves as a major game species, with the exception of the Cinder Cone and Yolla Bolly Areas. Among the State Hunting Areas, Honey Lake ("Pheasants") and Spenceville ("Quail") ordinarily give up good dove bags. All of the five military tracts noted under "Quail" have comparable dove shooting.

Whitewing shooting in California is restricted as to range, and spotty because these birds are early fall migrants into Mexico. The total California population is contained in a portion of the extreme southeast, in southeast San Bernardino, the eastern half of Riverside, all of Imperial, and a scant bit of eastern San Diego counties. The farm and desert country along the Colorado River is the prime whitewing range, and throughout the lower portions of the Coachella and Imperial valleys. A recent whitewing season in California was restricted to San Bernardino, Riverside, and Imperial counties. By mid or late September as a rule the birds have departed for Mexico.

Some of the best band-tailed pigeon shooting available is to be had in California during the southward fall and winter migrations of these birds. The bandtail is of barn-pigeon size, when properly fed on oak mast, various grain or fruit crops delectable eating, and it is a grand, swift flying game bird. It is a resident of the big timber of the high mountains, but it is exceedingly mobile and often comes down along the slopes and into the fruit or grain growing areas when food at higher elevations is scarce. It can be a menace to fruit growers and to growers of such crops as peas. The bandtail is exceedingly erratic because of its mobility, colonial habits, and the fact that its favorite (or only) food crops may have drastic seasonal ups and downs. Bandtails may appear in fantastic abundance here or there, then be as quickly gone, following the forage. In stable years when oak mast and wild foods are plentiful, they are more dependable, are found near such foods, or flying daily through certain mountain saddles or passes, or near springs or saltlicks in the mountains.

Bandtail seasons in northern California counties are usually held during late September and most of October. Del Norte, Butte, Glenn, Humboldt, Lassen, Mendocino, Modoc, Plumas, Shasta, Sierra, Siskiyou, Tehama, and Trinity counties usually get the early season. Later the birds have drafted on south, and the remainder of the state may be open during late December and early January. Limits lately have been ample—eight birds—which makes a hunt really worthwhile.

Annual kill in good years when migrations are steady runs from 275,000 to 325,000, with anywhere from 25,000 to 40,000 hunters participating. Comparison of hunters to kill make the bandtail, for its specialists, an important species in California. The best counties change erratically. However, some of the best remain fairly constant over many seasons. These are: Monterey and

San Luis Obispo among the very best, Santa Cruz, Shasta, Santa Barbara, Santa Clara following, Humboldt and Trinity fair, San Diego and Ventura likewise. During one recent season these produced about 85 percent of the total kill.

Numerous public lands offer bandtail shooting. Among the best are the National Forests (see early material in chapter). In the northwest, Six Rivers, Trinity, Mendocino are considered good. North-central Shasta rates likewise. In the east-central area, Plumas, El Dorado, Stanislaus, and Sierra offer good shooting. South-central Sequoia, south-coast Los Padres, and southern San Bernardino and Cleveland are the others.

Many BLM lands are bandtail havens. Those headquartered at Bakersfield, Redding, Folsom, Ukiah should be checked out (see chapter opening) and also the Special Kings Range Recreation Area ("Quail") in the Ukiah district. In the cooperative BLM-DFG lands, the Yolla Bolly ("Quail") is emphatically worthwhile. The four State Forests covered under "Quail" also are bandtail hangouts, and among the State Hunting Areas the Tehama Winter Deer Range ("Quail") in northern Tehama Co. is a good bet. Among the military lands, those in Monterey and San Luis Obispo counties have bandtails. These ("Quail") are Fort Ord, Hunter Liggett, Camp Roberts.

Over many years Monterey Co. has undoubtedly been the best all-out bet for migrating bandtails.

EXOTIC BIRDS

California has been active in trading native birds with foreign lands for exotics to be used as trial species for stocking. Valley quail were traded a year ago for seesee partridges from Pakistan. This is an arid-land bird to be tried on fringes of chukar range. Other exotics under trial: various chukars already mentioned, crested tinamou, several francolins, and several exotic pheasants. No seasons are yet open as this is written, but the DFG is hopeful.

WATERFOWL

California has excellent waterfowling for both ducks and geese. Historically the state had vast valley marshes with many millions of waterfowl wintering in them. Today much of the original wintering grounds are farmlands. A good National Refuge system has been built up, and state Waterfowl Management Areas supplement it. A difficult problem is that of depredation by waterfowl upon farm crops. Some Refuges must literally operate large food farms for the birds, to hold them away from farm crops. Some special hunts are conducted because of depredation problems.

Several species of geese winter in California and modest breeding flocks of several also summer there. Several subspecies of Canadas utilize the state in winter, some staying in the extreme northwest, others in the central valleys and along the Colorado River. Whitefronted geese are plentiful, chiefly in the central valley sector and in the Imperial Valley. The lesser snow goose is the most abundant species, wintering in vast flocks down through the interior. The Ross's goose, a small replica of the lesser snow, appears in the central valley and occasionally a few blue geese straggle in. The black brant, a small goose that migrates along the coast and that is hunted along the salt flats and sandbars and in the large bays, is abundant during the season.

Among the ducks, mallards are abundant residents and migrants. Pintails by millions come down from the north. Greenwing teal and gadwalls are common. Redheads are among the abundant diving ducks. There are also canvasbacks, scaups, and numerous lesser species.

The major share of the Pacific Flyway waterfowl harvest is collected in

California. Some 75 percent of all waterfowl in the Flyway go into California during winter. Approximately 50 percent of the ducks and 65 percent of the geese bagged in the entire Flyway are taken in the state. Winter surveys of waterfowl populations show as many as four million ducks, a million geese, half a million coots. Some seasons the figures are much higher. Waterfowl hunters average in number 150,000 to 200,000 each season. The statewide bag fluctuates as waterfowl nesting conditions in the north do. But generally at least two and a half million ducks are bagged. Goose kill averages around 250,000 to 350,000 but occasionally jumps almost to half a million. A good picture of where waterfowling ordinarily is best can be had from noting the top counties during one recent average season. Ducks: Merced, Colusa, Solano, Kern, Siskiyou, Yolo, Butte, Sutter, Imperial, Fresno accounted for approximately 65 percent of the total kill. Geese: Colusa, Siskiyou, Butte, Glenn, Modoc, Sutter, Imperial, Merced, Sacramento, and Yolo stood in that order regarding kill percentages, with better than 85 percent of the total bag. Colusa, Siskiyou, Butte together accounted for roughly 50 percent of the total goose kill.

There are numerous fee hunting locations for waterfowl, and there are also numerous clubs. Guided fee hunts, with decoys and blinds furnished, can be had throughout much of the north and the Central Valley and on down into the Imperial Valley. The Department cannot recommend guides and individuals operating such hunts, but can be instrumental in assisting hunters to locate them.

However, there is ample public hunting for waterfowl. There is shooting for both ducks and geese in the Modoc NF, the location of which is given early in the chapter. For specifics on waterfowl, write Modoc National Forest, 441 N. Main, Alturas, California 96101.

The National Wildlife Refuges and the State Hunting Areas listed as "Waterfowl Management Areas" also offer excellent shooting. Tule Lake NWR, Lower Klamath NWR, Sacramento NWR, Delevan NWR, Colusa NWR, Sutter NWR, Merced NWR, Kern NWR, San Luis NWR (see "Pheasant") are all prime locations for both ducks and geese, and also for coots.

Three other National Wildlife Refuges offering waterfowling have not yet been mentioned. Two are in Modoc Co. in northern California. These are: Modoc NWR (63), near U.S. 395 south of Alturus, and Clear Lake NWR (64), about twenty miles south of Tulelake via State 139. The third is in the south, in Imperial Co., Salton Sea NWR (65), reached via State 111 northwest of the town of Calipatria. Geese, ducks, and coots are available. Incidentally, each season there are apt to be special coot shoots on stipulated areas of both state and federal lands. These are crop depredation controls. Check with the Fish and Game Department.

State Hunting Areas offer quality waterfowling, too. In the north, Siskiyou Co. has two: Indian Tom Lake HA (66), almost on the Oregon border, near Dorris, U.S. 97; Sheepy Ridge HA (67), west of Tulelake. In Lassen Co., Honey Lake Waterfowl Management Area is a top choice; and in Butte Co., Gray Lodge WMA is also (see "Pheasant"). Sacramento Co. has Sherman Island, northeast of the city of Antioch. Grizzly Island WMA in Solano Co. is another good bet ("Pheasant"). In Solano and Napa Cos. are the Napa Marshes, west of Vallejo and near State 48.

Farther south there are several others. Los Banos in Merced Co. and Mendota in Fresno Co. have been noted under "Pheasant." The San Luis Wasteway (70) in Merced Co. lies northwest of Los Banos, near Volta, via State 33.

Imperial Co. has the Imperial WMA (71), in two tracts, the Wister Area near Niland, the Ramer Area near Calipatria. State 111 is the route for both. Incidentally, there is dove hunting on these tracts, too. Note that fees and hunter quotas are in force at some of the national and state areas mentioned.

Excellent ducks kills are made at almost all the national and state areas listed. Gray Lodge, Sacramento Refuge, Delevan Refuge, the Wister tract of Imperial furnished in one recent season the highest goose kills.

It is pertinent to call attention to the brant hunting along the coast. It is excellent, yet the sport is not pursued as diligently as it might be. There are endless stretches of public beach and public waters of bays and near bars where brant shooting may be enjoyed. The season usually lasts well into February, which actually gives an opportunity for "spring" hunting, since the migration by then has begun northward. Decoys should be set over eel grass beds or in the sand at the water's edge. An eel-grass diet assures the birds of excellent flavor. Driftwood or rocks make a good blind. Some good locations: Humboldt Bay, Morro Bay, Tomales Bay, Mission Bay, Drakes Bay.

Jacksnipe must also be mentioned here with waterfowl. They are abundant on all of the waterfowl marshes. There is ample public opportunity, and indeed a number of hunters do specialize in this sport. The estimated kill runs around 45,000 birds annually. More sport can be had with snipe if waterfowlers and others will pursue these agile targets on the marsh and mud flats. Although most of the state and federal areas furnish good shooting, jacksnipe are listed as a major species at Gray Lodge WMA mentioned above, likewise at Grizzly Island WMA, Los Banos, San Luis Wasteway, Mendota.

DEER

California has five subspecies of mule deer, plus the blacktailed deer, which is also one of the mule deer family. Occasionally there are reports of whitetails, but none have been verified over a number of years. Deer hunting is good, although the total bag is not large by standards in some of the other deer states of the mountain west. Seasons begin as early as August over most of the coastal counties. As a rule two bucks may be taken here. In the northwestern counties two bucks are the rule, in the northeast only one. Central California, the east and the south are almost entirely in one-buck range. There are also a number of special hunts annually. Check with the DFG regarding these. Some seasons there are as many as fifty, with upwards of 30,000 permits. A migratory herd along the Oregon border gets special attention; for example, in a co-op hunt between Oregon and California. Track counts are made, and a quota of antlerless deer taken. The summer range of this herd is in southern Oregon, the winter range in California.

Deer tag buyers in California average close to 450,000, but there have been serious fluctuations in deer numbers recently. In addition, California has had some difficulties getting what are considered accurate kill surveys. Hunter survey results usually show almost twice the kill shown by deer tag returns. Probably from 40,000 to 75,000 bucks are bagged annually. In recent seasons Humboldt Co. has ranked first, with the preponderance of the kill in the late season. Mendocino Co. was recently second, total kill in the early season. Siskiyou, entirely in late season, was third. Shasta and Trinity were fourth and fifth. Total kills range from 4386 in Humboldt down to 1868 in Trinity.

County kill averages over a period of years, including early and late season where both occur, show that the high-kill counties remain fairly consistent, as follows. Over 4000: Humboldt, Mendocino, Siskiyou. Between 2000 and 3000: Mono, Plumas, Shasta, Tehama, Trinity. Between 1500 and 2000: El Dorado, Fresno, Lake, Lassen, Monterey, Sonoma. Between 1000 and 1500; Alpine, Butte, Modoc, Napa, San Luis Obispo, Santa Barbara, Tulare, Tuolumne. While these statistics may be influenced slightly by hunting pressures near cities, they show nonetheless where most of the deer are.

Those who desire the Columbian blacktailed deer, smallest and most abundant of California's mule deer but a difficult trophy, should try the coast from the northern border down to Santa Barbara Co., or the west slope of the Sierra-Cascade ranges south to about Mariposa Co. The various subspecies of mule deer other than the blacktail are difficult for the layman to identify, and are scattered over various parts of the state. Second in abundance is the California mule deer. Third is the big Rocky Mountain mule deer common throughout the West. The Inyo mule deer, the southern mule deer, the burro deer have restricted ranges in Inyo Co., and in the extreme southwest and southeast.

There is no lack of public lands for deer hunting. The National Forests (see opening material in chapter) cover some twenty million acres and all have deer hunting of varying quality. Another twelve million acres of BLM lands are open to deer hunting. All districts (see front material) have deer on their ranges. The National Cooperative Land and Wildlife Areas (see "Quail") have deer on the following Areas: Mount Dome; Cinder Cone; Yolla Bolly; Clear Lake (three units); New Idria; Monache-Walker Pass; McCain Valley; Picacho. The four State Forests ("Quail") have good deer hunting. Among the military lands, Fort Ord, Hunter Liggett M.R., Camp Roberts offer deer hunting, and so does the Marine Corps' Camp Pendleton in San Diego Co., north of Oceanside on U.S. 101. Among state Hunting Areas, the Doyle Winter Deer Range, the Tehama Winter Deer Range ("Quail") are good possibilities. Nor should timber company lands be overlooked. These are noted in the front of the chapter. For example, the California Redwood Assn. has recently sponsored a 260,000 acre recreation program; 9373 deer hunters took 974 bucks.

A hunter who will check the public lands listed here against the counties with consistently big kills, and who will bear in mind that the best deer hunting will be found farthest from the crowd, will find exciting deer hunting in California.

BEAR

The black bear is fairly numerous in California. Bear tag sales show that from 30,000 to 35,000 hunters on the average try for a bear. Many bears are killed incidentally by deer hunters. Hunters should check restrictive regulations relative the use of dogs. Most of the state is open to bear hunting each fall, with a long season. The southern eight counties, or parts thereof, are closed. The annual bear kill probably averages from 700 to 1200.

During a recent season bears were bagged in thirty-six of the state's fifty-eight counties. Highest kills by counties remain rather consistent. Over several years the first six, in order, were: Siskiyou, Trinity, Shasta, Humboldt, Del Norte, Plumas. Tehama and Butte were next. Thus the northwest quarter, plus interior mountain terrain of the north, show as the black bear's stronghold. The first four counties are traditionally the top bear producers.

The National Forests of the northwest and north-central regions are undoubtedly the best public lands. Those in the northeast, east central, south central also have fair hunting. Check also BLM lands in the following districts: Susanville, Redding, Folsom, Ukiah. The Latour State Forest and the Moun-

tain Home State Forest ("Quail") are possibilities. And the cooperatively managed tract in Tehama Co., the Yolla Bolly Area ("Quail") is also a good choice.

ELK

Two varieties of elk are native to California. The Roosevelt elk of coastal
rain forests ranges down into Humboldt Co. The Tule or dwarf elk, smallest of
the elks, was native to valleys and interior foothills. A very small herd that
originated from transplanted animals clings precariously to existence in the
Owens Valley. Management plans call for this herd to be kept to around 250 to
300 animals, to tailor it to its range and avoid damage complaints. There have
been token hunts. Last counts of the animals found the herd somewhat short
and plans for a hunt were called off. Probably hunts will occur again. The
Rocky Mountain elk has been established here and there in small numbers in
California, but is not native, nor at this time hunted.

ANTELOPE

Many years ago the pronghorn occupied a vast range in California,
throughout most of the south and east and all of the central area. Slowly its
range was depleted until today there is only a small population in the extreme
northeast, with token bands here and there in surrounding counties. Airplane
counts over a ten-year period show that the total population has ranged from
just under 2000 to 2618. That high count turned up 1672 in Modoc Co., 746
in Lassen, 177 in Siskiyou, 23 in Shasta.

There have been limited hunts, by drawing, for several years past. Permits
usually number about 250. Several thousand applicants eagerly try for them. A
70 percent success figure is average. Check with the DFG regarding possible
season, and dates for application.

SHEEP

Mountain sheep of several subspecies were originally rather abundant in
California's mountains and southern deserts. They have been fully protected
since 1873. While there are several hundred sheep still in the state, they are
scattered in small bands from the Chocolate Mountains of eastern Imperial Co.
(desert bighorns) to others in remote portions of Death Valley National Monument and Joshua Tree National Monument. Still others (California bighorns)
are found in the high country of the Sierras. Careful and concentrated management is in progress. It is possible that a few permits may someday be available
for a hunt. No prediction, however, can presently be made.

WILD HOGS

European boars from a stock imported from Europe to North Carolina
were brought into the Carmel Valley, Monterey Co., and released about 1925.
They moved into the Santa Lucia range and became established, spreading to
the rough country west of King City and into Los Padres National Forest.
Today they are classed as game animals. They have crossed to some extent
with feral swine, and thus there are true Europeans, hybrids, and feral hogs.

In Monterey Co. there is a season and bag limit. The remainder of the
state is open without bag limit all year. While surveys tend to show several
thousand European boars annually bagged, this probably is not a true picture.
Undoubtedly several hundred are, although feral hogs outside Monterey Co.
may make up the difference. Guides may be obtained for hog hunting in the
Paso Robles and King City region. Much land is private, but guides generally

have hunting permission. Guide fees average around $30 per day per hunter, sometimes with a trophy fee—example, $20 per inch of tusk showing.

There are also hunts for wild hogs, wild goats, wild sheep on Catalina Island. These are privately operated, with no seasons.

MOUNTAIN LION

Two subspecies of mountain lion inhabit California: the California lion, which ranges sparsely in wilder areas over all but the general southwest; the Yuma lion, with a very restricted range along the Colorado River in extreme eastern Riverside and Imperial Cos. Probably no more than 500 to 700 lions exist in the state. These cling chiefly to remote ranges where deer are plentiful for food. The mountain lion as late as 1968 was not protected in California. Numerous states are putting it on the game list. California may in due time.

To arrange a lion hunt, which will almost certainly have to be guided, it is best to check for contacts via the DFG. The lion is listed as present in the Latour and Mountain Home State Forests ("Quail"), and is present in many of the National Forests.

SMALL GAME

Cottontails of several subspecies, pigmy and brush rabbits of several more, plus jackrabbits, and snowshoe or varying hares are found abundantly in California. Collectively they inhabit virtually all of the state's varied terrains. All have a regulated season and bag limit except the jackrabbits, blacktailed and whitetailed.

Hunting cottontails and the small and delicious brush rabbits is not as popular as it might be, although popularity appears to be growing. Some 700,000-plus are taken each season on the average. Snowshoe hares, which live in the high country of Modoc Co. and along the west slope of the Sierra Nevada, are not plentiful, and are also difficult to hunt in this steep terrain. Jackrabbits make up the big rabbit kill. Estimates place the average annual kill over two million.

It is not difficult to locate a place to hunt rabbits. Several of the National Forests list them as important game. Among these: Modoc, Lassen, Toiyabe, Inyo, Los Padres, Los Angeles, San Bernardino, Cleveland. Most of the state Hunting Areas have either cottontails or jacks or both. The same is true for most of the land cooperatively managed by BLM and the DFG. Other vast areas of BLM lands are excellent.

The small sooty-colored brush rabbits of the densely covered and tangled foothills are very sporty. The still smaller dark-tailed pigmy rabbit of the sage brush in extreme northeastern California is also an interesting experience. Best rabbit counties are to some extent based on the areas of heavy human population. One late survey showed 85 percent of the cottontail and brush rabbit bag from: Riverside, San Diego, Kern, San Bernardino, Orange, Los Angeles, Ventura, Fresno, Imperial, Santa Barbara. Some 60 percent of the total state kill came from the first four of those counties.

Squirrels are also fairly plentiful. The western gray squirrel is the important game species, and a large, handsome squirrel. Its range is throughout most of the mountain area of the state, from border to border. Some escaped eastern fox squirrels and eastern gray squirrels have established small domains.

The squirrel kill runs from 100,000 to 200,000 a season. The southern counties, the San Joaquin valley counties, and the northeast are currently closed to squirrel hunting. The bag limits also are low, 2 per day. Undoubtedly the low bag dampens general interest in squirrel hunting. National Forests and BLM lands in the open-season counties offer plentiful public hunting.

OTHER ANIMALS

Raccoons are fairly plentiful over most of the state up to elevations of 6000 feet. Hunting them at night with dogs is popular with specialists at this sport. There is no season or bag limit. Public lands have good populations.

Varmint enthusiasts hunt badgers to some extent. They are fairly plentiful in localized populations, where rodents are abundant.

There are gray foxes, and some red foxes from introduced animals. Grays range widely over the state and get some attention from animal-calling enthusiasts. Coyotes are present over almost all of the state in varying abundance. So is the bobcat. Both have a following among callers.

REGULATIONS

Game laws pertaining to seasons, bag and possession limits, areas to be hunted, special hunts, license fees all may have numerous changes from year to year. For current regulations, and for other specific queries, write to: California Department of Fish and Game, 1416 Ninth Street, Sacramento, California 95814.

OREGON

The original Indian word that eventually became corrupted to our word Oregon referred to water, and more specifically it is thought to the mighty Columbia River, which forms almost three-fourths of Oregon's northern border with the state of Washington. The water reference was apt. Oregon is dotted by high lakes, laced by scores of streams pouring either northward to join the Columbia on its trek to the Pacific, or roaring down from the coastal mountains to the ocean. The northern half of Oregon's eastern border, with Idaho, is also a river, the wild and beautiful Snake. The southern neighbor is California, and all of the western boundary is the long and often rocky and rugged beach fronting the Pacific.

The state is stunningly scenic, and full of contrasts of terrain and climate. Along the Pacific is the Coast Range with its rain forests, dense undergrowth, heavy rainfall, and torrential streams. On the east of this range is the fertile, beautiful Willamette Valley, draining north to the Columbia. North-south on the eastern edge of these broad lowlands the massive Cascades rise, with vast forests and snowy peaks, one of them the State's highest, 11,245-foot Mount Hood.

The Cascades drastically affect climate to the east. The mountains bar coastal moisture, stopping the flow of air eastward from the Pacific which gentles the climate of most of the west even in winter. On the eastern side of the Cascades the country is a high, dry plateau, much of it in the southeast a type of high, sparsely settled desert broken by the suddenly thrusting and isolated Steens Mountains, but rising toward the northeast to become the rugged Blue and Wallowa mountain ranges. These drastically differing terrains and climates offer habitats for game as diverse as the weather and altitudes.

There is ample room for wildlife. Approximately half of the state is heavily forested. Oregon, in fact, is first in the nation in forest products such as lumber and paper. Agriculture is also important, from vast wheat lands in the east to fruit in the moist interior valley. There is a prodigious amount of wild land and true mountain wilderness.

Oregon, with almost 97,000 square miles, ranks tenth in size among the states. The population is growing with astonishing swiftness. It is now well over two million. Nonetheless, there is little crowding if one really wishes to get away from the crowds. The coastal section and the valley have numerous good, fast highways. At least ten main highways cross the Cascades to join a north-south network based upon U.S. 97 on the east slope. All of eastern Oregon has good main highways, but there are vast open spaces here where only secondaries probe.

Much of the forest country in the western half and in the northeast is easily accessible. But there are numerous Wilderness Areas where no vehicular traffic is allowed. Oregon hunters can well use horses or 4WD vehicles to

693

get to many of the better back-in regions. Nonetheless, one can hunt all of the game birds and both deer and elk almost anywhere without special transport equipment. However, Oregon is a state where guides may be employed to great advantage in the wilder sections and for big game. The Game Commission can be helpful in locating guides in any sector but cannot recommend individuals. Air transport to large Oregon cities is good. Outlying smaller centers, particularly in mountain regions, may require ground travel. Travel distances are nominal. From north to south the average is a bit under 300 miles border to border and from east to west approximately 375. Mountain drives may stretch distances somewhat.

Hunter numbers, at present around 350,000, are growing steadily each year. Oddly, considering the good hunting, nonresident license sales are meager, hardly over 1 percent of the total. Hunting activities are diverse. There are coastal blacktail deer, mule deer, a few whitetails. Elk are numerous, and of two varieties. Token seasons for sheep, goat, antelope are held. There are abundant black bear, some lions. Waterfowl hunting is good. Upland birds include pheasants, chukars, Huns, three species of quail, blue and ruffed grouse, sage grouse, wild turkey, bandtailed pigeons and mourning doves. There are also numerous varmints and pests, such as crows, coyotes, foxes, bobcats, rockchucks, ground squirrels. And in small game there are rabbits, and the big silver gray squirrel. Deer and elk are the main attractions in big game for the majority, pheasants, chukars, ducks, bandtails top targets among the birds.

Public lands cover enormous expanses. Almost 50 percent of Oregon is in public ownership, which means over thirty million acres. National Forest and Bureau of Land Management lands are the most important. Each administers more than fifteen million acres. The National Forests are numerous. For maps and details on Oregon National Forests, write: U.S. Forest Service, Box 3623, Portland 97208.

The Oregon forests are listed below, by sectors where located. Following the name of the Forest is the headquarters town where the Forest Supervisor may be contacted. Maps of each forest, or of Wilderness Areas within individual Forests, may be acquired from the Regional Supervisor.

NORTHWEST: Suislaw NF (1), Corvallis, over 600,000 acres along coast; Mt. Hood NF (2), Portland, in northern Cascades, over 1 million acres; Willamette NF (3), Eugene, over 1.5 million acres, south of above in Cascades; Deschutes NF (4), Bend, over 1.5 million acres east of above; Ochoco NF (5), Prineville, nearly 850,000 acres east of Deschutes in central area.

NORTHEAST: Umatilla NF (6), Pendleton, over 1 million acres (some in Wash.); Wallowa NF and Whitman NF (7), Baker, 2¼ million acres; Malheur NF (8), John Day, nearly 1.5 million acres.

SOUTHWEST: Umpqua NF (9), Roseburg, nearly 1 million acres in Cascades; Rogue River NF (10), Medford, over 800,000 acres south of above; Winema NF (11), Klamath Falls, over 900,000 acres east of above two; Fremont NF (12), Lakeview, approximately 1¼ million acres east of two above; Siskiyou NF (13), Grants Pass, over 1 million acres near coast.

SOUTHEAST: parts of the Ochoco NF reach into the northwestern portion of this sector.

Bureau of Land Management lands are chiefly east of the Cascades, although there are large expanses elsewhere. Astonishingly, probably three-fourths of the southeast quarter of Oregon is administered by BLM. These lands stretch on north along the Snake and in greater acreage along the John Day River. Because BLM lands are not as compactly contained as the National Forests, and may be interspersed with private lands, hunters should acquire maps of, or information about, these lands in the areas where they wish to operate. Address: Bureau of Land Management, Regional Office, Box 2965, Portland 97208.

Some of the dozen National Wildlife Refuges in Oregon offer a modest amount of hunting. Corps of Engineers lands and Reclamation lands also are open to public hunting. State public lands, while far less important than federal lands, are still locally important. There are some State Forests, and approximately 110,000 acres in seventeen Game Management Areas. The latter are chiefly managed for waterfowl, and for experimental deer and elk range. Readers should not confuse these *Areas,* with Game Management *Units,* about which more presently.

While the millions of acres of federal lands are the important ones to hunters, the Oregon Game Commission looks ahead to years of still greater pressures and has been working hard to assure hunter access to some extent on private lands. This is important for bird hunting particularly, where game birds are by nature tied to agricultural habitats. To this end over recent seasons the Commission has been making game-habitat improvements on private lands, in return for signed agreements by the landowner permitting hunters on their lands. As much as 600,000 acres have been opened to hunters in this manner. The Commission can assist hunters in finding these lands.

Timber company holdings should not be overlooked. Thousands of acres allow hunting, with varying restrictions and regulations by the owners. As an example, Crown Zellerbach Corporation has over 300,000 acres available in Oregon, with deer, elk, bear the chief species. This firm cannot answer mail queries from hunters. Their open acreages are in the following counties: Clackamas; Clatsop; Lincoln; Columbia; Tillamook. Help in locating timber company lands open to hunters may be had from: American Forest Products Industries, 1835 K St., NW, Washington, D.C. 20006.

Several years ago the Game Commission launched a project that involved access to over 100,000 acres of private lands. The location for the pilot project was south of Heppner, in Morrow Co. in the northeast. "Welcome to Hunt" signs were posted, and Commission personnel furnished patrols for the area. Results were highly successful. Hunters should check with the Commission as to areas that may be open to public hunting under this plan each fall.

Game Commission administrative regions in Oregon are five in number. Boundaries do not in all cases exactly follow county lines. The Regions may be described roughly as follows: Region 1, Northwest; Region 2, Southwest; Region 3, Central, its western boundary along the ridge of the Cascades and the Region chiefly along the east slope; Region 4, Northeast; Region 5, Southeast and most of Lake Co. Reference to these administrative regions will assist hunters with queries to the Commission.

Big Game Management and regulation is by Big Game Management *Units.* These may in some cases, but do not necessarily, follow county lines. There are presently sixty-six of them, and they are referred to by names, not numbers. Hunters after big game must have a Management Unit Map current for the season in order to make sense of the regulations. Small-game management is for practical purposes statewide, and in following material either counties or Units may be referred to.

OREGON

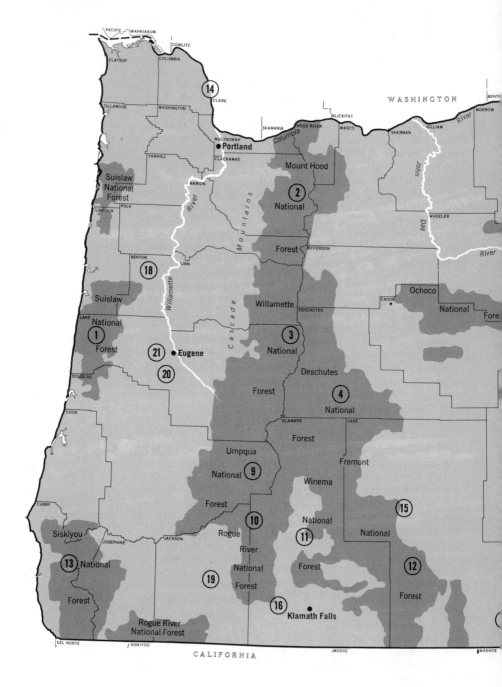

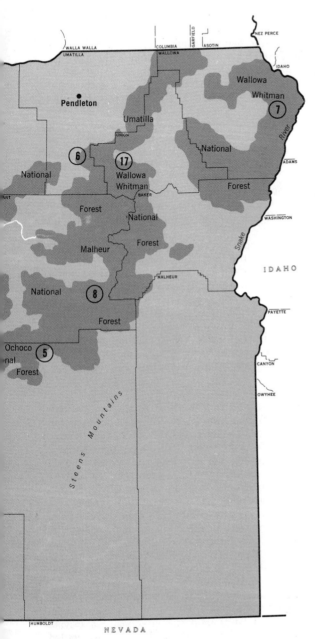

1. Suislaw NF
2. Mount Hood NF
3. Willamette NF
4. Deschutes NF
5. Ochoco NF
6. Umatilla NF
7. Wallowa NF; Whitman
   NF
8. Malheur NF
9. Umpqua NF
10. Rogue River NF
11. Winema NF
12. Fremont NF
13. Siskiyou NF
14. Sauvie Island GMA;
    Government Island
    GMA
15. Summer Lake GMA
16. Klamath GMA
17. Ladd Marsh GMA
18. E. E. Wilson GMA
19. Kenneth Denman GMA
20. Camas Swale GMA
21. Fern Ridge GMA
22. Warner Valley GMA

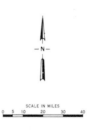

SCALE IN MILES

0   5   10   20   30   40

All management arrangements above become rather difficult to decipher when referring to Upland Game and Waterfowl Regulations. Hunters should carefully note in the law digest the definitions of Western Oregon, Eastern Oregon, Northwest Area, and Southwest Area. These are west or east of the Cascades summit in the first two instances, and by listed county groups in the last two. Also, although the popular term "Columbia Basin" may ordinarily refer to northern portions of Wasco, Sherman, Gilliam, Morrow, and Umatilla Cos. immediately adjacent to the Columbia River, by definition in the game-law sense (exceedingly important to waterfowlers) it means much of north-central and northeast Oregon plus all of huge Malheur Co. in the southeast. The counties it officially includes: Wasco, Sherman, Gilliam, Morrow, Umatilla, Union, Wallowa, Baker, Malheur.

Camping hunters will find hundreds of opportunities, in National Forests, on BLM lands, etc. BLM has an "Oregon Recreation Guide" (see address above); "Oregon Parks," another booklet, is available from the State Highway Department, Salem 97310. This state is far out front in numbers of State Parks and Wayside Parks (some 200) and County Parks (around 300). There are also several National Parks. Visitors might be cautious, however, about the sparsely settled southeast. Developed sites are few. There is no problem in finding motel and other accommodations along any of the main highways.

Weather is a problem. It all depends on where you are. The east can be hot and dry, or bitter cold and dry, the interior hot and humid, the coast wet and hot, or chilly and wet, the mountains cold. It is advisable to go prepared for any variety of weather, and especially on the west slope of the Cascades and the Coast Range to have rain gear. Arms and ammunition for the average hunter will be well covered by a good deer rifle in a caliber comparable to the .270, .30/06 or .308, plus possibly a .22, plus a shotgun with shells No. 7½ and 6 for the smaller birds and something heavier for waterfowl. Elk hunters may prefer magnum rifles, although well-selected heavy-deer calibers are perfectly adequate in the hands of good marksmen.

PHEASANT

It was in Oregon that the Chinese ringneck was first established successfully close to a century ago in the Willamette River Valley. The state has hunted pheasants longer than any other. The first season was in 1892, and it was reported that an estimated 50,000 birds were bagged on opening day. Today Oregon has good pheasant hunting, but not to compare with earlier years. Habitat is too swiftly being destroyed by urban encroachment and by changing agricultural use. Although pheasants will use sagebrush lands and foothill brush for hiding, they are irrevocably tied to agricultural lands.

Populations fluctuate. In the east weather conditions often deny a good hatch. However, hunter numbers and an average kill remain reasonably stable. It is estimated that some 75,000 hunters take 250,000 to 350,000 pheasants annually. While seasons with perfect conditions may skyrocket kill figures for peak years, it is doubtful that Oregon pheasant hunting under today's conditions can make any substantial upward trend.

By far the major share of pheasant hunting is on private lands, in the fruit growing and general farming valleys, and in the wheat areas. Nevertheless, in some of the best areas BLM lands in particular do adjoin private lands, and these will often harbor birds. Particularly in the sparsely settled portions of the east, permission on private lands is not difficult to obtain.

On the west side of the Cascades, the upper Willamette Valley is invariably best, with the mid-Valley close in quality. Farther south there are the Umpqua Basin of Douglas Co., and the Rogue Basin crossing coastward across Jackson, Josephine, and Curry Cos. These usually offer hunting slightly below the quality to the north.

East of the Cascades, the northern halves of counties lying along the Columbia and north of the Blue and Wallowa Mountains offer good shooting. The city of Pendleton is a good orientation point here. A bit to the west, the upper Deschutes River and all wheat-growing lands eastward are actually an addition to the Columbia "Basin" region. In the northeast, many places that in general follow the main highways offer good hunting. The regions around Wallowa and Elgin on U.S. 82, LaGrande at junction with U.S. 30, on south to Baker on U.S. 30, and farther on to Ontario and Vale near the Idaho border on U.S. 20-26 are important pheasant lands. In the general southeast sector, irrigated parts of Malheur Co. offer at times the best pheasant shooting in the state. Note that there are large expanses of BLM lands here, bordering or near irrigated croplands. The valley around Harney Lake south of Burns often has good pheasant populations. Westward in this quadrant, areas near Lakeview and Klamath Falls will offer fair hunting. See early portion of chapter regarding BLM lands.

There is some pheasant hunting on several of the State Game Management Areas. As noted earlier, most of these are developed mainly for waterfowl. On some there are wild pheasant populations, and on some pheasants are annually stocked. Sauvie Island and Government Island GMAs (14) are both north of Portland in the Columbia River. Summer Lake GMA (15), 17,400 acres, is south-central, in Lake Co., at the north end of Summer Lake, Klamath GMA (16), 7656 acres, is near Klamath Falls in Klamath Co. Ladd Marsh GMA (17) contains 3747 acres in the northeast, near U.S. 30 south of LaGrande. E. E. Wilson GMA (18), primarily for upland game bird production, has some hunting, particularly for juveniles, and for dog training. It contains 1625 acres north of Corvallis in the mid-Willamette Valley. Kenneth Denman GMA (19), 1920 acres, has pheasants released during season. It is in the southeast, near Medford, Jackson Co.

QUAIL

There are three species of quail presently in Oregon. The valley quail is most numerous. Mountain quail are next. Bobwhite quail are found in limited numbers. They are not native, but were introduced many years ago, the first ones in 1879.

Oddly, even during years when quail populations are high, few Oregon hunters appear interested in them. Most are taken as incidentals by pheasant hunters. The fact is, some excellent quail hunting is available in Oregon during peak years. From 25,000 to 30,000 quail hunters on the average bag at the highest perhaps a quarter-million birds in a good season.

Valley quail are found over much of the state, except in the timbered mountains. However, they are most numerous in the valleys and along stream courses. In general, best populations, sometimes in startling numbers, are in the southeastern counties. Other good populations are found in the so-called Columbia "Basin," along the river east of the Cascades. There are substantial numbers in the Willamette Valley, and in the southwestern sector in Josephine, Jackson, and Klamath Cos. The BLM lands and croplands of Malheur Co. are excellent. In all valley quail habitat the canyons and brushy foothills near agricultural lands will hold the heaviest concentrations.

In the southeast, the drainage of the Malheur River in Harney and

Malheur Cos. is good. The John Day River Basin of Crook, Wheeler, Gilliam Cos. is another prime spot. The Deschutes drainage between Wasco and Sherman Cos. also should be considered. Lake Co. in the south-central region and the area out of the city of Lakeview in the south of that county is excellent valley quail range. There is a small amount of quail hunting on some of the GMAs but other lands will generally be better.

Mountain quail, though abundant enough, live much of their lives in rugged terrain and are not pressured to any extent by hunters. The lower brushy slopes of all Oregon mountains have scattered populations of mountain quail, from the Coast Range through the Cascades and the Blue and Wallowa Mountains of the northeast. The unique Steens Mountains of southeast Harney Co. also contain a few. These birds do not to any extent inhabit the dense tall forests. Their habitat is along edges of clearings, in brushy draws, in burned-over places and in the rocky, steep slope expanses where good brush cover is available. It is very difficult to pinpoint concentrations. By counties, undoubtedly the best bets are: in the northwest in Tillamook Co. in the Coast Range well west of Portland; in Lane Co. to the south, also a Coast Range county, with the city of Eugene a focal point; both Coos and Douglas Cos. still farther south, with Roseburg in between on U.S. 99; Wallowa Co. in the extreme northeast.

Bobwhite quail are not numerous. Check laws to be certain if season is open. Bobwhites have not done well in Oregon, although numerous stockings have been made. There are some in the Willamette Valley. The region around Pendleton in Umatilla Co. in the northeast has some, and so does southeastern Malheur Co.

CHUKAR

The chukar partridge was first tried in Oregon in 1951. With continued stocking, it did very well. It has become an important uplander here. Virtually all suitable habitat has been stocked and chukars appear to be established wherever they match their habitat well. The rough, dry country of eastern Oregon is best suited to them, comparable to the region where the first stock originated, in India. The season is ordinarily open in "Eastern Oregon." By game-law definition this means all counties east of the summit of the Cascades, including all of Klamath County. Thus the eastern two-thirds of the state has open season.

Because chukars are arid-country birds, rather drastic population fluctuations occur. In an average year from 16,000 to 20,000 hunters take 75,000 to 130,000 birds. In one peak year (1963) almost 300,000 chukars were killed. This illustrates their solid establishment. The first season, in 1956, five years after introduction, showed less than 4000 bagged. The chukar season often is of several months duration.

Some of the best chukar areas are: along the lower Deschutes and the desert country to the east; the John Day River drainage, including barren-appearing and brushy, rocky hills along tributaries; the same types of terrain in the drainage of the Snake along the eastern border; the Owyhee River drainage and Canyon in the southeast in Malheur Co.; the Malheur River drainage in Harney and Malheur Cos.; the Steens Mountains which thrust abruptly from the desert floor in southeastern Harney Co.; the Imnaha River breaks. This last-named stream is in the extreme northeast, a tributary to the Snake which crosses much of eastern Wallowa Co. before joining the Snake at the border.

HUNGARIAN PARTRIDGE

The Hun was first stocked in eastern Oregon in 1900. It has established itself, is nowhere especially plentiful, and has not been especially popular with hunters. One recent survey showed approximately 17,000 hunters taking slightly over 22,000. More recently, only 4339 hunters participated, bagging 10,365 birds.

Huns are hunted concurrently with chukars, in eastern Oregon only, and are often taken in the same bag. In fact, bag and possession limits apply to these two species in the aggregate. This is because so few hunters purposely hunt Huns only, and because the two birds are often found in the same areas. However, the Hun is far more dependent upon agriculture and is likely to be found in coveys on wheat stubble lands and on rougher lands adjacent to farmlands. The counties of the northeast usually have the best populations. Some coveys are also found in the southeast, in sagebrush and bunch-grass habitat. See "Chukar" for drainages where it is plentiful. The Hun will be in many of the same places, but predominantly closer to croplands.

GROUSE

Blue, Franklin's, ruffed, sage, and sharptail grouse are all native to various parts of Oregon. The sharptail, once abundant in the short sage and the grass of eastern Oregon, has been all but wiped out by changing land use to grazing and agriculture. Remnants cling in portions of Baker Co. Several years ago another subspecies was introduced. The Franklin's grouse, a mountain grouse so trusting it has in numerous places been called "fool hen," is found in small numbers in a restricted range of the northeast, in portions of Baker, Union, and Wallowa Cos. It is not hunted.

Blue grouse, those large birds of the high-country timber, and sometimes of lower wooded slopes, are reasonably plentiful. Largest concentrations are in the Blue and Wallowa Mountains of the northeast. The Coast Range also has numerous blue grouse and so does the western Cascade slope, but they are exceedingly difficult to hunt except where logged areas and burns offer openings, in which and around the perimeters of which they consort.

The smaller but swift and erratic ruffed grouse, prime game species, is fairly plentiful in the lower thickets of willow or alder over much of the western Oregon mountains, the east slope of the Cascades, and up in the northeast in the Blue and Wallowa ranges. They, too, like the openings, the burns and the logged areas.

Blue and ruffed grouse appear in the game laws together, and are hunted together. The grouse season ordinarily differs somewhat in western and eastern Oregon. The bag is tallied in aggregate. A fair number of enthusiasts—from 10,000 to 20,000—avidly hunt these grouse each season. The combined bag, termed "forest grouse," runs from 25,000 to 35,000 or more. All told, the Blue and Wallowa ranges of the northeast usually offer the best hunting.

Sage grouse are found only in the southeast. Harney and Malheur Cos. have the most. A few are scattered over sage areas in other southeast counties. Sage grouse habitat is declining. Ten years or more ago fairly high kills were made each year. In 1958 over 21,000 were bagged by 7374 hunters. To illustrate fluctuations of the sage grouse population, 1964 saw only 3718 hunters out and a kill of 8669. Seasons are not opened each year. Check with the Commission as to possibility for any given year.

The whitetailed ptarmigan, grouse of altitudes above timberline and of the Arctic, have recently been introduced to some of the Oregon high country. Wild-trapped birds from British Columbia, Washington, and Colorado have been released in several plantings in the Wallowas. If the birds take hold, transplants will be made to the Cascades. It is far too early yet to forecast results.

WILD TURKEYS

Turkeys are not native to Oregon. Merriam's turkeys from Colorado, Arizona, New Mexico were brought in, the first ones in 1961. They were released in three different locations on the east slope of the Cascades. The birds quickly established themselves, and the first season was held in the fall of 1965, any sex, with the result sixteen gobblers and fifteen hens taken. A spring season was immediately announced, with 300 permits offered. Since then seasons have been held quite liberally, permits jumping first to 1000 and then to unlimited participation in the fall hunt in 1967. Some 4000 hunters participated, with the kill 150 birds in a three-day hunt.

Originally only the Wasco Management Unit was open. It is located in the region of the Dalles, in northern Oregon, Wasco Co., along and south of the Columbia River. In fall, 1968, the Sled Springs Unit also was opened. This is in the northeast, chiefly in Wallowa Co. It is quite likely that Oregon's turkey hunting may advance swiftly over the next few years. In an attempt to overlook no possibility, wild trapped turkeys of the eastern subspecies, brought from Tennessee, were released several years ago in the Rogue River Canyon, in the southwest. It is hoped this variety may adapt to the quite different climate.

DOVES AND PIGEONS

The mourning dove and the bandtailed pigeon are the two native species. Both are hunted. While fair dove populations exist, Oregon is at the northern part of dove range and thus cannot expect shooting such as states to the south enjoy, where migrating hordes of doves offer larger concentrations. In addition, the mourning dove is not as avidly hunted in Oregon as in many other states. Over a number of years, surveys have shown that an average of only about 16,000 hunters shoot mourning doves, and the kill over the past decade has exceeded 200,000 in only two seasons. It averages around 175,000. Compared to the total California kills of over four million, the Oregon kill is modest indeed.

The broad expanses of mountains and timberlands in Oregon prohibit large dove populations. The Willamette Valley has some. More are found east of the Cascades. Counties along the Columbia, and in the Columbia "Basin" (check early material in chapter to differentiate between the legal and popular connotations of this confusing term) usually have fair flights. Umatilla and Morrow Cos., and portions of Wasco, are good. So is Deschutes, and below it Lake Co. Both Harney and Malheur Cos. in the southeast are among the best. Hunters should keep in mind that shrub and grass lands and harvested croplands are the best areas for mourning doves, which do not feed from grain on the stalk but from fallen seeds.

The bandtailed pigeon is basically a bird of the high forest country, where it feeds on acorns, pine seeds, and on fruits of the lower slopes such as elderberries. It is highly mobile and migratory, and often when pressed for food comes to the valleys, where at times it concentrates and is rather destructive to fruit such as cherries and to field crops such as peas.

The bandtail is a summer nester over much of forested western Oregon. In fall birds from farther north begin to move south, and in most years Oregon has some very good bandtail shooting along the slopes of the coastal mountains and valleys. Bandtails habitually fly through saddles in the mountains and pass shooting in such spots is excellent. Salt has great attraction for these large pigeons. They fly along the coast to salt water, on tidal flats, and to mineral springs here and in the Willamette Valley. Flyway shooting along the beaches or near mineral springs is excellent, and in seasons when there are good fruit crops hunters stationed near such forage that the bandtails are utilizing will do well.

The entire state is generally open, with a worthwhile daily limit (8 birds), but the Coast and west Cascade slopes furnish most of the shooting. The National Forest lands make ample public sites available. Annual kill runs from 80,000 to 120,000 birds, with 9000 to 20,000 hunters participating. Feeding conditions, and weather, motivate the flocks. Cold weather or lack of ample forage will send them quickly southward. The season is usually in September.

WATERFOWL

Ducks and geese are important game in Oregon. Some 50,000 hunters follow this sport annually. A recent season kill showed over a half-million ducks and 51,000 geese taken. Numerous ducks and a fair number of geese are raised in Oregon. Others migrate through and some stay through the winter. Among the geese, snows and white-fronted (specklebelly) geese are abundant. Cackling geese are also numerous. For those who may be unfamiliar with this species, it is a very small dark-colored goose of the Canada clan. There are also large western Canada geese. Among the most highly prized ducks are mallards and pintails, both of which are abundant.

Oregon has two persistent problems regarding waterfowl. One is that periodic droughts in the southeast, best of the waterfowl areas, occasionally hinder both hatching and stopover of migrating birds. The other is that lakes and potholes in the best counties may freeze over so that the late seasons are hindered in those places. Nonetheless, the state may be considered excellent for waterfowl, the droughts are not common, and freeze-ups concentrate birds along the rivers.

The best places for hunting waterfowl are as follows: Harney County in the southeast contains large Harney Lake and Malheur Lake and the famous Malheur National Refuge surrounds them. Lake Co. west of and bordering Harney Co. has several large lakes heavily utilized by waterfowl. Klamath Co., bordering Lake on the west, is one of the best, with portions of the famous Klamath Refuges here. Marshlands in all three counties offer fine shooting for both geese and ducks. The Klamath Basin is especially productive. All three counties usually will be best during the early seasons. Freezes may occur later.

Along the northern half of the eastern border, the Snake River and the Wallowa Valley are considered among the best places in the northwest for mallards. The Owyhee River and the Malheur River and tributaries are excellent. The same is true of the Willamette Valley west of the Cascades. Pintails are also plentiful in the Willamette Valley. The grain counties along the Columbia—Sherman, Gilliam, Morrow, Umatilla—draw many geese, both the large Canadas and lesser Canadas. The coastal strip offers excellent shooting for both pintails and other ducks, particularly widgeons, and diving species such as scaup. The shooting in the coastal lowlands and the Willamette

Valley generally is slow at opening but improves as the season progresses into November and onward.

The several Game Management Areas developed for waterfowl furnish good shooting. Probably the best is Sauvie Island in the northwest. Nearby Government Island is also good. Others are Ladd Marsh, Summer Lake, and Klamath. See "Pheasant" for locations. Two others not so far mentioned are Camas Swale and Fern Ridge. Camas Swale GMA (20) has 2700 acres, is located in the west-central part of the state, south of Eugene, U.S. 99. Just west of Eugene is Fern Ridge Reservoir and the Fern Ridge GMA (21), often good for lesser Canada geese. In the southwest, near Medford, is Kenneth Denman GMA ("Pheasant"). Periodic checks should be made with the Commission regarding opening of other Areas or newly acquired Areas. Another choice waterfowl location is Warner Valley GMA (22). It is a Public Shooting Ground on the Warner Valley Stock Company lands. It is in the south near the California border about centered across the state. Key location town is Adel, east of Lakeview, Lake Co., State 140. On most of the GMAs, nominal fees are charged.

Oregon also has a number of National Wildlife Refuges with dense waterfowl populations, and on some of these portions are open at times to hunting. It is best to check with the Commission in any given season regarding the Refuges. The following generally offer shooting: Hart Mt. NWR, Lake Co.; Cold Springs NWR and McKay Creek NWR in Umatilla Co.; Upper Klamath and Klamath Forest NWRs, Klamath Co.; Deer Flat NWR, Malheur Co.; Malheur NWR, Malheur Co.; William Finley NWR, Benton Co.

Hunters should note that most of these Refuges have portions open for upland birds, and that Ankeny NWR, Marion Co. and Baskett Slough NWR, Polk Co., do also, although as this is written these two are closed to waterfowl shooting.

On most of the GMAs and other marsh and wetlands where waterfowl are hunted, fair to good snipe hunting is available. It gets almost no attention from hunters.

Black brant offer an excellent sport potential along the coast that is utilized by only a scattering of hunters. Brant are small marine geese. In Oregon the cackling geese mentioned earlier are often and erroneously called "brant." Black brant migrate along the coast, feed on eel grass, are excellent eating, and very sporty. This is specialized hunting requiring decoys to pull birds in to the tidal flats. Stormy days are best, to force the birds into sheltered bays. Brant arrive in late November. Best populations are found on the bays late in the long season—in December, January, and February. Best Oregon bays are Netarts, Tillamook, Yaquina, and Coos. Other bays that may have birds: Alsea, Nehalem, Siletz.

DEER

Oregon is an important deer state. And deer are tremendously important to Oregon hunters. More sportsmen hunt deer than any other animal or bird in the state. One recent season survey showed over 270,000 deer hunters, with the harvest 147,975 deer. There are seasons for bucks and special antlerless seasons. That year 107,757 buck deer and 40,218 antlerless were collected. By and large, hunter success hangs around 50 percent year after year, which is excellent.

Oregon has three varieties of deer. Mule deer are most numerous, and have the largest range. The Columbian blacktail which is actually a variety of mule deer but quite different in appearance, habits and habitat, is second.

There are a very few whitetails. Kill figures illustrate general abundance. One fall bag showed 87,180 mule deer, 54,820 blacktails, approximately 100 whitetails.

Range of the blacktail is in western Oregon chiefly in the Coast Range region and the Cascades. But it extends over the Cascades into Wasco and Jefferson Cos. in the north and into Klamath Co. in the south. Mule deer blanket the eastern two-thirds of the state, ranging from the summit of the Cascades eastward. The area northeast of Roseburg, in Douglas Co. in the southwest, harbors a few whitetails, which are exceedingly difficult to hunt and unusual trophies in this state. A few more are in the northwest along the Columbia north and west of Portland. Another remnant is in the far northeast, in Wallowa Co.

There is no problem finding a place to hunt. The National Forests and the BLM lands (see front material of chapter) offer millions of acres. Deer seasons, however, are set in a fairly complicated manner for careful management control. Therefore it is mandatory that prospective hunters acquire a Big Game Map (showing Big Game Management Units) and a booklet of the seasons, before planning a hunt.

In general, blacktails are found most abundant in logged or burned areas. They can also be hunted more successfully in such openings. In southwest Oregon, Douglas and Jackson Cos. are favorite blacktail spots. On the west Cascade slope Linn and Lane Cos. have consistently good populations, and on the coast Coos and Tillamook Cos. are considered prime.

For mule deer, virtually all of the southeast and the central portion of the state furnish good opportunities. Mule deer are found both in the high forests and in the juniper and sage. Among the National Forests, the Deschutes, Malheur, Ochoco, Fremont, Winema are good choices. The deserts of the southeastern counties, in the higher elevations—Harney and Malheur—offer more open hunting and many trophies. The Blue and Wallowa Mountains of the northeast are quality mule deer range, both in the scrub and the canyons and draws of the foothills and up in the timber. There is even good deer hunting along the fringe of the northeastern wheat lands. The southeast is difficult in some ways, for deer are fewer, but spots such as the Steens Mountains in southeast Harney Co. are good bets. Higher success percentages turn up in such drainages as the John Day, which is to the north along Wheeler, Wasco, Gilliam, and Sherman Cos.

In the Northwest, all Units generally show good kills. During the latest season as this is written the following Units had 50 percent-or-over hunter success in total deer killed: Alsea; McKenzie; Nestucca; Polk; Santiam; Suislaw; Willamette. Others fell slightly below 50 percent. However, there is actually little choice among Units, so far as kill figures over several seasons indicate.

In the Southwest, kill figures run so high in all Units that most seasons there is little choice. In the same season as noted above, Chetco, Dixon, Elkton, Evans Creek, Melrose, Powers, Sixes, Tioga Units all were 50 percent success or above. Dixon had 5180 hunters, a total all-seasons bag of 3480 deer. Elkton had 2020 hunters, a kill of 1510! Sixes, Melrose, and Powers Units were all well over 50 percent.

Central region: Fort Rock, Keno, Klamath, Maupin, Maury, Sherman, Sprague all were 50 percent or above. Sprague, usually a hot one, showed 5840 hunters and 4330 deer bagged. Deschutes and Ochoco were not far behind the 50 percent field.

All of the Units in the Northeast show such high success it is not necessary to name them. For example, of twenty Units here, over several years no more than four showed less than 50 percent and then only slightly less. Several, counting all deer killed in all seasons, consistently stack up astonishing success. Keating is one. Snake River, Sled Springs, Northside, Minam are others.

In the Southeast, much the same general situation occurs. Most show 50 percent or more. Among the best are: Beulah, Hart Mountain, Interstate, Silvery Lake, Steens Mountain, Wagontire (a large Unit with few permits but high success), Warner, Whitehorse (same situation as Wagontire).

On the overall picture, the Southwest and the Northeast may have a slight edge in overall success. Deer management in Oregon, however, is carefully supervised and hunting almost everywhere is good.

ELK

Oregon has two varieties of elk, the Roosevelt elk and the Rocky Mountain elk. The first ranges chiefly in the Coast Range but with some in the Cascades. The second is found in the northeast, in the Blue and Wallowa mountains and southward. Best herds of the Roosevelt elk are located in the northwestern coastal counties of Clatsop and Tillamook, and in southwestern coastal county of Coos. In the northeast, Morrow, Grant, Umatilla, Union and Wallowa Cos. contain the preponderance of the Rocky Mountain herd. Some Oregon elk hunting is possible via pickup truck or passenger car. Best hunting in most sections can be had by using horses and packing in.

It is odd indeed that Oregon is so little publicized nationally as an elk hunting state. Compared to several Rocky Mountain states highly touted as elk states, Oregon stacks up very well. Also, kill figures and success percentages in various areas remain extremely consistent. The average harvest, total, runs from 10,000 to 11,500 in round numbers, with 60,000 to 70,000 participant hunters. Of the kill total, adult bulls make up roughly 25 percent, yearling bulls about 50 percent, antlerless elk the remaining 25 percent.

Dividing the state into its five management regions, hunter success in the Northwest averages about 14 percent, in the Southwest 15 percent, in the Central region 8 percent, in the Northeast roughly 18 percent, in the Southeast variable from 12 to 17 percent. Depending on which species one wishes to hunt, and in which portion of the state, there appears to be little choice in Regions for Roosevelt elk, but the Northeast has a decided edge for Rocky Mountain Elk.

It is necessary for prospective elk hunters to check laws thoroughly to make sure they have the proper tag and to familiarize themselves with the permit system. Also, not all Units are open, and the list may change from season to season.

In the Northwest, the Clatsop Unit gets numerous hunters, has good consistent success. Wilson is next in number of hunters, with good average success comparable to Clatsop. Some of the Northwest Units with only a few permits, however, show annually very high success. In the Southwest, the Elkton Unit consistently shows late years the highest success, up to 24 percent. The Tioga Unit has the largest number of hunters and a consistently high success. The Central region has few permits, few hunters and low success. The Northeast gets the bulk of the hunters, at least two-thirds of the total. It also has numerous high-success Units. Those that remain consistently highest are as follows: Imnaha, Minam, Sled Springs, Snake River, Walla Walla, Wenaha. In the Southeast, the Beulah Unit is consistently highest.

Elk populations can undergo severe changes from season to season, or by change in habitat over a period of a few years. It is wise to check with the Comm. when planning an elk hunt to ascertain what their latest surveys indicate.

ANTELOPE

Oregon antelope herds are not large. They are found in the southeast, from portions of Deschutes, Crook, and Grant Cos. south over a bit of Klamath, plus much of Lake, Harney, Malheur. Presently only residents may apply for the limited number of permits offered. Over a period of years, permits have numbered from 500-plus to just under 1000. Success averages from 60 to 75 percent. It is not possible to pinpoint what may be the best Units, for there is little difference; permit numbers are decided upon by herd surveys, and it is not possible to tell which Units may or may not be open.

SHEEP

Bighorn sheep were gone from Oregon a good many years ago. In 1950 reestablishment was begun. Sheep were stocked on Hart Mountain in Lake County in the southeast. Transplants were made to the Owyhees, and to the rugged Steens Mountains. Biologists are considering other sites.

It is estimated that possibly a hundred or more sheep are now on Hart Mountain, and at least half that number in the Steens. A few permits were issued for seasons in 1965, '66, and '68. Eleven rams were taken by fifteen hunters. A season is not likely to be held each year. Only residents may apply, and permits will undoubtedly be restricted on these token hunts to less than a half dozen.

GOATS

A few mountain goats were brought for release to the Wallowas, in the Eagle Cap Wilderness Area, in 1950. Numbers are still small, but they have increased. Beginning in 1965, several token hunts, with a small number of permits offered to residents by drawing, have been held. In the 1968 season there were eight hunters, all saw goats, and five filled their permits with trophies. Up through that season twenty goats had been taken by twenty-three hunters. Token hunts will probably continue. The country is rugged, but success is high.

BEAR

Black bear are exceedingly plentiful in several parts of the state. It is imperative, however, that hunters be familiar with the laws. Bears are considered game animals in certain areas and are on the unprotected list elsewhere. Although kill figures differ in various reports, they appear to run from 2000 to almost 4000 annually, which makes Oregon one of the best black bear states. Much of the hunting, especially in the coastal region where cover is dense, is very difficult, requires hounds for any degree of success. This means a hunter will have his best chance by hiring a guide with a good hound pack. In fact, success on such hunts booked with a competent bear-hunter guide are extremely successful in Oregon. A few counties, some timber companies, and in some instances the Forest Service hire professional bear hunters to reduce the bear population. The animals do much damage by stripping the bark of young trees. Contact the Forest Service (address early in chapter) or the Commission or timber company people for assistance in lining up a guide. A few suggestions for hunt locations: the Mount Hood region; upper Rogue River region in Cascades, along the Umpqua; the Siskiyou Mountain area along the lower Rogue River; in the northeast the Wallowa Mountails and Wilderness Areas; the Snake River divide. Virtually all of the Coast Range is good bear territory and here the animals will be active all year.

LION

Traditionally the mountain lion has had no protection in Oregon, and until 1961 was bountied. Recently it has received status as a game animal. It is not at this time plentiful, but with protection may become so. Check with the Commission regarding new regulations and assistance in locating guides for hunting. An experienced hound pack is mandatory.

SMALL GAME

Oregon has very good rabbit (and hare) hunting, for several species. The snowshoe rabbit, more properly "hare," is found in all timbered parts of the state. The blacktailed jack ranges in greatest abundance east of the Cascades, in the sagebrush country. There are also whitetailed jacks, usually much larger than the blacktailed species. Some jackrabbits have invaded the country west of the Cascades, in the Willamette Valley.

Among the true rabbits Oregon has four varieties. Two of these are the Rocky Mountain and Oregon cottontails. In addition there are the smaller brush rabbit, and the still smaller pygmy rabbit. The eastern cottontail is primarily an inhabitant of the Willamette Valley. Some of these rabbits grow extremely large. The Oregon cottontail is found through most of the mountains and in the sagebrush of the east. The brush rabbit weighs at maximum about two pounds, inhabits the dense brush on the west side of the Cascades. The pygmy rabbit is seldom over one pound and is found in the dense sagebrush of the east.

The brush rabbits are invariably hunted with dogs. Otherwise they won't leave their havens. The big eastern cottontail, which was not native but introduced years ago, is most abundant roughly from Troutdale west to Deer Island and south to Salem. Snowshoe hares may be abundant during high cycles in any of the mountains—the Wallowa and Blue in the east, the Cascades, the Coast ranges. The Oregon cottontail is generally most abundant on the fringes of jackrabbit ranges, that is, along or on agricultural lands. In gullies and washes where there is brush they hang out, and others are found in high regions of heavy sage. Most of the pygmy rabbits, which are small but very sporty, and excellent eating, are found down in the southeastern corner of the state.

Oregon also has good squirrel hunting in some sections. The important squirrel species is the silver gray, or western gray squirrel. Some of them grow exceptionally large. Although they range in forests of western Oregon and along both slopes of the Cascades, there is usually an oversupply of them in the nutgrowing region of the northern Willamette Valley. Here, in specified areas of northwest Oregon, there is no closed season. This is to protect nut growers from squirrel depredation.

The eastern gray squirrel, and the fox squirrel, were introduced many years ago. These are not abundant nor important as game except in areas open to hunting.

OTHER ANIMALS AND PESTS

There are numerous targets in the varmint and pest category for year-round shooting. A hunting license is required. Ground squirrels are abundant in the Willamette Valley and in the wheat and sagebrush areas all over the east. Rockchucks (marmots) abound in the high, rocky regions of the east. Jackrabbits are abundant over much of the farm and sage expanse of the eastern two-thirds of the state. There are a good many coyotes in the east, and west of the Cascades foxes are fairly common in the valleys. In rocky rims of the east bobcats can be called, or run with hounds. All of these animals can be hunted on millions of acres of BLM and Forest Service lands. Magpie shooting is also an interesting sport. These shy pests are found throughout the east. Crows are also abundant. Several islands in the Columbia harbor vast roosts. The same is true of several other rivers—the Rogue, the Umpqua, Willamette, Snake have large rookeries nearby.

REGULATIONS

Game laws pertaining to seasons, bag and possession limits, areas to be hunted, special hunts, license fees all may have numerous changes from year to year. For current regulations, and for other specific queries, write to: The Oregon State Game Commission, 1634 SW Alder Street, Portland, Oregon 97208.

WASHINGTON

This state that forms the northwestern corner of the contiguous U.S. is a thrilling area of great contrasts. Its western boundary is on the Pacific, with several deeply indented large bays in the southwest, plus the broad mouth of the mighty Columbia River that forms much of the southern boundary with Oregon. Farther north, the broad Juan de Fuca Strait separates Washington from British Columbia's Vancouver Island, and here the intricately meandering arms of Puget Sound thrust deep into the interior of the state's northwestern quadrant. To the north British Columbia is the boundary neighbor, and on the east the border is with northern Idaho.

Washington is a state of sweeping forests dotted with thousands of lakes. Particularly in the coastal section there are torrential streams rushing to the Pacific. Along much of the Pacific Coast dense rain forests rise along the slopes of the Coast Ranges, and in the northwest these culminate in the Olympic Mountains that blanket much of the Olympic Peninsula. Rainfall in some coastal sections may be very close to 150 inches annually. The Puget Sound region forms a broad valley east of the coastal mountains, and to its east the Cascades rise, culminating in 14,408-foot Mount Rainier.

This high mountain range forms a barrier to moisture moving east. Thus, in much of eastern Washington there is drastically different terrain, temperature, and vegetation. Here plateaus and open country are given over to cattle and to wheat and other farming. The Columbia River snakes south and west from the northeast corner of the state, and down near the Oregon border the Snake joins it. On the east the land rises toward the Rockies. Lumber is king in the west. But in the valleys, and on the east slope of the Cascades, endless orchards put this state first in apple production. There is of course much industry and other farming. Nonetheless, the state is over 50 percent forest, with much true wilderness where hunters need guides and pack animals or 4WD to get in.

Roads are good, and air transport is adequate. There are, however, many large expanses of the Cascades and of eastern Washington where main roads are rather sparsely scattered. And the Primitive or Wilderness Areas with the several National Forests admit no travel except by horse or backpack.

Although Washington covers about 69,000 square miles, it is the smallest of the western states. It has by comparison a rather high population, well over three million at present and swiftly growing. By far the bulk of the population is concentrated along the eastern side of Puget Sound and southward into the valley below. Spokane Co. on the eastern border also has a large population, but many Washington counties have only about 10,000 residents, and several far less. With an extreme east-west distance across the state of about 345 miles, and a north-south mileage of approximately 225, there is plenty of room.

Approximately 10 percent of Washington residents are hunters. License sales of late average around 315,000 annually. Oddly, few nonresidents come to visit, in most seasons fewer than 2000. Considering the excellent hunting for a variety of game, this is surprising. There are abundant deer of several species and subspecies, two species of elk, plus mountain goats, black bear, cougar, a few mountain sheep. Game birds abound, in variety, with pheasants, quail, chukar, Hungarian partridge, several varieties of grouse, plus doves, bandtailed pigeons, and wild turkeys available to upland gunners. Ducks, geese, snipe, and brant along the coast, make up the waterfowl bag. There are several kinds of rabbits and a scattering of other small game, fur bearers, and predator animals.

Public lands, and private lands opened to hunting under various programs, are so numerous that there is little difficulty in finding a place to hunt, except in a few instances for birds in the more densely populated sections. The National Forests are as a group the most important public hunting lands. There are nine either entirely or partly within the state, with a total of some eleven million acres. The address of the Forest Service for this Pacific Northwest Region is Box 3623, Portland, Oregon 97208. Maps and information on the Washington Forests, and lists of packers and guides operating in them, can be obtained there. Or, via this headquarters office one may contact the Forest Supervisor for pinpoint information about any individual Forest. These Forests, plus the acreage of each in round numbers, general location, and the town where the individual headquarters is located, are listed below.

NATIONAL FOREST	ACRES	AREA AND NEAREST TOWN
1. Colville NF	1 million	Northeast, Colville
2. Kanisku NF	300,000	Northeast, Sandpoint (Idaho)
3. Okanogan NF	2 million	North-central, Okanogan
4. Mount Baker NF	1¾ million	North-central, Bellingham
5. Olympic NF	700,000	Northwest, Olympia
6. Wenatchee NF	2 million	Northwest, Wenatchee
7. Snoqualmie NF	1½ million	Northwest, Seattle
8. Gifford Pinchot NF	1½ million	South-central, Vancouver
9. Umatilla NF	300,000	Southeast, Pendleton (Oregon)

In addition to the above, there are some four and a half million acres of privately owned forest lands open to hunters each year. Of this total, approximately three and a half million are in western Washington, one million in the east. There are certain restrictions, and hunters should familiarize themselves with these. Among firms with such holdings are Crown Zellerbach, Weyerhaeuser, Longview Fibre, Northern Pacific Railway. There are numerous others. American Forest Products Industries, Inc., 1835 K St., NW, Washington, D.C. 20006, can be helpful to some extent in contacts with firms owning land open to hunting. Boundaries, however, are difficult to describe and it is best to check such private lands on a local basis. Most firms will provide maps, and some have been offered in the past under imprint of the Washington Forest Protection Assn. Check with Washington Game Department for further details.

The Department also has, as this is written, thirty-five Public Hunting Areas, or "Game Lands." These range in size from a few acres to the latest acquisition of almost 100,000 acres. Twenty-one of these are operated primarily as waterfowl management and hunting tracts. Others offer elk, deer, and upland birds. These lands are marked with green and white Game Department signs that state "Game Lands." Most will be noted under individual species. These are also called "Game Ranges."

There are several state programs in operation for opening of private lands to hunters under varying agreements. Current programs include private lands in the Regulated Hunting Program, marked by both red and green diamond-shaped signs; the Habitat Development Program on farms marked with green signs that state "Respect This Property"; the Farmer Sportsman Program with lands marked by signs stating "Hunting by Permission." During a recent season approximately one million acres of private lands were open under such programs, on both sides of the Cascades. Obviously, acreage and location may change from season to season. Check with the Game Department for local information.

Hunters should be familiar with the manner in which the Game Department has split up the state for management purposes. It is divided currently into ten Regions. These will be used later under species to indicate abundance, and thus are listed and located here.

Region 1, called Northeast and Palouse (indicating the Palouse River Area), takes in the northeast and east-central part of the state, contains Ferry, Stevens, Pend Oreille, Lincoln, Spokane, and Whitman Cos. Region 2, Columbia Basin, is to the west and southwest of the above, enclosing eastern Douglas Co., all of Grant, Adams, Franklin and the northern part of Benton Co. Region 3, Blue Mountains: southeast corner of state, with all of Walla Walla, Columbia, Garfield, Asotin Cos. Region 4, South Central, is located as named, contains Kittitas and Yakima Cos. and southern Benton Co. Region 5, North Central: Okanogan, Chelan Cos., and most of Douglas Co.

Region 6, Northwest, borders British Columbia, contains Whatcom, Skagit Cos., and the two counties made up of islands to the west, San Juan and Island Cos. Region 7, North Puget Sound, borders the Sound on the west and reaches across it, encompasses Kitsap, Snohomish and King Cos. Region 8, South Puget Sound, takes in the three counties of the valley below the Sound, Pierce, Thurston, Lewis. Region 9, Lower Columbia, is in the south, along the Columbia River, contains Wahkiakum, Cowlitz, Clark, Skamania, and Klickitat Cos. Region 10, Olympic Peninsula, is identified by that geographic name, with Clallam, Jefferson, Grays Harbor, Mason, Pacific Cos.

The above Regions should not be confused with the smaller divisions, called Units, used for setting deer, elk, goat, and sheep seasons. The Units are mapped in any current digest of hunting seasons and this map is mandatory for hunters after big game.

Camping hunters have no problems here. The National Forests, National Park campgrounds, the State Parks, plus unnumbered undeveloped places on public lands offer hundreds of sites. A State Park Guide can be obtained from the State Parks and Recreation Commission, 522 South Franklin, Olympia 98501. National Forest and National Park camping information is readily available from those sources. Motel and lodge accommodations are also numerous and well distributed.

Hunters not acquainted in Washington are advised to go clothed and prepared for variety. The coastal area will invariably be damp or rainy, and can be chilly. The high country of the Cascades and the Blue Mountains of the southeast and also the beginning of the Rockies in the northeast have weather conditions typical of high mountains everywhere. Early fall may be pleasant and crisp, but later seasons cold and snowy. The open country

WASHINGTON

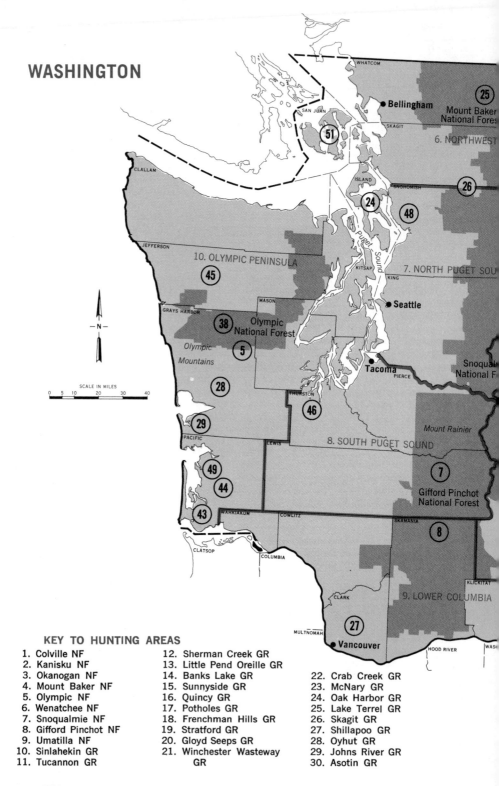

KEY TO HUNTING AREAS

1. Colville NF	12. Sherman Creek GR
2. Kanisku NF	13. Little Pend Oreille GR
3. Okanogan NF	14. Banks Lake GR
4. Mount Baker NF	15. Sunnyside GR
5. Olympic NF	16. Quincy GR
6. Wenatchee NF	17. Potholes GR
7. Snoqualmie NF	18. Frenchman Hills GR
8. Gifford Pinchot NF	19. Stratford GR
9. Umatilla NF	20. Gloyd Seeps GR
10. Sinlahekin GR	21. Winchester Wasteway
11. Tucannon GR	GR

22. Crab Creek GR	
23. McNary GR	
24. Oak Harbor GR	
25. Lake Terrel GR	
26. Skagit GR	
27. Shillapoo GR	
28. Oyhut GR	
29. Johns River GR	
30. Asotin GR	

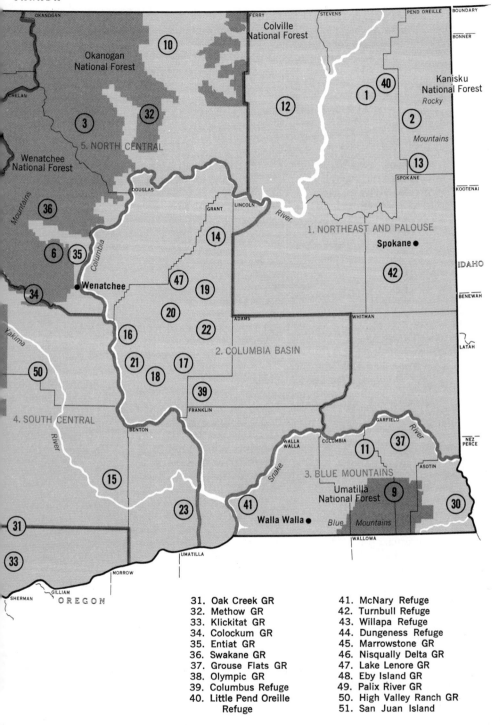

31. Oak Creek GR
32. Methow GR
33. Klickitat GR
34. Colockum GR
35. Entiat GR
36. Swakane GR
37. Grouse Flats GR
38. Olympic GR
39. Columbus Refuge
40. Little Pend Oreille
Refuge

41. McNary Refuge
42. Turnbull Refuge
43. Willapa Refuge
44. Dungeness Refuge
45. Marrowstone GR
46. Nisqually Delta GR
47. Lake Lenore GR
48. Eby Island GR
49. Palix River GR
50. High Valley Ranch GR
51. San Juan Island

of the east may be either hot and dry or chill and dry. By and large the climate is fairly temperate throughout, but altitude and proximity to the coast assure wide variety.

Arms and ammunition run the gamut, too, depending on the game. Deer hunters will need standard deer calibers. Elk hunters are far better armed with heavier ones, such as the several big-game magnums. Goat and sheep hunters need flat-shooting, hard-hitting calibers. Shotgunners can use No. 7½ and No. 6 as basic upland loads, with heavier shot for waterfowl and for wild turkey.

PHEASANT

Pheasant hunters are most numerous of all upland bird hunters in Washington, and the pheasant next to deer in popularity. The ringneck is the species. However, plantings have been made of both Reeves and green pheasants. Currently both are also legal. Both have been tried for several years on public lands where wild pheasants occur, and on some of the Public Shooting Areas. The Reeves pheasant may turn up as a trophy in the bag in the northeast and near Spokane, east-central. The green pheasant is presently stocked in the South Puget Sound Region, in Pierce, Thurston, and Lewis Cos.

The pheasant kill has for some seasons averaged close to 600,000 annually, with an average of 120,000 hunters participating. Region 2, the Columbia Basin, usually accounts for slightly less than half the entire state kill. Region 4, South Central, is second, with as much as one-fifth of the total. Region 1 is third, up in the northeast, and Region 3 in the southeast is fourth. South Puget Sound, Region 8, shows an average bag of possibly 25,000 birds, well above the other five not listed, but low compared to the foregoing. The lesser-kill Regions offer chiefly stocked birds, with wild stocks scattered and not dependable. See front material for counties in each Region.

All told, the Yakima Valley and the Columbia Basin are Washington's best pheasant areas, with Grant and Yakima Cos. showing highest consistent kills. Franklin, Adams, Whitman Cos. are next in line, with Spokane, Lincoln, Benton, and Walla Walla also important. While conditions may be somewhat crowded in these top areas, the programs (see opening of chapter) for making private land available to hunters are working well. Diligent, polite hunters have little trouble locating a place to hunt.

Here are listed a number of Public Hunting Areas, called Game Lands or more commonly Game Ranges, that offer fair to excellent pheasant shooting. While pheasants are not in general the primary species present, they are usually in good supply, the flocks in some cases enhanced by stocking. Regional offices of the Game Department, in Mt. Vernon, Seattle, Aberdeen, Yakima, Wenatchee, Ephrata, Spokane, Walla Walla, and Olympia can furnish detailed information and specific directions is to how to get to any of the Ranges in their area. Here only counties and acreages are given.

Sinlahekin GR (10), Okanogan Co., 12,491 acres; Tucannon GR (11), along border between Columbia and Garfield Cos., 11,286 acres; Sherman Creek GR (12), Ferry Co., 8086 acres; Little Pend Oreille GR (13), Pend Oreille Co., 43,395 acres. The foregoing are areas where deer or elk are the important species, with several upland bird species secondary.

The following tracts are all chiefly managed for waterfowl, but have pheasants next in importance. Banks Lake GR (14), Grant Co., 41,340 acres; Sunnyside GR (15), Yakima Co., 1639 acres; Quincy GR (16), Grant

Co., 12,210 acres; Potholes GR (17), Grant Co., 40,235 acres; Frenchman Hills GR (18), Grant Co., 3680 acres; Stratford GR (19), Grant Co., 5953 acres; Gloyd Seeps GR (20), Grant Co., 6022 acres; Winchester Wasteway GR (21), Grant Co., 1838 acres; Crab Creek GR (22), Grant Co., 20,918 acres; McNary GR (23), Walla Walla and Benton Cos., 8420 acres.

Note that all of the above are in the prime pheasant counties. In addition there are: Oak Harbor GR (24); Island Co., 589 acres; Lake Terrel GR (25), Whatcom Co., 1051 acres; Skagit GR (26), Skagit and Snohomish Cos., 12,164 acres; Shillapoo GR (27), Clark Co., 1456 acres; Oyhut GR (28), Grays Harbor Co., 682 acres; Johns River GR (29), Grays Harbor Co., 1137 acres. These are the tracts where stocked birds are more likely to be encountered.

QUAIL

Most quail hunting is done in eastern Washington. But on the whole quail are not especially popular with Washington hunters. This is unfortunate, since excellent quail hunting is available. Quail species are varied. The valley quail, sometimes called the California quail, is the important one. It is native to the coast and was established by introduction in eastern Washington, with most success in the southeastern quarter of the state. Bobwhite quail, nowhere native in the state, were also established thinly by introduction into eastern Washington. The mountail quail, found as a native along coastal mountains, is not especially plentiful. It was established by transplant in some mountainous areas of eastern Washington.

Quail in this state are not separated by species in the game laws. Seasons differ, however, between western and eastern Washington, with a long season in the east, a much shorter one in the west where quail populations are smaller. The total bag averages from 200,000 to 275,000, with fewer than 40,000 hunters participating. Leading counties in quail populations and kill are fairly consistent, and they are also rather scattered. Yakima, South Central, is a prime quail county. So is Okanogan, North Central, on the northern border. Whitman and Asotin in the southeast closely match these.

Some good areas by Regions are as follows. Region 1, in the northeast and east, the Snake and Palouse River drainages of Whitman Co., the Crab Creek drainage in southern Lincoln Co. Region 2, again the Crab Creek valley but in Grant Co., the Columbia River breaks below Grand Coulee Dam, the tri-city area in the south around Richland, Pasco, and Kennewick. Region 3, in the southeast corner, along the Snake, its tributary creeks and small rivers, and along the stretch of the Grande Ronde in the extreme southeast. Region 4, along the Yakima and its tributaries. Region 5, North Central, sagebrush flats and brushy draws near any of the main water courses, also most of the pheasant cover.

Although as noted, eastern Washington is best for quail, the islands of Region 6 in the northwest, such as Whidbey Island and the San Juans, usually hold good populations of valley quail. Region 9, in the south and southwest, offers good quail hunting in peak years in Klickitat Co., along the breaks of the Columbia, the Klickitat, and along Rock Creek in the eastern part of the county.

Some quail hunting is available on the State Game Ranges (Public Hunting Areas or Game Lands). The Asotin GR (30), southeast, in Asotin Co., 15,385 acres, offers good quail possibilities. Likewise for Sinlahekin GR ("Pheasant") in Okanogan Co. An extremely large one, Oak Creek GR (31), in Yakima and Kittitas Cos., 85,958 acres, is also good for quail hunting. So is Methow GR (32), Okanogan Co., 11,756 acres, and the Klickitat GR (33) in county of like name, 11,103 acres. One of the largest, Colockum GR (34), in Chelan and Kittitas Cos., contains 105,163 acres. Although quail are not a dominant species, much good hunting for quail is found in scattered portions. The Entiat GR (35) in Chelan Co., 11,343 acres, and the Swakane GR (36), same county, with 11,589 acres both offer fair quail shooting.

GROUSE

Several species of grouse are native to Washington. Blue, ruffed, and spruce or Franklin's grouse inhabit varying altitude levels in the mountains. Small flocks of both sharptail and sage grouse furnish a modest amount of hunting elsewhere. There are also ptarmigan, not currently listed in the game laws with an open season, above timberline in the Cascades. Grouse kills are not kept separate by species. A substantial interest is evidenced in the aggregate, however. An average of 250,000 to 300,000 grouse, total of all species, is annually harvested by some 90,000 bird enthusiasts.

Blue grouse are large grouse of high, timbered altitudes, in the Coast Ranges, the Cascades, the Blue Mountains of the southeast, and of mountainous sections of the northeast. Ruffed grouse are numerous but scattered, and range in the lower mountain altitudes, in alder and other thickets along the mountain stream courses. Spruce or Franklin's grouse live in the sub-alpine coniferous forests, and especially in the damper, more dense areas. There are some in the Cascades and in the extreme northeast. They are trusting birds, not very sporty. Blue and ruffed grouse are most popular. The sharptail is found in small numbers in the north, northeast, and east, in grass and brush areas east of the Cascades. To illustrate its present status, during one recent season the season limit was four birds. Sage grouse are found in extremely modest numbers chiefly in the southeast corner of the state. A season limit of two is average.

Surveys show Region 1, Northeast and Palouse River, as first in grouse kill. Region 10, the Olympic Peninsula vies for first, and is seldom far behind. Region 5, North Central, and Region 8, South Puget Sound, run about even for third place. This indicates a good grouse kill on the slopes of both Cascades and Coast Ranges. Lower Columbia, Region 9, in the south along the Columbia River, and North Puget Sound, Region 7, along the west Cascade slope in the north run fairly even for fourth and fifth spots. However, there is a fair to good grouse kill in all Regions except the Columbia Basin, which is top pheasant habitat. In variety and bird populations, Washington is an excellent grouse state, but hunting can be difficult in the mountain terrain. Three consistently good counties for the mountain species are Stevens in the northeast, Okanogan in the north-central, Lewis (Centralia and Chehalis are key cities) south of Puget Sound.

By Regions, here are a few choice locations.

Region 1: High country in Ferry, Stevens, Pend Oreille Cos. for blue grouse. Ruffed grouse in most of the northern portion of these counties. A few Franklin's grouse in northern Pend Oreille Co.

Region 2: This is sharptail and sage grouse country, with sage flats in Grant Co. and the region northwest of Coulee City in Douglas Co. best for sage grouse, and with sharptail prospects usually best in northern Douglas Co.

Region 3: Some blues in high areas of Blue Mts., ruffed grouse in brushy draws at lower elevations.

Region 4: All high areas in Yakima and Kittitas Cos. have limited number of mountain grouse.

Region 5: Sharptails are fair in Tunk Creek, Johnson Creek, Mount Hull areas of Okanogan Co. in sage adjacent to grain. Sage grouse appear in Mansfield and Withrow areas of Douglas Co. and elsewhere in this county. Blue grouse, which migrate up to higher altitudes in winter, are found in most high ridges during season. Ruffed grouse are in the brushy creek bottoms and draws. Spruce grouse in lodgepole pines at higher elevations. All told, Region 5 is a great area for hunting five grouse species on a single jaunt.

Region 6: Blues and ruffed grouse are both here, with Lake Shannon, Jackman Creek, Finney Creek, Deer Creek prime spots in Skagit Co., and Blue Mt., Sumas Mt., Maple Falls areas ditto in Whatcom Co.

Region 7: Both blue and ruffed along drainages of the Kitsap Peninsula; in King Co. there are huntable populations along the forks of the Snoqualmie and other streams. Numerous mountains and drainages in Snohomish Co. offer good prospects.

Region 8: Ruffed grouse are abundant in the upper Puyallup, and in the Black Hills and Winston Creek areas.

Region 9: The Grays River region of Wahkiakum Co., Yacolt Burn in Skamania and Clark Cos., drainages in Cowlitz Co. all have fair numbers of ruffed and blue grouse.

Region 10: Good grouse country for blues and ruffed grouse but seasonal. Black Creek, Grays Harbor Co., Nemah and Naselle area in Pacific Co., Snow and Penny Creeks in eastern Jefferson Co., and the Dickey area and the Sol Duc Burn in Clallam are among favorite places.

Sinlahekin Game Range ("Pheasant") has some grouse shooting. So does Methow GR ("Quail"), Sherman Creek GR ("Pheasant") and Little Pend Oreille GR ("Pheasant"). Two small GRs not previously noted that offer grouse are Grouse Flats GR (37), 640 acres in Garfield Co., and Olympic GR (38), 982 acres in Grays Harbor Co.

CHUKAR

In 1938 200 chukars were released in Douglas and Okanogan Cos. in north-central Washington. Continuing releases were made here for several years. Then in the '50s numerous other releases were made in Okanogan, Douglas Cos. and in neighboring Chelan Co. Meanwhile, the first season was held in 1949.

Washington was the second state to have chukar hunting. To date chukars have spread over a large area, from Wenatchee up the Columbia and the Okanogan to the Canadian border. Numerous valleys here contain excellent populations—along the lower Methow, the Similkameen, around Lake Chelan. Steep, dry areas of sage, scattered bunches of grass, and jumbles of rock are the prime chukar habitat. Washington authorities estimate they have at least half a million acres that are suitable. The birds are rather cyclic, with peak years and sudden lows.

Chukars have also been established in the southeast and south-central counties. There are excellent populations along the Snake, Grande Ronde, and Asotin Creek, for example, in the southeast corner of the state. This region is, in fact, one of the top areas in annual bag.

Annual total chukar kill has run from as low as 45,000 to a high of over 165,000. It averages around 100,000 birds, taken by an average of 25,000 hunters. By regions, best places are: Region 1, Snake River breaks; Region 2, Columbia River breaks in Franklin and Grant Cos., Snake in Franklin Co., Horse Heaven Hills, in Benton Co., from Coulee City to Quincy, Saddle Mountains, in Grant Co.; Region 3 (in preceding paragraph); Region 4, Columbia River slopes in eastern Kittitas Co., Rattlesnake Hills of Benton Co.; Region 5 (given in earlier paragraph for Okanogan Co., etc); Region 9, in Klickitat Co. along Columbia.

State Game Ranges offering chukar hunting: Asotin, Oak Creek, Klickitat, Colockum ("Quail"), Sinlahekin, Crab Creek ("Pheasant").

HUNGARIAN PARTRIDGE

The Hun has been established for some years over much the same range as the chukar. Huns are however to some extent more dependent upon grain. While they are hunted along with chukars, they do not really tolerate the more arid portions of chukar range. Few hunters are Hun specialists. The kill runs from 12,000 to 25,000 or more annually, with possibly 15,000 participant hunters.

In Region 1, north Lincoln, southeastern Whitman and southwestern Spokane Cos. have fair populations. Region 2 (Columbia Basin) birds are scattered and not numerous. Region 3, see "Chukar," and Region 4 likewise, but hunt close to water or grain for Huns. Region 9 has a few Huns in both Clark and Klickitat Cos. Kill surveys indicate that Region 1, Northeast & Palouse R., and Region 3, Blue Mountains in the southeast, offer best opportunities.

MOURNING DOVES AND BANDTAILED PIGEONS

Both the mourning dove and the bandtail are legal game and are present in substantial numbers. Neither draws heavy pressure. From 20,000 to 30,000 hunters pursue each sport annually. The bandtail bag averages around 150,000, doves about three times as many.

The North Central area (Region 5) and the South Central area (Region 4) have the highest dove bags, indicating that the birds follow the grain country out from the east slope of the Cascades. The Northeast (Region 1) is the third, also in farming valleys. The Columbia Basin (Region 2) has a modest kill. Other Regions rate much lower. Because of extreme mobility of the mourning dove, its dependence upon available food, and its rush to move south when inclement weather strikes, it is impossible to pinpoint good areas except broadly as above. Most dove shooting is on private lands, along stream courses and near or over harvested grain fields. Invariably the best dove hunting is during the first few days of September.

Bandtailed pigeons are birds of the mountains. They are plentiful along the coast and the slopes of the Cascades. Virtually all bandtail hunting is in western Washington. But they, too, are exceedingly mobile, whimsical regarding weather, and must seek food supplies. In Washington some favorite foods during hunting season are elderberries along the slopes, cascara, and dogwood. The birds also come into pea fields to feed. They seek mineral springs, congregate around them, making daily flights, and can at times be found flying to tidal flats along the coast. During a warm, dry fall the pigeons will stay chiefly in the higher mountains. Cool or wet weather will drive them lower, and also send them migrating south.

The Olympic Peninsula (Region 10), North Puget Sound (Region 7), South Puget Sound (Region 8) and the Northwest (Region 6) are the areas where bandtails are important game birds. Region 9, Lower Columbia in the south also generally has a fair kill.

Precisely where in each favored Region the birds may be during a given season cannot be guessed. However, each year the Game Department makes pre-season surveys of all game, and news releases are given out. Local newspapers in the bandtail counties offer this information, or one may contact the Department. The bandtail kill is ordinarily fairly consistent from season to season, but the flights of birds and their concentration places may change. If a hunt is planned, a check with the Game Department about two weeks prior to opening will result in specific information.

WILD TURKEYS

The wild turkey is not native to Washington. The Merriam's subspecies was introduced to several areas of eastern Washington in 1960. In 1965 the season was opened. There have been fall either-sex seasons since, and as this is written there is the possibility of a spring season also. A turkey tag is needed, but hunting is open to all, with no quota restrictions. An average of about a hundred birds per season have been bagged. Yellow pine areas of the east are the present habitat, with especially good results near grain-growing areas. There are currently huntable turkey populations in Stevens, Klickitat, Spokane, Chelan, Okanogan, Kittitas, Walla Walla, Columbia, and Douglas Cos.

Birds from Texas stock, of the Rio Grande subspecies, have been tried on some of the islands of western Washington—Protection, Orcas, and San Juan. Results appear very promising. It is believed that turkeys will eventually colonize all suitable habitats in the state.

WATERFOWL

There is excellent waterfowling in Washington. The annual duck bag averages from 600,000 to 800,000, with some seasons over a million. The goose kill runs from 40,000 to 60,000. Waterfowl interest among hunters is high. From 70,000 to 90,000 participate. All the management Regions of the state offer waterfowl hunting for both ducks and geese. The Columbia Basin, Region 2, has first place in both duck and goose kill. The Olympic Peninsula (Region 10), the Northwest (Region 6), North Puget Sound (Region 7), South Puget Sound (Region 8), South Central (Region 4), and the Northeast (Region 1) average fairly equal in duck kill, from 95,000 to about 150,000. The Northeast and Northwest are in second and third place as a rule for geese. The Olympic Peninsula and the Blue Mountain area of the southeast also turn up substantial goose kills.

The Columbia Basin is a natural for waterfowl, the flyway flocks surging down the Columbia and its many tributaries such as the Kettle, the Okanogan, the Wenatchee, and following in along the Snake from the east. Here in the Basin are several large impoundments and other lakes. Moses Lake and the Potholes Reservoir, southeastern Grant Co., form a huge resting place for both ducks and geese. To the north, the Coulee Dam region gathers in hundreds of thousands of waterfowl. The big buildup of waterfowl generally begins in earnest about November and continues on into December. One recent winter survey showed at the beginning of December a quarter-million ducks, predominantly mallards, and 30,000 geese from Coulee Dam to below

Moses Lake. As the goose season opened one recent season there were an estimated 55,000 geese on Stratford Lake in Grant Co.

Refuges throughout the Basin and elsewhere assist in holding birds. They offer hunting in the vicinity, and in some cases on portions of the refuges. The Columbia Refuge (39) is near Othello, in the Basin, in western Adams Co. It is a large acreage, draws heavy flights predominantly of mallards and Canada geese. Little Pend Oreille Refuge (40), over 40,000 acres, is near Colville, in Stevens Co., in the northeast. McNary Refuge (41) has its headquarters at Burbank, in the south almost to the Oregon border where the Columbia begins to turn to become the border. Turnbull Refuge (42) at Cheney, Washington, is in Spokane Co., southwest of that city. Willapa Refuge (43) has headquarters at Ilwaco, Washington, draws many Canada geese and also black brant. It is near the mouth of the Columbia River. Dungeness Refuge (44) is administered from Willapa. Hunters may contact Refuge Managers at the towns given for details of hunting on the refuges or in surrounding areas.

As mentioned earlier in the chapter, the Game Department manages a number of Game Ranges primarily for waterfowl. Excellent hunting is available on these. They are: Banks Lake, Sunnyside, Oak Harbor, Lake Terrel, Skagit, Shillapoo, Quincy, Oyhut, Potholes, Frenchman Hills, Stratford, Johns River, Gloyd Seeps, Winchester Wasteway, Crab Creek, McNary, all located under "Pheasant." There are in addition, small Marrowstone GR (45) in Jefferson Co.; Nisqually Delta GR (46) with 622 acres in Thurston Co.; Lake Lenore GR (47), 7690 acres in Grant Co.; Eby Island GR (48), 420 acres, Snohomish Co.; Palix River (49), 160 acres, Pacific Co.

Checking briefly by Regions, best in the state consistently is virtually all of Region 2 (Columbia Basin). Region 1 has declined late years (northeast and east), but there is fair although limited goose hunting along the upper Pend Oreille River and in southern Lincoln and Spokane Cos. Region 3 (Blue Mts.) has best shooting in the Walla Walla drainage, on the McNary GR, and with good goose hunting near Eureka and Burbank. Region 4 has many birds in the Yakima valley, but a lack of public hunting grounds for waterfowl. New lands recently acquired by the Fish and Wildlife Service offer some hunting along Toppenish Creek. Region 5, North Central, is not on the whole a top waterfowl area, but there is good late-season duck shooting on stubble lands in Okanogan Co., and good goose hunting along the Okanogan River.

Region 6 has fine shooting on the Game Ranges, and over croplands on Whidbey Island and Skagit Flats. Coastal black brant hunting, not so far covered, is excellent here, with best bet Padilla Bay and portions of the Sound. There is public access to Padilla at Bayview and March's Point. Regions 7, 8, 9, 10 have rather limited duck and goose shooting and in some cases all good shooting taken up by private clubs. Check locally.

Waterfowl hunters should not overlook snipe. They are abundant in marshy places on many of the waterfowling grounds. Few hunters try them, although a fair kill is bagged incidentally by duck and goose hunters— perhaps 30,000 a season. Avid snipe hunters number only about 5000. Region 6, Northwest, often has good snipe concentrations in salt marshes and on wet fields. Other shorebirds gather here, too, so a hunter must be able to identify his targets. In Region 8, South Puget Sound, there are plentiful snipe along the bottomlands such as Lincoln Creek, Chehalis, Nisqually, Hanaford. The public GRs in the Basin and elsewhere have good snipe flights.

DEER

Deer hunting is exceedingly popular. There are whitetails in some eastern counties, a scattering of the Columbian whitetail subspecies in a small part of the southwest. Eastern Washington's important species is the Rocky Mountain mule deer. The blacktail, a relative of the mule deer, ranges in the west, along the coastal mountains and the Cascades. The state deer herd probably numbers close to half a million animals. At least half are blacktails.

Total kill of deer averages around 60,000. Peaks of nearly 90,000 have occurred. Hunter numbers remain fairly stable, averaging around 220,000. Hunter success is excellent, from 30 to 35 percent. Deer are hunted in every Region of the state. The poorest is Columbia Basin. In general the Regions rate in order of kill about as follows: Northeast, North Central, Lower Columbia, Olympic Peninsula, South Puget Sound, Northwest, North Puget Sound. There is not any drastic choice among these, and deer herds have their ups and downs due to weather and other influences.

There is no great problem finding a place to hunt deer. As noted early in the chapter, there are millions of acres of National Forest lands, additional millions in privately owned forest lands open to hunters. The State Game Ranges add considerably to the total. While hunter pressure influences kills in any selected area, a fair idea of hunting quality can still be gained from checking figures of county kills and kills per square mile in any county during any season. Such statistics, compared to county area in square miles, can assist a hunter in selecting a spot.

For example, one recent season showed Island Co., area 206 square miles, with a kill of 1130 deer, or 5.48 per square mile! This obviously indicates an overpopulation. Some of the islands in the Sound do, indeed, have almost perennial overpopulation of deer. This shows in a kill of 5.06 per square mile the same season in small San Juan Co., another island county.

In alphabetical order, some counties with fairly consistent high kills per square mile are: Clark, Cowlitz, Kitsap, Klickitat, Lewis, Mason, Okanogan, Pacific, Pierce, Stevens, Thurston, Wahkaikum. In one survey these all had well over two deer per square mile harvested. Counties with slightly less, yet substantial kills: Asotin, Chelan, Clallam, Grays Harbor, Kittitas, Skagit. A few counties of large to extra-large size with high kills showing in the same survey: Chelan with a 5690 kill; Lewis and Klickitat each with over 5000; Okanogan, largest county in the state, with kill of 11,460; Stevens, almost 6000. Clallam, Cowlitz, Grays Harbor, Kittitas, Mason, Pacific, Skagit although varying broadly in size all had kills of from 2000 to over 3000. These figures give a good basic idea of where the deer are.

Hunters wishing to select a particular deer species or subspecies, should study the following figures. One season when 53,300 deer were killed, 31,700 were blacktails from an estimated blacktail herd of 210,000; 16,000 were mule deer, with a herd estimate of 160,000; 5600 whitetails came from an estimated herd of 55,000. Most seasons approximately 75 percent of the deer harvested are bucks. It is necessary that hunters acquire the Unit Map from the Department in order to orient their hunting. Each fall prior to season, usually about mid-September, the Game Department publishes last-minute surveys from each Region detailing herd conditions and the areas most likely to produce. Obviously these may change from season to season. The "Hunting Prospects" report is an invaluable aid to any Washington deer hunter. Pre-season queries to the Department about any specific Region will elicit most helpful replies.

ELK

There are two varieties in the state, the Rocky Mountain elk of the east, and the Roosevelt elk of the west. Both are considered originally native. The Rocky Mountain elk supposedly disappeared many years ago, was reintroduced in 1912. Although Washington gets little national publicity as an elk state, hunting is strikingly excellent. Annual kills have been steadily rising for many years. In one recent and exceptional season the total was 13,760. Elk hunting is popular. During that same season elk hunters numbered over 80,000. Hunter success of roughly 15 percent is established most seasons. The state elk herd is thought to number somewhere over 50,000 animals.

Although some Washington elk hunts are limited to permit holders, and are either-sex, an average total, all hunts, of three out of five animals taken are antlered. A hunter who draws a permit for a special hunt cannot apply again for three years. Most of the kill is during the regular bull season, open to all comers. Hunters after elk must familiarize themselves with the Unit map and with the carefully drawn regulations.

As with deer, there is no problem finding a place to hunt elk on public lands. The huge National Forests and commercial forests are by far the best of the elk habitat. While elk are hunted in a large percentage of Washington counties, they are by no means plentiful in all. Region 1 has a few, but extremely low kill. In that Region's Pend Oreille Co. there are a few moose and mountain caribou. Hunters should use extreme care in identifying targets. These animals are not legal game. Region 2 is not an elk habitat area.

Region 3, the Blue Mountains area of the southeast, is one of the four top areas, as a rule stands in either second or third place, with a kill of well over 2000 animals. This is a comparatively small Region, which indicates high success.

The high country and the slopes of the east Cascades with their expanses of National Forest and commercial forest lands in Region 4 form the best elk range in the state. This is chiefly in Yakima and Kittitas Counties. As many as 5500 elk have been harvested there in a single season. It is interesting to note that the first stocking of elk here was done in 1913, with fifty animals released in Yakima Co. and forty-five in Kittitas Co. Up through the 1965 season some 50,000 elk had been harvested from progeny of that original ninety-five. By now the total is considerably higher.

Region 5 is only fair, with the most animals in southern Chelan Co. A kill of 300 is considered high for the entire Region. The Northwest (Region 6) has an elk herd in difficult country on the south fork of the Noosack River and expanding from it. Second growth makes visibility poor. The kill amounts to only a few animals, chiefly because of the arduous hunting. Both of the Puget Sound areas, Region 7 and 8, have fair kills, with South Puget Sound best. The concentration of elk here is in Lewis Co. A recent kill during a high year was 910 elk for all of Region 8. Lower Columbia, Region 9, is a good bet, with kills ranging from 1000 to 1500 or better. Pressure is usually high in all of the west-Cascades ranges. Region 10, the Olympic Peninsula, is one of the three best in the state, with high elk populations in all counties along the coast and into the mountains—Clallam, Jefferson, Mason, Grays Harbor, Pacific.

While public hunting territory is not difficult to find, it should be noted that some of the State Game Ranges offer good opportunities. Asotin, Oak Creek, Colockum ("Quail"), Tucannon ("Pheasant"), Grouse Flats and Olympic ("Grouse") have elk as a primary game species.

There is a new, 100,000-acre State Game Range west of the Yakima River between Yakima and Cle Elum, called the High Valley Ranch (50), that elk hunters should not overlook. Deer hunters, chukar and grouse hunters should also make a note of this large expanse now owned by the state.

MOUNTAIN GOAT

The Cascades have a good population of goats and transplants have been made to the Olympic Mountains. Total goat population is estimated at 6000 to 8000. An average of 1000-plus permits are issued by drawing each season. Annual kill runs from 300 to 400 animals. Successful applicants cannot apply again for three years. Designated Units are open, with permits distributed to avoid concentration of hunters and to keep the goat population in balance. Washington has the largest number and kill of these animals of any of the contiguous states.

MOUNTAIN SHEEP

Bighorns, which disappeared from the state long ago, have been reintroduced from British Columbia. Between 100 and 200 animals are now estimated as a total population. Some of these are on the Sinlahekin Game Range in Okanogan Co. Others on the Tucannon GR in Columbia and Garfield Cos., and still more on the huge Colockum GR in Chelan and Kittitas Cos. A first season with a token number of permits by drawing was held in 1966. This was the first time since the early years of the century that sheep had been hunted in the state. A total of twenty permits was issued during a recent hunt. It is probable that token hunts for sheep may become regular fall occasions here.

OTHER HORNED AND ANTLERED GAME

There are a few moose and a few mountain caribou in Washington. Neither is presently of huntable abundance.

Antelope, once in the state but long erased, were reintroduced in the late 1930s. They did poorly. A few still hang on, and during 1968 a few more were brought in from Oregon and released in eastern locations. Antelope are not presently hunted. It is questionable if they ever will be.

MOUNTAIN LION

The mountain lion, or cougar as it is more often called in Washington, was finally made a game animal there in 1966. It is estimated that there are possibly as many as 500 to 600 in the state. Highest incidence appears to be in the Olympic Mountains, in Clallam and Jefferson Cos. Others are in the Cascades and scattered across northern Washington. Some counties have a 1-lion bag limit, others have none. Check with the Department. A guided hunt, with hounds, is practically the only successful hunting method. The Department can assist interested hunters in locating guides.

BEAR

Black bears are plentiful, in some regions to nuisance proportions. They can be extremely destructive to young trees on commercial and National Forests. The kill has been almost 9000 some years, but averages closer to

4000 or 5000. Hunters show an avid interest. Thirty thousand or more hunt bear each season. Western Washington currently has no bag limit but a tag is required, and there are stipulated seasons. In some counties there is a spring season beginning in April. In Clallam, Jefferson, Grays Harbor, Mason, and Kitsap counties, bears are at present classed as predators and unprotected. Eastern Washington has a 1-animal bag limit, and stipulated fall seasons.

Probably close to 30 percent of all black bears annually killed in the U.S. are bagged in Washington, which makes this the best black bear state in the Union. The Olympic Peninsula (Region 10) is by far the best location. The Northeast (Region 1) and Lower Columbia (Region 9) are next, and tie for second. North Central (Region 5), South Puget Sound (Region 8) and North Puget Sound (Region 7) are next in order.

There are guides with hounds in a number of Washington towns. Fees average around $100, but differ. Information about specific areas can be obtained from the Game Department. They can also assist in locating guides but of course cannot make recommendations. Numerous bears are killed as incidentals by deer and elk hunters. For a hunter specifically after bear, a good guide with a hound pack is practically mandatory.

RABBITS

The rabbit kill averages from 150,000 to 200,000, with possibly 35,000 hunters participating. There are cottontails, jackrabbits, and in the high country snowshoe hares.

Region 1 has fair snowshoe hunting in the northern part of the area, with cottontails plentiful along all drainages south of the Spokane River. In Region 2 the breaks of the Columbia and the Snake and Crab Creek Valley offer some of the best cottontail hunting. Region 3 hot-spot is along the Walla Walla River downstream from Lowden. There are snowshoes in small numbers in high areas of this Region. In Region 5, most brushy lowlands throughout the area furnish good cottontail shooting. In Region 6, thickets adjacent to farm lands are good cottontail cover in Island, Whatcom and Skagit Counties. Region 7 hunters evidence no great interest except incidentally, but there are both cottontails and hares present, especially along stream drainages. "Hare" may mean the Washington hare or coast brush rabbit, relative of the snowshoe. Region 8 has plentiful cottontails, with stocked cottontails doing well and expanding range in Thurston Co. Region 9 offers excellent cottontail populations along all the brushy stream courses where food is plentiful. Region 10 on the Olympic Peninsula has fairly abundant brush rabbits, or Washington hares. Though closely related to the snowshoe, they do not change to a winter coat of white.

There is unusual rabbit hunting on San Juan Island (51) in the northwest. Large Belgian hares were brought here years ago and are extremely plentiful. They weigh several pounds. The hares are such a nuisance and so prolific that there is no season, no limit, and no license is required. Night hunting with lights is not allowed. Lands here are almost entirely private. Hunting permission is not difficult to obtain, but there is traditionally a small charge.

OTHER ANIMALS, PESTS

There are bobcats, coyotes, foxes in varying abundance (Whidbey Island has excellent fox hunting), an occasional lynx in the mountains. Crows offer off-season shooting and in the east so do magpies. There are raccoons in many lowland regions. While there is no great interest in these animals, calling enthusiasts are growing swiftly in numbers. There are ample varmint species here to hunt.

REGULATIONS

Game laws pertaining to seasons, bag and possession limits, areas to be hunted, special hunts, license fees all may have numerous changes from year to year. For current regulations, and for other specific queries, write to: Washington State Game Department, 600 North Capitol Way, Olympia, Washington 98501.

Alaska
and the
Canadian
Provinces

ALASKA

To everyone living in the contiguous states of the U.S., Alaska has long been a kind of dream. Oddly, most sportsmen know more about it at least in a general way than they do about states in their own region. Occupying a vast area of the most northwestern portion of this continent, it is separated from the states to the south by Canada's British Columbia and the Yukon Territory. Alaska is at once a huge area of mainland, and a collection of islands.

Its terrain and its climate from region to region are exceedingly varied, and not always precisely visualized by those who have not visited the state. Beginning in the southeast, there is the so-called Panhandle. This is a narrow strip of coastline, islands, and fiords that might be described as geographically more properly a part of British Columbia. The climate here is rather mild, influenced by ocean currents, and the topography is comparable to that of coastal areas of Oregon and Washington. Here are fabulous, dripping rain forests, islands that heave up as rocky extensions of the mainland. This Panhandle may be considered a quasi-separate section of Alaska.

At the northern end of the Panhandle, Alaska's most massive and highest mountain ranges begin. They extend to the north and west, and curve in a tremendous arc around south and west at last to become a part of the Alaska Peninsula. This peninsula, streaming southwestward off that tip of Alaska, separates the Gulf of Alaska below and behind it, from the Bering Sea, and tapers off into the well known string of the Aleutian Islands. Within the great range described are series of mountains the names of which ring with romance for big-game hunters—the Talkeetna, Wrangell, Chugach.

Beyond this arc of towering mountains, to the north, lies the interior, with the Yukon River crossing east to west, and with scattered mountain chains in wilderness profusion. North of the Yukon Valley is the Brooks Range. It is this mountain barrier that separates the interior of Alaska from the Arctic. From the crown of Brooks, the terrain slopes down toward the Arctic Ocean.

Timber, oil, minerals, fisheries, furs are Alaska's chief industries. But this state differs from any to the south because the population is still so small that here is, indeed, true wilderness over hundreds of thousands of square miles. Roads are few, except the famed road leading there. The Alaska Highway up through Canada runs almost 2000 miles. A turn-off at Haines Junction leads to southeastern Alaska. Although roads are slowly being built and added to annually, at present the great share are those connecting Seward, Fairbanks, Anchorage. Others are being pushed out to smaller towns.

There is transport available via the 470-mile Alaska Railroad, connecting the cities named above. Timetables are uncertain, but hunters may arrange to be dropped and picked up again. Air transport is the most convenient and abundant means. A number of airlines take one into the state: Alaska, Pacific Northern, Pan Am, Scandinavian, Northwest Orient. Any travel agency in

731

any U.S. city can gather detailed information on flights. A good source of general travel information is the Alaska Travel Division, Box 2391, Juneau. There is also ferry transport up the coast from Seattle, or one can drive part way and ferry the remainder, from several ports en route. The Alaska Department of Public Works, Division of Marine Transportation, Box 1361, Juneau, will furnish information.

Almost all hunters going to Alaska will have booked guides or outfitters beforehand. It is important to book with one in the specific area of the hunt. In so large a state, guides from one region may be quite unfamiliar with another, or licensed to guide only in certain districts. The Alaska Game Department (address at end of chapter) issues a Guide Register listing master guides, registered and assistant guides. It states districts licensed in, gives addresses, species hunted, transport offered, and accommodations. From main airports where one may arrive, charter flights averaging around $20 to $35 per hour are available to get to the smaller places. From here bush pilots take one to the hunting grounds.

Alaska has been able to remain a great game area chiefly because of its size, remoteness, and lack of easy transport to every portion. This 49th State encompasses an area more than twice as large as the largest state (Texas) to the south. It spreads over 586,400 square miles. In this enormous area there are less than 300,000 people. These are of course concentrated almost entirely in the few cities and towns.

Hunters also are comparatively few. The average license sale runs only around 43,000. Although quite a number of nonresident hunters from southward make trips each year—approximately 3300 in a recent season— the major share of the licenses are held by residents. It is obvious that there is no crowding here. Nor is there any problem about public lands. Almost all of it is public. Game of great variety and in equal abundance is found almost everywhere. It has been estimated that among the big-game species there are probably well over a million head still today. Moose, caribou, Dall sheep, goat, grizzly, brown, black, and polar bears are the big-game species most commonly sought. There are also Sitka blacktailed deer, some elk in southern sections, plus bison and muskoxen. Seals and walrus are additional trophies.

While almost all nonresident hunters consider Alaska only for big game, there is excellent small-game hunting. Ptarmigan are abundant, there are blue, ruffed, spruce, and even sharptail grouse. Waterfowl, including ducks, geese, brant, are plentiful. There are snowshoe and Arctic hares, foxes, and trophies such as wolves and wolverines. Alaska is indeed still as close as one can come to the discovery of an unspoiled gameland.

The Game Department has divided Alaska for management purposes into (presently) twenty-six Management Units. Boundaries of course may change as deemed necessary. A map for the season in question is available from the Department, listing and describing these Units. The Units are placed in groups into five Guide Districts. These are as follows: A. Southeastern, Units 1 through 5; B. Southcentral, Units 6, 7, and 11 through 16; C. Southwestern, Units 8, 9, 10, 17; D. Central, Units 18 through 21, plus 24 and 25; E. Arctic, Units 22, 23, 26.

A study of this map is the beginning point for planning a hunt. But also one should carefully study the regulations for that season. Because of the variety of species, and the vast area, the laws are fairly complex. However, by checking the map and the regulations, and then studying the Guide Register, one can get a firm idea as to where and with whom he wishes to book a hunt.

This applies to many residents as well as nonresidents. While it is possible for many a resident to hunt deer or moose practically "in his backyard," others who wish to hunt species not in their area will invariably be better off, and more successful, with a good outfitter and guide.

Nonresidents are not required to have a guide for all hunting. As this is written guides are mandatory for hunting brown, grizzly and polar bear, and mountain sheep. This means either a registered guide, or a "relative within the second degree of kindred." And that phrase is defined as "relatives who are parents, grandparents, children, grandchildren, and siblings of the persons acting as guides." Without question all nonresidents will be well advised to hire registered guides. After perusal of the Register, one can then correspond with several, go on to contact references they give, and finally make a selection.

Basic expenses for those going to Alaska from the southern states can be gauged about as follows. From the East coast of the U.S. a round-trip flight will run between $600 and $700. From other points inland or from the northwest it will be progressively less. Charter flights mentioned earlier will add possibly another $100 to $200, depending on distance to the outfitter's scene of takeoff. Guide fees will average out, depending on services and quality of outfitter, from $50 to $150 per day. It is not always economical to see how cheaply the outfitter may be hired. Meals at restaurants in Alaska cost more than to the south, but hotel or motel charges are not very much above. However, with previously booked package hunts there is only minor need to consider these expenses.

Anyone going to Alaska must consider proper clothing as very important. Wet-weather gear and boots are mandatory. So are quality down and wool jackets and other warm clothing. Because terrain and climate differ radically from area to area and the climate from early to late seasons, it is best to go over in detail in correspondence with the outfitter precisely what wearing apparel and other gear he feels one should bring.

Rifles for big game should be of heavy calibers for the largest animals; magnums in the .300 or .375 category are commonly used for large bears and moose. Expert riflemen often do well, however, on most of the species with old favorites such as the .30/06 and comparable calibers. The 7mm magnum has done well recently on Alaskan big game. So has the .338. These calibers are given only as practical guidance. For deer of course the large calibers are not really needed. The best plan for a hunter new to Alaska is to take the advice of the outfitter beforehand as to what calibers he considers best for the game desired. In shotguns, gauges from 20 to 12 are fine, and loads can be as for grouse and ducks anywhere. A good compromise is No. 6 shot in express loads, with No. 4 short-magnum or No. 2 if any goose shooting is intended.

In the following material under species only rather general ranges of abundance will be given. What must be understood is that in a state so large, so sparsely settled, and indeed not even completely explored, it is not possible for game personnel to be aware of increase or decrease in many game populations widely separated. Many separate populations of individual species are not even hunted. The Department feels that in most cases the game populations in any given area are fairly static. But aside from general notes on what have proved to be good hunting areas for various big game, pinpoint locations are impossible to give. Success, and location of hunt, depend almost entirely on the guide. Also, where bird populations, for example, are concerned, only general ranges are known and annual harvest statistics in specific Units are not readily available.

To avoid disappointment, visiting hunters not familiar with the climate and the seasons should keep in mind that early openings such as in August may give a chance for enjoyment of fairly pleasant weather and excellent meat, but are not necessarily best for trophies among the big-game animals. To be sure that antlers are rubbed free of velvet and hardened, and that hides, such as goat, for example, are in prime condition, it is best to wait at least until September, even though a great many game seasons open as early as August 1.

UPLAND GAME BIRDS

Alaska can boast of seven members of the grouse family. There are three species of ptarmigan, the willow, rock, and whitetailed varieties. The willow ptarmigan, the state bird, is the largest of the three and the most abundant. The other grouses are the blue, spruce, ruffed, and sharptail.

The willow and rock ptarmigan are found throughout all of Alaska. However, populations are somewhat local and there are of course numerous areas where they do not exist. The whitetailed ptarmigan, a smaller bird, occurs in the Panhandle and the southeastern quarter of the main portion of Alaska. The high areas of the Alaska Range, the Kenai Mountains and the coastal ranges of the Panhandle are its home.

Ptarmigan are quite popular with resident hunters. Interest in big game among nonresidents overshadows the smaller species, but almost any big-game hunter coming to Alaska can get excellent ptarmigan hunting as a sideline activity. There are seasons in all Units, beginning in August and continuing through the winter and until the end of April. Presently limits are high, 20 per day, 40 in possession, and in the far northern Units there is no limit.

The willow ptarmigan, like all grouse, is quite cyclic, and reaches high population peaks followed by drastic declines. In coastal and foothill tundra it appears some years in startling abundance, and in winter often gathers in large flocks of a hundred or more. The rock ptarmigan lives in most instances in hilly regions above timberline. A few guides listed in the Register note that they specialize in ptarmigan hunting. However, most big-game guides will know areas within their Districts where ptarmigan are plentiful.

Generally speaking the ptarmigans, all three, are found most abundantly throughout country either beyond the tree line or above timberline. The coastal slopes and the far north, therefore, offer some of the best opportunities. These birds are not forest dwellers.

Next in general abundance and expanse of range is the spruce grouse. This rather naive grouse inhabits the evergreen timber area throughout the state. This means all of the interior and the north and south extremes of the Panhandle. It is lacking only on the western coastal slopes and the far north past the timberline. It is believed that at least one-half of the grouse harvest (among spruce, blue, ruffed, sharptail) in Alaska is made up of spruce grouse, or at least 25,000 to 30,000 or more. Most are bagged as incidentals by hunters after big game. Although this dark-meated grouse is not very sporty because of its inclination to tameness, it is good eating and is considered by the Game Department as a very important upland species.

The ruffed grouse and the sharptail grouse are found in the same general region in Alaska, although their habitat requirements are somewhat different.

They range throughout the Yukon River valley, and the valley of the Kuskokwim and their tributaries in the central and eastern interior. A few other local populations exist. The cover is broken, with openings, scattered deciduous hardwood thickets and shrubs, expanses of muskeg. Fires, land clearing, the changing of stream courses during floods all help to keep habitat suitable for these species. The sharptails will be found in the locations with much open area dotted with brush, and the ruffed grouse will be on the edges of the central-Alaska deciduous woodlands. Although both these grouse sustain some hunting, the pressure is light and probably the aggregate bag of the two is less than the kill of spruce grouse.

The blue grouse, largest of Alaska's uplanders, has the most restricted range. It is confined to the forests of the Panhandle. Only a small number are annually bagged. The kill is estimated at less than 2000. There has been experimentation in transplants of blue grouse to Kodiak Island.

It is interesting that grouse season (excluding ptarmigan) in the Panhandle Units runs as this is written from August 1 to May 15. These Units are of course in blue grouse range, and most of these birds are taken in spring during their "hooting" season. Their spring calls make them easy to locate in the timber. The Panhandle bag limit on the grouses, again not referring to ptarmigan, is lower than elsewhere, currently 5 per day. Elsewhere grouse season opens in August and runs into March. No hunting is allowed presently for any of the grouse family except ptarmigan in Unit 8, which is the group of islands that includes Kodiak east of the Shelikof Strait.

WATERFOWL

Vast numbers of waterfowl—geese, ducks, brant, snipe, sandhill cranes —breed in Alaska. Although there is some excellent waterfowl hunting, and far more is available that is never reached, the migration of most species results automatically in a very brief season.

The major species among ducks are mallards, pintails, baldpates (widgeons), green-wing teal, and shovelers. Canada geese, whitefronted geese, and black brant are abundant. Probably not over 100,000 ducks and 10,000 to 15,000 geese are annually harvested.

A large percentage of the brant that migrate down the Pacific Coast are produced in the delta of the Yukon and Kuskokwim rivers. Most brant bagged in Alaska are taken at Cold Bay, located at the base of the Alaska Peninsula. Far out at the end of the Peninsula there are large gatherings of brant, and of other waterfowl, prior to migration, and shooting here can be unbelievable, but of course the difficulty is in getting there.

Most of the waterfowl shooting of note is within the prime nesting areas: the Yukon-Kuskokwim Delta; the flats of the Yukon far upstream on the border between Units 20 and 25 between Fort Yukon and Stevens Village; the Copper River Delta in the southeast, which is quite accessible; the Minto Lakes area near Fairbanks. Of course, tens of thousands of birds that have nested on the huge coastal Arctic plain funnel down into these areas also during early migration.

The Stikine River Delta near Wrangell, which is well south in the Panhandle, is a gathering spot for migrating waterfowl as well as a nesting area. The Chickaloon Flats near Anchorage also are well known as a waterfowl shooting location. Some very good goose shooting can be had in the Cordova region on the Copper River Delta.

The fact is that waterfowl hunting has hardly had serious investigation over immense stretches of Alaska. Limits have been low and the season so brief before migration drains the birds away that only minor interest among hunters has so far been built up.

Lesser sandhill cranes have been legal game since 1961, with a 2-bird bag limit and 4 in possession. However, only a few hundred are taken each season. Snipe are plentiful on the wet flats where puddle ducks consort but there is little interest shown in hunting them.

EXOTIC GAME BIRDS

Both pheasants and chukar partridge have been introduced in various locations in experiments to attempt the establishment of local exotic bird populations. So far the experiments are not successful.

SMALL GAME

The only animals that can be considered in this category are the snow-shoe and Arctic hares. The Arctic hare is found in open tundra areas outside the tree limit, from the Peninsula north along the coast and across the Arctic. The snowshoe hare occupies the forested regions, but is most abundant in locations where the forest is not too dense. A few snowshoes are found down in the Panhandle on the river deltas outside the heavy timber. But they are by no means abundant, and here there is a stipulated season and a 5-a-day bag limit. Elsewhere throughout the state at this time there is no closed season on hares, and no limit. Transplants of snowshoes made some years ago have established this hare in Unit 8, the Kodiak Island group. There is no great amount of interest in hunting either species, but many are taken for food and as incidentals by hunters after other game. The total kill is probably not over 100,000 on the average in peak years.

DEER

The deer native to Alaska is a rather small relative of the mule deer, the Sitka blacktail. It was originally found only in the Panhandle. However, introductions have established it to the north and west on islands in Prince William Sound and on Kodiak Island. Estimates place the total deer herd at possibly a quarter million. The total annual kill varies from 10,000 to 20,000. At present and for some time a bag limit of 4 deer, either sex during part of the season, has been allowed in the Panhandle Units, and 3 in parts of Unit 8. The season extends over five months.

Hunting does no harm to the herd, but severe winters often do. The deer are driven down to the coast and confined to a rather small amount of range. Competition for food forces them some winters to eat seaweed, and starvation can take a heavy toll. The islands along the Panhandle generally have the highest population density of deer, but the deer on the Panhandle mainland are usually larger.

With the season opening August 1, deer extremely abundant, and the bag limit so high, this is a hunt that could be most interesting for numerous non-residents. Few avail themselves of it, however, because of interest in the larger species. There are a number of guides who specialize in deer hunting.

CARIBOU

The caribou is the most abundant big-game animal in Alaska and the most important, both for food and for sport hunting. The total herd is estimated at half a million animals, and the annual kill runs between 20,000 and 30,000. The species is the Barren Ground caribou. Although there have been reports of kills of woodland caribou in Alaska, none has ever been substantiated. A subspecies known as the Grant's caribou is found on the Alaska Peninsula. Over many years introduced reindeer, which are actually the domesticated caribou of Europe and Asia, have interbred with wild Alaskan caribou, but no detrimental effect has occurred.

The caribou of Alaska are separated into eleven fairly distinct herds. They are as follows. The largest is the Arctic herd of the western Arctic, and second in numbers is the herd of the eastern Arctic, the Porcupine herd, named after the Porcupine River. The Nelchina herd is third, and is estimated at 75,000 to 100,000 animals. This herd is fairly accessible to hunters because it ranges chiefly in the Talkeetna Mountain region north of Anchorage, in the area bounded by the Denali, Richardson, and Glenn highways and the Alaska Railroad. The herd fourth in size is called the Steese-Fortymile group. It winters across the line in Canada, but in Alaska is found in the triangle east of Fairbanks formed by the Yukon and Tanana rivers. This group is guessed at over 50,000 animals.

The other herds are much smaller. There is the McKinley-Minchumina herd, the Alaska Peninsula herd, Mulchatna-Rainy Pass herd, Delta-Wood River herd, Mentasta-Mount Sanford, Beaver Mountain, and Chisana-Wood River herds. Some caribou are scattered also in the Kuskokwim Mountains and near the Seward Peninsula.

For some years the kill of caribou, even with very liberal laws, has been far less than the natural addition to the herds. Most of the larger herds especially have been growing, and only some of the smaller ones have been kept stable by natural attrition. The caribou definitely needs more hunting, and game officials worry for fear it will outstrip its food supply. This will mean either that the herds, which are naturally seasonally migratory, must move, or will decline.

Although there are many local exceptions much of the caribou range where the largest groups are found is open all year to hunting. Hunters should check the current laws as to Unit exceptions, and these, because of the caribou situation, may change from year to year. The major share of the caribou killed annually are taken from the Arctic herds, mostly for food. The herd most easily accessible to the visiting—and many a resident—hunter is the Nelchina group, Unit 13. Along the Denali Highway here there is excellent hunting when the herd is on the move.

Other recommended areas are north of Mount McKinley National Park, portions of Unit 16, and of the Alaska Peninsula, which is Unit 9. The far north is of course excellent, for the Arctic herds are the largest. But the region is more difficult to get to, and the distance from civilization much farther.

MOOSE

The Alaskan moose is the largest of the species found anywhere in the world. It ranges over almost all of the state, from the Panhandle to the far north and along the Peninsula. Further, it has been extending its range into numerous sections where it was either rare or nonexistent a few years ago. The total herd is estimated to be at least 120,000. Moose hunting is exceedingly popular. As many as two-thirds of the paid license holders hunt moose each season, many for meat because of the size of the animal, and many for trophies. The kill averages from 8000 to 10,000.

Moose are fairly accessible to numerous hunters because they are commonly found along the railroads, the highways, and the rivers. Many live near the settled areas. Almost all Units are open, some for 2 moose, some for one of either sex, some for 1 bull only. At this writing only Unit 8 is closed. However, a careful study of the season regulations is mandatory because moose regulations are more complicated than for any other species. In some Units only specified portions are open. In many there is a split season, early and late.

Because moose are perhaps more evenly distributed over the state than any other big-game species, it is difficult to place one area as better than another. Hunting is excellent almost anywhere, but many good locations are not readily accessible. Aside from those who hunt the roads and railways on their own, and natives who hunt the river courses, most hunters will be guided and their chances of bagging a moose with any competent guide are excellent.

Some quality areas are the Lower Susitna (Unit 16), Nelchina (Unit 13), the southwestern part of Unit 20, portions of Unit 9 which is the Alaska Peninsula. The latter has recently been a 2-moose area. The far north, along the Brooks Range and the Arctic slope where moose are extending range is also very good.

As new roads are pushed through to remote areas, there will be virtually unlimited quality moose hunting. The Game Department estimates that a kill four times as high as at present can be sustained, given good distribution, without any harm to the moose population.

ELK

Many thousands of years ago elk were present in what is now Alaska. But that was in prehistoric times and elk were not native there in any modern era. In 1929 eight elk were brought from the Olympic Peninsula of Washington and transplanted to Afognak Island, which is in the Kodiak group. From that meager beginning elk established themselves there. Now there are somewhere between 1200 and 2000 elk on the island. In the early 1960s small transplants were made to an island off the Panhandle. There had been attempts in the southeast at about the same time as the Afognak stocking, but they were unsuccessful.

Whether or not the off-shore islands of the Panhandle will ever have elk hunting cannot now be predicted. But there have been elk seasons for some time to trim the herd on Afognak. The island is reached only by plane or boat, and fall hunting weather can make that precarious. In addition, getting to the elk herd, and getting a kill out, is a formidable task. Recently the season, which continues for five months beginning on August 1, has allowed 1 elk on most of the island and 2 elk on the Tonki Cape portion in the northeast. This is in Unit 8.

Only an average of 150 to 300 hunters make the attempt, and there are from 75 to 150 elk killed each season. Trophy hunters who are determined may indeed find some very large bulls here.

MOUNTAIN GOAT

The range of the mountain goat in Alaska is throughout the coastal mountains beginning at the southern end of the Panhandle and extending northward to the Talkeetna Mountains which lie north of Anchorage. Probably the entire goat population does not exceed 15,000. Transplants have been made to Kodiak Island, and to Baranof and Chichagof islands off the Panhandle.

At this time Units 1, 4, 5, 6, 7, 11, 13, 14, 15 (some in whole, some in part only) have open season, most allowing two goats. The season in all 2-goat Units is long, from five to six months. The kill, even with the 2-animal limit, is well under a thousand animals, most seasons probably about 600. There does not seem to be high interest except by trophy hunters, most of them nonresident.

Opportunities are excellent. Most of the goat population is within a modest distance of salt water and hunting via boat is a good way to spot trophies and then climb after them. The hunt, however, can be rugged. The Game Department to date has not shown any great interest in development of goat hunting, or in major transplants to new areas, probably because the mountain goat is, for hunters going long distances after larger trophies, to some extent at the bottom of the horned-game list.

MOUNTAIN SHEEP

The white Dall sheep is the most sought of all Alaskan trophies. It is the only wild sheep of Alaska, so far as is presently known. The Stone sheep, a gray or blackish subspecies, is found in British Columbia and the Yukon in mountain ranges adjacent to Alaska. But to date so far as is known none have been killed in Alaska.

The handsome Dall sheep ranges throughout most of the state's high mountain ranges except in the Panhandle. The Alaska Range and the northern end of the Aleutian Range, both of which lie northwest from Anchorage roughly in Units 19 and 16, offer a large sheep population. The Talkeetna Mountains, the Chugach, the Wrangell Mountains, all in the southeast region, are all famed sheep hunting locations. The Kenai and White Mountains, the Tanana Hills also furnish excellent opportunities. In the far north, the Brooks Range, though more difficult of access, has a large sheep population.

The estimated total sheep population is about 40,000. Seasons in various Units fall during August and September and only rams with three-quarter curl or larger may be shot. This means that rams must be at least five years old. An average season sees about 900 trophies collected. By far the majority of hunters go into the ranges in the Anchorage and Fairbanks areas and these southeastern mountains produce a high percentage of the kills. However, this is simply because access is easier. The far-northern Brooks Range is an excellent location. Chances of success in Dall sheep hunting are estimated to be about 25 percent. Nonresidents must be guided.

BISON

In 1928 twenty-three Montana bison, or buffalo, were transplanted to Alaska, on a range southeast of Fairbanks, the Delta-Clearwater area. It was hoped that a herd numbering in thousands might develop. The range, however, could not support more than a few hundred, as was evident over a period of years. Surplus animals have been hunted in special hunts, and some have been given to homesteaders who wished to try to establish them. Some others from the Delta herd were moved to the Chitina region to help establish a modest herd launched in 1950 from another stocking. This is now called the Copper River herd. There may be other small herds established elsewhere.

Hunts are set up only after careful surveys. During the first hunt, in 1961, fifty permits were issued. There were several thousand applicants. In a season just passed, removal of 10 mature bison from the Copper River herd was authorized. Interested hunters should contact the Game Department for details during any given season.

MUSK-OXEN

These curious animals were once native to what is now Alaska. They became extinct there over a hundred years ago. Thousands of miles away, in Greenland, there were existing herds, and thirty-four animals were brought from there to Alaska in 1930. A few years later, with only thirty-one animals remaining in the area where they had been held for observation near Fairbanks, the herd was taken to the National Wildlife Refuge on Nunivak Island which lies off the west coast, in Bering Sea, offshore from the Yukon-Kuskokwim Delta. Here over the years the herd did well, building to about 500 animals.

In 1964 a small herd was brought to the University of Alaska for experiments in domestication. Later more animals were brought to the mainland for the purpose of trying to establish a wild herd, with the hope that a harvestable surplus would eventually develop. It is therefore quite possible that limited hunting for musk-oxen may occur. As this is written there is no open season.

BEARS

Alaska is perhaps more famous for its bear hunting than for any other facet of sport. The huge brown and grizzly bears have long been coveted as trophies, and so have the polar bears. Black bears, while extremely plentiful in some locations, were until a few years ago classed as fur animals and far overshadowed in popularity by the larger species. The rare blue color phase of the black, called the glacier bear, also is found in the state.

The black bear, with total population estimate of around 20,000 and an annual bag of 1000 to 1500, ranges the timbered regions of Alaska. None are present on most of the southeastern islands north of Frederick Sound, nor are blacks found on the Aleutians or other islands beyond Prince William Sound. In the extreme southeast, Prince of Wales Island has a high black bear population. The same is true of the Kenai Peninsula.

The blue, or glacier color phase, is found in the extreme northern part of southeastern Alaska, in the region of Icy Cape and the Tyndall Glacier southeastward toward and inland from Yakutat Bay. Like the brown or cinnamon color phase of the black, these blue phases may be born in any litter, but apparently are not at all common. Only a very few are taken in any season. This is considered a rare and desirable trophy indeed.

Hunting for black bear, especially via boats that cruise the coastal locations with high density bear populations, is a sport worthy of more attention than it gets. This is particularly provocative because of the high bag limit. In most Units it is three. As this is written Unit 6 is restricted to two. In no Unit can more than one of the limit be a glacier bear. Spring hunting is possible, and the best time. The season runs through the end of June.

The huge brown bear and the grizzly, which scientists and hunters have argued about for years as to whether they were or were not different species or subspecies, are among the world's most sought big-game trophies. They are treated here, as they are in Alaska's game regulations, as one. Nonresident hunters must be guided to hunt them. Ordinarily bears of the interior and north are called "grizzlies," the larger coastal bears "browns." Records are established by geographic distinction also.

The total population estimate is placed at possibly 10,000. The annual kill averages around 600, split about evenly between resident and nonresident hunters and likewise between fall and spring hunting. Not all open Units allow spring hunting. Where it is possible, it usually offers the best chance of success. The chances of bagging a trophy brown or grizzly are difficult to predict, but they probably average around 25 percent and perhaps a bit better than that.

These large bears are found over virtually all of Alaska except the islands of the extreme southeast. About 75 percent of the annual kill comes from south-central Alaska. The remainder is split about evenly between southeastern Alaska and the interior and Arctic areas. In the far north the Brooks Range is a good location. The most popular hunting regions, chiefly because of the enormous size of the bears, is on the Alaska Peninsula (Unit 9) and on Kodiak and Afognak islands (Unit 8). Numerous outfitters have had a great deal of experience in these regions over the years and thus their knowledge gives guided hunters a better than average chance of success.

Popular bear hunting has been done for some years by plane, with hunters flown out mainly from Kotzebue, Point Barrow, Teller, Point Hope, Wainwright, going on the average upwards of seventy miles from the coast in order to find bears. Recently there has been much concern about the status of this huge bear of the ice. No one really knows how many are left in the world. And, bears born in Alaska it is thought may wander, and float on ice packs, for many thousands of miles.

Guesses have been made that perhaps as many as 20,000 polar bears still roam the Arctic world. A worldwide cooperative study is now underway to attempt to find out more about how precarious the position of the polar bear may be. The Alaska kill has run over past years an average of 150 to 250, sometimes higher. Many restrictions have been imposed. It is not impossible that polar bear hunting may be stopped for some years, or at least greatly restricted. The animal has been removed from the trophy list by the Boone & Crockett Club to discourage hunting. The present undetermined status makes it mandatory that hunters desiring to book a polar bear hunt—an expensive undertaking—check many months ahead with the Alaska Game Department as to what the situation may be.

MARINE MAMMALS

The walrus is an inhabitant of the Bering and Chuckchi seas along the western shores of Alaska. Whether the walrus should be considered a game animal is questionable. Residents may take walrus, with no closed season at this time, with no limit on bulls and with a fairly high limit on cows. These animals are taken for their commercial value. Occasionally a nonresident hunter desires to bag a walrus as an unusual trophy. Though there is no closed season, the limit is one adult bull. Probably not more than an average half dozen are collected in any year. Some traditional hunting centers, where spring hunting is best, are Diomede, King and St. Lawrence islands. Point Barrow and Point Hope hunters operate in summer. A few guides specialize in walrus hunting. The Units where walrus occur along the coast are 18, 22, 23, 26.

Beluga, sea lion, porpoise, and various seals also are covered by the game laws. While these animals are hardly game in the true sense, some hunters go after trophies, or the unusual hunting experience. It is best to study the regulations carefully and to correspond with the few outfitters who book such hunts. The beluga or white whale is utilized for food. There would seem to be no purpose whatever in killing the several porpoise species that range the Alaska coast.

OTHER ANIMALS

Wolves are numerous in portions of Alaska. So are wolverines. Both are now on the game list, although in the regulations booklet they are listed under fur animals. Both are considered by many big-game hunters as trophies, and are rather eagerly sought as incidentals during big-game hunts. Guides handling spring bear hunts offer wolf or wolverine as extras. There is a substantial amount of interest in aerial wolf hunting.

A number of Units have no closed season on wolves. In others aircraft hunting, ground hunting, and trapping each have specified seasons. Wolves range over most of the state, excepting the south-central and southwestern islands. Presently several hundred are taken annually by all methods.

The wolverine ranges as widely as the wolf but is by no means as abundant. Of several hundred taken each year, most are trapped. There is no limit, but there are differing specified seasons in a number of Units.

The red fox (and its color phases) is widely distributed. The white Arctic fox, and its blue color phase, is found coastally from the Aleutians on north. These are considered fur animals, and are trapped, during specified seasons. Some Units have no closed season. Occasionally a hunter collects one or another as an extra trophy.

There are some coyotes, but they are not numerous. Oddly, until the 1900s there were no coyotes in Alaska, or at least none were known to be present. During the early part of the century they came into the region and spread over almost all of the territory. After reaching a peak, the population leveled off and today, though not uncommon, they are nowhere populous.

The lynx reaches high peaks when hare cycles are up, and declines when the hares decline. Several thousand are taken annually by trappers. Hunters should be aware that there are specified seasons by Units for lynx, coyote, foxes. Thus they may not be indiscriminately shot. It is illegal to take sea otter at any time, anywhere.

REGULATIONS

Address all communications relative seasons, limits, licenses· and other queries to Alaska Department of Fish and Game, Subport Building, Juneau 99801.

YUKON TERRITORY

The Yukon Territory gained permanent worldwide fame in the late 1800s when the greatest gold rush of all times sent thousands of persons to Bonanza Creek and the Klondike River. The teeming activity was the spark that launched development of this northwesternmost portion of Canada. Soon there were steamers on the Yukon River, then came the Skagway to Whitehorse railway, and finally, in the early 1940s, there was the World War II rush to construct the Alaska Highway, which runs across the southern part of the Territory. All these developments joined over the years to make this remote land rather well known, at least in small part and by name, to thousands of Americans.

The Yukon borders Alaska on the west, the Northwest Territories on the east. The southern border is with northern British Columbia. The Territory is a rough triangle, its base to the south. The narrow, squared-off apex lies along a hundred miles of the shore of the Beaufort Sea, which is actually a part of the Arctic Ocean. The Yukon covers 207,076 square miles. The southern half is well forested with spruce, pine, and fir. As the conifers decline northward, the terrain is covered by low scrub, and this extends north until the tree line appears and the land continues as tundra on to the Arctic Ocean shores.

Much of the tundra area is flat to gently rolling. But the Yukon over much of its area is mountainous, and everywhere slashed by large rivers and their consequent valleys. Mightiest of these ranges is the St. Elias, in the southwest. Here are Canada's highest peaks, with Mount Logan soaring to just under 20,000 feet, Mount Elias to cover 18,000, Mount Lucania to above 17,000, and lesser peaks to 13,000 and 14,000. Here, too, in the south, are portions of the game-famous Cassiars. Other ranges—Pelly, St. Cyr, Campbell, Logan—march eastward across the southern portion of the Territory, and much of the eastern border with the Northwest Territories is marked by high ranges, the Selwyn and Richardson.

Production of gold, silver, lead, zinc are the chief activities of the Territory. Population is low, presently only about 15,000. There is of course no problem about public lands for hunting. Very little farming is done, due to severe climate and poor soil. Only small amounts of land are in private ownership. Except for Parks and Game Sanctuaries, residents may hunt anywhere. Nonresidents, both Canadians and aliens, are somewhat more restricted. The Yukon is not divided into Management of Game Zones, as occurs in the Northwest Territories. Rather, there are regions assigned to outfitters as their Registered Guiding Areas. Since a nonresident must book hunts (for big game) through an outfitter, and be accompanied by a registered guide, the result is that he is restricted for his hunting to the Area assigned to his outfitter.

Presently there are twenty-two Registered Outfitters, all of whom live in the Territory. A list is available from the Director of Game. There is also a map available which shows the assigned areas with the outfitters' names on them. Thus a person planning a hunt can first check the map to ascertain about where he wishes to hunt, and then contact the proper outfitter.

Transport into the Yukon, and within the Territory, is rather good, considering the remoteness of the region. One may drive via the Alaska Highway, entering from British Columbia at Watson Lake and traveling west and northwest to Whitehorse, Haines Junction, and to Beaver Creek on the Alaska border. Other roads reach north to portions of the southern interior and to Dawson. To date there are about 1300 miles of highway within the Territory. Eventually the now-planned Dempster Highway will reach from southeast of Dawson clear up across the northern interior and to Fort McPherson in the Northwest Territories.

Bus travel is also possible, from Edmonton, Alberta, and on north, and there are scheduled bus runs via Coachways Ltd. within the Yukon. However, most visiting hunters, and resident hunters also, will prefer to save time by utilizing air transport. Canadian Pacific offers daily service from Edmonton, Alberta, and from Vancouver, British Columbia, and scheduled flights to principal settlements within the Territory. Great Northern Airways Ltd. at Whitehorse has both charter and commercial inter-territorial flights. Once the sportsman has arrived at his commercial flight destination, then of course the outfitter takes over to fly him to his hunting area.

At the present time the major share of the Outfitter Areas are spread across the south and the central parts of the Territory. Only six Areas lie north and northeast of Dawson, and the Peel River in the mid-north is roughly the line at which Outfitter Areas cease. With the small population, one must bear in mind that most settlements are indeed small. Whitehorse, the largest, has roughly 5000 people, Dawson about 1000. Thus it is a good idea to go well supplied with basic necessities. Although summers are mild, and in the valleys even with rather hot days, the summers are also brief. Hunters will need the best in warm garments, footwear, and sleeping bags. Rifles for big game should be heavy, and it is a good idea to take advice of the outfitter as to what to bring. Since there is also some bird hunting, in proper season, it is a good idea to take a shotgun along. If one will be there before cold weather, ample insect repellent, to stave off attacks of mosquitoes and black flies, is a must.

Seasons for big-game begin either August 1 or August 15 and run through all or part of November. There are also spring seasons during April, May, and June, for both black and grizzly bears. Hunting for blacks is good, and for grizzlies fair. The Yukon grizzlies are known as a tough, cantankerous strain, not always huge, but often short tempered. There are polar bears along the northern coast, but only Eskimos are allowed to hunt them.

Other big-game includes moose and caribou, hunting for both of which is considered good. Only bull moose may be taken. In the mountains, especially in the south, there are Dall and Stone sheep. Rams only are legal. Sheep populations are plentiful and hunting chances good. There are also some mountain goats, but hunting is considered only fair. Caribou are abundant, and though migratory offer high chances of success dependent upon time and place. All the big-game species inhabit the major share of the entire territory. However, caribou predominate in the north.

Game birds include seven species of grouse: blue, spruce, ruffed, and sharptail, plus three varieties of ptarmigan, the rock, willow, and white-tailed. Sharptails are not abundant, except in scattered portions of the south. Blue, spruce, and ruffed grouse are found in the mountains. The blues are scattered in large timber and openings, ruffed grouse in the stream bottoms and brushy areas of the slopes and along the creeks, spruce grouse in dense stands of conifers, often in boggy locations. The several ptarmigans may be found almost anywhere in the open areas of high altitudes. The season for ptarmigan, sharptail, and spruce grouse is long, the five months beginning September 1 and extending through January. Blue and ruffed grouse may be hunted during September and October only. There are also abundant waterfowl—ducks, geese, snipe.

In addition to the above, there are plentiful snowshoe hares, and in the far north Arctic hares. These may be hunted at any time and without limit. The same is true for wolves, coyotes, and wolverine. But a hunting license must be in possession.

A fair picture of the wide-open wilderness hunting without any severe pressures anywhere may be gained from a brief study of average license sales and game-kill figures. During a recent season 2142 resident hunting licenses were sold. Resident trappers and natives numbered 429. Resident bird-hunting licenses were only 75. Nonresident hunters for birds only: 25. Nonresident alien big-game hunters numbered only 238, and there were only 3 non-resident alien spring bear hunters. Canadian nonresident big game: 37.

Although survey figures are not broken down by license types, total license sales in any game category, compared to total kill figures, illustrates chances of success. Bear in mind that nonresidents, guided by professionals, often gain a higher percentage of success than resident hunters on their own. During the same year noted for license sales above, there were 252 sheep bagged. Moose numbered 801, caribou 983. The goat kill indicates only fair abundance of these animals, plus rugged hunting. There were 45 killed. Bears were as follows: grizzlies, 80; black bears, 120. Game bird figures are given in aggregate among certain species. The total of timber grouse (blue, ruffed, spruce) and sharptails was 7608. Ptarmigan of all species: 1255. Ducks: 4783. Geese: 332. These figures do not of course reflect kills by natives living in part off the land, but only the kill which was mostly for purposes of sport.

There are some deer in the south and west. They appear to be making progress in building herds. But winters are difficult for them. Hunters should know that deer have full protection at this time. Elk also have been stocked, and so have buffalo. These, too, appear to be making slow buildups. But they, too, are fully protected.

License fees remain stable at this time, and are as follows. Resident, big game, and bird, $5, birds only, $2, general hunting and trapping, $5. Eskimos and Indians are given free licenses. Nonresidents, big game, and bird, $50, nonresident alien, $100. That license entitles the holder to two big-game trophies only. Additional trophies require a permit of $25 each. Spring bear licenses are $25 for British subjects, $50 for aliens. Birds only, nonresident: $10.

Some publications useful to prospective hunters are as follows: "Alaska Highway, Road to Yukon Adventure" is a booklet with numerous facts published by the Canadian Government Travel Bureau, Ottawa. "Your Yukon Guide to Outdoor Recreation" may be obtained from the Travel and Publicity Branch, Yukon Territorial Government, Whitehorse, Yukon. Another folder, "Facts About Canada's Yukon" is available from the same address.

Questions regarding game laws, seasons, outfitters and all other specific hunting queries should be addressed to: Director of Game, Yukon Territorial Government, Game Branch, Box 2703, Whitehorse, Yukon Territory, Canada.

NORTHWEST TERRITORIES

For the hunter, Canada's Northwest Territories hold a tremendous potential for the future, a sports resource only meagerly tapped to date. Only a very small portion of the vast region is presently open to non-residents, alien or otherwise. Native hunters, such as Eskimos and Indians, who must often live from the land, have first call on game resources. Resident sportsmen, who are few in number, come next. Nonresidents at this time may hunt only in two of the thirty-six Game Zones into which the Northwest Territories are divided.

This enormous region covers more than a third of the entire area of Canada. It takes in all lands (and water areas dividing some of the lands) north of the 60th parallel, excepting only the much smaller Yukon Territory, and the far northern tip of Quebec. This is a region of over one and one-quarter million square miles. To give a comparison so that one may at least partially visualize what that expanse means, these Territories are larger than half of the continental United States. Within that almost boundless Arctic there are currently only about 32,000 people, counting Eskimos, Indians, and other Canadians.

There is a high mountain range, the Mackenzie Mountains, along the western border, which on the mainland is entirely with the Yukon Territory. East of these mountains, mainland N.W.T. is a high plain that eases gently down toward Hudson Bay far to the east, and toward the far flung Arctic Archipelago to the northeast. There are other high mountains hundreds of miles distant from the mainland, along the eastern edges of Ellesmere, Devon, and Baffin islands. But hunters are hardly concerned with these remote lands, for few residents ever get that far, and no nonresidents are allowed to hunt there. To the south of the Territories, the boundary line is with the northern boundaries of the northeast British Columbia, all of northern Alberta, Saskatchewan, and Manitoba. Hudson Bay and Hudson Strait separate the Territories from far northern Ontario and Quebec.

At about the mouth of the Mackenzie River at the edge of the Arctic Ocean is the northern tree limit. The line runs in a southeasterly direction diagonally down across to Hudson Bay in northern Manitoba. Thus almost all of the mainland portion of the northeast N.W.T. is tundra, with countless lakes, and muskeg swamps. It is the region of the west in the Mackenzie Mountains area, however, west of the Mackenzie River, with which this chapter is chiefly concerned. For here is the relatively small expanse, of possibly 60,000 square miles of forest, steep slopes and river valleys, where visitors may hunt. Undoubtedly other Game Zones will be opened eventually. But there is not likely to be any swift expansion for years to come.

The two Zones in which visitors may arrange hunts are No. 12 and No. 19. The western boundary of each is the border with the Yukon Territory. In the northeast portion of No. 19, the northernmost of the two, the Mackenzie River forms a portion of the border. But other, narrow Zones are sandwiched to the west of the River from here on south. It is therefore mandatory that hunters acquire a map showing the two open Zones, before attempting to plan a hunt.

These Zones are roadless. There is a road under construction from Fort Nelson, British Columbia, running up to Fort Simpson on the Mackenzie, and beyond. There are also comparably short stretches of road farther east. One may, for example, drive to Hay River on the south shore of Great Slave Lake via the Mackenzie Highway, coming up from the south via Edmonton and Peace River, Alberta. This same highway continues on to the teeming small industrial settlement of Yellowknife. However, few visiting sportsmen will wish to drive so far only to have to fly in to their hunting grounds.

Air travel is efficient. Connecting with such national and international major Canadian terminals as Edmonton, Winnipeg, and Montreal there are regularly scheduled flights into the Territories, to main points like Yellowknife, and there are flights from these to outlying settlements. In addition charter craft are available to anywhere a hunter may wish to go or be legally allowed to go. For details, write TravelArctic, Yellowknife, N.W.T., Canada.

Traditionally the right to hunt in the N.W.T. was reserved for those who were long-time residents, plus the native Eskimo and Indian. Game has long been considered here a necessity for food. Sport was wholly secondary, and in fact sport hunting, for outsiders, has just been opened up during the past few seasons. Currently there are only an average of 3500 General Hunting Licenses issued annually. These allow the native hunter to take any game with very little restriction, anywhere. Other residents— a resident is construed now as one who has lived for an entire year in the N.W.T.—may hunt game birds, predators, small game anywhere in the Territories that seasons dictate. But for them big game, excepting caribou, has close restrictions by Zone and season. The nonresident, Canadian or alien, may hunt as noted only in Game Zones 12 and 19.

Such hunters must employ big-game outfitters. The outfitter in turn supplies guides, or does the guiding himself. The government of the N.W.T. will furnish a list of outfitters. As this is written there are only six outfitters licensed to operate in Zone 12, the southernmost of the two. All of these live outside the N.W.T. There are two who operate in Zone 19, one living in Yellowknife, the other in Inuvik, to which regular air flights reach.

License application forms are available either from the outfitters or from the government. For nonresident Canadians, the big-game hunting license is presently $100. Other persons: $150. There are no trophy fees. On the back of the folder listing outfitters is a sketch map of the two open Zones.

To give an idea of how remote these lands are and how minimal the hunting pressure, license sales average about as follows. Resident big-game, 350; resident bison, 50; resident game bird, 725. Nonresident licenses average: Canadian, big-game, 15; alien, big-game 150; Canadian, game bird, 135; alien, game bird, 30.

Quite obviously there is no problem in locating a place to hunt. The problem is one of accessibility, bookings with outfitters, and lack of exploration. Private ownership of lands in the N.W.T. is infinitesimal. Aside from that, and a few areas of Game Sanctuaries, all lands may be classed as public hunting lands. Hunters obviously must go well equipped with heavy rifles, and with the best equipment and clothing for severe low temperatures. Of the region open to visitors, only the Nahanni River Valley, where hot springs are found as well as a falls over 300 feet high, has been to any broad extent explored. This is in the southern part of Zone 12.

Seasons for big game open August 1 and run through November. The species in the two open Zones are black bear, grizzly bear, moose, caribou, Dall sheep, mountain goat. The sheep and goats are found predominantly in the western portions, in the Mackenzie Mountains, which run up to 9000 feet. There are areas of dense forest between the mountains and the river. Numerous other additional Zones are open for the resident, and contain the same game, with one addition: there are wood bison in certain localities, open to resident hunters on a special permit.

Some kill figures from a recent season may help give a basic picture. Counting all licenses—including native—big-game kills were as follows: caribou, 15,838 (mostly taken for meat); deer, 2; moose, 1355; goat, 1;

Dall sheep, 165; bison, 88; bears (aggregate of both varieties) 428. Although Zone 12 has been open to nonresidents since 1965, Zone 19 has more recently been opened. Kill figures for nonresidents, Zone 12, averaged, 1965 through 1968, as follows: Dall sheep, 86; caribou, 57; moose, 39; goat, 4; grizzly, 25; wolves, 7; wolverine, 2.

In addition to these animals, there are annual hunts held for sea mammals —seals and whales. There is a spring seal hunt on the ice, as a rule in May and June. There is a summer hunt, from boats, in late July and August. Dates vary, due to ice conditions. So do places along the Arctic coast where the hunts are held. Nonresidents are allowed to participate. There are special licenses. This hunting is under the control of the Federal Department of Fisheries, Ottawa. Hunters must take Eskimo guides and crewmen.

Both resident and nonresident hunters are allowed to take Arctic wolves, timber wolves, wolverine, and Arctic and snowshoe hares, which are fairly abundant, without license. The annual bag is very small.

A Game Zone map is available from the Government. A study of this, particularly for those who qualify as residents and who may hunt in Zones other than 12 and 19, is important. Orientation as to abundance of big-game species may be gained from the following listing. Moose are present in good numbers in Zones 3 through 24. Although caribou are migratory, they are found in all Zones, with woodland caribou present in Zones 5 through 22. Most portions of the Mackenzie Range have good populations of Dall sheep and also of grizzlies. This covers Zones 12, 19, 20, 22. Goats are not abundant, are scattered in small numbers in the southern part of Zone 12. Black bears are fairly common along the Mackenzie system and the Slaves River system. There are fairly substantial bison herds in Zones 3 and 5.

Hunters visiting or resident in the N.W.T. should not overlook the game birds. Ducks, geese, rails are found in abundance especially along the upper coast of Hudson Bay, and along the Mackenzie and the Slave. Bag limits for residents are high, 25 ducks and 15 geese. Nonresidents are restricted to 5 of each daily. Even though the season opens September 1, there is a short spate of good hunting, for most migratory waterfowl leave the Territories soon after the season begins.

Upland birds include ruffed and Franklin's (spruce) grouse, sharptail grouse, and ptarmigan. Nonresidents as well as residents are allowed to hunt these, in the proper Zones. Sharptails are not abundant, are found only in Zones 3, 5, 6, 7 in the central south below Great Slave Lake. Ruffed and spruce grouse are quite plentiful over the timbered regions, Zones 1 through 24, thus giving U.S. visitors a good opportunity. Ptarmigan are found in varying numbers throughout the N.W.T. Upland bird seasons open September 1 and run through April.

Total game bird harvest, all licenses, for a recent season were as follows: ptarmigan, 33,801; ducks, 24,208; geese, 5339, grouse (all species) 7895.

For other details on N.W.T. hunting, for regulations and pertinent queries, address the Superintendent of Game, Department of Industry and Development, Government of the Northwest Territories, Yellowknife, N.W.T., Canada.

BRITISH COLUMBIA

Westernmost of Canada's provinces, British Columbia with its complex frontage on the Pacific, its vast interior mountain chains, its limitless forests, and its many river valleys has long been known as one of the world's great game regions. Third largest of the provinces, it covers over 366,000 square miles of diverse and often awesomely rugged terrain. The Rockies range down the entire province forming great walls, sharp peaks deeply cut by glaciers. Peaks of 10,000 feet and more altitude are numerous.

A most unusual break in the topography is the Rocky Mountain Trench that divides the central and eastern portions. This corridor is narrow, from two to ten miles in width, and runs over a thousand miles. Here are the headwaters of many of the large rivers—the Kootenay, the Fraser, Columbia, Peace, Liard. Up in the far north the Stikine plateau lies between the game-famed Cassiar and Skeena mountains. To the south a broad upland sweeps on down, sinking in the middle of the province to the Basin of the Upper Fraser. Farther south are the Columbia and Cascade ranges, with the upland plateau tapered out and disappearing between them.

To the west there are the Coast Ranges, then the watery trail known as the Inner Passage where all of the coast is heavily cut and indented by bays and river mouths, and beyond all this lies the arc of far flung and scattered outer islands. Of the islands, Vancouver with over 12,400 square miles, is the most important. Second come the Queen Charlotte Islands farther north.

The enormous forest resources are the most important segment of the economy. Mining, some oil, and fisheries follow. In the south-central mainland and on southern Vancouver Island there is some agriculture. By far the major share of the population of the entire province is located in this arable area. Of some 1,900,000 people, about 900,000 are found in the Vancouver metropolitan region. British Columbia is indeed an uncrowded land, beautifully scenic, and with enormous stretches of total wilderness.

Uniquely, highway travel is possible all the way up to the border with the Yukon Territory. In the south there are numerous highways reaching north from the state of Washington. From this southern network a major highway runs on north to Prince George. Here it divides. Toward the northwest No. 16 leads up to coastal Prince Rupert. To the northeast the other route takes one to Dawson Creek, and thence far on north and back to the west via the Alaska Highway and at last to Whitehorse in the Yukon. Both of Canada's major rail lines, the Canadian Pacific and Canadian National furnish service in the south, and to Prince George and Dawson Creek.

However, most hunters will fly, because distances involved are long. Air service is excellent. Trans-Canada Air Lines services the largest southern cities. From Vancouver British Columbia Airlines runs flights to numerous interior towns, even up to Prince Rupert and from there to the Queen Charlotte Islands. Another line, Pacific Western, flies to Vancouver Island and runs numerous charters out of the city of Vancouver and also out of Prince Rupert in the northwest. Charter flights to anywhere in the interior are available via one or more of these lines, and of course bush pilots take up where these stop, to take hunters to their camps.

British Columbia has long been famous for the variety and excellence of its big-game hunting. There are mule deer, blacktail and whitetail deer, moose, mountain goat, Dall and Stone sheep plus bighorns, elk, caribou, both grizzly and black bear, and in addition there are cougers and wolves. There is also some excellent bird hunting. Among the species are grouse of several varieties, blue, ruffed, spruce, sharptail, three species of ptarmigan. There are some pheasants and quail, and also Hungarian and chukar partridge. Lesser animals such as coyotes, wolverines, foxes, and snowshoe hares are found here. Migratory waterfowl are abundant, and there are open seasons also for mourning doves and bandtail pigeons.

Hunting is popular here both for sport and for food. In an average season approximately 150,000 residents buy licenses. Nearly 6000 nonresidents hunted during the last season for which statistics are available at this writing. British Columbia has a licensing system somewhat different from most of the other provinces. There is a non-Canadian nonresident (that is, alien) license that covers all game. Currently is costs $25. The same type of license for nonresident Canadians is $15. A resident of Canada can also purchase a license for small game and game birds, for $4. Big-game hunters may of course hunt birds on their general licenses. But they must in addition purchase, before they start hunting, big-game tags for the desired species. These run from as low as 50 cents for black bear to $10 for grizzly. One who wishes, for example, to hunt only moose, or moose and sheep, purchases only the needed tags.

If a certain species for which a tag has been purchased is killed, then any nonresident must pay an additional trophy fee. Presently these fees are as follows: moose, $60; elk, $60; grizzly, $60; caribou, $60; goat, $40; sheep, $75; deer, $25; black bear, $5. Details on payment of such fees are contained in literature available from the Wildlife Branch, address at chapter end. All nonresident hunters must be accompanied by a guide, except when they are hunting wolf, coyote, cougar, or game birds. An up-to-date list of guides can be obtained from the Wildlife Branch. It lists them by Management Area, and by class of license each holds, and gives addresses.

There are presently twenty-eight Management Areas in British Columbia. A map with these Areas outlined and numbered is attached to the Game Regulations for any given season, and all seasons are set by use of these Areas. The Regulations folder also briefly describes the physical boundaries of each area. Because seasons may change and open Areas may change, it is mandatory that any hunter, resident or visitor, have a copy of the Regulations before planning a hunt. In the following material in this chapter Management Areas will be used where necessary as divisions to describe ranges or best hunting for any given species.

Since all nonresidents must be guided, there is certainly no problem for them so far as a place to hunt is concerned. Most residents after big game will also utilize guides. But for those who do not, or those who hunt birds only, there are few difficulties in finding ample public hunting grounds. Roughly 94 percent of all B.C. lands are Crown Lands, with free access except during fire or fire-hazard closures. In regions where there are private service roads leading to logging or mining operations, ordinarily hunters are allowed to use them, but they should check beforehand. In a few southern areas many private lands are posted. Usually permission to hunt is granted upon request. Regardless, there is so much Crown land available that seldom does one need access to private holdings.

There is a great deal of public hunting easily reached right from the highways, for those who do not wish to fly in or who do not need or wish to hire guides. There is a most useful booklet available from the Wildlife Branch titled "Hunting In British Columbia." It gives many details about procedures here, and also lists the species most common in each Management Area, and contains a map showing the Areas. Comparing the Management Areas map with an official British Columbia Road Map, obtained from the Department of Travel Industry, Parliament Buildings, Victoria, B.C., Canada, will orient any hunter, whether planning a guided or unguided trip. This map, incidentally, also lists campgrounds, for those who may wish to travel the highways.

British Columbia weather is varied. Coastal portions have generally mild winters and warm fall days. Fall bird hunters in the south will find the weather pleasant. Big game hunters in any season, especially in the central and northern parts, need to go prepared for extremely severe conditions, but also outfitted to be comfortable on the days that are mild. Good wool shirts, and down outer clothing, are essential. So are rugged hunting boots. It is advisable for all visitors not experienced in the region where they will hunt to ask and be attentive to advice of guides regarding their clothing and equipment.

Arms and ammunition here depend entirely on the activity. Hunters after moose, grizzly, goat, caribou, elk should use heavy calibers, either in the popular modern magnums or at least calibers such as the .30/06, .264, .270, preferably with heavy bullets. Deer hunters do not of course need large magnums, but can use any of the standard calibers, as above. For bird hunters, shot sizes of No. 7½ and 6 will fill most upland needs, with heavier shot for ducks, geese, brant.

In a province as large as this, with such variety both of game and terrain, and such huge wilderness expanses with little settlement, it is neither possible nor practical to attempt here to pinpoint small areas that are the best for each species. Many are not even known, and some not to date even discovered. However, success percentages, kill figures, and popularity of certain Management Areas indicate where opportunities are likely to be best. Even a careful study of the number of outfitters operating in certain Areas can be most helpful to one planning a trip in this famous big-game region. Hunters are advised to decide first which species is of most importance to them. Then if other big-game species are also desired, to try to select a general location where all are available, but hopefully with the most-sought species in heaviest population density. From there on, correspondence with several guides can step by step allow evaluation of precisely where the best opportunity may lie.

DEER

There are both mule deer and whitetail deer. The coast deer or Columbian blacktail, a mule deer subspecies, is found on Vancouver Island, along the lower coast and the adjacent islands. The Rocky Mountain mule deer ranges in the interior of the province. The Sitka deer, close relative of the coastal blacktail, has its range along the northern coast and on the Queen Charlotte and other northern islands. The whitetail deer, northwestern subspecies, is found in the Peace River region of the central-eastern border, in the Kootenay area of the southeast, and the Okanagan valley of the south-central part of the province.

Mule deer, which includes the blacktail subspecies, are presently hunted almost throughout the province, excepting in MA 26, which is in the central interior of the far north, east of the coastal slice of Alaska. Hunters desiring to hunt the Columbian blacktail should concentrate primarily on the west slope of the coastal mountains and on the coast and the islands, in densely forested regions of the southeast. MA 1, 3, and 17 are best choices. For the Sitka variety of coastal deer, one should move on north, into coastal portions of MA 23 and throughout MA 24, which is the Queen Charlotte Islands group.

Whitetails are presently hunted over much of the southeast, in MAs 5, 6, 7, 8, 9, 10, 11, 12, 13, 14, 15. They are also hunted in MA 20, the Upper Fraser, and in MA 28, the Peace River region. These Areas in general blanket whitetail range. Rocky Mountain mule deer are also found in parts of this range and along the interior.

Deer hunting in British Columbia is excellent, with extremely high success. An average of approximately 95,000 hunters participate. Most of these are residents. One recent season the resident deer harvest was 76,692, followed the next year by a kill of 70,534. Nonresidents bag an additional four or five hundred deer annually. In a number of MAs each season hunters are allowed three deer, in others two. Recently in the Queen Charlotte Islands there has been no bag limit. Here, one season recently 25 percent of hunters bagged three or more deer, over 36 percent bagged over two, and almost 28 percent bagged one. MA 1, which is Vancouver Island, also had an extremely high success record: one deer, 23 percent; two deer, 17½ percent; three deer, 16½ percent. Other MAs where success runs high for three deer: No. 2, 3, 4, 16. In the southeast, and south-central region, MAs where two-deer success has been very high are 7, 8, 10, 11.

The far northern Areas of course have the more moderate deer populations. Almost anywhere across the south and along the coast and its islands deer hunting is of high quality. The multiple bag does to some extent influence the overall success percentage, lowering it per hunter. Province-wide, around 22 percent of all deer hunters get their one deer each season. Another 11 percent bring in two, and over 5 percent additional take three or more. The high bag limit makes deer hunting in British Columbia highly attractive.

MOOSE

Trophy moose hunters should be aware that there are three subspecies in British Columbia, and should hunt in the territory where the one they desire is found. Most of the interior, but not the northwest and southeast corners of the province, is inhabited by the British Columbia moose. The Alaskan moose is found in the extreme northwest. In the extreme southeast is the Shiras, or Yellowstone, moose.

Some of the best moose hunting on the continent is found in this province. The kill is very high. Numerous MAs offer seasons for bulls only and later dates, often overlapping, for antlerless moose. A few Areas allow two moose to be taken. At this writing, MA 28 and part of MA 21 are in this category. Of course a second tag must be purchased. Virtually the entire province, excepting Vancouver Island and the Queen Charlottes, is open to moose hunting, although there may be seasonal exceptions.

Very nearly a third of British Columbia hunters hunt moose. Average license sales are around 40,000-plus. As a rule an additional five or six thousand nonresidents come to B.C. each year for moose. Over two recent seasons, the resident kill was nearly 20,000 animals, and the nonresident kill more than 3300. Thus the overall chances of success are close to 50 percent. Provincewide as a rule it runs about 40 percent.

In MA 26, in the northwest, the success is usually very high, to 55 percent or more, but the number of hunters here is low, possibly averaging around 125. The Peace River area, MA 28 shows excellent success, and so does the Liard River region to the north, MA 27. MAs 21 and 22 in the central interior run close to the others, and in the general southeast region Wells Gray, No. 12, and Big Bend, No. 9, also are usually high in kill success. Three other choice regions are the Upper Fraser, MA 20; Chilko in the south interior, No. 16; and MA 25, Skeena, inland from the north coast. All of these average in success around 40 percent or better. However, a late survey shows no Management Area open to moose with less than 20 to 25 percent success with the exception of MA 23, the North Coast, which averages slightly less.

The location of guide concentrations to some extent influences the kill of big game such as moose, for most hunters are guided and flown or packed in. To give an idea of how abundant moose are here, one season survey showed MA 20 with 6459 resident hunters taking 2853 moose, MA 22 with 7054 hunters and a kill of 3283, and MA 28 with 5250 hunters and 3294 moose. Good clues for nonresidents can be gleaned from both resident and nonresident kills. High MAs lately for nonresidents have been: 14, 16, 18, 19, 20, 21, 22, 25, 27, 28. Of these, 16, 18, 19, 22, 25 have run far past 50 percent success and in some cases over 75 percent. MA 13, in the southeast, has had but few nonresident hunters but an extremely high success percentage. In the extreme southeast, the East Kootenay MA, No. 11, gets numerous non-resident hunters, possibly because of easy accessibility from the U.S., but has been showing very low success.

ELK

Elk are not notably numerous in British Columbia, but there is a sub-stantial interest in hunting them. There are two subspecies, with ranges as follows: The Roosevelt elk of Vancouver Island, and the Rocky Mountain elk, chiefly of the extreme southeast, MA 11, East Kootenay, but also in scattered small herds in the interior.

From ten to twelve thousand or slightly more hunters annually purchase elk tags. The resident kill runs from 1700 to 2000. Thus, about 1 in 6 elk hunters is successful. Of nonresidents, one late season showed a success of about 27 percent in MA 11, East Kootenay, in the extreme southeast. This is for the Rocky Mountain elk. Nonresidents also took a modest number of elk in the northeast, MA 27, Liard, for a success of roughly 1 in 12.

In fact, all surveys show that MA 11 in the southeast gets the major share of the elk hunters and produces the largest kill. The Peace River, MA 28, is fair, and not heavily hunted by elk hunters. For Roosevelt elk, of course only MA 1, Vancouver Island, is worthwhile. But one's chances of success are only fair, possibly on the average about 10 percent.

CARIBOU

British Columbia has mountain caribou ranging in the mountainous por-tions of the southeast and similar habitat of the west-central region. There are also Osborn caribou in the north. At one time another subspecies was found on the Queen Charlotte Islands but is now presumably extinct.

A general picture of caribou status can be gained from hunter numbers and harvest over two seasons just passed. Resident hunters numbered 2160, killed 798 caribou the one year. The following year hunter numbers were over 3000 and the kill was 1191. Nonresidents during the last year bagged 492, but there is no accurate report on how many tags were sold. The best nonresident success on caribou is in the northeast. MA 27, Liard, where recently about 1 out of every 2 in the Area has bagged a caribou. Considering the fact that not all nonresidents may have had caribou tags or hunted caribou, the success is anywhere from about 50 percent on up. Resident success, as per the kill statistics above, averages somewhere around 35 percent.

A good portion of the southeast has open season, with MAs 9, 10, 11, 12, 13 all easily accessible from the U.S. and from Alberta. Much of the lower interior and east also is open: MAs 18, 19, 20, 21, 22, 23, 25, 28. In the north both 26 and 27 have open season. The largest harvest usually originates in the northeast, in Liard and Peace River, MAs 27 and 28. MA 26, in the northwest, has a higher success but a smaller number of hunters, almost all guided. Upper Fraser, MA 20 on the eastern border, shows a fair kill but about 25 percent success.

A careful study of the Management Area map, and of kill and hunter surveys, tends to show that a trophy hunter who makes meticulous plans and who selects his Area and guide with care can bring home a trophy. But such a study also shows that caribou hunting today is not in any northern region as successful as it once was, and that thoughtful planning and outfitter selection is most likely to bring success. Hunters should be cautioned, however, not to read into all harvest and success figures any open sesame to success. Some Management Areas, for example, have so few hunters, residents who have animals spotted, that a success percentage becomes meaningless. A good instance turned up during a recent survey that showed 60 percent success with caribou in MA 23, the North Coast. The fact was that only five resident hunters killed three caribou. None were killed by nonresidents that season, and in fact no nonresidents hunted them there.

MOUNTAIN GOAT

There are three subspecies in the province, although identification of each is of little consequence to hunters. Goats inhabit much of the mountainous area of British Columbia, but are not present on Vancouver, the Queen Charlottes or most coastal islands. From 3000 to 4000 residents hunt goats each season and the kill averages from 1500 to 1800. The nonresident kill runs somewhere between 500 and 600.

Usually all of the province except the islands (MA 1 and 24) is open to goat hunting. Over past seasons there has been a bag limit of two goats over all of the province excepting the MAs of the southeast: 5, 6, 7, 8, 10, 11. Hunter success province-wide averages about 33 percent, with an additional 5 percent of hunters successful in obtaining two. In MA 26, in the far northwest, one recent season success was 100 percent and 67 percent of the hunters took two goats. Hunter numbers here are, however, low, possibly twenty to thirty annually. Ratings on a few of the better MAs are as follows: No. 8, on the southern border, excellent; No. 19, Horsefly, in the Quesnel and San Jose watersheds of the upper southeast, almost as good; No. 21, west of Peace River, on a par with No. 19; the Central Coast, No. 17, and the Okanagan Valley, No. 6, both with at least 50 percent success. However, almost any guided hunt in any of the Management Areas offers fair to good opportunity in this high-altitude sport. Nonresidents have been doing best of late in the north, in MAs 25, 26, 27, especially in No. 26.

MOUNTAIN SHEEP

In this highly specialized endeavor, a hunter must decide which species or subspecies of sheep he desires and then formulate his hunting plan based on the range of the animal. British Columbia has two subspecies of bighorns. The California bighorn ranges over the southern interior part of the province. The Rocky Mountain bighorn is found only in East Kootenay (MA No. 11) in the extreme southeast, and in a small area near the Alberta border in east-central British Columbia, along Sheep Creek. The Dall sheep range is only in the extreme northwest. The Stone sheep, a subspecies of the Dall, is distributed over northern British Columbia.

During a typical season, an average of 1100 to 1200 residents take a total bag of approximately 225 rams. Nonresident hunters, many concentrating on sheep, often take a higher kill, up to around 400. Lately few bighorns are killed by visitors, but the thin-horned sheep of the north, the Dall and Stone, are the favorites. By far the major share of the nonresident kill is accomplished in MA 27, Liard, in the north and northeast. No. 26 in the northwest, the watersheds of the Stikine, Taku, and Atlin rivers, is second. Third on the list is the Peace River MA, No. 28. It is interesting to note that during one season recently passed, there were 451 nonresident hunters recorded in the Liard Area, No. 27, and of those—although the number of sheep tags held is not recorded—247 bagged rams.

Resident success follows somewhat the same patterns. MAs 26, 27, 28 show success from 27 to 36 percent. In the Skeena Area, No. 25, a small number of hunters has scored in the past as high as 100 percent. Bighorn success in No. 11 is generally low, but for the California bighorn, Nos. 4, 6, 7, 14, 16 rate as fair. In sheep hunting, guides thoroughly familiar with their hunting territory add immensely to the chance of success.

GAME BIRDS

The California quail ranges on Vancouver Island and in portions of suitable habitat in the southern interior. There are also a few mountain quail in the southern part of Vancouver Island. Both species were introduced, although there may have been mountain quail on the Island originally. It is possible that remnant introduced bobwhites may still survive on the U.S. border near Huntingdon but they cannot be considered, if existing, as at all important to hunters. There is little interest in quail hunting. As few as 1500 to 1800 hunters bag less than 10,000 quail annually. During a typical season, MAs 1, 6, 7, 14, 15 were open to quail hunting. Agricultural lands and brushy edges nearby are the prime quail range, with lower slopes best for mountain quail.

Pheasants are in fair supply in arable portions of the lower mainland and the southern interior, and on the southern part of Vancouver Island. Approximately 14,000 hunters try for pheasants, about half of them on the lower mainland. The kill averages 30,000 or a bit more.

Hungarian partridge are present in small and very scattered populations on the southern part of Vancouver Island and also in the Fraser Valley. The chukar is established in parts of the southern interior. It is of some consequence as a game bird, although the Hun, extremely local in distribution, is not important except to a few resident hunters who happen to be aware of coveys nearby. The chukar kill is relatively token, and somewhat cyclic. Under 2000 hunters bag from 3000 to upwards of 10,000 chukars. During a recent season, Management Areas 4, 6, 7, 13, 14, 15—the southern interior—were open.

Among them the various grouse species are the truly important game birds of the province, with the aggregate bag of blue, spruce (Franklin's), ruffed, and sharptail grouse running anywhere from half a million to a million birds. The blue grouse is found in mountain regions throughout the province, including the islands. The spruce grouse range is in dense forest of the Peace River region, the northwest, and the central and southern interior. Ruffed grouse are found along the stream courses and on the lower slopes over much of the province. Sharptail grouse are found in small numbers south and central in the interior, also in the Peace River district and in the extreme northwest. Three species of ptarmigan—willow, rock, whitetailed—also are found in the north, with the willow ptarmigan generally the most abundant.

Because of the immense range, the best key to where these various birds may be found is in the regulations covering the Management Areas. In a typical season the blue grouse is hunted throughout the entire province. During a season when the total grouse kill was roughly a million, blue grouse made up 186,000 birds in the aggregate bag. Spruce grouse are hunted everywhere except Vancouver and the Queen Charlotte Islands, and match or pass the blue in numbers bagged. Ruffed grouse are hunted everywhere but the Queen Charlottes, are the most important in numbers taken; slightly more than half the kill is of this species. Sharptails are open in most of their range, but the total bag during the season noted above when a million grouse in aggregate were bagged was less than 40,000. Ptarmigan have open season everywhere except the Queen Charlottes, are hunted chiefly by natives for food in the northern region and as incidentals by big-game hunters.

Mourning doves are open to hunting in a number of Management Areas across the south. There is a small amount of shooting in the agricultural regions. Bandtailed pigeons are often quite plentiful, and more important than the mourning dove as game birds here. They are found along the coast and the islands, have had open season lately on the Queen Charlottes, Vancouver, the north coast, central coast, south coast, and along the southwestern border in MA 2.

There is excellent hunting for ducks, geese, and brant all along the coast and along the numerous lakes and streams inland. The total duck kill amounts to about half a million birds each season, with well over half the bag originating along the lower mainland and Vancouver. The Okanagan Valley also is a good location, and the lakes of the southeast, the Kootenays, also turn in a fair kill. The upper coast and the Queen Charlottes have excellent possibilities but are not hunted to any extent except by local hunters. Goose hunting, for Canadas, whitefronted (specklebellies), snows, and Pacific brant is also excellent. The kill amounts to 25,000 or 30,000 geese each season. At least 15,000 hunters try for geese. By far the major bulk of the bag comes from the southern interior. The lower mainland is next. Both the Queen Charlottes and Vancouver also rate high for geese, and brant.

BEARS

Both grizzly and black bears are present. While plentiful, bears are scattered and guided hunts have by far the greater chance of success. Black bears occur throughout the province. There are seasons everywhere in late summer and early fall, and there are also spring seasons in numerous MAs. Hunters intent on trying for one of the rare white Kermode's bears should be certain to check special regulations pertaining to it. Grizzlies range, and there's open fall hunting for them, throughout the province, excepting at this writing the islands. Most Areas are also open in spring.

Bear hunting is not as popular with residents as with nonresidents who seek trophies. The kill is not high. One recent season nonresidents took 152 black bears, 181 grizzlies. Highest kills of grizzlies were made in: MAs 11,

26, 27, with 20, 17, 28, 25, and 8 following in that order. For blacks, No. 11 was first, followed by 22 and 27, then 25 and 19.

OTHER ANIMALS

The cougar, or mountain lion, is quite plentiful in British Columbia and has for many years been especially so on Vancouver. They are hunted in all Areas except No. 24, the Queen Charlottes. Most MAs are open all year. A few have seasons beginning in early fall and continuing through until March 31. There is no bag limit. Although guides for cougar hunting are not mandatory for nonresidents, in this specialized endeavor chances of success are slim without one who is a specialist at it.

Both wolves and coyotes range throughout most of British Columbia. Both are on the game list, but huntable all year in most places. A few Areas are closed part of the year.

Many trophy hunters are eager to collect a wolverine. While they are not rare, neither are they especially abundant or commonly seen. They are considered small game and subject to a season. All but the Islands are open, as a rule during the general big-game seasons.

There are also bobcats, some foxes and raccoons. These, too, are considered small game. Snowshoe hares are not on the protected list. Some seasons they are extremely abundant, particularly in the northern half of the province. There are also sea lions and hair seals along the coast. These are not covered by regulations. Hunters should carefully check with the Wildlife Branch regarding them. Magpies and crows are unprotected.

REGULATIONS

Address all queries regarding details of open seasons, guide list, etc., to The Department of Recreation and Conservation, Fish and Wildlife Branch, Victoria, British Columbia, Canada.

ALBERTA

Alberta is the westernmost of Canada's three so-called Prairie Provinces. Looking from west to east, this is where the Canadian prairies begin. But along its western border, which is entirely with British Columbia, Alberta has some of the most stunning mountain scenery, especially along the southern half of this border, to be found anywhere in Canada. The southern boundary is about 180 miles long, and is entirely with northwestern Montana. But at the point where Glacier National Park in the U.S. lies astride the crown of the Rockies and spills northward into Canada as the Watertown Lakes National Park, the Alberta border marches abruptly northwestward up the top of the Rockies almost to the 55th parallel and then turns directly north to the southern boundary of the Northwest Territories.

The northern boundary is with the Northwest Territories and on the east Alberta meets Saskatchewan. Along the southern portion of this boundary Alberta is chiefly a plain of 2500-feet altitude that rises slowly and gently westward until it breaks up in the foothills of the Rockies at some 4000 feet. From here on up the slope to the ridge of the mountains the country is violently broken and immense, with peaks near the British Columbia border rising to over 12,000 feet.

Southern Alberta is quite dry, and is almost entirely a treeless prairie, with much irrigated land on which wheat is produced. In the western foothills the wheat farms give way to cattle as the slopes become more and more forested. Northward from the vast prairie expanse there is a zone of poplar in scattered stands, with prairie interspersed. But as one moves farther north a mixed forest appears, with conifers, poplar, and birch. From here on forests become dense. Although there is crop farming and cattle raising in the interior, and lumber also is important, oil and gas have become the major products in vast and swiftly developed fields.

There is of course an immense amount of true wilderness, especially in the north. Alberta encompasses some 255,285 square miles. The total population at this time is not much more than 1.5 million. The two large cities of Edmonton and Calgary, both situated in oil- and gas-producing regions, now harbor between them at least half of the total population of the province.

There are good and numerous roads throughout all of southern Alberta, particularly across the east and in the central areas. Roads are rather sparse by comparison along the foothill region of western Alberta. Above Edmonton, settlement has reached out to Athabasca and to Lesser Slave Lake. West of Lesser Slave Lake there is fairly heavy settlement also, in the areas of Peace River, Grande Prairie, Spirit River, and Fairview, with consequently an adequate road network that reaches on across the British Columbia border to Dawson Creek. However, north of Peace River only one highway thrusts up across the northwest and into the Northwest Territories, and in the east a single highway runs only to Fort McMurray. The remainder of the northern half of the province is virtually roadless.

Thus, most visiting hunters and resident hunters can do very well with vehicular transport on the roads over the southern portion. In the north, however, charter planes are the main method of travel. There are also excellent scheduled air accommodations throughout the south, with connections to all of the larger cities.

Hunters have ample room. Even in the farming areas it is still not difficult to obtain permission to hunt on private lands. Alberta has a licensing system based on the purchase of a Wildlife Certificate. The price is the same (currently $2) for resident, nonresident, and nonresident alien. After the purchase of this certificate one may then purchase specific licenses for all or any species of big game, and one covering birds. Prices of these differ among resident, nonresident (which refers to residents of Canada but not of Alberta) and nonresident alien. Recent license sales indicate increases both in hunting interest and in population. Presently the certificate sale is moving up toward an average 150,000 annually. At least half of these hunters purchase bird licenses, and the purchase of a variety of big-game licenses by species is on an upward trend.

Nonresident Canadian and nonresident alien hunters should be aware that present license fees and regulations are so arranged that they do not automatically entitle one to all big-game animals. Canadian and alien nonresident fees differ, but a holder of either big-game license may kill one trophy sheep (check stipulation), one antlered animal (deer, moose, elk, or caribou), and one black or brown (not grizzly) bear. There is a special license for all nonresidents that allows kill of one whitetail deer, another special license for one moose in the northern Zone (Zone 1), another special license allowing, during a spring hunt, one grizzly and two black or brown bears. To avoid confusion or disappointment upon arrival, all nonresident visitors should be fully informed on these license stipulations.

Game is varied. There are both whitetail and mule deer, moose, elk, mountain sheep, caribou, and occasional seasons on mountain goats and antelope. There are both grizzly and black bears. Waterfowl are abundant. Upland birds include pheasants, Hungarian partridge, plus a variety of grouse: sharptail, ruffed, spruce, sage, blue, and two ptarmigans, willow and white-tailed. There are cottontails, snowshoe hares, jackrabbits, predators.

As noted, finding a place to hunt is not difficult. There are vast expanses of Crown lands and lands managed by the Forestry Division. Although hunters must have permission for hunting upon occupied lands, few locations in the province have yet had any excessive pressure to deny permission. In some ways it is easier for nonresidents and nonresident aliens, for there are regulations pertaining to the use of guides. In certain Big Game Zones a guide is mandatory, for hunting big game, and in others either a licensed guide or a resident of Alberta must accompany the visiting hunter. A list of both Class A and Class B guides (classes refer to their qualifications) can be obtained from the Department of Lands and Forests, address at chapter end. This list is kept updated, gives addresses.

Game management, and also hunting regulations, are handled in Alberta by Zones. There are currently fifteen Big Game Zones. These are divided into numerous smaller subdivisions that carry both letter and number, i.e. G-128, P-218. But these subdivisions do not necessarily refer by each letter only to one BG Zone. Big-game seasons are set by BG Zones for the General Season, and further by indication of various subdivisions for Extended Seasons. Bird seasons are also set by numbered Zones. However, these Zones do not correspond to the BG Zones. Nor are Upland Bird Zones and Waterfowl Zones the same. Presently there are five Upland Bird Zones and six Waterfowl Zones, but one of the latter (Zone 2) is divided into A and B sections, north and south of the Athabasca River, which for practical purposes makes seven Waterfowl Zones.

Because of this rather complicated system of regulations, it is extremely important that hunters obtain the "Summary of Game Regulations" for the year in question. It contains large maps showing the various Zones in each category and lists the current regulations for each.

Neither kill statistics by Zones nor success percentages by Zones is available for any game species in Alberta. Therefore, in the following material under various species headings, only general ranges can be given, plus in some instances an average total harvest.

Throughout all of the southern half of Alberta accommodations for hunters are in good supply. Since visitors from outside the province, as well as many residents, will be guided, lodging and food are easily arranged ahead of time via the outfitter. Camping enthusiasts will find this province highly geared to their needs. There are scores of campgrounds in Provincial Parks, at Government Highway Campsites and in the National Parks and the Forests. There are also a number of city and county campgrounds. The Alberta Travel Bureau at Edmonton can furnish complete lists of these camper accommodations. There is also a booklet, "Alberta Provincial Parks Guide Book," available from the Department of Lands and Forests.

Fall bird hunters in the south should expect crisp but enjoyable wool-shirt and jacket weather. Big-game hunters even during early seasons at higher elevations should go prepared for more severe weather. As the season progresses all hunters must be equipped for low temperatures.

Guns and ammunition cover a wide latitude here. Upland bird hunters can base their loads on No. 7½ and No. 6, but waterfowl hunters should use express No. 6 or short-magnum No. 4 for ducks, and magnum 4 or else No. 2 shot for geese. For big game, a good compromise is a caliber such as the .30/06. Moose, elk, and caribou hunters can utilize such a cartridge, but many will prefer heavier magnums. For deer, lighter calibers such as the 6mm will do nicely, but again, if a variety is sought, compromise should be made on a heavier caliber with a choice of loads.

PHEASANT

The ringneck was first introduced to Alberta in 1908. Original releases were in the Calgary area, in the southwestern part of the province. They spread widely and did well, but are dependent upon croplands for their livelihood, and thus the highest densities are in the irrigated portions of southern Alberta. Most of the prairie and the parkland south of an east-west line drawn through Edmonton has a fairly good distribution of pheasants, with density increasing southward. Above the North Saskatchewan River, which is north of Edmonton, only a few pheasants are found in scattered localities. The very best of the pheasant habitat lies within a large oval territory of the central south, inside a line drawn roughly from Brooks to Fort Macleod to Magrath to Foremost to Medicine Hat and on again to Brooks. In this oval the country in a line from Lethbridge to Medicine Hat has long been a favorite pheasant hunting ground.

Recently some severe years have brought a decline to pheasant populations in most of the Alberta range. An average season harvest by residents has been below 100,000 birds. Above Highway 1, which runs from Medicine Hat to Calgary, pheasant populations are low and probably will remain so.

HUNGARIAN PARTRIDGE

The Hun has for many years been a most important game bird here. Current harvests are higher than for pheasants, averaging above 100,000 birds. The Hun was brought to southern Alberta the same year as the ringneck, 1908. Apparently conditions were optimum for them and they swiftly established themselves and multiplied in such numbers that an open season was possible in 1913.

Although the Hun has drastic ups and downs of population from season to season, it is established over a huge area, from the Peace River clear to the Montana border. They are abundant in good years over the prairie and park-lands and have also moved into farming areas north of Edmonton. Apparently the Hun is far better equipped to survive the severe climate of Alberta than is the pheasant.

Huns mingle in the southern farmlands with pheasants. But some of the best Hun range is north of the best pheasant range. One of these high-density blocks is along and north of the Red Deer River, in the areas surrounding the villages of Drumheller, Hanna, Coronation, Oyen, Wardlow. North and east, along and for a short distance west of the Saskatchewan border, there is good Hun hunting in the region from Provost to Lloydminster, to Vermillion and Wainwright. To the west there is another major Hun distribution in a long strip lying east of Edmonton, running roughly from Red Deer in the south to St. Paul to the northeast.

SHARPTAIL GROUSE AND PRAIRIE CHICKEN

The sharptail is the most important upland game bird in Alberta, and probably the most populous, or at least the most populous and at the same time accessible. The kill exceeds 150,000 annually. The range of the sharptail within Alberta is vast. It can be found in open tamarack muskeg and sandhills in the north, in the poplar-studded parklands, on the grassy east slopes of the Rockies, and over almost all of the southern prairie.

In northern Alberta and in the west the sharptail often makes a winter migration to lower and more hospitable areas. Population density in the north is extremely cyclic but in the south remains reasonably stable. Some of the best sharptail hunting is found in the two easternmost areas noted above for Huns. But sharptails also inhabit much of the open country throughout the southern half of the province. Many visiting hunters are thus able to hunt pheasants, Huns, and sharptails all at the same time and in the same general area.

The sharptail is often colloquially called "prairie chicken" here. However, during early settlement of the province the true prairie chicken, or pinnated grouse, was exceedingly abundant. It was dependent upon large expanses of virgin grassland interspersed with some grain croplands that furnished winter sustenance. As the balance between grassland and cropland changed, with emphasis on crops, the prairie chicken declined rapidly. Today there is no hunting for it, and it may even be extinct in Alberta.

RUFFED GROUSE AND OTHER GROUSE

Most seasons the ruffed grouse kill is about even with or slightly less than the harvest of sharptails. This native woodland grouse is found throughout wooded regions of the southwest, central, and all of northern Alberta. Although there are pockets of abundance in many locations, and the western foothills and slopes where brushy stream courses are numerous furnish excellent shooting, probably the highest ruffed grouse density is in a half circle of range west of Edmonton. This quality range begins roughly at the North Saskatchewan River and swings north and east around Edmonton. Most ruffed grouse are bagged in Alberta by residents. Big-game hunters in the wooded regions take some, but the major share of the kill is by local hunters.

The large blue grouse is fairly populous in portions of Alberta, but is of lesser importance so far as sport hunting is concerned. It is a bird of the ever-green forests of the high country, and of alpine meadows. It ranges along the east slope of the Rockies all the way from the Smoky River near Grand Prairie down the western border to Montana. Because the blue grouse is not as easily accessible as aforementioned species, it is not much hunted. The total annual kill is probably only a few hundred.

There are also spruce grouse in Alberta, but these birds inhabit dense stands of conifers and are thus found chiefly in the west, along the Rockies chain, and in northern Alberta. They are not a popular game species, although there is a good potential. The kill is mostly by local hunters, and incidental by ruffed grouse or blue grouse hunters, or by big-game hunters.

The status of the big sage grouse is precarious in Alberta. This bird is a resident of open sage plains and dependent upon this habitat. In Alberta it is found today in appreciable numbers only in the extreme southeast. For many years there was a closed season. Then in 1967 a few permits were offered. About 250 birds were taken. Several other very restricted seasons followed.

However, the future of this game bird in Alberta is precarious and open seasons cannot be predicted.

There are two species of ptarmigan native to Alberta. The whitetailed ptarmigan lives in the high ranges above timberline in the Rockies in western Alberta. A study of the Big Game Zone map will show a number of western high-country subdivisions with the prefix letter "S." The whitetailed ptarmigan is found in most of these, but very few are bagged by hunters. A good potential exists, however. The willow ptarmigan is a bird of the north. In fact, it summers north of the Alberta border, then migrates for winter down into much of northern Alberta and as far south as Edmonton. It receives very little hunting pressure except sporadically from local hunters, but has great possibilities. In the Lesser Slave Lake, Lake Athabasca, and Fort McMurray areas it is often abundant during winter months. The weather during the stay of the ptarmigan is not conducive to large gatherings of hunters.

OTHER UPLAND BIRDS

In 1937 a few chukars were released near Midnapore, Alberta. Subsequent releases were made elsewhere in the province. None was successful. Presently there is no record of the existence of chukars from the experiments, and no open season is declared.

The Merriam's turkey, a subspecies native to western mountain forests, was tried in Alberta in the early 1960s, the stock brought in from South Dakota and placed in the Cypress Hills, in the extreme southeastern part of the province. There was an immediate increase, then over recent years a decline. The adverse winters seem to be a serious handicap to the birds. Other releases have been tried, without success. However, the Department feels that perhaps there is a possibility of eventually establishing the wild turkey and that further experiments may well be warranted.

WATERFOWL

Hunting for both ducks and geese is excellent in this province. Thousands of birds nest in the lake regions. The duck kill exceeds half a million, and as many as 60,000, sometimes more, geese are harvested annually. A vast number of geese that nest in the Arctic migrate down through Alberta. The wheat country is famed for its waterfowl shooting.

It is impossible to pinpoint specific waterfowling locations to any extent. They are widespread. Many pheasant hunters and other upland bird hunters will find large flights of both ducks and geese all across southern Alberta. Commonly waterfowl and upland birds are hunted during a single trip. Crop conditions and wetland conditions from season to season vary and it is therefore best for visitors to check with the Department prior to planning a hunt, to ascertain where the largest flights are expected.

There is much good shooting in the region of the upper southeast broadly surrounding the town of Hanna. Here are many large lakes and stream bottoms as well as open country into which the birds fly to feed. Another particularly good goose location is east of Edmonton and southeast from Elk Island National Park, in the Beaverkill Lake area. Good waterfowling is found in the north, but it is not easily accessible and there is little to hold the birds. The southern croplands and lake regions are better.

There are huntable numbers of jacksnipe present during the waterfowl season. Few hunters pay any attention to them.

SMALL GAME

Rabbits and hares are the only small-game animals, and they receive very little attention from hunters. Cottontails are distributed in limited numbers throughout the prairie river valleys in the south. Jackrabbits are common across the plains, foothills of the west, and the central parklands. Snowshoe hares are found in the forests of the north, to some extent in the central parklands and in the western mountains.

DEER

There are both mule deer and whitetail deer. Mule deer range throughout most of the province, excepting the extreme northwest corner. But this is somewhat deceiving, for mule deer populations have been declining for some time, particularly in the Alberta prairies and parklands. This species ranges in a wide variety of habitats, from the treeless plains of the southeast to the mountains of the west and in scattered numbers in the northern forests. In general the best mule deer hunting is in the southwestern quarter of the province, in the foothills and forests of the Rockies, and across the central parklands.

The whitetail has done far better in Alberta over recent years than the mule deer. It has been continually expanding its range, and it undoubtedly outnumbers the mule deer in all easily accessible locations. Whitetails are found over most of the southern half of Alberta, with the exception of the western mountains, where they are scarce. They have been extending their range through the central parklands and northward along the Athabasca River valley and westward into the Peace River region.

By and large, the best hunting for whitetails is found in the eastern and central parklands and opportunity here qualifies as excellent. Mule deer hunting also can be rated excellent along the eastern slope of the Rockies, especially in foothill situations.

ELK

Elk range is limited almost entirely to the western mountains. Sporadic occurrence of elk is noted reaching out some distance from the western foothills and north into the Grande Prairie region. There are pockets of elk distribution in several spots in east-central Alberta but no hunting there at present. Elk also are present now in the Cypress Hills area of the southeast. All these isolated populations derived from transplants. The prime elk hunting is in the foothills along the east slope of the Rockies. It deserves a rating of excellent.

MOOSE

Moose are found throughout all of the forest country of Alberta. They are plentiful across all of the north, and down the slopes of the western mountains. A few are now located, by transplant, in the Cypress Hills of the southeast. Northern Alberta offers the best moose hunting opportunities, mostly by fly-in to the camps of various outfitters.

For some years moose hunting was confined to residents, but in recent seasons numerous special nonresident licenses have been offered, and a substantial moose kill has resulted, particularly in the north. Success some seasons has run about 35 percent and total harvest of 14,000 to 15,000 animals appears average.

CARIBOU

Woodland caribou range over northern Alberta as far south as Lesser Slave Lake and Cold Lake. They are also found in the northern portion of Banff National Park. Outside the Rockies there are isolated herds in muskeg and spruce areas. Presently they are hunted only in Zone 1, which is the major share of the north, and in Zone 6, which lies north of Jasper National Park along the western boundary. Caribou hunting must be rated as only fair.

There are migrations of Barren Ground caribou into extreme northeastern Alberta, but there is no open season on them.

ANTELOPE

The position of the pronghorn is most precarious in Alberta. It is found presently only in the extreme southeast, most of the animals south of the Red Deer River. Over the past few years the herd, estimated in the early 1960s at about 18,000 animals, has declined to less than half that. Only residents may apply for the limited number of antelope permits offered, and it is not certain as this is written whether or not an open season will occur for any given year.

SHEEP

The Rocky Mountain bighorn ranges throughout the mountain area along the southwestern border. There is good hunting along the fringes of mountains bordering Jasper and Banff National Parks, and farther south below Banff National Park and along the British Columbia border. Recently there have been special hunts for residents termed "non-trophy" hunts, for ewes and for males under a year. These hunts were set to trim the sheep bands. How long they will continue cannot be predicted. All nonresident licenses, and the general sheep season for residents, are for trophy sheep. This is defined as a four-fifths curl, or with a horn which "can be intercepted at both the front of the horn base and the tip of the horn by a straight line drawn through the front of the eye."

MOUNTAIN GOAT

There are some goats along the top of the Rockies, in southwestern Alberta. As this is written there is no open season, although there have been special seasons in recent years. In 1967, for example, fifty-seven goats were taken by residents and sixty-nine by nonresidents. At present seasons are set only as "specifically authorized by the Lieutenant Governor in council by special order."

BUFFALO

Wood Buffalo National Park in the northeast is home to a herd of wood buffalo, and some are found adjacent to the park. Some buffalo are also in the several National Parks. At this time there is no hunting.

BEARS

The black bear and its brown color phase are both plentiful over much of northern Alberta, with the preponderance of the population found north of an east-west line drawn through Edmonton. The grizzly is found chiefly in the northwest, in the Peace River and Smoky River regions and along the eastern slope of the Rockies. There are both fall and spring bear seasons, for both species, in several Zones. Black bear hunting can be rated excellent and grizzly hunting as fair to good.

OTHER ANIMALS

The lynx is found sporadically across northern Alberta. There are red foxes and their color phases, and numerous coyotes. Coyotes range widely across the province, especially in the prairies. They have not been called to any extent and are rather naive when hunted by this method. Few hunters bother with any of these animals. Wolves, which once were common, have declined, but some remain in the north and in the mountains.

Pests such as ground squirrels, prairie dogs, crows, and magpies are found in the southern farm and prairie lands, and there are rockchucks along the southwestern mountain foothills. None of these species receives more than cursory attention from hunters.

REGULATIONS

Game laws pertaining to seasons, bag and possession limits, areas to be hunted, special hunts, license fees all may have numerous changes from year to year. For current regulations, and for other specific queries, write to: Alberta Department of Lands and Forests, Natural Resources Building, 109th Street at 99th Avenue, Edmonton, Alberta, Canada.

SASKATCHEWAN

Saskatchewan is the central one of Canada's three prairie provinces, flanked on the east by Manitoba, and on the west by Alberta. The northern border is with the Northwest Territories, in the south the province touches Montana and North Dakota. The shape of Saskatchewan is almost rectangular, with the long dimension north-south. Its area is vast, 251,700 square miles.

The southern one-third of Saskatchewan is a plains area, and consists chiefly of agricultural lands, privately owned. In the southwest, however, the Cypress Hills rise above the remainder of the high plain. To the north of the agricultural lands, the central third of the province is a mixture of aspen parkland and forest interspersed with numerous lakes. Above this section, the terrain becomes rocky, the forest is dense. Progressively northward the trees become smaller. This northern region is a welter of lakes large and small, and is cut by countless streams. Almost all of the northern two-thirds of the province is government owned, and most of these Crown lands are open to hunting. There are no specifically designated Public Hunting Grounds as in some provinces and states, but even on the private lands of the south permission for hunting is commonly granted upon request.

Southern Saskatchewan is Canada's greatest grain-producing region. There is also a substantial petroleum industry here. Farther north mixed farming with emphasis on livestock occurs in the settled areas. Copper, zinc, and uranium mining are important northern industries, along with forest products. Over most of the north the population is thinly spread, and there is much roadless wilderness. The total Saskatchewan population is about one million. At least a quarter of this total live in the two largest urban centers, Regina and Saskatoon. Most of the remaining population is spread across the southern prairie.

Roads in the south are plentiful, and good. North of Prince Albert, however, roads are few and mostly gravel. One route now runs toward the northeast, and to Flin Flon just across the border in Manitoba. Another reaches north to and slightly beyond Lac La Ronge. A third thrusts toward the northwest to Buffalo Narrows and La Loche. From here on throughout the north there are no roads, and travel is by air, mainly via float planes. A few air strips for wheeled planes are present, especially in the Lake Athabasca region of the far northwest. There are numerous lodges and camps in the roadless north to accommodate hunters, but they must all fly in. Air connections with the large cities are excellent, and there are numerous scheduled flights to the smaller provincial settlements, as well as charter services. Rail service via the Canadian National and Canadian Pacific covers the southern half of the province as far north as Prince Albert.

Saskatchewan hunting is excellent, varied, and, compared to the population, quite popular. About 50,000 resident and over 3000 nonresident bird hunting licenses are annually sold. Deer hunters number, total, an average of around 67,000 and during one recent season almost 12,000 moose licenses were purchased. Quite obviously, with the tremendous expanse of the province, there is ample room for those modest numbers of hunters to enjoy their sport.

Upland game birds are present in great variety. There are sharptailed grouse, Hungarian partridge, ruffed grouse, spruce grouse, pheasants, ptarmigan. Lowland birds include ducks, geese, snipe, sandhill cranes. Big game includes both mule and whitetail deer, moose, elk, woodland caribou, antelope, and bear. There are cottontails, snowshoe hares, and jackrabbits, plus foxes and coyotes. Deer, moose, waterfowl, sharptails, and Huns are the most important and popular species.

Saskatchewan is divided for game management purposes into numbered Zones. Presently there are thirty-seven of these, with several of them subdivided into A and B sections. Hunters familiar with these Zones in past seasons should be aware that in 1969 a number of Zone boundaries were changed. Seasons for all species are set by Zones. In the following material under individual species Zone numbers will be used to indicate the more specific high-density areas of game populations. Nonresident hunters planning a trip to Saskatchewan should carefully note the material here, and in copies of the hunting guide (digest of regulations) for any given year, regarding species restricted to hunting by residents only.

License laws are a bit different here from those in some other provinces. "Resident" as used for the game bird license means a resident of Canada, but there is an additional special pheasant license and this is issued only to residents of Saskatchewan. Other game bird licenses are nonresident alien, and they are valid for only ten days and only in specified zones. Big-game licenses are of three kinds: resident, meaning resident of Saskatchewan, nonresident Canadian, and nonresident alien. No hunting for any species is allowed in this province on Sunday.

For a list of outfitters and hunting camps in Saskatchewan, hunters should acquire the "Saskatchewan Travel Guide" for the year in question. It is available from the Saskatchewan Department of Industry and Commerce, Tourist Development Branch, Power Building, Regina. This is a very complete book, annually updated. It lists hotels, motels, campgrounds, parks. Guides are of course furnished by the outfitter selected.

Most upland bird and waterfowl seasons open in Saskatchewan in September. Weather at that time is mild over the south, where the bulk of this hunting occurs. Farther north heavier clothing is needed. And, for big-game seasons anywhere in the province one should be equipped with heavy outer clothing and insulated boots. Winters are of course severe. Upland bird hunters should be supplied with shot shells loaded with No. 6 and No. 7½ shot sizes as basic loads. Waterfowl hunters can use short-magnum No. 6 or else No. 4, and goose hunters will need No. 2 shot. For deer hunting any standard caliber such as the .270, .243, .30/06 serves well, but for moose it is best to use either a heavy bullet in a rifle such as the .30/06, or else to use one of the heavy magnum calibers.

SHARPTAIL GROUSE

The sharptail, a grouse of the mixed prairie and brush and aspen parklands, is the most numerous upland game bird of Saskatchewan, and has become an emblem of the province. It is the most popular uplander among hunters and in most seasons sustains the highest kill. Average seasonal sharptail bags over a five year period recently ran from a high of over 157,000 to a low of over 127,000.

The primary range of the sharptail is from the southern border up across the grassland region and the aspen grove region above Regina and across through the Saskatoon area to slightly south of Prince Albert. There are scattered pockets of sharptails north of Prince Albert far on up into northern Saskatchewan toward Lake Athabaska. Hunters seeking the greatest sharptail densities should concentrate on two locations. One is in the southeast near the Souris River. This is in the general area where the cities of Weyburn and Estevan are located. The other is over near the western border, above the village of Maple Creek in the region of sand hills on up to the South Saskatchewan River. Most of the hunting in either location will be on privately owned lands, but permission is usually not difficult to obtain, and there are accommodations in the regions for sharptail hunters, with guides available.

Although seasonal fluctuations may make one region better than the other and vice versa during certain years, a look at the high-kill Zones for a recent and quite typical season gives a good idea of where the birds are. Zones 11 and 13 were highest and almost identical in percent of kill, slightly over 10 percent of the total. Next came Zones 12 and 15, with slightly under and slightly over 8 percent each. Zones 14, 17, 25 were next, in that order.

Perhaps a more revealing statistic is the kill per square mile. The Zones stacked up in the following order: 12, which is along the South Saskatchewan River, was first; Zone 11 below it was second; then came Zone 15, Zone 13, Zone 8—which is east of 11 near Swift Current—Zone 1 in the southeast, then 14, 17, 25. While Zones 3, 4, and 6 in the southeast had a substantial harvest of birds, the kill per square mile was much less. The above statistics will be valid for almost any season in helping plan a hunt.

HUNGARIAN PARTRIDGE

The Hun, introduced in 1908 near Calgary, Alberta, spread eventually to Saskatchewan. The first nest was discovered there in 1922 near the village of Unity, which is near the western border southwest from North Battleford. In the 1930s the bird became extremely abundant over the agricultural area and much sought by sportsmen. Today it is second in abundance and popularity only to the sharptail. In fact, in some past seasons the kill has far exceeded that of the sharptail, having run above 200,000. The average is somewhat less, from below 100,000 to upwards of 150,000.

Huns favor croplands, prefer open fields, and require very little cover. Rolling plains with shallow valleys and some rather bare knolls on treeless farms are their prime habitat. Almost all of the cultivated part of Saskatchewan has this bird, with populations extending in lesser numbers clear to the forest region near the center of the province. Density of population is generally highest in the west.

Highest kill is usually in Zone 13. Curiously, this is the Zone just south of the spot where the first nest was discovered. Although high kills may differ with seasonal fluctuations in nesting success, recently they ran as follows: Zone 3 in the southeast was second, Zone 8 south of Swift Current in the southwest was third, followed by 11, 17, 6, 15, 1, 7, 14. This scattered incidence well illustrates the broad range of the bird.

However, kills per square mile do not quite follow the total kill figures given above. During one typical season lately they were as follows. Zone 8 was first, 13 second, 1 third. The remainder of the first ten were in the following order: 11, 3, 7, 12, 15, 17, 6.

RUFFED GROUSE

Although the ruffed grouse is quite common in portions of Saskatchewan, it is not as readily accessible to hunters as are the sharptail and Hun, and therefore not as popular. This is a bird of the forest edges. It is commonly called brush partridge or willow partridge in Saskatchewan. Its range is chiefly across central Saskatchewan, in the belt of aspen grove vegetation running from southeast to northwest from the eastern border across just north of Regina and roughly through Saskatoon, and in the belt of commercial forest in the next vegetation zone and pivoting on Prince Albert. The range extends onward into the next vegetation zone, the northern coniferous forest, but the density is lighter there. There is also a pocket of abundance down in the southwest, in the forest of the Cypress Hills. This area lies on the western border and extending out from in between Routes 1 and 13.

The annual ruffed grouse kill averages from 20,000 to 25,000, and on peak cycles shoots up to above 40,000. Zones 30, 25, and 32 in that order and lying up across the central part of the province often show high kills and fair density. Zone 27, northeast of Prince Albert, also often has a good supply of birds. During one season of late the first ten Zones in order of total kill were as follows: 30, 25, 32, 27, 29, 23, 14, 31, 33, 24.

SPRUCE GROUSE

The spruce grouse, a deep-forest bird, is found in Saskatchewan in the northern half of the province, where dense forest exists, and to some extent on into the far north transition zone where timber becomes dwarfed. Swampy regions along streams or bordering muskeg, where cedar, tamarack, or black spruce make dense thickets, are favored by this rather tame species. The birds are seldom hunted except as incidentals, and the kill is low, averaging from about 5000 to possibly 12,000 a season. The area to the northeast and northwest of Prince Albert shows the only sizable kill, probably because it is accessible from that city via road. The region corresponds to Zones 26, 27, 30, 33. Zone 25 to the southeast also is fair. Undoubtedly excellent hunting of a spotty nature exists still undiscovered in innumerable locations of the roadless north, but the so-called foolhen has no great appeal for sport because it has little fear of man.

PTARMIGAN

The willow ptarmigan, sometimes called "white partridge," is found in this province only north of the tree line in the tundra country. Only dwarf willows and birch grow in portions of their normal range. In winter scattered groups occasionally move as far south as the commercial forest region above Prince Albert. However, these migrations are uncertain. Thus, because of the arctic range of the bird in roadless country, few are taken by sportsmen. For those willing to brave the rigors of the far north in winter, excellent shooting is available. The kill at present is almost entirely by natives for food.

PHEASANT

The ringneck was introduced to this province, in the agricultural south, about 1900. It has been a popular game bird, but is present only in modest numbers. There has been a stocking program for many years. Winters are so severe that the birds often sustain high losses. Pheasants are fairly well distributed over the grassland vegetation zone of southern Saskatchewan, excepting the Cypress Hills forest area of the southwest. This range encompasses most of the cropland region. In the southeast, the Souris River course is an area of high density, and the same is true in the south-central sector, the Wood River region.

Presently pheasants are hunted only by residents of Saskatchewan, cocks only, under a special permit. One recent season opened at the end of September and ran through into early November. Almost half of the birds were bagged the first week, and the total kill was 10,564. In peak years it has been approximately double that. Ordinarily Zones 1 through 18 are open. Zones 7 and 3 show the bulk of the kill, well over 50 percent. Next in line are Zones 6 and 8. Along the South Saskatchewan River there is fair shooting, with Zones 12 and 16 next in line.

WATERFOWL

Some of the finest duck and goose shooting on the continent is offered in Saskatchewan. Compared to the number of hunters, the kill is extremely high. The duck bag has run as high in recent years as 750,000, but in most years between 400,000 and 500,000 are taken. The goose kill averages around 75,000, depending on leniency of regulations.

Because of its prairies and their sloughs and potholes, the province is a prime nesting ground for ducks. Mallards, one of the great favorites among duck hunters, make up at least two-thirds and sometimes more of the total harvest. Other ducks include pintails, blue- and green-winged teal, gadwalls, baldpates, shovelers, redheads, and canvasbacks.

The province makes a survey of the kill by weekly periods. This is valuable information for any hunter planning a waterfowl hunting trip. While weather during any given fall may change the timing somewhat, statistics show that in general the period from mid through late September in any normal season is fair to good for duck hunting, the first week of October brings the peak of the shooting, with a decline thereafter during the second week of October but still very good results. From there on the decline is steady.

The southern third of the province, south of Prince Albert, accounts for all but a minor percentage of the duck kill. There is much good shooting in scattered locations over most of this area, but the central portion of the west, and the central interior, furnish at least 75 percent of the ducks bagged. Zones 12, 13, 14 in the west, and Zones 17, 18, 25 in the interior are the most important. During one season just passed, Zone 13 furnished almost 20 percent of the total duck kill of the province, Zone 25 was next, with 12.85 percent, and Zone 17 third, with 11.09 percent.

Goose hunting is varied, with Canadas, whitefronted geese (speckle-bellies), snows, and blues. Canadas of three subspecies are found here, and they are dominant in the bag, with the whitefronts second. Of approximately 75,000 geese killed one season, 34,000 were Canadas, 29,000 whitefronts. Hunters should check regulations carefully. There have been restrictions on shooting snows in certain Zones until after a specified date, even when the season for other geese was open.

During a normal season the best weeks for goose hunting are the last week in September and the first week of October for Canadas and whitefronts, and the second two weeks of October for snows. Mid-September and late October are sometimes fair. Zone 13 is the quality goose hunting location. Some years it furnishes almost half of the total bag. Zone 12 just below it to the south may be qualified as good. There is also good goose hunting some seasons far to the north and east, along the Saskatchewan River in Zone 34.

There are several special goose-hunt regulations. Laws should be carefully checked.

SNIPE

There is an open season on jacksnipe, and they are plentiful in the prairie pothole region. They get very little attention from hunters except as incidentals. The bag limit is quite high—it has been 10 daily in recent seasons—and waterfowl hunters are well advised to add snipe shooting to their lowland activities. The better duck Zones are also the best for snipe.

SANDHILL CRANES

The lesser sandhill crane has long been a hazard in fall to grain farmers in the central portion of southern Saskatchewan. During late August and September the birds gather by thousands chiefly in the region north of Regina, at the northern end of Last Mountain Lake and in the vicinity of the Quill Lakes farther north. They are grain feeders, and their depredations are severe. For many years, beginning in 1918, the birds had full protection. Pressure built for an open season, but authorities were hesitant. This is a migration lane for the rare whooping crane, and also some greater sandhill cranes, which are by no means as numerous as the lesser sandhill cranes, pass through the area.

However, in 1964 a short season was instigated. It has been continued since. It is not set by Zone, but by specified highway and township boundaries. Recently it has occurred in early September for a two-week period, with a daily bag of 4 and a possession limit of 8. Hunters should note that if whooping cranes come into the area the season will be closed immediately.

Few hunters know the sandhill crane as a game bird. It is exceedingly wary, very sporty, and a superb table bird. Although birds are abundant in the hunting area, few hunters participate and only 2000 to 3000 cranes are bagged. This is a most interesting sport that many more hunters could enjoy without harming the crane population.

SMALL GAME AND PREDATORS

There are cottontails in southern Saskatchewan, with only fair density and mostly in the south-central border region and the southwest. The large white-tailed jackrabbit ranges over the plains of the province south of Prince Albert. The snowshoe or varying hare ranges throughout the province, but with highest density north of Prince Albert. Rabbits may be hunted throughout the year in the southern third of the province, but they receive very little attention.

The red fox is fairly common over the southern two-thirds of the province, excepting the extreme southwest. Coyotes range over all of the southern area and on a short distance above Prince Albert, are found very occasionally even farther north. Both foxes and coyotes are hunted all year in the south, but do not elicit much attention. However, interest in both is beginning to increase. Hunters using a predator call can do well in the prairie and plains region, for neither animal has to date had much experience with this method and most individuals are rather naive about the sound.

DEER

The province has both whitetail and mule deer. The whitetail is the most abundant and important big-game animal here. It ranges throughout all of the agricultural region of the southern half of the province where there is at least some cover, and the range extends to some extent to the north of Prince Albert. The mule deer is a species primarily of the southwestern corner of Saskatchewan, but it is also found in scattered and sparse population over all of the whitetail range.

Deer hunting is excellent, and extremely popular. License sales have averaged over recent years above 65,000, and the total kill exceeds 40,000. This indicates a very high success. Over two seasons lately it ran 63 percent. Some Zones offer 2-deer seasons, either-sex hunting is usual, and there are numerous special seasons offered each year, so the hunting guide (regulations) for the year in question should be carefully studied before a trip is planned.

Whitetails grossly predominate in the kill. Mule deer average from 5 to 10 percent of the total harvest. Over 60 percent of the total deer harvest are bucks. For some seasons Zone 2 in the southeast has turned in the largest kill, both in number of deer bagged and in number per square mile. The average is above 1.5 per square mile in this top Zone. During a recent special hunt, under permit, in the Moose Mountain Game Preserve in Zone 2, the kill ran almost seven deer per square mile.

Other Zones with high success are 1, 4, 19, 20. This indicates that the best deer hunting in the province is concentrated in the southeast, and is for whitetails. Mule deer range in the southwest, incidentally, has been declining in quality over a period of years and the future for that species is not too encouraging.

MOOSE

The Saskatchewan moose kill runs around 5000 animals per season. The range is over all of the province north of Prince Albert and to somewhat below that line in the east. As a rule there are several seasons: an early one beginning in September, a regular season in November, plus special Game Preserve seasons early and late. Success for residents and nonresident Canadians averages between 40 and 45 percent, but nonresident aliens do somewhat better, generally well above 60 percent, probably because all are guided. Invariably the major share of the kill occurs during the first week of the early season.

In a typical season approximately 13 Zones are open. These include 21, 22, 23, 24 in the east, then 27, 29, and 30, and the remainder of the north. Guided hunters with good outfitters have an excellent chance of success in any of the open Zones. A recent typical season showed the highest moose density, by kill per square mile, in Zones 34, 22, 21, 24, in that order. Zones 33 and 23 were next. Highest kills by number of animals bagged follow somewhat the same pattern. By Zones and in order they were: 22, 34, 32, 21, 33, 24, 23.

ELK

Elk are not plentiful in Saskatchewan, and their range has been diminishing for some years. They are found in the commercial forest zone that lies in a swath across the province to the north of Prince Albert and dipping down southward along the eastern border. There is also some elk range in the southwest, and the southeast. Only residents of Saskatchewan are allowed to hunt elk. Usually the hunt is for either sex, and the Zones follow fairly closely the commercial forest region—21 through 24, 27, 29, 30, 31, part of 32, and 33. There is some special hunting on several Game Preserves.

There is a special license for elk hunting, but to date it is not on a quota and drawing basis. Over recent seasons from 800 to 1100 hunters have participated in the regular season, with a kill of slightly under to a bit over 300 animals. In some of the Preserve hunts success is substantially higher. Total kill from all hunts in a recent, exceptional season was 436. Heaviest kill Zones that same season, in order, were: 30, 23, 27, 21, 33. As a rule this is either-sex hunting, with bulls making up approximately half of the kill.

WOODLAND CARIBOU

The range of the woodland caribou in Saskatchewan is mainly in the swath of commercial forest north of Prince Albert and on into the coniferous belt. They have been observed as far south along the eastern boundary as the town of Hudson Bay, south of the Saskatchewan River. Hunting is for residents of the province only, and there are even certain restrictions regarding nonresidents of some of the open Zones. There are usually several special Game Preserve seasons in addition to the regular season.

Success runs fairly high, with chances 1 in 3 to 1 in 2 or a bit better. Only an average of seventy-five to eighty animals are taken each season. For some time the heaviest kill has been in Zone 32, followed by 33. This is highly specialized hunting. Some seasons half the hunters see no caribou. The last few days of November and the first few of December appear to be the best in a normal season.

ANTELOPE

Antelope hunting also is only for residents of the province. The herd is not large, is restricted to the southwest and portions of the southern border. Because this region is at the northern fringe of antelope range, there is rather severe fluctuation in numbers of animals from year to year. Severe winters are hard on the antelope bands.

Each year an aerial survey is flown to determine the number of animals available as surplus. Then the number of permits is set, if a season appears possible. These are acquired by application and drawing. Lately applications have been required by mid-August. Interested hunters should contact the Wildlife Branch about mid-July to ascertain whether or not a season will be held, and to acquire an application form.

The kill is very modest, varying from under 1000 to a peak about ten years ago of approximately 4000. The open Zones depend upon herd condition. Ordinarily the ones expected to be open are 7, 8, 9, 10, 11, 12, 16. These cover the southwestern corner of the province. It is not possible to predict which Zones may be best in any given season. During one recently past, the first five in order were: 11, 9, 10, 12, 7.

BEAR

The black bear range of most consequence is the swath of commercial forest across the province immediately north of Prince Albert, and dipping southward along the eastern border. Bears range on north in lesser numbers.

Until 1967 residents of the province needed no license to hunt bear, and there was no bag limit. Presently residents as well as nonresidents must be licensed, and the bag limit has recently been 2 bear. The season is open both spring and fall. But during a certain period of the fall no person is allowed to hunt bear unless he has also purchased a deer, moose, elk, or caribou license valid in the Zone where he is hunting. Recently all Zones have been open to Saskatchewan residents, but only Zones 20 to 36 for nonresidents. There are some special Game Preserve hunts. These must be checked for the season in question.

Bear license sales are low, presently averaging total about 400. Most bear are killed during the regular big-game season, as incidentals. The kill is low, possibly averaging around a hundred per season. It is not possible to state which Zones are best. During one recent season the first five in order were: 32, 23, 22, 27, 31.

REGULATIONS

Address all queries regarding regulations, Zone maps, and other details to the Department of Natural Resources, Wildlife Branch, Government Administration Bldg., Regina, Saskatchewan, Canada.

MANITOBA

The Province of Manitoba has been described as the "heart of the continent, where east meets west and north meets south." It is almost exactly centered in North America. Called one of the three "prairie provinces," it is the easternmost, lying between Ontario and Saskatchewan. The northern border is with the Northwest Territories, and the northeast fronts on the western shores of Hudson Bay. The southern boundary is with North Dakota and Minnesota.

Manitoba covers a vast area, 251,000 square miles, with great diversity of terrain. In a triangle of the southwest are the upland prairies, with a general elevation of about 600 to 700 feet. Separating these uplands from Saskatchewan is the Manitoba Escarpment, a swath of hills and broken terrain reaching altitudes in places almost to 3000 feet. The southwest and much of southern Manitoba is farming country, with wheat a primary crop. East of the prairies and stretching in a broad corridor on a slant from northwest toward the southeast are the Manitoba Lowlands. Here the huge lakes—Lake Winnipeg, Lake Winnipegosis—and scores of lesser lakes are surrounded by forest, and rocky terrain once torn by glaciers begins. Above this, still on a slant across the province, is a region of dense forest with an endless welter of lakes and streams. The terrain eventually flattens out into the fourth and final climate-vegetation zone, the subarctic, where forest finally dwindles into tundra.

Much of Manitoba is wilderness. Total population is approximately one million. Over half this number are in the metropolitan area of Winnipeg, the largest city, and fourth largest in Canada. Over 80 percent of the total population of the province lives in a comparatively narrow belt across the south. This includes Winnipeg, and the farming region, roughly that portion south of Lake Manitoba and southern Lake Winnipeg.

Roads throughout this area are good, and numerous. A fair network of highways runs up the western border in the region west of Lake Manitoba and lower Lake Winnipegosis. These routes culminate at the town of Swan River. From here a good highway probes on north, along the western border, to The Pas, Cranberry Portage, locations famous among hunters, and finally to the mining town of Flin Flon. This is at the edge of the total wilderness of the far north. From it the Canadian National Railway reaches on to Lynn Lake, northwest of the Churchill River. Also from Flin Flon a newer and unpaved highway stretches east and northeast to the settlement of Thompson. The railway parallels this route, and goes on far across the northeast almost to the eastern border, and thence north to Churchill on the southwest shore of Hudson Bay.

For sportsmen who do not fly, this is the only highway and rail route into the far north, and the only one reaching as far north as the game lands near The Pas and Flin Flon. However, from Winnipeg in the southeast a main route runs northwest, up into the territory between Lake Winnipegosis and Lake Winnipeg. In the lower part of this region other roads reach out to settlements on the lakes. But throughout the northern half of the run the highway stretches through wilderness. All of the immense expanse east of Lake Winnipeg and from there on throughout the north is roadless and virtually unsettled, except for the crossing in the far north of the railway, already mentioned.

Air travel to and throughout the south is excellent, and there are scheduled flights to all the important outlying settlements, such as Flin Flon. Air travel into much of the wilderness, by charter and with bush pilots, is the chief means of transport. Adventuresome hunters, properly guided, can get to vast portions of the northern wilderness via canoe. Much of the northeast and north is a virtual maze of lakes and connecting streams. Many of the streams are large, and wild. This is in general not the kind of adventure for the casual hunter or one inexperienced in wilderness survival.

Quite obviously there is plenty of room to hunt, and enormous areas of open lands. Hunters are not numerous. For example, deer hunters, the largest segment of big-game hunters, number less than 40,000, and in one recent season about 43,000 bird hunting licenses were sold. Moose hunters numbered recently over 8000, but this number is divided between early and late seasons. And, the hunters are scattered over vast stretches of territory and among many guides and outfitters. The Wildlife Branch can furnish lists of licensed guides and their addresses. The lists are divided into southern Manitoba, and the northern region. In general the northern list is for guides from about The Pas on north.

Roughly 25 percent of the land area of Manitoba is owned by individuals or corporations. Almost all of this is in the south and developed for agriculture: the prairie uplands of the southwest, the southern and western portions of the Lowlands. More than 100 million acres in the province are Crown Lands, and of these only about two million are in National Parks, Indian Reservations, Refuges, etc. Thus there is no problem whatever in finding ample territory in which to hunt. However, visitors should be aware that for most bird hunting and some very good deer hunting privately owned lands of the south and southwest must be utilized, by permission. To date there is very little problem in obtaining it.

Because of its unusually diverse terrain and vegetation, and far-reaching latitudes, Manitoba has an impressively varied list of game species. Sharptail grouse, ruffed grouse, spruce grouse, rock and willow ptarmigan, Hungarian partridge are the uplanders. There are massive flights of ducks, geese, sandhill cranes. Among big game, whitetail deer are the most hunted. Moose are abundant, there is a small elk herd, plus a modest number of woodland caribou and black bear. Snowshoe hares, and various predators such as foxes, wolves, lynx, wolverine, range over much of the province.

While in several provinces of Canada it is mandatory that nonresidents use the services of a guide, it is not compulsory in Manitoba. Neither residents nor nonresidents are required to be guided, but certainly in remote areas it is advisable. The Wildlife Branch can be of assistance in locating guides, but of course cannot recommend them. Manitoba does have a new Hunter Safety Training law, with which residents must be familiar. It does not apply to non-residents.

For camping hunters who go to Manitoba during the early seasons, before winter temperatures make camping less inviting, there are numerous sites along the highways and in the Parks. A booklet listing all, titled "Manitoba Campgrounds," may be obtained from the Tourist Branch, Department of Tourism and Recreation, Legislative Building, Winnipeg. From this same address much printed matter about vacations in Manitoba may be obtained, as well as much specific information about areas and hunting. Guided hunters will of course be lodged in camps of outfitters. There are adequate facilities for food and lodging for hunters on their own in all the southern towns and also along the highways.

Manitoba weather in early fall is pleasant to crisp in the south, progressively colder as one moves north. In the north even during early big-game seasons warm clothing, rain gear, and good boots, both rubber and leather, are recommended. Later seasons require the warmest of clothing. Even southern Manitoba has extremely severe winters.

Weapons must be related to the game in question. Upland bird hunters will need shot sizes No. 7½ and No. 6 as standard loads. Waterfowlers should take heavier loads, larger shot sizes. Deer hunters do well with standard deer calibers anywhere from .243 and .30/30 to .308 and the milder magnums. For moose and bear the '06 and .308 and 7mm are good examples, with loadings of 180 to 200 grains.

Manitoba is divided into numbered Hunting Areas. Presently there are more than thirty-seven of these, with some subdivided (6, 6a). Numbers begin with Area 1 in the far north, and grow progressively larger southward, with the highest numbers in the southeast. Both residents and visitors must obtain from the Wildlife Branch a map showing these Areas, and study the laws pertaining to them and to which are open for the season in question. They should also be certain of the boundaries of the few Wildlife Refuges, and some twenty-six Game Bird Refuges where bird hunting is not allowed. These are all noted on the regulations map. Because it is not possible to predict from season to season which Areas will be open for which species, or exact Area boundaries, which may change from year to year, the following material under species headings will describe in general terms the location of the high density ranges for each species, but without mentioning Hunting Areas by number. By checking these ranges against the regulations map for a given season, readers can quickly establish where the most game of any variety is likely to be found. Guides of course are of immense assistance toward success, regardless of species.

SHARPTAIL GROUSE

Although much of Canada is renowned for its big game, some of the best upland bird hunting is found there, and especially so in the prairie provinces. The most important uplander in Manitoba is the sharptail grouse. Often confusingly and incorrectly called "prairie chicken" here, the sharptail is a bird of the prairies and the scrub aspen, of the open lands where second growth, grass, and farming are mixed, and of the large burns where brush and grass intermingle.

Manitoba sharptail seasons open in early September in the northern range of the bird, and progressively later, to about mid-October in the south. Limits in parts of the north are as high as 8 per day but only 3 or 4 per day near the southern border.

High-density areas for sharptails are chiefly over the southern large-lake region and the south. Near the town of Swan River near the western border at about latitude 52 degrees there is a small area of fair abundance. A large, long area east of the city of Dauphin, between Dauphin Lake and Lake Manitoba and running south between that lake and Riding Mountain National Park to the west is one of the best ranges. This range continues about to Spruce Woods Provincial Park. East, on the far side of Lake Manitoba and between it and lower Lake Winnipeg, in what is known as the Interlake region, this same high density exists. This is the area north of the city of Winnipeg, up to about Highway 68 east-west. There are patches of good range south and east of Winnipeg, centered about on the town of Steinbach, another large one south of Portage la Prairie. Possibly the best area is in the extreme southwest, in general along and south and west of the Assiniboine River, with the towns of Virden and Melita good location points.

Over all of the intervening region below an east-west line running through Swan River, fair to light sharptail populations are found. Farther north there is less suitable habitat and occurrences are scattered.

PRAIRIE CHICKEN

This grouse, also called pinnated grouse, moved into southern Manitoba with the coming of agricultural pursuits over a century ago. For a time it was abundant. But it was unable to tolerate concentrated land use and changing land uses, and is now considered all but extinct here. It is fully protected.

SPRUCE GROUSE

Spruce grouse are inhabitants of dense and usually boggy forests, where spruce and larch are in thick stands and there is much moss on the ground. Often called "fool hen" because of its lack of fear of man, it is nowhere here an important game bird but often shot incidentally by ruffed grouse hunters. It is found in the forests of eastern, central, and much of northern Manitoba, usually in rather scattered colonies, wherever suitable habitat is present.

RUFFED GROUSE

Over almost all of Manitoba ruffed grouse are present in sparse numbers, wherever proper forest edges, openings, and stream borders occur to supply their favored habitat. However, in several places in the south there are populations of much higher density. These expanses are where park lands of aspen, mixed forests, and brushy borders near farming lands form prime range. One such region lies south of Swan River, along and expanding east from the western border about to the town of Dauphin. Two other concentrations are on either side of Lake Manitoba, along and out from the shoreline, below the center point of that lake's constriction and, on the east side, south of Dog Lake. The southeastern corner of Manitoba, enclosed by lines running east and south from Winnipeg, also offers good ruffed grouse density. The same is true of a small area on the southern border well over toward the southwest, the Turtle Mountains.

PTARMIGAN

There are two species present, the rock ptarmigan, the willow ptarmigan. The rock ptarmigan is not an important game bird, but is used to some extent by natives of the far north. It is a bird of the arctic tundra which moves in winter down into the northern extremes of Manitoba. The vicinity of Churchill on Hudson Bay often gets a fair concentration. The birds summer farther north.

Willow ptarmigan are found in the mixed tundra and dwarf-tree zone of transition across northern Manitoba, but drift down into the forested region below tundra line during the winter. Occasionally they winter as far south as The Pas. Because ptarmigan densities are so far removed from most settlement, they are not important here as game birds. Moose hunters in the north, however, have an opportunity to hunt them. And with the season opening in early September hunters might easily plan special trips for ptarmigan, traveling via the Canadian National Railway north of Flin Flon or up toward Churchill. With a daily limit of 10 and 30 possession, this could be an attractive adventure.

HUNGARIAN PARTRIDGE

The Hun was introduced to southern Manitoba almost half a century ago. It has hit high peaks and at other times all but disappeared. There are a few over much of the southwest. In the southeast, between the Red River and the Sandilands Provincial Forest, there is a modest population. Best area for Huns, however, is in the far southwestern corner of the province, west of Deloraine and Hartney and south of Virden.

PHEASANT

A few pheasants are present in southern Manitoba near the border. Pheasants were first tried in the 1930s. Most have colonized from U.S. flocks. At time of this writing there is no open season, and none is expected. The birds are apparently at the fringe of their northern range and have not increased to huntable numbers.

WILD TURKEYS

The wild turkey was stocked experimentally in Manitoba some time ago. It has not made notable progress. Winters it is thought are too severe and food covered by too much snow. Some still remain but are for the most part dependent upon farmers who feed them with grain. There is not likely to be turkey hunting in the province within the foreseeable future.

WATERFOWL

For many years Manitoba has been world famous for its duck hunting. Numerous camps and lodges and guides specialize in duck hunting trips for both visitors and residents. This province is in the middle of the Mississippi Flyway and along the western border the Central Flyway overlaps. In addition, some of the most important duck breeding grounds on the continent are in Manitoba. The pothole district of the southwest, called the Minnedosa-Erickson district because of the towns south of Riding Mountain National Park on which it is based, has long been nationally important as a duck producing region. The same is true of the entire area from that surrounding The Pas down through the Basin of Lake Winnipegosis and Lake Manitoba. When in fall flights from farther north pour down the flyway, this entire region contains one of the great duck concentrations of the continent.

Mallards are the single most important species, making up over half the entire bag. Pintails are also very important. Bluebills, teal, redheads, canvasbacks also are numerous in the total duck bag.

All told, probably the best shooting area, and certainly the most spectacular, is the grainfield shooting in the southwest and the pothole region, where mallards and pintails are the dominant species. Some seasons duck depredations are a great nuisance to farmers. The Pas also has long been famous as a duck hunting location. So have the marshes around lower Lake Manitoba and Lake Winnipeg, and the wild rice areas of the southeast. Duck hunters shooting in southwestern Manitoba can usually make arrangements with farmers and have no difficulty finding birds. For shooting farther north, such as at The Pas or along the big lakes, it is desirable to hire a guide who knows the area and where the best flights occur. The Wildlife Branch can assist in locating proper guides.

A sizable percentage of the continent's goose flock also breeds in the far north. Only the Canada goose breeds in parts of Manitoba. In fall, blue and snow geese seldom pause in any concentration as they migrate south from their arctic breeding grounds. Some whitefronted geese (specklebellies) pass over western Manitoba and occasionally pause. Canada geese are the ones, in several of their varieties, that become concentrated in marshes, along the large lakes down the Basin, and in the grain region of the south and southwest. Hunting grounds are closely similar to the best one described for ducks. And again, guided hunts will invariably prove most successful. Hunters should carefully check special goose hunting restrictions.

There are open seasons on snipe and rails. These birds draw little attention. However, excellent snipe shooting is offered on wet prairies, around the potholes and marsh edges. Most of it is pursued as an incidental to duck hunting.

SANDHILL CRANE

Over the past few years there has been a hunting season allowed for lesser sandhill cranes in specified portions of the prairie provinces, among them Manitoba, where grain depredations have been severe. As this is written, only residents are allowed to hunt cranes, and in only a small area southeast of Riding Mountain National Park and between it and southern Lake Manitoba. This tract, designated on the regulations map as Area B, is bounded on the east by Route 50, on the north by 261, the west by 260, the south by 4.

SMALL GAME

There are a few cottontails in southern Manitoba but no important population of them. Snowshoe hares are present in suitable areas, are little hunted for sport. Manitoba does not issue a small-game license. Jackrabbits and snowshoes are not protected.

BEARS

The black bear is the dominant bear species in Manitoba, and ranges over all of the province except the south-central and southwest farming regions. A line drawn roughly from the west at the 51st parallel across to a bit south of Gimli on the western shore of Lake Winnipeg, thence around the southern end of that lake and then south a bit east of Steinbach to the U.S. border encloses to the vast north and east all of the black bear range. The range of medium to heavy density is somewhat farther south. It runs north to above the Churchill and Nelson Rivers, but does not include the far north or inland a good distance from Hudson Bay.

Black bears are nowhere especially abundant, and are not avidly hunted. They are taken as a rule additionally and by chance, by hunters after moose and deer. The kill is never high. Incidence of black bears around lumber and mining camps is fairly high, and near small and isolated settlements. Most of the province is open to hunting, and guides familiar with their areas are the best bet for successful black bear hunts. One recent season showed 385 blacks taken, most by trappers. The Whiteshell Provincial Park, Duck Mountain Provincial Park and Porcupine Provincial Forest Preserve are favorite bear hunting areas.

The grizzly, in its prairie form, once was found in Manitoba. It is now presumed to be extinct there.

Polar bears roam the edges of Hudson Bay, in the far northeast, spending the winters on pack ice, but drifting inland during late summer and early fall to establish denning areas along the pressure ridges. These bears, however, are fully protected.

ELK

Many years ago the southern Manitoba parklands with their aspen stands, open grasslands, and regions of mixed forest had an elk population of fair proportions. Elk, along with buffalo and antelope, were major wild "livestock" of this southern region. As settlement encroached on elk habitat, the animals were forced back into less suitable environments. Today, elk are not numerous. Remnant bands exist on protected lands. There are pockets of elk habitation north and south of Swan River on the lower western border, below the town of Dauphin in the upper southwest, and in a few small and scattered suitable localities. During a recent season a single Hunting Area, No. 18, had an elk season. This Area is on the western border and inland to the east, in the Duck Mountain region. It lies below Swan River and Routes 83 and 10 on the north and east, with Route 5 at the south. Season for residents only, a small number of permits by application and drawing, bulls only. Thus elk hunting in Manitoba is not an important pursuit except for a few residents who draw permits. Whether or not this elk herd can survive in huntable surplus over coming years is questionable.

CARIBOU

Two species are associated with Manitoba, the Barren-Ground caribou of the far north, which is habitually migratory by season, and the woodland caribou. The Barren-Ground caribou is not a sport-hunting species at this time in Manitoba. In past years it has been a prominent food source for arctic natives, wintering as far south as the Nelson River and Granville Lake in the north. Drastic decline in numbers is to date not fully explained.

Woodland caribou long ago came as far south in winter as southeastern Manitoba. Today only remnant herds are left, in small bands, with an estimated total of only a few thousand. They range north of Flin Flon and Gods Lake, with a fair winter population north and south of The Pas, others around Kississing Lake north of Flin Flon, and still more in the east, on the east side of Lake Winnipeg. Scattered bands appear elsewhere.

After years of closed season, there was a limited season for 1967. Seasons have continued since. In 1968 there were 32 caribou taken. The 1969 license issue was 350 resident, and 67 nonresident. Applicants may state their preference for open area, but all have low caribou populations, and there is little choice. The caribou herd, while small, appears to be stable.

MOOSE

The moose is second in importance, after deer, of big game in Manitoba. They are plentiful over a large territory, and kill success by both resident and nonresident hunters is high. There is an early season, generally bulls only, beginning in September, and a late season, in December, for any moose but over a much more restricted area. Statistics by seasons for a recent one give a good average picture.

Resident hunters for the early season numbered 1818, and the kill was 816. The winter season found 5321 resident hunters out, and a total estimated kill of 2723. Nonresidents, early season, 642, late season 450, kills of 207 and 232. Thus, 8231 hunters bagged 3978 moose for a success of close to 50 percent overall. Bulls-only seasons show slightly lower success.

Moose range in Manitoba is vast, and hunting is often best in the more inaccessible places. However, these present problems, both in getting hunters in and getting meat out. In the far north the moose range reaches up almost to Churchill in the northeast and to some distance north of Reindeer Lake (mostly in Saskatchewan) in the west. Few hunters are likely to go that far. Also, the best portions of range with highest moose populations are farther south.

One of these is immediately northwest of Granville Lake and south of the town of Lynn Lake to which the Canadian National Railway runs. This is on the western side of the province. South, beginning about at Kississing Lake and lying in a broad swath from there on south to Flin Flon, Moose Lake, and The Pas is another important area. To the east, in the Thompson region and southwest from it, is a third good range, accessible by rail or road. Still farther east, below the Nelson River and Split Lake, is a fourth region of substantial population. The CNR runs through this.

The remainder of the better moose range lies across the lake district south of The Pas, and in the southeast. Both north and south of Swan River on the western border are pockets of abundance, with good access. To the east, most of the area between Lake Winnipegosis and Lake Winnipeg is an important range. Some of the region straight across on the eastern border, about at the point where this border angles off to the northeast, is also important, but far less accessible. Most of the southeast, along the eastern shore of lower Lake Winnipeg roughly from Black Island to the Ontario border and in a corridor about this wide from both points south to the U.S. border, encompasses the remainder of the best moose territory. While moose occur all along and south of upper Lake Winnipeg, and there are scattered animals even south of Dauphin, none of the south-central or southwest or the Red River valley below Winnipeg is good hunting territory, and most of it has no moose population.

DEER

The whitetail deer is the most important big-game animal in Manitoba. When pioneers first came to the area, deer were all but unknown. Settlement, cutting and opening of forests, made habitat attractive to deer and slowly the deer population built up until today most of southern Manitoba has fair to dense occurrence. Close to 40,000 resident hunters follow the sport each fall, and success is high, on the overall average often up almost to 60 percent. Most Hunting Areas are open, for residents, for any-deer hunting. Nonresidents, who are discovering the excellent hunting possibilities, have recently been restricted to bucks only.

Although whitetails have colonized the region as far north as about to Flin Flon in the west and to slightly below the Berens River on the east side of Lake Winnipeg, most of these northern herds are sparse. The best whitetail ranges are as follows: in the southeast, from and north of the deep bend in the Winnipeg River south to the U.S. border; on the Lake Manitoba side of the Interlake region and also in the central portion of the Interlake; on the west side of northern Lake Manitoba; over much of the southwest. Neepawa, Brandon, Virden, Deloraine are all good general locations in the prime southwestern range. Much of the Assiniboine River region of the southwest is excellent. All of the country surrounding these high-density areas offers good hunting, and whitetails are becoming more abundant year by year. The herd now is estimated to be at least a quarter of a million.

At one time mule deer were fairly plentiful over much of the south. Settlement and agriculture, while amenable to the whitetail, seldom are to mule deer. Presently these deer, commonly called "jumpers" here, have practically disappeared from the province. It is possible that remnants remain in a small area on and spreading out from the western border north and south of the town of Swan River. The Porcupine Provincial Forest, Duck Mountain Provincial Forest, and Riding Mountain National Park encompass almost all of the last known remaining mule deer range. Mule deer may be taken during deer season and occasionally a hunter claims to have seen or shot one, but these reports are without confirmation.

OTHER ANIMALS

Although a number of predators and other common animals are native to Manitoba, most are considered fur bearers and treated as such. There is almost no sport hunting for them. There are wolves in modest numbers throughout much of the province, coyotes in the south. The lynx is fairly common in the forests, even down into the southeast. Bobcats apparently spread from the U.S. up into southeastern Manitoba within the past few decades.

There are red foxes and their color variations—black, silver, and cross. Arctic foxes prowl the tundra of the far north. Though not common, the wolverine ranges in the far north. There are a few badgers in the south and southwest and up the western side of the province to about the Duck Mountain region. Raccoons have over the past few years built up increasing numbers along the southern border, and there are whitetailed jackrabbits in the prairie sector. Animal calling, avidly followed by numerous hunters in the U.S., has not been tried with any concentration in Manitoba. The possibilities are exciting, for a variety of species.

REGULATIONS

It is important that any hunter planning a Manitoba hunt write for the map showing Hunting Areas. This applies both to birds and big game. As noted, open Areas may change from season to season. For this map, and other queries, write to: Department of Mines and Natural Resources, Wildlife Branch, 908 Norquay Bldg., Winnipeg 1, Manitoba, Canada.

ONTARIO

The province of Ontario is in many ways the focal province of Canada. Its extremely irregular boundaries encompass 412,582 square miles of territory lying between Quebec on the east and Manitoba on the west. In the south Ontario touches all of the Great Lakes except Lake Michigan, and in the north the entire boundary is with James and Hudson bays. Thus the province has approximately a fourth of its borders on fresh water and another fourth on salt water.

Ontario is like two separate provinces. North and west from the Great Lakes the great bulk of the region is typical of the vast, rocky plateau called the Canadian Shield. Here endless forests spread over the land, lakes are everywhere, streams slash the wilderness, and in the far north muskeg runs on toward Hudson Bay. From a high point of 2120 feet on northeastern Lake Superior the land tilts gently toward Hudson Bay, where there is a narrow shoreline strip called the Hudson Bay Lowlands averaging 500 feet above sea level.

The other geological face of the province is in the southeast. Here are the lowlands of the Great Lakes-St. Lawrence region. These extend over all of Peninsular Ontario, that portion that lies between Lake Huron and Lakes Erie and Ontario. Here the land is fertile farmland, an abrupt change from the rugged and rocky forests of the northwest. The climate is much milder, for the Peninsula thrusts farther south than any other part of Canada, reaching to the city of Windsor, across the Detroit River from Michigan. Because of the gentler landscape and climate, it is here that the wilderness of the north is exchanged for the most heavily industrialized and densely populated section of Canada.

The population of Ontario is presently about seven million. That is roughly 35 percent of the total population of Canada, and most of it is centered in this lowland Peninsular portion. Well over two million of the province total live in the Toronto area, a focal point of the industry of the province. Agricultural products of the south are diverse, and excepting the wheat-growing prairies of the western provinces this is the most important agricultural part of Canada.

The forested north and west amount to roughly 70 percent of the province. Only about 20 percent of the land area of Ontario is privately owned. Thus, there is almost endless hunting opportunity. But here again there are contrasts. The forest regions place few restrictions upon hunters, but Peninsular Ontario is already beginning to find public hunting lands severely limited and permission to hunt on private lands more difficult to obtain.

The road network of the populous portion is excellent. The Trans-Canada Highway and its connecting branches allow ready access to all of the southern part of the forested region clear to the Manitoba boundary, and spurs running north into the wilderness have opened up large areas there, too. However, most of the wilderness is roadless and the far north entirely so. Rail transport into and through much of the north is very good. The Canadian National Railway sweeps east-west on a long curve up into and across the wilderness; the Ontario Northland Line runs from contact with the CNR to Hudson Bay. From Sault Ste. Marie in the south the Algoma Central, sometimes dubbed the "Moose Meat Special," slashes up through the forest to intersect with the CNR. And, in the south the Canadian Pacific crosses east to west. Air transport throughout the populous region is excellent, and it is likewise to all of the cities across southern Ontario, to Kenora in the west. There are also numerous bush lines to transport hunters to the moose country of the north, and to the waterfowling on James Bay. Charter flights arranged by outfitters reach to a vast number of lodges and camps in the forests.

Ontario is one of the most important hunting grounds in Canada. Small-game hunters now average over 400,000 each season, and about 12,000 of those are nonresidents. Roughly 176,000 resident big-game hunters are licensed annually for one or another species, and a whopping additional 27,000 nonresidents on the average come into the province. Deer, moose, and black bear are the big-game species. Game birds include ruffed, spruce, and sharptail grouse, ptarmigan, Hungarian partridge, pheasants, bobwhite quail, waterfowl. There are some squirrels, plus cottontails, snowshoe hares, and imported European hares.

The various divisions of Ontario both for game management purposes and for civil administration may be somewhat confusing to hunters. However, maps printed with the hunting regulations each season show and describe these various divisions plainly. For example, the heavily populated Peninsular area is cut up into counties and townships. The remainder of the province, which means the major portion of it, is split only into large Districts, and these in turn are split into smaller Territorial Districts. Overlaying all of these administrative divisions are the Game Management Areas. Presently there are a dozen of these. In the north and west they are very large. In the populous south they are smaller.

License laws are also somewhat different here from those in other provinces. Some counties of the south have established township licenses. These are required in addition to the regular provincial license. Information on such licenses is available from the Department of Lands and Forests, address at chapter end.

The guide laws also differ here to some extent from some other provinces. Only in certain areas do guides have to be licensed, and only in one specific instance at present are hunters required to be accompanied by a guide. This pertains only to deer hunters in the District of Rainy River in the far west. Hunters should carefully distinguish between guides and outfitters. The latter must be bonded. The Department of Lands and Forests does not keep or furnish lists either of guides or outfitters. This information is handled by the Department of Tourism and Information, 185 Bloor Street East, Toronto.

Quite obviously the vast forested regions of Crown lands present no difficulties so far as places to hunt are concerned. But all hunters will be well advised to deal with an outfitter, or at least to hunt out of a reliable camp. There are hundreds of them. The railway lines will furnish lists of camps and the facilities of each along their right of way in roadless areas. Hundreds of ads for these camps also appear in outdoor publications.

In the Peninsula region of the south, by far the major share of the hunting is on private lands. Ontario is swiftly becoming aware of the need here for public hunting grounds. There are nine of these developed at present, chiefly for waterfowl and pheasant hunting, and there are currently six more under development. These are called Provincial Hunting Areas. It is presumed that this program will continue. These tracts will be noted individually under the species involved. There is a daily or seasonal fee for hunting on most of them.

For camp-out hunters there are ninety-five Provincial Parks available. There are also along the highways scores of excellent motel and cabin accommodations, and as noted there are a great many hunting camps and lodges back in the bush.

Hunters on the southern Peninsula will find fall weather pleasant, and even quite warm during the earlier seasons. Hunters going into any of the remainder of Ontario at any season should be equipped with plenty of warm clothing and good boots. An October moose hunt, for example, may be enjoyed in gently crisp weather, but a sudden storm may lay snow on the ground and drop the temperature considerably. Late seasons, as for moose, are usually severely cold.

Guns and ammunition cover a rather wide latitude, depending upon what one wishes to hunt. By and large the upland game birds can all be hunted with No. 7½ or No. 6 shot. For ducks No. 4 will be better, and for geese No. 2 is a standard load. Riflemen after deer can utilize any of the calibers considered standard, such as the .270, .30/06, .243, .30/30, etc. Bear hunters will use about the same list of calibers, although for large black bears nothing smaller than the .30/06 with 180-grain bullet, or something comparable, should be used. Moose hunters can do well with such calibers as the .308 with 200-grain bullet, or one of the several popular magnums. The .30/06 with heavy load, and the .270, are also used for moose. These are heavy animals with large bones and though a moose severely hit gives up rather easily, a heavy load is advisable for solidly and instantly anchoring a trophy.

RUFFED GROUSE

This is the most important game bird in the province. It inhabits virtually all forest areas. Ruffed grouse are cyclic birds anywhere, and the farther north they range, the more violent the population fluctuations from year to year. In Ontario much of the northern forest grouse hunting has these drastic seasonal ups and downs. Here the birds seem to quite closely follow a nine-year cycle, building up to great abundance and then falling sharply, from which they build up once more over the same cycle of years.

Ruffed grouse of the regions termed "south-central" and "southern" Ontario are not as cyclic. South-central Ontario is the area south of a line drawn west to east roughly from Sault Ste. Marie to the eastern border between Temagami and Mattawa, and north of a line west to east drawn across Georgian Bay to the eastern end of Lake Ontario and thence north to Ottawa. All of Peninsular Ontario below this line is termed southern Ontario.

The reasons for pointing out these regions are as follows. The southern region is agricultural, but also contains many wooded blocks which harbor abundant grouse. The south-central area is mostly in forest. However, both areas are much more heavily settled than all the vast remainder of the province, and grouse hunting compared as between the enormous north and the two regions described differs drastically. In these two southern regions ruffed grouse are wary, and superbly sporting shooting is available. Ruffed grouse of the sparsely settled areas of northern Ontario are rather naive. It is interesting to recall that when early settlers first hunted on the eastern coast of North America, the ruffed grouse—because it was almost tame—was called the fool hen. It is sometimes called similar names today in northern Ontario. There birds are often difficult to flush, will walk along a logging trail only a few feet from a hunter, and are commonly potted on the ground. They are trusting because they are unused to civilization, and are as "foolish" as the spruce grouse, which is usually still today called fool hen in numerous locations.

Ontario cannot easily check total bird kills per season because of the vast areas involved. However, in the more sporty shooting of the two southern areas noted, it is not uncommon during peak years to flush fifty to seventy-five grouse during a day's hunting in woodlots and agricultural areas. Over all of the region of the north where highways reach there is good grouse hunting almost anywhere. The best way to find it in the north is to walk logging roads or even along the railway right of ways. Forest openings are the best habitat for this bird, where scrub birch or poplar is interspersed openly with some conifers. The dense spruce of the north is not good ruffed grouse hunting.

During surveys made over recent years, some high successes have shown, often probably because of hunting pressure. Some of these areas are as follows. In southern Ontario: Kemptville, Pembroke, and Parry Sound vicinities; in northern Ontario: near White River, Gogama, Cochrane, Kapuskasing, Geraldton, Port Arthur, Fort Frances, Kenora. However, these are only samplings and ruffed grouse enthusiasts operating almost anywhere over the range of the bird in Ontario will find excellent hunting.

SPRUCE GROUSE

The spruce grouse is a dark-meated grouse, as opposed to the white-meated ruffed grouse. It is a bird of the dense black spruce and jackpine forests and in Ontario is most abundant in the northern and northwestern portions of the province. Spruce grouse in such wilderness regions are usually so tame that hunting them is not great sport, but they are good eating. Often they simply sit on a limb within a few feet of the hunter and can sometimes literally be knocked off a branch with a stick. However, they lend interest to bird hunting in the north and can be hunted in many places in combination with ruffed grouse. It is not possible to suggest any areas where they are especially abundant. Hunters traveling routes 11 or 17 up into the north, or any of the roads leading off from these, can usually find good spruce grouse shooting within walking distance of the highway, simply by locating dense stands of their favorite timber.

SHARPTAIL GROUSE

There are two subspecies of sharptail grouse in Ontario. These are birds primarily of the transition zone between forests and prairies, where grass and brush, or brush and open stands of small timber form broken cover.

The northern sharptail grouse is found on the lowland tundra of the James and Hudson bay region. They are often present in burns and northern blueberry bogs, and are nowhere abundant. Hunters along Route 11 from Cochrane to Kapuskasing to Geraldton ordinarily have a better chance at these birds than others elsewhere. Most are taken as incidentals by hunters after other species.

The prairie sharptail is found primarily in the Rainy River Territorial District of the west. This District lies just north of the U.S. border east of Lake of the Woods and the Manitoba border. Highway 11 crosses it east-west, and the city of International Falls, Minnesota, gives access from the states. Most of the birds are found on abandoned, brushy farmlands. The best area is west of Fort Frances. During average seasons this grouse is found in huntable abundance here, and there is also excellent ruffed grouse shooting in the same region.

PTARMIGAN

The willow ptarmigan is a grouse of the northern tundras and dwarf willows. It summers on the grassy tundra and on marshy flats, winters in protective low willows or other scrub arctic vegetation. The James Bay and Hudson Bay lowlands furnish good ptarmigan hunting. There are willow ptarmigan elsewhere across northern Ontario but few sport hunters ever reach them because of the roadless and totally unsettled expanses where they dwell. In the Hudson Bay Lowlands region, reached by rail and plane and famous for its goose camps, ptarmigan hunting is readily available as an added activity.

HUNGARIAN PARTRIDGE

The imported Hun has been established in scattered locations of the southern Peninsula for many years. The best populations, and probably the best in eastern North America, occur on farmlands of the eastern counties in the south, spreading out from Ottawa. Eastern Carleton Co., all of Russell Co., western Prescott, much of Dundas and Stormont Cos. offer the high densities of Huns. Good location by villages are near Russell in like-named county, Crysler in Stormont Co., Winchester, Chesterville and Iroquois in Dundas Co.

The hunting is almost entirely on private farmlands. Fortunately, little of it is posted, and permission is easily obtained. Numerous hunters come to the area purposely for Huns, and stay at farm homes year after year, paying for board and room in a most hospitable atmosphere. The fact that good ruffed grouse, woodcock, and waterfowl hunting in combination is available in the area makes this an attractive trip.

There are scattered Hun coveys in other parts of the south, but none are important except to local hunters who know their whereabouts.

PHEASANT

The ringneck range in Ontario is restricted to roughly two tiers of counties in the south along the Lake Erie shore, and to a marginal strip along western Lake Ontario. Even here pheasants have over recent seasons declined. The best hunting on the mainland today is found in only a few locations, as follows: along Lake Erie, all of Essex and Kent Cos., southern Lambton Co., southern Haldimand Co., all of Welland Co., eastern Lincoln Co.; along Lake Ontario, southern Peel and York Cos.

The best pheasant hunting, which is indeed very good, is found on Pelee Island at the western end of Lake Erie. Hunters have long dubbed it "Pheasant Island." It is offshore from Pelee Point, can be reached by ferry from several mainland locations, and by air from such large centers as Windsor, and Detroit, Michigan. As a rule there are two two-day hunts, with 10-bird limits for the two days. Hunters must have a regular small-game license, and in addition a Pelee Island Township license, which at this writing costs $50. Arrangements for licenses and accommodations can be made by contacting the Pelee Township Clerk, Pelee Island.

Elsewhere there are also township licenses involved for pheasant hunting. The regulations summary for any given year lists the townships where such are required.

There is a fair amount of pheasant hunting on the Provincial Hunting Areas noted early in this chapter. Of those already developed, all but one of which charge a fee by day or season, there are the following where pheasants are either the only game hunted or one of several primary species. The 350-acre Earl Rowe PHA is in Simcoe Co., two miles west of Alliston. Pheasants only are hunted here. The same is true of Sibbald Point, of 450 acres two and a half miles east of Sutton in York Co. The Darlington PHA, Durham Co., near Oshawa, contains 380 acres, has hunting for pheasants and waterfowl. This is also true of Presqu'ile PHA with 2170 acres three miles south of Brighton, Northumberland Co. Two other PHAs have hunting for all species in season, with pheasants one of the primary varieties. These are 2300-acre Tiny Marsh, at which there is presently no fee, near Elmvale, Simcoe Co., and Gananoque, near village of like name, 1041 acres, Leeds Co. This last-named PHA has a set fee.

As this is written there are three new PHAs, still under development and at this time without fees, where pheasants are one of the important species. On these all species may at present be hunted in season. These are: Brighton, near village of like name, Northumberland Co.; Aylmer Airport, also near like-named village, Elgin Co.; Fingal Airport, twelve miles southwest of St. Thomas, Elgin Co.

BOBWHITE QUAIL

Quail range is quite restricted in this province. The birds are hunted only in the extreme southwestern counties of the Peninsula. Quail are currently extending their range eastward somewhat from the open-season counties. Even though quite good hunting may be found, oddly there appears to be little interest. The counties open at this writing are: Essex, Kent, Lambton, Middlesex, Elgin. Human population is rather dense here and practically all the birds are on privately owned lands. However, gaining permission is not too difficult, and some good shooting can be had by those who will diligently pursue it.

DUCKS, GEESE, SNIPE

Some of the best waterfowling on the continent is found in widely scattered parts of Ontario. Undoubtedly the best is in the far north on James and Hudson bays. Here there are several camps for goose hunters. The geese are mostly snows, but there are also Canadas. In addition the Lowlands skirting the bays are filled with ducks, and snipe. Thus a package hunt here for all of the waterfowl is possible, and there are also ptarmigan. The goose hunting is the most famous of these activities. Three of the goose camps are operated by Cree Indians, famous for their ability to call geese. These camps are assisted by personnel of the Department of Lands and Forests. A brochure titled "Hunt the James Bay Lowlands With the Cree" is available from the Department with full details.

Inquiries concerning other package hunts in this northern outpost should be addressed to the James Bay Frontier Assn., Cochrane, Ontario. Hunters can fly to the area, or go by rail to Moosonee, from which point they are ferried either by freighter canoe or aircraft to the hunting grounds. There are other Indian-operated waterfowling camps on Hudson Bay at Fort Severn and Winisk. Contacts for these should be made via the District Forester, Department of Lands and Forests, Sioux Lookout, Ontario.

Although there is all but unlimited water over northern Ontario, the waterfowling is not especially notable with the exception of the above. The short season sends the birds farther south, and also there are much better forage conditions in the southern agricultural areas. Essex Co. in the south offers good goose shooting. There is also a goose management area near Morrisburg, located on Lake St. Lawrence of the St. Lawrence Seaway. Geese feed on privately owned stubble lands outside the refuge in this vicinity.

Duck hunting along the marshes of Lake Erie and Lake St. Clair is excellent, but much of this is privately owned. Walpole Island and vicinity in eastern Lake St. Clair is an excellent hunting ground for duck hunters, and arrangements can be made there with Indians. As the season wears on there is excellent lake shooting for the diving ducks over several areas of the south-central and south. Lake Nipissing, Georgian Bay, Broad portions of the lower Ottawa River, Lake St. Francis near Cornwall in the extreme east, the upper St. Lawrence all offer good shooting. The Bay of Quinte area on the eastern Lake Ontario shore, the Niagara River, the Long Point region of the Lake Erie shore, the Detroit River, Lake St. Clair and the St. Clair River all are good.

There are of course hundreds of other spots for duck hunting. The region around the North Channel and St. Joseph Island southeast from Sault Ste. Marie, the Manitoulin Island region are among these. In the west the Lake of the Woods region catches southbound flights. And there are thousands of beaver ponds scattered over the province, as well as thousands of lakes large and small that offer good shooting. However, the James Bay area and the various places in south-central and southern Ontario unquestionably furnish the great concentrations of ducks, geese, and snipe.

Of the Provincial Hunting Areas of the south, two noted under "Pheasant" also offer waterfowl shooting. These are Darlington and Presqu'ile. There are three other PHAs that are for waterfowling only. These are as follows: Holiday Beach, a 262-acre tract in Essex Co. near Amherstburg; Rondeau, near Morpeth, Kent Co., with 9200 acres; Long Point, near Port Rowan, Norfolk Co., with 1750 acres. All three are fee-hunt tracts. There is a manual titled "Regulations & Instructions for Hunting at Waterfowl Management Units" available from the Department of Lands and Forests. It gives all details concerning these three PHAs. Two new PHAs under development as this is written offer additional public waterfowl shooting. Winchester PHA is near Kemptville, Dundas Co., and Nonquon River PHA is near Port Perry, Ontario Co.

WOODCOCK

This is an under-harvested species in Ontario, but interest is growing. Opportunities for woodcock shooting are excellent. Southern Ontario, parts of south-central and northeastern Ontario also have abundant birds. Good general areas are the nine easternmost counties, all of the Lake Huron shoreline and the area bordering Georgian Bay and the North Channel. There is also an excellent concentration of woodcock, not much hunted, along the Quebec border in the New Liskeard and Englehart region. This is in northern Ontario, straight north of North Bay in the east, and easily accessible via Route 11. Undoubtedly there are thousands of woodcock in coverts of this area and the South that have yet to be discovered. Mid-October is usually when the flight brings the heaviest concentration to the south and south-central regions.

SMALL GAME

Ontario has cottontails in the south. Most of the hunting is on private lands. Some of the PHAs also furnish rabbit hunting. Among them are Gananoque, Winchester, Brighton, Nonquon River, Aylmer Airport, Fingal Airport, and a new one under development and not yet noted, Johnston Harbor, Bruce Co.

There are snowshoe hares farther north, and hunting them over much of what may be called central Ontario is very popular. Although the species is found farther north, there is not much interest in it there.

In the South there are also a modest number of European hares. These large hares were stocked years ago and were the cause of some uneasiness across the border in the U.S., for fear they might spread and become pests. Contact the Department for detailed information concerning this animal.

There are both fox and gray squirrels in modest numbers scattered over suitable portions of the south and south-central regions, where enough hardwoods and agricultural crops mixed with woodlots can sustain them. These squirrels are not present in the mixed poplar (aspen) and conifers farther north. Squirrels are not especially important game animals in the province.

DEER

Ontario has good whitetail deer hunting over limited portions of the province. There are three main areas where deer are found. The largest encompasses all of south-central and southern Ontario. Within this region the portions where deer are present in greatest numbers are as follows: Manitoulin Island; the counties of Parry Sound, Muskoka, Haliburton, Peterborough, Hastings, Lennox, northern Addington, Frontenac, Lanark, Renfrew, all of which spread out from and below Algonquin Provincial Park; portions of Middlesex, Haldimand, Welland, Wentworth, Halton, Peel, all of which are farther to the southwest on the Peninsula.

In western Ontario is found the next best deer concentration. It covers most of the Kenora and Rainy River Territorial Districts. Deer are abundant in the western end of the Rainy River District, and common farther to the east. They are abundant in the Kenora District around Lake of the Woods and spreading out into the interior of the District to and around Lac Seul and along the English River, and common along the fringes of this prime range. The third deer area is based on the northern Lake Superior shore in the southern Thunder Bay Territorial District from the Minnesota border north to southern Lake Nipigon and east along the Superior shore past Schreiber. They are not especially abundant in this area.

Deer hunting is popular. Recently over 150,000 hunters participated in a season. It is legal to use dogs for deer hunting, and many hunters do so. Hunting conditions vary a great deal from season to season, and in the northern deer areas severe winters can decimate herds. Over recent years, however, success percentages have averaged, throughout all of the deer range, above 20 percent. In the west, the region around Kenora has had high success, up to 34 percent. The Port Arthur area showed 28 percent during one recent season. The Sault Ste. Marie region averages about 23 percent. Farther east along the lake shore and in the vicinity surrounding Sudbury, deer are less numerous. But Manitoulin Island has a high deer population and averages around 25 to 30 percent hunter success.

The Parry Sound region is one of the better locations, with well above 30 percent success in good seasons. The eastern counties of the South all show success over 20 percent and as high as 28 percent. Hunters should check regulations carefully. In some areas dogs are not allowed, and in some only shotguns may be used.

MOOSE

Ontario is the most important moose hunting region on the continent. For a period of years the kill has run annually from 10,000 animals to almost 15,000. Recently 60,901 moose hunters participated. Of these, 48,565 were residents, 12,336 were nonresidents. The total kill was 13,207. Nonresident success averaged 34 percent and resident success almost 20 percent. The reason for the lower figure for residents is that many hunt without guides in areas where pressure is heavy, while numerous nonresidents fly in to hunt with guides in areas that are hunted very little.

The Ontario moose population is spread over much of the province, excepting the south, and the western shore of James and Hudson bays. There is excellent hunting all the way from the Quebec to the Manitoba border. Fortunately, a great deal of it can be reached via highway along either Route 11 or 17. Both, plus connecting highways, reach into a vast expanse of prime moose range, and there are numerous fly-in camps located along all these roads.

Western and central Ontario generally show the best success percentages. In the west, in the Kenora district, nonresidents have shown over a period of years success all the way from 41.6 up to 73.1. The Sioux Lookout district of the west has run even higher, and the Port Arthur region has not been far behind. However, over two recent seasons these have been, for nonresidents: Kenora 49.4 and 41.6; Sioux Lookout 54.7 and 47.7; Port Arthur 40.5 and 36.1.

Up in the central region the Geraldton area has run in past years over 80 percent success nonresident, and has had several seasons of over 50 percent. Over two seasons just past, it showed: 47.3 and 36.1 The Kapuskasing area averages very much the same. Farther east, toward Cochrane, and south to the Sault Ste. Marie, Sudbury and North Bay regions, one may expect success averages somewhat lower, but still from about 20 to 30 percent.

In much of the moose territory any moose is legal, but hunters should check by district for any given season. On the average, counting adult animals only, the take of bulls in any area stays fairly close to 50 percent, and nonresidents, who are perhaps more inclined to be seeking trophies, run between 50 and 60 percent. Adult cows average for all hunters somewhere around 35 percent, overall, of the kill. Calves make up the remainder, the take averaging over the various districts from 10 to 20 percent of the total.

Aerial surveys have shown that moose populations are high and quite stable almost everywhere within the range. High or low success is not always attributable in any sector to the number of animals present. The hunting method, whether by water, or walking log roads, whether there is snow or bare ground, etc., all influence the kill. Invariably a good outfitter or guide who has checked his hunting ground beforehand and knows pinpoint spots where the most moose are resident will make the difference between a successful or unsuccessful hunt.

BEAR

Black bear are abundant, are legal game from early September through until the end of June. In the fall some are taken incidentally by deer and moose hunters. Spring hunting, after the animals have come out from hibernation, is the most popular and most successful. The bears then hang around abandoned logging camps, cruise small streams seeking runs of spawning suckers or other fish, seek openings around old buildings or along log roads where they graze on newly sprouted grass.

Not until 1961 was the black bear made a full-fledged game animal in Ontario. Even now, however, there is no bag limit. Residents of Ontario show only very modest interest in bear hunting, with only about 600 licenses annually sold. Nonresidents come from throughout the entire U.S. for spring bear hunting here. Most seasons anywhere from 2000 to 3000 participate. Almost all hunt with guides or outfitters, setting up their hunts through ads appearing in outdoor magazines, or by writing to the Department of Tourism and Information for lists of bear-hunting camps and outfitters.

Bear hunters average at least 40 percent successful. Among the most popular bear hunting areas in recent years have been the Forest Districts with headquarters at Swastika, Gogama, Chapleau, Sault Ste. Marie, Kenora. Incidentally, offices of the District Foresters are located at these points and can be contacted for bear-hunt information. In those popular areas success has been running from about 35 to 49 percent. Although not as popular, the Districts based at Parry Sound, Cochrane, and Sudbury have shown higher success ratios. They were recently, in order of the above named, 85.7, 69.4, 59.5.

There is actually very little difference from one Forest District to another when percentages are averaged over a period of years. The addresses of all District Forester offices, incidentally, are given in the annual summary of hunting regulations. Annually, from 1000 to 1500 bears are bagged in the spring in Ontario. Again, as for moose, hunting with a competent guide who knows his area thoroughly greatly enhances the chance for success. Studies have shown that for several years the month of May has produced the highest percentage of the bear kill. Three different methods are in general favor. A few hunters use dogs. A few others like to stalk the lakeshores and log roads. The majority hunt from a blind, over bait.

OTHER ANIMALS

There are raccoons throughout the south, and red foxes here and farther north. Peninsular hunters do some raccoon hunting with hounds, and there is also some hound hunting, and calling, for foxes. Woodchucks are also present. Hunters should check laws pertaining to use of rifles in the heavily settled southern counties.

The most important non-game animals, considered trophies by many, are wolves and coyotes. There are two subspecies, possibly more, of wolves. One ranges along the tundra of Hudson and James bays. The other ranges over the forested region south as far as Lake Simcoe. It is estimated that at least 10,000 wolves are in the province. The greatest density is in the Algonquin Park and Parry Sound region, where one per ten square miles is estimated. In the north, where there is less forage, one for every hundred square miles is about average. The northern bay coasts have even less. Very occasionally a moose or deer hunter gets a shot at a wolf. A number of sportsmen hunt them with planes, or snowmobiles (permit required), and some others run them with dogs.

Coyotes have spread over Ontario during the past several decades. They are found in some farming areas, sparsely in the northern forests, and even clear to Hudson Bay. Great Lakes shores along Lakes Superior and Huron have a substantial coyote population. The animals range from the Manitoba border eastward clear to the Toronto area. There are occasional coyote-dog hybrids that show up in kills. The average annual kill of coyotes is about 800.

REGULATIONS

Address all queries regarding regulations or the various pamphlets mentioned in this chapter, to the Department of Lands and Forests, Fish and Wildlife Branch, Parliament Bldgs., Toronto, Ontario, Canada.

QUEBEC

Quebec with its hosts of French names and French-speaking people is the largest Canadian province. Approximately 15 percent of the total land area of Canada is within its boundaries. It spreads over 594,860 square miles. Hudson Strait and Ungava Bay in the Arctic form the northernmost watery boundaries, above the 60th parallel. Hudson Bay, James Bay, and eastern Ontario are the western boundaries. Portions of northern New York, Vermont, New Hampshire, Maine, and New Brunswick touch the south. The remainder of the southern land boundary is with the Gulf of St. Lawrence and the Strait of Belle Isle. On the Atlantic side to the east, the coast of Labrador lies between northeastern Quebec and the ocean.

In southern Quebec the St. Lawrence River cuts off a long, narrow strip that is rounded at its eastern end and in that region entirely surrounded by water. This is the Gaspé Peninsula. On past the end of this peninsula, and lying athwart the mouth of the St. Lawrence in the upper Gulf, is Anticosti Island, a part of Quebec and an important location for hunters.

There is a narrow strip of lowlands along the St. Lawrence, and here is where early settlement began and where the major share of the population is found still today. Here are farms, villages, and the large cities. Presently the total population of Quebec is slightly less than six million. Approximately 4.5 to 5 million of these residents are in the lowland strip and the eastern townships. Montreal alone is now over 2.5 million. It is thus easy to see that hunting in this huge expanse of northern forest and far-north tundra is far from crowded.

In fact, only a very small part of the province is served by roads. Most of the north and far-north is accessible only by plane, although several areas are cut by rail. The southern lowlands of course have a good network of roads, in the Montreal and Quebec City region and running out toward the Gaspé. The peninsula is adequately served by a coastal route that goes clear around it, and by several routes across the interior and a number of secondaries that reach short distances inland.

Ferry lines cross the river and its mouth in several places, and reach to Anticosti Island. On the north side of the St. Lawrence and its tributary the Allana River there is a good road in the west from Ottawa running north, a part of the Trans-Canada Highway, up to the Lake Abitibi area on the eastern Ontario border. A branch of this route also runs down to Montreal so the west is reasonably well served for those who wish to drive into game territory. From Trois Rivieres on the St. Lawrence a good route reaches north to La Tuque, which is an important outfitting center. Farther east, following Route 15 that parallels the St. Lawrence on the north shore, there is from Quebec City a good highway system (Route 54 chiefly) reaching far up to Lake St. John (Lac St. Jean) and the surrounding region.

One can drive in the west clear up to Matagami and to Chibougamau Lake. A rail line runs here, too. Much of the southeast, directly north of Anticosti Island, is nearly roadless. A rail line runs far north to Schefferville, on the western Labrador border, an important jump-off point for caribou hunting there and clear on north to Ungava Bay and the Whale River region.

While there are a scattering of other roads, and rail connections, virtually all of northern Quebec is reached only by plane. Main airlines of course reach Montreal and other large centers, and several short provincial lines reach north. Charters are numerous. Nonresident hunters are not allowed to hunt north of the 52nd parallel without being guided. This parallel runs slightly north of a line approximately through Matagami and Chibougamau and eastward to cut across the northern part of the Gulf of St. Lawrence, between the mainland and Anticosti Island.

The Department of Tourism publishes a booklet, "List of Outfitters," which locates all and explains what they offer and how to reach them. This publication splits the province into numbered Districts for easy reference. However, hunters should not confuse these with the Game Hunting Zones which are set for management and regulations purposes. A copy of the game laws, in both French and English, has a fold-out map showing the Game Hunting Zones, which are identified by letters.

Persons unfamiliar with this province—except that they possibly have toured the settled portion along the St. Lawrence—must realize that most of the remainder is a vast wilderness. Forests are dense and the rocky Canadian Shield north of the St. Lawrence lowlands is rugged country, reaching throughout an almost endless expanse of forests and lakes, with rough, narrow valleys cut by torrential streams. Near James and Hudson bays and on along the coast throughout the far north and along Ungava Bay, the terrain of course slopes down to the water and there are tundra and flat treeless stretches. South of the St. Lawrence, the northern portion of the Appalachian Mountains reaches into and along the peninsula, where in the Gaspé the highest points reach steeply above 3500 feet.

Quebec is Canada's largest producer of pulp and paper, and this bustling activity has opened up many localities of the north to entrance by hunters.

Mining is also important throughout much of the province. Copper, gold, iron, zinc are among the mining products.

License sales in recent seasons have run about 350,000. That figure, however, contains the aggregate of small- and big-game hunters. Small-game and waterfowl hunters number approximately 190,000, big-game hunters make up the remainder. A total of some 10,000 nonresidents purchase permits of one kind or another each season. Whitetail deer, moose, black bear, caribou are the big-game animals. Hares (varying or snowshoe), ruffed grouse, sharp-tail grouse, spruce grouse, ptarmigan, Hungarian partridge are the small-game species, plus waterfowl. There are wolves, coyotes, bobcats, some raccoons and woodchucks, and foxes.

Public hunting opportunities are everywhere, for the major portion of the entire province is in Crown Lands. On private lands, permission is easily gained, except in the very heavily settled location surrounding Montreal. In almost all cases nonresidents will be guided, or even if hunting only for birds will be staying at the establishment of an outfitter. Certainly this is the most successful arrangement, and it is just as good advice for residents who live in the lowland strip along the St. Lawrence and wish to go into the interior.

The camps of outfitters are in fact the most popular and abundant accommodations for the hunter. There are of course motels and hotels along the main routes, but one can get closer to his sport and be better advised about it by staying at a hunting camp selected from the booklet previously mentioned. For those who with to camp, the Provincial Parks and Reserves have good accommodations, and there are a great many private campgrounds.

Weather runs the gamut, depending on where one is and when. In the lower St. Lawrence Valley early fall is pleasant, with light frosts. But as fall eases into winter, even this region is cold. As one moves north, fall is certain to be chill and later the temperature plummets. The far north has little summer, and severe and early winters. No hunter should go to Quebec at any hunting season without being well supplied with down and wool garments.

Goose and duck hunters will need No. 2 and No. 4 shot. For the upland birds, No. 7½ or No. 6 is adequate and the latter, or No. 4, can serve for rabbits. For those who hunt deer only, much of the habitat is dense and any good forest-type rifle of standard deer caliber, from the popular old .30/30 to the .30/06 does the job. For moose and caribou heavier calibers are needed. A heavy load such as the 200-grain bullet in .308 is a good choice for moose. The 7mm, .338 and such calibers are favored by many moose hunters. Although caribou are not as large or heavy, a rifle such as the .30/06 or the 7mm is a good choice. Whatever one carries for the antlered game will do for black bear.

DEER

Whitetails range throughout the region south of the St. Lawrence and for some distance north of it. Severe winters can take their toll. Thus the deer kill does not remain constant season to season. Over the past decade the highest kill was over 16,000, the lowest slightly more than 6000. This is a registered kill. Undoubtedly many deer are killed that are not reported. During one recent season there was a total of roughly 92,000 deer licenses sold, and the kill was 6234. Bucks accounted for about 60 percent. Thus, though deer hunting can be locally excellent, success percentages on the overall are not high.

Very generally, the area south of the river is considered very good. Zone B, southeast and east from Montreal, with Sherbrooke and the country south and east of it a key location, is considered a good deer Zone, and so are Zones C and D which are farther east and include the Gaspé. Anticosti Island, Zone L, is considered very good, and there is a unique situation here. The season opens as early as July 1 and runs to the following January. Thus a summer hunt is feasible. Some high-kill counties recently have been Bonaventure, Compton, Frontenac, Gatineau, Labelle, Papineau, Pontiac, Rimouski, Timiscouata. These tallied better than half the total kill during the last season as this is written. Most of the country in the large Zones immediately south of the 50th parallel is closed to deer hunting. This is the fringe of the northern range.

MOOSE

Up until 1960, although moose were common in Quebec and much sought by hunters, no concentrated studies had been made of them aimed toward careful management. From the early 1960s onward much study has been applied to this popular game animal. During the preceding century moose were not as well distributed in Quebec as they are today. Much of the northern forest was too dense for good habitat. The range spread over the Gaspé and south of the St. Lawrence, and over the southwestern part of the province. Lumbering operations opened up much new habitat and created, and continues to create, far more congenial situations for moose. Today the range of abundance is roughly from the lower part of James Bay eastward across the province, with all areas south of that line having good populations except the western region south of the St. Lawrence River, which is too densely settled.

Game management personnel do not know how many moose may live in Quebec, but from studies so far they believe there are certainly from 50,000 to 75,000. This, if correct, means that 10,000 to 15,000 could be harvested annually while keeping the herd in good condition. The total kill probably approaches those figures now. Over the past few years it has run 8000 to 9000 in animals actually registered, but the total estimated kill has run close to 12,000. At this writing the last registered kill was 7190, but of course many moose are killed for food in outlying northern areas that never are reported. At any rate, undoubtedly more moose by far than deer are taken by hunters, and success is better, too. Total resident license sale in the season just noted was 53,850, and nonresidents numbered 1595. Thus, 55,000-plus hunters bagged over 7000 moose. This is roughly 12 percent success. Nonresidents, presumably because most are guided, have somewhat better success than the overall average. In that year it ran approximately 25 percent.

Greatest density of moose during the 1960s and apparently still continuing is north of the river and in much of the southwestern region. Zones currently recommended by the province game men are I, J, K, and H. These encompass the southwest and west up to the 50th parallel and eastward in the north about to Chibougamau, thence southeast to Roberval, south to Grand Mere, west to Route 11 and then south again to Ottawa. Zone G, which borders the above on the east beginning at Roberval and running east to the St. Lawrence at Tadoussac on the Saguenay River, is also a good area. The Gaspé, Zone D, is the final one of the recommended Zones.

Kill statistics for a recent season reflect these recommendations fairly well. Of the total of 7190 animals taken, Abitibi County (east portion) shows 1101, Laviolette 550, Pontiac 628, Saguenay 459, Temiscamingue 736, northern and southern Gaspé 442. Thus these counties furnished better than one-half of the total registered kill. All hunters will certainly have better than average chances of success by hunting with a good outfitter in the better moose range. The total kill, incidentally, is made up of both bulls and cows, with bulls accounting for roughly 60 percent of the total.

CARIBOU

Caribou are hunted north of the 50th parallel only, in Game Hunting Zone O, which includes all territory above that line. The kill is not high. The most recent showed a total of 488, with 614 resident and 221 nonresident licenses sold. Probably more caribou are killed by natives and not reported, but these statistics will give interested hunters a basic idea of what their chances of success may be. Lately nonresident visitors have been taking roughly half of the kill. For example, there were 172 bulls, 44 cows, 5 calves killed by nonresidents in the most recent season. The total of 221 animals exactly matches the licenses sold, which means a 100 percent kill, while resident hunters registered a kill of 267 for 614 licenses, or less than 50 percent success.

It is interesting to note that only within the past few seasons has the potential for fly-ins to fantastically good trophy caribou country been realized in this province. Some fabulous hunting has been experienced, with trophy animals, in the region of the far north, the Ungava Arctic in the Whale River region in particular. Numerous outfitters listed in the booklet previously mentioned offer caribou fly-in hunting.

BEARS

There is no open season on polar bears for hunters, although there have been trapping seasons.

Black bears are plentiful throughout most of the province. There are no restrictions on hunting them, that is, no limit and no closed season. Spring hunting over bait has long been the most successful and popular method. A few are killed as incidentals by moose and deer hunters, but the best way to bag a black bear in Quebec is by engaging an outfitter and arranging for a spring hunt. No annual kill statistics are kept by the game management people. Over 6000 residents and about 3000 nonresidents on the average purchase Quebec bear licenses each year. Hunting in the logged over regions, in areas near and at lumber camps, especially those abandoned for the summer, and along small streams where spawning runs of fish such as suckers occur in spring offer the best chances of success. Hunting is good to excellent throughout most of the province. There are no especially noticeable concentrations except on a very closely local scale.

UPLAND BIRDS

The ruffed grouse, or partridge as it is locally called, is the most important of Quebec's game birds. It ranges in good numbers throughout the province wherever forest conditions with brushy openings and stream edges are available, which means just about everywhere up to the tree line in the north. There are no special concentrations. Dozens of outfitters mention partridge among the game they can offer. The Game Department keeps no statistics on annual bag. In the vicinity of settlements, logging operations where openings and trails have been made, and usually in the vicinity of outfitter camps, and along the smaller streams is where most birds will be found.

The spruce grouse is occasional in the same areas where ruffed grouse occur. But it is a species predominantly of the moist spruce bogs where stands of timber are dense. This habitat, more specialized than that of the ruffed grouse, keeps the spruce grouse from widespread abundance. It is also a rather tame and trusting bird. Moose hunters commonly find the spruce grouse and kill a few for camp fare. There is little purposeful hunting for it.

The range of the sharptail grouse is in western Quebec, beginning along the lower eastern shore of Hudson Bay and continuing down along James Bay and southward roughly to the 50th parallel. It reaches eastward across the muskegs and brushy openings for some distance, well over toward the 75-degree longitude line. Because of this range outside populous portions of the province, few hunters become acquainted with it. Fair hunting can be found for those who go into the region.

The ptarmigan, grouse of the Arctic tundra, is most abundant above the 50th parallel and thence on north. Thus, Zone O is considered the best location. There are also ptarmigan below this line, in Zone K. This is in western Quebec and is bounded roughly as follows. The 50th parallel is the northern boundary. The eastern boundary runs from north to south roughly along a line drawn from a short distance east of Chibougamau down to La Tuque. The southern boundary runs from La Tuque westward through Parent, Sanneterre, Amos to La Reine and the Ontario border.

There is some hunting for Hungarian partridge. These birds are dependent to a great extent upon farm habitats. Most of the Quebec population is located south of the St. Lawrence, in the western portion of this strip, that is, the region south from Quebec City and Montreal. The species is important only locally.

HARE

The varying or snowshoe hare is widely distributed over the province. Hunting for it is good almost everywhere and numerous outfitters include it on their game lists. Many hares are snared by residents for food and under certain regulations the meat can be sold. There are restrictions on where and when snares may be used.

WATERFOWL

Ducks, geese, and snipe are abundant in numerous locations and some excellent hunting is available. Many outfitters guide for waterfowl. In the most easily accessible part of the. province, all of the southern border of western Quebec, which is formed by the Ottawa River, offers good waterfowling. Along the St. Lawrence clear to the Gulf of St. Lawrence there is more of the same. Some particular areas along this river are as follows: the vicinity of St. Anicet and Ste. Barbe on the south side of the river southwest from Montreal; the area of islands in the upper end of Lac St. Pierre, which is actually a widening of the river northeast from Montreal, near Sorel; points along the river between there and Quebec City, and, past Quebec City the Ile de Orleans region, and the Montmagny region on the south shore farther east. Some of the larger water areas in this vicinity and farther toward the Gulf offer shooting for geese, and there are flights of brant and sea ducks also.

Up in the Lake Abitibi region on the western border well below the

50th parallel there is good waterfowling. A vast amount of it exists through-out the northern lake areas, and much of it has never even been explored. Probably some of the best for those willing to go after it is on the flats along the shore of James Bay. Canada geese, snow geese and ducks are supremely abundant here. There are a number of outfitters who specialize in fly-ins here. Several have comfortable camps in the hunting area. The Department of Indian Affairs also cooperates in operating a lodge here that can accommodate a large number of hunters. For details, write to Department des Affaires Indiennes, Division de la baie James, 950 - 3e Avenue, Val-d'Or, P.Q., Canada.

OTHER ANIMALS

Occasionally hunters get a chance to bag a wolf or coyote, or bobcat. These animals are in fair supply and there is no restriction to taking them. There are also lynx in the north, and red foxes and their various color phases, and the white or Arctic fox in the far north. It is best to check regulations regarding these, for most such animals are taken by trappers and trapping laws may apply. Some raccoons and woodchucks are found in the St. Lawrence farming strip. They are not protected.

REGULATIONS

Game laws pertaining to seasons, bag and possession limits, areas to be hunted, special hunts, license fees all may have numerous changes from year to year. For current regulations, and for other specific queries, write to: Division of Tourism, Fish and Game Branch, Parliament Bldgs., Quebec City, Quebec, Canada.

NEWFOUNDLAND AND LABRADOR

Newfoundland is the newest province in Canada, having attained that status in 1949. Actually the province is made up of the Island of Newfoundland, plus a hugh mainland wilderness area to the north known as "the Coast of Labrador." The Island of Newfoundland lies in the Atlantic Ocean across the Gulf of St. Lawrence from the eastern coasts of Quebec and New Brunswick. It is a roughly triangular island averaging around 320 miles on each side, with a land area of approximately 43,000 square miles. It is heavily forested, rocky and barren, with numerous swamps, lakes, and rivers. Most of it is rather flat, but in the west there are the Long Range Mountains rising to a maximum of 2600 feet.

Forest products, fish, and minerals are the basis of the economy. The population of the Island is about half a million. Very nearly half of this modest population lives on the Avalon Peninsula, which juts from the southeast corner of the Island, and along the shores of the bays that separate that Penin-sula from the mainland. St. John's, which is the capital and the largest city, contains over one-fifth of the total population. The remainder is scattered along the coasts, where innumerable bays form harbors for fishing vessels and ports for shipping lumber products and minerals. Very few persons except those connected with lumbering and mining live in the interior, which is still for the most part wilderness.

It is the Island with which hunters are chiefly concerned, because Labrador has very little settlement. Natives hunt there, but nonresidents to date are heavily restricted. The Strait of Belle Isle separates the northern tip of the Island from "mainland Newfoundland," that is, the Labrador Coast. Labrador fronts on the northern Atlantic from that Strait all the way to Ungava Bay and the Hudson Strait. To the west and south the borders are with northern Quebec. Labrador, which is narrow at the top and thrusts inland in the south approximately 450 miles, spreads over some 113,000 square miles. It is remote, rocky, forested over much of its area, dotted with lakes and swamps. There is a high coastal ridge, and in the west the Torngat Mountains. This huge wilderness has a population, almost entirely in mining and in U.S. air base (Goose Bay) employees, of somewhere near 22,000. Over 4000 persons live at Happy Valley near the Goose Bay airport, and 5000-plus at Labrador City on the western border, which is a famed iron-mining region.

Hunters who visit Newfoundland will almost all be going to the Island. For those who wish to drive, it is possible to travel across New Brunswick to Nova Scotia's eastern shore, to North Sydney on Cape Breton Island. A ferry then takes one across Cabot Strait to Port-aux-Basques on the southwestern Newfoundland coast. From here the all-paved Trans-Canada highway stretches clear across the Island and to St. John's on the Avalon Peninsula. The distance is 565 miles. There are a number of side roads, mostly unpaved but passable in summer and some of them all year. By selecting the proper outfitter, a hunter thus may drive right to his hunting headquarters, or to the spot from which he will fly into the interior. An interesting trip via car can also be had by taking a new car-and-passenger ferry from Nova Scotia direct to southeastern Newfoundland. It is routed south of the Burin Peninsula and thence north up Placentia Bay to the port of Argentia on the west coast of the Avalon Peninsula. From here roads lead across the Peninsula.

By rail the route is about the same as by car across the Island. The Canadian National Railway takes one to North Sydney, Nova Scotia, then a ferry continues on to Port-aux-Basques, where regular train service continues across to St. John's. This also allows rail travel right to the location of a number of outfitters. Air travel is of course much faster, and connections are excellent. There are Air Canada flights connecting with flights from major centers in the U.S. and Canada. Once on the Island, Eastern Provincial Airways at Gander provides regional service. Charter planes are also of course available at several locations for wilderness runs.

For the few hunters going to Labrador, the easiest way is via plane to Goose Bay or else to Labrador City or to Schefferville, Quebec, on the western Labrador border much farther north. There is also a rail line running from Quebec north across western Labrador.

There is nothing crowded about hunting conditions in Newfoundland. An average total of big-game hunters may run around 15,000 to 17,000, although compilations do not always determine actual numbers, since one hunter may have several types of permits. Only a small amount of land is in private ownership. Most are Crown Lands, some of which are under lease by pulp and paper companies. However, most such lands are open to hunters. The companies have built numerous service roads, and these are ordinarily open to use by hunters, except when fire hazard is high.

Big-game hunting is for moose, caribou, and black bear. Newfoundland has in fact been famous for some years for its excellent moose hunting, and its carefully managed caribou herds. Small-game species include ptarmigan, spruce and ruffed grouse, snowshoe and Arctic hares, ducks, geese, and snipe. Nonresident hunters are required to have a guide who is registered and licensed. In a party of nonresident hunters, there must be at least one guide for each two hunters. Nonresidents with either moose or caribou license may hunt "partridge," the Newfoundland colloquial name for ptarmigan, and rabbits (hares) without the additional purchase of a small-game license.

The Wildlife Service does not offer lists of guides. However, there is a booklet, "Newfoundland and Labrador Hunting Guide," available from the Newfoundland and Labrador Tourist Development Office, Confederation Building, St. John's, Newfoundland, which contains a digest of all major regulations, and has an up-to-date where-to-hunt section. That section lists outfitters by their location—central Newfoundland, west coast, south coast, and western Labrador. Under each heading are paragraphs describing the location, address, telephone, services, prices, etc., of individual outfitters. There are presently upwards of seventy outfitting-guiding services on the Island and listed in the booklet, plus several in western Labrador. There is also much general information of importance to visiting hunters in this same publication. Regulations and game-area maps pertaining to moose, bear, and caribou may be obtained from the Wildlife Service, address at chapter end.

During September, when most big-game seasons open, many days may be warm or even quite hot. But this soon changes. Thus it is best to go prepared with clothing suitable for extremes each way. Light underwear and heavy underwear, a light jacket to put on over a wool shirt, plus heavy outer clothing also. Insulated rubber boots should be a part of the equipment, and also good leather hunting boots, preferably waterproof. Rain gear is essential. Rifles in the .270, .30/06, 7mm Magnum and comparable categories are necessary for moose and caribou. For small game, No. 6 and No. 7½ shot are good choices, except for waterfowl, which require heavier loads and larger shot sizes. Hunters should carefully study regulations. For example, shotgun hunters are not allowed to use guns capable of firing more than two shells. Pumps and automatics must therefore be permanently plugged to meet this requirement.

MOOSE

Moose are very abundant. The Island is divided into Hunting Zones and Moose Management Areas. General seasons are set by Zones and Areas. On the Management Areas, of which there are presently four spread across the interior, a quota system is in effect, to properly crop carefully managed herds. Licenses for these Management Areas are available from the Wildlife Service headquarters, unless at time of season opening some are left. Such leftovers are then available from officers at entry points to the Areas. General licenses can be obtained from Service headquarters or from vendors throughout the province. Presently the nonresident license is $75, resident, $15.

Resident moose license sales have risen over the past few years from less than 10,000 annually to around 14,000. Nonresident moose licenses have declined from a high of over 3000 to an average of well under 2000. Interestingly enough, although the annual moose kill fluctuates with hunter numbers from about 5000 some seasons to 8850 during the last season for which figures are available, the hunter success remains approximately stable.

It stays at from 53 to 58 percent, and the days hunted per kill hover around 3½ to 4. This is evidence of very good hunting indeed. Though separate figures are not available pertaining to nonresidents, success unquestionably runs for them above average, because of the mandatory guide law.

Selection of a location for moose hunting is, by and large, a toss-up, particularly for the visiting, guided hunter. The Moose Management Areas, when a permit can be obtained for one, offer excellent chances of success simply because the quota reduces hunter competition. By and large, Zones offering the longer seasons in reasonably accessible areas will offer the heaviest moose concentrations. A long season in a remote region may simply mean a moderate density of moose population. Hunters should be aware that some Zones may have hunting for bulls only, some for any moose.

At the present time the moose population is low on the Burin Peninsula in the southeast, and on the Baie Verte Peninsula and the northern portion of the Great Northern Peninsula in the northwest. All of the interior appears to have a stable moose population. In the southwest there is an intensive ecological study under way and it is probable that at this is read there will be a new Management Area there. The interior Management Areas currently being hunted are chiefly in logged-over areas and are partially accessible by road. At present no nonresident moose hunting is covered in regulations for Coast of Labrador.

CARIBOU

Caribou hunting in Newfoundland has drawn the interest of visiting hunters for a number of years. Although the animals are by no means as numerous on the Island as moose, careful management has made continued hunting, by quota and only in specified Areas, possible. During a recent season there was an estimated 25 percent increase in the herd, the greatest increase since the early 1950s. Authorities place the total herd now at over 12,000. Each season the Service holds a "caribou roundup" during which animals are captured and transplants made to various parts of the Island. As an example, one such current roundup succeeded in capturing and moving seventy-six animals. By this means the Service now has reestablished fifteen caribou herds throughout Newfoundland.

Only stags may be killed. In Area 5, part of the Avalon Peninsula, the season is brief, about two weeks, and hunting to date has been restricted to residents. Four other Areas, covering much of the southern part of the Island, south of the main highway and the Canadian National Railway (but not including the Burin Peninsula or coastal areas of east and west) are open to nonresidents as well as residents. The season is about six weeks. Area 1, La-Poile, is in the southwest; Area 2, Buchans, is north of it, lying between Grand and Red Indian Lakes; Area 3, Grey River, is south-central, and Area 4, Middle Ridge, is a large eastern Area. Although opportunity is about equal in all Areas, currently Areas 1 and 2 are considered to have an edge. The first three, at this writing, had 275 permits each for the current seasons. Area 2 had 100.

To give an idea of success percentages, the Service recently aimed at a kill of 450 caribou. There were 750 permits, total, issued. The actual kill was 419. This may be considered an average, as long as the herds continue to have seasonal increases. However, figures for the latest season available show a kill of 559. Such kills indicate that chances of drawing a license are just fair. Most seasons the distribution between residents and nonresidents is roughly even. Licenses are available only by application to Service headquarters. At this time they cost $100 nonresident, $15 resident.

There is some caribou hunting allowed for nonresidents in western Labrador. The season at this time is fairly long, opening in late August and continuing through November. Interested hunters should check with the Service for details, or with outfitters listed in the booklet mentioned earlier.

BEAR

The black bear is nowhere especially abundant in Newfoundland. Nor is it very popular with resident hunters. Seldom do more than fifty-odd resident hunters purchase bear licenses. Nonresidents purchase many more, simply because a hunter after moose can add a bear license for (at this time) an extra $10. The resident bear license is the same. Taking a late season as a sample, there were 54 resident bear licenses issued, and 465 nonresident, for a total of 519. The total kill was 39 bears, a success average of 14 percent.

The season on bear, and the hunting Areas, coincide with both for moose. Hunters should note, however, that bears are absent from the Avalon Peninsula. Bear hunters generally have the highest success in the Moose Management Areas, chiefly because active logging operations are located there. Bears are drawn to the vicinity of logging camps. They also fare better in opened territory.

WATERFOWL AND SNIPE

Hunting for these migratory birds is not good here, with the exception of sea ducks, for the region lies in general outside the heavily used flyways, and is so far north that many of the species do not appear in any concentration. During the period from January to March, however, vast numbers of sea ducks are found along the coastline, both of Labrador and the Island of Newfoundland. Seasons are long, and differ between northern and southern Labrador, and coastal Newfoundland. Most of the best shooting occurs in the late season, after the first of the year. Thus this hunting is for the most part confined to residents. Visiting big-game hunters have long since returned home. For hunters interested in making a special trip for this shooting, to Labrador, it is noteworthy that the present daily bag limit of scoters, eiders and old squaws is 25.

PTARMIGAN

In Newfoundland the ptarmigan is usually called "partridge." The range of both the willow and rock ptarmigan, grouse of the Arctic tundra and scrub willows, includes Newfoundland. With exceptions of several islands, ptarmigan season is open provincewide, for about six weeks on the Island but from October through April in Labrador. The ptarmigan is the only really important upland game bird in the province.

There are separate. licenses sold for game birds, and rabbits. Ptarmigan hunters currently number over 7000. Some hunting, however, is probably done by nonresident big-game hunters who are not required to purchase small-game licenses. The annual kill fluctuates broadly, because ptarmigan, like many other grouse, are highly cyclic. It averages anywhere from 25,000 to 50,000. Peaks of cycles seem to appear approximately every ten years. Studies tend to show that years ending in zero and one are generally the peaks.

Although ptarmigan are fairly generally distributed in all suitable habitats, the best hunting is found in two widely separated regions. These are: the southern shore of the Avalon Peninsula; the Long Range Mountains of the Great Peninsula up in the northwest part of the Island. No details can be given for ptarmigan in Labrador, since there is little hunting done for them except near the few settlements. Seasonal bag limit for ptarmigan is 50.

SPRUCE GROUSE

This grouse of dense and often boggy stands of spruce is found in the province, but at this time there is no open season on the Island. The season in Labrador corresponds with that for ptarmigan. There is no bag limit.

RUFFED GROUSE

The ruffed grouse is native to the southeast portion of Labrador, and has been introduced to the Island of Newfoundland. It is now definitely established on the Island in a number of scattered areas, some of which stretch over several hundred square miles. Other transplant areas have at this time uncertain populations. Further transplants to suitable habitats are continuing. The first season was held in 1968.

One of the original introductions was made near Badger, a settlement located in central Newfoundland on the railway and highway, and this has been the most successful one. The region has been heavily utilized for pulpwood cutting, there are numerous logging trails, and in general the more open habitat has allowed the birds to do well and to spread. They are now estimated to be established here in an area in excess of 3600 square miles. This is considered the best hunting area at this time. The season falls during late September and early October. Thus big-game hunters may participate.

HARES

There are two species of hares, the snowshoe and the Arctic hare. The snowshoe is generally spoken of here as a "rabbit." Both species are open to hunting in Labrador, but only the snowshoe may be hunted on the Island. There are no bag limits for either. These rabbits are important as food sources to numerous persons. Thus, sport hunting for them is almost nil. For the most part it is popular only in the vicinity of St. John's on the Avalon Peninsula of the Island. Most of both species are caught in snares. In fact, on both the Island and Labrador there are specified seasons for "shooting" and for "snaring."

The rabbit license is separate, costs at present $1 resident, $5 non-resident. Certainly there could be good snowshoe hunting for big-game hunters visiting the Island. But few residents participate. An indication shows in the following survey figures. Of an estimated kill one season of over 400,000 snowshoe hares on the Island, only about 8000 were shot. The rest were taken in snares. Total kill of hares in the province cannot be accurately determined but is at least 600,000 or more.

OTHER ANIMALS

The only non-game species hunted to any extent is the lynx. It is considered a fur animal as well as non-game. No one knows how many may be bagged by big-game hunters. The fur take tops 300 annually. The Wildlife Service discourages the killing by sport hunters of unprotected species that may be valuable to trappers for fur. There are foxes on the Island, but these are considered fur bearers and are not hunted to any extent for sport.

Wolves inhabit Labrador, have in the past been unprotected. However, that is changing. As this is written the wolf is being placed on the protected list, with a season. It may be that the new regulation will prohibit the shooting of wolves and consider them strictly as a fur animal, for trappers.

REGULATIONS

Address all queries regarding laws, licenses and game conditions to: Director of Wildlife, Wildlife Service, Department of Mines, Agriculture and Resources, St. John's, Newfoundland.

NOVA SCOTIA

Nova Scotia, one of the Maritime Provinces of eastern Canada, is a peninsula that barely missed being an island. Further, a portion of it is Cape Breton Island. The province touches only New Brunswick, and even there is nearly cut off from the mainland of Canada by the Missaquash River. All the remainder of its boundaries are water: The Bay of Fundy, Northumberland Strait, the Gulf of St. Lawrence, the Atlantic Ocean.

This is one of the smaller provinces, but it is a handsomely scenic one. The entire peninsula is about 380 miles long, and varies from 50 to 100 miles in width. Total area, including Cape Breton Island, is 21,425 square miles. Cape Breton Island is almost 4000 square miles in area. This Island gives the impression of being a series of other islands, for the entire center is cut almost in two and into numerous sectors by intrusion of salt water in the large Bras d'Or Lakes. This island is the more rugged portion of the province, well wooded and with steep ridges rising to the highest point in the province, slightly less than 1800 feet.

The Island is linked via causeway to the main portion of the province. There is much forested hill country on the mainland, too, with numerous ridges and low mountains averaging around 1000 feet in altitude. Very nearly two-thirds of Nova Scotia is forested. At least 75 percent of the forest lands are in private ownership, and the nonforested, cultivated areas are also in large part privately owned. Most lands, however, are open to hunting. Some cultivated lands are posted. The law states that one must obtain permission before carrying a firearm upon any land "used for the purpose of tillage or orchard or as land surrounding a dwelling house." Permission is usually granted. Forest lands may be zoned because of timber-cutting operations but otherwise are open to hunting.

The population of Nova Scotia is presently over 750,000. About 40 percent of the total live in the Sydney-Glace Bay region and the Halifax-Dartmouth region, the two large urban locations in the province. The remainder are scattered on farms and in small villages which are mostly along the coast. Thus there is ample room to hunt, and plenty of interior forest that is true wilderness.

Highways are excellent all along the coasts, including Cape Breton Island. There are a number of fine crossing highways running from northwest to southeast across the peninsula, too. But there is a great deal of interior country that has no main roads. Much the same situation occurs on Cape Breton Island. Hunters driving to Nova Scotia can come into the province near Amherst through New Brunswick, or via ferry from Bar Harbor, Maine, to Yarmouth at the western end of the province, or from Saint John, New Brunswick, via ferry-steamer to Digby in western Nova Scotia. The Canadian National Railway reaches to Halifax, and the Canadian Pacific reaches Digby via ferry service. Air service on numerous regular flights comes into Halifax, and inter-province air service is available from here.

Once in the province, nonresidents have little worry about getting to their hunting grounds, or for that matter obtaining permission to hunt. This is due to the Nova Scotia guide law. All nonresident hunters, whether hunting big or small game, must be accompanied by a licensed guide. Many of these guides live in small villages along the coast where settlement and wilderness are intermingled, and thus hunting areas are easily accessible. The Department of Lands and Forests, address at chapter end, will furnish a list of registered guides. The list gives addresses, telephone numbers, notes the species guided for (including upland game birds and small game), lists the counties in which each guide operates, and the accommodations and equipment offered. This very complete listing makes it easy for a hunter to select not only the type of accommodation and guide he wants, but to see what combinations of game, in overlapping seasons, he will be able to hunt.

Hunting conditions are far from crowded. Currently the number of big-game licenses sold amounts to between 50,000 and 60,000 resident, and less than 1000 nonresident. Small-game licenses average under 30,000 resident. Very few nonresident small-game hunters visit the province. One recent season only 127 licenses were sold. There is excellent opportunity here in that field, and nonresidents would do well to investigate it.

Big-game species are whitetail deer, black bear, and moose, but moose at this time may be hunted only by residents. Upland game birds are ruffed grouse, pheasant, Hungarian partridge. There are woodcock, snipe, ducks, including sea ducks, plus geese and brant. Snowshoe hares are abundant. Raccoons, bobcats, red foxes, lynx, woodchucks are the other animals available. Deer, snowshoes, and ruffed grouse are the most popular and abundant species, with the black duck and sea ducks next in importance.

Because there are no specific Public Hunting tracts as there are in some states and provinces, and no Game Management Zones or Units except by county and highway boundaries, the material under species will be handled by counties. Nova Scotia is roughly divided into three regions: western; eastern; Cape Breton Island. To assist in orientation, the counties in each region are as follows: western Nova Scotia—Digby, Yarmouth, Shelburne, Annapolis, Queens, Kings, Lunenburg; eastern Nova Scotia—Cumberland, Hants, Halifax, Colchester, Pictou, Guysborough, Antigonish; Cape Breton Island—Inverness, Victoria, Richmond, Cape Breton. Note that the last-named is a county on island of like name. This is sometimes confusing.

Hunters who wish to visit Nova Scotia with a recreational vehicle, and to camp, should contact the Nova Scotia Travel Bureau, Box 130, Halifax, for a booklet, "Nova Scotia Camp and Trailer Sites." The listing and details on each campground are very complete. Other accommodations are abundant and include hotels, motels, cabins, lodges. The booklet "Nova Scotia, Where To Stay" can be obtained from the Travel Bureau. It also gives very detailed listings, and indicates accommodations from which hunting is available.

Although the climate of Nova Scotia is more moderate than continental areas of the interior, nonetheless game seasons can be quite cold. Most open either in October or November. Stormy winters are the rule on the Atlantic coast, and there is generally much fog. It is advisable to go prepared with warm clothing and waterproof outer wear. Any of the standard deer calibers will do for deer and bear hunters. Moose hunters should be prepared with heavy loads, certainly nothing less than a cartridge comparable to the 180-grain .30/06, or 200-grain .308. Upland gunners will need shot sizes from No. 6 to No. 7½, with No. 8 preferable for small birds such as snipe and woodcock. Duck hunters will need high-base No. 6 or else No. 4, with No. 2 advisable for geese.

RUFFED GROUSE

This is the favorite game bird of Nova Scotia hunters. The ruffed grouse is distributed throughout all of the province. Because ruffed grouse like open forest, stream margins, hedgerows, apple orchards, abandoned fields with scrub woods nearby, much good grouse shooting is available on the edges of the cultivated lands which are easily accessible.

Kill surveys indicate that there is really not much difference in success on any hunting locations. Grouse do show up or down cycles in the west, the east, or on Cape Breton Island that are not always the same in any given year. The overall picture indicates that the most grouse are shot in eastern Nova Scotia, and the least on Cape Breton Island. The statistics are probably meaningless, however, and only reflect more, or less, hunters in one or the other regions. Total annual bag averages anywhere from 50,000 to 65,000 birds.

SPRUCE GROUSE

As this is written the spruce grouse is fully protected in Nova Scotia. It is fairly numerous in the dense stands of conifers, especially where boggy situations occur. A survey several years ago indicated that on Cape Breton Island about 17 percent of the grouse population were spruce grouse. In eastern Nova Scotia they made up about 9 percent of the grouse population, and in western Nova Scotia 4 percent. It is not unlikely that Nova Scotia may open a season on this bird, giving hunters a chance for mixed-bag grouse shooting.

PTARMIGAN AND SHARPTAILED GROUSE

Neither of these birds is native to Nova Scotia. However, willow ptarmigan are being tried in suitable habitat. Although the bogs and barrens on which they thrive in Newfoundland are not extensive here, there is some hope that the introduction may be successful.

As this is written, northern sharptails are being obtained from Ontario for trial in Nova Scotia. It is not possible to predict the outcome of this experiment.

PHEASANT

Pheasants were successfully introduced into Nova Scotia during the late 1930s. There is not a vast amount of suitable habitat, and their hold has been rather precarious. Some releases are made each year. But there definitely is a wild breeding population of pheasants scattered in proper agricultural habitat throughout the province. The kill is very modest. It presently is averaging slightly more than 6000 birds a season. Best counties are: Kings,

Hants, Annapolis. The area called the "Annapolis Valley," in northern Annapolis Co. and along the river of the same name, is one of the top areas. This is a region internationally famed for its apple orchard.

HUNGARIAN PARTRIDGE

The Hun was introduced about the same time as the pheasant. It is not as widely established as the pheasant, and the annual bag is low, currently running from 1500 to 2500 birds. The Annapolis Valley counties as above under "Pheasant" are the best, and there are some Huns in Pictou, Colchester, and Cumberland counties. These birds favor open farmland. In the Annapolis Valley there is a large acreage that is diked to keep salt water out, and similar habitat around the Minas Basin and along parts of Northumberland Strait. Huns favor such locations.

WOODCOCK

Woodcock are very abundant in Nova Scotia. In fact, the province is one of their prime nesting grounds. There is also a phenomenal flight into some western counties during migration. However, hunter interest is extremely low. Most seasons only a couple of thousand hunters concentrate on woodcock, and the kill has averaged over several past years less than 7000 birds.

Alder swamps with sparse grass below, scrub poplar and birch stands are favorite habitat for woodcock here. Most of mainland Nova Scotia has high woodcock nesting populations. The best counties for hunting are Cumberland, Kings, Hants, Annapolis, Digby, Yarmouth. The two last-named counties are probably best, for during migration time some phenomenal concentrations gather there. Yarmouth Co. has the highest kill of any county.

SNIPE

Snipe are plentiful, but draw even less attention than woodcock. Wet pastures, open bogs and marshes are the preferred hangouts for these birds, and the counties noted as best under "Woodcock," above, are also the best locations for snipe hunters. Not more than 1500 hunters annually try this sport, and they harvest about 5000 snipe. The potential for snipe hunting in Nova Scotia is high for those who will pursue the sport.

WATERFOWL

The black duck is the most popular and abundant of Nova Scotia's waterfowl. Annual bag is usually between 20,000 and 30,000, with possibly 5000 to 6000 hunters participating. Best counties are in the west and in the south-central mainland, although black ducks are found generally throughout the province. Yarmouth, Shelburne and Halifax counties are the preferred locations.

Sea ducks—that is, the scoters and eiders—are abundant along Nova Scotia shores, and a more favorable season than previously is now in effect, to give hunters a better chance at these birds. Sea ducks make up about a third of the total bag. One recent season almost 22,000 were taken. The sport is a bit specialized, and only about 3000 hunters follow it. The southwest counties of the mainland offer the best sea duck shooting along their shores. Queens and Shelburne are the top locations. Of the two, Shelburne is favored. Approximately half of the total sea duck bag comes from the coastal area of this county.

The kill of other varieties of ducks runs anywhere from 20,000 to almost

30,000, with possibly 4000 hunters interested in them. Teal, ringnecked ducks, golden eyes, greater scaup and bufflehead are among the varied species. These ducks are found along all of the shores and scattered unevenly over lakes within the province. It is interesting to note that "tolling dogs" are still used in Nova Scotia to attract ducks. The dogs are taught to run up and down a shore, arousing the curiosity of ducks and causing them to swim into range.

Canada geese and brant winter along the south coast, and migrate across the province and along its shores. The total goose kill depends much on weather and erratic migration buildups. Over a period of several years it has fluctuated from a low of about 1600 birds to a high of slightly more than 5000, with about 2000 hunters annually participating. The best counties for geese are as follows: Halifax, Cumberland, Shelburne, Colchester, Yarmouth, Kings. During one recent season over 80 percent of the geese were taken in the counties of Halifax, Cumberland, Shelburne, Colchester, in that order.

SNOWSHOE HARE

The snowshoe hare, commonly called a "rabbit," is the only small-game animal in Nova Scotia. It is extremely abundant, and popular. It is found throughout the province. High and low cycles occur, and these sometimes differ markedly from one part of the province to another. In peak years hunters take over 350,000 snowshoes. The average is around 250,000. At least two-thirds of the resident small-game license buyers hunt these hares. Of the total kill, however, a great many are snared on their runways. There is no valid choice of one hunting area over another. Snowshoe hares during their upward cycles are abundant in all counties.

DEER

Whitetail deer hunting draws more interest here, as is evidenced by the high license sale to big-game hunters, than does any other type of hunting. The whitetail is the most abundant big-game animal in the province. Deer were not native, but were introduced in 1890. For almost half a century the animals slowly built up a modest population and dispersed over the province. About 1940 the deer population began to advance swiftly, and so did the interest in hunting. The catapulting of the deer population, in fact, might well have done great damage to their range but has been brought under partial control over recent years by either-sex hunting.

The average total kill now runs between 20,000 and 25,000 deer annually. In 1960 a peak kill of over 34,000 occurred but for some years now the lower average appears fairly stable. At this writing the license allows 1 deer in western Nova Scotia, 2 in the east, 2 on Cape Breton Island. The east has an edge so far as total kill is concerned. But Cape Breton Island has the most deer, possibly because of fewer hunters. (Statistics in the following paragraph will illustrate.) Over two recent seasons kill figures were as follows: west, 6040 and 5509; east, 9123 and 10,010; Cape Breton Island, 4512 and 6332.

Because all counties have fair to excellent hunting, it is difficult to make choices among them. However, the kill per square mile over a period of several years is a good indicator of the deer population. In the counties of the west, Lunenberg has for six out of nine consecutive years had a kill between 1 and 1.5 deer per square mile, and shows the best record of the seven western counties. In the east, Colchester and Hants counties show the same type of record for seven out of nine years, and Cumberland for four out of nine. On Cape Breton Island, all four counties had kills of well over 1 deer per square mile for all nine consecutive years. Cape Breton Co. showed a kill of over two deer per square mile for three of the nine years. Richmond Co. had kills of over two deer per square mile for six of the nine years and had two seasons with over three per square mile. Inverness Co. had over two per square mile for seven out of nine seasons, and over three per square for two of those seasons. Victoria was the low county among the four, never running much above 1.5 per square mile. That is still very good. All the above paragraph illustrates plainly where the deer are in Nova Scotia.

The ratio of bucks to does killed runs fairly even. In most years more bucks than does have been bagged, by one to two thousand each season. To show a hunter how his chances of success stack up, of a total of 57,799 big-game licenses sold for a recent season, there were 22,079 deer brought in. This is quite a bit better than 1 chance in 3. Although, as noted earlier in the chapter, nonresidents are only a small percentage, they undoubtedly fare better because they must be guided. Nova Scotia deer hunting can be considered as some of the best on the continent.

MOOSE

Moose are not plentiful, but are scattered over many locations. The season was closed from 1937 until 1964. That year 400 permits were issued, for residents only, and there was a total harvest of 183 animals. The next season occurred in 1966, with 800 resident permits and 361 animals killed. Since then permits have numbered 1000. Total bag—any moose—averages upwards of 300 animals.

Originally only Cumberland, Colchester, Pictou, Antigonish, all in eastern Nova Scotia, were open. More recently Guysborough has been added. Permits are given out on an application-and-draw basis. As many as 15,000 applicants try for the 1000 permits. This means a 1 in 15 chance of being drawn, and about a 1 in 3 chance if drawn, of bagging a moose. Colchester Co. has consistently attracted the most hunters, and shown the highest kill. Cumberland Co. is second on both counts, and Pictou third. Again, this hunting is for residents only.

BEAR

For many years black bears were bountied in Nova Scotia. They are widely scattered over the province, but reach their highest incidence in the western counties. In 1966 the bounty was removed, and the bear was placed on the game list, with hunting only during deer season. Although the bear kill has declined since removal of the bounty, this undoubtedly indicates not fewer bears but a high population level for the trophy hunter. The kill during the first year of protection was 221, followed the next season by 165.

Shelburne Co. is by far the best bear county so far as kills are concerned. About half the trophies have come from there. Approximately a third have been taken from Queens, Annapolis and Yarmouth counties, in that order. The four counties mentioned also had the highest bear kills when the bounty was in effect, and thus are placed as the best bets for hunters. Other kills occur erratically in scattered locations across the province. Some counties report no kills at all.

CARIBOU

Once common in Nova Scotia, caribou became extinct there during the 1920s. During 1968 transplants were made to Cape Breton Island using animals from Quebec, and it is hoped that eventually the caribou may be restored, at least in limited numbers.

OTHER ANIMALS

Raccoons are quite common on the mainland, have recently established themselves in a few locations on Cape Breton Island. Although there is a season on them, there is no bag limit. Night hunting for this animal is by permit.

The red fox is also quite common, especially in settled areas. It is protected by a season, but as with the raccoon there is no bag limit.

The same is true of the lynx, but the lynx is rare on the mainland and appears only in modest numbers in remote forested areas of Cape Breton Island.

Bobcats are fairly plentiful on the mainland, but rare or nonexistent on Cape Breton Island. Some municipalities have for years paid bounties on foxes, bobcats, and raccoons. There is some trapping for these animals for fur, but to date there is no great amount of sport hunting for them.

Some woodchucks live on the mainland, especially in the agricultural sectors. They are not abundant, nor hunted for sport to any extent.

REGULATIONS

Address all queries regarding laws or details about hunting in any part of the province to: Director of Wildlife Conservation, Department of Lands and Forests, P.O. Box 516, Kentville, Nova Scotia, Canada.

NEW BRUNSWICK

New Brunswick is the largest of the three eastern Maritime Provinces of Canada, with an area of roughly 28,000 square miles. The western border is with Maine, much of the northern one with the Gaspé Peninsula of Quebec. In the extreme southwest New Brunswick very briefly touches northern Nova Scotia. All the remainder of the province fronts on water, the Bay of Fundy to the south, Northumberland Strait and the Gulf of St. Lawrence along the east, and Chaleur Bay over much of the northeast.

During its days of early settlement, the waterways formed the "roads" of this province, and thus almost all of its settlement still today is along the coast, and along the major river valleys such as the St. John in the west, which is the most important lowland and farming area. This is scenically a beautiful province, heavily forested over at least 85 percent of its territory. Fishing, mining, lumbering are the chief activities.

The land is undulating, slashed deeply in numerous places by large rivers. In the northwest the elevation is up to 1500 feet. Centrally there are highlands, stretching up ruggedly to somewhat above the northwest plateau, with the highest point Mount Carleton, 2690 feet. From here the land slopes gently toward the south until it reaches the lesser highlands and ridges near the coast.

Roads along the coast, and down the St. John's Valley, and spreading out from the region of the capitol, Fredericton, are excellent. There are also two good highways, No. 8 and No. 109, across the interior, and another, No. 17, across the northwest and connecting with the coastal system. There are numerous highway entry points from eastern Maine, and one in the north, from Quebec, Route 6 (Quebec), connecting with 17 and 11 in New Brunswick. Free ferries take vehicles across the several rivers where crossings are necessary. Air transport is good to the three main airports, Fredericton, Moncton, St. John. The two large Canadian railways, the Canadian National and Canadian Pacific, both run lines into New Brunswick.

Much of central and northern New Brunswick is without highways, very sparsely settled, and over large expanses total wilderness. Outfitters take hunters into these regions by charter flight, or by canoe or small craft. However, with such a modest population, at present not over 625,000, and with the cities and towns of medium to very small size, there is much good hunting right on the edges of the settled areas to which one may drive.

Hunting is never crowded. Total license sales average just over 75,000 annually. Usually about 3000 of these are nonresidents. Whitetail deer are abundant, and the most important big-game animal. There are moose and black bear. Ruffed grouse, spruce grouse, woodcock offer excellent shooting, and waterfowl are plentiful. New Brunswick differs from some other provinces and states in having all its wildlife listed under varying types of licenses. Any birds or animals not specifically listed as "game" are protected. Thus a nonresident Class 1 license (currently $35.50) covers deer, bear, rabbit, upland and migratory birds, plus lesser species such as bobcat, fox, raccoon, etc. A Class 2 nonresident license (now $25.50) covers upland and migratory birds, rabbit, and certain specified lesser species. A special game license (nonresident $10) is for bear, and also for rabbit, bobcat, fox, and such lesser varieties. Resident licenses follow the same general pattern, only of course at lower fees. The moose license, for residents only, is separate.

Nonresident hunters must be accompanied by a licensed guide. Two hunters, but not more than two, may share one guide between them. There are certain exceptions: a nonresident who has at one time been a resident for five years or more in New Brunswick, persons who own camps in the province and intend to spend at least two weeks hunting there. These may apply to the Wildlife Branch for permission to hunt without a guide.

Outfitters are numerous. A booklet, "New Brunswick, Canada, Fish & Hunt" may be obtained from the New Brunswick Travel Bureau, P.O. Box 1030, Frederiction. This publication contains an up-to-date directory of outfitters and the accommodations they offer, and indicates which ones are members of the New Brunswick Outfitters Association.

There is no problem finding places to hunt. Although the province does not have public hunting areas as such, over 40 percent of the entire province is in Crown Lands. Some privately owned forest lands are posted, but many are not. There is no real access problem anywhere for hunters, and visitors in particular have no problems, since they will be guided anyway.

For general orientation when selecting outfitters, hunters should know that New Brunswick is divided into Management Zones. There are five. Zone

1 takes in the northwest and north-central region, Zone 2 all of the central region plus the northeast. Zone 3 spreads across the south. Zone 4 encompasses the southern offshore islands of the Grand Manan group, excepting Campobello. Zone 5 is Campobello Island.

The province is divided into fifteen counties. These will be used to some extent later on under species. There are a few Game Refuges scattered across the province, their boundaries plainly marked. They are also prominently shown on the official tour map available from the Wildlife Branch or the Travel Bureau. For visiting or resident hunters who wish to camp, this map also lists and describes all sites.

Although the weather here is basically continental, there are moderating influences from the sea. Early and mid-fall are crisp; late fall and winter can be very cold, and somewhat damp. Wool shirts and light jacket and light long underwear are adequate for bird shooting in October, but for November and December heavier clothing is mandatory. Good boots with insulation should be worn, and for snowtime hunting rubber-bottomed pacs with high leather tops are a good choice. Obviously hunters after waterfowl should have hip boots or waders, and insulation in such footwear is an excellent choice.

Nothing very specialized is needed in guns and ammunition. Shotgunners will use shot sizes of No. 7½ or No. 8 for woodcock and grouse, although some may prefer a size larger. No. 6, for grouse. Waterfowl hunters will require No. 4 as a basic size. Big-game hunters after deer should carry rifles in the .243 to .30/30 to .30/06 categories. The .270, '06 or facsimile does well for black bear. Moose hunters should use either magnums, or else such calibers as the .308 with 180- or 200-grain load, or .30/06 in the same load class.

RUFFED AND SPRUCE GROUSE

The ruffed grouse is abundant, is often called "birch partridge" here because of its fondness for stands of birch and its habit of feeding on birch buds. It ranges throughout the province, but is most abundant where mixed cover is available, and where woods trails, burns, and openings offer its favorite habitat. The spruce grouse, or "spruce partridge," seeks the more dense stands of coniferous timber, often where boggy situations with heavy ground moss occur. Thus it is more abundant in the wilderness north and central area than southward. Restigouche Co. and Gloucester Co. in the far north, Madawaska, Victoria, Northumberland reading from west to east just below them, and northern York Co., which thrusts up into the same general region, cover the best of the spruce grouse habitat.

The seasons are set by Zones, as a rule with the entire mainland having the same season dates and the southern islands a shorter hunting period. Daily and possession limits are set without regard to species, that is, by aggregate of both together. Currently these limits are 6 and 12. Both birds are hunted usually at the same time, simply as a hunter comes upon habitat suitable for each. The ruffed grouse is by far the most common, or at least the more popular. Over a period of ten years the total grouse kill has run annually from a low of about 77,000 to a high of roughly 178,000. The spruce grouse invariably makes up an average 20 percent of the total grouse bag.

It is interesting to note that few nonresidents avail themselves of the excellent grouse hunting, and the mixed-bag hunting that occurs by commonly finding woodcock in the same coverts. Of the total grouse kill, aggregate of the two species, only from 2000 to 4000 birds are taken by visitors. Virtually all guides and outfitters are able to show one to fine grouse shooting, either by itself, or as an adjunct to deer or bear hunting.

PHEASANT

Excepting preserve shooting, there is at this writing no open season on pheasants. Some stocking has been done at times in the farming region. But it is doubtful that much emphasis on pheasants will materialize or that habitat suitable for them in any quantity will ever be available.

WOODCOCK

New Brunswick has a large nesting population for woodcock, and excellent shooting. Birds are found about evenly distributed throughout the province except in the densely forested portions unsuitable for them. To avoid confusion, hunters should be aware that because these are migratory birds and thus come under federal jurisdiction, the seasons, though set by Zones, have the Zones arranged quite differently from the *province* Zones already noted. Thus, Zone 1 is made up of parts of St. John and Charlotte Cos. in the extreme south. Zone 2 takes in some of the southern islands. Zone 3 includes the five northernmost counties: Restigouche, Gloucester, Madawaska, Victoria, Northumberland. Zone 4 is the remainder of the province. In the north the season usually opens around mid-September. There are later openings for all of the central and south portions and the islands.

Because woodcock migrate as soon as hard frosts strike, interested hunters will ordinarily have the best shooting by being on hand when the season opens. All of the stream courses, from smallest to largest, will furnish the best habitats. Oddly, though woodcock are plentiful, the kill is never high, mostly because of lack of interest. It fluctuates from as low as 5000 birds to as high as 15,000. Nonresidents account for an average 30 percent of the kill.

WATERFOWL AND SNIPE

Over recent seasons a Canadian migratory game bird hunting permit has been required in addition to the regular hunting license. It is sold at post offices. Waterfowl hunting is excellent, especially along the southern and southeastern coasts, and in the lake region of the southwest and along the St. John River valley. However, hunter participation is not very high, and this in turn means that while hunting may be good, the total bag is modest. In a recent season there were only 8340 permits sold to residents of Canada, and less than 300 to aliens. A few less than 28,000 ducks were killed, and a few over 2000 geese. The average runs somewhat higher, however, to anywhere from 37,000 to 70,000 ducks over the past decade, and as high as approximately 5000 geese.

The black duck is the most abundant and popular duck here. Good hunting for this species, and other ducks, is found on the southern shore along the Bay of Fundy, along the lower St. John and the lake region to the south and westward of it between the St. John and the St. Croix. The mouth of the St. Croix in the southwest is an excellent location.

Canada geese are found in these same areas also, and along the eastern shore. The Tabusintac region of the coastal northeast with its lagoons furnishes good shooting for Canada geese, for black ducks, and along the shore for brant. Some geese and brant can also be found in the region of the Tantramar marshes, but these marshes are primarily known for black ducks and pintails. They are located in the southeast, between the city of Moncton and the border with Nova Scotia.

Scaup swarm into the lake region of the southwest, and onto Grand Lake east of Fredericton, late during migration. Sea ducks, such as scoters and eiders, are found plentifully along the eastern shore. They are also especially abundant around the Charlotte Co. islands of the southwestern coast. The sea duck season runs late in winter, to about the end of February. Most years these ducks are very abundant at that time.

Jacksnipe are found in fair abundance in all suitable places already noted for waterfowl. Albert Co. in the southeast and marsh edges along the eastern shore are particularly noted for them. The Tantramar marshes mentioned above are among the best jacksnipe locations.

SMALL GAME AND OTHERS

By continent-wide standards, the rabbit, in this instance the snowshoe hare, would be considered the only genuine small-game animal. However, in New Brunswick, as mentioned earlier, all species with open seasons are spoken of as game. Licenses are so arranged that some of these species, under proper license, can be hunted around the entire year. In addition to rabbits, the animals and birds in question are bobcats, crows, foxes, porcupines, raccoons, skunks, cormorants, and groundhogs.

The rabbit season extends over five months, through to the end of February. Rabbits are found in good supply in all Zones. They are the most important by total bag of all the above-mentioned species. But rabbits are not as much hunted in New Brunswick as they are trapped. The take by trappers is at least double that of the gun hunter.

Hunting under the Special Game License for all of the above animals has become fairly popular among residents. About 5000 such licenses are now annually sold, and of course some of the same species are killed under the other types of licenses. Bobcats and red foxes are in fair abundance, raccoons modestly so in the farming regions. However, on the overall picture none of these lesser species, excepting the rabbit, is especially popular with sport hunters. Few nonresidents hunt under the Special Game License. The average is not over 150 annually.

DEER

Whitetail deer are abundant, and extremely popular with New Brunswick hunters. Over a period of years the kill has remained remarkably consistent, averaging about 22,000 animals annually, with roughly 20,000 bagged by residents, the remainder by nonresidents. Some seasons have been higher, but the balance between resident and nonresident remains roughly the same.

Hunters can get a good general picture of deer hunting here by several sets of statistics gathered by the Wildlife Branch. For example, under a program of either-sex hunting, with a 2-deer bag per license, and all Zones except five (Campobello Island) open, the kill runs about 60 percent bucks. During seasons that continue, according to the Zone hunted, from October 1 through November 30, the last two weeks of seasons shows a higher percentage of success than the other three two-week periods. The first two weeks, and the third two weeks, are a bit better than the second two weeks. These findings may assist hunters in timing a hunt. Overall success, based on the resident kill, which is of course much greater in total than nonresident, shows that an average of slightly more than 25 percent of hunters bag their deer. This is an excellent showing on whitetails. Of these 25 percent, about one-third to one-fourth on the average are successful in bagging the 2-deer limit.

While the various counties do not always show the same success percentages, regardless of total kill the hunter success over a recent two-year period rates them about as follows: Restigouche, hunter success 45 to 50%; Gloucester, 15 to 20%; Northumberland, 25%; Kent, 15 to 20%; Westmoreland, about 20%; Albert (in the southeast) 50% or more; St. John, roughly 16%; Charlotte, approximately 50%; Kings Co., 60% or more; Queens Co., 75% or more; Sunbury Co., about 50%; York Co., about 40%; Carleton Co., slightly above 30%; Victoria Co., very high success, up to 80% or more; Madawaska Co., about 25%. These percentages, while variable, should ·give both resident and visiting hunters solid clues as to where they should select their hunting grounds.

MOOSE

In 1960, after a closed season on moose since 1936, New Brunswick began experimental controlled harvesting of its modest moose population. There has been an open season each year since then. However, the hunting is for residents only. As a rule all Zones are open, and a hunter may take either bull or cow. Annual harvests have run from a low of 174 animals to a high of 606.

Originally less than 400 permits were issued. Recently the system has operated as follows. Each fall 1000 names are randomly selected from the applications, which average over 16,000. After the selection, an additional 100 names are drawn and held as a waiting list, to be used in case some of the original 1000 fail to obtain their moose license. A hunter is not allowed to receive a moose license in any two consecutive years. Recently the season has been held during the final week of September. This is done so that it does not coincide with the opening of deer season, to discourage party hunting where several hunters are actually hunting moose but only one carries a license.

A study of kill distribution over several years shows that the Fundy Highlands of southeastern New Brunswick have the highest density of moose population. Albert and Kings counties show consistently high kills. In the north, Northumberland Co. is best. Lowest kills are in the counties of the north (Restigouche, Gloucester), and in the west (Madawaska, Victoria, Carleton). All other counties are about equal, with an average annual kill of from fifteen to thirty animals.

BEAR

The black bear population is substantial. In fact, prior to 1961 bear were not protected and were bountied in New Brunswick. They are hunted under two types of license: the regular hunting license, the Special Game license. Both residents and nonresidents are allowed to hunt, and under the two licenses this means hunting both fall and spring. Trappers also account for numerous bears each year. The total bear kill by all methods and licenses average around 1000, although some seasons it has been nearly 1500. Trappers take approximately 15 to 20 percent of these, and residents account for the major share of the remainder.

No records are kept showing which counties furnish the best bear hunting. Outfitters in Victoria Co., in the Plaster Rock and Riley Brook areas have over the past few years specialized to some extent in bear hunting. In general, spring hunts are more successful than fall hunts, and a good guide adds greatly to the chance of success.

REGULATIONS

For copies of game laws, and for any special information, write to the Department of Natural Resources, Fish and Wildlife Branch, Fredericton, New Brunswick, Canada.

PRINCE EDWARD ISLAND

The "Garden Province" is the term that has attached itself to Prince Edward Island, smallest of Canada's provinces. It is indeed a beautiful spot, with its rolling garden-like farms with woodlots interspersed, and with the heavily indented shoreline showing a scalloped pattern of blue bays.

Prince Edward Island is separated from the mainland of New Brunswick and from Nova Scotia by the Northumberland Strait. On the east the Island looks out upon the Gulf of St. Lawrence. Because of its unique geographical position the climate is rather mild. This combined with rich soil long ago invited heavy settlement and intense agricultural pursuits. Grain, potatoes, stock farms, growing of fruit and vegetables for canning and freezing utilize at least 70 percent of the land area.

The Island is small by standards of the other provinces. It has 2184 square miles. At its narrowest point it is only four miles wide, and at the widest about forty. It is approximately 140 miles in length. The terrain is gently undulating and the highest point roughly 450 feet above sea level.

At last census there were 110,000 residents. Since the capital, Charlottetown, is home to 17,000, this means that settlement is fairly dense and well distributed over the island. Roads are good and 3000 miles of them reach to every corner of the small province. There is also railway service to the larger towns, and commercial flights to both Charlottetown and Summerside. A ferry reaches the Island at Port Borden from the termination of Route 16 in New Brunswick, and another comes from Caribou, Nova Scotia, to the southeast coast at Wood Islands.

There are all but limitless accommodations on the Island, for it has long been a haven for tourists. The P.E.I. Travel Bureau, Charlottetown, can furnish lists of lodgings and restaurants. There are also numerous campgrounds in the Provincial Parks and National Parks. The Travel Bureau will also furnish a booklet listing these.

Prince Edward Island is a delightful place to visit in fall because of its beauty and its mild Indian summer climate. Only a light shirt and a jacket are needed for October. Later seasons make heavier clothing welcome. Unfortunately, however, this is not an especially important location for hunters. Opportunities are exceedingly limited.

As this is written there is a government program slowly getting underway to attempt redevelopment of the resources of the province, including game. But to date this is only in the planning stage, and the effects of careful game management, especially with the Fish and Wildlife Division severely cramped for funds, will be some time in maturing. To date there has been very little formal game management, and a licensing system that exempts most rural residents handicaps such a system.

There is no big game on the island. Originally there was some, but heavy settlement and lack of management long ago wiped it out. The snowshoe hare is perhaps the most abundant common game species. Figures on annual kill are not available, but in good years the harvest by both gun and snare is quite high. There are red foxes, but they are considered pests by the rural population. Raccoons are fairly plentiful, though not popular with hunters. There are a few gray squirrels, plus the small red squirrel. Hunters have little interest in these.

Among game birds, woodcock are moderately plentiful and there are jacksnipe (Wilson snipe) found in the marshes in fall, but these, too, seem to attract only minor interest. Upland game birds have severe problems at present. The ruffed grouse is native but not really abundant. It is estimated that not more than 500 are bagged in a season. This bird, however, could tolerate more hunting pressure. Both the ringneck pheasant and the Hungarian partridge were introduced some years ago, the latter in 1930. After the Hun became established, there was excellent hunting into the 1950s, at which time the species abruptly declined. Presently both pheasant and Hun are at such low population levels that there is no open season. Some put-and-take hunting is currently experimental, and the Division is hoping to find a suitable exotic to successfully replace the Hun.

Probably the best hunting is for waterfowl. A recent survey shows estimates for a season of over 19,000 ducks bagged, excluding sea ducks. Some 22,000 sea ducks also were taken, plus 6000 geese. Chief species are the Canada goose, the black duck, blue- and greenwinged teal. Salt marshes, and the many inland ponds and marshes offer good shooting, with sea ducks added on the saltwater bays and around the points. It is interesting to note that waterfowl furnish the bulk of the hunting for all hunters. In a recent season there were 3649 federal stamp sales for hunting migratory birds, 3622 resident all-game, and 44 nonresident.

This Province has no guides or outfitters. None is necessary. At this writing a game distribution map is in the planning stage, which will assist visitors or residents in finding best locations for what is available. Practically all land is in private ownership. Hunter-landowner relationships, as elsewhere in heavily settled areas, appear to show a downward trend. However, most visitors will find landowners willing to allow trespass, if common courtesy is exercised.

For current regulations, and for other specific queries, write to: Department of Tourist Development, Fish and Wildlife Division, Charlottetown, Prince Edward Island, Canada.

Directory of
Shooting Preserves

This directory of shooting preserves was compiled for *Outdoor Life* by the North American Game Breeders and Shooting Preserve Association. A good shooting preserve offers an exciting variety of gunning, and topnotch dogwork for your enjoyment and success afield.

Some shooting preserves charge for birds bagged, others charge for birds released, and some sell a sporting chance to harvest game birds. Know the system of charging, and the rate, before you go afield. Prices are more reasonable than you think.

The North American Game Breeders and Shooting Preserve Association has the following minimum standards for shooting preserves:

1. The area should look like good hunting country, with a blend of natural and cultivated cover.

2. Pheasants, quail, and chukars should be full-plumaged, more than sixteen weeks old, and of the same color and conformation as their wild counterparts.

3. Mallards should be similar in weight and plumage to wild mallards, and capable of strong flight between release site and rest pond.

4. Well-trained dogs should be available for the guests and to reduce crippling loss of game.

Most shooting preserve operators will clean and package your birds, and most states offer a special nonresident hunting license at reduced rates for shooting preserve hunters. Check on ammunition and hunting license requirements while you are making your reservations.

P = Pheasant   **Q** = Quail   **M** = Mallard   **C** = Chukar   **T** = Turkey
Bg indicates stocked big game, mostly exotic species

Nearly every shooting preserve operator offers a free brochure, with a map showing the preserve's location, which he will be happy to send you. Always make reservations well in advance before driving to a preserve.

ALABAMA
October 1-March 31
Nonresident game bird license $10.15

Barbour County
TROPHYLAND HUNTING PRESERVE   205: 687-2831   QMTBg
C. F. (Pete) Lunsford, Eufaula 36027

Bullock County
HALL HUNTING PRESERVE   205: 485-2621   Q
Jeff Hall, P.O. Box 17, Midway 36053

DeKalb County
LITTLE RIVER CANYON SHOOTING   205: 845-2939   PQ
PRESERVE
J. O. Crow, 110 SE 8th St., Fort Payne 35967

Macon County
QUAIL HAVEN HUNTING PRESERVE   205: 738-2367   Q
S. B. Bledsoe, Armstrong 36002

ARIZONA
January 1-December 31
No hunting license required

Pinal County
MAGMA SHOOTING PRESERVE   602: 868-4600   PC
Forrest Cooper, Jr., Rt. 1, Box 20,
Florence 85232

Yavapai County
VERDE VALLEY SHOOTING PRESERVE   602: 634-5900   PQC
G. E. McPaland, P.O. Box 1044,
Cottonwood 86326

ARKANSAS
October 1-March 31
Special nonresident license $5; $2 (1 day)

Baxter County
SCOTT VALLEY DUDE RANCH   501: 425-5136   Q
Gene Scott, Rt. 2, Mountain Home 72653

Benton County
OAK RIDGE GAME FARM   501: 291-3314   PQCM
Max Crawley, Rt. 2, Gravette 72736

Faulkner County
TRIANGLE J RANCH   501: 849-2048   QC
Jim James, Mount Vernon 72111

Hot Springs County
WAG'S GAME PRESERVE   501: 356-3614   PQM
R.R. 1, Bonnerdale 71933

Lonoke County
MARTI'S QUAIL FARM   501: 676-2431   Q
Marti Roush, Rt. 2, Box 145, Carlisle 72024

Prairie County
HESTIR GAME PRESERVE   501: 256-4546   PQ
J. "Max" Hestir, Rt. 1, Griffithville 72060

St. Francis County
CROWLEY RIDGE SHOOTING RESORT   501: 633-3352   PQ
Dale Horton, Rt. 1, Box 133, Forrest City
72335

Woodruff County
LOST ACRES GAME BIRD FARM   501: 733-2228   QC
Samuel Hay, Rt. 4, Box 176D, McCrory 72101

CALIFORNIA
Season varies by zones
Special nonresident license $5 (1 day)

Amador County
CAMANCHE NORTH SHORE HUNTING RESORT 209: 763-5144 PQCM
Larry Skinner, Rt. 1, Ione 95640
IONE VALLEY PHEASANT CLUB 209: 274-2554 P
Richard Searcy, R.F.D., Box 154, Ione 95640

Butte County
BUTTE CREEK PHEASANT CLUB 916: 743-6803 PC
Leonard Shippen, 2110 Walnut Ave., Marysville 95901
HILL'S PHEASANT CLUB 916: 476-2603 P
Ronald Hill, Rt. 1, Box 63, Arbuckle 95912

Colusa County
EL RANCHO CHICA GAME BIRD CLUB 916: 458-4586 PM
Leo Yates, P.O. Box 182, Colusa 95932
FLYWAY RANCH 415: 447-0678 PM
Warren Davison, 1712 Sixth St., Livermore 94550
NORTHERN CALIFORNIA BRITTANY PHEASANT CLUB 916: 476-2490 P
Elmer Flack, Rt. 1, Box 15, Arbuckle 95912
SYCAMORE CLUB 916: 489-2648 P
Bob Reedy, P.O. Box 21-4152, Sacramento 95821

Contra Costa County
HOLLAND TRACT GAME BIRD CLUB 415: 684-2193 PQCT
John Mass, P.O. Box 134, Knightsen 94548

Fresno County
ORO LOMA GUN CLUB 209: 392-2477 P
Henry Tietgens, Rt. 1, Box 194-B, Dos Palos 93620

Kern County
MILLS SHOOTING PRESERVE 805: 858-2498 PC
Carl Mills, 401 Fuller Dr., Bakersfield 93307

Lassen County
SEVEN UP PHEASANT CLUB 916: 827-2359 P
F. M. Rowland, Doyle 96109

Los Angeles County
RITTER PARK SPORTSMAN'S CLUB 805: 947-1742 PC
Ewell Moffett, 7200 Elizabeth Lake Rd., Palmdale 93550

Madera County
COTTONWOOD PHEASANT CLUB 209: 674-2071 PC
Frank Bergon, P.O. Box 1211, Madera 93637

Marin County
CIRCLE S RANCH 707: 762-4962 P
Bill Souza, 1740 Tomales Rd., Petaluma 94952
PIERCE POINT PHEASANT CLUB 707: 823-9684 PQC
James Johnson, P.O. Box 375, Inverness 94937
ST. VINCENT'S GUN CLUB 415: 479-4420 P
George Caesari, P.O. Box M, San Rafael 94903

Nevada County
NORTH STAR SHOOTING PRESERVE 916: 273-3786 P
Ray Conway, Rt. 1, Box 553, Grass Valley 95945

Orange County
CLUB DE CAZA 714: 586-0761 PQCM
Robert Sanchez, Box 438, Trabuco Canyon 92678
EL TORO GAME BIRD CLUB 714: 837-0522 PC
H. E. Asmus, 24755 Trabuco Rd., El Toro 92630
IRVINE LAKE HUNTING PRESERVE 714: 633-1520 PQCM
Russell Cleary, Star Rt., Box 38, Orange 92668

Placer County
PHEASANT ACRES HUNT CLUB 916: 442-1583 P
Thomas Eastus, 5604 Kingston Way, Sacramento 95822
REESER'S PHEASANT CLUB 916: 878-2710 P
J. A. Reeser, Sr., P.O. Box 206, Applegate 95703

Riverside County
C. V. WILD GAME PROPAGATION CLUB 714: 347-5932 PC
C. K. McCasland, P.O. Box 1603, Indio 92201
HIDDEN VALLEY GUN CLUB 714: 689-5100 PCM
John Laughlin, 6209 Arch Way, Riverside 92504
THE LAKEVIEW RANCH 714: 654-7270 PQC
Roy Evans, P.O. Box 71, NE Davis Rd., Lakeview 92353
ROYAL RINGNECK CLUB 714: 658-8673 PC
John Reed, Hiway 71, Aguanga 92302

Sacramento County
NICOLAUS RANCH HUNTING PRESERVE 916: 443-1610 PQ
Wendel Flint, 1845 Second Ave., Sacramento 95818

San Bernardino County
LAS FLORES RANCH HUNTING PRESERVE 714: 389-2205 PQCM
E. E. "Bill" Tate, Star Rt., Summit 92387
ROBBIE'S GUN CLUB 213: 636-8420 PQC
James Robinson, P.O. Box 3004, Compton 90222

San Diego County
PEPPER'S HUNTING CLUB 714: 789-0169 PC
B. A. Pepper, Ramona 92065

San Luis Obispo County
RIGHETTI ROD & GUN CLUB 805: 543-3445 PQC
Ernest Righetti, Rt. 3, Box 267, San Luis Obispo 93401

San Mateo County
ROLLING HILLS ROD AND GUN CLUB 415: 879-0211 P
Jesse Nunziati, Pescadero 94060

Santa Clara County
GREEN VALLEY HUNTING PRESERVE 408: 842-8546 PC
Leonard Ekelund, 111 Waverly Oaks, Palo Alto 94301

Shasta County
FLYING "H" RANCH SHOOTING PRESERVE 916: 378-2463 PQCBg
Harold Espinosa, Star Rt. Box 345, Millville 96062
JIM MACE SHOOTING PRESERVE 916: 474-3150 PQC
Jim Mace, P.O. Box 23, Shingletown 96088

Solano County
CACHE SLOUGH PHEASANT HUNTING PRESERVE 916: 678-5912 P
Roy Saucerman, P.O. Box 128, Dixon 95620
GRIZZLY ISLAND RANCH HUNTING PRESERVE 707: 425-3905 PQC
Ralph Lang, P.O. Box 326, Suisan 94585
HASTINGS ISLAND HUNTING PRESERVE 707: 374-2779 P
Jack Klingle, 110 Hastings Rd., Rio Vista 94571
PETERS POCKET PHEASANT CLUB 707: 644-4963 P
Leo Braito, 2278 Tennessee St., Vallejo 94590
LINK RAAHAUGE PRESERVE 707: 425-4158 P
Link Raahauge, P.O. Box 698, Fairfield 94533

Sonoma County
BLANCK POINT GAME BIRD CLUB 707: 763-0076 P
Mike Sutsos, 7711 Lakeville Rd., Petaluma 94952
SPLENDID GAME BIRD CLUB 707: 224-1917 PQ
Jim Splendid, 1138 First Ave., Napa 94558

Stanislaus County
PARADISE HUNTING CLUB 209: 529-1440 PQC
George Haney, P.O. Box 162, Empire 95319
WARNER PHEASANT CLUB 209: 874-2645 PC
T. M. Warner, 336 Denton Rd., Hickman 95322

Sutter County
GURRY GAME BIRD CLUB 916: 332-2385 P
Fred Gurry, 4905 Hemlock, Sacramento 95841
BOB HAHN'S HUNTING CLUB, Nos. 1 and 2 415: 664-4006 P
R. Hahn, 1657 Twelfth Ave., San Francisco 94122
McGRATH GUN CLUB 916: 735-6217 P
Jim McGrath, Star Rt., Knights Landing 95645

Tehama County
DYE CREEK PRESERVE 916: 527-3588 Bg
Wayne Long, P.O. Box 308, Red Bluff 96080

Ventura County
GREEN HEAD HUNTING CLUB 805: 526-7161 PQCM
Thomas Williams, P.O. Box 291, Simi 93065

Yolo County
WILLOW SLOUGH PHEASANT CLUB 916: 662-1310 PQC
Larry Chriss, 125 Buckeye St., Woodland 95695

Yuba County
SEVEN MILE PHEASANT CLUB 916: 743-6803 PC
Leonard Shippen, 2110 Walnut Ave., Marysville 95901

COLORADO
October 1-March 31
Special nonresident license $5 (calendar year)

Adams County
GUNNER'S MARK GAME PRESERVE 303: 288-1928 PCM
David Howe, Rt. 1, Henderson 80640

CONNECTICUT
September 15-March 15
Nonresident game bird license $11.35

Fairfield County
MOHEGAN GAME FARM 203: 929-0165 PQC
George Boehm, 140 Far Mill St., Shelton 06484

Litchfield County
BENEDICT FARMS GAME PRESERVE 203: 266-7505 P
Samuel Benedict, Hard Hill Rd., Bethlehem 06751

DELAWARE
October 15-March 31
Special nonresident license $3

Kent County
KENT GUN CLUB AND GAME PRESERVE 302: 697-7642 Q
R.D. 1, P.O. Box 136, Magnolia 19962

LOUIS DE MARIE SHOOTING PRESERVE 302: 734-5213   **PQM**
P.O. Box 108, Dover 19901

FLORIDA
October 1-April 20
Special nonresident license $5.50

Alachua County
HATCHETT CREEK HUNTING   904: 372-3908   **PQT**
PRESERVE
John Titus, R.F.D. 2, Box 364, Gainesville
32601

Citrus County
RIVERSIDE VILLAS HUNTING   904: 795-3491   **PQC**
PRESERVE
B. J. Dixon, P.O. Box 258, Homosassa 32646

Hernando County
P K RANCH   904: 796-3040   **PQCMT**
P. K. Smith, Rt. 3, Box 445, Brooksville 33512

Highlands County
JAYS HUNTING PRESERVE   305: 685-2453   **QT**
J. M. Messana, 14080 NW 20th Crt.,
Opa-Locka 33054

Lee County
ARGO FARMS   813: 334-1333   **PQCT**
Thomas Baker, P.O. Box 1812, Fort Myers
33901
STATON PRESERVE   813: 642-5161   **Q**
Arvil Staton, 734 5th Ave. S, Naples 33940

Marion County
BIRD NUTS LODGE   904: 787-6090   **PQC**
Ed Bell, Box 418, Leesburg 32748

Okaloosa County
WARD'S DEER RANCH   904: 682-2434   **Bg**
Hervis Ward, P.O. Box 697, Crestview 32536

Palm Beach County
BONNETTE SHOOTING PRESERVE, INC. 305: 746-7378   **PQT**
Wm. Bonnette, 5309 Hood Rd., Lake Park
33403
LOXAHATCHEE SHOOTING PRESERVE   305: 683-2100   **PQCMT**
S. A. Belcher, III, P.O. Box 176, Loxahatchee
33470

Pasco County
SARAN RANCH SHOOTING PRESERVE 904: 588-3809   **PQMT**
John Hammer, Rt. 2, Box 242, Dade City
33525

Sarasota County
V. O. SHOOTING PRESERVE   813: 929-5151   **QT**
Paul Carson, Rt. 2, Box 869, Arcadia 33821

Washington County
EL RANCHO HUNTING & FISHING   904: 638-1353   **M**
PRESERVE
Rex Yates, Chipley 32428

GEORGIA
September 1-March 31
Special nonresident license $5.25 (one preserve);
$12.50 (ten days—all preserves)

Bacon County
ALMA QUAIL FARM & HUNTING   912: 632-4449   **Q**
PRESERVE
Jack Kinlaw, 314 20th St., Alma 31510

Baker County
NOTCHAWAY HUNTING PRESERVE   912: 758-3313   **Q**
Dr. T. W. Rentz, 205 W. Main St., Colquitt
31737

Bulloch County
MARSH HUNTING PRESERVE   912: 587-5727   **Q**
Troy Marsh, R.F.D. 3, Statesboro 30458

DeKalb County
HUTCHINS HUNTING PRESERVE   404: 482-6572   **Q**
Herschel Hutchins, P.O. Box 328, Lithonia
30058

Glyn County
BRUNSWICK QUAIL FARM   912: 265-1348   **Q**
J. W. Harrington, 433 Old Jesup Hy.,
Brunswick 31520

Gordon County
EDGEWOOD KENNELS & HUNTING   404: 629-8154   **PQCM**
PRESERVE
W. A. Elsberry, P.O. Box 1406, Dalton 30720

Harris County
CALLAWAY GARDENS HUNTING   404: 663-2281   **Q**
PRESERVE
Dutch Martin, Pine Mountain 31822

Jackson County
SANDY CREEK SHOOTING PRESERVE   404: 367-5798   **Q**
Robert Howard, Rt. 1, Jefferson 30549

Jasper County
MARBEN FARM HUNTING PRESERVE   404: 786-3331   **PQC**
Billy Hester, Mansfield 30235

Johnson County
PRICE HUNTING PRESERVE   912: 864-3642   **Q**
Samuel Price, Wrightsville 31096

Lamar County
REDBONE FARMS HUNTING PRESERVE 404: 358-1658   **Q**
Newton Moye, Rt. 2, Barnesville 30204

Lowndes County
INDIANOLA HUNTING CLUB   912: 242-0903   **Q**
Thomas Hodge, Rt. 4, Box 80, Valdosta 31601
KINDERLOU FOREST HUNTING   912: 242-6391   **Q**
PRESERVE
Russell Howell, P.O. Box 980, Valdosta 31601

Mitchell County
RIVERVIEW PLANTATION   912: 294-4058   **Q**
C. B. Cox, Camilla 31730

Pulaski County
PULASKI HUNTING PRESERVE   912: 893-7041   **PQ**
Wilbur Slade, Box 34, Hawkinsville 31036

Walker County
CEDAR SPRINGS FARM   404: 539-2427   **Q**
John Frierson, Rt. 1, Kensington 30727

Wayne County
SPORTSMAN SHOOTING PRESERVE   912: 427-3350   **QMT**
James Tootle, P.O. Box 32, Jesup 31545
WAYNE COUNTY HUNTING PRESERVE 912: 427-9180   **Q**
H. E. Ogden, Jesup 31545

ILLINOIS
October 15-March 31
Special nonresident license $5

Bureau County
HICKORY GROVE HUNTING CLUB &   815: 699-2603   **PQCMT**
CAMPING
Edward Wirth, R.F.D. 1, Wyanet 61379
LEN-A-LONG CLUB   309: 364-2136   **M**
Leonard Longman, 1100 Warren St., Henry
61537

DeKalb County
VALLEY SPORTSMEN'S CLUB   312: 695-4650   **P**
David Trimm, 551 Sunset Dr., Elgin 60120

DuPage County
PIONEER VALLEY GUN ASSOCIATION   312: 668-1607   **P**
Dean Rawlings, O.N. 350, Pleasant Hill Rd.,
Wheaton 60187

Edgar County
MAPLE MOUND GAME FARM   217: Paris 463-9677   **PQC**
W. S. Logan, Dennison 62423

Franklin County
INGRAM'S ACRES   618: 629-2701   **Q**
Carl Ingram, Ewing 62836
WILD ACRES HUNTING AREA   618: 937-1548   **Q**
Orba Blades, R.R. 1, Thompsonville 62890

Hamilton County
MOORE'S SHOOTING PRESERVE   618: 728-3200   **Q**
James Moore, Macedonia 62860

Jefferson County
LACEY'S SHOOTING PRESERVE   618: 735-2435   **QCM**
James Lacey, Box 122, Woodlawn 62898

Jo Daviess County
RUSH CREEK GAME FARM   815: 598-2547   **PQC**
Donald Fitzgerald, 5875 N. Lincoln Ave.,
Chicago 60645

Kane County
BEVERLY KENYON AREA   Elburn 9819   **M**
E. T. Samuelson, 414 Babcock, Elburn 60119

Lake County
WINDY ACRES HUNT CLUB   312: 395-1458   **P**
Albert Dax, Wadsworth 60083

La Salle County
FLYING FEATHERS HUNTING CLUB   815: 695-5647   **PM**
Russell Hanson, Box 424, Newark 60541

Lee County
ROGERS HUNTING CLUB, INC.   815: 379-2427   **PCM**
Howard Rogers, R.F.D. 2, Ohio 61349

Macoupin County
HAMMANN'S HUNTING PRESERVE   217: 839-2862   **PQC**
Leonard Hammann, R.R. 1, Gillespie 62033
WYNCHESTER SHOOTING PRESERVE   217: 753-4717   **Q**
Chester Jacoby, Chesterfield 62630

Madison County
PIASA POINTER & SETTER CLUB   **PQ**
Loyd Carson, Godfrey 62035

Marshall County
AUTUMN FLIGHT GAME FIELDS   815: 452-2004   **P**
Gilbert Holz, Toluca 61369
ROBERT A. BARNES   309: 246-8481   **M**
Robert Barnes, Box 68, Lacon 61540

McHenry County
HILLENDALE HUNT CLUB   815: 678-2861   **P**
Arnold May, 9622 Hideaway Lane, Richmond
60071
HUNTLEY GAME FARM   312: 669-5600   **P**
Peter Exner, 10308 Crystal Lake Rd., Huntley
60142
LAKEFIELD FARM   312: 639-7286   **PM**
George Bates, P.O. Box 37, Cary 60013
THUNDERBIRD LAKE HUNTING &   815: 459-6223   **PQ**
FISHING CLUB
Gene Johnson, 2209 N. Ringwood Rd.,
McHenry 60050

TWIN PONDS HUNT CLUB, INC.   312: 669-5784   PC
John Oliver, R.R. 1, Box 50, Algonquin 60102
Pulaski County
KAY'S LAKE HUNTING PRESERVE   618: 745-6475   M
Donald Humphrey, Box 254, Mounds 62964
Randolph County
ELM SHADE FARM   618: 282-2492   PQC
Adolph Hitzemann, Rt. 2, Red Bud 62278
Tazewell County
WINGFEATHER HUNTING PRESERVE   309: 244-7230   PQ
H. G. Friedrich, Delavan 61734
White County
P. D. Q. ACRES   618: 382-8406   PQC
Raleigh Pollard, R.R. 2, Carmi 62821
Winnebago County
FLASHING FEATHERS GAME FIELDS   815: 389-2749   PQCMT
Addison Foss, R.R. 1, Roscoe 61073

INDIANA
September 1-March 31
Special nonresident license $2.50 (calendar year)
Delaware County
HI-LAKES HUNT CLUB   317: Parker 3783   PQCM
Dick Arnold, R.R. 1, Parker 47368
ROY MARTIN AND SONS HUNTING   317: 284-8939   PQC
PRESERVE
Roy Martin, R.R. 7, Box 243, Muncie 47302
Owen County
ROLLING ACRES HUNTING AND   317: 795-4444   PQC
FISHING CLUB
Wayne Staley, R.R. 1, Quincy 47456

IOWA
September 1-March 31
Special nonresident license $5
Clarke County
BUFFALO VALLEY SPORTS CLUB   515: 447-2308   PQC
Hal Pearson, Rt. 2, Murray 50174
Clinton County
ARROWHEAD HUNTING CLUB, INC.   319: 577-2267   PQCMT
John Mullin, Rt. 1, Box 28, Goose Lake 52750
Delaware County
LOGAN'S SPORTS FARM   319: 922-2516   PM
Marvin Kreutner, Delhi 52223
Jasper County
OAK VIEW GAME FARMS   515: 994-2094   PQCM
Ronald DeBruin, Rt. 1, Prairie City 50228
Mahaska County
BIRD LAYNE FARMS   515: 637-2364   PQCM
Ed Lloyd, Rt. 1, New Sharon 50207

KANSAS
September 1-March 31
Special nonresident license $3; upland game
bird stamp $1; total, $4
Ford County
COBB'S GAME FARM AND SHOOTING   316: 227-3554   PQ
PRESERVE
Charles Cobb, Wright 67882
Harvey County
SAND HILLS, INC.   316: 283-1029   Q
Irvin Toevs, 801 E. 4th St., Newton 67114
Lyon County
J & F SHOOTING PRESERVE   316: 884-3185   PQC
Jesse Johnson, Bushong 66841
Ottawa County
BLUE LINE CLUB   913: 488-3785   PQC
Bernie Janssen, Rt. 2, Solomon
Saline County
SUN SHOOTING PRESERVE   913: 827-9661   PQCT
Thelma Sundgren, P.O. Box 856, Salina 67401
Wabaunsee County
MAIKE PHEASANT FARM &   913: 765-3820   PQCMT
SHOOTING PRESERVE
J. R. Maike, Rt. 2, Alma 66401

KENTUCKY
October 1-April 15
Special nonresident license $5 per preserve
Barren County
BARREN RIVER SHOOTING PRESERVE   502: 646-2046   PQC
Marshall Kinslow, Rt. 3, Smiths Grove 42171
Christian County
PEMBROKE SHOOTING PRESERVE   502: 475-4490   Q
Richard Mullins, Rt. 2, Pembroke 42266
Jefferson County
PRESTON HIGHWAY HUNTING   502: 969-1616   PC
PRESERVE
Frank Quick, 6304 Mt. Washington Rd.,
Louisville 40229
Lyon County
BARKLEY LAKE SHOOTING PRESERVE   502: 388-7013   Q
Kenneth (Ted) Scott, Kuttawa 42055
Muhlenberg County
McCLELLAN SHOOTING PRESERVE   502: 754-2655   PQ
Charles McClellan, Rt. 1, Central City 42330
Nelson County
ROYAL ACRES HUNTING PRESERVE   502: 252-4331   PQCM
J. W. Royalty, R.R. 1, Bloomfield 40008

Webster County
WATSON SHOOTING PRESERVE   502: 639-5202   Q
Glen Watson, Dixon 42409
Woodford County
WOODFORD COUNTY SHOOTING   606: 873-4438   PQ
PRESERVE
Jess Jones, Versailles 40383

LOUISIANA
October 1-March 31
Nonresident license $25 (per season);
$5 (5 days)
East Feliciana Parish
OLD SOUTH HUNTING PRESERVE   504: 629-5522   PQCMT
Robert Lee, Norwood 70761
Natchitoches Parish
WOODS LODGE SHOOTING PRESERVE   318: 875-2233   PQC
Thomas Hall, Box 96, Campti 71411
Tangipahoa Parish
WILD WING HUNTING PRESERVE   504: 796-3017
AND KENNELS
Abele Dutreil, Rt. 1, Folsom 70437
West Feliciana Parish
ROSEMOND SHOOTING PRESERVE   504: 635-3096   QC
Mrs. R. E. Nelson, Rt. 5, Box 650-A,
St. Francisville 70775

MARYLAND
October 1-March 31
Special nonresident license $4.50
Calvert County
HUNTING CREEK PHEASANT FARM   M
J. Dorman Hall, Prince Frederick 20678
Caroline County
TUCKAHOE ROAD PRESERVE   301: 364-5241   Q
George Wood, Rt. 3, Box 12, Denton 21629
Charles County
BRYANTOWN HUNTING CLUB   301: 274-3427   PQ
Walter Langley, Box 96, Bryantown 20617
Howard County
RIVER HILL FARM   301: 737-7215   PQM
Ed Mougin, 10221 Wincopin Circle,
Suite 303, Columbia 21043
Kent County
SANDY HILL GAME FARM   301: 778-1834   QM
Vincent Raimond, Warton 21678
Montgomery County
OLD FORT HILL SHOOTING PRESERVE   703: 525-1662   PQ
Dr. Beno Vajda, Rt. 2, Dickerson 20753
Prince George County
BLACK SWAMP CREEK   301: 579-6859   M
C. Morton Peed, Rt. 3, Box 192-M,
Brandywine 20613
Queen Anne's County
WYE RIVER SHOOTING CLUB, INC.   301: 827-8710   PQCM
Lee Knight, Queenstown 21658
Somerset County
KRAFT'S GAME BIRD FARM   301: 651-2353   PQC
Ralph Kraft, Princess Anne 21853
Talbot County
FRIENDSHIP FARM   301: 745-2153   Q
Samuel Leonard, Royal Oak 21662
TALBOT SHOOTING PRESERVE   301: 479-0640   PQ
Thomas Swann, R.F.D. 3, Box 95,
Denton 21629
Washington County
GAME "A" PLENTY   301: 842-2917   P
Charles Shank, R.D. 4, Hagerstown 21740
HEPBURN'S ORCHARDS, INC.   301: 678-6147   PQ
Edward Hepburn, R.F.D. 1, Hancock 21750

MASSACHUSETTS
September 15-April 1
Nonresident game bird license $16.25
Berkshire County
MILL POND GAME BIRD FARM   413: 229-8814   PM
William Gilligan, Sheffield 01257
Essex County
ROWLEY SHOOTING PRESERVE   617: 948-2593   PQCM
Carl Savage, Jr., Hammond St., Rowley 01969
Middlesex County
ARROWHEAD FARMS   617: 369-6025   P
AND SHOOTING PRESERVE
Elizabeth Mattison, 321 Williams Rd.,
Concord 01742

MICHIGAN
August 15-April 30 pheasant, mallard
August 15-December 15 bobwhite quail
Special nonresident license $5
Cass County
INDIGAN   616: 663-2340   PQCM
Earl Koldyke, P.O. Box 111,
Edwardsburg 49112
Clinton County
WILD ACRES   417: 862-5076   PQ
Morris Farr. Rt. 1, Elsie 48831

Eaton County
MICHIGAN PUBLIC HUNT CLUB 517: 372-0094 PQC
Jerry Donovan, 6634 Picketts Way,
Rt. 2, Lansing 48917

Genesee County
GLENDALE SHOOTING PRESERVE 313: 636-7100 PC
H. V. Burrow, 12174 Green Rd.,
Goodrich 48438

Grand Traverse County
JAXTON CREEK HUNTING PRESERVE 616: 263-5577 PQCM
Bob Stinson, 7116 Hency Rd., Kingsley 49649

Iron County
SMOKY LAKE PRESERVE 715: 545-2300 PQCMTBg
P. C. Christiansen, Phelps, Wisc. 54554

Kalamazoo County
ROY A. KERBS SHOOTING PRESERVE 616: 731-4632 P
Ray Kerbs, R.F.D. 1, Augusta 49012
RED WING SHOOTING PRESERVE 616: 629-9057 PQ
William Crane, Rt. 1, Box 252,
Richland 49083
ROCK-N-PINE SHOOTING PRESERVE 616: 679-5784 PM
Harold Havens, R.R. 2, W Ave.,
Schoolcraft 49087
RUMZ SHOOTING PRESERVE 616: 648-9892 PQC
Fred Rumz, East Y Ave., Vicksburg 49097

Lapeer County
SECORD GAME INC. 313: 796-3660 PQM
Larry Hammond, 5664 Secord Lake Rd.,
Dryden 48428

Menominee County
FAITHORN PHEASANT FARM & Faithorn 2803 PQCM
SHOOTING PRESERVE
M. A. Garrison, R.R. 1, Vulcan 49892
WALLACE PHEASANT FARM & 906: 788-4453 P
SHOOTING PRESERVE
Wesley Eland, Wallace 49893

Oakland County
R & C PHEASANT RANCH 313: 684-4915 PQCM
Ron Strohl, 1335 Robblee, Milford 48042

St. Joseph County
CUPP'S M-66 SHOOTING PRESERVE 616: 432-3591 P
Philip Cupp, 718 Colon Rd., Rt. 2,
Mendon 49072
HAPPY'S HUNTERS HAVEN 616: 432-3996 PC
Frank Walters III, R.R. 2, Mendon 49072

Washtenaw County
JOHN L. AREND SHOOTING PRESERVE 313: 429-4149 P
John Arend, 10052 Michigan Ave.,
Saline 48176
DEXTER LAKES CLUB, INC. 313: 663-2377 P
Parker Pennington III, 1906 Peppermill Way,
Ann Arbor 48103
KEMETER'S SHOOTING PRESERVE 313: 428-8356 PQ
Joe Kemeter, 9761 Noggles Rd.,
Manchester 48158

MINNESOTA
September 1-March 31
Special nonresident license $3 (possible increase to $5)

Anoka County
ARMSTRONG RANCH, INC. 612: 421-3602 PCM
William J. Crolley, Box 76, Rt. 2, Anoka 55303
HAMILTON SHOOTING PRESERVE 612: 434-6103 PQCM
Jim Hamilton, R.R. 1, Box 107, Cedar 55011

Clay County
HUNTING UNLIMITED PRESERVE 218: 498-6916 PCMT
Dr. Gordon B. Magill, 1206 S. 9th St.,
Fargo, N.D. 58102

Cottonwood County
IDEAL GAME FARM 507: 793-2775 PCM
Glenn Peterson, Heron Lake 56137

Mahnomen County
RECREATIONAL RANCH 218: 435-5385 P
Mrs. B. L. Smith, 515 N. Foss Ave.,
Fosston 56542

Morrison County
LE BLANC SHOOTING PRESERVE 612: 745-3232 PQCMT
Bert LeBlanc, Little Falls 56345

Scott County
WILD OUTDOORS, INC. 612: 447-2145 PCMT
J. M. Olsen, 6531 Cambridge St., Suite 206,
Minneapolis 55426

Stearns County
GOLD MEADOWS GAME FARM 612: 347-2747 PQCM
Ralph Doubek, Rt. 1, Richmond 56368

Todd County
LONG PRAIRIE SHOOTING PRESERVE 612: 732-3311 PM
Gary Hotzler, Rt. 1, Box 188, Burtrum 56318

Wabasha County
BREMEN SHOOTING PRESERVE 507: 798-2022 PM
Gunther Rankenburg, Millville 55957

Washington County
HARDWOOD CREEK SPORTS CLUB 612: 464-5522 PQCMT
Ray Lemmons, Rt. 1, Box 329,
Forest Lake 55025
WILD WINGS OF ONEKA 612: 439-4287 PQCM
Lyle "Pop" Lehner, Rt. 2, Hugo 55038

Wright County
HOWARD LAKE GAME FARM 612: 543-4894 PM
Louis Klingelhoets, Howard Lake 55349

Yellow Medicine County
GRANITE FALLS GAME FARM 612: 564-3626 PM
Carl Aus, Granite Falls 56241

MISSISSIPPI
September 1-March 31
Special nonresident license $3.25

Adams County
ELLISLIE SHOOTING PRESERVE 601: 442-6563 QC
J. Earl Bufkin, Natchez 39120

Alcorn County
HATCHIE HILLS SHOOTING PRESERVE 601: 462-4115 PQ
Harvey Crow, Rt. 5, Corinth 38834

Clay County
WEBBER BROS. GAME PRESERVE 601: 494-5881 Q
Malcolm Webber, R.F.D. 1, West Point 39773

Harrison County
LONG BEACH PRESERVE 601: 864-1876 Q
T. L. Necaise, R.R., Box 142-H,
Longbeach 39560

Lamar County
BLACK CREEK SHOOTING PRESERVE 601: 796-3151 PQ
Darnell Thomas, P.O. Box 233,
Lumberton 39455

Rankin County
SIX W RANCH, INC. 601: 362-9691 PQC
L. D. Worley, Box 16075, Jackson 39206

Wayne County
YELLOW CREEK QUAIL PRESERVE 601: 735-9060 Q
Jim West, Rt. 1, Box 252A, Waynesboro 39367

MISSOURI
October 1-March 31
Special nonresident license $3.30 (3 days)

Cass County
BAIER'S DEN KENNELS & 816: 758-2345 PQC
SHOOTING PRESERVE
Bud Baier, Peculiar 64078

Lewis County
NOEL SMITH SHOOTING PRESERVE 314: 655-4674 PQC
Noel Smith, Taylor 63471

Montgomery County
GOOD EARTH CONTROLLED 314: 564-2076 PQCM
SHOOTING
Joe Keshner, Rt. 1, New Florence 63363
RANCH ROY-L HUNTING CLUB 314: 585-2211 PQCM
Jim Longstreet, High Hill 63350
REUST ROOST PHEASANTS & 314: 252-4301 PQC
SHOOTING PRESERVE
Lawrence Waldo, New Florence 63363

St. Charles County
SORENSON KENNELS & 314: 828-5149 PQ
SHOOTING PRESERVE
Tom Sorenson, Rt. 1, Wentzville 63385

St. Francois County
RAINES' KENNELS & SHOOTING AREA 314: 756-5463 Q
Sam Raines, P.O. Box 351,
Farmington 63640

Texas County
RESTLESS FEATHERS HUNTING 417: 967-3838 PQC
PRESERVE
Warren Ragsdale, Rt. 2, Cabool 65689

Warren County
MISSOURI GUN & QUAIL CLUB, INC. 314: 739-0717 PQ
Lacy Lewton, 12721 San Clemente Dr.,
Bridgeton 63042

Washington County
HORN AND HOOK RANCH 314: 469-3440 PQ
C. K. Reynolds, Rt. 2, Conway Rd., Box 485,
Chesterfield 63017

NEBRASKA
September 1-March 1
Special nonresident license $5 + $1 Upland
Game Stamp

West Cherry County
POLE CREEK GAME FARM & 308: 53-W-1 PQC
SHOOTING PRESERVE
Ned Fair, Gordon 69343

NEVADA
August 1-April 30
No hunting license required

Clark County
HIDDEN VALLEY RANCH 702: 642-7507 P
Don Ferguson, P.O. Box 560, Las Vegas 89101

Douglas County
HARVEY'S JAMES CANYON RANCH 702: 782-2600 PCT
Red Roberts, Genoa 89411

Lyon County
LOGAN DENISON'S WILD WIND 702: 882-0423 PC
KENNELS & SHOOTING PRESERVE
Logan Denison, Box 167, Dayton 89403

Nye County
MASTERS GAME BIRD SHOOTING   702: 870-0554   PC
PRESERVE
Daniel Masters, 5498 Sheila, Las Vegas 89108
Pershing County
VALLEY GUN CLUB   702: 273-2247   P
Bill Milich, P.O. Box 780, Lovelock 89419

NEW JERSEY
September 1-March 15
Special nonresident license $2.15 (1 day)
Hunterdon County
AMWELL SHOOTING PRESERVE   609: 397-2285   PQCM
Duncan Dunn, R.D. 1, Stockton 08559
RINGNECK FISH & GAME CLUB   201: 925-5970   PQ
Frank Castellano, 116 Raritan Rd., Linden
07036
ROCK-ERRA   201: 996-2095   PQC
E. S. Ecker, R.D. 2, Stockton 08559
Middlesex County
FEATHER DUSTERS SHOOTING   201: 247-1730   PQ
PRESERVE
Milton Clark, 1392 How Ave.,
North Brunswick 08902
Salem County
WINSLOW FARM   609: 935-1230   PQCM
Earl Wood, Hook & Winslow Rds.,
Pennsville 08070
Sussex County
BIG SPRING GAME FARM   201: 875-3373   P
John Eby, R.D. 3, Sussex 07461
KYMER'S GAME FARM   201: 875-3167   PQC
Frank Kymer, R.D. 2, Branchville 07826

NEW MEXICO
September 1-March 31
Special nonresident license $5.25
Lea County
WILAGLEN FARMS   806: 376-9678   PQ
Hollis Harris, 711 Kentucky, Amarillo, Texas
79106
Torrance County
NEW MEXICO UPLAND SHOOTING   505: 384-2833   PQC
PRESERVE
Ralph Dial, Star Rt., Box A4A, Estancia 87016

NEW YORK
September 1-March 31
No hunting license required
Albany County
OLD MACDONALD'S GAME FARM   518: 861-2864   P
Robert Macdonald, Box 325, Altamont 12009
Allegany County
VALHALLA SHOOTING PRESERVE   607: 478-8188   PQC
Ed Van Stine, R.R. 2, Andover 14806
Cattaraugus County
TEE JAY GAME FARM   716: 372-3648   PQ
Tom Banfield, Four Mile Rd., Allegany 14706
Chautauqua County
BUTTON VALLEY PRESERVE   716: 782-3894   PC
Ernest Button, Panama 14767
Chenango County
GREENACRES SHOOTING PRESERVE   607: 656-4926   P
Robert Marcy, R.D. 2, Box 350, Greene 13778
Columbia County
DUTCH ACRES FARMS, INC.   518: 766-2081   P
Edward Light, Jr., North Chatham 12132
MACEDONIA GAME PRESERVE   518: 392-9439   P
Charles Briggs, Jr., R.D., East Chatham 12060
Cortland County
COLD BROOK GAME FARM   607: 749-4000   PM
Donald Steger, R.D. 1, Homer 13077
Dutchess County
COX GAME PRESERVE   914: 855-1280   PQCM
Mrs. Helen Cox, Box 173, Pawling 12564
EAST MOUNTAIN SHOOTING PRESERVE 914: 877-4611   PQC
Victor D'Avanzo, Mountain Rd., Dover
Plains 12522
LAUREL HILL FARM PRESERVE   914: 226-6669   PQC
Walter Klein, Stormville 12582
RING-NECK LODGE GAME PRESERVE   914: 373-9665   PQC
John Spucches, Smithfield Rd., Millerton
12546
SAW KILL GAME PRESERVE   914: 758-6411   PQCM
W. G. Schreiber, R.D. 2, Box 158, Red Hook
12571
T-M-T HUNTING PRESERVE   914: 266-5108   PQC
Mrs. Thomas Mackin, School House Rd.,
Box 204-B, Staatsburg 12580
Genesee County
WEST BERGEN GUN CLUB   716: 494-1599   P
Francis Oberer, 7244 Buffalo Rd., Rt. 33,
Bergen 14416
Greene County
VALLEY GAME FARM   518: 945-1429   P
Wm. Rositzke, R.D. 2, Catskill 12414

Jefferson County
S'NO FUN SHOOTING PRESERVE   315: 629-4392   PQC
James Cowick, P.O. Box 86, Evans Mills 13637
Monroe County
PHEASANTS UNLIMITED, INC.   716: 334-2212   PQCM
Gerald Doyle, 1458 Middle Rd., Rush 14543
Montgomery County
MOHAWK VALLEY GAME PRESERVE   518: 922-5288   PC
Albert Fiorenza, R.D. 2, Randall 12142
Orange County
BRAE-BURN KENNELS   914: 361-3511   PQM
Jasper Briggs, Box 235, Circleville 10919
STONEGATE FARM KENNEL &   914: 427-2115   PQC
SHOOTING PRESERVE
Herm Levee, Day Rd. & Rt. 207, Campbell
Hall 10916
Otsego County
QUAPHEGRO GAME FARM & PRESERVE 315: 858-1492 PQCM
J. A. Hammerle, P.O. Box 91, Schuyler Lake
13457
Steuben County
VALHALLA SHOOTING PRESERVE   607: 478-8188   PQC
Ed Van Stine, R.D. 2, Andover 14806
Suffolk County
SPRING FARM   516: 725-0038   PQCM
George Schellinger, Sag Harbor 11963
Tioga County
MILE LANE SHOOTING PRESERVE   607: 589-4521   P
Joseph Bergman, R.D. 1, Box 68, Lockwood
14859
Westchester County
TWIN ELMS GAME FARM   914: 232-4373   PQC
Mike Pender, Box 239, Goldensbridge 10256

NORTH CAROLINA
October 1-March 31
Special nonresident license $5.25
Bertie County
PINE VALLEY HUNTING PRESERVE   703: 622-5869   QC
Brock Jones, Lewiston 27849
Cleveland County
PAUL ANTHONY'S QUAIL SHOOTING   704: 487-7502   Q
PRESERVE
Paul Anthony, Jr., Rt. 2, Shelby 28150
Cumberland County
CARVERS CREEK SHOOTING PRESERVE 919: 488-4256   Q
A. L. Maynor, P.O. Box 5543, Fayetteville
28303
Currituck County
BAY POINT SHOOTING PRESERVE   919: 429-6939   Q
Edwin Fentress, P.O. Box 113, Knotts Island
27959
Davie County
HUNTER'S PARADISE SHOOTING   704: 492-7262   Q
PRESERVE
Glenn Foster, Rt. 5, Mocksville 27028
Iredell County
QUAIL HATCHERY SHOOTING   704: 592-2935   PQCM
PRESERVE
Paul Harmon, Rt. 5, Box 163, Statesville 28677
Johnston County
WILDWOOD SHOOTING PRESERVE   919: 772-0461   Q
H. M. Jackson, 606 E. Garner Rd., Garner
27529
Madison County
BRIGMAN HUNTING PRESERVE   704: 649-2143   PQ
Wayne Brigman, P.O. Box 85, Marshall 28753
Mecklenberg County
SQUASH HILL SHOOTING PRESERVE   704: 376-6137   Q
M. N. Ballard, Box 9381, Charlotte 28205
Moore County
PINE LAKE SHOOTING PRESERVE   919: 947-5302   QCM
Jack Myrick, Rt. 1, West End 27376
WHISPERING PINES SHOOTING   919: 947-5888   QCM
PRESERVE
Kenneth Clayton, P.O. Box 383, Whispering
Pines 28327
Orange County
NORMAN'S SHOOTING PRESERVE   919: 732-2053   Q
Norman Walker, Rt. 2, Rougemont 27572
Randolph County
PARKS AND WRIGHT SHOOTING   919: 857-2196   Q
PRESERVE
Ervin Parks, Rt. 5, Asheboro 27203
VONCANNON'S SHOOTING PRESERVE 919: 629-9253   PQCT
Nolan Voncannon, Rt. 1, Box 335,
Asheboro 27203
Stanly County
SCOTT QUAIL AND CHUKAR FARM   704: 483-4375   QC
M. W. Scott, Rt. 1, Stanfield 28163
Stokes County
DAN RIVER SHOOTING PRESERVE   919: 342-1775   PQ
L. W. Hanes, 209 McCoy Rd., Reidsville
27320
Union County
SQUASH HILL SHOOTING PRESERVE   704: 376-6137   Q
Mack Ballard, Box 9381, Charlotte 28205

Wake County
TARA FARM SHOOTING PRESERVE   919: 833-3617   QC
Dr. V. Watson Pugh, Raleigh Rd. 2016,
Raleigh 27609

OHIO
September 1-April 30
Special nonresident license $5.35

Ashland County
TALLMADGE PHEASANT FARM AND   419: 368-6653   P
SHOOTING PRESERVE
James Tallmadge, R.D. 2, Box 106,
Jeromesville 44840

Ashtabula County
BOB WILLIAMS SHOOTING PRESERVE   216: 255-4229   PQC
Robert Williams, 8527 Forestview Dr.,
Mentor 44060

Clinton County
CHERRYBEND PHEASANT FARM   513: 584-4269   PQ
"Holly" Hollister, R.R. 4, Wilmington 45177

Columbiana County
VALLEY VIEW HUNT CLUB   216: 424-7237   PQ
G. V. Weinstock, P.O. Box 225, Lisbon 44432

Crawford County
ELKHORN LAKE SHOOTING   419: 562-6131   PQCT
PRESERVE, INC.
Charles Baehr, R.R. 2, Bucyrus 44820

Hancock County
DRAY'S SHOOTING PRESERVE   419: 358-6170   PQC
James Dray, R.R. 1, Bluffton 45817

Logan County
INDIAN LAKE HUNTING AND   513: 843-3667   PQ
SHOOTING PRESERVE
Lowell Howard, McCalla Rd., Lewistown
43333

Washington County
MILLER'S UPLAND HUNTING   614: 989-2227   PQ
PRESERVE
Charles Miller, R.D. 1, Little Hocking 45742

Wayne County
CEDAR VALLEY HUNTING PRESERVE   216: 264-7192   PQC
Harold Mowrer, R.D. 6, Wooster 44691
PRAIRIE LANE SHOOTING PRESERVE   216: 262-6823   P
Lester (Red) White, R.D. 4, Prairie Land Rd.,
Wooster 44691
W. D. & P. CLUB   216: 262-8015   P
Louie Carter, 470 Carter Dr., Wooster 44691

OKLAHOMA
January 1-December 31
Special nonresident license $1 (1 day)

Delaware County
BIRD ISLAND RESORT   918: 782-3571   PQC
Buck Hogan, Rt. 2, Afton 74331

Oklahoma County
D & D HUNTING RESORT   405: 277-3395   PQ
Jimmy Palmer, Rt. 1, Luther 73054

PENNSYLVANIA
September 1-March 31
Special nonresident license $3.15 (3 days)

Adams County
TWIN HEMLOCK PHEASANT FARM   717: 642-8622   PM
Dale Showvaker, R.D. 2, Fairfield 17320

Armstrong County
LOG CABIN HUNTING PRESERVE   412: 461-0379   PQCM
Ray Waugaman, 4443 Kennywood Blvd.,
West Mefflin 15122

Bedford County
BEDFORD HUNTING LODGE   814: 623-5075   PQM
Harry Beegle, R.D. 2, Bedford 15522

Berks County
READING REGULATED SHOOTING   215: 582-4516   P
AREA
H. Weldon Weidner, R.D. 1, Birdsboro 19508

Bucks County
DARK HOLLOW SHOOTING PRESERVE   215: 766-8621   PQC
Robert Lerch, Pipersville 18947
GAYBIRD FARMS   215: 297-5553   P
Barney Berlinger, Carversville 18913

Cambria County
GOLDEN ACRES HUNTING CLUB   814: 495-5897   PQCT
Stan Golden, R.D. 2, Box 769, Portage 15946

Centre County
HIDDEN VALLEY SHOOTING PRESERVE   814: 237-7175   P
R. E. Stover, 557 Glenn Rd., State College
16801

Chester County
BLUE ROCK ENTERPRISES   215: 696-8717   PQ
John McKee, R.D. 4, West Chester 19380
COX PHEASANT PRESERVE   215: 273-3840   PQC
James Cox, R.D. 2, Honey Brook 19344
HAHN'S REGULATED SHOOTING   215: 932-8428   P
PRESERVE
W. A. Hahn, R.D. 1, Box 214, Oxford 19363
MURPHY GAME FARM   215: 469-6448   P
John Murphy, Harmonyville Rd. Star Rt.,
Pottstown 19464

Crawford County
LITTLE SUGAR TROUT FARM   412: 425-5222   Q
Ben Forker, R.D. 1, Box 212, Cochranton
16314

Dauphin County
SUNRISE GAME FARM   717: 362-8413   PQCM
Joe Stetson, R.D. 1, Elizabethville 17023

Fayette County
NEMACOLIN TRAIL HUNTING   412: 329-5552   PQCM
RESERVE, INC.
Lou Scarnecchia, Rt. 40, Box 67, Farmington
15437
RICH HILL SPORTS HAVEN   412: 929-5700   PQCT
John Hutchinson, R.D. 3, Box 112,
Belle Vernon 15012

Indiana County
MAHONING VALLEY HUNTING   412: 783-6360   PC
GROUNDS
Robert Wagner, 221 Fourth St., Sagamore
16250

Juniata County
HIGH VALLEY PHEASANT FARM   717: 737-9089   P
G. H. Plank, R.D. 2, East Waterford 17021

Lancaster County
WATERS GAME FARM   717: 786-7237   P
M. D. Waters, Sr., R.D. 1, New Providence
17560

Luzerne County
WILD ORCHARD SHOOTING PRESERVE   717: 639-5453   PQ
J. Elgaway, R.D. 2, Shickshinny 18655

Mercer County
COLONEL HUNTER FARM   412: 932-5114   PM
Edward Smith, R.D. 2, Jamestown 16134
SAGULLA HUNTING GROUNDS   814: 786-7368   PM
Joseph Sagulla. R.D. 1, Jackson Center 16133

Monroe County
FIELDCREST KENNELS & HUNTING   717: 992-4509   PQ
PRESERVE
Gordon Latzko, R.D. 1, Box 74, Saylorsburg
18353
PHEASANT VALLEY HUNTING   717: 629-0367   P
PRESERVE
Walter Gould, Effort 18330

Schuylkill County
LA-DA-JO PINES   215: 779-3343   PQC
Larry Delp, 218 N. 25th, Mount Penn 19606

Tioga County
TIOGA BOAR HUNTING PRESERVE   717: 835-5341   TBg
Omar Swift, Mannshill Rd., R.D. 1, Tioga
16946

Venango County
CROSS CREEK HUNTING & FISHING   814: 823-9645   P
PRESERVE
Thomas Harman, R.D. 3, Titusville 16354

Washington County
BIG COUNTRY RANCH RESORT   412: 428-3546   PQ
Bernard Bailey, R.D. 2, West Finley 15377

RHODE ISLAND
September 1-April 15
Special nonresident license $3.25

Newport County
BOYS TOWN HUNTING RANCH   401: 683-0074   P
William Conroy, 349 Huntington Ave.,
Providence 02909

Washington County
PEACE DALE SHOOTING PRESERVE   401: 783-7137   PQC
Edward Frisella, Rose Hill Rd., Peace Dale
02883

SOUTH CAROLINA
September-March (180 days)
Special nonresident license $5

Aiken County
CAROLINA SHOOTING PRESERVE   803: 648-3489   Q
A. K. Lain, P.O. Box 2103, Aiken 29801
QUAIL COUNTRY   803: 568-4121   Q
Frank Poole, Jr., Rt. 2, Swansea 29160

Beaufort County
HILTON HEAD SHOOTING PRESERVE   803: 785-3529   QT
J. Pringle Scheider, P.O. Box 1014,
Hilton Head Island 29928

Berkeley County
SPRING GROVE PLANTATION   803: 553-1121   PQC
Wm. Baldwin, Mount Holly 29463

Clarendon County
SANTEE HUNTING PRESERVE   803: 435-8776   Q
Jay B. Potter, Jr., P.O. Box 192, Manning
29102

York County
TAR-SAND HUNTING PRESERVE   803: 366-3908   PQC
E. A. Covington, Rt. 1, Box 194, Rock Hill
29730

SOUTH DAKOTA
September 1-March 31
Nonresident general hunting license $1

Pennington County
HUNTERS HAVEN   605: 342-0977   PQ
Joe Lytle, 915 12th St., Rapid City 57701

TENNESSEE
October 1-April 1
Special nonresident license $5

Cumberland County
CARYONAH HUNTING LODGE   615: 484-5377   TBg
Lawrence Cary, Rt. 1, Box 188, Crossville 38555

RENEGADE HUNTING RANGE   615: 484-6072   PQCTBg
Ben Burton, P.O. Box 304, Crossville 38555

Fayette County
W & W GAME PRESERVE   901: 867-2226   Q
Sam Wilson, Box 310, Arlington 38002

Hickman County
PINE RIDGE SHOOTING PRESERVE   615: 446-8602   PQC
Sterling Holt, Rt. 2, Bon Aqua 37025

Lewis County
QUAILRIDGE SHOOTING PRESERVE   615: 832-9649   Q
Charles Sanders, 310 Lawndale Dr., Nashville 37217

McMinn County
TELLICO JUNCTION HUNTING   615: 887-7819   TBg
PRESERVE
F. L. Satterfield, Hog Hollow Rd., Englewood 37329

Sullivan County
CHEROKEE SHOOTING PRESERVE   615: 247-2141   PQ
Louis Milhorn, Rt. 11, Kingsport 37663

Sumner County
MEADOWBROOK GAME FARM   615: 888-2411   PQC
G. B. Denning, Westmoreland 37186

TEXAS
October 1-March 31
Special nonresident license $3.15

Austin County
HILLSIDE GAMEBIRD FARM   713: 885-3829   PQ
Frank De Fratus, Box 1, Sealy 77474

Bastrop County
SANDY CREEK SHOOTING RESORT   512: 478-1346   Q
Dr. Ray Jones, 307 Buckeye Trail, Austin 78701

Bee County
PAPALOTE SHOOTING RESORT   512: 287-3329   PQC
Charles Griffith, Box 1335, Sinton 78387

Caldwell County
4 JACKS SHOOTING RESORT   512: 444-5573   PQ
Herman Neusch, 2700 Metcalfe, Austin 78741

Edwards County
RANCHO DE CONTENTO   512: 234-3342   PQCT
Carlton Ward, Barksdale 78828

Ellis County
LAKE CLOPTON SHOOTING RESORT   214: 937-2439   PQC
Pete Clopton, Rt. 1, Waxahachie 75165

LONGHORN SHOOTING RESORT   214: 875-3987   PQ
John Wheelock, Jr., Box 881, Corsicana 75110

Grimes County
ISBELL'S SHOOTING RESORT   713: 394-5176   PQC
W. A. Isbell, Rt. 2, Iola 77861

MYERS' GAME BIRD FARM &   713: 894-2383   PQ
SHOOTING PRESERVE
H. E. Myers, Rt. 2, Box 193, Navasota 77868

Kaufman County
WILD WING HUNTING RESORT &   214: 887-6606   PQ
KENNEL
Afton Flowers, Rt. 1, Box 44, Mabank 75147

Kerr County
Y-O RANCH   512: 654-2076   TBg
Robert Snow, Jr., Box 27, Mountain Home 78058

Robertson County
PUCKETT'S DAM RANCH   214: 742-3631   PQC
Dr. Joseph Puckett, 517 Medical Arts Bldg., Dallas 75201

San Augustine County
FAIRWAY FARM HUNTING &   713: 275-2145   PQCM
GOLF CLUB
J. C. Benedum, Drawer T, San Augustine 75972

Shelby County
HAWKEYE HUNTING CLUB   713: 598-3825   PQCM
Jerry Waters, P.O. Box 27, Center 75935

UTAH
September 1-March 31
Nonresident hunting license $20

Cache County
ANDERSON SHOOTING PRESERVE   801: 563-6251   P
Jim Anderson, R.F.D., Smithfield 84335

Morgan County
BROWNING SHOOTING PRESERVE   801: 399-3481   PQC
David L. Peterson, Rt. 1, Morgan 84050

Washington County
RANCHO VUE DESERT   801: 673-2280   PQC
Bud Branham, P.O. Box 27, Hurricane 84737

VERMONT
September 15-December 31
Nonresident game bird license $10.50

Orange County
WILD HILL PRESERVE   802: 333-9171   PC
Webster Keefe, Ely 05044

VIRGINIA
October 1-March 31
Special nonresident license $3

Charlotte County
HOLLOW LOG HUNTING LODGE   703: 735-3466   PQCMT
J. Acree Devin, Wylliesburg 23976

Chesapeake County
CEDAR RIDGE FARM   703: 622-3255   Q
W. H. Belanga, P.O. Box 6225, Norfolk 23508

LAKE DRUMMOND GAME PRESERVE   703: 426-2857   Q
Willie Fentress, Rt. 4, Box 4013A, Virginia Beach 23457

Chesterfield County
QUAILWAY GAME FARM   703: 739-2113   PQ
Charles Barger, Rt. 2, Box 286, Midlothian 23113

Dinwiddie County
WOODSTOCK SHOOTING PRESERVE   703: 733-7529   PQCM
George Smith, Jr., Rt. 4, Box 495, Petersburg 23803

Fauquier County
GRANVILLE SHOOTING PRESERVE   703: 347-1333   PQ
James Nash, Box 260, Warrenton 22186

Hanover County
CEDAR LANE SHOOTING PRESERVE   703: 449-6408   Q
Conway Nuckols, Rt. 1, Box 106, Montpelier 23192

SOUTH ANNA SHOOTING PRESERVE   703: 883-6886   PQ
Wm. Brown, Rt. 1, Box 27, Montpelier 23192

Louisa County
CAMPBELL SHOOTING PRESERVE   703: 967-0395   Q
Roy Campbell, R.F.D. 2, Louisa 23093

Pulaski County
NEW RIVER SHOOTING PRESERVE   703: 674-5438   PQ
Ronald Simpson, Rt. 2, Box 302, Dublin 24084

Richmond County
BELLE VISTA LODGE & SHOOTING   703: 443-3738   PC
PRESERVE
Howard Reisinger, P.O. Box 655, Tappahannock 22560

Rockbridge County
THUNDER RIDGE SHOOTING PRESERVE   703: 291-3536   PQC
R. N. Horn, P.O. Box 68, Natural Bridge Station 24579

Smyth County
APPALACHIAN SHOOTING PRESERVE ·   703: 646-3387   PQ
Jack Haga, Rt. 2, Chilhowie 24319

MOUNTAIN EMPIRE SHOOTING   703: 783-7701   PQ
PRESERVE
Fred Rupard, Sr., 302 Virginia Ave., Marion 24354

Washington County
MEADOW LANE SHOOTING PRESERVE   703: 496-7029   PQC
R. G. Rexroad, Box 15, Saltville 24370

Wythe County
BRIARPATCH SHOOTING PRESERVE   703: 228-4309   PQC
Frank Otey, Jr., Rt. 2, Wytheville 24382

WASHINGTON
January 1-December 31
No hunting license required

King County
CHERRY VALLEY SHOOTING PRESERVE   206: 885-3605   PQC
R. C. Shoemaker, 4235 148th NE, Bellevue 98004

Lewis County
LINCOLN CREEK HUNTING CLUB   206: 736-6609   PQM
Corky Smith, Rt. 2, Box 250, Rochester 98579

San Juan County
WEST VALLEY SHOOTING PRESERVE   206: 378-4711   P
Brian J. Ingoldsby, Rt. 1, Box 171, Friday Harbor 98250

Whitman County
PHEASANT VALLEY PRESERVE   509: 657-3692   P
Fay Wiedrich, Box 161, LaCrosse 99143

WEST VIRGINIA
October 1-March 31
Special nonresident hunting license $3 (5 days)

Jackson County
PLEASANT VALLEY GAME FARM   304: 372-8395   PQCM
Edward Ball, Given 25245

Marshall County
FRANKLIN HUNTING & FISHING CLUB   304: 455-3797   PM
Paul Yoho, Rt. 1, Proctor 26055

Preston County
BIG SANDY WILDLIFE CLUB   304: 379-3221   PQ
Bill Bowermaster, Bruceton Mills 26525

MOUNTAIN TOP VACATIONLAND, INC.   304: 789-2111   **PQCMT**
Rt. 1, Terra Alta 26764

Tyler County
   HOLLY FARMS   304: 758-2758   **P**
   H. M. Gillespie, Jr., Rt. 1, Friendly 26148

WISCONSIN
October 18-February 28
Special nonresident license $5

Ashland County
   MADELINE ISLAND GAME FARM   715: 747-3483   **PM**
   Roy Burrow, LaPointe 54850

Columbia County
   WHITE TAIL ACRES   608: 253-3771   **P**
   Roland Baryenbruch, Box 1, Wisconsin
   Dells 53965

Fond Du Lac County
   MILLERS SHOOTING PRESERVE   414: 589-2291   **P**
   Darwin Miller, 5975 Triangle Rd., Pickett
   54964
   A. V. ORTH SHOOTING PRESERVE   414: 922-7370   **P**
   A. V. Orth, 104 S. Main St., Fond Du Lac
   54935
   PHEASANT CITY   414: 324-5813   **PM**
   Leo Scallon, Rt. 1, Markesan 53946

Green Lake County
   SPRING VALLEY SHOOTING PRESERVE   414: 294-6213   **P**
   Edward Bartel, Green Lake 54941

Kenosha County
   PHEASANT VALLEY HUNTING CLUB   414: 694-2474   **PQCMT**
   Edward Halter, Rt. 5, Box 614, Kenosha
   53140

Manitowoc County
   LAZY ACRES INC.   414: 776-1733   **P**
   Erwin Van Calster, R.R. 1, Mishicot 54228
   THUNDERBIRD GAME FARM AND   414: 853-5343   **PQM**
   KENNEL
   Leonard Leberg, Rt. 4, Chilton 53014
   TUMBLIN WEED INC.   414: 682-4188   **P**
   Halvor Halvorsen, 1015 N. 15, Manitowoc
   54220

Marquette County
   HI LO SHOOTING PRESERVE   608: 587-2510   **P**
   Loyed Koenig, Endeavor 53930

Oneida County
   STEFONEK'S SHOOTING PRESERVE   715: 272-5172   **P**
   B. V. Stefonek, R.R. 2, Box 104, Rhinelander
   54501

Outagamie County
   K & S GAME FARMS   414: 986-3326   **PQC**
   Dave Duffey, P.O. Box 227, Appleton 54911

Ozaukee County
   OZAUKEE COUNTY FISH AND GAME   414: 692-2114   **P**
   ASSN.
   M. Hochstein, Rt. 1, Box 176, Fredonia 53021

Portage County
   MILL ROAD FARMS   715: 423-0122   **P**
   Dr. John Schaller, 280 Shore Acres, Wisconsin
   Rapids 54494

Price County
   TALL PINE GAME FARM   715: 339-2683   **PQCMT**
   Dave Hill, Phillips 54555

Racine County
   EAGLE LAKE SHOOTING PRESERVE   414: 637-6577   **P**
   Samuel Myers, 727 Wisconsin Ave., Racine
   53403
   LANE'S LAKEVIEW KENNEL   414: 895-7838   **PQ**
   John Lane, Rt. 3, Box 140, Muskego 53150

Rock County
   BLONHAVEN HUNTING PRESERVE   608: 868-3176   **P**
   Donald Millis, R.R. 1, Milton Junction 53564

St. Croix County
   GAME UNLIMITED HUNTING   715: 246-6456   **PQCMT**
   CLUB, INC.
   Robert Swanson, Rt. 2, Hudson 54016

Sauk County
   BEAVER SPRINGS SHOOTING PRESERVE   608: 254-6871   **P**

Russell Tollaksen, Rt. 1, Box 17,
   Wisconsin Dells 53965

Sheboygan County
   HAWE HUNTING CLUB   414: 668-3400   **PQCM**
   Thomas Hawe, Rt. 1, Oostburg 53070
   SUE-GAR-DA SHOOTING PRESERVE   414: 564-3218   **P**
   Norman Koeppe, R.R. 1, Oostburg 53070
   SUNSET FARM   414: 894-3318   **PM**
   William Maass, P.O. Box 54, Elkhart Lake
   53020

Vilas County
   SMOKY LAKE RESERVE   715: 545-2300   **PQCMTBg**
   P. C. Christiansen, Phelps 54554

Walworth County
   FLASHING FEATHERS GAME FIELDS   414: 275-3512   **PC**
   Addison Foss, Belvidere Park, Fontana 53125
   RAINBOW SPRINGS COUNTRY CLUB   414: 642-7311   **PCM**
   Larry Mitten, Mukwongo 53149

Waukesha County
   OCONOMOWOC GAME FIELDS   414: 965-2715   **P**
   I. J. Perkins, Rt. 3, Sunset Dr., Oconomowoc
   53066
   WILSHER KENNELS AND GAME FARM   414: 965-2380   **PQCMT**
   Sam Wileman, 5357 Hwy. ZC, Dousman
   53118

Winnebago County
   NIEMUTH'S GAME FARM &   414: 446-3358   **PM**
   SHOOTING PRESERVE
   Robert Niemuth, Rt. 2, Alpine Rd., Fremont
   54940

Wood County
   MARSHFIELD PHEASANT RANCH   715: 676-2162   **PM**
   Natter-Thompson, Inc., R.R. 2, Marshfield
   54449

WYOMING
October 1-January 28
Special nonresident license $3 (3 days)

Johnson County
   CRAZY WOMAN VALLEY 41 RANCH   307: 684-2375   **P**
   George Nimick, Buffalo 82834

Sheridan County
   DLMRS BIRD FARM   307: 674-9441   **P**
   John Destefano, 1555 S. Thurmond,
   Sheridan 82801

NEW BRUNSWICK
January 1-December 31
Special nonresident license $1

Kent County
   ST. NICHOLAS RIVER   506: 523-6163   **PM**
   PHEASANT SHOOTING PRESERVE
   W. A. Robertson, R.R. 2, Rexton

ONTARIO
September 1-March 31
Special nonresident license $5.25

Carleton County
   RIDGEWAY HUNTING PRESERVE   613: 824-3282   **P**
   Alex Komaromi, Box 46, R.R. 9, Ottawa

Lambton County
   HARD OIL SHOOTING PRESERVE   519: 882-0659   **PQC**
   Clayton Shain, Rt. 3, Petrolia

Lincoln County
   BRUCE DALE GAME FARM   416: 892-2277   **PQC**
   Jack Ross, R.R. 4, Fenwick
   TWENTY VALLEY HUNTING PRESERVE   416: 562-4281   **PQC**
   Dean Wismer, R.R. 1, Jordan Station,
   Vineland

Northumberland County
   GRAFTON GAME FARM   416: 349-2264   **P**
   Jack Reymes, Grafton

Ontario County
   BRENDEAN GAME FARM &   416: 985-7465   **PC**
   SHOOTING PRESERVE
   Fred Plunkett, R.R. 4, Uxbridge

Oxford County
   CRAWFORD GAME FARM   519: 424-9232   **PQ**
   John Crawford, R.R. 2, Burgessville

Hunting Area Locator

All hunting areas numbered in the text and on the maps of this book are arranged below in alphabetical order. The first listing after the name of the area is the state in which it is found. The second listing is the number that locates the area on the map of that state. *The number is not a page number.* The same number appears in the text after the first mention of the area.